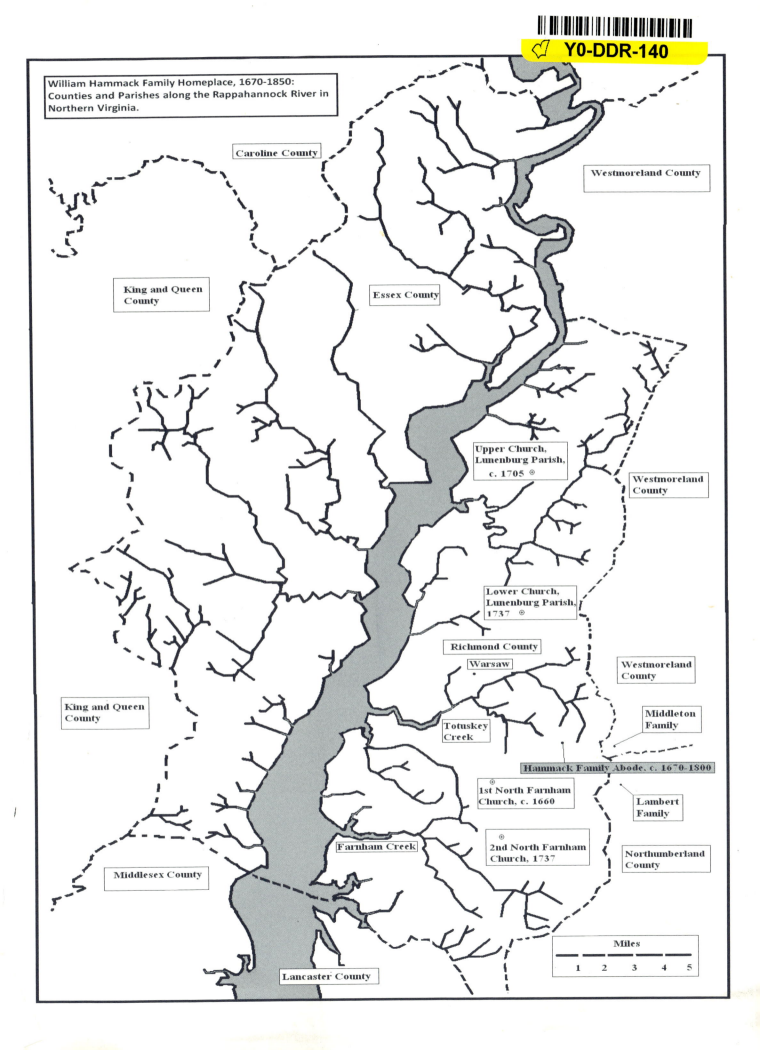

William Hammack Family Homeplace, 1670-1850:
Counties and Parishes along the Rappahannock River in
Northern Virginia.

Caroline County

Westmoreland County

King and Queen County

Essex County

Upper Church, Lunenburg Parish, c. 1705 ⊕

Westmoreland County

Lower Church, Lunenburg Parish, 1737 ⊕

Richmond County

Warsaw

Westmoreland County

King and Queen County

Totuskey Creek

Middleton Family

Hammack Family Abode, c. 1670-1800

1st North Farnham Church, c. 1660 ⊕

Lambert Family

Farnham Creek

2nd North Farnham Church, 1737 ⊕

Northumberland County

Middlesex County

Lancaster County

Miles

1   2   3   4   5

Hammack Cousins:

Hammack and Hammock Families in England and America, 1569-2010

by

Thomas Daniel Knight

PENOBSCOT PRESS

First Printing March 2011

This book is available from:

Felix Maben Hammack
1169 NW Constellation Dr
Bend, OR 97701-5471

Manufactured in the United States of America
Printed on 50# acid-free paper

∞

Sponsor's Introduction

As a youngster growing up on a farm in central Mississippi, only my paternal grandmother and great-grandmother, nee Sallie Elizabeth Cates and Abbie Doxey Brown, besides my parents, were still living. They were advanced in age and we seldom saw them even though they lived within two miles of us. Their concerns with the Civil War and Reconstruction seemed to take precedent over ancestral history. Our great grandmother was a school teacher during and after the War, and she was a featured lecturer at the local school when that period in our nation's history was being covered.

The most prominent written record about our family's history was the date of death of our grandfather, William S. Hammack, on December 25, 1899, scratched on the inside surface of an old pendulum clock that ticked out the time on the mantle piece of the room where our father was born in 1884. Our father, George C. Hammack, Sr., died in 1963 in the same room where he was born seventy-nine years prior. The house was built in the late 1840s and is now listed on the National Register of Historic Places as the "Cates House," recognizing that it was built and continuously owned by descendants of the Cates line.

There were numerous uncles, aunts and cousins from both sides of our family living within a radius of 100 miles, but my mother and her brothers and sisters were the only relatives to promote family gatherings. These mostly annual gatherings took place under the Bankston banner around Thanksgiving, and they served to promote a cohesiveness that was lacking on the Hammack side.

I didn't appear on the scene until 1928, and learning who the Hammacks were didn't spark my interest until about 1990 during a visit with two of my brothers, George, who lives in Jackson, Mississippi, and James, who lives in the "Cates House" located near Brownsville, about twenty miles northwest of Jackson. During this visit with brothers George and James, we decided to take a trip to the state archives to initiate a search for our "roots." In so doing, we came across a listing of certified researchers, among whom was the late Mrs. Ruth Land Hatten, then of Jackson. On further investigation, we learned that she was present at the premises that day, and we sought her out. We had a good discussion with Mrs. Hatten and engaged her services for some exploratory searching of available records. She provided some trail-blazing work that whetted our appetite for going further. She continued with our project for more than a year until she felt she had exploited most of the locally available sources and thereupon provided a written summary of her findings.

Before the completion of Mrs. Hatten's report on our Hammack ancestors, our niece, Caroline Babb Glover, told me about a very able young man who had recently completed high school in LaGrange, Georgia, where she also lived. Caroline had heard him give talks about matters of historical importance and suggested that I get to know him as a possible researcher. I made a telephone call to Thomas Daniel (Danny) Knight and engaged his services to complete what Mrs. Hatten had started. Danny exceeded all our expectations in navigating through the ancestral cobwebs. He maintained his research during twenty years while he finished school, obtained first one university degree and then another, and was ultimately awarded a Ph.D. by Oxford University in England. The volume before you is a summary of Danny's findings. Thank you, Dr. Knight. This project could not have been completed without you.

Felix Maben Hammack
Bend, Oregon
1 November 2010

Direct Descendants of John Hammack (Hammock, Hammick, Hammot)

John Hammack (Hammock, Hammick, Hammot)

John Hammocke — **Joane Sparkwill**

William "O" Hammack — **Grace [------]**

William "The Elder" Hammack — **Christian Middleton**

Robert Hammack — **Anne Lambert**

Robert Hammack — **Millenor Jackson**

William T. Hammack — **Mary Felts**

Simeon J. Hammack — **Elizabeth Jane Moore**

John T. Hammack — **Louisa Templeton**

William Simms Hammack — **Sallie Elizabeth Cates**

George Cleveland Hammack — **Mary Almedia Bankston**

Felix Maben Hammack

Author's Preface

This work sets out to chronicle the family history of William Hammack, who arrived in Virginia about 1656. It follows several lines of his descendants but focuses primarily on the lineage of his son William, his grandson Robert, and his great-grandson Robert, who left Southside Virginia and settled in Wilkes County, Georgia, just before the American Revolution. It incorporates a narrative history of the lives of the people involved and attempts to place them generally in the broader context in which they lived.

My interest in the Hammack and Hammock families began in 1984, when I first encountered Benedict Hammock while studying the Kettle Creek community in Wilkes County, Georgia. I became actively involved in researching the family in 1991 after having been contacted by Felix Maben Hammack, now of Bend, Oregon, a descendant of Robert and Millenor Jackson Hammack of Wilkes County, Georgia. In the course of this work, I have uncovered several connections linking individuals in my own family to such figures as John Hammack of Granville County, North Carolina, Philip and Abigail Hammack Combs of Wilkes County, Georgia, John and Martha Hammock Combs of Wilkes County, Georgia, and Joel and Rebecca Hammack Culpeper of Harris County, Georgia.

From these examples, it should be clear that the American descendants of William Hammack of Richmond County, Virginia, employ both the spellings Hammack and Hammock. In the main text, I have usually used the spelling Hammack, but in the genealogical appendices, when I have known that a particular family preferred the spelling Hammock, I have tried to use that form instead. I have located few colonial records bearing original signatures to indicate which spelling a given individual preferred; in general, scribes recorded the name however they heard it and employed many different spellings. By the middle nineteenth-century, however, certain families had often come to use one spelling as opposed to the other. In actual fact, though, spelling often differed within individual families. For instance, in the family of Simeon and Elizabeth Jane Hammack, almost all of the Hammack descendants who remained in Mississippi retained the spelling Hammack. Descendants of Simeon's son Alfred Washington, who moved to Ashley County, Arkansas, used the spelling Hammock instead.

In England, I have discovered a number of other common spellings not generally used in the United States. These spellings, and the possible evolution of the surname itself from older English surnames, are discussed in the second and third chapters of the text, before returning to the narrative of the family's activities in America. In recognition of the plural spellings of the same surname, Felix M. Hammack and I have chosen the title *Hammack Cousins: Hammack and Hammock Families in England and America, 1569-2010* to include all American descendants of the immigrant William. The date 1569 was chosen because in that year an individual identified in the written record as John Hamot, perhaps father of another John Hamot of Ermington Parish in Devonshire (whose name is spelled in written records as Hamot, Hamat, Hamack, Hameck, Hamock, Hamoak, Hammick, Hammack, Hammock, and many other ways), appears as a bowman on a militia list for that portion of eastern Cornwall near its boundary with Devonshire in southeastern England. This is the earliest and only known legal appearance of the individual who may be the ultimate progenitor of the American Hammack and Hammock families today. The designation "America" rather than "United States" in the title reflects the migration of the family not only from Virginia on the Atlantic Coast to California, Oregon, and Washington on the Pacific Coast but also the migration in the early twentieth century of many of the children and grandchildren of John Robert Hammack and Emma Christiane Beal Hammack, formerly of Mississippi and the Dakotas, into southern and western Canada.

As a precursor to this work, I first generated research reports on each individual or family group studied. These reports included lengthy transcriptions of legal records as well as efforts to reconstitute individual family groups based on the analysis of primary sources. These individual reports constitute at present approximately 5,000 typed pages and cover not only the Hammack and Hammock families but many associated families in England, Pennsylvania, Virginia, the Carolinas, Georgia, and the southeastern

United States. After consolidating these reports, I then used them as the evidentiary background to write the narrative that follows. Those readers desiring further information on certain individuals may wish to contact me for additional data.

During the course of the past two decades, I have undertaken research on Hammack and allied families in the following archives and libraries:

The National Archives, Kew, Richmond, England;
The Bodleian Library, Oxford, England;
The Society of Genealogists Library, London, England;
The National Art Library, Victoria and Albert Museum, London, England;
The British Library, London, England;
The Kensington and Chelsea Public Library, Kensington, London, England;
The Maryland Hall of Records, Annapolis, Maryland;
The Library of Virginia, Richmond, Virginia;
The Virginia Historical Society, Richmond, Virginia;
The John D. Rockefeller Library, The Colonial Williamsburg Foundation, Inc., Williamsburg, Virginia;
The North Carolina Department of Archives and History, Raleigh, North Carolina;
The Hillsborough, North Carolina, Public Library, Hillsborough, Orange County, North Carolina;
The Person County, North Carolina, Public Library;
The Caswell County, North Carolina, Public Library;
The South Carolina Archives, Columbia, South Carolina;
The South Caroliniana Library, The University of South Carolina, Columbia, South Carolina;
The Newberry County, South Carolina, Public Library, Newberry, South Carolina;
The Laurens County, South Carolina, Public Library, Laurens, South Carolina;
The Georgia Department of Archives and History, Morrow, Georgia;
The Washington Memorial Library, Macon, Georgia;
The Troup County Archives, LaGrange, Georgia;
The Bradley Memorial Library, Columbus, Georgia;
The Wilkes County Public Library, Washington, Georgia;
The Alabama Department of Archives and History, Montgomery, Alabama;
The Cobb Memorial Archives, Valley, Alabama;
The Mississippi Department of Archives and History, Jackson, Mississippi;
The Calhoun City Public Library, Calhoun City, Mississippi;
The Canton Public Library, Canton, Mississippi;
The Jackson Public Library, Jackson, Mississippi;
The Oklahoma Department of Archives and History, Oklahoma City, Oklahoma.

Staff members at all of these libraries and archives have been unfailingly polite, and I could not have completed this research without their assistance. I had completed research for this book before coming to The University of Texas – Pan American in Edinburg, Texas, but I have benefited from the university library, the expertise of the university librarians, and my many knowledgeable colleagues in the Department of History and Philosophy as I wrote and revised the manuscript.

I am also indebted to the county officials who staff the following county court houses and who have assisted me during my visits there: Richmond County, Virginia; Pittsylvania County, Virginia; Amelia County, Virginia; Lunenburg County, Virginia; Orange County, North Carolina; Caswell County, North Carolina; Person County, North Carolina; Union County, South Carolina; Newberry County, South Carolina; Laurens County, South Carolina; Wilkes County, Georgia; Greene County, Georgia; Taliaferro County, Georgia; Upson County, Georgia; Crawford County, Georgia; Macon County, Georgia; Meriwether County, Georgia; Pike County, Georgia; Troup County, Georgia; Muscogee County, Georgia;

Chambers County, Alabama; Washington County, Alabama; Clarke County, Alabama; Hinds County, Mississippi; Madison County, Mississippi; Copiah County, Mississippi; Webster County, Mississippi; Grenada County, Mississippi; Calhoun County, Mississippi; Choctaw County, Mississippi.

Among the many individuals whose kindness and generosity have benefited this work, I must also acknowledge the following individuals: Mrs. JoAnn Griffin of LaGrange, Georgia, who has provided encouragement throughout this project; Mrs. Maureen Mason of Kensington, London, England, who has provided encouragement and a home in which to research and write while in England; Mrs. Carolyn Hardin Goudie of Lunenburg, Virginia, who generously shared with me her research on Jesse and Robert Moore of Lunenburg County, Virginia; Mrs. Anne Martin Haigler of Birmingham, Alabama, who generously opened to me her research files on the Bankston, O'Neal, and Stewart families; Mrs. Sarah Hallum and the late Miss Imogene Springer of Calhoun City, Mississippi, both of whom generously introduced me to the local records available in Calhoun County, Mississippi; Mr. Willard Rocker, former director of the Genealogy and History Room of the Washington Memorial Library, Macon Georgia, who has for more than a decade generously indulged me during visits to his institution; Mrs. Muriel Jackson, present head of the Genealogy and History Room of the Washington Memorial Library and archivist of the Middle Georgia Archives, and Dr. Christopher Stokes, formerly staff historian of the Genealogy and History Room, for their kind assistance over many years; Larry Hammack of Chandler, Arizona, who many years ago kindly provided me with copies of Henry Franklin Hammack's series, *Wandering Back;* Thomas McBryde, of Austin, Texas, who kindly shared information on the family of John Hammock of Talbot County, Georgia; Glenda Brack of Escondido, California, who generously shared her research on the Tallapoosa County, Alabama, Hammocks and their connections; Kaye Lanning Minchew, Forrest Clark Johnson, III, and Randall Allen, of the Troup County Archives, LaGrange, Georgia, who have also provided valuable assistance; and Mrs. Miriam Syler and her staff at the Cobb Memorial Archives in Valley, Alabama, who have helped me on many occasions. I also wish to thank Lewis Rohrbach and Candy Perry at Penobscot Press, who have provided much valuable guidance over the past two and a half years.

My greatest debt is to Felix Maben Hammack of Bend, Oregon, who has sponsored this work since its inception in 1991. All those who profit from this book will also be indebted to him. I also wish to thank my wife, Kathryn, and my children, LeeAnn and Joshua, who have lived with this work for as long as I have known them. LeeAnn was particularly obliging in employing her computer skills to help generate many of the maps included in this volume and in restoring the old photographs included here. We thank her for her assistance.

> Thomas Daniel Knight
> Edinburg, Texas
> 1 November 2010

Felix Maben Hammack: Felix Maben Hammack was born on March 5, 1928 on a farm about twenty miles northwest of Jackson, Mississippi, near the small community of Brownsville. The sixth son and eighth of ten children in the family of George Cleveland Hammack and Mary Almedia Bankston Hammack, he attended through the tenth grade in Brownsville and Bolton before transferring to Lake Providence, Louisiana for completion of high school in 1945 while living with his oldest sister's family.

Mr. Hammack took advantage of a military engineering scholarship at Clemson A & M College in Clemson, South Carolina, beginning July 3, 1945, but the program was disbanded following surrender of the Japanese. He then enlisted for active duty in the Army Air Corps for three years service in Occupied Germany after being trained as a cryptographer. He was honorably discharged in November, 1948, upon completion of a tour of duty culminating with participation in the Berlin Airlift.

Mr. Hammack entered as a freshman at Louisiana Polytechnic Institute in the School of Chemical Engineering in February, 1949. He was graduated, magna cum laude, with a B. S. degree in Chemical Engineering in January, 1953. Working experiences included Phillips Petroleum in Borger, Texas; Buckeye Cellulose in Louisville, Kentucky and Memphis, Tennessee and Foley, Florida; Crossett Paper Mills in Crossett, Arkansas; Western Kraft in Albany, Oregon; Temple-EasTex in Evadale, Texas; Willamette Industries in Portland, Oregon; and Valmet Builders (a Finnish company) in Charlotte, North Carolina.

After retiring in May, 1990, in Charlotte, Mr. Hammack and his wife Mary Ann returned to Oregon where they remain near three of their four children. Principal activities since retirement have been traveling and pursuit of his "roots."

Thomas Daniel Knight: Thomas Daniel Knight was born on August 25, 1970 in LaGrange, Georgia. The second son and youngest child in the family of Thomas Leon Knight and Juanita Sue Duke Knight, he was educated in Georgia's Troup County school system and was graduated from Troup county Comprehensive High School in 1988 as class valedictorian. He holds a B.A. degree from Washington and Lee University in Lexington, Virginia, from which he was also graduated as class valedictorian in 1992 with a double major in history and classics. He also holds Master of Studies (M.St.), Master of Literature (M.Litt.), and Doctor of Philosophy (D.Phil.) degrees in American and English history from The University of Oxford in England.

Dr. Knight was a Fulbright Scholar in 1992 and 1993 and a Slosson Fellow at the University of Michigan from 1994 to 1996. He has published several family histories, co-authored two books on Troup County, Georgia, and served as editor of the series *Troup County, Georgia, and Her People*. He was employed by the Troup County Archives as a research assistant from 1985 until 1992 and held an internship within the Department of Historical Research at the Colonial Williamsburg Foundation, Inc., in 1991. In the course of researching this book, he uncovered a hitherto unknown connection to his own family, proving that he is an eighth generation descendant of John and Mary Ann Hammack of Granville County, North Carolina, and Wilkes County, Georgia.

In addition to family history, Dr. Knight's research interests include the transatlantic connections between England and her North American colonies during the colonial period and the settlement and development of the Southeastern United States. He is currently Assistant Professor of History at the University of Texas – Pan American, where he has also served as Assistant Chair of the Department of History and Philosophy.

Dr. Knight divides his time between homes in Edinburg, Texas, and LaGrange, Georgia. He and his wife Kathryn have two children.

Descendants of John Hammack (Hammock, Hammick, Hammot)

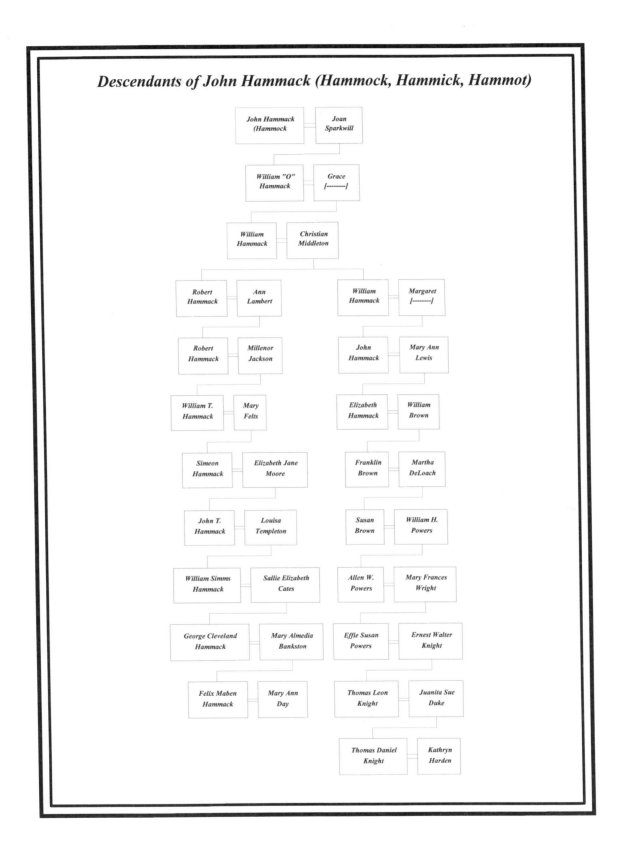

Direct Descendants of John Hammack (Hammock, Hammick, Hammot)

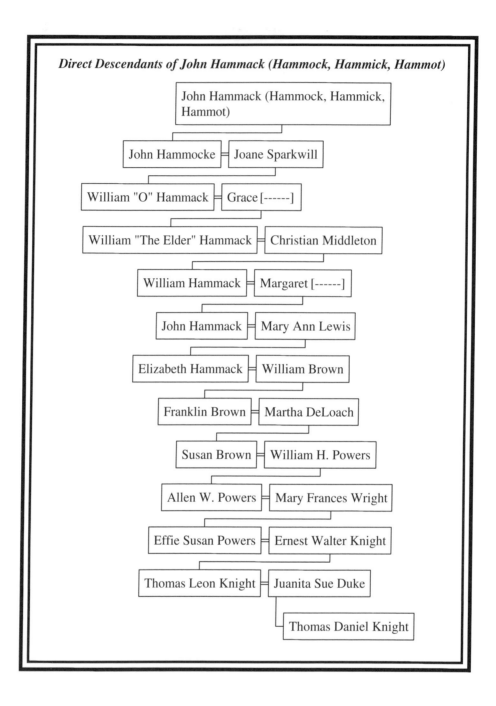

Contents

Illustrations

Chapter 1:

William Hammack's Immigration to Virginia

The exact date of William Hammack's arrival in Virginia, as well as the identities of the ship on which he travelled and its passengers, are mysteries that probably will never be solved. Few passenger manifests from the seventeenth-century have survived, and, among those that are known to exist, his name does not appear. Some researchers have thus theorized that he was born in Virginia and that it was his father, not he, who was the immigrant.[1]

Certainly, William was not the first Hammack in America. The late Henry Franklin Hammack argued at length that William was likely the son of Allen Hammack, whose name is found on a passenger list from the 1630s and who likely also settled in Virginia. Henry Franklin Hammack, however, was researching and writing in the 1940s and 1950s, at which time many surviving records were inaccessible; moreover, at the time he wrote, the study of Virginia's colonial history had been largely focused on leading individuals and key events. Since that time, an array of social historians have developed in enormous detail the history of many Virginia settlements and developed an understanding of life in early Virginia that goes far towards explaining the social world of men like Allen Hammack and William Hammack. Since that time, also, a significant portion of previously inaccessible early Virginia records have been archived and extracted, making them available either through microfilmed copies of the originals or through access to published transcriptions that are widely available today throughout the United States.[2]

Thus it is that we can write with a fair degree of certainty that Allen Hammack likely left no descendants in the New World, at least through the male line. Although there is clear evidence that he embarked for Virginia, there is no evidence that he lived long after he arrived in the colony. Further, there is nothing to suggest that he acquired land, that he married, or that he left a family. Historians of seventeenth-century Virginia stress the high mortality rate the colony experienced during its first decades. Many settlers died within months of their arrival. The causes of mortality were many. The earliest settlements along the James River unwittingly made their inhabitants vulnerable to salt poisoning. The Jamestown settlement of 1607 was believed to be far enough inland that its inhabitants would have a safe water supply, but this was not the case. In addition to the contaminated water supply, many colonists experienced what they called the "seasoning." This was an illness that struck colonists within a few months of arrival. Its symptoms included an extremely high fever, nausea and diarrhea, disorientation, and other flu-like symptoms. Many colonists died as a result of the seasoning, and those who survived often complained that they never possessed the strength and vigor they had formerly experienced.[3]

A host of other problems contributed to Virginia's high mortality rate. Inadequate knowledge of nutrition, problems adapting to the landscape and climate of Virginia, and lost convoys meant that early settlers lacked key nutrients that may have contributed to suppressed immune systems. Confrontation with Native Americans -- in particular two massacres in 1622 and 1644 that the Powhattan Confederacy intended to obliterate European settlement in the colony -- took a severe toll.[4]

Also, during the colony's first decades, those fortunate enough to acquire land and servants often abused them through overwork and inadequate maintenance. Once John Rolfe realized in 1614 that west Indian tobacco would grow, and perhaps even thrive, in the colony, many planters began cultivating the crop. The Virginia Company of London, which had established the colony, had thus far not been able to

---

[1] For this view, see especially Henry Franklin Hammack, *Wandering Back* (2 vols., Beebe, AR, 1954-1961). See also Adeline Evans Wynne, *Southern Lineages: Records of Thirteen Families* (Aberdeen, MS, 1940), pp. 98-130.

[2] Hammack, *Wandering Back*, Vols. 1 - 2.

[3] See R. L. Heinemann, J. G. Kolp, A. S. Parent, Jr., and W. G. Shade, *Old Dominion, New Commonwealth: A History of Virginia, 1607-2007* (Charlottesville and London, 2007), pp. 19-40.

[4] Edmund S. Morgan, *American Slavery, American Freedom: The Ordeal of Colonial Virginia* (New York, 1975), pp. 75 et seq.

make it a productive enterprise. Planters had begun to move away from the core settlements around Jamestown, and, as they acquired tracts along the James River to the north and south, they began to focus almost exclusively on tobacco cultivation. Reforms initiated by George Sandys in 1619, and aimed at making the disorganized colony more orderly, more productive, and more appealing to Englishmen in the mother country, included the creation of a headright system whereby an individual could acquire a fifty acre headright for each person whose passage he paid to the colony. A person of means in England with a wife and five children who sailed to the colony could thus immediately obtain a right to three hundred acres of land upon arrival in Virginia. Although some immigrants did come in family groups, the typical immigrant of this generation was a lone adventurer seeking to improve his or her status in the new world before ultimately returning to England. Thus many young men with modest means came to the colony while not yet married, obtained a small plantation, and began importing indentured servants into the colony.

The institution of indentured servitude was a combination of two older English systems. One was the system of apprenticeship, whereby an individual was apprenticed to learn a skill or a trade. The second was a system of short term husbandry, whereby individuals became servants of nearby families to learn farming skills or, in the case of females, the necessary skills to maintain a productive and efficient household. Indentured servants in the new world, in exchange for the payment of their passage, thus traded their labor for a longer time than usually did Old World servants. If an individual was highly valued or could contribute partially towards the expense of travel to the colony, he or she might be given a shorter indenture; an ordinary servant without any financial means might serve an indenture of seven or more years. However long the indenture, during this period the servant was vulnerable to extreme exploitation. Masters controlled every aspect of daily life -- the hours worked, the living and sleeping conditions, how many days per week a servant would labor, the amount of food and the nature of clothing a servant would be given, as well as the punishments that might be meted out for disobedience or dawdling. In some instances, a skilled servant with a kind master might be well treated; in others, servants might be harshly abused, sometimes beaten or worked to the point of physical exhaustion and even death.[5]

The expansion of the system of tobacco cultivation in the colony meant that most planters were eager to acquire additional lands in order to grow more tobacco. Rather than build elaborate houses during these early decades, they focused almost all profit made into the economic process. They imported more servants, acquired additional lands, opened new quarters, and grew even more tobacco.[6] Those who were fortunate in time became very rich; many achieved a comfortable sustenance that would have been beyond what they would probably have experienced in England. But for servants during the early decades, this equated to harsh, exploitative conditions that, when combined with the other problems the colony experienced, often meant early death without marriage or procreation. Despite the fact that well over 100,000 immigrants arrived in the colony before 1700, at that date -- nearly 100 years after the colony's settlement -- its population hovered at around sixty thousand, and much of this increase took place in the last three decades of the century. Thus it was that the overwhelming majority of immigrants, especially those who came as servants, died at young ages, most without offspring in the colony. In mid-seventeenth-century Virginia, an old man was one who had reached the age of about thirty-three years; those who had passed forty were often described as "ancient" in legal documents.[7]

This means that the weight of historical evidence suggests that Allen Hammack probably died without issue within a year or two of settling in the colony, if not earlier. At least some records have survived for most of the early plantations and counties, and there are no known references to Hammacks in Virginia before William Hammack's arrival about 1656.

---

[5] Richard Middleton, *Colonial America: A History* (3rd ed., Malden, MA, 2002), pp. 63-66.

[6] C. Carson, N. F. Barka, W. M. Kelso, G. W. Stone, D. Upton, "Impermanent Architecture in the Southern American Colonies," *Winterthur Portfolio* 16 (1981), pp. 135-196.

[7] Heinemann et. al., *Virginia*, p. 378; see also Morgan, pp. 158-180, 395-433.

Second, the fact that William Hammack is listed in 1656 on a list of headrights for James Price is proof that he had been transported into Virginia from overseas. This does not exclude the possibility that he could have been born in the colony and was returning in 1656 from a trip to England. The evidence suggests, however, that he had only recently arrived, and for the first time at that. When James Price patented a tract of land in Virginia's Northampton County, he did so based on the transportation of six individuals (not including himself) into the colony. According to the headright system, in return he claimed 300 acres on Matchotanke Creek in Northampton that was joined on the South by lands of Matilda Scarborough, a wealthy Eastern Shore widow.

Virginia's Eastern Shore is the peninsula of land on the eastern side of the Chesapeake Bay that extends along the Atlantic Coast. Today it is often called the Delmarva Peninsula, for it includes lands located in all three of these original colonies -- Delaware, settled by the Swedes in the 1630s; Maryland, settled by Lord Baltimore and his Catholic followers at about the same date; and Virginia, which had seen its first permanent settlement in 1607. Within a decade of founding Jamestown, Englishmen had begun to establish plantations on Virginia's Eastern Shore. Somerset County, on Maryland's Eastern Shore, did not see its first settlers until the middle 1650s. The records of Accomack and Northampton Counties -- Virginia's only two Eastern Shore counties -- are exceptionally complete, and those for Somerset County, Maryland, are also extensive. No known references in any of these counties exist for William Hammack from 1656 until he appears across the bay in Rappahannock County in 1668. James Price had several plantations in the area, and the weight of evidence suggests that William Hammack spent most of the decade after he arrived in the colony working as a servant on one of Price's plantations. If he had spent seven or eight years working off his indenture, Hammack would have been released about 1663 or 1664. It was customary for planters to hire back servants at a wage after their release if the association had been a pleasant one. The typical pattern would then be for a former servant to work for wages for three or four years before accumulating enough money to buy or rent a tract of his own. Once this occurred, the former servant himself would enter the ranks of the small planters, focusing on tobacco cultivation and the acquisition of additional property.[8]

The known facts concerning the life of William Hammack in Virginia adhere to just this pattern. He entered the colony about 1656 and appears in no known record afterward until 1668. In that year he was living in Rappahannock County, when he witnessed a deed on 8 June from George Greene to James Samford.[9] A little over four years later, Hammack purchased 300 acres of land in Rappahannock County from Thomas Freshwater.[10] Notably, Freshwater's wife Joanna had witnessed the 1668 transaction with William Hammack. In that first record, Hammack had signed his name by mark. This indicated that William Hammack could not write, at least well enough to sign his name. The mark that he used was the letter "O", a sign that he would use regularly until his death more than thirty years later.

---

[8] See J. R. Perry, *The Formation of a Society on Virginia's Eastern Shore, 1615-1655* (Chapel Hill and London, 1990), pp. 1-27. See also R. T. Whitelaw, *Virginia's Eastern Shore: A History of Accomack and Northampton Counties* (2 vols., Richmond, VA, 1951) and C. Torrence, *Old Somerset on the Eastern Shore of Maryland: A Study in Foundations and Founders* (Richmond, VA, 1935).

[9] Virginia Land Patent Book No. 4, p. 62, in N. M. Nugent, ed., *Cavaliers and Pioneers: Abstracts of Virginia Land Patents and Grants* (3 vols., Richmond, VA, 1929-1934), Vol. I, p. 338; Old Rappahannock County, VA, Deed Book 3, 1663-68, pp. 477-79

[10] Old Rappahannock County, VA, Deed Book 1672-76, pp. 89-90.

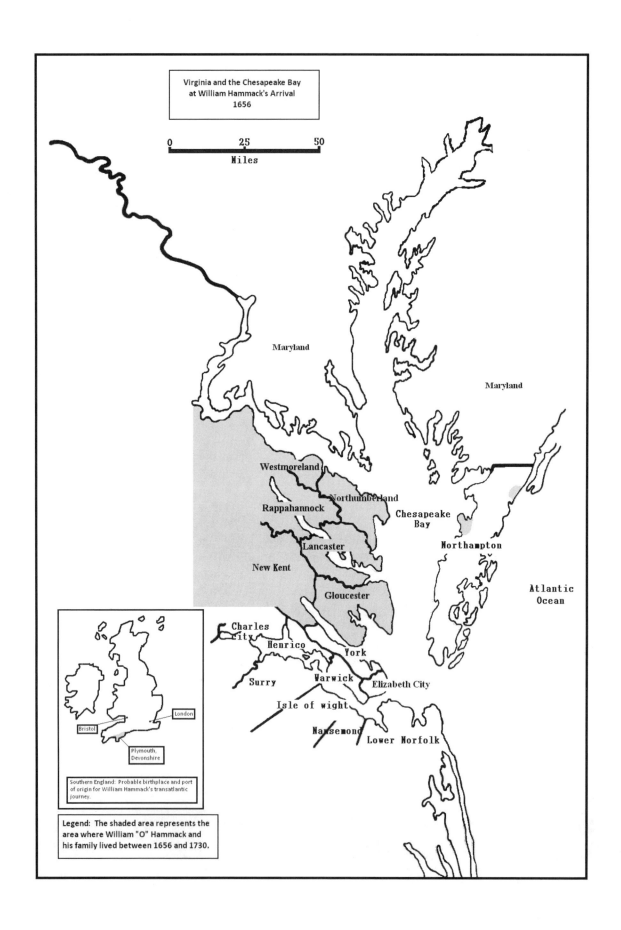

Virginia and the Chesapeake Bay
at William Hammack's Arrival
1656

0   25   50
Miles

Maryland

Maryland

Westmoreland

Northumberland

Rappahannock

Chesapeake
Bay

Lancaster

Northampton

New Kent

Atlantic
Ocean

Gloucester

Charles
City

Henrico

York

Surry

Warwick

Elizabeth City

Isle of wight

Nansemond

Lower Norfolk

London

Bristol

Plymouth,
Devonshire

Southern England: Probable birthplace and port
of origin for William Hammack's transatlantic
journey.

Legend: The shaded area represents the
area where William "O" Hammack and
his family lived between 1656 and 1730.

Chapter 2:

The Origins of William Hammack

Before discussing William Hammack and his life in Virginia, another matter needs to be considered. The question in this instance is whether anything can be learned about William Hammack's identity in England, his social background, and the origins of his family. As is the case with many Virginia families, this is not an easy question to answer.

The vast majority of early immigrants to the Chesapeake came as bonded laborers. They were recruited from villages across the south and west of England. Many, although born in rural areas, had already moved first to metropolitan areas -- London or Bristol, for instance -- in search of opportunity before making the decision to cross the Atlantic.[11]

In seventeenth-century England, several related factors encouraged Englishmen to seek their fortunes abroad. Population was increasing, and a variety of legislation made it more difficult for ordinary Englishmen to survive in the kingdom without inherited estates. The fear that Charles I was moving the Anglican Church towards Catholicism in the early 1600s had caused many Separatists and Puritans to establish colonies in New England; the outbreak of the English Civil War in 1642, and then the execution of the King in 1649, caused many who were loyal to him and his policies to fear reprisals from the Puritan forces led by Oliver Cromwell, who ruled England from 1649 until his death in 1658.

The exact date on which William Hammack left England is unknown; it was probably in the middle 1650s, and certainly prior to 1656. The reasons for his migration to the Chesapeake are also unclear. He may have been a man of mature years seeking a new start abroad, perhaps having suffered economic difficulties under the Puritan government; on the other hand, he may have been a youth seeking adventure and riches abroad.[12]

In his study, *Wandering Back*, the late Henry Franklin Hammack proposed that William Hammack was of Welsh origins and that he descended from Halmarack, a Norman settler who reached the British Isles following the Norman Conquest of 1066. It has been impossible to refute his claims, but there are certainly other scenarios meriting serious consideration.[13]

To date, the only William Hammack located in parish entries before 1650 was found in Ermington, Devonshire. "William Hamick, son of John Hamick," was baptized 11 July 1623 in Ermington, located in southwestern England near Plymouth, a larger urban center. This William was the youngest known child of John, who, with wife Joane, had also baptized several older offspring: John Hamick in 1619, Henry Hamicke in 1610, and Johane Hammecke in 1608.[14]

In evaluating whether this William "Hamick" might be the man who appears in Virginia three decades later, several factors need to be considered. These include whether "Hamick" might be the same surname as "Hammack," whether there is additional evidence regarding this William in Devonshire, whether there is reason to believe that this William may have left the area, and whether there are other possible candidates to be the William Hammack who settled in Virginia. These items will be considered in sequence below.

---

[11] See Morgan, *American Slavery*, pp. 108-158; see also D. H. Fischer, *Albion's Seed: Four British Folkways in America* (Oxford, 1989), pp. 207-419.

[12] Virginia county court records often contain legal depositions giving the age of those testifying. Unfortunately, records for Rappahannock, Richmond, and Northumberland Counties contain no such document giving William Hammack's age.

[13] See Hammack, *Wandering Back*, Vol. I.

[14] Ermington Parish Register Transcripts, 1603-1850. This volume includes baptisms and burials from 1603 to 1850 and marriages from 1606 to 1838. All references to individuals born or married in Ermington are from this volume. The original records are held in the Exeter Public Library, Exeter, England. They were microfilmed in 1973 by the Genealogical Society of Utah and are available in that form from The Church of Jesus Christ of Latter-Day Saints.

A. Is "Hamick" the same name as "Hammack" and "Hammock"?

It was not uncommon for spelling to alter as individuals crossed the Atlantic from their native regions in the British Isles or continental Europe; further, it was not uncommon for spellings to alter over time even within a confined geographical area. The evidence located strongly supports the conclusion that the surname "Hamick" is the same surname as "Hammack" and "Hammock."

Within the parish records at Ermington, we find several different spellings of the name: Johane Hammecke in 1608, Henry Hamicke in 1610, Joane Heamicke in 1625, Joan Hamich in 1645, and Penticost Hammick in 1646, for instance. John Hammock, son of John Hammock, was baptized at Ashburton, Devon, in 1692, and Thomazin Hammack, daughter of John Hammack, at Ermington on 9 April 1708. Wills proven within the Prerogative Court of Canterbury establish that multiple spellings can be used for the same individual: "Henry Hammack, Mariner, of Ermington, Devonshire" wrote his will in 1698; he is probably the same man baptized as "Henrie Hamicke" in Ermington in 1653.

The case of John and Thomazin Hammick of Ermington is instructive with regard to multiple spellings of a given surname within the same family. John and Thomazin were the parents of five children, all baptized at Ermington: Henery Hammick in 1699, John and Mary Hamack in 1701 and 1703, and Charles and George Hammack in 1706 and 1709. Charles Hammack and wife Mary moved from Ermington to Stoke Damerel, also in Devonshire. Their first known son, John, was baptized at Stoke Damerel in 1739 under the spelling "Hamilk." Of the six children born to him and wife Grace between 1763 and 1774 in Stoke Damerel and Plymouth, three were spelled Hammick (1763, 1764, 1767) and three were spelled Hammack (1765, 1770, 1774).[15]

The evidence seems to indicate conclusively that individuals found in one document with the surname Hamick might be found in another with the surname Hammack or Hammock. In all likelihood, the pronunciation was very similar but spelling differed according to the knowledge and understanding of the individual clerk recording the record. Thus, in terms of nomenclature, there is no reason to believe that William Hamick of Ermington might not be William Hammack of Virginia (whose name is also found spelled in a variety of ways there, including Hamock and Hammock).

B. Is there additional evidence concerning William Hamick in Devonshire?

To date, no further information concerning William Hamick has been found in Devonshire. Anglican parish records begin in the 1530s following the creation of the Church of England by Henry VIII. Records survive for a cluster of parishes in Devonshire during the seventeenth-century; in none of those consulted is there any record of the marriage or death of William Hamick. This finding is all the more significant because there are numerous entries for individuals with this surname in these same records. While it is possible that this particular William left the region and married or died elsewhere in England, no documented evidence has been found to support this possibility.

C. Is there reason to believe that William Hamick may have left Devonshire?

Although the information is speculative, there are several reasons that might explain why William Hamick would leave Devonshire and settle in Virginia. William seems to have been the youngest of at least four children; there may have been older Hamick offspring for whom no record has been located. He had at least twelve nieces and nephews baptized in Ermington before 1655, reducing the possibility that he might inherit a residual interest in any property owned by his father John Hamick. Thus, there was little economic motivation for him to remain within the area.

---

[15] All references to Hammack (Hammick, etc.) baptisms or burials in places outside of Ermington, Devon, are taken from the International Genealogical Index, Version 5.0, The Church of Jesus Christ of Latter-Day Saints.

In England and its American colonies, the law of primogeniture held that the bulk of an individual's properties were concentrated in the oldest male heir and his direct bloodline. Thus, the larger the family, the smaller the likely inheritances of younger offspring (if they received bequests at all). In some instances, older children might die childless, and properties inherited by them might then fall to younger siblings who initially stood to inherit little. In William's case, the fact that his older siblings were genetically productive, and that by 1655 he had at least six nephews, significantly reduced the likelihood that he might inherit any family properties.

At this point, we must consider the wealth of John Hamick, William's father. No probate records for John Hamick have been found. From hearth tax records, however, it is clear that he was a man of at least modest property. Hearth tax returns indicate that John Hamick's home had three hearths. The very poorest were exempt from the hearth tax, and ordinary husbandmen usually had only one hearth. Those with two and three hearths were usually tradesmen, craftsmen, and prosperous yeoman farmers, while those with four or more hearths were usually wealthier tradesmen and merchants. Thus, it seems likely that John Hamick possessed at least modest real and material property that he might have passed on to his heirs and from which William, by virtue of his birth order and the existence of a second generation of potential heirs, would probably have been excluded.

Hence, the decision of William Hamick to leave Ermington seems financially rational. As the youngest child, his prospects in Ermington were limited, and he stood to inherit little, if any, property from his father. He may have initially taken to the sea, as did his nephew Henry, a mariner. On the other hand, he may have moved for a time to Bristol or London, which were drawing immigrants from across the isle. The puzzling issue is why, at more than thirty years of age, he may have decided to cross the Atlantic in the early 1650s? No record has been found to suggest that he married in England or had offspring there, although that is certainly possible. If he had a wife and children who died, or if he suffered some economic or social reversal during the troubled 1640s or 1650s, he may have decided to venture west in search of opportunity.[16]

D. Are there other possible candidates to be William Hammack of Virginia?

Given that the name William was so common among the American descendants of William "O" Hammack (he even gave this name to **two** surviving sons), it is striking that so few references to individuals named William Hammack have been found in the British Isles. It must be emphasized, however, that some parish registers and public records were destroyed by bombs during World War II and that the bulk of remaining documents -- especially legal records -- remain unindexed. As part of their religious mission, the Latter Day Saints have made significant progress at transcribing and indexing early parish registers, although this task also is still incomplete.

Apart from the William Hamick baptized at Ermington in 1623, the only other Williams located are as follows: William Amocke, who in 1583 baptized a daughter Elizabeth in Ripon, Yorkshire; William Hamma, who in 1589 baptized children Elizabeth and Justinian at Kingston Upon Thames in Surrey[17]; William Emeces, who in 1634 baptized a daughter Sarah in Selborne, Hampshire; William Hamox, who in 1663 baptized a daughter Alice in Peterchurch, Hereford; William Hamack, who in 1677 baptized a daughter Jane in Ashburton, Devonshire; William Hamocke, baptized at St. Botolph Without Aldersgate, London, in 1689; William Hammock, baptized at St. Olave, Southwark, in 1692; William Hamick, baptized in 1692 at Totnes, Devonshire; William Hamack, baptized in 1716 at Ermington, Devonshire;

---

[16] Another possibility is that he first went to one of Britain's island colonies -- perhaps Bermuda or Barbados -- before venturing to Virginia.

[17] Other records for a William "Hammande" are found there in 1591, but a family of Hammocks is also found there from 1714 until 1736.

William Hamocke, son of William Hamocke, baptized at Madeley, Staffordshire, in 1718[18]; William Hammock, baptized at St. Dunston, Stepney, in 1724; William Hammock, baptized in 1733 at Marldon, Devonshire; William Humock, baptized in 1763 in Stannington, Yorkshire; William Hammock, baptized at Southwark, Surrey, in 1768; William Hammock, baptized in 1770 at Plymouth, Devonshire; William Hammocks, baptized in 1790 at Hammersmith, London; and William Hammock, baptized in 1799 at Southwark, Surrey.

The preceding references indicate that there were more than a dozen men living in England with the last name Hammack (and its variations) and the first name William between roughly 1600 and roughly 1800. This suggests that the name William was comparatively rare among individuals in England with the surname Hammack; moreover, it is notable that only two of them were living during the same years when William Hammack was likely living in England. William Emeces who baptized a child in 1634 was probably born by 1610; he could not have been the William Hammack who died in Richmond County, Virginia, in 1702, nor could he have been William Hamick of Ermington, Devonshire. William Hamox was living in Peterchurch, Hereford, in 1663, when he baptized daughter Alice, and William Hammack was living at Ashburton, Devonshire, in 1677, when he baptized a daughter Jane. Neither of these men could be the William who died in Richmond County, Virginia, in 1702, as he was living in Virginia by 1656. It seems unlikely -- although not impossible -- that William Hamick of Ermington was the father of either or both of these children. Hereford is about 150 miles northeast of Ermington, and there were other Hammack families in that area to which William of Peterchurch might have belonged. William of Ashburton in Devonshire is more problematic; the parish is a short distance from Ermington, and the Hammacks in both parishes were clearly related. Since this is the only reference to a William Hammack found after 1650 in Devonshire, it seems likely that this man was probably born in the 1650s and a grandson of John, Richard, or Leonard Hamick of Ermington.

What must be stressed, however, is that birth records have not been located for William Emeces of Hereford or William Hamox of Hampshire or William Hamox of Peterchurch. Most likely they were baptized in southeastern England in parishes whose registers have not survived or have not been indexed. Hence, the Ermington parish entry alone cannot be taken as positive proof that William Hammack of Richmond County, Virginia, is identical with William Hamick of Ermington, Devonshire. Yet, based on the available evidence, he seems the most promising candidate to have been this man.

Two other pieces of evidence should be considered. The first is that William Hammack of Richmond County, Virginia, fathered four known sons: William ("the elder"); John; Richard; and William ("the younger"). All three given names are found in among the Hamick, Hammack, and Hammock entries at Ermington before 1640. The second is that, of the Hammack families located in England in the 1841 and 1851 census returns, the majority indicated that they had originated in southeastern England, in either Devonshire or Cornwall.[19] Cumulatively, these two factors suggest that even if William Hammack of

---

[18] This William appears often in records from 1717 to about 1721. There is some evidence that his name may also have been spelled "Halmarak" and "Hamarik".

[19] England's 1841 Census showed sixteen individuals bearing the surname Hammack. They originated in the following locations: Lincolnshire (2); Devonshire (2); Kent (2). The other ten were born in Middlesex, Surrey, Essex, and Cornwall. The same census showed twenty-seven individuals bearing the surname Hammock. They originated in the following locations: Middlesex (14); York (1); Surrey (2); Suffolk (1); Staffordshire (2); Essex (3); Cheshire (1); Surrey (2); Lincolnshire (1).
In addition to these individuals, the following table summarizes alternative spellings:

Spelling	County	Number
Hammoc	Somerset	3
Hammac	Essex	1
Awmack	Yorkshire	7
Hammick	Devonshire	48
Hammick	Middlesex	9
Hammick	Surrey	1
Hammick	Lincolnshire	3

Richmond County, Virginia, was not the man baptized in Ermington in 1623, he was likely a member of this family and that his origins probably lie in southeastern England.

This more general conclusion leads us to a consideration of the Hammack surname and to the possibility of a common origin for English Hammack and Hammock families. In the pages that follow, we shall investigate the linguistic origins of Hammack and related surnames.

E. Hammack: Origins of the Name

Several possibilities exist for the origins of the surname Hammack or Hammock, depending on whether the name originated as a personal name or as a place name. The modern spelling Hammack may also have evolved over the centuries from another surname as regional pronunciations and spellings changed.

C. W. Bardsley, in *A Dictionary of English and Welsh Surnames With Special American Instances* (London, 1901), classified most English surnames beginning with "Ham" as either deriving from a baptismal name -- the son of Hamo -- or from a local name, 'of the ham,' which could refer to a particular dwelling (a home) or to a particular place (i.e., a parish name in the dioceses of Canterbury, Salisbury, Rochester, and elsewhere). Bardsley cites instances such as a Johannes Hamme in Yorkshire in 1379 and a Robert de la Hamme of Sussex in 1273 and John de Hamme of Wiltshire in the same year. Similar instances can be found in Cambridgeshire and Somerset during the reign of Edward III. Such surnames as Hamblett, Hamblett, Hamlet, Hamlett, Hamlin, Hamling, Hymlyn, Hamblin, Hambling, Hamman, Hammand, Hammett, Hammatt, Hammitt, Hammon, Hammond, Hammondson, Hammons, Hammonds, Hamnett, and Hamonet he classes in this category as meaning either "the son of Hamon" or deriving from a place name. In the case of Hamnet, for instance, Bardsley defines the meaning as "son of Hamon," from the diminutive Hamon-et, which was soon shortened to Hamnet. Another diminutive of the same name was Hamlet (Hamelot). Bardsley argues that "frequently both forms are ascribed to the same individual. In discussing Hammett, Hammatt, and Hammitt, Bardsley suggests that the surname means "son of Hamon" and is a modified form of Hamnet.[20]

The Surnames of Oxfordshire[21] offers a different evolution for this series of names. "There are consequently some topographical names that are found in East Anglia during the Middle Ages, and are at least not particularly in that region, but which have not been found in Oxfordshire during the same period. There are similarly surnames which occur in Oxfordshire, and often in the adjoining counties as well, but which have not been found in Norfolk. The surname *Hamme*, for instance, is derived from a word for a meadow or water-meadow, a word widely used in Oxfordshire field names, and occurring in field names over a wide area in the south of England and the southern part of the Midlands. *Hamme* occurs as a surname in Oxfordshire during the Middle Ages, though it is not particularly common, and it also occurs fairly frequently in some other southern and south Midland counties in the same period. It has not, however, been found in Norfolk during the Middle Ages. Significantly, the surname Meadow (atte Medwe, etc.) was fairly common in medieval Norfolk, but has not been found in Oxfordshire at that

---

The following spellings were not found in the 1841 census: Hammuck, Ammack, Ammic, Ammick, Ammock, Ammoc. Note that, of the various spellings shown, three Williams were found in Devon; the only other William was found in Middlesex.
Source: 1841 Census of England Database, The National Archives, Kew, Richmond, Surrey, TW9 4DU.

[20] C. W. Bardlsey, *A Dictionary of English and Welsh Surnames With Special American Instances* (London, 1901), pp. 1-8, 43, 57, 267. Most of these names came into existence early. The name Hamblett and its variations existed by the sixteenth-century; Hamlett was in use earlier. Bardsley cites examples in Cheshire of a reference in 1311 to "the wife of Richard, son of Hamelot." Hamelin de Humpton was living in the time of Henry III, and William Hamelin and Walter Hamline are found in Lincolnshire in 1273 and one Robertus Hamely in Yorkshire in 1379. Hamund le Mester was living in Huntingdonshire in 1273, and Hammund de Cursun in Shropshire. There are references to the name in Oxfordshire, Lincolnshire, London, and elsewhere during the thirteenth and fourteenth-centuries.

[21] R. McKinley, *The Surnames of Oxfordshire* (London, 1977), pp. 46-47.

period."[22] Hence, local linguistic customs may have given rise to very different surnames possessing a common meaning. If Hammack originated in southern England as a place name, a different word for the same geographical feature may have been used elsewhere in Britain.

The only possible match found at this point for the origins of William Hammack of Virginia is the William Hammick baptized in Devon in 1623. His death has not been found in the register for the parish in which he was born, and no record of a marriage or of offspring there has been located either. This leads one to suspect that he left the parish for one reason or another; he may have moved elsewhere in England, or he could be the immigrant to Virginia. Sir William Addison, in *Understanding English Surnames*[23] discusses nomenclature in Devon and surrounding areas, commenting on the tendency to reverse normal trends in shortening names and, instead, to add extra letters to preexisting names. This custom took place through the addition of letters in cases like Greenaway for Greenway and Hannaford for Hanford. Addison argues that in "the West of England the ear cannot endure a harsh conjunction of consonants." In that region, he suggests, Englishmen "played fast and loose with consonants as well as vowels," often adding a consonant at the end of a name as well. As evidence of this trend, Addison cites such examples as Simond for Simon, Hammond for Hamon, and Perking for Perkin. He also writes that, although some occupational names do occur, "it is the rural character of Devonshire that has determined its main surname structure."[24]

Since the greatest single concentration of references to this surname (Hammack, Hammock, Hamick, and the like) occur in southwestern England, it seems likely that the surname is of Devonshire origin. One should, then, ask the nature of its creation. Addison posits that, in "contrast to those of East Anglia, Devonshire surnames derived from places are not overwhelmingly those of towns or villages, but of local topographical features which would be known to everyone living in the community in which they arose. Most of them are notably earthy." As examples of this tendency he offers Clampytte for claypit, Fosse for ditch, Furzen for furze, Gribble for crab tree, Haye for hedge or enclosure, Knappe for hill summit, Heird for sheep farm, Kurne for mill, Twitchen for a place where a road forks. Twitchen, he notes, became a "common name in Devonshire," with its variants including the better known Tichner. Such dialectical modifications became common over time. "Fosse may be Forse, Vos, or Vose in the Doulting or Shepton Mallet districts of Somerset," he suggests. Many such Devonshire families taking their names from local geographical features predate the Norman Conquest of England in 1066, descending from the ancient

---

[22] Ibid., pp. 46-47, pp. 239-244. Regarding Hammond, Amund, and similar names, he writes: "The distribution of surnames derived from personal names, even as late as the 16th and 17th centuries, is undoubtedly due to the relative popularity, from region to region, of the personal names concerned at the period, basically from the 12th to the 14th century in the South, the Midlands, and East Anglia, when most such surnames were formed. Seman, for example, was one of the most popular masculine personal names in both Norfolk and Suffolk during that period, and it is no surprise that surnames derived from it are subsequently numerous in the same counties. Estimating the frequency of the name Hammond, he found 6 instances in Buckinghamshire (1523 subsidy), 6 in Dorset (1662-1664 Hearth Tax Returns), 27 in Norfolk (1522-25), 6 in Oxfordshire (1641-42 Protestation Returns), 3 in Oxfordshire (1665 Hearth Tax Returns), 2 in Staffordshire (1670, Hearth Tax Returns for two hundreds only), 42 in Suffolk (1523 subsidy), 34 in Surrey (1664 Hearth Tax Returns), 19 in Sussex (1523 subsidy), and 1 in Wiltshire (1576 lay subsidy). He writes: "The large number of Olivers in 17th century Dorset may be due to the growth of one prolific family, since many of the Olivers in that county lie closely grouped together, and a similar cause may lie behind some other cases in which surnames are especially numerous in one particular locality. It is difficult, however, to suppose that this explains the distribution of a name like Hammond, which was already a widespread surname in East Anglia in the early 14th century. In the Suffolk subsidy for 1327, for instance, there are 20 persons called Hammond, in 18 different places. In the Norfolk subsidy roll for 1329-30 there are 14 persons called Hamond or Ammund (and one more called Hamon), in fourteen different places. It cannot be supposed that a surname so widespread at such an early period could be due to the ramification of a single family, or even several families. The great number of Hammonds in Norfolk, Suffolk, and some other counties such as Surrey, can only be caused by an exceptional popularity in those counties, during the formative period of surnames, of the personal name from which the surname was derived."

[23] W. Addison, *Understanding English Surnames* (London, 1978), pp. 53-69.

[24] Addison, p. 63. He also notes that Devonshire was one of three counties particularly favored by settlers from across the Channel.

populations resident in the area before the West Saxons incorporated it into the kingdom of Wessex.[25]

If Hammick, Hammack, or Hammock were the original surname spelling, an origin as a Devonshire place name appears probable. One problem with that scenario, however, is the scarcity of references to the surname prior to the early seventeenth-century. Were Hammick (or some similar spelling) the original form of the name, one might expect earlier references to the surname as well as a greater concentration of individuals with this surname throughout southern England. Almost no reference to this surname has been found prior to 1600. Might Hammick then have been derived from another, older surname?

One strong possibility is that Hammick was a variation of Hammett, a far more common surname throughout the region.[26] The Devonshire Protestation return of 1642 for Ermington shows Arthur Hammocke, Henry Hammocke, John Hammocke, Sr., John Hammocke, Jr., John Hammocke, Leonard Hammocke, and Richard Hammocke. These entries are the only ones for this surname by any spelling found in the protestation return. Yet neither the name Hammack nor any immediate variation is present in the 1569 Muster Rolls of Cornwall, Devon, Dorset, or Somerset seventy years earlier.[27]

Ermington records clearly demonstrate that even in the seventeenth-century the surname Hammick was sometimes spelled Hammett. A lay subsidy role for Ermington from 1655 contains a reference to "John Street and his tenant Richard Hammett."[28] The 1674 Hearth Tax Return for Ermington shows that John Hammett was taxed with two hearths, while Henry Hammacke, John Hammacke, and "Leonard Hammett" were each taxed with a single hearth. Even the marriage record for John Hammick and Joane Sparkwill -- the parents of William Hammick baptized in 1623 -- give the groom's name as "John Hammat."

The muster rolls of 1569 are perhaps the best source for tracking the movement of surnames throughout southern England. The surname Hammett does not appear in the muster rolls for Dorset or Somerset, but, moving west, the surname appears in both Cornwall and Devon. At Powder, Fowey, Cornwall, in 1569 "John Hammet" was enumerated with a bow and twelve arrows. At Stratton, Poughyll, was another "John Hamett" with a bow and four arrows, while a third "John Hamatt" at Stratton, Stratton, also was mustered with a bow and four arrows. At Devon, in Harpforde Venotterye, East Budleigh, Richard Hamott was a billman, while at Tyverton, Tyverton Parish (very near to Ermington) Richard Hukley and "John Hamott" were mustered together while another John Hamot" was a pikeman.

Hammett, as we have seen, was often a diminutive form of the Old French personal name Hamo. Reaney gives the example of William Hamet in 1297 in Stoke Climsland, Cornwall.[29] This place, however, was one of three in Cornwall that contain Hammett as a minor place name, which suggests that, contrary to what the surname dictionaries indicate, these places are the source of the name and that, in

---

[25] Addison notes, however, that many post-Conquest families crossed the Channel and settled in Devon, among them the well known Courtenay family. The earliest known example of a surname similar to Hammack is from the Patent Rolls, 15 May 1322 to 11 May 1324, mentioning "John Hammok of Chechele," a reference to Chicheley in Buckinghamshire. John is not shown in the 1332 Lay Subsidy for Buckinghamshire, and the surname is not found in the 1522 Buckinghamshire muster. The line may have perished with his death. See Addison, p. 63, 242.

[26] This possibility was first suggested to the author by London researcher J. C. B. Sharp in 1999 (J. C. B. Sharp to Thomas Daniel Knight, 13 April 1999).

[27] The Protestation Return was taken as grievances concerning King Charles I intensified in England. On 3 May 1641, every member of the House of Commons was required to declare loyalty to the King and Parliament. This declaration was called their Protestation against "an arbitrarie and tyrannical government". Another order required every rector, churchwarden, and overseer of the poor make a similar Protestation Oath before the Justices of the Peace in the hundred in which they lived. This oath was to be a statement of their belief in "the Protestant religion, allegiance to the King and support for the rights and privileges of Parliament." Once they had taken the Protestation Oath, these men then returned to their own parishes, where they required the same oath of allegiance from all men over the age of eighteen. Individuals who refused to take the oath were to be noted and were assumed to be Roman Catholics. The 1641/2 Devonshire Protestation Return thus functions as a census of all males aged 18 and over in 1642. For a discussion of the Protestation Oath, see D. Cressy, "The Protestation Oath Protested, 1641 and 1642," *The Historical Journal*, 45 (2002): 251-279.

[28] Devonshire Lay Subsidy, 1655, 57 (PRO: E 179/245/11).

[29] L. M. Midgley, ed., *Ministers' Accounts of the Earldom of Cornwall, 1296-1297*, 2 vols. (Camden Society, 3rd ser., vols. 66, 68, 1942-1945), 68: 225.

these areas, at least, it has nothing to do with Hamo. The other two locations are in St. Neot and in Quethiode.[30] All these are towards the eastern end of Cornwall, an area whose inhabitants would naturally spread into Devon. Certainly the name does not seem to have originated in Devon as there are no examples at all in the 1332 Lay Subsidy.[31]

Hence, there exists a strong possibility that the family at Ermington moved there late in the sixteenth century, probably from Cornwall. Their name was perhaps originally Hammett, which was transformed into Hammack.[32]

In general, research into the origins of the Hammack surname leads to four overall conclusions. First, the surname Hammack may have been a diminutive form of another name. Among American researchers, Henry Franklin Hammack was the first to introduce this possibility. He wrote that William Hammack of Virginia had come from Wales and that he was a descendant of Halmarack, a Saxon lord living in England before the Norman Conquest.[33]

Evidence does suggest that the surname Hammack might have been a diminutive of Halmarack or of some similar name. Reaney and Wilson discuss diminutive forms of surnames that may be related to the surname Hammack, although they do not discuss the Hammack surname specifically.[34] Reaney and Wilson write that most English surnames evolved as local place names; as surnames indicating a relationship; as surnames indicating an occupation or office; and as surnames indicating a nickname.

Regarding diminutive surnames, it is useful to consider the following examples, which Reaney and Wilson suggest all derive from the Old French given name Hamo, a popular Norman name:[35]

> Hamlet, Hamlett, Hamblet, and Hamblett. Reaney and Wilson argue that these surnames evolved as a double diminutive of the given name Hamo (or Haim). The name first evolved into Hamel or Hamil by adding the suffix -el, producing Ham-el, a name meaning "little Hamo." Later, the suffix -et was added to produce Hamel-et, meaning "little Hamel."

> Hamelin, Haimelin. This name originated also as a diminutive form of Haimo. Modern

---

[30] O. J. Padel, *Cornish Place-Name Elements* (1985). This volume was published as volumes LVI-LVII of the *English Place Name Society* series.

[31] The most common forms of this surname are Hammet and Hammot. Further evidence of this relationship between Hammett and Hammack can be found in Exeter. A John Hammett was taxed in the 1674 Hearth Tax rolls for Combe Martin in Exeter, while Exeter marriages indicate that John Hamocke of Combemartin, Esquire, married Margaret Ball of Kentesberry, spinster, in 1665.

[32] If this analysis is correct, it might also be possible for the surname to change forms between England and America. Given that the surname almost always appears with the ending "ck" in Virginia, it seems likely that this spelling had been used before William left England. J. C. B. Sharpe noted that William Hammack, Elder Adkin, Ann Smith, Barbara Matthews, Elizabeth Eaton, and William Barker were listed together in 1656 as headrights of James Price. Eaton, like Hammack, is a fairly distinctive surname, and Sharp noted that it appeared commonly in Devonshire near Exeter. He located both surnames near Exeter, Barnstable, and Totnes in the period shortly before William Hammack appears on the importation list. Sharp argued that, using the hypothesis that William Hammack's name might also be written Hammet, Hammett, or Hammatt, Totnes, Exeter, and Barnstable might also be considered as possible places of origin for William since the surnames Barker and Eaton are both found there also. Sharp noted the following possibilities: William Hammet, son of William, 1623, Coleridge, Dartmouth, St. Saviour; William Hammot, son of William and Edeth, 1637, Black Torrington, Holsworthy; William Hamett, son of Henry, 1637, Teignbridge, Moretonhampstead; William Hammett, son of George, 1643, Teignbridge, Moretonhampstead; William Hamatt, son of Richard and Johan, 1643, Crediton, Newton St. Cyres, Exeter; William Hammett, son of Richard, 1632, Shebbear, Alwington, Barnstable; William Hamott, son of William, 1645, Barnstable, Shebbear, Alwington; William Hamott, son of William and Elinor, 1638, Shebbear, Northam, Barnstable; and William, son of William and Elinor, 1642, Shebbear, Northam, Barnstable.

[33] Hammack, *Wandering Back*, 1: 1.

[34] P. H. Reaney and R. M. Wilson, *A Dictionary of English Surnames*, pp. 214-215.

[35] The authors note that English surnames reflect the many different cultures present in the British isles in the medieval period. They argue that the suffix "uc" or "ock" is Old English in origin and appears in names like Haddock, Whitlock, and Willock. French diminutives include -ot, -et, -un, -in, and -el, and appear in surnames such as Philpot, Hewett, Dickens, and Pannel. Double diminutives are not uncommon. The most frequently seen combinations are "-el-en" as in Hamlin; "-el-ot" as in Giblett; "-in-ot" as in Adnett; and "-et-in" as in "Turketine."

spellings include Hamlin, Hamlen, Hamlyn, Hamblen, Hamblin, and Hamlin. "Robertus filius Hamelin" is recorded in Devonshire as early as 1130.

Hammett, Hamet, Hamat, Hammatt. This surname evolved as a diminutive of Hamo also. William Hamet is recorded as early as 1297.

Hamnet. This surname derived also as a double diminutive of Hamo. It became first Ham-un and then Ham-un-et. Hamonet of Waltham is recorded as early as 1180. Other surnames derived in a similar fashion include Hammon and Hammond. The given name Hamandus, a diminutive of Haimo and Haimund, is found in Norfolk as early as 1145.

As noted, the surname Hammack (and its variants) may have evolved in the fifteenth and sixteenth centuries from Hammatt, as the final "tt" was transformed into "ck", reflecting regional differences in pronunciation from one location to another.[36]

Second, the surname Hammack may have originated as a place name. Many English surnames derived as indicators of place. For instance, Robert de la Hamme is recorded as early as 1255, and variants of this name included Ham, Hamm, Hamme, and Hami. A contemporary understanding of this name would have been Robert "who dwells in the flat, low-lying land by the stream." John Hammyg is recorded in Worcester in 1275 and James Hammyng in Sussex in 1327; here the surname had already evolved but meant "dweller in the Hamme." Scholars of Devonshire nomenclature have noted a large number of surnames deriving from place names indicating residence in or near a stream and thus having "Ham" as their root; the suffix -ic or -uc was often used as a diminutive in Devonshire. Thus one derivation of Hammack could be an evolution of Ham-m-ic, meaning dwelling in or around the Ham.

Third, it is probable that there were multiple evolutions of this surname and that not all Hammacks, Hammocks, and Hammicks are related. Two possible derivations of the surname Hammack have been discussed. One may have occurred as Hamo became Hammatt and then Hammack. The other may have evolved as a form of the place name Ham, meaning a dweller in the low-lying area near a stream.[37]

There are also at least two other possible sources for the surname. Reaney and Wilson indicate that many surnames evolved as nicknames. Examples cited in their study include Hallmark and Allmark. Forms of this surname include Allmark, Almack, Awmack, and Halfmark. Robert Alfmarck is found in the 1279 Rotuli Hundredorum living in Huntingdonshire, near present-day Cambridge. Adam Alfmark is found in Worcestershire in 1296 and Emma Halmark as early as 1324. John Awmack of Yorkshire appears a century later. Reaney and Wilson argue that this group of related surnames derived from "Half-a-mark," being a surname having to do with accounting and possibly indicating the value of an individual's landholding. Names such as Halfmark and Tenmark are traceable to the Germanic ancestry of modern English.

Fourth, in its modern renderings, the surname probably did not exist before the fifteenth century. Reaney and Wilson indicate that English surnames evolved slowly during the twelfth, thirteenth, and fourteenth centuries before becoming fixed. In heavily populated areas, surnames were adopted earlier; in

---

[36] Reaney and Wilson, *Dictionary*, pp. 214-215.

[37] Similarly, it is likely that not all American Hammack and Hammock families are related. Most American Hammacks and Hammocks descend from William "O" Hammack of Richmond County, Virginia. There was another, much smaller Hammack (also spelled Hammock and Hammick) family group that lived in Connecticut and upstate New York. That group clearly descends from a different immigrant, a person whose English progenitors may or may not be related to those of the Virginia Hammacks. Even within Virginia, there is no clear evidence -- although it is possible -- that the family of Rudolph Hammack of Frederick County, Virginia, was related to the family of William "O" Hammack of Richmond County. With the unusual given name Rudolph, it seems likely that the Frederick County Hammacks were German. Further, there is evidence of late nineteenth and early twentieth century families of Germanic descent living near the United States - Canada border whose surnames were anglicized as "Hammack" or something similar. With the exception of the line of Rudolph Hammack of Frederick County, Virginia, virtually all American Hammacks and Hammocks south and west of Maryland, from the Atlantic to the Pacific, do seem to descend from William "O" Hammack.

areas with a low population density, individuals were often designated by their given name only. Likewise, a surname might evolve slowly over several generations, differing slightly with each successive bearer. Hammack might then have been the final stage in the surname's evolution across several centuries.

F. English Origins: Conclusion

The surname Hammack and its variants -- including Hammock and Hammick -- was less common in England than it has been in North America, where the three surviving sons of the immigrant William Hammack produced a numerous progeny.

Based on the research conducted in England, it has been impossible to identify the immigrant William Hammack conclusively. Cumulatively, the evidence suggests that William's family probably originated in southwestern England, probably in Cornwall and Devon. There is a strong possibility that he was William Hammic, son of John Hammic (whose name was also spelled Hammack, Hammock, and Hamat), whose birth is recorded at Ermington in 1623.

The evidence suggests multiple origins for the surname Hammack. It might have originated as a diminutive form of the given names Halmarak or Hamo. Another explanation is that it may have originated as a nickname indicating the value of a family estate -- Halfmark -- which evolved into Awmack, Ammack, and possibly Hammack. A third explanation is that it may have been a place name, indicating a group of people who dwelt in the ham -- the low-lying flat land near a river or stream.

Those who have studied the Devonshire family suggest that the Hammicks, Hammocks, and Hammacks of Devonshire may originally have borne the surname Hammett. The surname Hammick and its variants have not been found in southwestern England much before 1600, and there is evidence during the seventeenth-century in villages such as Ermington -- where the spelling Hammick and Hammic was most common -- that the name was also written Hammett. Nowhere in southwestern England is the surname Hammick (by any spelling) found in the 1569 Muster Rolls, and Hammett does not appear in Dorset or Somerset. But six examples of the name are found in Cornwall and Devonshire:

John Hammet, in Powder, Fowey, Cornwall
John Hamett, in Stratton, Poughyll, Cornwall
John Hamatt, in Stratton, Stratton, Cornwall
Richard Hamott, in East Budleigh, Harpforde Venotterye, Devon
John Hamott, in Tyverton, Tyverton Parish, Devon
John Hamot, in Tyverton, Tyverton Parish, Devon

Tyverton Parish, Devonshire, is located near Ermington, where the family of John Hammick was living as early as 1607. It may be that the Ermington Hammacks descended from John Hamot who was living at Tyverton in 1569 and earlier from members of the same family living in eastern Cornwall.

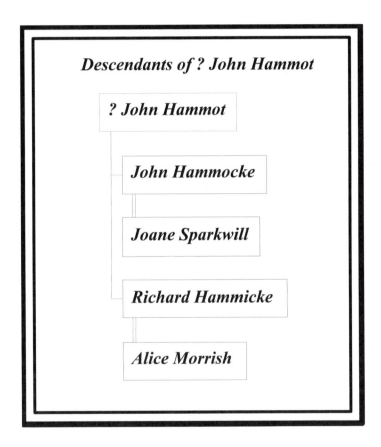

Descendants of ? John Hammot

? John Hammot

John Hammocke

Joane Sparkwill

Richard Hammicke

Alice Morrish

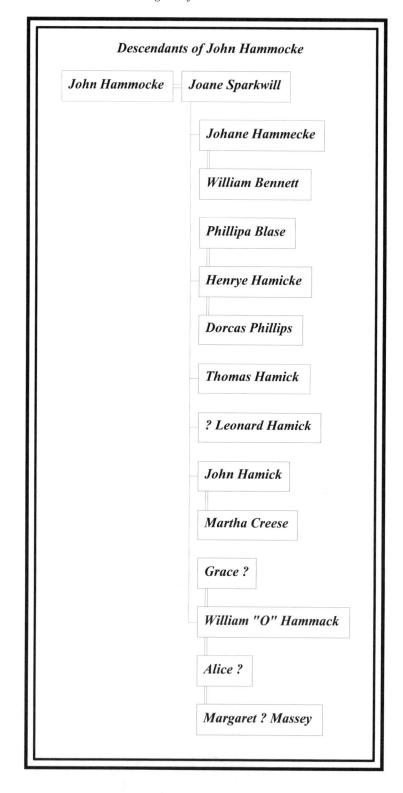

Descendants of John Hammocke

John Hammocke	Joane Sparkwill

Johane Hammecke

William Bennett

Phillipa Blase

Henrye Hamicke

Dorcas Phillips

Thomas Hamick

? Leonard Hamick

John Hamick

Martha Creese

Grace ?

William "O" Hammack

Alice ?

Margaret ? Massey

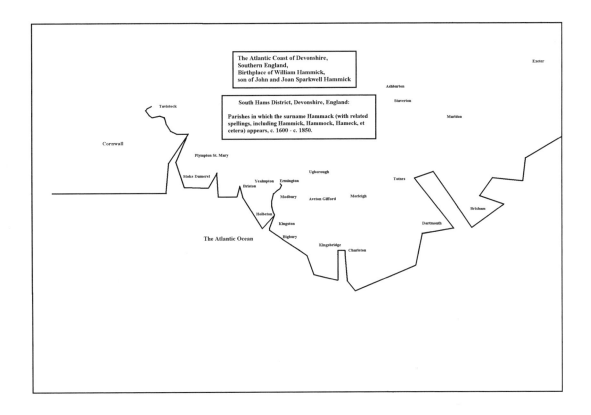

The Atlantic Coast of Devonshire,
Southern England,
Birthplace of William Hammick,
son of John and Joan Sparkwell Hammick

South Hams District, Devonshire, England:

Parishes in which the surname Hammack (with related
spellings, including Hammick, Hammock, Hameck, et
cetera) appears, c. 1600 - c. 1850.

Exeter

Ashburton

Staverton

Marldon

Tavistock

Cornwall

Plympton St. Mary

Stoke Damerel

Yealmpton   Ermington   Ugborough

Briston

Modbury

Aveton Gifford   Morleigh

Totnes

Brixham

Holbeton

Kingston

Dartmouth

Bigbury

The Atlantic Ocean

Kingsbridge   Charleton

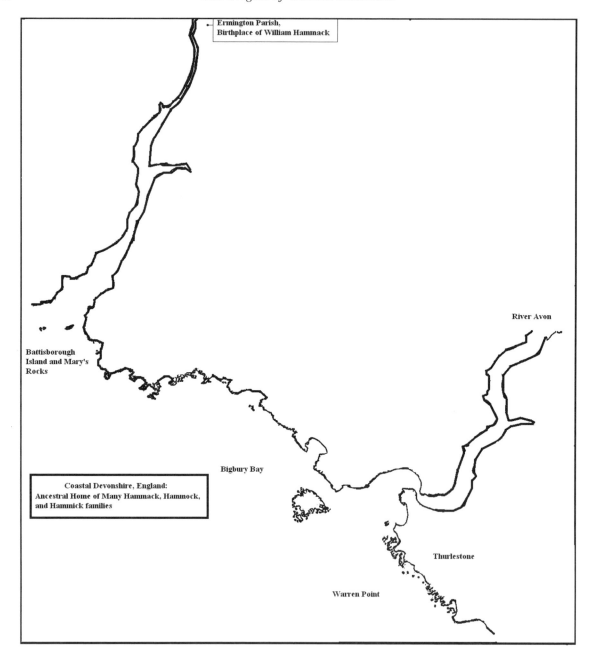

Ernington Parish,
Birthplace of William Hammack

River Avon

Battisborough
Island and Mary's
Rocks

Bigbury Bay

Coastal Devonshire, England:
Ancestral Home of Many Hammack, Hammock,
and Hammick families

Thurlestone

Warren Point

Chapter 3:

Hammacks of Ermington, Devon

There were three Hammack (Hammick, Hammock, Hammocke) families living in Ermington Parish, Devonshire, England, between about 1600 and 1650. John Hammick, Richard Hammick, and Leonard Hammick headed these families. Based on nomenclature and residence, it appears that these three men were closely related, but the available records do not allow us to determine their precise relationship. A summary of the information known about these men and their families appears below.

A. John Hammat (Hammick, Hammack, Hammocke).[38]

As "John Hammat," John married Joane Sparkwill on 23 November 1607 in Ermington, Devon. Both John and Joane were probably born about 1585. It seems likely that John and Richard Hammicke who married Alce Morrish at Ermington in 1611 may have been relatives -- probably brothers. Leonard Hammack was probably another brother, son, or nephew whose birth is not found in the Ermington records; he baptized six children at Ermington between 1644 and 1655. Another probable family member is Barnard Hammocke who married Elizabeth Rowse 27 July 1621 at Modbury, Devon[39]; note that Barnard Haimek, son of John Haimek of St. Mabyn, Cornwall, was born the same year.

Children of John Hammocke (Hamicke, Hammat) and Joan Sparkwell were:[40]

1. Johane Hammecke (5 October 1608, Ermington, Devon --). She may be the Joane Heamicke who married 22 February 1625, Ermington, Devon, William Bennett. (A Joan Hamich married Thomas Mounden there 23 August 1645.)

2. Henrye Hamicke (20 March 1610, Ermington, Devon --). He appears to have m. (1) 17 May 1636,

---

[38] In 1996, the author contracted Mrs. Jeannette Court to do research on the origins of this family. She wrote: "From the research already completed, you may well have tracked down the right family in Ermington, Devon, but we need a little more proof it at all possible. Just a few thoughts at this stage....I know you searched Hammack/ock/ick, but did you try Ammack/ock/ick? The addition and dropping of the H at the beginning of a name is so common, and A is a long way from H in alphabetical listings.

The Hearth Tax returns were dated 1662-1670. I must disagree with the preface to the printed edition of Devon returns in one respect. In my own experience and from Roger Fieldhouse's definitive survey, various classifications of hearth numbers have been proposed. Briefly these state 1 hearth for husbandmen, and the poorest members of society liable for the tax (remember that the very poor were exempt), 2-3 hearths most craftsmen, tradesmen and yeomen, 4-7 hearths for wealthier tradesmen and merchants, 8+ hearths for gentry and nobility. This can only be a rough guide since (for instance) many lesser gentry are to be found in houses with fewer than eight hearths. There was no-one in our parish with more than one!

From this I would think that John Hammack was probably in some sort of trade and could, perhaps, have left a will. The other tack to take might be to try to disprove William bap. 1623. If his burial or a will can be found, or a marriage for him and children baptized after 1656 -- then it can't be him. Rather a negative approach, but we must take a pragmatic view of research in this difficult period.

[39] Modbury is the parish joining Ermington, and several references to descendants of John Hamick are found there.

[40] The majority of Hammack references in Devon are found in Ermington. Isolated references to Hammacks have been found in several other Devon parishes. It is clear from the surviving Ermington records that either they are incomplete or that Hammack references must also be recorded in adjoining parishes. For instance, many of the Ermington Hammicks vanish from the Ermington registers; a few appear later in surrounding parishes. Likewise, there are marriages in Ermington for Hammacks who do not appear elsewhere in the surviving parish registers:

Elizabeth Hamick married John Quick, 2 April 1646, Ermington, Devon.
Piety Hammick married Anthony Shinner 25 October 1677, at Ermington, Devon.

There are marriages for Margaret Hamack at Ringmore by Kingsbridge in 1733; for Ruth at Upottery in 1655; for Johan (possibly of Ermington) at Ugborough in 1668; and for Henery (also possibly of Ermington) at Staverton in 1690.

Ermington, Devon, Phillipa Blase, who died after 1642, and (2) 27 May 1645, Ermington, Devon, Dorcas Phillips.

By first marriage:

1. Joan Hamick (29 March 1637, Ermington, Devon --). She may be the Johane Hamick who married Thomas Elwill at Yealmpton, Devon, on 18 November 1657. Note that Michael Hammack reared a large family at Yealmpton, where his descendants remained for several generations.

2. Dorrytye Hamick (1 January 1639, Ermington, Devon --). She may be the Dorothy Hammick who married Daniel Ball 1 October 1675, Ermington, Devon.

3. Thomas Hamick (22 April 1642, Ermington, Devon --). As Thomas Hammick, he m. 15 May 1671, Ermington, Devon, Agnes Reckwood. He seems likely to be the Thomas Hammick who with wife Agnes baptized the following children:

> 1. Phillippa Hammick (8 March 1671/72, Ermington, Devon --). She may be the Phillipa Hammick who married 7 May 1700, Ermington, Devon, John Hutchins. She may also be the Phillippa Hammick, a single woman, who was mother of:
>
>> 1. Elizabeth Hamick (14 April 1689, Ugborough, Devon --).
>
> 2. Sarah Hammick (22 June 1675, Ermington, Devon --).
> 3. Thomas Hammick (28 January 1679, Ermington, Devon --).
> 4. Christopher Hamick (25 December 1684, Ermington, Devon --).
>
> 5. Michael Hamick (25 December 1684, Ermington, Devon --), m. 23 November, 1707, Yealmpton, Devon[41],
>
>> 1. Agnis Hammack (24 June 1709, Yealmpton, Devon --).[42]
>>
>> 2. Michael Hammick (2 April 1713, Yealmpton, Devon --). His mother's name is not shown in the christening record. He fits to be the Michael Hammick who with wife Elizabeth began baptizing children at Yealmpton, Devon, in 1733. Offspring:
>>
>>> 1. Agnes Hammick (8 March 1733, Yealmpton, Devon --).
>>>
>>> 2. Michael Hamick (26 April 1736, Yealmpton, Devon --). He is likely the Michael Hammick with wife Mary who baptized the following children:
>>>
>>>> 1. Michael Hammick (27 December 1765, Yealmpton, Devon --). He is probably the Michael Hammick who married Frances and reared a family at Yealmpton, Devon. Michael may have married

---

[41] One Johan Hamock married Thomas Elwill 18 November 1667 at Yealmpton, Devon.
[42] One Agnes Hamick married John Chaffe 9 June 1709 at St. Mary Arches, Exeter, Devon.

(2) Ann, with whom he christened five children at St. Petrox, Dartmouth, Devon, between 1797 and 1807.

1. John Hammick (23 September 1788, Yealmpton, Devon --). He fits to be the John Hammick who with wife Mary began baptizing children at Yealmpton in 1814. The name was spelled Hemmick, Hammick, and Hamick.

1. John Hemmick (20 May 1814, Yealmpton, Devon --). He may be the John Hamach or Hamack who with wife Mary baptized these children at St. Columb Minor, Cornwall:

1. Mary Julia Anna Hamach (22 April 1854, St. Columb Minor, Cornwall --).

2. Julia Hamack (2 July 1857, St. Columb Minor, Cornwall --).

2. Michael Hammick (27 October 1816, Yealmpton, Devon --).

3. Betsey Hamick (13 September 1818, St. Columb Minor, Cornwall, Devon --).

4. Mary Anne Hammick (5 November 1820, Brixton and Yealmpton, Devon --).

5. Richard Hammick (17 August 1823, Brixton and Yealmpton, Devon --).

2. Mary Hammick (19 October 1790, Yealmpton, Devon --).

Michael Hammick and wife Ann baptized five children at St. Petrox, Dartmouth, Devon, between 1797 and 1807:

3. Mary Ann Hammick (22 January 1797, St. Petrox, Dartmouth, Devon --).

4. Agness Hammick (14 April 1799, St. Petrox, Dartmouth, Devon --).

5. Michael Hammick (21 June 1801, St. Petrox, Dartmouth, Devon --).

6. Elizabeth Hammick (21 October 1804, St. Petrox,

Dartmouth, Devon --).

7. Robert Paterson Hammick (11 January 1807, St. Petrox, Dartmouth, Devon --).

2. Mary Hammick (22 January 1768, Yealmpton, Devon --).

3. John Hamick (7 September 1740, Yealmpton, Devon --).

6. Elizabeth Hamick (25 December 1684, Ermington, Devon --).
7. Ann Hammick (18 May 1688, Ermington, Devon --).

By second marriage:

4. Penticost Hammick (2 April 1646, Ermington, Devon --).

5. John Hamick (22 May 1648, Ermington, Devon --). He might be the John Hammick who married Elizabeth Slevell at Ermington on 2 February 1669. The first child identified as an offspring of John and Elizabeth Hammick was John, baptized 13 June 1673, but they may also have been the parents of Henry Hammick, baptized 5 November 1670, who is shown as son of John Hammick. On that basis he is listed below as eldest son:

1. Henry Hammick (5 November 1670, Ermington, Devon --).

2. John Hammick (13 June 1673, Ermington, Devon --). He was of an age to have been the John Hammack who in 1692 baptized a son John Hammock at Ashburton:

1. John Hammock (28 February 1692, Ashburton, Devon --).

3. Stephen Hammicke (10 June 1677, Ermington, Devon --). He may be the Stephen Hammick who with wife Jane baptized the following children:

1. Johannah Hammick (12 August 1711, Ermington, Devon --).

2. Stephen Hammick (27 April 1714, Ermington, Devon --). He may be the Stephen Hammick who with wife Prudence baptized the following children:

1. Stephen Hammick (31 August 1744, Ermington, Devon --).

3. William Hammick (19 October 1716, Ermington, Devon --).
4. Jane Hammick (7 August 1719, Ermington, Devon --).
5. Joan Hammick (30 May 1722, Ermington, Devon --).
6. Amy Hammick (9 January 1724, Ermington, Devon --).

4. Mary Hammick (11 February 1680, Ermington, Devon --).
5. Samuel Hamick (16 January 1683, Ermington, Devon --).
6. George Hamick (5 November 1685, Ermington, Devon --).

6. Dorcas Hamick (4 February 1650, Ermington, Devon --). She may be the Dorcas Hammick

who married John Gunnett 29 November 1672 at Ermington, Devon.

7. Henrie Hamicke (9 August 1653, Ermington, Devon --). He may be the "Henry Hammack, Mariner, of Armington, Devon," who wrote his will 18 September 1693. He appointed Elizabeth Byles, wife of John Byles, of Bermondsey, Mariner, lawful attorney.[43]

He could be the Henry Hammick who was father of:

    1. Henry Hammicke (24 May 1683, Totnes, Devon --).

8. Arthur Hamick (8 November 1655, Ermington, Devon --). He is likely the Arthur Hammack who reared a large family at Totnes, Devon, the oldest of whom was baptized in 1683:

    1. Agnes Hamocke, "daughter of Arther" (28 August 1683, Totnes, Devon --).

    2. Arther Hammacke, "son of Arther" (19 August 1685, Totnes, Devon --). He seems likely to have been the Arthur Hammick who was father of:

        1. Arthur Hammick (27 September 1723, Marldon, Devon --).

        2. Nicholas Hammick (4 March 1726, Marldon, Devon --).

        3. John Hammick (26 April 1728, Marldon, Devon --).

        4. Charity Hammick (26 February 1731, Marldon, Devon --).

        5. William Hammick (11 December 1733, Marldon, Devon --).

        6. Samuel Hammick (13 April 1736, Marldon, Devon --).

        7. Honiwell Hammick (15 March 1739, Marldon, Devon --). Honiwell Hammack and wife Elizabeth baptized at least one child, a son:

            1. Samuel Hammack (14 February 1772, Brixham, Devon --), who with wife Elizabeth [------] had several children also baptized at Brixham:

                1. Elizabeth Hammick (25 September 1806, Brixham, Devon --).

                2. Samuel Hammack (20 August 1809, Brixham, Devon --).

                3. Ann Hammack (9 June 1811, Brixham, Devon --).

                4. Horatio Honniwill Hammick (14 March 1816, Brixham, Devon --).

                5. Anna Mary Hammick (24 July 1817, Brixham, Devon --).

---

[43] Prerogative Court of Canterbury, Will of Henry Hammack, Mariner, Probate 11/416.

      6. Eliza Elizabeth Hammick (4 February 1819, Brixham, Devon --).

      7. John Wotton Hammick (7 December 1820, Brixham, Devon --).

   8. Thomas Hammick (30 January 1742, Marldon, Devon --).

  3. William Hamicke, "son of Arthur" (20 April 1692, Totnes, Devon --).

9. Samuel Hamick (19 March 1657, Ermington, Devon --).

10. Michael Hamick (2 January 1660/1, Ermington, Devon --).

Michael came of age and married in Ermington. He was a son of Henry Hamick and Dorcas Phillip of Ermington. Michael Hamick married Susannah Godfree 1 January 1683/84 at Ermington, Devon. The Ermington registers show only one child, Richard, born in 1684, but there may have been others:

  1. Richard Hamick (5 September 1684, Ermington, Devon --). He fits to be the Richard Hammick who with wife Agnes began baptizing children at Ermington in 1717, although he could also have been the son of John and Marie. Offspring of Richard and Agnes Hammick:

    1. Mary Hammick (3 January 1717, Ermington, Devon --).
    2. Tomasin Hammick (8 March 1722, Ermington, Devon --).
    3. John Hammick (7 October 1726, Ermington, Devon --).

3. Thomas Hamick (c. 1612, Ermington, Devon -- 1636, Ermington, Devon).

4. John Hamick (6 February 1619, Ermington, Devon --). He likely married 25 November 1645, Ermington, Devon, Martha Creese (28 February 1620, Ermington, Devon --), daughter of Nicholas Creese. He seems likely to have been the John Hamicke/Hamick who with wife Martha (also shown as Mathew) baptized these children:

  1. John Hamicke (1646, Ermington, Devon -- 1646, Ermington, Devon).

  2. Sarah Hamicke (10 December 1647, Ermington, Devon --). Her mother's name is shown as Mathew, which often appears among women as a misrepresentation of the name Martha. She fits to be the Sarah Hammick who married Bartholomew Fox 20 October 1674, Ermington, Devon.

  3. Marye Hamicke (31 December 1650, Ermington, Devon --).

  4. Christopher Hamick (29 April 1653, Ermington, Devon --), probably m. (1) 5 May 1679, Ermington, Devon, Mary Lambert, m. (2) 30 January 1679, Ermington, Devon, Mary Revell. They were the parents of:

    1. Martha Hammick (30 January 1680, Ermington, Devon --).

    2. Hannah Hamick (30 May 1682, Ermington, Devon -- 1751, Modbury, Devon), m. 18 March 1704, Modbury, Devon, Abraham Lethbridge (26 December 1682, Modbury,

Devon --).

3. John Hammick (10 February 1687, Ermington, Devon --).

5. Elizabeth Hamicke (31 July 1655, Ermington, Devon --). She may have married John Ellis, 13 April 1681, Ermington, Devon.

6. Thomas Hamick (2 October 1657, Ermington, Devon --). He seems likely to be the Thomas Hammick who with wife Mary baptized the following children:

    1. Mary Hammick (23 March 1679, Ermington, Devon --).
    2. Robert Hamick (17 January 1681, Ermington, Devon --).
    3. Mathew Hamick (8 April 1683, Ermington, Devon --).

7. John Hamicke (29 July 1662, Ermington, Devon --). His mother's name is shown as Mathew. He may be the John Hammick who married Mary Stevens in 1680 and who with wife "Marie" baptized at least one child:

    1. Richard Hamick (18 May 1683, Ermington, Devon -- 1742).

This John Hammick may be the same individual who married a woman named Thomazin and baptized six children in Ermington between 1699 and 1709:

    2. Henery Hammick (10 November 1699, Ermington, Devon --).
    3. John Hamack (11 March 1701, Ermington, Devon --).
    4. Mary Hamack (11 November 1703, Ermington, Devon --).

    5. Charles Hammack (10 April 1706, Ermington, Devon --). He fits to be the Charles Hammack who was of age by 1739 with wife Mary when they began baptizing offspring at Stoke Damerel, Devon. Children:

        1. John Hamilk (20 May 1739, Stoke Damerel, Devon --). He is likely the John Hammick who with wife Grace baptized the following children:

            1. Elizabeth Hammick (11 May 1763, Stoke Damerel, Devon --).

            2. John Hammick (6 October 1764, Stoke Damerel, Devon --).

            3. John Hammack (7 October 1765, Batter Street Presbyterian Church, Plymouth, Devon --).

            4. Elizabeth Hammick (7 December 1767, Batter Street Presbyterian Church, Plymouth, Devon --).

            5. William Hammack (27 March 1770, Batter Street Presbyterian Church, Plymouth, Devon --).

            6. John Hammack (11 April 1774, Batter Street Presbyterian Church, Plymouth, Devon --).

    2. Mary Hamick (25 January 1740, Stoke Damerel, Devon --).
    3. Charles Hamick (2 November 1743, Stoke Damerel, Devon --).
    4. Catherine Hammick (11 June 1749, Stoke Damerel, Devon --).

    6. Thomazin Hammack, "daughter of John" (9 April 1708, Ermington, Devon --).

    7. George Hammack (28 January 1709, Ermington, Devon --).

5. William Hamick (11 July 1623, Ermington, Devon --). No further record of him has been found in the Ermington Register or any other English source. He may be the William Hammack who went to Virginia in or before 1656 and who died there about 1703.

B. Richard Hammicke (Hammeck, Hammack, Hamecke).

Richard Hammicke married Alce Morrish on 18 November 1611 at Ermington, Devon. They were the parents of at least five children baptized at Ermington between 1614 and 1624:

1. Richard Hammick (2 December 1614, Ermington, Devon --).

2. Arthur Hamecke (27 July 1616, Ermington, Devon --). He may have been the Arthur who lived at Ashburton and was father of:[44]

    1. Richard Hammeck (23 September 1648, Ashburton, Devon --).
    2. Edward Hamecke (4 October 1654, Ashburton, Devon --).

3. John Hammeck (23 May 1619, Ermington, Devon --).

4. Sara Hamick (12 August 1621, Ermington, Devon --).

5. Joan Hamick (16 April 1624, Ermington, Devon --). Her mother's name is shown as Alce.

C. Leonard Hamick (by c. 1620 --) and Marye [-----].

Leonard was of an age to have been a son of John or of Richard Hamick. His connection to the other Hammick families has not been established, however.

1. Alice Hamick (2 March 1644, Ermington, Devon --).

2. Remond Hamick (8 February 1645, Ermington, Devon --).

3. Anne Hamick (28 March 1647, Ermington, Devon --). She may be the Ane Hammicke who married John Feasant 5 May 1668, Ermington, Devon.

4. Mary Hamicke (16 October 1649, Ermington, Devon --). She may be the Mary Hammick who married Samuel Wakeham, 24 October 1676, Ermington, Devon.

---

[44] One William Hammack also lived at Ashburton, where he baptized at least one child. Based on baptismal records, he was probably born about 1655. His daughter Jane Hammack was christened at Ashburton on 30 September 1677.

5. Samuel Hamicke (23 July 1652, Ermington, Devon --).

6. Isett Hammicke (5 May 1655, Ermington, Devon --).[45]

D. Conclusion.

The families of John, Richard, and Leonard Hammick (Hammack, Hammock, Hamecke) were living in Ermington Parish, Devonshire, England, from the during the first half of the seventeenth-century. John Hammick's family was the largest numerically, and many of his descendants remained in Devonshire into the nineteenth and twentieth centuries. William Hammack of Richmond County, Virginia, may have been the William, son of John and Joane Sparkwell Hammick, who was baptized in Ermington, Devonshire, in 1623.

---

[45] Isett was apparently a daughter.

Descendants of John Hammack (Hammock, Hammick, Hammot)

John Hammack (Hammock, Hammick, Hammot)

- **John Hammocke**
- **Joane Sparkwill**
- **Richard Hammicke**
- **Alice Morrish**

Joane Sparkwill
- Johane Hammecke
- William Bennett
- Phillipa Blase
- Henrye Hamicke
- Dorcas Phillips
- Thomas Hamick
- ? Leonard Hamick
- John Hamick
- Martha Creese
- Grace ?
- William "O" Hammack
- Alice ?
- Margaret ? Massey

Alice Morrish
- Richard Hammick
- Arthur Hamecke
- John Hammeck
- Sara Hamick
- Joan Hamick
- ? Elizabeth Hamick
- John Quick

Chapter 4:

William "O" Hammack in Virginia,
1656 - 1702

The earliest known reference to William Hammack dates from 1656, when he was among a group of six individuals claimed as headrights by James Price. According to the headright system created in 1619, any Virginian might claim fifty acres for each person whose passage into the colony he or she paid. In all likelihood, the six persons for whom Price claimed 300 acres were all indentured servants whom Price intended to use as labor on his plantations. On 9 October 1656, Price patented 300 acres on Matchotanke Creek.[46]

For the next decade, records are silent concerning William Hammack, his whereabouts, and his activities. As an indentured servant, he was required to serve seven to nine years for his master, depending on the terms of his indenture. If the 1656 date corresponds to his arrival in the country, he likely acquired his freedom between 1663 and 1666. Although we do not find William in legal records until several years after this, it is clear that he was still in the colony and married by about 1668 or 1669, when his eldest known son, William, was born.

As an indentured servant, William likely led a hard life. Virginia in the seventeenth century was notoriously harsh. Tobacco had been the colony's dominant cash crop since John Rolfe discovered that it would thrive in Virginia's rich soil in 1614. The colony experienced a boom in the 1620s and 1630s, and tobacco continued to be a path to enrichment for several decades thereafter. The key ingredients in this formula -- since tobacco was land and labor intensive -- were large tracts upon which to grow tobacco and a large number of workers to cultivate it.[47]

Because the environment in Virginia was so unlike that in England, English settlers in the colony experienced heavy mortality during the first half-century of settlement. In 1619, when the House of Burgesses -- the first representative political assembly in North America -- met for the first time, the minutes record that Burgess Shelley died while the assembly broke for lunch. Death was a common incident in the colony. Accidents were frequent, but more common were illnesses such as typhus or death as a result of the "seasoning" that new settlers experienced within a few months of reaching the tobacco colony.[48]

As a result of this high level of mortality, slavery did not become common in the Chesapeake until the late seventeenth century. Slaves cost about five times as much as servants, and, although a slave's labor would belong to the master for life rather than for a fixed term, servants and slaves were equally likely to die within a couple of years of reaching the colony. Hence most settlers with means purchased indentured servants for a fixed term, and for each servant they brought into the colony they also received a headright of 50 acres. A planter wealthy enough to bring twenty servants into the colony would thus receive a grant for 1000 acres of land. If he turned a profit, he would likely bring more servants to the colony and, in turn, receive even more land.[49]

Until mid-century, it was thus possible, perhaps even common, for ordinary planters to amass a substantial plantation within a few years, and many industrious servants who survived their indentures went on to acquire considerable estates as well as political and social eminence. In such a situation, planters hungry for wealth often abused their servants in order to maximize profits, and under the best of circumstances a servant's life was rigorous. Often servants slept in a loft or barn; although they generally ate with their masters and their families, the provisions were often simple -- corn-based products, pork meat, bread, and, along the coast, fish and oysters. To drink most early Chesapeake settlers relied on beer,

---

[46] Nugent, *Cavaliers and Pioneers*, I: 302.
[47] Middleton, *Colonial America*, pp. 47-54.
[48] Morgan, *American Slavery*, pp. 101-102, 115.
[49] Ibid., 94.

cider, or wine, for, given the colony's tainted water supply, fermented beverages were safer for consumption than natural ones.[50]

The biggest threat to servants was an unscrupulous master who would require tremendous amounts of labor from them. In 1678, a servant along the James River named Thomas Herriot murdered his master and mistress with an ax. Not only had they overworked Herriot, but Mistress Williamson had also scolded him constantly. In a confession penned shortly before his hanging, Herriot told how his mistress had harangued him constantly with her "sharp tongue." Given the circumstances in which he lived and worked, Herriot at length decided the best course of action was to murder the Williamsons and attempt an escape. His plan was foiled when he became lost in Virginia's thick forests and was forced to ask other settlers for directions. He was apprehended, tried, and executed. Unfortunately, many settlers who came to Virginia with great expectations found them frustrated, either by the harsh climate or the unscrupulous Virginia settlers with whom they were forced to deal. All too often an early death was the result.[51]

Another problem that servants encountered was an attempt to prolong their periods of indenture. Servants who successfully completed their contract usually received a gun, a suit of clothing, and basic provisions for a year; they were then often hired back by their former masters at a fixed wage for a year or more. Under these conditions, in time they might acquire land and servants of their own.

In order to get additional labor from these vulnerable workers and to diminish the pool of settlers vying for a limited land supply, masters found ways legally to extend indentures. The most common extensions occurred as a result of some real or alleged violation on the part of a servant. Female servants who became pregnant often had their terms extended by several years to make up for time lost while with child as well as for the trouble caused the master by the whole affair. Servants who were responsible for damage to their master's property, who ran away, who stole property belonging to their master, or who were guilty of fornication or fathering children out of wedlock often had their contracts extended as well.[52]

The records are silent regarding James Price's relations with his servants, but William Hammack's life as a servant was almost certainly a harsh one; at best, he would have worked long hours in the colony's tobacco fields while living in the simplest of ways.

Yet fortune smiled on the immigrant William. Unlike many of his peers, he lived to fulfill the entire period of his indenture, to acquire his freedom, and to live for another three decades in the colony. He acquired land and servants himself and in some measure fulfilled the dream that drew most migrants to the Chesapeake during the seventeenth century.

Twelve years after Price's land grant named William Hammack as one of his headrights, the former servant appears on the west side of Chesapeake Bay in what was then Rappahannock County. Named for a group of Native Americans who were part of the powerful Powhattan Confederacy, the Rappahannock River is the third of Virginia's four great rivers that shape the state's topography. The fourth, the Potomac, forms the boundary between Virginia and Maryland. The swath of land between the Rappahannock and Potomac Rivers forms Virginia's Northern Neck. In 1649, days before his execution, King Charles I of England had granted the entire Northern Neck to a group of loyal supporters; after the Restoration of Charles II to the English throne in 1660, the proprietors appointed an agent to supervise land grants and the collection of annual land taxes, called quitrents. One of the new counties formed in this area was Rappahannock, and, like Lancaster, it spanned both sides of the mighty river.[53]

William Hammack settled on the north bank of the Rappahannock in the region that in 1692 would become Richmond County, where William's descendants have resided for more than three centuries. The

---

[50] Ibid., pp. 182-183.

[51] T. H. Breen, J. H. Lewis, and K. Schlessinger, "Motive for Murder: A Servant's Life in Virginia, 1678," *William and Mary Quarterly*, 3rd Ser., xl (1983): 116-117.

[52] For more on this theme, see J. R. Pagan, "Law and Society in Restoration Virginia" (D. Phil. Thesis, University of Oxford, 1996) and J. R. Pagan, *Anne Orthwood's Bastard* (Oxford, 2004).

[53] Old Rappahannock Co., VA, DB 3, pp. 477-479; Morgan, *American Slavery*, pp. 244-245.

first recorded reference to him there dates from 1668, when he witnessed a property transaction. At that time, James Samford -- who would be a neighbor for the next quarter of the century -- purchased several cows, calves, and yearlings from George Greene. Livestock transactions were common in the Chesapeake, and, next to tobacco and land, livestock were one of the most valuable commodities in the colony. Together with Johanna Freshwater, William Hammack was one of the two witnesses to the transaction. This is also the first known instance in which he used his mark, "O", to sign a legal instrument. The use of a mark suggests that William could not write, at least well enough to sign his name. Precisely why he chose to use "O" is not known; often settlers used the first letter of their surnames or given names, and the mark likely had some personal significance for William. He continued to use the same mark for the rest of his life, the last time being when he signed his will in 1701.[54]

Having researched the chronology of William Hammack's life, it is difficult to resist concluding that this initial entry into the records involving Johannah Freshwater is not significant. Evidence suggests that for the next decade Hammack had some close relationship with the Freshwaters. He likely was living on their plantation as a hired laborer when he signed the deed in 1668, and over time there may have been some family connection between the two. No documentary evidence exists to prove what this connection may have been, but Hammack may have married a female relative of one of the Freshwaters.[55]

On 3 March 1672/3, Thomas Freshwater of Rappahannock County deeded to "William Hamock" a tract of 300 acres of land in Rappahannock County. According to the terms of the deed, Hammack had already conveyed to Freshwater 3000 pounds of tobacco as payment. It seems likely that, upon receiving his freedom, Hammack had begun working for the Freshwaters. Afterwards, he likely rented a portion of the Freshwater lands and then, with tobacco grown there, acquired enough money over several years to purchase the tract he had previously been renting.[56] Johannah Freshwater joined her husband Thomas in the deed and then on the same day in a separate transaction appointed "Mr. Henry Clerke" her attorney to acknowledge her dower release.[57]

The land that Thomas Freshwater conveyed to Hammack had been patented 24 August 1664 by Thomas Freshwater, John Webley, and Robert Davis. Baptized in England in 1633, Thomas Freshwater was a son of Edward Freshwater of Oxfordshire; in 1649 he was apprenticed to the Oxford Guild and in

---

[54] Old Rappahannock Co., VA, DB 3, pp. 477-479.

[55] Some have concluded that William Hammack was Johanna Freshwater's son by a previous marriage, but this seems impossible. Why researchers have reached this conclusion should be addressed, however. On 3 March 1672/3, "Joane Freshwater the Lawfull Wife of Thomas Freshwater of the County of Rappa. and Parrish of Farnham" did "make and appoint Mr. Henry Clerke my true and lawfull attorney for me and in my place to acknowledge a parcell of land containing three hundred acres *sold by aforesd Husband William Hamock* as by Deed of Writing from under both our hands and seals will appear at the County Court abovesaid next held ratifying and confirming the same to be as authentick as if I myself were personally present." A cursory examination of this document has led some researchers to conclude that Johanna had first married the indentured servant William Hammack, that he had acquired land in Rappahannock, that he was deceased by 1673, and that the William Hammack alive in Rappahannock in 1673 was her son. This scenario is impossible for several reasons. First, born Joanna Haslelock, Johannah Freshwater was baptized 28 May 1649 at St. Lawrence Jewry in London. She was married to Thomas Freshwater by 1666, when she first appears in the colony. She could not therefore have had an adult son by 1673. Apart from chronology, however, a careful study of the transactions explains what is obviously a clerical error. In a 1672/3 deed immediately preceding this item, Thomas Freshwater had deeded property to William Hammack. In this instrument, Johannah is releasing any legal rights she had to this property. The "aforesaid husband" was Thomas Freshwater, who had just made the deed to William Hammack. Thus, the clerk had omitted "to" when copying the original handwritten deposition into the minute book. If rendered *sold by aforesd. Husband to William Hamock"* this statement is perfectly consistent with the deed immediately preceding it. Since the publication of *Index to Marriages, Old Rappahannock & Essex Counties, Virginia, 1655-1900*, which appears to "document" the Hammack-Freshwater marriage, incautious researchers have regarded William Hammack as the son of a hypothetical earlier William Hammack and wife Johannah. This was manifestly not the case.

Note that the North Farnham Parish Registers document only two Freshwater children: Michael, in 1672, and Joanna in 1677. Deed records establish that Thomas -- born by about 1675 and perhaps earlier -- was also a son. He married Mary Hudson, who married (2) William Linton, another Hammack neighbor.

If a Hammack-Freshwater connection existed, the likeliest scenario is that Grace [----] Hammack may have been a servant of the Freshwaters or a relative of one of them who had recently come from England.

[56] Old Rappahannock County, VA, Deed Book 1672-76, Part I, p. 89-90.

[57] Old Rappahannock County, VA, Deed Book 1672-76, Part I, p. 89-90.

1655 -- a year before William Hammack appears in the colony's records -- he, too, had come to Virginia as an indentured servant, evidently in the employ of Humphrey Booth. By 1664, he was a free man. Together with John Webley and Robert Davis, by 1664 he had amassed enough resources to import 145 persons into the colony, earning the trio the right to 7,220 acres of land in Rappahannock and Northumberland Counties.[58] Later, in 1673, Freshwater deeded 250 acres of this land to Dennis Swellivant, who already owned land adjacent the Freshwater holdings in Rappahannock.[59]

William Hammack's land is mentioned again in a 1678 deed[60], but Hammack himself does not appear in legal records again until 1682. On 28 May 1682, in consideration of 2,000 pounds of tobacco, he deeded fifty acres of the tract purchased from Freshwater to Francis Elmore. James Tarpley and William Barber witnessed the deed. Grace Hammack, William's wife, signed with him.[61]

Several times in 1690 and 1691, William Hammack served as a juror to hear cases in Rappahannock County. The seventeenth-century method of jury selection was to empanel individuals who were often at court to prosecute or testify in other pending suits, and such individuals tended to include friends and neighbors who were involved in a common court suit. Thus, those serving as jurors with William included William Morgan and Samuel Samford -- son of the earlier James -- who lived on plantations near William's own in western Rappahannock County. One case involved disputed ownership of a horse and another involved a charge of assault and battery. In a third matter, Henry Pickett was found guilt of "from time to time...[having] exposed & disposed of Diverse quantities of Rum & Syder in his House in a Retayling manner contrary to the 9th Act of Assembly made at James Citty the 17th: day of 7br: 1668."[62]

At the time of his jury service, Hammack was at court to attend a personal matter, the circumstance that led to his jury service in cases not involving him. At some point after 1682, Hammack's wife Grace had died, and he had remarried, before 1687, to a woman called Alice. Something about Alice's character or behavior caused comment throughout the neighborhood, and William and Alice ultimately resorted to legal action. They chose to sue "John Jones & Alice his Wife, Defts., for scandalous words spoken by the sd Alice Jones against the sd Alice Hammack." Apparently, William and Alice were able to establish the falsehood of Alice Jones's statements. The verdict was a favorable one: "Wee of the Jury do find for the Plts. Fifteen hundred pounds of Tobb: or else three Duckings according to Law with cost of suit."[63] The exact nature of the statements made by Alice Jones is unclear, but the legal references do provide one tantalizing piece of evidence. At the conclusion of the matter, the court

> Ordered that Doctr: Robert Clarke be payed for Twelve dayes attendance according to Act by Wm. Hamock being by him Subpena'd an Evidence in the suit between the sd Wm. Hamock & Alice his Wife and John Jones & Alice his Wife, Defts; [and] Ordered that John Lewis be payed for Twelve days attendance according to Act by Wm: Hamock being by him Subpena'd an evidence in the suit between the sd Wm: Hamock & Alice his Wife & Jno: Jones & Alice his Wife, Defts.[64]

Since Robert Clarke is here identified as a doctor, the designation suggests that a medical issue may in some way have been involved. From the registers of North Farnham Parish, we know that William Hammack the younger -- only known son of William and Alice -- had been born on 15 March 1688/9.

---

[58] For background on Freshwater, see C. Edelblute, R. Freshwater and H. Freshwater, *Freshwater Families: Research and Genealogy* (2nd ed., Richmond, 1990); Virginia Patent Book D-8, p. 273.

[59] Old Rappahannock County, VA, Deed Book 1672-76, Part I, p. 150-51.

[60] Old Rappahannock County, VA, Deeds & Wills, 1677-1682, Part I, p. 187-88.

[61] Old Rappahannock County, VA, Deed Book 1682-86, p. 56-57.

[62] Old Rappahannock County, VA, Orders, 1689-92, p. 183-4, 203, 205.

[63] Old Rappahannock Co., VA, Orders, 1689-92, p. 209-10.

[64] Ibid.

The case was ultimately resolved on 5 March 1690/1, a little less than two years after William's birth, but had been filed months earlier. Thus it seems likely that there was some connection between the birth of young William Hammack and the "scandalous words" spoken by Alice Jones.

In societies where a majority of the inhabitants are illiterate, the value of spoken language is regarded as greater than that of written language. A man or woman's reputation is thus what it is acknowledged to be within the community in which he or she lives. If a miller is accused of diluting his flour with sawdust, if a maiden is accused of immodest conduct, or if an elderly spinster is accused of witchcraft, such charges have potent force throughout the community. The miller's business fails, the maiden's prospects for a successful marriage diminish, and the elderly lady finds herself shunned and suspected. Thus William Hammack and wife Alice chose a court suit to restore her reputation; given the public nature of community life in seventeenth-century America, it seems likely that Alice Jones had in some way questioned Alice Hammack's chastity or virtue, and the Hammacks chose to vindicate her reputation with a legal judgment.[65]

Until 1692, William's residence on the north shore of the Rappahannock River rendered him and his community on the fringes of life in Rappahannock County. The court house lay south of the river, and in order to prosecute a matter an individual had to be ferried from one side to the other. The journey was costly and, in difficult weather, perilous. Because of increased population growth on the northern shore, however, in 1692 the Virginia House of Burgesses created a new county, Richmond, formed from the northern half of Rappahannock. Thus, the new county had a new county seat, and William's close residence to the new town of Warsaw (originally called Richmond Courthouse) meant that he became a frequent participant in legal matters.

In June 1692, Hammack was sued by a neighbor, John Lewis, perhaps over a debt; Lewis dropped the charges, however, and failed to ever appear at court.[66] In February 1693, William was chosen by the county court as surveyor to clear and improve a road "over Totaskey Mill leading to Westmoreland County formerly in part cleared by Tho: Colley, Survayor, [but]... now grown up with bushes turned by fences & bad in severall places."[67] A 1694 deed indicates that Edward Lewis of Richmond and John Cralle of Northumberland had purchased portions of the Freshwater lands joining Hammacks and were now his near neighbors.[68] In August of that year, he again served as grand juror, apparently without any other pending legal obligations.[69] On 18 December 1694, one William Hammack -- either this man or his eldest son, who had recently reached legal age -- patented 300 acres on Totuskey Creek in Richmond County.[70] If the immigrant William, this patent almost doubled his landholdings, bringing them to 581 acres.

In August 1695, William found himself attending Richmond County court as a witness in another neighborhood dispute. Robert Clarke -- who five years earlier had served as a witness for William Hammack -- was now suing Hammack's neighbor Daniel Swellivant, who also owned a portion of the original Freshwater tract. Dr. Clarke's horse had grazed on Swellivant's land while Clarke was attending a matter in the neighborhood, and Swellivant, "out of an evil and malitious intent in or about the month of September in the year of our Lord 1694 in the County aforesaid did cause the said Mare to be taken up and with Whip Cord to be hard lyed about the footlock by reason whereof the said Mare came by her death to the damage three thousand pounds of tobacco for which he craves Judgment with costs."[71] Hammack's testimony must have helped Clarke, for Clarke won his suit; he was, however, awarded only

---

[65] R. St. George, "'Heated' Speech and Literacy in Seventeenth-Century New England," in D. G. Allen and D. D. Hall, *Seventeenth-Century New England* (Boston, 1985), pp. 275-322.

[66] Richmond Co., VA, Orders, 1692-1694, p. 20.

[67] Richmond Co., VA, Orders, 1692-1694, p. 64.

[68] Richmond Co., VA, Deeds, 1692-94, pp. 26-28.

[69] Richmond Co., VA, Orders, 1692-94, p. 136.

[70] Northern Neck Land Grants, No. 2, 1694-1700, pp. 100-101.

[71] Richmond Co., VA, Orders, 1694-97, p. 73.

1,000 pounds of tobacco in damages.[72] Such was the nature of early American justice that on the day following the verdict Hammack and Swellivant themselves were among the jurors who heard another case before the Richmond Court.[73]

Hammack and Swellivant were again involved in a legal matter in 1699, this time involving one of Hammack's servants. On that occasion, Hammack brought charges that his servant woman Margaret Jones had given birth to an illegitimate child. The father, she alleged, was Daniel Swellivant's overseer Arthur King. Although Jones, "upon the Holy Gospell of God made oath" that King was the "true father," for reasons that are not entire clear William Hammack's son Richard "confessed Judgement to the Churchwardens of North Farnham Parish for the use of the Parish for Five hundred pounds of good tobo: in cask being the Fine due for committing the sin of fornication by Margrett Jones." Margaret was ordered to serve William Hammack an extra year for the trouble caused him and then to serve an additional six months to compensate Richard Hammack for paying her fine to the parish.[74]

As events transpired, William Hammack found himself back at court eight months later, on 6 March 1699/1700, involving the same matter. The document itself is worth quoting at length:

> Whereas the Court have been circumvented in the grant of an order passed to Richard Hammock for one halfe years service of Margtt: Jones for paying her fine to the Parrish of Farnham for committing the sin of ffornication, And for as much as the said Margarett is a Servant to Wm. Hamock, Father to said Richard, And her said master being willing to pay the said fine in case the said Servant shall be ordered to serve him the said terme, and for that the said Richard is unable to pay the said fine. The Court upon the humble petition of Wm. Colston, one of the Church Wardens of the said Parish, do order that the said Margarett Jones do serve the said Wm. Hammock or his assignes the full term of halfe a year after her time by Indenture or Custome be fully expired, he the said William paying her fine as aforesaid.[75]

It would appear that Richard Hammack, enamored of young Margaret, had volunteered to pay her fine, believing that he was the father of her child. Rather than admit that she had slept with her master's son, Margaret named Arthur King as her child's father. William Hammack had gone to court intending to charge Arthur King in the manner when Richard, inspired by the ardor of youth, had upset the whole matter by confessing his indiscretion. To make matters worse, however, he found himself unable to pay the fine, and his father had to step in. Ultimately the elder Hammack paid the fine, and Margaret worked for him a year and a half beyond her initial indenture. Sadly, the records do not indicate whether the child was male or female or what became of it.

The suit over Margaret Jones's pregnancy was William Hammack's last personal appearance in the legal life of Richmond County. He died on 2 July 1701 at his home on Totuskey Creek in western Richmond County. He was somewhere between sixty and eighty years old.[76]

In his will, William Hammack bequeathed 200 acres of land to his youngest son William Hammack, born in 1688. He also stated that his daughter Elizabeth was to be of age at 16 years and that she was residual heir in case William died without issue. Thus it seems likely that Elizabeth may also have been William's daughter by Alice Hammack. The will mentions son Richard, who was named as executor, and

[72] Richmond Co., VA, Orders, 1694-97, p. 73.

[73] Richmond Co., VA, Orders, 1694-97, p. 77.

[74] Richmond Co., VA, Orders, 1697-99, p. 407.

[75] Richmond Co., VA, Orders, 1699-1701, p. 17-18.

[76] G. H. S. King, *The Registers of North Farnham Parish, 1663-1814, and Lunenburg Parish, 1783-1800, Richmond Co., VA* (Fredericksburg, VA, 1966), pp. 79-82. All subsequent specific references to dates of burials, births, and christenings for Hammacks and Hammocks in Richmond County during the period from 1663 to 1814 are from this source. The register also contains several Hammack and Hammock marriages, which are also included and supplemented in G. H. S. King, *Marriages of Richmond Co., VA, 1668-1853* (Fredericksburg, VA, 1964). Whenever a specific dated reference to a Hammack marriage in Richmond County before 1853 appears, it is from this source.

son William, who was bequeathed only one shilling. The fact that William's eldest son was not listed as an heir is significant and needs explanation. By 1701, William Hammack was more than thirty years of age and had been married and living independently for ten to fifteen years. For most if not all of that time he had been living in Westmoreland County, where he had acquired a sizeable plantation. William may have assisted his son with the initial land acquisition. Unlike many Virginians, then, he chose in his will to favor his young offspring, who would not reach legal age for many years, in disposing of his estate.[77]

William's will makes two curious omissions. He apparently had at least one additional child, John Hammack, who may have still been a minor in 1701; John died in 1708, leaving one surviving child, another William, who seems to have died as a boy. Another curious omission is William's failure to mention his wife directly. It is not until a chancery suit was filed two years later, in May 1703 in neighboring Westmoreland County, that we learn that William's wife Alice had predeceased him and that he had married for a third time before his death to Margaret Macey, a widow with several young offspring. In William's defense, however, may be the circumstances of his death; the will was written the same day it was entered for probate, indicating that he may have taken ill rather suddenly.[78]

William Hammack's name appears in the legal records of Richmond and Westmoreland County more frequently in the decade following his death than it did in his own lifetime. John Bohannan and John Hartley both testified that they had witnessed William sign his will, and Richard Hammack entered upon his duties as the document's executor in July 1701. Charles Barber, Dr. Robert Clarke, Mr. George Glasscock, and William Lambert were ordered to meet together and appraise the personal property of William Hammack.[79]

In 1702, Richard Hammock found himself party to a legal action involving Patrick Moggee. Moggee had made a contract with William Hammack, apparently as a tenant, to produce a crop of tobacco in 1699. William Hammack died before the crop had been harvested, and Moggee wanted his portion of the proceeds. Moggee and Hammack settled the matter amicably before the court could rule, however.[80] At the same time, William Colston sued the estate for a debt owed by William Hammack at his death. In the following months, there were various suits filed by Francis Lynch, Rawleigh Travers, Henry Williams, Captain John Cralle, and Colonel John Tarpley. Most of these were small matters involving modest amounts of tobacco owed as part of the local neighborhood's system of debt obligation; Hammack had likely bartered for goods and services on the promise to pay once his tobacco had been harvested and marketed, as was the method used throughout the Chesapeake. It is notable that never in his own lifetime had William Hammack been charged with failure to pay his debts, as was common in Virginia. Since most of these matters were settled with minimum legal action, it seems likely that in the event of the elder Hammack's death his creditors wished only to make a legal statement that Hammack owed them for services rendered. Given what seems to have been a reputation for honesty, it may even have been that some of these obligations had never been written in what was still a predominately oral culture within the colony.[81]

The two exceptions to this rule were matters involving Francis Lynch and John Cralle. On 25 August 1703, Francis Lynch was awarded 953 pounds of tobacco for his claim against the Hammack estate. The matter had stretched on for two years through five different hearings at court. Initially the matter had abated in 1702 because of inconsistencies between the writ and declaration. Lynch filed charges once more, alleging that the Hammack estate owed him 2,000 pounds, and Richard Hammack was briefly detained by Sheriff Lewis Markham to answer Lynch's charges. Markham repeatedly attempted to force Hammack to respond to the charges, but Hammack remained evasive. In a single instrument, Hammack

[77] Headley, *Wills of Richmond Co., VA* (Baltimore, 1983), p. 7.

[78] Westmoreland County, VA, Order Book, 1698-1705, p. 192a.

[79] Richmond Co., VA, Orders, 1699-1701, p. 134, 137, 138, 147, 150, 159, 170, 188, 197, 213; Westmoreland Co., VA, Orders, 1698-1705, pp. 168a, 174, 192, 192a, 195a, 199a.

[80] Richmond Co., VA, Orders, 1699-1701, p. 134.

[81] Richmond Co., VA, Orders, 1699-1701, p. 134, 137, 138, 147, 150, 159, 168A, 170, 174, 188, 197, 213.

was required to respond to Lynch on one matter, to John Cralle on another, and to Thomas Newton on another.[82]

By this time, Richard Hammack had settled in Westmoreland County, where he remained for many years. With the joint "bill...being duely served" in June 1702, and with Richard Hammack "contemptuously refuseing to make answer," the Westmoreland County court ordered a writ of attachment which directed the Sheriff to issue an order " commanding him to have Richard Hammock at the next Court to answer for his contempt."[83]

From this point onwards, Richard Hammack seems to have been more obliging. Although the court did find in Lynch's favor, it awarded him less than half the amount he claimed, indicating that he may have been fraudulently attempting to extract more from the estate than he was owed.

The matter involving Hammack's neighbor John Cralle was more complicated. The evidence suggests that William Hammack and John Cralle enjoyed a harmonious relationship. Their lands lay near the joint boundary of Westmoreland, Richmond, and Northumberland Counties, and Cralle owned additional large tracts in Northumberland County, where he sat as a county justice. On 25 May 1703, his suit was heard by the Westmoreland County court:

> John Cralle of the County of Northumberland, Gent., by his bill in chancery exhibited against Richard Hammock, executor of Wm. Hammock, setting forth that hee became security to the Worshippfull Court of Northumberland with Margrett Macey, relict of Henry Macey late of the County of Northumberland, for Margret's due administration of her husband's estate, that some short tyme after Margrett intermarried with Wm. Hamock who removed Macey's estate into Richmond, which by appraisement was found to amount to 9,390 pounds of tobacco, and afterwards died leaving his son Richd. Hamock his executor, who inventoryed Macey's estate with his father's without distribution, that Cralle upon two of Macey's daughters coemeing to age and applying themselves to him for such part of their father's estate as of right belonged to them, hee to avoid trouble at law paid the two daughters, Ruth and Mary, their respective fifth parts of Macey's estate, which being divided into five equall parts betwixt his four children and their mother amounted to 1,878 pounds of tobacco each, well hopeing Wm. Hammock would honestly refund and reimbusrst the same to him againe. But Hammock departing this life, no part of the tobacco beinge repaid Cralle, and Macey's estate being removed from county to county, so that Cralle could not come at his debt or the knowledge where Macey's estate was lodged by the strict rules of the common law, therefore prayed her Majestie's writt to cause Richd. Hammock to discover to this Court what hee knew of Macey's estate and whether the same or any part came to the hands of Wm. Hamock and if it appeared there was sufficient to pay the orator's disbursements or any part thereof, prayed a decree for the same. Richd. Hamock neglecting to appeare or put in any answer to the orator's bill, the same was continued till next Court, and now Hammock appeareing but refuseing to make any anwer and Cralle produceing severall receipts amounting to 2,534 pounds of tobacco, it is decreed that Richard Hamock doe pay to John Cralle 2,534 pounds of tobacco out of Wm. Hamock's estate.[84]

Oddly, this is the first we hear of William Hammack's marriage to Margaret Macey. Given the known evidence about his life and activities, it seems likely that he married her only a short time before his death. From Northumberland records we learn that Henry Macey (whose name was also spelled Massey and Massie) died at some point after 1688 and that his children included Ruth, born in 1682; Mary, born

---

[82] Westmoreland Co., VA, Orders, 1698-1705, pp. 168a, 174, 192, 192a, 195a, 199a.
[83] Westmoreland County, VA, Order Book 1698-1705, p. 168a.
[84] Westmoreland County, VA, Order Book, 1698-1705, p. 192a.

in 1684; and William, born in 1688.[85] Otherwise, the lives and activities of Henry and Margaret Macey and their offspring seem mysterious. After William Hammack married the widow Macey, he had joined her husband's estate from Northumberland with his own in Richmond, and then upon his death Richard Hammack had transferred this property into Westmoreland County. Richard Hammack presumably followed the Westmoreland Court's ruling and paid the Macey heirs their due, for we read no more of their case in Richmond and Westmoreland Counties.

By August 1703, it seems that all disputes arising from the estate of William Hammack had been settled. His life -- nearly five decades spent in Virginia and perhaps another three in England before that -- had been a long and eventful one. Although he came to the colony as a servant, he amassed nearly 300 acres of land between 1670 and 1700, a substantial holding. His selection as a road surveyor, juror, personal attorney, and legal security suggests that he was a man of integrity worthy of trust within his community. The fact that he lived for three decades in Rappahannock and Richmond without once being prosecuted for debt suggests that he valued and honored his obligations and his reputation, also indicated by the suit he filed -- and won -- against John and Alice Jones in 1691.

At his death, William left four sons and at least one daughter. Young Elizabeth Hammack may have died young, for no records concerning her have been found. When William Hammack the younger -- youngest son of the immigrant -- came of age in 1710, he deeded one-half of his 200 acre inheritance to his brother, William Hammack the elder. No mention in the deed is made of Elizabeth as a residual heir (as per his father's will), suggesting that she was already deceased.[86]

William Hammack was not the only Hammack immigrant to reach the American shores. Twenty years before he came, Allen Hammack had set sail from London to America; he apparently died without issue, perhaps before he reached the colonies. At least one Hammack immigrant settled in colonial New England, founding a very small family in Connecticut and New York. In the mid nineteenth-century, several immigrants from German states settled in Michigan, Wisconsin, Illinois, Ohio, and other northern states, anglicizing their name to Hammock, Hammack, or Hamack. Rudolph Hammack -- probably also of German extraction, and possibly originally surnamed Hammacher -- settled in Augusta County, Virginia, and established a small family in the Shenandoah Valley. But from the three surviving sons of William Hammack sprang the vast majority of all American Hammacks and Hammocks. Within a century of his death, they lived in Maryland, Virginia, North and South Carolina, Tennessee, and Kentucky. Within another five decades, they would reach the Pacific Ocean.

---

[85] See the transcriptions of St. Stephen's Parish Register, Northumberland Co., VA, in B. Fleet, *Virginia Colonial Abstracts: The Original 34 Volumes Reprinted in 3* (3 vols., Baltimore, 1988).

[86] Richmond County, VA, Deeds, 1708-1711, p. 179-181.

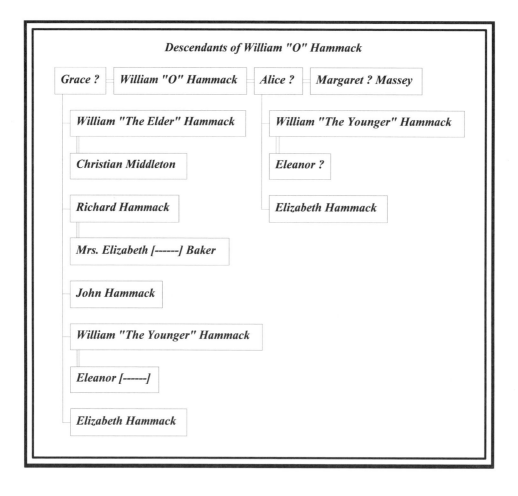

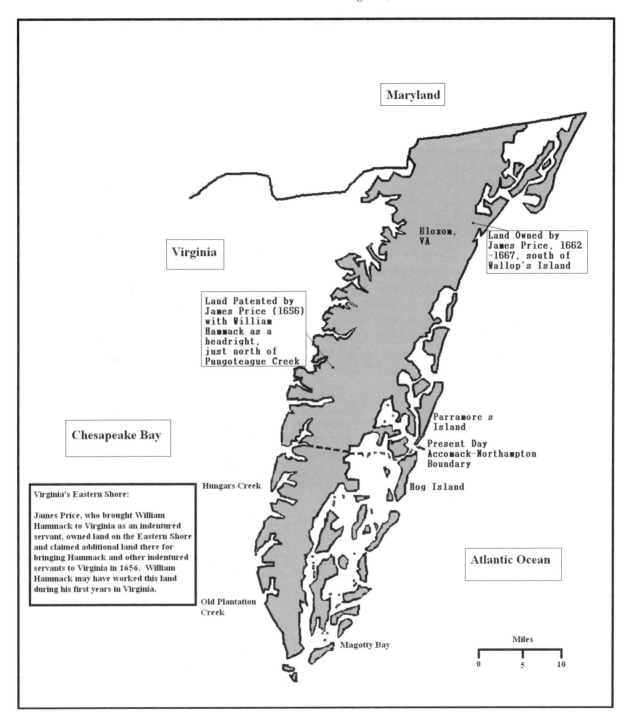

Maryland

Virginia

Bloxom,
VA

Land Owned by
James Price, 1662
-1667, south of
Wallop's Island

Land Patented by
James Price (1656)
with William
Hammack as a
headright,
just north of
Pungoteague Creek

Parramore s
Island

Present Day
Accomack-Northampton
Boundary

Chesapeake Bay

Hungars Creek

Hog Island

Virginia's Eastern Shore:

James Price, who brought William
Hammack to Virginia as an indentured
servant, owned land on the Eastern Shore
and claimed additional land there for
bringing Hammack and other indentured
servants to Virginia in 1656. William
Hammack may have worked this land
during his first years in Virginia.

Atlantic Ocean

Old Plantation
Creek

Magotty Bay

Miles

0   5   10

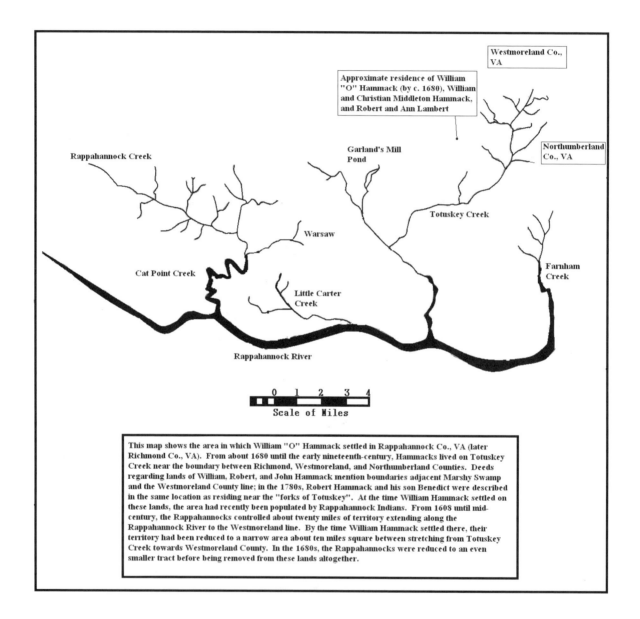

Westmoreland Co., VA

Approximate residence of William "O" Hammack (by c. 1680), William and Christian Middleton Hammack, and Robert and Ann Lambert

Garland's Mill Pond

Northumberland Co., VA

Rappahannock Creek

Totuskey Creek

Warsaw

Cat Point Creek

Farnham Creek

Little Carter Creek

Rappahannock River

0   1   2   3   4
Scale of Miles

This map shows the area in which William "O" Hammack settled in Rappahannock Co., VA (later Richmond Co., VA). From about 1680 until the early nineteenth-century, Hammacks lived on Totuskey Creek near the boundary between Richmond, Westmoreland, and Northumberland Counties. Deeds regarding lands of William, Robert, and John Hammack mention boundaries adjacent Marshy Swamp and the Westmoreland County line; in the 1780s, Robert Hammack and his son Benedict were described in the same location as residing near the "forks of Totuskey". At the time William Hammack settled on these lands, the area had recently been populated by Rappahannock Indians. From 1608 until mid-century, the Rappahannocks controlled about twenty miles of territory extending along the Rappahannock River to the Westmoreland line. By the time William Hammack settled there, their territory had been reduced to a narrow area about ten miles square between stretching from Totuskey Creek towards Westmoreland County. In the 1680s, the Rappahannocks were reduced to an even smaller tract before being removed from these lands altogether.

Chapter 5:

Hammacks in Virginia, 1700-1776

The immigrant William Hammack produced four surviving sons: William the elder, Richard, John, and William the younger. John died in Richmond County in 1708, leaving one surviving son, William Hammack. Although there were several later William Hammacks in Virginia, no clear references have been found to John's son William Hammack. It is therefore presumed -- but not proven conclusively -- that he died young and without issue.

Of the three other sons, William Hammack the elder remained in Richmond County, where he died in 1732. William Hammack the younger remained in Richmond as late as 1740 and may also have died there. Richard Hammack left Richmond County and moved southwest into the Piedmont region of Virginia. His family was found in the newly settled territory of Louisa and later Albemarle County. The only surviving son of William Hammack the younger, John Hammack (who married Mildred Lambert), moved to Lunenburg County, where he died about 1780.

Many American families have legends indicating that they were established by several immigrant brothers. According to the tenor of these stories, one brother usually traveled south to establish one family line. Another headed west, and another headed north. Although there was only one early Hammack immigrant in this line, such a story might hold true for the next generation of Hammacks and Hammocks. The offspring of Richard moved westward into Tennessee, Kentucky, and ultimately into middle America. From this family descend the Hammacks and Hammocks of Missouri, Iowa, Kansas, and the first Hammacks to settle in California, Oregon, and Washington. The descendants of William Hammack the younger remained in the Virginia Southside at least until the middle nineteenth century. The descendants of William Hammack the elder pressed ever southward, populating the American "cotton belt" that stretched along the gulf coast from Georgia to east Texas. These later migrations will be discussed below; before we proceed, however, the lives of the four surviving sons of the immigrant William Hammack will be examined.

A. The Second Generation: The Sons of William Hammack, Sr.

William Hammack, the elder, of Westmoreland and Richmond Counties, Virginia.

Records of North Farnham Parish, Richmond County, Virginia, establish that Richard Hammack was born in 1674 and that William Hammack the younger was born in 1688. The births of William Hammack the elder and of John Hammack were not recorded and may have taken place before the register began or outside North Farnham Parish.

The earliest known reference to William Hammack the elder dates from 1693; if he were of legal age by this time, then he was born prior to 1672.[87] Based on the birth dates of his offspring, it seems likely that he was slightly older and probably born about 1670, either in Old Rappahannock County, Westmoreland County, or on Virginia's Eastern Shore. He grew up on his father's Richmond County plantation along Totuskey Creek, and it was in this region -- near the boundary with Westmoreland County -- that William lived his life.

William Hammack was already married to Christian Middleton when he first appears in Westmoreland County records. On 29 November 1693, he conveyed a tract of land to Thomas Lamkin, apparently as payment for another tract Lamkin and his wife Susannah were conveying to William

---

[87] Westmoreland Co., VA, Order Book 1690-98, p. 112.

Hammack. The deed for the tract which Hammack was conveying to Lamkin has not been located.[88]

William seems to have married Christian Middleton, daughter of Robert Middleton, a prosperous Westmoreland County planter, about 1688 or 1689. No one single piece of evidence exists to establish the marriage, but the cumulative evidence is strong. On 29 July 1695, Thomas and Susannah Lamkin conveyed a tract of Westmoreland County land to Simon Robins. The land -- perhaps that deeded to him in 1693 by William Hammack -- was a tract of sixty acres on Yeocomico Creek. Susannah Lamkin appointed Benedict Middleton as her legal attorney to acknowledge her release of her legal rights in this property to Robins, and John and Elizabeth Middleton witnessed the deed.[89] William Hammack and his sons appear frequently in legal transactions with members of the Middleton family, and he served as executor of John Middleton's will. These associations, and the fact that William named two of his three sons Middleton names -- Benedict and Robert, strongly suggest a family connection. The likely scenario is that William Hammack married Christian Middleton, daughter of Robert Middleton and sister of Benedict Middleton of Westmoreland County.[90]

Between 1697 and 1730, William Hammack was involved in several land transactions in Westmoreland and Richmond Counties. Described as William Hammack, "Cooper," with wife Christian, he acquired 161 acres in Yeocomico Forrest on 28 June 1697. The property joined Robert Middleton, George Harrison, and John Wright. It included thirty acres where William Hammack was already residing. On 25 April 1698, William Hammack "of Youcomoc in Westmoreland County" deeded 131 acres of this land to John Headley by prior arrangement, apparently in consideration of payment Headley had been working off for Hammack.[91]

On 31 January 1699, William patented 214 acres in Westmoreland County's Yeocomico Forrest.[92] This property, too, joined the lands of Robert Middleton. A decade later, on 1 April 1710, William purchased 100 acres from his younger half-brother, William Hammack the younger. This had been the younger William's inheritance, which he apparently sold upon reaching legal age in 1709. On 19 November 1715, along with Peter Cornwall and Myrty Hogan, William Hammack obtained a grant for 524 acres in Stafford County; this grant was apparently an investment, and William then conveyed his portion to Wansford Arrington of Westmoreland County.[93]

The net balance of these transactions was that William Hammack owned approximately 345 acres of land when he wrote his will in 1730. Of that land, thirty acres went to his grandson John and the remainder to his son Benedict; in each case, the bequests were to follow the death of William's widow Christian. The personal property on the plantation likewise went to Christian during her lifetime for her maintenance and for the support of William's three orphaned grandchildren; following Christian's death, the personal property was to be divided among all of William's surviving children or their heirs. Robert Hammack, William's younger son, was given a residual right to inheritance should Benedict and his son John die without heirs. He may already have received an inheritance from his father in establishing his own plantation along Totuskey Creek, but William's will was written consistent with the English tradition of primogeniture, whereby the bulk of the estate went to support the eldest surviving son and his family.[94]

---

[88] Westmoreland Co., VA, Order Book 1690-98, p. 112.

[89] J. F. Dorman, ed., *Westmoreland Co., VA, Deeds and Wills No. 2, 1691-1699* (Washington, D.C., 1965), pp. 51a-52a.

[90] Northern Neck Land Grants, No. 2, 1694-1700, p. 309-310; Westmoreland Co., VA, Deeds and Wills No. 3, 1701-07, pp. 425-27, 433-434; Westmoreland Co., VA, Order Book, 1705-07, p. 37a; A. B. Fothergill, *Wills of Westmoreland Co., VA, 1654-1800* (Richmond, 1925), pp. 17-18.

[91] Westmoreland Co., VA, Deeds and Wills No. 2, 1691-99, pp. 190-190a. See also Gray, *Northern Neck Land Grants, 1694-1742*, p. 20. Hammack received a formal grant for this land on this date. It joined lands owned by Clay, Robert Middleton, George Harrison, and John Wright. Ten days earlier, John Hartley of Westmoreland County had received a grant for 699 acres in Richmond and Westmoreland counties joining Mr. Robert Middleton, Dennis Corniles, and George Harrison.

[92] Northern Neck Land Grants, No. 2, 1694-1700, p. 309-310. A published extract is found in Gray, *Northern Neck Land Grants, 1694-1742*, p. 22. John Bailey's land also joined the tract.

[93] Gertrude E. Gray, *Northern Neck Land Grants, 1694-1742*, p. 62.

[94] Richmond Co., VA, Will Book 5, 1725-1753, p. 155.

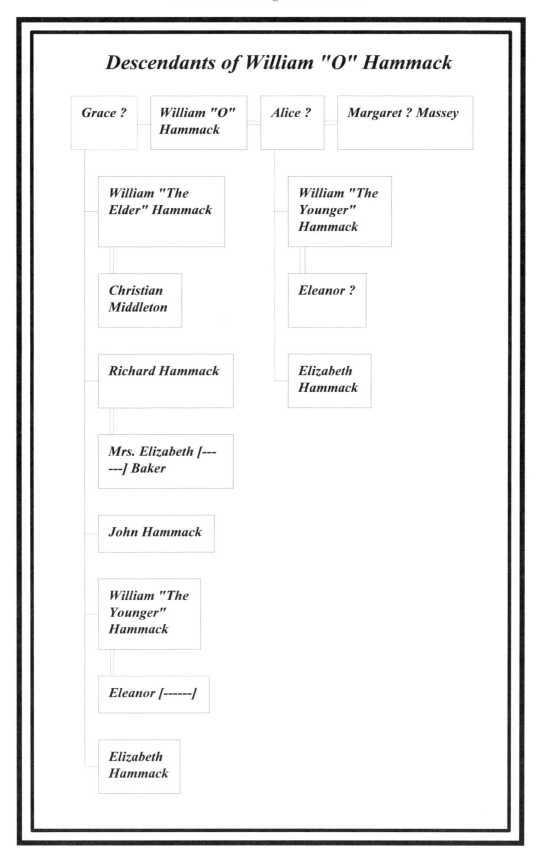

Descendants of William "O" Hammack

Grace ? — William "O" Hammack — Alice ? — Margaret ? Massey

William "The Elder" Hammack

Christian Middleton

Richard Hammack

Mrs. Elizabeth [------] Baker

John Hammack

William "The Younger" Hammack

Eleanor [------]

Elizabeth Hammack

William "The Younger" Hammack

Eleanor ?

Elizabeth Hammack

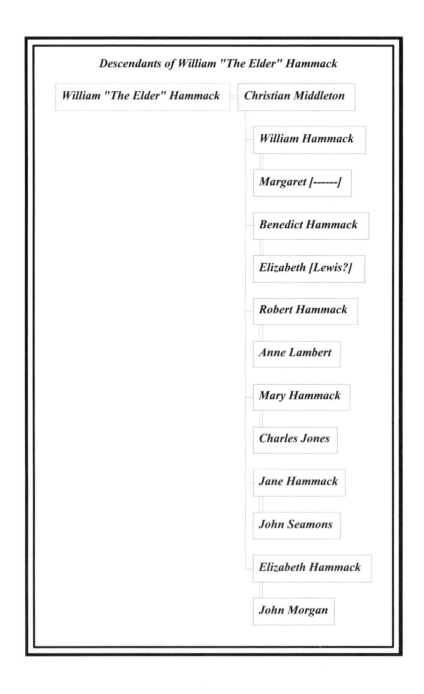

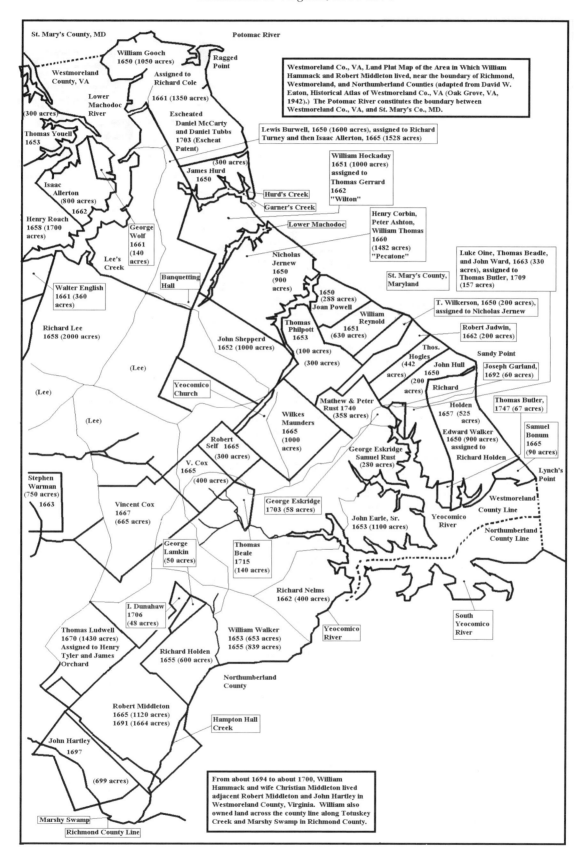

St. Mary's County, MD

Potomac River

William Gooch
1650 (1050 acres)

Ragged
Point

Westmoreland
County, VA

Assigned to
Richard Cole

1661 (1350 acres)

Lower
Machodoc
River

Escheated
Daniel McCarty
and Daniel Tubbs
1703 (Escheat
Patent)

(300 acres)

Westmoreland Co., VA, Land Plat Map of the Area in Which William
Hammack and Robert Middleton lived, near the boundary of Richmond,
Westmoreland, and Northumberland Counties (adapted from David W.
Eaton, Historical Atlas of Westmoreland Co., VA (Oak Grove, VA,
1942).) The Potomac River constitutes the boundary between
Westmoreland Co., VA, and St. Mary's Co., MD.

Thomas Youell
1653

Lewis Burwell, 1650 (1600 acres), assigned to Richard
Turney and then Isaac Allerton, 1665 (1528 acres)

Isaac
Allerton
(800 acres)
1662

James Hurd
1650

(300 acres)

William Hockaday
1651 (1000 acres)
assigned to
Thomas Gerrard
1662
"Wilton"

Henry Roach
1658 (1700
acres)

Hurd's Creek

Garner's Creek

Lower Machodoc

Henry Corbin,
Peter Ashton,
William Thomas
1660
(1482 acres)
"Pecatone"

George
Wolf
1661
(140
acres)

Lee's
Creek

Nicholas
Jernew
1650
(900
acres)

St. Mary's County,
Maryland

Luke Oine, Thomas Beadle,
and John Ward, 1663 (330
acres), assigned to
Thomas Butler, 1709
(157 acres)

Walter English
1661 (360
acres)

Banquetting
Hall

1650
(288 acres)
Joan Powell

William
Reynold
1651
(630 acres)

T. Wilkerson, 1650 (200 acres),
assigned to Nicholas Jernew

Richard Lee
1658 (2000 acres)

John Shepperd
1652 (1000 acres)

Thomas
Philpott
1653

Robert Jadwin,
1662 (200 acres)

(Lee)

(100 acres)

(300 acres)

Thos.
Hogles
(442
acres)

John Hull
1650
(200
acres)

Sandy Point

Joseph Garland,
1692 (60 acres)

(Lee)

Yeocomico
Church

Mathew & Peter
Rust 1740
(358 acres)

Richard

Holden
1657 (525
acres)

Thomas Butler,
1747 (67 acres)

(Lee)

Wilkes
Maunders
1665
(1000
acres)

Edward Walker
1650 (900 acres)
assigned to
Richard Holden

Samuel
Bonum
1665
(90 acres)

Robert
Self 1665
(300
acres)

George Eskridge
Samuel Rust
(280 acres)

Lynch's
Point

Stephen
Warman
(750 acres)
1663

V. Cox
1665
(400 acres)

George Eskridge
1703 (58 acres)

John Earle, Sr.
1653 (1100 acres)

Yeocomico
River

Westmoreland
County Line

Northumberland
County Line

Vincent Cox
1667
(665 acres)

George
Lamkin
(50 acres)

Thomas
Beale
1715
(140 acres)

Richard Nelms
1662 (400 acres)

South
Yeocomico
River

I. Dunahaw
1706
(48 acres)

Thomas Ludwell
1670 (1430 acres)
Assigned to Henry
Tyler and James
Orchard

Richard Holden
1655 (600 acres)

William Walker
1653 (653 acres)
1655 (839 acres)

Yeocomico
River

Northumberland
County

Robert Middleton
1665 (1120 acres)
1691 (1664 acres)

Hampton Hall
Creek

John Hartley
1697

(699 acres)

From about 1694 to about 1700, William
Hammack and wife Christian Middleton lived
adjacent Robert Middleton and John Hartley in
Westmoreland County, Virginia. William also
owned land across the county line along Totuskey
Creek and Marshy Swamp in Richmond County.

Marshy Swamp

Richmond County Line

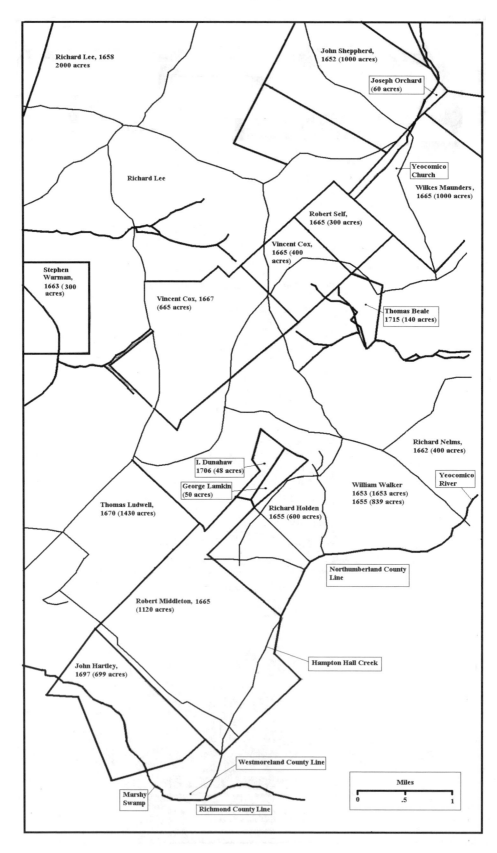

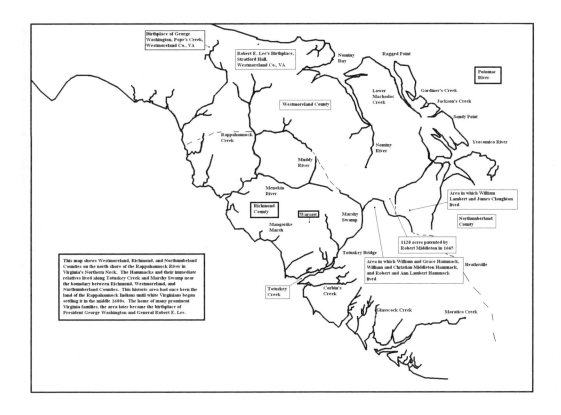

This map shows Westmoreland, Richmond, and Northumberland Counties on the north shore of the Rappahannock River in Virginia's Northern Neck. The Hammacks and their immediate relatives lived along Totuskey Creek and Marshy Swamp near the boundary between Richmond, Westmoreland, and Northumberland Counties. This historic area had once been the land of the Rappahannock Indians until white Virginians began settling it in the middle 1600s. The home of many prominent Virginia families, the area later became the birthplace of President George Washington and General Robert E. Lee.

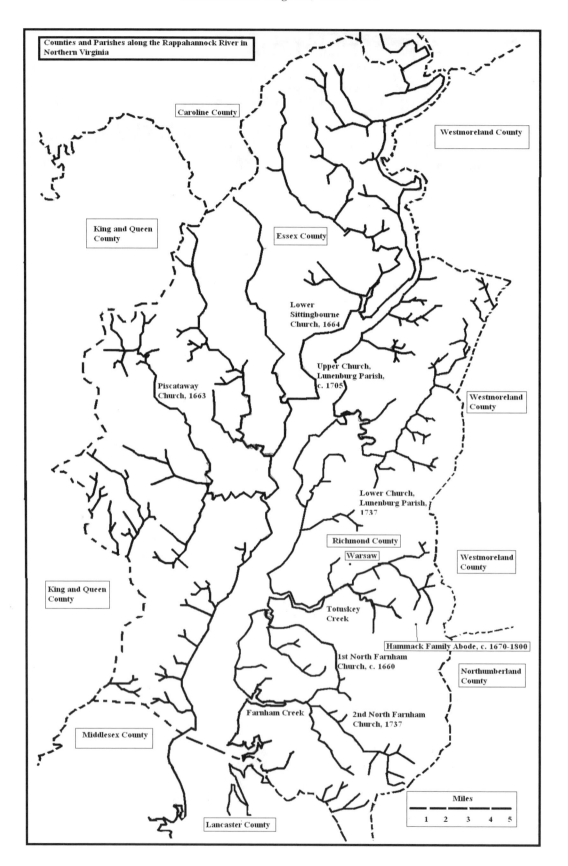

Counties and Parishes along the Rappahannock River in Northern Virginia

Caroline County

Westmoreland County

King and Queen County

Essex County

Lower Sittingbourne Church, 1664

Upper Church, Lunenburg Parish, c. 1705

Piscataway Church, 1663

Westmoreland County

Lower Church, Lunenburg Parish, 1737

Richmond County

Warsaw

Westmoreland County

King and Queen County

Totuskey Creek

Hammack Family Abode, c. 1670-1800

1st North Farnham Church, c. 1660

Northumberland County

Farnham Creek

2nd North Farnham Church, 1737

Middlesex County

Miles
1 2 3 4 5

Lancaster County

A home tract of 345 acres was sufficient to establish William Hammack as a prosperous yeoman planter. Surviving tithable records from eastern Virginia taken in the year 1704 reveal that most ordinary planters owned tracts that varied in size between 300 and 700 acres. Very modest landholders owned smaller tracts ranging from only a few acres to more than 200, and the wealthiest owned tracts that ranged from 800 or 900 acres to many thousands. While William Hammack was thus not among the "Great Planters" who dominated Virginia's society, he was among the rank of self-sufficient middling planters engaged in the commercial production of tobacco for the European market.[95]

William's personal property and social activity in Westmoreland and Richmond Counties was consistent with such a ranking. An inventory of his estate was made 25 August 1730 in Richmond County. His personal property amounted to £164.17.04. This inventory included five slaves -- valued at £75 altogether and the largest financial investment on Hammack's plantation. In addition to livestock, there were also Cooper's tools and a large number of plantation implements necessary for the cultivation of wheat, corn, other vegetables, and tobacco.[96]

In addition to these implements, there were also traces that Hammack was living in a prosperous fashion consistent with a man rising through the ranks of society. He owned a case of pistols, holsters, a breast plate, and an old belt that would have been used during local militia service and in defense of his home and plantation. He owned 130 pounds of pewter that was likely used for serving in the household, twelve new spoons, and thirteen old spoons. Many of the personal items would have been used in cooking.

In terms of fashion, William owned one "suit of cloth Clothes," two pair of shoes, and two pair of stockings, valued at £4.16.00. He also owned two pair of worsted hose and two pair of cotton hose, a cotton vest, caps, gloves, boots, and numerous other clothing items indicating a family that valued its appearance. Altogether, the cloth and clothing owned by the Hammack family was worth about £15, nearly one-tenth of the total value of William's personal estate.

Among the household furniture were four feather beds, one of them described as "large," bedsteads, curtains, rugs, and other items. While many planters lived in the simplest of ways, Hammack's inventory evidenced attempts at refined living: among his possessions were several small gilt boxes, a green rug, a silk rug, a red rug, curtains, a valens, a looking glass, five old leather chairs, two Russia leather chairs, several tables, and perhaps a dozen chests. All-purpose items in seventeenth and eighteenth century Virginia, chests could be used for storage, as tables, and as extra sitting during family and business gatherings. There is evidence, too, that William was both literate and pious. He owned a pair of spectacles and a parcel of books, among which was Richard Allestre's *The Whole Duty of Man*, a Psalter, a testament, a religious primer, and a Bible. Including the books, looking glass, and spectacles, the value of Hammack's ordinary household furnishings came to almost £25. In addition, there were a number of blankets, pillows, table cloths, and napkins that would have added to the family's comfort and, with the pewter, gilt boxes, and Russian leather chairs, would have provided an elegant veneer.

The level of comfort evidenced by William Hammack's household inventory is significant. The immigrant William had acquired a modest plantation during his four decades in the colony; no household inventory of his possessions survives, although most seventeenth-century dwellings were spartan owing to Virginians' desire to concentrate all of their available wealth in the acquisition of land and slaves. Hammack himself never held high office, but he moved in good society. His brother-in-law Benedict Middleton was a justice on the Westmoreland County court -- sitting in office when George Washington was born on Pope's Creek a few miles from his home plantation, and Hammack had business dealings with members of the county court in Richmond County and neighboring Westmoreland County.

Hammack served as a grand juror in Westmoreland County in 1695.[97] A few months later he served

---

[95] See T. J. Wertenberger, *Planters of Colonial Virginia* (Princeton, 1922), esp. pp. 183-247.
[96] Richmond Co., VA, Will Book, 1725-1753, pp. 159-160.
[97] Westmoreland Co., VA, Order Book, 1694-98, p. 184a.

as power of attorney for Mary Laughon.[98] With his brother-in-law Benedict Middleton, he was executor of John Middleton's estate in March 1706 and overseer of the estate while Middleton's children remained minors.[99] This position brought him in contact with other of Westmoreland's leading citizens. George Eskridge and Daniel McCarty, both of whom were county justices, entered into bond with Hammack and Middleton to execute the estate.[100] In 1706, Hammack again served as grand juror[101]; he also witnessed a deed with Benedict Middleton involving part of an 1,100 acre tract that had once belonged to his father-in-law Robert Middleton.

Although William seems to have lived for much of his adult life in Westmoreland County, his lands apparently lay along the county line, with a portion of them lying in Richmond County. The 1710 deed in which he purchased land from his younger brother marks his first appearance as a Richmond County landowner.[102] A 1712 deed places Hammack's land more exactly; when Charles Lewis was granted 200 acres, it was described as "adj. William Lambert, Charles Lund, Capt. John Tarpley, William Hammock, Richmond County line, and Clark's line."[103] When Charles Lewis sold this land in 1719, it was described as "bounded by ye lands of William Lambert, Charles Lund, Collo: John Tarpley and William Hamock."[104] At some point between 1710 and 1727, Hammack seems to have relocated onto his Richmond County lands[105]; on 2 November 1727, with Hugh Lambert and Thomas Lewis he appraised the estate of Patrick Short of Richmond County.[106] In 1729, he entered into a bond with Daniel Hornby -- a Richmond County Justice -- and John Elmore to serve as security for Elmore while he administered the estate of Robert Grigg, deceased.[107]

Hammack appeared in Richmond County court on 7 May 1729; ten months later, on 3 July 1730, he wrote his will. He had apparently become ill only recently, and William likely drafted his will knowing that he would not live long. The register of North Farnham Parish records that he died four days later on 7 July; he was likely not much more than sixty years old.[108]

William had already outlived one son -- William, likely his firstborn -- who died in 1724 in Westmoreland County.[109] Two other sons, Benedict and Robert, survived him, in addition to three married adult daughters.

Richard Hammack of Richmond, Westmoreland, and Louisa Counties, Virginia.

Richard Hammack was the only child of William and Grace Hammack whose birth was recorded in North Farnham Parish; he entered the world on 4 March 1674, probably on the tract his father had purchased from Thomas Freshwater a year earlier.

Richard Hammack seems to have been more contentious than his father. He first appears in legal

---

[98] Westmoreland Co., VA, Order Book 1703-05, p. 250a.

[99] Westmoreland Co., VA, Deeds and Wills No. 3, 1701-07, pp. 425-27.

[100] Westmoreland Co., VA, Order Book, 1705-07, p. 37a. Eskridge later served as guardian for a young girl named Mary Ball; after her marriage to Augustine Washington, she would name her infant son George – the future first President of the United States – in his honor.

[101] Westmoreland Co., VA, Order Book, 1705-07, p. p. 42.

[102] Richmond County, VA, Deeds, 1708-1711, pp. 179-181.

[103] Gray, *Northern Neck Land Grants, 1694-1742*, p. 51.

[104] Richmond County, VA, Deeds, 1714-20, pp. 486-87.

[105] The births of only two of William's children are recorded in the North Farnham Parish Register. These were of Jane Hammock in 1711 and of Elizabeth Hammock in 1714. All three daughters married in Richmond County. In 1727, Jane wed John Seamons, and Mary wed Charles Jones. In 1729, Elizabeth -- the youngest child -- married William Morgan. Granddaughter Christian (daughter of Benedict) was baptized in Richmond in 1723 and grandson William (son of William, Jr.) in 1724. William -- eldest child of Robert Hammack -- was baptized in 1726 in Richmond, as were almost all of Robert's younger offspring.

[106] Richmond Co., VA, Account Book, Part I, p. 18-19.

[107] Richmond Co., VA, Deeds, 1720-33, pp. 487-88.

[108] Richmond Co., VA, Deeds, 1720-33, pp. 487-88; Richmond Co., VA, Will Book 5, 1725-1753, p. 155.

[109] Westmoreland Co., VA, Order Book 1724-1726, pp. 74, 124.

records on 3 March 1698/9, when he was sued for debt by Thomas Newton.[110] Three months later, he confessed to having impregnated his father's servant Margaret Jones and nobly offered to pay her legal fines, but, nine months later, when he admitted his inability to do so, his father fulfilled the obligation.

Despite these indiscretions, the immigrant William Hammack retained sufficient trust in his young son to appoint him sole executor of his estate as he lay dying in 1701. Richard's record as administrator is similarly ambiguous. He repeatedly evaded claims against the estate. He removed from Richmond County to Westmoreland and ignored the charges of both courts to respond to his legal obligations. He was detained by the Westmoreland Sheriff for finally delivering a "contemptuous" response to the court's instructions. In addition to complaints involving his father's estate, Richard was personally sued by John Griffin in 1702.[111] Otherwise, to his credit, most of his other legal actions during these years involved his behavior as his father's executor rather than personal debts and obligations.

Perhaps marriage brought maturity and stability to Richard. He had at least two children -- William and Richard, both of whom seem to have been born about 1700 -- and in 1703 he became guardian to his stepson John Baker, indicating perhaps that Richard's first wife had died and that he had remarried an older woman.[112]

From this point onwards, Richard seems to have lived consistently in Westmoreland County. In 1704, he was on a committee to appraise John Ware's estate[113] and the following year Mary Laughon appointed him as her personal attorney to acknowledge release of her dower rights when her husband sold land.[114] In April 1705, Richard, his wife Elizabeth, and her son John Baker sued Francis Morris for trespassing on Baker's lands in Westmoreland, and cutting down several oak trees from Baker's property.[115] Apparently, Morris had earlier leased these lands from the Baker estate, but for five years had failed to pay rent. Richard and Elizabeth sued Morris for 2,000 pounds of tobacco due in back rent.[116] The court ultimately resolved the matter in Hammock's favor, and he and Morris were ordered to divide the court costs among the two.[117]

It seems that by 1709 Richard Hammack had married again, this time to the widow of Peter Duncan, and was serving as administrator of the Duncan estate.[118] Hammack was sued for debt in 1712 by Willoughby Allerton, Gent., and William Robottom. Richard was ordered to pay Allerton 450 pounds of tobacco and 542 pounds to Robottom.[119]

In 1717, Richard Hammack was arrested, although this time for what would today be considered a just cause. He was one of a group of local men -- Richard Organ, Thomas Harper, William Harper, Matthew Haile, George Newton, Jonas Hartley, Anthony Morgan, and Joseph Simmons -- arrested and ordered to appear before Justice Willoughby Allerton. The charge was that "of conveneing themselves (under pretence of religious worship) in company with divers other persons in conventicles contrary and repugnant to law being read and heard." George Eskridge, a Westmoreland attorney, handled the prosecution on behalf of Nathaniel Pope, Esquire, the authorized attorney.

---

[110] Richmond Co., VA, Orders, 1697-99, p. 389.
[111] Richmond Co., VA, Orders, 1699-1701, p. 154.
[112] Westmoreland Co., VA, Order Book 1701-03, p. 201a.
[113] Westmoreland Co., VA, Order Book 1703-05, p. 231a.
[114] Westmoreland Co., VA, Deeds and Wills No. 3, 1701-07, pp. 286-87.
[115] Westmoreland Co., VA, Order Book 1703-05, p. 260a.
[116] Westmoreland Co., VA, Order Book 1705-07, p. 32.
[117] Westmoreland Co., VA, Order Book, 1705-07, p. 46a.
[118] Westmoreland Co., VA, Order Book 1709-11, p. 128.
[119] Westmoreland Co., VA, Order Book 1711-13, pp. 183, 184, 190, 195.

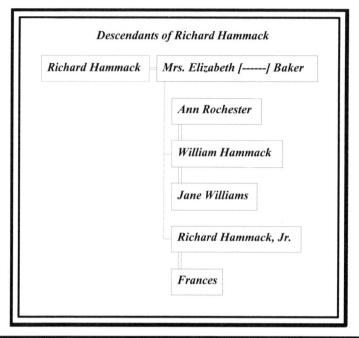

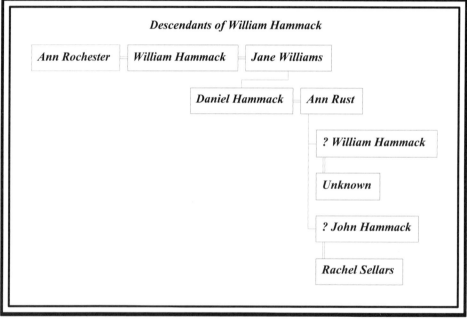

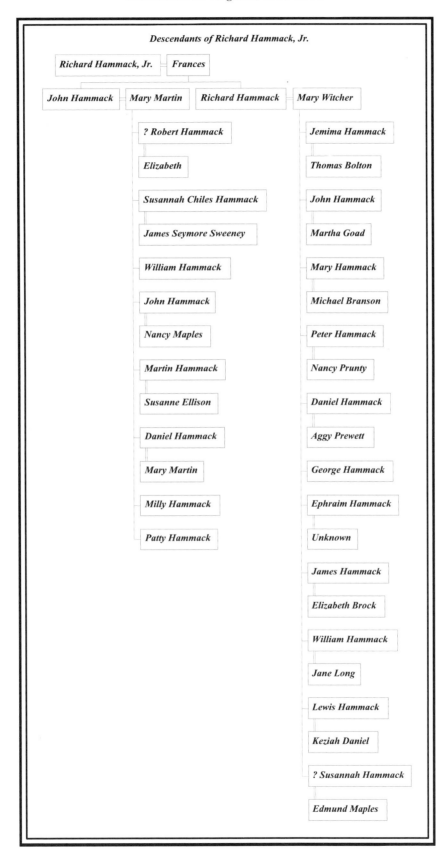

Descendants of Richard Hammack, Jr.

Richard Hammack, Jr. — Frances

John Hammack — Mary Martin — Richard Hammack — Mary Witcher

? Robert Hammack

Elizabeth

Susannah Chiles Hammack

James Seymore Sweeney

William Hammack

John Hammack

Nancy Maples

Martin Hammack

Susanne Ellison

Daniel Hammack

Mary Martin

Milly Hammack

Patty Hammack

Jemima Hammack

Thomas Bolton

John Hammack

Martha Goad

Mary Hammack

Michael Branson

Peter Hammack

Nancy Prunty

Daniel Hammack

Aggy Prewett

George Hammack

Ephraim Hammack

Unknown

James Hammack

Elizabeth Brock

William Hammack

Jane Long

Lewis Hammack

Keziah Daniel

? Susannah Hammack

Edmund Maples

The defendants were convicted and faced the following punishment:

Upon mature consideration it is their opinion that the prisoners have been guilty of the crime laid to their charge and thereupon do order that each and every of the prisoners do severally in the presence of the persons congregated at Yeocomico Church on the next Lord's day that divine service shall be celebrated there own their fault and acknowledge their error in the following words: I do acknowledge and confess before God and in the presence of this congregation that I have been guilty of convening and meeting in unlawfull assemblies and I doe humbly ask God and this congregation forgiveness of my offence therein and do also promise never to committ the like againe, as also that they do enter into bond with good and sufficient security in the sum of £40 sterling a piece to our Sovereign Lord the King for their good behaviour herein for the future.

Within a generation, the Church of England would be under assault throughout the Tidewater and Piedmont from dissenting evangelical groups. Richard Hammack's participation at this time may reflect the first seeds of religious dissent in the Northern Neck. Following the instructions of the court, he entered into bond with Richard Organ and Peter Dunkan -- probably his stepson -- for his obedience and good behavior in the future.[120]

Richard Hammack lived in Westmoreland County for nearly four decades; apparently he rented his farm and never became a landowner there. The 1733 will of William Walker makes clear that Walker owned the land on which Richard's family was living. To his son William he left "one hundred and fifty acres of Land lying in Nomini Forest whereon Richard Hammack, Junr., now liveth," and to his son Daniel he bequeathed "Eighty acres of Land lying in Nomini Forest whereon Old Richard Hammack now liveth."[121]

Richard's relations throughout his community seem to have been neighborly for the most part. In 1716, with Hugh Dunnahaw and Sampson Demouvel, he witnessed a deed from John Pyecraft to John Gorum for sixty acres in Westmoreland County.[122] In 1727, he and Morris Murfey witnessed the will of Moses Hopwood, and Elizabeth Hammack -- probably Richard's wife -- in 1733 witnessed William Walker's will.[123] In 1735, Richard was one of a large number of witnesses -- including Benjamin Walker, John Freshwater, Hugh Thomas, James Thomas, Jr., and John Bailey, Jr. -- who signed a deed from Elizabeth Bailey, widow of John Bailey, Sr., and her son William to William Lane.[124] In 1736, along with John Freshwater and John Sutton, Richard again witnessed a transaction for Elizabeth Bailey. This time she was deeding land to her son John.[125]

Richard's last known appearance in the records of Richmond and Westmoreland County occurs in 1737 and 1738, when he sued John Bowyer for trespass. Hammack alleged that Bowyer had detained a mare belonging to him worth £8. To support his claim, William Hammack of Westmoreland County and Peter Dunkan of Westmoreland County both made several appearances at the Richmond County court. Both Hammacks claimed they had traveled seven miles from their Westmoreland County home to the Richmond Court and then seven miles back; Richard Hammack, Jr., claimed he had lost fourteen days attending the Richmond Court on behalf of the suit. Bowyer pleaded not guilty, but the court ultimately found in Hammack's favor. The Richmond County court awarded him one pound and five shillings in

---

[120] Westmoreland Co., VA, Order Book 1717-18, pp. 323-323a. It is not immediately clear to which dissenting group these men belonged. The date -- 1717 -- predates the first flowering of the "Great Awakening" by nearly two decades. It is possible that these men were Quakers. Louisa County, to which Richard later removed, had a significant Quaker population by the middle eighteenth century. The Presbyterian and Baptist faiths are also possibilities.

[121] Westmoreland Co., VA, Deeds and Wills, 1723-38, pp. 212-212a.

[122] Westmoreland Co., VA, Deeds and Wills, 1723-38, pp. 574-80.

[123] Westmoreland Co., VA, Deeds and Wills, 1723-38, pp. 50, 212.

[124] Westmoreland Co., VA, Deeds and Wills, 1723-38, p. 274-274a.

[125] Dorman, Westmoreland Co., VA, Deed & Will Abstracts, 1736-40, pp. 314a-315a.

damages, and he was, in turn, to reimburse William Hammack 522 pounds of tobacco and Peter Dunkin 422 pounds of tobacco for costs incurred appearing on his behalf.[126]

Just when Richard Hammack left Westmoreland County is unclear, as is the probable date of his death. In 1742, Louisa County was formed from Hanover County, located southwest of the Rappahannock River about forty miles from Richmond County. Two years later, in 1744, the Virginia Assembly created Albemarle County -- later home to many of Richard's descendants -- from Louisa and Goochland Counties. The last located reference to Richard Hammack dates from 10 July 1750, when Richard Hammack, Sr., and Richard Hammack, Jr., witnessed the will of Robert Wells in Fredericksville, Louisa County, Virginia. Although Richard may have lived for several more years, no additional references to him have been discovered. He was survived by two sons, William and Richard, who moved with him westward into the Virginia frontier.[127]

William Hammack, the younger, of Richmond County, Virginia.

Just why the immigrant William Hammack chose to name a second son William is unknown. Such actions were not entirely unusual. In England, families that desired to perpetuate a particular name sometimes gave that name to more than one child, often with a second name used to distinguish two siblings. The Gawdy family of Norfolk, England, in which the name Thomas was often used, is an example. And, in William Hammack's instance, perhaps the reasoning was similar. In any case, his elder son William lived across the county line in Westmoreland, and William's new wife Alice may have wished to give her first son her husband's name.[128]

William Hammack the younger, only known son of William and Alice Hammack, was born on 15 March 1688 in North Farnham Parish, Richmond County, Virginia. He was perhaps twenty years younger than his older brother, William Hammack, the elder, and he was a lad of only thirteen years when his father died in 1701, leaving him in the care of his elder brother Richard and of his stepmother, Margaret Macey Hammack.

William probably grew up in Westmoreland County on the rented farm of his brother Richard Hammack, who may also have managed the 200 acres bequeathed to William in 1701 by their father. He may also have lived for a time with his brother William Hammack the elder, who seems to have moved from Westmoreland County back into Richmond County about 1710.

The reasons are unclear, but William's first action upon reaching adulthood was to deed one half of his inheritance from his father to his elder brother. In a deed dated 1 April 1710 -- only two weeks after he reached his maturity -- William Hammack the younger, of North Farnham Parish in Richmond County, conveyed to William Hammack the elder, of Cople Parish in Westmoreland County, the eastern portion of a 200-acre tract left him by the immigrant William Hammack. In exchange for the land, William Hammack the elder paid his younger brother 3,000 pounds of tobacco. Dr. Robert Clarke and Benedict Middleton witnessed the deed.[129]

Like his father, the younger William Hammack seems to have lived a quiet and uncontentious life. He seldom appears in legal records of any sort. He may be the William Hammack who on 2 July 1718 in Richmond County bound with Eliza McKenney and William Gupton to administer the estate of Cormack McKenney, deceased.[130] He is probably also the William Hammack found on a 1741 poll record in

---

[126] Richmond Co., VA, Order Book, 1732-1739, pp. 579, 585.

[127] Louisa Co., VA, Will Book A, p. 23.

[128] For more on aristocratic nomenclature, see D. Cressy, *Birth, Marriage, and Death: Ritual, Religion, and the Life Cycle in Tudor and Stuart England* (Oxford, 1997) and F. Heal and C. Holmes, *The Gentry in England and Wales, 1500-1700* (Basingstoke, 1994). For the Gawdy example, see P. Millican, "The Gawdys of Norfolk and Suffolk," in *Original Papers of the Norfolk and Norwich Archeological Society*, 26 (Norwich, 1946): 335-347, and 27 (Norwich, 1947): 30-43, 70-73.

[129] Richmond County, VA, Deeds, 1708-1711, p. 179-181.

[130] Richmond Co., VA, Deeds, 1714-20, p. 299.

Richmond County who cast his vote for John Woodbridge, a candidate for the House of Burgesses.[131]

Just when or where William Hammack the younger died has not been determined, and no probate on his estate has been found. He may have died legally unnoticed, with his property passing by right of primogeniture to his son John. Certainly, William seems to have lived continuously from 1710 to at least 1739 in North Farnham Parish. By 1714, he had married a woman named Eleanor -- who may have been related to the Lambert family; between 1715 and 1739, they baptized six children in North Farnham Parish: Alice (1715); John (1718); William (1720); Alice (1724); Elizabeth (1734); and Eleanor (1739).

Of these offspring, John Hammack married Mildred Lambert in 1741; by 1748, they had settled in Lunenburg County on the southern frontier, probably accompanying Mildred's Lambert relatives as they moved southward.[132] No clear trace of William Hammack, son of William and Eleanor, has been found. He may have died young.

It is worth noting that by the 1730s there were several men named William Hammack living in Richmond and Westmoreland Counties:

> William Hammack the elder, who died in 1730;
> William Hammack, Jr., son of William Hammack the elder, who died in 1724;
> William Hammack, son of William Hammack, Jr., and wife Margaret, born in 1724 and a reared
>   by his grandfather William Hammack the elder, who named him as an heir in his 1730 will;[133]
> William Hammack, son of Richard Hammack, who was married by 1719 to
>   Ann Rochester, and who probably was Richard Hammack's witness in
>   1738;
> William Hammack the younger, who lived in Richmond County from 1715
>   to 1739, with wife Eleanor who was alive during all of this period;
> William Hammack, born in 1720, who was son of William and Eleanor;
> William Hammack, born in 1726, son of Robert and Ann Lambert Hammack,
>   who apparently died young;
> William Hammack, born between 1726 and 1730, son of Benedict and Elizabeth
>   Hammack, who moved to Amelia County, Virginia, and Wilkes County,
>   Georgia.
> William Hammack, son of John Hammack, who was named as a minor in his
>   father's 1708 will. No clear reference to him has been found after that
>   date.

One minor mystery is the identity of the William Hammack who was by 7 December 1732 married to Joan Williams, daughter of David and Elizabeth Williams.[134] Joan was baptized 19 August 1709 in Richmond County and was about twenty-three when she married William Hammack. He sued the

---

[131] Richmond Co., VA, Account Book I, pp. 174-177.

[132] 1748 Lunenburg Co., VA, Tithe List, Hound's Creek to Meherrin River, Library of Virginia, Richmond, VA.

[133] This William was born about the time of his father's death and christened in North Farnham Parish, Richmond County, by his mother Margaret Hammack. Westmoreland Co., VA, Order Book 1724-1726, pp. 74, 124, clarifies this relationship. On 30 September 1724, "William Hammock next of kinn to Wm: Hammock junr decd came into court & made oath that the sd dec departed this life without making any Will so farr as he knows or believes and upon his motion and his performing what is usual in such cases certificate is granted him for obtaining Letters of Administration upon the said Williams estate in due form (Margtt his relict having certified her relinquishment thereof to this court) George Eskridge gentl & Bennedict Middleton assumeing in court to be security's for his faithful administration according to law. Ordered that Bennedict Middleton, John Middleton, Benja: Middleton and Frances Self or any three of them being first sworn before a majestrate of the sd county do sometimme before the next court to be held for the county aforesaid value & appraise the sd estate in money & make report thereof to the said court." This document refers to William Hammack, Sr., of Richmond County, who became administrator for his son's estate and then reared the children of William Hammack, Jr., and wife Margaret.

[134] Richmond Co., VA, Order Book, 1732-1739, p. 20.

Williams estate to claim her inheritance from her parents from 1732 until 3 April 1739, when the court ordered her former guardian Benjamin Rust to hand over her share of her father's estate.[135]

Based on the Hammack chronology, only William Hammack -- son of Richard -- or William Hammack -- son of John -- could be this individual. The likeliest scenario seems to be that this was a second marriage for William Hammack, husband of Ann Rochester, since no clear references to John's son William have been located.

B. The Third Generation: Grandchildren of the Immigrant William Hammack

From 1668 to 1740, the saga of the American Hammacks unfolded within a couple of miles of Totuskey Creek in what is today eastern Richmond County, Virginia. There the immigrant William settled upon receiving his freedom from servitude. There his children and all of his grandchildren were born. If there is a single theme that characterizes the third and fourth generation of American Hammacks, however, it is migration. The grandchildren and great-grandchildren of the immigrant William Hammack would end their lives as far away as Kentucky, Tennessee, North Carolina, and Georgia.

In the paragraphs that follow, the third generation of American Hammacks will be discussed briefly, separated by family group.

The sons of William Hammack the elder.

William Hammack and Christian Middleton were the parents of three sons and three daughters: William Hammack (by c. 1698 -- c. 1724); Benedict Hammack (by c. 1702 -- c. 1767); Robert Hammack (by c. 1704 -- 1786); Mary Hammock Jones (c. 1706 – c. 1750); Jane Hammack Seamons (c. 1711 -- c. 1729); and Elizabeth Hammack Morgan (c. 1714 -- aft. 1735).

Of the offspring of William and Christian, all grew to maturity in Richmond County. By mid-century, however, many of his descendants had begun to leave the Northern Neck and settle in the Virginia Southside, the region south and west of the James River stretching from the Tidewater westward into the Piedmont.

A growing population and an increasing need for fertile land were the two primary determinants that pushed the physical expansion of eighteenth-century Virginia. A labor intensive crop, tobacco also quickly exhausts the soil in which it grows. Every three or four years, existing fields must be abandoned in favor of new, more productive ones. By the early eighteenth-century, much of the eastern Tidewater was declining in productivity, and Virginia's planters were eager to acquire additional lands to the south and west.[136]

In addition, since the 1660s Virginia's mortality rate had been declining. Virginians were living longer, and they were producing larger families, as is exemplified by the demographics of the immigrant William Hammack's own family. Only three of William's children lived into adulthood. Yet these three produced at least fourteen grandchildren, including at least nine who reached adulthood and left offspring of their own. Although William Hammack had acquired in his lifetime a farm of perhaps 300 acres which was sufficient to provide for himself and his offspring, it had long since ceased to support the dozens of descendants who were living in Richmond and Westmoreland Counties by the 1730s. This phenomenon was taking place throughout the colony, pressuring the House of Burgesses to create new counties from the lands on the western frontier.

In 1720, the Virginia Assembly established Brunswick County from Prince George, Surry, Isle of Wight, and the unsettled lands to the west of them. Lunenburg was created from Brunswick in 1746 and

---

[135] Richmond Co., VA, Order Book, 1732-1739, p. 705.

[136] For studies of western expansion and its social and political consequences, see R. Isaac, *The Transformation of Virginia, 1740-1790* (New York, 1982) and R. Beeman, *The Evolution of the Southern Backcountry: A Case Study of Lunenburg Co., VA 1746-1832* (Philadelphia, 1984).

Amelia in 1734 from Brunswick and Prince George. These were originally huge counties from which all or part of Pittsylvania (1766), Halifax (1752), Campbell (1781), Bedford (1753), Charlotte (1764), Prince Edward (1753), Mecklenburg (1764), Nottoway (1788), Franklin (1785), and Henry (1776) were later formed. By the time the Assembly established Brunswick County, it was already being populated by settlers from the north and east, including many residents of the Northern Neck.[137]

It was not until after 1740 that the progeny of the immigrant William Hammack began arriving in the Southside. Benedict Hammack, son of the William and Christian, left the Northern Neck for Amelia County in 1743.[138] Hugh Lambert, father-in-law of two grandsons of the immigrant William Hammack, began acquiring land in Brunswick County in 1748 while still living in Richmond County. He was living in Brunswick County with his grandson Robert Hammack, Jr., throughout the 1750s, while his son-in-law John Hammack (who had married Mildred Lambert in 1741) was living further west in Lunenburg as early as 1746.[139] His contemporary, another John Hammack, remained in Richmond County into the 1760s before venturing even further South, into Granville County, North Carolina.[140]

Benedict, son of William and Christian Hammack.

Benedict Hammack was the second son of William Hammack and Christian Middleton; he was named for his uncle Benedict Middleton, who was a prominent local figure in Westmoreland County, Virginia. Although the date of Benedict's birth is uncertain, his firstborn child was born in 1723 -- the same year that he makes his first appearance in the legal records of Richmond County. Hence, he was probably born in or just before 1702, in Westmoreland County, Virginia. About 1710, he moved with his father to Totuskey Creek in Richmond County, and there he married and began his family. Benedict's wife was named Elizabeth, and some have suspected that she may have been a member of the Lewis family who lived on a farm adjoining the Hammack plantation.

On 30 April 1723, Benedict Hammack purchased fifty acres of land from George Sisson; he paid 3,000 pounds of tobacco for the property.[141] No deed has been found in which Benedict disposed of this property; he may have sold it privately in an instrument no longer recorded, but he probably lived on this land, and that inherited from his father William in 1730, until about the time he left Richmond County in 1743.

On 6 September 1744, Benedict patented a tract of 396 acres on Hurricane Creek in Amelia County.[142] Rather than write a will, Benedict apparently chose to dispose of his landed estate through deeds of gift to his offspring. Between 1756 and 1768, he deeded 244 acres in Amelia County to his sons and son-in-law. All of this land lay in contiguous tracts located along Hogpen Branch and Long Branch; neighbors in Amelia included John Hames, Charles Connally, Samuel Bentley (his son-in-law's brother), John Seamon (a relative from Richmond County), James Jackson, Henry Green, and George Hill.[143]

After 1758, Benedict thus retained about 150 acres of his original 1744 grant. In 1765, probably preparing to leave the county, his son William Hammack and wife Elizabeth Hames Hammack deeded 110 acres to Mary Wainwright of Dinwiddie; Benedict Hammack joined his son at this time and also sold another ninety-five acres of his 1744 grant to Wainwright. In 1766, Benedict and wife Elizabeth deeded the final ninety acres of his holdings to William Holloway of Dinwiddie. What became of him after that

---

[137] For a concise study of the formation of Virginia counties, see W. M. Everton et al., *The Handy Book for Genealogists* (7th ed., Logan, UT, 1981), pp. 296-307.

[138] Richmond Co., VA, Deeds, Book 10, p. 8.

[139] Brunswick Co., VA, DB 3, p. 497, 504; Lunenburg Co., VA, Deed Book 5, p. 405-6; Brunswick Co., VA, Will Book 2, pp. 426-429.

[140] Richmond Co., VA, Deeds, Book 10, p. 537; Granville Co., NC, Deed Book L, pp. 219-221.

[141] Richmond Co., VA, Deeds, 1720-33, pp. 196-98.

[142] Amelia Co., VA, Deed Book 8, p. 606. See also VA Land Office Index, Patent Book No. 35, 1762-64, p. 304. This was the neighborhood in which John Jackson, grandfather of Millenor Jackson Hammack, began acquiring land as early as 1738.

[143] Amelia Co., VA, Deed Book 5, p. 464, and Deed Book 6, pp. 142, 204, 241, 246.

date is unclear; he may have died soon afterwards in Amelia, or he may have moved with his adult children to Onslow County, North Carolina, and died there.[144]

In terms of landholdings, Benedict seems to have possessed more than enough property to support his family and probably generate a modest profit from tobacco cultivation. As each of his children came of age and married, he was able to gift them with a small plantation that served to give them an economic foothold as well.

In terms of Benedict's standing within his community, he seems to have been respected as a solid and dependable neighbor. He was a juror in Richmond County in 1733[145], 1736[146], 1739[147], and 1740[148]. He was security for William Abshone in 1734 when he was sued by Thomas Osborne,[149] and he appears on Richmond County voting lists in 1735 and 1741.[150] In 1736 and 1737, he was security for his father's old neighbor William Hartley when he was sued by Richard Barnes, Gent.[151] In 1737, with John Clark, his brother Robert Hammock, and Robert's father-in-law Hugh Lambert, he appraised the estate of William Grady.[152] The same year, along with William Hammack, he was security for John Morgan when he became guardian of Joshua Morgan.[153] In 1738, he was named to survey all roads from the Beaver Dam to Totuskey Mill[154], and, along with his cousin Robert Middleton and Hugh Lambert, he in 1740 was named to lay out a new road from Totuskey "between the Secretary's Fence and the Governor's Spring to the said Middleton's Mill." Along with John Oldham, Jr., Hammack was then to supervise the construction of the road.[155]

Although friends and neighbors could rely on Benedict Hammack for assistance in times of need, Benedict did on occasion utilize the court system for himself. In 1734, he sued John Spragg for a debt and was awarded 455 pounds of tobacco.[156] The next year, with his brother Robert Hammock, he sued John Brown for another debt and was awarded 325 pounds of tobacco.[157] In 1736, he filed suit against Tobias Purcel and Richard Meeks for trespass, but the case was soon dropped when Hammack declined to prosecute.[158]

The evidence suggests that Benedict Hammack had a particularly close relationship with his brother Robert and Robert's father-in-law Hugh Lambert. The men were involved in several legal transactions together, and in the 1740s Lambert also began investigating recently settled areas in the Southside.[159] Hugh Lambert waited until the 1750s to move southward, however, and his son-in-law Robert Hammack remained in Richmond County until his death. Yet Benedict Hammack, the eldest of the Hammack siblings, chose to leave Richmond County; as noted above, in 1744 he received a substantial land grant in Amelia County and settled there.[160]

---

[144] Amelia Co., VA, Deed Book 9, p. 191.

[145] Richmond Co., VA, Order Book, 1732-1739, p. 154.

[146] Richmond Co., VA, Order Book, 1732-1739, p. 373.

[147] Richmond Co., VA, Order Book, 1739-1746, p. 37

[148] Richmond Co., VA, Order Book 1739-1746, p. 82.

[149] Richmond Co., VA, Order Book, 1732-1739, p. 161.

[150] Richmond County Poll List, Huntington Library, San Marino, CA, from negative photostats at the Library of Virginia, and Richmond Co., VA, Account Book I, pp. 174-177.

[151] Richmond Co., VA, Order Book, 1732-1739, pp. 406, 439, 455-456.

[152] Richmond Co., VA, Order Book, 1732-1739, p. 519.

[153] Richmond Co., VA, Order Book, 1732-1739, p. 547.

[154] Richmond Co., VA, Order Book, 1732-1739, p. 631.

[155] Richmond Co., VA, Order Book, 1739-1746, p. 90.

[156] Richmond Co., VA, Order Book, 1732-1739, p. 164.

[157] Richmond Co., VA, Order Book, 1732-1739, p. 305.

[158] Richmond Co., VA, Order Book, 1732-1739, p. 383.

[159] See, for instance, Richmond Co., VA, Order Book, 1732-1739, p. 519; Richmond Co., VA, Order Book, 1739-1746, p. 90.

[160] The close association might be partly attributable to a kinship between their wives. As noted previously, Benedict's wife may have been Elizabeth Lewis. Hugh Lambert's mother-in-law Anne Morgan may also have been a Lewis before marriage. Both were likely related to John, Thomas, Charles, and Edward Lewis, who owned tracts adjoining William Hammack, William Lambert, and William Morgan. Hence it may be that Elizabeth (Lewis?) Hammack and Anne (Lewis?) Morgan were aunt and niece, thus making

Less is known of Benedict's activities after settling in Amelia. Although many Northern Neck families were moving southward, immigrants were also coming from other parts of the Tidewater as well as from older settlements east of Amelia and Brunswick. Benedict probably also acquired prominence in his neighborhood, but we know less of his activities in Amelia County.

Benedict may have inadvertently played a significant role in the future of another Hammack relative. His lands in Amelia joined those of William and James Jackson, and it was into this Jackson family that Benedict's nephew Robert Hammack married a decade later when he took Edward Jackson's daughter Millenor as his wife. It is worth noting that documents pertaining the Hammacks, Jacksons, and allied kin appear simultaneously in Amelia, Lunenburg, and Brunswick Counties; the Hammacks lived near the common boundary shared by all three counties in the vicinity of what is today Nottoway County, created from Amelia County's Nottoway Parish in 1788.[161]

John, grandson of William and Christian Hammack.

Demography favored the eighteenth-century Hammacks, so much so that distinguishing between the many William Hammacks and John Hammacks residing in the same neighborhoods has become a challenge for modern researchers. This situation has complicated the correct identification of William Hammack's grandson John Hammack.

When William Hammack wrote his will in 1730, he left the care of his grandchildren -- William, Mary, and John -- to his wife Christian during her widowhood. The will does not identify the father of these offspring, but he appears to have been the William Hammack who died in Westmoreland County in 1724. Further, he was apparently also the William with wife Margaret whose son William Hammack was baptized the same year in Richmond County.

Of these three orphaned children, Mary married Francis Elmore on 23 November 1739 in Richmond County. He belonged to a neighboring Richmond County family with connections in Amelia and Lunenburg Counties in the Southside as well. What became of the grandson William Hammack is less clear; no record of him other than the reference in his grandfather's will has been found.

John Hammack, the other grandson of William and Christian, became an adult in Richmond County in the early 1740s. At the same time, his father's first cousin, another John Hammack, born in 1718 to William Hammack the younger and wife Eleanor, came of age. One John Hammack married Mildred Lambert in 1741 and moved to Lunenburg County by 1746; the other married first a woman called Susannah and second a woman called Mary Ann and moved to Granville County, North Carolina, where he died in 1776.

It is believed that the grandson of William Hammack and wife Christian Middleton was the John Hammack who with wife Mary Ann moved about 1761 or 1762 to Granville County, North Carolina. One reason for this belief is that Mary Ann Hammack, John's widow, subsequently moved to Wilkes County, Georgia, where she was a near neighbor of Robert Hammack (husband of Millenor Jackson). She seems to have had a prolonged, close relationship with Robert and Millenor Hammack which is indicative of a close connection between her husband and Robert Hammack.[162]

---

the wives of Benedict Hammack and Hugh Lambert first cousins.

[161] Amelia Co., VA, Deed Book 4, pp. 304, 314.

[162] Along with Benedict, Robert Hammack, Sr., had in 1730 been charged with rearing William Hammack's three orphaned grandchildren and overseeing their estate. Benedict Hammack left the county in 1743, but Robert remained until he died in 1787. Thus, Robert Hammack, Sr., may have been a "father figure" to John during his youth and early manhood. If so, John and Robert Hammack, Jr. (husband of Millenor Jackson) may have had a close relationship, possibly explaining why Mary Ann Hammack and her family chose to settle near Robert's family in Georgia.

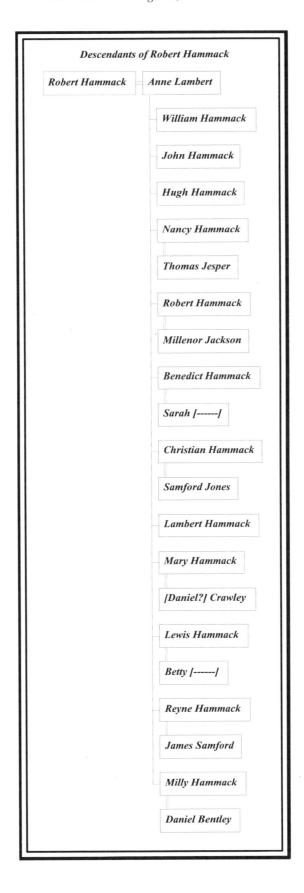

Descendants of Robert Hammack

Robert Hammack — Anne Lambert

William Hammack

John Hammack

Hugh Hammack

Nancy Hammack

Thomas Jesper

Robert Hammack

Millenor Jackson

Benedict Hammack

Sarah [------]

Christian Hammack

Samford Jones

Lambert Hammack

Mary Hammack

[Daniel?] Crawley

Lewis Hammack

Betty [------]

Reyne Hammack

James Samford

Milly Hammack

Daniel Bentley

Descendants of Milly Hammack

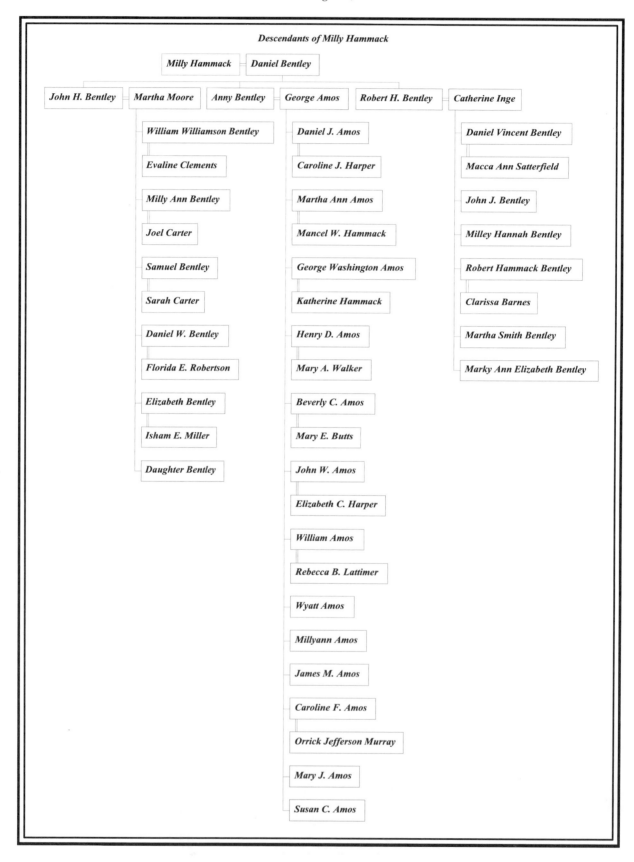

Milly Hammack — Daniel Bentley

John H. Bentley — Martha Moore — Anny Bentley — George Amos — Robert H. Bentley — Catherine Inge

William Williamson Bentley
Evaline Clements
Milly Ann Bentley
Joel Carter
Samuel Bentley
Sarah Carter
Daniel W. Bentley
Florida E. Robertson
Elizabeth Bentley
Isham E. Miller
Daughter Bentley

Daniel J. Amos
Caroline J. Harper
Martha Ann Amos
Mancel W. Hammack
George Washington Amos
Katherine Hammack
Henry D. Amos
Mary A. Walker
Beverly C. Amos
Mary E. Butts
John W. Amos
Elizabeth C. Harper
William Amos
Rebecca B. Lattimer
Wyatt Amos
Millyann Amos
James M. Amos
Caroline F. Amos
Orrick Jefferson Murray
Mary J. Amos
Susan C. Amos

Daniel Vincent Bentley
Macca Ann Satterfield
John J. Bentley
Milley Hannah Bentley
Robert Hammack Bentley
Clarissa Barnes
Martha Smith Bentley
Marky Ann Elizabeth Bentley

Another factor supporting this identification is the fact that this John Hammack heired thirty acres in 1730 from his grandfather William Hammack. The land is described as adjacent Sullivant and Cralle and was a portion of the original tract that had belonged to John's great-grandfather, the immigrant William Hammack. On 12 March 1749/50, John and Susannah Hammack sold 200 acres to John S. Webb; the land is described as "bound by Mr. John Crawley, Hugh Lambert, Robert Hammack, the Drinking Swamp, and sd. Webb." It is not clear how John Hammack acquired this land; it may have included the thirty acres he had heired from his grandfather plus additional lands purchased by himself later.[163]

North Farnham Parish records establish that John and Susannah were married before 1745, when their son Charles was baptized on 29 January 1744/45. After Charles came William (born 1747), Mary (born 1753), and Caty (born 1755). There may also have been a son named David (born c. 1750). Susannah apparently died about 1755, and John then married a woman named Mary Ann, who may have been the daughter of Thomas Lewis (1692-1744) and his wife Elizabeth who was baptized on 23 April 1733. They had a large family, which included John (born 1756), Ann (born 1758), three unidentified daughters (born c. 1760 – c. 1764), Elizabeth (born c. 1770), Lewis (born c. 1772), William (born c. 1774), James (born c. 1776), and probably Thomas (born c. 1766) and Willoughby (born c. 1768).

At some point between 1762 and 1769, John and Mary Ann Hammack left Richmond County, Virginia and settled in Granville County, North Carolina. He was living there on 24 November 1769, when he purchased 200 acres from Joseph and Nancy Miller.[164] John Hammack wrote his will in Granville on 4 November 1776; it was proven days later.[165] Therein, John names wife Mary Ann and son John, Jr., and alludes to additional offspring. John, Jr., at this point was about twenty years old and probably already married to Phoebe Paschall. A 1771 militia list had shown John Hammack, David Hammack, Charles Hammack, Elisha Paschall, and John Paschall as soldiers in Nutbush District of Granville County,[166] and all except John signed an oath of allegiance to the new government there in 1775.[167]

Soon after John Hammack, Sr., died, Mary Ann moved her large family a short distance north to Pittsylvania County, Virginia. She may have had relatives of her own there. She was taxed in Pittsylvania County in 1785 with eight white souls in her household. In 1787, Thomas Hammack, probably her son, was taxed in the household beside her; he had in 1786 sold land in Granville County, North Carolina, before joining his mother in Virginia.[168]

Mary Ann and Thomas were both taxed in Pittsylvania County as late as 1790, when they probably moved south. In 1791, Thomas Hammock was found living along Kettle Creek in Wilkes County. Mary Ann settled a few miles to the southwest, along Rocky Creek in what is today Taliaferro County. She was taxed there from 1792 until 1802, when she sold her land and disappeared from the records.[169]

Robert, son of William and Christian Hammack.

One of the largest groupings of American Hammack families was sired by Robert Hammack, son of William Hammack and Christian Middleton. He seems to have been named for his uncle, Robert Middleton, a leading citizen of Westmoreland County who operated Middleton's Mill near the boundary between Westmoreland and Middlesex. William and Christian apparently favored family names for their

---

[163] Richmond Co., VA, Deed Book 10, p. 537. Richmond County Court Orders distinguish this man from his cousin by calling him "John Hammack (the freeholder)" indicating that he was a landowner. His cousin, the son of William Hammack the younger, apparently rented rather than owned property in his own right.

[164] Granville Co., NC, Deed Book L, pp. 219-221.

[165] Z. H. Gwynn, *Abstracts of Wills and Estate Records of Granville Co., NC, 1746-1808* (Rocky Mount, NC, 1973), p. 148.

[166] *The Colonial and State Records of North Carolina* (26 vols., Raleigh, NC, 1886-1907), 22: 160.

[167] Ibid., 22: 175.

[168] Z. H. Gwynn, *Court Minutes of Granville Co., NC, 1746-1820* (Rocky Mount, NC, 1977), p. 47.

[169] F. P. Hudson, *Wilkes Co., GA, Tax Records, 1785-1805* (2 vols., Atlanta, GA, 1996). See especially the lists for 1792, 1793, 1795, 1797, 1799, 1801, and 1802.

offspring. Their first son William was likely named for the immigrant William Hammack. Benedict, the second son, was named for Christian's brother. Robert, the third son, was named for his grandfather, Robert Middleton.

Because he was born in Westmoreland County, no precise date of birth for Robert Hammack is known. He was of age by 7 June 1727, when, with Hugh Lambert, he made bond to Thomas Morgan.[170] By this point, he was already married to Ann Lambert, daughter of Hugh Lambert and Ann Morgan, for their first child was baptized in North Farnham Parish on 10 September 1726. If Robert were of legal age when he and Ann married, then he was probably born by about 1704. Ann may have been slightly younger but in any case was probably born no later than 1710.

When William Hammack died in 1730, Robert was given a residual interest in lands left to Benedict Hammack. He was also given the land on which Benedict Hammack was in 1730 living, with the provision that it revert back to Benedict should Robert die without legal heirs. Robert and his brother Benedict were charged with rearing William's three orphaned grandchildren and with caring for Christian Middleton Hammack during her old age; they were also given an equal share in William Hammack's personal property.

The exact acreage of the tract Robert inherited from his father in 1730 is unknown. He supplemented it with another 200 acres in 1743 when he purchased land joining William Lambert, John Tarpley, William Hammack (deceased), and Charles Lund from John Cavenaugh. John Hammack, Charles Jones, John Elmore, and Robert Stadder witnessed the deed.[171] Robert apparently retained all of this land until he died in the fall of 1786.

During the course of his long life -- which probably spanned more than eight decades -- Robert Hammack played many roles in the community around Totuskey Creek. He seems to have remained for most of his life a loyal communicant of the Church of England, baptizing children in North Farnham Parish from 1726 until 1758. That he continued to have grandchildren baptized in the English church suggests that his family retained the Anglican faith at least into the Revolutionary era.[172]

In terms of his relations with his neighbors, Robert seems to have played a role in the local community similar to that of his elder brother Benedict. He was a juror in 1735[173], the same year that he and his brother Benedict successfully sued John Brown for debt.[174] With Benedict Hammack, Hugh Lambert, and John Clark he appraised the estate of William Grady in 1737.[175] In 1741, he witnessed a deed from his wife's uncle William Lambert to her father Hugh Lambert. His name appears on Richmond County voting lists for 1741[176], 1752[177], and 1758.[178] On 12 March 1749/50, he was a witness when his nephew John Hammack sold land in Richmond County,[179] along with Robert Croff and David Hammack. In 1768, he, William Headley, and George Clarke helped settle Anne Headley's estate[180], and in 1772 and 1773 he served as witness in a court case involving Thomas Taffe.[181] Robert also served as surveyor of roads, district constable, and, at times, jailor for Richmond County.[182]

---

[170] A. E. Wynne, *Southern Lineages: Records of Thirteen Families* (Atlanta, GA, 1940).

[171] Richmond Co., VA, Deed Book 10, pp. 171, 174.

[172] See Isaac, *Transformation of Virginia*, for the decline of the established church and the rise of evangelical denominations in Virginia.

[173] Richmond Co., VA, Order Book, 1732-1739, p. 288.

[174] Richmond Co., VA, Order Book, 1732-1739, p. 305.

[175] Richmond Co., VA, Order Book, 1732-1739, p. 519.

[176] Richmond Co., VA, Account Book I, pp. 174-177.

[177] *Magazine of Virginia Genealogy*, Vol. 24 (1986), pp. 66-68.

[178] Richmond Co., VA, Order Book 14.

[179] Richmond Co., VA, Deed Book 10, p. 537.

[180] Richmond Co., VA, Account Book II, p. 540.

[181] Richmond Co., VA, Order Book 17, 1769-1773, p. 524, and Order Book 19, 1773-1776, and 1784-1786, p. 10.

[182] Richmond Co., VA, Order Book 11, 1740-1747, pp. 275, 507; Richmond Co., VA, Order Book 12, 1748-1752, pp. 246, 360.

As was required of all adult male Virginians, Robert Hammack performed militia service in Richmond County for much of his adult life. Although he was too old for active military duty, during the Revolutionary period he supported the American Continental troops as they struggled to create a new nation. In 1782, Robert and his son Benedict made record that they had supplied 225 pounds of beef and other supplies to aid the patriot forces.[183] At the same time, Robert's sons and grandsons on the Georgia frontier were aiding the Continental troops through military service.

Robert Hammack's land seems to have lain along the boundary that separated Richmond County from Westmoreland County, where he had been born. When Benedict Middleton of Westmoreland County purchased 185 acres of land in Westmoreland County in 1737 from John and Hannah Hartley, the property is described as lying on Totuskey Creek and "binding on the several lands of Crawley, George Harrison, deced., Thomas Brown, deceased, and Robert Hammock, and so up the Marshy Swamp the several courses and meanders thereof to the beginning".[184] Likewise, in 1755, when Robert and Mary Middleton sold 185 acres to their son Benedict, the land was described in a Westmoreland deed as "joining Robert Middleton and Robert Hammack, John Bailey, land of Robert Middleton, deceased."[185] A 1783 tax list describes Robert Hammack and son Benjamin as living in the "Forks of Totuskey," apparently near the point at which the Totuskey shifts into Westmoreland County.[186]

Robert Hammack was more than eighty years old when he wrote his will on 1 October 1785 in Richmond County, and he and wife Ann had been married for sixty of those years. To her, he bequeathed:

...the land I now live on during her natural life. I give to my loving wife my Negro woman Mary and Negro Child James. I give to my loving wife my desk and trunk that stands upon it. I give to my loving wife two of my best Beds and furniture. I give to my loving wife my large Chest and lock and key. I give to my loving wife one of my best Butter potts and Cream pott and my two earthen plates and mug and Spice mortar and pestle. I give to my loving wife half of the stock of Cattle and hogs. I give to my loving wife half of all my pewter and my warming pan and my Box Iron and heaters. I give to my loving wife my Horse and her Saddle and my two leather Chairs and my large table and looking Glass, all these things, I do give to my loving wife to do as she thinks proper at my death.[187]

Between 1726 and 1757, Ann Lambert Hammack, daughter of Hugh Lambert and Ann Morgan, gave birth to twelve children; several of them seem to have predeceased their parents. Robert's will names only Benedict Hammack, Lewis Hammack, Rayne Samford, Nancy Jesper, Christian Jones, Robert Hammack, and Mary Craughley. To his son Benedict, he left the land where Robert then lived as well as a Negro slave and personal property. Lewis, Rayne, Nancy, and Christian also received slaves. Robert's personal property was to be equally divided between Benedict, Lewis, Robert, Rayne, Nancy, Christian, and Mary. At the time Robert wrote his will, Lewis was living in Charlotte County, Virginia, and Robert Hammack, Jr., was living in Wilkes County, Georgia. Of the Virginia Hammacks, only Benedict Hammack, son of Robert and Ann, remained near his father in the Northern Neck.[188]

Robert Hammack named Thomas Jesper, Benedict Hammack, and Daniel Brown as his executors; William Hammack, Benedict Hammack, and Thomas Brown witnessed the will. The document was

---

[183] Janice L. Abercrombie and Richard Slatten, eds., *Virginia Revolutionary Public Claims* (3 vols., Athens, LA, 1992), 3: 817.

[184] Westmoreland Co., VA, Deeds & Wills, 1723-38, pp. 330-31.

[185] Westmoreland Co., VA, Deeds and Wills, 1753-1756, pp. 202-204.

[186] 1783 Richmond Co., VA, Tax List, Library of Virginia, Richmond, VA.

[187] Richmond Co., VA, Will Book 7, 1767-1787, pp. 527-528.

[188] Milly Hammack Bentley, daughter of Robert and Ann, was also then living in Lunenburg County, but she is not named in her father's will.

proved at Richmond County Court on 2 October 1786, although other court documents show that Robert was deceased before 4 May 1786.[189]

An inventory of Robert Hammack's estate was returned 2 April 1787. The inventory reveals a total estate value estimated at £245. Robert owned five slaves appraised at £170. His remaining personal property was valued at £75, of which £21.05 consisted of cattle and hogs. Four beds, bedsteads, and accompanying furniture were valued at £22. Robert also owned a desk, an oval table, five old tables, four chests, and one trunk, the value of which was almost £5. In addition to Robert's oval table, four leather chairs and a brass candlestick in the main room evidence an attempt at polite and refined, if not genteel, living. Robert also owned a "Great Bible" and "eight other books." As compared with his father sixty years before, Robert owned only four pieces of pewter and no gilt. Most of his serving items were earthenware and tin. Of the remaining £30 or so of Robert's inventory, a significant portion was used in household and agricultural production. Among these items were a flax wheel, three spinning wheels, a weaving loom, two pair of sheep shears, a scythe, two baskets, a quantity of lumber, "a parcel of carpenter's tools," eight sickles, five hoes, two iron wedges, and two ox chains. Four butter pots, two milk pans, and nine jugs give evidence of dairy activity as well. The presence of a scythe and several sickles is significant, for it reveals that, like many planters in the Northern Neck, Robert Hammack had also shifted at least partially from tobacco cultivation to wheat and grain production.[190]

Prolonged depression in the tobacco market, and an accompanying high level of debt, had prompted many Virginia planters in the late colonial period to abandon the colony's traditional staple. In the 1760s, as colonists formulated strategies to confront the Sugar Act, the Stamp Act, and the Townshend Duties that taxed paint, tea, and a variety of other items, they adopted wide-scale boycotts -- termed "Nonimportation Agreements" in the parlance of the day -- intended to eliminate much of the luxury spending of the early eighteenth-century. Luxury, the colonists reasoned, had been the problem all along. The desire for finery had corrupted their simple republican ways and caused them to purchase costly items intended only for display. Thus, beginning at mid-century and extending throughout the Revolutionary era, Virginians cut back, and imports of silver, pewter, crystal, velvet, and brocade became scarce. Replacing them was the simple homespun of the Revolutionary period; even such women as Abigail Adams, wife of the second President, took up weaving their own cloth on looms like those Robert Hammack owned.[191] Hence, while the value of Robert's estate and the quantity of his possessions is similar to that of his father six decades earlier, the quality does differ. To some extent this may reflect the privations of the 1760s coupled with the colonial distress of the 1770s and 1780s as the new national and state governments struggled for survival. But to an equally great extent, it is indicative of a different economic and social reality, one in which colonists shifted from one staple to another and adopted simple republican ways in the face of indebtedness and oppression.

Ann Lambert Hammack, Robert's widow, was still alive on 2 June 1795 when she was plaintiff in a court case involving her grandson Benjamin Hammack and Francis Morgan. The date of her death is not known. Since her eldest son had been baptized on 10 September 1726, Ann must then have been in her late eighties or early nineties when the case was filed.[192]

Together, the lives of Robert Hammack and his wife Ann Lambert Hammack spanned almost the entire eighteenth-century. They were born British subjects in England's most prosperous colony. They died American citizens in a new nation, one whose formation they had supported with material aide and

---

[189] Richmond Co., VA, Order Book 19, 1773-1776, 1784-1786, p. 327; Richmond Co., VA, Order Book 20, 1786-89, p. 30.

[190] Richmond Co., VA, Will Book 8, 1787-1794, pp. 9-11.

[191] On consumerism and debt in colonial Virginia, see: T. H. Breen, *Tobacco Culture: The Mentality of the Great Tidewater Planters on the Eve of the Revolution* (Princeton, 1985); T. H. Breen, ed., "Baubles of Britain": The American and Consumer Revolutions of the Eighteenth Century, in P. D. Morgan, ed., *Diversity and Unity in Early North America* (London, 1993), pp. 227-253; W. Holton, *Forced Founders: Indians, Debtors, Slaves, and the Making of the American Revolution in Virginia* (Chapel Hill and London, 1999).

[192] Richmond Co., VA, Order Book 22, 1795. There are no page numbers, but the items pertaining to this court were heard at court on 2 June 1795.

for whom their sons and grandsons had fought. Although they died within a mile or two of their birthplaces, their children and grandchildren were already spread more than six hundred miles along the southern frontier from Virginia's Northern Neck to the thick forests of the Georgia frontier. Yet, despite this significant geographical expanse, the intellectual and cultural distance they had traveled in the years following 1763 was even greater.

The family of Richard Hammack.

Richard Hammack seems to have possessed an independent spirit; the records of Richmond and Westmoreland Counties show that he was no conformist. Thus it seems no surprise that of the four sons of the immigrant William Hammack he was the only one known to have left the Northern Neck and to have begun his family's migration southward and westward. That independence of thought and spirit he bequeathed to his offspring; his descendants would be the first Hammacks to push westward to the Pacific, settling in Nevada and California in the 1840s and 1850s and Oregon in the 1850s and 1860s.

Because neither Richard nor his sons is known to have left a will, the family's genealogical outlines are more difficult to sketch. Richard lived the bulk of his adult life in Westmoreland County, where the parish registers for Cople Parish do not survive. Thus we cannot with absolute certainty identity all of his offspring and their ages.

Based on the records of Richmond, Westmoreland, and Louisa Counties, it seems that Richard had only two sons: William Hammack, husband of Ann Rochester (and perhaps of Joan Williams) and Richard Hammack, whose wife was named Frances.

William, son of Richard Hammack.

This William Hammack was born about 1695 in Westmoreland County, Virginia; he may have been living in Albemarle County, Virginia, as late as 1779. The first known reference to him dates from 1715, when he was indebted to the estate of Benjamin Eattle in Westmoreland County.[193]

By 1719, William had married Ann Rochester, daughter of Nicholas Rochester of Cople Parish, Westmoreland County. On 26 May 1719, Nicholas Rochester made a deed of gift to his son William. After William's death, his son John was to be the heir; if John died without issue, then his brother William Rochester, Jr., would inherit the property. Should both die without issue, the property devolved upon their aunt Ann Rochester Hammack, wife of William Hammack. The property deeded consisted of 100 acres in Nomini Forest of Westmoreland County. Benedict and Elizabeth Middleton witnessed the deed.[194]

On 3 March 1734, William Hammack, Elizabeth Hammack, and John Baker were listed among those indebted to the estate of Thomas Shrewsbury in Westmoreland County.[195] On 3 March 1737, William Walker -- from whose family the elder Richard Hammack rented his property -- deeded to William Lane 150 acres of land in Nomini Forrest. William (W) Hammock, William Rochester, John Rochester, George Dunbar, Samuel Morris, and Robert Tidwell witnessed the deed.[196] Two years later, in 1739, the same group of witnesses proved another deed involving Lane and Walker.[197]

The identification is not certain, but this William Hammack may be the one who married Jane Williams, daughter of David and Mary Williams, before 5 October 1736.[198] Jane was one of six children born to David and Mary Williams in North Farnham Parish between 1707 and 1721. Baptized on 19

---

[193] Westmoreland Co., VA, Deeds & Wills No. 5, 1712-16, p. 410.

[194] Westmoreland Co., VA, Deeds and Wills No. 6, 1716-20, pp. 482-83.

[195] Richmond Co., VA, Account Book Part I, p. 76.

[196] Westmoreland Co., VA, Deeds and Wills, No. 8, 1723-38, pp. 331-331a. This land had been patented by William Carr and bequeathed to his daughter Mary Walker, who was William's mother. William's wife was Phillis Walker.

[197] Westmoreland Co., VA, Deeds and Wills, 1749.

[198] Richmond Co., VA, Order Book 1732-1739, p. 469. Her name also appears as Joan.

August 1709, she was almost eighteen when her parents died in 1727.[199] Soon after she married William Hammack, he filed suit to obtain her share of her parents' estate, which had been committed in trust to Benjamin Rust as guardian. After three years of litigation, on 3 April 1739, Rust was ordered to settle his account with the Williams heirs and to pay Jane Hammack her portion of her father's estate. Landon Carter, Gentleman, one of the wealthiest men in the colony and a Richmond County justice, was ordered to arbitrate the dispute; he found that Rust owed the Hammacks two pounds, eight shillings, and nine pence.[200]

This chronology is consistent with a first marriage for William to Ann Rochester. Ann may have died about 1734 or 1735, at which time William may have remarried to Jane Williams. Since no other evidence of William's residence is found in Richmond County records for this time period, the probability is great that the William who married Jane Williams was living in Westmoreland County at the time of the marriage.

By 1748, William Hammack had apparently settled in Albemarle County, just beyond Louisa, where his father Richard was living. On 9 June 1748, he applied for letters of administration on the estate of John Strosbury.[201] On 8 February 1758, he deeded to Daniel Hammack for "value received and in hand paid" 100 acres "on the north side of ye Little Mountains" in Albemarle. John Henslee, John Hammack, and David Watts witnessed the deed, which sounds suspiciously like a deed of gift from father to son.[202]

On 7 August 1761, William received a patent for 400 acres on the north side of Ballenger's Creek of Rivanna River in Albemarle.[203] On 14 August 1765, he deeded 290 acres to Alexander Baine. The deed describes the land as "being the land and plantation whereon he now lives," in addition to one other tract of land on the head of Ballenger's Creek, containing 400 acres, joining Hays, Giles Letcher and William Murrill, being land purchased from Samuel Henderson. David Ross, Robert Clark, Samuel Woodson, and Richard Woods witnessed the deed, which was signed William "W" Hammack -- the same mark William had used years earlier in Westmoreland County.[204] William was mentioned as an adjacent landowner in 1766 when David Watts deeded 200 acres adjacent Hammack, Sandadge, Carr, and others to his new son-in-law, William Watson.[205] On 27 November 1771, William Hammack is mentioned as owing money to the estate of Nicholas Easton in Albemarle County,[206] and on 10 April 1772 he is named as an adjacent landowner when Thomas Terry deeded property to William Watson.[207] On 17 March 1773, with wife Jane[208] and signing his name as "W", William Hammack of Albemarle sold 290 acres joining Carr and Key to William Ragland of Louisa; Andrew (A) Beck, William Harris, and John Robinson witnessed the deed.[209]

This final deed is significant for several reasons. In two transactions dated 1737 and 1739 involving members of the Rochester family, William Hammack had signed his name in Westmoreland County with the mark "W". In this deed, his wife is named as Jane, consistent with the idea that he is the same William Hammack who about 1736 married Jane Williams. Alone, this deed does not prove that William of Albemarle was the William who married Ann Rochester as his first wife; cumulatively, however, these transactions do support this theory.

Finally, the deed suggests that William may once more have been on the move. If so, just where he went is unknown. He may be the William Hammack who on 30 July 1779, purchased from the estate of

[199] Richmond Co., VA, Will Book 5, 1725-1753, p. 35.

[200] Richmond Co., VA, Order Book, 1732-1739, p. 705.

[201] Albemarle Co., VA, Court Orders, *Magazine of Virginia Genealogy*, 29:123.

[202] Albemarle Co., VA, Deed Book 2, 1758-61, p. 1-2.

[203] Virginia Land Patents No. 34, 1756-62, p. 929.

[204] Albemarle Co., VA, Deed Book 1764-68, pp. 224-25.

[205] Albemarle Co., VA, Deed Book 1764-68, p. 374.

[206] Whitten, *Bedford Co., VA, Abstracts, 1754-1787*, p. 37.

[207] Albemarle Co., VA, Deed Book 5, 1768-1772, pp. 458-59.

[208] Again, this record strengthens the argument that this is the William Hammack who married Jane Williams.

[209] Albemarle Co., VA, Deed Book 1772-76, pp. 112-14.

William Arnold in Bedford County, Virginia.[210] There is also the possibility that he may have moved into Augusta County, where in 1773 one "William Hammack, Jr." was living when he sold land in Albemarle County.[211]

No proof of William's offspring's names has been found. Given the 1758 deed, it seems likely that he was the father of Daniel Hammack. This deed establishes that Daniel was likely born in or before 1736; he might be the son of William by Jane Williams. Daniel appears as witness with Richard Hammack in 1762[212] and with William Hammack in 1763.[213] In 1767, he sold the land in Albemarle deeded him a decade earlier by William Hammack and apparently moved south into Bedford County.[214] Before 1772, he had married Ann Rust, daughter of George Rust of Bedford County;[215] Daniel was in Campbell County in 1781,[216] Fluvanna in 1782,[217] and Campbell in 1784.[218] What became of him afterwards is a mystery; the Rust and Middleton families moved into Burke County, North Carolina, and then Tennessee. It may be that the Hammacks and Hammocks of Chatham County, North Carolina, and Overton County, Tennessee, descend from Daniel and Ann Rust Hammack.

Richard Hammack, son of Richard Hammack.

Richard Hammack was the second known son of Richard Hammack of Westmoreland and Louisa Counties. The earliest known reference to him is dated 20 September 1722, the occasion on which Richard Hammack and his wife Frances chose to baptize their son John Hammack. Thus it is presumed that Richard was born about 1701, probably in Westmoreland County.

In 1733, both Richard and his father were renting land from the family of William Walker in Westmoreland County; in the same year, "Richard Hamock Junr. of Westmoreland County" was summoned to the Richmond County Court in the case of Frederick Blake versus Christopher Dominick Jackson.[219] Either he or his father was the Richard who in 1736 and 1737 sued John Bowyer for trespass in Richmond County.[220]

By the early 1740s, Richard had apparently decided to move his family westward into the Piedmont. On 20 August 1741, he patented 400 acres in Hanover County joining Christopher Clark and Major Carr.[221] On 11 February 1743, his property in Louisa County was mentioned as being adjacent a tract Benjamin Hensley was selling to John Hensley.[222] On 15 March 1744, Richard's Louisa lands were identified as adjacent those of Nicholas Meriwether and Christopher Clark.[223] From a deed dated 5 June 1746, we learn that Richard's property lay along the boundary between Louisa and Goochland, along

---

[210] Whitten, *Bedford Co., VA, Abstracts, 1754-1787*, p. 97.

[211] Albemarle Co., VA, Deeds, 1772-1776, pp. 332-333.

[212] Albemarle Co., VA, Deed Book 3, pp. 244-45.

[213] Albemarle County, VA, Deed Book 3, pp. 387-89.

[214] Albemarle Co., VA, Deed Book 1764-68, pp. 412-13.

[215] Bedford Co., VA, Will Book I, 1763-87, p. 238. George Rust's older brother Matthew Rust (c. 1697 -- 1751) had married (2) Frances Garland Middleton (c. 1696 -- c. 1761), who was widow of Thomas Middleton, Christian Middleton Hammack's nephew. Another brother was Benjamin Rust (c. 1700 -- c. 1754) of Westmoreland County, who married Eleanor Branham Greene and Sarah Metcalfe; he was the Benjamin who acted as Jane Williams Hammack's guardian. Hannah Rust, sister of Matthew, George, and Benjamin, married George Eskridge, son of Col. George Eskridge and Rebecca Bonum. Col. George Eskridge was King's Attorney in Westmoreland County and was guardian for Mary Ball, mother of George Washington. If the relationships posited here are correct, Ann Rust Hammack's uncle Benjamin Rust was guardian of her mother-in-law Jane Williams Hammack in Richmond County.

[216] Campbell Co., VA, Deed Book 1, 1782-84, p. 38.

[217] *The Virginia Genealogist.*, 28 (1985): 193.

[218] Campbell Co., VA, Deed Book 1, p. 253.

[219] Richmond Co., VA, Order Book, 1732-1739, p. 84.

[220] Richmond Co., VA, Order Book, 1732-1739, pp. 466, 485, 500.

[221] Virginia Patent Book 19, p. 1092. See also *The Virginia Genealogical Society Quarterly*, 25 (1987): 74.

[222] Louisa Co., VA, Deed Book A, pp. 125-27.

[223] *Magazine of Virginia Genealogy*, 26 (1988): 308.

Key's Mill Swamp. Apart from the county line, other boundaries were formed by the lines of Major Carr and Captain Clark.[224]

On 25 November 1749, Richard Hammack of Fredericksville Parish, Louisa County, Virginia, deeded 100 acres in Louisa to his son John Hammack; John paid his father £20. The land was part of Richard's earlier 400 acre grant and was located on both sides of Red Bird Branch. Benjamin Henslee, John Maccalley, and Richard Sarcey witnessed the deed.[225] John Hammack, the purchaser, was then about twenty-seven years old and had probably recently married, perhaps leading his father to sell him a homestead.

On 10 July 1750, Richard and his father witnessed a Louisa County transaction together; in the same year, a Louisa County deed identified Joseph Martin of Louisa as owner of a tract adjacent Richard Hammack's land.[226] This association is significant, for Joseph Martin's daughter and granddaughter would both marry Richard's descendants. Son John had probably already married Mary Martin, Joseph's daughter; a generation later, John's son Daniel Hammack would marry his first cousin, another Mary Martin, Joseph's granddaughter.

On 27 August 1751, Richard Hammack deeded the remaining 300 acres of his 400 acre grant to David Watts; Watts paid him £80.[227] Watts and Hammack remained neighbors, and Watts had dealings with Richard's brother William's family also. In fact, for the next century a close bond would exist between the Hammack and the Watts families, one transferred from Virginia into Tennessee and then into Missouri and Texas.[228]

On 9 May 1753, Richard Hammack patented a new tract in Louisa County, this one comprising 240 acres.[229] The land was near that he had earlier owned, on Red Bird Creek, and neighbors were Major Carr, Edward Clark, and Captain Joseph Martin.[230] A 1760 deed reveals that Richard still owned this tract adjacent Edward Clark and Nicholas Easton, with whom William Hammack also had dealings.[231]

About this time, records become more difficult to interpret, for a younger Richard Hammack -- probably this Richard's son -- appears on the scene. On 11 November 1768, Richard Hammack, Daniel Witcher, and Mary Hammack witnessed the will of John Sloan in Pittsylvania County,[232] and on 26 July 1770 one Richard Hammack of Pittsylvania purchased fifty acres on the south side of the Pigg River from Richard Adkinson. William Witcher, William Adkinson, and Levi Shockley witnessed the deed.[233] On 25 February 1771, Richard Hammack, John Long, and Nathan Swanson witnessed a Pittsylvania County deed from Peyton and Judith Smith to Robert Garrett for land on Pigg Creek in Pittsylvania.[234]

It is not clear which, if any, of these last references refer to the older Richard Hammack. Born about 1701, he could well have lived into the 1770s. According to family tradition, however, the younger Richard Hammack married Mary Witcher, and it seems likely that the transactions involving both Hammacks and Witchers involve the younger man.

No will or administration for Richard Hammack, son of Richard of Westmoreland, has been found; he likely died after 1760 in Albemarle or Pittsylvania County. If he had already disposed of his landed property, he may have had no substantial wealth to bequeath. Almost certainly he had daughters, but their

---

[224] *Magazine of Virginia Genealogy*, 26 (1988): 120.

[225] Louisa Co., VA, Deed Book A, pp. 406-7.

[226] Louisa Co., VA, Deed Book A, p. 393.

[227] Louisa Co., VA, Deed Book A, p. 434.

[228] Often where such bonds lasted for generations, they indicate a pre-existing familial connection. Since nothing is known of the daughters of Richard Hammack (born 1674), it is possible that an early Hammack-Watts marriage had already united the two families.

[229] *Magazine of Virginia Genealogy*, 31: 321.

[230] *Magazine of Virginia Genealogy*, 31: 321.

[231] Louisa Co., VA, Deed Book C, pp. 51-52.

[232] Pittsylvania Co., VA, Deed Book 1, p. 249.

[233] Pittsylvania Co., VA, Deed Book 1, p. 492.

[234] Pittsylvania Co., VA, Deed Book 2, p. 490.

names have not been located. The only two sons for whom evidence exists are John Hammack, born in Richmond County in 1722, and Richard Hammack, who was probably born about 1732. John Hammack married Mary Martin and sired a large family in Albemarle; Richard Hammack married Mary Witcher and sired an equally large family in Pittsylvania. Together, these two families would move into Tennessee, Kentucky, and Missouri as they began the long trek westward to the Pacific.

The family of William Hammack the younger.

The second son of the immigrant William Hammack to bear his father's name, William Hammack the younger was born in 1688; between 1715 and 1739, he and wife Eleanor baptized six children in Westmoreland County: Alice (1715); John (1718); William (1720); Alice (1724); Elizabeth (1734); and Eleanor (1739). They may also have been the parents of Caty Hammack (1735) and of a son David who was born by about 1732.

William Hammack was probably alive in 1741 and may have been deceased by 1745 when a Richmond County deed mentions property of "William Hammack, dec." Of his offspring, the fate of none of his daughters is known. Nor is there any clear evidence of what became of his son William, who was born in 1720. He may have died as a child since no trace of him has been found elsewhere in Virginia or the Carolinas. If David Hammack was William's son, he did survive to adulthood; he witnessed a deed in Richmond in 1748 and is mentioned in court proceedings as late as 1760. No trace of him has been found after that date, however.[235]

William's son John Hammack, baptized 14 December 1718 in North Farnham Parish, survived and reared a large family. As noted previously, there were two contemporary John Hammacks in Richmond County about 1740. They were about the same age, and they lived in exactly the same location. Hence, it is difficult to distinguish between them. One married twice, first to Susannah and second to Mary Ann, and moved to Granville County, North Carolina, where he died in 1776. Richmond County Court Orders call him "John Hammack (the freeholder)" to distinguish him from his landless cousin.[236] The other John married Mildred Lambert in 1741 and moved to Lunenburg County. As noted previously, the John who married Susannah and Mary Ann almost certainly was the grandson of William and Christian Middleton Hammack; the John who married Mildred Lambert, therefore, was the son of William and Eleanor Hammack and first cousin once removed of the other John Hammack.

If William Hammack the younger died about 1745, his death may explain why young John Hammack decided to try his fortune in a distant part of the colony. Many other Northern Neck families were moving southward, among them members of the Bentley and Lambert families as well as John's cousin Benedict Hammack, who settled about 1743 in neighboring Amelia County.

Before discussing the life of this John Hammack, the subject of his marriage should be addressed. Many researchers have confused the nature of the Hammack and Lambert connections in Richmond County. Hugh Lambert, son of William Lambert and Ann Claughton, married Ann Morgan, daughter of William Morgan and Ann Lewis[237]; the Lambert, Claughton, Morgan, and Lewis families all lived in Richmond and Northumberland Counties from the 1690s onward. Hugh Lambert about 1748 began acquiring land in Brunswick County, but he remained in Richmond County for almost another decade. Ultimately, he did move to Brunswick County, where he died testate about 1765. His will reveals that he sired a large family, among whom were daughters *Mildred Hammack* and *Ann Hammack*. Mildred had married John Hammack in 1741; her much older sister Ann had married Robert Hammack about 1725. Their spouses were first cousins, Mildred's John being the son of William Hammack the younger and

---

[235] Richmond Co., VA, Deeds, Book 10, p. 537.

[236] See, for instance, Richmond Co., VA, Order Book 12, p. 72, 3 August 1747. John Hammack "freeholder" was named surveyor of highways in room of John Oldham on this date.

[237] Richmond Co., VA, Wills and Inventories, 1709-1717, pp. 247-248; Richmond Co., VA, Will Book B, 1725-1753, pp. 33-34; Brunswick Co., VA, Will Book 2, pp. 426-429.

Ann's Robert being the son of William Hammack the elder. By marriage, however, John Hammack and Robert Hammack were brothers-in-law, and their children were first cousins on the Lambert side as well as second cousins on the Hammack side. Hence, there seems to have existed a close tie between the family of Robert and Ann Hammack and that of John and Mildred Hammack; Lunenburg County emerges as a crucial location linking Hammacks in the Northern Neck with those living far southward on the Georgia frontier well into the nineteenth-century.

After leaving Richmond County, John and Mildred Hammack first appear in Lunenburg County about 1748. They were still in North Farnham Parish, Richmond County, in 1742 and 1745 when son William and daughter Ann were baptized. In 1748, John was living in the district of Lunenburg identified as being between "Hound's Creek and Meherrin River." He was taxed with only one tithable -- himself -- indicating that he was the only white male aged over sixteen years in the household. Neighbors in the same district included Edward Jackson (father of Millenor Jackson, who would marry John's nephew Robert Hammack about 1758), James Amoss (whose descendants would intermarry with John's children as well as with the descendants of Robert and Millenor in Georgia), Robert Moore and the widow Ussery (whose descendants would likewise intermarry for several generations with offspring of John and Mildred Hammack as well as of Robert and Millenor Hammack), and Robert Leverett (whose family would live near the Hammacks later in Wilkes and Lincoln Counties, Georgia). For the next century, in Virginia and in Georgia, this small group of family's would maintain intimate ties of kinship and friendship.[238]

In 1749 and 1750, John Hammack paid for one white tithe and six slaves. In 1752, he was taxed with two tithes, himself and his wife's brother Lewis Lambert, who apparently was living with the family. The next surviving tax list dates from 1764, when John is identified as a resident of Cumberland Parish, Lunenburg County; he paid tax on two tithes and 350 acres. The second tithable is identified as "John Hammack his son." In an adjoining household was William Hammack -- baptized in Lunenburg in 1742 -- indicating that he was then head of his own household.[239]

The land on which John Hammack paid tax in 1764 included two tracts he had purchased from his neighbor Robert Moore. Originally from New Kent County, Robert Moore had acquired a tract of more than 4,000 acres in Lunenburg when he settled there in the late 1740s; this land he apparently acquired for speculative purposes and then sold in smaller tracts over the next several years. On 18 May 1759, John Hammack purchased 150 acres from Robert Moore; the land was described as adjacent "Hammack's Spring Branch, Hugh Lambert, Col. Bird, Mathew Hubbard, John Askew, Nathaniel Owen." John Moore, Robert Moore, Jr., and Ambrose Williams witnessed the deed.[240] Ten months later, on 19 March 1760, John purchased a second tract from Robert Moore. This time he purchased 100 acres "down from Thomas Weaver to Henry Daniel, John Askew's spring branch, [and] John Hammock." Witnesses included John Moore and William Ussery.[241]

The next Lunenburg tax list to report acreage owned was compiled in 1769; that list, too, showed John Hammack with 350 acres of land. He was taxed with three white tithables -- himself, John Hammack, Jr., and Hugh Hammack. The next name after John's was that of his son William Hammack. Two names after William Hammock's name was that of Robert Hammack, John and Mildred's nephew, who had married Millenor Jackson several years earlier. Robert at this time owned no land and paid for only one white tithe. John Hammack and sons John, Hugh, and William were taxed in 1772, 1774, 1775, and 1776.[242]

Just when John Hammack and wife Mildred died is not clear; no trace of Mildred has been found in the Lunenburg records. The 1776 tax list shows John Hammack and son John Hammack, Jr. The younger

[238] 1748 Lunenburg Co., VA, Tithe List, Library of Virginia, Richmond, VA.

[239] 1749, 1750, 1752, 1764 Lunenburg Co., VA, Tithe Lists, The Library of Virginia, Richmond, VA.

[240] Lunenburg Co., VA, Deed Book 5, pp. 405-406.

[241] Lunenburg Co., VA, Deed Book 6, pp. 88-90.

[242] 1769, 1772, 1774, 1775, 1776 Lunenburg Co., VA, Tithe Lists, The Library of Virginia, Richmond, VA.

John was first taxed in 1764 and therefore was probably born about 1747 or 1748. He apparently was still living in his father's household in 1776 and may not yet have married.[243]

One of the two John Hammacks seems to have died or left the county soon after 1776. On 29 January 1778, Thomas Jones of Brunswick sold to John Hammack of Lunenburg a tract of sixteen acres on the "south side of Crooked Run, adj. Byrd, Hammack, [and a] small branch."[244] Witnesses were Hugh Williams, John Jones, and John Hammack. On 15 March 1782, one John Hammack was reimbursed for supplying 250 pounds of beef to the Continental troops during the Revolution.[245] This reference probably refers to John Hammack, grandson of John and Mildred Lambert Hammack, for Lunenburg County Court Orders indicate that the will of John Hammack, deceased, was proven and ordered to be executed on 8 February 1781.[246]

The 1783 tax list shows only John Hammack, Hugh Hammack, and William Hammack. Since the elder John Hammack would, by this point, have been about 65 years old, however, he would no longer have been liable for his own tithe. This reference, combined with the 1781 probate reference, suggests then that it was the elder John Hammack who died in 1780 or 1781 and that it was his grandson who supported the Revolutionary cause, was compensated in 1782 for beef he had supplied, and was taxed in 1783.[247]

What is clear, however, is that John Hammack left a large family in Lunenburg when he died. His sons William and Hugh both died there, William in 1785 and Hugh in 1804. William left at least five children, all of whom remained in Lunenburg with their families well into the nineteenth-century. Hugh and wife Elizabeth left another six offspring when Hugh died in 1804.[248]

The fate of John Hammack's son John Hammack, Jr., is unclear. He was still living in his father's household as late as 1776 and was probably unmarried at that time. About this time, Lunenburg records cease to distinguish between John Hammack, Sr., and John Hammack, Jr. To complicate matters, however, the eldest son of William Hammack -- also named John -- came of age in the early 1760s. He was aged eighty-three at the time of the 1850 census, but he may have been slightly older than that; although his age was given in 1840 as 70-80, when he died in 1856, the death registry reported his age as ninety-six. He married for the first time on 6 August 1791 in Lunenburg County.[249] Lunenburg County tax records were examined from 1783 to 1807, and at no point during these years do the tax lists show two John Hammacks in the county at the same time. Since William Hammack's son John was born at least by 1766 or 1767, he should have been taxed from 1782 onwards. Hence, the reasonable conclusion seems to be that John Hammack, Junior -- son of John Hammack and Mildred Lambert -- either died or left Lunenburg County between 1776 and 1782. Perhaps he was a casualty of the American Revolution, or perhaps he moved southward; no clear evidence of him has been found after 1776, however, leading one o conclude that he likely died soon afterwards.

---

[243] 1776 Lunenburg Co., VA, Tithe List, Library of Virginia, Richmond, VA.

[244] Lunenburg Co., VA, Deed Book 13, p. 82.

[245] Abercrombie and Slatten, *Virginia Revolutionary "Publick" Claims*, p. 648.

[246] Lunenburg Co., VA, Order Book 14, 1777-1781, p. 71. The will has not been found, and the names of the executors are not included in the order book.

[247] 1783 List of Taxable Property and Souls, Lunenburg Co., VA, Library of Virginia, Richmond, VA; 1783 and 1784 Lunenburg Co., VA, Personal Property Tax Lists, Library of Virginia, Richmond, VA.

[248] Lunenburg Co., VA, Will Book 3, p. 235; Lunenburg Co., VA, Will Book 6, p. 93.

[249] Lunenburg Co., VA, Register of Deaths, 1 April 1856, Library of Virginia, Richmond, VA.

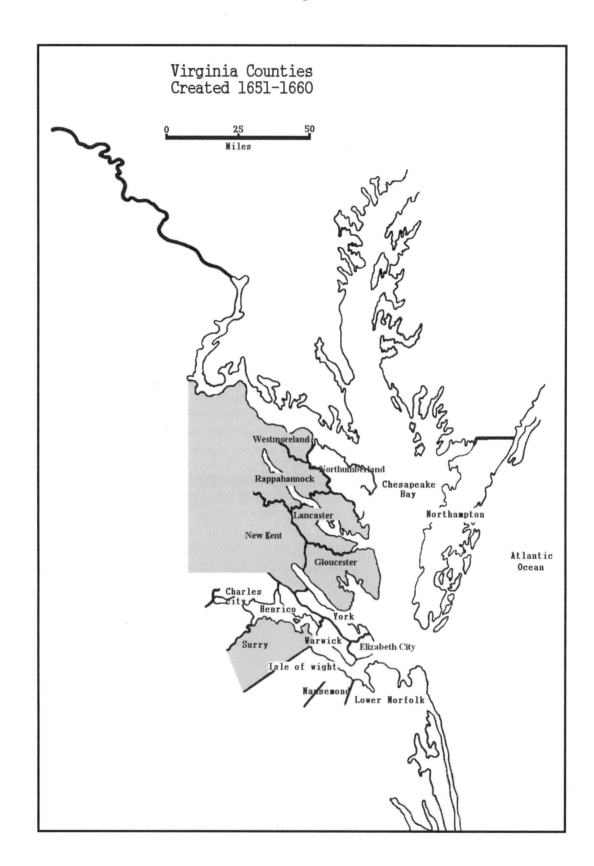

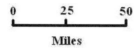

Virginia Counties Created Between 1660 and 1670

1=Possible Residence of William Hammack, c. 1656 - c. 1666
2=Residence of William Hammack, c. 1670-c. 1701

0   25   50

Miles

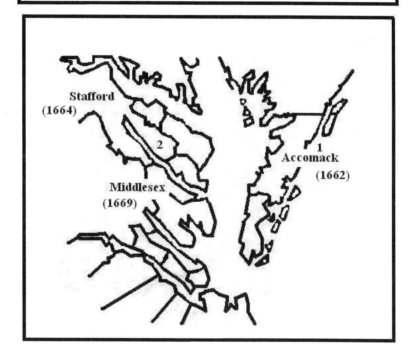

Stafford
(1664)

2

Middlesex
(1669)

1
Accomack
(1662)

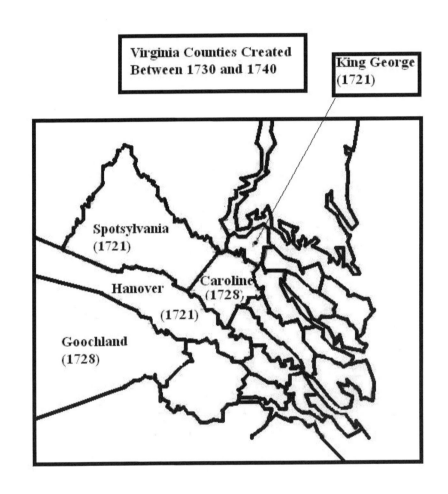

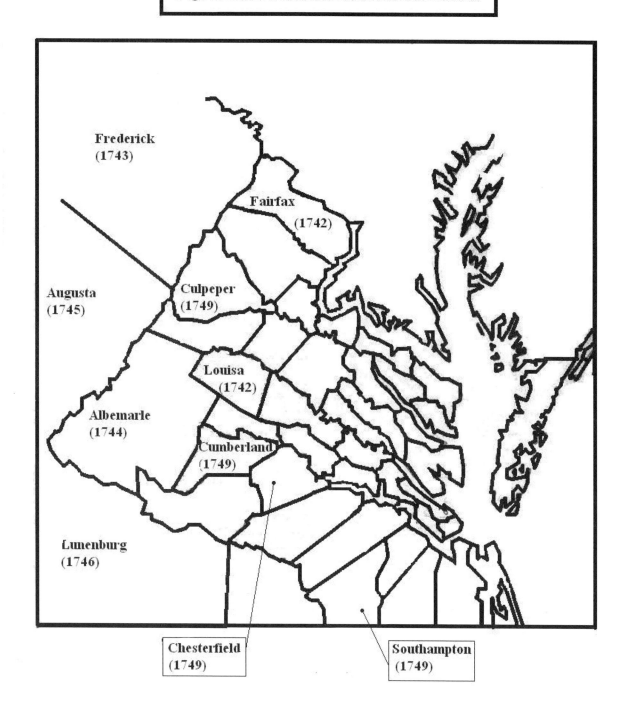

Virginia Counties Created Between 1740 and 1750

Frederick
(1743)

Fairfax
(1742)

Augusta
(1745)

Culpeper
(1749)

Louisa
(1742)

Albemarle
(1744)

Cumberland
(1749)

Lunenburg
(1746)

Chesterfield
(1749)

Southampton
(1749)

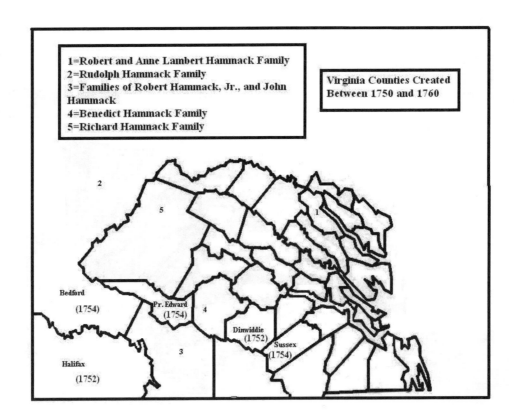

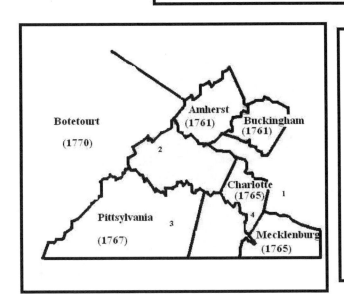

Virginia Counties Created Between 1760 and 1770

1=Families of Robert Hammack, Jr., and John Hammack (Lunenburg County)

2=Family of Daniel and Ann Rust Hammack (Bedford County)

3=Family of Richard and Mary Witcher Hammack and family of Mary Ann Hammack

4=Family of Lewis Hammack (son of Robert and Ann Lambert Hammack)

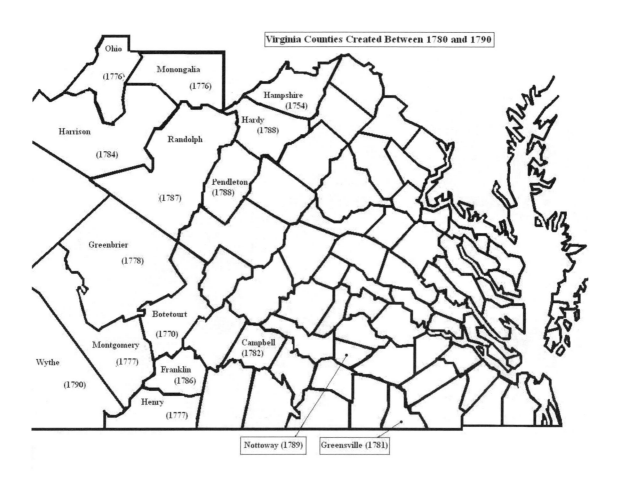

Virginia Counties Created Between 1780 and 1790

Ohio (1776)

Monongalia (1776)

Hampshire (1754)

Hardy (1788)

Harrison (1784)

Randolph (1787)

Pendleton (1788)

Greenbrier (1778)

Botetourt (1770)

Campbell (1782)

Montgomery (1777)

Franklin (1786)

Wythe (1790)

Henry (1777)

Nottoway (1789)   Greensville (1781)

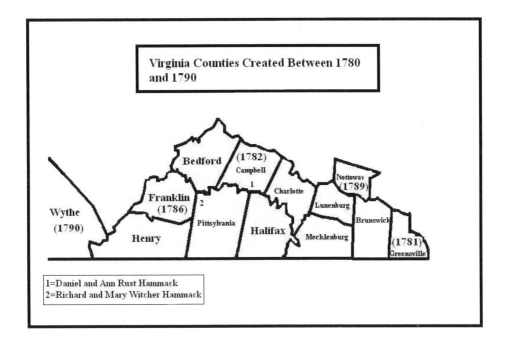

Virginia Counties Created Between 1780 and 1790

1=Daniel and Ann Rust Hammack
2=Richard and Mary Witcher Hammack

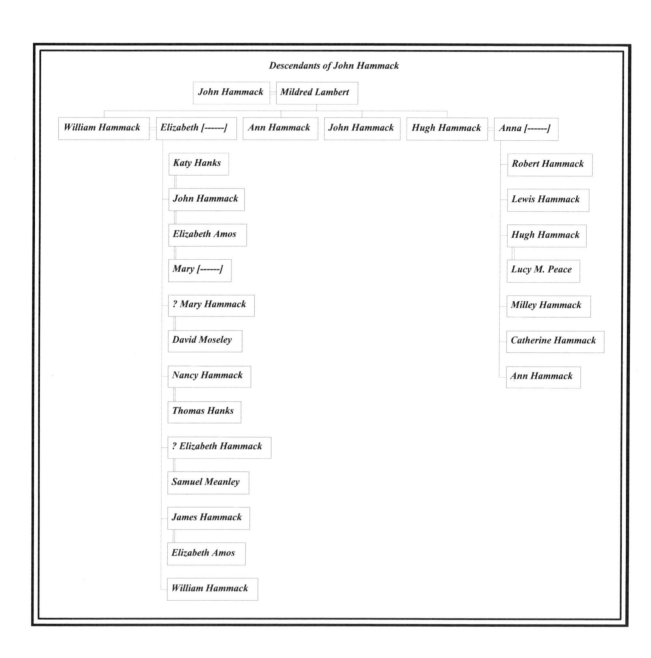

Descendants of John Hammack

John Hammack — Mildred Lambert

William Hammack | Elizabeth [------] | Ann Hammack | John Hammack | Hugh Hammack | Anna [------]

Katy Hanks

John Hammack

Elizabeth Amos

Mary [------]

? Mary Hammack

David Moseley

Nancy Hammack

Thomas Hanks

? Elizabeth Hammack

Samuel Meanley

James Hammack

Elizabeth Amos

William Hammack

Robert Hammack

Lewis Hammack

Hugh Hammack

Lucy M. Peace

Milley Hammack

Catherine Hammack

Ann Hammack

Chapter 6:

Tennessee, Kentucky, and the Heartland

Most Hammacks and Hammocks to settle in Tennessee and Kentucky were descendants of Richard Hammack of Westmoreland and Louisa Counties. Richard was born in 1674, and his family were the first of the Hammack fold to move from Richmond County into the Piedmont. In the next generations, they became trailblazers, pushing ever more westward across the middle regions of the new nation.

The one exception to this rule, and perhaps the first Hammack to reach Kentucky, was William Hammock, who moved there from Georgia. This man was a native of Virginia and was reared in North Carolina; his parents were William and Betty Ann Hames Hammack, natives of Richmond County, and his grandparents were Benedict and Elizabeth Lewis Hammack. William was born 15 June 1760 in Amelia County, Virginia, and at the age of nine he moved with his parents and other relatives to Onslow County in eastern North Carolina. He first enlisted in the Anson County, North Carolina, militia during the early days of the Revolutionary struggle. He was stationed at Hanging Rock and also fought during the Revolution at the Battle of Eutaw Springs. Tories captured William, and he was imprisoned by the British at Cheraw Hills along South Carolina's Congaree River. After some time, he escaped from the British, only to sign up for another eighteen month tour of duty as a militiaman. In a third period of enlistment, William was among a troop sent to deal with the Creek Indians along the Georgia frontier.[250]

William's Revolutionary service along the frontier may have given him the notion to settle in Georgia; certainly other Hammacks -- among them the family of his uncle Benedict and of his father's cousin Robert -- were doing so about this time. William and his parents were living in Wilkes County, Georgia, by the time the Revolution ended; although his father remained there until his death, William Hammock chose to push further into Kentucky. About 1798, he moved to Christian County, Kentucky, where he remained until 1803.[251] He then settled in Caldwell County and finally, between 1810 and 1820, in Union County, Kentucky, where he died "in his 89th year" in 1849.[252] For part of this migration, William's sister Charity Hammock and her husband Abraham Hammons also accompanied the family; the Hammons family ultimately moved beyond Kentucky into Vermillion County, Illinois, where Abraham died in 1844 and where Charity was still living in 1846 when she applied for his Revolutionary War Pension.[253]

William Hammock and his wife Nancy Brown produced a large family, most of whom remained in Union County, Kentucky. Sons William, Morgan, Daniel, and Jeremiah were prosperous farmers and tradesmen in Union County before the Civil War; daughters Ruth Hammock Sullivant, Winnie Hammock Gregory, and Nancy Hammock Anderson all married and lived in Union County. Nancy's sons and grandsons became bankers who operated the Morganfield Bank in Morganfield, Kentucky. Although he is not named in the Bible record preserved among the Anderson family, Benjamin Hammack (1791, Wilkes County, Georgia -- aft. 1870, Saline County, Illinois) was probably the eldest son or a nephew. He was living near William's family at the time of the 1820 census, had been present in Kentucky before 1812, and seems to have had a close connection with William's offspring. By 1830, however, he had moved from Union County, Kentucky, across the line into Gallatin County, Illinois. He was living in Saline

---

[250] Revolutionary War Pension Application of William Hammock, S15442, National Archives, Washington, D.C., Microfilm Series M805, Roll 393.

[251] See 1798, 1800, 1803 Christian Co., KY, Tax Lists, Kentucky State Library and Archives, Frankfort, KY.

[252] 1810 Caldwell Co., KY, Census, p. 16; 1820 Union Co., KY, Census, p. 168; 1830 Union Co., KY, Census, p. 41; Hammack, *Wandering Back*, 2: 156-164.

[253] Revolutionary War Pension Application of Abraham Hamman, W10088, National Archives, Washington, D.C., Microfilm Series M805, Roll 398.

County, Illinois, by 1850 and remained there until at least after 1870. The other descendants of William Hammock and Nancy Brown, however, remained in Union County, Kentucky, for several generations.[254]

About the same time that Benedict Hammack's grandson William moved to Christian County, Kentucky, descendants of Richard Hammack began settling in Tennessee. These Hammacks included the offspring of John Hammack and Mary Martin Hammack, the offspring of Richard and Mary Witcher Hammack, and John and William Hammack of Chatham County, North Carolina, who may have been children of Daniel and Ann Rust Hammack of Virginia. Many of their descendants would use the spelling Hammock as well as Hammack. John Hammack who married Mary Martin and Richard Hammack who married Mary Witcher were brothers; Daniel Hammack who married Ann Rust was their first cousin. These given names would be repeated many times in the coming generations as their descendants moved westward across the country.

Of the children of John Hammack and Mary Martin, Susannah Hammack Sweeney and Martin Hammock moved westward beyond the Shenandoah Valley but remained in what was then Virginia. Martin Hammock's family settled in Kanawha County and Susannah Sweeney's family in Monroe County. Martin, another Revolutionary soldier, was living as late as 1838;[255] Susannah Hammack Sweeney was still alive in 1850, when the census reported her age as 105 years.[256] When Virginia seceded from the United States during the Civil War, the present state of West Virginia seceded from Virginia. The region beyond the Shenandoah Valley is mountainous, and the soil is often gravely; plantation-style agriculture never really thrived there, and slavery was uncommon. Thus the Hammacks and Hammocks in that region were small scale self-sufficient farmers and artisans; many of their descendants remain in Kanawha County, West Virginia, and surrounding areas to this day.

Of the other sons of John and Mary Martin Hammack, John (born about 1755) and Daniel (born about 1762) both settled in Tennessee. Another Revolutionary soldier and pensioner, John Hammock married Nancy Maples about 1780 in Pittsylvania County, Virginia. He served in the Virginia militia during the Revolution and ultimately returned to his bride in Pittsylvania County when the conflict ended; members of the Maples family were already moving South and West, for Nancy had a sister in South Carolina and a brother in Greenbriar County, Virginia. John and Nancy Maples Hammock chose to move to Greenbriar County, where they lived from about 1790 to about 1805. By this point, the Maples relatives in South Carolina had begun to settle in Tennessee, and John and Nancy chose to follow them. John Hammock reported in his Revolutionary War pension application in 1840 that he had resided in Grainger County, Tennessee, for more than 33 years.[257]

John and Nancy Maples Hammock had at least six children; there may have been others, for John left no will recording all of their names. Many of their descendants would use the spelling Hammock as well as Hammack. Sons John and William both remained in Grainger County. Son Martin settled in nearby Claiborne County, and, after he died in 1839, his descendants moved into Marion County, Tennessee, and northern Alabama and Georgia. Daniel Hammack, another son, founded a large Hammack grouping in Union County, Tennessee. Ephraim Hammack, still another son, married Jane Long, daughter of Elder Isaac Long; he died in Indiana in 1855, but most of his family returned to Tennessee before 1860. Several

---

[254] Hammack, *Wandering Back*, 2: 156-164. My placement of Benjamin as William's son is circumstantial; he certainly had a close relationship with William and traveled from Georgia to Kentucky with him. For later details of Benjamin, see 1830 Gallatin Co., IL, Census, p. 291; 1850 Saline Co., IL, Census, p. 43; 1860 Saline Co., IL, Census, p. 803 ; 1870 Saline Co., IL, Census, p. 409.

[255] Revolutionary War Pension Application of Martin Hammock, R4529, National Archives, Washington, D.C., Microfilm Series M805, Roll 366.

[256] 1850 Monroe Co., VA, Census, p. 800.

[257] Revolutionary War Pension Application of John Hammock, S2601, National Archives, Washington, D.C., Microfilm Series M805, Roll 364.

of his children settled in northern Arkansas, while others remained in Union and Grainger Counties of Tennessee.[258]

Daniel Hammack, probably the youngest child of John and Mary Martin Hammack, was only about eight years old when his father died and when he and his siblings were bound out in 1770 to learn trades. He followed relatives into Henry and Pittsylvania Counties, and about 1789 he had married his first cousin, Mary Martin, daughter of Joseph Martin and Sarah Lucas. By 1790, Daniel and Mary were living in Greenville County, South Carolina, where their small family was enumerated in the federal census. They then moved into Georgia, where they lived in Franklin County from about 1794 to about 1798. By 1800, Daniel, Mary, and their young children had settled in Union County, Tennessee, where they both died. Daniel died there on 16 July 1829, in his sixty-seventh year. His widow Mary died 21 August 1852, when she was about eighty-two years old. Both are buried in a small family cemetery in Smith County, Tennessee; as early as 1820, their sons had begun to leave Tennessee and settle in Missouri.[259]

Smith County, Tennessee, would also be the temporary destination for members of the family of Richard Hammack and Mary Witcher; their eldest son, another John, married Patsy Goad in Pittsylvania County, Virginia, also during the Revolutionary era. They remained in Pittsylvania and died there, as did most of their offspring. One son, Toliver, moved with his family to Smith County, Tennessee, where he settled. Other offspring of John and Patsy Goad Hammack remained in Pittsylvania until past 1850, but by the early 1860s John and Patsy had grandchildren scattered throughout Tennessee, Illinois, and Indiana.[260]

This John Hammack's younger siblings did not remain in Pittsylvania as did he; instead, just after the turn of the century, they began to settle in Tennessee and Kentucky. The reasons are unclear. John was the eldest son, and he had married into an old and established family with considerable property in the region. His father Richard Hammack died in Pittsylvania or nearby Franklin County in the early 1790s, by which time a couple of John's brothers had come of age and married. Between about 1788 and 1802, all of the remaining Hammack siblings reached maturity and married in Pittsylvania, Franklin, and Henry Counties of Virginia. By about 1804, almost all of them were living in Tennessee.

Peter Hammack, who married Nancy Prunty in Franklin County, Virginia, in 1788, seems to have been the first to move. He was living in Grainger County, Tennessee, by 1799. He lived there until at least 1809; by 1812, he was in Knox County, Tennessee, and by 1820 in Giles County, Tennessee, where he died after 1830. By 1805, Peter's brothers James, Daniel, and William had joined him in Grainger County, as had his cousin John Hammack, son of John and Mary Martin Hammack.[261]

Several of these Hammacks remained in Tennessee only briefly. By 1810, Daniel, William, Ephraim, and Lewis were all living in the same neighborhood of Madison County, Kentucky. Daniel died about 1819 in Knox County, Kentucky; his children and grandchildren were living in Indiana, Illinois, and Iowa by the 1830s and 1840s.[262] Ephraim was in Pittsylvania as late as 1805 and in Kentucky by 1810; he died

---

[258] Identification of the children of John and Nancy Maples Hammock is based on a study of Grainger Co., TN, census records between 1820 and 1860 and of Grainger Co., TN, legal documents and tax lists. Additional detail is set forth in the genealogical summary at the end of this work.

[259] This family is detailed in G. P. Omahundro, *Ancestors and Descendants of Brice Wiseman Hammack* (Santa Ana, CA, 1986). See also Hammack, *Wandering Back*, 2: 16, 77, 175-178, 238.

[260] 1820 Pittsylvania Co., VA, Census, p. 51; 1830 Smith Co., TN, Census, p. 67; 1840 Smith Co., TN, Census, p. 289; 1850 Macon Co., TN, Census, p. 154. John's grandson William Hammack was enumerated in Henry Co., IN, in 1860 and his widow and family in Madison Co., IN, in 1870 and Henry Co., IN, in 1880. Oliver Hammack, another grandson, was living in Madison Co., IN, in 1870 and in Hancock Co., IN, in 1880. Spencer Hammack, another grandson, was living in Henry Co., IN, in 1860. Toliver Allen Hammack, another grandson, was enumerated in Pope Co., IL, in 1860, 1870, and 1880.

[261] See 1804, 1805, and 1809 Grainger Co., TN, Tax Lists and 1812 Knox Co., TN, Tax List, Tennessee State Library and Archives, Nashville, TN.

[262] Children of Daniel Hammack and Aggy Pruitt are believed to have been John Hammack (1791-aft. 1840) of Posey Co., IN; Nancy Hammack (1793-); Mary Hammack Fox (1796-aft. 1850) of Macon Co., MO; Ephraim Hammack (1798-1855) of Perry Co., IN; Daniel Hammack (1800-1855) of Mercer Co., IL; Isaiah Hammack (1804-aft. 1830) of Knox Co., KY; James Marion Hammack (abt. 1815-1890) of Union Co., OR. Some researchers also believe that Frances Hammack Esray (abt. 1796-1851) of Perry Co., IN,

in Garrard County after 1830. While his younger children and their families remained in Garrard for several generations, his older children seem also to have moved west.[263] James Hammack, another brother, left Pittsylvania between 1803 and 1805 and settled in Grainger County, Tennessee, where he died about 1809. His children were living in Indiana by 1836.[264]

Other siblings were William Hammack, who died about 1814 in Kentucky, and Lewis Hammack. William left Pittsylvania after 1803 but was in Madison County, Kentucky, by 1810; two children remained in Kentucky, but one died in Indiana and another in Missouri.[265] Lewis Hammack, perhaps the youngest brother in this large group, married in 1802 in Pittsylvania and was taxed there in 1803; by 1810, he, too, was in Madison County, Kentucky. Some researchers believe he died in Warren County, Tennessee, but the Lewis who died there seems to have been a different individual. It may be that Lewis died in Madison County, Kentucky, at some point after 1816, when he was last taxed there. His children settled in Missouri and Illinois, and Judge Lewis Hammack of Pinckneyville, Illinois, a prominent lawyer and jurist, was his grandson.[266]

An important issue to consider at this point was what was fueling this intensely high volume of migration. For the first ninety years of their American experience, the Virginia Hammacks had confined themselves chiefly to a neighborhood surrounding Totuskey Creek in Richmond County, Virginia, although their landholdings lay along the county's boundaries with both Westmoreland and Northumberland Counties. Beginning in the 1740s, however, Hammacks had begun leaving the Northern Neck in search of large, fertile, inexpensive tracts of land on the frontier. During the next century this quest for property would propel them across the nation. In the Pennyroyal Barrens of south-central Kentucky between the Green and Cumberland Rivers, public lands were selling during the 1790s for $30 for every hundred acres surveyed. Better quality lands in the rich Bluegrass region might sell for $100 an acre. That area drew wealthy planters and investors, but families on the make sought out inexpensive tracts that might offer them not only a sustenance but over time economic and social advancement as well. That quest drove them southward into the Georgia frontier after the Revolution as well as westward into Tennessee and Kentucky. In time it would push them north of the Ohio River into Illinois and Indiana as well as beyond the Mississippi.[267]

In terms of our consideration of Tennessee and Kentucky Hammacks, there was one other large grouping of Hammacks and Hammocks in this region, and that was the family which settled after 1800 in Overton County, Tennessee. John Hammock had married Rachel Sellers in Chatham County, North Carolina, in 1795, and he settled in Overton County about 1805 or 1806. The identity of this group is less certain than that of the others. John Hammock was living in Chatham County by August 1792, when he was mentioned among a group named to work the local roads.[268] The 1800 Chatham County, North Carolina, census showed John Hammock and William Hammock on the same page. Both were aged 26-45 and hence born between 1755 and 1774. From later census reports, we can deduce that John Hammock

---

was also a daughter.

[263] Children of Ephraim Hammack and his unidentified wife are believed to have been William Hammack (1798-1873) of Franklin Co., MO; Martin Hammack (abt. 1807 - 1857) of Parke Co., IN; James Hammack (abt. 1815-1845) of Franklin Co., MO; Elizabeth Hammack Glenn (1810-1877) of Pettis Co., MO; George Washington Hammack (1817-1859) of Garrard Co., MO. Some researchers also believe that Ephraim Hammack was father of Daniel Hammack (abt. 1812-1862).

[264] James Hammack and Elizabeth Brock's offspring are believed to have been William Hammack (1800-1858) of Hamilton Co., IN and John Brock Hammack (abt. 1806-aft. 1880) of Mills Co., IA.

[265] William Hammack and Jane Long's offspring are believed to have been James L. Hammack (1801-1862) of Mercer Co., MO; Elizabeth Hammack Murphy (1803-1843) of Garrard Co., KY; George Hammack (1806 - 1880/1882) of Vigo Co., IN; Daniel Hammack (1811-1888) of Anderson Co., KY; and Fanny Hammack Murphy (abt. 1814-aft. 1831) of Garrard Co., KY.

[266] Lewis Hammack and Keziah Daniel's offspring are believed to have been Coleman Hammack (abt. 1802-bef. 1843) of Monroe Co., MO; Benjamin Hammack (abt. 1804-1875) of Marion Co., IL; and two daughters, whose names have not been determined.

[267] Norman Risjord, *The Romantics* (Lanham and Oxford, 2001), pp. 289-305, for a case study of one family's migration during this period.

[268] Chatham Co., NC, Court Minutes, Volume May 1790-August 1792.

was born between 1770 and 1774 and that William was born between 1760 and 1765. The likelihood seems to be that they were brothers.

In terms of the known chronology of Hammack families, there seem to be few possibilities concerning their parentage. They might be offspring of John Hammack, son of John and Mildred Hammack of Lunenburg County; that John was aged sixteen or more by 1764, and he appears on Lunenburg tax lists from 1764 to 1776. Still, there is no clear evidence that he lived beyond 1776 or that he left offspring.

Among the descendants of Richard Hammack, there seem to be two possibilities. One is that they were sons of William Hammack, son of John and Mary Martin Hammack, who was bound out as an orphan in 1770. If John and William of Chatham County were brothers, this seems unlikely, since William, son of John Hammack and Mary Martin, was still a minor in 1770. The strongest possibility seems to be that they were sons of Daniel Hammack who married Ann Rust. Daniel was an adult in 1757, and he could well have fathered both William and John.[269] Further, he had moved from Albemarle County southwest into Bedford and then into Campbell County, where the last known references to him are found about 1784. He and Ann Hammack were both alive at that time, but Daniel is conspicuously absent from Virginia's comprehensive 1787 tax survey. That absence strongly suggests that he had died between 1784 and 1787 or that he had left the state. Further, in 1784, he and Ann were selling the fifty acres they had inherited from her father George Rust twelve years earlier; this action strongly suggests that they were preparing to leave the county. No record of either of them has been found after 1784.[270]

In Campbell County, the Hammacks and Rusts lived on Mollie's Creek near Rustburg, the present county seat, which was named for Ann Hammack Rust's brother Jeremiah Rust. Rustburg is located about fifteen miles north of where the Roanoke River separates Campbell County from Pittsylvania and Halifax Counties.[271] It is about thirty-eight miles north of the boundary between Virginia and North Carolina and perhaps eighty miles due north of Chatham County, North Carolina. In terms of timing and geography, had Daniel and Ann Hammack left Campbell County, Virginia, about 1784 heading south, Chatham County, North Carolina, would have been a likely destination.

This, unfortunately, does not prove that John and William Hammock of Chatham County were sons of Daniel and Ann Rust Hammack; it only supports the possibility, not the probability. Of these two Chatham County Hammocks, William remained in Chatham County, where he died at an advanced age after 1840; he was apparently the father of John Hammock, who was enumerated in Chatham County, North Carolina, in 1850, 1860, and 1870.[272] John Hammack who was enumerated in Chatham County in 1800 moved to Overton County, Tennessee, about 1806. He received a small land grant there in 1818 and was enumerated there in 1830 and 1840. John died between 1840 and 1850, but his widow Rachel was still living in 1850, when she was enumerated at age seventy-five. John and Rachel produced a large family, including William, James, John, Laird, David, Rachel, and Anne. Members of this family remained in Overton County into the twentieth-century.[273]

Another challenge confronting the study of the Overton County, Tennessee, Hammack family is the enumeration in 1850 of a William Hammock, age seventy, a Virginia native, living near Rachel Sellars Hammock. The 1850 census showed in his household Milly, age 50, a Virginia native; Thomas, age 26, a Tennessee native; Mary, age 22, a Tennessee native; Susan, age 20, a Tennessee native; and Jerusha ("Jericia") Quarles, age 76, a Virginia native.[274] Milly Quarles, daughter of John Quarles and Jerusha

---

[269] Albemarle Co., VA, Deed Book 2, 1758-61, pp. 1-2.

[270] Campbell Co., VA, Deed Book 1, p. 253.

[271] Bedford Co., VA, Will Book 1, 1763-87, p. 238.

[272] 1800 Chatham Co., NC, Census, p. 203; 1810 Chatham Co., NC, Census, p. 349; 1820 Chatham Co., NC, Census, p. 31; 1830 Chatham Co., NC, Census, p. 440; 1840 Chatham Co., NC, Census, p. 140.

[273] 1800 Chatham Co., NC, Census, p. 203; Overton Co., TN, DB P, p. 573; 1830 Overton Co., TN, Census, p. 212; 1840 Overton Co., TN, Census, p. 3; 1850 Overton Co., TN, Census, p. 45.

[274] 1850 Overton Co., TN, Census, p. 46.

Ferris, had married William Oakley on 14 June 1811 in Henry County, Virginia. The family then moved to Overton County, Tennessee, where John Quarles died between 1840 and 1850. Milly Quarles Oakley seems to have married William Hammock as her second husband. Strangely enough, they are not found prior to the 1850 census, nor are any members of the family found in later enumerations. The identity of this William Hammock is unclear. He was not the William enumerated in Chatham County, North Carolina, from 1800 to 1840. One possibility is that he was the son of Robert Hammack of Albemarle County, Virginia, and Surry County, North Carolina; Robert's will names a son William who had apparently already left Surry County, North Carolina, when Robert died in 1823.[275] This Robert Hammack was also of the lineage of Richard Hammack, for he first appears in Albemarle County, Virginia, in 1779.[276]

Between 1790 and 1830, a large number of Hammacks and Hammocks moved into Tennessee and Kentucky. Although one line descended from Benedict Hammack of Amelia County, Virginia, most of these Hammacks and Hammocks were of the lineage of Richard Hammack of Richmond and Westmoreland Counties, Virginia. In coming generations, they and their descendants would carry the surname across the continent.

[275] Census records for Surry County, North Carolina, 1786 and 1790, both indicate a son born before 1786 who was apparently Robert's son William. Robert's only other proven son, Bartlett, was born about 1796. The 1790 census does indicate a second son born between 1786 and 1790. Surry is southwest of Henry County, Virginia; both Henry County, Virginia, and Surry County, North Carolina, border Patrick County, Virginia, which was formed in 1790 from Henry County.

[276] Albemarle Co., VA, DB 7, p. 291; Albemarle Co., VA, DB 7, p. 297; 1785 Albemarle Co., VA, Tax List.

Chapter 7:

"Westward I Go Free": Texas, California and Oregon[277]

Throughout American history, the frontier has lured settlers looking for better lives to press westward in search of better lands and greater economic opportunity. The Louisiana Purchase of 1803 doubled the size of the United States, extending its lands to the eastern boundary of Texas and giving it a claim to the present states of Oklahoma, Kansas, Nebraska, and the Dakotas. In 1819, the Transcontinental Treaty, negotiated by then Secretary of State John Quincy Adams, added Florida to the United States and gave the nation a legal claim to a western boundary on the Pacific Ocean. The United States and England would jointly occupy the northwestern territories that today comprise the states of Washington and Oregon, and the area below the treaty line -- which included portions of modern California, Utah, Colorado, New Mexico, Arizona, and Texas -- would remain a part of New Spain.[278]

After a decade of struggle, Mexico achieved its independence from Spain in 1821. In order to promote settlement on its remote northern frontier, Mexico welcomed immigration from the United States into the Mexican province of Tejas. By the end of the decade, thousands of Americans -- mostly slave-owning southerners in search of better plantation lands -- had entered Mexican territory. Nominally they conformed to the two requirements placed upon them by the Mexican government -- the abolition of slavery and the conversion of new settlers to Catholicism -- but most retained both their enslaved African property and their Protestant faith. In 1836, a coup began near San Antonio, led by an unlikely group of Revolutionaries that included the Tejano hero Juan Seguin and former American citizens Sam Houston and Davy Crockett, both of whom had come to Texas via Tennessee.[279]

After successfully concluding their Revolution with the capture of Santa Anna and his army at the Battle of San Jacinto in 1837, Houston, Seguin, and others established the Republic of Texas. Almost immediately, however, the former American citizens who comprised the majority of Texas residents began pressing for annexation by the United States. To their surprise, however, the land-hungry Americans were less than enthusiastic about adding the vast Texas territory to their country. The Missouri Compromise of 1820 had settled the bitter question of the future of slavery in the Louisiana Purchase. It had added Maine to the Union as a free state and Missouri as a slave state, and it had declared that all states formed from the Louisiana Purchase below the 36' 30° line would be slave states; those formed above that line, with the exception of Missouri, would be free states.[280]

Many Americans feared that annexation of Texas would reopen the bitter question of slavery's expansion in the American nation. For a decade the Texans and many pro-slavery southerners, including former President Andrew Jackson of Tennessee, pressed for annexation. Another Tennessean, Democrat James Knox Polk, made annexation of Texas a plank of his presidential platform during the 1846 election; days before Polk would take office, his opponent, sitting President John Tyler, would issue an order adding Texas to the union. Mexico, which had only tenuously accepted Texas's claim to independence, objected, and the task fell to Polk to defend the American claim. From 1846 to 1848, the United States of America battled the Mexican nation in a war that would end only after General Winfield Scott captured Mexico City itself.[281]

---

[277] Henry David Thoreau wrote: "Eastward I go by force, but westward I go free." The quotation appeared originally in Thoreau's posthumous essay, "Walking," published in the *Atlantic Monthly* (June 1862), p. 266. A modern version appears in L. Hyde, *The Essays of Henry D. Thoreau* (London, 2002), p. 158.

[278] D. W. Howe, *What God Hath Wrought: The Transformation of America, 1815-1848* (Oxford, 2009), pp. 108-110, 805-811.

[279] D. E. Chipman, *Spanish Texas, 1519-1821* (Austin, 1992), pp. 238-240; Howe, *What God Hath Wrought*, pp. 658-701, esp. 663-666.

[280] Ibid., pp. 147-160, 663-666.

[281] Ibid., pp. 658-701, 744-792.

For a while it seemed that Polk would find himself fighting two wars at once. Although England and the United States had shared joint occupation of Oregon and Washington for decades, they nearly came to blows in the middle 1840s over the precise boundary between the two nations. Through diplomatic negotiation, the United States acquired sole possession of the Oregon Territory in 1848; at that time, the region embraced all of present Washington and Idaho and parts of Wyoming and Montana. There were about 13,000 inhabitants in Oregon in 1850; the territory became the thirty-third state in the union in 1859. Washington was organized as a territory in 1853 and remained such until 1889, when it was admitted as the forty-second state.[282]

As American diplomats were negotiating over the Oregon territory, however, American troops were heading south into Texas and Mexico. After Scott captured Mexico City, American victory was assured. In 1848 the Treaty of Guadalupe-Hidalgo formally ended the conflict, adding to the United States all of the present state of Texas as well as the territory that became New Mexico, Arizona, California, and parts of Utah and Colorado. When Zachary Taylor became President of the United States, southerners believed he would identify with their region; after all, he was a slaveholding plantation owner from Louisiana who belonged to one of Virginia's oldest planter families. Taylor surprised many Americans by pushing for California's admission to the Union in 1850 as the thirty-first state. Unlike Texas, which had in 1845 originally been annexed as a slave state, California became a free state. For the next decade, an ever more intense debate would rage about the future of slavery in the territories of the Mexican cession as well as in the remaining territories of the Louisiana Purchase. This debate would, in 1861, degenerate into Civil War.[283]

As the nation moved westward beyond the Mississippi, Hammacks and Hammocks were among the vanguard of expansion. While Congress debated Missouri's admission to the Union in 1820, at least four Hammack families were already living in the new territory, which had first been organized in 1812.[284] All of these men and their families had come from Smith County, Tennessee, and were of the bloodline of the first Richard Hammack. His great-grandson Daniel Hammack who married Mary Martin had settled in Tennessee about 1799 after leaving Franklin County, Georgia. By 1820, Daniel's sons Brice, Martin, and William were all living in Lincoln County, Tennessee, where they were heads of household. Another William Hammack had already settled in Franklin County, Missouri; he was of the family of Richard Hammack and Mary Witcher and had come there via Grainger County, Tennessee, and Madison County, Kentucky. Soon afterwards, they would be joined by another William Hammack and James Daniel Hammack, both of whom moved westward from Smith County, Tennessee. By the 1880s, apart from Virginia, Georgia, and Alabama, Missouri would have one of the single largest concentrations of Hammacks in the nation.

The first Hammack known to settle in Texas was Reddick P. Hammack, formerly of Laurens County, Georgia, who was of the bloodline of Benedict Hammack, Sr. Reddick was living in Texas by 1835 and took part in the Revolution of 1836. He was among Fanning's troops who were not massacred at the Alamo. Reddick remained in Texas for several years but returned to Georgia prior to 1840, where he lived the remainder of his days. Throughout the 1850s, his widow Sarah pressed for land grants in Texas based on his earlier residence and service.[285]

Likewise, the first Hammack in California was a migrant rather than a permanent settler. Jesse Harvey Hammack, son of Lewis Hammack and Sarah Harvey, had been born in Warren County, Tennessee, after his parents left Charlotte County, Virginia. He was of the bloodline of Robert Hammack

---

[282] Ibid., pp. 715-721.

[283] Ibid., pp. 744-792, 837-856.

[284] French settlements in Missouri long predate the American ones. American settlers began filtering into Missouri immediately after the Louisiana Purchase. William Clark and Meriwether Lewis launched their famous expedition in 1804 from St. Louis, and throughout the next decade fur traders venturing as far as the Pacific used St. Louis as the point from which to begin their westward journeys. The early Hammacks thus had ample motivation to seek their future in this new land beyond the Mississippi.

[285] T. L. Miller, ed., *Bounty and Donation Land Grants of Texas, 1835-1888* (Austin and London, 1967).

and Ann Lambert, his grandfather Lewis Hammack being a brother of Robert Hammack who married Millenor Jackson and settled along the Georgia frontier during the Revolution. Jesse Harvey Hammack traveled to California in 1848 as a miner during the legendary Gold Rush and was enumerated there in 1850; soon afterwards, however, he returned to his family in Benton County, Arkansas, and then later in life moved to Hunt County in eastern Texas, where he died.

During the 1840s, several Hammacks arrived as permanent settlers in Texas. These included Henry Hammack from Jones County, Georgia, and John and James Hammack, single men, from Tennessee and Kentucky. Susannah Hammack Stringfield, a widow from Lincoln County, Georgia, settled in the Republic of Texas with her three orphaned sons long before statehood; she remained there until her death, and her son became a prosperous merchant and trader in Brazoria County.

Between 1853 and 1855, the family of Brice Wiseman Hammack would relocate from Lincoln County, Missouri, to Coryell County, near Austin, in central Texas. Brice sold out his Missouri property in 1853 and immediately headed south; a prosperous farmer, he was a local justice in both Missouri and Texas. Although some of Brice's offspring remained in Missouri, most relocated to Texas. Son Daniel (1822-1909) was county surveyor for more than twenty years, and grandson Daniel Leroy Hammack -- the first Hammack to be born in Wisconsin -- was a well-known livestock breeder in central Texas. In the 1880s, Brice's nephew -- Dr. Elijah Hammack, a real estate developer and physician -- would live briefly in Texas before settling among his cousins in Oregon.

Brice Wiseman Hammack died in Coryell County in 1867; by that time, his elder brother Martin had been living in California for more than fifteen years. Martin had been born during his parents' brief sojourn in South Carolina. The family lived in Franklin County, Georgia, when Brice was born in 1796. They soon afterwards settled in Dixon and Smith Counties, Tennessee, where both Daniel and Mary Martin Hammack died. Martin Hammack lived in Lincoln County, Missouri, for more than thirty years before setting out for Texas. Martin's wife Eleanor was a niece of Missouri's first governor, Alexander McNairy, and had been raised as a member of his household. In Lincoln County, Missouri, Martin seems to have been prosperous, if not wealthy. His sons John and Brice are said to have gone west in search of gold in 1847 and to have returned to Missouri the following year filled with alluring tales. For a man of Martin's station, brighter prospects in California must have beckoned.

Martin Hammack and his family left Missouri in April 1852. The trek westward was a long one. Migrants generally left Missouri in early spring and traveled for six to eight months by foot across the country, reaching their destinations on the Pacific coast in early autumn of the year. According to legend, Martin Hammack's family were the first white settlers of Lake County, California. After leaving Missouri, they

travelled along the Oregon Trail to California, coming by way of the Nevada line and on down the trail along the Humboldt River. They branched off the trail just before reaching Lassen Meadows in Nevada, going by Honey lake on the Nobles cutoff -- opened in the spring of 1852 -- passing north of Lassen's peak, and entered the Sacramento Valley at Fort Reading above Battle Creek. This road skirted the Snake River Desert and the lava fields of modern Lassen County. The party spent the first winter at Middletown, four miles from old Shasta City. The next spring (1853) they moved down the Sacramento River to near where Colusa city now stands. While there they heard of Lake County, and five of the men rode horseback with an Indian guide to where they could look down from the mountains into Clear Lake. The following spring (1854) the party made their way into Lake County with the Indian guide, building their own roads and paths, and arrived in April. There were fourteen wagons in the Hammack train and only three men outriders. Martin Hammack refused to join a big train or to guide a big train across the plains, as he was urged to do. They started with over four hundred head of fine cattle and horses, and drove oxen (two wagons) across the plains. Martin Hammack went back to his old home in Tennessee to get some especially fine blooded horses, five mares and a stallion, to add to his own good stock in Missouri, to bring to California. The family planned on having fine stock farms in California. They arrived in Lake County with about 300 head of cattle and horses intact after the trip from Missouri.[286]

Martin was enumerated in Napa County in 1860 and Lake County in 1870; although his eldest son John returned to Missouri, the others remained in California. Brice's family was enumerated in Napa and Lake Counties from 1860 until 1920. The two youngest sons, William and Robert, never married but lived long lives; William was living in Mendocino County at the age of eighty-two in 1920 while Robert was living in Lake County at the age of seventy-seven.

In the 1850s and 1860s, other Hammack families began pressing westward also. By 1860, George and Davis Hammack had settled in Toulumne County, California, where they were farming and mining. Both had come west from Missouri. Martin and son Brice M. Hammack were in Napa County, and another Brice M. Hammack, also from Missouri, was living in Siskiyou County's Scott Valley, where he was mining.[287] M. R. Hammack, a twenty-eight year old farm laborer from Illinois, was living in Yolo County, and Calvin Hammack, son of John Brock Hammack of Tennessee and Iowa, was living on Sutter Creek in Amador County. In 1880, the family of Martin Hammack remained in Lake County, the family of George Hammack in Stanislaus, and Brice M. Hammack was still working in Siskiyou.[288] By the end of the century, many descendants of Richard Hammack and Mary Witcher would settle in Los Angeles and surrounding counties, traveling by way of Missouri, Indiana, Illinois, Kansas, and Iowa to the west coast. Daniel M. Hammack, a descendant of Richard's son Ephraim, would become a Los Angeles attorney by the turn of the century[289], and in 1900 Hammacks would be living in Amador, Lake, Butte, San Diego, Sacramento, San Bernardino, and Humboldt Counties.[290]

As noted, Oregon was admitted to the Union in 1859, eleven years after being organized as a territory in 1848. By the early 1860s, Hammacks began arriving in Oregon from Indiana and Iowa. All of these Hammacks came from the line of Richard Hammack who married Mary Witcher in Virginia. George Hammack, a twenty-four year old miner born in Illinois, was living in Shasta Precinct, Baker County, Oregon, in 1870. In Union County were James Hammack, age fifty-five, a native of Kentucky; James was farming in Orodell District. His son John W. Hammack was living two doors away, also farming; the census enumeration indicates that the family had left Iowa after 1864 and had arrived in Oregon by 1866. In Hillsboro District, Washington County, Oregon, was twenty-one year old George Hammack, an Indiana native, living with James and Meary Gerrish, who had recently arrived from Missouri. By 1880, the Oregon Hammacks were concentrated in Marion and Union Counties. George Hammack, age thirty-eight, from Iowa, was living with his small family in Labish, Marion County, where he was farming near his brother Fred. Andrew and Sarah Hammack, aged sixty-three and seventy-one, natives of Tennessee, were farming in Union County's Indian Valley. The James Hammack family was now living in Island District; James and Elizabeth were sixty-five and sixty-two, both born in Kentucky. Living with them was forty year old son Daniel, also born in Kentucky, and two doors away was Ephraim, age thirty-five, born

---

[286] Hammack, *Wandering Back*, 2: 177-178, quoting Elizabeth Hammack Cross.

[287] He was aged 27 and born in TN with real estate valued at $1600. He was living with J. A. Free, age 29, IL. He was shown in Scott Valley in 1870 as H. B. Hammock, 35, OH, a shingle maker. In 1880, he was still in Scott Valley: Brice M. Hammack, 44, Laborer, TN/VA/VA. He was living with Frank W. Hooper, 19, CA. As late as 1880, this Brice seems to have been unmarried.

[288] Interestingly, there was a family of Indian Hammacks living in the Indian Village of Upper Lake Valley in Lake Co., CA. Jim Hammock, 60, and wife Leesy, 48, natives of CA, were living among a large number of Native Americans.

[289] He was aged 42, an Illinois native, with wife Isabella and son Daniel, both natives of Iowa, in 1900. The elder Daniel was a lawyer, and the younger Daniel was then at school. See 1900 Los Angeles Co., CA, Census, Los Angeles Township, Precinct 30, p. 191.

[290] Ephraim Hammack (1825-1901) settled in Audubon Co., IA, where he died. His widow Ellen was in Burleigh Co., ND, in 1910 but back in Henry Co., IA, by 1920, at which time she was ninety years of age. Their son Daniel settled in Los Angeles County. Son William moved from Harlan Co., Nebraska, to San Bernardino Co., CA, before 1920. Son Ephraim was living in San Diego Co., CA, by 1900, as was his brother Nottley S. Hammack.

in Missouri. Thomas, age forty-two, Missouri, was near them in Island City, and James W., age forty-five, Kentucky, was living in Summerville. George Hammack from Illinois was still farming in Wapato Precinct, Washington County, with his new wife and young daughter. They would be joined within the decade by another cousin, Dr. Elijah Hammack, who moved from Franklin County, Missouri, to Texas before settling in Oregon about 1884.

Almost without exception, the first Hammacks and Hammocks to populate the Pacific states of California, Oregon, and Washington were descendants of Richard Hammack, son of the immigrant William. The first Hammock enumerated in Utah would be John P. Hammock, born about 1832 in Illinois, who was living in Jack's Valley, Carson County, by 1860. No Hammacks are found in early Nevada census reports, but Oregon and California enumerations show Hammack births there in the 1870s.

The only notable exception to this westward migration of Richard Hammack's descendants was the migration of John Robert Hammack into North Dakota. John was born in Macon County, Georgia, and reared in Calhoun County, Mississippi, a son of John T. and Louisa Templeton Hammack and a descendant of Robert Hammack and Millenor Jackson. He left Mississippi after 1880 and settled in North Dakota, where he married Emma Beale. At the time of the 1900 McLean County Census, John was aged forty-two and working as a rancher. Emma was aged twenty-six, a Dakota native of Swedish extraction; members of this family would move later into Oregon and Canada.

Richard Hammack's descendants moved westward as new lands became available; like many other pioneers, they pressed into unsettled territories, staking claims and waiting for the nation to move westward after them. Richard's sons were the first Hammacks to leave the Northern Neck. His grandsons and great-grandsons pressed beyond the Blue Ridge Mountains into Tennessee, Kentucky, and modern West Virginia. They settled in Missouri while it was a fledgling territory, and they were the first Hammacks to settle permanently in California and Oregon. Less than two centuries after the first William Hammack crossed the Atlantic Ocean to settle in a still largely unexplored continent, his descendants reached the Pacific.

Descendants of Martin Hammack and his brother Brice Wiseman Hammack, sons of Daniel and Mary Martin Hammack, were among the early Hammacks and Hammocks to head west. Brice settled in Texas and Martin in California.

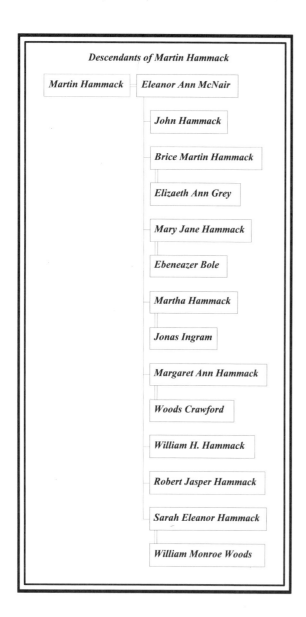

Descendants of Martin Hammack

- Martin Hammack — Eleanor Ann McNair
  - John Hammack
  - Brice Martin Hammack
  - Elizaeth Ann Grey
  - Mary Jane Hammack
  - Ebeneazer Bole
  - Martha Hammack
  - Jonas Ingram
  - Margaret Ann Hammack
  - Woods Crawford
  - William H. Hammack
  - Robert Jasper Hammack
  - Sarah Eleanor Hammack
  - William Monroe Woods

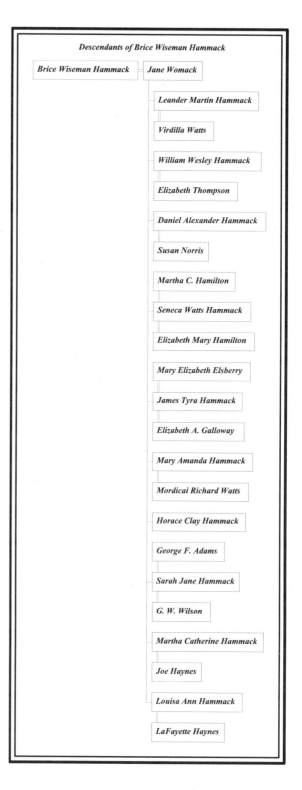

Descendants of Brice Wiseman Hammack

- Brice Wiseman Hammack — Jane Womack
  - Leander Martin Hammack
  - Virdilla Watts
  - William Wesley Hammack
  - Elizabeth Thompson
  - Daniel Alexander Hammack
  - Susan Norris
  - Martha C. Hamilton
  - Seneca Watts Hammack
  - Elizabeth Mary Hamilton
  - Mary Elizabeth Elsberry
  - James Tyra Hammack
  - Elizabeth A. Galloway
  - Mary Amanda Hammack
  - Mordicai Richard Watts
  - Horace Clay Hammack
  - George F. Adams
  - Sarah Jane Hammack
  - G. W. Wilson
  - Martha Catherine Hammack
  - Joe Haynes
  - Louisa Ann Hammack
  - LaFayette Haynes

Chapter 8:

The Virginia Southside

To Virginians, the term "Southside" refers to the area below the James River, spreading west into the Piedmont towards the backcountry. Most of its early settlers moved west from Surry, Prince George, and Isle of Wight Counties or south from the Northern Neck and middle peninsula. Although scions of some of the colony's most powerful families established prosperous plantations in Lunenburg and Brunswick Counties, most of the settlers were yeomen and planters seeking to improve their fortunes.

After 1800, there were four primary groupings of Hammacks left in Virginia. One was centered in Richmond County in the Northern Neck, and another was centered in Lunenburg County in the Southside. The two remaining groups -- both from the line of Richard Hammack -- were centered in Pittsylvania County (originally a portion of Lunenburg) and in Kanawha and Monroe Counties, areas that later became a portion of West Virginia.

A small but significant group of Hammacks remained in the Northern Neck after 1800. This group descended from Benedict Hammack (1740 -- 1815), son of Robert Hammack and Ann Lambert. Benedict and wife Sally had a large family, including several sons: Benjamin (1765/70 -- c. 1801), husband of Molly Scutt and Patty Scutt; John (c. 1780 -- aft. 1830), husband of Anna Beale; William; and Lewis (c. 1796 --), husband of Lucy Clarke. Of these sons, Benjamin was the father of William Hammack of Northumberland County, who married Judith Clarke Sydnor. This William had sons William and John who settled in Natchez, Mississippi, between 1840 and 1860, and a third son, Benjamin, who lived in Alexandria, Virginia, and Washington, D.C.

Lewis, another son of Benedict and Sally, married Lucy Clarke, a descendant of Dr. Robert Clarke who had been a close associate of the immigrant William Hammack and his offspring. Among their offspring was Rodham Clarke Hammack (c. 1818 - 1874) who fathered a large family in Richmond County. The second son of Lewis and Lucy was Benedict Hammack (1814 -- 1895), who married Ellen Ball Polk (1818 -- 1855) and Jane E. Muire (c. 1820 -- 1898). Ellen Ball Polk Hammack was a daughter of Charles Peale Polk and Ellen Ball Downman, a great-niece of the painter Charles Willson Peale, and a distant cousin of Mary Ball Washington, mother of the president. Rodham Clarke Hammack and Benedict Hammack left many descendants in Richmond and Northumberland.

The Hammacks of West Virginia, descendants of Richard Hammack's grandson Martin Hammack, have already been outlined. The two remaining Virginia families after 1800 were those of Martin's cousin John Hammack of Pittsylvania County and of John and Mildred Lambert Hammack of Lunenburg. As noted previously, Richard and Mary Witcher Hammack moved from Albemarle County into Pittsylvania County in the 1770s; their eldest son, John Hammack, came of age about 1785. In May 1784, he married Patsy Goad, daughter of William and Taby Goad. In 1785, he was shown on the Pittsylvania tax list between the names of William Goad and John Goad. William Goad's family contained ten white souls. John Hammack's contained three white souls, and John Goad's contained four white souls. John remained in Pittsylvania for the rest of his life, although most of his siblings -- and perhaps his mother -- moved to Tennessee and Kentucky after 1800. He died in late 1844, when he must have been past eighty years of age, and his widow Patsy survived him for a decade.[291]

Of the offspring of John and Patsy Goad Hammack, their son Toliver settled in Smith and Macon Counties, Tennessee. By 1860, his children were living in Illinois and Missouri. Spencer, Coleman, and John T. Hammack remained in Pittsylvania County, where they produced large families. Spencer's sons William, Oliver, and Spencer, Jr., all moved to Indiana after 1850, but Lewis, Toliver, and John Alfred remained in Pittsylvania County, where their descendants live today.

---

[291] Pittsylvania Co., VA, Order Book 38, pp. 193-94. Martha was shown as ninety in 1850 but as eighty when she died in July 1855.

The largest group of Virginia Hammacks at this time were those who lived in Lunenburg County. John Hammack and Mildred Lambert had at least two surviving sons: William Hammack (1742 -- 1785) and Hugh Hammack (by c. 1753 -- 1804). A third son was John Hammack (by c. 1748 -- aft. 1776) whose fate has not been determined. Of John and Mildred's offspring, William wrote his will in 1784 and Hugh in 1804. William left a widow named Elizabeth and sons John, James, and William. He seems also to have left several daughters, whom he did not name in his will. Hugh's will names wife Anna, sons Lewis, Robert, and Hugh, and daughters Milley, Caty, and Anna. Both William's family and Hugh's family remained in the same neighborhood of Lunenburg; their offspring seem to have been more like siblings than first cousins, and legal records indicate that they associated closely together. Of William's offspring, John (c. 1765 -- 1856) married Katy Hanks and Ann Amos. James married Elizabeth Amos. William seems not to have married. Elizabeth Hammack who married Samuel Meanley in 1796, Nancy Hammack who married Thomas Hanks in 1791, and Mary Hammack who married David Moseley in 1789 were probably all daughters. Interestingly, Katy Hanks and Thomas Hanks were distant cousins of Nancy Hanks Lincoln, mother of President Abraham Lincoln.

Hugh Hammack was his brother's executor and was active in many legal transactions in Lunenburg before he died in 1804; in 1792, he served as administrator of Milley Bentley, widow of Daniel Bentley, and daughter of Robert Hammack and Anne Lambert. Milley was Hugh's second cousin on the Hammack side and his first cousin on the Lambert side. Mildred was a sister of Robert Hammack who married Millenor Jackson and moved to Wilkes County, Georgia, and after 1800 her children -- along with many Lunenburg cousins -- relocated to Wilkes County, Georgia.[292] Among these families were the families of Robert Moore (for whom in 1794 Hugh served as a witness)[293] and Ussery Moore, whose land in 1802 joined that of Samuel Peace, James Moore, and Jesse Moore.[294]

Of Hugh's offspring, Ann, Caty, and Lewis seem never to have married, although they lived well into adulthood. Robert and Milly may have died young. Only Hugh Hammack (c. 1799 -- 1860) seems to have reared a family. Hugh married Lucy Peace in 1825. Lucy was a daughter of John Peace and a granddaughter of Samuel Peace; her father's sisters Susannah Peace and Elizabeth Ann Peace were the first two wives of Jesse Moore (1759/60 -- 1842), brother of Ussery Moore of Lunenburg County, Virginia, and Wilkes County, Georgia. These were only two of many ties uniting the Hammacks and Moores of Lunenburg County and their descendants. Among Jesse Moore's fourteen children by four wives, Elizabeth Moore and husband John Hobson Fallin, Elisha Moore and wife Elizabeth Jennings Gee, and John Robert Moore and Martha Inge all settled in Taliaferro County, Georgia, where they were neighbors of James Moore (son of Ussery Moore) and his wife Sarah Hammack (daughter of William and Mary Hammack, and sister of Simeon Hammack who married Elizabeth Jane Moore).

Cumulatively, with the Hammack, Lambert, Bentley, and Amos connections on the one hand and the Moore and Peace connections on the other, the evidence suggests that the family of Hugh Hammack of Lunenburg County, Virginia, had a particularly close relationship with the family of William and Mary (Felts) Hammack of Georgia. Their offspring were related in myriad ways, and those connections proved important as the two sets of families migrated across Georgia together and often intermarried in later generations.

---

[292] Milley was the mother of John H. Bentley who married Martha Moore and settled in Crawford County. He was a neighbor of Simeon Hammack; Martha Moore Bentley and Elizabeth Jane Moore Hammack may have been sisters. Milley was also the mother of Anny Bentley who married George Amos. George Amos was related to Elizabeth Amos Hammack, who married John Hammack in 1815, and Elizabeth Amos Hammack, who married James Hammack in 1805. Anny Bentley Amos's son George W. Amos married Simeon Hammack's sister Catherine Hammack.

[293] Lunenburg Co., VA, Deed Book 16, p. 475.

[294] Lunenburg Co., VA, Deed Book 19, p. 31.

William "O" Hammack, the Immigrant: The Families of his Three Surviving Sons Followed Different Migration Routes Across the Country. Descendants of Richard Hammack reached the west coast about 1855.

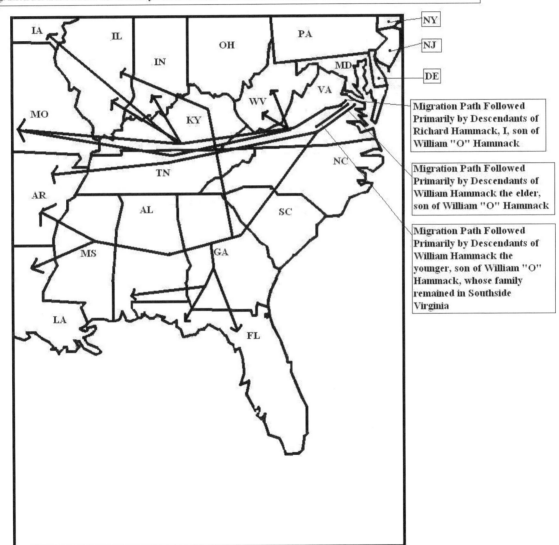

NY

NJ

DE

Migration Path Followed Primarily by Descendants of Richard Hammack, I, son of William "O" Hammack

Migration Path Followed Primarily by Descendants of William Hammack the elder, son of William "O" Hammack

Migration Path Followed Primarily by Descendants of William Hammack the younger, son of William "O" Hammack, whose family remained in Southside Virginia

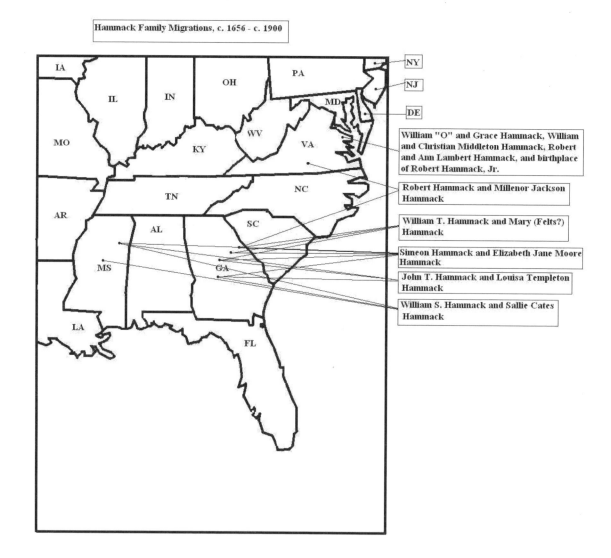

Hammack Family Migrations, c. 1656 - c. 1900

NY

NJ

DE

William "O" and Grace Hammack, William and Christian Middleton Hammack, Robert and Ann Lambert Hammack, and birthplace of Robert Hammack, Jr.

Robert Hammack and Millenor Jackson Hammack

William T. Hammack and Mary (Felts?) Hammack

Simeon Hammack and Elizabeth Jane Moore Hammack

John T. Hammack and Louisa Templeton Hammack

William S. Hammack and Sallie Cates Hammack

Chapter 9:

"A Turn in the South": The Carolinas, Georgia, and Alabama[295]

Virginians settling along the Georgia frontier were known to be more genteel and refined than settlers pouring in from South Carolina and North Carolina. As a rule, they came later than families who had already moved into the Carolinas in search of improving fortunes, and, unlike many of the Carolinians, they rapidly acquired land and often brought with them slaves and substantial property. It was these Virginians, conventional wisdom goes, who brought culture to the frontier.

Three large Hammack groupings settled on the Georgia frontier before 1800. These were the families of Benedict and Elizabeth Hammack, Benedict's nephew Robert and his wife Millenor Jackson, and Benedict's nephew John Hammack and his wives Susannah and Mary Ann. All three of these families settled in Wilkes County, Georgia, and their children and grandchildren remained in Georgia until past 1820; in the decades between 1820 and the beginning of the American Civil War, they spread into Alabama, Florida, Mississippi, Louisiana, and Texas. Each family will be treated briefly below.

A. Benedict and Elizabeth Hammack of Richmond and Lunenburg Counties, Virginia.

The first Benedict Hammack died either in Lunenburg County, Virginia, or in Onslow County, North Carolina, where his offspring began settling in the 1760s. He was the father of Benedict Hammack, Junior; William Hammack; John Hammack; and Christian Hammack Bentley. All four families relocated to Georgia just after the American Revolution

Christian Hammack, eldest child of Benedict and Elizabeth Hammack, was born in 1723. She married John Bentley in Lunenburg County, Virginia, before 1756. By 1769, they had settled in Onslow County, North Carolina, where John was taxed with sons James and William. On 24 March 1774, William and John Bentley sold 183 acres in Onslow to Edward Howard, and on the following day they sold 182 acres of the same 365 acre tract to John Jarrett.[296]

Within a year, William Bentley was living in Wilkes County, Georgia. On 13 January 1775, his uncle Benedict Hammack patented 200 acres in Wilkes County on the north fork of Little River joining lands owned by William Bentley. John Bentley -- probably Christian's husband -- was living in Wilkes County by 1786. In that year, he was taxed with 787 acres and two slaves. His nearest neighbors were Balaam Bentley and William Bentley. John was taxed consistently in the same district with the same tract of land until 1796, when he disappears from the tax records. He may be the John Bentley who on 13 January 1797 conveyed land in Lincoln County to William Moncrief; if so, Christian had died prior to that date, for John's wife on two 1797 deeds is identified as Temperance Bentley.

The two proven offspring of John and Christian Bentley were James and William Bentley; James is named in the will of John Bentley's step-father James Spicer in Brunswick County, Virginia, and was living as late 1786. William is probably the man who married Jane Hammond -- whose family had also moved from Richmond County, Virginia, to Lunenburg County, Virginia, to Onslow County, North Carolina -- on 8 October 1774 in Onslow County, North Carolina. As noted above, he was in Wilkes County, Georgia, by January 1775. He lived there until 1791, when he wrote his will, naming as heirs wife Jane and children John, Lewis, Susannah, James, and Catherine.

Balaam Bentley, who appears consistently in Wilkes County near William and John, may have been another son of John and Christian. His will was proven in Lincoln County, Georgia, in 1816, naming offspring John, Benjamin, Vincey, and Keziah. Some researchers believe that John Holmes's wife Chloe was another child of John and Christian Hammack Bentley.

---

[295] The quotation is also the title of a travel narrative by V. S. Naipaul: *A Turn in the South* (New York, 1989).
[296] Onslow Co., NC, Deed Book I, p. 78-79.

B. William Hammack and Betty Ann Hames of Lunenburg County, Virginia, Onslow County, North Carolina, and Wilkes County, Georgia.

The birth date of William Hammack is unclear, but he was the second known child of Benedict and Elizabeth Hammack. He was probably born between 1726 and 1730. On 25 April 1767, he patented 100 acres in Onslow County, North Carolina.[297] He was taxed there in 1769 and 1770, when he patented another 135 acres in Onslow.[298] He later conveyed this tract to Hezekiah Jones[299], and on 8 November 1775 he sold the original 100 acre tract in Onslow to Edward Starkey.[300]

William apparently settled in Anson County, North Carolina, where his son William, Jr., enlisted as a Revolutionary War soldier. By 1785, he was living in Wilkes County, Georgia, where he remained for the rest of his life. In that year, he was taxed with four polls, six slaves, and 400 acres in Wilkes County. William Hammack, Jr., was taxed with 1 poll and 200 acres. The names are adjacent on the tax list. Nearby families included Robert Hammack, Philip Combs, Benedict Hammack, and William Bentley.

William Hammack was granted 700 acres in 1787. On 26 September 1791, with Sarah Thornton -- who later married his cousin John Hammack -- he witnessed the Wilkes County will of William Bentley. William was taxed with 600 acres in Wilkes County in 1804. Two years later, on 10 March 1806, he and wife Betty Ann sold 250 acres of land to their son-in-law Abraham Hammons.[301] William died before 16 March 1808, when his estate was inventoried in Wilkes County.[302]

By the time William Hammack died, his offspring had begun to move beyond Wilkes County. His son William -- born in 1760 -- settled in Christian County, Kentucky, before 1799. Daughter Charity married Abraham Hammons in 1784, probably in Wilkes County, and they later moved into Kentucky and Indiana, where Abraham died in 1844 and where Charity was still living in 1846. There is no clear evidence that William and Betty Ann had additional offspring, but some researchers suggest they had two additional children, Benedict (born 1762) and Ruth (born 1764). After William's son William reached Kentucky, he and his descendants generally used the spelling Hammock rather than Hammack.

Benedict Hammack, Jr., the third son of Benedict and Elizabeth, was born in 1732 in Richmond County, Virginia. He was deceased by 1787 in Wilkes County, Georgia. His widow Mary -- whom family lore indicates was a Combs before marriage -- died about 1811 in Greene County, Georgia. Benedict seems to have settled in Onslow County, North Carolina, by 1768;[303] he was taxed there in 1769 and 1770. On 12 October 1772, he and William Bentley witnessed a deed from Martin Hammond to Edward Hammond.[304]

Soon thereafter, Benedict settled in Wilkes County, Georgia. In 1774 or 1775, he and William Bentley signed a petition by the inhabitants of Wilkes County that the tracts ceded by the Creek Indians be granted according to the headright system. Balaam Bentley and Thomas Leverett signed the petition with him.[305] On 13 January 1775 -- indicating that he was removing from North Carolina -- Benedict applied for 200 acres on the south side of Little River adjacent William Bentley. Benedict's petition specified that he then had a wife and five sons and one daughter, aged seventeen years to two years. This suggests that Benedict and Mary had married about 1757. The daughter, possibly Benedict's oldest child, was Patsy Hammack Leverett. The five sons included Benedict, Robert, John C., and Benjamin.

---

[297] NC Patent Book 23, p. 29.

[298] NC Patent Book 20, p. 575

[299] Onslow Co., NC, Deed Book J, p. 67.

[300] Onslow Co., NC, Deed Book J, p. 75.

[301] Wilkes Co., GA, Deed Book WW, p. 61; Robert S. Davis, Jr., *The Wilkes Co. Papers, 1773-1833* (Easley, SC, 1979), p.73

[302] Davidson, *Early Records of Georgia: Wilkes County*, II: 234

[303] Onslow Co., NC, Deed Book H, p. 60.

[304] Onslow Co., NC, Deed Book H, p. 60.

[305] Davis, *Wilkes County Papers*, p. 292.

In 1784, Benedict was granted 287.5 acres in Wilkes County.[306] On 24 September 1785, Benedict Hammack and John Bentley were identified as elders of the "Baptist Society at Upton's Creek," when Gideon Anderson deeded them two acres where their meeting house was then located.[307] On 5 November 1785, he purchased 400 acres on Little River from John Beal; this land, too, bordered William Bentley's property.[308]

The 1785 Wilkes County tax digest shows Benedict with 287.5 acres and another 200 acre tract. Later, in 1786, he was granted 500 acres on Little River and Rocky Creek joining John and Phillip Combs.[309] Cumulatively, these real estate transactions indicate that Benedict was a prosperous farmer; like many, he may also have been engaging in frontier land speculation, acquiring vacant tracts whose value he expected to increase over time. But Benedict's ambitions were cut short. He was deceased by 1787, when his son Robert Hammack was taxed with 287.5 acres belonging to "Benedict Hammack, deceased." Although Benedict did leave a will, it was recorded in Wilkes County's now lost Will Book DD, which spanned the period from 1779 to 1792. An inventory of his estate, dated 31 July 1787, survives, listing property he had left to son Benedict and daughter Betsy.[310] Benedict's wife Mary survived until about 1811, when she died in Greene County, where her estate was administered by Benjamin and John C. Hammack.[311]

Although no complete listing of the offspring of Benedict survives, tax digests, his inventory, the deeds by his executor Robert Hammack, and family documents preserved by his descendant Adeline Evans Wynn indicate that he was the father of at least seven children. Many of Benedict's descendants adopted the spelling Hammock rather than Hammack. Benedict Hammock, III, died about 1826 in Jones County, Georgia. Betsy Hammock, wife of William Evans, died after 1820 in Wilkes County, Georgia. Benjamin Hammock died after 1850 in Jasper County. Robert Hammock married his cousin Nancy Combs and died about 1839 in Wilkes County. John C. Hammock died about 1813 in Greene County. William Hammock may have died young. Patsy Hammock, wife of Robert Leverett, who was living in Lincoln County, Georgia, when Robert wrote his will in 1807. The offspring of these children lived in several Georgia Counties (Wilkes, Butts, Jasper, Walton, Coweta) as well as in Alabama, Mississippi, and Texas.

John Hammack, the youngest known son of Benedict and Elizabeth, was born 17 August 1736 in Richmond County, Virginia. He moved to Amelia County, Virginia, with his father as a boy and remained there until about 1765, when he purchased 125 acres on Edgecombe County, North Carolina's Tyanscoca Creek from John Barnes.[312] Ten years later, on 25 January 1776, John Hammack sold this land to Stephen Watkins; witnesses were Archabald Laman, Dun Lamar, and another John Hammack, probably his son.[313]

No clear reference to John Hammack has been discovered after 1776; by 1784, however, one Samuel Hammack was of age in Edgecombe County, and, by 1786, all of the Edgecombe Hammacks had left the county. It would appear that Samuel Hammack was John Hammack's son, and that John Hammack also had offspring named John, William, Jesse, and Emanuel. The family settled first in Burke County, Georgia, and is subsequently found in Washington, Jefferson, and Telfair Counties. Emanuel Hammock was living as late as 1850, at which time he was enumerated as being seventy-two years of age and a native of North Carolina. Tax records document John, Jesse, Samuel, and William as residents of Burke and Jefferson Counties before 1810. The trail becomes less clear after that point. John Hammack, Jr., may

---

[306] GA Land Plats, Book B, 1784-85, p. 19, No. 53. Of this land, 200 acres on Rocky Creek were sold to heirs of Benjamin Hendricks by Robert Hammack, executor. (Wilkes Co., GA, Deed Book NN, pp. 70-72, in Davis, *Wilkes County Papers*, p. 73.)

[307] Davidson, I: 236.

[308] Davidson, I: 241.

[309] Wynn, 87.

[310] Davidson, II: 234.

[311] Greene Co., GA, Executions and Administrations Book G, 1811.

[312] Edgecombe Co., NC, Deed Book C, p. 376, in Wynn, *Southern Lineages*, 86.

[313] Edgecombe Co., NC, Deed Book 3, p. 84.

have been the John Hammack who was living in Monroe County, Alabama, due west of Jefferson County, Georgia, by 1819. Samuel Hammack was in Jefferson County, Georgia, from 1799 until at least 1807. He seems to have moved to Laurens County, Georgia, shortly after this point. He was in Laurens County until about 1826, when he may have died. It seems probable that he was the father of the several Hammacks -- John, Reddick, and Sarah -- who appear in Laurens County during these years. He could also have been the father of George and Jackson Hammock who were found in adjacent Pulaski County, Georgia, before they settled in Florida.[314]

Jesse Hammack was found in Jefferson County, Georgia, from 1799 until at least 1807. No record of him in Georgia has been found after that date. He may have been the Jesse Hammack enumerated in Bedford County, Tennessee, in 1820, with five sons under age 16 and four daughters under age 16. While the connection remains tentative, Jesse may have moved from Tennessee into South Alabama after 1820. According to tradition among the South Alabama Hammacks, Joshua Hammac and George W. Hammac were brothers. Joshua was born in 1807 in Georgia, and George was born in 1812 in Tennessee. George named a son Jesse, and Joshua seems also to have had a son named Jesse. Further, Joshua named a son Willoughby Hammac, and in Kentucky after 1830 appear Willoughby and Hugh Hammack who were both born before 1810 in Georgia. It may be that Jesse Hammack was the father of all of these men, with two of his older sons remaining in Tennessee and Kentucky after the rest of the family relocated to Alabama.[315]

The youngest known child of Benedict and Elizabeth Hammack was Abigail Hammack, baptized in 1739 in North Farnham Parish, Richmond County, Virginia. There is a strong probability that she married Phillip Combs. In 1762, Phillip Combs was taxed in the household of Benedict Hammack, Jr. In 1763 and 1764, he was taxed in the same neighborhood as head of his own household. He was found in Lunenburg County from 1771 to 1775, and on 27 November 1775 Phillip Combs and wife Abigail sold 150 acres in Lunenburg County to John Elmore, whose family was related to the Hammacks.[316] Phillip was in Fairfield District, South Carolina, from 1778 to 1781, and he first patented land in Wilkes County, Georgia, in 1784.[317] In 1785, he was taxed with 950 acres; at that time, his name appears between those of Robert Hammock -- his future son-in-law, and son of Benedict Hammack, Jr., with whom Phillip was living in 1763 -- and Abraham Hammons, who was married to Charity Hammack, niece of Benedict, Jr. Phillip appears consistently from 1791 until at least 1805 on the same tax lists as the children of Benedict Hammack, Jr. The 1794, 1795, and 1796 tax digests indicate that Phillip Combs and John Hammack owned adjoining tracts of land on Rocky Creek in western Wilkes County.

It is not clear whether Abigail Combs lived long after 1778; no subsequent references to her have been found, but there is no evidence that Phillip took a second wife in Wilkes County. Therefore, it appears that Abigail was probably the mother of all of Phillip's children. Phillip was alive as late as 1822, when he was probably at least 83 years old; he was deceased by 1838. Deeds of gift, tax digest entries, and returns on his estate indicate that he was the father of Nancy Combs Hammack, Phillip Combs, Jr.,

[314] See Edgecombe Co., NC, DB 4, p. 363; 1796, 1799, 1802, 1806, 1809, and 1810 Jefferson Co., GA, Tax Digests, 1805 Georgia Land Lottery Registration Lists, and 1807 Georgia Land Lottery Fortunate Draws (Wilkinson County), Georgia Department of Archives and History, Morrow, GA; Marilyn Davis Hahn, *Old Cahaba Land Office Records & Military Warrants, 1817-1853* (Easley, SC, 1981), pp. 29, 81; Marilyn Davis Hahn, *Old Sparta & Elba Land Office Records and Military Warrants, 1822-1860* (Easley, SC, 1983), pp. 21, 27, 31, 65; 1820 Tattnall Co., GA, Census, p. 117; 1840 Tattnall Co., GA, Census, p. 242; 1850 Tattnall Co., GA, Census, p. 365. Many references to these families are also found in A. Thomas, *Laurens Co., GA, Legal Records, 1807-1857* (2 vols., Roswell, GA, 1991).

[315] 1820 Bedford Co., TN, Census; 1830 Monroe Co., AL, p. 44, Census; 1840 Conecuh Co., AL, Census, pp. 262-263, 267; 1850 Conecuh Co., AL, Census, pp. 351, 363, 364, 371.

[316] 1762, 1763, and 1764 Amelia Co., VA, Tithable Lists and 1771-1775 Lunenburg Co., VA, Tithable Lists, Library of Virginia, Richmond, VA; Lunenburg Co., VA, Deed Book 12, p. 479.

[317] Georgia Patent Book EEE, p. 281, cited in S. E. Lucas, Jr., ed., *Index to the Headright and Bounty Grants of Georgia, 1756-1909* (Vidalia, GA, 1970).

James Combs, Martha Combs Jackson, Enoch Combs, a daughter who married James Woodruff, and probably John Combs, Sterling Combs, and Thomas Combs.[318]

B. John Hammack and wives Susannah and Mary Ann, of Richmond County, Virginia, Granville County, North Carolina, and Wilkes County, Georgia.

John Hammack, grandson of William and Christian Middleton Hammack and nephew of Robert and Ann Lambert Hammack, moved to Granville County, North Carolina, where he died in 1776. His first wife, Susannah, had died about 1755 in Richmond County, Virginia; John's second wife, Mary Ann, survived him, and relocated first to Pittsylvania County, Virginia, and then about 1791 to Wilkes County, Georgia, where she was taxed in 1792 with 300 acres of land. Mary Ann settled in southwestern Wilkes County in what is now Taliaferro County. She lived just north of the boundary between present-day Taliaferro and Hancock Counties; there she lived for the rest of her life, dying about 1804.[319]

The family of John Hammack seems to have had a close relationship with that of his cousin Robert Hammack, Jr., husband of Millenor Jackson. Mary Ann Hammack's and Robert Hammack's family were neighbors in Wilkes County for almost two decades; a second connection, the marriage of her son James to Robert's daughter Lucy, served to further unite the two groups. Likewise, Mary Ann's children seem to have had a close relationship with their unmarried half-sister Caty, who apparently lived with Mary Ann, and with their married half-sister Mary Hammack Paschall, who lived in the eastern portion of Wilkes County.

Of John Hammack's offspring, two of his children by Susannah settled in Georgia. Mary Hammack had married William Paschall in Granville County, North Carolina; she and William settled in Wilkes County about 1783, in the western portion that later became Lincoln County. Caty Hammack -- who was baptized in 1756 on the same day as her younger half-brother, John Hammack, son of John and Mary Ann -- came to Wilkes County about 1790 with her step-mother Mary Ann; Caty did not marry until about 1812, when she was nearly sixty years old, at which time she married a widower named William Simmons in Jones County, Georgia. After Simmons died about 1826, Caty moved to Crawford County, where she lived near the family of her cousin William T. Hammack, son of Robert and Millenor Jackson Hammack. She spent the final years of her long life -- dying at more than ninety years of age -- in the family of William's son Mansel Womack Hammack, who administered Caty's estate in Crawford County.[320]

About the same time that William and Mary Hammack Paschall settled in Wilkes County, Mary's half-brother John Hammack (1756-1832), who had married her husband's sister Reliance Paschall, settled in the same neighborhood of eastern Wilkes County. John lived in eastern Wilkes County and western Lincoln County until his death in 1832. After Reliance died, John married second, about 1786, to a woman named Phoebe and then, following her death, in 1807 to Mrs. Sarah Thornton, widow of William Thornton, Sr. John owned several hundred acres in Wilkes and Lincoln Counties and left a lengthy will. Many of John's descendants would use the spelling Hammock as well as Hammack.[321]

John Hammack outlived two of his eleven offspring; his sons Samuel and John both predeceased him, leaving several grandchildren with families of their own by the time John died in 1832. Of Samuel's

---

[318] Davidson, *Early Records*, 2: 210; S. Q. Smith, *Early Georgia Wills and Settlements of Estates: Wilkes County* (Washington, GA, 1959), pp. 14, 32, 33.

[319] 1792 Pittsylvania Co., VA, Land Tax Roll, Library of Virginia, Richmond, VA; for Mary Hammack's Wilkes County, GA, tax digest entries, see Hudson, *Wilkes County Tax Records*.

[320] Crawford Co., GA, Will Book 2, pp. 124-125; Crawford Co., GA, Inferior Court Minutes, 1838-49, pp. 95, 102, 104, 145; Crawford Co., GA, Returns Book F, pp. 291, 299; Crawford Co., GA, Returns Book I, p. 53; Jones Co., GA, Deed Book D, p. 81; Jones Co., GA, Deed Book E, p. 232; 1814 Jones Co., GA, Tax Digest, Georgia Department of Archives and History; Bibb Co., GA, Deed Book A, p. 281.

[321] See R. L. P. Paschal, *Some Paschal Ancestors, Descendants and Allied Families* (Wolfe City, TX, 1969); Lincoln Co., GA, Will Book D, p. 250.

children, John remained in Wilkes County, Thomas settled in Chambers County, Alabama, and Susannah Hammack Stringfield relocated to Brazoria County, Texas, where her son became a prosperous merchant. Of the children of John Hammack, Jr., Simeon and William settled in eastern Alabama. John G. Hammack removed to north Georgia, and Elizabeth Hammack Moncrief and her children settled in south Georgia before relocating to Arkansas.[322]

Of the nine children who survived John Hammack, William and his large family settled in Chambers County, Alabama; his children later lived in Alabama, Mississippi, Louisiana, and Texas.[323] Pheriby Hammack Mumford remained in Lincoln County, where her husband Robert died in 1852.[324] Reverend Elijah Hammack moved to Wilkinson County, Georgia, and then late in life to Marion County, Georgia, near Columbus.[325] Paschall Hammock lived in Twiggs County, Georgia, before settling in Randolph County, Georgia; his family spread across southern Georgia.[326] Margaret Hammack Green was living in Jasper County, Georgia, as late as 1860.[327] Charles Hammack died after 1850 in Houston County, and his family remained in South Georgia and southeastern Alabama.[328] Thomas Hammack settled in Barbour County, Alabama, where he died after 1860,[329] and David Hammack settled in Houston County, Georgia. His widow Sally later moved to Henry County, Alabama, near her brother-in-law Thomas and his family.[330] The two youngest daughters, Elizabeth Hammack Rowland Powell and Reliance Hammack Steadham, both remained in Lincoln County.[331]

John Hammack was the eldest child born of his father's marriage to Mary Ann Lewis. The younger children included Ann, Thomas, Lewis, Elizabeth, William, and James. There were probably three other children born between Ann's birth in 1758 and Thomas's birth about 1766. Two may have been daughters, possibly including Ellida Hammack who married William Cunningham in Warren County, North Carolina, in 1782. Willoughby Hammock, who later lived in Wilkes, Warren, Clarke, and Newton Counties, may have been a son also; he was likely named for Willoughby Lewis, a cousin of Mary Ann Lewis.[332]

Of these offspring, Thomas removed to Wilkes County with his mother Mary Ann, although he settled on Kettle Creek several miles northeast of Mary Ann's residence on the Ogeechee River. Thomas died about 1806 after being struck by a falling tree; he left a large family, including sons who settled in Kemper County, Mississippi, Paulding County, Georgia, and Upson County, Georgia. Most of Thomas' descendants would adopt the spelling Hammock rather than Hammack.[333] Lewis Hammack, son of John and Mary Ann, moved from Wilkes County to Jones County by 1820 and was living in Bibb County, Georgia, near his brother James Hammack in 1830; Lewis probably then moved to Marion County, Georgia, where his widow Elizabeth was enumerated at the time of the 1840 census.[334]

Elizabeth Hammack married William Brown; William's father Waller Brown lived just across the Ogeechee River in Hancock County from Mary Ann Hammack's farm in southwestern Wilkes County. He apparently crossed the river to work as a farm laborer on Mary Ann's property and married her young

---

[322] Lincoln Co., GA, Will Book A, p. 49; "Jeremiah Hammack Family Bible," *Tap Roots*, Vol. 7, No. 3 (1970): 123-125.

[323] "William Hammack Family Bible," *Tap Roots*, Vol. 24 (1987).

[324] Lincoln Co., GA, Will Book 3, p. 98.

[325] 1840 Early Co., GA, Census, p. 122.

[326] 1830 Twiggs Co., GA, Census, p. 68; 1840 Twiggs Co., GA, Census, p. 377; 1850 Randolph Co., GA, Census, p. 376; 1860 Randolph Co., GA, Census, p. 704.

[327] 1860 Jasper Co., GA, Census, p. 282.

[328] 1840 Houston Co., GA, Census, p. 373; 1850 Houston Co., GA, Census, p. 376.

[329] 1840 Barbour Co., AL, Census, p. 84; 1850 Barbour Co., AL, Census, p. 147; 1860 Barbour Co., AL, Census, p. 425.

[330] 1840 Houston Co., GA, Census, p. 377; 1850 Randolph Co., GA, Census, p. 430; 1870 Barbour Co., AL, Census, p. 329.

[331] R. S. Davis, Jr., and J. E. Dorsey, *Lincoln County Genealogy and History* (Swainsboro, GA, 1987), pp. 253, 255.

[332] Identification of the younger offspring of John and Mary Ann is inferred from their first appearances in Wilkes Co., GA, tax records. See Hudson, *Wilkes County Tax Records*.

[333] Thomas Hammock Estate File, Wilkes Co., GA, Loose Estate Papers, Georgia Department of Archives and History.

[334] 1830 Bibb Co., GA, Census, p. 70; 1840 Marion Co., GA, Census, p. 75.

daughter about 1795. They afterwards moved to Hancock County, Georgia, and then to Laurens County, Georgia. After William Brown died, Elizabeth Hammack Brown and her four young children moved to Jones County, Georgia. Elizabeth's sister Caty Hammack had drawn a tract in Jones County during the 1807 land lottery; Caty, middle-aged and unmarried, relocated with her younger siblings to the land about 1809 before marrying William Simmons in 1812 when she was nearly sixty. Just after the marriage, Caty's husband William deeded fifty acres of the tract to Elizabeth Brown, probably for the maintenance of Elizabeth and her children. She lived there on a small farm adjacent to William and Caty Simmons until her children were grown; she then settled with them in Upson County, where she died about 1830.[335]

The two youngest children of John and Mary Ann were William and James. William seems to have had a close relationship with his mother; she conveyed land to him, and he appears as her agent on tax rolls. He may have been the last of her children to marry, and he seems to have had only a small family. He lived in Wilkes County as late as 1820 before relocating to Ware County in southern Georgia.

The youngest child of John and Mary Ann was James Hammack. He married, probably about 1802, his cousin Lucy Hammack, daughter of Robert Hammack and Millenor Jackson. James moved to Jones County with his sister Caty and seems to have initially lived on her land; later his brother-in-law William Simmons also deeded him property. About this time, his wife's mother Millenor Jackson Hammack and several of her married children followed them to Jones County, where they remained as neighbors for nearly twenty years. Lucy Hammack, James's wife, died between 1820 and 1826 after rearing a large family; James later relocated to Bibb County, where he married and began a second family. James was living in Bibb County as late as 1830 and in Pike County shortly afterwards; he probably died in the mid-1830s. His younger children later appear in Muscogee County, although his older children born from his marriage to Lucy Hammack scattered across Georgia and Alabama.[336]

Millenor Jackson Hammack, Lucy's mother, in 1829 made a deed of trust to Lucy's children; Lucy was then deceased, and James had remarried in 1827. Millenor deeded a male slave to her son Lewis, who in turn was to pay $100 to Lucy's children when the youngest reached maturity.[337]

James and Lucy reared a large family; it seems almost certain that they were the parents of Celia Hammack who in 1817 married Harrison Hammack in Jones County. In 1825, Catherine Hammack Simmons made a deed of gift to "Elizey" Hammack, eldest daughter of Harrison and Celia.[338] In 1824, Harrison witnessed a deed in which James Hammack conveyed land.[339] On 18 January 1821, James Hammack conveyed to his son Abel Hammack 101 acres in Jones County, "the same where Harrison Hammock now lives."[340] Since Harrison was born about 1795 and Celia about 1803, the likeliest scenario is that Celia was the daughter of James and Lucy Hammack; Celia's husband Harrison was probably her first cousin, most likely the son of James's older brother Lewis Hammack. Harrison and Celia are particularly noteworthy in Hammack annals, for they were the grandparents of Henry Franklin Hammack of McRae, Arkansas, who devoted two decades to seeking out his Hammack ancestry. Henry Franklin Hammack died without ever conclusively sorting out his Hammack lineage. It appears that he was twice a descendant of John and Mary Ann Hammack and once a descendant of Robert and Millenor Jackson Hammack.[341]

---

[335] Jones Co., GA, Deed Book D, p. 81; 1807 Georgia Land Lottery, Fortunate Drawers, Georgia Department of Archives and History; 1814 Jones Co., GA, Tax Digest; 1820 Jones Co., GA, Census. Elizabeth Hammack Brown was the ancestor of Thomas Daniel Knight.

[336] 1811 and 1814 Jones Co., GA, Tax Digests; Jones Co., GA, Deed Book E, p. 232; Jones Co., GA, Deed Book L, p. 316; Bibb Co., GA, Deed Book A, pp. 163, 281; 1820 Jones Co., GA, Census, p. 3; 1830 Bibb Co., GA, Census, p. 61; 1831 Pike Co., GA, Tax Digest.

[337] Jones Co., GA, Deed Book P, p. 205.

[338] Bibb Co., GA, Deed Book A, p. 281.

[339] Bibb Co., GA, Deed Book A, p. 163.

[340] Jones Co., GA, Deed Book L, p. 316.

[341] Hammack, *Wandering Back*, 1: 44, 303-305.

Willoughby Hammock was living in Georgia as early as 1788, when Micajah Williamson was charged in Wilkes County Superior Court with assaulting him.[342] Two years later, as "Wilby Hammer" he was taxed in the same district as Micajah Williamson, still in Wilkes. In 1795 and 1799, "Willibe Hammack" is mentioned as an adjacent landowner in Warren County deeds involving land located near the southern boundary of Wilkes County.[343] Yet Willoughby is found in Franklin County, in northeastern Georgia, as early as 1795,[344] and he seems to have remained always in that area despite owning land in Warren County. He was taxed in Jackson County -- formed from Franklin -- in 1799 and served as a juror in Clarke County -- formed from Jackson -- in 1801. He lived in Clarke County until after 1815 but was enumerated in Jasper County in 1820. By 1822, he was in Newton County, where he was already serving as a Justice of the Inferior Court.[345] He died there before 9 October 1823, when his son Thomas Hammock and son-in-law John Barnes Garrett were granted temporary administration of his estate.[346]

Willoughby's identity is uncertain. In terms of age, he fits to have been a son of John and Mary Ann; he was likely born after 1760 but before 1765. In terms of location, he fits also. He was living by 1788 in southern Wilkes County in the same area where Mary Ann settled two years later. His name also seems significant. Willoughby Allerton, a prominent resident of Virginia's Northern Neck, seems to have been the first Willoughby in northeastern Virginia. Between 1680 and 1730, a number of families named offspring for him, including Mary Ann Lewis's uncle William Lewis.[347]

Beyond this, however, there is nothing concrete to link Willoughby to John and Mary Ann Hammack. As noted earlier, John Hammack -- son of Benedict and Elizabeth -- seems to have settled in nearby Burke County and Washington Counties with his offspring in the 1780s. And, if the family reconstitution is correct, there was a Willoughby Hammack in Kentucky and another in South Alabama who may have been his descendants. Hence, it may be that Willoughby was a son of John Hammack of Edgecombe County, North Carolina, who pushed north and west on his own after the family reached Georgia.[348]

Whatever his placement in the Hammack and Hammock annals, Willoughby sired a large clan. Elizabeth Hammock married John Barnes Garrett and died in Heard County, Georgia. Louisiana Hammock married Benjamin Hodnett and died in Rapides Parish, Louisiana. Sally Hammock married Thomas Garrett and died in DeKalb County, Alabama. Thomas Hammock, Aaron G. Hammock, and Willoughby Hammock likewise both relocated to DeKalb County, Alabama, where they died. Matilda Hammock Muncy and Levisey Hammock Thornton are later found in Harris County, Georgia; Jackson Hammock was living in Crawford County, Georgia, in 1835. Willoughby's widow, Levisey Hammock, married James Garrett in Fayette County, Georgia, in 1826. She accompanied her children to North Alabama, where she died in 1848.[349]

---

[342] Davis, *Wilkes County Papers*, p. 186.

[343] Warren Co., GA, Deed Book B, p. 43, 53.

[344] M. W. Acker, *Franklin Co., GA, Court of Ordinary Records, 1787-1849* (Birmingham, 1989), p. 3.

[345] Newton Co., GA, Historical Society, *History of Newton Co., GA* (Covington, 1988), p. 38.

[346] J. L. Bruno, *Newton County, GA, Estate Records, 1822-1900* (2 vols., Covington, 1996), 1: 133-134.

[347] Davis, *Wilkes County Papers*, p. 186. For more on Allerton, see J. F. Dorman, ed., *Adventurers of Purse and Person in Virginia, 1607-1624* (3rd. ed., Richmond, 1987), p. 692. Willoughby Lewis's birth is recorded in the register of St. Stephen's Parish, Northumberland Co., VA.

[348] Henry Franklin Hammack identified Willoughby as a son of Hugh Hammack, son of Robert and Ann Lambert Hammack, because the given name Hugh was used on at least one occasion by his descendants. This, too, is possible, although no evidence has been found to indicate that Hugh Hammack had offspring. Born in 1732, he was taxed in 1771 in Surry Co., NC, and his estate was administered in Wilkes Co., GA, about 1783, probably by his cousin Robert Hammack. See Hammack, *Wandering Back*, 2: 192, 237, 271.

[349] Bruno, *Estate Records*, 1: 134-135.

Chapter 10:

Robert Hammack and wife Millenor Jackson,
Of Lunenburg and Amelia Counties, Virginia, and Wilkes County, Georgia

Robert Hammack was baptized 17 October 1737 in North Farnham Parish, Richmond County, Virginia, where he spent his youth. About the time he reached manhood, he relocated with his grandfather Hugh Lambert to Brunswick County, Virginia, where he lived near his aunt and uncle, John and Mildred Lambert Hammack.

The first known reference to Robert Hammack after he reached adulthood dates from 18 November 1764, when his grandfather Hugh Lambert wrote his will in Brunswick County, Virginia. Hugh named each of his children and then included a special bequest to his grandson Robert Hammack, to whom he left a Negro boy named Frank.[350] Probably Robert Hammack was then living in Brunswick County on his grandfather's property; five years later, in 1769, Robert appeared on the Lunenburg County, Virginia, tithable list. His name appeared two entries after that of his uncle John Hammack (who had married his mother's sister Mildred Lambert), two names before his uncle Lewis Lambert, and three names before that of Robert Moore, whose offspring would play an important role in Robert's family later. In 1764, the name of Edward Jackson had appeared two entries after that of John Hammack on the tax roll for the same district; a note indicated that Edward himself was levy free and that he was taxed only with 280 acres of land in the district and no poll tax.[351]

Lewis Hammack, eldest son of Robert Hammack, was born about 1765. It would appear then that Robert Hammack moved from Brunswick into Lunenburg about 1764, where he married Edward Jackson's daughter Millenor, who was probably born about 1745. The next known reference to Robert occurs in 1770, when, on 23 May, Edward and Abigail Jackson deeded eighty-one acres on Little Hurricane Creek in Amelia County. The deed was made in return for five shillings and "natural affection and love for son-in-law and his wife."[352]

Robert and Millenor Hammack seem to have remained in Amelia County, Virginia, until about 1774. On 29 September 1773, Robert Hammack, Daniel Jackson, and John Bailey witnessed a series of deeds involving Travis McKinney and William Spain.[353] On 25 November 1773, Robert and Millenor sold the eighty-one acres on Little Hurricane Creek that Edward Jackson had given them to John Wilkes.[354] They probably headed south soon after this, for in a testimony given many years later Millenor Hammack indicated that they were living in Wilkes County prior to 1779.[355] At that date, Millenor recorded, the Hammacks were among a group of Patriot families who were attacked by Tories and Indians along the Georgia frontier.

Robert Hammack and his family supported the American cause during the Revolutionary conflict in deed as well as in word. The Georgia frontier was a particularly violent place. Creek and Cherokee Indians on the frontier added to the tensions experienced by the settlers; much of the state lay in British hands, and bands of Tory sympathizers regularly struck out at patriots in the area called by contemporaries "The Hornet's Nest." On 15 September 1780, a list of "Officers and Soldiers who fled the Protection of the British and took refuge in other states and did their Duty faithfully Under the Command of Collo. Wm. Candler from the 15th Septr. 1780 Untill the Reduction of the British Troops in Augusta" was begun. Robert Hammack appears as a private in the second battalion.[356]

---

[350] Brunswick Co., VA, Will Book 2, pp. 426-429.

[351] 1764 and 1768 Lunenburg Co., VA, Tax Lists, Library of Virginia, Richmond, VA.

[352] Amelia Co., VA, Deed Book 11, p. 125.

[353] Amelia Co., VA, Deed Book 12, p. 148, 152.

[354] Amelia County, VA, Deed Book 12, p. 164.

[355] Donna B. Thaxton, C. Stanton Thaxton, eds., Georgia Indian Depredation Claims (Americus, GA, undated), p. 410.

[356] The name actually appears twice, and, from this document, it would appear that father and son served in the same company. This list is taken from the Keith Reed Collection, Manuscripts, University of Georgia Library, Athens, GA, as cited in George F. Whatley, *The Families of Whatley, Persons, Roop and Fields* (St. Petersburg, FL, 1989), p. 40.

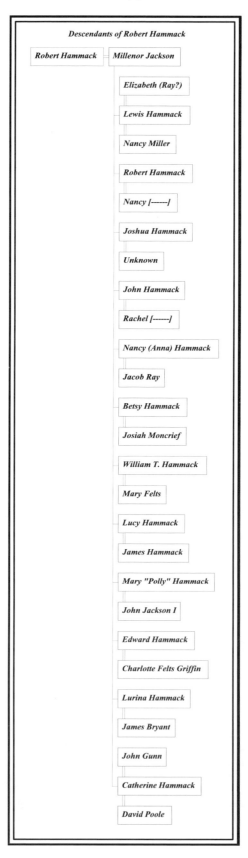

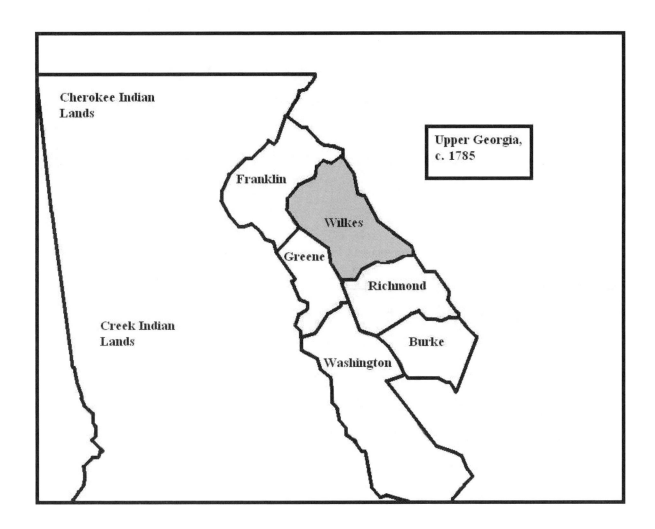

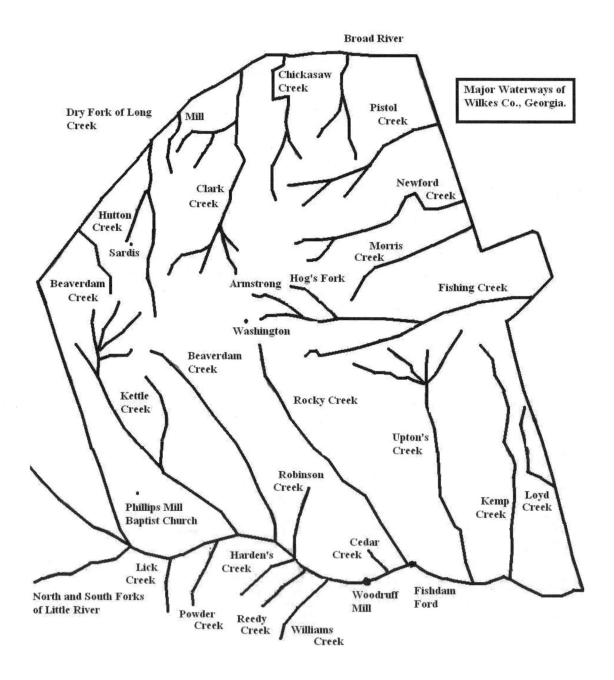

Broad River

Chickasaw
Creek

Pistol
Creek

Major Waterways of
Wilkes Co., Georgia.

Dry Fork of Long
Creek

Mill

Newford
Creek

Clark
Creek

Hutton
Creek

Morris
Creek

Sardis

Beaverdam
Creek

Armstrong

Hog's Fork

Fishing Creek

Washington

Beaverdam
Creek

Kettle
Creek

Rocky Creek

Upton's
Creek

Robinson
Creek

Kemp
Creek

Loyd
Creek

Phillips Mill
Baptist Church

Cedar
Creek

Lick
Creek

Harden's
Creek

North and South Forks
of Little River

Woodruff
Mill

Fishdam
Ford

Powder
Creek

Reedy
Creek

Williams
Creek

1=Residence of William Hammack, John Hammack of Lincoln County, and Travis McKinney; area designated by F. P. Hudson as District "G".

Wilkes Co., GA: Primary Residencces of Hammack Family Members, c. 1785 - c. 1820.

2=Residence of family of Robert and Millenor Jackson Hammack, Mary Ann Hammack, and Ussery and Martha Bishop Moore; designed by F. P. Hudson as "HH" (1785) and "II" (1804). By 1804, Hudson also recognizes "RR" (west of "II") and "MM" (north of "II").

4=Residence of Thomas Hammack, Kettle Creek; area designed by F. P. Hudson as District "M", 1785-1804.

3=Residence of family of Benedict Hammack (settled about 1773), Robert and Nancy Combs Hammack, and Phillip and Abigail Combs; area designated by F. P. Hudson as District "I" in Wilkes County Tax Digests, 1785-1804.

5=Residence of Willoughby Hammack, c. 1786-c. 1790; area designed by F. P. Hudson as Districts "HH" and "LL" in 1785.

NOTE: Lincoln, Taliaferro, northern Warren, Greene, and northern Hancock were all part of Wilkes County until after 1785.

6=Residence of John Hammack, son of Robert and Millenor Hammack, about 1800; members of the families of Mary Ann Hammack and William T. Hammack later settled here. This district along Powell's Creek was designed as District "QQ" by F. P. Hudson in 1785. The northern portion of Hancock later became part of Taliaferro County.

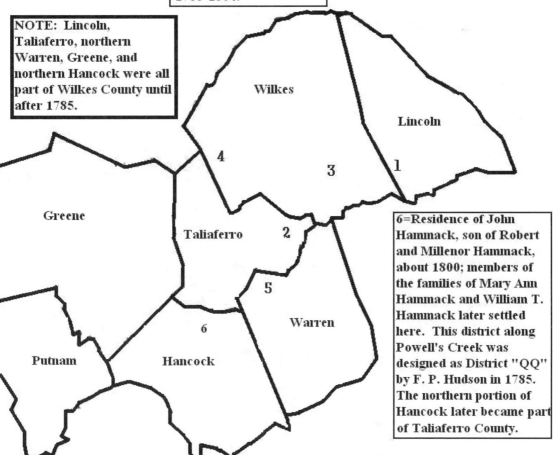

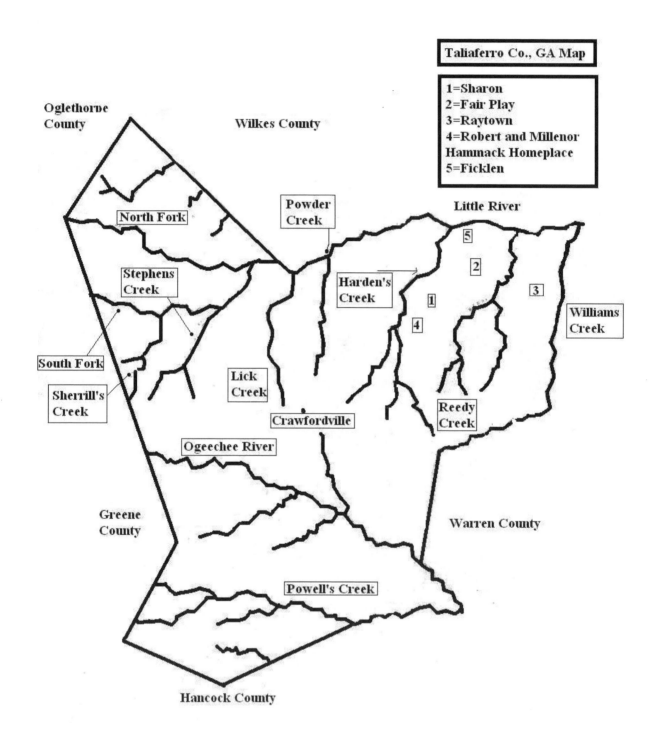

After the Revolutionary conflict had established American Independence, Robert Hammack quickly obtained a series of land tracts in Wilkes County, probably land that he and his family had been homesteading since they settled along the frontier. On 12 July 1784, he received a grant for 200 acres on the waters of Hardin's Creek.[357] Three months later, on 10 September 1784, he received another 200 acres located south of the initial tract.[358] Additional grants in the summer of 1785 awarded him another 558 acres on Harden's Creek, bringing his holdings to a combined total of 958 acres.[359] Three years later, in 1788, Robert purchased a slave Dolly from Alexander Moss.[360]

Sometimes between 1785 and 1790, Robert seems to have disposed of part of the property he had already patented in Wilkes County. In 1790 he was taxed with 550 acres and in 1793 with 558 acres. In the 1790 listing, he was also taxed with two polls -- his sons Robert and Lewis, who had recently come of age but who as of yet owned no land.

Living near Georgia's western frontier, local citizens were required to perform militia service in their defense. Several skirmishes in the early 1790s provoked warfare between the Creeks and the Americans, and local battalions marched across the state to confront the Creeks. Wilkes County militia records indicate that in 1793 Lewis Hammack was a Sergeant and his brother Joshua Hammack a private in Samuel Alexander's Regiment; in 1794, Robert Hammack's name also appears on the list.[361]

Robert Hammack wrote his will in Wilkes County on 9 July 1799, at which time he was sixty-two years of age.[362] Two years earlier, in 1797, he had purchased a final 225 acres from Thomas Stuart.[363] When Robert wrote his will, he followed the traditional English custom of identifying his sons by birth order.[364] During her lifetime, he left the bulk of his personal property and a share of his real estate to his wife Millenor. Lewis, Robert's "first son," received the property where he was living. Robert, the second son, received 100 acres joining son Lewis and their neighbor Joshua McFarland. Joshua, the third son, received 100 acres joining Robert's land, and "fourth and fifth sons John and William" received 200 acres from the 1797 Stuart survey. Edward, the sixth son, received 200 acres, and daughter Catherine received the remainder of "my survey and the Stewart survey." Although not named in the original will, three additional daughters and daughter Catherine are named in a codicil in which Robert left to them the "residue of moveable effects" after their mother's death; these daughters were Anna, wife of Jacob Ray; Betsy, wife of Josiah Moncrief; Lucy, wife of James Hammack; and Catherine Hammack, who was still, like her brother Edward, a minor.

Robert Hammack's will was proven 24 February 1800 in Wilkes County, Georgia. The widow Millenor and her son Lewis were granted administration on the estate, and two months later, in April 1800, an inventory of Robert Hammack's estate was taken in Wilkes County. Robert's land and slaves were not included in the inventory, but his other property was valued at approximately $620. Like his father and grandfather before him, the bulk of Robert's estate was invested in tools and livestock intended to support his family and generate a modest profit for the market. The single most valuable item he owned was a wagon and wagon gear valued at $50.00; this wagon could have been used for farm work as well as for traveling. Robert also owned two sows, twelve young hogs, sixteen adult pigs, three swarms of bees, twenty-one geese, eight sheep, four horses, twelve cows, three calves, two steers, one bull, and three yearlings. Altogether, the livestock was valued at $312. In addition, Robert owned three muskets, a variety of carpenter's tools, cooper's tools (some of which may have been inherited from his grandfather), blacksmith's tools and a quantity of iron, shoemaker's tools and leather, a grinding stone, and an

[357] Wilkes Co., GA, Plat Book C, p. 295.
[358] Wilkes Co., GA, Plat Book C, p. 296.
[359] Wilkes Co., GA, Plat Book C, p. 113; Grant Book HHH, p. 170, 184.
[360] Davidson, *Early Records*, I: 254.
[361] M. J. Clark, *American Militia in the Frontier Wars, 1790-1796* (Baltimore, 2003), p. 250.
[362] Robert Hammack Estate File, Wilkes Co., GA, Loose Estate Papers, Georgia Department of Archives and History.
[363] Wilkes Co., GA, Deed Book QQ, p. 181.
[364] This custom had, however, become less common in the more egalitarian Revolutionary era.

assortment of axes and hoes. These items altogether came to approximately $70. Robert also owned a still, still cap, and still worm valued at $45.[365]

In terms of landownership and agricultural tools and implements, Robert owned a substantial plantation, carved out of uncultivated land that until the 1770s had belonged to Native Americans. His household furnishings, while not lavish, indicate that he and his family lived well and comfortably. Three beds, bedsteads, and furniture were valued at $60. Other furnishings consisted of a chest, a pine table, and six chairs valued altogether at $6.50. Robert and his family must have spent some time entertaining, for they owned two black bottles, two decanters, four small punch bowls, twelve cups, fifteen saucers, a cream pot, four pewter basins, three pewter dishes, eight pewter plates, forty pewter spoons, five knives, seven forks, a tin pepper box, two teapots, one wine glass, and one candlestick. Altogether, these items were valued at approximately $20. In addition, Robert owned six old books and five plays valued at $4.50.[366]

After Robert's death, Millenor and her children remained in Wilkes County for more than a decade. It appears that the only children unmarried when Robert wrote his will were son Edward, daughter Catherine, and perhaps daughter Lucy, who married her cousin James Hammack sometimes around 1800. Millenor, in 1801, was taxed with 283 acres of land on Hardin's Creek, while sons Robert, Lewis, and William were each taxed with 100 acres inherited from their father. Millenor apparently was then holding the land in trust for Edward and Catherine; in 1805, the next digest that shows the family, Lewis Hammack was taxed as agent for his brother Edward, who owned 200 acres, and for his sister Catherine, who owned ninety-five acres.

In 1807, Millenor Hammack, of Young's District, Wilkes County, drew a tract of land in Baldwin County, Georgia. The land was identified as land lot 85, land district 12, and later became a portion of Jones County. On 7 January 1808, Millenor appointed her "trusty friend David Satterwhite" of Jones County to sell the tract for her.[367] Millenor was still a resident of Wilkes County on 27 May 1808 when David Satterwhite sold the land to his brother Stephen; Millenor received $600 for the land.[368]

Tax digests for 1809 and 1812 show that Millenor Hammack owned no land but did own two slaves inherited from her husband. Edward Hammack paid tax for his mother on both occasions. The Wilkes County 1816 tax digest indicates that Millenor then owned three slaves, that her son Robert owned four, and that her daughter Catherine owned one. Sons John, Edward, and William owned no slaves. The same year, in the first of a series of deeds of gift, Milly conveyed one slave to her son John Hammack.[369]

Millenor was still living in Wilkes County in 1821. On 5 November, she entered a claim that "that in 1779 or 1780 her husband had one horse, valued at $80.00, stolen by the Indians". In a second affidavit on the same date, Milly Hammock "claims that Indians stole several horses from her late husband, Robert Hammock. She says that John Danielly, a neighbor, saw one of the horses in the possession of Creek Indians. The robbery took place in Richmond County, Georgia."[370]

Soon after giving this deposition, Millenor moved to Jones County. The move may have been influenced by her fortunate draw in the 1807 land lottery, but, since Milly chose to sell that land rather than relocate then, it probably played only a minor role in her ultimate decision to move. Of more importance, however, and perhaps more closely linked with Millenor's 1807 draw, was the fact that several of her children and grandchildren had begun, as early as 1807 and 1808, to settle in Jones County. By the early 1820s, at least as many of Millenor's relatives were living in Jones County as in Wilkes County.

---

[365] Robert Hammack Estate File, Wilkes Co., GA, Loose Estate Papers, Georgia Department of Archives and History.

[366] Ibid.

[367] Jones Co., GA, Deed Book A, pp. 327-28.

[368] Jones Co., GA, Deed Book A, pp. 355-56.

[369] Jones Co., GA, Deed Book O, p. 273.

[370] Thaxton, ed., *Indian Claims*, p. 410.

In 1825 and 1826, then in Jones County, Millenor was taxed with five slaves. In 1827, she was taxed with six slaves. Two years later, she deeded a seventeen year old slave girl and her six month old child to daughter Catherine Hammack Pool.[371] Later that same year, she deeded a slave named Feriby to daughter Nancy Ray[372] and a slave named Ann to son Joshua, provided that he pay her daughter Mary Jackson $10 after Millenor died.[373] Just before the year ended, on 30 December, she deeded a four year old slave girl to her grandson Mansel Womack Hammack.[374] In 1829, Millenor executed three other deeds of gift. To son Edward she deeded a twelve year old slave girl, and to daughter Mary Jackson she deeded a thirty-three year old slave woman. On 17 September, Millenor deeded to son Lewis a slave boy named Nathan provided that he pay $100 to the heirs of her deceased daughter Lucy, wife of James Hammack.[375]

With this final deed of gift, Millenor Hammack disposed of the remainder of her worldly estate and vanished from the written record. She was likely still living at the time of the 1830 census when she was enumerated, aged 80-90, in her son Lewis's home. She was probably then at least eighty-five years of age and possibly older. She likely died soon after 1830, for no further record of her has been discovered.[376]

Of the twelve children who were born to Robert Hammack and Millenor Jackson between 1765 and 1785, all of them seem to have remained in Georgia. In increments between 1805 and 1832, the frontier pushed westward until by 1832 the entire southeast, from coastal Georgia to the Texas Gulf, was open to contiguous European-American settlement. Although Millenor's children remained in Georgia, her grandchildren would push westward across the country.

A. Lewis Hammack, first son of Robert and Millenor Jackson Hammack, of Wilkes and Jones Counties, Georgia.

Lewis Hammack was born about 1765 in Lunenburg County, Virginia; he died more than eighty years later in Jones County, Georgia. As a youth, he moved from Amelia County, Virginia, to the Georgia frontier, where he was reared in southwestern Wilkes County on lands ceded by the Creek Indians in 1777.

Lewis probably married about 1790 to Elizabeth Ray, a daughter of Sanders and Christiana Ray, former neighbors from Lunenburg County who had also moved to the Georgia frontier. It was the first of many alliances between members of the Ray and Hammack family. Soon afterwards, Lewis's sister Nancy would marry Elizabeth's brother Jacob Ray. Three of Jacob Ray's sisters would marry sons of Ussery Moore, whose son James married Lewis's niece Sarah Hammack. These families would live together in a tightly knit community in southwestern Wilkes County until they began moving to Jones County after 1807.[377]

Lewis Hammack owned no land until he inherited 100 acres from his father in 1800. With his mother Millenor, in 1800, he served as administrator on his father's estate. In 1803, he served as a surety when Martha Montcrief applied for letters of administration on her husband Samuel Montcrief's estate. Martha was another daughter of Jacob and Christiana Ray, and she soon married Robert Moore, another son of Ussery Moore.[378]

In 1808, with his brother-in-law Jacob Ray, Lewis Hammack applied for a passport to pass through the Creek Indian lands to the west and travel into Mississippi territory. This was the first known migration of any member of Robert Hammack's family west of Georgia, although Lewis and Jacob did not long

[371] Jones Co., GA, Deed Book O, p. 141.

[372] Jones Co., GA, Deed Book O, p. 149.

[373] Jones Co., GA, Deed Book O, p. 154.

[374] Jones Co., GA, Deed Book O, p. 158.

[375] Jones Co., GA, Deed Book O, pp. 167-168, and P, p. 205.

[376] 1830 Jones Co., GA, Census, p. 451.

[377] Washington Co., AL, Deed Book A, p. 203.

[378] In 1796, Lewis had been a surety when Solomon Ray married Jane Echols. See Davidson, *Early Records*, 1: 114, 168, 312, 317, 325.

remain in the Mississippi area. Sanders Ray had, as early as 1796, settled in Washington County, Alabama, and he died there about 1805. Jacob and Lewis may have been traveling into Alabama to attend to matters arising from Sanders Ray's estate.[379]

By 1809, Lewis was back in Georgia, when he was taxed in Wilkes County. In 1811, he purchased fifteen acres of Wilkes County land on Hardin's Creek from his brother Edward Hammack.[380] In 1814, still a resident of Wilkes County, he sold 202.5 acres in Jones County which he had drawn in the 1807 land lottery.[381] Soon afterwards, he chose to migrate to Jones County, where he lived for the remainder of his life. He was enumerated there in 1820, and from that point onwards was taxed consistently with two tracts of land totaling 303.75 acres. By 1830, he had also acquired two tracts in Crawford County for which he was taxed in Jones County, but he chose to remain in Jones rather than to relocate to the new land.[382]

In 1831, Lewis deeded fifty acres of his Jones County property to his son-in-law Mason Miller.[383] The following year, he paid tax on the remaining 253 acres on Wolf Creek in Jones County as well as 355 acres in Crawford County. In addition, Lewis was taxed with sixteen slaves of his own. He also paid tax on one lot in Carroll County on behalf of his daughter Christiana Moore and on two lots, one in Wayne and one in Wilkinson, for his son Jacob Hammack. In 1834, Lewis deeded a portion of the Jones County lands as a gift to his son John M. Hammack.[384] The 1834 digest showed Lewis taxed with lots in Jones, Crawford, and Cherokee Counties totaling 620 acres and fourteen slaves. By 1840, he was taxed with 717 acres and seventeen slaves. He also paid tax on 692 acres belonging to his son Jacob Hammack and on one slave belonging to his son-in-law Elijah Smallwood. Lewis was taxed with seventeen slaves in 1841, eighteen in 1842 and 1843, and nineteen in 1844. The same digest showed that he owned 820 acres and that he was still paying tax on 692 acres for his son.

By the standards of his day, Lewis Hammack would have been considered a prosperous farmer or, perhaps, a modest planter. As a rule, "planters" of the Old South were those slaveholders whose holdings included twenty or more slaves altogether. By the end of his life, Lewis had nearly reached this number, and the acreage he was cultivating also corresponded the economic profile indicated by the size of his slaveholding. Yet this level of prosperity came at the end of Lewis's life, not the beginning, and his wealth would soon be redistributed among his heirs.[385]

The long life of Lewis Hammack drew to a close in late 1845 or early 1846. His inventory was filed on 7 April 1846 with his son-in-law Beauford Stallsworth serving as administrator. The estate was valued at $7,465.[386] A division on 16 November identified six heirs: Nancy Hammack, the widow; Beauford and Christiana Hammack Moore Stallsworth; Talbot and Milly Hammack Davidson; Jacob Hammack; Mason and Mary Hammack Miller; and the children of John M. Hammack, deceased.[387] The widow who survived Lewis Hammack was his second wife. His first wife Elizabeth had died in 1840 or 1841, and Lewis married in December 1841 to a neighboring widow named Nancy Miller. Nancy was the mother of

[379] M. G. Bryan, *Passports Issued by Governors of Georgia, 1785 to 1820* (Washington, D.C., 1977) and D. W. Potter, *Passports of Southeastern Pioneers, 1770-1823: Indian, Spanish, and other Land Passports for Tennessee, Kentucky, Georgia, Mississippi, Virginia, North and South Carolina* (Baltimore, 1982).

[380] Wilkes Co., GA, Deed Book ZZ, p. 494.

[381] Jones Co., GA, Deed Book F, p. 15.

[382] 1820-1845 Jones Co., GA, Tax Digests, Georgia Department of Archives and History, Morrow, GA. All subsequent references to Jones Co., GA, tax digests between 1811 and 1855 refer to the volumes held by the Georgia Department of Archives and History and will not be cited individually.

[383] Jones Co., GA, Deed Book O, p. 43.

[384] Jones Co., GA, Deed Book P, p. 254.

[385] See Howe, pp. 58-60; W. J. Cooper and T. E. Terrill, *The American South: A History* (2 vols., 4th ed., Lanham, 2008), 1: 31-57, 285-315. For general studies of the period, see J. W. Blassingame, *The Slave Community: Plantation Life in the Antebellum South* (New York and Oxford, 1972) and J. Boles, *The South Through Time* (New York, 1995).

[386] Jones Co., GA, Annual Returns 1842-47, p. 461.

[387] Jones Co., GA, Annual Returns 1842-47, p. 493.

Mason Miller, who had, long before, married Lewis Hammack's daughter Mary. Nancy Miller Hammack survived Lewis, dying in 1848.[388]

Of Lewis Hammack's offspring, all but Jacob remained in Georgia. Jacob died after 1850 in Perry County, Alabama, and his widow Hannah moved to Lauderdale County, Mississippi, a few years later.[389] In the years after 1850, several of Lewis's other children and grandchildren would join them there, where they would often spell the surname Hammock as well as Hammack. Lewis's great-great-grandson, William Thomas Hammock, served as Arkansas State Senator; Mayor of Quitman, Arkansas; Judge of Cleburne County, Arkansas; and Arkansas State Tax Commissioner in 1927.[390]

B. Robert Hammack, second son of Robert and Millenor Jackson Hammack, of Wilkes, Warren, and Taliaferro Counties, Georgia.

The longevity enjoyed by Millenor Jackson Hammack and her husband's parents Robert and Ann Lambert Hammack passed to the sons of Millenor and Robert; their second son, Robert Hammack, Jr., died in Warren County, Georgia, in 1862, "aged 96." He was born in Lunenburg or Amelia County, Virginia, and reared on the Georgia frontier; militia rosters indicate that he served with his father as a frontier guard during the American Revolution. He was probably only fifteen or sixteen years old at that time.[391]

Robert remained in Wilkes County when his mother and siblings moved into Jones County. He was still living in the area when Taliaferro County was formed in 1826, and he remained there for most of his remaining years. He was enumerated there in 1827, 1830, and 1840. Tax digests for intervening years show that he was never a large landowner. In 1834 and 1835, he was taxed with three slaves and forty acres of land in Cherokee County, a tract which in 1836 he deeded to his son Doctor T. B. Hammack in return for "means of support while we live".[392]

Robert's wife died after 1840, and he chose to spend his remaining years with his son Gustavus Hammack a few miles away in Warren County. The 1850 census gave his age as eighty-two; at the time of the 1860 census enumeration, Robert reported that he was ninety-four years old.[393]

Robert Hammack reared a large family. The son to whom he deeded land in 1836 predeceased him and died without heirs. Two other sons, John Hammack and Gustavus Starling Hammack, survived him, as did two daughters: Martha Hammack, wife of William Frank, and Sarah Hammack, wife of Richard Rhodes.[394]

Although Robert Hammack himself never amassed substantial property, his offspring prospered. His son John was a mechanic who specialized in repairing cotton gins. In time, he served as county commissioner, tax receiver, and inspector of roads and bridges. John acquired a modest estate through careful management of his resources, and he died testate in 1872, naming sons Joseph and Henry and daughters Julia and Nancy as heirs. Joseph Davis Hammack (1822-1899) was a gin maker and merchant, as was his brother Henry. Both married and reared offspring in Taliaferro County. Henry's daughter

---

[388] Bruno, *Newton County*, p. 133.

[389] Crawford Co., GA, Returns Book H, p. 69; 1860 Lauderdale Co., MS, Census, p. 289.

[390] *Who's Who in Governnment* (3 vols., New York, 1930).

[391] Wynne, *Southern Lineages*, pp. 92-98.

[392] Taliaferro Co., GA, Deed Book 1, p. 197. This son was not a physician; his name was Doctor. All references to Taliaferro County tax digest data are from Taliaferro Co., GA, Tax Digests, 1827-1860, Georgia Department of Archives and History.

[393] 1840 Taliaferro Co., GA, Census, p. 247; 1850 Taliaferro Co., GA, Census, p. 148; 1860 Warren Co., GA, Census, p. 19.

[394] Wynne, pp. 92-98; the placement of the daughters is inferred from tax and census records and has not been conclusively documented.

Lucinda Frances Hammack (1849-1945) married Dr. Linton Alexander Stephens (1845-1894), who was a nephew of Confederate Vice President Alexander Hamilton Stephens.[395]

Joseph Davis Hammack became a leading citizen of Taliaferro County. A biographical sketch of his life was contributed to *Biographical Souvenir of the States of Georgia and Florida* which gives details of his character:[396]

He was brought up on the farm to the age of fifteen. He was then apprenticed to the trade of cotton-gin making, which business he has followed continuously since. His early education was limited, but fortunately he had a natural taste for books. He early formed the habit of reading, study and observation, which has furnished him with an abundant store of information, and has served to make up the deficiency in his youthful training. He has been a man of remarkably sturdy character, distinguished for great deliberation of mind, and scrupulously honest and exact in the discharge of his duties as a citizen and public official. He has held some public position nearly all his life. When quite a young man he was elected justice of the inferior court, and held that office until the court was abolished. Then he was elected and held the office of justice of the peace for thirteen years. He was tax-collector for two years. In 1864 he was elected ordinary, and while serving in this office, was elected clerk of the superior court and treasurer of the county, all three of which offices he held simultaneously, and for some years. He resigned the office of ordinary in 1871, and that of superior court clerk in 1887. He continues to serve as county treasurer. He has many times in life been importuned to offer himself for other positions, but he has uniformly refused, preferring the peaceful ways of private life to the turmoil and uncertainties of a public career. He was a neighbor and warm personal friend of the late Hon. Alexander H. Stephens, and it may be added that he was the recipient of many of that distinguished statesman's most valued confidences.

Joseph D. Hammack's leading position in Taliaferro County was continued by his son Dr. William T. Hammack, a physician who succeeded his father as Clerk of Court in 1886.[397]

Of the daughters of Robert Hammack, the tendency towards longevity passed to his daughter Martha Hammack Frank. On 23 July 1894, the *Washington Chronicle*, local newspaper of Wilkes County, Georgia, carried an article about Martha and her family:

On Sunday last our respected young citizen Mr. Edward Markwalter went up to Greensboro accompanied by Mr. Hodgson the photographer to be present on an interesting occasion. It was the 100th birthday of his great-grandmother Mrs. Frank and there was a gathering of her descendants in honor of the occasion. They had a barbecue picnic near Siloam in Greene County. Thirty-three of the family were present and Mr. Hodgson took a picture of the group. There were on the picture five generations. Mrs. Frank, aged 100; her daughter Mrs. John Winter, aged seventy who is Ed Markwalter's grandmother; his mother Mrs. M. Markwalter of Greensboro, aged 49; his sister Mrs. George Smith, aged twenty-six, who lives near Crawford, GA; and finally little Theodore Smith one year old, who is Ed Markwalter's nephew. Mrs. Frank was born in Wilkes County between Washington and Crawfordville, and was a Miss Hammack. Her husband was killed in the Indian Wars of Florida. She is perfectly sound in health and able to walk about.[398]

---

[395] Taliaferro Co., GA, Will Book 3, p. 55. For many deeds involving this family, see Taliaferro Co., GA, Deed Books E, H, and J. R. M. Bell, *The Alexander Stephens Family: Pennsylvania-Georgia* (Washington, PA, 1981), Stephens File, Georgia Department of Archives and History, details the Stephens-Hammack connection.

[396] *Biographical Souvenir of the States of Georgia and Florida* (Chicago, 1889), pp. 363-364.

[397] Ibid.

[398] *Washington Chronicle*, 23 July 1894, Wilkes County Public Library, Washington, Georgia.

The children and grandchildren of Robert Hammack remained in Taliaferro and Warren Counties for generations, living near the lands initially patented by Robert Hammack in the 1780s.

C. Joshua Hammack, third son of Robert and Millenor Jackson Hammack, of Wilkes, Clarke, and Newton Counties, Georgia.

Joshua Hammack, third son of Robert Hammack and Millenor Jackson, inherited the longevity of his Hammack grandparents. Born in Virginia about 1769, he was enumerated in 1850 as being eighty-one years old and in 1860 as being ninety-one years old. Family tradition among his descendants indicates that he was alive as late as 1864, at which time he was ninety-five years of age.[399]

Joshua first appears in Wilkes County, Georgia, tax records in 1791, when he paid the poll tax in the district where his parents were living. He probably married soon thereafter to an unknown woman from the same community; a family reconstitution suggests that his first child was probably born about 1796. Joshua remained in Wilkes County until at least 1800, when he was taxed with 100 acres on Hardin's Creek in John Bethune's District. His name appears near those of his siblings, who, like himself, had recently inherited a portion of his father's real estate. The tract for which Joshua was taxed had been granted to his father and joined the lands of his brother Robert Hammack.

Soon after 1800, Joshua Hammack began moving his family from the region. In 1803, he was involved in a Hancock County in a land transaction with Mansel Womack, who lived across the Ogeechee River from the Hammacks.[400] The following year, he purchased a tract of land in Clarke County, about sixty miles northwest of Hardin's Creek, where he soon settled.[401] At the time, Clarke had recently been created from Jackson County and was still largely unpopulated. This move northward would separate Joshua and his offspring from their other Hammack kin for the duration of Joshua's life and beyond. There is, however, no evidence of friction between the families; oral tradition passed down among other Hammack families recalled details of Joshua's family, and his mother later deeded property to him. Perhaps the family of Joshua's unknown wife influenced his decision to pursue a migration route not followed by his near kin.

Joshua Hammack was taxed in Clarke County from 1804 until 1818. At the time of the 1804 digest, Joshua paid only poll tax, but by 1806 he was taxed with the tract he had purchased when he settled in the county. It was on this tract of ninety-three acres located along the Appalachee River that Joshua lived for more than a decade and reared his family. Joshua was taxed with this property in 1817 but sold it to Abner Whatley on 29 January 1818; he seems to have left the county immediately afterwards.[402] By 1820 he was living in nearby Walton County. At the time of the census enumeration, he and his wife were both enumerated as being more than forty-five years old. Joshua's household at the time consisted of three sons and one daughter, all below twenty-six years of age. When Newton County was created from Morgan and Walton Counties in 1821, Joshua then appears there.[403]

As a resident of Newton County, in 1825 Joshua Hammack, Sr., deeded land lot 64, land district 10, to his son John Hammack.[404] In 1830, Joshua's son Jesse, who had also settled in Newton County, deeded him a small portion of the same land lot.[405] Joshua retained this and additional acreage in land lot 64 until 1846, when he deeded the same to his sons Jesse, John, and Joshua. He also transferred to them his

---

[399] 1850 Newton Co., GA, Census, p. 433; 1860 Newton Co., GA, Census, p. 509; W. E. Nuss, *My Hammock Family, 1656-: A History of the Ancestors and Descendants of George Bartlett William Hammock (1825-1862)* (Cullman, AL, 1997).

[400] Hancock Co., GA, Deed Book E, p. 184.

[401] Clarke Co., GA, Deed Book C, p. 253.

[402] All Clarke Co., GA, tax digest data is taken from M. H. Abbe and L. W. Parr, *Clarke Co., GA, Tax Digests, 1802-1830* (3 vols., Athens, GA, 2005-2006). See Abbe and Parr, 1: 77, 120, 146, 231, 259; Abbe and Parr, 2: 27, 73, 113, 140, 192, 223, 271, and 311; and Clarke Co., GA, Deed Book L, p. 126.

[403] 1820 Walton Co., GA, Census, p. 518.

[404] Newton Co., GA, Deed Book A, p. 489.

[405] Newton Co., GA, Deed Book D, p. 117.

personal property and a seventeen year old slave girl in exchange for care from them during the remainder of his life.[406] John seems to have lived with his son John in Newton County for the remainder of his life. Neither the 1850 nor the 1860 census indicated that he owned any property, although for most of his life he had been a self-sufficient farmer working his own tract.[407]

Of the three sons of Joshua Hammack, Jesse was the oldest. Tax records indicate that he was born in 1796; he was alive as late as 1850, although he has not been located in the federal census for that year and was probably missed in the enumeration of Cobb County. Jesse married Polly Jones in 1813 in Clarke County and remained there for a time with her relatives after his father moved to Walton. By 1830, however, Jesse had joined his father in Newton County and remained there until settling in Cobb County more than a decade later. Census records indicate that Jesse, who seems to have used the spelling Hammock, had two sons -- probably including Robert Hammock of Clay County, Alabama -- and several daughters.[408]

Born about 1798, Joshua Hammack, Jr., was his father's second son. He left Newton County after 1850 and settled in Carroll County, Georgia, where he left a large family, most of whom spelled the surname Hammock. Either this Joshua or his father held several local offices in Newton County; among these was service as county coroner from 1830 to 1838 and again in 1840 and 1841. Age would suggest that it was Joshua, Jr., who served as coroner, although this is by no means conclusive.[409]

John Hammack, born about 1802, was his father's third and youngest son. He married Piety Day and sired a large family in Newton County. John's offspring retained close links with their uncle Joshua, and several of them moved into Carroll County, Georgia. From that location, John's descendants – who used the spelling Hammock as well as Hammack -- spread throughout northern Georgia and northern Alabama.[410]

The 1820 Georgia census indicates that Joshua Hammack had only one daughter. At that time she was aged sixteen to twenty-six. She was almost certainly Susannah Hammack, born about 1804, who married John Day on 10 October 1823 in Newton County. Susannah was living in Newton County with her large family at the time of the 1850 census.[411]

D. John Hammack, fourth son of Robert and Millenor Jackson Hammack, of Wilkes, Hancock, Jones, and Talbot Counties, Georgia.

The will of Robert Hammack identifies John Hammack as his fourth son. Biographical data concerning his brothers and Wilkes County, Georgia, tax lists indicate that John was born about 1770, probably in Lunenburg County, Virginia. He was taxed in Littleberry Little's District in southern Wilkes (now Taliaferro) County as late as 1804, when he owned two slaves and 100 acres on Hardin's Creek. This land was part of the Stuart tract mentioned in his father's will and joined property owned by S. Hendrick.

About this time, John Hammack acquired property interests in Hancock County, and he may have lived briefly in Clarke County.[412] John was a resident of Jones County, however, on 25 February 1810

---

[406] Joshua's mother Millenor had in 1828 made him a deed of gift. Nancy, who was described as 17 in 1846, was probably the child of slaves deeded by Millenor Hammack in 1828. See Jones Co., GA, Deed Book O, p. 154; Newton Co., GA, Deed Book D, p. 117; and Newton Co., GA, Deed Book F, p. 232.

[407] The 1846 deed mentions 140 acres of land lot 10 and land lot 140.

[408] 1830 Newton Co., GA, Census, p. 41; 1840 Newton Co., GA, Census, p. 21; Newton Co., GA, Deed Book I, p. 519.

[409] 1850 Carroll Co., GA, Census; 1860 Carroll Co., GA, Census, p. 561; *History of Newton Co., GA*, p. 47.

[410] See Nuss, *Hammock Family*, p. 12 et seq.; 1840 Newton Co., GA, Census, p. 44; 1850 Newton Co., GA, Census, p. 433; 1860 Newton Co., GA, Census, p. 509; 1870 Newton Co., GA, Census, p. 176; 1880 Rockdale Co., GA, Census, p. 68C.

[411] 1850 Newton Co., GA, Census, p. 433.

[412] Hancock Co., GA, Deed Book G, p. 18 (1804), and Deed Book I, p. 4 (1809). One John Hammack of Robinson's District, Clarke County, drew land in Wilkinson (now Twiggs) at the time of the 1807 land lottery. If John did settle in Clarke, he does not appear in the deed or tax records. The entry might actually be for his brother Joshua, who was in Clarke at the time. Yet Joshua was

when he purchased land lot 12, land district 8, from Charles Groom.[413] Months later, on 19 March 1811, John purchased another tract in Jones County from Henry K. Jones. This additional tract of 150 acres was located in land lot 175, land district 12.[414] Both tracts were located on Falling Creek, and, at the time of the 1811 Jones County tax digest, both were still owned by John Hammack.[415] The following year, John purchased another 202.5 acres in land district 12 from Harrison Bury.[416] He paid a total of $1,450 for a combined total of 557.5 acres. By 1813, he also owned two slaves.

John seems not to have retained the 1813 purchase for long, although record of its disposal has not been found. In 1817 and in 1825 he was taxed with the initial two tracts, totaling 355 acres, on Falling Creek. He may have conveyed portions of the tract to his sons as they came of age; by 1825, Jackson, Lewis, and John P. Hammack were all of legal age and heads of their own households.

By 1828, John Hammack had left Jones County and settled in newly opened Talbot County, about forty miles southwest. He remained there for the rest of his life. From his sons John P. and Lewis, he purchased land lot 133, land district 16, in Talbot County.[417] At the time of the 1830 census, John Hammack was aged 50-60 with a wife aged 60-70. The 1840 Talbot County census showed him aged 60-70 with a wife aged 70-80. These data are consistent with the 1850 census, which showed John's widow Rachel as aged eighty-two years. Rachel was apparently about four years older than her husband. They probably married in the mid-1790s in Wilkes County, but record of the marriage -- and Rachel's maiden name -- have not been discovered. Significantly, however, the 1850 census indicates that Rachel was a native of Pennsylvania, a clue that might help determine her biological family connections in early Wilkes County.[418]

At the time of the 1840 Talbot County census, John's sister Catherine Hammack Gunn Poole lived only a few households from him; otherwise, his nearest neighbors were his married adult children and their in-laws.[419]

After John settled in Talbot County, the family often used the spelling Hammock. As John Hammock, he wrote his will 24 August 1843 in Talbot County. He was probably about seventy years old at the time. John was then living on a 300-acre farm in land district 16; he also owned another 202.5 acre tract in Carroll County and seven slaves. Hope Hull Hammock was to provide for his mother during her life and to take control of his father's estate -- including also two horses, thirty-six head of cattle, twenty-eight head of hogs, oxen, a crop of cotton, plantation tools, a threshing machine, household furniture, and notes and personal accounts -- until Rachel Hammock died. After both parents died, Hope Hull Hammock was to satisfy his father's debts before inheriting the bulk of his father's real and personal estate. Small bequests -- ranging from $2.50 to $5 -- were left to the other sons of John Hammock, while daughters Elizabeth Adams and Nancy Childers each inherited a slave woman. John Hammock must have died after a brief illness; his will was proven on 4 September 1843, ten days after he wrote it. Given that probate usually followed a testator's decease by several days, John probably passed away soon after he wrote his will.[420]

---

never taxed in Clarke with this tract. One possibility is that several members of the family lived briefly in Clarke before settling elsewhere. Twiggs County joins Jones County, and John may have left Clarke -- where he owned no land -- to settle first on the new tract in Twiggs. By 1810, he was living in Jones County.

[413] Jones Co., GA, Deed Book B, p. 470.

[414] Jones Co., GA, Deed Book C, p. 106.

[415] 1811 Jones Co., GA, Tax Digest.

[416] Jones Co., GA, Deed Book D, p. 326.

[417] Talbot Co., GA, Deed Book A, p. 180.

[418] 1830 Talbot Co., GA, Census, p. 135; 1840 Talbot Co., GA, Census, p. 223.

[419] Ibid.

[420] Talbot Co., GA, Will Book A, p. 135-38.

Of John Hammock's offspring, Robert B. Hammock (c. 1795, GA --) moved to Pike and Carroll Counties.[421] Son William Hammock (c. 1797, GA --) remained in Talbot County but died about 1848.[422] Daughter Rebecca Hammock (1799-1883) and her husband Ransom McBryde (1797-1860) both remained in Talbot County, as did most of their offspring.[423] Son John P. Hammock married Sarah Ussery, whose family had also come to Jones County from Lunenburg County, Virginia, and moved from Jones County to Tallapoosa County, Alabama, before 1850. After his death, Sarah Ussery Hammock returned to Jones County, where she was living with her sister Sophia Maddox's family in 1870.[424]

Jackson Hammock (1801-1873), son of John and Rachel, moved to Talbot County between 1825 and 1830 and to Tallapoosa County, Alabama, between 1840 and 1850. He remained in Tallapoosa County for the rest of his life and was enumerated there in both 1860 and 1870.[425] Elizabeth Hammock (c. 1803 -- 1895) married Caleb Adams in Jones County in 1825; they also moved to Talbot County before settling in Chambers County, Alabama, where Caleb died in 1844. Elizabeth reared her family in western Chambers and Eastern Tallapoosa Counties. She later moved to Texas, however, dying in Hunt County in 1895.[426]

Nancy Hammock (c. 1806 --) and husband John Childers moved to Talbot County before settling in Schley County; they had fourteen children between 1822 and 1853.[427] Lewis Hammock (c. 1805 -- aft. 1870) married Amanda Davenport in Jones County in 1829; he was still in Jones County in 1830 but in Marion County by 1840. At the time of the 1850, 1860, and 1870 census enumerations he was living in Columbus, Muscogee County, Georgia. The 1860 census indicated that Lewis was a farmer, but the 1870 census showed that he was a night watchman in a cotton mill. Lewis had at least ten children; several remained in western Georgia, although his son Edmund Harper Worrell Hammack lived in Texas from about 1866 until his death in 1933.[428]

E. Nancy Hammack Ray, daughter of Robert Hammack and wife of Jacob Ray, of Wilkes and Taliaferro Counties, Georgia.

A close connection existed in Virginia and in Georgia between the Hammack and Ray families. According to Robert Hammack's will, Nancy Ray was his eldest daughter. She was still living at the time of the 1850 Taliaferro County, Georgia, census, which indicated that she was born in 1772 or 1773.[429]

Nancy Hammack was married when her father wrote his will. Her husband Jacob Ray first appears as a taxable in Wilkes County digests in 1791, suggesting that he was born in 1769 or 1770. It was probably about this time -- 1791 -- that he and Nancy Hammack married. Interestingly, Nancy and Jacob had been born on adjoining farms in Lunenburg County, Virginia, where Jacob's parents Sanders and Christiana Ray were then living. The Rays headed south in the 1780s, settling in Wilkes County. Later in the 1790s, Sanders Ray relocated to south Alabama, dying about 1800 in Washington County, Alabama. Jacob Ray, his mother Christiana, and several married siblings remained behind in eastern Georgia. When the Ray estate was settled in 1808, additional heirs were identified as John Moore (husband of Jane Ray), Robert Moore (husband of Martha Ray Moncrief), Bishop Moore (husband of Sarah Ray), and Ussery Ray

---

[421] 1850 Carroll Co., GA, Census, p. 33; Pike Co., GA, Deed Book E, p. 303.

[422] 1840 Talbot Co., GA, Census, p. 229.

[423] Son Mansel Theodore B. McBryde died in 1896 in Bell Co., TX.

[424] 1850 Tallapoosa Co., AL, Census, p. 55; 1870 Jones Co., GA, Census, p. 265.

[425] 1840 Talbot Co., GA, Census, p. 224; 1850 Tallapoosa Co., AL, Census, p. 61; 1860 Tallapoosa Co., AL, Census, p. 73; 1870 Tallapoosa Co., AL, Census, p. 196.

[426] 1850 Tallapoosa Co., AL, Census, p. 55.

[427] 1860 Schley Co., GA, Census, p. 31.

[428] 1850 Muscogee Co., GA, Census, p. 316; 1860 Muscogee Co., GA, Census, p. 350; 1870 Muscogee Co., GA, Census, p. 772; On-line Texas Death Certificate Index, 1933, Church of Jesus Christ of Latter Day Saints.

[429] 1850 Taliaferro Co., GA, Census, p. 331. Nancy was living with William G. Moody and his wife Elizabeth, who was probably Nancy's granddaughter.

(husband of Jincy Kelly). Christiana "Kitty" Ray was still living at this time.[430] It seems that three of Jacob's sisters had married members of the family of Ussery and Martha Bishop Moore of Lunenburg County, Virginia, and Wilkes County, Georgia. Ussery Moore had been another neighbor and associate of the Hammack family in Virginia. In Georgia, family ties would become even more complex when his son Matthew Moore married Mary Ray, daughter of Jacob Ray and Nancy Hammack, and when Ussery's granddaughter Elizabeth Jane Moore married Simeon Hammack, nephew of Nancy Hammack Ray.[431]

The Hammack and Ray properties lay in southern Wilkes County. Today the area is in Taliaferro County and lies near the boundaries of Warren and Hancock Counties. On 10 October 1796, Jacob Ray purchased land in Warren County from John Harris.[432]

On 10 February 1810, Nancy Ray, Polly Moore (daughter of Nancy, and wife of Matthew Moore), and Patsy Moore (sister of Jacob Ray, and wife of Robert Moore) became members of Williams Creek Baptist Church, located about half-way between present-day Crawfordville and Warrenton. Nancy was still a member as late as September 1828, at which time her daughter Mary Ray Moore transferred her membership to a church in Jones County.[433]

Jacob Ray was a farmer and a hatter; he seldom appears in court records, but he lived comfortably on a 300-acre farm in Wilkes and Taliaferro Counties. He was sued in 1816 by Thomas Scott and then purchased land from Martin Pitts later the same year. He and Nancy were enumerated in Wilkes County in 1820 with two sons and three daughters; they were in Taliaferro County in 1830, aged 60-70 and 50-60 respectively, with two young females, probably granddaughters, living in their household. The 1840 census found them in Taliaferro County as well; at that time they had a host of individuals, probably including several adult children and grandchildren, living with them. Jacob Ray was aged 70 to 80 at the time and must have been about seventy-eight when he died in 1847.[434]

Jacob Ray owned 327 acres of land in Taliaferro County, and an inventory filed by his administrator, Aaron M. Grier, indicated that he owned personal property worth $474. Not all of his material possessions are identified.[435] The family must have had a comfortable existence, however, for the following year the widowed Nancy Ray deeded to Aaron Grier several personal effects, including two beds and bedsteads, a brass clock, a looking glass, a spinning wheel, several chairs, a book case, three chests, livestock, and several other items.[436]

No references to Nancy Ray have been found after 1850; she may have died soon after the census. No single document identifying all of her offspring have been found, but based on census records, estate records, and family associations, it appears that Nancy Hammack and Jacob Ray probably had at least eight children. These included Mary Ray (c. 1792 --), wife of Matthew Moore[437]; Elizabeth Ray (c. 1794 --), wife of Martin Pitts; Samuel Ray; Lucy Ray, wife of Thomas Trouton; and Jane Ray, wife of Edmund McLoughlin. It is possible that Martha Ray who married Simeon Felts in 1824 in Jones County was also a daughter. Chesley Ray (who married Lucy Ray in 1826) was a neighbor and may also have been a son.[438]

---

[430] Washington Co., AL, Deed Book A, p. 203.

[431] Ray researchers believe that Sanders and Christianna Ray were also parents of Elizabeth, wife of Lewis Hammack.

[432] Warren Co., GA, Deed Book C, pp. 45-46.

[433] K. J. Brantley, ed., *Records of the Church of Christ at Williams Creek, 1787-1840* (Powder Springs, 1995), pp. 45, 113, 116.

[434] 1820 Wilkes Co., GA, Census, p. 212; 1830 Wilkes Co., GA, Census, p. 293; 1840 Taliaferro Co., GA, Census, p. 242; Taliaferro Co., GA, Deed Book A, p. 232; Taliaferro Co., GA, Returns Book A, 1827-1850; Taliaferro Co., GA, Inventories, Appraisals, Sales, and Divisions of Estates, Book B, 1834-1850, pp. 477-478.

[435] Taliaferro Co., GA, Inventories, Appraisals, Sales, and Divisions of Estates, Book B, 1834-1850, pp. 477-478.

[436] Taliaferro Co., GA, Deed Book D, p. 323.

[437] 1912 Arkansas Census of Confederate Veterans, Welborn Moore, Arkansas State History Commission, Little Rock, AR.

[438] See Davidson, *Early Records*, 2: 352, 357.

F. Elizabeth Hammack Moncrief of Wilkes County, Georgia.

The will of Robert Hammack -- written 9 July 1799 -- identifies two married daughters, Nancy Hammack Ray and Betsy Hammack Moncrief. It further identifies Nancy Ray as Hammack's eldest daughter. It would therefore seem that Betsy Hammack Moncrief must have been born about 1774 or 1775 and that she likely married between 1792 and 1799.

Records concerning Betsy Hammack Moncrief are scarce. The evidence suggests, however, that she married Josiah Moncrief. On 7 February 1816, Zilpha and Noah Moncrief executed a deed "to my father and mother, Josiah and Elizabeth Moncrief," for "land on Hardin's Creek waters where they now live."[439]

Josiah is found in Wilkes County as early as 1791. At the time of the 1791 tax digest, as "Josiah Moncreaf" he was taxed as a defaulter in Captain McCormick's District, Wilkes County. He appears in the same vicinity regularly for more than twenty years. In 1807, as a resident of Hendricks' District, Wilkes County, Josiah Moncrief drew land lot 165, land district 12, Baldwin County.[440]

Josiah Moncrief apparently had little property in Wilkes County. In 1816 and 1817, he was allotted $20 per year for his support from the poor fund. In 1818, he was allotted $36, and from 1819 to 1824 there were regular payments "for Josiah Moncrief and wife". In 1825, Elizabeth Moncrief -- apparently a widow -- received $50 from the county poor fund for her support.[441]

Moncrief family researchers believe that Josiah Moncrief was the sire of the Wilkes County Moncrief family. An immigrant from North Carolina, he was probably born about 1739 in Currituck County, North Carolina, a son of William Moncrief and Elizabeth Simmons. Josiah had apparently married first in North Carolina to an unknown woman; she probably died shortly after the family settled in Wilkes County, and Josiah then married Elizabeth Hammack in the early 1790s.[442]

There is no evidence that Josiah Moncrief and Elizabeth Hammack Moncrief had children together; Moncrief genealogists suggest -- apparently without firm supporting data -- that Josiah and his first wife were the parents of several children born between about 1765 and 1787, including Noah Moncrief, John M. Moncrief, Zilpha Moncrief, Samuel Moncrief, Thomas Moncrief, Josiah Moncrief, David Moncrief, Laban Moncrief, Austin Moncrief, and Martha Moncrief. Of these children, Samuel Moncrief married Martha Ray (sister of Jacob Ray), who then remarried to Robert Moore (son of Ussery and Martha Bishop Moore). Noah and Zilpha joined together in the 1816 deed to Josiah and Elizabeth Moncrief.[443]

If this analysis is correct, then, Josiah Moncrief was married to two women named Elizabeth. On 22 June 1766, Josiah Moncrief, Elizabeth Moncrief his wife, and Elizabeth Moncreaf, widow, all of Currituck County, North Carolina, deeded to William Moncrief, also of Currituck County, eighty-nine and one-half acres of land in Currituck, being half of a tract of 179 acres. The elder Elizabeth is identified as widow and mother of Josiah Moncrief. In a deed dated 1 July 1768 Josiah Moncreefe is identified as "eldest son and heir to William Moncreef, deceased,' who had conveyed land to him by a deed of sale on 22 March 1762. Josiah Moncreaf was in Currituck County as late as 1779 and was taxed in Wilkes County as early as 1785. At that time, he and wife Elizabeth Moncrief were members of Phillips' Mill Baptist Church.[444] Josiah was taxed with 200 acres of land in Captain George Heard's District in 1786,

---

[439] Wilkes Co., GA, Deed Book BBB, p. 247.

[440] 1807 Georgia Land Lottery Records, Fortunate Draws, Georgia Department of Archives and History, Morrow, GA.

[441] These amounts varied per year: $50 for 1819, $75 for 1820, $75 for 1822, $70 for 1823, and $70 for 1824. See Wilkes Co., GA, Poor Fund Distributions, 1816-1825, in Wilkes Co., GA, Miscellaneous Minutes, Overseers of the Poor, 1800-1850.

[442] Erick Montgomery, "Josiah Moncrief" (2002) (http://searches2.rootsweb.ancestry.com /th/read/MONCRIEF/2002-05.)

[443] Ibid.

[444] Ibid. Moncrief researchers report that Elizabeth Moncrief was a member of Phillips' Mill Baptist Church when it was formed on 10 June 1785 at the home of George Lea. A membership roster from 1785 shows Elizabeth and Josiah as members along with Marcy Moncrief and Elizabeth Moncrief, Jr. Another Elizabeth Moncrief joined the church on 8 January 1791. Perhaps this third Elizabeth Moncrief was Elizabeth Hammack Moncrief. See Minutes of Phillip's Mill Baptist Church, Georgia Department of Archives and History, Morrow, GA.

and on 10 July 1790 he deeded this land, along with household furniture, horses, cows, and "all his estate" to Noah Moncrief.[445]

There were marriages in Lincoln County, Georgia, between members of the Hammack and Moncrief families. William Moncrief, son of Austin Moncrief and Nancy Hamrick and grandson of Josiah and Elizabeth Moncrief, married Elizabeth Hammock, granddaughter of John Hammack of Lincoln County. If the above analysis is correct, he would have been a step-grandson of Elizabeth Hammack Moncrief.[446]

Minutes of Phillip's Mill Baptist Church, Wilkes County, Georgia, contain the following notation:

11 September 1824: "Brother Josiah Moncrief deceased."

Moncrief had been a member of this congregation since 1790, but his association with the church was tumultuous. He was frequently expelled for drinking, cursing or arguing, and then after a heartfelt repentance would be readmitted to fellowship.[447]

Because Moncrief family records are not conclusive, the information here is subject to revision. At present, however, it appears that Josiah Moncrief moved to Wilkes County with his large family and that, about 1792 or 1793, following the death of his first wife, he married Elizabeth Hammack. They apparently had no offspring. Elizabeth was still living in Wilkes County as late as 1825 but has not been located after that date.

G. Lucy Hammack Hammack, daughter of Robert and Millenor Jackson Hammack, wife of James Hammack, of Wilkes and Jones Counties, Georgia.

Lucy Hammack was probably born about 1775 in Virginia. She moved with her parents to Georgia as a child, and it was there that she married her cousin James Hammack, son of John and Mary Ann Hammack. Mary Ann Hammack had as a widow settled in Wilkes County in the early 1790s; she had first moved from Granville County, North Carolina, to Pittsylvania County, Virginia, and then with her eldest son Thomas to Georgia.

James Hammack and his family have already been discussed in the context of John and Mary Ann Hammack and their family. He and Lucy were married for nearly thirty years and may have reared as many as ten children. Lucy was deceased by 2 August 1827 when James Hammack married Mary Pollard in Bibb County. James Hammack then began a second family with his new wife in Bibb, Pike, and Muscogee Counties, Georgia.

The offspring of James and Lucy Hammack are discussed above; the evidence is strong that they were the parents of Celia Hammack, who married her cousin Harrison Hammack on 1 December 1817 in Jones County. Celia and Harrison were the grandparents of Henry Franklin Hammack, the early family researcher who authored the series *Wandering Back* from 1958 to 1961.

H. Mary Hammack Jackson, daughter of Robert and Millenor Jackson Hammack, wife of John Jackson, Sr., of Wilkes and Jones Counties, Georgia.

Mary Hammack Jackson was an unmarried minor at the time her father wrote his will in 1799; she married less than a year later, on 12 August 1800 in Wilkes County, to John Jackson, who may have been

---

[445] Wilkes Co., GA, Deed Book GG, p. 511.
[446] Davis and Dorsey, *Lincoln County*, p. 252.
[447] See Minutes of Phillip's Mill Baptist Church, Georgia Department of Archives and History, Morrow, GA.

her cousin. It seems likely that Mary was born about 1784 in Wilkes County; she died prior to the 1850 census, by which time her husband had remarried -- probably about 1847 -- and begun a second family.[448]

Little specific information is known concerning Mary. She and John Jackson spent their early years together in the Hardin's Creek area of Wilkes County. They moved prior to 1829 to Jones County, for in that year Mary's widowed mother Millenor Hammack deeded to "daughter Polly, wife of John Jackson of Jones County" a slave woman named Chloe.[449]

After Mary's death, John Jackson married a much younger woman named Martha Moye; they were enumerated in Jones County in 1850 and had at least one child, Wiley, by the time that John Jackson died in Monroe County in 1859.[450]

John and Mary Hammack Jackson had a large family, most of whom remained in Jones County and surrounding areas well past 1850. Their children included the following: William P. Jackson (c. 1803 -- aft. 1870, Jones County, Georgia), husband of Frankie Murphy and Temperance Lane; Thompson Jackson (c. 1805 -- aft. 1870, Jones County, Georgia), husband of Mary Lane; Edward Jackson (c. 1808 -- 1894, Jones County, Georgia), who probably never married; Lucy Jackson (c. 1810 --), who may have married Samuel Morgan in 1834[451]; Wilkins Jackson (c. 1812 -- aft. 1850, Jones County, Georgia), husband of Lively Adams Hammack[452]; John Jackson (1815 -- 1868), who married Littie Rowe and settled in Macon County, Georgia; Andrew Jackson (1816 -- 1903), who was unmarried in 1850; and Lewis Jackson (1820 -- 1865), husband of Margery Carmichael (1822-1871).[453]

I. Edward Hammack, son of Robert and Millenor Jackson Hammack, of Wilkes and Jones Counties, Georgia.

Edward Hammack was the youngest son of Robert and Millenor Jackson Hammack; his father's will made special provision for him and his sister Catherine Hammack. Both were minors, and their estate was entrusted to the care of their mother Millenor and their eldest brother Lewis, who managed affairs on their behalves for several years.

Edward married, probably about 1808, Charlotte Felts (c. 1790 - c. 1856), widow of William Griffin.[454] He appears regularly on Wilkes County tax digests living in the vicinity of Harden's Creek. In 1816 he and John Bryant were securities for his sister Catherine Gunn when she filed for administration on the estate of her deceased husband John Gunn in Wilkes County.[455] He was still living in Wilkes County in 1821 when he drew 202.5 acres in Monroe County in the state land lottery. At the time, he was a resident of Bryant's district and drew land lot 56, land district 12, in Monroe County.[456]

By 1825, Edward had joined his mother and siblings in Jones County, and he remained there for the rest of his life. From 1825 to 1828, he consistently paid tax on the tract drawn in 1821. In the 1827 land lottery, he won a tract in Lee County, also containing 202.5 acres.[457] In 1826 and 1827, Edward Hammack also paid tax on 162 acres in Taliaferro County. In 1829, Edward's mother deeded him one slave girl named Sophia. Edward may have owned additional slaves obtained through other means, or Sophia may

---

[448] Carolyn White Williams, comp., *History of Jones County, Georgia: For One Hundred Years, Specifically 1807-1907* (Macon, GA, 1957), pp. 631-633.

[449] Jones Co., GA, Deed Book O, pp. 167-168.

[450] Williams, *Jones County*, pp. 631-633.

[451] After Lucy died, Samuel married Kittie Hammack, Lewis Hammack's granddaughter.

[452] She was Lewis Hammack's daughter-in-law.

[453] Williams, *Jones County*, pp. 631-633. Lewis and Margery had several daughters. These daughters never married and lived together in Jones County until they died. All are buried in the "Jackson Girls Cemetery" near Round Oak in Jones County.

[454] Jones Co., GA, Will Book D, p. 97.

[455] Davidson, *Early Records*, 1: 191.

[456] 1821 Georgia Land Lottery Records, Fortunate Draws, Georgia Department of Archives and History, Morrow, GA.

[457] 1827 Georgia Land Lottery Records, Fortunate Draws, Georgia Department of Archives and History, Morrow, GA. The land fell first into Lee County (land lot 147, land district 12) and then later into Terrell County.

have borne children who supplemented Edward's labor force. By 1840, he was paying tax on six slaves and 303.75 acres in Jones and Lee Counties.[458]

Edward Hammack apparently died in late 1840 or early 1841. The 1840 census enumeration for Jones County showed that Edward was aged 50-60 and that his wife Charlotte was aged 40-50. The only other members of their household were two male slave and four female slaves, all of whom were under age ten.[459] When tax data was recorded for 1841, Edward Hammack was already deceased. Allen Wheeler paid tax on behalf of Charlotte Hammack, who was assessed with the 303 acres and six slaves. Charlotte apparently disposed of the Lee County acreage soon after Edward's death. From 1842 onwards, she was taxed only with 101.25 acres in Jones County. The number of slaves she owned continued to increase, however. She was taxed with seven slaves in 1842 and with eight in 1843; by 1857, when her estate was inventoried, she owned twelve slaves.[460]

Although no marriage record has been found to document the marriage of Edward and Charlotte Hammack, documents in Jones County establish that she was Charlotte Felts, daughter of John Felts of Wilkes, Jones, and Putnam Counties. There is a strong possibility that Charlotte was a sister of Mary Hammack, wife of Edward's brother William T. Hammack. From the time of Edward Hammack's death, Allen Wheeler acted as Charlotte's agent in legal records. On 10 April 1847, she deeded ten acres of land lot 10, land district 9, Jones County, Georgia, to her nephew William A. Felts; the land was bounded by other property owned by Charlotte Hammack, John Bryant, and John Felts. When Charlotte wrote her will on 6 February 1847, she bequeathed $800 to her nephew Allen Wheeler and his seven children and the remainder of her property to her nephew William A. Felts, who was to execute Charlotte's will. The will was proven 12 June 1857.[461] An inventory recorded 29 October 1857 revealed that Charlotte's estate -- including twelve slaves and a warrant for 160 acres of land -- was valued at $9,483.50.[462] The high valuation testifies to the enhanced value of young slaves in the years immediately preceding the opening of the American Civil War. By the time Charlotte's inventory was recorded, her nephew William A. Felts had died; his widow Margaret served as Charlotte's administrator and continued to file documents regarding her estate until it was finally settled in 1864.[463]

When Charlotte Felts Griffin Hammack wrote her will, in addition to bequests to her nieces and nephews, she provided $200 to "be expended in a suitable enclosure around the graves of myself and deceased husband." If the graves were marked, they have not been found. Both Edward and Charlotte Hammack seem to have died childless.[464]

J. Catherine Hammack Gunn Poole, daughter of Robert and Millenor Jackson Hammack, wife of John Gunn and David Poole, of Wilkes, Taliaferro, and Talbot Counties, Georgia, and Russell County, Alabama.

Catherine Hammack seems to have been the youngest child of Robert and Millenor Jackson Hammack; she was born about 1792 in the family homestead along Hardin's Creek in southern Wilkes County. She was alive as late as 1860 in Salem, Russell County, Alabama, and may have lived for several years thereafter.[465]

---

[458] Jones Co., GA, Deed Book O, p. 167.

[459] 1840 Jones Co., GA, Census, p. 137.

[460] Jones Co., GA, Returns Book T, pp. 93, 455; Jones Co., GA, Returns Book U, p. 390; Jones Co., GA, Returns Book V, p. 49; Jones Co., GA, Returns Book X, p. 457.

[461] Jones Co., GA, Will Book D, pp. 97-98.

[462] At the time of the 1850 Jones Co., GA, Slave Schedule, Charlotte owned ten slaves, including three males, aged three to seventeen, and seven females, aged three to thirty-five.

[463] Jones Co., GA, Returns Book T, p. 93, 455; U, p. 390; V, p. 49; X, p. 457.

[464] Jones Co., GA, Will Book D, p. 97.

[465] 1860 Russell Co., AL, Census, p. 1058.

Catherine was only a small girl when her father Robert died, and his will evidences particular care for her and her brother Edward, who was probably the closest to her in age. Catherine married John Gunn in Wilkes County on 5 August 1810; he was deceased by 6 May 1816, when Catherine Gunn applied for letters of administration on her husband's estate with Edward Hammack and John Bryant as her securities.[466] She seems to have remained in Wilkes County when her siblings moved to Jones County and was still living in the area when Taliaferro County was created in 1825. Catherine's daughter Sicily married John Wynne on 9 July 1826 in Taliaferro, and her son George Gunn married Nancy Doster there on 22 May 1831.

Why Catherine Hammack Gunn remained in Taliaferro when most of her natal family had left the area is unknown. Her husband belonged to a large family in southern Wilkes County, and her children had many Gunn relatives throughout the area. John Gunn had inherited real estate from his father William Gunn, and it seems that Catherine and her children lived there until after they both came of age.[467]

Once Catherine's children reached adulthood, the compulsion to remain in Taliaferro County may have lessened. She had remarried, by 23 July 1828, when her mother deeded her a slave, to a man named David Poole.[468] Her second marriage may also have played a role in her decision to head west. By 1840, Catherine was living in the same Talbot County, Georgia, community as her older brother John Hammack and his large family. At that time, her household consisted of two sons aged 5-10 and an older son aged 10-15.[469]

By 1850, Catherine Hammack Gunn Poole had settled in Russell County, Alabama. She was then aged fifty-eight, and in her household were sons William Poole and David Poole, aged sixteen and eighteen. Living near her, on Hog Island in Russell County, was her daughter Sisley Catherine Gunn Wynne and her family. George and Nancy Doster Gunn were also in Russell County in 1860, although they have not been located in 1850.[470]

Catherine Poole was still living in Russell County at the time of the 1860 census. Her son William had recently married, and he, his wife, and their two children were living with Catherine. Next door was son David Poole, his wife Frances, and their two daughters.[471]

The time and place of Catherine Hammack Gunn Poole's death is unknown. Her daughter Sisley Wynne and family remained in Russell County, where their descendants live to this day. Between 1860 and 1870, George and Nancy Doster Gunn moved west into Talladega County, Alabama. David Poole and his family were still living in Russell County, Alabama, in 1870. William Poole's whereabouts have not been determined later than the 1860 census. John J. Poole, eldest son of David and Catherine, had married prior to the 1850 census. He settled first in Elmore County, Alabama, but ultimately moved to Henderson, Rusk County, Texas, where he died in 1908. Whether Catherine Hammack Gunn Poole remained in East Alabama or whether she moved west with her son John J. Poole has not yet been determined.[472]

K. Conclusion: The Family of Robert and Millenor Jackson Hammack

Robert Hammack (1737-1800) married Millenor Jackson (c. 1745-aft. 1830) about 1763 or 1764, probably in Amelia County, Virginia. They remained in the Virginia Southside, where most of their

[466] Davidson, *Early Records*, 1: 191.
[467] Robert R. Gunn, *The Gunns* (Crawfordville, GA, 1925), pp. 94-98.
[468] Jones Co., GA, Deed Book O, p. 141.
[469] 1840 Talbot Co., GA, Census, pp. 223-224.
[470] 1850 Russell Co., AL, Census, p. 36.
[471] 1860 Russell Co., AL, Census, p. 1058.
[472] 1870 Talladega Co., AL, Census, p. 449; 1870 Russell Co., AL, Census, p. 216; 1880 Calhoun Co., AL, Census, p. 621; 1880 Lee Co., AL, Census, p. 91D. John Pool was enumerated 6 August 1870 in Henderson, Rusk Co., TX. He was still living there at the time of the 1880 census (22 June 1880) as well as in 1900 (7 June 1900). See 1870 Rusk Co., TX, Census, p. 456; 1880 Rusk Co., TX, Census, p. 207; 1900 Rusk Co., TX, Census, p. 184.

children were born, until moving to the Georgia frontier, settling there between 1773 and 1779. Robert acquired several tracts of land along Hardin's Creek in what was then southern Wilkes County. He had become a prosperous farmer by the time he died in 1800.

Robert's widow, Millenor Jackson Hammack, survived him for more than three decades. She died between 1830 and 1840 in Jones County, Georgia, at which time she was between eighty-five and ninety-five years of age. Millenor may have inherited her longevity from her grandfather John Jackson, who, Albemarle Parish, Virginia, records note, was ninety years old when he died in 1770. The family tendency towards longevity was evidenced among several of Millenor's descendants. Sons Robert and Joshua both lived to be ninety-five, and her granddaughter Martha Hammack Frank celebrated her one-hundredth birthday in 1895.

Robert Hammack left land and slaves in Wilkes County to support his wife and children; the lands ultimately passed to Robert's minor children, but Millenor had full control of the slaves bequeathed her by her husband. In a series of deeds of gift between 1810 and 1829, Millenor deeded these slaves and their increase to several of her children and grandchildren. All of Millenor's sons became prosperous farmers, and Lewis, William, and Edward owned enough land and slaves to have been considered cotton planters by the standards of their time.

Robert Hammack and Millenor Jackson had six sons and four daughters who lived to adulthood; while there may have been infant deaths, no record of them has survived. A careful family reconstitution suggests that all ten children were born between 1765 and 1784, a birthrate that indicates a new birth every two years. Millenor apparently outlived one and possibly two of her daughters, Lucy Hammack (who married her cousin James Hammack) and died prior to 1827 and Betsy Hammack Moncrief, who married a widower named Noah Moncrief and had no children of her own. Millenor's youngest son, Edward Hammack, also had no children of his own. Her eight offspring who married and left issue produced at least fifty-three grandchildren, many of whom were married with families of their own when Millenor died.

All of the children of Robert Hammack and Millenor Jackson died in Georgia and Alabama; many of their grandchildren headed west, settling in Mississippi, Louisiana, Arkansas, and Texas. By the time that the American Civil War began, their descendants -- who then numbered in the hundreds -- lived in six Confederate states. Although some were modest farmers, others were wealthy planters. Without exception, they seem to have supported the Confederacy and southern independence, a stance whereby many southerners -- slaveholders and the slave-less -- cast themselves as the true defenders of the liberty and independence that men like Robert Hammack had supported during the American Revolution.

Of the offspring of Robert and Millenor Jackson Hammack, sons Lewis and John had large families. Robert Hammack remained in Taliaferro County, where he left sons John, Gustavus Sterling, and Dr. T. B. Hammack. Joshua settled in Newton County, leaving sons Jesse, John, and Joshua. As discussed in the following chapter, William settled in Crawford County, where he left a large family. Lewis Hammack died in Jones County, and his brother John in Talbot County. Another son, Edward, died childless. Descendants of these five brothers – using both the Hammack and Hammock spellings – spread throughout the southern states.

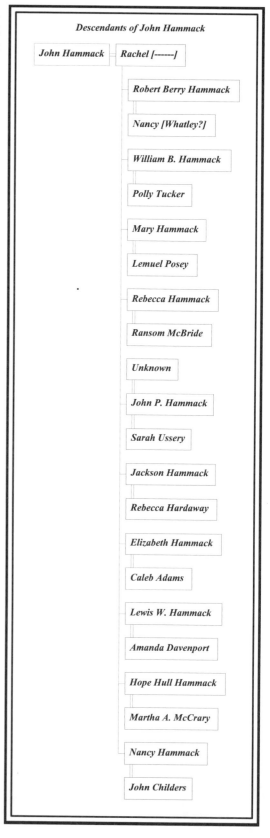

Descendants of John Hammack

John Hammack — Rachel [------]

- Robert Berry Hammack
- Nancy [Whatley?]
- William B. Hammack
- Polly Tucker
- Mary Hammack
- Lemuel Posey
- Rebecca Hammack
- Ransom McBride
- Unknown
- John P. Hammack
- Sarah Ussery
- Jackson Hammack
- Rebecca Hardaway
- Elizabeth Hammack
- Caleb Adams
- Lewis W. Hammack
- Amanda Davenport
- Hope Hull Hammack
- Martha A. McCrary
- Nancy Hammack
- John Childers

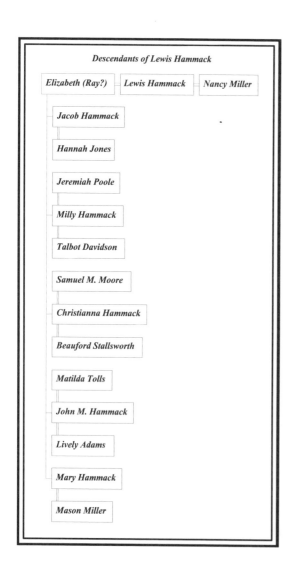

Descendants of Lewis Hammack

Elizabeth (Ray?) — Lewis Hammack — Nancy Miller

- Jacob Hammack
- Hannah Jones
- Jeremiah Poole
- Milly Hammack
- Talbot Davidson
- Samuel M. Moore
- Christianna Hammack
- Beauford Stallsworth
- Matilda Tolls
- John M. Hammack
- Lively Adams
- Mary Hammack
- Mason Miller

Chapter 11:

The Family of William T. Hammack,
son of Robert and Millenor Jackson Hammack,
and husband of Mary Felts Hammack,
of Wilkes, Jones, and Crawford Counties, Georgia

When Robert Hammack wrote his will on 9 July 1799, he left "to fourth and fifth sons John and William 200 acres in the Stewart survey." William was probably born about 1777, a date which would make him about five years younger than his brother John and about seven years older than his brother Edward (who is identified in Robert Hammack's will as "my sixth son".)

The lack of precision in identifying William T. Hammack's birth date is due to the fact that he and another William Hammack lived in the same community and were almost exactly the same age. Contemporaries even confused the two men in court records. Differentiating between William Hammack, son of Robert and Millenor, and his cousin William Hammack, son of John and Mary Ann, in early Wilkes County is difficult. It seems that William, son of John and Mary Ann, was slightly older. He is probably the William Hammack who paid poll tax in Captain Joseph Morrow's District in 1794. This record suggests that he was born about 1773 and had just come of age as he was appearing in the digest for the first time. He paid poll tax again in 1796 in Hiram Howard's District; his name appears immediately below that of Mary Ann Hammack, suggesting that he was then living in her household. In 1797, the names of Mary Ann Hammack, William Hammack, and James Hammack appear in sequence. James may already have been married to Robert Hammack's daughter Lucy, but he -- and his brother William -- seem to have still been living in their mother's household. The 1798 digest for Hiram Howard's District is missing, *but the 1799 digest showed both William Hammacks in the same district*, which was then headed by John Bethune. At that time, William, son of Mary Ann, paid poll tax only, while William, son of Robert and Millenor, paid tax on eighty acres along Rocky Creek. By 1800, Robert Hammack had died, and his property had been distributed among his heirs. In that year, William Hammack paid tax on the eighty-acre tract on Hardin's Creek as well as the 100 acre Stuart Survey bequeathed him by his father.[473] William Hammack, son of Mary Ann, paid poll tax only.

The records become more confusing in 1801, apparently due to a clerical error confusing the two Williams. As noted above, William, son of John and Mary Ann, was taxed as early as 1794 and was thus born by 1773. William, son of Robert and Millenor, was taxed in 1799 and thus born by 1778 or 1777. Yet, in 1801 Robert and Millenor's son William is called "William Hammack, Sr." when he paid tax on the two tracts he owned, while "William Hammack, Jr.," son of John and Mary Ann, still owned no property. The same pattern appeared in 1802, with William Hammack, Jr., still owning no land. The 1803 digest is missing, and by 1804 land purchases and sales had altered the listing for each man. William Hammack, son of Robert and Millenor, in 1803 had sold sixty-eight and one-half of his eighty acres on Rocky Creek. In 1804, he was shown as "William Hammack, Jr.," and taxed with 295 acres on Hardin's Creek joining William Smith and originally granted to Thomas Stuart. The 1805 digest for Captain Young's District showed William Hammack taxed with 100 acres on Harden's Creek joining Hendrick and granted Stuart, this being the tract bequeathed him five years earlier by his father.[474]

---

[473] William had purchased this eighty-acre tract on 8 November 1800 from James Kelly for $50. Both were residents of Wilkes County. The land lay on "Hales' old line" and extended to the creek bank and down the creek to the road. It had been granted to Joseph McCormack on 9 April 1792. (Wilkes Co., GA, Deed Book UU, p. 172.) On 20 May 1803, William Hammack sold 68.5 of these acres on Rocky Creek "joining Hail's old line and the Spring Branch" to Drury Goyne. The land is again identified as part of Joseph McCormack's 9 April 1792 grant. William received $275 for the land, a handsome return on his $50 investment. (Wilkes Co., GA, Deed Book UU, p. 254.)

[474] Thomas Stuart was living in Greene County in 1797 when he sold this land to Robert Hammack. Robert's will refers to the tract as the "Stewart survey". At this time, the spellings Stuart (which was the original form) and Stewart (the modern variant) were used interchangeably.

Descendants of William T. Hammack

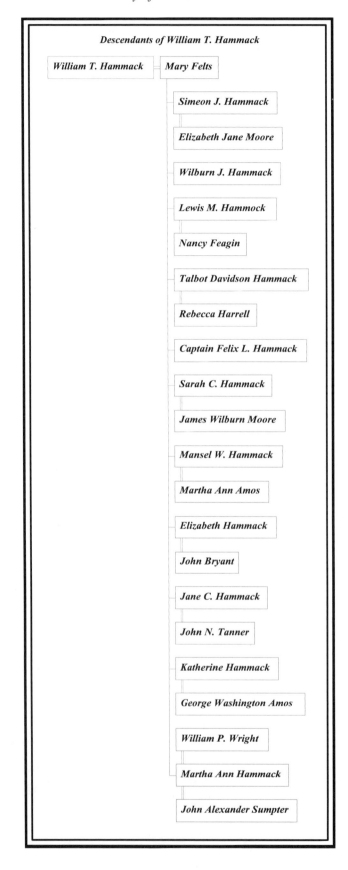

William T. Hammack — Mary Felts

Simeon J. Hammack

Elizabeth Jane Moore

Wilburn J. Hammack

Lewis M. Hammock

Nancy Feagin

Talbot Davidson Hammack

Rebecca Harrell

Captain Felix L. Hammack

Sarah C. Hammack

James Wilburn Moore

Mansel W. Hammack

Martha Ann Amos

Elizabeth Hammack

John Bryant

Jane C. Hammack

John N. Tanner

Katherine Hammack

George Washington Amos

William P. Wright

Martha Ann Hammack

John Alexander Sumpter

Mary Ann's son William can similarly be traced by his landholdings. On 14 August 1802, Mary Ann Hammack had sold a tract along the Ogeechee to her son William Hammack. The land was granted 8 July 1793 to David Bryan as a tract of 243 acres. Mary Ann's deed to William, for which William paid $100, was for "one half made less by fourteen acres" of Bryan's tract. Depending on how one interprets the deed, it would seem that William purchased either 114.5 acres (243 acres minus fourteen acres, divided by half) or 107.5 acres (243 acres halved, minus fourteen acres).[475] At the time of the 1804 digest for Littleberry Little's District, he was shown as "William Hammock, Sr." and taxed with 128 acres on Rocky Creek joining M. Little and granted D. Bryan. Although the acreage does not correspond perfectly with the 1802 deed, this is the tract sold by Mary Ann Hammack to her son William Hammack. He was taxed with the same 128 acres on Rocky Creek -- joining Little and granted Bryan -- in Captain Young's District in 1805. As William Hammack, Sr., he paid tax on this same 128 acres joining Little and granted Bryan in 1806; he paid tax on the same tract in 1809 as William Hammack without any other designation. He was still in Wilkes County as late as 1816, when he was taxed in Solomon Perkins' District; the land at that time was described as 128 acres joining Edward Stephens on Rocky Creek and granted D. Bryan. This man was still in Wilkes County as late as 1820 but moved afterwards to Ware County, Georgia.[476]

William Hammack, son of Robert and Millenor, was also taxed in Wilkes County in 1806. At that time he paid tax on 100 acres on Harden's Creek joining Hammock and granted Stewart as well as twelve acres on Rocky Creek joining Little and granted to an unknown person. By 1809, however, he had apparently left Wilkes County. This William Hammack was taxed in Jones County in 1811, at which time he owned one slave and several tracts of land. These lands included 202.5 acres in Jones County granted Hammack and joining Davis on Wolf Creek; eighty-four acres in Jones County granted Herrington and joining Stokes on Walnut Creek; and 100 acres in Wilkes County granted Stewart and joining Gunn on Walnut Creek. This latter entry conclusively identifies William Hammack of Jones County as the man who heired the Stewart Survey in Wilkes County from his father Robert Hammack. At the time of the 1811 digest, William was also serving as executor of Joshua Williams, on whose behalf he was taxed with two slaves, 101.25 acres in Jones granted Herrington and joining Stokes on Walnut Creek, and 202.5 acres in Wilkinson County granted Williams on Big Sandy Creek.

In 1815, William Hammack was taxed with most of these same properties. He owned two slaves and 202.5 acres in Jones County on Wolf Creek granted Hammack and joining Davis. He still owned the 100 acres of the Stewart survey in Wilkes County, and he had acquired a new forty-five-acre tract in Putnam County granted Felts and joining Wright on Rooty Creek. William was still serving as executor of Joshua Williams and paid tax on three slaves, 101.25 acres in Jones County, and 202.5 acres in Wilkinson County.[477] As late as 1825, William was taxed in his son Felix Hammack's district of Jones County. At that time he owned 449 acres in Jones County including the tract granted to himself on Wolf Creek and two 202.5 acre tracts in Crawford County's land district 1.[478]

Because of the specificity of Robert Hammack's will, it is possible to trace his son William Hammack in records consistently through his ownership of the Stuart survey. Although he was taxed from 1801 and 1802 as William Hammack, Sr., in 1804 and 1806 Mary Ann's son William was taxed as William Hammack, Sr. The purpose of the designations "Jr." and "Sr." was not to differentiate between father and son but, rather, to differentiate between two men with the same name who were living in the same area. The term merely meant that one was older than the other but implied nothing about kinship between the two men. In this instance, it appears that Mary Ann's son was really older and born about 1773 and that Robert and Millenor's son William was slightly younger and born about 1777. Mary Ann's son William appears alone from 1793 to 1796 and then in 1799 both Williams appear. Thereafter, for two years, they

---

[475] Wilkes Co., GA, Deed Book UU, p. 15.

[476] 1820 Wilkes Co., GA, Census, p. 254; 1830 Ware Co., GA, Census, p. 217; Taliaferro Co., GA, DB A, p. 6.

[477] At this time, Allen Felts' name appeared two lines after that of William Hammack.

[478] These tracts were land lot 85 and land lot 112. Surrounding names on the digest were Edward Hammack, Samuel Moore, and Simeon Hammack.

were confused, but after 1802 the situation was corrected. From 1804 onwards, so long as both men remained in the county, Mary Ann's William was referenced as William Hammack, Sr. He was still living in Wilkes County in 1820 when his age was recorded as being more than 45 years, hence indicating a birth date before 1775. His cousin William T. Hammack was enumerated in that year in Jones County; his age is recorded as being less than 45 years, consistent with a birth date of 1777 or 1778.

When William Hammack settled in Jones County, he was already a married man with a large family. Specific details concerning his marriage have not been located. Based on a family reconstitution study, it appears that William probably married about 1797 or 1798. No single record has been located which identifies the maiden name of William's wife, but the preponderance of evidence suggests that she was Mary Felts, daughter of John Felts of Warren County, North Carolina, Wilkes County, Georgia, and Putnam County, Georgia. The 1830 and 1840 Crawford County, Georgia, census enumerations indicate that Mary was born after 1780 but before 1790. She was probably born about 1780 or 1781. Simeon Hammack, born about 1798 along Hardin's Creek in Wilkes County, was thus the oldest son of William and Mary. When Simeon was born, William was perhaps twenty years old, and Mary was probably about eighteen.

The identification of Mary Hammack as Mary Felts, daughter of John Felts, is circumstantial. A summary of the relevant supporting data follows. John Felts came to Wilkes County from Warren County, North Carolina, settling there about 1790. He was taxed as a poll in 1791 and 1792 in Captain Anthony's District. At that time, he was living in central eastern Wilkes County near the future boundary with Lincoln County. He does not appear in Wilkes County tax digests again until 1799, when he was living in Captain John Bethune's District. The 1798 digest for this district is missing, so it may be that John settled there in 1797 and was also taxed there in 1798. In 1799, he paid only poll tax, and his name was recorded as "John Phetts."[479] His adult son "John Felts, Jr." was also assessed in this district, as were Robert, Lewis, Robert (Jr.), William, Lewis, William, James, and Mary Ann Hammack. In Bethune's District in 1800 as "John Fetts" he again paid only poll tax; two households away was William Hammack with 100 acres on Harden's Creek ("the Stuart survey") and eighty acres on Rockey Creek. In 1801, John Fetts appears in Bethune's District paying only the poll tax; his name appears immediately following that of "William Hammack, Sr." who was taxed with the same two tracts, suggesting that Felts may have been a renter living on Hammack's land.[480] Fetts again paid poll tax in the same district in 1802; his name appears three lines from that of William Hammock.

By 1804, Littleberry Little had become captain of this militia district, and Felts was taxed with twelve acres on Rocky Creek joining Tabor and granted an unknown person. William Hammack was taxed in the same district with a combined total of 295 acres, including the Stuart survey. By 1805, Captain Young was the district commander. John Felts was still taxed with twelve acres, land that this time was identified as being adjacent Goyne and granted to an unknown person. William Hammack paid tax on the Stuart survey, and Joseph Felts was assessed with the poll tax. In 1806, John Felts paid poll tax only, while William Hammack was taxed with the 100-acre Stuart survey and twelve acres on Rockey Creek.

Note that on 8 November 1800 William Hammack, son of Robert and Millenor, had purchased an eighty-acre tract on Rockey Creek from James Kelley.[481] Two years later, on 20 May 1803, he sold sixty-eight of these acres to Drury Goyne.[482] In 1804 and 1805, William Hammack paid tax on 100 acres only, while Felts paid tax on twelve acres described as joining lands owned by Tabor and Goyne. Cumulatively, this suggests that Felts had been a neighbor and possibly a renter from William Hammack

---

[479] The name is also spelled "Fitts" in Warren County, North Carolina.

[480] The next name on the list was that of William Evans, who owned 250 acres in Jackson County. Felts' name thus appeared between those of William Hammack and William Evans. Evans may have rented lands in Wilkes County also. The next name was that of Peyton Smith, who owned 200 acres in Wilkes. Thus Fetts must have been renting from Hammack or Smith.

[481] Wilkes Co., GA, Deed Book UU, p. 172.

[482] Wilkes Co., GA, Deed Book UU, p. 254.

and that about 1803 he made some contractual obligation to purchase twelve acres from William Hammack. For some reason, Felts reneged, and the land returned to Hammack in 1806.

John Felts had owned land in Warren County, North Carolina, but he seems not to have prospered after settling in Georgia. Perhaps economic hardship had forced him to sell the North Carolina properties and relocate to Georgia. Felts was of an age to have been Mary Hammack's father, and he lived very near William Hammack at the probable time of Hammack's marriage. Moreover, there is evidence of a continuing association between the two families long after both had left Wilkes County. As residents of the same district, Hammack and Felts had both registered for the 1805 land lottery. Felts had a successful draw and won a lot in what became Putnam County. He moved there and lived there for several years, possibly until his death.[483] On 23 November 1814 in Putnam County, John Felts, Sr., deeded to William Hammack "both of county and state aforesaid" a tract of thirty-two acres granted to Felts on 16 October 1805. The land was located adjacent David Bazemore and Asa Wright.[484] Hammack paid $50 for the land. Shortly afterwards, on 27 December 1814, John Felts, Sr., of Putnam County deeded to John Felts, Jr., and William Felts, both of Putnam County, ninety acres of this same tract.[485] The two men paid $500 for the land. The only other known land transaction involving John Felts took place on 1 February 1812 when, as John Felts, Sr., of Putnam County he conveyed eighty acres of the same grant to Allen Felts of Jones County. Allen Felts paid $350 for the land, described as lying in lot 222 of former Baldwin but then Putnam County.[486] Considering each of these transactions, William Hammack paid less than $2 per acre, while John and William Felts paid nearly $6 per acre. Allen Felts paid more than $4 per acre. Since Baldwin County lots were 202.5 acres, in these three transactions Felts conveyed the entire tract of land.

The deeds from John Felts to John, William, and Allen Felts and William Hammack might have been a form of estate division intended to provide for some of Felts' offspring. From other records, it is clear that Felts had children to whom he did not deed land. Simeon Felts was a proven son, and Mary Wheeler and Charlotty Hammack were also daughters. Felts may have provided for them in another fashion. It may be that William Hammack had originally sold, given, or rented the twelve-acre tract in Wilkes County to his father-in-law; when John Felts drew the land in Baldwin County and decided to move, they then voided the transaction. Later Felts deeded a small portion of his Putnam lands to William Hammack in order to provide for Mary Hammack and Felts' Hammack grandchildren.

Putnam County's 1815 tax digest showed that John Felts, John Felts, Jr., Simeon Felts, and William Felts were living in the same district,[487] while in 1816 Allen Felts and James Felts were living in Jones County. Association between the Hammack and Felts families continued long after the 1815 deed. John Felts, Jr., died about 1846 in Putnam County.[488] William Felts lived until 1862, dying in Jones County.[489] Simeon Felts -- born about 1790 in North Carolina -- died in 1845 in Putnam County; he had married Martha Ray, possibly a daughter (and almost certainly a relative) of Nancy Hammack's husband Jacob Ray.[490] Allen Felts moved with Mary and William Hammack to Crawford County, where he was living as

---

[483] 1805 Georgia Land Lottery Records, Registrants and Fortunate Draws, Georgia Department of Archives and History, Morrow, GA.

[484] Putnam Co., GA, Deed Book D, p. 26.

[485] Putnam Co., GA, Deed Book D, p. 25.

[486] Putnam Co., GA, Deed Book C, pp. 46-47.

[487] 1815 Putnam Co., GA, Tax Digest, Georgia Department of Archives and History, Morrow, GA.

[488] His will, written 4 March 1835, and proved 8 December 1846, is found in Putnam Co., GA, Wills Book B, pp. 212-213. He names brothers William and Simeon Felts and niece Mary Wheeler.

[489] His will names deceased brother Simeon Felts and his wife Martha; Simeon's son William Felts; and William's son John S. Felts. Also mentioned was niece Mary Wheeler Simpson. The will was written 10 March 1861 (Jones Co., GA, Will Book D, p. 138).

[490] Simeon wrote his will in Putnam County on 6 November 1844. He identifies wife Martha Felts and son William A. Felts. He also makes reference to other children. (Putnam Co., GA, Miscellaneous Book Q, p. 102). Born about 1794 in Georgia, Martha Ray Felts died of smallpox about 15 March 1866 in Jones County. It is entirely possible that she was a daughter of Jacob and Nancy Hammack Ray. At least one of her offspring married a proven grandchild of Jacob and Nancy Ray Hammack. Further, William A. Felts, son of Simeon and Martha, seems to have been particularly favored by his aunts and uncles. Charlotte Felts Griffin Hammack named him as her primary heir in 1857, and she had first deeded him land in 1848. William's daughter Martha (1847-1891) married

late as 1860.[491] Charlotty Felts Hammack died about 1858 in Jones County. Her will names nephew William A. Felts and nephew Allen Wheeler and his seven children. As Charlotty Felts, she had married, on 5 January 1808 in Putnam County, William Griffin; when Griffin died, she then married Edward Hammack.[492]

It would thus seem that the Felts and Hammack families remained in close contact from about 1797, when John Felts settled near the Hammack lands in southern Wilkes County, until after 1860, when Allen Felts was living in Hammack's District of Crawford County. If the scenario proposed is the correct one, then William Hammack probably met Felts' daughter Mary sometimes in 1797. They married in late 1797 or early 1798, and their first child, Simeon J. Hammack, was born on or prior to 29 September of that year. Simeon was aged fifty-two at the time of the 1850 census and sixty-two at the time of the 1860 census, which was taken 29 September 1860. It is probably significant that one of John Felts' sons was Simeon J. Felts, born about 1790 in North Carolina.[493]

As noted, William Hammack moved from Wilkes County to Jones County after 1807. At the time of the 1807 Georgia Land Lottery, he was living in Young's District of Wilkes County when he drew land lot 10, land district 9, Baldwin County. At the same time, his mother drew land lot 85, land district 12, Baldwin County, and his brother Lewis drew land lot 296, land district 8, Wilkinson County.[494] On 5 January 1808, William Hammack purchased eighty-four and one-fourth acres of land lot 9, land district 9, from Joshua Williams; he paid $400 for this land, and John McKenzie and Allen Felts witnessed the deed. Hammack apparently had a close relationship with Joshua Williams; he paid tax on Williams' behalf as his agent, and on 15 February 1811 he was named as executor in Joshua Williams's will. The other executor, Samuel Stokes, had been a neighbor from Wilkes County. Stokes had married Tellithy Rogers, whose sister Sarah had married Mansel Womack.[495]

William Hammack lived for nearly two decades in Jones County's ninth district. Tax digests document his residence in the county as well as his changing land ownership. These data are summarized briefly in the table below:

Year	Slaves	Taxpayer	Acreage	Granted	Joins	Creek
1805		William Hammack	100 acres, Wilkes County	Stewart	Hendricks	Hardin's Creek
1811		William Hammack	202.5 acres	Hammack	Davis	Walnut Creek
			84.25 acres	Herrington	Stokes	Walnut Creek
			100 acres, Wilkes County	Stewart	Gunn	Hardin's Creek
		William Hammack, as executor of J. Williams	101.25 acres, Wilkinson County	Williams		B. Land Creek
			101.25 acres, Jones County	Herrington	Stokes	Walnut Creek
1814	2 slaves	William	202.5 acres,	Hammack	Davis	Walnut

Felix Theodore Bryant, a grandson of William T. and Mary Felts Hammack.

[491] On 5 January 1810, Allen Felts witnessed a deed from Joshua Williams to William Hammack in Jones County (Jones Co., GA, Deed Book C, p. 80). On 24 July 1816, he sold 101.25 acres to Lewis Hammack with William Hammack as witness (Jones Co., GA, Deed Book H, p. 401). On 11 January 1821, he deeded 101.25 acres to James Hammack, husband of Lucy Hammack (Jones Co., GA, Deed Book L, p. 265). He was enumerated in Crawford Co., GA, in 1850 and 1860 near the family of William and Mary Felts Hammack.

[492] Jones Co., GA, Will Book D, p. 67.

[493] 1850 Macon Co., GA, Census, p. 124; 1860 Choctaw Co., MS, Census, p. 421.

[494] 1807 Georgia Land Lottery Records, Fortunate Draws, Georgia Department of Archives and History, Morrow, GA.

[495] Jones Co., GA, Deed Book C, p. 80; Jones Co., GA, Will Book A.

		Hammack	Jones			Creek
			100 acres, Wilkes	Stewart	Hendrick	Hardin's Creek
			45 acres, Putnam	Felts	Wright	Rooty Creek
	3 slaves	William Hammack, as executor of J. Williams	101.25 acres, Jones	Herrenton	Cook	Anderson Creek
			202.5 acres, Wilkinson	Williams	Kemp	Big Sandy Creek
1825	19 slaves	William Hammack	449 acres, Jones	Self	Cock	Wolf Creek
			202.5 acres, Crawford, LD 1, LL 85	Self		
			202.5 acres, Crawford, LD 1, LL 112			
	5 slaves	William Hammack, for Milly Hammack				
1826	19 slaves	William Hammack	450 acres, Jones County		Cook	Wolf Creek
			405 acres, Crawford County, LD 2 and LD 1			

In 1817, as Josiah Williams' executor, William Hammack had sold 101.25 acres of land lot 9, land district 9, Jones County, and another 122 acres of land district 3 in Wilkinson County. He had also supervised the sale of three slaves belonging to the Williams estate.[496] In 1821, for $700, he purchased another 101.25 acres in Jones County; this land was located in land district 8, land lot 11.[497] On 4 June 1822, for $1,000, he purchased another 202.5 acres from James McInvale; this land was located in land district 8, land lot 117.[498]

In 1824, William Hammack began acquiring the Crawford County properties to which he would soon relocate. When William had first settled in Jones County, it was Georgia's western frontier. During the two decades he resided there, additional lands in central Georgia had been purchased from the Creek Indians, surveyed, and distributed to Georgia residents through land lotteries in 1820 and 1821. Many Jones County inhabitants were relocating to the newly settled lands southwest of Jones County, and William Hammack was among them. On 3 January 1824, for $200, he purchased land lot 88, land district 1, Crawford County, from Thomas W. Hughes, Jr.[499] Two days later, perhaps already contemplating the move to Crawford, he sold fifty acres of his Jones County lands located in land lot 8, land district 11, to Lewis M. Hammack. Lewis paid $350 for the land.[500] William does not appear in the 1827 tax digest, and he probably moved to Crawford County sometimes after paying tax in 1826. A notice on 1 January 1827

---

[496] Evans, *Jones Co., GA, Newspaper Abstracts*, p. 55.
[497] Jones Co., GA, Deed Book M, p. 222.
[498] Jones Co., GA, Deed Book M, p. 103.
[499] Crawford Co., GA, Deed Book B, p. 421.
[500] Jones Co., GA, Deed Book M, p. 385.

indicated that there was an unclaimed letter for him being held at the post office in Clinton,[501] and on 14 April 1827 his wife Mary was received as a member of Mt. Carmel Primitive Baptist Church in Crawford County, Georgia.[502]

After moving to Crawford County, William Hammack continued to own property in Jones County. He lost a portion of his Jones County lands as a result of a lawsuit in which Joseph Chiles sued him. On the first Tuesday in December 1828, the Jones County Sheriff auctioned off 202.5 acres of land belonging to William Hammack on which Mansel W. Hammack was then living.[503] It would seem that William Hammack was still alive when notice of the sale was given on 27 October, but he was deceased by 15 November 1828 when Mary Hammack, Talbot D. Hammack, and Mansel W. Hammack gave notice to his creditors so that they could begin settling his estate.[504] The public sale of his property in Crawford and Jones Counties took place the following month.[505]

At the time of the 1830 census, Mary Hammack was living in Crawford County with her son Wilborn. Her age was reported as being between forty and fifty years, indicating a birth between 1780 and 1790. Wilborn Hammack's name appeared beside that of his brother Talbot and six lines from that of his brother Simeon; Allen Felts, probably Mary Hammack's brother, appeared on the same page.[506] Mary was still living in Crawford County in 1840, at which time she headed her own household. She was then aged between fifty and sixty years; two young men, probably grandsons, were living with her. Mary's name appeared next to that of her son Simeon and three entries away from that of Allen Felts. In the same community was son Mansel Womack Hammack and son-in-law William P. Wright.

Mary Hammack lived for nearly fifteen years following the death of her husband. An enterprising woman, she seems to have operated a mercantile business in western Crawford County as well as to have supervised her plantation affairs. She drafted her will on 5 March 1842 and died prior to its probate on 3 October 1842.[507] She indicated that all property was to be sold by her executor Talbot D. Hammack and that her son Simeon was to be paid $200 more than her other children because he "took care of her during her widowhood." Mary's other children were to have equal shares of her estate, which consisted primarily of her husband's lands, seven slaves, household furniture, and plantation tools and implements. Two sons -- Wilborn and Felix -- had predeceased Mary, and these names would become prominent given names among her descendants for many generations. Living children mentioned in Mary's will were Simeon Hammack, Lewis Hammack, Talbot Davidson Hammack, Mansel Womack Hammack, Sarah Hammack Moore (wife of James Moore), Betsy Hammack Bryant (wife of John Bryant), Jane Hammack Tanner (widow of John Tanner), Catherine Hammack Amos (wife of George Washington Amos), and Martha Hammack Wright (widow of William P. Wright). Mary appointed her son Talbot D. Hammack to serve as trustees for his sisters Sarah Moore, Betsy Bryant, Jane Tanner, and Martha Wright in order to keep their shares free from the control of their present husband or future husbands.[508]

Following Mary Hammack's death, in 1845 her administrators sold land lot 2, land district 9, to Allen Felts for $1020. The annual returns also mention ownership of lot 24 in the same district. Mary's entire personal estate was appraised on 27 November 1843 by Nathan Mobley, George Moore, James Harris, Washington Cleveland, and Allen G. Simmons at $3,153.62. Not included was a forty-acre lot in Cherokee County drawn in the 1832 land lottery. Of the total value, Mary's slaves were appraised at $2,525. Like many wealthy planters, Mary had apparently frequently loaned money to close relatives and

---

[501] T. Evans, *Jones Co., GA, Newspaper Abstracts, 1810-1888* (2 vols., Savannah, GA, 2001), 1: 218.

[502] Mt. Carmel Baptist Church Records, Georgia Department of Archives and History, Morrow, GA

[503] *Georgia Journal*, Issue of 27 Oct., 1828.

[504] Evans, *Jones Co., GA, Newspaper Abstracts*, 1: 259.

[505] Evans, *Jones Co., GA, Newspaper Abstracts*, 1: 258.

[506] 1830 Crawford Co., GA, Census, p. 410; 1840 Crawford Co., GA, Census, p. 371.

[507] Minutes of Mt. Carmel Primitive Baptist Church dated 15 September 1843 lists "Polla Hammack" among the three members who had died within the past year; at her death, Mary was apparently the last remaining of the original members at the church's founding.

[508] Crawford Co., GA, Will Book A, p. 48.

friends; among the notes owed her estate were amounts borrowed by Greenberry Felts, James E. Hammack, Mansel Hammack, William T. H. Hammack, Simeon Hammack, and Daniel D. Taylor (husband of Mary's granddaughter Sarah Hammack Taylor).[509] When Mary's property was sold at a public sale on 1 January 1844, most of the purchasers were her sons and sons-in-law. Greenberry Felts was probably a nephew; Seaborn Jolly, Lucy Mobley, Nathan Mobley, Anderson Grant, John Martin, and John Whittington were neighbors, but several of them were also related through marriages of Mary's children and grandchildren to members of their families.[510]

At the 1844 sale, Mary's property sold for significantly more than its appraised value. Her son Simeon purchased slaves Sally, George, Betty, and a child named Monroe for $2,228. Son-in-law James Moore purchased Peter for $751. Son Lewis M. Hammack purchased Ann Elisa for $450, and son-in-law John Bryant purchased Becca for $481.[511]

Following Mary's death, family relations between Simeon Hammack and his siblings may have soured. Simeon had purchased four slaves from his mother's estate, but he later attempted to claim that he did not owe the money because of monies he had spent on his mother's behalf during her final years. A lengthy lawsuit followed, the results of which are unclear. Talbot D. Hammack employed Poe, Nesbett, Hall, and Wimberly as attorneys to represent the estate's claim. A receipt dated 2 May 1847 shows a payment to the attorneys for $200, suggesting that the estate won its claim and that Simeon was forced to pay the $2,228 he owed for the slaves.[512]

Mary and William Hammack were buried in a family cemetery on their own property. The cemetery is today located about three miles east of the boundary between Upson and Crawford Counties, near US Highway 80. Mt. Carmel Primitive Baptist Church, where members of the Hammack, Bentley, Moore, and Carter families worshiped, is northeast of the Hammack Cemetery on State Route 69, just south of the boundary between Crawford, Upson, and Monroe Counties. The Bentley Cemetery, where William Hammack's cousin John Bentley's family are buried, is located in the extreme northwestern corner of Crawford County, near the boundary with Upson County.[513]

William T. and Mary Felts Hammack were the parents of eleven known children, two of whom lived to adulthood but predeceased their mother Mary. These children will be discussed briefly below. Simeon Hammack, the eldest son, and his family will be the subject of a later chapter.

A. Wilborn J. Hammack of Jones and Crawford Counties, Georgia.

Wilborn J. Hammack was the second-born of William and Mary Hammack's offspring; he was probably born in 1800 and died unmarried and childless prior to 14 January 1834, when his estate was appraised in Crawford County.[514]

At the time of the 1830 Crawford County census, Wilborn headed a household in Crawford County that consisted of himself, his brother Felix, their mother Mary, and Mary's young daughters Jane, Katherine, and Martha.[515]

Wilborn himself had already begun to acquire a modest estate; he owned a portion of land lot 112, land district 1, which he sold to his brother Mansel Hammack in 1830.[516] He was engaged in 1832 in a

---

[509] Crawford Co., GA, Returns Book D, p. 182.

[510] Crawford Co., GA, Returns Book D, pp. 182, 313; Crawford Co., GA, Returns Book E, pp. 44, 124.

[511] *Ibid.*

[512] Hammack v. Hammack, 1845, Crawford Co., GA, Loose Court Papers, Georgia Department of Archives and History, Morrow, GA.

[513] Arthur Curtis Carter, *Carter and Kinsmen: Folmar - Rodgers - Sanders - Bryan* (1990). Samuel Bentley and several members of the Curtis and Carter families lived just south of the Bentley Cemetery in the area between there and the Hammack Cemetery, northeast of US 80 and SR 69.

[514] Crawford Co., GA, Inferior Court Minutes, County and Court Purposes, 1830-1846, p. 12.

[515] 1830 Crawford Co., GA, Census, p. 410.

[516] *Inferior Court Records, County and Court Purposes, 1830-1846*, p. 12.

business transaction with Alison M. Greathouse; Greathouse owed Hammack $50, and Greathouse was ordered to pay.[517] When Wilborn died in 1834, he owned one slave, Aaron, who sold to Wilborn's brother Simeon for $813. Wilborn also was owed money by his brothers Simeon and Mansel, and he owned town lots 48 and 74 in Knoxville.[518]

B. Lewis M. Hammack of Jones and Sumter Counties, Georgia.

Born about 1801, Lewis M. Hammack was probably the third child of William and Mary Hammack. He married Nancy Feagin on 3 August 1820 in Jones County. They settled first in Crawford County and then in Sumter County, where Lewis died 2 September 1867 and where Nancy died about 1870.

Lewis Hammock was head of household in Jones County in 1820, 1830, and 1840. By 1850, he had settled in Sumter County. At the time of the 1860 census, Lewis's widow Nancy Feagin Hammack was head of a household in Americus, Sumter County. Her property at that time was valued at $1,800.[519]

Lewis and Nancy Feagin Hammack reared a large family. Their children and grandchildren remained in Jones and Sumter Counties, Georgia.

C. Talbot Davidson Hammack of Jones and Crawford Counties, Georgia.

Talbot Davidson Hammack was born 2 October 1802, probably at his parents' home along Hardins' Creek in southern Wilkes County. He lived in Wilkes throughout his early boyhood but was reared in Jones County. About 1828, Talbot married Rebecca Harrell, daughter of Hardy and Susan Harrell.

At the time of the 1820 land lottery, Talbot D. Hammack of Jones County drew land lot 71, land district 1, Houston County. This land lay in what became Crawford County and was probably one of the reasons Talbot's father William eventually relocated.[520] Talbot and Rebecca Harrell Hammack joined Mt. Carmel Church in Crawford County on 16 August 1829; they remained members for the rest of their lives. Talbot seems to have been consistently of a more religious temperament than his siblings. In 1835 he was named to the church building committee and in 1836 was ordained a deacon. By 1841, he had also become church clerk.[521]

Talbot's primary economic activity seems to have been farming, although he may have engaged in trade as well. He was enumerated in Crawford County in every federal census from 1830 until 1870. At the time of the 1830 enumeration, he had only one child, a daughter who had been born in 1829. By 1850, he had ten children living at home. Marriage shrunk Talbot's family to seven children at home in 1860 and three in 1870.[522]

Financially, Talbot seems to have prospered and, unlike many of his generation, to have survived the Civil War with much of his wealth in tact. At the time of the 1850 census, he was enumerated as a planter with an estate valued at $5,000. At that time, he owned sixteen slaves. By 1860, his real estate was valued at $5,700 and his personal property -- largely slaves -- at $19,500. The 1870 census listed the total value of his real and personal property as $17,000, an impressive sum given that the emancipation of slaves and the physical destruction caused by Civil War had bankrupted many former planters. Talbot was then sixty-eight years old and a resident of Hickory Grove Precinct of eastern Crawford County. Only a year after the census enumeration, on 27 December 1871, Talbot wrote his will. To five daughters he left $400

---

[517] *Inferior Court Records, County and Court Purposes, 1830-1846* , p. 12.

[518] Crawford Co., GA, Annual Returns, Book A.

[519] 1830 Jones Co., GA, Census, p. 428; 1840 Jones Co., GA, Census, p. 135; 1850 Sumter Co., GA, Census, p. 198; 1870 Sumter Co., GA, Census, p. 282.

[520] 1820 Georgia Land Lottery Records, Fortunate Draws, Georgia Department of Archives and History, Morrow, GA.

[521] Mt. Carmel Baptist Church Records, Georgia Department of Archives and History, Morrow, GA.

[522] 1830 Crawford Co., GA, Census, p. 410; 1840 Crawford Co., GA, Census, p. 372; 1850 Crawford Co., GA, Census, p. 399; 1860 Crawford Co., GA, Census, p. 941; 1870 Crawford Co., GA, Census, p. 452.

each in addition to a bed, bedstead, and additional furniture. He also left each daughter two cows and calves and 400 pounds of pork or its equivalent in cash. To Talbot's older daughters, who had married earlier, he left smaller bequests: $200 to Malinda Parham and $150 to Sarah Wright. Wife Rebecca received land lot 70 (located on the north side of the road to Macon), land lot 71 (which Talbot had drawn fifty-two years earlier) and part of land lot 88, totaling in combination 430 acres. Rebecca also received a substantial amount of livestock and tools and utensils necessary to operate Talbot's substantial farm: five horses, six cows and calves, hogs, farming utensils, a cotton gin and gin belts, a two-horse wagon, a buggy and harness, blacksmiths and carpenters tools, and enough corn and grain to support her for at least a year. Talbot included additional bequests in cash and livestock to two young granddaughters and his daughter Rebecca before stipulating that his remaining real estate -- including part of land lot 87 and an interest in 360 acres in Alabama which he owned jointly with Dr. W. P. Wright -- be sold and the profits divided among his nine living daughters. Talbot's son-in-law (and nephew) Dr. W. P. Wright was named to execute the will, which was proved at May Court, 1873.[523]

Talbot D. Hammack passed away on 8 March 1873 and was buried near his parents in the Hammack Cemetery; his wife Rebecca survived him for more than a decade, dying 24 May 1886. Her will -- written seven days before her death -- ordered that her remaining property be sold and divided between her two unmarried daughters.[524] The 1880 census had shown Rebecca as a head of household; living with her were four unmarried daughters, a granddaughter, and a black servant.

Talbot and Rebecca Harrell Hammack were the parents of eleven children; their two sons both died before them. William Wilborn Hammack died 8 October 1857 at the age of twenty-six; he left a young widow and two daughters. Talbot Hammack, Jr., a soldier in Company C, 6th Regiment, Georgia Volunteers, from neighboring Houston County, died on 16 May 1864 at Drury's Bluff, Virginia. Of the daughters of Talbot and Rebecca Harrell Hammack, two never married. The remaining daughters married into the Fowler, Parham, Wright, Roberts, and Graddick families; they lived the remainder of their lives in Crawford, Macon, and Bibb Counties of central Georgia.

D. Sarah Hammack and James Wilborn Moore of Wilkes and Taliaferro Counties, Georgia.

The oldest daughter of William and Mary Hammack, Sarah was born in 1804 in Wilkes County; she married James Wilborn Moore, a widower, on 4 December 1823 in Jones County. Sarah seems to have lived all of her married life in Taliaferro County, although she and her children had close ties to Jones County.

Sarah's marriage to James Wilborn Moore deserves comment. James Wilborn Moore (1787 - 1856) was a native of Lunenburg County, Virginia, and settled in Wilkes County about 1804 with his parents Ussery Moore and Martha Bishop. It was in Wilkes County that James married Jane Irwin, his first wife. When she died about 1822, he traveled to Jones County to marry Sarah Hammack. The complicated connections that existed between the Hammack, Moore, and Ray families probably explain the marriage. James Moore's brothers Bishop Moore, John Moore, and Robert Moore had all married daughters of Sanders and Christiana Ray; Jacob Ray, brother of these three Ray sisters, married Nancy Hammack, sister of William T. Hammack, and their daughter Martha Ray married Matthew Moore, another brother of Bishop, John, Robert, and James Wilborn. All of these marriages took place prior to 1820, when Simeon Hammack -- son of William Hammack and Mary Felts -- married Elizabeth Jane Moore. Simeon, although residing in Jones County, had returned to Wilkes County to marry Elizabeth Moore. Elizabeth may have been the youngest child of Ussery and Martha Bishop Moore, but she was probably the daughter of their older son Robert and the step-daughter of his wife Martha Ray Moncrief Moore. When James Moore's wife Jane Irwin Moore died, then, his Moore, Ray, and Hammack relatives probably

[523] Crawford Co., GA, Will Book B, p. 66.
[524] Crawford Co., GA, Will Book B, p. 174.

suggested that he court young Sarah Hammack, who was just shy of her twentieth birthday. Their marriage lasted for thirty-three years and ended only with James's death in 1856; Sarah remained a widow for twenty years more, dying in Taliaferro County in 1878, only a few miles from the place of her birth.[525]

Sarah's husband James Moore was a prosperous landowner and cotton planter; his property in 1850 was valued at $2,500, but when he died in 1857 the appraisal of his personal wealth was $14,978.91.[526]

Sarah Hammack and James Moore were the parents of seven sons. Of these, Felix and Richard became prominent attornies. Captain James W. Moore (1827-1907) operated stage coach lines in Taliaferro and Hancock Counties and served as tax collector and sheriff for Hancock County. He was elected to three terms in the Georgia Legislature and, after the Civil War, he cultivated a 1,500 acre plantation in Hancock County, Georgia.[527] James W. Moore was the father of Judge Richard Welborn Moore, Mayor of Sparta and Judge of the Sparta City Court in Hancock County. George W. Moore died in battle near Richmond, Virginia, during the Civil War. Like his brother James, Richard H. Moore also lived at Culverton in Hancock County, where he was postmaster, express agent, and owned a general store. A prosperous peach planter, Moore was also a founder of Hancock Canning Corporation. He was also the father of Dr. Terrell Moore, the well-known historian educated at Johns Hopkins University and a faculty member at Columbia University.[528] Owen Moore (1839-1910) married his first cousin Mary Bryant (1839-1906), daughter of John and Elizabeth Hammack Bryant, in Jones County in 1859; they returned to Taliaferro County, where Owen was a prosperous farmer and merchant, and lived there the remainder of their lives.

E. Mansel Womack Hammack of Jones and Crawford Counties, Georgia.

Mansel Womack Hammack was born about 1805 along Hardin's Creek in southern Wilkes County; he was given the unusual name of Mansel Womack, a friend and associate who lived across the Ogeechee River in Hancock County.

Mansel lived from about 1832 until his death around 1865 in Crawford County, Georgia. Prior to moving to Crawford, he settled in Hancock County about the time of his marriage and lived there for several years. At the time of the 1827 land lottery, when Mansel drew lots of land in Lee County, he was a resident of Jones County. He seems to have still been living there in 1828 when his grandmother Millenor Hammack deeded him a slave girl on 30 December 1828, but by 1830 he had settled in Hancock County. It was probably his marriage to Martha Ann Amos of Hancock County on 7 November 1826 that was the deciding factor in his decision to relocate.[529]

As in the case of Mansel's other siblings, family connections may have influenced Mansel's choice of mate. Martha Ann Amos Hammack was his second cousin, her grandmother Mildred Hammack Bentley having been Mansel's great-aunt. In addition, Martha's uncle John H. Bentley had married Martha Moore -- probably a sister of Elizabeth Jane Hammack Moore -- and they had relocated from Wilkes County to Crawford County, where they were neighbors of William and Mary Felts Hammack. A year later, in 1831, this web of kinship would be strengthened again when Mansel's sister Katherine married Martha Ann's brother George Washington Amos. Such alliances among families across generations were common, providing a network of solidarity and social support against the hardships of the time.

---

[525] E. W. Smith, *The History of Hancock Co., GA* (Sparta, GA, 1974), 2: 114; Southern Historical Association, *Memoirs of Georgia* (2 vols., Atlanta, GA, 1895), 2: 1040-1041.

[526] Taliaferro Co., GA, Annual Returns, p. 150.

[527] John Rozier, *The Houses of Hancock, 1785-1865* (Decatur, GA, 1996); *Memoirs of Georgia*, 1: 1040.

[528] Forrest Shivers, *The Land Between: A History of Hancock County, Georgia, to 1940* (Spartanburg, SC, 1990), p. 203.

[529] Jones Co., GA, Deed Book O, p. 158; 1827 Georgia Land Lottery Records, Fortunate Draws, Georgia Department of Archives and History, Morrow, GA; 1830 Hancock Co., GA, Census, p. 155.

On 14 September 1832, Mansel and Martha Ann Hammack joined Mt. Carmel Church in Crawford County. Mansel remained a member until he requested his letter in 1848, although Martha remained in fellowship after this date.[530]

Mansel seems not to have prospered to the degree that his brother Talbot did, but he also became a successful farmer. Unlike Talbot, the Civil War seems to have hit Mansel's family hard financially. At the time of the 1850 census, Mansel owned property valued at $1,000.[531] By 1860, his total wealth was valued at $8,200; it divided almost equally between land and personal property, suggesting that he owned several slaves. By 1870, when Mansel was already deceased, Martha's wealth was valued at only $610; of that amount, her real estate was valued at $400.[532]

In one curious record, Mansel Hammack on 29 October 1850 served as trustee in a deed from his brother Simeon Hammack, who was then living in Macon County, Georgia. Simeon executed the deed in order to provide for his cousin Milly Hammack Davidson, who was a daughter of Lewis Hammack of Jones County. Simeon deeded fifty acres of land lot 46, land district 2, Crawford County to Mansel on behalf of Milly Davidson; Milly herself had paid Simeon Hammack $250 and was purchasing the land to provide for her grandchildren Lewis Sheppard Smallwood, Jacob W. Smallwood, and Milly Smallwood Hammack. The deed included a condition that if William H. Smallwood were to pay the sum of $250, then Mansel W. Hammack was to execute a deed to him conveying the property in exchange for his taking care of Milly Davidson in her final years. A son of Lewis M. and Nancy Feagin Hammack, William Henry Clifton Hammack had on 15 May 1845 married Milly Smallwood, another grandchild of Milly Hammack Poole Davidson.[533] The deed is significant for several reasons. Apart from representing the importance of kinship within the tangled Hammack cousinhood, it suggests that Mansel W. Hammack was a person that both his brother Simeon and his cousin Milly could trust to satisfy the terms of the obligation without attempting to defraud Simeon, Milly, or any of Milly's descendants. Further evidence of this tendency to support kin can be found in Mansel's relationship with his elderly cousin Catherine Hammack Simmons; a middle-aged spinster when she married a widower named William Simmons, Catherine had no children of her own. Although she was Mansel's grandfather's cousin, Catherine's younger brother James Hammack had married Mansel's aunt Lucy Hammack. One of these relationships probably explains how Mansel knew Catherine Simmons, who would have been a near neighbor when he was growing up in Jones County. But in addition to the family tie, Mansel's good nature may explain why he took Catherine in when there were relatives with a closer biological connection who did not. Catherine came to live with Mansel in the late 1840s and remained there until she died about 1849, when she was in her middle nineties.[534]

Mansel Womack Hammack died at some point between 1860 and 1870. Martha's final years were probably sad ones; in 1876 she was declared a ward of the court due to a mental impairment, perhaps senility. Her son James became her guardian; just when Martha died is unclear, but it may have been before 1877, when George White, administrator of Mansel W. Hammack, sold 110 acres in land lots 147 and 180 of district 1 belonging to the estate.[535]

Mansel and Martha Ann Amos Hammack were the parents of eight (or possibly nine) children. Son Felix Wilborn Hammack died about 1862 while serving in the Confederate Army. Son William Henry Hammack married his cousin Catherine Hammack, also of Crawford County. Aurelius, James Mansel, and John Hammack remained in Crawford and Houston Counties, as did sister Caroline Hammack

---

[530] Mount Carmel Baptist Church Records, Georgia Department of Archives and History, Morrow, GA.

[531] In 1850, Mansel owned three slaves, a male aged 26 and two females aged 23 and 24.

[532] 1850 Crawford Co., GA, Census, p. 299; 1860 Crawford Co., GA, Census, p. 935; 1870 Crawford Co., GA, Census, p. 443.

[533] Crawford Co., GA, Deed Book U, p. 103.

[534] Crawford Co., GA, Inferior Court Minutes, 1838-49, pp. 95, 102, 104, 145; Crawford Co., GA, Returns Book F, pp. 291, 295; Crawford Co., GA, Returns Book I, p. 53.

[535] Crawford Co., GA, Deed Book O, p. 319. In 1875, Mansel's administrator had also sold or mortgaged a larger tract, 278 acres, located in lots 147, 179, and 180, to Aurelius H. Hammack. See Crawford Co., GA, Deed Book 27, p. 249.

Hamrick and her husband William. Nothing more is known of Martha, Mary, and Robert Hammack; they may all have died young.

F. Elizabeth Hammack and John Bryant of Jones County, Georgia.

Born 4 May 1809, Elizabeth was the second daughter of William and Mary Felts Hammack; she married John Bryant on 2 April 1829 in Crawford County, but the couple returned to Jones County, where they spent the remainder of their lives.

John Bryant was at least a dozen years older than Elizabeth Hammack; no evidence has been found that he had been married previously, although it is possible that he had. There is also the possibility that he may have been a relative of James Bryant who had married Raney Hammack in Clarke County about 1807.

On 28 November 1834, Jane C. Hammack of Crawford County deeded 85 acres of land to her brother-in-law John Bryant of Jones County; the land was located in land lot 10, land district 9, and Lewis and Simeon Hammack witnessed the deed. Exactly how Jane acquired the land, or why she conveyed it to John Bryant, are unclear. It was rare at that time for a single woman to control or convey property in her own right, and the land may have been deeded to Jane by another relative.[536]

John Bryant seems to have been deceased by 11 December 1854, when his administrator William A. Lane deeded to Robert V. Hardeman 730 acres in land district 8. The properties joined lands owned by Charlotte Felts Hammack, Joseph Stallsworth (whose son Beauford married Christiana Hammack), Mary Sumner (a daughter of Bishop Moore and Mary Ray Moore), and Allen Wheeler (a grandson of John Felts, Sr.).[537] Bryant apparently operated a prosperous farm in Jones County; at the time of the 1850 census, he owned 14 slaves, including six males and eight females ranging in age from infancy to fifty years.[538]

The profits from the sale of the land -- $4,326, or $5.93 per acre -- were used to settle the accounts of the estate and to provide for John's children, most of whom were still minors. At the time of the 1860 census, Elizabeth Hammack Bryant owned additional real estate which was valued at $2,200 and personal property valued at $8,500.[539] No record of Elizabeth Hammack Bryant has been found after 1870. At that time, she was enumerated in the Jones County, Georgia, census. Like her brother Talbot, she seems to have weathered the 1860s in good circumstances. Her property was then worth $7,900, including personal property valued at $1,900.[540]

Elizabeth and John Bryant had ten known children. William died of typhoid fever while serving as a Confederate soldier in Danville, Virginia, in 1862, and James died in 1865 as a Confederate soldier in Richmond, Virginia. Martha married but apparently predeceased her mother, who reared her young children. Cornelius was living in Jones County as late as 1873. Mary (1839-1906) married her first cousin Owen Moore and moved to Taliaferro County. Felix Theodore Bryant survived the Civil War despite being wounded at Richmond, Virginia, in 1862; he married his distant cousin Martha Elizabeth Felts (1847-1891) and remained in Jones County. Nothing more is known of Louisiana and Josephine Bryant, but their sister Malissa married James W. Slocumb and remained in Jones County.

Elizabeth Hammack Bryant died on 11 September 1871; she was buried in the Bryant-Slocumb Cemetery in Jones County near her husband John and Malissa Bryant Slocumb and her family.

G. Jane Hammack and John Tanner of Jones County, Georgia.

---

[536] Jones Co., GA, Deed Book P, p. 418.
[537] Jones Co., GA, Deed Book S, p. 72.
[538] 1850 Jones Co., GA, Census, p. 198A.
[539] 1860 Jones Co., GA, Census, p. 560.
[540] 1870 Jones Co., GA, Census, p. 225.

Born about 1813 in Jones County, Georgia, Jane C. Hammack married John Tanner on 29 January 1837 in Crawford County; he was deceased by 17 November 1840, and Jane remained a lifelong widow, dying in 1889.

Soon after reaching adulthood, probably about the time of her twenty-first birthday, Jane deeded eighty-five acres in Jones County to her brother-in-law John Bryant.[541] Two years later, she married John Tanner. She was a widow on 17 November 1840 when her brothers Talbot and Mansel were named as administrators on the estate of John N. Tanner, deceased.[542]

Jane was enumerated in Crawford County as head of household in 1850 and 1860; although apparently a resident there until her death, she has not been found in the census reports of 1870 and 1880. In 1850, her property was valued at $1,000[543], and in 1860 at $3,600, including $2,000 in personal estate.[544] Curiously, in both enumerations Anderson Grant, who was born about 1800, was a resident in Jane's household; there is no known family connection between the Hammacks and Grants, but Anderson Grant also performed work for William and Mary Felts Hammack and is mentioned in their estate returns.

Jane and John Tanner had only two children, both daughters. Mary married Dr. George M. Bazemore on 17 November 1859 in Crawford County; she apparently died soon thereafter, for in 1861 Dr. Bazemore remarried Rhoda Simmons, the daughter of Allen Gassaway Simmons and step-granddaughter of Catherine Hammack Simmons.[545] Sarah Tanner, who was born about 1840, was enumerated in Jane's household in 1850 but not in 1860. If she married, no record of it has been found.

Jane C. Hammack Tanner joined Mt. Carmel Church in Crawford County on 8 September 1876; a membership roster dated 15 September 1889 includes the notation "died 1889" beside her name. She was probably buried in the Hammack Cemetery in Crawford County.[546]

H. Katherine Hammack and George Washington Amos of Jones and Talbot Counties, Georgia, and Coffee and Pike Counties, Alabama.

Katherine Hammack was born 8 May 1817 in Jones County, Georgia. On 24 August 1831, at the age of fourteen, she married her second cousin George W. Amos in Hancock County. Born 9 February 1812 in Hancock County, George Amos was a son of George and Anny Bentley Amos of Lunenburg County, Virginia, and Hancock County, Georgia, and a grandson of Daniel and Mildred Hammack Bentley. The Amoses lived in Georgia until 1852, when they moved to Pike County, Alabama. Both are buried at Union Springs Primitive Baptist Church in Pike County, although Katherine died in adjoining Coffee County on 8 October 1886 and George in the same location on 1 April 1889.[547]

Katherine and George Amos seem never to have moved to Crawford County. Instead, they followed a different migration route across central Georgia into eastern Alabama. They moved first to Talbot County, where Katherine's uncle John Hammack and aunt Catherine Hammack Gunn Poole, were then living. At the time of the 1850 census, George, Katherine, and their eight children were living in Talbot County. They were enumerated in Pike County, Alabama, in 1860, 1870, and 1880.[548]

---

[541] Jones Co., GA, Deed Book P, p. 418.

[542] Crawford Co., GA, Annual Returns, Book C.

[543] The 1850 slave schedule showed that Jane owned three slaves, a male and female aged fifty-two and fifty-one, and a twelve year old female. See 1850 Crawford Co., GA, Census, p. 489.

[544] 1860 Crawford Co., GA, Census, p. 930.

[545] Dr. George Monroe Bazemore (1834-1910) was educated at New York University and The University of Nashville. He married first, in 1857, Rachel Johnson (1840-1859), who is buried in the Hammack Cemetery. He married second, ten months after his wife's death on 9 January 1859, Mary Tanner. He married third, on 17 December 1861, Rhoda Simmons. They moved to Cleveland, Tennessee.

[546] Mount Carmel Baptist Church Records, Georgia Department of Archives and History, Morrow, GA.

[547] For more information on this family, see the Amos Family File and the George Amos Family Bible Record, Fort Smith Public Library, Fort Smith, AR.

[548] 1850 Talbot Co., GA, Census, p. 68; 1860 Pike Co., AL, Census, p. 297; 1870 Pike Co., AL, Census, p. 378; 1880 Pike Co., AL, Census, p. 154.

Katherine and George Amos were the parents of fourteen children, many of whose descendants remain in Pike and Coffee Counties, Alabama. Their sons William Wilborn and Beverly Amos both died in 1863 as Confederate soldiers. Daughter Susan died as an infant in 1841. Nothing more is known of Elizabeth, Mary, and Jane, who may all have died young. Mary Ann married Thomas Bryant Allen, Sarah married John Hetson, and Becky married Buchanan Wise. Henry died in Coffee County in 1889, leaving a large family. William Greenbury died in Coffee County, Alabama, in 1916, as did his sister Martha Amos Paul in 1916. John Zachariah died in Pike County in 1915, and Isaac LaFayette in Coffee in 1917. George Washington Amos (1845 - 1916) left Pike County about 1872 and settled in Sebastian County, Arkansas, a popular destination for migrants from eastern Alabama in the 1870s. He reared a large family there, and his descendants today live in and around Fort Smith, Arkansas.[549]

I. Martha Ann Hammack and husbands William P. Wright and John Sumpter of Jones and Crawford Counties, Georgia.

The youngest child of William and Mary Felts Hammack, Martha Ann Hammack was born about 1822 in Jones County. She was only about four years old when her family made the move to newly settled Crawford County and only a few months older when her father died.

Martha Ann was reared by her mother Mary Felts Hammack, probably with a considerable amount of assistance from her elder brothers Wilborn, Simeon, Felix, Talbot, and Mansel, all of whom lived in the same community and two of whom were still living at home when their father died.

When she was only about fourteen, Martha married William P. Wright on 24 November 1836. Wright was deceased by 4 January 1842, and Martha had remarried by 1844 when she is identified in legal records as Martha Sumpter, wife of John A. Sumpter.[550]

Martha's first husband William P. Wright belonged to a prosperous local family. When he died in 1842, his father Robert M. Wright and his brother-in-law Simeon Hammack administered his estate. Less than a month after they entered administration on 4 January 1842, William's father Robert M. Wright wrote his will. He identifies his deceased son William and William's three orphaned children, Mary Ann, Adaline Jane Missouri, and William Robert Simeon Wright. To them Robert Wright left 101.25 acres of land lot 53, land district 1, Crawford County. At the death of Robert's widow Nancy, there was to be a second division of personal property in which William's three orphans would share with their uncles Washington Bazemore and Edmond Walpole.[551] Returns on the estate of William P. Wright revealed that he also owned local tracts in the neighborhood, including twenty-five acres of land lot 69, land district 1, and at least one slave, whose name was Charity.[552] Simeon Hammack served as administrator of the estate until 1851, when he resigned because of a conflict with Martha's new husband John A. Sumpter; Simeon, who as administrator was legally responsible for the management of the estate, claimed that he feared John Sumpter was mismanaging the property and wished to escape liability.[553] Sumpter, on the other hand, claimed that Simeon Hammack had not properly accounted for all of the monies coming in and out of the estate; Hammack was ordered to pay the estate $170 that he had failed to credit in interest. At the same time, Sumpter became guardian for his three stepchildren who had been under the legal guardianship of Simeon Hammack until then.[554]

Despite the prior guardianship, it does not seem that William P. Wright's orphans had ever resided with Simeon Hammack, however. Simeon left Crawford County in the late 1840s and settled in nearby Macon County. At the time of the 1850 census, more than a year before Sumpter received legal

[549] George W. Amos Family File, Vertical Files, Fort Smith Public Library, Fort Smith, AR.
[550] Crawford Co., GA, Will Book A, p. 40.
[551] Crawford Co., GA, Will Book A, p. 40.
[552] Crawford Co., GA, Deed Book E, p. 696.
[553] Crawford Co., GA, Annual Returns Book F, and *Miscellaneous Estate Records of Crawford Co., GA.*
[554] Ibid.

guardianship of his stepchildren, they were enumerated in his household. At that time, Sumpter was thirty-five years old and working as a millwright in Crawford County. In addition to himself and wife Martha, his household included the three Wright children and two children born since his marriage to Martha, a daughter named Sarah and a son named John. The Sumpters also owned five slaves -- an adult couple and three children aged under five years.[555]

John and Martha Hammack Wright Sumpter have not been traced after 1851. They presumably remained in Georgia, however, for one of Martha's children, Dr. William P. R. S. Wright, left a clear documentary trail.[556] Wright married his first cousin Sally Hammack and was head of household in Crawford County in 1870 and in Pike County in 1880. At the time of the 1880 census, the Wrights had four children aged between thirteen years and one year old.[557]

---

[555] 1850 Crawford Co., GA, Census, p. 396.

[556] Wright apparently had several names. Annual Returns Book F, Crawford Co., GA, 7 January 1850, identifies him as "W. M. P. R. Wright." His grandfather's will identifies him as "William Robert Simeon Wright." His full name may have been William M. P. Robert Simeon Wright, perhaps named for his father William P. Wright and his grandfather Robert M. Wright.

[557] 1860 Crawford Co., GA, Census, p. 941; 1870 Crawford Co., GA, Census, p. 453; 1880 Pike Co., GA, Census, p. 111D.

Descendants of John Felts

John Felts

John Felts

Mary Felts

William T. Hammack

Daughter Felts

[-------] Wheeler

William Felts

Allen Felts

Elzy [------]

Charlottey Felts

Edward Hammack

Simeon Felts

Martha Ray

Chapter 12:

Simeon Hammack and His Descendants:
Central Mississippi, 1850-1950

The same forces that drew Hammacks into Texas, the Midwest, and California impelled Simeon Hammack and his family westward also. Born about 1798 in Georgia, Simeon Hammack lived the bulk of his life east of the Mississippi. Georgia in 1800 was still a narrow swath of land, most of which lay east of the Oconee River. Simeon's birth took place on land his grandfather had patented a generation earlier in the region of Harden's Creek in what is today southern Wilkes, northern Warren, or northeastern Taliaferro County. He grew to boyhood there on Harden's Creek surrounded by kin, most of whom had moved from the Virginia Southside after the Revolution.

Family connections would shape Simeon's life from birth to death. He entered a world on Harden's Creek that consisted of his parents, all of his father's siblings, his mother's Felts relations, his paternal grandmother, and several of his grandmother's Jackson kin. Nearby lived Mary Ann Hammack and her children, his father's cousins who had come to Wilkes County by way of Granville County, North Carolina. A few miles westward along the boundary of Wilkes and Lincoln Counties lived another cousin and contemporary of Simeon's grandfather, John Hammock, and John's sister Mary Paschall. In addition to all of these blood kin, several other interrelated families -- including the Moore family of eastern Lunenburg with Hammack connections of their own -- lived along Harden's Creek. Over time, the Moores would come to play a crucial role in Simeon's life.

From 1798 until about 1811, Simeon and his parents lived in the Harden's Creek community; between 1811 and 1820, much of the community moved westward and settled together in Jones County, Georgia, on lands newly ceded by Creek Indians. This initial migration was the first step in a long chain of movements that would draw Simeon Hammack ultimately to Choctaw County, Mississippi. The historical forces that made those migrations possible deserve attention.

The Creek cession of 1773 had opened much of what later became Wilkes County to American settlement; it was in these ceded lands that Simeon's grandfather Robert settled during the American Revolution. The next large Creek cession did not occur until after 1800. Between 1800 and 1832, the remainder of what is the present state of Georgia would be ceded to the United States, most of it coming from the Creeks and the northwestern portion of Georgia coming at last from the Cherokees.[558]

Unique among southern states, Georgia adopted a system of land distribution called the lottery system. Newly ceded tracts were surveyed into uniformly sized and shaped lots, which were recorded by lot number into large districts. Several districts formed a single county. Once surveyed, the lands were distributed by lottery to Georgians who met a residence requirement and certain other eligibility standards. Lotteries in 1805, 1807, 1820, 1821, 1827, and two in 1832 distributed hundreds of thousands of acres taken between 1800 and 1832 from Native Americans. Although the loss devastated native tribes, for white Americans searching for opportunity during these years, the possible rewards were rich. Many without means to purchase land acquired "fortunate draws" that enabled them to establish successful farms; for some, this initial foothold led to still greater wealth and enhanced success.[559]

At the time of the 1807 land lottery, several Wilkes County Hammacks drew lots in what became Jones County. The lands distributed by the 1807 lottery lay between the Oconee and the Ocmulgee Rivers. Those distributed in 1820 lay mostly south of the Altamaha River and north of the Florida border. The 1821 lottery distributed lands between the Ocmulgee and the Flint River, and the 1827 lottery distributed lands between the Flint and the Chattahoochee, which comprised the western boundary of the state.[560]

---

[558] C. D. Saggus, *Agrarian Arcadia: Anglo-Virginian Planters of Wilkes County, Georgia* (Washington, GA, 1996), pp. 1-20.
[559] "Land Lottery System," The New Georgia Encyclopedia (http://www.georgiaencyclopedia.org).
[560] Ibid.

163

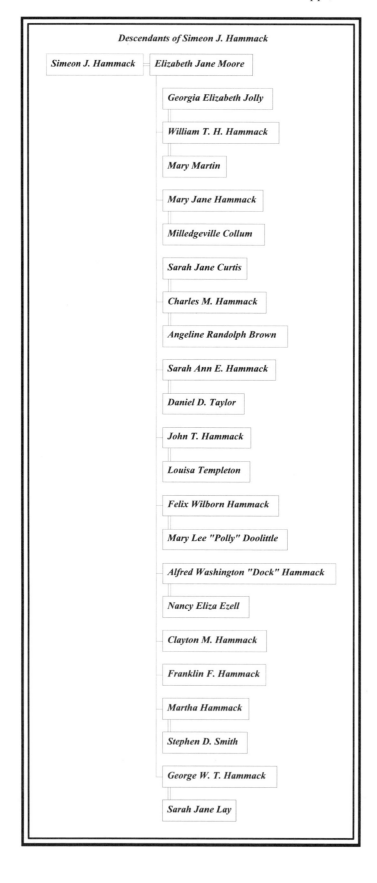

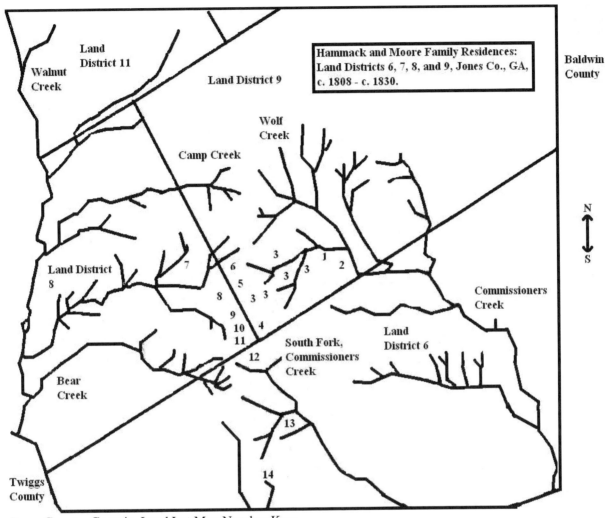

Jones County, Georgia, Land Lot Map Number Key:

1. Bishop Moore, uncle of Elizabeth Jane Moore Hammack, Land Lot (LL) 59, Land District (LD) 9.
2. Bishop Moore and John Bentley, son-in-law of Robert Moore and son of Milly Hammack Bentley, LL 60 and LL 61, LD 9.
3. Lewis Hammack, LL 11, LL 12, LL 14, LL 34, LL 35, LL 38, LD 9.
4. Allen Felts, son of John Felts, LL 12, LD 9.
5. John Bryant, husband of Elizabeth Hammack, LL 10, LD 9.
6. William T. Hammack, father of Simeon Hammack, LL 9, LD 9.
7. William T. Hammack, father of Simeon Hammack, LL 7, LD 8.
8. Edward Hammack, brother of William T. Hammack, and Talbot D. Hammack, son of William T. Hammack, LL 10, LD 8.
9. William T. Hammack and Lewis M. Hammack, LL 11, LD 8.
10. James Hammack, husband of Lucy Hammack, LL 12, LD 8.
11. Lewis M. Hammack, LL 12, LD 8.
12. William Simmons, husband of Catherine Hammack, and James Hammack, brother of Catherine Hammack Simmons, LL 53, LD 7.
13. Lewis Hammack, LL 56, LD 6.
14. James Hammack, LL 32, LD 6.

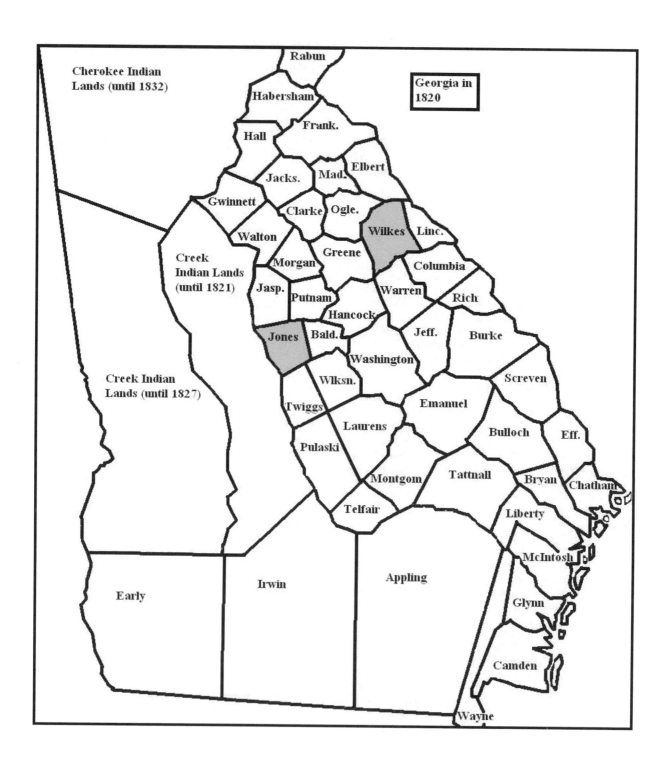

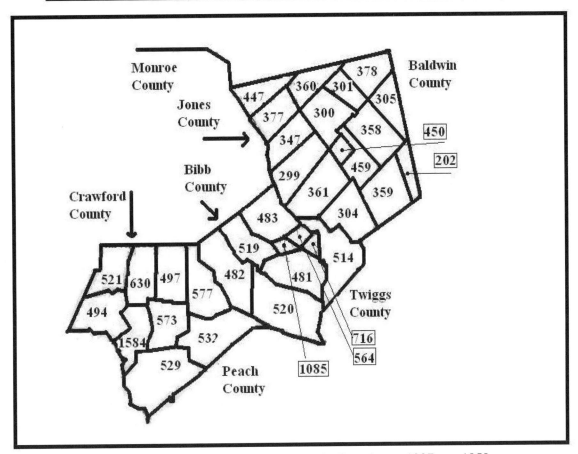

Hammack and Moore Residences, Jones, Bibb, and Crawford Counties, GA

Hammack and Moore Family Residences in Central Georgia Counties, c. 1807 – c. 1850:

Simeon Hammack, William Hammack, Bishop Moore, Matthew Moore, and Robert Moore:
        GMD 359 and GMD 459, Jones Co., GA, c. 1807 – c. 1824.
Simeon Hammack, William Hammack, and Hammack and Moore kin:
        GMD 521, Crawford Co., GA, c. 1824 – c. 1850.
James Hammack, Johnston Hammack, and Lewis Hammack:
        GMD 482, GMD 716 and 564, and GMD 519, Bibb Co., GA, c. 1828 – c. 1835.
Bishop and Matthew Moore and families:
        GMD 359 and GMD 459, Jones Co., GA, c. 1824 – c. 1850.

While Georgia was expanding westward during these years, significant developments took place in Alabama and Mississippi that would ultimately affect Simeon Hammack and his connections. Although Simeon was only a boy when the war of 1812 began, the war would eventually have a huge impact on Simeon and his kin.

The war of 1812 began as a response to a prolonged trading crisis. England and France had been at war since 1804, and the issue actually dated to the same trade tensions that during George Washington's administration had necessitated the Neutrality Act and during John Adams' administration the Quasi War. Neither country recognized the rights of the United States to trade in foreign waters as a neutral carrier. England demanded an American alliance before the United States could trade in European waters, and France similarly pressed for American support against Britain. Both countries seized American ships and cargoes. To make matters worse, England between 1804 and 1812 impressed several thousand American sailors into the Royal British Navy, a grievance that fueled American hostility. Thomas Jefferson's response as president from 1801 to 1809 was to institute an embargo by which the United States voluntarily suspended all foreign trade. Jefferson believed that such an act would eliminate European meddling with American trade and inspire American self-sufficiency in the process. Instead, the Embargo of 1807 nearly wrecked the country's finances before it was repealed a year later.[561]

As president from 1809 to 1817, James Madison inherited a nation with serious financial woes and one which was militarily weak owing to financial retrenchment Jefferson had instituted during his first administration. Despite continued aggression from England and France, Madison avoided war until 1812. In March of that year, he finally yielded to John C. Calhoun, Henry Clay, and the other War Hawks and asked Congress for a Declaration of War against England. In addition to impressment and the rights of neutral carriers, the War Hawks feared that England was provoking Native Americans in the Great Lakes region to strike at American settlements there, and they desired to expand the country's size by taking Canadian territory from England.[562]

As it turned out, Great Britain had not yet significantly aided the Natives to the west, although Tecumseh and his brother Tenskwatawa, better known as "The Prophet," had long been rallying native peoples to unite and organize in order to resist American expansion. News of their activities in Illinois and Indiana spread south throughout the Mississippi River basin to the five civilized tribes of the Southeast, leading white Americans to fear that a great Indian uprising was imminent.[563]

Americans feared that these Indians, too, might receive help from the British to strike at settlements in the new Louisiana Purchase and along the Gulf of Mexico, west of Spanish Florida and north of Pensacola. To defend this region came thousands of Tennessee militia under the command of a then as yet largely unknown frontier figure, a young Scots-Irish warrior named Andrew Jackson. Jackson, born in South Carolina in 1767, had read law in a frontier law office in Salem, North Carolina, before moving into Tennessee in the 1790s. He became a wealthy land speculator and planter and served both as Congressman and Judge before his military service during the war of 1812; but it was Jackson's role in the war, and his exploits as an Indian fighter, that made him famous.[564]

Jackson in 1813 moved his men into Central Alabama. When the militia threatened to mutiny because their periods of enlistment were almost up, Jackson ordered any man who left his post shot. He pressed on with his force of frontier soldiers and at a bend in the Coosa River broke the power of the Creek nation. The Battle of Horseshoe Bend was a landmark in American confrontations with Native Americans. The bloodshed and loss of life were remarkable; so too was the absoluteness with which Creek power in central Alabama was destroyed. Although it would not see its full fruition until a quarter of a century later, near the end of his presidency, Jackson had at Horseshoe Bend set in motion the forces that would

---

[561] For the background and course of the war, see R. H. Brown, *The Republic in Peril: 1812* (New York, 1971) and R. V. Remini, *Andrew Jackson and His Indian Wars* (New York, 2001), pp. 1-61.

[562] J.N. Rakove, *James Madison and the Creation of the American Republic* (3rd ed., New York, 2007), pp. 177-203.

[563] N. K. Risjord, *Representative Americans: The Revolutionary Generation* (Lanham, MD, 2001), pp. 284-307.

[564] R. V. Remini, *Andrew Jackson* (New York, 1969), pp. 17-49.

claim hundreds of thousands of acres in Alabama and Mississippi for white Americans, that would lead to the relocation of the Five Civilized Tribes of the Southeast, and that would make Alabama and Mississippi rich, powerful, cotton-producing states during the peak years of the Old South.[565]

A boy on Georgia's western frontier in 1813, Simeon Hammack could not then know the impact that events a hundred miles to the west would have on him and his family. But at no time in the next half a century could the powerful forces unleashed by the Battle of Horseshoe Bend not impact his life.

For the next decade, however, Simeon's life was by all accounts a quiet one. From 1813 until the mid-1820s, he lived in Jones County, Georgia, during the formative years when the county took shape. In 1820, he chose to marry and begin a family. Rather than marry a girl from a neighboring farm, he returned to the community in Wilkes County where he had been born. His choice for a bride was Elizabeth Jane Moore, who came from a family long familiar to Simeon's.

It is difficult to escape the conclusion that family ties played a crucial role in Simeon's choice as a marriage partner. The Moores had settled in Lunenburg County, Virginia, in the 1740s, about the time Hammacks began moving there from the Northern Neck. In the eighteenth-century, there were several indirect connections between the two. Both Hammacks and Moores intermarried with the Peace family, and both had connections with the Amos and Bentley families. After Ussery Moore brought his large family to Wilkes County about 1804, the connections became more complex. Three of Ussery's sons -- Bishop Moore, Matthew Moore, and Robert Moore -- married daughters of Sanders Ray; Jacob Ray, Sanders' son, married Nancy Hammack, Simeon's aunt. Samuel Moore, probably a son of Ussery, had married Christiana Hammack, Simeon's first cousin.

While the Hammacks remained in Jones County, they apparently kept in regular contact with their Wilkes County kin. By 1820, Samuel Moore had settled in Jones County, where he lived on a farm next to Simeon Hammack. Ussery Moore, Bishop Moore, Matthew Moore, Robert Moore, John Moore, and Jacob Ray remained neighbors in Wilkes County. Simeon had known the Moores before his family moved to Jones County, but he and Elizabeth were only children then. We cannot know now whether they remained in contact after the Hammacks moved west or whether Simeon met Elizabeth afresh on a visit to his aunt and uncle in 1819 or 1820; we do know, however, that Simeon and Elizabeth married in 1820 in Wilkes County but were living together in Jones County by the time of the 1820 census. Elizabeth at the time of her marriage to Simeon was at most sixteen years of age and in all likelihood only fourteen or fifteen.[566]

The evidence concerning Elizabeth's place of birth is conflicting. Some of the Lunenburg Moores had moved to Wilkes County in the 1790s, but Ussery Moore himself did not move south until 1804 or 1805, about the time of Elizabeth's birth. Census reports for Elizabeth and her offspring variously list her place of birth as Virginia or Georgia; she may not have been positive of the location herself. In either case, she seems to have been born about the time Ussery and his sons Robert, James, John, Matthew, and Bishop all settled in Wilkes County.

Elizabeth and Simeon were not themselves related, but they had many kin in common. Elizabeth's stepmother was Martha Ray Moncrief Moore, who was Jacob Ray's sister. Thus Elizabeth and Simeon shared Jacob and Nancy Ray as uncle and aunt. Further, Martha Ray Moncrief Moore had been married to Samuel Moncrief, who was stepson of another of Simeon's aunts, Betsy Hammack Moncrief. In later years, Simeon's sister Sarah would marry Elizabeth's uncle James Moore, and Elizabeth's sister Martha Moore would marry Simeon's cousin John Bentley (who was an uncle of George and Martha Amos, the spouses of Simeon's siblings Katherine and Mansel). Within their Jones County and Wilkes County neighborhoods, almost every surrounding family was related as closely to Elizabeth as they were to Simeon.

---

[565] Ibid., pp. 49-80.
[566] 1820 Jones Co., GA, Census, p. 134.

Elizabeth and Simeon lived the first years of their marriage in Jones County, but the forces that would move them further into central Georgia were already at work when they married in 1820. Georgia's 1820 land lottery -- authorized by an act of 15 December 1818 -- distributed the lands south of the Altamaha River. Living in Samuel's District, Jones County, Simeon Hammack and his uncle Lewis both drew lots of land Early County. Although Simeon himself probably never lived on the Early County land, its sale gave him the wherewithal to purchase property of his own, and its location -- in extreme southwestern Georgia -- may have caused Simeon to look carefully at the newly settled lands.[567]

In 1821, a lottery distributed the lands between Georgia's Ocmulgee and Flint Rivers. The western boundary of Jones County lay along the Ocmulgee, which until 1821 alone had separated Jones on the Georgia frontier from the Creek Indians and their lands to the west. Among the lands distributed in 1821 was what would become Crawford County, with its westward boundary along the Flint River. Crawford was formed in 1822 from Houston, one of the original counties created in 1821 from the ceded lands. Its position along the Flint River was analogous to that of Jones County on the Ocmulgee from 1807 until 1821, the years when Simeon grew to manhood there. Moreover, only Bibb County -- about twenty miles in width -- separated southwestern Jones County from northeastern Crawford. The Hammacks in Crawford County would be no more vulnerable than when they had settled in Jones a decade earlier, and, as with the earlier move, they would be only a short distance away from their established kinship networks in Jones County and in Wilkes County. Had they taken up residence on the Early County lands, however, they would have had to have moved more than one-hundred miles to the southwest, across much of the Creek Nation, to a location itself bounding upon the Creek lands in Alabama and near to sparsely settled northwestern Florida, which had only recently become a part of the United States.[568]

So it was that in the early 1820s William T. and Mary Hammack began moving their large family from Jones County to Crawford County. About this time, Simeon Hammack acquired the first tract of land known to have been owned by him. During the 1820 land lottery, he drew land lot 385, land district 2, Early County. Early County deeds do not reveal what became of the land, but Simeon likely sold it and used the profits to purchase other tracts elsewhere. Simeon seems not to have owned land in Jones County before moving to Crawford, although he apparently was well known throughout his community. By 1825 he was serving as a Justice of the Peace, and he may have held this position until moving to Crawford County in 1827.[569]

Soon after moving to Crawford County, Simeon Hammack's father William Hammack died; as the eldest son, Simeon apparently became head of the family. His mother and younger siblings did not live with him, however, for they were enumerated at the time of the 1830 census in the household of Simeon's younger, unmarried brother, Wilborn Hammack. Simeon was enumerated six households away with wife Elizabeth and their four young children. That Simeon played a leading role in supporting his widowed mother and younger siblings is made clear by Mary's estate records, including a court case chronicling a dispute between Simeon Hammack and his brother. These items will be discussed shortly.

There is very limited evidence concerning Simeon Hammack and his religious beliefs. Most of his relatives were committed Baptists, many of whom endorsed the Primitive Baptist doctrine when that group split from other Baptists after 1837. Unlike his mother and siblings, Simeon apparently never joined Mt. Carmel Church in Crawford County, and there is no record of him as a church member among the surviving church registers for Calhoun and Choctaw Counties, Mississippi. Simeon's wife Elizabeth Jane Hammack appears as a member of Mt. Carmel Church on 17 August 1839, although the date on which she joined the congregation has not been preserved. She remained a member until 18 August 1847, when she was dismissed, probably in preparation for the family's move from Crawford County. Later she

---

[567] 1820 Georgia Land Lottery Records, Fortunate Drawers, Georgia Department of Archives and History, Morrow, GA.

[568] For a general history of the period, see N. V. Bartley, *The Creation of Modern Georgia* (2d. ed., Athens, GA, 1990), pp. 1-45.

[569] 1820 Georgia Land Lottery Records, Fortunate Drawers, Georgia Department of Archives and History, Morrow, GA; Henry Co., GA, Deed Book J, p. 68.

belonged to Baptist congregations in Mississippi as well; yet no clear evidence has been unearthed to suggest that Simeon Hammack formally embraced religion, at least while he lived in central Georgia.[570]

Instead, Simeon seems to have focused his energies on economic enterprise. Records for Crawford County, Georgia, suggest that he was an active and prosperous planter with diversified business interests. In addition to cotton planting, Simeon Hammack seems to have had mercantile interests and to have worked along with his mother, who also was a general trader in Crawford County. On 31 July 1832, Simeon Hammack purchased 197.5 acres from Seaborn Bryan; the land was located in lot 9, district 1, and lay adjacent a two-acre tract Simeon already owned. Hammack paid $125 -- about seventy-five cents per acre -- for the land. Less than two months later, on 18 September, Simeon sold a one acre tract of the same property to J. B. Kirkland for $25.[571] Two months later, on 19 November, a road order named Asa Jolly, William Jordan, and James Roberts "Commissioners to see and mark out a road leading from Macon to Calhoun's Ferry, through Crawford County as far as it extends through Captain Simmons District be and the same is hereby established a public road . . . as the old road run except the new one cut out by Simeon Hammack from below the store of Mary Hammack, and that it the said new road be established a public road . . . in lieu of the old road."[572]

During the next decade, Simeon Hammack continued to speculate in real estate. He also became a leading citizen in Simmons' District of western Crawford County, a district headed by his cousin Catherine Hammack Simmons's stepson, Judge Allen Simmons. Simeon purchased land from his brother-in-law James Moore in 1832[573], and he sold 202.5 acres in land lot 117, land district 1, to Joseph Thompson in 1833. Thompson paid $600 for the land.[574] In 1835, Simeon purchased a slave from the estate of his deceased brother Wilborn Hammack, and in 1838 he sold 170 acres, land district 1, land lot 9, to his uncle Allen Felts. The land was described as lying "on [the] public road from Macon to Blountsville by way of Hammack's grove against Hammack's house lot, adj[acent] Mobley, [the] Dist[rict] line, Mathis, Jolly Curtis, and Felts."[575] Simeon sold the land for $1,400, nearly $7 an acre -- a handsome return on his 1832 investment. It was not until 1847 -- following his falling out with his brother Talbot -- that Simeon liquidated his remaining Crawford County properties. At that time, on 25 January, he conveyed to John Martin a tract of thirty-six acres in district 1, lot 9. Hammack received $270 for the land, which lay "on [the] Main Road from Mitchell's Ferry on the Flint River to Macon, adj[acent] Eleazar Stephens, to the Dist[rict] line, adj[acent] reserve of 1/4 acre made by Talbot D. Hammack and Mansel W. Hammack, adm[instrator] on the estate of William Hammack, late of Crawford Co., dec'd. by deed to Allen Felts."[576] Simeon was probably already preparing to move to Macon County, for less than a year later his wife Elizabeth requested her letter from Mt. Carmel Church.

During these same years, Simeon seems to have been actively engaged within his community in western Crawford County. He was security for the administration of neighbor James Tanner's estate in 1834.[577] In 1836, along with Thomas Feagin and Asa Jolly, Simeon was named a Commissioner to examine two roads leading from Knoxville towards Houston County to see if one road could be eliminated.[578] A year later, he served on a board of commissioners who were to lay out a road to Culloden in Monroe County.[579] In 1838 and 1839, he served as security on two separate occasions involving administration of the estates of Burton Hill and Thomas Feagin and in 1843 for the estate of Joshua

---

[570] Mt. Carmel Baptist Church Records, Georgia Department of Archives and History, Morrow, GA; Bethel Baptist Church Minutes, Calhoun Co., MS, transcription, Calhoun City Library, Calhoun City, MS.

[571] Crawford Co., GA, Deed Book A, pp. 289, 301.

[572] Crawford Co., GA, Inferior Court Records, County and Court Purposes, 1830-1846.

[573] Crawford Co., GA, Deed Book B, p. 423.

[574] Crawford Co., GA, Deed Book B, p. 53.

[575] Crawford Co., GA, Deed Book C, p. 451.

[576] Crawford Co., GA, Deed Book E, p. 703.

[577] Crawford Co., GA, Estate Records.

[578] Inferior Court Records, County and Court Purposes, 1830-1846.

[579] Inferior Court Records, County and Court Purposes, 1830-1846.

Rowe. In 1842, he served as administrator of the estate of his brother-in-law William P. Wright, about the same time as he appraised the estate of neighbor William Rowell.

Between 1842 and 1847, much of Simeon Hammack's efforts focused on settling the estate of his mother, Mary Felts Hammack. Mary's will, dated 5 March 1842, gave Simeon Hammack $200 above his "equal share" in return for his assistance to her during her widowhood. Mary died on 4 September 1843, and Talbot D. Hammack, Simeon's brother, began settling the estate. Mary's slaves were sold at auction on 1 January 1844; Simeon Hammack purchased Cassa, Sally, George, Betty, and Monroe for $2,228. The total value of slaves sold at the sale was $4,148.51. Subtracting Simeon Hammack's added $200 legacy, each child should then have received $438.72 as their legacy from the sale of slaves.[580]

On 28 June 1845, Simeon Hammack appealed for an injunction against his brother Talbot Hammack to prevent him from collecting $2,700 Simeon owed the estate for the purchase of slaves and personal property. He claimed that he had provided services to his mother Mary Hammack during her widowhood for $2,700 and that he was owed this money from her estate before any legacies could be paid. In effect, Simeon suggested that his debt to the estate should be cancelled in return for services rendered between 1830 and 1843. Talbot Hammack responded to Simeon's charges on 8 July 1845; Talbot hired as attorneys Hall and Wimberley and Poe and Nesbitt, who claimed that Simeon's bill had been "trumped up." Simeon responded by elaborating on the circumstances that led to the indebtedness. He claimed that after William Hammack died:

> MARY HAMMACK the mother of your orator and widdow of the Said deseased being then a resident of the county of Crawford she became desirous that your orator should live with her and attend to her business during her life for which the said Mary promised and agreed to pay your orator whatever your orators services might be reasonably worth. Your orator agreed to take upon himself the trouble and expence so requested of him and moved to the county of Crawford and settled there...near her and [she] then and there engaged the services of your orator to attend to her said business. Your orator then and there to wit on or about the first of January 1829 carried the attention of said business and continued the same from that time untill the death of the said Mary Hammack which was the --- day of 1844[581]. Your orator charges that he during all that time attended strictly to all the business of the said Mary and furnished to the said Mary large amounts of provisions and other necessary things (for your orator charges that her family was composed of young Negroes and [illegible] mostly which prevented its making it support her for the most of the time...your orator prays [that this assistance] may be taken as a part of this bill... [and] further charges and says that the said Mary Hamack at all times during her life [recognized] your orator's claim against her and at all times expressed herself well satisfied with your orator's conduct and management of her business, and at all times expressed a desire that your orator should be compensated for his said services and she at all times during her life as your orator believes considered and wished that your orator might be compensated out of her property after her death....Your orator further charges and says that the said Mary Hammack left a will...[with] Talbot Hammack the executor in which said will she acknowledged that said estate was due your orator for said services...Your orator charges and says that the said Mary Hammack was quite old at the time she made her will and did not know the amount of your orators just account against her and in fact did not know the worth of your orators services rendered to her or the amount furnished; and whether She was influenced [by others] Your orator cannot say but your orator charges that either from a want of a knowledge of your orators

---

[580] See Crawford Co., GA, Returns Book D, pp. 182, 313; Crawford Co., GA, Returns Book E, pp. 44, 124.
[581] The actual date was 1843.

account, or from some undue and unaccountable influence the said Mary Hammack did not [stipulate] a sufficiency by a large amount to satisfy the demand of your orator against her and now against said estate - Your orator further charges and says that after the death of the said Mary Hammack her said executor pressed an order to Sell the property belonging to Said estate and when said Sale came on your orator believing that his said account was just against said estate and knowing that it was the only debt against said estate and believing that the said executor would not refuse to pay the same, and even permit your orator to purchase property and credit his account with the amount or not attempt to press your orator for the amount of your orators purchases...Your orator purchased at said sail a large amount of property amounting in the aggregate to the sum of seventeen hundred & ninety two dollars & sixty eight and three fourth cents or thereabout....Your orator notes for the same but would leave the same to set off the demand of your orator when your orator should become the amount of your orators account which your orator avers is a larger amount than the amount of the demand against your orator, your orators account being for the sum of Twenty seven hundred Dollars. But your orator charges and says that shortly after said purchases by your orator the said executor demanded of your orator your orator's notes for the same. Your orator charges [and] says that he refused to sign said notes and informed the said Executor that as said estate was not indebted accept [for] your orators demand that it would be unjust for your orator to give said notes and subject himself to a suit on this before your orator could [illegible word] on his said account yet your orator, notwithstanding, was forced to give his notes for the amount but as your orator then and now believes with the understanding that your orator was not to be pressed to pay the same untill your orator could...your orator charges & says that said notes were made due and payable on the twenty fifth day of December 1844 and your orator could not file his suit untill August 1849 - which enabled the said executor to file suit six months before your orator.

Your orator charges and says that notwithstanding said estate is not in debt save your orators account, and, notwithstanding, the notes your orator gave for said debt are perfectly good and likely to remain so and that your orator is willing to allow his account to be credited and that your orator believed that he would not be pressed on said notes until he could prove a judgment on his said account, and, notwithstanding the premises, The said Talbert Hammack executor as aforesaid has.... [regarded the said notes as presently due and] returnable to the February Term of the Superior Court of said county 1845....all of which will more fully appear by reference to the records & files of said court to which your orator begs leave to refer as often as may be nesasry - Your orator further charges and says that if the said executor is permitted to receive judgment on said demand at the next term of said court and press the same against your orator (which your orator believes he will do) Your orator's property must be sacrificed and your orator thereby wholly received and your orator not being informed which he believes that the said Executor intends to defend your orator's suit against him which is now coming returnable to the next superior court in said county and with an order to postpone your orator's suit against him, as early as possible your orator charges that he will [illegible words] that the said Executor would [illegible word] your orators account credited with the amount of your orators notes and settle the matter which your orator much denied. But now so it is as may it pleas your Honor that the said Executor, continuing now to harass offend cheat and defame your orator in All of which actings and doings of the said Executor are contrary to good conscience and to the manifest [harm] of your orator....in as much as your orator is remediless at the common law and must nesasarely be oppressed harassed & wholly reviled without the intercession of your Honor's high remedial restraining Equitable powers - To the end therefore, that the said Talbot Hammack may upon his aforesaid oath answering the business... may it please your Honor to grant unto your orator the state's most gracious writ of Injunction to be directed to the said Talbot Hammack Executor as aforesaid commanding and enjoining him under a certain penalty to seize and desist from the further prosecution of said common law action untill your orator can obtain a judgment on his said account; and that the judgment and cost of said cases may be at the same time and of Equal date and grant unto your orator such other...relief as the nature of his case deserves, the equity may he...grant the state's writ of subpoena order a certain penalty for the said Talbot Hamack Executor as aforesaid to be and appear at the next term of the superior court to be held in and for the said county then & there to stand to and abide such ordinances as may be heard in the [illegible word] and as in [illegible word] your orator will ever pray.[582]

To support his claim, Simeon submitted a bill outlining his services to the estate during the last fifteen years of Mary Hammack's life.

Mary Hammack To Simeon Hammack DR

1829	To services rendered ~~in taking care~~ attending to the Business of the said Mary and attending to her $100 ~~premises the same 100~~				$100.00
1830	Attention to business	$100.00			$100.00
1831	Do	$100.00			$100.00
1832	Do	$100.00	+ $100.00	Provisions Furnished	$200.00
1833	Do	$100.00	+ $100.00	Do	$200.00
1834	Do	$100.00	+ $100.00	Do	$200.00
1835	Do	$100.00	+ $100.00	Do	$200.00
1836	Do	$100.00	+ $100.00	Do	$200.00
1837	Do	$100.00	+ $100.00	Do	$200.00
1838	Do	$100.00	+ $100.00	Do	$200.00
1839	Do	$100.00	+ $100.00	Do	$200.00
1840	Do	$100.00	+ $100.00	Do	$200.00
1841	Do	$100.00	+ $100.00	Do	$200.00
1842	Do	$100.00	+ $100.00	Do	$200.00
1843	Do	$100.00	± $100.00	Do	$200.00
					[$2,700.00]

Effectively, Simeon Hammack charged that he had supported his mother during the last fifteen years of her life and that he was owed $2,700 for his trouble. Simeon argued that Mary acknowledged the debt but undervalued it; her will stipulated that he should receive $200 more than his siblings in return for his efforts. Because of her age and incapacity, Simeon suggested, Mary had failed to recognize the true value of his assistance. Simeon further charged that when he agreed to purchase the slaves from Mary's estate, he expected that his brother would not attempt to collect the debt from him until he had received the money he was owed for assisting Mary from 1829 until she died. Instead, Talbot ruthlessly pursued the claim, damaging both Simeon's reputation and his financial well-being.[583]

---

[582] Hammack v. Hammack, 1845, Crawford Co., GA, Loose Court Cases, Georgia Department of Archives and History, Morrow, GA.

[583] Ibid.

Talbot Hammack, in turn, responded with a lengthy statement of his own. Talbot attempted to justify his own behavior and to refute Simeon Hammack's charges.

The Answer of Tolbert D. Hammack Executor of the last will & testament of Mary Hammack late of Crawford County deceased, defendant to the bill of complaint of Simeon Hammack complainant

This defendant now & at all times hereafter saving & reserving to himself all benefit & advantage of Exception which can or may be had or taken to the many errors, uncertainties, & other imperfections in the said complainants said Bill of Complaint contained for as sworn thereunto or unto so much & such parts thereof as this defendant advised in or on material for him to make answer unto, this defendant answering says.

That William Hammack the father of the said complainant departed this life sometime in the month of April 1828 intestate, and that Mary Hammack the widow of said William Hammack deceased, was at the time a resident of the County of Crawford and that the said complainant was then a resident of the County of Jones — that sometime during the month of January or February 1829 the said complainant left his residence in the County of Jones and came to the residence of the said Mary Hammack in the County of Crawford and commenced living with her as this defendant is informed & believes not at the desire of the said Mary Hammack but at his the said complainants own suggestion this defendant does not know nor does he believe that there was any contract entered into at that time between the said complainant & the said Mary Hammack, that the said complainant should live with the said Mary Hammack during her life & attend to her business or that the said Mary Hammack promised & agreed to pay the said Complainant whatever the said Complainants services might be reasonably worth.

This defendant admits that the said Complainant did about that time commence attending to the business of the said Mary Hammack & that he continued attending to said business until the death of the said Mary Hammack which took place on the 4th day of September 1843, but this defendant says that during the years 1829 & 1830 the said complainant worked for & received a part of the crop & that during the remainder of the time the said Complainant lived with the said Mary Hammack she employed her hands upon his farm & disposed of the produce thereof & only did not allow the said Mary Hammack a sufficient support out of the proceeds of the same, but appropriated the same to his own purposes, which was more than a fair recompense for any service which he rendered in attending to her business

This defendant denies that the said Complainant did attend strictly to the business of the said Mary Hammack during all the time the said complainant lived with her, but says that he was very careless and negligent & that the interest of the said Mary Hammack was greatly injured & suffered in consequence of his negligence and inattention & this defendant knows nothing of the said complainant furnishing the said Mary Hammack with large amounts of provisions or other necessary things, but believes if any such provisions or other necessary things were furnished that they were purchased with the means of the said Mary Hammack

This defendant further answering says that there was on the plantation of the said Mary Hammack during most of the time the said Complainant lived with her a sufficient force to have yielded if prudently managed an ample and abundant support & more besides for he says that during the time that the said Mary Hammacks Negroes were young & unable to work, that she hired able bodied hands to work on the farm - that the said complainant had a large family & derived a support for himself & family from the proceeds of the farm of the said Mary Hammack & that in addition thereto he had ample time allowed him to attend to his own concerns.

This defendant does most explicitly deny that the said Mary Hammack did at all times, during her life recognize the said complainants pretended claim or account of Twenty seven hundred Dollars against her & that she did at all times express herself well satisfied with the said

Complainants conduct, management of her business, and that she at all times expressed a desire that the said Complainant should be compensated (at least in any such fashion as his said pretended account calls for) for his said services; and that she at all times during her life, considered & wished that the said Complainant might be compensated out of her property after her death & that she ever recognized the said Complainants account as a necessary account against her but insists that she had capacity sufficient to understand accounts & attend to the settlement of claims against her - this defendant because of the facts above set forth says that it is true as charged in complainants bill that the said Mary Hammack did not know the amount of said Complainant accounts against her, but denies that she did not know the worth of his work, or the amount of provisions furnished her, in truth, this defendant insists that the said plaintiff had long before the death of the said Mary Hammack been amply paid for all the work he ever did for the said Mary, all the provisions (if any) which he ever furnished her. This defendant further answering says that he has been informed and verily believes that the said Mary Hammack at the time of making & executing her said last will & testament was subjected to no improper & illegal influence & that she did not intend the extra legacy of Two hundred Dollars given by her will to the said Simeon Hammack as a satisfaction of the pretended claim of the said Simeon.

This defendant further answering says that at the November Term 1843 of the Court of Ordinary of Crawford County he procured from said Court an order to sell the property belonging to the estate of the said Mary Hammack deceased & that afterwards after giving due notice of the time & place of said sale he proceeded in conformity with said order & the provisions of said will, on the first Monday in January 1844 at the late residence of Mary Hammack to dispose of the perishable property belonging to said estate, & on the first Tuesday in February before the Courthouse door in the town of Knoxville to dispose of the Negroes belonging to said estate - that the said Simeon Hammack purchased property at said sale, to the amount of Twenty two hundred & forty five Dollars & 68 3/4 cents or thereabouts.

This defendant admits that the said Complainant refused to comply with the terms of said Sale & to give his notes for the amount but he does not believe that the said Complainant expected to set off his said account against said notes for at that time the said Complainant had not notified this defendant of his having said account but pretended to set up a claim to said property - but the said Complainant did eventually comply with the terms of said Sale & on the 14th day of February 1844, he and one John L. Woodward as his Security did make & deliver to this defendant their sundry joint & several promissory notes amounting in the aggregate as near as this defendant now recollects to the sum aforesaid -- then he gave this defendant verbal notice of said account -- this defendant denies that there ever was any understanding that the said complainant should not be forced to pay said notes until he could obtain a judgment on said account for this defendant says that he has never consented to pay said account or admitted that it was in any aspect just & this defendant further says that since said notes became due the complainant has paid Four hundred & fifty dollars on the same.

This defendant says that the said Complainant was laboring under no legal disability to bring suit against him for the amount of said account before the said notes became due on the Twenty fifth day of December 1844 because this defendant says that he took out Letters Testamentary on said Estate at the November Term 1843 of the Court of Ordinary of said County of Crawford as will fully appear by references to the date of said letters now in court ready to be shown and the minutes records of said Court.

And this defendant further answering admits that he did commence suit on said notes returnable to the February Term 1845 of the Superior Court of Crawford issuing against the said Complainant & the said John L. Woodward & that said Suit is now pending in the said Court & this defendant will hope to obtain a judgment on said notes at the next August Term of said Court.

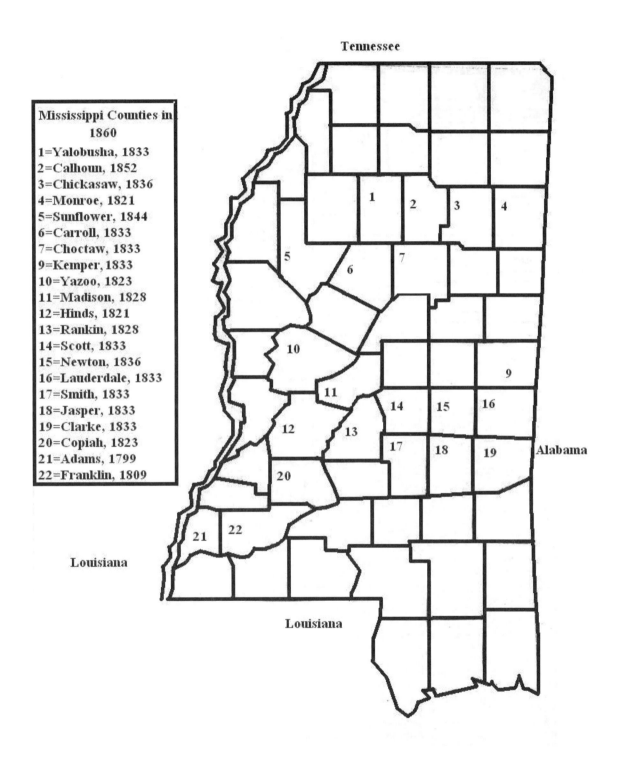

Mississippi Counties in 1860

1=Yalobusha, 1833
2=Calhoun, 1852
3=Chickasaw, 1836
4=Monroe, 1821
5=Sunflower, 1844
6=Carroll, 1833
7=Choctaw, 1833
9=Kemper, 1833
10=Yazoo, 1823
11=Madison, 1828
12=Hinds, 1821
13=Rankin, 1828
14=Scott, 1833
15=Newton, 1836
16=Lauderdale, 1833
17=Smith, 1833
18=Jasper, 1833
19=Clarke, 1833
20=Copiah, 1823
21=Adams, 1799
22=Franklin, 1809

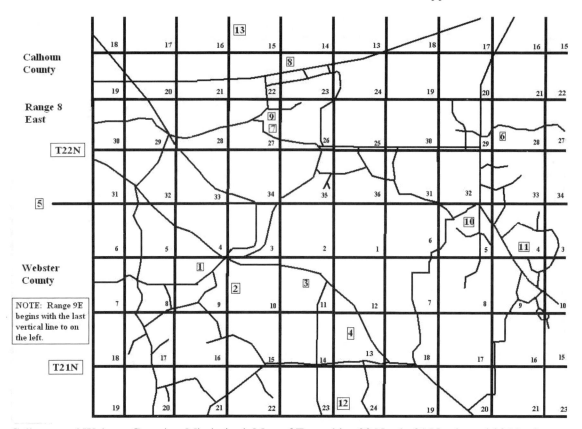

Calhoun and Webster Counties, Mississippi, Map of Townships 20 North, 21 North, and 22 North, Range 8 East, Number Key:

1.   Cadaretta (1860 Residence of Simeon Hammack).
2.   Philadelphia Baptist Church & Cemetery (Elizabeth Jane Moore Hammack and children were members here, c. 1866).
3.   Doolittle Chapel School.
4.   Spring Hill Church & Cemetery.
5.   Boundary between Webster and Calhoun Counties.
6.   Slate Springs (1870 Residence of John T. Hammack).
7.   Dentontown.
8.   Sabougla Baptist Church & Cemetery (Felix W. Hammack was a charter member here.)
9.   Bethel Church & Cemetery (Felix W. and George W. Hammack and spouses are buried here.)
10.   New Hope Cemetery.
11.   New Hope Church.
12.   Hammack Springs. Homeplace and family cemetery of Simeon and Elizabeth Jane Moore Hammack.
13.   Felix W. Hammack Homeplace, Section 15, Township 22 North, Range 8 East. Note that the George W. Hammack Homeplace was about one mile northwest of Felix's home, located in contiguous sections 4, 9 and 10 of Township 22 North.

This defendant admits that he intends defending the said Complainant suit as the said Complainant has been informed, because this Defendant has other demands gainst said complainant amounting to a considerable sum & because said Complainants demand is wholly unfounded as this defendant is advised & believes this defendant further answering says that he requested said Complainant to sue him on said demand at the last February Term of said Superior Court & that the said Complainant refused to do so & requested this defendant to sue on the demand upon which this defendant has commenced suit - This defendant admits that said Estate is not now in debt & says that he is now ready & willing & has always been ready & willing to credit the demand which he holds against said Complainant with the amount due the said Complainant as his legacy under said Will.

And this defendant denies all & all manner of unlawful combination & conspiracy which he is by the said bill charged; without this there is not any other matter cause or thing in the said complainants said bill of complaint for this defendant to make answers unto ...[584]

Unfortunately, statements from witnesses -- if they existed -- have not survived, and the final disposition of this case is unknown. The evidence suggests, however, that Talbot Hammack may have won the suit. If this were the case, the reasons are unclear. Perhaps Simeon was unable to demonstrate to the court's satisfaction that he had in fact expended $2,700 on his mother's case and that he had not been compensated for the same. Perhaps the case embodies an element of sibling rivalry and economic competition as well. Even Talbot admitted that Simeon had cared for Mary Hammack and managed her estate during the final decade of her life, although he suggested that Simeon had not been asked to do so and that his motives were base and self-serving. Yet, if Simeon's claim were true, paying the $2,700 owed him would have greatly diminished the estate's value and would have reduced each child's potential inheritance from $438.72 to less than $160.

To further support Simeon's claim, legal records suggest that his reputation remained in tact during the years he was at odds with his brother and his mother's estate. In 1844, he appraised the estate of John Collum, his son-in-law Milledgeville's father, and in 1850 his cousin Milly Hammack Davidson involved him and his brother Mansel W. Hammack in a complex legal instrument whereby she provided an inheritance for her grandchildren Lewis S. Smallwood, Jacob W. Smallwood, and Millie Smallwood Hammack. If Simeon's reputation had been badly damaged by the affair, it seems unlikely that he would have continued to hold positions of authority within the community or of trust within his extended family circle, especially since he had already moved from Crawford County to Macon County by the time of the latter instrument.[585]

Nevertheless, it is difficult to escape the conclusion that a direct link existed between Simeon's falling out with his brother and his decision to leave Crawford County, and perhaps even the state. Many early Macon County deeds have been destroyed, making it impossible to determine when Simeon first purchased property there. But, given the sale of Simeon's land in 1847 and the granting of Elizabeth's letter from Mt. Carmel Church the same year, it seems likely that Simeon Hammack moved his family to Macon County sometimes that year. They were enumerated there at the time of the 1850 census, living in GMD 1002. Simeon was then aged fifty-two and Elizabeth forty-five; both were reported as natives of Georgia. Living at home were seven children, six sons and a daughter ranging in age from twenty to two years; the eldest of these was son John T. Hammack, although several older children had already married and begun to head west.[586]

The 1852 Macon County tax digest shows Simeon Hammack living in GMD 1070. He was taxed with 500 acres in that district as well as a tract of forty acres in Cherokee County. Hammack's land was valued at $3,140 and his seven slaves and personal property at $3,610, for a combined value of $6,950.

---

[584] Ibid.

[585] Crawford Co., GA, Deed Book U, p. 103; Crawford Co., GA, Inferior Court Records, 1830-1848, p. 112.

[586] 1850 Macon Co., GA, Census, p. 124.

John T. Hammack, who had recently married, was living as head of his own household; he owned no land and was probably renting from his father or father-in-law at the time.[587]

About 1854, Simeon Hammack and his son John T. Hammack relocated to Mississippi, probably settling first in Choctaw County. Before 1850, Simeon's son-in-law Milledgeville Collum had settled in Yazoo County, Mississippi. His son Charles was at that time living in Choctaw County, and son William T. H. Hammack settled in Madison County. Simeon may have settled briefly in Yazoo or Madison, but, by the mid-1850s, he had settled permanently in Choctaw County. There is in 1856 and 1857 record of an Elizabeth Hammick or Hamrick who transferred her letter from Mulberry Creek in Choctaw County to Old Concord Baptist Church in the same location (but now Webster County).[588]

Although little is known about Simeon Hammack's early years in Choctaw County, the following sketch of his neighbor Sterling Doolittle (1814-1883) may reflect conditions similar to those experienced by Simeon and Elizabeth Hammack and their family.

The attractive possibilities of the rich soil in Mississippi drew them near to Slate Springs, Calhoun County[589], in a central part of that state....[They] were a splendid couple and substantial, thrifty farmers, and like so many of our people, they were pioneers and settled in the southern pine country. He cleared the forest from his farm with, in those days, strenuous labor and which few of our time could endure. Their first home in Mississippi was of logs he hewed from the forest. Their chimney was made of clay and sticks. Those were primitive times in that then backwoods country with no roads and only bridle paths through the woods to other settlements miles away. Their products for marketing were taken sixty miles to Greenwood, Mississippi, on the Yazoo River, a tributary of the Mississippi, and there shipped on rafts to New Orleans. For supplies they had to undergo great difficulties of a long rough journey of a hundred miles to Memphis, Tennessee, requiring several months to go and come in that undeveloped region of early days. All their wearing apparel was home made. They even had to spin their yarns and weave their own cloth...However, their old-homestead was a social center of the community where the young folks often gathered and enjoyed many happy evenings of merriment long to be remembered, such as popular corn-huskings and jolly quilting bees followed by generous revels in plantation goodies, with many a captivating dish of famous southern cooking. In their pioneer experience it was not uncommon for bears and wolves to prowl about the home at night and even

---

[587] 1852 Macon Co., GA, Tax Digest, Georgia Department of Archives and History, Morrow, GA.
Considering the children of William T. and Mary Hammack, Simeon seems to have been a farmer of substantial economic standing but not extremely wealthy. The following table illustrates the relative wealth of Simeon and his siblings in terms of slave-ownership about 1850.

T. D. Hammack	16 slaves
John Bryant	14 slaves
Simeon Hammack	7 slaves
John Sumter	5 slaves
Mansel W. Hammack	3 slaves
Jane Tanner	2 slaves

Simeon owned more slaves than three of his siblings, including brother Mansel, but not as many as brother Talbot D. Hammack or brother-in-law John Bryant. Simeon Hammack's seven slaves are as reflected in the 1852 Macon Co., GA, tax list, not the 1850 census. Data for the other siblings comes from the 1850 Georgia Slave Schedule.

[588] Old Concord Baptist Church Records, Choctaw Co., MS, transcript, Calhoun City Library, Calhoun City, MS; 1850 Choctaw Co., MS, Census, p. 3; 1850 Yazoo Co., MS, Census, p. 506.

[589] Slate Springs in Calhoun County is "located nine miles south of Calhoun City; the place took its name from the springs located west of town on the Slate Springs-Grenada Road. The exact settlement date is uncertain, but it is thought by local people to be older than Pittsboro. If this is true, then Slate Springs could possibly the oldest settlement in the county. Slate Springs appears to have been a trading center in the early 1800s. At that time, in addition to the saloons, there were two stores, the first one probably being operated by a man named Woodward. Between 1880 and 1890, a post office, flour mill, and two churches were added. Also at this time the Fox College was opened, with Fuller Fox as the first teacher." James W. Brieger, *Hometown Mississippi* (2nd ed., no publisher, no date), Mississippi Department of Archives and History. Calhoun County was formed in 1852 from Lafayette and Yalobusha Counties. Lafayette and Yalobusha counties were formed in 1833.

come up on the porch. Sometimes they would go up on the roof and then...more logs [would be added] on the hearth fire to keep them from coming down the chimney.[590]

The 1860 Choctaw County Census showed Simeon Hammack residing in Township 21, Range 8 East, Cadaretta Post Office, in what is now southern Calhoun County.[591] Simeon was aged sixty-two and Elizabeth aged fifty-six; both were shown as natives of Georgia, and the enumeration indicated that Elizabeth was illiterate. With the exception of married son John T. Hammack, all six of the children shown in the 1850 Macon County, Georgia, census were still living at home with Simeon and Elizabeth. Almost all early Choctaw County legal records have been destroyed, but it seems likely that Simeon Hammack acquired property soon after settling in Choctaw. The 1860 Choctaw County agricultural census showed him with 150 improved acres and 170 unimproved acres. The combined total value of the two tracts was $3,500. John T. Hammack did not, according to the 1860 census, own any real estate, but the agricultural census indicated that he was farming a tract of eighty improved acres and 150 unimproved acres valued together at $1,380. It may be that John was renting a portion of his father's land; if so, this would increase Simeon's total holdings to 230 improved acres and 320 unimproved acres, with a total value of $4,880. The figures match well with the value -- $5,000 -- of Simeon's real estate as reported in the population schedule for that year; in addition, Simeon owned slaves valued at $2,000, including one female slave working on his own farm and another four that had been rented to son-in-law Daniel D. Taylor.[592]

For Simeon Hammack's family, as for the nation at large, the years immediately after 1860 were tumultuous ones. In Simeon's instance, however, the hardships faced by the nation were compounded by his own declining health. Unfortunately, the date of his death has not been preserved, but he probably died in 1861 or 1862. The 1863 Choctaw County, Mississippi, Personal Property Tax list shows "Mrs. E. Hammack" taxed with one slave under age sixty. No further references to Simeon Hammack have been located.[593]

Seven of Simeon Hammack's eight sons served in the Confederate Army between 1861 and 1865; two -- Franklin and Clayton -- lost their lives in the conflict that divided the nation. Whether Simeon lived to know that his sons had perished is unknown. At his death, Simeon was buried on the family homestead at Hammack Springs in what is now northern Webster County, Mississippi, near the line between present-day Webster and Calhoun Counties. Whether the bodies of Franklin and Clayton were returned there for burial is unknown. Of the other sons, Felix is buried at nearby Sabougla, while George is buried at Bethel Baptist Church near Cadaretta. William is buried in Madison County, Mississippi, and Alfred is buried in Ashley County, Arkansas. The burial places of John T. and Charles are unknown; both

---

[590] W. F. Doolittle, *The Doolittle Family in America* (Cleveland, OH, 1901), p. 591.

[591] 1860 Choctaw Co., MS, Census, p. 421. Cadaretta in Webster County is "located six miles northwest of Embry; the date of founding is thought to have been in the 1830s and is known to have been a trading post earlier than 1850. There is also no record of how the place got its name; some older citizens contend that it was named for a young lady while others say the Indians named it. Until 1868, there was a school located there which is said to have been the best in the county at that time. About 1896 there was another school built one mile north of Cadaretta and operated successfully until it was consolidated with Springhill. A church was built at Cadaretta about 1872 by public subscription which was known as the Philadelphia Church. The post office, which was established soon after the founding of the village, was abolished in 1912. Two businessmen of the town in 1868 were Steve Herrod and J. T. Moore, who did a good mercantile business. See J. W. Brieger, *Hometown Mississippi* (2nd ed., no publisher, no date), Mississippi Department of Archives and History. Webster County was formed in 1874 from Montgomery and Choctaw. From 1874-1882, it was known as Sumner County. Cadaretta, which lies on the present Webster/Calhoun county line, is within this county. Choctaw County was formed in 1833 from the Choctaw Indian Cession of 1833. Choctaw's first county seat was Chester, which burned several times and has no extant records. The courthouse in Ackerman, the second county seat, burned in 1880. Some records are found in the adjacent counties of Montgomery and Webster.

[592] 1860 Choctaw Co., MS, Slave Schedule, p. 58; 1860 Choctaw Co., MS, Agricultural Schedule, p. 50; 1860 Choctaw Co., MS, State Census, p. 59.

[593] 1863 Choctaw Co., MS, Personal Property Tax Roll, Auditor's Records, RO17-B23-S4-03618, p. 21, MS Department of Archives and History, Jackson, MS.

apparently died in Calhoun County and could be buried at either Hammack Springs or at Bethel Church.[594]

Elizabeth Jane Moore Hammack survived her husband for several years; she probably died prior to 1870 in Calhoun or Madison County, Mississippi, although a record of her death has not been discovered. One Elizabeth Hammack was received by experience at Bethel Baptist Church in present-day Calhoun County on 13 September 1862; this is probably Sarepta Elizabeth Hammack, Charles's daughter, for Elizabeth Moore Hammack should have been received by letter rather than experience since she was already an established member of Baptist congregations in Georgia. Records of Philadelphia Baptist Church, located near the line between Choctaw and Calhoun Counties, are lost prior to 1860; the surviving minutes, however, show that Elizabeth and Martha Hammack were dismissed from membership on 1 September 1862 and that Elizabeth was received again in October 1862. Martha must also have rejoined, for, in October 1866, letters of dismissal were received for George Hammack, Elizabeth Hammack, Martha A. Hammack, and Sallie Taylor.[595]

It is difficult to resist the conclusion that letters were requested by Elizabeth and her offspring in 1866 prior to or immediately following a move to Madison County. Martha Hammack, Simeon's youngest daughter, married Stephen Smith on 28 July 1868 in Madison County, and Sallie Hammack Taylor and her family were enumerated near Martha Hammack Smith and William T. H. Hammack in Madison County, Mississippi, in 1870. Moreover, son John T. Hammack was listed on the 1868 Madison County, Mississippi, tax list, suggesting that he had also accompanied his mother and siblings southward.[596]

If the family did move to the Madison County area, George Hammack had returned to Calhoun County by 1870. He married Sarah Jane Lay there about 1871 and remained in Calhoun County for the rest of his life, with his family burying him there at Bethel Church in 1893. Although the records are inconclusive, Elizabeth Jane Moore Hammack may have returned with George to Calhoun County. One Elizabeth Hammack was received as a member of Bethel Baptist Church in October 1872; no record of her dismissal is found, suggesting that she remained a member until her death. If this were Elizabeth Jane Moore Hammack, however, no record of her has been found in the 1870 federal census. She may have been in the process of traveling from Madison County to Calhoun County at the time; in any case, with the exception of the 1872 reference, no clear record of her has been found after 1866, and it seems likely that she had died at least by the middle 1870s.

Elizabeth Jane Moore Hammack seems to have died in Calhoun County and to have been buried with Simeon Hammack at Hammack Springs. Roscoe Davis, a native of Calhoun County and a descendant of the couple, recalled family reunions at the Hammack Springs home place in what is today Webster County, Mississippi. Hammack Springs is located in the southwestern corner of Section 23 and the southeastern corner of Section 22, Township 21 North, Range 8 East. It is near the Spring Hill Community and a short distance from Philadelphia Cemetery. The property is southeast of Cadaretta and about four miles south of the line between Calhoun and Webster Counties. It lies about six miles southwest of Slate Springs and about nine miles southeast of Sabougla.

A newspaper clipping from 1938 preserved by Hammack descendants in Calhoun County provides further details concerning Hammack Springs:[597]

> On Sunday morning, September 25th, members and friends of the Hammack family met at
> the home of Dr. W. W. Gore, near Spring Hill, who accompanied the party to the old

[594] Mississippi Confederate Military Rosters, Captain McCord's Company and 3rd Battalion, Company D, Mississippi Department of Archives and History, Jackson, MS.

[595] Philadelphia Baptist Church Minutes, Choctaw Co., MS, transcription, Calhoun City Library, Calhoun City, MS; Bethel Baptist Church Minutes, Calhoun Co., MS, transcription, Calhoun City Library, Calhoun City, MS.

[596] 1868 Madison Co., MS, Personal Property Tax List, Mississippi Department of Archives and History, Jackson, MS.

[597] "Hammack Family Enjoys Picnic at Old Homestead," *Calhoun Monitor-Herald*, 25 September 1938.

homestead of the Hammack family -- better known as Hammack Springs. The party viewed the remains of the old pioneer homestead, in Webster County, and with bowed heads listened to a short narrative of the lives of the early settlers.

Being present on this occasion recalled to Dr. Gore's mind a picnic which he attended seventy-five years ago at the same place.[598] The purpose of the earlier meeting was to organize a regiment to wear the gray in the War Between the States. After speeches had been made by both men and women, a regiment of volunteers was organized and drilled for the first time in an open glade nearby.

At noon a bountiful lunch was spread under the giant boughs of the ancient trees. The fine food was enjoyed to the fullest extent by all present.

Immediately after lunch the family and friends sat together and discussed reminiscences of the Hammacks of ante-bellum days. The members of the family then gathered souvenirs of the home of their forefathers.

Descendants of the family present were: F. F. Hammack and small daughter, L. L. Hammack, Mrs. J. M. Tucker, Mrs. A. E. Parker, Mrs. J. A. Lominick, Mrs. Lay Davis, Mrs. Charlie Fulton, Mrs. Roane Lovorn, Roane Lovorn, Jr., Ralph Davis, James Davis, and George Hammack. Dr. Gore and Edward Love were guests of the party. The family parted hoping that they would be spared to enjoy another picnic next summer at the old home.

From the article, it seems that a strong sense of family identity and kinship existed among the descendants of Simeon and Elizabeth Jane Hammack long after their deaths. The hardships faced by the family in the decades immediately after the American Civil War may have reinforced family bonds, for in those years not only did sons Franklin and Clayton die in the Confederate Service but Simeon and Elizabeth Jane Hammack also passed away. Moreover, by 1880, Charles M. Hammack, Sarah Curtis Hammack, Angeline Randolph Hammack, John T. Hammack, and Louisa Templeton Hammack had all died. Sarah Curtis Hammack had died just before the Civil War began, but the deaths of two sons and two daughters-in-law of Simeon and Elizabeth between 1870 and 1880 are noteworthy. John T. Hammack himself died in 1870 as a result of debilitated health which was probably brought on by his service in the Confederate Army. The reasons for the deaths of Charles, Angeline, and Louisa are unknown, but a powerful yellow fever epidemic hit northern Mississippi and western Tennessee during the 1870s. Deaths were reported in Calhoun and Choctaw Counties, and it may be that Charles, Angeline, and Louisa succumbed to the disease as well.

In the years after 1880, descendants of Simeon and Elizabeth Jane would scatter. By 1880, daughter Mary Collum was living in Navarro County, Texas. Following the deaths of John T. and Louisa Templeton Hammack, their surviving children would move to Madison County, where they lived near Hammack kin there. During the 1880s, Alfred Hammack and his family would relocate to Ashley County in southern Arkansas. The children and grandchildren of Charles M. Hammack, Felix W. Hammack, and George T. Hammack would remain in Calhoun County well into the twentieth-century, and it was they who comprised the core of the group who visited Hammack Springs in 1938 to reminisce about Simeon, Elizabeth Jane, and the ante-bellum Hammack heritage.

The sections that follow will briefly examine each of the children of Simeon and Elizabeth Jane Moore Hammack and their families before focusing on son John T. Hammack, his offspring, and his descendants.

---

[598] The date would have been on or about 25 September 1863.

A. William T. H. Hammack and wives Georgia Elizabeth Jolly and Mary Martin, of Madison County, MS.

Simeon Hammack named his eldest son for his father, William T. Hammack. In adulthood, William often signed his name William T. H. Hammack. The name for which either initial stood is not known, although the initials were probably first used to distinguish William from his several cousins with the same given name.

William T. H. Hammack grew to manhood in Crawford County, Georgia; he married Georgia Elizabeth Jolly there on 16 January 1842. They remained in Crawford County after Simeon and his family moved to Macon County, possibly because of Georgia's Jolly family connections in the area as well as William's kinship ties. Soon after 1850, the family headed west, settling in Yazoo County, Mississippi, near Milledgeville and Mary Hammack Collum. It was there that Georgia Jolly Hammack died near Benton on 23 June 1855.[599]

Georgia's death left William Hammack with six small children, the youngest of whom was about three years old. When William chose to remarry, he returned -- for an unknown reason -- to Crawford County, Georgia, taking as his wife Mary Martin. The couple was married 29 October 1859 in Crawford County, but they were enumerated eight months later in Madison County, Mississippi, where they were living in Canton District.[600]

As noted previously, many members of Simeon Hammack's family were heading west during these years. Children and grandchildren of Simeon's uncle Lewis Hammack had also begun to settle in Alabama and Mississippi in the 1840s and 1850s. Why family members chose particular locations is unclear, however. The Collum family settled first in Yazoo County, and several of Simeon's family seem to have first settled there before moving more permanently to other locations. From research in Madison County, one can speculate that there may have been another tie that led the family to that destination. In Wilkes and Taliaferro Counties, the Hammack family and the Semmes family had been neighbors, and land records of James Moore and Sarah Hammack Moore, sister of Simeon Hammack, in Taliaferro County, Georgia, show that their land bordered tracts owned by Ignatius Semmes. The Semmes family had settled in Madison County in the 1840s but left kin in Taliaferro County. Buried three miles west of Canton, near the residence of William T. H. Hammack and family, is "Mrs. Mary, relict of Dr. Ignatius Semmes, formerly of Wilkes County, Georgia, born St. Charles County, Maryland, and departed this life 19 December 1854, aged 71, Madison County, Mississippi." Perhaps members of the Semmes family commended Madison County to their Taliaferro County, Georgia, kin, who in turn recommended it to Sarah Hammack Moore and her family.[601]

Whatever the reason for the choice, Madison County, Mississippi, became the seat of William T. H. Hammack's family for more than a century. In time, he would be joined there by his mother and several siblings; of these, Sallie Hammack Taylor and Martha Hammack Smith would remain in the area for many years. Following the deaths of John T. Hammack and his wife Louisa Templeton Hammack in Calhoun County, their surviving offspring would also relocate to Madison County, where they would remain well into the twentieth-century.

William T. H. Hammack -- who was forty when the American Civil War began -- is not known to have served in the Confederate Army, although all of his other brothers and several of his sons did. At the time of the 1860 census, William was working as an overseer for John Robinson, who owned five plantations in Madison County at that time[602]; William owned real estate valued at $100 and personal property valued at $200. On Robinson's behalf he was supervising 1,400 acres and eighty-three slaves. William was taxed in Madison County in 1861 and 1868; both tax lists noted that among his property was

---

[599] 1850 Crawford Co., GA, Census, p. 299; *The Weekly American Banner*, published in Yazoo City, MS, Issue of 27 June, 1855.

[600] 1860 Madison Co., MS, Census, p. 823.

[601] Old Sulphur Springs Catholic Cemetery, Madison Co., MS; *Agrarian Acadia*, pp. 144-145.

[602] Other overseers included J. N. Tanner, J. R. Tucker, R. Slocumb, and T. Y. Bains.

a watch valued at $10.[603]

William seems to have worked most of his life as an overseer for others and to have accumulated little real property of his own. The 1870 census showed him with no real estate but with personal property valued at $200.[604] William died landless in 1880[605]; the 1880 Madison County, Mississippi, agricultural schedule showed that Mary Martin Hammack was farming twenty-five acres which she rented in return for part of the produce. This arrangement -- sharecropping -- became the dominant land and labor arrangement in the south during Reconstruction and persisted throughout the region for decades.[606]

At William Hammack's death, Mary Martin Hammack was left with a large family to rear. She and William had several children following their marriage in 1859; George Thomas, Maggie, Laura, and Josephine were all still living at home when their father died, and George, the eldest, had only just turned twenty-one. Two other children, born in 1873 and 1874, had died as infants. They are buried in a small cemetery with only two known markers in Madison County. William and Mary Martin Hammack may have also been buried there, but they were more likely interred near Flora in the Mt. Olympus Cemetery (also known as the Hammack Cemetery), where several of William's other sons and their families are buried. No record of Mary Martin Hammack's death has been located.

William T. H. Hammack and Georgia Elizabeth Jolly Hammack had six children. The eldest, James Wilburn Hammack, died at Vernon, Madison County, Mississippi, in 1917, when he was seventy-four years old. He had married a widow named Jeffersonia Collum Briggs, who was his uncle Milledgeville Collum's half-sister. James became a prosperous farmer in Madison County, farming more than 1,500 acres at the time of the 1880 census.[607] He was a charter member and one of the first two deacons of Flora Baptist Church in 1887.[608] James and Jeffie reared three sons and three daughters who lived in and around Flora, Mississippi; their daughter Lena Hammack married a distant cousin, John Samuel Hammack, son of Wilson and Martha Hammack.

Charles Jolly Hammack, second son of William T. H. and Georgia Elizabeth Jolly Hammack, moved to Mississippi with his parents. He enlisted in the Confederate Cavalry at Brownsville, Mississippi, in 1863;[609] no subsequent record of him has been found, and he may have died during the American Civil War.[610]

Mary Hammack, eldest daughter of William T. H. Hammack and Georgia Elizabeth Jolly, married John M. Ward in 1867 in Madison County, Mississippi. Ward had in 1860 been living with John T. and Louisa Hammack in Choctaw County, and had likely moved south with the other Hammacks during the early 1860s. Ward enlisted in the Confederate Cavalry in 1864 in Brandon, Mississippi, and served until the war ended. His mother Nancy Templeton Ward was a sister of Louisa Templeton Hammack, meaning that his offspring were nieces and nephews of both John T. Hammack and his wife Louisa Templeton

---

[603] 1860 Madison Co., MS, Census, Canton, p. 823; 1861 and 1868 Madison Co., MS, Personal Property Tax Lists, Mississippi Department of Archives and History, Jackson, MS. The 1861 list showed two watches valued together at $25.

[604] 1870 Madison Co., MS, Census, p. 95.

[605] The 1880 Mississippi Mortality Schedule showed that William died the preceding March; he was fifty-nine years old and a native of Georgia. Paralysis, perhaps a stroke, was the cause of death.

[606] 1880 Madison Co., MS, Census, p. 117; 1880 Madison Co., MS, Agricultural Schedule, p. 9.

[607] This land apparently came from the Briggs estate. Madison Co., MS, Deed Book OO, pp. 283, and 634-635, contains deeds from the estate of A. A. E. Briggs to Jeffie A. E. and Cora Hammack on 27 July 1880 and from Jeffie and James W. Hammack to Cora and John A. Hammack on 20 July 1881.

[608] C. L. Mead, *The Land Between Two Rivers: Madison Co., MS* (Jackson, 1987), p. 70.

[609] "Located on the old Bolton-Cox Ferry Road about eight miles north of Bolton, Brownsville in its early days boasted five stores and a jail. It is said to have been one of the wildest sections of the county during the open saloon days and a number of men were killed in the free-for-alls that took place here. A post office was opened in 1905, and the community received its name from its first postmaster." J. W. Brieger, *Hometown Mississippi* (2nd ed., no publisher, no date), Mississippi Department of Archives and History, Jackson, MS.

[610] Mississippi Confederate Military Rosters, Co. F, Ballentine's Cavalry Regiment, Mississippi Department of Archives and History, Jackson, MS.

Hammack.[611]

John Asa Hammack, third son of William T. H. and Georgia Elizabeth Jolly Hammack, was born in Crawford County, Georgia, in 1847 and died in Madison County, Mississippi, in 1917. On 20 December 1876, he married Cora Augusta Briggs, daughter of Arthur Eugene Briggs and Jeffersonia Collum Briggs Hammack. John Asa thus became his brother James's stepson-in-law, and his children were triple relations of Milledgeville and Mary Hammack Collum. Cora Briggs Hammack owned a tract of 520 acres in Madison County that she inherited from her father's estate. It seems likely that her step-father James Wilburn Hammack acquired much of his financial resources through his marriage to Jeffersonia Collum Briggs as well. At the time of the 1887 Madison County, Mississippi, tax list, James W. Hammack and Cora Briggs Hammack were the only two Hammack landowners shown within the county.[612]

John and Cora were charter members of Flora Baptist Church in 1887.[613] They reared nine children born between 1878 and 1894. Their eldest daughter Ethel Hammack (1878-1966) married H. W. O'Neal, a cousin of Mary Almedia Bankston, wife of George Cleveland Hammack. Their daughter Corille Hammack Lane (1901-2000) died two months before her 100th birthday.

Of the remaining children of William and Georgia Jolly Hammack, son Simeon Hammack died in boyhood. William M. Hammack (1851-aft. 1910) seems never to have married. At the time of the 1910 census, he and his first cousin Felix W. Hammack, son of John T. Hammack and Louisa Templeton, were farming together near Flora, Mississippi. No subsequent record of him has been found.[614]

By his second marriage to Mary Martin, William T. H. Hammack fathered four additional offspring between 1860 and 1870.

George Thomas Hammack (1861-1937) became a Primitive Baptist elder. He married Viola Sanderford (1866-1944) and reared a large family in Hinds and Copiah Counties. Their son William Howard Hammack married Mary K. Gary, a distant cousin of H. W. O'Neal and Mary Almedia Bankston Hammack.

George's sister Laura Hammack married G. W. Sanderford in Madison County in 1881. Margaret Hammack (1864-) married Thomas Lorance, son of John and Elizabeth Cates Lorance, in 1882. Thomas Lorance was thus a first cousin of Elizabeth Cates who married William S. Hammack, son of John T. and Louisa Templeton Hammack. Claude Lorance, a nephew of Thomas Lorance and grandson of John and Elizabeth Lorance, married Minnie Hammack, granddaughter of William T. H. and Georgia Jolly Hammack.

Josephine Hammack (1869-1930) was the youngest child of William T. H. and Mary Martin Hammack. Madison County marriages show that one Josephine Hammack married J. F. Baker in 1888; Collum family researchers, however, indicate that William's daughter Josephine Hammack (1869-1930) married Benjamin Franklin Collum (1865-1941) and reared a large family in Biloxi and Gulfport, Mississippi.[615]

B. Mary Jane Hammack and Milledgeville Collum of Yazoo and Holmes Counties, Mississippi, and Navarro County, Texas.

Mary Jane Hammack, elder daughter of Simeon Hammack and Elizabeth Jane Moore, was born about 1824 in Jones County, Georgia. She married Milledgeville Collum on 14 April 1842 in Crawford County,

---

[611] 1850 Randolph Co., GA, Census, p. 775; Mississippi Confederate Military Rosters, Co. D, 3rd Mississippi Cavalry, Mississippi Department of Archives and History, Jackson, MS.

[612] 1887 Madison Co., MS, Land Tax, Mississippi Department of Archives and History, Jackson, MS.

[613] Mead, *Land Between*, p. 70.

[614] 1910 Madison Co., MS, Census, p. 228.

[615] The date of the marriage of Josephine to J. F. Baker is 19 December 1888; the date of the marriage to Collum is 20 December 1888. It appears that the Collum marriage is the correct one. Benjamin F. Collum was a son of John Collum and Hester Ashley and a cousin of Jeffersonia Collum Briggs Hammack, Cora Briggs Hammack, and Milledgeville Collum.

Georgia.

The Collum family would play a significant role in the Hammack family's move westward. Milledgeville Collum's father John Collum had moved from Edgefield District, South Carolina, to Georgia in the 1820s. In the 1830s, Milledgeville's elder siblings would begin the move westward into Alabama and Mississippi, and Milledgeville and his younger siblings would follow them in the 1840s and 1840s. Absalom Collum and Elbert Collum both settled in Yazoo County, Mississippi, before 1850. Miranda Collum Dillard and her husband Manning Dillard also settled in Mississippi. Among Milledgeville's younger half-siblings was Jeffersonia A. E. Collum, born about 1835, who married first Arthur E. Briggs and second James W. Hammack and lived in Madison County, Mississippi.

Milledgeville and Mary Jane Hammack Collum left Georgia for Mississippi about 1843. The 1850 Yazoo County, Mississippi, census indicated that seven year old daughter Mary was born in Georgia while six year old son John was born in Mississippi.[616] By 1860, the Collums were neighbors of the William T. H. Hammack family in Madison County, Mississippi. They were living in Tehula, Holmes County, Mississippi, at the time of the 1870 census and in Corsicana, Navarro County, Texas, in 1880. Mary Hammack Collum died about 1880, and Milledgeville Collum remarried, beginning a second family. He was enumerated, age seventy-eight, in Navarro County in 1900; living with him was his second wife, Mary, age forty-six, and sons Milton, age nineteen, and Ollie, age eighteen.[617]

While living in Mississippi, Milledgeville Collum served during the Civil War in Company C, 39th Mississippi Infantry. Wounded in 1863, Milledgeville was sent from Port Hudson, Louisiana, to New Orleans. Muster Rolls for 1863 and 1864 list him as a Prisoner of War, indicating that he was being held in Sandusky, Ohio, and Baltimore, Maryland. A Captain in his unit, Milledgeville was exchanged on 3 March 1864 but was soon afterwards sent to hospital in Atlanta on 28 June 1864. The records do not indicate whether he continued to serve after his release from the hospital in 1864 or whether he received a medical discharge.[618]

Milledgeville and Mary Hammack Collum were the parents of six children. Mary Collum, born about 1843 in Georgia, was enumerated with her family in 1850; she had either died or married by the time of the 1860 census. John Simeon Collum, born about 1844 in Mississippi, was living with wife Nettie and two small children in Navarro County in 1880. William J. Collum, born about 1846 in Mississippi, served in the Confederate Army while living in Madison County; he was living with his parents in Navarro County as late as 1880. Milledgeville Clayton Collum, born about 1848 in Mississippi, married Mary Ella Lane in 1878; they were living in Navarro County in 1880. Cicero Simon Collum, born about 1851 in Mississippi, married Pauline Kelley; they were living in Corsicana, Navarro County, in 1880, 1900, and 1910. Simon had apparently died by the time of the 1920 census, but Pauline lived until 9 May 1932, when she died in Corsicana.[619] Eugene Collum, born about 1853 in Yazoo County, Mississippi, died 5 April 1920 in Navarro County, Texas. He and his wife Anna were enumerated in Navarro County in 1910.[620]

C. Charles M. Hammack of Calhoun County, Mississippi.

Charles M. Hammack was born about 1824, probably in Jones County, Georgia. He died prior to 1 April 1879 in Calhoun County, Mississippi.[621]

---

[616] 1850 Yazoo Co., MS, Census, p. 506.

[617] 1860 Madison Co., MS, Census, p. 822; 1870 Holmes Co., MS, Census, p. 243; 1880 Navarro Co., TX, Census, p. 504; 1900 Titus Co., TX, Census, p. 152.

[618] Mississippi Confederate Military Rosters, Co. C, 39th Mississippi Infantry, Mississippi Department of Archives and History, Jackson, MS.

[619] The 1930-32 Mortality Schedule, Corsicana, Navarro Co., Texas.

[620] 1910 Navarro Co., TX, Census, p. 157; Texas State Death Index, 1920, Texas State Archives, Austin, TX.

[621] Calhoun Co., MS, Land Abstract Book 1 East.

Little is known of Charles Hammack's early life. He married Sarah Jane Curtis, daughter of Thomas G. and Sarepta Curtis, on 15 December 1844 in Crawford County, Georgia. Between 1846 and 1849, Charles and Sarah moved with the Thomas Curtis family to Choctaw County, Mississippi. They were enumerated there on 21 October 1850.[622]

In 1859, Charles Hammack acquired 160 acres, Township 22, Range 8 East, Section 36, from T. H. Flowers and wife, Benjamin Flowers, W. N. Flowers, Sterling Doolittle and wife, T. R. Davis and wife, and Thomas Johnson and wife. The land apparently was part of an estate settlement in which a group of Flowers heirs disposed of inherited property.[623] The 1860 tax list for Calhoun County showed Charles Hammack as owner of three slaves; at the time of the 1860 census, he owned real estate valued at $1,000 and personal property valued at $500.[624]

In August 1859, Charles Hammack united with Bethel Baptist Church in Calhoun County. His wife Sarah Curtis Hammack also became a member, and the church minutes note that she died on 6 April 1861. Charles remained a member of the congregation for a decade, but the minutes reveal that in the late 1860s he experienced a serious conflict with his brethren. Between November 1868 and April 1869, Charles faced discipline for not attending services and for reports that he had been swearing. Charles refused to answer the complaints and was finally excluded from membership in April 1869. He was finally restored to membership in October 1873 after a gap of more than four years.[625]

Charles soon remarried Angeline Randolph Brown, a native of Kentucky whose family had recently settled in Calhoun County.[626] Although their first surviving child was not born until about 1866, there might have been older offspring who died in infancy.

During the Civil War, Charles Hammack served as a private in Company F, 2nd Partisan Rangers, and Company D, 8th Battalion, Mississippi Infantry. He enlisted 19 October 1863 at Brownsville, MS, under Captain J. G. Ballentine. He was present on muster rolls throughout 1863 but by 1864 was noted as "absent without leave." Charles apparently returned home in December 1863 and never returned to active service; although initially listed as absent without leave following 13 December 1863, later muster rolls indicate that he deserted on that date.[627]

In November 1865, Charles and Angeline Hammack sold a portion of Section 36, Township 22, Range 8 East, to Samuel Frank. Perhaps through marriage to Angeline, Charles acquired an interest in Section 9, Township 22, Range 8 East.[628] The 1870 Calhoun County agricultural schedule shows that Charles was cultivating twenty acres and had an unimproved 140-acre tract.[629] He owned no horses but

---

[622] 1850 Choctaw Co., MS, Census, p. 2: Thomas G. Curtis, 45, GA; Sarepta, 42, GA; Isabella M., 18, GA; John F., 14, GA; James W., 12, GA; William H., 9, GA; Josephine A., 6, GA; Martha A., 4, GA; Charles M. Hammack, 27, GA; Sarah J., 24, GA; Sarepta E., 4, GA; Mary J., 2/12, MS.

[623] Calhoun Co., MS, Land Abstract Book 1 East.

[624] 1860 Calhoun Co., MS, Personal Property Tax List, Mississippi Department of Archives and History, Jackson, MS; 1860 Calhoun Co., MS, Census, p. 40.

[625] Bethel Baptist Church Minutes, transcription, Calhoun City Library, Calhoun City, MS.

[626] Angelina was sister of Sarah Elizabeth, wife of Thomas Macon; Orpha Randolph; and Virginia Randolph, wife of John Mordecai Cook. There are several ties between the Hammacks, Lays, Cooks, and Davises. The Randolphs trace back through Kentucky to Henrico County, Virginia. Angeline Randolph Brown Hammack was a direct descendant of William and Mary Isham Randolph and a distant cousin of President Thomas Jefferson (1743-1826), Chief Justice John Marshall (1751-1835), and the controversial legislator John Randolph of Roanoke.

[627] Mississippi Confederate Military Rosters, Company D, 8th Battalion, Mississippi Department of Archives and History, Jackson, MS.

[628] Calhoun Co., MS, Land Abstract Book 1 East.

[629] 1870 Calhoun Co., MS, Census, pp. 445-446. The following table briefly summarizes Hammack landholdings in Calhoun County in 1870:

had two mules, ten cows, and fifteen swine valued together at $500. During the preceding year, Charles's farm had yielded 400 bushels of Indian corn, three bales of cotton, twenty bushels of peas and beans, fifteen bushels of Irish potatoes, ninety bushels of sweet potatoes, 200 pounds of butter, two tons of hay, $50 in home manufactures, and meat from slaughtered animals valued at $130. The census taker estimated that the total value of Charles's farm production for the year 1869-1870 was in excess of $1,100.

Charles apparently began to experience financial difficulties in the middle 1870s. On 10 January 1875, he and wife Angeline mortgaged a portion of Section 9 to Oscar Holden for $554.[630] They apparently failed to repay the note, for a list of forfeited lands shows that in 1875 Charles Hammack lost 160 acres in Section 9 for failure to pay taxes on the tract.[631] The following year, Oscar Holden sold the land to B. E. Davis.[632] No record is found of Charles from 1875 until 1879, when a deed from A. B. Davis describes the land being sold as "adjacent the house of the late Charles Hammack."[633]

Charles and Angelina Hammack may have both died during the Yellow Fever epidemic that gripped much of Tennessee and Mississippi in the late 1870s. At the time of the 1880 census, their two orphaned daughters were living with their aunt and uncle, John M. and Virginia Randolph Davis, and their grandmother, Eliza Randolph, in Slate Springs.[634]

Charles Hammack was the father of six known offspring, three by his first marriage and three by his second marriage. His eldest child, Sarepta Hammack (1846-1919), was named for her grandmother Sarepta Curtis. She married Samuel Doolittle (1846-1914), from whose father Sterling Doolittle Charles Hammack had purchased land in 1859.[635] They reared a large family, and many generations of their family resided at Slate Springs. Both Samuel and Sarepta were active in Bethel Church, and both are buried in the church cemetery.

Mary J. Hammack was Charles's second daughter; she was born in early 1850, after the family settled in Choctaw County, Mississippi. Mary was alive in October 1864 when she joined Bethel Church; no record of her dismissal has been found. She may have married, but, if so, the identity of her husband has not been determined.

Isabella M. Hammack (1852-1884) was the third daughter of Charles and Sarah Jane Curtis Hammack. She married William Stoddard (1857-1886) and had an only known child, William, born in 1878. Both Isabella and her husband died at young ages and are buried together in Bethel Cemetery; the fate of their offspring is uncertain.[636]

By his second marriage to Angeline Randolph Brown, Charles Hammack fathered one son and two

Name	Improved	Unimproved	Farm Value	Livestock Value	Home Manufacturers	Slaughtered Meat	All Products
Charles Hammack	20	140	$800	$550	$50	$150	$1100
William Hammack	40	60	$400	$50	$30	$50	$1100
Alfred Hammack	30	50	$250	$200	$20	$75	$450
Felix W. Hammack	60	100	$800	$450	$30	$100	$750
George Hammack	30	50	$300	$250	$0	$200	$700

[630] Calhoun Co., MS, Land Abstract Book 1 East.
[631] Lands forfeited to the State of MS for Taxes, RG 29, Vol. 38, MS Dept. of Archives and History, Jackson.
[632] Calhoun Co., MS, Land Abstract Book 1 East.
[633] Calhoun Co., MS, Land Abstract Book 1 East.
[634] 1880 Calhoun Co., MS, Census, p. 607.
[635] Calhoun Co., MS, Land Abstract Book 1 East.
[636] 1880 Calhoun Co., MS, Census, p. 607.

daughters. Charles Hammack, Jr. (1867-bet. 1897/1900) married and had three children, Lester, Annie, and Joe. The family lived in Calhoun and Sunflower Counties, Mississippi.[637] Orva Hammack, whose name is also spelled Orphie, was named for her aunt Orpha Randolph. Born about 1868, Orva became a member of Bethel Church in 1887, and her name appears on membership lists until 1891. It would seem likely that she died or married soon afterwards.[638] Naomi Hammack, the youngest child of Charles Hammack, was born about 1874. She and her sister Orva were enumerated with their aunt Virginia Randolph Cook and their grandmother Eliza Randolph at the time of the 1880 census. Naomi, who seems to have been known as "Omma", married J. A. Wasson on 14 May 1891 in Sunflower County, Mississippi. She was deceased by 1899, when J. A. Wasson remarried Leila Lamberson of Kemper County.[639]

D. Sarah Hammack and Daniel D. Taylor of Calhoun and Madison Counties, Mississippi.

Sarah Ann Hammack, Simeon's second daughter, was born about 1826 in Jones County, Georgia. On 24 December 1844, she married Daniel D. Taylor in Crawford County, Georgia. With her new husband, Sarah moved to Sumter County, Georgia, where she was enumerated at the time of the 1850 census living near her uncle Lewis Hammack. Between 1851 and 1854, she and Daniel Taylor moved their family to Mississippi, where they were living in Choctaw County at the time of the 1860 census.[640]

Daniel D. Taylor worked as a farmer cultivating a modest holding. He seems to have owned no land in his own right and may have rented both land and slaves from his father-in-law Simeon Hammack. The 1860 Choctaw County slave schedule showed that Taylor had one male and three female slaves.[641] The 1863 Choctaw County Personal Property Tax list showed him with three slaves under age sixty.[642]

Daniel Taylor died between 1863 and 1870, perhaps as early as 1866. Sallie Taylor was listed alone at the time of the 1870 census, but records of Philadelphia Baptist Church show that, in November 1866, Sallie Taylor received a letter of dismissal along with "Bro. George Hammock and Sisters Elizabeth and Mat. A. Hammock."[643] The group apparently moved to Madison County, Mississippi, where Sallie was enumerated at the time of the 1870 census and where she apparently lived the remainder of her life.[644]

In 1870, Sallie was living near her Hammack kin. The census showed her living in Vernon District, aged forty-four, and keeping house. She owned no taxable property, although her son John did own property valued at $500.[645] No references to Sallie have been found after 1870; she presumably died prior to the 1880 federal census.

Sallie Hammack and Daniel Taylor were the parents of seven children. Mary Taylor (c. 1846-) was enumerated with her parents in 1850 and 1860; no other records of her have been found. Record of her marriage may have been among the now lost Choctaw County marriages for the period 1860 to 1866. John Taylor (c. 1849 -) married F. J. Lard on 14 February 1873 in Madison County. They were living in Vernon, Madison County, Mississippi, with two small children at the time of the 1880 census.[646] Amanda V. Taylor (c. 1851-) married William Sanderford in 1869 in Madison County. They were enumerated in Vernon in 1870 and 1880 but moved to Texas between 1880 and 1884. At the time of the 1900

---

[637] 1900 Calhoun Co., MS, Census; 1920 Sunflower Co., MS, Census, p. 280.

[638] Bethel Baptist Church Minutes, transcription, Calhoun City Library, Calhoun City, MS.

[639] Two of the three children of Omma Hammack and J. A. Wasson lived to adulthood. Ruth Wasson married John Frank Wise, and Charles Randolph Wasson (probably named for Charles Hammack and Angeline Randolph) married Jewell Sharp. They lived in Greenville, Mississippi. See 1900 Sunflower Co., MS, Census, p. 217; 1920 Sunflower Co., MS, Census, p. 94.

[640] 1850 Sumter Co., GA, Census, p. 148; 1860 Choctaw Co., MS, Census, p. 421.

[641] 1860 Choctaw Co., MS, Slave Schedule, p. 58.

[642] 1863 Choctaw Co., MS, Personal Property Tax Roll, taken from original document at Mississippi Department of Archives and History, Auditor's Records, RO17-B23-S4-03618, p. 21 is original number but later renumbered as p. 16.

[643] Philadelphia Baptist Church Records, Webster Co., MS, transcription, Calhoun City Library, Calhoun City, MS.

[644] 1870 Madison Co., MS, Census, p. 95.

[645] Ibid.

[646] 1880 Madison Co., MS, Census, p. 97.

Henderson County, Texas, Census, Amanda Taylor Sanderfer was a widow with four sons in her household. Living next door to her was married son Charlie Sanderfer and his family. No references to Amanda have been found after 1900, although son Charlie Sanderfer was still living in Henderson County in 1910 and son Robert M. Sanderford was living in Jack County in the same year.[647] Sallie Taylor (c. 1854 --) apparently married a son of Manning Dillard after the 1870 census; she was a widow in Madison County in 1900 with several children[648], among them a son Robert Neal Dillard who was listed as a nephew of Daniel Taylor at the time of the 1910 census.[649] Daniel W. Taylor (c. 1859-) married Martha M. "Patsy" Sanderfer on 29 January 1881 in Madison County, Mississippi. He and his sister Laura, both unmarried, were living together at the time of the 1880 Madison County census. The Madison County agricultural schedule indicated that he was renting 124 acres of improved land and sixty acres of unimproved land at that time.[650] Daniel and Pattie were members of Flora Baptist Church when it was organized in 1887 and were enumerated with seven children at the time of the 1900 census for Vernon District. They were living in Madison County in 1910 and 1920, and several of their children remained in the county well afterwards.[651] Marcus Taylor, youngest son of Daniel and Sarah Taylor, was three years old at the time of the 1870 census; he has not been located after that date.

E. Felix Wilborn Hammack of Calhoun County, Mississippi.

Born about 1834 in Crawford County, Georgia, Felix Wilborn Hammack moved with his parents from Macon County, Georgia, to Choctaw County, Mississippi. Felix was living at home, unmarried, with his parents in 1860.

Felix W. Hammack enlisted in Company D, 3rd Mississippi Infantry. He enlisted 2 November 1861 in Grenada, Mississippi, and, by the end of the year, had served as 3rd and 2nd Lieutenant. By 1862, he was serving in Company D, 45th Mississippi Regiment. Felix was hospitalized in Georgia due to illness from 13 October to 13 November 1863. He was serving as the company's Lieutenant at the time of the Battle of Shiloh.[652]

About 1866, Felix W. Hammack married a local widow, Mary Lee Doolittle May, sister of Sarepta Hammack's husband Samuel Doolittle. Mary had married William T. May about 1860; the couple had four children -- William, Samuel, Elijah, and Jane -- before William May died about 1866. Soon after May's death, Mary married Felix Hammack, recently returned from the Confederate service, and he became administrator of her husband's estate.[653]

Felix seems to have been a well-to-do farmer. Slightly younger than his brother John, he did not marry until significantly later. But with marriage Felix acquired an interest in the estate of his wife Mary Lee May's first husband, including an already functional and prosperous farm. Thus, at the time of the 1870 census, Felix had only been farming on his own for about four years, but the agricultural schedule suggests that he was already prospering.[654] In that year, Felix controlled 160 acres of land valued at $800,

---

[647] 1870 Madison Co., MS, Census, p. 95; 1880 Madison Co., MS, Census, p. 105; 1900 Henderson Co., TX, Census, p. 80; 1910 Henderson Co., TX, Census, p. 125.

[648] 1900 Madison Co., MS, Census, p. 114.

[649] 1900 Madison Co., MS, Census, p. 114 ; 1910 Madison Co., MS, Census, p. 185.

[650] 1880 Madison Co., MS, Agricultural Schedule, p. 15.

[651] 1880 Madison Co., MS, Census, p. 105; 1900 Madison Co., MS, Census, p. 115; 1910 Madison Co., MS, Census, p. 185; 1920 Madison Co., MS, Census, p. 110.

[652] Mississippi Confederate Muster Lists, Company D, 45th Mississippi Regiment, Mississippi Department of Archives and History, Jackson, MS; Dunbar Rowland, *The Mississippi Official and Statistical Register of 1908* (Jackson, 1908). Rowland states that Felix was a Captain before his unit merged.

[653] Doolittle, *Doolittle Family*, p. 591.

[654] 1870 Calhoun Co., MS, Census, p. 446. William May's father Thomas died prior to 1860, leaving significant landholdings and several children. Estate records of Thomas T. May, originally filed in Report Book B, p. 264-65, but surviving now only in abstract form in Calhoun County, shows that he was the father of William T. May. At the division of the May property, Virginia May received SW 1/4 NE 1/4, Section 22, Township 22, Range 8 East and James May received NW 1/4 NE 1/4, Section 22, Township

including sixty acres of improved farm. His livestock was valued at $450 -- $100 less than that of his brother Charles but a sum greater than that of any of his siblings -- and consisted of two horses, three milk cows, five head of cattle, and thirty hogs. The farm produced 200 bushels of Indian corn, two bales of cotton, thirty bushels of peas, fifty bushels of sweet potatoes, and 200 pounds of butter. Felix had also produced twenty tons of hay and twenty pounds of molasses. He had produced household manufactures valued at $30 and slaughtered meat valued at $100; the total value of his farm produce was $750, less than that of his older siblings Charles and John but greater than that of his younger siblings Alfred and George.[655]

At the time of the 1880 census, Felix was working twenty-five acres of tilled land but owned another 195 acres of woodland. The land, livestock, and farm implements were together valued at $1,240, and in 1879 the farm had yielded produce valued at $375.[656] Felix reported that he owned 160 acres in Section 15, Township 22, Range 8 East, in 1883[657] and 120 acres in the same location in 1887.[658] On 19 December 1884, Felix and Mary, along with J. W. May, had deeded forty acres of Section 15 to Oscar Holden, a trustee for J. T. Parker.[659] Felix and Mary deeded additional property to Holden and Parker in 1892,[660] and by 1902 Felix owned no land in his own right. At that time, tax records show that Simeon's children and step-children Sam May, Gertrude Nolen, and Sid Hammack owned a cumulative total of 220 acres in Sections 13, 14, and 15.[661]

Religion played a significant role in the life of Felix Hammack and his family. Felix joined Bethel Baptist Church by experience in October 1869.[662] Several times the church named Felix to visit members who were in violation of church discipline. Yet Felix himself had a brief clash with the church elders in 1878, when reports circulated that he had hosted a dance at his own home. Hammack testified that the dance had occurred, but that it had taken place contrary to his own wishes. After his testimony, the church "agreed to bear with him."[663] In October 1883, Felix and several of his neighbors received letters of dismissal from Bethel Church to organize "themselves into a Church at Sabougla". In addition to Felix and Mary Hammack, George W. and Sarah Hammack William May, and several members of related families -- including John W. and Mary Jane Davis and W. D. and Mary Susan Cooke -- received letters at the same time.[664] Felix played a leading role in establishing the church at Sabougla and attended it for the rest of his life.

Mary Lee Doolittle May Hammack died about 1900 in Calhoun County. Her tombstone, which does not record her date of death, reveals that she was sixty years old when she died. The 1860 and 1880

22, Range 8E. Thomas T. May in 1857 had patented W 1/2 NE 1/4 and NE 1/4 NE 1/4, Section 28, Township 22, Range 8E. On 22 Dec., 1854, with Cash Certificate No. 37248, May had entered the claim for this land, in all 200.23 acres. At the time of the 1860 census, Dr. Jonathan May, age 21, was living with his brother William. Also in that household were Mary, 14; Benjamin, 12; and James, 6. All were natives of Mississippi except for William and Jonathan, who were born in Alabama. With the value of land and personal property combined, William May's estate was worth $8,300. Respective values for his siblings were $8,000 for Jonathan, $7,720 for Mary, $7,200 for Benjamin, and $7,600 for James. Several members of this family are buried at Bethel Cemetery: Thomas T. May (2 Sept., 1800 - 30 July, 1859); Mary A. C. May (2 Aug., 1817 - 30 July, 1856); James H. May (12 Feb., 1855 - 14 Aug., 1861); Harriet May (24 Oct., 1849 - 8 May, 1855); Martha A. May (15 Sept., 1853 - 6 Feb., 1855); Joseph T. May (7 May, 1851 - 3 June, 1852); Francis A. E. May (5 Feb., 1838 - 9 Sept., 1851). John W. Magness, a neighbor and associate of Felix W. Hammack, was also his brother-in-law of sorts. Magness married Mary Virginia May, who died 29 October 1870, aged twenty-four, and was buried in the Magness Cemetery. J. W. Magness died 7 January 1889, aged fifty-six.

[655] 1870 Calhoun Co., MS, Agricultural Schedule, pp. 11-12.

[656] 1880 Calhoun Co., MS, Agricultural Schedule, p. 21.

[657] 1883 Land Tax Roll, Township 22, Range 8 East, Calhoun Co., MS, Mississippi Department of Archives and History, Jackson, MS.

[658] 1887 Calhoun Co., MS, Land Tax Roll, Mississippi Department of Archives and History, Jackson, MS.

[659] Calhoun Co., MS, Land Abstract Book 1 East, vol. 2, page 185, col. 2, SW 1/4, Section 15, Township 22, Range 8 East.

[660] Calhoun Co., MS, Land Abstract Book 1 East, vol. 2, page 185, col. 2, SW 1/4, Section 15, Township 22, Range 8 East.

[661] 1902 Calhoun Co., MS, Land Assessment List, Mississippi Department of Archives and History, Jackson, MS.

[662] Bethel Baptist Church Minutes, transcription, Calhoun City Library, Calhoun City, MS.

[663] Ibid.

[664] Ibid.

census records reveal that she was twenty and forty years old respectively, while the 1870 census indicates that she was thirty-four years old. Mary is buried next to Felix Hammack in Bethel Cemetery, with the inscription noting that "She lived and she loved trusting in God."[665]

At the time of the 1900 census, Felix was living at home in Sabougla, with his adult children Jennie and Sidney.[666] Felix was alive at the time of the 1903 Personal Property Tax List for Sabougla District, Calhoun County.[667] He does not appear in subsequent lists and probably died in 1903 or 1904. Felix W. Hammack was buried beside his wife Mary Lee Doolittle May Hammack in Bethel Cemetery. Felix's great-grandson Roscoe Davis recalled that Felix's home place was near the Sabougla Church, just northwest of Sabougla Cemetery.[668]

Of the offspring of William T. May and Mary Lee Doolittle, William M. May was living in Texas in 1922. Samuel May married Josephine Shaw and was living near Slate Springs in 1922. Elijah May and Jane May are not mentioned in the 1922 *Doolittle Family History* and presumably died without offspring prior to that date.[669]

Felix Wilborn Hammack and Mary Lee Doolittle May had six children. Of these, Gertrude A. Hammack (1867-1945) married William Nolen (1864-1900). They are buried in Bethel Cemetery, Calhoun County, Mississippi. Simeon S. "Sim" Hammack (1870-1887) died as a teenager and was buried at Bethel Church. Betsy Ann Hammack (1872-1941) married James Lay Davis and lived at Sabougla, Mississippi, where she reared a large family. Her obituary described her as a "splendid Christian woman" whose "abiding faith in God and her daily deeds of goodness endeared her to every one who came in contact with her."[670] Sidney W. Hammack (1875-1943) married Grace Fox (1882-1900). By 1910, Sidney was living in Washita County, Oklahoma. He was living in Custer County in 1920 and in Oklahoma City when he died in 1943.[671] Mary Elizabeth Hammack (c. 1877 -- 1945) married Samuel Yeager; she was living in Harrison, Arkansas, in 1941. Martha Virginia ("Jennie") Hammack (1882-1959) married James Ellis Riley (1880-1954); they lived in Weatherford, Custer County, Oklahoma, from 1920 until their deaths.

F. Alfred Washington Hammock of Calhoun County, Mississippi, and Ashley County, Arkansas.

Alfred Washington Hammock was born 17 June 1838 in Crawford County, Georgia. He moved with his parents to Mississippi and was living at home, unmarried, at the time of the 1860 Choctaw County, Mississippi, Census.

Alfred was taxed in Madison County, Mississippi, in 1861. He subsequently enlisted in Company D, 8th Mississippi Infantry, serving until the end of the war. Called Dock, Alfred returned to Choctaw County by 1864, when he joined Bethel Church.[672] Two years later, he was charged by the church with dancing, admitted the charge, and was pardoned. In October 1866, however, he left the church by letter[673], although he seems not to have left the area.

---

[665] 1870 Calhoun Co., MS, Census, p. 446; 1900 Calhoun Co., MS, Census, p. 245.

[666] 1900 Calhoun Co., MS, Census, p. 245.

[667] 1903-1907 Calhoun Co., MS, Personal Property Tax Lists, Mississippi Department of Archives and History, Jackson, MS.

[668] Davis indicated in 1996 that he himself grew up just east of the cemetery, about half-way between the cemetery at Sabougla and the church at Sabougla.

[669] W. F. Doolittle, *Doolittle Family in America* (revised ed., Cleveland, OH, 1922). A copy of this monograph may be found in the Calhoun City Library, Calhoun City, MS.

[670] *The Monitor-Herald*, Calhoun County, MS, 17 July 1941. Jennie had seven children. Her son Robert Sidney Davis was Chancery Clerk in Pittsboro, MS. William Roscoe Davis (1893-1959) married Bertha May Vance (1892-1946). They were the parents of William Roscoe Davis, Jr., who supplied much information about this family.

[671] 1910 Washita Co., OK, Census, p. 210; 1920 Custer Co., OK, Census, p. 70; Obituary of Sidney W. Hammack, *Weatherford (OK) News*, 24 August 1943, p. 1.

[672] Mississippi Confederate Muster Lists, Company D, 8th Mississippi Infantry, Mississippi Department of Archives and History, Jackson, MS; Bethel Baptist Church Minutes, transcription, Calhoun City Library, Calhoun City, MS.

[673] Bethel Baptist Church Minutes, transcription, Calhoun City Library, Calhoun City, MS.

Alfred married Nancy Elizabeth Ezell on 12 August 1869 in Webster County, Mississippi. Born 3 May 1852, Nancy was a daughter of William A. Ezell (1822-1865) and Pernicey Risenhoover (1825-1855). Through her mother, Nancy descended from the French Huguenot immigrant Cyprian Prou (1663-1712), who settled in Richmond County, Virginia. The Ezells moved from Pickens County, Alabama, to Choctaw County, Mississippi, following Pernicey's death in 1855.[674]

Of the Calhoun County Hammacks in 1870, Alfred was the least prosperous. Like his brother George, he was farming an eighty acre tract that consisted of thirty improved acres and fifty acres held in reserve. His farm, however, was valued at $250, whereas George's was valued at $300. Alfred also owned a horse, a milk cow, two other cows, and fourteen hogs, altogether worth $200. The farm in the preceding year had produced 100 bushels of Indian corn, significantly less than that produced by any other Calhoun County Hammack. Alfred's other produce suggests that he was a less successful farmer than his siblings. His farm produced only one bale of cotton, twenty pounds of sweet potatoes, fifty pounds of butter, and $20 pounds of molasses. Including meat slaughtered the preceding year worth $75, the total value of Alfred's farm production during the preceding year was only $450, while the farms of his other brothers all yielded a product valued at more than $700.[675]

During the 1870s, Dock rejoined Bethel Church, and his wife Nancy became a member following a conversion experience in 1875.[676] Alfred attended church irregularly, however, and in 1878 a committee was appointed to consult with him on this matter. After failing to make amends, the church formally excluded Alfred from membership in December 1878.[677] After a period of reflection, the church welcomed Alfred back to membership, however, and in 1885 he was among the group granted letters from Bethel Church to establish a new church at Sabougla. Other charter members of the new church included his brothers Felix and George and their families.[678]

Alfred was enumerated in Calhoun County at the time of the 1880 census and taxed there in 1884 and 1885.[679] He does not appear in Calhoun County tax records for 1887, 1889, or 1892. Apparently Alfred and Eliza left Calhoun County soon after 1885, settling in Ashley County, Arkansas, where Alfred died on 18 July 1898 and was buried at Old Union Cemetery. After settling in Arkansas, Alfred and his descendants generally used the spelling Hammock rather than Hammack.

As a widow, Eliza applied for a Confederate pension in 1902 based on her husband's military service during the War Between the States. She indicated that her husband had served honorably until his discharge in 1864 and that he had died in 1898, leaving her with young children and in need of financial assistance.[680] The 1910 Ashley County census showed Eliza living with her married daughter Jennie Ferguson. Although Jennie herself was deceased by 1920, Eliza was still with the family at that time, helping care for Jennie's young children.[681]

Nancy Eliza Ezell Hammock, called "Little Granny" by her descendants, lived until November 1941; she died six months prior to her ninetieth birthday. Alfred's granddaughter Lois Hagood recalled him as a "large, fat man" who died of dropsy, a nineteenth-century term for congestive heart failure. Alfred died at home while sitting in a chair; after working the fields, Eliza came in and found him dead. Of Nancy Elizabeth Ezell Hammock, her great-granddaughter recalled: "I remember Little Granny, as we called her. Everyone that knew her loved and respected her. She was a very jolly person and never complained about anything. I used to read to her out of a New Testament that belonged to her Daddy. It was older than the

---

[674] L. H. Hagood, *The Elusive Ancestor* (Crossett, AR, 1992) provides a detailed account of the family history of Nancy Ezell Hammock.

[675] 1870 Calhoun Co., MS, Agricultural Schedule, pp. 11-12.

[676] Bethel Baptist Church Minutes, transcription, Calhoun City Library, Calhoun City, MS.

[677] Ibid.

[678] Ibid.

[679] 1880 Calhoun Co., MS, Census, p. 632; 1884 and 1885 Personal Property Tax Lists, Calhoun Co., MS, Mississippi Department of Archives and History, Jackson, MS.

[680] Arkansas Confederate Pension Application No. 14582, Arkansas History Commission, Little Rock, AR.

[681] 1910 Ashley Co., AR, Census, p. 276; 1920 Ashley Co., AR, Census, p. 150.

Civil War....Granny was always willing to join in the games we played as children. She would dress up in old sheets and false faces and scare us. She had a deep compassion for girls that got into trouble where most people condemned them. I feel that she developed a heart of gold due to her life. I think she had to live among different relatives while growing up. After marrying, she had problems. She lost three children in a measles epidemic. One died with a heart attack after a tornado, one daughter died in childbirth. Out of nine children, she survived all but the eldest son, Felix. She was eighty-nine years old at her death and always had a very good strong mind. She pieced and quilted quilts all the time, always giving them to one of her grandchildren and a great grandchild. She was a wonderful little old lady."[682]

Alfred Washington Hammock and Nancy Elizabeth Ezell Hammock produced nine children; Nancy outlived all but one. Felix A. Hammock (1869-1946) married Annie J. Carman (1874-1939) in 1893; he was the only child of Alfred and Eliza who survived his mother. Felix and Annie had four children who left many descendants in Ashley County, Arkansas. Bettie Hammock (1872-1891) married Ben Morman; she left an only child, Gertrude Mormon Dillon (1888-1975), and several grandchildren. Jeffie Hammock (1875-1937) married Charles Wesley Roberts (1864-1942) in 1893; they reared a large family -- ten children -- and remained in Ashley County until they died. William Hammock (1876-1882), Ambrose Hammock (1879-1891), Willie Hammock (1882-1892), Austin Hammock (1884-1891), and Grover Lee Hammock (1888-1892) all predeceased their parents. Margaret Virginia "Jennie" Hammock (1886-1917), the youngest daughter, was born before the family left Calhoun County. Jennie married William Ferguson in 1900 and, following his death, William Peden. She predeceased her mother but left five children, who were partially reared by their grandmother.[683]

G. Clayton M. Hammack of Calhoun County, Mississippi.

Clayton M. Hammack, born about 1840 in Crawford County, Georgia, was living at home with his parents at the time of the 1850 and 1860 census enumerations. He served in Captain McCord's Company, enlisting in Slate Springs, Mississippi, in 1861. Clayton apparently died in the Confederate service as no further information has been discovered concerning him.[684]

H. Franklin F. Hammack of Calhoun County, Mississippi.

Franklin F. Hammack, born about 1843 in Crawford County, Georgia, was living at home with his parents at the time of the 1850 and 1860 census enumerations. He served in Company D, 3rd Mississippi Infantry, in the Confederate Army and died 8 October 1862 at Graysville, Georgia.[685]

I. Martha Hammack and Stephen D. Smith of Madison County, Mississippi.

Martha Hammack, born about 1845 in Crawford County, Georgia, was living at home with her parents at the time of the 1850 and 1860 census enumerations. She joined Philadelphia Church in Choctaw County, Mississippi, prior to 1862 and, along with her mother, was dismissed from membership on 1 September 1862. Between 1862 and 1866, however, Martha rejoined the church, and in November 1866, with her mother, her brother George Hammack, and her sister Sallie Taylor, she received a letter of dismissal from Philadelphia Church.[686] This receipt of letters apparently occurred in anticipation of the family's removal to south central Mississippi. It was there, living in the same neighborhood as her brother

---

[682] Hagood, *The Elusive Ancestor*, p. 36.

[683] Ibid.

[684] Mississippi Confederate Muster Lists, Captain McCord's Company, Mississippi Department of Archives and History, Jackson, MS.

[685] Mississippi Confederate Muster Lists, Company D, 3rd Mississippi Infantry, Mississippi Department of Archives and History, Jackson, MS.

[686] Philadelphia Baptist Church Minutes, Webster Co., MS, transcript, Calhoun City Library, Calhoun City, MS.

William T. H. Hammack, that Martha married Stephen D. Smith on 23 July 1868.

At the time of the 1870 census, Martha and Stephen were living in Vernon, Madison County, Mississippi, with their infant daughter Luanna.[687] By 1880, Martha and Stephen were still living in Vernon, where Stephen was farming and Martha was keeping house. By this point, their family had grown to include four additional daughters born between 1872 and 1878. The Madison County agricultural schedule for that year showed that Stephen Smith was farming twenty-three acres but that he owned a total of 108 acres altogether.[688]

Stephen and Martha Smith were still living in Madison County at the time of the 1900 census.[689] One Stephen sold land in Canton, Madison County, Mississippi, on 24 September 1906, although this was not in the area where Stephen and Martha were living in earlier years; by 1908, Stephen D. Smith's name had disappeared from Madison County tax records. No record of Stephen and Martha has been found after the 1906 deed.[690]

Martha Hammack and Stephen D. Smith were the parents of seven known children. Luanna, born about 1869, married Sam Cagle on 20 December 1890 in Madison County. They were living near Luanna's parents at the time of the 1900 census enumeration.[691] By 1910, they had moved to Yazoo County, where they were enumerated.[692] Of the other Smith children, Mary, Lula, Josephine, Lida, Estis, and Belle were all born in Madison County between 1872 and 1885.

J. George W. T. Hammack and Sarah Lay of Calhoun County, Mississippi.

George W. T. Hammack, born 6 October 1847 in Crawford County, Georgia, was the youngest child of Simeon and Elizabeth Jane Moore Hammack. He moved with his parents to Mississippi as a small child and was reared in Choctaw County, where he lived until early adulthood. He may have temporarily removed with his mother and siblings to Madison County about 1863, but he was soon back in Choctaw County, where, with his mother and sisters, he was a member of Philadelphia Baptist Church. He joined Bethel Baptist Church in September 1869 and remained a member there for the rest of his life.[693]

George W. T. Hammack married about 1871 to Sarah Jane Lay (16 December 1848-14 December 1903), daughter of Jesse G. Lay (1816-1869) and Barbara Cooke Lay (1820-1888), whose family had moved to Choctaw County from Greene County, Alabama. The Lays, Cookes, Ottersons, and Foxes belonged to a group of related families that had moved together from coastal Virginia into South Carolina and ultimately into Alabama and Mississippi. As an extended network of kin, they settled together in Choctaw County in the 1830s and 1840s, and Sarah Lay Hammack was reared amongst a large group of relatives.[694]

Choctaw and Calhoun County legal records present a difficulty in tracing George W. T. Hammack. In addition to George W. T. Hammack, there was a second George W. Hammock -- this man descended from Lewis Hammack of Jones County, Georgia -- who married Mary Sibley and was living in the

[687] 1870 Madison Co., MS, Census, p. 90.

[688] 1880 Madison Co., MS, Census, p. 105; 1880 Madison Co., MS, Agricultural Schedule, p. 15.

[689] 1900 Madison Co., MS, Census, p. 147.

[690] Madison Co., MS, Deed Book PPP, p. 359. One Martha J. Hammack (5 December 1846 -- 26 May 1901) was buried at Pocahontas Methodist Church Cemetery in Hinds County (S3 T7 R1W). Pocahontas in Hinds County is "located fourteen miles northwest of Jackson; the little town of Pocahontas had its beginnings in 1884 when J. E. Lane donated land for the railroad right-of-way. Section houses and a depot were built and a number of homes and businesses soon followed. The station was called Pocahontas for two Indian mounds nearby. Other early settlers were the Skidmore, Hull, Whitfield, Graves, Middleton, and Bell families." James W. Bridger, comp., *Hometown Mississippi* 2nd ed. (no publisher, no date). The Martha Hammack buried at Pocahontas was probably the wife of Wilson Hammack.

[691] 1900 Madison Co., MS, Census, p. 147.

[692] 1910 Madison Co., MS, Census, p. 22.

[693] Philadelphia Baptist Church Minutes, Webster Co., MS, transcript, Calhoun City Library, Calhoun City, MS; Bethel Baptist Church Minutes, Calhoun Co., MS, transcript, Calhoun City Library, Calhoun City, MS.

[694] For the family of Jesse and Barbara Lay, see M. M. Wilkinson, *Genealogy of the Wilkinson and Allied Families* (Shelby, MS, 1949); Will of Samuel Otterson, Greene Co., AL, Will Book B, p. 199.

Hopewell area of Calhoun County by 1870. That George and his family later moved to northeastern Arkansas, where his son because a state senator and a judge.

At the time of the 1870 census, George Hammack (who, unmarried, was then living with his brother Felix) was one of the five Hammacks operating a farm in Calhoun County. He farmed thirty acres of improved land with another fifty acres of unimproved land in reserve; the total value of his real estate was $300. He also owned a horse, a milk cow, two working oxen, five cattle, and fifteen hogs, all of which was valued at $250. George's farm had produced 200 bushels of Indian corn, one bale of cotton, fifty bushels of peas, twenty bushels of sweet potatoes, forty tons of hay, 600 pounds of butter, and forty pounds of molasses.[695]

In 1871, George W. Hammack purchased the SW 1/4 NE 1/4 Section 10, Township 22, Range 8 East.[696] In 1876, he mortgaged this land to W. T. Smith and H. C. Horton.[697] By 1879, he had apparently satisfied these obligations, for he was taxed with 150 acres in the SW 1/4 of Section 4 and twenty-five acres in the SE 1/4 of the NW 1/4 of Section 9.[698]

At the time of the 1880 census, George was farming twenty acres of cultivated land but also owned 155 acres of woodland and forest. This land was valued at $600. George also owned farm implements valued at $10 and livestock (including horses, cows, calves, swine, and poultry) valued at $130. In 1879, his farm had produced goods valued at $395. The farm had produced fifty dozen eggs, 150 bushels of Indian corn (grown off eight acres of fields), six bushels of cotton (grown off ten acres of fields), and ten cords of wood.[699]

In 1885, George and Sarah Hammack left Bethel Church to join other friends and relatives in establishing Sabougla Baptist Church. At Bethel, George had been an active member, serving to discipline other members, acting as representative of the church to district associational meetings, and in 1881 serving as singing clerk.[700]

In the 1880s and 1890s, George and Sarah began to experience financial difficulties. They mortgaged one tract in 1883[701] and another in 1890.[702] George W. Hammack died on 23 December 1893 in Calhoun County; he was buried near his wife's family in Bethel Cemetery.

Sarah Lay Hammack resided in Calhoun County for the rest of her life. She and her son Leslie continued to mortgage land throughout the 1890s, with deeds in 1896 and 1897 using tracts in section 4 and section 9 as collateral.[703] At the time of the 1903 tax roster, George's estate still owned 146 acres in Section 4 and thirty acres in Section 9. Sarah and her children mortgaged twenty acres of this land in 1903[704] and sold timber rights on the land in 1917.[705] In a series of deeds in 1927 and 1928, Sarah conveyed other Calhoun County properties to her sons Folsom and Leslie.[706]

Sarah Lay Hammack lived until 16 September 1931, when she died at her son's home. Her obituary in the *Calhoun Monitor* recorded:

---

[695] 1870 Calhoun Co., MS, Census, p. 446; 1870 Calhoun Co., MS, Agricultural Schedule, pp. 11-12.

[696] Calhoun Co., MS, Land Abstract Book 1 East, vol. 2, page 174, col. 1, NE 1/4, Section 10, Township 22, Range 8 East.

[697] Calhoun Co., MS, Land Abstract Book 1 East, vol. 2, page 175, col. 2, SW 1/4, Section 10, Township 22, Range 8 East.

[698] 1879 Calhoun Co., MS, Land Tax. Twenty acres of this land had been purchased in July 1880. Calhoun Co., MS, Land Abstract Book 2 East, p. 163, col. 2, SW 1/4, Section 4, Township 22, Range 8 East, and p. 172, col. 2, NW 1/4, Section 9, Township 22, Range 9 East.

[699] 1880 Calhoun Co., MS, Census, p. 608; 1880 Calhoun Co., MS, Agricultural Schedule, p. 21.

[700] Bethel Baptist Church Minutes, Calhoun Co., MS, transcript, Calhoun City Library, Calhoun City, MS.

[701] Calhoun Co., MS, Deed Book R, p. 183, as Calhoun Co., MS, Land Abstract Book 8 East.

[702] Calhoun Co., MS, Land Abstract Book 2 East, p. 163, col. 2, SW 1/4, Section 4, Township 22, Range 8E.

[703] Calhoun Co., MS, Land Abstract Book 2 East, page 163, col. 2, SW 1/4, Section 4, Township 22, Range 8E, and page 172, col. 2, NW 1/4, Section 9, Township 22, Range 8E.

[704] Calhoun Co., MS, Land Abstract Book 3 East, page 163, col. 2, SW 1/4, Section 4, Township 22, Range 8E.

[705] Calhoun Co., MS, Land Abstract Book 2 East, page 163, col. 2, SW 1/4, Section 4, Township 22, Range 8E.

[706] Calhoun Co., MS, Land Abstract Book 2 East, page 162, col. 2, NW 1/4, Section 4, Township 22, Range 8E.

Mrs. S. J. Hammack Dies, Buried at Bethel 17th. We regret to hear of the death of one of Calhoun's pioneer ladies, Mrs. S. J. Hammack, whose death occurred at the home of her son, F. F. Hammack, at Tutwiler, Mississippi, last Wednesday evening at 9 o'clock. She was near eighty-three years of age, and had lived in this county until a few years ago, when her sons moved to the Delta and she went with them. She was a lovable Christian lady. She leaves three sons and four daughters to mourn her passing. They are: L. L. Hammack, of Big Creek; J. G. and F. F. Hammack of Tutwiler; Mesdames J. M. Tucker of this City; A. E. Parker, of Big Creek; J. A. Lominick of Tutwiler; and J. T. Bracht, of Cincinnati, Ohio. Her body was brought to this county and laid to rest in the cemetery at Bethel Church by her husband who preceded her near thirty-eight years. Funeral services were conducted by the Revs. John McPhail and Joel Dorroh, attended by many sorrowing relatives and friends.[707]

George and Sarah Lay Hammack were the parents of ten children. Leslie L. Hammack (c. 1871- bef. 1961) and wife Fannie were living in Calhoun County as late as 1931. Barbara Hammack (1874-1961) married Walter Gable and then, after Gable's death, J. M. Tucker. She died at her brother Folsom's home in Tutwiler but was buried in Bethel Cemetery. Walter Hammack (1876-1901) died unmarried. Ella Hammack (1878-1947) married J. A. Lominick. She lived in Tutwiler, Mississippi. Sara Hammack (1880-1973) married J. T. Bracht; she was living in Cincinnati, Ohio, in 1931 and in Tampa, Florida, in the 1960s. Jesse G. Hammack (1882-1959) married Debbie Swindoll (1889-1946); they remained in Calhoun County and are buried in Bethel Cemetery. Mary Clevie Hammack (1885-1939) married Arthur E. Parker (1881-1942); she lived in Grenada County but was buried at Bethel Cemetery in Calhoun County. Ola Hicks Hammack (1887-1889) died as an infant. Folsom Francis Hammack (1890-1968) married Marjorie Ruth Miles (1897-1976); they lived at Tutwiler in Tallahatchee County, Mississippi, leaving three children and seven grandchildren. Vene Hammack (1893-1893), the youngest child of George and Sarah Lay Hammack, died two months before her father.

---

[707] *Calhoun Monitor*, 24 September 1931, p. 1.

Chapter 13:

John T. Hammack and Louisa Templeton Hammack,
of Macon County, Georgia, and Calhoun County, Mississippi

The third son and fifth child of Simeon and Elizabeth Jane Moore Hammack, John T. Hammack was reared in Hammack's District of Crawford County, Georgia, among an extended network of kin that included his grandmother Mary Felts Hammack and many aunts, uncles, and cousins. Born about 1830, John was a teenager when the financial dispute over his grandmother's estate prompted his father to remove their family to Macon County, Georgia.

Had it not been for the move to Macon County, John T. Hammack's life would no doubt have developed differently than it did. There he met and married Louisa Templeton, daughter of Milton Templeton and Martha Fuller, about 1851. Louisa came from a prosperous family, and her father's death had left her with a modest inheritance that benefited Louisa and her husband financially.

At the time of the 1852 Macon County, Georgia, Tax Digest, John T. Hammack owned no taxable real estate. His wife inherited a tract of land from her father Milton Templeton on which John T. and his family lived until leaving for Mississippi.[708] On 13 January 1857, John T. Hammack sold 272 2/5 acres of LL 4, LD 1, Macon County. The 1852 tax digest reveals that this had been land owned by Milton Templeton.[709]

John T. and Louisa Hammack had apparently moved to Mississippi about 1854, lived there for two years, and then returned to Georgia. The 1860 Choctaw County, Mississippi, census indicated that Martha Hammack and Felix Hammack were born in Mississippi about 1854 and 1856 while William S. Hammack and John R. Hammack were born in Georgia in 1852 and 1858. It may be that John and Louisa returned to Georgia to oversee the settling of the Templeton estate; whatever the motivation, they were living near John's father Simeon Hammack at the time the 1860 Choctaw County, Mississippi, census was taken on 29 September 1860. Living with the family in 1860 also was Louisa's twenty-seven-year old nephew John Ward, who would later marry John's niece Mary Hammack in Madison County. Employed as a farm laborer, Ward was apparently helping John T. Hammack to farm the tract he was renting from his father Simeon.[710]

Choctaw County's 1860 agricultural schedule indicated that Daniel D. Taylor and John T. Hammack were both farming portions of a larger tract of land owned by Simeon Hammack. Simeon himself was farming a 320-acre tract valued at $3,500, while John T. Hammack was farming a 230-acre tract -- eighty acres improved and 150 acres unimproved, valued at $1,200.[711] Simeon's farm, with 150 acres improved, was worth more than twice John's farm. John owned livestock valued at $580, including mules, cattle, and swine (but no horses). Between September 1859 and 1860 he had produced eighteen bales of ginned cotton, six bushels of peas and beans, 500 pounds of Indian corn, 151 pounds of sweet potatoes, sixty pounds of butter, meat valued at $125, and manufactured products worth $80. Such a promising beginning suggests that, had the Civil War not intervened, John might have soon become more successful than his father, again perhaps aided by the substantial inheritance his wife received from the estates of her parents and brothers.[712]

---

[708] 1852 Macon Co., GA, Tax List, Georgia Department of Archives and History, Morrow, GA.

[709] Macon Co., GA, Deed Book A, p. 571.

[710] 1860 Choctaw Co., MS, Census, p. 421.

[711] 1860 Choctaw Co., MS, Agricultural Schedule, Cadaretta Township, p. 50.

[712] Ibid. Simeon's farm had in the previous year produced 38 ginned bales of cotton, fifty pounds of wool, $160 worth of home manufactures, and $345 worth of meat. He also owned livestock valued at $1,160.

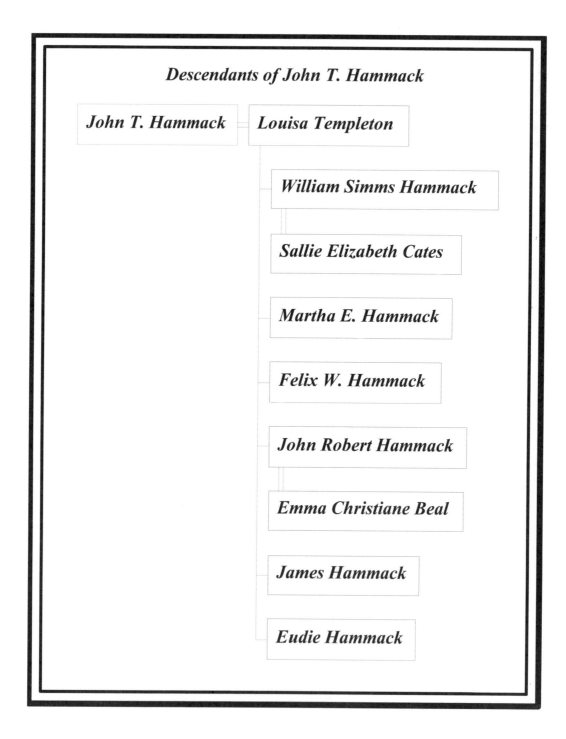

Descendants of John T. Hammack

John T. Hammack — Louisa Templeton

- William Simms Hammack
- Sallie Elizabeth Cates
- Martha E. Hammack
- Felix W. Hammack
- John Robert Hammack
- Emma Christiane Beal
- James Hammack
- Eudie Hammack

But the Civil War did come. John T. Hammack enlisted on 14 January 1863 at Oakley, Hinds County, Mississippi. He served until June of 1863, when he was hospitalized, and was discharged on account of disability on 5 August 1863 upon orders from General Bragg. At the time of his discharge, John was stationed near Dalton, Georgia.[713]

The Hammacks had apparently moved south to Madison County about 1863, possibly following Simeon's death, and it was there that John T. and Felix W. were living when they enlisted in the Confederate service (and there that John Ward married Mary Hammack). As previously noted, they seem to have returned to Choctaw County by the end of the war, although Elizabeth and several of her children may have again moved to Madison County about 1866 or 1867. John T. Hammack was taxed in Madison County, Mississippi, in 1868, alongside his brother William T. H. Hammack and his nephew James Wilburn Hammack. This listing indicated only taxable personal property, not real estate, but land records for Madison County provide no evidence that John T. Hammack owned land there.[714]

By 1870, John T. Hammack had returned to Calhoun County. He died there in January 1870 as a result of pneumonia, possibly related to his extended hospitalization and discharge in 1863.[715] When the federal census was taken on 13 August 1870, Louisa Templeton Hammack was living in Township 22, Range 8 East, Slate Springs, Calhoun County, Mississippi. She indicated in that year that she owned real estate valued at $400 and personal property valued at $200.[716] Although Calhoun County land records (which begin with the county's formation in 1852) do not contain any trace of this land and its disposition, it may be possible that John T. inherited this tract from his father Simeon.[717] The 1870 Calhoun County agricultural schedule lists this property under the name of William Hammack, indicating that he was then managing his father's estate. At that time, William was nineteen.[718]

A neighborhood comparison between the 1860 and 1870 census enumerations make it clear that John T. Hammack had moved between census years. In 1860, he was probably renting land and slaves from his father Simeon Hammack. Following Simeon's death, John apparently moved briefly with his mother and siblings about 1863 to Madison County, where his brother William T. H. Hammack was then living. He may, in fact, have moved between Madison and Choctaw Counties more than once; but by the late 1860s, John T. had settled in Calhoun County and was apparently living there when he died. William Simms Hammack, eldest son of John T. Hammack, apparently took over his father's farming enterprises and was considered head of household when the agricultural schedule for that year was produced.

At the time of the 1870 census, William -- probably to support his mother and younger siblings -- was farming forty acres of improved land with sixty acres of unimproved land in reserve. The property was valued at $400.[719] He also owned one horse, two cows, and twenty swine, worth a combined value of $50. In the preceding year, John T. Hammack's farm had produced 150 bushels of Indian corn, eight bales of

---

[713] Mississippi Confederate Muster Lists, Company D, 45th Regiment Mississippi Infantry, Mississippi Department of Archives and History, Jackson, MS. He could be the John Hammack who enlisted at Brownsville, MS, on 16 October 1863, although this could be his nephew or cousin of the same name. This man served in Company F, Ballentine's Regiment, but deserted on 18 February 1864. Charles Hammack, son of William T. H. Hammack, also served in the same unit and also deserted.

[714] 1868 Madison Co., MS, Personal Property Tax Lists, Mississippi Department of Archives and History, Jackson, MS.

[715] John T. Hammack's military records, Mississippi Confederate Muster Lists, Company D, 45th Regiment, Mississippi Department of Archives and History, Jackson, MS, indicate that he suffered from varicose veins, a condition which necessitated his discharge.

[716] 1870 Calhoun Co., MS, Census, p. 445.

[717] Calhoun was formed in 1852 from Yalobusha and Lafayette Counties. Calhoun's records burned in 1922 and all early deeds were lost, but the title book abstracts, which summarize the early land conveyances, survived. Webster County, adjacent Calhoun, was formed in 1874 from Choctaw and Montgomery Counties.

[718] 1870 Calhoun Co., MS, Agricultural Schedule, pp. 11-12. The Hammacks had apparently not moved far between 1860 and 1870. Slate Springs is actually in Range 9 East, while the 1870 census recorded the family in Range 8 East. This suggests that they were not actually living in Slate Springs but that that was the nearest post office. Range 8 East, which is where surviving land records place Felix W. Hammack and George W. Hammack, was very near the area where Simeon Hammack lived in 1860. Philadelphia Church, where Elizabeth Hammack worshipped, lay inside Choctaw County. It seems likely that John T. and his family were living just north of where they had resided in 1860, but inside Calhoun County rather than Choctaw or Webster.

[719] 1870 Calhoun Co., MS, Census, p. 445.

cotton (significantly more than any of the other Hammacks), fifteen bushels of peas, and 100 pounds of butter. The family's household manufacturers were valued at $30, and meat slaughtered on the farm during the preceding year was valued at $50. Of the Calhoun County Hammacks, only Charles approached John T. Hammack's family in terms of cotton production; his farm had produced three bales, while the other Hammacks produced one bale of less. It may have been the extra bales of cotton that gave John's family an economic edge, for -- with only 40 improved acres and a total of 100 acres altogether -- his farm had produced goods worth $1,100 during the preceding year, a value equal to that of Charles Hammack, who had a considerably greater quantity of both land and livestock.[720]

Widowed by the time she was thirty-five, Louisa was left with five children younger than William to rear. Martha was sixteen, while Eduie, the youngest daughter, was only three. Family lore is sketchy regarding Louisa after John T. Hammack died. Since many Calhoun County records perished in courthouse fires, there is no record of her or John T. Hammack's estate settlement; nor is there record of any real estate transfer by which John T. Hammack's land was sold or distributed. A county tax list from 1875 survives but does not include Louisa, John T.'s estate, or William Hammack, suggesting that the land had been sold, or perhaps lost to debt, by this point. No trace of Louisa has been found after the 1870 census. Family stories did not contain any information concerning Eduie or James, who was six in 1870. The likeliest scenario is that James, Eduie, Louisa, and possibly Martha all died between 1870 and 1880. In 1878, a tremendous yellow fever epidemic gripped the northeastern portion of Mississippi and western Tennessee and Alabama. Published newspaper accounts indicate that scores of individuals in and around Calhoun County perished at this time, including whole families. It may be that Louisa and her two youngest children died as part of this outbreak.

Of the offspring of John T. Hammack and Louisa Hammack, William Simms Hammack, their eldest child, will be discussed later. Of the other children, nothing more is known of James and Eduie, who were born about 1864 and 1867 respectively. Martha E. Hammack, just younger than William S., was born about 1854 in Mississippi. She was living at home with her parents in 1860 and with her widowed mother in 1870; she was alive in Calhoun County in October 1871 when she joined Bethel Baptist Church by experience. The minutes contain no date on which Martha was dismissed, indicating that she died while still a member there. While it is possible that Martha married, family tradition is silent concerning her, suggesting that she may have died young, perhaps at the same time as her mother and younger siblings.[721]

Felix W. Hammack, the second son of John T. and Louisa Templeton Hammack, was born 29 July 1856 in either Mississippi or Macon County, Georgia. He died, unmarried, on 15 January 1938 in Flora, Madison County, Mississippi.[722] Felix was still living in Calhoun County in 1880 (when his brother William had already settled in Madison County) and was enumerated with his younger brother John Robert Hammack as a field hand working on a farm owned by James J. Criss. The Crisses were near neighbors of Felix's uncle George Hammack and were enumerated only a few households from them at this time.[723] The agricultural schedule for that year indicated that Felix and John "rent for [a] share of products," the labor form known as sharecropping that became common throughout the South after Reconstruction. At that time, Felix was tilling eighteen acres while John R. Hammack was working thirteen acres. Felix had six cows valued at $30, and John had two cows valued at $10.[724]

---

[720] 1870 Calhoun Co., MS, Agricultural Schedule, pp. 11-12; Bethel Baptist Church Minutes, Calhoun Co., MS, transcription, Calhoun City Library, Calhoun City, MS.

[721] Bethel Baptist Church Minutes, Calhoun Co., MS. Martha has not been found in the 1880 or any later census enumerations. Neither have Louisa, James, or Eduie Hammack.

[722] Death Certificate of Felix W. Hammack, Rankin Co., MS, Microfilm, MSDAH. Felix W. was a farmer, aged eighty-five years, five months, sixteen days; born Macon, Georgia, unmarried. Parents were John and Louisa T. Hammack, both natives of Georgia.

[723] 1880 Calhoun Co., MS, Census, p. 608.

[724] 1880 Calhoun Co., MS, Agricultural Schedule, ED 16, p. 1.

Felix remained in Calhoun County until about 1885. He was taxed there, in Sabougla District, in 1884 near his uncles Felix, George, and Dock.[725] In 1885, he was dismissed from Bethel Baptist Church in Calhoun County, and by 1887 he had settled in Hinds County, more than 100 miles to the south.[726] On 17 September 1887, Felix purchased ninety-eight and three-fourths acres auctioned by the state for delinquent taxes. He paid $81 for the land.[727] On 2 January 1890, Felix purchased lots one, three, and four of section 14, Township 8, Range 3 West. He paid $339 for the land.[728] On 27 February 1894, Felix mortgaged these three lots for $319.[729] Felix began purchasing the first of several tracts in Madison County in 1895, acquiring four complete lots and several partial tracts over the next two years.[730] In order to satisfy a series of promissory notes totaling $1,160, Felix on 4 February 1897 put up as collateral "my entire interest in any and all crops of cotton, corn, cotton seed, and all other agricultural products raised or caused to be raised by me or any hands I may employ during the year 1897-1898 and 1899, in Madison County, Mississippi, and all of the rents issues and profits arising from or growing out of the property hereinafter described, also N 1/2 of Lot 2, and all of Lot 3, and N 1/2 of Lot 4 and fifty acres of North end Lot 6 in Section 4, Township 8, Range 2 West, and Lot 6, Sec. 33, Township 9, Range 2 West, also the following lands in Hinds County, Mississippi, Lot 8 in Section 1 and Lot 1 in Section 12, Township 8, Range 3 West, and all mules, horses, wagons and cattle that I now own and possess." If Felix satisfied his obligations to W. H. Powell and H. D. Priestly, then the property was to be returned to him in tact.[731] A note by Powell indicates that Felix succeeded in satisfying the obligation and kept his property.

Between 1900 and 1935, Felix farmed his lots in Madison County and operated a small general store at his premises. He continued to buy, sell, and mortgage lands in Madison and Hinds Counties as he increased his holdings.[732] In all, Felix borrowed more than $1,600 between 1900 and 1905 as he expanded his cotton planting. Each time he mortgaged land, crops, and livestock, and each time he successfully repaid the obligations.[733] Felix retained his properties for much of the rest of his life, although in the years immediately preceding his death he sold tracts to neighbors in the local community.[734]

Although both of Felix's parents apparently died before reaching forty years of age, Felix's own life spanned twice that amount of time. He died on 15 January 1935 in his eighty-second year. His obituary in the *Madison County Herald* read:[735]

> Funeral services were held at the Mount Olympus Cemetery[736] near here Sunday afternoon at three o'clock for Mr. Felix W. Hammack. Mr. Hammack was eighty-five years old and came to this community from the northern part of the state when he was a

---

[725] 1884 Calhoun Co., MS, Personal Property Tax List, Mississippi Department of Archives and History, Jackson, MS.

[726] Bethel Baptist Church Minutes, Calhoun Co., MS, transcription, Calhoun City Library, Calhoun City, MS.

[727] Hinds Co., MS, Deed Book 58, p. 275.

[728] Hinds Co., MS, Deed Book 60, p. 344.

[729] Hinds Co., MS, Deed Book 64, p. 582.

[730] Madison Co., MS, Deed Book EEE, p. 555, and FFF, p. 186. He purchased Lot 6, Section 33, Township 9, Range 2 West, and N 1/2 Lot 4 and fifty acres off the north end of Lot 6, Section 4, Township 8, Range 2 West, and N 1/2 Lot 2, and all lot 3, Section 4, Township 8, Range 2 West in 1895 and N 1/2 Lot 2 and all Lot 3 and N 1/2 Lot 4 and fifty acres off the north end of lot 6, Section 4, Township 8, Range 2 West, and Lot 6, Section 33, Township 9, Range 2 West in 1897.

[731] Madison Co., MS, Deed Book 67, pp. 297-300.

[732] Madison Co., MS, Deed Book 75, pp. 38-41.

[733] Hinds Co., MS, Deed Book 76, pp. 68-69; Madison Co., MS, Deed Book 75, pp. 38-41.

[734] Madison Co., MS, Deed Book 9, p. 509, Deed Book 10, p. 240.

[735] "Flashes from Flora," *Madison County Herald*, 21 January 1938.

[736] W. W. Wellington, *Cemeteries of Madison County, Mississippi* (1995), p. 431, identifies this cemetery as the Hammack Cemetery, located at SW 1/4 of NE 1/4 of SE 1/4, Section 22, Township 8, Range 1 West, Madison Co., MS. From the intersection of Hwy 22 and SE Railroad Avenue go south to Railroad Avenue then 2.1 miles to Mt. Leopard Road on left. Turn left (East) and go .4 miles on Mt. Leopard Road. The cemetery is on the right up an embankment about 150 feet off the road. The Cemetery is grown up in a wooded area and is not currently being used. It was charted by Mr. Wellington on 31 July, 1995. The grave of Felix W. Hammack is marked only by a funeral marker that states that he died 15 January, 1938, aged eighty-five years, four months and sixteen days. Also buried in this cemetery are John Asa and Cora A. Briggs Hammack and George T. and Viola Hammack.

young man. He had been confined in a Jackson Hospital for several weeks. The rites were conducted by the Rev. Mr. Howard Spell, pastor of the Flora Baptist Church, of which the deceased had been a member. Mr. Hammack had no close relatives and is survived only by nieces and nephews,[737] they being Mrs. Clara Belle Burgess and Mrs. Dolly Burgess of Flora; Mrs. Alice Lehman of Monroe, Louisiana, B. B. Hammack and Cleveland Hammack of Flora, Robert Hammack of Bentonia and Ed Hammack of Jackson. He is, in addition to these, survived by one sister-in-law, Mrs. S. E. Chapman of Clinton.[738]

John Robert Hammack, the only other surviving brother of William Simms Hammack, was born 13 May 1858, probably in Choctaw County, Mississippi. John lived in Choctaw County until at least 1880, but he apparently left the county between 1880 and 1885. Unlike his two surviving siblings, who headed south and settled among their kin in Madison County, John Robert Hammack headed instead north and west. He was living in the Dakota territory -- still the home of Native American tribes and the site of bloody conflicts between natives, settlers, and United States military forces -- by the early 1890s, and it was there that he met and married Emma Christiane Beal, daughter of Swedish immigrants. John and Emma ranched in the Dakotas for the remainder of their lives, he dying on 11 February 1919 in Stanton, North Dakota, and she on 9 June 1920, in Bismarck, North Dakota.[739]

John Robert and Emma Christiane Beal Hammack were the parents of nine children, who lived in the northwestern United States and southwestern Canada. LaVelle Hammack Salisbury (1894-1970) remained in North Dakota. Myrtle Louise Hammack Telenga (1896-1978) moved from her native North Dakota to Bengough, Saskatchewan, Canada, leaving six children and many grandchildren. Romey Hammack (1898-1976) married Agnes Gunderson and settled in Minot, North Dakota. Harry Herbert Hammack (1900-1936) married Wallena Warterude (1903-1965) and died in Ward County, North Dakota. Willie Hammack (1904-1907) died as a small child as a result of burns while the family was living in Stanton, North Dakota. Eugene Hammack (1905-1986) married Flora Albers (1908-) and died in Stanley, North Dakota. Wilbon Hammack (1907-1987), whose name traces back for more than a century to James Wilburn Moore, son of Ussery Moore and Martha Bishop, married Margaret May (1912-1995) and settled in Portland, Oregon. Irene Hammack Cassiday Branton (1910-1990) settled in Houston, Texas. Jonas Alan Hammack (1914-2007) married Annie Bilodeau (1921-1992) and settled in Bend, Oregon.

---

[737] George Cleveland and Mary Almedia Bankston Hammack named their son Felix Maben Hammack, born 1928, in honor of his great-uncle Felix W. Hammack.

[738] The obituary erroneously calls his sister-in-law Mrs. S. E. Trotman rather than Chapman.

[739] 1900 McLean Co., ND, Census, p. 31. John Hammack, aged forty-two, was a rancher born in Georgia. Emma, aged twenty-six, was a housewife born in North Dakota. Emma's brother Nels Beal, a native of Sweden, was living with the family. 1910 McLean Co., ND, Census, p. 162. John R. Hammack, aged fifty-two, was a farmer and a rancher born in Georgia. Emma, aged thirty-five, was shown as a housewife born in Sweden who had immigrated to the United States in 1886. 1920 Mercer Co., ND, Census, p. 264. Emma Hammack, aged forty-five, a widow born in Sweden, was working as a general farmer. Both the 1910 and 1920 census reports indicated that John and Emma were farming their own land. Emma had immigrated to the United States in 1889 and naturalized in 1896.

Chapter 14:

William Simms and Sallie Elizabeth Cates Hammack
of Calhoun and Hinds Counties, Mississippi.

Born 14 April 1852 in Macon County, Georgia, William Simms Hammack was the eldest child of John T. and Louisa Templeton Hammack. He moved to Mississippi with his parents while still a small child and was reared in Choctaw and Calhoun Counties, where he grew to manhood.[740]

William was not quite eighteen years old when his father died in January 1870. As the eldest child, he took responsibility for the family's farming enterprises and probably also assumed an important role in rearing his younger siblings. The 1870 agricultural schedule indicated that William was working the family's 100-acre farm, which grew corn, potatoes, peas, and beans for sustenance as well as cotton for commercial marketing. In addition, the family raised livestock, including horses and mules used on the farm as well as poultry, swine, and cattle, which yielded not only meat but also milk, eggs, and butter.[741]

As suggested above, Louisa Templeton Hammack, her son James Hammack, and her daughter Eduie may all have died in 1877 or 1878 as a yellow fever epidemic gripped the northeastern portion of the state. The loss of his mother and siblings may have prompted William to leave northern Mississippi. In May 1877, he was granted letters of dismissal from Bethel Baptist Church -- which he had joined by experience in October 1873.[742] Although his brother John remained in Calhoun County until at least 1880 and his brother Felix until about 1885, William seems to have moved to Madison County about 1877 or 1878. By 1880, he was working as a farm laborer on the 840-acre farm of his uncle's neighbor and associate, W. B. Jones, in Madison County.[743]

On 20 December 1883, William S. Hammack married Sallie Elizabeth Cates (1863–1951) in Hinds County. Sallie belonged to a prosperous local family, and her grandparents had all settled together in Mississippi after leaving North Carolina about 1832. Shortly before her marriage, on 4 December 1883, Sallie had joined her mother and siblings in conveying a portion of the Cates estate to Charles B. Hawkins. Although single at the time the deed was executed, she was married when she acknowledged her signature on the document several weeks later.[744] In 1885 and 1886, Sallie joined her siblings on several additional deeds, all related to the distribution of her father and grandmother's estate in Hinds County. (Sallie's grandmother had divided her estate between Sallie and her brother, although the birth of two younger children after the deed complicated the property transfer.)[745]

On 1 February 1893, William S. Hammack purchased ninety-eight and three-fourths acres of land in Hinds County from his brother Felix W. Hammack. William paid $100 for the land; at the time, he was already living in Hinds County, while Felix was residing in Madison County.[746] This is the first known real estate purchase for William S. Hammack. He had probably been living since his marriage on land owned by the Cates family, thus making it less necessary that he purchase land in his own right. Although the terms of the deed are not clear, Sallie's family may have put up all or some of the money to fund the

---

[740] Note that there continues to be some uncertainty concerning the middle name of William S. Hammack. Descendants remember that it was Sims, Simms, or Simmons. One possibility is that he was called "Sim" for his grandfather Simeon Hammack. Another possibility is that he was named William Simmons Hammack; if so, he may have been named for a distant cousin, Catherine Hammack of Jones County who married William Simmons. A prominent Semmes family in Madison County had come from Taliaferro County, Georgia. In Georgia, they had been neighbors of James Wilborn Moore and his wife Sarah Hammack, and in Mississippi they were neighbors of Sarah's nephew William T. H. Hammack. Another possibility is that William was named for William Gilmore Simms, a prominent southern writer and intellectual of the 1850s.

[741] 1870 Calhoun Co., MS, Agricultural Schedule, pp. 11-12.

[742] Bethel Baptist Church Minutes, Calhoun Co., MS, transcription, Calhoun City Library, Calhoun City, MS.

[743] 1880 Madison Co., MS, Census, p. 120A.

[744] Hinds Co., MS, Deed Book 54, p. 435.

[745] Hinds Co., MS, Deed Book 55, pp. 489-91.

[746] The land lay in Lot 8, Section 1, Township 8, Range 3 West, and Lot 1, Section 12, Township 8, Range 3 West. See Hinds Co., MS, Deed Book 65, p. 128.

land purchase. Less than a year later, on 5 January 1894, acknowledging himself "legally and justly indebted to Sallie E. Hammack," William put up as collateral for his debt this ninety-eight and three-fourths-acre tract along with livestock, hay, a wagon, and a cane mill.[747] William at this time was obligating himself to pay Sallie $1,000, but, three months later, on 8 April, Sallie joined William in putting up another thirty acres of land, apparently from the Cates estate, as collateral to satisfy a $73 promissory note.[748] On 5 March 1896, Sallie and William put up another tract of land as collateral for three other notes, altogether totaling $321.25. This deed makes more explicit the circumstances that gave rise to the series of transactions. Following the American Civil War, as the sharecropping system developed throughout the South, many individuals became indebted to local storeowners and landowners for seeds and supplies necessary to cultivate their lands. Apparently William and Sallie were borrowing money to finance their farming enterprises, using their land as collateral to satisfy obligations which were satisfied at harvest time. As the deed indicates, the "parties of the first part expect the said J. T. Downs to advance them money and sell supplies and merchandise during the year 1896, at such prices as may be agreed upon at the time of delivery, or at the unusual customary credit prices, and whereas said parties of the first part, have agreed to secure the payment of said indebtedness, as also any further amounts that may be advanced as aforesaid." In exchange for the cash advanced, William and Sallie offered

> their entire interest in any and all crops of cotton, corn and other agricultural products planted or to be planted to be raised by them and any hands they may employ during the year 1896, on land belonging to them and land of Mrs. Cates now leased and occupied by them or any other land they may rent and cultivate during said year, and any and all cotton and corn that may be due said parties of the first part, or rent for said year, and upon the following land situated in Hinds County and in District 2, towit: E1/2 NE 1/4 Section 20 Township 7 Range 2 West and upon the following stock, towit: one brown horse named Robin, one bull face bay mare named Nedia, one dark bay mare named Daisy, one sorrel bull face colt named Nancy, one bay horse colt named Albert, one blue and white cow named blue, one black and white cow named spot, one red and white cow named Jane, all of said cattle are marked with over bit in left ear and underslope in right ear.

William and Sallie had until 15 November 1896 to satisfy the obligation without penalty. Should they default on the obligation, Downs could seize the property placed as collateral and sell it for cash at public auction.[749] William and Sallie Hammack, like William's brother Felix, seem to have been successful at repaying their obligations. For scores of southerners, however, transactions like this meant permanent enmeshing within a web of debt and credit that ultimately caused them to lose their farms and their financial independence.[750]

William Simms Hammack died on 25 December 1899 in Hinds County, Mississippi. He was buried with his wife's relatives in Brownsville Cemetery. Sallie Elizabeth Cates Hammack lived for many years as a widow, although she later remarried, on 23 September 1913, to Louis E. Chapman. She again became a widow with Chapman's death on 3 June 1925.

---

[747] Hinds Co., MS, Deed Book 64, pp. 430-31.

[748] Hinds Co., MS, Deed Book 68, p. 59.

[749] Hinds Co., MS, Deed Book 70, p. 68.

[750] They successfully paid the obligation. See Hinds Co., MS, Deed Book 72, p. 201. Downs signed a receipt attesting to payment of the obligation on 20 December 1899, five days before William S. Hammack died. In 1897, Sallie Hammack conveyed for $500 the ninety-eight and three-fourths acres deeded her by her husband in 1894. She sold this land to William's brother Felix for $500. The reasons for this deed are not clear, but it would seem that, since William did not sign the deed, the land was then Sallie's alone (although she may have been holding it still as collateral). It may be that William and Sallie decided to sell this tract in order to raise funds to satisfy their other obligations. See Hinds Co., MS, Deed Book 67, 285.

Descendants of William Simms Hammack

William Simms Hammack — Sallie Elizabeth Cates

George Cleveland Hammack

Mary Almedia Bankston

Robert Felix Hammack

Katie Campbell

Little Dollie Hammack

Alice Williams Hammack

E. L. Lehman

Drury Brown "Dooley" Hammack

Mary Ann Tanner

Clara Belle Hammack

Algey Louis Burgess

Dollie Clifford Hammack

Harley Cleveland Burgess

Mattie Elizabeth Hammack

Edd Brown Hammack

M. Marjorie Hardy

John William Watts Hammack

Although Sallie conveyed the ninety-eight and three-fourths-acre tract purchased from Felix Hammack in 1893 back to him in 1898, she and her offspring continued to live on the Cates family lands at Brownsville following William Simms Hammack's death in 1899. At the time of the 1900 census, Sallie indicated that she was a thirty-seven year old widow, that she was fully literate, and that she owned her own farm without any encumbrances. She further indicated that she then had living nine children, one child having died in infancy.[751] Although widowed at a young age, Sallie lived on for many years, dying in 1951 when she was nearly ninety. She was buried beside her husband and parents in Brownsville Cemetery.

William Simms Hammack and Sallie Elizabeth Cates Hammack were the parents of ten children. George Cleveland Hammack (26 October, 1884, Hinds County, Mississippi - 17 November, 1963, buried Brownsville Community Cemetery, Hinds County, Mississippi) married Mary Almedia Bankston and lived for most of his life in Hinds County. Robert Felix Hammack (15 Oct 1885, Hinds County, Mississippi - 2 April 1949) married Katie Campbell on 24 March 1910 in Hinds County. "Little Dolly Hammack" (5 November, 1886, Hinds County, Mississippi - 31 December, 1886, buried Brownsville Community Cemetery, Hinds County, Mississippi) died when she was about seven weeks old. Alice Williams Hammack (8 November, 1887 - 1949) married E. L. Lehman on 12 January 1920. Drury Brown "Dooly" Hammack (11 September 1889 -) married Mary A. Tanner on 21 February 1916 in Hinds County. Clara Belle Hammack (10 April 1892, Hinds County, Mississippi - 21 April 1989) married Algey Louis Burgess (1890-1959) on 17 June 1918. Dollie Clifford Hammack (1 March 1894 - October 1977) married Harley C. Burgess on 11 February 1912. Mattie Elizabeth Hammack (11 October 1895 - 27 September 1907) died while still a young girl; she was buried near her father and grandparents in Brownsville Cemetery. Edd Brown Hammack (24 December 1897 - May 1981) married Marjorie Hardy on 23 December 1933. John William Watts Hammack (18 November 1899 - 19 December 1912) died of pneumonia while still a young boy; he, too, was buried near his father and grandparents in Brownsville Cemetery.

William Simms Hammack (1852-1899), husband of Sallie Elizabeth Cates and father of George Cleveland Hammack, moved from Macon County, Georgia, to Choctaw County, Mississippi, as a child. He died in Hinds County, Mississippi.

---

[751] 1900 Hinds Co., MS, Census, p. 166.

Hammack Residences

The following map indicates the communities in which Hammack family members lived in Hinds and Madison Counties, Mississippi. Shown are the towns in which William T. H. Hammack, William Simms Hammack, and George Cleveland Hammack all lived.

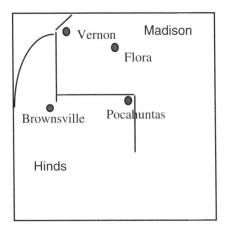

Hammack Residences in Hinds and Madison Counties, 1860-1935

William T. H. Hammack came to Madison County by 1 Jun 1860, with J. N. Tanner; both were overseers for John Robinson. (John Cates bought his Brownsville property from Ransom Robinson.) William T. H. Hammack lived in Vernon, four miles northwest of Flora, in 1870. Tax records indicate that Elizabeth Jane Moore Hammack and her children were living there in 1863 and that John T. Hammack was living there in 1868. William T. H. Hammack never left the area, dying there in 1880. In 1880, William Simms Hammack was living with his uncle's neighbor and business associate W. B. Jones in Vernon, Madison County, Mississippi.

William S. Hammack married Sallie E. Cates in 1883 and lived in Brownsville. Since William S. Hammack was working as a farm laborer in 1880, he may have moved into Brownsville in search of work on the Cates farm, thus meeting Sallie Elizabeth Cates. Given the nearness of Brownsville and Vernon, other possibilities to explain their meeting include business dealings between Anderson Bradley Cates and William T. H. Hammack and religious revivals, which often drew crowds from miles around.

Wilson H. Hammack and Martha married in 1875 in Madison County; they lived in Pocahontas from 1880 onwards. Wilson's son John S. Hammack married the granddaughter of William T. H. Hammack.

Felix W. Hammack lived in Flora from about 1885 until the time of his death in 1935. At the time of the 1910 census, William Hammack, son of William T. H. Hammack, was living with Felix W. Hammack, son of John T. Hammack; the census indicated that the two men were cousins.

Following his marriage to Sallie Cates in 1883, William Simms Hammack lived on the Cates farm at Brownsville. He died there in 1899 and his son George in 1973. The land remains in the Hammack family today.

Descendants of Anderson Bradley Cates

Anderson Bradley Cates — Abbie Doxey Brown

Drury John Cates

Cora A. Chapman

William Simms Hammack

Sallie Elizabeth Cates

Louis E. Chapman

Eunice Cates

Thurman Edgar Bardin

Fannie Mae Cates

Richard Albert Moore

Chapter 15:

George Cleveland Hammack and Mary Almedia Bankston Hammack of Hinds County, Mississippi

George Cleveland Hammack (26 Oct 1884, Hinds County, Mississippi - 17 November 1963, Hinds County, Mississippi, buried Brownsville Community Cemetery, Hinds County, Mississippi) was the eldest son of William Simms Hammack and Sallie Elizabeth Cates. He was born in the home of his grandfather Anderson Bradley Cates at Brownsville, Hinds County, Mississippi, and died in the same room seventy-nine years later.

George married Mary Almedia Bankston (3 Apr 1894, Hinds County, Mississippi - 9 December, 1974, Hinds County, Mississippi, buried Brownsville Community Cemetery, Hinds County, Mississippi) on 19 February 1911 in Hinds County, Mississippi. Mary Almedia Bankston, whose ancestry will be discussed later, was a descendant of Anders and Gertrude Rambo Bankston of Pennsylvania; her Bankston and O'Neal ancestors had moved from North Carolina into Georgia in the late eighteenth-century and then moved to Mississippi from Georgia and Alabama in the 1850s.

George and Mary were the parents of ten children, four daughters and six sons. They and their families are discussed briefly below.

Sadie Lucile Hammack (21 February 1912 - 16 November 1996), eldest daughter of George and Mary Almedia Bankston Hammack, married Alton Babb on 20 August 1933 in Lake Providence, Louisiana. They were the parents of six children, Mary Katherine Babb Bull, Almedia Lee Babb Lueg, Carolyn Babb Glover, Frances Ann Babb Lawler, Sadie Ruth Babb Pena, and John Alton Babb.

William Bankston Hammack (24 October 1913 - 10 April 1989), eldest son of George and Mary Almedia Bankston Hammack, married Aline Lancaster on 26 July 1937 in Yazoo City, Mississippi; they lived in Jackson, Hinds County, Mississippi. They were the parents of three children, Mary Ann Hammack Lee, Carol Kay Hammack Kirkland, and William Bankston Hammack, Jr.

Mary Mildred Hammack (7 August 1915 - 29 August 2003), second daughter of George and Mary Almedia Bankston Hammack, married Thomas Joseph Sitton on 11 April 1937 in Lake Providence, Louisiana. Mildred and Tom were the parents of four children, Dorothy Lucille Sitton White, Mary Elizabeth Sitton, Joseph Paul Sitton, and Thomas Stribling Sitton.

Edgar Hendricks Hammack (20 October 1917 - 28 December 1986), second son of George and Mary Almedia Bankston Hammack, married Avis Myrdell McFarland on 15 February 1940. They were later divorced after rearing sons John Eugene Hammack and Edgar Hendricks Hammack, Jr. Edgar subsequently married Mariam Franklin. They lived for many years in Atlanta, where Edgar died.

George Cleveland Hammack, Jr. (17 May 1922 -), third son of George and Mary Almedia Bankston Hammack, married Margaret Mitchell Goode on 2 November 1946 in Lake Providence, Louisiana. They later divorced after rearing children George Cleveland Hammack, III, Annette Hammack Martello Santos, and David Mitchell Hammack. George C. Hammack, Jr., remarried Frances Reynolds on 13 August 1983 in Jackson, Mississippi, where they still live.

James Wilson Hammack (28 May 1924 -), fourth son of George and Mary Almedia Bankston Hammack, married Martha Johnson on 20 June 1948 in Lake Providence, Louisiana. James and Martha have four children, Daphne Jean Hammack, James Wilson Hammack, Jr., Lisa Joy Hammack, and Marcus Charles Hammack.

Daniel Clement Hammack (13 April 1926 -), fifth son of George and Mary Almedia Bankston Hammack, married Viola Sullivan on 1 July 1949 in Lake Providence, Louisiana. They later divorced after rearing children Daniel Clement Hammack, Jr., Janet Celeste Hammack Nolan, and Pamela Louise Hammack Johnson. Daniel Clement Hammack, Sr., subsequently married Mary Christine Jordan of Oak Grove, Louisiana, on 30 June 1984. Since Christine's death, Dan has resided near his daughter Janet and her family.

Felix Maben Hammack (5 March 1928 -), sixth son of George and Mary Almedia Bankston Hammack, married Mary Ann Day on 31 August 1952 in Union Parish, Louisiana. Felix and Mary Ann have four children, Charlotte Christmas Hammack Nitcher, Denise Hammack Finch, Philip Steven Hammack, and Frederick Nathan Hammack. Felix and Mary Ann live in Bend, Oregon.

Celeste Almedia Hammack (24 March 1932 - 12 October 1951), third daughter of George and Mary Almedia Bankston Hammack, married Lloyd Lebane Clements on 1 January 1950 in Lake Providence, Louisiana. She was killed in a head-on automobile collision with a drunken driver near Alexandria, Louisiana. Celeste left one daughter, Elizabeth Gayle Clement Causey, who was reared by her father and step-mother.

Allie Jo Hammack (1 November 1934 - 11 October 1966), fourth daughter of George and Mary Almedia Bankston Hammack, married Frank Herman Shulte (1927-2002) on 1 September 1957 in Lake Providence, Louisiana. Allie Jo died as a result of a tumor and abscess formed in her brain; an unsuccessful surgery left her in a long vegetative state in a Memphis, Tennessee, hospital, where she died. Allie Jo left one adoptive son, Frederick Bernard Schulte, and two natural daughters, Laura Ann Schulte Carroll and Emily Irene Schulte Sherrill.

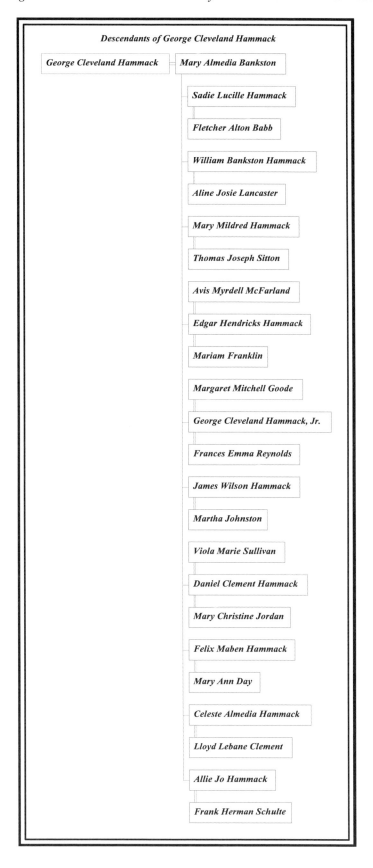

Descendants of George Cleveland Hammack

George Cleveland Hammack — Mary Almedia Bankston

- Sadie Lucille Hammack
- Fletcher Alton Babb
- William Bankston Hammack
- Aline Josie Lancaster
- Mary Mildred Hammack
- Thomas Joseph Sitton
- Avis Myrdell McFarland
- Edgar Hendricks Hammack
- Mariam Franklin
- Margaret Mitchell Goode
- George Cleveland Hammack, Jr.
- Frances Emma Reynolds
- James Wilson Hammack
- Martha Johnston
- Viola Marie Sullivan
- Daniel Clement Hammack
- Mary Christine Jordan
- Felix Maben Hammack
- Mary Ann Day
- Celeste Almedia Hammack
- Lloyd Lebane Clement
- Allie Jo Hammack
- Frank Herman Schulte

John Manly Bankston (1857-1922) moved from Bibb County, Alabama, to Hinds County, Mississippi, where he married Abi Doxey O'Neal (1870-1899). Of Swedish extraction, his ancestors had moved from Pennsylvania to the Carolinas and then Georgia. Abi's family – of mixed Scots, Irish, and English origins – had lived primarily in North Carolina before moving further south. John Manly and Abi Doxey O'Neal Bankston were the parents of Mary Almedia Bankston (1894-1974), who married George Cleveland Hammack (1884-1963).

Descendants of John Manly Bankston

Abi Doxey O'Neal	John Manly Bankston	Elizabeth Ludlow

James Rederick Bankston

Leoda (Lolo) Reneau

Andrew Jackson (Jack) Cates

Joan Bankston

William Henry Maben

John Malcolm Bankston

Jennie Lea Miller

Thomas Hendrix Bankston

Mary Almedia Bankston

George Cleveland Hammack

Allie Gertrude Bankston

James Monroe Martin

Alvin Watts Bankston

Lucille Cook

Chapter 16:

Hammack Conclusion: Ermington, Devonshire, England, to Mississippi

The preceding pages have chronicled four centuries of Hammack heritage, from the family's emergence in southeastern Devonshire in the late sixteenth-century to the present day. William "O" Hammack arrived in Virginia about 1656 and lived there for the next fifty years; he left four sons, from whom virtually all American Hammacks and Hammocks descend.

During the century and a half following William Hammack's death, his descendants spread across the continent, reaching California before 1850 and Oregon before 1860. The descendants of William Hammack's son Richard moved through southwestern Virginia into Tennessee and Kentucky, where they became modest farmers. In the next generation, they moved into Missouri, Illinois, Indiana, Kansas, and Iowa, where they became prosperous mid-western farmers. Most of these Hammacks were self-sufficient farmers; few of them owned slaves, and many of them supported the Union during the American Civil War.

Many of the descendants of William Hammack, eldest son of the immigrant William, remained in North Farnham Parish, Richmond County, Virginia. They still live today within a few miles of where the immigrant William made his first documentable appearance in 1668.

But members of this family, too, left the Northern Neck. Robert Hammack, Jr., son of Robert and Anne Lambert Hammack and grandson of William and Christian Middleton Hammack, settled in Lunenburg and Brunswick Counties of Southside Virginia. His cousin John Hammack, another grandson of William and Christian, settled in Granville County, North Carolina. Benedict Hammack, Robert's uncle, settled in Amelia County, Virginia. Robert's cousin and, through his mother's side, his uncle as well, another John Hammack, settled in Lunenburg County, where he sired a large family. The Lunenburg Hammacks remained in the Southside throughout the nineteenth-century, but descendants of John Hammack of Granville County, Benedict Hammack of Amelia County, and Robert Hammack, Jr., moved south and west. By and large, they produced the many Hammack and Hammock families of Georgia, Florida, Alabama, Mississippi, and Louisiana.

Descendants of these three Deep South Hammack families included several wealthy cotton planters before the American Civil War. Many of them were slave owners, and most supported the Confederacy. More than a dozen descendants of William and Christian Middleton Hammack gave their lives serving in the Confederate Army between 1861 and 1865.

Simeon Hammack, on whom much of this study has concentrated, was the son of William T. and Mary Felts Hammack and the grandson of Robert and Millenor Jackson Hammack. His parents and grandparents were prosperous farmers, and, by the end of his life, William T. Hammack, like his brother Lewis, owned enough real estate and slaves to have been considered a member of the proverbial "planter class" of the Old South. Yet, in each instance, death and inheritance weakened the concentration of real and personal property. Like the majority of southern slaveholders, Simeon Hammack himself seems to have owned only a few slaves, and they probably toiled alongside Simeon and his sons in the cotton fields of central Georgia and northeastern Mississippi.

Simeon Hammack did amass a substantial amount of real estate during his lifetime; because estate records for Choctaw and Calhoun Counties have not survived, we do not know whether this land was distributed among his heirs after Simeon died about 1862 or whether it was sold in the aftermath of the American Civil War. Four of Simeon's sons -- Charles, John, Felix, and George -- remained in Calhoun County, Mississippi, although John and Charles both died not long after the Civil War. George died in 1893, and Felix lived until 1903. Of the remaining sons, William T. H. Hammack settled in Madison County, where he died in 1880, and seems never to have lived in Choctaw or Calhoun Counties. Alfred Washington Hammack, one of the younger sons, left Mississippi in the 1880s and settled in Ashley County, Arkansas, just north of Louisiana, where he died in 1898.

Although Simeon's son William T. H. Hammack was a plantation overseer and seems never to have owned land of his own, Simeon's other sons became modest farmers, owning tracts that ranged between thirty and 200 acres. Although nothing is known about the religious affiliation of William T. H. and John T. Hammack, Simeon's other sons seem, like their mother, to have been faithful members of the Baptist church. Their religious activism and their landed wealth seem to have established them as leaders in their local communities, although none of them became individuals of great wealth or prominence. Felix Wilborn Hammack, who died in 1903, was probably the most successful of Simeon's sons, working a substantial farm (part of which he had acquired through marriage to Mary Lee Doolittle May, a young widow) and taking an active role in both Bethel Baptist Church and Sabougla Baptist Church, of which he was a charter member.

John T. Hammack, Simeon's third son, married Louisa Templeton in Georgia. Although John survived the Civil War, his health failed him during the Confederate service. John was hospitalized in 1863 and may never have completely recovered. He died in 1870, leaving a young widow and several children. Louisa seems to have died soon after John, possibly as a result of the 1878 Yellow Fever epidemic that killed thousands in Mississippi, Tennessee, and Alabama.

Only three of the children of John T. and Louisa Templeton Hammack are known to have survived to adulthood. Felix W. Hammack outlived all of his siblings, dying childless in 1935. John Robert Hammack died in 1919 in North Dakota, having pursued an unusual migration path that took his descendants into the northwestern United States and southwestern Canada. William Simms Hammack, older than both Felix and John, left Calhoun County about 1878 and moved to Madison County, where his brother Felix later settled. William worked first as a farm laborer and perhaps as a sharecropper, marrying Sallie Cates of nearby Brownsville, Mississippi, in 1883. They produced a large family, although his death in 1898 left Sallie with several young children to rear on her own.

The descendants of John T. and Louisa Templeton Hammack overcame many obstacles. Having lost both parents at an early age, they depended on their own resourcefulness and the kindness of more distant relatives to gain a foothold in life. Yet all three surviving sons prospered. John Robert Hammack ranched for many years in the Dakotas,[752] and Felix W. Hammack owned substantial real estate and had mercantile interests as well around Flora, in Hinds County, Mississippi. William S. Hammack died more than two decades before either of his brothers. Prior to his death, he had purchased a small tract of land which was amplified by his wife's inheritance from her Cates relatives. The twentieth-century descendants of John and Louisa Templeton Hammack and of their son William S. and his wife Sallie Cates Hammack built on this heritage and included many successful professionals as well as agriculturalists.

In each generation, the Hammack achievements have been aided by Hammack foremothers as well as forefathers. These women brought personal traits and values that shaped subsequent generations, as well as kinship connections and sometimes property that physically and materially affected the success of their spouses and offspring. It is to the families of these women that we now turn.

We shall begin first with Grace Hammack, like her husband probably an indentured servant who settled in Virginia in the seventeenth-century. In the next two generations, Christian Middleton Hammack and Anne Lambert Hammack brought significant connections in Virginia's Northern Neck; each woman belonged to a prosperous and well-established family resident in the colony since the 1640s, and the economic legacy of that success likely also contributed to the good fortune of their husbands and children. In the fourth generation, Millenor Jackson Hammack also brought real property to her marriage that no doubt aided her husband in his economic pursuits.

---

[752] Jonas Hammack, John Robert's son, indicated that John Robert never owned a home or land but instead rented and often relocated. He is said to have participated in a ferry venture across the Missouri River with his eldest son-in-law prior to the outbreak of World War I, about which time the son-in-law, Jacob Jerome "Jack" Telenga (1889-1957), moved to Canada. The 1910 and 1920 North Dakota census, however, indicates that John and Emma Hammack farmed their own land, perhaps indicating tracts they rented rather than working for others.

Anne Lambert Hammack and Millenor Jackson Hammack left another important legacy -- longevity -- that positively impacted future generations. Both women lived past eighty, and possibly past ninety, as did several of their children and grandchildren. In an age when early death was common, the long lifespans of these women were notable, both in terms of longevity as well as in terms of the stability, continuity, and unity which they may have provided to their families. Their influence was felt among their descendants for generations.

So far as is known, the first five generations of Hammack foremothers were of primarily English stock. Christian Middleton, Anne Lambert, Millenor Jackson, and Mary Felts all belonged to English families that had begun their American saga in eastern Virginia. Grace Hammack, Christian Middleton, and Anne Lambert all originated in the Virginia's Northern Neck, while the ancestors of Millenor Jackson and Mary Felts both trace to families that settled in Albemarle Parish, Sussex County, Virginia, in the late seventeenth-century.

In the sixth generation, Elizabeth Jane Moore Hammack similarly enriched the family gene pool. Her ancestors had come out of Hanover, Prince George, and Charles City Counties into Lunenburg and Brunswick Counties in the 1740s and 1750s. Robert Moore became a substantial landowner in Lunenburg in the 1740s and 1750s, but hard times seem to have pressed the Moores, like the Felts family, to Georgia. The Virginian Ussery Moore and the North Carolinian John Felts seem to have owned little property after settling in Georgia, although both later drew lots in the state land lotteries that may have benefited their Hammack descendants.

In the seventh, eighth, and ninth generations, as the Hammack family spread south and west, the Hammack foremothers introduced new genetic strains into the family's heritage. Leaving Tidewater and Southside Virginia, the early Hammacks encountered families of different ethnic origins who introduced new cultural and genetic elements into the family's history. On her father's side, Louisa Templeton Hammack descended from Scots-Irish migrants who had settled in Pennsylvania in the 1720s; they had been among the very first European settlers in southwestern North Carolina in the 1740s, where they became leading citizens on the frontier. Louisa's daughter-in-law Sarah Elizabeth Cates Hammack was a native of Hinds County, Mississippi, but all four of her grandparents had come to Mississippi from Person County, North Carolina. From Person County, they trace back to eastern Virginia, although several of them descended from families prominent in Virginia's history. Sallie's ancestors William Coxe and Christopher Calthorpe were both "Ancient Planters" who had settled in Virginia prior to the end of the Virginia Company's control of the colony in 1624; Christopher Calthorpe belonged to a noble English family traceable to the eleventh-century in Norfolk.[753]

In the tenth generation, Mary Almedia Bankston Hammack's ancestry added further diversity to the family. Her Bankston, Rambo, and Boore ancestors all came from Sweden and Finland to New Amsterdam and New Sweden -- later New York, Delaware, and Pennsylvania -- in the middle seventeenth-century. Anders Bengston became a prominent citizen in New Sweden, where his son Andrew and his grandson Lawrence -- the southern migrant -- were born. Mary Almedia Bankston's ancestors Hiram Mitchell and Mourning Dove added further Scots-Irish heritage to the family, along -- possibly -- with a trace of Native American heritage. Her O'Neal and Stewart ancestors were Irish and Scots-Irish, while her Gary, West, Melton, Stephens, Brewer, and Parker ancestors were of English descent. Through her great-grandmother Mary Lanier Bankston and an earlier ancestor Sarah Lanier Brewer, Mary Almedia Bankston twice descended from Nicholas Lanier, a native of Rouen, France, and his wife Lucretia de Bassano, whose parents had moved from their native Venice, Italy, to London in the early sixteenth-century.

It is to these allied families, their heritages, and their genetic and material legacies that this study now turns.

---

[753] This lineage is produced, with appropriate citation, in the appendix.

Part II:

Hammack Maternal Line Ancestors

Chapter 17:

Grace [------] Hammack of Richmond County, Virginia

Grace was the first known wife of William "O" Hammack, sire of the American Hammack family. Her maiden name is unknown. She likely married William Hammack about 1666 -- possibly in Northampton County, Virginia, but more likely in Old Rappahannock County. Grace and William were married for more than a decade, from about 1666 until 1682 or afterwards. She had died by 1688 when William Hammack and his second wife, Alice, baptized their son, William Hammack the younger. Grace Hammack was apparently the mother of William, John, and Richard Hammack, the three eldest sons of the immigrant William Hammack, while Alice was the mother of Elizabeth and William Hammack the younger.

Grace Hammack was probably either an indentured servant who came to Virginia to work on a plantation near the one where William Hammack was then working or she was the sister or daughter of a neighboring planter. If Grace arrived in the colony as a servant, she likely traveled there alone, probably for the same reasons as William. Indentured servants during the first half of the seventeenth-century were predominately men who came to the colony willing to do hard labor in order to improve their fortunes. Nevertheless, from the 1620s, the colony attracted a steady stream of female servants as well. These women, too, sought better lives. Most did the same work as men. They worked tobacco fields and tended to livestock; some performed domestic chores as well, and many were vulnerable to sexual exploitation by unscrupulous masters and their male kin. If Grace came to the colony as a servant, she probably left her kin in England and had no further communication with them. She and William probably met after he completed his indenture and may have married soon after she became a free woman.[754]

Another possibility, however, is that William married the daughter of a neighboring planter. Many male former servants after their indentures married women who were the daughters, sisters, or widows of successful planters, many of whom began their own careers in the colony as servants. This path to stability and financial success was so well recognized in the seventeenth-century that one sojourner in the colony quipped that "wealthy widows are the best commodity the country affords." Marriage to a widow or daughter with a dowry of any sort could be an asset for a rising planter in the seventeenth-century.[755]

There is no evidence that William Hammack acquired any property by virtue of his marriage to Grace. If she did belong to an established local family, she probably brought only a small dowry to the marriage. But she may have provided another important asset, kinship and friendship ties in a society that was primarily composed of unattached, often transient individuals.

There is no clear indication of a family connection between William Hammack and any other settlers in Old Rappahannock County, but William certainly maintained a close connection with Thomas and Johanna Freshwater and another neighbor, Daniel Swellivant. It may be that Grace was a female relative of one of these individuals or a servant brought by them to work on their lands.[756]

Grace Hammack was probably born about 1650; if she lived until 1687, she was probably no more than thirty-eight years old when she died, perhaps as a result of childbirth. During the years that she was married to William Hammack, she probably worked with him on the small homestead in Rappahannock

---

[754] See Pagan, *Anne Orthwood's Bastard*, pp. 1-20, and Morgan, *American Slavery*, pp. 95, 163, 235, and 310, regarding female immigrants to seventeenth-century Virginia. K. M. Brown, *Good Wives, Nasty Wenches, and Anxious Patiarchs: Gender, Race, and Power in Colonial Virginia* (Chapel Hill and London, 1996), esp. pp. 75-103, provides a scholarly account of Virginia women during this period.

[755] Ibid., pp. 247-283.

[756] Some researchers have concluded, erroneously, that William Hammack married Thomas Freshwater's widow. This is a result of misreading the evidence. But William did for more than two decades maintain a steady association with the Freshwaters that may be indicative of some other connection. His ties to Swellivant were not as close or prolonged, but they are also noteworthy.

County in addition to her work in the home and her childrearing responsibilities. Her life probably involved few comforts, but she helped erect a stable foundation upon which future generations of Hammacks prospered.[757]

---

[757] There were significant regional variations in the lives, expectations, and obligations of colonial women. For an account of women outside the colonial Chesapeake, see L. T. Ulrich, *Good Wives: Image and Reality in the Lives of Women in Northern New England, 1650-1750* (New York, 1982). D. B. and A. H. Rutman, *A Place in Time: Middlesex Co., VA, 1650-1750* (New York and Oxford, 1984), esp. pp. 94-108, 104-113, places the lives of individual women in the context of the time and place in which they lived. Middlesex County lies just across the Rappahannock River from Richmond County, ancestral home of the Hammack family.

Chapter 18:

Christian Middleton Hammack of Westmoreland and Richmond Counties, Virginia

The identification of William Hammack's wife as Christian Middleton is based on three factors. First, the will of John Middleton appoints William Hammack as one of two men named to execute the document. The men are called "brothers," a term that in the seventeenth and eighteenth century could refer to the spouse of a sister.[758] Second, Middleton family names -- Robert and, especially, Benedict -- recur in each Hammack generation from the marriage of William and Christian for the next two centuries. Third, Westmoreland and Richmond County, Virginia, records indicate that the Hammacks and Middletons were neighbors and long-term associates. Living in the same neighborhood increases the possibility that a marriage could have occurred between the two families, while a prolonged association between them seems to suggest that some kinship tie did in fact unite them.

The Middleton family in England was a prominent one, and in the seventeenth and eighteenth century Middletons appear in Maryland, Virginia, and South Carolina. Several of these men can be proven to connect to the English Middleton family which can then be traced back several generations. Certainly there were Middletons present in Virginia by the early 1630s, but no proven connection has been discovered to link them with the Middletons of the Northern Neck.[759]

The earliest Middleton in the Northern Neck family was Robert Middleton, who was mentioned in the 16 November 1655 Lancaster County will of Arthur Dunn.[760] On 5 April 1658, a deed for a cow he had purchased from Mr. Rowland Burnham of Lancaster County was confirmed by Henry Corbin, who had since married Burnham's widow.[761] On 15 September 1658, he and Thomas Willys purchased 200 acres from Samuel Matthews.[762] On 23 August 1659 and 22 October 1659, Middleton witnessed transactions in which Henry Corbin sold land in Lancaster County.[763] On 12 September 1660, Robert Middleton and "Mary my wife" delivered a power of attorney to John Harris to formally convey the land earlier deeded by him to Willys.[764] Three months later, the Middletons named Corbin as power of attorney to convey a 260-acre tract in Lancaster County to Thomas Kidd.[765] The land was on Burnham's Creek, which had been named for Corbin's wife's first husband.[766] The connection between Corbin and Middleton may be

[758] Westmoreland Co., VA, Deeds and Wills 1701-07, p. 425-27.

[759] Daniel B. Lloyd, *The Middletons and Kindred Families of Southern Maryland* (Bethesda, MD: 1975), p. 379-382. This book deals primarily with the family of Robert Middleton (c. 1651-c. 1708, Prince George's Co., MD), who left sons John, James, Thomas, Robert and William Middleton. The origin of this Robert is unidentified, but he may have been related to Robert of Westmoreland. This volume extensively examines early Middleton families in England and their trans-Atlantic connections. Note that one Robert Mydleton died in 1616 and was buried 13 June 1616 at St. Dunston's in the East, London. He was a merchant of Mincing Lane and an investor in the Virginia Company of London. He was Member of Parliament for Melcombe Regis in 1603 and for the City of London in 1614. He was a son of Richard and Jane Dryhusrt Middleton and was one of several London Middletons with economic interests in Virginia.

[760] Fleet, 1: 104.

[761] Fleet, 1: 124.

[762] Fleet, 1: 164. Mary was apparently the widow of Andrew Butcher. On 12 March 1661/2, a notice was filed at Lancaster Court indicating that "there is a Heyfer belonging to the Orphan of Andrew Butcher (deced.) runninge upon the Plantacon of Mr. Cut: Potter. It is ordered that the sd. Heyfer been delivered to Robt. Middleton, Father in Law to the sd. Orphan, or to his order." The seventeenth century term "Father in Law" was analogous to the modern "stepfather." Lancaster Co., VA, Order Book, 1656-1666, p. 90, 28 September 1659, indicates that "Mary Butcher, Widd., the Relict of Andrew Butcher, late deced., relinquishing her right of administracon, upon her peticon is ordered (wth: the consent of the Administrator) to have & enjoy her wearing apparel, bedd & furniture, wth: the crop of Corne planted by her Husband towards the sustenacon of her selfe & Childe." Andrew "Butchart" was alive on 27 May 1657 when he purchased a heifer from Robert Chowninge (Lancaster Co., VA, Order Book, 1656-1666, p. 23). Butcher's name appears as a tithable on 30 November 1659 on Henry Corbin's list (Lancaster Co., VA, Order Book, 1656-1666, p. 104).

[763] Fleet, 1: 161.

[764] Fleet, 1: 164.

[765] Fleet, 1: 137.

[766] Fleet, 1: 137.

significant, for Corbin was one of Lancaster's leading men. The fact that Robert Middleton frequently appeared in connection with him may suggest that he was involved in a business relationship with either Corbin or Burnham; further, the fact that Middleton could name Corbin -- a person of considerable prominence -- as his power of attorney suggests that Middleton was himself a man of status in the local community.

Sometimes after 1660, Middleton seems to have moved to the northern side of the Rappahannock River, settling in Westmoreland County. He does not appear in Lancaster County Court Orders after 1662 except for 1671, when on 8 March 1670/71 a runaway servant belonging to "Robt. Middleton of ye County of Westmoreland" was seized by the Lancaster Court and ordered to be returned to Middleton. The man may have been trying to return to family or friends he had known before Middleton left Lancaster County.[767] Middleton had been granted 1,120 acres in Westmoreland County on 21 May 1666 at the head of the main branch of Yeocomico River and near the Machotick Horse Path, including 300 acres originally granted to him on 26 September 1665.[768] This was itself a renewal of an earlier grant dated 17 May 1662 for 300 acres on Yeocomico.[769]

Robert Middleton lived the remainder of his life on the Westmoreland County tract, writing his will there on 1 February 1696/7, at which time he must have been nearly seventy years old. The will identifies only two children, sons John and Benedict.[770] Land records from 1697 and 1699 indicate that Robert Middleton's Yeocomico tracts then joined land owned by William Hammack.[771]

Of the sons of Robert and Mary Middleton, John Middleton died in 1706 in Westmoreland County. He appointed his "loving brothers Benedict Middleton and William Hammack both of this county of Westmoreland, overseers and executors in trust" to fulfill the terms of his will.[772] Probate was issued to them on 25 September 1706.[773] Middleton's estate was valued at 47,225 pounds of tobacco, including four Negroes valued at 22,500 pounds of tobacco.[774] On 26 November 1706, William Hammack returned the inventory to Westmoreland Court.[775] John's widow Elizabeth Middleton survived until 1733, writing her will on 9 February 1732/3.[776] Children of John and Elizabeth Middleton included the following: John Middleton (-- 1726, Westmoreland or Northumberland County, Virginia), who married Eleanor Rogers, later wife of Allen Harvey; Robert Middleton, probably the individual who wrote his will in 1739 and died childless about 1754; Thomas Middleton, who married Leasure [-----] and was deceased by 1755 in Westmoreland County; Benjamin Middleton, who married Jemima and died about 1756 in Westmoreland County; Elizabeth Middleton, about whom nothing more is known; Mary Middleton, who died unmarried and childless about 1763; and Alice Middleton, who died unmarried and childless about 1772.[777]

Benedict Middleton, the other proven son of Robert Middleton, married Elizabeth Rogers and died about 1730 in Westmoreland County. He was surveyor of highways for Westmoreland in 1719, vestryman of Cople Parish in 1727, a churchwarden of Cople Parish in 1729, and for many years Justice of the Westmoreland County Court. William Hammack witnessed a deed on 22 February 1708/9 in which Benedict Middleton purchased 100 acres (which had been originally included within his father's 1,120 acres) from William Landman.[778] Benedict and Elizabeth Middleton in 1719 witnessed a deed from

[767] Lancaster Co., VA, Order Book 1666-1680, p. 188.

[768] Nugent, *Cavaliers and Pioneers*, 2: 4. For the earlier grant, see Ibid., 1: 565.

[769] Ibid., 1: 565.

[770] A. B. Fothergill, *Wills of Westmoreland Co., VA, 1654-1800* (Richmond, 1925), pp. 17-18.

[771] G. E. Gray, *Northern Neck Land Grants, 1694-1862* (4 vols., Baltimore, 1987-2008), 1: 20-22.

[772] Westmoreland Co., VA, Deeds and Wills 1701-07, pp. 425-27.

[773] Westmoreland Co., VA, Deeds and Wills 1701-07, pp. 425-27.

[774] Westmoreland Co., VA, Deeds and Wills, 1701-07, pp. 433-34.

[775] Westmoreland Co., VA, Deeds and Wills, 1701-07, pp. 433-34.

[776] The will was probated on 27 March 1733. See Fothergill, p. 96.

[777] See Fothergill, pp. 117, 141, 153, 166.

[778] Westmoreland Co., VA, Deeds and Wills No. 4, 1707-09, pp. 166-69.

Nicholas Rochester to his son William Rochester, mentioning Nicholas's daughter Ann Rochester Hammack and her husband William Hammack.[779]

Benedict and Elizabeth Rogers Middleton were the parents of Benedict Middleton, Jr. (d. 1783, Westmoreland County, Virginia), who married Hannah Lane; William Middleton, who may have died intestate and without issue in Westmoreland in 1757; Robert Middleton, who died in Westmoreland in 1773; Mary Middleton; Elizabeth Middleton, who married Daniel Tebbs; and Jane Middleton, who married John Crabb and died in Westmoreland in 1779. Of Benedict's sons, Captain Benedict Middleton, Jr., followed in his father's footsteps. He was vestryman and churchwarden of Cople Parish and surveyor of roads in Westmoreland. During the Revolutionary conflict, he was a member of the Committee of Safety for Westmoreland County.[780]

The Middletons of Westmoreland continued to be a family of regional prominence throughout the eighteenth century. By marriage, they had family connections to several families in Northumberland and Richmond Counties who intermarried with the descendants of William ("O") Hammack in the Northern Neck.

---

[779] Westmoreland Co., VA, Deeds and Wills No. 6, 1716-20, pp. 482-83.
[780] T. R. B. Wright, L. Washington, R. H. McKim, and G. W. Beale, *Westmoreland Co., VA* (Richmond, 1912), p. 51.

Standard Pedigree Tree

Robert Middleton

b:
m:
d: Abt. 1698 in Westmoreland Co., VA

Christian Middleton

b: Abt. 1675 in Westmoreland Co., VA
m: Bef. 29 Nov 1693 in UNKNOWN
d: Aft. 1730 in Richmond Co., VA

Mary ?

b:
d:

Notes:

Chapter 19:

Ann Lambert Hammack of Northumberland and Richmond Counties, Virginia

Robert Hammack, son of William and Christian Middleton Hammack, married Ann Lambert, daughter of Hugh Lambert and Ann Morgan. The marriage took place in the late 1720s; the ancestors of Ann Lambert Hammack had at that time been living in the Northern Neck since the 1650s.

Hugh Lambert, father of Ann Lambert Hammack, was a son of William and Ann Claughton Lambert of Northumberland and Richmond Counties. William Lambert himself was probably born about 1665; he may have been connected to John Lambert who lived in Rappahannock County during the 1670s, but there is no clear evidence to support a connection. The earliest known reference to William dates from 19 September 1692, when with Hugh Harris and Alexander Swann he witnessed a deed from Richard and Abigail Winter of Richmond County to Richard Adams of Northumberland County for land along Totuskey Creek in Richmond County.[781] On 12 January 1694/5, as William Lambert of Bowtreay Parish, Northumberland County, he purchased 300 acres in Richmond County from Daniel Swellivant. James Richardson and John Claughton witnessed the deed.[782]

William Lambert married as the first of three wives -- all named Ann -- Ann Claughton. The marriage is documented by a court petition dated 20 July 1698 in Northumberland County in which

> Motion... [was made by] John Claughton, William Lambert, and Edward Smyth on behalfe of their wives and Middleton Claughton by her brother the aforesaid John Claughton, Commission of Administration to them on the estate of James Claughton their deceased father.[783]

By 20 June 1700, Middleton Claughton had married Robert Smith, and he joined John Claughton, William Lambert, and Edward Smyth as co-defendants in a debt suit filed by John Turbeville in Northumberland County.[784]

Ann Claughton Hammack, daughter of James Claughton, was mother of Hammack ancestor Hugh Lambert. Ann's grandfather James Claughton was one of the earliest settlers in the Northern Neck, dying in 1648 in Northumberland County.[785] A mariner, Claughton and wife Jane had settled first on Kent Island, in Maryland, before relocating to Northumberland. His estate inventory, valued at 3,536 pounds of tobacco, was filed in August 1648. Claughton owned one old satin petticoat, two black hoods, one mask, one pair of stockings, one black neck cloth, a small parcel of lace, a taffeta petticoat, three books, a wainscot chest, and other furniture. From the inventory, it would seem that Claughton and his family lived well.[786]

---

[781] Richmond County, VA, Deed Book 1692-94, p. 86-90. Some researchers have concluded that William Lambert came from Charles Co., MD, and that he was William Lambert, son of John and Ellinor Lambert, baptized there 27 February 1669. See E. G. Jordan, *Abstracts of Charles Co., MD, Court and Land Records, 1685-1694* (Baltimore, 2007), pp. 63, 123. John Lambert's wife was Ellinor, daughter of John Nevill. Other children of this John were John (baptized 1664), Elizabeth or Ellinor (baptized 1667), and Samuel (baptized 1671). All were living in 1672, and William was still living on 1 March 1680, apparently in Charles County.

[782] Richmond County, VA, Deed Book 1695-1701, pp. 187-8.

[783] Northumberland Co., VA, Order Book 4, p. 830, in B. Fleet, *Virginia Colonial Abstracts*, Series 2, Vol. 1, Northumberland Co., VA, 1678-1713 (34 vols., Baltimore, 1961), p. 51.

[784] Northumberland Co., VA, Order Book 5, p. 101, in Fleet, *Virginia Colonial Abstracts*, Series 2, Vol. 1, Northumberland Co., VA, 1678-1713, p. 72.

[785] Northumberland Co., VA, Records, 1652-55, p. 5, 7, in Fleet, *Virginia Colonial Abstracts* (1988), 1: 369-71.

[786] Ibid., 1: 371.

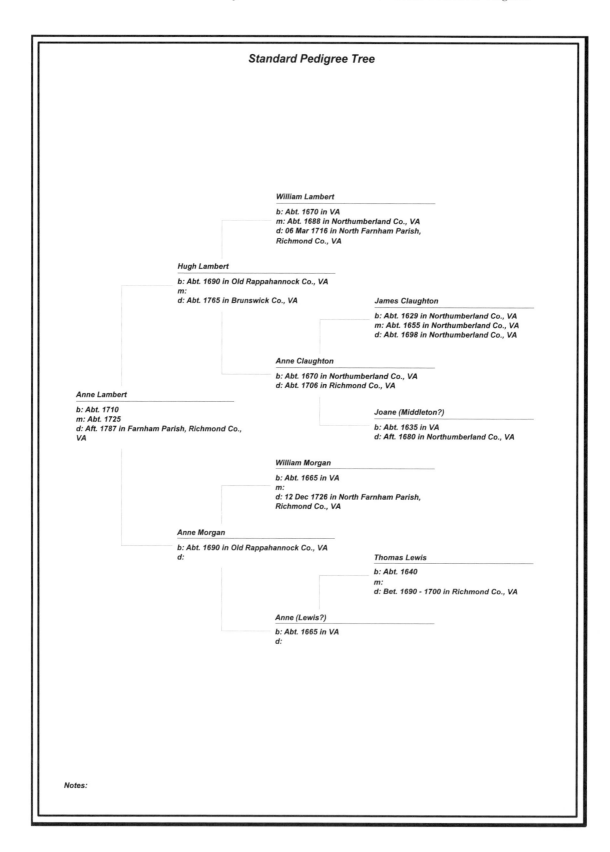

Standard Pedigree Tree

William Lambert

b: Abt. 1670 in VA
m: Abt. 1688 in Northumberland Co., VA
d: 06 Mar 1716 in North Farnham Parish, Richmond Co., VA

Hugh Lambert

b: Abt. 1690 in Old Rappahannock Co., VA
m:
d: Abt. 1765 in Brunswick Co., VA

James Claughton

b: Abt. 1629 in Northumberland Co., VA
m: Abt. 1655 in Northumberland Co., VA
d: Abt. 1698 in Northumberland Co., VA

Anne Claughton

b: Abt. 1670 in Northumberland Co., VA
d: Abt. 1706 in Richmond Co., VA

Anne Lambert

b: Abt. 1710
m: Abt. 1725
d: Aft. 1787 in Farnham Parish, Richmond Co., VA

Joane (Middleton?)

b: Abt. 1635 in VA
d: Aft. 1680 in Northumberland Co., VA

William Morgan

b: Abt. 1665 in VA
m:
d: 12 Dec 1726 in North Farnham Parish, Richmond Co., VA

Anne Morgan

b: Abt. 1690 in Old Rappahannock Co., VA
d:

Thomas Lewis

b: Abt. 1640
m:
d: Bet. 1690 - 1700 in Richmond Co., VA

Anne (Lewis?)

b: Abt. 1665 in VA
d:

Notes:

Two years after the elder Claughton died, his son James, born about 1629, came of age. James patented 250 acres on Claughton's Creek in Northumberland on 20 December 1650.[787] To this he added an interest in 300 acres in 1652,[788] 496 acres in 1653,[789] an interest in 600 acres in 1657,[790] 345 acres in 1661,[791] and seventy-two acres in 1663.[792] Claughton, who gave his age as twenty-three in a 1652 deposition[793], married prior to 26 January 1657 to a woman named Joan.[794] Claughton's close relationship with Robert and Ann Bradshaw and their daughter Ann Bradshaw (later Ann Bradshaw Bradley Lambert) suggests a close family relationship. It may be that Claughton married Bradshaw's sister or vice-versa; another closely related couple with whom Claughton had dealings were Robert and Mary Sechs. Robert testified on 4 August 1665 that he was aged "thirty-four years or thereabouts;"[795] Robert's wife Mary, on 15 October 1660, had appointed "my loveing Brother, James Claughton," as her lawful attorney to acknowledge a deed from her husband.[796] The evidence does not clearly indicate whether Mary Sechs was the biological sister of James Claughton or of his wife Joan.

James Claughton had a long and active life in Northumberland County; he appears frequently in legal records as a participant in court suits, sometimes suing to collect delinquent debts and occasionally sued by creditors for the same reason. One telling reference, from 1651, reveals that he was called a "mischief maker" by some of his neighbors. Apparently, Claughton had taken it upon himself to tell another neighbor, George Thompson, that Thompson's wife had been sleeping with a nearby planter.[797] The records do not indicate whether the charges were substantiated. Otherwise, Claughton seems to have avoided controversy, serving often as an attorney for friends and neighbors and from time to time as a juror and estate appraiser. Claughton would probably have been about seventy when in 1698 his heirs received an order from the Northumberland Court to divide his property.[798]

About 1700, William Lambert moved from Northumberland County into Richmond County, settling on Totuskey Creek. In 1701, he was sued by James Tarpley for an unpaid debt.[799] On 2 July of the same year, along with Charles Barber, Dr. Robert Clark, and Mr. George Glascock, Lambert was named to the commission to inventory the estate of William Hammack.[800] In 1703, Lambert was involved in a legal dispute with Francis Lynch of Richmond County.[801]

Lambert's first wife, Ann Claughton, had died by about 1705, and he had remarried to Mrs. Ann Bradshaw Bradley, daughter of George Bradshaw and widow of Robert Bradley. Ann's father, Robert Bradshaw, a son of George and Ann Bradshaw, was baptized 1 November 1622 at St. James Garlickhithe, London. He was living in Northumberland County, Virginia, by 21 January 1651/2, at which time he and James Claughton -- father of William Lambert's first wife -- were jurors in Northumberland.[802] Bradshaw and Claughton seem to have had a close relationship, and by 1655 they were co-owners of a tract in

[787] Ibid., 1: 378.

[788] Ibid., 1: 378-9.

[789] Ibid., 1: 377.

[790] Northumberland Co., VA, Record Book 1652-58, p. 136.

[791] Northumberland Co., VA, Deeds & Wills, 1706-20, pp. 87-88.

[792] Fleet, I, p. 512.

[793] Fleet, I, p. 369.

[794] Northumberland Co., VA, Record Book, 1658-62, p. 43; Northumberland Co., VA, Record Book 1662-66, p. 143.

[795] Northumberland Co., VA, Records Book 15, p. 161, and 3, p. 51, in Fleet, *Virginia Colonial Abstracts* (1988), 1: 605.

[796] Northumberland Co., VA, Records Book 15, p. 53.

[797] Fleet, *Virginia Colonial Abstracts* (1988), 1: 618.

[798] Northumberland Co., VA, Order Book 5, p. 101, in Fleet, *Virginia Colonial Abstracts*, Series 2, Vol. 1, Northumberland Co., VA, 1678-1713, p. 72. Interestingly, Claughton's son John Claughton married Anne Pemberton. They were the ancestors of Pemberton Claughton, with whom John and William C. Hammack moved from Northumberland and Richmond Counties, Virginia, to Amite Co., MS, in the late 1840s.

[799] Richmond Co., VA, Order Book 1699-1701, p. 89.

[800] Richmond Co., VA, Order Book 1699-1701, pp. 110-11.

[801] Richmond Co., VA, Order Book 1702-04, pp. 270, 279.

[802] Northumberland Co., VA, Deeds & Orders, 1650-52, p. 71.

Northumberland which they sold to Richard Rice and Thomas Walker.[803] Bradshaw and Claughton patented another tract together in 1657, which they sold to Thomas Shepherd and wife Rose in 1660.[804] Bradshaw wrote his will in 1660, naming wife Ann Bradshaw and daughter Ann Bradshaw. The will was witnessed by James Claughton, who proved the will on 20 January 1661.[805] Claughton then on 9 June 1661 deeded his right to 250 acres to "Ann Bradshaw, daughter of Robert Bradshaw, late of Matta Ponii in the county of Northumberland, deceased."[806] This Ann Bradshaw married by 1676 Robert Bradley of Northumberland County; John Bradley, the eldest of their four known children, was baptized 30 November 1676 in St. Stephen's Parish, Northumberland County.[807] The elder Bradley was deceased by 16 November 1699, at which time Ann was wife of Charles Dermott of Northumberland County.[808] Dermott's will, written 4 April 1703, was proven 17 May 1703.[809] Ann had remarried William Lambert by 17 December 1707. On that date, as "William Lambert of North Farnham Parish, Richmond County, Virginia, and Ann his wife, daughter of Robert Bradshaw, deceased," they sold 100 acres in Mattapony Neck to Matthew Myers.[810]

On 4 May 1708, William Lambert of Richmond County conveyed to his stepson Robert Bradley a tract located on the "East side of the Road that cometh from Potowmack to Totuskey Mill, wch: said land is part of a tract of land containing three hundred acres which William Lambert purchased of Daniell Swellivant the twelfth day of Janry. one thousand Six hundred and ninety four."[811] A land grant to Charles Lewis, dated 26 May 1712, indicated that William Lambert, Captain John Tarpley, and William Hammack were adjacent landowners and that their tracts joined the line between Richmond and Northumberland Counties.[812] On 4 January 1713, Samuel and William Samford of Richmond County conveyed 141 acres in Richmond County for 8,520 pounds of tobacco.[813] On 23 July 1713, William Lambert, Edward Jones, Sr., and Edward Jones, Jr., witnessed a deed from Samuel Samford to Samford Jones. The land lay "on the South side of Totuskey Creek betweene the Ferry Road and Totuskey Mill, being part of a greater Devident by Patent to James Samford, Father to the aforesd. Samll. Samford, and bounded, beginning at the head of a Branch of Swamp comonly knowne or called the Schoole House Swamp by the Ferry Road near the Plantation of John Shaproone and runing downe the Ferry Road to the line of John Williams, thence by and alongst the said line of William Barber, thence along his line to the Schoole House Swampe." In addition to documenting William Lambert's landed wealth, these deeds also locate the Richmond County lands on which William Hammack and his son Robert, future husband of Ann Lambert, lived.[814]

Ann Bradshaw Bradley Lambert was deceased by May 1715, when William Lambert married for the third time, this time to a widow named Ann Bailey.[815] Although not mentioned in Lambert's will, she apparently survived him, dying testate in 1742.

---

[803] Northumberland Co., VA, Record Book, 1652-58, p. 81.

[804] Northumberland Co., VA, Record Book, 1658-62, p. 43.

[805] Northumberland Co., VA, Record Book, 1658-62, p. 53.

[806] Northumberland Co., VA, Record Book 1658-62, p. 57.

[807] For the Bradley births, see Northumberland County, Record of Births, 1661-1810, in Fleet, *Virginia Colonial Abstracts* (1988), 1: 408-9. Robert Bradley, Jr., lived for a time in Richmond County, probably explaining the gap in his children's births in the parish record. In addition to John, other children of Robert and Anne Bradshaw Bradley were James (baptized 5 April 1679); Robert (baptized 10 May 1682); and Elizabeth (baptism not located). John and James were both apparently deceased by 1703, although their siblings Robert and Elizabeth were living at that date.

[808] Ibid., 1: 521.

[809] Ibid., 1: 521.

[810] Northumberland Co., VA, Record Book 17, pp. 130-35, as cited in *Ibid.*, 1: 561.

[811] The land had originally been patented by Thomas Freshwater and joined lands of Edward Lewis. The deed was witnessed by Edward Brady, Hugh Lambert, and Samuel Churchill. See Richmond Co., VA, Deed Book 1705-1708, pp. 130a-131a.

[812] Gray, *Northern Neck Land Grants*, 1: 51.

[813] Richmond Co., VA, Deed Book 1714-15, pp. 215-16.

[814] Richmond Co., VA, Deed Book 1714-15, pp. 217-18.

[815] Richmond County, VA, Deed Book 1714-15, in Ruth and Sam Sparacio, Virginia County Court Records, *Deed Abstracts of Richmond County, VA, 1714-15* (McLean, VA, 1993), p. 55.

William Lambert's third marriage was a brief one. He wrote his will on 9 January 1715/6 in Richmond County; it was probated there on 4 April 1716, although the North Farnham Parish Register reveals that William died on 4 March 1715/6.[816] William's will, quoted in detail below, gives an overview of the size and complexity of his real and personal estate in the Northern Neck, documents details of his religious faith, and identifies his many children:

> In the Name of God, Amen. I William Lambert of the County of Richmond in Virginia being Sick and Weak of Body but of perfect Sense and Memory praysed bee Allmity God Doe make this my Last Will and Testament in name and form hereafter specifyed. Imprimis, I Commit my Body to the Earth from whence it Came to be Dessently Buried by my Executors hereafter named and my Soule I Bequeath to Allmyty God my Heavenly father hoping through the Merits of my Blessed Saver to Receive it againe att the time of my Resurrection and as for what Worldly Goods it hath pleased God to Bestowe upon me, I Give and Bequeath of as followeth.

> Imprimis, I Give to my Sonn Hugh Lambert a hundred Acres of Land wherein he now Liveth, Lying on the North side of a Branch that Divides the said Land from the Plantation I now live upon, Being up the said Branch to the main Road and to all the said Courses and Bounds upon the North side of the said Branch be the same a hundred acres more or less.

> Imprs. I give to my Sonn William Lambert the Plantation whereon I now Live with all the appertances thereunto belonging.

> Imprs. I give to my sonn John Lambert a hundred and forty one acres of Land that I Bought of Samuel Samford and his Sonn William Samford.

> Imprs. I give to my Daughter Elizabeth Lambert fifty Acres of Land which I Bought of John Pound Lying oun the west side of Totaskey Creek.

> Imprs. I Give to my Daughter Ann Ellmor a Negro Girl called An[817] during her Naturall life But in Case my said Daughter Ann Dyeth without issue then my Will is that the said Negro Girl shall be my Sonn Hughes and after her Death I Doe Give him the said Negro, Imprimis in case the said Negro Girl shall live to bring a Child I give it to my Daughter Elizabeth to be deliver to her when it is twelve month ould Imprimis I give to my sonn Hugh Lambert One Negro Man Called Sam my said Sonn paying fifteen hundred pounds of tobacco to my sonn William and fifteen hundred pounds of tobacco to my sonn John in Lew of there shares of the said Negro within three years after my Dessease.

> Imprimis. I Give to my Sonn William and to my Sonn John and to my Daughter Elezebeth each of them a ffeather bed with also what furniture belongeth to them and as for the Rest of my Estate I Give it to be Eaquelly deveyded amongst all my Children that is to say, Hugh, Mary, Ann, William, John and Elizabeth each to have a Eaqle share. Imprimis my will is that my son William and my sonn John and my Daughter Elizabeth shall live with my Sonn Hugh and [three words illegible] the age of seventeen Years. For

---

[816] Headley, *Wills of Richmond County*, pp. 31, 32.

[817] This bequest is ambiguously worded and very difficult to read. Ann's name was Ann Elmore ("Ellmor"), not Ann Elinor. There are two other references in the will in which Ann is mentioned, and there is no reference to Elinor. This means that William Lambert did not have two daughters -- Ann and Eleanor -- as some researchers have suggested.

the true performance of this my Last Will and Testament I constitute and make my loving Sonn Hugh Lambert whole and sole Executor of this my Last Will and testament Revoking and Disannulling all former Wills and Testaments by me maid. Witness my hand and seal this nine day of January Anno Domini 1715. Signed: William Lambert. Witnesses: John Hartley, Robert Gaille, Sarah (H) Hutchins. Att a Court held for Richmond County the fourth Day of April 1716 This will was proved in open Court by the oaths of Robert Gaille and Sarah Hutchins two of the witnesses thereto, and admitted to Record. Test. M. Beckwith, C. Cur.

Although the evidence is not conclusive, William's third wife Ann Bailey Lambert may have been the Ann Lambert who wrote her will on 14 March 1742/3 in Richmond County. John and Andrew Morgan witnessed the will, and Ann mentions a married daughter Elizabeth Adkins, a son-in-law William Dunn, and grandchildren Lambert Morgan, Elizabeth Morgan, and Ann Jones in the will.[818] The will was proven on 7 November 1743 with Hugh Lambert, Andrew Morgan, and John Morgan inventorying the estate on 5 December 1743.[819]

Of the offspring of William Lambert, daughter Ann (baptized 14 February 1699) married John Elmore in Richmond County. She apparently died in 1725, and her husband remarried to Ann Reynolds in 1728. John Elmore and Ann Lambert had several children, including Francis Elmore (baptized 12 December 1716) who married Mary Hammack on 23 May 1738. John Lambert (baptized 25 November 1702) and wife Frances remained in Richmond County until at least 1744, when he and his brother Hugh conveyed land that had formerly belonged to their father William Lambert.[820] John settled in Lunenburg County as early as 1749 and lived there as late as 1763; he died about 1765 in Brunswick County, leaving at least seven children -- all baptized in North Farnham Parish. Elizabeth Lambert (baptized 4 December 1704) married Robert Christie on 23 April 1731 in Richmond County; they moved to Brunswick County, where Christie wrote his will on 15 January 1749.[821] William Lambert, baptized 1 August 1711 in Richmond County, was his father's youngest known child. William, John, and Elizabeth Lambert were all minors under age seventeen when their father died, and the elder man's will directed that they would live with their brother Hugh Lambert until attaining their majority. William Lambert was alive in Richmond County as late as 11 April 1741, when he conveyed to his brother Hugh Lambert seventy acres. The land had been purchased by his father William Lambert from Dennis Swellivant and was located on the east side of Totuskey Creek, bound by John Cralle and lands that had once belonged to Edward Lewis. Robert Hammack and David Morgan witnessed the deed.[822]

---

[818] Headley, *Wills of Richmond County*, p. 86.

[819] *Ibid.*, p. 86. Lambert Morgan was baptized 11 May 1720, son of William Morgan and Elizabeth Lambert, who was baptized 4 December 1704 in North Farnham Parish, a daughter of William Lambert and Anne Bradshaw.

[820] Richmond Co., VA, Deed Book 10, p. 208.

[821] Brunswick Co., VA, Will Book 1739-1750, pp. 183-185. Christie appointed William Samford and John "Lamberth" as his executors. Note that William Samford in 1744 had purchased the tract sold by John Lambert and Hugh Lambert that had belonged to their father William Lambert. Many individuals have expressed confusion, however, concerning the marriage of Elizabeth Lambert, and the problem is not easily solved. The wife of William Morgan, Jr., was named Elizabeth, and William and Elizabeth Morgan named their child (born in 1720) Lambert Morgan. Elizabeth is identified in the will of her mother Ann Lambert as Elizabeth Adkins, for following William Morgan's death she had remarried to William Adkins. A thorny problem arises here and requires further research. William Lambert married first Anne Claughton and second Anne Bradshaw Bradley. Still, his will mentioned no wife, and there is a marriage for a William Lambert to a Mrs. Anne Bayley around the time of William Lambert, Sr.'s death. If Anne Bayley was the third wife of William Lambert, it would appear that Elizabeth Morgan Adkins was her daughter by her first marriage. Alternatively, if it were not William, Sr., who married Anne Bayley, then Elizabeth Morgan Adkins could have been a daughter of William Lambert's second wife Anne Bradshaw Bradley by her previous marriage. Possibly, however, the Anne who died in the 1740s was not the widow of William at all, as the records cited in the following note would seem to indicate that there was another, probably related, set of Lamberts living in North Farnham Parish at the same time.

[822] Richmond Co., VA, DB 10, p. 8. Note that there was one William Lambert in North Farnham Parish in the 1720s and 1730s who was born by c. 1702. The will of William Lambert, Sr., above, states that his son William was under seventeen years of age at the time that the will was written. If William Lambert (born 1711) died as an infant, it is possible that William Lambert's will is

As previously indicated, much misinformation has confused the identity of Hugh Lambert and his daughter Ann Lambert Hammack. Earlier researchers believed that Robert Hammack's wife Ann Lambert was a daughter of William Lambert, Sr., and identified her date of birth as 1699. Although later research corrected Ann's parentage, some researchers still persist in identifying Ann's date of birth as 1699, thus suggesting that her father Hugh was born prior to 1678. Others speculate from the date of birth of Ann's first known child -- 1725 -- that she was born about 1705 and that Hugh Lambert was born about 1685. Again, there is no evidence that the birth dates were this early. The eldest known child of Robert and Ann Lambert Hammack was baptized on 10 September 1726. Robert Hammack appears in a legal record the following year, 7 June 1727, when he made a bond to Thomas Morgan along with his father-in-law Hugh Lambert.[823] If Robert were of legal age when he and Ann married, then he was probably born by about 1704; if he were only eighteen when their first child was born, he might have been born as late as 1708. Ann may have been slightly younger but in any case was probably born no later than 1710. A conservative estimate would then put Hugh Lambert's birth no later than 1692; in any instance, he was probably not born much before 1690. The only two children of Hugh whose births are not found in the North Farnham Register were Ann and Mildred, who married Robert and John Hammack. The next child was Hugh, born 4 March 1718. Since the earliest known legal record for Hugh Lambert dates from 4 December 1717,[824] it seems reasonable to conclude that Hugh Lambert was probably born about 1690. He was likely about twenty when Ann Lambert was born around 1710 and about twenty-seven when he first appears in Richmond County legal records. If this estimate is correct, he was probably about seventy-five years old when he died in Brunswick County in 1765.

Hugh Lambert entered a bond with Ann Loyd to administer the estate of Joshua Lawson on 4 December 1717.[825] He was then probably living on land inherited from his father William in 1715, and 4 February 1723/4 he and his brother John together sold a tract that they had heired from their father's estate.[826] Hugh seems to have lived on lands belonging to his father until about 1740, when he purchased 100 acres joining Robert Clarke, John Cralle, and the estate of William Morgan, deceased, from Edward and Elizabeth Spencer.[827] He paid 5,000 pounds of tobacco for the land. A year later, on 11 April 1741, he purchased seventy acres from his brother William Lambert; Hugh paid 1,400 pounds of tobacco for the land.[828] On 24 March 1743/4, with his brother John Lambert, Hugh sold "about seventy-one acres" of land formerly belonging to their father to William Samford, who paid 6,025 pounds of tobacco for the land.[829] On 6 April 1746, Hugh Lambert and wife Ann sold 100 acres in Richmond County to William Garland, Jr. Garland paid £38 for the land, which had once belonged to Dr. Robert Clarke.[830]

The 1746 deed was likely executed as Hugh and Ann prepared to move from Richmond County to Brunswick County in Virginia's Southside. On 4 October 1748, Hugh Lambert, still a resident of North Farnham Parish, purchased 604 acres in Brunswick on the south side of Crooked Run from Thomas and

---

referring to an older son William. (Note that William "O" Hammack fathered a son William Hammack the elder by his first marriage and a son William Hammack the younger by his second marriage.) If William Lambert had two sons named William, it is possible that the elder one was born about 1700 and still a minor when his father wrote his will. He would have been of an age to be the William whose children's baptisms are discussed further in this note. At this point, however, this is speculation. The William Lambert, born by c. 1702, baptized the following children in North Farnham Parish: son John on 25 Jan., 1723/4; son William, 25 Sept., 1726; daughter Mary, 28 Jan., 1727; son Hugh, 27 July, 1729; daughter Anne, 14 Aug., 1731; son James, 8 April, 1736; son Joseph, 22 Sept., 1741; daughter Sarah, 28 March, 1744. Since William and Frances and William and Sarah both baptized children in the period 1741-44, there seems to be two Williams -- both probably related.

[823] Wynne, *Southern Lineages*, pp. 91-110.
[824] Richmond County, VA, Deed Book, 1714-20, pp. 251-52.
[825] Richmond County, VA, Deed Book, 1714-20, pp. 251-52.
[826] Richmond County, VA, Deed Book, 1720-33, pp. 236-37.
[827] Richmond Co., VA, Deed Book 9, p. 623.
[828] Richmond Co., VA, Deed Book 10, p. 8.
[829] Richmond Co., VA, Deed Book 10, p. 208.
[830] Richmond Co., VA, Deed Book 10, pp. 400-403.

Mary Jones and Charles and Susannah Irby. The Lamberts paid £390 for the land.[831] The following day, Hugh and Ann purchased another 200 acres on Rocky Run from Matthew and Judith Matthews. They paid £35 for the land.[832] Lambert's lands apparently lay near the boundary between Lunenburg and Brunswick, for a Lunenburg deed dated 1759, involving Robert Moore, John Hammack, and Robert Moore, Jr., names Hugh Lambert as an adjacent landowner.[833]

Hugh Lambert married Anne Morgan, daughter of William and Ann Lewis Morgan. The couple probably married about 1708, shortly before the birth of Ann Lambert Hammack. Ann's father William Morgan settled in Richmond County about 1690, locating along Totuskey Creek. William formed business dealings with several members of the large Lewis family that lived in Northumberland and Richmond Counties; circumstantial evidence suggests that he married Ann Lewis, whose father was one of his business associates.[834] A deed, dated many years after William Morgan died, reveals the complexity of the family connections. On 1 April 1745, Lambert Morgan, grandson of William Morgan, sold a tract of land that lay adjacent lands owned by his uncle Hugh Lambert. The land was described as:

> 200 acres bounded by a corner near Andrew Morgan's corn field, Robert Clark, Hugh Lambart, Mr. Robert Middleton's Mill road, Hog Island near the run of the Marchey Swamp, the mouth of Old William Morgan's Spring branch the Grand Father of said Lambert Morgan, thence up the said branch to Andrew Morgin's Spring, thence up the valley crossing the Main Road, including the land that said Garland purchased of Joshua Morgan, the son of William Morgin, deceased, which land is part of a patent granted to Thomas Lewis, Charles Lewis and the said William Morgan, deceased, by patent dated 21 August, 1691, and the said 200 acres was where the aforesaid Lambart Morgan lived, he claiming right under his father, Will'm Morgan, Jr., the son of William Morgan that said land was granted to. And he, being the right heir at law of the said William Morgan the Elder, and grandson to him, and now making sale to the said William Garland, Jr.[835]

William Morgan (by c. 1670 -- 12 December 1726, North Farnham Parish, Richmond County, Virginia) makes his first known appearance in Virginia records on 20 January 1688 when he, along with Paul Thilman and William Darnell, witnessed a deed from John Curtis to Christopher Robinson.[836] On 7 August 1690, with William Hammack and Samuel Samford, Morgan served on a jury in Rappahannock County.[837] At the same time, he, William Hammack, and Edward Lewis were together sued by Peter Nicholls.[838] On 21 August 1691, William Morgan, Edward Lewis, and Thomas Lewis together patented 360 acres in Richmond (then Rappahannock) and Northumberland Counties. The land joined Thomas Freshwater's tract.[839] On 2 March 1691/2, Morgan deeded his interest in the tract to Edward and Thomas Lewis. These deeds link William Morgan closely with Edward and Thomas Lewis; they also indicate that all three men were near neighbors of William Hammack and his family.[840]

---

[831] Brunswick Co., VA, Deed Book 3, p. 504.

[832] Brunswick Co., VA, Deed Book 3, p. 497.

[833] Brunswick Co., VA, Deed Book 3, p. 504.

[834] If this analysis is correct, it would also explain the introduction of the given name Lewis into the Lambert and Hammack families. Anne may have been a daughter of Thomas and Mary Lewis or a sister of Thomas and Edward Lewis.

[835] Richmond Co., VA, Deed Book 10, p. 280.

[836] Old Rappahannock Co., VA, Deed Book 8, 1688-1692, pp. 49-51. The land had once belonged to John and George Haslewood, relatives of Johanna Freshwater.

[837] Old Rappahannock County, VA, Order Book, 1689-1692, p. 183.

[838] Old Rappahannock County, VA, Order Book, 1689-1692, p. 185.

[839] Richmond Co., VA, Deed Book 1695-1701, pp. 182-183.

[840] Richmond Co., VA, Deed Book 1695-1701.

A deed dated 8 March 1704/5 reveals that Edward and Thomas Lewis had also patented 528 acres in Richmond (then Rappahannock) and Northumberland in their own right. The land was being sold by Symon and Elizabeth Taylor, Thomas and Anne Jesper, and Christopher and Mary Pridham.

William Morgan, on 1 June 1709, sold 100 acres in Richmond County to Theophilus King for 1000 pounds of tobacco. The deed mentions "John Morgan's Spring Branch" and "Edward Lewis's Swamp."[841] William Morgan wrote his will on 6 December 1726 in Richmond County, naming wife Elizabeth Morgan, sons Joshua, William,[842] John, Thomas, and Robert, and daughters Ann Lambert, Mary Harris, Ann Morgan, Elizabeth Morgan, and Judith Morgan.[843] He died 12 December 1726, and his will was filed 1 February 1726/7.[844]

Edward Lewis had begun acquiring land in the Totuskey area as early as 20 February 1662, when he and Thomas Robinson patented land which they then sold to William Landman. Edward was deceased by 1698, at which time his wife may have remarried to [------] Hammond.

A Richmond County deed (Deed Book 1734-1741, p. 186) dated 20 April 1735 indicates that Anthony Linton was selling 100 acres "entered by Edward Lewis, deceased, and thence descended to his son, John Lewis, deceased, then 100 acres descended to Johanna Lewis, sister and co-heir of said John Lewis." Johanna Lewis married William Linton, deceased, father of said Anthony, and the land descended to him as next heir-at-law.

The North Farnham Parish Register shows that Edward and Mary Lewis baptized Elizabeth (1674) and Joanna (1676).

Known children of Edward and Mary Lewis were: John Lewis, who died prior to 1704/5 without issue; Johanna Lewis, who married William Linton; Anne Lewis, who married Thomas Jesper; Elizabeth Lewis, who married Simon Taylor; and Katherine Lewis, who married Joseph Deeke.

Another Edward Lewis died about 1698 in Richmond County; he may have married twice. He had land interests in both Northumberland and Richmond. He was the father of Lucretia Lewis (1689), William Lewis (who may have died in Lancaster County in 1733), Charles Lewis (born about 1691), Edward Lewis (c. 1692 - aft. 1714), Jane Lewis (1693), and Lewis ap Lewis (1695-1734).

Thomas and Mary Lewis baptized Benjamin (1685), Thomas (1692), and William (1695). There may have been older children whose baptisms do not appear in the register; descendants of Benjamin Lewis, Thomas Lewis, and William Lewis remained in Richmond and Northumberland County for generations.

John Lewis of Northumberland County, who died about 1697, may have been a cousin (or perhaps even brother) of Edward and Thomas Lewis. John Lewis married Mary Garner, who married (2) Richard Price. Mary Garner Lewis Price died testate in Northumberland County in 1726 (Northumberland County Record Book 1718-1726, page 388). John Lewis was living in Northumberland County by 1675. Mary Garner Lewis Price was a daughter of John Garner and Susannah Keene of Northumberland County; and is named in John Garner's 1702 Westmoreland County will. Offspring of John and Mary Garner Lewis were John Lewis (30 September 1683, Northumberland Co., VA -- May 1735, Northumberland Co., VA); William Lewis (6 Jan., 1685 -- by 30 September 1719); Elizabeth Lewis, who married Mark Tune; James Lewis (-- 11 January 1747, Northumberland Co., VA), who married Hannah [------] and lived at Mundy Point; and Mary Lewis, who married Pemberton Claughton, son of John and Ann (Pemberton) Claughton. Mary Garner Lewis Price was also mother of a daughter who married Joseph Damerill and of Arjalon Price of Northumberland County. See *John Lewis, "The Lost Pioneer," His Ancestors and Descendants* (1670 - 1970), by Daniel Reid Long, Jr. (Privately Printed, 1971).

[841] Richmond Co., VA, Deed Book 1708-1711, pp. 94-95. John Morgan, whose wife was named Barbara, was apparently about the same age as William Morgan. Both appear together in Rappahannock County before Richmond County's creation. They may have been brothers. John Morgan was a blacksmith living on Totuskey Creek in 1695. (Richmond Co., VA, Deeds, 1695-1701, pp. 231-233), at which time his land joined the lands of Edward Lewis. On 2 May 1692, Mary Lewis, wife of Edward Lewis, named her "very good friend John Morgan" to serve as her power of attorney. (Richmond Co., VA, Deed Book 1692-1694, pp. 29-30.) Thomas Lewis's wife, who also signed the deed, was named Mary Lewis, too. The earliest known legal reference to John Morgan dates from 1685/6 (Old Rappahannock Co., VA, Order Book, 1685-1687, p. 4). He and Barbara baptized a daughter Barbara (1686) and a son John (1687) in North Farnham Parish.

[842] The Morgan family is difficult to reconstitute. It appears that two William Morgans -- father and son -- died within a few months of one another in late 1726 and early 1727. Both men had wives named Elizabeth, and both men appear to have had first wives named Anne. Guardians -- Hugh Lambert, Daniel Hornby and Robert Hammack -- were appointed for the estates of William's two children by his first wife, William and Thomas. If this analysis is correct, both Williams had children named Joshua, Judith, Elizabeth, Anne, William and Thomas. More research should be done to verify that this analysis is correct. Children of William and Anne Morgan were William (2 May 1715) and Thomas (1 June 1716), who were wards of Hugh Lambert, Daniel Hornby, and Robert Hammack. Children of William and Elizabeth Morgan were Anne (1718), Lambert (1720), Joshua (1720), Betty (1722), Leannah (1722), Joyce (1724), Judith (1724), and Elizabeth (1727). These are the dates of baptism, not birth. If Lambert Morgan was his grandfather's heir-at-law, then William and Thomas must both have died prior to 1745.

[843] See Headley, *Wills of Richmond County*, p. 58. Of these offspring, Joshua Morgan was still in Richmond in 1743 when he sold land belonging to his deceased father William Morgan. William Morgan, Jr., died 28 April 1727, leaving a widow and several children (among them Lambert Morgan). John Morgan married Elizabeth Hammack on 21 August 1729. He was still in Richmond in 1743 when he sold land left him by his father. One Thomas Morgan married Sarah Pannell about 1718; he may have been William Morgan's son. Elizabeth Morgan may have married Joseph Hall on 21 April 1729. No clear record of the other children named in William Morgan's will has been discovered.

[844] Headley, *Wills of Richmond County*, pp. 58-59.

Hugh Lambert seems to have enjoyed a close relationship with his Morgan in-laws. He was guardian for his wife's nephews following the death of William Morgan, Jr., about 1727. An additional connection occurred in 1729, when John Morgan married Elizabeth Hammack, a relative of Ann Lambert's husband Robert Hammack.

Hugh Lambert and Ann Morgan Lambert lived most of their lives in Richmond County; both must have been in their late fifties or early sixties when they relocated to Brunswick County, Virginia, after 1748. Although they lived in Brunswick County for more than a decade, they appear in few legal records there. Perhaps Hugh's advancing age was partially responsible for this decline in activity. Hugh Lambert wrote his will on 18 November 1764 in Brunswick County. Describing himself as "of perfect sense and memory," Lambert provided for his wife, children, and several grandchildren:

> Imprimis. I lend my beloved wife during her Natural life the use of my Negroes, viz. Jacob, Solomon, Jenny, Vag, and all my stock of cattle, Hogs, Horses, sheep and all my Household furniture.

> Item. I give and bequeath to my son William Lambert two Negroes, Viz., Jacob and Cate only my desire is that my Wife have the use of Jacob during her natural Life to him and his heirs forever.

> Item. I lend to my daughter Ann Hammock during her natural Life after my Wife's Death the use of my Negro Solomon.

> Item. I give to my grandson Hugh Hammock after my Wife's and Daughter's Death my Negro Solomon.

> Item. I give to my daughter Mildred Hammock two hundred acres of Land whereon she now lives according to the bounds already made to her and her heirs forever.

> Item. I lend to my daughter Mildred Hammock during her and her Husband's lives one Negro Girl name Suck and at their Death the said Suck and her Increase to be equally divided between the heirs of my Daughter.

> Item. I give and bequeath to my son Lewis Lambert the land the north side his Spring Branch to the line of Mildred Hammock containing two hundred and fifty acres more or less to him and his heirs forever and two Negroes at my Wife's Death, Viz., old Jenny and Agg.

> Item. I give and bequeath to my daughter Lorana Kirke all the remainder part of my Land on Crooked Run not already given containing one hundred and fifty acres more or less to her and to her Heirs forever.

> Item. I lend to James Kirke and his Wife during their natural Lives one Negro Girl named Pat and at their Death the said Pat and her increase to be equally divided between the Heirs of my Daughter Larana Kirke.

> Item. I lend to my son Richard Lambert during his Life and to his wife during her natural Life of Widowhood two Negroes on Marriage I give the said two Negroes and their Increase to be equally divided between the Heirs of my said son Richard.

Item. I give and bequeath to my son Hugh Lambert at my Wife's Death two Negroes named Hannah and Ned them & their Increase to him and his Heirs for ever.

Item. I give and bequeath to my grandson Robert Hammock one Negroe child named Frank to him and his Heirs forever.

Item. My will and desire that my Negro Woman called old Nan choose either of my Children to live with but if neither of my Children will maintain her for her Labour my Desire is she be maintained by all my Children.

Item. I give and Bequeath to my son Richard Lambert all my wearing apparel and at my wife's Death my Bed and furniture that I lie on.

Item. I give and bequeath to my son Thomas Lambert the land and plantation whereon I now live and three Negroes, Viz., James and Prince and Little Jenny and all my stock of what kind or Quantity whatsoever at my Wife's Death, also all my Household furniture to him and his Heirs forever.

Item. My will and desire is that not any of my Negroes be taken off my plantation til Christmas or the Crop finished in the Year 1765, which Crop I give to my son Thomas Lambert.

Item. My will and Desire is that all my Children bear an equal part in paying Lewis Lambert eleven pounds current Money and he to bear a part with the rest.

Item. My will desire is that if any Just or Lawful Demands comes against my Estate that all my Children bear an equal part in discharging them.

Item in Will I devise that my Estate be not appraised. I make and ordain constitute and appoint my son Thomas Lambert my whole and Sole Executor of this my last Will and Testament utterly disannulling revoking all other Wills by me made in Testimony whereof I hereunto set my Hand and fix my Seal this eighteenth Day of November, 1764.[845]

Lambert's will was proven in Brunswick County on 24 June 1765.[846] Months later, on 3 January 1766, Anne Morgan Lambert and her son Thomas Lambert entered into an agreement whereby she transferred to her son all right to her inheritance in exchange for maintenance during the remainder of her life. The deed is significant, for elderly parents often chose instruments such as this to ensure that they were cared for during their declining years:

Whereas Hugh Lambert, Decd., by his last Will and Testament bearing date the 18th Day of November 1765 lent to his Wife during her natural Life four Negroes Named Jacob, Solomon, Jenny and Agg and all his Stock of Hoggs, Horses, Sheep and Cattle, and all his Household furniture intended for the support and maintainance of his said Wife and she the said Anne Lambert do hereby agree to and with her son Thomas Lambert that if said Thomas shall have the Command of all the Property that Shall arise from the above

---

mentioned Slaves, Stock and Household furniture during his life in consideration whereof the said Thomas Lambert is hereby obliged himself his Heirs Exers. Admrs. and Assigns that the said Thomas Lambert will Maintain and Keep his said Mother from Want of Meat, Drink, Cloathing, Lodging, Washing and Apparel Suitable to the Legacy lent.[847]

Thomas Lambert may have been favored by his mother, particularly since he was one of the younger children. On the other hand, enterprising offspring sometimes struck deals such as this to provide themselves with an extra legacy that might enrich themselves in the long run. Unfortunately, we know nothing more of the motivations of Thomas or of Ann, or of the outcome of the arrangement. Since no legal cases were filed for breach of contract, presumably Thomas lived up to his end of the obligation, maintaining his mother comfortably for the remainder of her life.

Of the children of Hugh and Anne Morgan Lambert, Ann Lambert Hammack remained in Richmond County, Virginia, dying there at an advanced age. Her son Robert Hammack, Jr., apparently moved with his grandparents to southern Virginia. He received a small legacy in his grandfather's will and settled in neighboring Lunenburg and Amelia Counties before relocating to Georgia. Mildred Lambert Hammack and her husband John left the Northern Neck, settling in Lunenburg County when her father moved to Brunswick. Hugh Lambert, Jr. (baptized 4 March 1718) married Elizabeth Smith and was living in Brunswick County as late as 1778.[848] William Lambert (baptized 15 June 1720) and wife Mary were living in Richmond County as late as 1767[849]; they baptized six children between 1741 and 1757 in North Farnham Parish. John Lambert was baptized 19 April 1722 in North Farnham Parish; he is not mentioned in his father's will and may have predeceased his parents. Lewis Lambert (baptized 19 August 1724) was living in Lunenburg County as late as 1772, when he was taxed with son William Lambert in his household; he probably remained there until at least 1800, for Lewis Lambert, Sr., and Lewis Lambert, Jr., appear in Lunenburg deeds and tax records during the 1780s and 1790s.[850] Thomas Lambert (baptized 1 October 1726) had legal dealings with his mother in Brunswick County in 1765 and with his brother Lewis Lambert there in 1766.[851] Lurana ("Rana") Lambert (baptized 5 August 1729) married James Kirk; they were living in Brunswick County in 1764 and in Lunenburg County in 1767.[852] Richard Lambert, named in his father's will, was not baptized in North Farnham Parish; he was deeded land by his father in Brunswick County in 1752 but has not otherwise been traced.[853]

---

[847] Brunswick Co., VA, Deed Book 8, pp. 357-58.

[848] Brunswick Co., VA, Will Book 1739-1750, pp. 157-160; Brunswick Co., VA, Deed Book 5 , pp. 453-456; Brunswick Co., VA, Deed Book 13, pp. 219-20. He may be the Hugh who died testate in Mecklenburg County in 1781 (Mecklenburg Co., VA, Will Book 2, p. 1).

[849] Lunenburg Co., VA, Deed Book 11, p. 172.

[850] Lunenburg Co., VA, Deed Book 18, p. 259.

[851] Brunswick Co., VA, Deed Book 8, pp. 357 - 59.

[852] Lunenburg Co., VA, Deed Book 11, p. 172.

[853] Brunswick Co., VA, Deed Book , pp. 453-456.

Chapter 20:

Millenor Jackson Hammack of Lunenburg and Amelia Counties, Virginia,
and Wilkes and Jones Counties, Georgia

Three generations of American Jacksons preceded Millenor Jackson Hammack in Virginia. Her great-grandfather, William Jackson, first appears in Surry County, Virginia, on 24 September 1685, when he was fined for failure to attend church services.[854] A list of freeholders dated 2 August 1687 lists his name adjacent those of Richard Jackson and Robert Crawford, possibly suggesting a family connection.[855] On 3 January 1687/8, he was listed as a freeholder in Lawne's Creek Parish.[856]

Jackson lived in Surry County until his death in 1710. He appears as an administrator of the estate of William Meade in 1696[857] and, with Robert Crawford and William Chambers, of John Rodwell's estate in 1702.[858] In 1707, William Jackson served as a constable in Surry County.[859] Based on his service at the local level, Jackson appears to have been a respected neighbor and a man of some consequence in his community.

Jackson may have become ill suddenly in early 1710/11. The verbal will he gave indicates that it may have been composed in haste, possibly as Jackson knew he was dying. Jackson made reference to his wife but did not identify her; he provided for his four sons, John, George, William, and Samuel. William and Roger Nicholls witnessed Jackson's oral statements, and, following his death, on February 1710/11, the court named John Jackson as administrator to settle his father's estate.[860] The Surry Court named William Nichols, William Chambers, and William Newsome to inventory the estate.[861]

John Jackson, probably his father's eldest child, was born about 1680, presumably in Surry County. He lived to an advanced age, dying on 12 October 1770 in Sussex County, Virginia. He lived all of his ninety years south of the James River, dying only a short distance from the parish in which he was born and reared.[862]

John Jackson first appears in legal records for Surry County in February 1710/11 when he, James Sammon, and John Freeman were named to inventory the estate of Richard Gourd.[863] John also served as his father's administrator in 1710 and 1711.

About this time, John Jackson began acquiring lands in Surry and adjacent counties. Because the name John Jackson was a common one, it is difficult to know how many acres this John Jackson patented, but records of Brunswick and Sussex County make it clear that he owned substantial tracts of land. Among the early grants to individuals named John Jackson were grants for 140 acres on "Mockerson" Neck in Surry in 1715,[864] to 335 acres on Gallay Swamp in Surry in 1722,[865] to 200 acres on Meherrin

---

[854] Surry Co., VA, Court Records, 1682-1691, Book IV, p. 515.

[855] Surry Co., VA, Court Records, 1682-1691, Book IV, p. 600.

[856] Surry Co., VA, Court Records 1682-1691, Book IV, p. 622.

[857] E. T. Davis, *Wills & Administrations of Surry Co., VA, 1671-1750* (Smithfield, VA, 1955; repr., Baltimore, MD, 1980), p. 94.

[858] Surry Co., VA, Court Records, 1700-1711, Book VI, p. 238.

[859] Surry Co., VA, Court Records 1701-1711, Book VI, p. 302.

[860] Surry Co., VA, Will Book 6, p. 46, as shown in E. T. Davis, *Wills and Administrations of Surry Co., VA, 1671-1750*, p. 77; Surry Co., VA, Court Records 1701-1711, Book VI, p. 357.

[861] Surry Co., VA, Court Records 1701-1711, Book VI, p. 357.

[862] Albemarle Parish Register, Surry and Sussex Counties, VA, p. 321.

[863] Surry Co., VA, Court Records 1701-1711, Book VI, p. 355.

[864] Virginia Patent Book No. 10, p. 275.

[865] Virginia Patent Book No. 12, p. 161.

River near Ralph Jackson in 1724,[866] 145 acres on Blackwater Swamp in Isle of Wight in 1725,[867] 125 acres in Brunswick County in 1726,[868] 525 acres on Reedy Creek in Brunswick in 1728,[869] 1,000 acres on Nottoway River between "Mockerson" Neck Creek and Gallay Swamp in Surry County,[870] 195 acres on Nottoway River joining Edward Achols in 1730,[871] 1,740 acres on Burchen Swamp in Prince George County in 1735,[872] 395 acres on Little Hurricane Creek in Amelia County in 1738,[873] 4,440 acres in Prince George and Amelia County on Burchen Swamp in 1741,[874] 260 acres on Burchen Swamp in Amelia County in 1747.[875]

John Jackson's 1770 Sussex County will identifies his children, and land records executed between 1746 and 1770 identify many of these tracts as belonging to this particular John Jackson. On 15 November 1746, he deeded 600 acres on Burchen Swamp to Charles Jackson "for love and affection."[876] This deed identifies John Jackson as a resident of Surry County. On 15 November 1746, he also deeded 500 acres on Hurricane Swamp to James Jackson, also "for love and affection."[877] On the same date, John gifted 1,000 acres on Burchen Swamp in Amelia and Prince George Counties to son William Jackson. The deed describes the grantor as a resident of Surry County and identifies adjacent landowners as Thomas, Robert, and Charles Jackson.[878] Two other deeds dated the same day were to sons Edward and Thomas Jackson. Edward Jackson received 600 acres on both sides of Little Hurricane Creek.[879] Thomas Jackson received 500 acres on Burchen Swamp.[880]

By 1747, John Jackson and his wife Mary were living in Albemarle Parish in what would soon become Sussex County. As residents of that location, on 1 October, they deeded to son John Jackson 195 acres on Reedy Branch in St. Andrew's Parish, Brunswick County.[881] The land joined property owned by Edward Echols, who, on the same date, with wife Mary (Jackson) Echols, sold another 400 acres in Brunswick to John Jackson, Jr.[882] One John Jackson, either father or son, purchased 390 acres joining Richard Ward in Amelia in 1752 from Joseph Motley.[883] The elder John Jackson, in 1752, while a resident of Albemarle Parish, deeded to son William another eighty-three acres granted to him in 1751. He sold his son this land for £8.[884] On the same date, he sold son Edward Jackson 284 acres for £28; Edward was identified as of Nottoway Parish in Amelia while his father was of Albemarle Parish in Surry.[885] Sussex County was formed from Surry in 1753, and John Jackson's residence there fell into the new county. On 21 February 1755, as a resident of Sussex, he gifted 100 acres in Amelia on Little

[866] Virginia Patent Book No. 12, p. 448. At least some of these patents may belong to a John Jackson, who may have been a sibling of Ralph Jackson of Prince George and Brunswick Counties. See W. J. Jackson, *Ancestral Notebook of Jackson and Related Families* (no place of publication; undated), p. 21. A copy of this work is housed in the Georgia Department of Archives and History, Morrow, GA.

[867] Virginia Patent Book 12, p. 448.

[868] Virginia Patent Book No. 12, 1724-26, p. 520.

[869] Virginia Patent Book No. 14, 1728-32, p. 63.

[870] Virginia Patent Book No. 14, p. 127.

[871] Virginia Patent Book No. 14, p. 127.

[872] Virginia Patent Book No. 17, p. 109.

[873] Virginia Patent Book No. 18, 1738-39, p. 82.

[874] Virginia Patent Book No. 20, 1741-43, p. 52.

[875] Virginia Patent Book No. 28, 1746-49, p. 281.

[876] Amelia Co., VA, Deed Book 2, p. 452.

[877] Amelia Co., VA, Deed Book 2, p. 454.

[878] Amelia Co., VA, Deed Book 2, p. 456. This land is today in Nottoway County.

[879] Amelia Co., VA, Deed Book 2, p. 458.

[880] Amelia Co., VA, Deed Book 2, p. 460.

[881] Brunswick Co., VA, Deed Book 3, p. 346.

[882] Brunswick Co., VA, Deed Book 3, p. 347.

[883] Amelia Co., VA, Deed Book 4, pp. 306-7.

[884] Amelia Co., VA, Deed Book 4, p. 311.

[885] Amelia Co., VA, Deed Book 4, p. 316.

Burchen Swamp to his son Thomas Jackson.[886] Two years later, John deeded Thomas another 100 acres in the same location.[887] He deeded lands to John Echols in 1765,[888] to Robert Jackson in 1769,[889] and to Charles Jackson in 1770.[890]

John Jackson wrote his will in Sussex County on 22 August 1770. He identifies daughters Mary Echols and Susannah Tucker[891] and sons James, Charles, Thomas, Robert, John, Edward, and William. Thomas Jackson had predeceased his father, and Thomas's wife Amy and children are named as heirs in his stead. John also provided for a grandson John Jackson, son of Charles Jackson, and for Mary Waller, probably a domestic servant, "who now lives with me."[892] James Greenway, otherwise unidentified, was appointed to execute the document, which James Butler, Reuben Jackson, Joel Tucker, and William Wilkerson witnessed.[893] The will was proven on 18 October 1770. The same month, Robert Jackson reported to the parish clerk that his father John Jackson, aged ninety, had died on 12 October.[894]

Mary Jackson, wife of John Jackson, was named as a daughter in the will of John Woard of Surry County on 30 August 1715. Another daughter, Jane Ellis, who had presumably had already received a bequest, inherited one shilling only. To daughter Mary Jackson, "wife of John Jackson," Woard bequeathed "all of my estate" and named her as the document's executrix.[895]

Edward Jackson, father of Millenor Jackson Hammack, was probably born about 1715. He appears as a tithable in Amelia County in 1744 and 1746 and on 15 November 1746 was gifted 600 acres on Little Hurricane Creek in Amelia County by his father John Jackson. Richard Jones, Robert Ferguson, and John Bridgeforth witnessed the deed.[896] Jackson appears regularly in Amelia County tithable records until at least 1763. On 20 March 1752, while living in Amelia, Edward received another 284 acres from his father John Jackson.[897] In 1755, Edward witnessed two deeds from Edward Echols to Robert Echols and Thomas Echols.[898] In 1763, Edward Jackson, Samuel Bentley, and Benedict Hammack all witnessed a deed from John Bentley of Onslow County, North Carolina, and Benedict Hammack, Jr., to William Hancock for land in Amelia County.[899]

Edward Jackson is said to have married first Lucy Parrish, who was the mother of most his children, and second Abigail James. No records have been located to confirm the maiden identity of either wife,

---

[886] Amelia Co., VA, Deed Book 5, p. 539.

[887] Amelia Co., VA, Deed Book 2, p. 454.

[888] Sussex Co., VA, Deed Book C, p. 193.

[889] Sussex Co., VA, Deed Book D, p. 73.

[890] Sussex Co., VA, Deed Book D, 1768-72, p. 285.

[891] John Jackson on 30 March 1752 deeded to William Tucker 333 acres on Rocky Branch for £100. The land had been patented in 1751. It joined lands deeded to James and John Jackson; Edward, Charles, and William Jackson witnessed the deed. William Tucker then lived in Bath Parish, Prince George County. William was Susannah's husband. On 29 March 1770, John Jackson entered a deed in Sussex Court setting free an Indian servant named Ben at John Jackson's death (Sussex Co.., VA, Deed Book D, 1768-72, p. 285). On 2 November 1770, William Tucker, Mary Eckles, William Jackson, Charles Jackson, Edward Jackson, and James Jackson consented to the deed (Sussex Co.., VA, Deed Book D, 1768-72, p. 285).

[892] Sussex Co., VA, Will Book B, 1764-71, pp. 275-77.

[893] Sussex Co., VA, Will Book B, 1764-71, pp. 275-77.

[894] Sussex Co., VA, Will Book B, 1764-71, p. 275; Albemarle Parish Register, Sussex Co., VA, p. 321. Robert Jackson was the only son of John and Mary Jackson to remain in Sussex County. He died there on 8 April 1772.

[895] Surry Co., VA, Will Book 6, p. 264, and Will Book 5, p. 264, in Davis, *Wills and Administrations of Surry Co., VA*, p. 144. Note that Evelyn Duke Brandenberger and Clara Jackson Martin, "The Jacksons of Lower Virginia," *The Virginia Genealogist*, 33 (1990): 294-304, propose an alternative identity for Mary Jackson's father: "It seems quite likely that John Jackson's father-in-law was not John Word (Ward) as the Surry records seem to read, but rather John Werrell or Warrell, son of Joseph Werrell (Warrell) who had, by patent on 28 October 1702, 142 acres in the Upper Parish of Nansemond County adjoining William Jones, granted for the transportation of Daniel Sullivan, William Jackson, and Robert Wilmout. Warrell already owned 166 acres adjoining the land of William Jones who witnessed the will of John Word (Ward or Warrell) in 1715/16." Since no other references to John Woard have been located, Brandenberger's theory seems reasonable. It is possible that "Woard" was a mistranscription of "Woarl."

[896] Amelia Co., VA, Deed Book 2, p. 458.

[897] Amelia Co., VA, Deed Book 4, p. 316.

[898] Amelia Co., VA, Deed Book 6, pp. 103-5; Amelia Co., VA, Deed Book 6, p. 341.

[899] Amelia Co., VA, Deed Book 8, p. 262.

although Edward and Abigail were married by 23 May 1770 when they deeded 150 acres on Little Hurricane Creek in Amelia to Daniel and Elizabeth Jackson and eighty-one acres in the same location to Robert Hammack and Milley, his wife. The deed to Daniel and Elizabeth Jackson was executed in consideration of "natural love and affection for my son and his wife," while the deed to the Hammacks was issued "in consequence of affection for my son-in-law and his wife." Charles Connally, Benjamin Bridgeforth, Charnel Hightower, and John Bailey witnessed the deeds.[900] On 29 September 1773, Robert Hammack and Daniel Jackson, along with John Bailey, witnessed a deed from Travis and Ann McKinney of Amelia County to William Spain of Dinwiddie.[901] Hammack, Jackson, and McKinney afterwards all appear in Wilkes County, Georgia.

Edward Jackson lived until 1789, dying in the recently formed county of Nottoway. He apparently supported the American cause during the Revolution, for in a pension application his grandson Thomas Jackson recalled that "It may be necessary to say that my Father was a volunteer in the war as he was only sixteen years old when he entered it, two older Brothers were enlisted by the recruiting officer, when he said he would go too if his Father [Edward Jackson] would let him, and the old man told him to go and do his country all the service he could." The document indicates that, although the elder Jackson himself did not render military service during the struggle, he favored the American cause and supported his children's active participation therein.[902]

Two of the last records referring to Edward Jackson, both dating from the Revolutionary period, involve deeds to his offspring. On 6 March 1778, Edward Jackson deeded 200 acres to his son William Parrish Jackson, and on 20 July 1781 he deeded 100 acres "joining Parish Jackson" to Edward Jackson, Jr.[903] Jackson lived for several years afterwards, but his advancing age and the fact that his Amelia lands fell into the new county of Nottoway (which has suffered significant records loss) probably explains Edward's decline in legal activity during the final decade of his life.

The recorded version of Edward Jackson's will was lost in a courthouse fire in Nottoway County, but a handwritten copy was preserved in the Revolutionary War Pension file of Edward's son John E. Jackson of Nottoway County. The will is quoted below:

> In the name of God, Amen. I Edward Jackson, Sen., of Nottoway County in the State of Virginia aged, Infirm and weak in Body, and being sensible that it is appointed for all men once to die, do in my right mind memory and senses make this my last Will and Testament, Imprimis, that is, First, I bequeath my Soul to Almighty God who gave it me, hoping and fully trusting that I shall be received into the Heavenly Choir, through the merits of my dear redeemer Jesus Christ who suffered for me and all mankind, My Body I commit to the Earth from whiche it came, to be therein buried in Christian like manner by my Executors hereafter named. And as to what Worldly Estate it hath pleased God to possess me with, I give and dispose of in form and manner as follows. (To wit)--
>
> Item. First of all, I leave all my Just Debts and Burial Expenses to be paid out of the most wasteful part of my Estate.
> Item. I lend to my wife Abigail Jackson during her Widowhood, one hundred and eight Acres of my Land which I now possess to be taken off where she pleases so that she Joins the old line, excepting my Land that lyeth on the north side of the Haw branch: also four Negroes named James, Amey, Tom and Robin, together with all my Stock of Horses, Cattle and Hogs, and all my House hold and Kitchen furniture.

[900] Amelia Co., VA, Deed Book 11, pp. 123-125.
[901] Amelia Co., VA, Deed Book 12, p. 151.
[902] Revolutionary War Pension Application of Mrs. Jane Bailey Jackson, widow of John E. Jackson, W3823/BLWT36721-160-55, National Archives, Washington, D.C., Microfilm Series M805, Roll 465.
[903] Amelia Co., VA, Deed Book 14, p. 304, and Deed Book 16, p. 17.

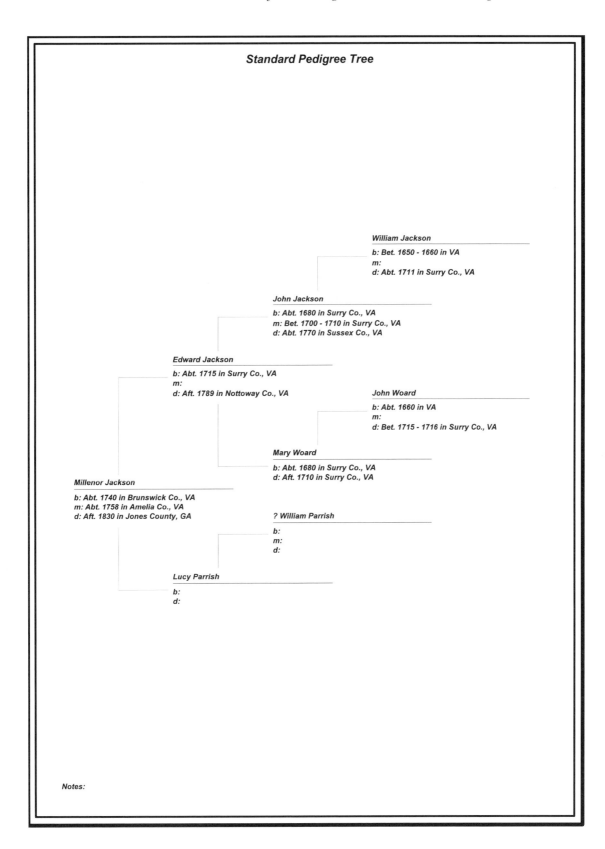

Standard Pedigree Tree

William Jackson
b: Bet. 1650 - 1660 in VA
m:
d: Abt. 1711 in Surry Co., VA

John Jackson
b: Abt. 1680 in Surry Co., VA
m: Bet. 1700 - 1710 in Surry Co., VA
d: Abt. 1770 in Sussex Co., VA

Edward Jackson
b: Abt. 1715 in Surry Co., VA
m:
d: Aft. 1789 in Nottoway Co., VA

John Woard
b: Abt. 1660 in VA
m:
d: Bet. 1715 - 1716 in Surry Co., VA

Mary Woard
b: Abt. 1680 in Surry Co., VA
d: Aft. 1710 in Surry Co., VA

Millenor Jackson
b: Abt. 1740 in Brunswick Co., VA
m: Abt. 1758 in Amelia Co., VA
d: Aft. 1830 in Jones County, GA

? William Parrish
b:
m:
d:

Lucy Parrish
b:
d:

Notes:

Item. I give to my son Daniel Jackson five shillings specie at the division of my Estate.

Item. I give to my daughter Millenor Hammock five shillings Specie at the division of my Estate.

Item. I give to my son Edward Jackson one hundred acres of Land adjoining the Land of Wm. Parrish Jackson, John May and Charles Sallard which Land he hath a Deed for on record, to him and his Heirs and assigns forever.

Item. I give to my daughter Lucy Jackson five shillings specie at the Division of my Estate.

Item. I give to my son William Parrish Jackson Two hundred acres of Land adjoining the lands of William Spain, Lamme Hobbs and John May, which Land he hath a Deed on record, also one Negro Girl named Aggy and her Increase, to him and his Heirs or assigns forever.

Item. I give to my Daughter Mary Howard five shillings specie at the Division of my Estate.

Item. I give to my son John Jackson all my Lands and plantation that I now possess, also one Negro man named Moses, one Negroe woman named Hannah with all her future increase, one Cow and Calf, one feather Bed and furniture, one Sorrel mare which was got by Granby, and my Still, to him and his Heirs or Assigns for ever, also my Beaufatt whiche he has the House.

Item. I give to my Daughter Silvaner Frank one Negroe Girl named Liddy and her Increase, to her and her Heirs or Assigns for ever.

Item. I give to my Daughter Phebe Whitesides one Negroe girl named Winney and her Increase, which girl she has in possession with a Deed of gift for the same on record, to her and her Heirs or Assigns forever.

Item. I give to my son Benedick Jackson one Negroe Girl named Lucy and her Increase which he has now in possession to him and his Heirs Assigns for Ever.

Item. I give to my Son Moses Jackson five shillings specie at the Division of my Estate.

Item. I give to my Son Ephraim Jackson one Negroe woman named Phebe with all her future Increase, to him and his Heirs for ever.

Item. I give to my son Woody Jackson one Negroe boy named Jeremiah to him and his Heirs or Assigns for ever.

Item. I give to my Son Ambrose Jackson one Negroe girl named Charlott and her Increase, to him and his Heirs or Assigns for ever.

Item. I give to my son Reuben Jackson one Negroe girl named Judah and her Increase to him and his Heirs or Assigns for ever.

Item. I give to my five Sons to wit, Benedick Jackson, Ephraim Jackson, Woody Jackson, Ambrose Jackson and Reuben Jackson all my Negroes which I have lent to my Wife Abigail, after the expiration of her Widowhood to be equally divided amongst them and to remain to them and their Heirs or Assigns for ever.

Item. I give all my Stock of Horses, Cattle and Hogs and all my Household and Kitchen furniture which I have lent to my Wife Abigail, after the expiration of her Widowhood, to my four Sons, to wit, Ephraim Jackson, Woody Jackson, Ambrose Jackson and Reuben Jackson to be equally divided amongst them, and to remain to them and their Heirs or Assigns for ever.

Item. My will is, that if my Wife Abigail Jackson doth not stand to and abide by this my Will, but chooses and takes any thing else in preference, then, in that case, I give to my Son William Parrish Jackson all that part of my Estate which I have before given to my five Sons, towit, Benedick Jackson, Ephraim Jackson, Woody Jackson, Ambrose

Jackson and Reuben Jackson except the sum of five shillings specie each, and to remain to him the said William Parrish Jackson his Heirs or Assigns for ever.

Item. Lastly, I constitute, leave and appoint my three Sons, to wit, William Parrish Jackson, John Jackson and Benidick Jackson my whole and sole Executors to execute this my last Will and Testament, and I do by these presents make void all and every other Will or Wills made by me or for me heretofore, In Witness whereof I have hereunto set my hand and affixed my Seal this nineteenth day of October in the year of our Lord Christ one thousand seven hundred and Eighty Nine.

Signed, Sealed and Acknowledged in the presence of -- Lamme Hobbs, Jno. Wm. Connally, Stephen Mayes, John Manson.

Signed: Edward Jackson.[904]

The identification of Edward Jackson's first wife as Lucy Parrish is traditional; Millenor Jackson Hammack named one daughter Lucy (a name not otherwise used by the Hammack and Lambert families), while Edward Jackson named one son William Parrish Jackson. Both names suggest that the traditional identification may be correct. Most of the early Parrishes of Brunswick, Amelia, and Lunenburg Counties came from New Kent and Hanover Counties; while the leap is purely speculative, it may be that Edward Jackson married Lucy, daughter of William Parrish, formerly of Hanover County.[905]

According to his will, Edward Jackson fathered fifteen children. Many of them have not been traced. Son John E. Jackson remained in Nottoway County; he married Jane Bailey and died there in 1810. Millenor and Robert Hammack moved during the 1770s to Wilkes County, Georgia. Edward's son Daniel Jackson is probably the Daniel Jackson who in 1784 received land on Dry Fork in Wilkes County. He died there in 1794 with Edward Echols, probably a cousin, serving as appraiser of his estate.[906] He apparently left a will, now lost, naming Robert Jackson and Jeremiah Reeves as executors. Annual returns indicate that Robert left children named Daniel, Joshua, John, William, and Gabriel Jackson.[907]

Three generations of American Jacksons preceded Millenor Jackson Hammack. From at least 1685 until 1789, the family resided in several contiguous counties in Southside Virginia. Millenor's grandfather John acquired landholdings that significantly exceeded those of his own father William; a portion of these he passed on to his son Edward Jackson, who in turn provided Millenor Jackson Hammack and her new husband Robert with an eighty-three-acre farm. A few years earlier, about the time of his marriage, Robert's grandfather Hugh Lambert had left him an adult male slave. These two bequests together provided the foundation on which Robert and Millenor in time built a substantial holding that, in turn, benefited the next generation of Hammacks.

---

[904] The only known copy of Edward Jackson's will is found in the Revolutionary War Pension Application of his daughter-in-law Betty and son John E. Jackson: Revolutionary War Pension Application of Mrs. Jane Bailey Jackson, widow of John E. Jackson, W3823/BLWT36721-160-55, National Archives, Washington, D.C., Microfilm Series M805, Roll 465.

[905] One William Parrish, with wife Amy, was living in Amelia County at the time of its formation. He died about 1734. Charles Parrish, formerly of Brunswick County, also settled in Amelia and Lunenburg; Charles was a neighbor of both the Hammack and the Jackson family, and John Hammack witnessed his Lunenburg County will. Both Charles and his father died testate, and their wills identify a multitude of Parrish kin. Neither will contains any reference to William Parrish or to Lucy Parrish Jackson, although there might be some as of yet undetermined connection.

[906] Davidson, *Early Records*, 1: 110.

[907] Davidson, *Early Records*, 2: 243. One might conclude that this John Jackson was the man who married Mary Hammack, daughter of Robert and Millenor Jackson Hammack, on 12 August 1800 in Wilkes County were it not for the fact that John Jackson, "being above fourteen years old," chose Jeremiah Reeves to serve as his guardian on 22 February 1801. (See Davidson, *Early Records*, 1: 116.) This man is probably the John Jackson who married by 1818 Jane, daughter of Sherwood Wise, and died in Wilkes County in before 1822 (See Davidson, *Early Records*, 2: 182, 314). John's brother Joshua (who was deceased by 1829) married Eleanor Wise. (See Davidson, *Early Records*, 2: 243-244). J. H. Austin, *The Georgians: Genealogies of Pioneer Settlers* (Baltimore, 1984), p. 190, incorrectly identifies John Jackson who married Mary Hammack as Daniel Jackson's son.

Descendants of Edward Jackson

Edward Jackson — **Lucy Parrish**

- **Millenor Jackson**
  - **Robert Hammack**
- **Daniel Jackson**
- **Edward Jackson**
- **Lucy Jackson**
- **William Parrish Jackson**
- **Mary Jackson**
  - **[-------] Howard**
- **John Jackson**
  - **Jane Bailey**
- **Silvaner Jackson**
- **Phoebe Jackson**
  - **[-------] Whitesides**
- **Bendeict Jackson**
- **Moses Jackson**
- **Ephraim Jackson**
- **Woody Jackson**
- **Ambrose Jackson**
- **Reuben Jackson**

Chapter 21:

Mary Felts Hammack of Warren County, North Carolina,
and Wilkes, Jones, and Crawford Counties, Georgia

As previously indicated, the identification of Mary Hammack, wife of William T. Hammack, as Mary Felts is circumstantial and based on the close association between 1797 and 1850 of members of the family of William and Mary Hammack and those of the family of John Felts. Based on this extended association, it appears that John Felts was probably Mary Hammack's father.

The Felts family was established by Humphrey Felts (c. 1648 - c. 1713) who settled about 1680 in Surry County, Virginia. Humphrey appears on Surry County tithable records but was seldom involved in legal disputes or land transactions. In 1709, he sold a tract of land to William Land; Humphrey's wife Helen, whose name also appears as Eleanor and Helenor, released her dower rights, allowing the land to change hands.[908]

Humphrey Felps wrote his will in Surry County on 19 September 1713. He names his wife Eleanor and three sons "that are gone from me," namely William, Humphrey, and Richard. To these three sons he left "all the estate of mine that they have in their hands". Sons John, Thomas, and Nathaniel Felps were each to receive fifty pounds of tobacco at age twenty-one, and son "Callepe" Felps was given a cow. Daughter Mary Felps was to receive a Bible and wife Eleanor Felps and son Francis Felps were named to share equally in the remaining estate. Witnesses were Jestes Willison and John Lanier. The will was proved 20 January 1715.[909]

Of the offspring of Humphrey Felts, Francis, William, Humphrey, and Richard were presumably all above twenty-one years of age when their father wrote his will in 1713 and hence born prior to 1692. The chronology fits well with Humphrey's appearance in Surry County about 1680. If he married soon after he arrived in the area, he could well have fathered four sons during the intervening decade. Of the offspring, Humphrey, William, and Richard had left Surry County before 1713. Two sons had apparently moved southwest, into coastal North Carolina, where Humphrey Felts and William Felts were each taxed with one tithable on the southwest side of Perquimans River in Perquimans County on 16 December 1715.[910] Richard Felts may have accompanied his brothers into North Carolina; if so, he returned to Surry County, where he reared five children.

John Felts, Thomas Felts, and Nathaniel Felts were all minors when their father wrote his will in 1713; they may have, in fact, been quite young. Thomas Felts, Jr., the eldest known child of Thomas Felts, was born about 1725, suggesting that his father was likely born between about 1700 and 1703. Agnes Felts, the oldest known child of Nathaniel Felts, was born about 1732, suggesting that Nathaniel could have been born as late as 1710.

John Felts of Wilkes County, Georgia, is believed to have been a son of John Felts of Sussex County, Virginia, a grandson of Thomas Felts of Surry County, Virginia, and a great-grandson of Humphrey Felts. Thomas Felts and wife Jane were the parents of Thomas Felts (c. 1723-); Nathaniel Felts (c. 1725-); John Felts (c. 1727-); Ann Felts (c. 1729-); and Sarah Felts (c. 1731-), wife of John Bullock. Of these children, John Felts and wife Mary baptized seven children in Albemarle Parish between 1746 and 1757: Andrew (19 July 1746-); Sukey (11 February 1747-); John (7 August 1749-); Jordan (16 July 1751-);

---

[908] Surry Co., VA, Court Records, 1701-1711, Book VI, p. 338.

[909] Surry Co., VA, Records Book 6, p. 251, as found in Eliza Timberlake Davis, *Surry County, Virginia Wills, 1671-1750*, p. 33.

[910] Humphrey Felts, Jr., died testate in Perquimans Co., NC, with a will proved in July 1726. The will names son John and daughter Elizabeth. William Long executed the document, which was witnessed by Edward Standin, Joshua Long, and Samuel Wiatt. (J. B. Grimes, *Abstract of North Carolina Wills, 1690-1760* (Raleigh, 1910), p. 119.) William Feps died in Beaufort County with a will written on 11 January 1753 and proved in June 1754. He names sons William, Nathaniel, and Josiah and daughters Molle Feps, Sarah Feps, and Lu. Rainer. Mary Feps, William's wife, executed the document (Ibid., p. 119).

Molly (1 April 1753-); Nathaniel (25 January 1755-); and Allen (19 July 1756-). Godparents of John Felts (7 August 1749-) included Thomas Felts, Thomas Felts, Jr., and Anne Rolland. Godparents for his siblings included members of the Felts, Bulloch, Seats, Cooper, Hix, Adkins, and Harris families.

Thomas Felts, Sr., wrote his will in Albemarle Parish on 6 December 1765. The will, proven 15 June 1769, names sons Nathaniel, John, and Thomas Felts and daughters Ann (wife of Robert Seat) and Sarah (wife of John Bullock). Thomas Felts, Jr., executed the document, which James Bell, John Whitehorn, Samuel Bullock, and David Mason witnessed.[911] In four deeds dated August 1757, Thomas Felts deeded 100 acres "for love and affection" to William Harris, 370 acres "for love and affection" to son Thomas Felts., Jr., 300 acres "for love and affection" to son John Felts, and 300 acres "for love and affection" to son Nathaniel Felts.[912] The tract left to John Felts lay on the long fork of Poplar Swamp and joined tracts owned by Thomas Felts, Robert Berry, and John Barnes.[913] Members of the Felts family began to appear in Bute (later Warren) County, North Carolina, as early as 1764,[914] and by the time of the 1800 census there were eight Felts households there.[915]

The younger John Felts may be the man who in 1779 -- the same year Warren County was formed out of Bute -- purchased a tract of land from Thomas Young with William Roland as witness.[916] He was taxed in 1781, 1782, 1783, 1784, and 1785 in Jordan Harris's District of Warren County. The 1784 and 1785 tax lists showed that he owned 400 acres at that time.[917] At the time of the 1785 Warren County tax list and census, John Felts, Jordan Felts, Francis Felts, William Felts, Rowland Felts, Isham Felts, Nathaniel Felts, and Randolph Felts headed households in Warren County. John Felts was at that time an adult man with a wife, a young son, and a young daughter. He was taxed in Warren County from 1786 to 1790, each year paying tax on 400 acres of land. One John Felts briefly appears in Wilkes County, Georgia, from about 1790 to about 1792; it is not clear whether he was the same man.

The John Felts who seems to have been Mary Hammack's father was living in Wilkes County by about 1798. He was taxed in Wilkes County until 1805, at times owning a twelve-acre tract which he rented to William Hammack, but leaving soon afterwards for land he had drawn on 16 October 1805 in what became Putnam County. On 23 November 1814, he deeded thirty acres of this tract to William Hammack.[918] He deeded ninety acres of the same tract to John Felts, Jr., and William Felts on 27 December 1814.[919] The remaining 80 acres had gone to son Allen Felts of Jones County on 1 February 1812.[920] John Felts, Sr., and John Felts, Jr., were both taxed in Putnam County in 1815; no record of the elder man has been found after this date.

Based on deed records, tax records, estate records, census documents, and prolonged association, it appears that John Felts fathered William Felts (c. 1780, NC -- c. 1862, Jones County, Georgia); Mary Felts (c. 1781, NC --), wife of William T. Hammack; John Felts, Jr. (c. 1782, NC -- c. 1835, Putnam County, Georgia); Simeon Felts (c. 1790, NC -- c. 1845, Putnam County, Georgia), who married Martha Ray; Allen Felts (c. 1790, NC[921] -- aft. 1860, Crawford County, Georgia), who married Elzy [-----];

---

[911] Sussex Co., VA, Will Book B, 1764-1771, p. 205.

[912] Sussex Co., VA, Deed Book A, 1754-1759, pp. 234, 235, 237, 238.

[913] Sussex Co., VA, Deed Book A, p. 237. The land had been granted to Thomas Felts on 20 August 1747.

[914] Bute Co., NC, Deed Book A, p. 55.

[915] One John Felts was a head of household in Warren County in 1800; he is probably not the father of Simeon, Allen, John, William, Charlotty, and Mary Felts of Wilkes County, as their father seems to have been in Wilkes County at least by about 1797. Yet the evidence suggests that John Felts had come from North Carolina, and Warren County seems to have housed several different Felts families before 1800. In 1800, there were also Felts in Wilkes, Wake, Duplin, and Northampton Counties. One John Felts died testate in Warren County in 1802, leaving children Needham and Mary.

[916] B. H. Holcomb, *Bute Co., NC, Court Minutes, 1767-1779* (Columbia, SC, 1988), p. 342.

[917] D. B. Gammon, *Tax Lists of Warren County, NC, 1779-1790* (Raleigh, NC, 1994), pp. 14, 24, 33, 42, 51, 60, 71, 83, 87, 95.

[918] Putnam Co., GA, Deed Book D, p. 26.

[919] Putnam Co., GA, Deed Book D, p. 25.

[920] Putnam Co., GA, Deed Book C, pp. 46-47.

[921] The 1860 Crawford Co., GA, Census, p. 940, Hammack's District, indicated that he was seventy years old and a native of North Carolina. At that time, he owned real estate valued at $10,100 and personal property valued at $21,700.

Charlotte Felts (c. 1790, NC -- c. 1858, Jones County, Georgia), who married first William Griffin and then Edward Hammack; and a daughter, who was the mother of Mary Wheeler (wife of Joseph Simpson) and of Allen Wheeler (c. 1807 --), husband of Nancy Bryant and Mary Elizabeth Hutcheson. In the early nineteenth-century, family connections between the Felts, Hammack, and Moore families became complicated, with several intermarriages linking the three family groups.

Although the Felts family had been owners of substantial tracts in both Sussex County, Virginia, and Warren County, North Carolina, John Felts may have fallen upon hard times in the early 1790s. The decade after the American Revolution ended witnessed much economic instability, and financial problems may have caused him to lose the tract he had purchased in Warren County. By the time he reached Georgia, John Felts owned no land, and the only property he possessed during the remainder of his life seems to have been the tract he drew in 1807 and then later divided among his offspring. As noted previously, however, Felts deeded a portion of this tract to William T. Hammack at a bargain rate. This tract, probably intended as an inheritance for his daughter Mary Hammack, in time became one of several tracts owned by William Hammack and his offspring in central Georgia.

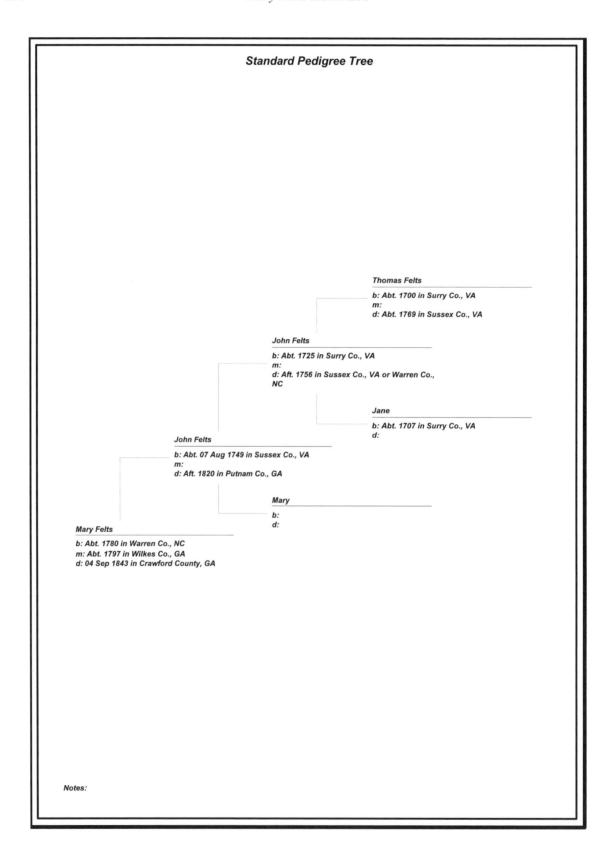

Standard Pedigree Tree

Thomas Felts
b: Abt. 1700 in Surry Co., VA
m:
d: Abt. 1769 in Sussex Co., VA

John Felts
b: Abt. 1725 in Surry Co., VA
m:
d: Aft. 1756 in Sussex Co., VA or Warren Co., NC

Jane
b: Abt. 1707 in Surry Co., VA
d:

John Felts
b: Abt. 07 Aug 1749 in Sussex Co., VA
m:
d: Aft. 1820 in Putnam Co., GA

Mary
b:
d:

Mary Felts
b: Abt. 1780 in Warren Co., NC
m: Abt. 1797 in Wilkes Co., GA
d: 04 Sep 1843 in Crawford County, GA

Notes:

Chapter 22

Elizabeth Jane Moore Hammack of Wilkes, Jones, Crawford and Macon Counties, Georgia, and Choctaw, Calhoun, and Madison Counties, Mississippi

The Moore lineage is exceedingly complex and has been difficult to reconstruct. Elizabeth Jane Moore was born about 1804, probably in the Harden's Creek area of Wilkes County, Georgia. Like her future husband Simeon Hammack, her own family had lived in Virginia for generations before relocating to Wilkes County; unlike her husband's family, however, the Moore family had come to Georgia a generation later, settling not in a frontier community but instead in a prosperous farming enclave in southeastern Wilkes County, a region that had by then been settled for more than three decades.

There are documentary difficulties in reconstructing and verifying Elizabeth Jane Moore's ancestry, but there is sufficient evidence to make a strong argument that she was a daughter of Robert Moore (c. 1775, Lunenburg Co., VA - aft. 1850, Crawford Co., GA) and a granddaughter of Ussery Moore (c. 1748, Lunenburg Co., VA - aft. 1820, Jones Co., GA) and Martha Bishop. The evidence also suggests that an exceedingly complex web of family relationships existed between Simeon Hammack and his wife Elizabeth.

The earliest Moores in this particular family were James, Robert, and John Moore, probably brothers, who baptized children in St. Peter's Parish, New Kent County, Virginia, between 1711 and 1738. James Moore and wife Agnes baptized sons James, John, Robert, and daughters Mary and Rebecca between 1718 and 1734. Robert Moore and wife Mary baptized sons John, David, and Thomas between 1730 and 1738. John Moore -- whose wife is not identified -- baptized sons Robert and John and daughter Sarah between 1711 and 1724. The New Kent registers indicate that Enoss, an Indian man, died at Robert Moore's home in 1726, suggesting that he was an adult at that time and probably born before 1705. Hence, we can speculate that John Moore was born about 1690, James Moore about 1696, and Robert Moore prior to 1705.[922]

One Robert Moore appears in Lunenburg County, Virginia, as early as 1748. By that time, he was an adult man with what seems to be grown or nearly grown children, suggesting that he was likely born by 1709/1710, if not earlier.[923] Studying the Lunenburg County records for the period between roughly 1748 and 1775 reveals many individuals bearing the surname Moore. While it is possible to identify what seem to be rough kinship groups, it nevertheless appears that the kinship group to which this Robert belonged was already large and complicated when its members first began settling in Lunenburg in the 1740s and 1750s. Between 1740 and 1797, men named Robert Moore had land or other dealings with James Moore, Valentine Moore, David Moore, John Moore, Jesse Moore, Ussery Moore, and another Robert Moore, many of which individuals were designated "Senior" or "Junior" to distinguish them from another person in the community bearing the same given name. Since almost no Lunenburg document before 1780 seems to specify who was the father of whom -- no will, estate settlement, or clearly identifiable deed of gift, on the basis of these records alone it would seem almost impossible to identify family relationships among this group.

The first Robert Moore of Lunenburg maintained a close association with members of the Ussery and Blackwell families which, however, suggests that there may have been a kinship tie there; the argument is strengthened by the emergence to manhood in the late 1760s of an individual named Ussery Moore, a name that suggests at least one marriage between the Ussery and Moore families before about 1748, when Ussery Moore seems to have been born. Although the marriage may have occurred in Lunenburg, families usually moved together from one location to another, maintaining ties of kinship and association across time and place. The Ussery and Blackwell families, already related, can be traced back to St.

---

[922] Register of St. Peter's Parish, New Kent Co., VA, The Library of Virginia, Richmond, VA.
[923] 1748 Lunenburg Co., VA, Tithables List, The Library of Virginia, Richmond, VA.

Peter's Parish, New Kent County, where they were residents by the late 1690s.[924] Living there in the same community between circa 1700 and circa 1735 were the aforementioned individuals named Robert Moore, James Moore, and John Moore, who seem to have been near neighbors of John Ussery and James Blackwell.[925]

While the evidence is only speculative, it may be that John Moore (born by c. 1690), James Moore (born by c. 1697), and Robert Moore (born by c. 1705) were brothers. An Edward and Frances Moore also appear in the register with son John born in 1718 and son Edward in 1718, but whether they were related to John, James, and Robert is unclear. In addition to members of the Ussery and Blackwell families, members of the Peace family with whom Robert Moore's clan had dealings in Lunenburg are also found in the register: John Peace baptized a son Joseph in 1700 and a daughter Susannah shortly afterwards, and the families appear together in many early documents. What became of John Moore is unclear, but his son Robert (born 1711) may be one of the other Roberts found later in Southside Virginia.

Among the early references to the Moores is an entry from the parish vestry book dated 4 May 1689, authorizing the processioning of lands. Among those whom the processioners -- men who were charged with verifying local land boundaries -- were to visit were John Epperson, Samuel Weaver, *James Moore, James Blackwell, and John Peace*. The vestry book is missing between 1691 and 1698, but when the vestry book and register resume we learn that John Moore baptized a daughter Mary in 1698, that James Moore baptized a son William in 1699, that John Moore baptized a son John in 1699, and that James Moore baptized a daughter Mary in 1700. Several Moore references appear later. One learns that in 1703 William Moore was called "A Sick and Lame man" whose care the vestry had to provide and that for at least the following year his food and lodging were provided by the parish. Edward Moore emerges as a man prominent in parish affairs, his name appearing often in the vestry minutes for service in different capacities. Thomas Moore likewise is frequently mentioned before 1730, but few other references appear to James, John, and Robert.[926]

A large county, New Kent saw its original territory divided and sub-divided several times. King and Queen was carved from it in 1691, and King William from King and Queen in 1701. In 1720, Hanover was formed directly from New Kent. Most records for all four of these counties were destroyed during the Civil War. In Hanover's case, like New Kent, some Anglican church records do survive. Although the Moores are not mentioned there, the records do reveal that the Ussery, Blackwell, and Peace families were all in the area between 1730 and 1743. Joseph Peace, John Blackwell, William Blackwell, James Blackwell, John Ussery, John Blackwell, Jr., and Samuel Peace are all mentioned regarding the processioning of lands in their neighborhood in 1731-1732 and 1735, and a 1739 return of processionings again mentions Joseph Peace, John Blackwell, William Blackwell, James Blackwell, John Ursury, John Blackwell, Jr., and Samuel Peace as landowners in the same neighborhood, stating that Joseph Peace's land had been divided between John and William Peace and that Arthur Hopkins had conveyed land to John Orsery and that James Blackwell had to Mr. John Thompson. A 1743 return of processioning mentions John Peace, William Peace, John Ursery, John Blackwell, William Blackwell, John Blackwell, Jr., and Samuel Peace. A 1759 processioning order mentions land of John Ussery's heirs adjacent Samuel Peace, John Peace's heirs, John Blackwell, Josias Blackwell, Micajah Blackwell, and James Blackwell's heirs, indicating that, while many family members moved into Lunenburg, others remained in Hanover.

[924] The Moores also had dealing with the Elmore family, a family sometimes associated in Lunenburg and Richmond Counties with the Hammack family. Lyle Elmore speculates that the early Elmores may also have been related to the Moore family. See L. Elmore, *An Elmore Odyssey* (not published, undated, c. 1995). A copy of this work is held in The Library of Virginia, Richmond, VA.

[925] Ibid. In addition to the parish register, see also the Vestry Book of St. Peter's Parish, New Kent Co., VA, The Library of Virginia, Richmond, VA, which documents activities of many parishioners within the parish.

[926] The Parish Register and Vestry Book of St. Peter's Parish, New Kent Co., VA, The Library of Virginia, Richmond, VA.

The record further suggests that John Ussery retained some of his Hanover properties after settling in Lunenburg.[927]

Robert Moore may have remained in the Hanover-New Kent area until the 1740s, but the absence of any reference to the family in the parish register or vestry book after the early 1730s suggests that he may have moved on about that time. Possibly he settled first in Brunswick or even Hanover before appearing in the late 1740s in Lunenburg. Certainly, when he does appear there he is in the company of members of the Ussery and Blackwell families, and he continued to associate with them for several years.

The fate of this particular Robert Moore is unclear. The Lunenburg estate records never mention his death, and there is no clearly identifiable deed that indicates that he was selling his property and moving elsewhere. A court order from 1769 mentions that the suit of William Clopton against Robert Moore had abated because of the defendant's death; this almost certainly refers to the Robert who had sold the lands patented by Clopton in the 1750s and who may have still owed commissions on those lands to Clopton, but was this Robert, Jr., or Robert, Sr.?[928]

Although the evidence is not as clear as it might be, one can argue that Robert Moore, Sr., is the same Robert Moore who still appears in Lunenburg in the 1790s, in 1791 conveying 100 acres to Jesse Moore and in 1797 disposing of his remaining 100 acres and dropping silently from the Lunenburg records. Certainly one Robert Moore between 1782 and 1797 paid tax consistently on the same tract of land, and the deed records establish that this was the Robert Moore with wife Mary who in 1797 disposes of his remaining land.[929] Given the long chronological span, it seems more likely that Robert Moore, Sr., died in 1769, aged about sixty-four or sixty-five years, and that the Roberts found in the 1780s and 1790s are younger men. Careful study of the evidence also seems to indicate that this was the case. The original deed from Clopton to Moore in 1758 does not indicate whether the purchaser of the large Clopton tract was Robert Moore, Sr., or Robert Moore, Jr. Certainly the very favorable terms of the deed -- just over £90 paid for more than 4,000 acres -- indicates that something more than a straightforward land transaction was occurring.[930] Likely, Robert Moore sold the land for Clopton as part of some pre-existing agreement, promising to pay commission or a larger sum at some point in the future. That obligation, and a failure to keep it, may have generated the 1768 lawsuit -- a decade after the original deed from Clopton to Moore was executed.[931]

Studying all subsequent Lunenburg land transactions involving men named Robert Moore reveals that, in several of the deeds disposing of the above tract of 4,142 acres, the grantor was identified as Robert Moore, Sr. In others, the grantor was identified only as Robert Moore, but Robert Moore, Jr., was a witness to the transaction, indicating that Robert Moore, Sr., was the grantor. Further, study of deeds for adjacent landowners -- Matthew Turner, Thomas Riddle, Daniel Askew, Moses Hurt, and others -- indicates that Robert Moore, Sr., was the individual who owned the adjacent lands. Hence, it seems likely that if the 1769 Clopton suit related to some obligation stemming from the 1758 deed, then the Robert Moore who died in 1769 must have been the same Robert Moore who purchased the Clopton lands in 1758 -- that is, *Robert Moore, Senior.*[932]

---

[927] Among the few surviving Hanover Records is Court Record Book 1733-1735, which contains a deed dated 3 May 1734 from Joseph Peace of St. Paul's Parish to brother William Harmon Peace of St. James Parish, fifty acres, south side of Pamunkey River, a place commonly called Harmon's old plantation. John Usery, Samuel Peace, and James Balfour witnessed the deed, and Mary Peace relinquished her dower.

[928] Lunenburg Co., VA, Order Book 1766-1769, p. 274; Lunenburg Co., VA, Deed Book 16, p. 475.

[929] 1782-1797 Lunenburg Co., VA, Personal Property Tax Lists, The Library of Virginia, Richmond, VA;

[930] Brunswick Co., VA, DB 9, p. 313. Note that William Clopton patented this land on 10 April 1758. The entire tract consisted of 5,145 acres on Crooked Run and Cedar Creek, adjacent George Green, Williams, Robert Lambert, Robert Pleasants, Jonathan Mote (land purchased by John Ussery), William Rivers (purchased by Blackwell), Hubbard, Jones, Dickerson, and Cary Wills Daniel (Virginia Patent Book 33, pp. 428-429.)

[931] Brunswick Co., VA, Deed Book 6, pp. 338, 341, 343, 395, 396, 398; Lunenburg Co., VA, Deed Book 5, pp. 403-406, 409-410, 418-420, 423-427, 433-435; Lunenburg Co., VA, Deed Book 7, pp. 72-90, 486-488; Lunenburg Co., VA, Deed Book 11, pp. 28-30; Lunenburg Co., VA, Deed Book 14, p. 417.

[932] Ibid.

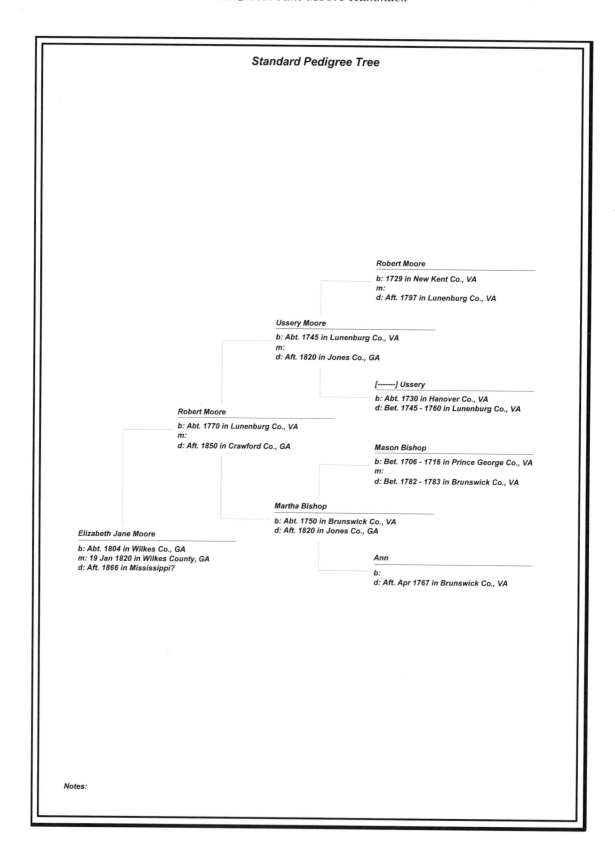

Standard Pedigree Tree

Robert Moore
b: 1729 in New Kent Co., VA
m:
d: Aft. 1797 in Lunenburg Co., VA

Ussery Moore
b: Abt. 1745 in Lunenburg Co., VA
m:
d: Aft. 1820 in Jones Co., GA

[-------] Ussery
b: Abt. 1730 in Hanover Co., VA
d: Bet. 1745 - 1760 in Lunenburg Co., VA

Robert Moore
b: Abt. 1770 in Lunenburg Co., VA
m:
d: Aft. 1850 in Crawford Co., GA

Mason Bishop
b: Bet. 1706 - 1716 in Prince George Co., VA
m:
d: Bet. 1782 - 1783 in Brunswick Co., VA

Martha Bishop
b: Abt. 1750 in Brunswick Co., VA
d: Aft. 1820 in Jones Co., GA

Elizabeth Jane Moore
b: Abt. 1804 in Wilkes Co., GA
m: 19 Jan 1820 in Wilkes County, GA
d: Aft. 1866 in Mississippi?

Ann
b:
d: Aft. Apr 1767 in Brunswick Co., VA

Notes:

Moore Family Migrations, c. 1700 - c. 1805

1=New Kent County, residence of James and Robert Moore, c. 1690 - c. 1730
2=Hanover County, residence of Robert Moore, c. 1730 - c. 1740
3=Goochland County
4=Cumberland County
5=Amelia County, residence of Robert Moore, c. 1760
6=Lunenburg County, residence of Robert Moore, Sr., and Jr., and of Ussery Moore, c. 1745 - c. 1805
7=Dinwiddie County, residence of Ussery Moore, c. 1780
8=Brunswick County, residence of Robert Moore (c. 1760) and of Ussery Moore (c. 1783)

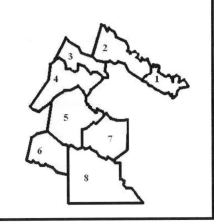

Lunenburg deeds also indicate that the Robert Moore who in 1756 patented a 400-acre tract was also Robert Moore, Senior. This conclusion also was reached by studying the relevant deeds and transactions involving adjacent property owners. Precise citations appear in a separate manuscript which includes annotated abstracts of the relevant deeds. Hence it was Robert Moore, Sr., who also sold 200 acres of this tract to his son John Moore in the late 1750s.[933]

At this point, it is necessary to ask how many adult Robert Moores there were appearing in Lunenburg records between 1745 and 1795 and which, if any, of these was the father of Ussery Moore. Lunenburg records make it clear that during the late 1740s, 1750s, and early 1760s there were at least two -- Robert Moore, Sr., and Robert Moore, Jr. What is not clear is whether these men were father and son or uncle and nephew. The New Kent register indicates that that Robert Moore, son of James and Agnes, was born in December, 1729, and that John Moore, eldest known child of Robert and Mary Moore, was born 23 January 1729/30 and baptized two months later. The New Kent registers are largely complete for this period, but the possibility always exists that entries are missing: a torn page could obliterate key references, or a brief residence in another county could have produced baptisms recorded in another parish. If Robert and Mary Moore had an older son named Robert Moore -- born say 1727/1728 -- and if he were the oldest son of Robert Moore, then by intestate law of the period he would have automatically inherited the bulk of his father's property had the older man died without a will. Hence this hypothetical eldest son could be the Robert Moore, Jr., shown in Lunenburg references, while the Robert Moore, Jr., shown in Brunswick references would be the son of James Moore.

Although the possibility of an older son named Robert Moore, Jr., cannot be entirely dismissed at this point, there is little evidence for the existence of such an individual. References to Robert Moore as "Junior" and "Senior" chiefly occur from about 1750 to the late 1760s and seem to end about 1769, when the elder Robert Moore died. Lunenburg, Brunswick, and Amelia deeds and tithable records for the period contain no known evidence indicating that there were two younger men named Robert Moore in the community. The line between Lunenburg and Brunswick was an artificial boundary of the community in which Robert Moore, Sr., and James Moore, Sr., and their offspring lived after moving to the area from New Kent County. The Clopton - Moore tract lay in both Lunenburg and Brunswick, and references to the relevant deeds are filed in the county in which a specific mini-tract lay; still, the individuals involved appear simultaneously in transactions in both counties. Many of the deeds indicate that the tracts in Lunenburg lay adjacent the county line and were bounded by parcels in Brunswick County owned by Valentine or James Moore or William Martin. There is no evidence in the deeds of two younger men named Robert Moore. For instance, in the 1780s, when distinguishing between multiple Jesse Moores, one was regularly referenced as Jesse Moore of Stoney Creek and the other as Jesse Moore of Cedar Creek. In other situations, where several individuals bearing the same given name and the same surname are found, it is not uncommon to find them distinguished by a notation as to their paternity -- i. e., John (of William), John (of John), and John (of Robert). The clerks of Lunenburg and Brunswick do not seem to have grappled with such a difficulty. Moreover, there is no conflicting evidence indicating that two younger Robert Moores with the same name were active at the same time. References to Robert Moore, Jr., occur in Lunenburg throughout the 1750s. He is mentioned in only a few Brunswick deeds as an adjacent landowner. In 1763 and 1764, he was in Amelia County, and then probably later in 1764 he moved into Lunenburg County, where he apparently remained until the 1790s.[934]

---

[933] See T. D. Knight, *Early Moore Families of Wilkes, Jones, Greene, Hancock, and Taliaferro Counties, Georgia: The Quest to Identify Elizabeth Jane Moore Hammack* (unpublished manuscript, 2004), pp. 48-62. This manuscript -- in excess of 400 pages -- includes all relevant information on the Moores of New Kent Co., VA, Lunenburg Co., VA, and Wilkes, Greene, Hancock, and Taliaferro Counties, GA. For Moore's 303-acre grant, see Virginia Land Patent Book 36, 1764-1767, page 696. See Lunenburg Co., VA, Deed Book 5, pp. 433-35, and Virginia Patent Book 34, p. 96, for Moore's land on Cedar Creek and Horsepen Branch.

[934] Lunenburg County Order Books further confirm these data. Order Book 8, p. 8, April Court 1762, recorded that the suit of Richard Hanson v. Robert Moore, Jr., had abated, because the "defendant is not an inhabitant of this county." Robert Moore, Jr., was back in Lunenburg by about 1764. Like land records, tithable records for colonial Virginia constitute an important source for tracing early Virginians. The Church of England, the established, state-supported religious institution in the colony, collected an annual tax --

Once one understands that it was Robert Moore, Sr., who died in 1769, the references during and after the 1760s seem clearer. In 1764, Robert Moore was taxed with one tithe and no land in Lunenburg. If this is Robert Moore, Sr., this reference indicates that the entire Clopton tract and the 1756 patent had both been disposed of. The tithable list was dated 10 June 1764, and on 24 September 1764 Robert Moore patented 303 acres beginning at a corner "of James Moore on Cedar Creek." This land joined the Connally lands and lay along the Lunenburg - Brunswick County line where Cedar Creek flows from one county to another.[935] Thus the adjacent tract was land owned by James Moore in Brunswick. Later Lunenburg deeds indicate that this is the property being sold in the 1770s by Robert and Rachel Moore of Lunenburg to Christopher Hinton, George Connally, and James Moore, all of whom were then or had been residents of Brunswick County. Since this land was not sold until the 1770s, then the patentee must be Robert Moore, Jr., apparently the son of James Moore, Sr., of New Kent and Brunswick. He had appeared in early Lunenburg tithables but then was absent from the county for several years, apparently while residing in Brunswick and then, in 1763 and 1764, in Amelia.[936]

Robert Moore appears in 1763 and 1764 in Nottoway Parish of Amelia County taxed with land and slaves; he was surrounded by familiar families, including that of Charles Connally whose son George married first a daughter of Charles Matthews (another of Matthews's daughters married Matthew Bishop, Ussery Moore's brother-in-law). Moreover, the Revolutionary War Pension Application of David Moore of Missouri indicates that he was born in Amelia County in 1763 but reared in Lunenburg County, where at the time of the Revolution he enlisted as a substitute *__for his father Robert Moore.__* The Lunenburg records from c. 1776 - c. 1783 make no distinction between Robert Moores, indicating that there was only one adult Robert Moore in the county at that time. Hence it would seem that the Robert Moore in Lunenburg between 1776 and 1782 was the father of David Moore and that he was the Robert who was selling Lunenburg lands during this time *__and__* that he was the Robert who in 1764 patented those lands as the 1764 patent included acreage sold in 1776 and subsequent years by Robert and Rachel Moore.[937]

This indicates that the Robert Moore who was grantor in the 1776 deeds was the man born in December 1729. Note that the Robert Moore, Sr., who first moved into Lunenburg would have by the late 1760s passed the tithable age.[938] At the time of the 1769 tithable list, only one Robert Moore appeared. The older man may have already died or not been shown at all because of his exemption. The only Robert Moore who was shown was head of a household that included James Moore, an adult son; yet Robert was charged with only one tithable -- indicating that he himself was exempt. He was also charged with 300 acres -- apparently the tract patented by him in 1764. If James had just reached tithable age, this suggests a likely birth date for him of 1748 -- the year Robert Moore, Jr., turned nineteen. Yet Robert Moore, Junior, would only have been forty years old in 1769; hence it would appear that he was the Robert

---

called a tithe -- from Virginia's inhabitants. Adult white males, and male and female slaves of certain ages, were taxable unless they had been declared exempt by local officials due to age or disability. Hence, a man's tithables on a tithable list were the individuals for whom he was legally required to pay a tithe. This money was used for the support of the local church and its minister. In the years before the American Revolution, when dissenting sects such as the Baptists, Methodists, and Presbyterians became common, the established church came under fire from many sectors. Once declaring their independence, Virginians quickly disestablished the Anglican Church. New forms of taxation followed in the post-Revolutionary period but were not linked to the maintenance of any one religious group.

[935] Virginia Patent Book 34, p. 96.

[936] Lunenburg Co., VA, Deed Book 12, pp. 92, 477; Lunenburg Co., VA, Deed Book 13, pp. 16, 78, 90-91, 133, 207; 1782 and 1783 Lunenburg Co., VA, Personal Property Tax List, The Library of Virginia, Richmond, VA; 1787-1790 Lunenburg Co., VA, Land Tax Lists, The Library of Virginia, Richmond, VA.

[937] 1762-1764 Nottoway Parish, Amelia Co., VA, Tithables Lists, The Library of Virginia, Richmond, VA; Revolutionary War Pension Application of David Moore, S16980, The National Archives, Washington, D.C., Microfilm Series M805, Roll 594.

[938] In February 1769, Robert Moore was "discharged from the payment of the county's public levies for the future." See Lunenburg Co., VA, Order Book 13, p. 229. The same order book, p. 279, indicates that the suit of William Clopton v. Robert Moore, defendant, in Chancery, had abated "it appearing to the court that the defendant is dead." This record was dated July 1769. From these records alone, it is not clear which Robert Moore received the exemption. As argued above, it may be that Robert Moore, Sr., had died and that Robert Moore, Jr., had received an exemption because of some disability.

Moore for whom exemption from the levies was granted in February 1769. Such an exemption at age forty would have been unusual and likely caused by some health problem; hence the entry in the court order books recorded it for future reference should questions arise in later years. This exemption also explains the absence of Robert Moore from tithable lists during the 1770s and 1780s when land records indicate he was residing in Lunenburg and possibly his need for a substitute during the Revolution.

Note that Connally family Bible records identify Frances Connally, wife of George Connally, as a daughter of Robert Moore and indicate that she was born in 1754. Her marriage in the middle 1770s corresponds well with the deeds to George Connally from Robert and Rachel Moore in 1776, and a similar deed from the Moores to Christopher Hinton and wife Ann (who were for many years associates of the Connallys in Brunswick, Lunenburg, and Halifax Counties, Virginia, and Caswell County, North Carolina) suggests that Ann Hinton may have been another Moore daughter. James Moore (born 1747), Frances Moore Connally (born 1754), Ann Moore Hinton (born prob. c. 1752-1756), and David Moore (born 1763) all fit as probable children of Robert Moore, Jr., of Brunswick, Amelia, and Lunenburg.[939]

To this list Ussery Moore (born 1748/1749) and Jesse Moore (born 1760) should probably also be added. Ussery first appears in Brunswick in 1770 as an insolvent for the year 1769, and he seems to have also been taxed in Lunenburg in 1769. Throughout the 1770s and early 1780s, he seems to have been in Brunswick County on Cedar Creek living adjacent George Connally and Christopher Hinton. Thomas Tarpley, brother-in-law of Ussery's wife Martha Bishop Moore, appears in numerous transactions along with Connally and Hinton and is often found with Ussery Moore. Likewise, Connally's first wife was a sister of the wife of Matthew Bishop, who was himself a brother-in-law of Thomas Tarpley and Ussery Moore. It seems probable that James Moore of Cedar Creek in Lunenburg also married into this group; Martha Bishop Moore's sister Hannah married Humphrey Garrett, and their daughter Jane Garrett Moore was of age by 1793 and possibly well before. Although it is speculative, the Mason Moore shown adjacent James of Cedar Creek in personal property tax lists and census enumerations and identified as an adjacent landowner in deed records may have been a son of James Moore named for his uncle Mason Garrett and for his great-grandfather Mason Bishop. Another Garrett sibling married Joseph Peace, whose sisters Susannah and Elizabeth were the first and second wives of Jesse Moore (born 1760). A third Peace sister married Littleberry Moore in Brunswick, and John Peace, their brother, was the father of Lucy, wife of Hugh Hammack of Lunenburg. This Hugh, in turn, was involved in legal transactions with his cousin Mildred Hammack Bentley, on whose business Jesse Moore's son Elisha ventured to Wilkes County, Georgia, about 1815.[940]

Cumulatively, the evidence is strong to suggest that Jesse, James, and Ussery Moore were closely related, and the linkages of their wives to the Bishop - Garrett - Peace - Matthews kinship group is significant. Note that Jesse Moore's third wife is alleged by Thomas family descendants to have been Mary Thomas, sister of the Martha Thomas who in 1789 married Robert Moore, Jr., of Lunenburg, and his fourth wife was Rebecca Laffoon Matthews, whose husband's family ties to the Charles and Drury Matthews family. Before George Connally was Robert Moore's son-in-law, he was Matthew Bishop's brother-in-law, and at that time Bishop's sisters Martha and Susannah seem already to have been married to Ussery Moore and Thomas Tarpley. Hence one observes a very tight, multi-faceted web of kinship existing among the parties to the 1770s deeds involving Robert and Rachel Moore, Christopher and Ann Hinton, George and Frances Connally, and Ussery, James, and Jesse Moore.

---

[939] George Connally Family Bible, The Library of Virginia, Richmond, VA; Lunenburg Co., VA, Deed Book 12, p. 92; Lunenburg Co., VA, Deed Book 13, pp. 90-91, 207, 355, 357.

[940] This group of families was heavily interconnected; the bonds seem to have endured for generations, as is suggested by the 1815 transaction involving Jesse Moore on behalf of Mildred Hammack Bentley. If this analysis is correct, Mildred's son John Bentley married Martha Moore, sister of Elizabeth Jane Moore Hammack. John Bentley was Simeon Hammack's first cousin. John's sister Annie married George Amos, and their son married Simeon Hammack's sister Katherine Hammack. These connections are explored more fully in Knight, *Moore Family*, above. See especially Lunenburg Co., VA, Deed Book 16, pp. 123, 475; Lunenburg Co., VA, Deed Book 19, p. 120; Lunenburg Co., VA, Deed Book 20, p. 3; 1783 Lunenburg Co., VA, Tithables List, The Library of Virginia, Richmond, VA; and 1784-1805 Lunenburg Co., VA, Personal Property Tax Lists, The Library of Virginia, Richmond, VA.

Lunenburg deeds indicate that Robert and Rachel Moore disposed of 325 acres of land in deeds to the Hintons, Connallys, and James Moore. The puzzling thing is that, since Robert Moore held no land before patenting the 303 acres in 1764, there is no record of where the additional 22 acres conveyed in the series of deeds came from. A second puzzle hinges on Lunenburg County, Virginia, land tax records that show Robert Moore taxed continuously from 1782 - 1790 with 200 acres of land in Lunenburg while Lunenburg deeds do not show the purchase of this land until **1786**! Moore may have rented the land prior to purchase, and, likewise, the original 303 acre patent may have been found to be larger upon resurvey. Another possibility is that the conditions of the deeds were never met and some of the properties deeded by Robert Moore and wife Rachel in the 1770s reverted back to Robert Moore. These are issues that warrant further investigation. Court orders from the period 1766 to 1780 appear to shed no light on these issues. But, taken together, the Lunenburg deeds and land tax records for the period after 1770 do indicate that the same Robert Moore resided in the county during these years and continued to own lands in the Cedar Creek area. He seems to have been Robert Moore, Jr., son of James Moore of New Kent and Brunswick Counties, and the evidence is strong that he was the father of Ussery, James, Frances, Ann, Jesse, David, and perhaps others. (Littleberry Moore who married Lucy Peace and Benjamin Moore who married Elizabeth Laffoon may both connect in some way.)

This Robert Moore's first wife was probably a daughter of "Widow Ussery" who was taxed adjacent Robert Moore in 1748 and a member of the Ussery family of New Kent, Hanover, and Lunenburg. Robert Moore's dealings with the Weaver family (also apparently from New Kent), and the presence of a Rachel Weaver witnessing these transactions, and then of Robert Moore with wife Rachel in the 1770s deeding land to his adult children, is striking. Was Rachel Weaver the second wife of Robert Moore? And was the Mary Moore shown with him in Lunenburg deeds during the 1790s his third wife? Finally, what became of Robert Moore after he vanished from Lunenburg deeds about 1797? He was then sixty-eight years old. Did he go to North Carolina, Georgia, or perhaps to Kentucky with son David? These remain questions with no clear answers at this point.[941]

Based on this analysis, we can present the following probable pedigree for Elizabeth Jane Moore Hammack:

Generation I: James Moore, flourished 1689, New Kent County, Virginia.

Generation II: James Moore (by c. 1696, New Kent County, Virginia -- by 11 August 1761, Brunswick County, Virginia), m. Agnes [------].

---

[941] There were three adult Robert Moores in Wilkes County in the 1790s. On the surface it seems possible that one of the early Wilkes County Robert Moores was the man who was active in Lunenburg in the 1770s, 1780s, and 1790s; certainly after selling the Lunenburg tracts, Robert Moore seems to have disappeared. But the timing does not seem to fit for him to have been identical with any of the three contemporary Robert Moores of Wilkes. Robert of Greene, Walton, and Paulding was in Georgia continuously from 1793 and could not be the Robert selling Lunenburg lands in 1797. Likewise, Robert of Warren, Wilkes, and Taliaferro was also in Georgia by 1794-1795 and so could not be the Robert in Lunenburg at the same time. Robert of Wilkes, Jones, Marion, and Crawford Counties was too young, for the evidence indicates that the Robert selling the properties in 1797 was an adult in Lunenburg well before 1782. Hence, while the three adult Robert Moores found in Wilkes County records between 1793 and 1822 likely all originated in Lunenburg, none of them appears to be the Robert Moore with wife Mary selling land in 1797; where that Robert went is still an unresolved question.

Generation III: Robert Moore (8 December 1729, New Kent County, Virginia -- after 1797, Lunenburg County, Virginia)[942], m. (1) c. 1747, Lunenburg County, Virginia, prob. [-------] Ussery[943], m. (2) Rachel [Weaver?], m. (3) Mary [-------].

Generation IV: Ussery Moore (c. 1748/9, Lunenburg County, Virginia -- after 1821/22, Jones County, Georgia), m. Martha Bishop (c. 1750, Brunswick County, Virginia -- after 1832, Jones County, Georgia).[944]

---

[942] Note that as Robert Moore, Jr., he was a tithable in Lunenburg County in 1751. He had just turned 21 years of age. The next five sets of names on the list are those of William Pettey, Richard Brooks, Robert Moore, Sr., Thomas Weaver, and William and John Ussery. A 1759 deed identifies Robert Moore as a neighbor of "William Essary" (Lunenburg Co., VA, DB 5, pp. 403-4).

[943] She was probably a daughter of John Ussery (c. 1700 - c. 1748), who moved from New Kent County to Lunenburg, where he died testate. John married Sarah Blackwell, probable daughter of James Blackwell (by 1683 -- aft. 1748), who was taxed in New Kent County in 1704 and who later settled in Lunenburg. He may have been the son of James Blackwell (c. 1660/65 -- by 1719), the grandson of Captain Robert Blackwell (c. 1640/45 --), the great-grandson of Capt. Joseph Croshaw (1612 - by 1671/2), and the great-great-grandson of Raleigh Croshaw, Ancient Planter, who arrived in Virginia as part of the Second Supply of April 1608 and who was dead by 27 December 1624. Ussery researchers have maintained for generations that John Ussery married Sarah Blackwell, daughter of James Blackwell. For the Blackwell-Croshaw connection, see John Frederick Dorman, ed., *Adventurers of Purse and Person in Virginia, 1607-1624*. John Ussery was probably also the father of William Ussery (by 1727 --); John Ussery (by 1728 --); Thomas Ussery (by 1740 --); and Sarah Ussery, who married Athanatius Elmore about 1765. John Ussery (d. 1748) was likely a brother of William Ussery (by 1710 --) who settled in Lunenburg and had, according to Lunenburg tithables, at least two sons, John (by 1729 --) and William (by 1731 --). These men may have been sons of an earlier John Ussery who was living in New Kent Co., VA, before 1686.
Lunenburg records (Lunenburg Co., VA, Order Book 2, pp. 348, 461, 467) show:

At Oct. Court, 1750, Sarah Ussery, widow of John Ussery, deceased, was summoned to show cause why she has not administered on the estate of her deceased husband.

At Oct. Court, 1751: Ordered that John Williams, Reps Jones, William Rivers and Robert Moore, or any three of them, do appraise the personal estate of John Ussery, deceased.

At Oct. Court, 1751, William Ussery was granted administration on the estate of John Ussery with John Tabor and John Blackwell as his securities.

Likewise, the 1748, 1749, and 1750 tithables list show a close geographic connection.

1748, Lunenburg Co., VA, Tithables between Hound's Creek and Meherrin River:
William Burgame	
Henry Moor	3
John Blackwell	2
At Widow Userey's	
William Userey	2
Robert Moore	2

1749, Lunenburg Co., VA, Tithables between Hound's Creek and Meherrin River:
William Burgame		
James Blackwell	2	6
William Usery		
John Usery	3	
John Blackwell	2	6
Robert Moor	1	6
Henery Moor	1	

1750, Lunenburg Co., VA, Tithables taken by Hugh Lawson:
John Blackwell	2
Henerey Moor	1
William Burgame	
James Blackwell	3
William Userey	2
Robert Moor	1

Ussery Moore first appears in 1769, suggesting that he was born about 1748. Cumulatively, this would seem to suggest that Robert Moore had a close relationship with the family of John and Sarah (Blackwell) Ussery about 1748; the most likely explanation is probably that he married their daughter as the first of at least three wives.

[944] Martha's ancestors John and Elizabeth (Booker?) Bishop were living in Virginia prior to 1643. Their son John Bishop (bef. 1643 - 1716) and wife Sarah reared a large family in Prince George Co., VA. Their son Harmon Bishop died before his father John wrote his will in 1716. Harmon Bishop was the father of Mason Bishop (bef. 1716 -- 1782/83, Brunswick Co., VA), who married

Generation V: Robert Moore (c. 1771, Lunenburg County, Virginia -- after 1850, Crawford Co., GA), m. (1) poss. Martha Thomas, m. (2) c. 1805/6, Wilkes County, Georgia, Martha Ray Moncrief, daughter of Sanders and Christiana Ray and widow of Samuel Moncrief.

Generation VI: Elizabeth Jane Moore (c. 1804, Wilkes Co., GA -- 1867/70, Webster Co., MS), m. Simeon Hammack.

Elizabeth Jane Moore Hammack would, therefore, be a great-great-great-granddaughter of the James Moore who was active in St. Peter's Parish, New Kent Co., VA, by 1689, and a granddaughter of Ussery Moore, who brought his family from Lunenburg Co., VA, to Wilkes Co., GA, about 1804.

Ussery Moore and his family were first discovered by studying the Moore families who appeared in the same Jones County, Georgia, neighborhood as members of the family of William and Mary Felts Hammack and in the same Wilkes County, Georgia, neighborhood in which Simeon Hammack married Elizabeth Jane Moore in 1820. This technique meant studying not only census records but also tax digests to learn which Moores might have temporarily lived in the area for a few years between census enumerations as well as Moores who lived in the community for a longer time. When all information was gathered and analyzed, clear evidence of a migration from Brunswick and Lunenburg Counties, Virginia, to Wilkes County, Georgia, and surrounding counties, and then to Jones and Crawford Counties, Georgia, emerged. The migration appears to have occurred in three stages. First, about 1785-1793, one group of Lunenburgers settled in western Wilkes County. These included members of the family of Sanders Ray and Robert and Millenor Hammack, as well as possibly Robert Moore (husband of Betsey Edwards) and John Moore, Sr. (husband of Jean Irwin and Susannah Walker) as well as David Moore and John and Mary Moore. These individuals seem to have all known one another and to have had pre-existing social, economic, and family connections that ante-dated their migration to Georgia.

A second wave of migration occurred in 1804 and 1805. Ussery Moore and his offspring left Lunenburg County for Wilkes County, Georgia, sometimes in 1804. Ussery might already have had older, grown offspring or siblings living in Wilkes County. In 1804, Ussery and several children -- apparently including son Robert, son James Wilborn, son John, Jr., son Bishop, son Matthew, and daughter Elizabeth -- moved to Wilkes County, where Ussery lived most of the rest of his life. With them was Charles Fallin and his son, John Hobson Fallin, a son-in-law of Jesse Moore of Lunenburg. They all settled in the southwestern corner of Wilkes County in the region that ultimately became Taliaferro County -- Georgia Militia District 172, then located along the boundary with Warren County and near the line with Greene County. Both earlier Robert Moores, John Moore (husband of Jane Irwin and Susannah Walker), Sanders Ray, Jacob Ray (who married Nancy Hammack), and Robert and Millenor (Jackson) Hammack were all well established residents of the community, having lived there for a decade or more when Ussery and his family arrived. Prominent citizens of this community included Andrew B. Stephens -- father of Confederate Vice President Alexander Hamilton Stephens -- and Stephens's brother-in-law Robert Grier, the Justice of the Peace who performed many local marriages -- including that of Simeon Hammack and Elizabeth Jane Moore -- and who also founded *Grier's Almanac.*

A third wave of migration took place a decade later, about 1815. At that time, Elisha Moore, a son of Jesse Moore of Lunenburg County and a nephew of Ussery Moore, moved with his wife Elizabeth Gee

first Ann (living April 1767) and second Jane (living 1782). Mason Bishop appears consistently in Brunswick County records from at least 1744 until he wrote his will in 1782. The will was recorded 24 February 1783, including bequests to wife Jane and children: Hannah Garratt, Susannah Tarpley, Martha Moore, Lucy Thomason, Rebecca Lewis, William Bishop, Matthew Bishop, Mary Reese, and Sarah Oldham. Also mentioned were Mary Thompson and John Garratt. Captain John Bishop (whose name was often spelled Bishopp) was a man of considerable prominence in Virginia before 1650 and had marital ties to George Menefie and Roger Booker, other leading men in the colony. See B. B. Weisiger, *Prince George Co., VA, Records, 1713-1728*, pp. 13, 33, 79, for the wills of John and Sarah Bishop. See Brunswick Co., VA, Order Book 2, p. 386, for the will of Mason Bishop. Additional information on the earlier Bishop lineage is found in Dorman, *Adventurers*, pp. 487-488, and Fleet, *Virginia Colonial Abstracts* (1988).

Moore and their family to the same community in Wilkes County where Ussery Moore and his family were living. John Bentley, son of Mildred Hammack Bentley, and George Amos and wife Anney Bentley Amos, sister of John, also arrived in the neighborhood about the same time, fresh migrants from Lunenburg County. In all likelihood, the three families made the 300-mile trip together.

Based on deed, census, tax, estate, and marriage records, it would appear that the following Moores in Wilkes, Taliaferro and Jones Counties were closely related. Ussery Moore and Elisha Moore had fairly unique names and left a clear paper trail in Lunenburg County, Virginia, documenting their move to the Georgia frontier. Evidence concerning Robert Moore (husband of Betsey Edwards) and Robert Moore of Taliaferro (husband of Martha [-----]) and John Moore, Sr. (husband of Jane Irwin and Susannah Walker) is compelling, but exactly how they fit into the family is still unclear. Further study of Lunenburg tax lists from c. 1795 to c. 1807 and Lunenburg Court order books from c. 1775 - c. 1804 may help clarify the situation. It appears that both of these Robert Moores were in Georgia by 1793-1795 and that John Moore was in Georgia by 1796, when first taxed with the poll tax in Wilkes County. John probably came of age in 1796 and was hence born about 1775. It is entirely possible that he had been in Wilkes County for several years at that point, not appearing in tax lists because he was too young to pay the poll tax and was living in the household of his parents or other relatives. These men may have come from Lunenburg at the same time as Sanders Ray and others, possibly offspring of one of Ussery Moore's brothers or cousins who disappear from the Lunenburg records in the 1770s.

In reconstructing the Ussery Moore family, tax digests and secondary accounts were essential because Ussery left no will or estate settlement. Ussery Moore also owned no property in Georgia except for a lot in Walton County that he drew in the 1820 land lottery and sold to Thomas Hutchins (stepson of John Irwin, and step-brother-in-law of James Wilburn Moore and John Moore, Sr.). Had he owned land when he died, that property would have generated a paper trail that might have identified his heirs; as it was, the legal record was silent at his demise.

Tax Digests, deed records, marriage records, census records, and evidence of common association and group migrations all played a role in reconstituting Ussery Moore's family. Helpful also were an account in *Memoirs of Georgia* (1895) stating that James Wilborn Moore, husband of Sarah Hammack and [-----] Irwin, was a son of Ussery Moore, and an account in Carolyn Williams's *History of Jones County, Georgia* which identifies Samuel Moore, Bishop Moore, and Joseph Moore as brothers who moved from "near Petersburg" Virginia to Wilkes and Jones Counties in the early 1800s.[945] In addition to James Wilborn Moore (married Sarah Hammack), Samuel Moore (married Christiana Hammack, daughter of Lewis Hammack and probable granddaughter of Sanders and Christiana Ray), Bishop Moore (husband of Sarah Ray, sister of Jacob Ray who married Nancy Hammack), and Joseph Moore (probably the otherwise unidentified man for whom James Wilborn Moore paid tax in Wilkes County), the evidence suggests several other offspring for Ussery Moore:

> Robert Moore (possibly born as early as 1771 in Virginia), who was living in Georgia in 1804, who married Martha Ray Moncrief (another sister of Jacob Ray), and who was taxed with 100 acres in Wilkes on Hardin's Creek before losing it in a court suit between c. 1818 and c. 1822, thereafter removing to Jones County (where he resided from c. 1823 to about 1841) and then Crawford County (where he resided from c. 1842 to after 1850), where in 1850 he was enumerated in the household of John Bentley (son of Daniel and Mildred Hammack Bentley of Lunenburg) and Martha (Moore) Bentley;

> Jincey Moore (born between 1775 and 1780 in Virginia), who married Samuel Kelley in Wilkes County (Kelley's family having been involved with the Hammacks since the

---

[945] Carolyn W. Williams, *History of Jones Co., GA, 1807-1907* (Macon, GA, 1957).

1790s) and moved to Jones County about 1820 and thereafter to Crawford County, Georgia;

John Moore (probably born about 1783 in Virginia), called "Junior," in almost all Wilkes County documents, who came of age about 1804 and probably married in 1805 Elizabeth Davis (possible sister of Nancy Davis, who married Elisha Smallwood, and was the grandmother of Milly Smallwood, who married William Hammack in Jones County) of Warren County;

Matthew Moore (born about 1790, Virginia), who married Mary Ray (daughter of Jacob Ray and Nancy Hammack) and moved to Jones County, Georgia, in the early 1820s;

and Elizabeth Moore (born between 1790 and 1795 in Virginia), who in 1813 married James Edge in Wilkes County and who remained in Taliaferro County near James Wilburn Moore and Robert Moore for the remainder of her life, dying there after 1860.

This group of individuals associated almost exclusively with one another and with other Lunenburg families in Wilkes and Jones Counties. Other than transactions involving siblings and their spouses, most associated families -- witnesses, grantors and grantees in deeds, et cetera -- included members of the Hammack, Ray, Edge, and Irwin families.

In addition to this group, Elisha Moore and Elizabeth Gee Moore of Taliaferro had close dealings with the Ussery Moore family. Elisha came to Georgia about 1815 as agent for Robert H. Bentley, one of the three children of Mildred Hammack and Daniel Bentley of Lunenburg, in a court suit to recover slaves that Mildred had taken along with or had allowed her son John to take to Wilkes County, Georgia.[946] This is the son John Bentley who appears in Wilkes tax digests before 1820 and who was in Wilkes and Jones Counties throughout the 1810s, 1820s, and 1830s before settling in Crawford County, Georgia. In 1850, John Bentley and wife Martha Moore Bentley were in Crawford County, and Robert Moore (aged seventy and born in Virginia) was living with them. This Robert Moore appears to be the son of Ussery and Martha Bishop Moore of Virginia; his date of birth is uncertain, but he was probably born about 1771. Martha Moore Bentley (born about 1795 in Virginia) was likely his eldest daughter.

Elisha Moore and Elizabeth Gee Moore lived near Ussery and family in Lunenburg and then in Wilkes County, Georgia; Elisha remained near James Wilborn Moore in Taliaferro County until he died, sharing ownership in Moore's Mill with Ussery's son James Wilborn Moore (husband of Sarah Hammack) and being involved in several land transactions with James Wilborn Moore and Elizabeth Davis Moore, widow of John Moore, Jr. Charles Fallin and John H. Fallin appear frequently in transactions with this group, and Charles Fallin, Jr., eventually married Sarah Edge, daughter of James and Elizabeth Moore Edge. Elisha Moore and Betsey Moore Fallin were children of Jesse Moore of Lunenburg, who had married first Susannah Peace and second Elizabeth Ann Peace. Jesse's third wife is unidentified, but Thomas family researchers maintain that she was Mary Thomas, sister of Martha Thomas who in 1789 married one Robert Moore in Lunenburg County, Virginia. Jesse's fourth wife was Rebecca Laffoon Matthews. After Jesse died in 1842, Rebecca moved to Taliaferro County, Georgia, with her only son by Jesse, John Robert Moore, who remained in Taliaferro for the remainder of his life.

It is interesting, and probably significant for Georgia events, that Jesse Moore's first two wives were sisters of Joseph Peace (husband of Elizabeth Garrett, sister of Jane (Garrett) Moore of Lunenburg, and niece of Martha (Bishop) Moore), of Lucy Peace who in 1799 married Littleberry Moore in Brunswick (one Littleberry Moore appears in Taliaferro County, Georgia, c. 1830 - c. 1840), and of John Peace, who

---

[946] Wilkes Co., GA, DB CCC, p. 42.

died leaving an only daughter, Lucy Peace, wife of Hugh Hammack of Lunenburg County, Virginia. Hence, when Ussery Moore and family settled in Wilkes County in 1804 and when Elisha Moore and family settled there a decade later, they were rejoining friends and relatives who were members of the parent community in Lunenburg and who had settled in Georgia during the previous two decades. The Moores and Hammacks were hardly strangers when Ussery Moore settled along Hardin's and Williams's Creek in 1804; rather, they had been in almost constant association since about 1750.

Given his singular name, Ussery Moore is a somewhat easier figure to follow than his father Robert Moore, Jr. Ussery is listed on the 1769 Lunenburg County, Virginia, Tithables list, indicating that he was born in 1748.[947] The second reference to him dates from the same time period; significantly, the listing also includes the name of Robert Hammack, and it indicates that both Hammack and Moore had left Lunenburg County:

Anthony Street's List of Insolvents, taken 9 November 1770 and compiled for the year 1769:[948]

List I:

Insolvents's Names	Bad	Returns
James Elmoore	1	**Removed**
Jno. Gunn	1	No effects Come at
Wm. Hall	1	not known
Robert Hammock	1	**Removed**

List II:

Jno. Moore junr. *not Gent. Jno.*	1	**not known**
[skip four names]		
Ussery Moore	1	**Removed**

On 23 June 1776, Ussery Moore purchased sixty-two acres on Cedar Creek in Brunswick County from Thomas and Susannah Tarpley; Susannah Tarpley and Martha Moore, Ussery's wife, were daughters of Matthew Bishop of Brunswick.[949] This deed probably followed the marriage, for it appears that Ussery Moore's eldest offspring were born in the early 1770s. Three years later, Ussery sold to John Tarpley a fifty-acre tract adjacent Christopher Hinton's land on the county line; his brothers-in-law Matthew Bishop and Thomas Tarpley witnessed the deed.[950]

By 1782, Ussery Moore had returned to Lunenburg County, where he appears on both the land tax and the personal property tax rolls for that year; he owned 175 acres of land at that time and headed a household including only one male -- himself -- over the age of twenty-one years. Lunenburg's 1783 tax list shows that Ussery headed a family consisting of "seven white souls" and no blacks; of this number,

---

[947] 1769 Lunenburg Co., VA, Tithables List, The Library of Virginia, Richmond, VA.

[948] There are actually two lists, one of about seventy individuals initially compiled on which the names of Robert Hammock and James Gunn are found, and then one of a further twenty-four individuals, this group appearing roughly in alphabetical order, on which the names of John Moore, Jr., and Ussery Moore appear. I am grateful to Carolyn Hardin Goudie for sharing this list with me in 1996. It was found in Lunenburg County Judgments/Causes determined - Box 27 - in a bundle labeled "1764 - 1789". Also found was a list of sheriffs costs returned by Anthony Street. The list was apparently compiled to assist with collecting judgement awarded by the court; Moore and Hammock had apparently left the county by the time the judgments were issued. Both may have moved into Brunswick County for a time as Ussery Moore appears there during the 1770s.

[949] Brunswick Co., VA, DB 12, p. 236.

[950] Brunswick Co., VA, DB 13, p. 331. Note that Ann Moore Hinton was probably a daughter of Robert and Rachel Moore. Ussery paid £25 for sixty-two acres but sold the tract in 1779 for £1 per acre.

there was only one tithable, himself, the only white male over age twenty-one. The record is significant, for it suggests that Ussery and Martha had five children at this point. One can posit the births of these offspring as follows: 1779-1781, 1777-1779, 1775-1777, 1773-1775, and 1771-1773 -- all consistent with a man who came of age about 1769.[951]

From 1782 to 1803, Ussery Moore was consistently taxed with 175 acres of land in Lunenburg; after 1784, he also paid tax on one slave -- a woman named Bett -- who was probably the slave Bettey that Mason Moore left his daughter Martha Bishop Moore in 1783.[952] Ussery and James Moore, along with Hugh Hammack, witnessed a 1787 deed from John Meredith to Josiah Reese[953], and in 1789 both were mentioned as neighbors in deeds from Richard Ferguson to John Potts and from John Potts to George Potts.[954] In 1791, Robert Moore -- probably Ussery's father -- deeded 100 acres on Cedar Creek to Jesse Moore; the tract was described as lying adjacent land of Ussery Moore. Robert's wife Mary Moore signed the deed, and another David and Mary Moore witnessed it.[955]

Ussery Moore appears regularly in property tax lists for Lunenburg from 1782 to 1803 as well as in the land tax. A significant occurrence took place, however, between the timing of the 1791 and 1792 listings. In the latter document, Ussery was taxed with two free white males over age twenty-one, whereas until that point he had been taxed with only one. This document suggests that Ussery's eldest son -- probably Robert Moore, born about 1771 -- had just come of age and was still living at home with his father. Ussery was taxed with two adult males in 1793 and with three in 1794 and 1795. By 1796, Ussery was taxed with only two white males, suggesting that one of his sons had begun living independently at this point.[956]

Ussery and John Moore and James Parrish, Sr., witnessed the will of James Thompson in 1794[957]; a 1796 deed from Parrish to Ralph Maddox lists Ussery Moore as a neighbor.[958] In 1801, Ussery Moore, Jesse Moore, Samuel Peace, and Hugh Hammock (Peace and Hammock were related to Jesse Moore by marriage) served as jurors when William Mize and his daughter Louisa were charged with murder.[959]

Although the records are not clear, one senses that Ussery's circumstances may have changed for the worse after 1800. In 1801, with Theodorick Love as trustee, he mortgaged Bettey -- the slave left his wife Martha in 1783 by her father Mason Bishop -- and a Negroe boy Dick -- probably Bettey's son -- to James MacFarlane and Company.[960] The mortgage is puzzling, for it suggests that Ussery had debts he could not pay or that he needed cash for some business venture. The following year, Samuel Peace deeded to him for £1 and fifteen shillings -- surely a token sum -- the tract of 175 acres on which he had been living for two decades. Apparently Ussery had leased the land from Peace and been paying for the property gradually in anticipation of outright ownership. Located on Cedar Creek, the land was adjacent property owned by Jesse Moore, Hugh Hammock, James Parrish, and James Moore, to whom Samuel Peace also conveyed 125 acres on the same day.[961] Perhaps Ussery Moore had mortgaged the slaves in an effort to secure the remaining money needed to settle his debt to Peace.

Whatever the reason, Ussery Moore's days in Lunenburg were numbered. On 10 April 1804, he conveyed sixteen acres adjacent Hugh Hammock to Jesse Moore for £16; tax rolls for 1804 show that he thereafter paid tax on only 159 acres of the former 175-acre tract. Then, on 10 August 1804, Ussery

---

[951] 1782 Lunenburg Co., VA, Land Tax List; 1782-1783 Lunenburg Co., VA, Personal Property Tax Lists, The Library of Virginia, Richmond, VA.

[952] 1782-1804 Lunenburg Co., VA, Personal Property Tax Lists, The Library of Virginia, Richmond, VA.

[953] Lunenburg Co., VA, Deed Book 14, p. 420.

[954] Lunenburg Co., VA, Deed Book 15, pp. 413, 423.

[955] Lunenburg Co., VA, Deed Book 16, p. 123.

[956] 1782-1803 Lunenburg Co., VA, Personal Property Tax Lists, The Library of Virginia, Richmond, VA.

[957] Lunenburg Co., VA, Wills, Book 4, p. 60.

[958] Lunenburg Co., VA, Deed Book 17, p. 123.

[959] Lunenburg Co., VA, DB 19, p. 2.

[960] Lunenburg Co., VA, Deed Book 19, p. 45.

[961] Lunenburg Co., VA, Deed Book 19, 1801-04, p. 120.

Moore -- "of Lunenburg County, Virginia" -- conveyed 169 acres in Lunenburg to John Peace for 103 pounds, one shilling, and four pence. William Peace, Joseph Peace, and Littleberry Moore witnessed the deed.[962] This reference is the last one to Ussery Moore known to exist in Lunenburg County; he presumably moved in the following months to Wilkes County, Georgia, where in 1806 he was taxed with no land and two slaves -- perhaps Bettey and Dick from the 1802 deed.

It seems likely that Ussery's sons Robert, James, and John may have preceded him to Georgia. The evidence suggests that Ussery may have been planning a move for some time, sending his older sons in advance while he mortgaged his slaves to pay off his land deed and then worked for another two years to satisfy his obligation to MacFarlane and Company. With the exception of a tract drawn in Georgia's 1820 land lottery, Ussery seems never to have owned land in Georgia, and he probably lived on the tracts owned by his sons.

Ussery Moore was taxed in Wilkes County until 1822.[963] Ussery was enumerated in the 1820 Wilkes County census and taxed in Wilkes County in 1820 and 1821; also in 1820 he drew land lot 58, land district 1[964], in newly created Walton County, a tract for which he was taxed in 1821 before selling it to Thomas Hutchins on 16 July 1821.[965]

No record of Ussery Moore has been found after 1822; he presumably died about that time. Martha Moore, widow of a Revolutionary soldier, registered for the 1827 Georgia land lottery as a resident of Jones County.[966] She may have been the female, aged 70-80, enumerated near Bishop Moore in Joseph Moore's Jones County household in 1830. It is possible that she was the Martha Moore enumerated in Jones County at the time of the 1840 census.[967]

The offspring of Ussery Moore have not been documented, but the research summarized here suggests that he fathered a large family. Key sources for identifying his children include the 1783 Lunenburg tax listing indicating that Ussery and Martha Moore then had five children, Wilkes and Jones County, Georgia, tax digests from 1800 to 1830, Wilkes and Jones County, Georgia, marriage records from 1800 to 1830, and the network of associations observed in Virginia and Georgia during these years. As noted above, Robert Moore (c. 1771 -- aft. 1850) was probably Ussery's eldest son; he may be the Robert Moore who married Martha Thomas in Lunenburg County, Virginia, on 5 November 1789, with Robert Moore, Sr., as security.[968] Based on the 1783 listing, there were probably four additional children born before 1783. These likely included Jenny Moore (c. 1780 -- before 1848, Crawford Co., GA), who

---

[962] Lunenburg Co., VA, Deed Book 20, p. 88A.

[963] Ussery may have briefly lived in Jones County. One "Tusley" Moore -- otherwise unidentified -- drew land in Dooly County in 1821 as a resident of Cabaniss' District, Jones County.

[964] 1820 Georgia Land Lottery Papers, Fortunate Drawers, Georgia Department of Archives and History, Morrow, GA.

[965] Walton Co., GA, Deed Book A/B, p. 148.

[966] F. M. Abbott, *History of the People of Jones Co., GA* (16 vols., Macon, GA, 1977), 11: 35.

[967] 1840 Jones Co., GA, Census, p. 145. If this were in fact Martha Bishop Moore, she was nearly 90 years old, while this Martha Moore was shown as aged 60-70. Given the evidentiary problems associated with census enumerations, however, such an error is possible. This Martha was then living very near other members of the Ussery Moore family group. She could, however, be a widow of another relative of Ussery Moore.

[968] Martha was living in 1795, when she and Robert Moore joined her siblings in deeding property bequeathed to them by their brother John Thomas of Nottoway County. Martha's siblings included: Mary Thomas, wife of Jesse Moore; Spencer Thomas, husband of Nancy Stanback; Elizabeth Thomas, wife of William Overstreet; William Thomas, husband of Eliza Bass; David Thomas, husband of Martha Hurt; Joshua Thomas, husband of Patsy Chappell; John Thomas (c. 1760/62 -- bef. 1795); Robert Thomas, husband of Sallie Wilkes; Samuel Thomas (aft. 1756 -- 1791/95); Woodlief Thomas, husband of Sarah Williams; and Athanatius Thomas. Several of these children moved to Davidson and Williamson Counties, TN, while others remained in Lunenburg and Nottoway Counties, Virginia. They were children of Samuel Thomas (1728 - 1791) and Susannah Woodlief (1730/32 - 1801). John was a son of John and Sarah Thomas who moved from Gloucester Co., VA, to Amelia Co., VA, about 1739 and a grandson of Samuel Thomas and Mary Spencer of Gloucester Co., VA. Susannah "Sukey" Woodlief Thomas was a daughter of Joshua Woodlief (c. 1694 - bef. 1746) of Prince George Co., VA, and a granddaughter of John Woodlief (c. 1650 - c. 1737) and Mary Wynn, daughter of Robert and Mary Wynn. John's grandfather John Woodlief had immigrated from Buckinghamshire to Virginia; that John's father, Drew Woodliffe, was implicated in the murder of the English playwright Christopher Marlow. For additional data on the Woodlief family, see Dorman, *Adventurers*, 4: 705-712.

married Samuel Kelly (c. 1784 -- aft. 1850, Crawford Co., GA) in Wilkes County in 1816; the 1820, 1830, and 1840 census reports consistently indicate that Jenny was older than Samuel and born between 1775 and 1780. John Moore (by 1783 -- c. 1825) was probably also one of these children; possibly one of the first of the Ussery Moore clan to migrate to Georgia, John was taxed in Wilkes County in 1804 before marrying Elizabeth Davis in Warren County in 1805. The fourth and fifth children of Ussery Moore born before 1783 may have been daughters; one of these daughters seems still to have been living at home, unmarried, as late as 1820, while the other may have married about the time the family settled in Georgia, but no firm evidence to identify these children has been found.

Given that Ussery Moore moved to Georgia after 10 August 1804 but before the time of the assessment for the 1806 Wilkes Co., GA, tax digest, any male offspring of Ussery Moore born after 1785 should have appeared in Wilkes County, Georgia, tax digests as they came of age. Thus we can identify Bishop Moore (c. 1785 - 1844), James Wilborn Moore (c. 1787 - aft. 1850), Matthew Moore (c. 1789 - c. 1852), Samuel Moore (c. 1797 - aft. 1820), Joseph Moore (c. 1800 - aft. 1830)[969], and perhaps Charles Moore (c. 1788 -- aft. 1850)[970] as probable offspring of Ussery Moore. It seems likely, also, that Ussery was the father of Elizabeth Moore (c. 1791, Lunenburg County, Virginia -- after 1860, Taliaferro Co., GA), who married James Edge on 31 March 1813 in Wilkes County. James Edge appears near Ussery Moore in Wilkes County tax records, and he and Elizabeth lived near James Wilburn Moore in Taliaferro County.

At the time of the 1820 Wilkes County, Georgia, Census, Ussery's household consisted only of himself and two women aged over forty-five years, presumably Martha Bishop Moore and an unmarried daughter born prior to 1775. Thus, considering the cumulative sum of the evidence, one may be reasonably confident that one has correctly identified the sons, and at least two of the daughters, of Ussery Moore; it is possible that Ussery Moore fathered one or more daughters whose identities have not been learned, but the listing proposed may be correct without addition.

Considering the offspring of Ussery Moore and Martha Bishop, several interesting connections emerge that prove significant for the marriage of Simeon Hammack to Elizabeth Jane Moore in 1820. First, Robert Moore (who may have married Martha Thomas in 1789) married second, sometimes in late 1805 or early 1806, Martha Ray Moncrief, widow of Samuel Moncrief and probable daughter-in-law of Josiah Moncrief (whose second wife Elizabeth Hammack was Simeon Hammack's aunt)[971]. Bishop Moore married Sarah Ray, sister of Martha Ray Moncrief. Matthew Moore married Mary Ray, daughter of Jacob Ray and Nancy Hammack. Jacob Ray was another brother of Martha Ray Moncrief Moore and Sarah Ray Moore; Nancy Hammack Ray was a sister of Elizabeth Hammack Moncrief and another aunt of Simeon Hammack. James Wilborn Moore married as his second wife Sarah Hammack, sister of Simeon Hammack; he had been first married to a daughter of David Irwin, by whom he had several older children. Samuel Moore married Christiana Hammack, daughter of Lewis and Elizabeth Hammack; Christiana was named for Christiana Ray, wife of Sanders Ray, and mother of Martha Ray Moncrief Moore, Sarah Ray Moore, and Jacob Ray. Jenny Moore married Samuel Kelley, whose sister Nancy Kelley in 1804 married Ussery Ray. Many of these individuals, or their offspring, moved to Crawford County, Georgia, where they were neighbors of Robert Moore and Martha Ray Moncrief Moore and of Simeon Hammack and Elizabeth Jane Moore Hammack.

---

[969] Note that in 1825 James Wilburn Moore was taxed for himself and for Joseph Moore.

[970] Charles Moore (c. 1788, Virginia -- after 1850, Taliaferro County, Georgia), m. 22 December 1813, Warren County, Georgia, Elizabeth Ellington. He appears first in Wilkes Co., GA, in the same district as Ussery Moore lived, although he appears consistently near Robert Moore (husband of another Martha, and father of Anderson), who is known to have had only one child, Anderson Moore. Elizabeth Edge also appears near Charles and Robert in tax digests. Charles married Elizabeth Ellington -- also of a Lunenburg family -- and had a son Wellborn Moore, born 1817. Thus far, all references to the name Welborn or Wilborn found in the Moore family group relate to descendants of Ussery Moore and his son James Wilburn Moore.

[971] The marriage of Martha Ray and Samuel Moncrief took place in 1793 with one Robert Moore as witness.

Based on the available evidence, the writer has concluded that Elizabeth Jane Hammack Moore was a daughter of Robert Moore, eldest son of Ussery and Martha Bishop Moore. Robert was born between 1770 and 1780 in Virginia; if he were the adult son living with Ussery Moore between 1792 and 1795, he was probably born in 1771. As noted, he may be the Robert Moore who married Martha Thomas in 1789 in Lunenburg County, Virginia, although this is by no means conclusive.[972] It does appear, however, that Robert Moore was married before about 1795, when his first known child was born. It was probably this wife who accompanied him to Georgia, dying shortly before his marriage to Martha Ray Moncrief in 1805.

With so many Robert Moores in Lunenburg in the 1790s, it is difficult to identify this man positively; he does not appear to have owned land, although he may be one of the Robert Moores who appears in Lunenburg Personal Property tax lists after 1790 and before 1804.[973]

Of the Lunenburg Moores who moved to Wilkes County after 1800, John Moore -- called Junior to distinguish him from another John Moore in the same neighborhood -- was in Georgia by 13 June 1804. He seems to have been the first of the group to travel south. Robert Moore may have been the next, leaving Lunenburg in 1804 and arriving in Georgia later that year, in time to be taxed in Gammage's district in 1805 as a defaulter. Within months of this event, Robert Moore's first wife seems to have died, and he remarried to a local widow, Martha Ray Moncrief.

Martha Ray Moncrief was a daughter of Sanders and Christiana Ray. In the 1790s, Sanders Ray had left his family in Georgia and relocated to southwestern Alabama, where he settled in Washington

---

[972] There were three other adult Robert Moores living in Wilkes County before 1800. One of them also had a wife named Martha. At least two of the other three Robert Moores seem to have been from Lunenburg. Hence, there were several contemporary Robert Moores, any one of whom could have married Martha Thomas. There seem to have been three Robert Moores in Lunenburg who were all about the same age: Robert, son of David, who was mentioned without a guardian in a 1787 court document; Robert, son of Ussery, who was born in the 1770s; and Robert, probable son of Robert (b. 1729), who may be the Robert appearing in Wilkes - Warren Counties from 1793 on. Robert Moore (1729 - aft. 1797) was also in Lunenburg at the time, but he had a wife named Mary at the approximate time when Robert Moore married Martha Thomas.

[973] The following personal property tax listings for men named Robert Moore have been found in Lunenburg after 1790:

1789	Robert Moore	2 adult tithables
1790	Robert Moore	1 adult tithable
1791	Robert Moore	1 adult tithable
1792	Robert Moore	1 adult tithable
1793	Robert Moore	1 adult tithable
1794	Robert Moore	2 adult tithables
1795	Robert Moore	2 adult tithables
1796	Robert Moore	2 adult tithables
1797	Robert Moore	2 adult tithables
1798	Not shown	
1799	Not shown	
1800	Not shown	
1801	Robert Moore (Cedar)	1 adult tithable
1802	Not shown	
1803	Not shown	
1804	Not shown	
1805	Not shown	
1806	Robert Moore	1 adult tithable
1807	Robert Moore	1 adult tithable

The 1806 and 1807 Robert Moores appear to be Robert of Stoney Creek, who was taxed with several slaves in both enumerations. Note that the number of tithables referred to men over age sixteen. The Robert taxed in 1789, 1790, 1791, 1794, 1795, and 1797 had no blacks over age sixteen in his household, while the Robert taxed in 1792, 1793, and 1796 did. The explanation may be that these were hired workers.

County.[974] There he acquired a tract of land which passed to his heirs when he died about 1806. On 7 October 1808, an instrument was filed in Washington County, Alabama, concerning this property:

> We, John Moore and Jane his wife, Robert Moore and Martha his wife, Bishop Moore and Sarah his wife, Kitty Ray widow of the deceased Sanders Ray, Ussery Ray son of the deceased Sanders Ray, appoint Jacob Ray, co-heir with us and representative of the said Sanders Ray, our attorney. In testimony whereof we have herewith set our hands and affixed our seals.

The instrument was signed by John Moore, Jane Moore, Robert Moore, Martha Moore, Bishop Moore, Sarah Moore, Kitty Ray, and Ussery Ray. William Thompson and James Patterson, both Justices of the Peace, witnessed the instrument.[975] Although no record of the marriage of Robert Moore and Martha Moncrief is known to exist, the marriage must have taken place in 1805 or 1806. At the time of the 1805 Wilkes County, Georgia, tax digest, Martha Moncrief was shown as a resident of Captain Hendricks's District in that portion of Wilkes County later known as militia district 170. Martha was taxed with 100 acres of land on Hardin's Creek joining Ogletree and granted to an unknown person. In 1806, Robert Moore paid tax on this same tract of land, which he owned for more than a decade. Thus, Robert Moore must have married Martha Moncrief at some time between the dates when the 1805 and 1806 digests were compiled. Robert was taxed with this tract consistently until 1818; the digests for 1816 to 1818 all indicate that the land was drawn by W. Parker and bounded variously by J. Edwards, R. Towns, and J. Harden.

On 15 July 1819, describing themselves as "Robert Moore, Jr., and wife Martha Moore," Robert and Martha conveyed this 100-acre tract to Henry B. Thompson as security for twenty notes worth $25, each payable 1 November 1819. The land was described as "a certain tract of land in Wilkes County, waters of Hardin's Creek, adjoining lands of John Gresham, Uriah Farmer, and the widow Edwards, containing 100 acres,[976] being the place whereon I now live." In addition to the property itself, Moore conveyed "all the crop of corn and cotton with the profits arising from the same for the present year, also two grey mares, two colts, one horse cart, five head of cattle, fourteen head of hogs, fifteen head of sheep, ten geese, one gin stone, four feather beds and furniture, one cupboard, one chest, two trunks, five pots, one kettle, one slides, one pair stillyards, one loom, two tables, ten chairs, two wash tubs, four pails, two men's saddles, and other property." The land and personal property were both to be forfeited if the notes were not repaid with legal interest by 1st November 1819.[977] Robert Moore signed the document, and Martha Moore

---

[974] Sanders Ray was recorded on the 1797 census in the Spanish Territory of San Esteban de Tombeche, later Mississippi and Alabama. At that time, he had a wife and two children living with him. Some believe that Sanders Ray was also the father of Elizabeth Ray, who may have married Lewis Hammack. Lewis Hammack signed as surety for the marriage of Solomon Ray, son of George Ray, to Jane Echols in 1796. Lewis's sister Nancy married Jacob Ray. Lewis Hammack named a son Jacob Hammack and a daughter Christiana Hammack. It does appear that Sanders Ray had additional offspring not named in the 1808 deed, for on 10 October 1801 Sanders Ray and son Jonas Ray were granted passports to travel to the Tombigbee Settlement. See Davidson, *Early Records*, 1: 138, 145, and 299, for more on Sanders and Christiana Ray.

[975] Washington Co., AL, Deed Book A, p. 203.

[976] The 1816 digest described Robert Moore's 100 acres on Hardin's Creek as adjacent John Edwards.

[977] Wilkes Co., GA, DB EEE, p. 264.

signed by mark.[978] Witnesses to the document were Jane (X) Mulkey,[979] Samuel Moncrief,[980] and Robert Grier, JP.[981]

Robert Moore retained legal ownership of this tract for a couple of additional years. He was taxed with this tract in 1819 and 1820, but, on 7 March 1820, William Smith, Sheriff of Wilkes County, sold seventy acres of the tract to Bishop Moore for $56. The deed stipulates that "whereas Uriah Farmer, constable in one of the districts of the said county levied sundry executions issued from a Justices Court on a certain tract of land in the said county containing seventy acres more or less on the waters of Hardin's Creek, joining Uriah Farmer and the said Executor being in the name of Robert Simpson[982] versus Robert Moore's land, the said tract of land being levied on as the said Robert's property to satisfy the executions and the said land being returned to me by the said Uriah Farmer Constable." Farmer confirmed that Moore owned no property other than this tract. Sheriff William Smith then took control of the tract and sold it at public auction. Richard Willis and Robert Grier, J.P., witnessed the deed.[983] Shortly afterwards, on 23 January 1821, Bishop Moore of Wilkes conveyed the land to Henry B. Thompson of Warren County for $90. In the deed the tract is described as located on the "waters of Hardin's Creek, adj. Uriah Farmer, Mrs. Edwards, and others, it being the tract of land sold at sheriff's sale on the first Tuesday in December Eighteen hundred and nineteen as the property of Robert Moore containing fifty acres more or less, it being one half of the tract of land on which the above mentioned Robert Moore now lives....." J. H. Bradley and Abner Darden witnessed the deed, testifying in 1822 before Justice Aaron Grier that they witnessed Bishop Moore affix his signature. Robert Moore was still taxed with the tract in 1821, but he is not found on any subsequent Wilkes County digest.[984]

It is clear by 1821 that Robert Moore had lost most, if not all, of his tract, probably as a result of the growing indebtedness he was experiencing in 1819. At the time of the 1820 census, he was enumerated in Wilkes with a large family -- five sons born between 1802 and 1820, and two daughters born during the

---

[978] Note that this is the only document identifying this Robert Moore's wife. Robert of Taliaferro County, in earlier documents called "Robert Moore, Sr.", was older than this Robert. The 1830 census indicates that Robert of Taliaferro was born between 1760 and 1770, whereas Robert of Wilkes, Jones, and Crawford Counties was born between 1770 and 1780. This land also seems to be the 100 acre tract owned by the younger Robert Moore. He had lost this land by about 1822, when he moves to Jones County.

[979] William Parker, to whom Robert Moore's 100 acres was originally granted, died about 1805, leaving his second wife as widow. His offspring included Delilah Parker Gammage, Nancy Parker, and Jesse Parker. Jesse Parker died about 1816 with Jacob Ray as his administrator. James Mulkey was guardian of the Parker orphans. John Mulkey had married Annis Parker, daughter of William, in 1793. William Parker had m. (2) 24 October 1792 Mary Cripp/Crief/Grief. There was some Parker - Moncrief connection as is evidenced by Wilkes County deeds and the use of a common and unusual given name by both families -- Maesey.

[980] Samuel Moncrief who married Martha Ray in 1793 died about 1803. This younger Samuel was a member of the same family, probably a son or nephew of the older Samuel.

[981] Robert Grier was a local Justice of the Peace and founder of *Grier's Almanac*. He performed the marriage of Simeon Hammack and Elizabeth Jane Moore in 1820.

[982] This is the only evidence of an association between the Simpson and Moore families located thus far, but it is interesting that Robert Moore apparently named a son Simpson Moore. The origins of the Simpson family have not been investigated, but the will of John Nelson may be relevant. Nelson wrote his will 15 December 1808 in Wilkes County naming grandsons John and Charles, son of deceased son William, and daughter-in-law Elizabeth Nelson, relict of deceased son William. Annexed to the will was a statement appointing nephews William Simpson, Robert Simpson, and David Simpson executors. Archibald Simpson, Charles Phillips, and Samuel Rice witnessed the will. (Davidson, *Early Records*, 1: 49.) Note that at least one secondary source identifies the wife of James Stewart, son of Henry Stewart (who is discussed in a later chapter), as Margaret Nelson.

[983] Wilkes Co., GA, DB FFF, pp. 22-24.

[984] The deed refers to the property as "being one half of the tract of land on which the above mentioned Robert Moore now lives." This would appear to be the 100 acre tract on which Robert Moore was taxed 1806 - 1821. This evidence suggests that this is the Robert Moore who in 1827 drew land in Muscogee County as a resident of Jones County; who was taxed on that land in Jones as late as 1833; who was taxed with the same land, then in Marion County, in 1835; and who was in Jones County in 1840 and in Crawford County in 1850. This information is important, for it distinguishes this Robert Moore from another man with the same name resident in the same area. The other Robert Moore -- who owned 218.5 acres on Harden's Creek and continues after 1821 to appear in Wilkes tax digests -- apparently remained there, fell into Taliaferro County, died there between 1830 and 1840, and was survived by a wife Martha, whose 1841 will bequeaths property to her son Anderson E. Moore and grandchildren. Her will is consistent with having only one son, an individual born 1805 - 1810, in the 1820 and 1830 census reports. That individual would be Anderson E. Moore, born c. 1807/1809, who in 1833 married Nancy Peek in Taliaferro County.

same time period. Robert and wife Martha were both shown as being aged between 26 and 45 years, indicating a birth around 1775. Robert Moore has not been located between 1823 and 1826, although he may have settled in Jones County as early as 1822.[985] By 1826, both Robert and Bishop Moore had settled in Jones County, however. At that time, they were living in Captain Thomas Davis's District, where Bishop Moore was taxed with five slaves, 120 acres on Wolf Creek in Jones County, and 250 acres in Rabun County. Robert Moore's name appears adjacent that of his brother, but he was taxed only with the poll tax, indicating that he then owned no property. The two men were listed alongside Allen Felts, probable brother of Mary Felts Hammack. In adjoining Hammack's District were Simeon Hammack, John Bentley, Matthew Moore, and many other members of the Hammack family. Robert Moore, Bishop Moore, Samuel Kelley, and Allen Felts were all shown as neighbors in Thomas Low's District in 1827; Moore still owned no taxable property.[986]

At the time of the 1827 Georgia Land Lottery, Robert Moore of Davis's District, Jones County, Georgia, drew land lot 196, land district 3, Muscogee County. This land was taken from Georgia's Creek cession and lay in the southwestern portion of the state. Originally a large county, Muscogee County today is located along the boundary between Georgia and Alabama, which is marked by the Chattahoochee River. The portion of Muscogee in which Robert Moore's tract lay, however, soon became a new county, Marion, located east of the present Muscogee County.[987]

About this time, many members of the Hammack, Moore, and kindred families began migrating to Crawford County, Georgia. As noted previously, William Hammack's widow, Mary Felts Hammack, settled there about this time, and she was soon followed by Simeon Hammack and her other offspring. Bishop and Matthew Moore never left Jones County, but John Bentley -- son of Mildred Hammack Bentley and son-in-law of Robert Moore -- did. Bentley was still in Jones County in 1830, at which time he was taxed with 175 acres on Wolf Creek in Jones County and 202.5 acres in District 12 of Lee County.

Robert Moore likely left Jones County between 1827 and 1832, probably settling for a time on the land he had drawn in the land lottery. He has not been identified in the 1830 census or in Jones County tax digests for this period.[988] He was back in Jones County by 1832, when he registered for the state land lottery as a resident of that county.[989] The 1835 Jones County tax digest, Cox's District, GMD 459, shows John Bentley and Robert Moore as neighbors. Moore was taxed with land lot 196, land district 3, the lot he had drawn in 1827.[990] Robert Moore, again taxed with the Marion County tract, Ussery Moore (probably Robert's son), and John Bentley were all in Cox's District in 1836. In 1837, Simpson Moore -- who had since 1835 appeared in neighboring district 359 -- was taxed with 140 acres in his own name, 202.5 acres in Marion County, land district 3, land lot 46, belonging to Ussery Moore, and 202.5 acres in

---

[985] Tax digests for this period are incomplete, and much of the 1823 digest -- including the districts where the Moores and Hammacks lived -- is missing.

[986] Matthew Moore, Simeon Hammack, and John Bentley were in adjoining Weldon's District, the area called Hammack's District in 1826.

[987] 1827 Georgia Land Lottery Records, Fortunate Drawers, Georgia Department of Archives and History, Morrow, GA.

[988] Those Robert Moores indexed for the 1830 Georgia census were examined. None fits. Robert Moore of Clarke County was aged 20-30 with three males 0-5 and one 5-10 and one female 20-30 (1830 Clarke Co., GA, Census, p. 321.) Robert H. Moore, also of Clarke County (p. 316), was aged 20-30 with females aged 0-5, 15-20, 40-50. Robert Moore of Walton County was aged 50-60 with a son aged 20-30 and one female aged 50-60, one female aged 15-20, and one aged 20-30. Neighbors included Israel Moore, Charles Broach, Joseph James, Christopher Ross, John Bailey, Jesse C. Pawlet, Nancy Chappell, William Dillard, Samuel Lee, Nathan Whitley, Winston Bennett, David Myres, Terrey Comby, Timothy Bradford, Thomas B. Moon, Moses Park, Elisha Ellis, Jesse Barber, James Scott, Henry Butts, Richard Cox, James Bentley, John Grammell, Hiram Williams, Eli Bentsch, and Benjamin Woodruff. One Robert Moore was found in Habersham County, page 21; he was aged 20-30 with a wife aged 15-20. An individual indexed as Robert Moore of Jackson County (p. 321) was actually Robert Moon, age 20-30. Robert Moore of Monroe County (p. 212) was also a young man, aged 20-30. The only other Robert Moore indexed in Georgia was Robert of Taliaferro County, p. 316, who appeared in Wilkes County in 1820. It may be that Robert Moore of Jones (c. 1827 - 1840) was living in Jones or Monroe County in the household of a child.

[989] 1832 Georgia land Lottery Records, Registrants, Georgia Department of Archives and History, Morrow, GA.

[990] The land is today in Schley County, it having been formed in 1857 from Taylor and Marion Counties.

Marion County, land district 3, land lot 196, belonging to Robert Moore. Descendants maintain that Ussery Moore and Simpson Moore were brothers, and the tax evidence strongly suggests that Robert Moore was their father.[991] Simpson paid tax in 1838 for himself and Robert Moore; in 1839 and 1840, Robert Moore was taxed alone, with poll tax only, first in GMD 359 and then in GMD 360. At the time of the 1840 census, he was shown as being aged sixty to seventy, and thus born between 1770 and 1780.[992]

There is no clear evidence of Robert Moore in Jones County after 1840; the only reference to a man who might be him is from 1843, when Simpson Moore paid poll tax for Robert M. Moore. In no other record is Robert shown as Robert M. Moore, and this document may refer to a younger man. At some point between 1840 and 1850, Robert Moore seems to have moved to Crawford County, Georgia, where he settled in Hammack's District. At the time of the 1850 census, he was living with his daughter Martha Moore Bentley and her husband John Bentley. They were enumerated in HH 156. The census indicates that Robert Moore was born in 1780, although other evidence suggests that he was several years older.[993]

No record of Robert Moore has been found after the 1850 census. He likely died in Crawford County, Georgia, shortly afterwards and may be buried in the John Bentley Family Cemetery in western Crawford County, near the border with Upson County.

It is believed that Robert Moore and his first, unknown wife -- who may have been Martha Thomas -- were the parents of at least four children: Martha Moore (c. 1794, Lunenburg County, Virginia - after 1850, Crawford County, Georgia), wife of John H. Bentley; Elizabeth Jane Moore (c. 1804, Wilkes County, Georgia - after 1860, Choctaw County, Mississippi), wife of Simeon Hammack; an unknown

---

[991] Simpson Moore's son Winfield Taylor Moore is said by descendants to have stated that Simpson Moore was a son of John Robert Moore and Martha Sinclair of Virginia. The names Robert and Martha appear to have been correct, although there is no evidence that Robert was named John Robert. Likewise, there is no documentary evidence that suggests a Sinclair connection. Simpson was in Jones County in 1850 but in Quitman County by 1860. He died there 27 March 1883. Winfield Taylor Moore (11 September 1847 -- 11 June 1928) was likely too young to have personal knowledge of his grandparents, although his older siblings probably remembered them well. Taylor Co., GA, DB D, 1866-1873, pp. 234-5, contains a deed from Ussery Moore to his brother Simpson Moore. A copy of the Simpson Moore family Bible record is found on microfilm at the Georgia Department of Archives and History, Morrow, Georgia.

[992] 1840 Jones Co., GA, Census, p. 146. Robert Moore was living near Mason Miller (stepson of Lewis Hammack), who in 1832 was taxed twenty-five names after Beaufort Stallsworth (son-in-law of Lewis Hammack, and husband of Christiana Hammack Moore) and John Bentley. James Miller's name appeared eight names after John Bentley in 1832, beside Bentley's in 1835, and seven names before Robert Moore's in the same year. This suggests that the Robert Moore of the 1840 census is likely the man taxed in the district in 1835 and 1836.

[993] The enumeration shows John Bentley, age 65, VA, $1200; Martha Bentley, age sixty, born in Virginia; Robert Moore, age seventy, born in Virginia. Robert Moore owned no property. It seems likely that Robert Moore was born closer to 1772 and that Martha Moore Bentley was born closer to 1793. The 1820 Wilkes Co., GA, Census shows that John Bentley's wife was aged 16-26, and thus born between 1794 and 1804. The 1830 Jones County census shows her age as 30-40, as does the 1840 Crawford Co., GA, census. Nearby households included Rhoda Cleaveland (HH 151); Allen G. Simmons (HH 149); John Ray (HH 161); Samuel Kelley (HH 221); John and Martha (Hammack) Sumpter (HH 224). Note that at the time of the 1820 census, John and Martha Bentley had three children -- two sons and one daughter -- under age 10. A. C. Carter, *Carter and Kinsmen* (1990), discusses the family of John Bentley. The three children shown in 1820 were Amelia Ann "Milly" Bentley (c. 1817 -- 1841), wife of Joel Carter; William Williamson Bentley (c. 1815 --); and Samuel Thomas Bentley (7 June 1816, Wilkes Co., GA -- 19 May 1887, Upson Co., GA). Younger children of John H. Bentley and Martha Moore were Evaline Bentley; Daniel Walter Bentley; and Caroline Elizabeth Bentley (1827-1885), who married Isham Miller in Crawford County, GA, in 1844. When John H. Bentley died in Crawford County about 1858, Talbot D. Hammack, Mansel W. Hammack, and Washington C. Cleaveland were named to distribute his estate (Crawford Co., GA, Annual Returns Book J, 1858-1870, pp. 525-528).

The autobiography of Samuel T. Bentley was published in a religious newspaper, *The Gospel Manager*, Volume 6, No. 5 (May 1884). There Bentley states: "I was born in Wilkes County, Georgia, June 7, 1816. My father and mother, John Bentley and Martha Moore, were born in Lunenburg County, Virginia, and were married in Wilkes County, Georgia. My father had only one brother who remained in Virginia and one sister who married George Amos in Hancock County. My mother joined the church at Williams' Creek, Warren County, Georgia, and was baptized by Elder Thomas Rhodes, at the age of about sixteen years. My father joined the Church at Mount Carmel, Crawford County, Georgia, and was baptized by Elder James Mathews, in about 1840. My father moved to Jones County, Georgia, in 1823, and in 1837 to Crawford County, Georgia."

daughter - born about 1800 - who married after the 1820 census; and a son born between 1802 and 1804.[994]

Robert Moore married the widow Martha Ray Moncrief in Wilkes County in late 1805 or early 1806.[995] It may be that his wife died during childbirth or as a result of birthing complications following the birth of Elizabeth Jane Moore. Martha Ray Moncrief was then about thirty years old; she had married Samuel Moncrief in 1793, and they were the parents of three children for whom Robert Moore became guardian: Sanders Moncrief (c. 1797, Wilkes County, Georgia - after 1860, Sumner County, Tennessee), who married 17 January 1817, Wilkes County, Georgia, Susannah Phillips; Drucilla Moncrief (c. 1799, Wilkes County, Georgia - after 1860, Fayette County, Tennessee), who married Reuben Hamrick on 26 June, 1819, in Wilkes County, Georgia; and William Moncrief (c. 1802, Wilkes County, Georgia - after 1889, Fayette County, Tennessee), who married Sarah Jane Bailey 14 November 1819, Wilkes County, Georgia.

Based on the research presented here, it appears that Robert Moore and Martha Ray Moncrief were the parents of several children. The 1820 census showed that their household included three males under age ten; one male aged 10-16; one male aged 16-18; one female under age ten; and one female aged 16-26. It would thus appear that Robert and Martha Moore had a son born between 1804 and 1810, three sons born between 1810 and 1820, and a daughter born between 1810 and 1820. These children probably included Ussery Moore (c. 1808, Georgia -), who married Sarah Reaves on 26 November 1826, Talbot County, Georgia,[996] and Simpson Moore (29 May 1811, Georgia - 27 March 1883), who married Cynthia Cane on 19 August 1827 in Jones County, Georgia. Robert M. Moore, for whom Simpson Moore paid tax in 1843, might have been another son. Jane Moore, who married William Emmerson on 17 April 1832 in Jones County, might also have been a daughter.[997]

Having been reared in a community full of biological kin, Elizabeth Jane Moore and Simeon Hammack left this kinship group behind when they chose to migrate to Mississippi in the 1850s. So far as is known, there was no prolonged contact between the Georgia Moore family and the Mississippi Hammack family after Simeon and Elizabeth left the area. In Jones and Crawford Counties in Georgia, however, Moores, Hammacks, Bentleys, and other kin continued throughout the nineteenth and early twentieth century to have a close relationship. Its roots stretched back nearly two centuries, to the 1740s, when Robert Moore migrated from New Kent County, Virginia, to Lunenburg County, where he first encountered the early Hammacks on their trek southward.

---

[994] This daughter may have been Lucynthia Moore, who married Tyre Freeman in Jones County on 8 January 1826. Tyre Freeman married (2) 27 December 1832, Jones Co., GA, Lucy Fallen, who may have been a granddaughter of Jesse Moore of Lunenburg County. He married (3) 1 October 1840, Jones Co., GA, Keziah Morris. Lovick P. Jordan married Malinda A. Freeman on 6 October 1844. In 1843 he paid pole tax for Simpson Moore, who himself paid pole tax for Robert M. Moore. The association may have been purely coincidental, but perhaps there was some connection between Malinda Freeman and Tyre Freeman. Descendants of Elijah and Mary (Moore) Moore, who moved from Delaware to Jones Co., GA, identify Lucynthia as their daughter, however. Tyre Freeman died in 1854 in Chambers or Pike Counties, Alabama.

[995] See Davidson, *Early Records*, 1: 114, 168, 312, 317, 325. The estate of Samuel Montcrief was inventoried 6 March 1804 with Henry Garland and John Langdon appraisers. The sale took place on 13 October 1805 with Martha Montcrief as administratrix. Martha, Isaiah, William, and Noah Montcrief were purchasers. Montcrief was apparently deceased as early as 6 December 1803 when Martha Montcrief was named administratrix with John Hendrick and Lewis Hammack as securities. Samuel Montcrief registered in 1803 for the 1805 land lottery, but Robert Moore registered in 1806 for the 1807 land lottery as trustee for the orphans of Samuel Moncrief, deceased. It would seem that the marriage of Robert Moore to Martha Moncrief took place after 13 October 1805 but before the assessment for the 1806 tax digest and the 1806 land lottery registration.

[996] Sarah Reaves had previously lived in Jones and Hancock Counties in Georgia. Her Reaves relatives also removed to Choctaw and Calhoun Counties, Mississippi.

[997] Miles Kelley, son of Jenny Moore Kelley, and nephew of Nancy Kelley Ray, was trustee for William Emmerson at the time of the 1843 Crawford Co., GA, tax digest. Miles Kelley had married Martha Emmerson on 24 January 1833 in Jones County.

Descendants of Ussery Moore

Ussery Moore — Martha Bishop

Robert Moore

Bishop Moore

Sarah Ray

Matthew Moore

Mary Ray

Samuel Moore

Christiana Hammack

Joseph Moore

James Welborn Moore

Sarah Hammack

Jenny Moore

Samuel Kelley

John Moore

Elizabeth Davis

? Charles Moore

Elizabeth Ellington

? Elizabeth Moore

James Edge

Chapter 23:

Louisa Templeton Hammack of Morgan and Macon Counties, Georgia, and Calhoun County, Mississippi

Louisa Templeton Hammack was born about 1833, probably in Morgan County, Georgia. She married John T. Hammack about 1851 in Macon County, Georgia, where her parents had settled during her girlhood. With John Hammack, she soon removed to Choctaw County, Mississippi. During the Civil War, Louisa and her family settled southwards in Madison County, but after the war they relocated to the newly formed Calhoun County.

Louisa was left a widow when John T. Hammack died in January 1870 of pneumonia. She was living in the Slate Springs area with several young children at the time of the 1870 census. No further record of Louisa has been found, and no family oral tradition records her fate. Calhoun County deed, probate, newspaper, and tax records have all be searched in an effort to learn more about her; likewise, all available church records were examined for clues as well. No trace of Louisa and her two youngest children, Jim and Eduie, has been found after the time of the 1870 census. The likeliest explanation is that all three died between 1870 and 1880, probably as a result of the Yellow Fever epidemic that claimed many lives in eastern Mississippi and western Tennessee during 1878 and 1879.[998]

Louisa Templeton was the first Hammack foremother to introduce non-English roots into the family gene pool. Earlier generations of Hammacks had all married women whose families hailed from eastern Virginia, like that of William "O" Hammack himself and his immediate descendants. All were descendants of English colonists who had come to the Chesapeake in search of improved fortunes in the seventeenth-century.

Louisa Templeton Hammack was a daughter of Milton Templeton and Martha Fuller; her parents married there 23 February 1817 and lived there for more than a decade before settling in Macon County, Georgia. Milton Templeton died shortly before 1850 in Macon County, and his widow outlived him by several years, dying on or about 13 January 1857.[999] Although Louisa moved to Mississippi with her husband John T. Hammack and his Hammack relatives, she had ties to Mississippi as well. Her nephew John Ward accompanied the Hammacks to Mississippi and was living with John T. and Louisa at the time of the 1860 census; likewise, her father's brother Zephaniah Templeton had settled near Madison County in Copiah County, where he reared a large family. The presence of Templeton kin in Copiah may have played a role in John T. and Louisa's decision to relocate their family to that area during the Civil War.[1000]

Milton Templeton belonged to a large Scots-Irish family that had settled first in Pennsylvania. David Templeton (c. 1690, Northern Ireland -- after 1742, Harmony Ridge, Lancaster County, Pennsylvania) had come from Ireland to Pennsylvania in the early eighteenth-century. The Scots-Irish were descended from Scots Presbyterians who had settled in Northern Ireland in the seventeenth-century; like their descendants who came to America, they had made the initial move to Ireland in search of better living conditions. Some married into local Irish families, but most of the Scots-Irish maintained their own ethnic identity by marrying Scots women from neighboring families. When the Scots-Irish began coming to America in large numbers after 1717, family ties proved extremely important in the migrations that

---

[998] The epidemic began in New Orleans and made its way upriver to Memphis. There were more than 120,000 documented cases of yellow fever in the Mississippi Valley and more than 20,000 deaths there as a result. See K. J. Bloom, *The Mississippi Valley's Great Yellow Fever Epidemic of 1878* (Baton Rouge, 1993). The epidemic became the subject of "The Great Fever," an episode of PBS's "American Experience" series.

[999] Macon Co., GA, Returns Book A, pp. 59, 79.

[1000] 1841 Copiah Co., MS, Personal Property Tax Roll, Mississippi Department of Archives and History, Jackson, MS; 1850 Copiah Co., MS, Census, p. 230, HH 312; Copiah Co., MS, Estate Book C, p. 937.

brought them to the British colonies. They traveled in family groups, and each new wave of migration brought additional relatives to join the existing enclaves.[1001]

Understanding the Templeton family relationships is complicated by the fact that the Scots-Irish tended to repeat a limited number of given names in each generation. There were several men in each generation named James Templeton, David Templeton, George Templeton, and Samuel Templeton. Once the family reached North Carolina, the name Thomas Templeton became common -- perhaps as a result of marriage into a neighboring family there -- and by 1800 there were half a dozen men named Thomas Templeton in Rowan and Iredell Counties, North Carolina.

The Templetons became somewhat prominent in the Scots-Irish community of Lancaster County, Pennsylvania, holding several local offices before they began migrating to North Carolina in the early 1740s. Although eastern North Carolina had been settled since the 1660s, the western portion of the colony was, by European standards, relatively undeveloped until the middle of the eighteenth century. A network of Indian trails extended across the frontier, facilitating trade and travel among the native peoples. Increasingly after 1720, these trails came under the control of the white settler population, and descendants of European colonists began to move into the backcountry areas.[1002]

The Templetons were among the very first settlers in what was to become Rowan County, North Carolina. Three men -- all believed to be sons of David Templeton who had come from Ireland to Pennsylvania -- settled in North Carolina during the 1740s. David Templeton (by 1720, Pennsylvania or Ireland -- after 1761, Mecklenburg County, North Carolina), John Templeton (by 1724, Pennsylvania or Ireland -- 1788, Rowan County, North Carolina), and James Templeton (by 1726, Pennsylvania or Ireland -- after 1800, Iredell County, North Carolina) all settled together along the Carolina frontier in the middle 1740s, along with the Davidsons, Grahams, and other Scots-Irish families.[1003]

Robert W. Ramsey, then professor of history at Hollins College, near Roanoke, Virginia, published *Carolina Cradle: Settlement of the Northwest Carolina Frontier, 1747-1762*, in 1964. Mastering an abundance of primary sources for not only North Carolina but also Virginia and Pennsylvania, Dr. Ramsey wrote of the first settlers of western North Carolina -- defined by him as the region between the Yadkin and Catawba Rivers north of the 1746 Granville line. The Great Wagon Road crossed Virginia and entered Carolina, intersecting at the Yadkin River with an Indian Trading Path coming southwest through Northampton, Granville, and Orange Counties out of eastern Virginia. Crossing the Yadkin, the lands extended south and northwest, and their travelers peopled Dr. Ramsey's Carolina frontier. Of these migrants, many led the vanguard of settlement in western South Carolina, Georgia, Tennessee, and other locations.[1004]

The Scots-Irish Templetons of North Carolina figure prominent in Ramsey's account, apparently coming in what he terms the "third wave" of settlement. The initial Irish settlement occurred between 1747 and 1749 south of the Yadkin River, and the Bryan settlement took shape at roughly the same time near the intersection of the Great Wagon Road and the Yadkin River, just northwest of Linville's Creek and Panther Creek. Begun in 1748, the Davidson's Creek settlement, where the first Templetons located, was even further west.[1005]

[1001] J. G. Leyburn, *The Scotch-Irish: A Social History* (Chapel Hill, 1962), pp. 3-62, discusses the Scots heritage before the migration to Ulster. P. Griffin, *The People With No Name: Ireland's Ulster Scots, America's Scots-Irish, and the Creation of a British Atlantic World, 1689-1764* (Princeton, 2001) places the Scots-Irish within the larger Atlantic world. D. H. Fischer, *Albion's Seed: Four British Folkways in America* (Oxford, 1989) provides a rich and lively account of the Scots-Irish in the Carolina backcountry, the area in which Louisa's ancestors settled.

[1002] Leyburn, *Scotch-Irish*, pp. 172, 186, 210-218, 236, 252-254.

[1003] See R. W. Ramsey, *Carolina Cradle: Settlement of the Northwest Carolina Frontier, 1747-1762* (Chapel Hill, 1964), p. 25. Of these three, John and James seem both to have had sons named Thomas, and David had at least one grandson named Thomas.

[1004] Ibid., pp. 1-14.

[1005] Ibid., pp. 25, 35-47, 188-189.

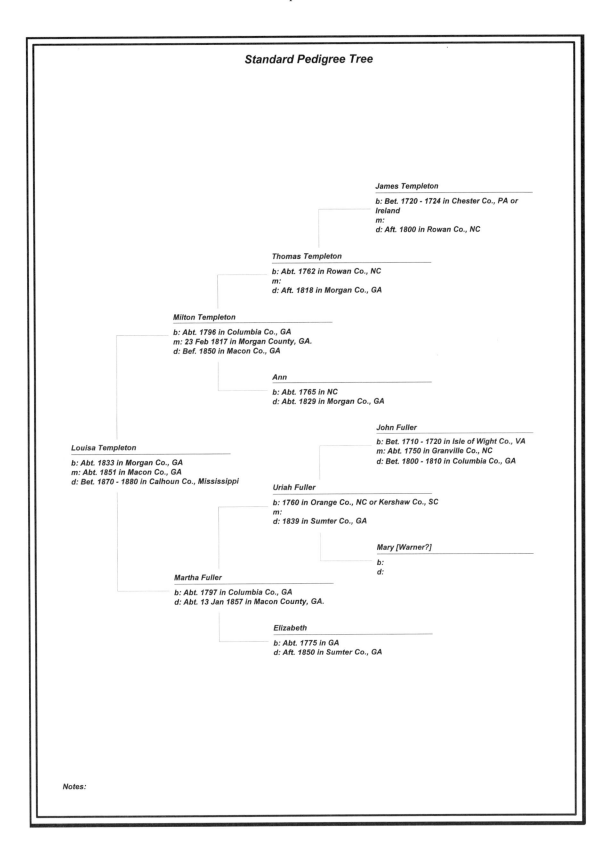

Standard Pedigree Tree

James Templeton

b: Bet. 1720 - 1724 in Chester Co., PA or Ireland
m:
d: Aft. 1800 in Rowan Co., NC

Thomas Templeton

b: Abt. 1762 in Rowan Co., NC
m:
d: Aft. 1818 in Morgan Co., GA

Milton Templeton

b: Abt. 1796 in Columbia Co., GA
m: 23 Feb 1817 in Morgan County, GA.
d: Bef. 1850 in Macon Co., GA

Ann

b: Abt. 1765 in NC
d: Abt. 1829 in Morgan Co., GA

John Fuller

b: Bet. 1710 - 1720 in Isle of Wight Co., VA
m: Abt. 1750 in Granville Co., NC
d: Bet. 1800 - 1810 in Columbia Co., GA

Louisa Templeton

b: Abt. 1833 in Morgan Co., GA
m: Abt. 1851 in Macon Co., GA
d: Bet. 1870 - 1880 in Calhoun Co., Mississippi

Uriah Fuller

b: 1760 in Orange Co., NC or Kershaw Co., SC
m:
d: 1839 in Sumter Co., GA

Mary [Warner?]

b:
d:

Martha Fuller

b: Abt. 1797 in Columbia Co., GA
d: Abt. 13 Jan 1857 in Macon County, GA.

Elizabeth

b: Abt. 1775 in GA
d: Aft. 1850 in Sumter Co., GA

Notes:

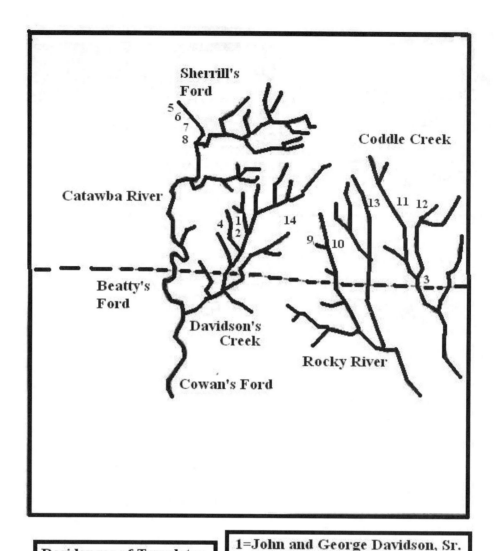

Residences of Templeton and associated families, Davidson's Creek Settlement, Rowan Co., NC, c. 1748 - c. 1751

1=John and George Davidson, Sr.
2=George Davidson, Jr. (before 1759)
3=David Templeton
4=James Templeton
5=Adam Sherrill
6=Ute Sherrill
7=William Sherrill
8=Abenton Sherrill
9=John Bravard
10=Robert Bravard
11=Walter Carruth
12=Adam Carruth (before 1762)
13=Jane Carruth (before 1756)
14=Centre Church

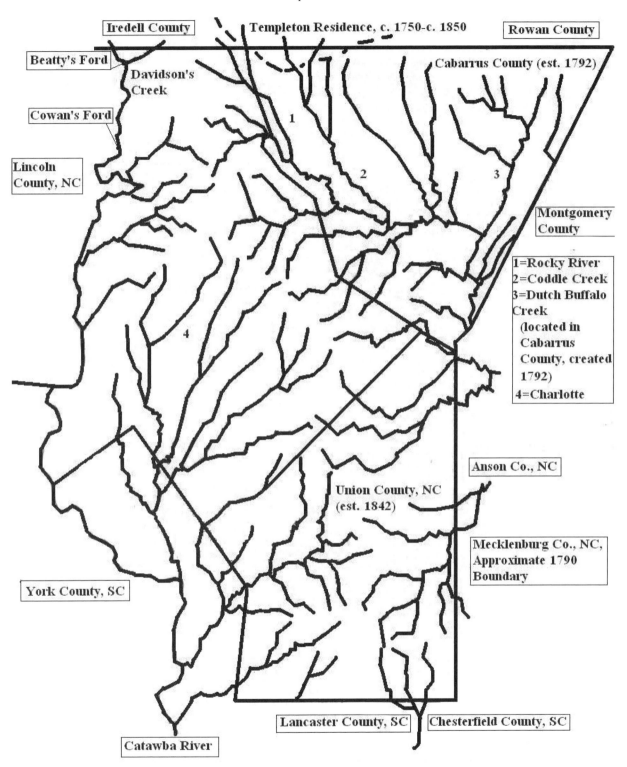

Iredell County

Templeton Residence, c. 1750-c. 1850

Rowan County

Beatty's Ford

Davidson's Creek

Cabarrus County (est. 1792)

Cowan's Ford

1

Lincoln County, NC

2

3

Montgomery County

1=Rocky River
2=Coddle Creek
3=Dutch Buffalo Creek
 (located in Cabarrus County, created 1792)
4=Charlotte

4

Anson Co., NC

Union County, NC (est. 1842)

Mecklenburg Co., NC, Approximate 1790 Boundary

York County, SC

Lancaster County, SC

Chesterfield County, SC

Catawba River

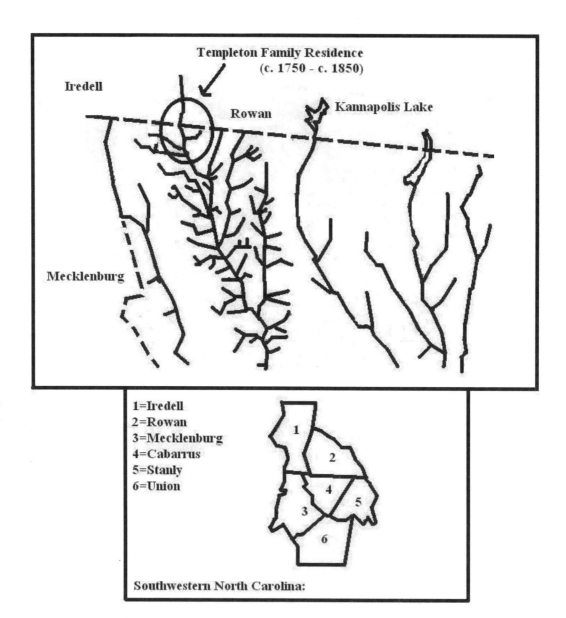

Southwestern North Carolina:

Louisa Templeton Hammack   281

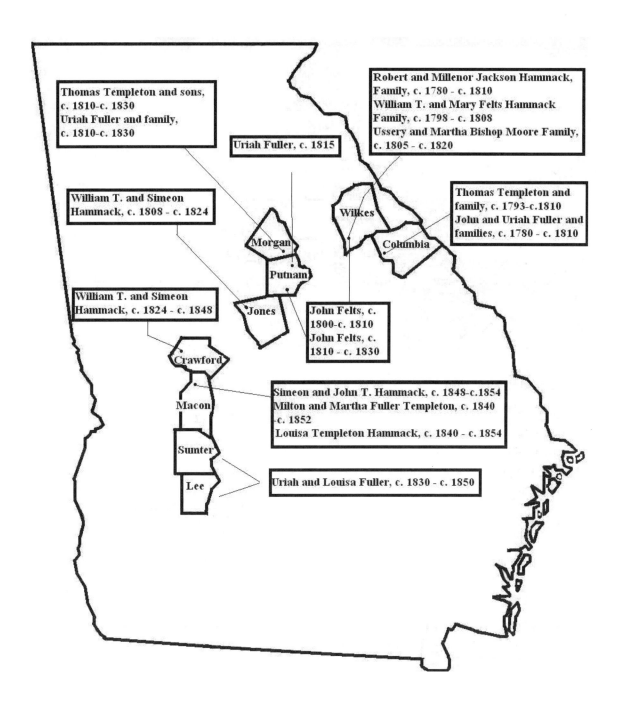

Thomas Templeton and sons,
c. 1810-c. 1830
Uriah Fuller and family,
c. 1810-c. 1830

Uriah Fuller, c. 1815

Robert and Millenor Jackson Hammack,
Family, c. 1780 - c. 1810
William T. and Mary Felts Hammack
Family, c. 1798 - c. 1808
Ussery and Martha Bishop Moore Family,
c. 1805 - c. 1820

William T. and Simeon
Hammack, c. 1808 - c. 1824

Thomas Templeton and
family, c. 1793-c.1810
John and Uriah Fuller and
families, c. 1780 - c. 1810

Wilkes

Columbia

Morgan

Putnam

William T. and Simeon
Hammack, c. 1824 - c. 1848

Jones

John Felts, c.
1800-c. 1810
John Felts, c.
1810 - c. 1830

Crawford

Simeon and John T. Hammack, c. 1848-c.1854
Milton and Martha Fuller Templeton, c. 1840
-c. 1852
Louisa Templeton Hammack, c. 1840 - c. 1854

Macon

Sumter

Uriah and Louisa Fuller, c. 1830 - c. 1850

Lee

In discussing the settlement period between 1747 and 1751, Ramsey speculates that David and James Templeton were among the initial arrivals[1006]; certainly they were present within a year or two of the first settlement. "James and John Templeton were neighbors of George and Samuel Davidson in East Nottingham Township," Ramsey writes. "David Templeton was tax collector for Harmony Ridge (Lancaster County) in 1742. Members of this family trekked to Carolina with the Davidsons. James Templeton's land adjoined that of John and George Davidson, while David Templeton settled on Coddle Creek, six miles to the eastward."[1007]

James Templeton was in North Carolina by 26 November 1748, when he and George Davidson were chain carriers for the survey of a 650-acre grant issued to John Davidson.[1008] Ramsey pinpoints David and James Templeton as living in the Davidson's Creek Settlement between 1748 and 1751; David lived on the north side of Coddle Creek near Walter Carruth, Thomas Cook, Adam Carruth, and James Huggen. James Templeton lived west of David, past Rocky River and on a northern branch of Davidson's Creek off of the Catawba River. John and George Davidson were his nearest neighbors, but John McConnell, Samuel Baker, and Edward Given also lived in the neighborhood.[1009]

Ramsey writes that in 1755 Reverend Hugh McAden of the New Castle County, Delaware, Presbyterian congregation "set out on a missionary tour of the southern frontier."[1010] His journal documents his travels into the neighborhoods in which the early Carolina Templetons settled. On 3 September, McAden arrived at Henry Sloan's residence at the Yadkin Ford, where he remained until the Sabbath. McAden lamented the loss of many Presbyterians to the burgeoning Baptist congregations in the Backcountry. On 12 September, McAden crossed the Yadkin and traveled about 10 miles to James Allison's. During the following week, he made several short trips, remaining with Walter Carruth until 21 September. Then, while en route to David Templeton's residence, "about 5 miles from Mr. Carruth's", McAden met a group of settlers who had fled from the region of the Calfpasture River in the valley of Virginia because of Indian depredations. He spent that night with William Denny before reaching David Templeton's residence on Tuesday, 23 September. McAden, Templeton, and others spent Wednesday in "fasting and prayer", after which McAden rode to the meetinghouse and preached. He then went home with Captain Alexander Osborne," a distance of about six miles, where he remained for a week.[1011] From McAden's journal we learn that the North Carolina Templetons had retained their Presbyterian faith, at least until mid-century. The distances indicated in McAden's journal -- five or six miles traveled a day -- also indicate that David Templeton's residence was isolated and that he lived several miles from other Scots-Irish Presbyterians in the area.

The lands on which the Carolina Templetons first settled in western Rowan County largely fell into Iredell County upon its creation in 1788. Today Coddle Creek lies southeast of Mooresville, near the line separating Davidson County (created in 1822) from Iredell. Both border Mecklenburg to the south, and across the Catawba River lie Wilkes County, Burke County, and Lincoln County. Sherrill's Ford across the Catawba, named for the early Indian traders who left Pennsylvania and Maryland for the Shenandoah in the 1730s, marks the northern boundary of the portion of Iredell in which the early Templeton's settled.

[1006] Ibid., p. 25.

[1007] Ibid., pp. 25, 47, citing Chester Tax Lists, 1737-1738; Lancaster Minute Book, p. 58; North Carolina Land Grants, VI, 139, and X, 304. East Nottingham borders West Nottingham, West Fallowfield, Londonderry, and New London in Chester County and Sudbury, Colerain, and Little Britain across the Octorano Creek in Lancaster County. It also lies on the line dividing Chester County from Cecil County, Maryland, near both New Castle Co., Delaware, and the Susquehanna River as it crosses from Pennsylvania into Maryland.

[1008] Ibid., p. 46. The original survey is found in the George F. Davidson Collection, 1748-1887, Duke University Library, Durham, NC. George Davidson, brother of John, was father of William Lee Davidson, a Whig general who was killed at Cowan's Ford in 1780.

[1009] The Brevards later settled on the headwaters of Rocky River, between the Davidson and Templeton families. Ibid., pp. 25, 44-47.

[1010] Ibid., pp. 188-189.

[1011] Ibid., pp. 188-189.

Most of their properties lay south of the road from Salisbury in Davidson County to Mooresville in Iredell and then southwest to Beatty's Ford along the Yadkin River, between Mecklenburg and Lincoln Counties. Understandably, as the family grew numerically, each of these counties became significant to the Templeton family's development.[1012]

By the 1780s, members of these families began moving South onto the Georgia frontier. John Templeton and his wife Rosanna Mackey Templeton, originally from Burke County, North Carolina, settled in Wilkes and Elbert Counties in the early 1780s[1013]; John may be the same John Templeton who lived briefly about 1787 in that portion of Richmond County which would become Columbia County.[1014] About this time, George Templeton -- probably one of the Georges found in Rowan and Iredell Counties -- appears in that portion of southern Wilkes County that later became Warren County.[1015]

Thomas Templeton, grandfather of Louisa Templeton Hammack, first appears in this area about 1795. He appears less than a mile from land purchased by John Templeton in the 1780s and only a short distance from the area where George Templeton was living at about the same time. Probably all three men left southwestern North Carolina and settled in Georgia at about the same time; since no subsequent record of George has been found, he may have returned to North Carolina after his sojourn in Georgia.[1016] Based on the family reconstitution of Thomas Templeton, we can estimate that he was born at least by about 1766. It seems likely that he is the young Thomas Templeton taxed in Rowan County, North Carolina, in 1782 and that he had only recently reached taxable age.[1017] At that time he was probably not yet married, but he probably married in North Carolina before settling in Georgia.[1018]

After studying the chronology of the North Carolina Templeton family, it seems most likely that Thomas Templeton of Georgia was a son of James Templeton (born by 1726, in Ireland or Pennsylvania, and living in 1800, Iredell County, North Carolina). This man was apparently called James Templeton, Sr., by 1778, when a James, Jr., was also taxed in Rowan. Since George (taxed in 1778) later sells property patented by James in 1761, it may be that he was a son of James Templeton, Sr. Ramsey speculates that James and David Templeton arrived together from Pennsylvania as early as 1747,

---

[1012] Ibid., pp. 187-188.

[1013] In 1790, John Templeton was taxed with his Mackie in-laws in what later became Madison County. He owned a 2,000-acre tract located in Franklin County, Georgia, and 400 acres in Wilkes County. See B. M. Doughtie, *The Mackeys (Variously Spelled) and Allied Families* (Decatur, GA, 1957), p. 589

[1014] G. G. Davidson, ed., *Historical Collections of the Georgia Chapters, Daughters of the American Revolution, Records of Richmond County, Georgia (formerly Saint Paul's Parish)* (Macon, 1929), p. 291, shows that, on 25 September 1787, John Templeton and Jesse Sanders witnessed a deed from Elizabeth Lee, widow of Greenberry Lee, to Thomas Carr for 400 acres on Germany's Creek in Richmond County. The land had been granted to John Lee in 1771. Greenberry Lee married Elizabeth, daughter of William Few; she married (2) after 1787 a man named Thomas Bush and was still living in Columbia County in 1802. Thomas Templeton was living in Germany's Creek when he first appears in the records of Columbia County. The only known John Templeton in the area at this time was the man who married Rosannah Mackie, although the 1787 John Templeton could be another man.

[1015] George was taxed in Medlock's District in 1790. Today this land is in Glascock Co., GA, but became Warren County when first ceded by Wilkes County. This district lay southwest of the area where Thomas Templeton settled in Columbia County. See Hudson, *Wilkes County Tax Records*, Volume 1.

[1016] Georgia Land Grants, Book NNNN, p. 721.

[1017] J. W. Linn, *Rowan Co., NC, Tax Lists, 1757-1800: Annotated Transcriptions* (Rowan, NC, 1995), pp. 10, 17, 51, 149-150, 192, 234, and 283. In 1759, Robert and James Templeton were taxed. John, Archibald, and David Templeton all signed petitions in Rowan in 1759. A military roster shows James and Robert as soldiers at the same time. James Templeton was taxed in 1761. The most complete surviving digest appears to be the 1778 one. In Captain Davidson's District were George Templeton, James Templeton, Sr., James Templeton, Jr., John Templeton, and Joseph Templeton. Joseph Templeton paid poll tax in 1778 and Thomas Templeton in 1782, indicating that he had recently come of age.

[1018] Some researchers believe that he is the Thomas Templeton who married Ann Hamilton in Scotland. I find no evidence to support this statement. There seems to be nothing to indicate that Thomas and Ann Templeton came directly from Scotland to America, and no immigration lists have been found from that time period (when such records are fairly common) that show individuals with these names as passengers for America. There were, however, Scots-Irish Templetons still coming into South Carolina at this time. It is difficult to resist the conclusion that these Templetons, who settled in South Carolina, were related to those in Rowan County, North Carolina. They had similar names and may even have dealt with one another.

indicating a birth date of at least 1726. James is documented to have been in North Carolina by 1748.[1019] Jo White Linn notes:[1020]

> James Templeton was a constable by 1755 and proved the will of James McCulloch in 1758[1021] and witnessed the 1758 will of George Davidson. He had received a Granville Grant for 400 acres on Davidson's Creek adjacent McCulloh, George Davidson, Jr., and John McConnell surveyed 6 February 1753 and can be identified in then Anson County by 1748.[1022] The 1800 Iredell County Direct Tax showed him with 600 acres. There is no record of division of his estate. He was originally from Chester County, Pennsylvania, as were his neighbors.[1023]

On 4 April 1762, James Templeton witnessed a deed with John McConnell from William and Dinah Mcrea to Catherine Barry for £25; involved was 432 acres on Davidson's Creek on the east side of Catawba River and adjacent John McConnell.[1024] He was an adjacent owner on 10 January 1762 when George Davison was granted 403 acres joining James Templeton, Moses Andrews, and Andrew Allison.[1025] On 15 July 1767, Moses Peares was appointed overseer of the road in the room of Thomas Carson, and Patrick Hamilton was appointed overseer of the road in the room of James Templeton.[1026] On 25 January 1776, James Templeton had conveyed to George Templeton for £5 proclamation money, 200 acres on Davidson's Creek joining James McCullough, part of a tract granted him 9 January 1761. George Davison and Robert Byars witnessed.[1027] On 26 March 1783, James Templeton deeded to Joseph Templeton a 200-acre tract near Davidson's Creek joining John McConnell and George Davidson for £5; he had been granted this land in 1761. George Templeton and James Willson witnessed the transaction.[1028] If Linn's analysis is correct, the James Templeton enumerated in Iredell County in 1790 and taxed there in 1800 was James Templeton, Sr., born by 1726 in Ireland or Pennsylvania.

Thomas Templeton had probably settled in Georgia by the early 1790s.[1029] He first appeared in the Columbia County records in 1795, when he claimed a seventy-eight-acre tract on Germany's Creek.[1030] Columbia had been formed from Richmond County in 1790, but Thomas does not appear between 1790 and 1795 in the surviving Columbia County records. He maintained his seventy-eight-acre tract until he left the county two decades later, paying tax on it in 1806 and 1808. In 1806, the land was described as

---

[1019] See J. W. Linn, *Abstracts of the Minutes of the Court of Pleas and Quarter Sessions, Rowan County, North Carolina, 1753-1762* (Salisbury, NC, 1977), pp. 35, 39, 57, 67, and 82, and J. W. Linn, *Abstracts of the Minutes of the Court of Pleas and Quarter Sessions, Rowan County, North Carolina, 1763-1774* (Salisbury, NC, 1979), pp. 69, 142, 147, and 153, which includes references to James, John, and Robert Templeton.

[1020] Iredell County, NC, 1815 Tax List, North Carolina Department of Archives and History, Raleigh, NC.

[1021] Linn, *Rowan Court Minutes, 1763-1774*, pp. 64, 205.

[1022] M. Hoffmann, *Colony of North Carolina, 1735-1764: Abstracts of Land Patents* (Raleigh, 1982), 3: 107 and 4:10.

[1023] Linn is assuming that the James taxed in 1800 is the James present in 1748; this is possible but not established.

[1024] Rowan Co., NC, Deed Book 4, p. 687.

[1025] Rowan Co., NC, Deed Book 5, p. 407

[1026] Linn, *Minute Abstracts, 1763-1774*, p. 69.

[1027] Rowan Co., NC, Deed Book 9, p. 331.

[1028] Rowan Co., NC, Deed Book 9, p. 288.

[1029] One Thomas Templeton, a single man, was enumerated in Iredell Co., NC, in 1790. Iredell County deeds indicate that he was the son of John and Margaret Graham Templeton of Iredell Co., NC, and York Co., SC. He later moved to Tennessee. Another Thomas Templeton married Mary Wigfield in Surry Co., NC, in 1792. Mary likely had a connection to Benjamin Wigfield who lived on North Hunting Creek in southern Surry County near the boundary with Iredell County. The area where Wigfield and Templeton lived has been Yadkin County since 1851. It seems likely that this Thomas who married Mary Wigfield was Thomas of Iredell County. NOTE that Thomas Mackie, father of Rosannah Mackie Templeton of North Carolina and Georgia, also lived on Hunting Creek.

[1030] Georgia Land Grants, Book NNNN, p. 721.

joining tracts owned by Hambleton and Scott. At that time, Thomas Templeton also owned land lot 183, land district 4, Baldwin County, which he had drawn in the 1805 land lottery.[1031]

Sometimes between 1806 and 1811, Thomas Templeton removed his family from Columbia County to Morgan County; he retained ownership of his Columbia County tract until 1815, however, when he sold it to Benjamin Crabb for $285.[1032] By 1811, Thomas was taxed in Morgan County, paying tax on the 202.5 acre tract he had recently drawn as well as on seven slaves. By 1812, Greenberry Templeton -- apparently Thomas' eldest son -- had come of age. Thomas continued to be taxed in Morgan County until 1818, at which time he owned fifty-nine and one-fourth acres adjacent Hudson Wade and granted himself. Apparently as Thomas's sons came of age, he had given them control of a portion of the larger tract, for Greenberry and Milton Templeton were each taxed with forty-seven and one-fourth acres originally granted to Thomas Templeton. Thomas had apparently died by 1820, when Greenberry Templeton paid tax as agent for Ann Templeton, who was assessed on the same fifty-nine and one-fourth acres of land on which Thomas had been taxed in 1818. Greenberry Templeton continued to pay tax for Ann Templeton in 1824, 1826, and 1829.[1033]

Ann Templeton was probably deceased by 1829, when, on 17 November, Thomas Templeton's heirs conveyed the fifty-nine-acre tract owned by him to William F. Starke. The deed conveyed the tract "where Ann Templeton formerly lived", located on Sugar Creek adjacent Moody and Pennick, for $150. The heirs of Thomas Templeton signed as grantors: Richard Mathias of Randolph County, Greenberry Templeton of Morgan County, Milton Templeton of Morgan County, Zephaniah Templeton of Morgan County, and Dovey Templeton of Morgan County.[1034] Joseph Pennick and Hudson T. Ware witnessed the deed.

Thomas and Ann Templeton were the parents of five known children. Dovey Templeton, born before 1790, never married; she may have had some disability, for her siblings usually represented her in legal matters.[1035] Greenberry Templeton, born about 1790, married Elizabeth Matthews in 1811 and moved to Stewart County, where he died after 1830.[1036] Zephaniah Templeton, born about 1794, married Sarah Watson in Morgan County in 1817; he settled in Mississippi about 1840 and died in Copiah County in 1859.[1037] Milton Templeton will be discussed below. Nancy Templeton, born about 1800, married Richard Matthews in Morgan County in 1818; they also moved to Stewart County, where Nancy died about 1837.[1038]

The father of Louisa Templeton Hammack, Milton Templeton was born about 1797 in Columbia County, Georgia. He was reared on the seventy-eight-acre homestead his father owned along Germany's Creek in Columbia County, but he was only about ten years old when the family relocated to the larger tract his father had drawn in Morgan County. Several neighboring families -- including the Matthews and Fuller families -- also moved to Morgan at this time, so the Templetons had familiar neighbors in the new land.

Milton Templeton married Martha Fuller on 23 February 1817 in Morgan County. Like Milton, Martha was probably also a native of Columbia County, where she was born about 1797. The evidence suggests that Martha was a daughter of Uriah and Elizabeth Fuller and a granddaughter of John and Mary Warner Fuller. Many Fuller historians believe that John Fuller was born in Isle of Wight County, Virginia, a son of Ezekiel and Deborah Spivey Fuller. Ezekiel Fuller wrote his will in Isle of Wight

---

[1031] 1805 Georgia Land Lottery Records, Fortunate Drawers, Georgia Department of Archives and History, Morrow, GA.

[1032] Columbia Co., GA, Deed Book P, p. 452.

[1033] 1811-1829 Morgan Co., GA, Tax Digests, Georgia Department of Archives and History, Morrow, GA.

[1034] Morgan Co., GA, DB I, p. 33.

[1035] The 1840 Stewart Co., GA, Census gives her age as 60-70, suggesting that she was born between 1770 and 1780. If this date is correct, she was probably several years older than her other siblings. It lends further credence to the idea that Thomas Templeton was born by 1766, if not earlier.

[1036] 1840 Stewart Co., GA, Census, p. 41.

[1037] Copiah Co., MS, Estate Book C, p. 937.

[1038] Matthews remarried, on 5 January 1837 in Stewart County, to Susan Cooper.

County; it was proven there in November 1722. His widow Deborah, who was a daughter of John and Sarah Littleton Spivey of Nansemond County, survived him for more than two decades, dying about 1744 in Isle of Wight. Ezekiel Fuller's will names several sons, including John Fuller. By the 1750s, most of these sons were living in the vicinity of Granville County, North Carolina, where John Fuller also appears.[1039]

Between 1750 and 1780, John and Mary Fuller lived in several different locations. Legal records place them in Granville County, North Carolina; Orange County, North Carolina; Kershaw County, South Carolina; and Richmond County, Georgia. It was probably in Orange County, North Carolina, that Uriah Fuller was born about 1760.[1040] By the early 1770s, the family had settled in Kershaw County, South Carolina, and they resided there at the time of the Revolution. The Revolutionary War Pension Application of John Fuller, Jr., who lived to be nearly 100 years of age, indicates that his father, John Fuller, Sr., supported the American cause during the Revolutionary struggle. It also alleges that John Fuller, Sr., may have been a centenarian when he died after 1800 in Columbia County.[1041]

By about 1782, the Fullers had settled along the Georgia frontier. It was there, while living in Richmond County in 1782, that John Fuller, Sr., deeded property to his son Joshua Fuller. Isaac Fuller and John Youngblood, a neighbor from South Carolina, witnessed the deed.[1042] John Fuller was living in Columbia County as late as 1806, when he was taxed with 145 acres on Cain Creek and sixty-five acres, adjoining Hambleton and Jones, on Germany's Creek. John Fuller, Jr., also owned land on Cain Creek.[1043]

Uriah Fuller was probably born in Orange County, North Carolina. He appears with the family as an adult in Columbia County, Georgia, during the 1790s. He appears along with John and Abner Fuller on a 1793 Columbia County, Georgia, militia list as "Riah" Fuller. By 1813, he had moved westward into Putnam County, where he was taxed in 1813 and 1815. On 9 October 1817, Uriah witnessed a deed in Morgan County from Barna Woolbright to Hudson T. Ware.[1044] In the same year, he was listed as a resident in Fears' District, Morgan County, paying tax on a 101.5 acre tract on Indian Creek.[1045] On the same page was Milton Templeton -- who on 23 February 1817 had married Martha Fuller.[1046] Uriah Fuller was also taxed in the same district in 1818, but he owned no land at that time.[1047] At the time of the 1820 census, Uriah was enumerated on the same page as Zephaniah Templeton, Richard Matthews,[1048] and

---

[1039] K. F. Mitchell, *Early Southern Fullers* (Easley, SC, 2004), pp. 1-40. Mitchell chronicles the descendants of Ezekiel Fuller through several generations, detailing John Fuller and his migrations through South Carolina into Georgia.

[1040] John Fuller was in Orange County from at least 1755 until after 1761. See Orange Co., NC, Court Minutes, 1752-1761, pp. 103, 193, 410, 434.

[1041] Revolutionary War Pension Application of John Fuller, R3835, The National Archives, Washington, D.C., Microfilm Series M805, Roll 343.

[1042] Davidson, ed., *Historical Records of Georgia, Richmond County*, pp. 244-245.

[1043] 1806 Columbia Co., GA, Tax Digest, Georgia Department of Archives and History, Morrow, GA.

[1044] Farmer, Morgan Co., GA, Deed Abstracts, p. 291. The land was described as "adjoining Douglas." Thomas Templeton's land also joined "Douglas" (See the 1812 Morgan Co., GA, Tax Digest). The land in question -- LL 155, LD 4, along Morgan County's Indian Creek -- was nine land lots from the Putnam County line.

[1045] 1817 Morgan Co., GA, Tax Digest, Georgia Department of Archives and History, Morrow, GA. This land was also described as "adjoining Douglas." Milton Templeton's name appeared six lines below. He paid poll tax for himself and tax on one slave; he owned no land at that time.

[1046] Jesse Thomas, who performed the Fuller-Templeton marriage, was also shown. He owned 192 acres on Indian Creek. Frances Douglas, William Douglas, and S. Douglas were all shown with land on Sugar Creek taxed in Fears' District.

[1047] 1818 Morgan Co., GA, Tax Digest, Georgia Department of Archives and History, Morrow, GA. The same neighbors were shown. Greenberry Templeton appeared nearby for himself and as agent for Milton, Thomas, and Dovey Templeton with land adjacent Douglas and Wade on Indian Creek.

[1048] Note that Richard Matthews who married Nancy Templeton may have been a first cousin of Martha Fuller who married Milton Templeton. Catherine Fuller married Richard Matthews in Columbia County in 1792. Richard Matthews was taxed there as late as 1806 but was deceased by 1808; one Richard Matthews was in Putnam County by 1815. In 1818, in Fears District, next to Thomas Templeton, Richard Matthews was taxed with 100 acres on Greenbriar Creek in Columbia County. Jesse Thomas also appeared beside the Templetons.

Hudson T. Wade.[1049] Uriah and his wife were both aged more than forty-five years at that time; their family included a son born between 1804 and 1810 and three sons and a daughter born between 1810 and 1820.[1050]

About 1826, Uriah Fuller moved from Morgan County to Lee County. He was enumerated there at the time of the 1830 census but was deceased in Sumter County by about 1832. His widow Elizabeth Fuller survived him for nearly two decades; in 1850, she was living in Sumter County, Georgia, with her daughter Louisa Fuller Faust and her son-in-law William Faust.[1051]

Tax digests, deed records, and census records establish that Uriah Fuller was a near neighbor of Milton, Thomas, and Greenberry Templeton from at least 1817 until after 1820. Moreover, he was the only Fuller known to be living in the neighborhood. Both Fuller and the Templetons had land dealings with Hudson T. Wade, and both owned tracts located adjacent lands owned by William and Robert Douglas. Moreover, Uriah Fuller named his youngest daughter Louisa Fuller, and Martha and Milton Templeton named one daughter Nancy -- probably for Milton's sister -- and another Louisa -- probably for Martha's sister. Based on the available evidence, Uriah Fuller appears to have been the father of Martha Fuller Templeton.

Uriah Fuller left no will, and no returns on his estate have been found. Based on location, association, and family traditions, it is believed that Uriah Fuller fathered the following children: Martha Fuller Templeton; James Fuller; Amos Enoch Emmanuel Fuller; Walton W. Fuller; John D. Fuller; Asa Jefferson Fuller; Francis A. Fuller; Louisa Fuller Faust; Multrie Fuller; and Juriah Fuller.[1052]

After his marriage to Martha Fuller, Milton Templeton resided in Morgan and Macon Counties, Georgia. Prior to his marriage, but while living in Morgan, Milton Templeton served as a soldier in the War of 1812, enlisting with his brother Greenberry Templeton in Wimberley's Division.[1053] Later, in 1820, as a resident of McClendon's District, Morgan County, he drew land lot 254, land district 5, Appling County. A year later, on 11 May 1821, when he chose to sell the forty-seven and three-fourths acres of land conveyed to him by his father, it was to friend and neighbor Hudson Wade that he sold it. Wade paid Templeton $357.75 for the tract, which was described as adjoining the land of Greenberry Templeton.[1054]

Milton Templeton was still living in Morgan County in 1829 when he joined his siblings in the deed disposing of the lands of Thomas and Ann Templeton; he has not been located in the 1830 census, although he may already have moved to Lee or Sumter Counties, where Uriah Fuller and his family had settled. By 1840, Milton was living in GMD 470, Macon County, Georgia, where he was enumerated with two sons aged 10-15, a daughter aged 0-5, and a daughter aged 5-10. Milton and his wife Martha were both aged 40-50 years.[1055]

Milton Templeton seems to have been a prosperous farmer. By 1848, he owned two shares in the Macon and Western Railroad. He died between 4 December 1848, when the list of stockholders was made, and the time of the 1850 census, when Martha Fuller Templeton, age fifty-three, a widow, was enumerated as head of household.[1056]

A courthouse fire destroyed most early Macon County legal documents, so deeds, wills, and marriages no longer exist to document the first years of the Templeton residence in Macon County. An 1851 deed establishes that Martha Templeton's land lay along the road from Oglethorpe, the Macon

---

[1049] Hudson T. Wade appears as a neighbor in many transactions. He married Virginia Ware in Morgan County in 1816 and Mary Ware in Morgan County in 1828.

[1050] 1820 Morgan Co., GA, Census, p. 136.

[1051] Mitchell, *Early Southern Fullers*, pp. 797-798.

[1052] Ibid.

[1053] J. S. Kratovil, *Index to War of 1812 Service Records for Volunteer Soldiers from Georgia* (Atlanta, GA, 1986), p. 135.

[1054] Morgan Co., GA, DB GG, p. 258, Georgia Department of Archives and History, Morrow, GA.

[1055] 1840 Macon Co., GA, Census, p. 13.

[1056] 1850 Macon Co., GA, Census, p. 150.

County seat, to Pond Town[1057]. The earliest surviving Macon County tax digest dates from 1852; it reveals that Milton Templeton owned 200 acres in land lot 4, land district 1, Macon County, valued at $4,000, and other property valued at $5,910. This property included two slaves still owned by the estate. A preliminary division had already taken place, for Martha Templeton owned one slave valued at $750. Robert Templeton and William Augustus Templeton each paid tax on one slave also.[1058]

Martha Templeton outlived her husband by nearly a decade. On 29 April 1857, A. H. Greer entered returns in Macon County Court of Ordinary as executor of Milton Templeton and as administrator of Martha Templeton. The return indicates that Martha V. Templeton, a daughter of Milton and Martha, had married David Ward. The return on Martha Templeton's estate provides proof of the marriage of John T. Hammack to Louisa Templeton. A receipt dated 29 March 1856 was included, reading:

> Voucher No. 4: Received this 29 day of March, 1856, of Allen H. Greer, administrator on the estate of Martha Templeton, deceased, fifty-six dollars, twenty cents in full payment of my distributive share of said estate in right of my wife Louisa.

The document was signed by John T. Hammock with Joel B. Griffin and John M. Greer as witnesses.[1059]

The returns on Martha Templeton's estate provide evidence that the family maintained a comfortable existence during the life of Milton Templeton and after his death. The estate paid for such items as Webster's *Defense*, Darus' *Arithmetick*, and the *New York Review*. Other payments included sums for "1 pair of gloves, .25, 1 pair of shoes, $1.18 3/4, 9 yards, presents for daughter" in 1851. The date for that receipt is 27 May 1851 and may reflect preparations for the marriage of Louisa Templeton to John T. Hammack about that time. The date of Martha Templeton's death is not shown, but she seems to have been deceased by 29 March 1856, when John T. Hammack signed his receipt.[1060]

The relationship of Allen H. Greer (1819-1888) to the Templeton family is unclear. Executors and administrators were often close relatives of the deceased; Greer may have been a son-in-law or perhaps business associate of the Templetons. His wife Caroline (1819-1871) is buried with him in the Oglethorpe Cemetery, Macon County, Georgia, but her maiden name is not indicated.[1061] There may have been other offspring whose marriages are not documented by the surviving estate returns. The documented offspring of Milton Templeton and Martha Fuller were:[1062] Martha Templeton (c. 1817-after 1850), who married David Ward; William Augustus Templeton (c. 1827-c. 1857), who died unmarried, Robert M. Templeton (c. 1827-c. 1856); Louisa Templeton (c. 1833-after 1870), who married John T. Hammack; and Nancy Templeton (c. 1837-before 1860), who married Joseph J. Mashburn.

Martha Templeton married David Ward prior to 1840; at the time of the 1850 Randolph County, Georgia, census, they had four children aged 10 to 15. The eldest of these was John M. Ward, who by 1860 was living in Choctaw County, Mississippi, with his uncle John T. Hammack and family. On 16 December 1858, David Ward conveyed to Carlton McKenzie his "undivided interest, being 1/6 part" of land lot 321, land district 28, "originally Lee, now Macon County, Georgia." Felix W. Hammack and A.

[1057] Macon Co., GA, DB A, pp. 34-35.

[1058] 1852 Macon Co., GA, Tax Digest, Georgia Department of Archives and History, Morrow, GA. Allen H. Greer served as Milton Templeton's executor; he may have been another son-in-law, but no proof has been found.

[1059] Macon Co., GA, Returns Book A, p. 79.

[1060] Ibid.

[1061] The International Genealogical Index of the Latter Day Saints includes information submitted by descendants of Allen H. Greer indicating that he married Caroline Templeton.

[1062] Although no final settlement was located for Milton, Martha, Robert or William Augustus Templeton it would appear that there were only six children who survived to adulthood in this family, for the deeds by which the Templeton estate were sold all speak of an "undivided 1/6 interest." This being the case, all six heirs are identified through the census, deed and estate records. See Macon Co., GA, Returns Book A, p. 79.

H. Greer witnessed the deed.[1063] At the same time, Ward appointed his son John M. Ward "power-of-attorney" to receive from Allen H. Greer his portion of the estate of William A. Templeton, deceased.[1064] William A. Templeton, brother of Louisa Hammack, had died unmarried, leaving an estate valued in excess of $1,500.[1065]

Like his brother William, Robert Templeton also died young, at about thirty years of age. He had recently married, however, and he left a young widow and an only child when he died in 1856. Mrs. Caroline Templeton remarried in November 1856 to Thomas H. B. Fleming, who became guardian for her young son, Robertus Templeton,[1066] and who served as administrator for the estate of Robert Templeton himself.[1067] No record of Thomas and Caroline Fleming, or of Robertus Templeton, has been found following the last record of Robert Templeton's estate in 1859.

Nancy Templeton, the youngest child of Milton and Martha, was thirteen at the time of the 1850 census enumeration. She had married Joseph J. Mashburn by the time her mother died in 1856. Nancy herself apparently died at a young age, leaving two children, Augustus and Mary, who were both born about 1855. The 1860 census of San Augustine County, Texas (located along the boundary between Texas and Louisiana), showed that Joseph Mashburn had remarried to a twenty year old woman named Lucy, a native of Florida.[1068] By 1870, Joseph, Lucy, and their large family were living near Wheelock in Robertson County, Texas. Joseph had by that time become a minister, an occupation he followed for the rest of his life.[1069]

Based on the evidence located, Louisa Templeton's paternal ancestors were self-sufficient farmers who moved from Northern Ireland to Pennsylvania and then to North Carolina and Georgia. Her grandfather, Thomas Templeton, owned first a modest tract of seventy-eight acres in Columbia County, Georgia, and then a larger tract of 202.5 acres in Morgan County, which he divided among his children. Milton Templeton prospered, owning an even larger tract and half a dozen slaves in Macon County. His wife, Martha Fuller, came from English stock, but her ancestors were also small farmers, owning tracts that ranged from the 101.5 acres owned by Uriah Fuller in 1817 to the several hundred acres each owned by his father John and his grandfather Ezekiel. Milton and Martha seem to have prospered after settling in Macon County, Georgia, and the annual returns filed on their estates as well as those of sons William Augustus Templeton and Robert M. Templeton evidence a polite and refined existence.

[1063] Macon Co., GA, DB A, p. 279.

[1064] Macon Co., GA, DB A, p. 394. David Ward was then living in Clay Co., GA.

[1065] Macon Co., GA, Annual Returns, Book A, pp. 522-24.

[1066] Macon Co., GA, DB A, p. 591.

[1067] Macon Co., GA, Annual Returns, Book A, pp. 345-46.

[1068] 1860 San Augustine Co., TX, Census, p. 362. Joseph and the two children were both born in Georgia.

[1069] 1870 Robertson Co., TX, p. 278. Augustus was shown as Giles, age twelve, and Mary was shown correctly, but as age thirteen.

Descendants of Thomas Templeton

Thomas Templeton — Ann

- Milton Templeton
- Martha Fuller
  - Martha Templeton
  - David Ward
  - Caroline Templeton
  - Allen H. Greer
  - Robert M. Templeton
  - Caroline [------]
  - William Augustus Templeton
  - Louisa Templeton
  - John T. Hammack
  - Nancy Templeton
  - Rev. Joseph J. Mashburn
- Dovey Templeton
- Greenberry Templeton
- Zepheniah Templeton
- Nancy Templeton

Chapter 24:

Sallie Elizabeth Cates Hammack of Hinds County, Mississippi

Sallie Elizabeth Cates Hammack was born 14 January 1863 in Hinds County, Mississippi, and died there 30 April 1951, aged eighty-eight years. She married William Simms Hammack on 20 December 1883 in Hinds County. Widowed sixteen years later, Sallie survived her husband by more than half a century.

Sallie's parents, Anderson Bradley Cates and Abbie Doxey Brown, were both natives of Mississippi. Anderson Bradley Cates was born 31 July 1834 and died 26 April 1884, both in Hinds County. He married Abbie Doxey Brown there near Raymond on 19 September 1860. A lifelong resident of Hinds County, Abbie Doxey Brown Cates was born 10 November 1841 and died 1 January 1940, in her ninety-eighth year.

The parents of Anderson Bradley Cates and Abbie Doxey Brown migrated together in one extended kinship group from Person and Caswell Counties, North Carolina, where they had lived for three generations. In fact, a kinship tie existed between them. Colonel Drury J. Brown was a son of Alfred Brown and Judith Nichols; Alfred Brown died at an early age, leaving a widow and several children, and Judith Nichols Brown remarried to a young widower named John Cates. John Cates had first married Elizabeth Foster, by whom he had a son John Foster Cates. Thus, John Foster Cates and Drury J. Brown -- the two grandfathers of Sallie Elizabeth Cates -- were step-brothers, and they had half-siblings in common. Judith Nichols Brown Cates, maternal great-grandmother and paternal step-great-grandmother of Sallie Elizabeth Cates Hammack, lived to an extended age, dying when Sallie was a young girl in Hinds County.

The four grandparents of Sallie Elizabeth Cates Hammack will be discussed briefly below; natives of Person and Caswell Counties, North Carolina, they descended from families that had settled in eastern Virginia during the seventeenth-century and later moved into North Carolina as new lands became available.

A. John Foster Cates.

The Cates family lineage begins with Robert Cate, Sr. (by c. 1668, possibly England - c. 1729, Surry County, Virginia), who was living in Henrico County, Virginia, by 30 September 1689, when he apprenticed himself for four years to Peter Wyke. Wyke was to teach Cate to be a shoemaker, and in return for learning this skill Cate obligated himself to work for Wyke for four years.[1070] By 1 April 1695, Cate was a free man, and at that time he announced his intention to leave Henrico County.[1071] Prior to this, he had for a period of time been leasing a plantation from Edward Matthews of Henrico County.[1072]

No record of Cate has been found between his avowed departure in 1695 and 1701, but by late 1701 he was back in Henrico County. He had, prior to this date, converted to the Quaker faith, and in 1701 he signed a certificate as a member of Curles Monthly Meeting in Henrico County. As early as 1695, he had leased a plantation next to lands owned by John Pleasants, a prominent Quaker, and in 1713 Pleasants received a certificate for paying Cate's transportation into the colony. By Virginia law at that time, a man was entitled to fifty acres for each individual whose transportation into the colony he financed. Pleasants may have been responsible for bringing Cate to the colony in the 1680s, or he may have financed a later trip to England. In either case, he claimed 1,385 acres for bringing twenty-eight people into the colony.[1073]

[1070] Weisiger, *Henrico Co., VA, Deeds, 1677-1705*, p. 54.
[1071] Ibid., p. 88.
[1072] Ibid., p. 92.
[1073] Patent Book No. 10, p. 94, as cited in, Nugent, *Cavaliers and Pioneers*, 3: 133.

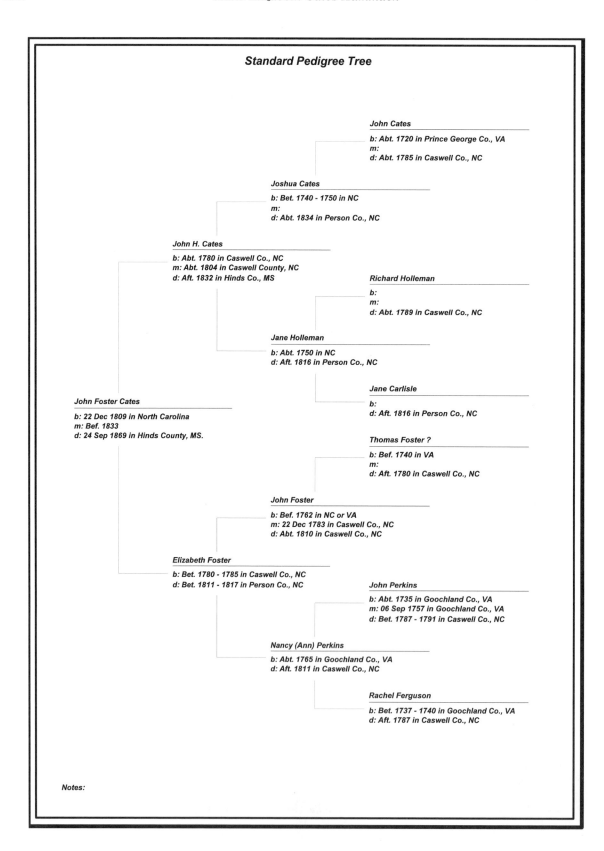

Standard Pedigree Tree

John Cates
b: Abt. 1720 in Prince George Co., VA
m:
d: Abt. 1785 in Caswell Co., NC

Joshua Cates
b: Bet. 1740 - 1750 in NC
m:
d: Abt. 1834 in Person Co., NC

John H. Cates
b: Abt. 1780 in Caswell Co., NC
m: Abt. 1804 in Caswell County, NC
d: Aft. 1832 in Hinds Co., MS

Richard Holleman
b:
m:
d: Abt. 1789 in Caswell Co., NC

Jane Holleman
b: Abt. 1750 in NC
d: Aft. 1816 in Person Co., NC

Jane Carlisle
b:
d: Aft. 1816 in Person Co., NC

John Foster Cates
b: 22 Dec 1809 in North Carolina
m: Bef. 1833
d: 24 Sep 1869 in Hinds County, MS.

Thomas Foster ?
b: Bef. 1740 in VA
m:
d: Aft. 1780 in Caswell Co., NC

John Foster
b: Bef. 1762 in NC or VA
m: 22 Dec 1783 in Caswell Co., NC
d: Abt. 1810 in Caswell Co., NC

Elizabeth Foster
b: Bet. 1780 - 1785 in Caswell Co., NC
d: Bet. 1811 - 1817 in Person Co., NC

John Perkins
b: Abt. 1735 in Goochland Co., VA
m: 06 Sep 1757 in Goochland Co., VA
d: Bet. 1787 - 1791 in Caswell Co., NC

Nancy (Ann) Perkins
b: Abt. 1765 in Goochland Co., VA
d: Aft. 1811 in Caswell Co., NC

Rachel Ferguson
b: Bet. 1737 - 1740 in Goochland Co., VA
d: Aft. 1787 in Caswell Co., NC

Notes:

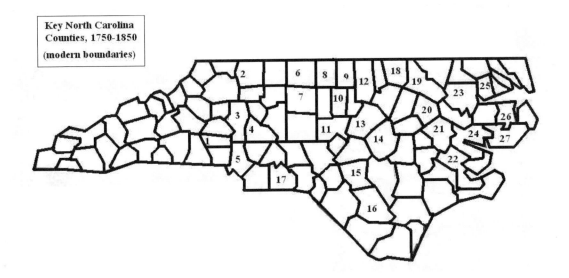

North Carolina County Map
Key: Significant Counties for Hammack-Cates Ancestry

1. Lincoln	10. Orange	19. Halifax
2. Surry	11. Chatham	20. Edgecombe
3. Iredell	12. Granville	21. Pitt
4. Rowan	13. Wake	22. Craven
5. Mecklenburg	14. Johnston	23. Bertie
6. Rockingham	15. Cumberland	24. Beaufort
7. Guilford	16. Bladen	25. Chowan
8. Caswell	17. Anson	26. Tyrell
9. Person	18. Warren	27. Hyde

Cates Ancestors in Virginia, c. 1608 - c. 1750

1=Burch Family, King and Queen Co., VA, c. 1710 - c. 1750
2=Nichols Family, Norfolk and Princess Anne Counties, VA, c. 1650 - c. 1730
3=Cates Family, Henrico Co., VA, c. 1690 - c. 1720, and Perkins Family, Henrico Co., VA, c. 1650 - c. 1730
4=Perkins, Whitfield, and Towler Families, Goochland Co., VA, c. 1730 - c. 1770
5=Jones Family, Isle fo Wight and Southampton Counties, VA, c. 1680 - c. 1740
6=Calthorpe Family, York Co., VA, c. 1650 - c. 1740
7=Jones and Calthorpe Families, Southampton Co., VA, c. 1750 - c. 1775
8=Brown Family, Mecklenburg and Amelia Counties, VA, c. 1750 - c. 1770

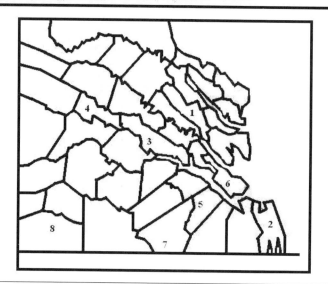

Cates Family Residence, Hinds Co., MS
Established c. 1835

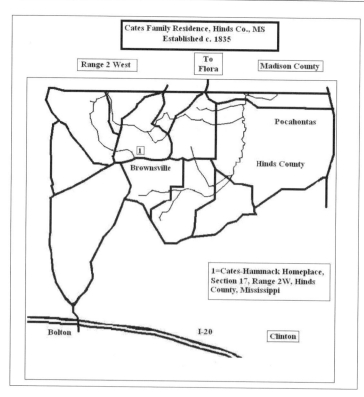

Range 2 West

To Flora

Madison County

Pocahontas

Brownsville

Hinds County

1=Cates-Hammack Homeplace,
Section 17, Range 2W, Hinds
County, Mississippi

Bolton   I-20   Clinton

AGREEMENT WITH FREEDMEN.

This Agreement, made this 23rd day of June A. D., 1865, by and between John G. Cates of the County of Hinds and State of Mississippi, of the first part, and the persons hereinafter named and undersigned, Freedmen of the same place, parties hereto of the second part,

Witnesseth, That for the purpose of cultivating the plantation known as the farm of John G. Cates in the County aforesaid, during the year commencing on the 23rd day of June A. D. 1865, and terminating on the 1st day of January, 1866. The said John G. Cates party of the first part, in consideration of the promises and conditions hereinafter mentioned on the part of the parties of the second part, agrees to furnish to the said laborers and those rightfully dependent on them, free of charge, clothing and food of good quality and sufficient quantity; good and sufficient quarters; medical attendance when necessary, and kind and humane treatment.

Henry his mark Cates.   Sarah her mark Cates.   Patsy her mark Cates John F. Cate
William his mark Cates.   Harriet her mark Cates. Sal her mark Cates
Calvin his mark Cates.   Jane her mark Cates.   Hester her mark Cates
Moses his mark Cates.   Rhody her mark Cates.   Steven his mark Cates

And it is further agreed, That in case the said party of first part shall fail, neglect, or refuse to fulfil any of the obligations assumed by him, or shall furnish said parties of the second part with insufficient food or clothing, or be guilty of cruelty to them he shall, besides the legal recourse left to the party or parties aggrieved, render this contract liable to annulment by the Provost Marshal of Freedmen. And it is agreed on the part of the parties of the second part that they will each well and faithfully perform such labor as the said party of the first part may require of them for the time aforesaid, not exceeding ten hours per day in summer and nine hours in winter, and in every respect be dutiful and faithful servants; and in case any laborer shall voluntarily absent themselves from, or shall neglect, or refuse to perform the labor herein promised, and the fact shall be proven to the satisfaction of the proper officer, the party so offending shall be punished in such manner as the Provost Marshal of Freedmen shall deem proper.

In Testimony Whereof, The said parties have affixed their names to this Agreement at the plantation of J. G. Cates, Hinds Co., State of Mississippi, on the day and date aforesaid.

Executed in Presence of

J. G. Williams

16 Dependents.

This document was prepared by John Foster Cates following the emancipation of Mississippi slaves at the end of the American Civil War. Labor contracts like this were one form of agreement by which former masters and slaves attempted to come to terms with the reality of life in the post-emancipation South.

From 1720 to 1728, Robert Cate appeared in Prince George and Charles City County records, south of the James River and east of Henrico County. By late 1728, he had settled east of Prince George County in Surry County, and he was deceased there by 18 February 1729/30, when his widow Anne qualified as his administrator and Christopher Tatum, William Tomlinson, and Edward Davis were ordered to appraise the estate.[1074]

The offspring of Robert Cate have not been documented, but Henrico and Prince George County legal documents suggest that he was the father of John Cate, Richard Cate, and Robert Cate, Jr. Of these offspring, John Cate was of age by 1 October 1707 in Henrico County, where he was living as late as 1749; he had at least one child, a son named Curtis Cates who was living in Henrico as late as 1735.[1075] Richard Cate was of age by 14 April 1720, when he witnessed a document in Prince George County along with his brother Robert Cate, Jr.; he was living there as late as 1759.[1076] Some researchers believe that Robert Cate may also have been the father of men named Thomas, Benjamin, and William Cate, who were living in Orange County, North Carolina, by about 1754.

Robert Cate, Jr., was living in Prince George County, Virginia, as late as 1720 but afterwards settled in Granville and Orange Counties, where he was living as late as 1754. He apparently settled there with three of his brothers and several of his nephews, as the presence of several men named John, Thomas, Richard, and Robert Cate -- all contemporaries -- suggests. Bernard Cates, involved in a legal proceeding in Orange County in 1769 with Thomas and Charles Cate, may have been named for Bernard Sykes, who had legal dealings with Richard Cate in Prince George Co., VA.[1077]

Surviving Orange County legal records do not document the offspring of Robert Cate, Jr., although a careful study of such records suggest that he probably had several sons, among them Thomas Cate (born by about 1720), who died testate in 1764[1078], and John Cate (born by about 1722), who died testate in Caswell County in 1784. Thomas Cate and Robert Cate are mentioned together as early as 1754, and Thomas's will indicates that he was the father of Thomas Cate, Jr. (living, Orange County, North Carolina, 1790); Joseph Cates (living, Orange County, North Carolina, 1799); Reuben Cate; Sarah Cate; and John Cate. Thomas may also have had a son named Richard who was not named in his will.[1079]

John Cate (c. 1722-c. 1785) was the ancestor of the Cates family of Hinds County, Mississippi. He was living in Orange County, North Carolina, by 20 March 1753, when he was granted 200 acres on Flat River in what was then Granville County.[1080] On 4 December 1753, he received a survey for 227 acres on the south side of the south fork of Flat River in what was by then Orange County.[1081] In April 1754, the Orange County Court named him commissioner to supervise the construction of a road across Flat River;

[1074] B. B. Weisiger, III, *Prince George Co., VA, Wills and Deeds, 1713-28* (Richmond, 1973), p. 55; W. W. Hinshaw, *Encyclopedia of American Quaker Genealogy* (6 vols., Ann Arbor, MI, 1936-1950), 6: 162; Weisiger, *Prince George 1713-28*, p. 117, 119; B. B. Weisiger, III, *Charles City Co., VA, Wills and Deeds, 1725-31* (Richmond, 1984), p. 24; L. H. Hart, III, *Surry Co., VA, Wills, Estates and Inventories, 1730-1800* (Easley, SC, 1983), p. 2.

[1075] B. B. Weisiger, *Henrico Co., VA, Deeds, 1706-1737* (Richmond, 1706-1737), pp. 7, 49; B. B. Weisiger, III, *Charles City Co., VA, Records, 1737-1774, with several 17th Century Fragments* (Richmond, 1986), p. 113; Fleet, *Virginia Colonial Abstracts*, 21: 412. This volume deals with Henrico County and the Southside.

[1076] Weisiger, *Prince George 1713-28*, p. 55; B. B. Weisiger, *Prince George Co., VA, Records, 1733-92* (Richmond, 1975), pp. 41, 62, 70.

[1077] Weisiger, *Prince George 1733-92*, p. 70. Descendants of Bernard Cates claim that he was a son of Thomas and Rebecca Sykes Cate and a grandson of Bernard Sykes of Prince George Co., VA.

[1078] There were several contemporary men named Thomas Cates in Orange County. One might have been a son of Robert Cate, Sr., of Henrico and Prince George Counties.

[1079] Orange Co., NC, Will Book A, p. 66.

[1080] M. M. Hoffman, *The Granville District of North Carolina, 1748-63: Abstracts of Land Grants* (5 vols., 1988-1995), Vol. 4, No. 2521.

[1081] W. D. Bennett, *Orange Co., NC, Records* (19 vols., Raleigh, NC, 1987 -), 1: 5. This may be the same 227 acre tract on Flat River for which Cate received a grant in 1759. See Hoffman, *Granville District, 1748-63*, Vol. 4, No. 3778. This land is mentioned again in a 1767 deed. See Orange Co., NC, DB 2, p. 514.

Lawrence Bankston, one of the Orange County Justices, served as his supervisor.[1082] Soon afterwards, on 9 May 1755, Cate received another grant for 191 acres in Orange County.[1083] On 14 February 1760, Cate entered a claim to 600 acres in Orange County on Flat River.

John Cate lived on these tracts along Flat River until his death in 1784. When Caswell was formed from Orange, the land fell into the new county. As early as 1771, John Cate had begun to provide for family members. On 23 October 1771, he deeded seventy acres on Flat River to John Pyron, and on 25 January 1772 as John Cate, Sr., he deeded seventy-six acres, also on Flat River, to John Cate, Jr. John Pyron and Joseph Aldridge, who appears frequently with John Cate in legal transactions and as a neighbor of Cate's in deed records, witnessed the instrument.[1084] Joshua Cate, John's son, witnessed the 1771 deed from Cate to Pyron.

At the time of the 1777 Caswell County, North Carolina, tax list, Joshua Cate, Thomas Cate, and John Cate were taxed together in St. Luke's District. Joshua was taxed with 506 acres, Thomas with 160 acres, and John with 144 acres. Joshua may have been paying tax on portions of his father's land then under his control but still legally belonging to his father, for no legal transfer seems to have taken place until after the elder man's death in 1785.[1085]

An Orange County court order dated March 1757 identifies John Cate's wife as Margery; they were at that time present in court to give evidence at the suit of Berry v. Gibb.[1086] They had a large family, including several children named in John Cate's 1785 will. Of these, Margery Cate married John Pyron, who had several legal dealings with members of John Cate's family in Orange and Caswell Counties. Nancy Cate Griffin and Elizabeth Cate Berry were also married when their father named them in his will; Nancy may have married Thomas Griffin and Elizabeth may have married William Berry, both of whom were neighbors and associates of Cates family members. John Cate, Jr., born about 1745, may have been the man of that name who moved to Jefferson County, Tennessee, dying in the Damplin Valley about 1828. Joshua Cate, born about 1750, remained in Caswell County, North Carolina. Thomas Cate, identified in John Cate's will as his father's youngest son, was probably born by 1756. He was taxed with 160 acres in 1777 and on 18 June 1784 received a deed from his father for 121 acres on Flat River.[1087] He was taxed in St. Luke's District in 1784 and mentioned in Thomas Vanhook's inventory in 1791.[1088] Robert Cate of Flat River, who owned 200 acres of land adjoining the lands of John Cate, Sr., may have been a son not named in his father's will, possibly because he had already been gifted land.[1089]

The first known reference to Joshua Cate dates from 1771, when he witnessed a deed from his father to his brother-in-law John Pyron. From that time until his death in 1834, he appears regularly in Caswell and Person County, North Carolina, legal records. He purchased land in Person County on Aldridge's Creek of Flat River in 1791 from James Jones[1090] and was taxed in St. Luke's District, Person County, in 1795, along with Thomas Cates, William Cates, Matthias Cates, James Rimmer, James Farquhar, Josiah Browne, and William Browne. This land in 1795 was identified as an adjacent tract when Miles Wells of Granville County, grandfather of Sarah Wells Brown, purchased 353 acres on Aldridge Creek.[1091]

[1082] R. H. Shields, *Abstracts of the Minutes of the Court of Pleas and Quarter Sessions of Orange Co., NC, 1752-1766* (Chapel Hill, NC, 1965), p. 144.

[1083] Hoffman, *Granville District, 1748-63*, Vol. 4, No. 3788.

[1084] Orange Co., NC, DB 3, pp. 355, 464.

[1085] 1777 Caswell Co., NC, Tax List, North Carolina Department of Archives and History, Raleigh, NC; Caswell Co., NC, Will Book B, p. 84.

[1086] Shields, *Orange Co., NC, Court Minutes*, p. 212. Many researchers list her name -- without cited documentation -- as Margery Lawrence.

[1087] Caswell Co., NC, Deed Book C, p. 31.

[1088] Caswell Co., NC, Will Book B, p. 422.

[1089] Caswell Co., NC, Deed Book C, p. 154.

[1090] Person Co., NC, DB C, p. 318.

[1091] Person Co., NC, DB B, p. 103.

In 1805, Joshua Cate, Sr., was taxed with 640 acres, while Isaiah Cate, John Cate, Jr., and Matthew Cate were taxed with 300 acres, 250 acres, and 330 acres respectively.[1092] On 6 December 1806, Joshua deeded to James Thomson a tract on Aldridge's Creek, including the land where Isaiah Cate then lived.[1093] In 1813, Joshua deeded 122 acres on Flat River to Robert Wallis, and in 1814 he deeded 116.5 acres on Flat River to Charles Cates and 161.5 acres to John Cate, Jr..[1094] In May 1814, Joshua deeded 161.5 acres on Aldridge's Creek to John Cate, Jr.[1095] Based on these deeds, it would appear that Joshua was attempting to provide for his children and grandchildren, perhaps anticipating his own demise. By the time of the 1823 Person Co., NC, tax digest, Joshua Cate, Sr., was taxed with no property, while Joshua, Jr., owned 345 acres; Charles owned 116 acres; Robert owned 120 acres; and John owned 162 acres himself and also controlled 102 acres for the orphans of Alfred Brown.[1096]

Legal records and religious ones link the Cates family with the Brown family into which they would later marry. Both families attended Wheeley's and Flat River Primitive Baptist Churches, and land records indicate that they owned contiguous tracts. Estate records suggest that they had other associations as well. In August 1814, when the heirs of James Farquhar (great-grandfather of Colonel Drury J. Brown) auctioned off his personal estate, members of the community assembled to bid on and purchase items. Among these individuals were Miles Wells, John Brown (grandfather of Drury Brown), Joshua Cate, Sr., Joshua Cate, Jr., James Cate, Sr., Charles Cate, and John Cate, Jr.[1097]

At the time of the 1820 Person County, North Carolina, census, eight Cate households were enumerated. Joshua Cate and his wife were both aged over forty-five years, while a male and female aged 16-26 were living with them. Joshua's wife apparently died between 1820 and 1830. At the time of the 1830 Person County census, Joshua Cates, Sr., was enumerated as aged 80-90 years old. At that time, he was residing with Joshua Cates, Jr., aged 30-40, and two households away from his son John Cates, Sr., aged 40-50.[1098]

Although Joshua Cate had disposed of his lands in 1814, he retained possession of several slaves until near the end of his long life. In 1829, he deeded two slaves to his son Charles,[1099] and, in 1831, he deeded another two to his son John,[1100] one to his grandson James F. Cates,[1101] and seven to his son James H. Cates, at which time he confirmed to James the title to 160 acres.[1102] Joshua was still alive as late as 31 January 1835 -- at which time he was more than eighty-five years old -- when he conveyed one slave to his son Richard Cates.[1103]

Joshua Cates married, probably about 1775, Jane Holeman, a daughter of Richard and Jean Carlisle Holeman who had moved to Orange County, North Carolina, from Maryland. Richard Holeman died about 1789 in what was then Caswell County; his widow survived him until 1816. On 4 May 1816, an inventory of her estate was filed, and, in November 1816 in Person County, Joshua Cates and Richard Holeman entered a motion requesting the county court to appoint commissioners to appraise and divide the Negroes of Jean Holeman, deceased. The commissioners on 27 November 1816 reported that the estate had been settled through the division of the Negroes between Richard Holeman, Joshua Cates, and the children of Elizabeth Persons. It would seem that when Richard Holeman died in 1789, he must have

---

[1092] 1805 Person Co., NC, Tax List, North Carolina Department of Archives and History, Raleigh, NC.

[1093] Person Co., NC, DB D, p. 38.

[1094] Person Co., NC, DB D, pp. 392, 395, 398.

[1095] Person Co., NC, Deed Book D, p. 398.

[1096] 1823 Person Co., NC, Tax Digest, North Carolina Department of Archives and History, Raleigh, NC.

[1097] Person Co., NC, Record Book 6, pp. 227-237.

[1098] 1820 Person Co., NC, Census, pp. 252-253.

[1099] Person Co., NC, DB K, pp. 37-38.

[1100] Person Co., NC, DB K, p. 130.

[1101] Person Co., NC, DB K, p. 121.

[1102] Person Co., NC, DB K, p. 139.

[1103] Person Co., NC, DB L, pp. 337-38.

requested that his estate fall to his wife for the remainder of her life and remain undivided until after her death or remarriage.[1104]

Joshua Cate and Jane Holeman reared a large family in Caswell and Person Counties. Richard Holeman Cates (c. 1779-c.1870) married Lucy Perkins Grant, a first cousin of Elizabeth Foster Cates, who married Richard's brother.[1105] John Cate married first, on 25 September 1804, Elizabeth Foster and second, on 21 June 1817, Judith Nichols Brown. Joshua Cates, Jr., seems to have predeceased his father, dying about March 1834 in Person County.[1106] Charles H. Cates was living in Person County as late as 1830; he married Charlotte Wilson and died en route to Tennessee in 1833. Robert H. Cates died about 1825 in Person County, leaving five orphans who became wards of their uncle James H. Cates. James H. Cates (1792-1852) remained in Person County, where he married Edith Moore in 1828 and Frances Hudgins in 1844.[1107] Elizabeth Cates, who married Isaiah Cates on 6 August 1800 in Person County, may have been Joshua Cate's daughter.[1108]

John Cates, son of Joshua Cates and Jane Holeman, married twice, first, on 25 September 1804 in Person County, to Elizabeth Foster and second, on 21 April 1817 in Person County, to Mrs. Judith Nichols Brown. John's brother Richard served as bondsman when he married Elizabeth Foster in 1804; Richard's wife Lucy Perkins Grant and John's wife Elizabeth Foster were cousins. Elizabeth died sometimes between 1811 -- the date of her father's estate division -- and 1817, the date of John Cates's second marriage. In 1818, Cates became guardian for his step-children, Drury J. and Malinda Brown.[1109] He served in this capacity until near the time when wards reached their majority.[1110] Court documents reveal that Cates was a conscientious guardian, providing regularly for Drury Brown's education and managing the lands and slaves inherited from Brown's father Alfred to the benefit of his two wards.

John Cates was enumerated in Person County in 1820 and 1830 as head of household. In 1820, he headed a family that included himself, wife Judith, six males born between 1802 and 1820, and two females born between 1804 and 1820.[1111] In 1830, Cates was aged 40-50, hence born between 1780 and 1790, and head of a household that included Judith, two males born between 1815 and 1825, and five females born between 1820 and 1830.[1112] The 1823 Person County tax list indicates that John was during these years living on a tract of 161 acres on Flat River and managing another tract of 102 acres held for the orphans of Alfred Brown. John's own lands -- 161.5 acres on Aldridge's Creek of Flat River -- had

---

[1104] Note that the two slaves deeded to James H. Cates by Joshua in 1831 were the two slaves he inherited from the estate of Jean Holeman in 1816. See also the will of Charles Holeman, dated 1813, Person Co., NC, Records Book 7, p. 2, which identifies his mother Jane Holeman and names nephews Charles Holeman and James Holeman, sons of Richard Holeman. The will also mentions property in Wilson Co., TN. Person Co., NC, Records Book 7, p. 273, contains the recorded division of Jean Holeman's slaves. Joshua Cates received Francis, Elisha, and Jinny. In 1831, Joshua Cate, Sr., deeded Frances and her three children, Elisha, Tim, and Americas to James H. Cates (Person Co., NC, Records Book 11, p. 139). Richard Holeman may have been a son of Daniel Holeman and Elizabeth Cartley, who settled in Fairfax Co., VA.

[1105] Lucy was born 11 December 1774 in Goochland Co., VA, a daughter of John Perkins, Jr. She married first, 23 September 1793, Caswell Co., NC, Cornelius Grant.

[1106] Person Co., NC, Estate Book 1831-37, p. 260-62.

[1107] C. C. Moore, probably Elizabeth's brother, died in Hinds Co., MS, in 1853. His will (Hinds Co., MS, Will Book A, p. 319) names the following heirs: nephew, Legrand H. Whitfield of Christian Co., KY; nephew, Thomas Oakley, son of Henderson Oakley; nephew, William Tapp; Nephew, Columbus Cates; nephew, John Cates; nephew, James Cates. Moore states that he was to be buried with Masonic Honors in the town of Brownsville.

[1108] The names Joshua, Josiah, and Isaiah are often confused and sometimes mistranscribed. Isaiah Cates lived on Joshua's land; he was probably a son or son-in-law. One Isaiah was a son of Thomas Cates of Orange Co., NC, but it is not clear that this was the same man.

[1109] Person Co., NC, Guardian Accounts Book A, 1810-19, p. 174.

[1110] Person Co., NC, Guardians Accounts Book B, p. 45; Person Co., NC, Guardians Accounts Book B, pp. 73-74; Person Co., NC, Guardians Accounts Book B, p. 142.; Person Co., NC, Guardians Accounts Book B, p. 212;

[1111] 1820 Person Co., NC, Census, p. 454.

[1112] 1830 Person Co., NC, Census, p. 29.

been deeded him by his father Joshua Cate, Sr., in May, 1814;[1113] he held this land until 1832, when, on 11 September, he sold this tract to Peter Wood for $300. Joshua Cates, either his father or brother of the same name, witnessed the transaction.[1114]

Several factors indicate that John Cates and his family in the fall of 1832 were contemplating a move to Mississippi. Cates' sale of the tract he had owned for two decades and on which he had reared his family is significant. Also, at the October 1832 meeting of Flat River Baptist Church, Isaac and Minerva, an enslaved couple belonging to John Cates, requested letters of dismissal from the church, indicating that they, too, were preparing for a move.[1115] Finally, oral tradition records the migration of a group of kindred families from Person County, North Carolina, to Hinds County, Mississippi, in 1832. Richard Rimmer is said to have sold his lands in Person County at this time and to have joined a wagon train for Mississippi, together with his wife and ten children. According to descendants, "they were accompanied by James and Leonard Hargis, Stephen Wells, Wright Nichols, John Cates, and John Farquhar, who settled in Hinds County."[1116]

John Cates lived for six years after settling in Mississippi, dying in 1838 when he was probably in his late fifties. Two years after the move to Mississippi, on 11 August 1835, Cates executed a deed to his adult son, John Foster Cates, for forty acres in Hinds County, Mississippi, bordering lands owned by John Cates, Josiah Chatman, and William Wells. John Cates and his wife Judith Nichols Brown Cates signed the deed.[1117] Five months later, in January 1836, Cates purchased 200 acres from Lee and Budy Grayson in Hinds County. He paid two thousand dollars for the tract, whereas his son John had paid him only $200 for a tract one-fifth as large. Perhaps the senior man had sold the land to his son at a discounted rate as part of his inheritance.[1118]

John Cates was taxed in Hinds County in 1836, 1837, and 1838. He was deceased prior to 10 September 1838, at which time Judith Cates and C. C. Spann gave bond for $20,000 to initiate the administration of the estate of "John H. Cates, deceased."[1119] The estate was taxed in 1839, and afterwards Judith Cates, widow, was taxed in her own right. On 29 July 1847, Cates and Spann gave notice of their intention to make a final distribution of Cates' estate. The document identifies the offspring of John Cates by both of his marriages:

> ...It appearing to the satisfaction of the Court that Susan Cates and Augustus V. Cates, children and heirs at law of said decedent, are minor without any legal guardian to protect their interest in this behalf, It is thereupon ordered that James W. Daughtery be and he is hereby appointed guardian ad Litem for said minors in their behalf -- and that a citation issue citing the said guardian ad Litem, and also John F. Cates, Elizabeth Lorance, and her husband John Lorance, Eliza Jane Burton and her husband David Burton, and Wilson

---

[1113] 1823 Person Co., NC, Tax List, North Carolina Department of Archives and History, Raleigh, NC; Person Co., NC, Deed Book D, p. 398.

[1114] Person Co., NC, Deed Book K, p. 389.

[1115] Flat River Primitive Baptist Church Minutes, Vol. 1, 1786-1890, Microfilm, Person Co., NC, Library.

[1116] C. Mead, *The Land Between Two Rivers: Madison Co., MS* (Canton, MS, 1998), p. 364.

[1117] Hinds Co., MS, DB 10, p. 288.

[1118] Hinds Co., MS, DB 5, p. 33.

[1119] Some Hinds County estate books are missing. Many records survive to document the administration of this estate, however. According to the Hinds Co., MS, Index to Estates, the following items were filed regarding the John Cates estate: Minutes Book 2, pp. 275 (Bonds and Letters), 281 (Inventory and Appraisement and Order to Sell), 294 (Citation to Sell Slaves); Minutes Book 3, pp. 64 (Time Allowed), 83 (Annual Settlement), 283 (Citation), 308 (Citation), 337 (Continuance), 340 (Report), 579 (Citation), 595 (Attachment), 596 (Citation), 615 (Petition to sell land), 616 (Citation to Heirs), 621 (Attachment Dismissed); Minutes Book 4, pp. 5 (Citation vs. Heirs Dismissed), 14-16 (Continuance), 44 (Citation to Sell Land), 54 (Order to Sell Real Estate), 236 (Report of Sale), 245 (Report of Sale), 344 (Citation), 367 (Continuance), 383 (Continuance), 417 (Continuance), 426 (Application for Final Settlement), 480 (Settlement Continued), 495 (Citation), 527 (Continuance), 565 (Attachment), 600 (Attachment), 624 (Continuance), 641 (Continuance), 672 (Continuance); Annual Reports Book 4, pp. 63 (Annual Return), 71 (Report of Sale), 120 (Inventory and Appraisement); Annual Reports Book 5, pp. 540 (Annual Return).

Cates, other distributees residing in this County, and Sophia Crawley and her husband C. S. Crawley in Simpson County, to be and appear before the court on the 4th Monday in October next, then and there to show cause if any they can why the final account of said administrators should not be allowed and a decree made thereupon accordingly. And it further appearing to the satisfaction of the Court that James F. Cates and Mary Burton and her husband Jno. Burton, other distributees of said estate are non residents of this state -- It is thereupon ordered that publication be made for the space of sixty days in the *Raymond Gazette* a public newspaper printed and published in the Town of Raymond in this County, citing the said non resident distributees to be and appear before this Court on the 4th Monday of October next then and there to show cause if any they can why the final account of said admr. and admx. should not be allowed and a decree made thereupon accordingly.[1120]

On 16 November 1846, as part of the preparation for the estate's final division, the lands of John Cates were put up for auction at the Hinds County courthouse:

> before the door of the Court House in the town of Raymond...at Public Sale to the highest bidder [were offered] the following land belonging to the estate of said Cates, towit: The N 1/2 W1/2 NW 1/4 of Section 28 Township 7 Range 2 West, the W 1/4 Section 29, the W 1/2 NE 1/4 and W 1/2 SE 1/4 and W 1/2 E 1/2 SW 1/4 except forty acres sold to J. F. Cates, the E 1/2 SW 1/4 of Section 15, the E 1/2 NW 1/4 of Section 22, the S 1/2 W 1/2 NE 1/4 of Section 22, all in Township 7 Range 2 West, at which sale Thomas J. Wharton of said county and state being the highest and best bidder, became the purchaser at and for the sum of one hundred and fifty dollars.[1121]

Although Wharton purchased these lands on 27 March 1847, he and his wife Mary J. Wharton for $330 deeded to Judith Cates "the following tracts or parcels of land situated in said County towit, the N 1/2 W 1/2 NW 1/4 of Section 28, Township 7, Range 2 West, the W 1/4 Section 29, the W 1/2 NE 1/4 and W 1/2 SE 1/4 and W 1/2 E 1/2 SW 1/4, except forty acres, sold to J. F. Cates, the E 1/2 SW 1/4 Section 15, all in Township 7 Range 2 West..." The second conveyance may have been a planned exchange initiated as part of the original purchase agreement before Wharton bought the lands.[1122]

On 20 December 1850, Judith Cates deeded to the heirs of John Williams for $500 "for their use and benefit the following described tract or parcel of land, Towit, the west half of the east half of the south west quarter of Section twenty-one, Township seven, Range two west, except so much of the said tract or parcel of land as was conveyed by Jno. H. Cates and Judith Cates to John F. Cates, the amount conveyed by these presents being one hundred and fifty acres more or less."[1123] On 5 June 1851, Judith Cates deeded to her daughter Susan Cates a four year old slave girl named Lavinia.[1124] On the same day, she deeded to her son Wilson Cates "the North West fourth of the west fourth of Section twenty-eight and the north east fourth of the north east fourth of Section twenty-nine all in Township seven Range two West containing eighty acres more or less." Wilson paid his mother $200 for the property.[1125]

Judith Cates was enumerated in Hinds County in 1850, 1860, and 1870. At the time of the 1850 census, she was head of Household 1233. Judith was fifty-five years old, a widow born in North Carolina with an estate valued at $800. In her household were three adult children, Wilson, Susan, and Augustus,

---

[1120] Hinds Co., MS, Probate Minutes Book 4, 1846-48, pp. 426-27.

[1121] Hinds Co., MS, DB 18, pp. 294-5

[1122] Hinds Co., MS, DB 18, pp. 295-6.

[1123] Hinds Co., MS, DB 20, pp. 656-57.

[1124] Hinds Co., MS, DB 21, p. 195.

[1125] Hinds Co., MS, DB 21, p. 196.

aged between twenty-five and eighteen years. In Household 1234 was Eliza Cates Burton and her family, while in Household 1412 was John Foster Cates. S. A. Wells, fifty-six, a North Carolina native, was in Household 1380, while William Wells, forty-four, was in Household 1419.[1126] At the time of the 1860 census, she was living alone but near her married daughter Elizabeth Lorance. Judith was shown as being sixty-five years old; she owned real estate valued at $2,000 and personal property valued at $6,000.[1127] In 1870, Judith was enumerated in Household 242, living with her son Wilson Cates and his wife Martha Elizabeth Slay Cates. Judith was a widow, aged seventy-six, a native of North Carolina, with real and personal property valued at $1,600 altogether. This considerable sum suggests that Judith had survived the American Civil War with a significant amount of property in tact.[1128]

Judith Nichols Brown Cates died prior to 1 September 1877, at which time a Chancery Notice was issued regarding the distribution of her estate.

Chancery Notice

In the Chancery Court of the second district of Hinds County, Mississippi, before the Clerk in Vacation.

In the matter of the original and amended petitions of John D. McConnell, administrator of the estate of Judith Cates, deceased, for the sale of the real and personal estate of the deceased.

Upon reading and filing the original and amended petitions of John D. McConnell, administrator of the estate of Judith Cates, deceased, praying a sale of the real and personal estate of the said decedent, to pay the debts due by her estate, the same having been sworn to by the said administrator, and it appearing to the satisfaction of the Court, that the following parties, defendants to said petitions, are non-residents of the State of Mississippi, and have their residences and post offices as follows, to-wit: Wilson Cates, of Pleasant Hill, DeSoto Parish, State of Louisiana; George Burton, whose residence and post office is unknown; Robert Burton, whose residence is in the Indian Territory, but whose exact place of residence and post office is unknown, after diligent search to find out the same; and it further appearing that there are the following heirs of the said deceased, whose names and residences and post offices are unknown to the petitioner after diligent search made therefore, to wit: the unknown children of Malenia, a daughter of the said deceased, by her husband, the late John G. Chandler, supposed to be in the state of Kentucky; the unknown children of Susan, another daughter of the said decedent, by her second husband, Thomas Williams, living, it is supposed, in Morehouse Parish, State of Louisiana; all the children of Sophia, another daughter of the decedent, by her husband, ---- Cauley or Crawley, except Drury B. and Bettie Cauley or Crawley, supposed to be living in East Mississippi, or in the State of Texas; and Green Smith and Henry and Jimmy Smith, supposed to be living in Holmes County, Mississippi, but who cannot be found after repeated and diligent search; and that there may be other heirs and distributors, of the said decedent, or claiming to be such, whose names and residences are unknown to the said petitioner.

It is therefore ordered by the court that the said non-resident and unknown heirs and distributors, do appear and plead, answer or demur, to the said original and amended petitions of the said Jno. D. McConnell, administrator aforesaid, at rules, to be held in the office of the clerk of the Chancery Court of Hinds County, at his office in Raymond, for the second district of said county, on Monday, the 13th day of November, 1877; that this order be published once a week for four consecutive weeks

---

[1126] 1850 Hinds Co., MS, Census, pp. 197-198.
[1127] 1860 Hinds Co., MS, Census, p. 580.
[1128] 1870 Hinds Co., MS, Census, p. 676.

in the *Hinds County Gazette*; and that the clerk of this Court transmit by mail, postage paid, to each one of said non-residents whose residence is known, a copy of this order. Ordered and recorded this the first day of September 1877. S: W. T. Ratliff, Clerk.

Although many of Judith's children and step-children continued to reside in Hinds County, the document indicates that, in the years after the close of the American Civil War, the descendants of Judith had become separated and in some instances estranged. The surviving Mississippi court records do not indicate whether the heirs were located or not.[1129]

Judith Nichols Brown Cates will be discussed further later inasmuch as her son Drury J. Brown was the father of Abbie Doxey Brown Cates; Judith was thus grandmother of Abbie Doxey Brown Cates and step-grandmother of Abbie Doxey's husband Anderson Bradley Cates.

Elizabeth Foster Cates, first wife of John H. Cates, was the mother of John Foster Cates. Elizabeth was a daughter of John Foster and Nancy Perkins, who married 22 December 1783 in Caswell County, North Carolina. Her paternal grandfather was probably Thomas Foster, who was taxed in Caswell County in 1780. At that time, Thomas was living in Caswell District but owned no land. Neighbors included James Perkins, John Perkins, John Perkins, Jr., and Abraham Perkins. Four years later, in 1784, Thomas Foster and John Foster were living in Caswell District; Thomas owned 110 acres, while John, whose name appears adjacent Thomas', owned no land. The listing suggests that John was Thomas's son, perhaps born about 1764, who had recently come of age. Thomas Foster has not been traced before he appeared in Caswell Co., NC, but it is possible that he was the Thomas Foster who lived near the Perkins family in Goochland County, Virginia, before they removed to Caswell.[1130]

John Foster died about 1810 in Caswell County. On 11 January 1811, a division of his lands took place. In addition to the widow, Nancy Perkins Foster, there were ten other heirs. Of these, "John Cates and Betsy his wife" received sixty-six and one-half acres adjacent Moon's Creek and the widow's dower.[1131]

Nancy Perkins Foster descended from Nicholas Perkins, who settled in Charles City County, Virginia, in the middle seventeenth century. Perkins died about 1655, leaving a widow Mary, who remarried Dr. Richard Parker of Nansemond County.[1132] Nicholas is said to descend from Thomas Perkins, who was living at Hillmorton, Warwickshire, England, in the fourteenth-century. Nicholas was living in Henrico County, Virginia, as early as 10 October 1641, when he is mentioned in a land patent for Bryant Smith, who claimed to have financed Nicholas's transportation into the colony.[1133] Nicholas may have arrived as an indentured servant, but, if so, he had completed his indenture and married by the

---

[1129] Judith Cates Chancery Notes, 1877, Cates Vertical File, Mississippi Department of Archives and History, Jackson, MS.

[1130] 1780 and 1784 Caswell Co., NC, Tax Lists, North Carolina Department of Archives and History, Raleigh, NC. It is also possible that Thomas was one of the several Thomas Fosters found in Halifax and Mecklenburg Counties, Virginia, shortly before this Thomas Foster appears in Caswell County. One Thomas Foster, however, in Goochland County baptized a daughter Catherine Graves Foster in 1782, while the Caswell Co., NC, Graves family were neighbors of John Foster. Individuals named Thomas Foster also appear in Surry, Sussex, and Amelia Counties, Virginia, prior to 1780. No clear connection with Caswell County could be demonstrated.

[1131] Caswell Co., NC, Deed Book Q, pp. 186-91. The other heirs were Robert Foster, who married Elizabeth Grant on 5 September 1805 in Caswell County; Thomas Foster, who married Polly Haralson; Susannah Foster, who married Richard Gunn on 30 October 1810 in Caswell County; Polly Foster, who married Richard Jones on 9 December 1811 in Caswell County; John Foster, who married Elizabeth Perkins on 29 July 1816 in Caswell County; Jesse Foster, who married Polly Adkins on 3 November 1817 in Caswell County; Richard Foster, who married Lucy Hobbs on 28 February 1821 in Caswell County; Azariah Foster, who married Nancy King on 30 June 1828 in Caswell County; and Sally Foster, who married James Mitchell on 3 October 1826 in Caswell County.

[1132] This Dr. Richard Parker was ancestor of Mary Almedia Bankston Hammack; see below. Charles City Records, 1655-65, pp. 62, 87, proves the marriage, which took place before September 1656 (when Richard Parker was granted administration on Nicholas's estate) and after 31 July 1656. The classic work on this family is William K. Hall's *Descendants of Nicholas Perkins of Virginia* (Ann Arbor, MI, 1957).

[1133] Virginia Land Patent Book 1, p. 783.

late 1640s. On 30 August 1650, he patented 170 acres in Bermuda Hundred, Henrico County, Virginia, in exchange for transporting four individuals, including his wife Mary, into the colony.[1134]

Nicholas Perkins, Jr., born about 1647, married Sarah Childers, who was probably a daughter of Abraham Childers, Sr., of Henrico County, Virginia. Nicholas died testate in Henrico County in 1712; Sarah survived him for nearly a decade, dying prior to January 1722 when her will -- no longer extant -- was entered for probate in Henrico County.[1135] Philemon Perkins, probably named for Sarah's brother Philemon Childers, inherited all of his father's land between Springey Branch and Abraham Childers' line in Henrico County. Born about 1680, Philemon lived in Henrico County until Goochland was formed from Henrico in 1746; he died there in 1769, at which time he was nearly ninety years old. In April 1769, Obedience Cox Perkins came "into Court and makes oath that Philemon Perkins deceased died without any will as far as she knows or believes & on her motion Certificate is granted her for obtaining Letters of Administration thereof in due form."[1136] The following year, on 6 September 1770, Obedience wrote her will in Goochland County. She died in Goochland prior to 15 April 1771, when her will was probated there.[1137] John Perkins (c. 1718-1791) married Rachel Ferguson on 6 September 1757 in Goochland County; he was named in the will of his father's brother Abram Perkins (who bequeathed him "one middling large table") in Henrico County in 1743. Along with his father Philemon, John became a resident of Goochland County when it was created. On 16 March 1772, John and Rachel Perkins sold 200 acres on Beaverdam Creek in Goochland County to George Smith.[1138] They probably moved soon afterwards to North Carolina; in any case, they were living in Caswell County by 1777, when John was taxed in Caswell District. On 29 December 1787, John wrote his will in Caswell County, naming wife Rachel and several children, including daughter Ann Foster, to whom he left a slave named Jacob.[1139]

Obedience Cox Perkins, grandmother of Nancy Perkins Foster, descended from two of Virginia's oldest families. The term "Ancient Planter" was used in early Virginia to refer to those individuals who settled in the colony during the company period, prior to the royal take-over by James I in 1624. Two years before this event, in 1622, Powhattan Indians had attacked the settlers, reducing the colony's population by more than a third. Of those settlers living in Virginia after the massacre of 1622, only about one hundred individuals have documented descendants living today. One of those individuals was William Coxe, who arrived in Virginia in 1610, aged twelve, aboard the Godspeed. Coxe traveled in the party of Thomas West, 3rd Lord De la Warr.[1140] In February 1624/5, Coxe was listed in the colony's muster with Thomas Boulding at Elizabeth City. On 20 September 1628, he received a grant for 100 acres "within the precincts of Elizabeth City," bounded on the south by the James River, on the east by Dictoris Christmas, planter, and Christopher Calthropp, Gentleman. In 1636, he received a patent for 150 acres in

---

[1134] Virginia Land Patent Book 2, p. 262.

[1135] Henrico Co., VA, Records, 1710-1714, Part 1, p. 185; Henrico Co., VA, Records, 1710-1714, Part 2, p. 299; Henrico Co., VA, Court Minutes, 1719-1724, p. 226.

[1136] Goochland Co., VA, Order Book, April, 1769; Goochland Co., VA, Deed Book 9, p. 204.

[1137] Goochland Co., VA, Deed Book 10, p. 122.

[1138] Goochland Co., VA, Deed Book 10, p. 196.

[1139] John and Rachel had several children. James Perkins married Judith Whitlow on 1 November 1764 in Goochland Co., VA. He died in Green Co., KY, in 1817. Susannah Perkins married John Baker on 5 January 1767 in Goochland County. Sarah Perkins married David Maddox on 11 September 1768 in Goochland County. John Perkins married Ursley Richardson on 12 October 1768 in Goochland County; she married (2) William Cannon in Caswell Co., NC, in 1783. Richard Perkins was born 6 September 1757 in Goochland Co., VA. Abraham Perkins was born 1 March 1760 in Goochland Co., VA, and was killed during the American Revolution on 5 March 1778. Nancy Perkins married John Foster. Jesse Perkins was born 26 June 1764 in Goochland County. Martin Perkins was born 10 March 1767 in Goochland County; he married Dicey Sawyer on 21 August 1787 in Caswell Co., NC. All of these children are either named in the will of John Perkins or otherwise documented by entries in W. K. Jones, *The Douglas Register: Detailed Register of Births, Marriages, and Deaths as Kept by the Rev. William Douglas, from 1750 to 1797* (Richmond, 1928) for Goochland Co., VA. It is possible that there were children not named in either source.

[1140] Lord De La Warr's brother Robert West married Elizabeth Coxe, daughter of Sir Henry Coxe of Broxburn, Herefordshire, and this relationship may suggest a connection between William Coxe of Virginia and Sir Henry Coxe of Broxburn, Herefordshire. See J. F. Dorman, ed., *Adventurers of Purse and Person in Virginia, 1607-1624* (3rd. ed., Richmond, VA, 1987), pp. 211-216.

Henrico County, about two and a half miles above Arrowhattocks ("Harroe Attocks"), to which land his family subsequently relocated. He was probably the William Cocke who served as a Burgess for Henrico County in 1646; he was deceased by 1656, when a land patent mentioned lands "belonging to the orphans of William Coxe."[1141]

John Cox, son of William Coxe, died in Henrico County in 1696. John married twice, first to an unknown woman and second, by license dated 22 September 1682, to Mary Kennon or Cannon. As John Cox of Arrowhattocks, he patented 550 acres in Henrico County on 29 March 1665. He wrote his will in Henrico on 19 February 1691/2, naming six sons. Mary Kennon Cox was still living on 1 February 1696 -- the date of John Cox's probate, when she filed suit against her stepsons (Henry, John, William, George, and Bartholomew Cox) in order to obtain the dower rights.[1142]

Born in 1683, Richard Cox was the only son of John Cox's marriage to Mary Kennon. He held 300 acres in Henrico at the time of the 1704 quit rent list. Richard wrote his will in Henrico on 13 July 1734, naming three sons and six daughters. To daughter Obedience Cox, for whom he had probably already provided, he left one shilling. The will, proved in February 1734/5, left to his wife Mary Trent Cox personal property and named her as executor.[1143] Cox's inventory and appraisal, filed on 7 April 1735, with John Whitlow, William Whitlow, and Abraham Bailey as commissioners, was valued at £8.[1144] When Mary Trent Cox's undated will was proven on 2 February 1735, it was found that Mary left "clothing" to daughter Obedience Perkins.[1145]

Mary Trent Cox was herself a daughter of Henry Trent, Sr., who died testate in April 1701 in Varina Parish, Henrico County, Virginia. Trent wrote his will on 8 January 1700, leaving one gold ring to daughter Mary, wife of Richard Cox. Trent left 109 acres each to his four sons and provided for his other three daughters with bequests of 2000 pounds of tobacco each.[1146] His widow, Elizabeth Sherman Trent, survived him, entering probate on the will in April 1701 before remarrying to Henry Gee of Henrico County.

Indirectly, marriage into Henry Trent's family gave Richard Cox's children ties to the Jefferson family of Henrico County, ancestors of President Thomas Jefferson. Henry Trent, brother of Mary Cox, married Edith Harris, whose mother Mary Jefferson Harris was the president's aunt.[1147]

An additional tie to the Jefferson family came through Mary Trent Cox's mother, Elizabeth Sherman Trent, daughter of Henry Sherman and Mrs. Cicely Hutchins of Henrico County. Henry Sherman died testate in 1695; he had married, about 1657/8, a widow named Cicely Hutchins, who became the mother of his children. Many researchers believe that she was Cicely Farrar, daughter of Mrs. Cicely Baley Jordan Farrar. The elder Cicely came as a widow to Virginia, where she married twice, both time to "Ancient Planters." After her husband Samuel Jordan died, Cicely married William Farrar, born 28 April, 1583, Croxton, Lincolnshire, third son of John Farrar the elder (died 1628) of Croxton and of St. Mary, Aldermanbury, London, and his wife (married 25 August, 1574, St. Sepulchre's Without Newgate, London) Ciceley Kelke, daughter of William Kelke (died 1552) of Barnetby-le-Wold, Lincolnshire. William Farrar's father was of an ancient family of Ewood, in Midgley, Halifax, Yorkshire. He was a relative of Nicholas Ferrar, Sr. (1544-1620), a merchant and a leading member of the Virginia Company. William Farrar left London on 16 March, 1617/8, in the Neptune with Lord De La Warr and reached Virginia in August, 1618. In 1623/4, when the census was taken, he was living at Jordan's Journey, where, aged thirty-one, his muster was recorded jointly with that of Mrs. Sisley Jordan, aged 24, 1624/5.

[1141] Ibid.
[1142] Ibid. Weisiger, *Henrico Co., VA, Wills, 1654-1737* (Richmond, 1976), p. 46.
[1143] Ibid., p. 143.
[1144] Ibid., p. 144.
[1145] Ibid., p. 148.
[1146] Ibid., pp. 54-55.
[1147] Dorman, *Adventurers*, pp. 97, 137, 215, 275, 469.

He had been appointed administrator of the estate of her husband, Samuel Jordan, 19 Nov., 1623. As Dorman states in *Adventurers of Purse and Person in Virginia*,[1148]

> His interest in the widow Cicely Jordan thrust him into considerable prominence in colonial records since she, within three or four days of her husband's death, seemingly, agreed to become, in due course, the wife of the Rev. Greville Pooley, who sought to hold her to her promise. But William Farrar was also a contender for her hand, and the successful one, causing the first breach of promise suit in America of record. The case reached London where the Council for Virginia returned it to Virginia 'not knowinge how to decide so nice a difference' and desired 'the resolution of Civill Lawiers.' The matter was resolved in January 1624/5, when Mr. Pooley withdrew his suit and gave bond that he would make no further claim. Thereafter Farrar and Mrs. Jordan were married for, as at court held 2 May, 1625, Farrar's bond as administrator was ordered cancelled.

William Farrar was appointed to the Virginia Council on 14 March, 1625/6, and served for the rest of his life. He was also named in August, 1626, as a commissioner "for the Upper Partes kept above Persie's Hundred," with authority to determine whether court should be held at Jordan's Journey or at Shirley Hundred. The appointment was affirmed 7 March, 1627/8. He had returned to London briefly when, on 6 September, 1631, he sold to his brother Henry Farrar, of Reading, Berkshire, a tract of land left him in the will of his father John Farrar the Elder in 1628. He soon returned to Virginia, where he was deceased by 1637, when on 11 June his young son William received a patent as his heir.[1149]

William Farrar and Cicely Baley Jordan Farrar named their first daughter, born about 1625, Cicely. She is believed to have first married Isaac Hutchins and then Henry Sherman as her second husband. Isaac Hutchins and wife Cicely had a son Robert who died as a minor without producing offspring. Henry Trent and Cicely had two sons and two daughters. One daughter, Elizabeth, married Henry Trent. A second daughter, Anne, married Christopher Branch of Henrico County, grandson of Christopher Branch, Ancient Planter, who was the earliest American ancestor of Thomas Jefferson. Christopher Branch, husband of Anne Sherman Crowley, was the brother of Mary Branch, who married as her first husband Thomas Jefferson (who was deceased by 1697, Henrico County); she became the maternal great-grandmother of Thomas Jefferson, third United States President.[1150]

Offspring of John H. Cates and Elizabeth Foster included James F. Cates, who was living outside the state of Mississippi at the time of his father's death; John Foster Cates, who married Elizabeth Rimmer; and Mary Cates, who married John Burton and was living outside Mississippi at the time her father died. Offspring of John H. Cates and Judith Nichols Brown Cates included Alfred Brown Cates, who died 2 January 1845 in Hinds County, Mississippi; Wilson Cates, who married Martha Elizabeth Slay on 16 July 1841 and was living in DeSoto Parish, Louisiana, in 1877; Elizabeth F. Cates (c. 1822-after 1870),[1151] who married John Lorance on 13 May 1850 in Hinds County; Eliza Ann Cates, who married David Burton on 3 February 1842 in Hinds County; Sophia Cates, who married Christopher S. Crawley on 14 April 1842 in Hinds County; Susan Cates, who married Thomas Williams and was living in Morehouse Parish, Louisiana, in 1877; Augustus V. Cates, who was living in Hinds County, Mississippi, in 1850. All of these children were born in Person County, North Carolina.

John Foster Cates (22 Dec., 1809, Person County, North Carolina -- 24 Sept., 1869, buried Brownsville Cemetery, Hinds County, Mississippi) married Elizabeth W. Rimmer on 30 January 1829 in

---

[1148] Ibid., p. 264.

[1149] For more on all of these families, see Dorman, *Adventurers*, pp. 137-138, 275, 558.

[1150] Ibid.

[1151] Elizabeth was the grandmother of Claude Waverly Lorance (1874-1937), who married Minnie E. Hammack (1871-1952), daughter of James Wilburn and Jeffersonia A. E. Collum Briggs Hammack.

Person County, North Carolina. At the time of the 1830 Person County census, he was enumerated as John Cates, Jr., living in a household adjacent that of his father. Both John and his wife were aged 20-30; they had no offspring at the time of the census enumeration.[1152]

John and Elizabeth accompanied other members of the Rimmer, Wells, Brown, and Cates families to Mississippi during the winter of 1832-1833. On 3 May 1834, he purchased forty acres of land in Hinds County from Ransom Robinson. The land was located in the south one-half of the east one-half of the southwest one-fourth, Section 21, Township 7, Range 2 West.[1153] The following year he also purchased forty acres of land from his father John H. Cates. John F. Cates appears consistently in Hinds County tax digests between 1835 and 1850. In 1844, he and Elizabeth sold eighty acres in Section 22, Township 7, Range 2 West, to Anderson Snipes. Snipes paid $200.[1154] On 1 January 1847, Cates paid $1,500 to purchase Mary Thomas's interest in the west one-half of the southeast one-fourth and the east one-half of the southwest one-fourth and the south one-half of the east one-half of the southeast one-fourth of Section 17 and the west one-half of the northeast one-fourth of Section 20, all Township 7, Range 2 West, 280 acres in Hinds County, Mississippi.[1155] A month later, in August 1847, he and Elizabeth conveyed one acre of Section 17, Township 7, Range 2 West, to Franklin White for $6.[1156] On 27 November 1849, Cates purchased another 160 acres from Robert S. Young,[1157] to which he added another 160 acres in 1851,[1158] forty acres in 1856,[1159] and eighty acres in 1858.[1160]

John Foster Cates apparently owned several slaves at the end of the American Civil War. Like many former plantation owners, he was forced to negotiate alternative labor arrangements to restore the productivity of his holdings. On 23 June 1866, he entered into a legal contract with Henry Cates, William Cates, Calvin Cates, Moses Cates, Sarah Cates, Harriett Cates, Jane Cates, and Rhody Cates, whereby he hired them as wage laborers to work his lands for the following year. Afterwards, on 21 February 1867, Cates conveyed to Joseph Robertson "the East half of South East quarter and West half of South West quarter of Section Sixteen, the south east quarter and east half of south west quarter section Seventeen, the North East quarter of Section Twenty, the west half of north west quarter of Section Twenty-one all in Township Seven Range Two West, also one dark mare mule, one dark horse, one mouse colored mule, one mouse colored horse, one Gray horse, also eighty head of sheep." The purpose of this conveyance was to secure a debt for $3,000 which Cates had owed his son Anderson Bradley Cates since 1861; if, by 1869, John Foster Cates had failed to fully satisfy his obligation to his son, Anderson Bradley Cates was to order Robertson to auction the property in order to satisfy the debt.[1161]

John Foster Cates died 24 September 1869 in Hinds County. His obituary appeared a month later in the *Hinds County Gazette*:

> Died At his residence near Brownsville, in this county, on the 24th of September 1869, Mr. John F. Cates, aged 59 years, 9 months. The deceased was an old and highly respected citizen of Hinds County, and for over 40 years a member of the Baptist Church. He died in full assurance of faith, saying in his last moments, "I wish all the world felt as ready and as willing to die as I do." "Blessed are the dead who die in the Lord. Yea, saith the spirit, that they may rest from their labors, and their works do follow them." May his

---

[1152] 1830 Person Co., NC, Census, p. 29.

[1153] Hinds Co., MS, Deed Book G, p. 583.

[1154] Hinds Co., MS, DB 17, p. 379.

[1155] Hinds Co., MS, Deed Book 18, p. 449.

[1156] Hinds Co., MS, DB 19, p. 125.

[1157] Hinds Co., MS, Deed Book 20, pp. 186-87.

[1158] Hinds Co., MS, DB 20, pp. 730-31.

[1159] Hinds Co., MS, DB 24, p. 242

[1160] Hinds Co., MS, DB 26, pp. 149-50.

[1161] Hinds Co., MS, DB 30, p. 141.

friends be comforted in this assurance, and may they follow him as he followed Christ, that their last end may be peaceful as his was. [1162]

Although Cates died in 1869, administration of his estate was not begun until 1875. On 5 February 1875, Anderson Bradley Cates entered a bond for $1,000 qualifying him to administer the estate of John Foster Cates, who had died without a will.[1163] According to the petition,

> John F. Cates departed this life on the 24th day of September, 1869, in said second district intestate so far as your petitioner is advised and believes, leaving him surviving a widow and relict, Mrs. Elizabeth W. Cates and your petitioner as his only heirs at law and distributees. That said widow is now very feeble in mind and body and wholly unable to attend to any business whatever. That all the debts due by said intestate have been paid and satisfied. That the claims due to said intestate are utterly worthless except as will be hereafter set forth. That there is now no personal property belonging to the estate of said decedent. That said estate has a claim against the U. S. Government upon what it is not hoped to realize more than one thousand dollars. That said claim cannot be prosecuted without a legal representative of said estate. Your petitioner therefore prays that letters of administration of the goods & c. of said decedent may be granted to him and be qualified as such administrator.[1164]

This instrument began what would become the lengthy process of settling the estate of John Foster Cates.

Soon after Anderson Cates filed for administration on his father's estate, the widowed Elizabeth Rimmer Cates executed a deed of gift to her grandchildren on 8 December 1876:

> The State of Mississippi, Hinds County. Know all men by these presents, that I, Elizabeth W. Cates, for and in consideration of the natural love and affection which I have and do bear my beloved grandson D. J. Cates and Granddaughter Sallie E. Cates, have this day given and granted and delivered and by these presents doth grant and deliver unto my said grandchildren the following property, towit, all my real estate as follows, the north east quarter of section seventeen, Township seven, Range two West, the North East quarter of Section Twenty, Township Seven, Range two west, and the west half of North West quarter, Section Twenty-one, Township seven, Range two west, to be equally divided between them when the said D. J. Cates arrives at the age of twenty-one, to have and to hold the same unto my grandson D. J. Cates and granddaughter Sallie E. Cates and to their heirs and assigns forever. In testimony whereof I, the said Elizabeth W. Cates, have hereunto set my hand and seal this the 8th day of December A. D. 1876. Signed: E. W. Cates. Acknowledged 8 Dec., 1876, before J. B. Robertson, JP.[1165]

Elizabeth Rimmer Cates was living in Tinnin Township, Hinds County, Mississippi, with her son Anderson Bradley Cates and his family at the time of the 1880 federal census.[1166] She died 5 March 1885 in Hinds County, Mississippi, and was buried in Brownsville Cemetery.

[1162] Hinds County Gazette, 3 November 1869. A note instructs the *Vicksburg Herald* to "please copy," indicating that Cates had family or business associates outside the immediate area who would be interested to learn of his death.
[1163] Estate File of John F. Cates, Loose Papers, Chancery Court, Hinds Co., MS, Court House, Raymond, MS.
[1164] Estate File of John F. Cates, Loose Papers, Chancery Court, Hinds Co., MS, Court House, Raymond, MS.
[1165] Hinds Co., MS, Deed Book 48, p. 231.
[1166] 1880 Hinds Co., MS, Census, p. 196.

John Foster Cates and Elizabeth W. Rimmer Cates had two children, an unusually small family for the times in which they lived. Anderson Bradley Cates, the eldest son, will be considered below. John T. Cates, the second son, was born 2 December 1836 in Hinds County, Mississippi, and died there 23 August 1853, when he was 17 years old. He was buried in Brownsville Cemetery.

Anderson Bradley Cates, firstborn child and only surviving son of John Foster Cates and Elizabeth W. Rimmer, was born 31 July 1834 in Hinds County. On 19 September 1860, he married Abbie Doxey Brown (10 November 1841-1 January 1940) in Copiah County.[1167] On 26 April 1884, Anderson Bradley Cates died in Hinds County; he was buried near his father and brother in Brownsville Cemetery, where his mother was interred the following year.

The American Civil War began in April 1861, and on 29 November 1861 Anderson Bradley Cates enlisted for sixty days as a Confederate soldier in Company D, 3rd Regiment Mississippi Volunteer Army, also known as the "Brownsville Fencibles". Cates' first months in the service were difficult ones. His fellow soldier, Clay Sharkey, recalled that on 28 January 1862 "We reached Granada...I attempted to walk -- but found that my feet had been frozen -- so that I was taken to the Hotel as there was no hospital in Granada then and we, Peyton Dismukes, Bradley Cates & myself mustered out of the service -- but I could not travel as the bottoms of my feet and balls of my toes had become raw sores. My two friends left me in the hotel and went home."[1168] Soon afterwards, Cates re-enlisted, serving from 7 March 1862 onwards in Company K, 36th MS Infantry, under the command of his father-in-law, Colonel Drury J. Brown. Cates was captured at Vicksburg, Mississippi, and paroled following the capitulation on 4 July 1863.[1169]

Preserved in the Confederate Widow's Pension Application of Abbie Doxey Brown Cates is a letter written at the time of Anderson Bradley Cates' capture:

Vicksburg, Mississippi, July 7th, 1863.

To all whom it may concern, Know ye that:

I A. B. Cates, Private of Co. K, 36th Regiment, Mississippi Volunteers, C.S.A., being a prisoner of War, in the hands of the United States Forces, in virtue of the capitulation of the city of Vicksburg and its Garrison, by Lieutenant Gen. John C. Pemberton, S. C. A., Commanding, on the 4th day of July 1863, do in pursuance of the terms of said capitulation, give this my solemn parole under oath. That I will not take up arms again against the United States, nor serve in any military, police, or constabulary force in any Fort, Garrison, or field work, held by the Confederate States of America, against the United States of America, nor as guard of any prisons, depots, or stores nor discharge any duties usually performed by Officers of soldiers against the United States of America, nor as guard of any prisons, depots, or stores nor discharge any duties usually performed by Officers or soldiers against the United States of America, until duly exchanged by the proper authorities.

A. B. Cates.

[1167] Abbie Doxey Brown Cates, Confederate Widows' Pension Application, Mississippi Department of Archives and History, Jackson, MS. The application, dated 25 June 1924, gave the place of marriage.

[1168] George C. Osborn, ed., "Notes and Documents: My Confederate History -- Clay Sharkey," *The Journal of Mississippi History*, Vol. 4 (1942): 225-232.

[1169] Mississippi Confederate Muster Lists, Co. K, 36th Mississippi Infantry, Mississippi Department of Archives and History, Jackson, MS.

The document was sworn to and subscribed before John O. Dow, Captain, 4th Illinois Volunteers, at Vicksburg on 4 July 1863.[1170]

At the time of the 1870 Hinds County census, A. B. Cates and family were living in Brownsville. Cates owned real estate valued at $6,400 and personal property valued at $1,000, a considerable amount for a former planter in the early years of Reconstruction.[1171] On 28 April 1876, in order to secure a note for $500 plus ten percent interest, A. B. and Abi Doxey Cates deeded 320 acres of the west one-half of the southwest one-fourth of Section 16 and the southeast one-fourth of the east one-half of the southwest one-fourth of Section 17, Township 7, Range 2 West, in Hinds County.[1172]

On 4 December 1883, the four grandchildren of John Foster and Elizabeth Rimmer Cates deeded a tract of land to Charles B. Hawkins in return for $250. The land sold was described as "Twenty acres of land off the north end of the north half of the north east quarter of the north east quarter of section 17 Township 7 Range 2 West in Hinds County, State of Mississippi." D. J. Cates, Sallie E. Cates Hammack, and E. H. Cates signed the deed. On 22 July, 1884, John D. McConnell, Mayor of Brownsville, and Justice of the Peace, acknowledged that he saw "Sallie E. Hammack (nee Cates) who having now become of age acknowledged that she signed sealed and delivered" the deed to Hawkins.[1173] Two years later, on 18 July 1885, "D. J. Cates and Sallie E. Cates Hammack, parties of the first part," deeded to "Eunice Cates and Fanny May Cates their Sisters parties of the second part," for $1 and "the great love and affection which the parties of the first part have and hold for their sisters the parties of the second part," the east one half of the north east quarter of Section 17, Township 7, Range 2 West, less twenty acres off the north end the same being the property of C. B. Hawkins also the west one half of the northwest quarter of Section 21, Township 7, Range 2 West."[1174] Finally, on 18 July 1885, D. J. Cates and Sallie Hammock deeded to "A. D. Cates their mother party of the second part," in return for $1 and "the love and affection which the parties of the first part have and hold for their mother, the party of the second part," the west one half of the north east one quarter of section Seventeen, Township Seven, Range two west.[1175]

On 28 April 1890, in consideration of $10 "as the further consideration of a fair and equitable division of our deceased father's estate, we hereby convey, release and quit claim to our brother D. J. Cates, the following land situated in Hinds County, Mississippi, viz.: the west one half of the north east quarter of Section Twenty of Township seven of Range Two West." Mrs. A. D. Cates, Eunice Cates, and Fannie May Cates signed the deed.[1176] At the same time and in exchange for the same consideration, the same grantors also deed to "our sister Sallie E. Hammack" the "following land situate in Hinds County, Mississippi, viz.: East one half of the North east quarter of Section Twenty Township Seven of Range Two West."[1177]

Mrs. Abbie D. Cates applied for a Confederate Widow's Pension in Clinton, Hinds County, Mississippi, on 25 August 1910, at which time she was sixty-eight years old. She noted that her husband "served till the close of the war and was honorably discharged about the time of Lee's surrender. The cause of his discharge was the surrender at Vicksburg of the 36th Mississippi. He served until this

---

[1170] Abbie Doxey Brown Cates, Confederate Widows' Pension Application, Mississippi Department of Archives and History, Jackson, MS.

[1171] 1870 Hinds Co., MS, p. 676. The family was enumerated at Brownsville Post Office, HH 227/228.

[1172] Hinds Co., MS, DB 48, pp. 272.

[1173] Hinds Co., MS, Deed Book 54, p. 435.

[1174] Hinds Co., MS, DB 55, pp. 489-90.

[1175] Hinds Co., MS, DB 55, p. 490. Sallie E. Cates Hammack on 5 January 1886 issued a quit claim for the W 1/2 of the NE 1/4, Section 20, Township 7, Range 2 West, in exchange for which Drury J. Cates issued a quit claim to her for the E 1/2 of the NE 1/4, Section 20, Township 7, Range 2 West. See Hinds Co., MS, DB 55, p. 491. In exchange for D. J. Cates's quit claim to this property, Sallie then issued a quit claim to D. J. Cates for her interest in the W 1/2 of the NE 1/4, Section 20, Township 7, Range 2 West. Hinds Co., MS, DB 55, p. 491.

[1176] Hinds Co., MS, DB 61, p. 127.

[1177] Hinds Co., MS, DB 61, p. 127.

surrender and then returned home. He died at his home near Brownsville, Mississippi. Mrs. Cates indicated that she was not then receiving any pension for her husband's service and that she owned her own home, valued at $500 and located near Brownsville. At the time of application, she lived with an unmarried daughter and had living one son and three daughters. The application was denied because of an inability to document the service details, and Mrs. Cates applied again on 23 August 1916 and 25 June 1924.[1178]

Abbie Doxey Brown Cates lived until 1 January 1940, dying in her ninety-ninth year. She was buried beside her husband in Brownsville Cemetery.

Anderson Bradley Cates and Abbie Doxey Brown were the parents of four children. Drury John Cates (23 October, 1861, Hinds County, Mississippi-14 March, 1937, Warren County, Mississippi) married Cora A. Chapman (10 April, 1857-21 January, 1883, Hinds County, Mississippi, buried Brownsville, Hinds County, Mississippi) on 20 October 1881 in Hinds County. Following Cora's death, Drury married Ella Blanche Cohn (24 December, 1860, Mississippi-6 August, 1935, Warren County, Mississippi).[1179] Sallie Elizabeth Cates (14 January, 1863, Hinds County, Mississippi-30 April 1951, Hinds County, Mississippi, buried Brownsville Cemetery, Hinds County, Mississippi) married 20 December, 1883, Hinds County, Mississippi, William Simms Hammack (14 April, 1852, Macon County, Georgia-25 December, 1899, Hinds County, Mississippi, buried Brownsville Cemetery, Hinds County, Mississippi) on 20 December 1883 in Hinds County. After her first husband died, Sallie married as her second husband, on 23 September 1913, Louis E. Chapman, who died 3 June 1925. Eunice Cates (24 September, 1878, Hinds County, Mississippi-1 February, 1939, Hinds County, Mississippi, buried Flora Cemetery) married Thurman Edgar Bardin (8 April 1883-31 January 1939, Hinds County, Mississippi, buried Flora Cemetery) in July 1906. Fannie Mae Cates (1881, Hinds County, Mississippi-1960, Hinds County, Mississippi, buried Brownsville Cemetery), apparently the unmarried daughter with whom her mother was living in 1910 and 1916, married Richard Albert Moore (1879-1954, Hinds County, Mississippi, buried Brownsville Cemetery, Hinds County, Mississippi).

B. Elizabeth Rimmer Cates.

The North Carolina Rimmer family is believed to trace to Hugh Rimmer who was living in eastern Maryland by the early eighteenth-century. Born about 1695, Hugh and wife Mary settled in Dorchester County, where Hugh died about 1745 at Hogg Range.[1180] Their son James Rimmer married Anne Taylor and died in Dorchester County about 1774, leaving an adult son named James Rimmer. It is this James Rimmer who is believed to be the individual of the same name found in Caswell County, North Carolina, from 1784 onwards.[1181]

James Rimmer of North Carolina likely married about 1775; no record of the marriage has been found, but his wife was named Phoebe, and many descendants claim that she was a Ruffin before

---

[1178] Abbie Doxey Brown Cates, Confederate Widows' Pension Application, Mississippi Department of Archives and History, Jackson, MS. Abbie Doxey Brown Cates spent her remaining years in the Cates family home, which was then owned by her son-in-law and daughter, R. A. "Dick" Moore and Fannie Mae Cates Moore. In the 1950s, Fannie Mae Cates Moore ceded title to the family homestead to George Cleveland and Mary Almedia Bankston Hammack in return for her keep. George Cleveland and Mary Almedia Bankston Hammack later conveyed the home and land to their son James Wilson Hammack in exchange for his commitment to care for them until their deaths. James Wilson Hammack lives in the now remodeled Cates family home, which was placed on the National Register of Historic Places in 1985 (National Register of Historic Places, Building No. 85001076). Family legend holds that the house, situated on the highest hill in the area, was used by a Union officer as his headquarters for several days during the closing of the noose around the Confederate States Army at Vicksburg.

[1179] Drury settled in Warren Co., MS, before 1900. He was the father of Andrew Jackson "Jack" Cates (26 Mar., 1889, Hinds Co., MS-20 Oct., 1919, Memphis, TN, bur. Div. C, Square 9, Lot 2, Cedar Hills Cemetery, Vicksburg, Warren Co., MS), who married 29 Jan., 1910, Joan Bankston (1 May, 1889, Hinds Co., MS -). Joan m. (2) aft. 1919, William Henry Maben.

[1180] Hugh was also the father of Jane Rimmer and Margaret Rimmer, wife of Daniel Jones.

[1181] Dorchester Co., MD, Accounts, Liber 22, folio 247. Individuals named William Rimer, Nicholas Rimer, and David Rimer all appeared in Rowan Co., NC, in the 1750s and 1760s. See Linn, *Rowan Co., NC, Tax Lists, 1757-1800*, pp. 14, 28, 32, 46.

marriage. James and Phoebe were certainly married by 1777 or 1778, when John Rimmer, their oldest known son, was born. James Rimmer witnessed a legal record in Caswell County in 1784 and was enumerated there in 1790.[1182] In the same year, he purchased 200 acres of land from Joseph Farrar of Caswell County. He was taxed with this tract in 1794; the following year he purchased another 200 acres of land from Risdon Fisher.[1183] A 1797 deed from Josiah Brown to Ephraim Hawkins provides additional details about the location of Rimmer's properties, indicating that they lay on the Bushy Fork of Flat River adjacent lands owned by James Farquhar and John Brown.[1184] In 1802, James sold 200 acres of his lands to Ephraim Hawkins.[1185]

James Rimmer joined Wheeley's Primitive Baptist Church in Person County in 1802.[1186] Apart from documented land purchases, he seldom appears in the Caswell or Person County legal records. Rimmer was deceased by 1 June 1809, when his estate was inventoried in Person County. Purchasers included Phoebe Rimmer, John Brown, Henry Burch, Miles Wells, Wright Nichols, Baylor Burch, James Farquhar, Samuel Rimmer, Polly Rimmer, and Thomas Rimmer.[1187] Phoebe Rimmer was still living in Person County in 1820, at which time she was aged more than forty-five years and headed a household including two females aged sixteen to twenty-six. She was living near her adult sons, Richard and Samuel Rimmer.[1188]

James and Phoebe Rimmer reared a large family. Although several of their offspring remained in North Carolinas, others moved westward, settling in Tennessee, Mississippi, Missouri, and Illinois. John Rimmer, their eldest son, married Mary Whitfield in 1800. Thomas Rimmer married Jemima Jacobs in 1800 and moved to Illinois, where he died in Madison County after 1850. Jenny Rimmer married Nathan Hargis in Person County in 1799. James Rimmer married Polly Nelloms in Person County in 1810. Elizabeth Rimmer married Stephen Ellis in Person County in 1803.

Samuel Rimmer married Elizabeth Blalock in Person County in 1812. Jeremiah Rimmer moved to McNairy County, Tennessee, where he was still living in 1852. Richard Rimmer married Jane Farmer and moved to Mississippi with the Cates family in 1832; he died there in 1858. Polly Rimmer married Samuel Jordan in Person County in 1821. Phoebe Rimmer married Anderson Blalock in Person County in 1821.

John Rimmer, eldest son of James and Phoebe Rimmer, is believed to have been the father of Elizabeth Rimmer Cates. John was born about 1778, probably in North Carolina, and died between 1840 and 1850 in Tennessee or Missouri. He was taxed in Caswell County in 1798 and enumerated in Person County with seven children in 1810.[1189] He appears in Person County legal records as late as 1825 but was living in Sullivan County, Tennessee, by 1830, at which time he was aged 50-60, with three sons aged 15-20 and one son aged 5-10. His wife was aged 30-40, and they had living with them two daughters under age five and two daughters aged 5-10.[1190]

Mary Whitfield Rimmer, whom John married by bond dated 21 February 1800 in Orange County, North Carolina, was still living as late as 1850, at which time she was enumerated, aged seventy-four years and a native of Virginia, in LaClede County, Missouri. She was living with her daughter Sarah Jane Rimmer Bildenbrack and near her son Jeremiah Rimmer. Sarah Jane was aged twenty-four, and Jeremiah was aged thirty-three; both children were born in North Carolina.[1191]

[1182] 1790 Caswell Co., NC, Census, p. 6.

[1183] 1794 Caswell Co., NC, Tax List, North Carolina Department of Archives and History, Raleigh, NC; Person Co., NC, Deed Book B, p. 164-65.

[1184] Person Co., NC, Deed Book C, p. 203.

[1185] Person Co., NC, Deed Book C, p. 551.

[1186] Wheeley's Primitive Baptist Church Minutes, Person Co., NC, Library.

[1187] Person Co., NC, Record Book 5, p. 128.

[1188] 1820 Person Co., NC, Census, p. 239.

[1189] 1798 Caswell Co., NC, Tax List, North Carolina Department of Archives and History, Raleigh, NC; 1810 Person Co., NC, Census, p. 167.

[1190] 1830 Sullivan Co., TN, Census, p. 345.

[1191] 1850 LaClede Co., MO, Census, p. 135.

John Rimmer seems never to have owned any substantial property in North Carolina; he probably rented the lands on which he lived and reared his family. If the census records are correct, he may have fathered as many as ten children born between 1800 and 1830.[1192] These children are believed to have included the following: James Wesley Rimmer (born 1801), who married Malinda Combs in 1824 and moved to South Carolina and Mississippi; William Rimmer (born 1802), who married Mary A. Whitfield in 1825; Elizabeth Rimmer (born 1805), who married John Foster Cates; Lewis Rimmer (born 1807), who married Mary Whitfield and moved to Tennessee and Illinois; Ann Rimmer, who married Ben Roberts; Jeremiah Rimmer (born 1816), who moved to Missouri and Iowa; and Sarah Rimmer Bildenbrack (born 1825), who moved to Missouri.[1193]

Mary Whitfield Rimmer (c. 1776, Goochland County, Virginia - after 1850, LaClede County, Missouri) was a daughter of William Whitfield and Mary Towler, who married 14 December 1772 in Goochland County, Virginia.[1194] William enlisted in the Revolutionary service in Goochland County on 16 February 1778 and served for a year, participating in military service at Valley Forge, Pennsylvania, and Middlebrook, New Jersey. William lived in Goochland County as late as 1787, but, by 1793, he was living in Person County, North Carolina. He lived there until his children reached adulthood, and in his later years he relocated to Alabama; on 25 November 1829, as a resident of St. Clair County, Alabama, he applied for a Revolutionary pension. He indicated that he had moved to Alabama about 1818 after living in Pendleton District, South Carolina. He was living in Shelby County, Alabama, in 1835.[1195]

William Whitfield's Revolutionary War Pension Application indicates that he fathered twelve children, eleven of whom were living in 1829.[1196] Not all of these children have been identified. Person County, North Carolina, legal records indicate, however, that four of the children of William Whitfield and Mary Towler maintained a close association in Person and Caswell Counties. These children were George Whitfield, James T. Whitfield, Mary Whitfield Rimmer, and William Whitfield. The births of these four children are documented in Reverend Douglas's Register of Goochland County, Virginia. George Whitefield (20 September 1773, Goochland County, Virginia - 1826, Person County, North Carolina) married Elizabeth Burch on 25 October 1793; they remained in Person County, where they were members of Wheeley's Primitive Baptist Church. James Towler Whitfield (17 May 1777, Goochland County, Virginia - 14 April 1850, Person County, North Carolina) married Susannah Minchew on 4 January 1798 and Elizabeth Robertson on 9 August 1832. Mary Whitfield (21 March 1782, Goochland County, Virginia - after 1850, LaClede County, Missouri) married John Rimmer in Orange County, North Carolina, in 1800. William Whitfield (4 August 1783, Goochland County, Virginia -) also settled in North Carolina.[1197]

[1192] Thomas Rimmer, John's brother, married Jemima Jacobs in 1800 but was living in Sumner Co., TN, by 1820, and in Madison Co., IL, by 1828. James Rimmer, Jr. (born about 1783) did not marry until 1810. Samuel Rimmer (born about 1785) did not marry until 1812. Jeremiah Rimmer (born about 1788) did not marry until 1810. Richard Rimmer (born 1790) did not marry until about 1816. Of the offspring of James Rimmer in Caswell and Person Counties, it seems that only John or Thomas could have fathered Elizabeth Rimmer Cates. Given that Thomas Rimmer left the county a decade before Elizabeth married, it seems unlikely that he was her father. Location, timing, and family association indicate that John and Mary Whitfield Rimmer were most likely her parents.

[1193] Other offspring may have been Diannah Rimmer Clinkingbeard (wife of John Reed Clinkingbeard), Phillip B. Rimmer, Phoebe Rimmer (wife of Wright Farquhar, whom she married in 1828), John Marion Rimmer, Bedford Rimmer, Anivy Rimmer, and Andrew Rimmer.

[1194] Jones, *Douglas Register*, p. 50.

[1195] Revolutionary War Pension Application of William Whitefield, File S38466, The National Archives, Washington, D.C., Microfilm Series M805, Roll 862.

[1196] Ibid.

[1197] Jones, *Douglas Register*, p. 317.

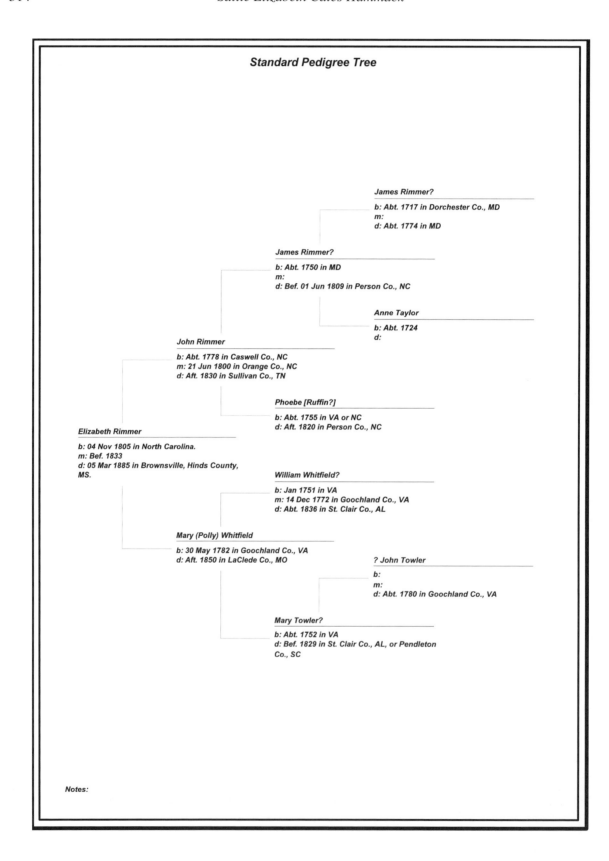

Standard Pedigree Tree

James Rimmer?

b: Abt. 1717 in Dorchester Co., MD
m:
d: Abt. 1774 in MD

James Rimmer?

b: Abt. 1750 in MD
m:
d: Bef. 01 Jun 1809 in Person Co., NC

Anne Taylor

b: Abt. 1724
d:

John Rimmer

b: Abt. 1778 in Caswell Co., NC
m: 21 Jun 1800 in Orange Co., NC
d: Aft. 1830 in Sullivan Co., TN

Phoebe [Ruffin?]

b: Abt. 1755 in VA or NC
d: Aft. 1820 in Person Co., NC

Elizabeth Rimmer

b: 04 Nov 1805 in North Carolina.
m: Bef. 1833
d: 05 Mar 1885 in Brownsville, Hinds County,
MS.

William Whitfield?

b: Jan 1751 in VA
m: 14 Dec 1772 in Goochland Co., VA
d: Abt. 1836 in St. Clair Co., AL

Mary (Polly) Whitfield

b: 30 May 1782 in Goochland Co., VA
d: Aft. 1850 in LaClede Co., MO

? John Towler

b:
m:
d: Abt. 1780 in Goochland Co., VA

Mary Towler?

b: Abt. 1752 in VA
d: Bef. 1829 in St. Clair Co., AL, or Pendleton
Co., SC

Notes:

Mary Towler Whitfield's parentage has not been documented, but, on 10 October 1782, William Whitfield made a claim in Goochland County for reimbursement for losses experienced during the American Revolution. He made a claim for himself and another claim as administrator of John Towler, deceased, indicating that John Towler may have been Mary Whitfield's father.[1198]

C. Colonel Drury J. Brown.

Colonel Drury J. Brown became a leading citizen of Copiah County, Mississippi, serving as a Colonel during the American Civil War and also as a local court justice and Sheriff in Hinds County. Born in 1813 in Person County, North Carolina, Brown died in Copiah County in 1868, just after the close of war and at the comparatively young age of 55.

Drury Brown's ancestors trace to Francis Browne (c. 1630-c. 1691) who was living in Rappahannock County, Virginia, by about 1654. Browne's legal transactions reveal that he was an active and prosperous tobacco planter. On 19 May 1654, Francis Browne patented land on Cox's Creek in Rappahannock County.[1199] On 18 January 1657/8, Francis Browne witnessed a Rappahannock County deed from William Johnson to Richard Stephens and John Burnett.[1200] Rappahannock deeds reveal that Browne held a patent with Oliver Seager and was involved in business dealings with Seager as well.[1201]

Although Francis Browne must have been married by about 1652, the first known documented reference to his wife Elizabeth dates from 13 February 1660/1, when he and Elizabeth acknowledged a deed to William Richards.[1202] Browne appears frequently in the deed and court records of Rappahannock and Essex Counties, Virginia, as a witness and litigant as well as a direct participant in real estate transactions. A 1665 deed describes him as of Piscatacon in Rappahannock County, but by 1666, he was described as of Farnham Parish.[1203] On the latter date, Richard Glover paid the Brownes 3,600 pounds of tobacco for a tract of land adjacent Browne's "now dwelling plantation, being at the head of Piscatacon Creek on the South side of the Rappahannock River." In addition to cash paid, other consideration provided by Glover included "one years schooling for my Daughter Sarah Browne wch is already performed by the aforesd Richard Glover."[1204] The following year, the Brownes conveyed to Thomas Goodrich 700 acres of land[1205] and to William Richards another 200-acre tract.[1206]

Although Browne appeared in court documents during intervening years, the next known real estate conveyance for him dates from 27 May 1687, at which time he deeded to his son Daniel Browne 300 acres in Farnham Parish. In exchange for the land, Daniel conveyed to his father a "Man Servant." The land was described as lying near the "King's High Road," indicating the main thoroughfare of the time linking settlers from as far away as New England with the southern colonies. Although the deed is not clear, given the value of such a tract of land, the man conveyed by Daniel Browne to his father was more likely an African slave than a white indentured servant, whose value would at that time have been comparatively low.[1207]

[1198] "Revolutionary War Public Service Claims," *The Virginia Genealogist*, Vol. 30 (1986), No. 4. John Towler and his wife Mary may have been parents of Mary Towler Whitefield. One John Towler (possibly Mary's brother) and wife Sarah Thomas married in Goochland County in 1762 and moved to Orange Co., NC, before 1789. The elder John Towler's inventory, valued at £6,067.10, was recorded in Goochland Co., VA, Deed Book 13, p. 94.

[1199] Rappahannock Co., VA, Deed Book 1656-1664, Part I, pp. 35-36.

[1200] Rappahannock Co., VA, Deed Book, 1656-1664, Part I, p. 120.

[1201] Rappahannock Co., VA, Deed Book 1656-1664, Part I, p. 146.

[1202] Rappahannock Co., VA, Deed Book 1656-1664, Part I, pp. 141-142.

[1203] Rappahannock Co., VA, DB 1665-1677, pp. 5-6; Rappahannock Co., VA, Deed Book 3, pp. 188-191.

[1204] Rappahannock Co., VA, Deed Book 3, pp. 188-191.

[1205] Rappahannock Co., VA, DB 3, pp. 201.

[1206] Rappahannock Co., VA, Deed Book 1668-1672, pp. 249-250.

[1207] Rappahannock Co., VA, DB 1686-1688, pp. 359-361.

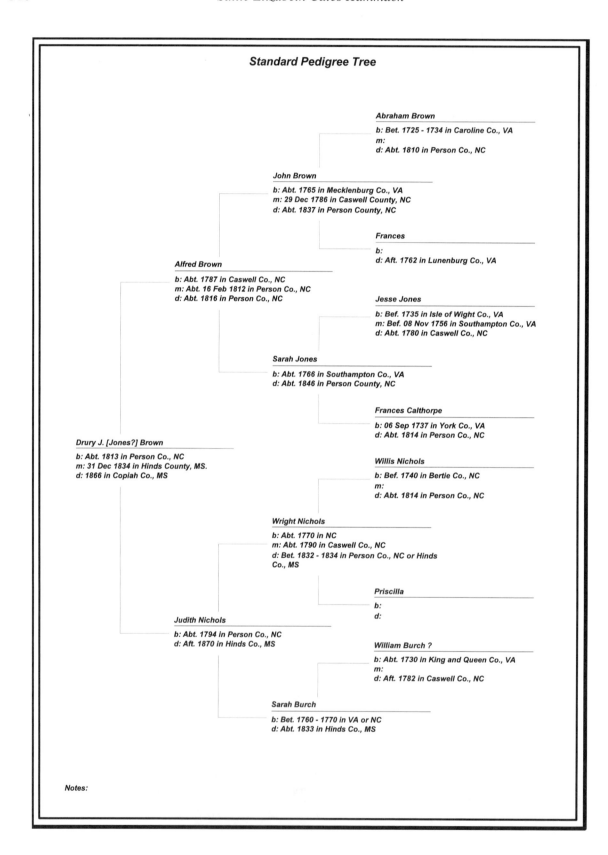

Standard Pedigree Tree

Abraham Brown
b: Bet. 1725 - 1734 in Caroline Co., VA
m:
d: Abt. 1810 in Person Co., NC

John Brown
b: Abt. 1765 in Mecklenburg Co., VA
m: 29 Dec 1786 in Caswell County, NC
d: Abt. 1837 in Person County, NC

Frances
b:
d: Aft. 1762 in Lunenburg Co., VA

Alfred Brown
b: Abt. 1787 in Caswell Co., NC
m: Abt. 16 Feb 1812 in Person Co., NC
d: Abt. 1816 in Person Co., NC

Jesse Jones
b: Bef. 1735 in Isle of Wight Co., VA
m: Bef. 08 Nov 1756 in Southampton Co., VA
d: Abt. 1780 in Caswell Co., NC

Sarah Jones
b: Abt. 1766 in Southampton Co., VA
d: Abt. 1846 in Person County, NC

Frances Calthorpe
b: 06 Sep 1737 in York Co., VA
d: Abt. 1814 in Person Co., NC

Drury J. [Jones?] Brown
b: Abt. 1813 in Person Co., NC
m: 31 Dec 1834 in Hinds County, MS.
d: 1866 in Copiah Co., MS

Willis Nichols
b: Bef. 1740 in Bertie Co., NC
m:
d: Abt. 1814 in Person Co., NC

Wright Nichols
b: Abt. 1770 in NC
m: Abt. 1790 in Caswell Co., NC
d: Bet. 1832 - 1834 in Person Co., NC or Hinds Co., MS

Priscilla
b:
d:

Judith Nichols
b: Abt. 1794 in Person Co., NC
d: Aft. 1870 in Hinds Co., MS

William Burch ?
b: Abt. 1730 in King and Queen Co., VA
m:
d: Aft. 1782 in Caswell Co., NC

Sarah Burch
b: Bet. 1760 - 1770 in VA or NC
d: Abt. 1833 in Hinds Co., MS

Notes:

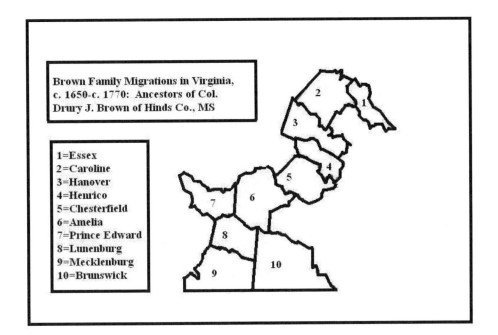

Brown Family Migrations in Virginia,
c. 1650-c. 1770: Ancestors of Col.
Drury J. Brown of Hinds Co., MS

1=Essex
2=Caroline
3=Hanover
4=Henrico
5=Chesterfield
6=Amelia
7=Prince Edward
8=Lunenburg
9=Mecklenburg
10=Brunswick

Three years later, on 10 November 1690, Francis Browne, Sr., wrote his will. He had been in the colony for forty years or more. Describing himself of South Farnham Parish and being "very sick and weake of body butt of perffect sence and memory", Browne made his last will and testament. Browne began with a customary religious preamble, indicating that he bequeathed "my soule unto Almighty God that gave it me with a sure and certayne hope of a joyfull Resurrection through the merits of my Blessed Lord and Saviour Jesus Christ and my body unto my mother the earth to be decently interred." Like most Virginians at the time, Browne was a member of the Church of England and would regularly have attended services at the South Farnham Parish church. After the will's preamble, Browne set about to provide for his wife and children in several specific bequests:

I give and bequeath unto my son ffrancis Brown after mine and my Loving wife Elizabeth decease, all that necke of Land Lying on the north side of my devident of Land I now live on bounded as followeth, that is to say, strayt away through an ould field from the Run of the deviding branch to the mill road, which goes to my son Daniel goes over & for a small branch neare my ould dwelling house, called by the name of the spring branch, which sayd Land I give and bequeath unto my said son ffrancis to him and his heirs forever.

I also give and bequeath unto my son Daniel Brown after my and my Loving wife Elizabeth decease, all that Rest of my land I am now possessed with, all my plantation and housing to him and his heires to have and to hould in fee simple for ever also itt is my will and desier that my household goods be equally divided between my two sons ffrancis and Daniel, both in quality and goodness to them and their heirs to have and to hould in fee simple for ever, also it is my will and desier there be a row of orchard trees planted along ye sayd ould field to devide the above sayd Land. I also give and bequeath unto my sons ffrancis and Daniel my parcell of Land Lying on the south side of pescataway Creeke called by the name of ye wading place poynt, equally between them and their heires forever, I alsoe give and bequeath unto my fower daughters, Elizabeth, Sarah, Mary and Rebecca, one shilling apeace to be payd them by my lawful executor or executrix. I also give and bequeath unto Daniel Brown the son of my son Francis Brown one feather bed with the furniture belonging unto itt, to him and his heirs forever, after my and my wife's decease.

I give and bequeath unto my Loving wife Elizabeth all the Rest of my moveable Estate that I am now possessed with, to have and to hould without any Lett or molestation to her and her heirs forever, I also give and bequeath unto my fower Godsons that is Joseph and John Edmondson and ffras Brown, the son of Daniell Brown senior, my neighbour and ffras Graves, the son of ffras Graves, deceased, to every one of them, one pocket Bible of five or six shillings price, to be truly payd them after my decease by my Lawfull executor or executrix, I alsoe apoynt my Loving wife Elizabeth my sole and whole executrix of this my last will and testament and this my Last will, to cut off and disannull all former wills whatsoever, as witness my hand and seal this 10th day of novber 1690.

The will was proven 3 February 1691/2, more than forty years after Browne first appeared in the colony. In a century in which immigrants to the Tidewater tended to die young, Browne's life had been a long one; he had prospered in the colony, and he had founded a family that would long remain in northern and eastern Virginia.[1208]

Of the children of Francis and Elizabeth Browne, Francis Browne, Jr., died in Essex County in 1709, leaving a widow (also named Elizabeth) and children Daniel and Anne. No evidence has been found to suggest who Francis Browne's four daughters -- Elizabeth, Sarah, Mary, and Rebecca -- married. Of the

---

[1208] W. M. Sweeny, *Wills of Rappahannock Co., VA, 1656-1692* (Lynchburg, VA, 1947), pp. 147-148.

two remaining sons, Abraham Browne died in 1692/3, leaving one known child -- an "Orphant Girle" -- named Elizabeth.[1209]

Daniel Browne, the other son of Francis and Elizabeth Browne, was of age in Rappahannock County by 1683. His appearance in legal records at that time suggests that he was born at least by 1662 and perhaps several years prior to that date. Two deeds from 1683 indicate that Browne owned a tract of land adjoining George Morris's property; in one of the deeds, Browne purchased a second tract, joining the first one, from Morris in exchange for another tract of land promised him by Stephen Bembridge. The deed did not specify the relationship between Bembridge and Browne; Browne appointed his friend James Vaughan as his "true and lawful attorney" to receive the deed from Morris, and Francis Browne and Robert Berkeley witnessed the instrument.[1210]

Apart from these initial land transactions, Browne seldom appeared in the records of Rappahannock or Essex Counties. On 27 June 1685, he witnessed a deed from Nathan Baxter involving land that joined his father's property,[1211] and, on 23 December 1698, along with Francis Browne, John Farguson, and James Fullerton, he was named to appraise the estate of John Moss, deceased.[1212] The next record of him is his last will and testament, dated 18 January 1707/8. Still a young man, Brown described himself as "very sick and weake of body." Browne was deceased by 10 September 1708, when his widow and executrix entered the will with Richard Jones and William Price as her securities.[1213]

At the time of his death, Daniel Browne was probably between forty-five and fifty-five years old. His will indicates that he fathered a large family and that he was a substantial planter in Essex County. Daniel took care to provide for his offspring, leaving the bulk of his estate to his older sons but providing as well for his minor children. While Daniel's real estate went mostly to his sons, he left a tract of land to his daughter Sarah Boughan but bequeathed livestock to his other children:

> To my eldest son Abraham Brown my old plantation through the old field bounding upon the line of Daniel Brown, Junr. by the old mill path on the side of the dividing branch...side of the middle branch near unto Mr. Thomas Edmondson's old field, dividing the land of my son Henry Brown and Abraham Brown...Unto my son Henry Brown my now dwelling plantation and all of my land lying between the dividing branch and the middle branch...Unto my son Francis Brown, all the remainder of my land lying on the upper side of the middle branch... Unto my daughter Sarah Boughan, land beginning at the bridge and so up the branch to a spring in Thomas Wood's old field...to a dividing corner tree of Francis Brown, Senr...to the middle branch...Unto my son Abraham Brown, one shilling...Unto my daughter Sarah Boughan, one shilling... Unto my son Henry Brown, one cowe when he comes to the years of twenty-one... Unto my son Francis Brown, one cowe when he comes to the years of twenty-one... Unto my daughter Mary Brown, three cowes, upon her wedding day, and a young mare the same day... All the remainder unto my loving wife Jane Brown and at her decease unto my two daughters Jane and Elizabeth Brown, and appoint her my sole executrix.[1214]

Henry Broune, Jean Broune, and Alexander Younger witnessed the will, which was signed "10 7ber 1708". Although in earlier documents his name appears spelled as Browne, when Daniel signed his will

---

[1209] Essex County Deeds & Wills, 1692-1693, pp. 143-144.

[1210] Rappahannock Co., VA, Deed Book 1682-1686, pp. 45, 113

[1211] Rappahannock Co., VA, DB 1682-1686, pp. 186-187.

[1212] Essex Co., VA, Order Book, 1695-1699, p. 119.

[1213] Essex Co., VA, Deeds and Wills, Book 13, 1707-1711, pp. 148-149.

[1214] Essex Co., VA, Deeds and Wills, Book 13, 1707-1711, p. 148.

in 1707/8, he did so as "Daniell Brown." Most references to his family from this point onwards use the spelling Brown rather than Browne.[1215]

Identified as his father's eldest son, Abraham Brown was of legal age when his father wrote his will in January 1707/8. A deed dated 17 November 1718 reveals that he was working as a cooper when he sold 150 acres in South Farnham Parish, Essex County, to William Gatewood. Gatewood paid £62 for the land which "was left to the said Abraham Brown by his father's last will till it meets the antient line of Francis Browne deceased." Abraham's wife Mary relinquished her dower in the deed, which was witnessed by Joseph Baker, Thomas Bryan, and Thomas Wheeler.[1216] In 1723, Abraham and Mary sold 150 acres purchased from Richard Holt and Peter Treble to John Pette of South Farnham Parish. Pette paid 4,800 pounds of tobacco and ten pounds sterling to Brown, who is identified as a carpenter in the deed.[1217] Mary relied on Thomas Bryant to act as her power of attorney on the legal documents regarding the 1723 deed.[1218]

Caroline County was formed in 1727 from Essex, King and Queen, and King William Counties. Whether Abraham Brown's land fell into the new county at its creation or whether he moved southwest into Caroline is unclear, but he was living in Caroline when his will -- no longer extant -- was written. On 14 February 1734/5, Mary Brown, widow of Abraham Brown, presented the will for probate with her son Daniel Brown as her fellow executor. George and Dianah Trible witnessed the original will and testified to its veracity. William Brown, James Collins, James Terrill, and William Terrill were named to appraise the estate,[1219] and an inventory was filed on 14 March 1734/5.[1220] One of Abraham's sons, John Brown, died about the same time as Abraham, and on 14 March 1734/5, Mary Brown, mother of John Brown, petitioned for letters of administration on his estate with the two Terrills, John Sutton, and Thomas Ham as appraisers.[1221]

Because Abraham's will has not survived, owing to the destruction of many early Caroline County records, the names of his offspring are undocumented. Strong evidence exists, however, to suggest that he was the father of William Brown; Abraham Brown, Jr.; John Brown; Daniel Brown; and George Brown.

Of these offspring, Abraham Brown, Jr., was probably born about 1725 in Essex County. He grew to adulthood in Caroline County, where he remained until moving to Amelia County about 1746. On 18 July 1746, as Abraham Brown of St. Margaret Parish, Caroline County, he purchased 200 acres from Matthew Womack of Raleigh Parish, Amelia County. Brown paid £8 for the tract, which was described as "bounded in part by lines of Daniel Brown and Burk's mill branch of Sandy River, being on the branch where Charles Burk's mill stands."[1222] In 1751, Daniel Brown and Abraham Brown witnessed an Amelia County deed in which George Brown of St. Margaret's Parish, Caroline County, purchased 200 acres in Nottoway Parish from James Dyer of Spotsylvania County.[1223] These deeds document the removal of several of Abraham Brown's sons from Caroline County into the Southside. Prince Edward County was created from Amelia County in 1753, and Abraham Brown appeared there as early as 1756, when he was named Constable in place of George Stubblefield. Daniel Brown, Abraham Brown, and George Brown all appeared together in Prince Edward County from 1756 onwards,[1224] and it appears from Prince George deeds that their Amelia County properties fell into Prince Edward at its creation.

[1215] Ibid.

[1216] Essex Co., VA, Deeds and Wills, 15, 1716-1718, pp. 239-243, 244.

[1217] Essex Co., VA, Deed Book 17, pp. 186-191.

[1218] Essex Co., VA, Order Book, 1716-1723, p. 771.

[1219] Caroline Co., VA, Order Book, 1732-1746, p. 275.

[1220] Caroline Co., VA, Order Book, 1732-1740, p. 279.

[1221] Caroline Co., VA, Order Book 1732-1740, p. 280.

[1222] Amelia Co., VA, DB 2, 1742-1745, p. 354.

[1223] Amelia Co., VA, Deed Book 3, 1747-1753, p. 322. Thomas Foster of Amelia was owner of a tract adjacent the one Brown purchased, and he is mentioned with Abraham Brown in several transactions.

[1224] Prince Edward Co., VA, DB 1, p. 87b.

About 1760, Abraham Brown moved from Prince Edward County southward into adjoining Lunenburg County. On 2 February 1761, he purchased 400 acres on Bluestone Creek in Lunenburg County from William Evans of Amelia,[1225] and on 7 September 1762, as Abraham Brown of Lunenburg County, he sold 200 of these acres to Elizabeth Stone of Halifax County.[1226] On 11 October 1762, Abraham sold the remaining 200 acres of the 400 acre tract to Daniel Stewart of Amelia County.[1227] He is probably the Abraham Brown taxed in St. James's Parish, Lunenburg County, in 1764 with 200 acres of land; Stephen Evans and others mentioned in deeds involving Abraham appear also in this district. Brown still owned his lands on Bluestone Creek in 1768 and 1771, when he was named as an adjacent landowner. On 14 December 1772, as a resident of Mecklenburg County -- directly south of Lunenburg, and directly north of Caswell County, North Carolina -- Abraham Brown sold to Abraham Forrest of Amelia County 200 acres on Bluestone Creek, then in Mecklenburg County, it being the land on which Abraham Brown then lived and which was patented in 1754.[1228]

Fourteen months after selling his lands on Bluestone Creek in Mecklenburg County, Abraham Brown first appears in the legal records of Orange County, North Carolina; he may have been in the area for several months before appearing in legal documents, either renting or homesteading the land he was soon to purchase. On 18 February 1774, as Abraham Brown of Orange County, North Carolina, he purchased 220 acres on the Bushy Fork of Flat River in what was soon to become Caswell County. He appeared on the earliest surviving Caswell County tax list, that for 1777, and appeared consistently in the area until he died three decades later. Brown was granted another 200 acres in 1780 and purchased an additional seventy-one acres in 1792, by which time his lands had fallen into newly created Person County.[1229]

In 1792 and 1793, already in his late sixties and perhaps anticipating his own death, Abraham Brown initiated a series of deeds of gift to his children in Person County. On 18 September 1792, he deeded to his son John Brown 160 acres on the Bushy Fork of Flat River, and, on 20 March 1793, he deeded to his son Josiah Brown two slaves, livestock, and furniture. In two separate deeds, both dated 20 March 1793, Brown deeded to his daughter Sarah two slaves and furniture and to his daughter Margaret another two slaves, furniture, and a calf.[1230] Another possible explanation for the series of deeds of gift is that Abraham Brown had remarried, although there is no clear evidence to support this idea. The earliest known reference to Abraham Brown's wife is from 1762, when his wife Frances Brown joined him in conveying property to Elizabeth Stone.[1231] This wife may have been the mother of his children; Person County records do not identify the name of his wife during his residence there.

At the time of the 1794 tax list for St. Luke's District, Person County, Abraham Brown paid tax on 190 acres of land, one white poll, and five black polls. Son John Brown was taxed with 160 acres of land and one white poll in the same neighborhood. The white poll in Abraham's house was likely his adult son Josiah, since Abraham himself would have been exempt from poll tax because of age. Neighbors included Drury Jones, George, Henry, John, Philip, and Richard Burch, James Rimmer, Thomas Cates, and Goodrich and Francis Jones.[1232] On 9 August 1794, after the tax list was compiled, Abraham Brown deeded the 190 acre tract he owned on the Spring Branch of Bushy Fork to his son Josiah Brown.[1233]

No additional references to Abraham Brown have been found until 1810. Having disposed of his landed property and too old to pay poll tax, he did not appear in the surviving tax records or in land

---

[1225] Lunenburg Co., VA, DB 6, p. 356.

[1226] Lunenburg Co., VA, DB 7, pp. 374-375.

[1227] Prince Edward Co., VA, DB 2, p. 125a. A deed dated 9 September 1763 from Stephen Evans, Sr., to Stephen Evans, Jr., both of Lunenburg County, identifies Abraham Brown as an adjacent landowner. See Lunenburg Co., VA, DB 9, pp. 257-259.

[1228] Mecklenburg Co., VA, DB 3, p. 499. Mecklenburg had been formed from Lunenburg County in 1764.

[1229] 1777 Caswell Co., NC, Tax List, North Carolina Department of Archives and History, Raleigh, NC; Caswell Co., NC, Deed Book A, p. 503; Person Co., NC, DB A, pp. 43-44.

[1230] Person Co., NC, Deed Book A, pp. 44, 226; Person Co., NC, Deed Book B, pp. 30-31.

[1231] Lunenburg Co., VA, DB 7, pp. 374-375.

[1232] 1794 Person Co., NC, Tax List, North Carolina Department of Archives and History, Raleigh, NC.

[1233] Person Co., NC, Deed Book B, pp. 4-5.

deeds. The 1793 deed of gift to his daughter Margaret had reserved the use of one of the slaves to Abraham during his life, although legally the slave belonged to Margaret Brown.[1234] Not until February 1810 did references to Abraham Brown again appear among Person County's legal documents; at that time, an inventory of his estate was filed, and on 19 March 1810 a sale of his property took place. Josiah Brown served as administrator for his father, and he, John Brown, Richard Holsomback, L. V. Hargis, and William Joplin purchased at the estate sale. The total value of the sale, which included only personal items, was $28. In November 1812, Josiah Brown made a final return on his father's estate, and Abraham Brown vanishes from the Person County legal records.[1235]

Abraham and Frances Brown were the parents of four known children. John Brown, born by about 1760, married Sarah Jones in 1786 and remained in Person County, North Carolina. Josiah Brown, born by about 1770, was living in Person County as late as 1811. Sally Brown, born by about 1770, married James Key Daniel on 17 February 1794 in Person County; they moved to Missouri, where Sally died in Jackson County in 1849 and James in 1851. Margaret Brown, Abraham's fourth known child, was apparently an adult when her father deeded her property in 1793; no further record of her has been discovered.

John Brown, probably born about 1760 in Prince Edward County, Virginia, lived in Mecklenburg County before settling in what was then Orange County, North Carolina, with his father about 1773. On 29 December 1786, he married Sarah Jones in Caswell County. As mentioned above, John Brown's father Abraham deeded him 160 acres on Bushy Fork in 1792. John paid tax on this land in 1793. In 1794, John Brown joined his mother-in-law Frances Calthorpe Jones and his wife's siblings Drury Jones and Wilson Jones in deeding a slave named Nancy to Goodrich Jones, another brother of Sarah Jones Brown.[1236]

Unlike his father Abraham Brown, John Brown appeared frequently in legal records, both as a party in real estate transactions as well as a witness in these and other sorts of legal records. On 9 September 1796, he purchased 181 acres on Flat River from Jesse Womack, and eleven days later he deeded this tract to his brother Josiah Brown.[1237] Ten days after this, Josiah Brown deeded to John 137 acres on Bushy Creek. Because the currency varies from deed to deed -- $500 in the first deed, £140 in the second one, and £71 in the third one -- it is difficult to evaluate the financial aspects of the transaction, but it seems probable that these deeds were part of a planned real estate swap between the two brothers. In 1797, John purchased 212 acres from Thomas Farmer[1238] and twenty-one acres from Benjamin Joplin[1239]. In 1804, he deeded twelve acres to Stephen Wells[1240] and in 1806 100 acres adjoining this tract to Ephraim Hawkins.[1241] Alfred Brown, John's teenage son, witnessed the transaction.

In 1812, John Brown deeded a slave to Nathaniel Norfleet,[1242] and in 1819 he sold fifty-one acres on Flat River joining Ephraim Hawkins to Asa Hudgins.[1243] Brown deeded another seven acres to Hawkins in 1822[1244] and fifty-seven acres to Stephen Wells in 1825.[1245] This was the first of four separate transactions between 1825 and 1828 in which Brown deeded to Wells a total of 194 acres on Bushy Fork.[1246]

[1234] Person Co., NC, Deed Book B, p. 31.

[1235] Person Co., NC, Estate Book, 1807-1811, p. 182; Person Co., NC, Estate Book 1807-1811, p. 191; Person Co., NC, Estate Book 1811-1815, p. 102.

[1236] Person Co., NC, Deed Book B, p. 4-5.

[1237] Person Co., NC, Deed Book B, pp. 294-295, 315-316.

[1238] Person Co., NC, Deed Book C, pp. 64-65.

[1239] Person Co., NC, Deed Book C, pp. 63-64.

[1240] Person Co., NC, Deed Book C, pp. 468-69.

[1241] Person Co., NC, Deed Book D, p. 274.

[1242] Person Co., NC, Deed Book D, p. 325.

[1243] Person Co., NC, Deed Book E, pp. 152-53.

[1244] Person Co., NC, Deed Book F, pp. 284-85.

[1245] Person Co., NC, Deed Book G, pp. 305-6.

[1246] Person Co., NC, DB I, pp. 166, 219, and K, p. 77.

Like his father, John Brown seems to have disposed of the bulk of his personal property through deeds of gift, and the evidence suggests that he had a particularly close relationship with his son Alfred Brown. On 1 February 1809, John deeded to his son Alfred for "natural love and affection" 108 acres on Bushy Fork.[1247] The next day, he deeded a slave girl to his daughter Elinor Brown.[1248] In 1812, for $150, he sold a slave girl named Chainey to his son Alfred Brown, and the following year he sold another slave to Alfred for $275.[1249] In 1823, again for "love and affection," John Brown deeded to his daughter Elizabeth Brown a slave named Clara.[1250] When Brown died intestate in 1837, his inventory listed personal property, livestock, and seven other slaves still belonging to the estate.[1251] The sale, which was recorded at March Term 1838, recorded items valued altogether at $3,068.90, although slaves represented the most valuable portion of the property sold.[1252]

At his death, John Brown had not disposed of all of his real estate. On 18 September 1837, Green W. Brown, James Wood, Asa Hudgens, William Terry, and James Bradsher, "heirs at law of John Brown," deeded fifty acres of land to John's widow Sarah Brown for her support during her widowhood. This included the tract where Sarah then lived.[1253] Sarah Jones Brown was alive in Person County as late as 1849, when her son Green W. Brown deeded her forty-seven acres on Flat River.[1254]

John's marriage to Sarah Jones gave descendants of John and Sarah Jones Brown descent from several prominent Virginia families, as well as from English gentry in Norfolk, England. Sarah Jones Brown was a daughter of Jesse Jones and Frances Calthorpe Jones, who had moved from Southampton County, Virginia, to Caswell County, North Carolina, in the 1770s. Jesse Jones's ancestors settled in Isle of Wight County, Virginia, in the middle seventeenth-century, when Edward Jones, an English merchant working in Barbados, settled in the colony. The Jones family traces to Robert Jones, of Oldland in the parish of Bitton, Gloucestershire, who was buried in the church of Bitton on 13 November 1604, aged about sixty years.[1255] Edward Jones, Jr., grandfather of Jesse Jones of Caswell County, married Deborah Exum; her father William Exum had settled south of the James River in Isle of Wight County about 1665, dying there in 1701. Jesse's parents William and Elizabeth Jones were living in Isle of Wight County in 1749 when Southampton was created from it; it seems likely that Jesse, born about 1730, lived in this area until he and his wife Frances left Virginia in the 1776.[1256]

Jesse's wife Frances Calthorpe Jones was baptized 6 September 1737 in York Parish, York County, Virginia, a daughter of Charles and Eleanor Butts Calthorpe of York County. The Calthorpe lineage traces to Walter de Calthorpe who was living in Norfolk, England, during the thirteenth century. Christopher Calthorpe, who settled in Virginia in 1622, was a son of Christopher Calthorpe (1581-1626) and Maude Thurton (1584-). Both of Christopher's parents descended from Walter de Calthorpe, for his mother Maude Thurton's maternal grandmother was Prudence Calthorpe, daughter of Edward and Thomasine Gaval Calthorpe. Prudence married as her first husband Ralph Shelton, and their daughter Grace Shelton, baptized 2 August 1554, at Broome, Norfolk, married John Thurton there in 1582. Edward Calthorpe's grandmother Elizabeth Stapleton, wife of Sir William Calthorpe, was a direct descendant of Joan Plantagenet, daughter of Edward I, King of England, and Eleanor of Castile, through Joan's marriage to Gilbert de Clare, 3rd Earl of Gloucester and 7th Earl of Hereford. Their daughter Elizabeth de

---

[1247] Person Co., NC, Deed Book D, p. 160.

[1248] Person Co., NC, Deed Book D, pp. 159-60.

[1249] Person Co., NC, Estate Book 1811-1815, p. 201.

[1250] Person Co., NC, Deed Book F, pp. 326-27.

[1251] Person Co., NC, Wills, Inventories and Lists of Tithables, 1835-37, p. 214.

[1252] Person Co., NC, Estate Book 14, 1838-41, p. 2.

[1253] Person Co., NC, Deed Book N, p. 269.

[1254] Person Co., NC, Deed Book R, p. 71.

[1255] J. A. Brayton, "The Ancestry of Edward Jones of Isle of Wight County, Virginia," *The Virginia Genealogist*, Vol. 45, No. 1 (January-March 2001): 67, citing P. Carlyon-Britton, comp., *The Register of Hanham and Oldland, Gloucestershire, 1584-1681* (The Parish Register Society, v. 63; Exeter, 1908).

[1256] Southampton Co., VA, DB 5, pp. 240, 242, 243.

Clare and her husband Roger, 1ˢᵗ Baron Damory, were the great-great-grandparents of Sir Miles Stapleton, father of Elizabeth Stapleton Calthorpe.[1257]

Christopher Calthorpe settled in Virginia in 1622, during the Company Period, arriving aboard the Furtherance with Lieutenant Thomas Purefoy. Calthorpe obtained a grant for 500 acres on the York River in 1630. Calthorpe called the tract "Thropland" for the family home in Norfolk; located in what was then New Poquoson Parish but later York Parish, the land remained in the Calthorpe family for more than a century, and it was there that Charles and Eleanor Calthorpe were probably living when they baptized their daughter Frances in 1737. Christopher's son James Calthorpe was a Justice in York County; his son, Elestrange Calthorpe (1680-1726) married Mary Butts (1684-1718), daughter of Anthony and Mary Rookesbury Butts of Charles Parish.[1258] Their son Charles Calthorpe (1709-1763) married Eleanor Clifton (1714-1775), daughter of Benjamin Clifton (1682-1728) and Sarah Hay (c. 1686-1719), also of Charles Parish.[1259]

Charles and Eleanor Calthorpe were still living in York County, Virginia, on 23 January 1740/41, when son James was baptized in York Parish. On 4 April 1742, Charles Calthorpe purchased 400 acres in Isle of Wight County from the Nottoway Indians. Calthorpe then moved his family to the tract, which in 1749 fell into newly formed Southampton County. It was there that he drafted his will on 8 November 1756.[1260]

Charles Calthorpe's widow Eleanor Clifton Calthorpe survived him for more than a decade, writing her will 7 April 1772 in Southampton County. The document was proved there on 12 January 1775. Perhaps with Eleanor's death in 1775 came a lessened sense of family obligation for Jesse and Frances Jones. In any case, during November 1776, in three separate deeds, they disposed of 105 acres on Roundhill Swamp granted Jesse Jones on 12 May 1759,[1261] 297 acres granted Jesse Jones on the same date as the land disposed in the previous deed,[1262] and another fifty acres which had been patented at the same time.[1263] Jesse and Frances seem immediately to have moved to Caswell County, North Carolina, where they were taxed in 1777.[1264] Jesse Jones entered claim for 1,240 acres on Double Creek in Caswell County on 7 August 1778.[1265] He was deceased by December 1780, leaving widow Frances, daughter Sarah, and sons Drury, Goodridge, and Wilson as survivors.[1266] At the time of the 1794 Person County tax

---

[1257] The Calthorpe lineage is treated in detail in the appendix to this work. See Dorman, *Adventurers*, pp. xxviii, 54, 149-152, 177, 212, 499. This lineage was researched by J. A. Brayton and published as "A Royal Descent For Christopher Calthorpe of York Co., VA," *The Virginia Genealogist*, pp. 67-70. Brayton notes that Generations 1 - 8 are as presented by Frederick Lewis Weis in *Ancestral Roots of Sixty Colonists Who Came to New England Between 1623 and 1650* (6ᵗʰ ed., W. L. Sheppard, Jr., ed., Baltimore, 1988), pp. 13, 226, 227. From this generation onwards, the source is Rev. James Lee-Warner, "The Calthropes of Burnham," *Norfolk Archaeology*, v. 9 (1884), pp. 1-19. Other sources include "Shelton of Shelton", in W. Harvey, Clarenceux King of Arms, *The Visitation of Norfolk in the Year 1563, ed. by Brigadier General Bulwer* (2 volumes; Norwich, 1895) and W. Rye, ed., *The Visitation of Norfolk, Made and Taken by William Hervey, Clarenceux King of Arms, Anno 1563, Enlarged with Another Visitation Made by Clarenceux Cocke, with Many Other Descents; and Also the Visitation Made by John Raven, Richmond, Anno 1613* (Harleian Society, Publications, v. 32; London, 1891), pp. 63-67. Birth and baptismal records for descendants of Christopher Calthorpe are found in L. C. Bell, *Register of Charles Parish, York Co., VA: History and Register of Births, 1648-1789, and Deaths, 1665-1787* (Richmond, 1932).

[1258] Anthony Butts (c. 1660-1687, Charles Parish, York Co., VA) is believed to have married Mary Rookesby, daughter of Anthony Rookesby (-24 December 1677, Charles Parish, York Co., VA) and wife Elizabeth (-abt. 2 March 1687, Charles Parish, York Co., VA).

[1259] Eleanor was a granddaughter of Benjamin Clifton (c. 1650-1713, Charles Parish, York Co., VA) and wife Eleanor (bef. c. 1666-1717, Charles Parish, York Co., VA).

[1260] Southampton Co., VA, Will Book 2, pp. 30-31. Eleanor's will, written 7 April 1772, was proved there 12 January 1775. See Southampton Co., VA, Will Book 3, p. 118

[1261] Southampton Co., VA, Deed Book 5, p. 240.

[1262] Southampton Co., VA, DB 5, p. 242.

[1263] Southampton Co., VA, DB 5, p. 243.

[1264] 1777 Caswell Co., NC, Tax List, North Carolina Department of Archives and History, Raleigh, NC.

[1265] A. B. Pruitt, *Abstracts of Land Entries: Caswell Co., NC, 1778-95, 1841-1863, and Person Co., NC, 1792-1795* (Raleigh, 1990), Nos. 567-568.

[1266] Caswell Co., NC, Will Book A, pp. 104, 120.

digest, Frances -- who lived until about 1813[1267] -- was taxed with the 640-acre tract on Double Creek, while Drury Jones and Goodrich Jones each owned half of the 600-acre tract on Double Creek. Wilson Jones owned no land at the time.

John Brown and Sarah Jones Brown were the parents of six known children. Alfred Brown, born about 1787, was the eldest son and the oldest known child. Levina Brown married Asa Hudgens in 1818. Elizabeth J. Brown married William Terry in 1824. Sally Brown married James Bradsher in 1818. Green W. Brown married Judith Briggs in 1821. One daughter -- possibly Polly or Ellinor -- married James Wood, who was named as an heir of John Brown in 1838.

Of these children, Alfred Brown, John's eldest son and the only one who did not join the 1838 deed as an heir-at-law, predeceased his father. Alfred Brown, born about 1787, witnessed his father's deed to Ephraim Hawkins on 31 December 1806 when he was still a minor.[1268] Two years later, on 1 February 1809, Alfred's father John deeded him 108 acres on Bushy Fork.[1269] In 1811, Alfred sold this land, for $140, to Ephraim Hawkins.[1270] In 1812, Alfred purchased a slave named Chainey from his father for $150, and, in January 1813, he purchased 112 acres on Double Creek, near the lands of his grandfather Jesse Jones, for $140.[1271]

The cause of Alfred Brown's death is unknown, but he was still a young man -- not yet thirty -- when he died in 1815. An inventory, taken 31 May 1815 in Person County, included furniture, farm implements, livestock, and several notes for money loaned to neighbors and relatives. Wright Nichols served as administrator of the estate.[1272]

A marriage bond exists documenting the marriage of Alfred Brown and Judith Nichols; the bond was dated 16 February, but the section recording the year of marriage is torn. It seems likely that the marriage occurred in 1810 or 1811, for, from 1811 onwards, Alfred's legal transactions usually involved Wright Nichols or other members of the Nichols family.[1273] Following Alfred's death, on 29 January 1816, Judith was allotted thirty-four and one-sixth acres out of a 100-acre tract owned by Alfred Brown.[1274] The remainder of the land was held in trust for Alfred's two children, Malinda Brown (who married John Chandler) and Drury J. Brown (who married Sarah Wells). The orphans became wards first of their grandfather Wright Nichols and then later of their stepfather, John H. Cates, with whom they moved to Hinds County, Mississippi, in 1832.

Judith Nichols Brown Cates was a daughter of Wright Nichols and Sally Burch, who married about 1790 in Caswell County, North Carolina. Both moved to Mississippi with the Cates, Rimmer, and Wells families in 1832, and both died there about 1833. On 29 June 1833, in Hinds County, Mississippi, an order was issued to appraise the goods of Wright Nichols' estate. Sarah was still living on 17 September 1833 in Hinds County, when she relinquished her dower rights on her husband's lands and claimed only a child's portion of the estate.[1275] She wrote her will in Hinds County on 17 October 1833, mentioning her deceased husband Wright Nichols, her "beloved granddaughter Malindy Chandler and beloved grandson Drury J. Brown," who were to receive one third of her undivided portion of her husband's estate. Sarah appointed her grandson Drury J. Brown as executor of her will. Significantly, Sarah's primary concern was to provide for the children of Alfred Brown, for the orphaned children of her daughter Nancy Farquhar, and for her daughter Susan Nichols Wells, wife of James Wells. She mentions no other heirs in

---

[1267] Person Co., NC, Record Book 6, p. 176. Frances was deceased by August 1813, when Goodrich Jones, Wilson Jones, Drury Jones, and John Brown (for his wife Sally) were named as her heirs.

[1268] Person Co., NC, Deed Book D, p. 274.

[1269] Person Co., NC, Deed Book D, p. 160.

[1270] Person Co., NC, Deed Book D, p. 391.

[1271] Person Co., NC, Deed Book D, p. 353.

[1272] Person Co., NC, Record Book 7, pp. 23-24.

[1273] Person Co., NC, Deed Book D, p. 391.

[1274] Person Co., NC, Deed Book D, p. 462.

[1275] Loose Papers, Estate of Wright Nichols, Chancery Court, Hinds Co., MS.

her will.[1276] The date of Sarah's death is unknown, but she was deceased by 23 June 1834 when Drury J. Brown appeared in Hinds County Court as her administrator.[1277]

Wright Nichols, Judith's father, was born about 1768 or 1770 in North Carolina. He first appeared in Caswell County records in September 1792, when an orphan girl was bound out to him by the county court.[1278] Wright's parents Willis and Priscilla Nichols had come to Caswell County from Bertie County, appearing in Caswell County as early as 1779.[1279] Willis, who was taxed in Bertie County as early as 1757, was probably born about 1735; he deeded land to his son Micajah Nichols in 1794 and to his son Wright Nichols in 1796.[1280] Willis Nichols died about 1814 in Person County, leaving sons Wright, Micajah, Willis, and Matthias. In addition, Willis and Priscilla Nichols had at least one known daughter, Mary Nichols, who married Archibald Ingram in Person County in 1802.

Earlier generations of the Nichols family had spelled their surname Nicholas. About 1650, three brothers settled in Norfolk County, Virginia. Henry Nicholas, "son of Henry Nicholas of Oxenbury in Huntingdonshire", married Ann Harding and died in Norfolk County about 1677. Andrew Nicholas, "Seaman," was living in Norfolk County by 1647; he died there before May 1655, naming Henry Nicholas in his will.[1281] Richard Nicholas first patented land in Isle of Wight County in 1639.[1282] In 1650, he deposed that he was aged thirty or thirty-two and that he had lived in the colony for fourteen years "& declaring himself to bee of Oxenbury[1283] in Huntingtonshire, a Taylor & sonne of Hen: Nichols of ye same place, living at ye sign of ye White House".[1284]

Descendants of these three brothers lived in close proximity in Lower Norfolk and Princess Anne Counties for the next century. Certain given names -- Henry, Richard, Matthias, John, Eleanor -- recur frequently, making conclusive identifications difficult. It appears, however, that Willis Nichols who died in 1814 in Person County, North Carolina, was a son of Willis Nichols who died after 1760 in Bertie County, North Carolina. That man was a son of Richard Nickles who died in 1721 in Princess Anne County, Virginia; a grandson of Henry Nicholas who died about 1694 in Norfolk County, Virginia; and a great-grandson of Henry Nicholas, the immigrant, who died about 1677 in Norfolk County, Virginia.

About 1660, the immigrant Henry Nicholas converted to the Quaker faith.[1285] His will, written "ye 28th day of ye 10th month, called decembr 1676" indicates that he retained the Quaker faith at his death.[1286] Henry Nicholas, Jr., "being bound for the sea," wrote his will on 20 April 1694, naming a son Richard Nicholas, a minor under age eighteen, who was to inherit his lands on the eastern branch of the Elizabeth River.[1287] This Richard wrote his will on 20 January 1721 in Princess Anne County, Virginia; he was dead three months later. Like his father, Richard was still a young man -- perhaps no older than forty -- when he died. His will names wife Martha Nicholas and two sons, Nathaniel and Willis, both of whom moved to Bertie County, North Carolina.[1288] Nathaniel Nicholas was taxed in Norfolk County as late as 1735[1289]

[1276] Loose Papers, Estate of Wright Nichols, Chancery Court, Hinds Co., MS.

[1277] Loose Papers, Estate of Sarah Nichols, Chancery Court, Hinds Co., MS.

[1278] Person Co., NC, Compilations, p. 37.

[1279] Caswell Co., NC, Deed Book A, p. 221.

[1280] Person Co., NC, Deed Book A, pp. 253-54; Person Co., NC, Deed Book B, p. 212.

[1281] Norfolk Co., VA, Book C, f. 157.

[1282] Nugent, *Cavaliers and Pioneers*, 1: 115.

[1283] Unfortunately, there seems not to have been an Oxenbury in Huntingdonshire. The closest name to "Oxenbury" in Huntingdonshire is Alconbury, which was originally Aukingbury. The 1641-42 Protestation Returns for Huntingdonshire shows four men named Henry Nichols, one in Farcett, one in Alconbury Cum Weston, one in Molesworth, and one in Gransden Magna. There were also two men named Richard Nichols, one in Leighton and one in Alwalton.

[1284] Norfolk Co., VA, Court Minutes, f. 143.

[1285] Hinshaw, *Encyclopedia of American Quaker Genealogy*, 6: 11.

[1286] Norfolk Co., VA, Book 4, f. 15.

[1287] Norfolk Co., VA, Book 5, ff. 229-232.

[1288] Princess Anne Co., VA, DB 3, pp. 382, 472.

[1289] E. B. Wingo, *Norfolk Co., VA, Tithables, 1730-1750* (Norfolk, 1974), p. 152

but present in Bertie County by 8 December 1736, when he witnessed a deed there.[1290] He appears consistently in Bertie County from that point onwards, orally deposing a will on 17 September 1755 that named two sons and three daughters. Willis Nicholas, either the testator's brother or his nephew, witnessed the will.[1291] Willis Nicholas, probably the younger son of Richard Nicholas, was born by at least 1713 and perhaps earlier; he witnessed two deeds on 6 March 1732 from George Nicholson to Anthony Webb (both families were later associates of the Nichols family in Bertie County).[1292] He has not been found in the 1732 or 1733 Norfolk County tax lists, although his brother Nathaniel and other family members were shown both times in Indian Creek Canton.[1293] The two sets of documents together indicate that Willis was approaching adulthood in 1732 but not yet of legal age; he was, however, old enough to be taxed by 1734, when his name appeared on a list from "Ferry Point to the Great Bridge," indicating that he was born about 1713. At that time, Willis was enumerated with James Jamson, Smith Whitehurst, and Richard Scott, near his relatives John Matthias and Richard Nicholas. The fact that Willis was not living independently may suggest that he was still unmarried and working as a laborer in the employ of one of the men with whom he was grouped.[1294] Willis was shown in the same district, with the same group of men, in 1735; he and Nathaniel do not appear in the tax records after that date. He may have moved to Bertie County with his brother Nathaniel, but the first documented reference to him there dates from 12 November 1740 when he purchased land on Ahontskey Swamp from John Wynns.[1295] Willis witnessed real estate transactions in 1757, 1758, and 1767.[1296] In each instance, he was involved with individuals connected with Nathaniel Nicholas and with whom the Nicholas family had had dealings since the 1730s.[1297] Willis Nichols, Sr., apparently died intestate, probably after 1767; he seems to have been the father of Willis Nichols of Person Co., NC, as well as (perhaps) of Wright Nichols (by c. 1760-1844) of Bertie County.[1298]

The Nichols family lived for nearly a century in Norfolk and Princess Anne Counties, Virginia, where they were mariners involved in the coastal trade as well as in tobacco production. When Willis and Nathaniel Nichols settled in Bertie County, they entered a region isolated from the sea but in the heart of the North Carolina tobacco country. Many of the families settling in this region had come south from central Virginia, and among them was the Burch family into which Wright Nichols married in 1790. The parentage of Judith Nichols' mother Sarah Burch Nichols has not been determined, but Caswell and Person County legal records are sufficient to document several members of her family and to allow one to reach fairly certain conclusions regarding her immediate ancestry. Several related Burch families moved to Orange County, North Carolina, from King and Queen County, Virginia, in the late eighteenth-century. Among these were the parents of Sarah Burch Nichols. Sarah was apparently a close relative of Richard, George, John, William, Baylor, and Pemberton Burch, who lived near her and her husband John Brown along the Bushy Fork of Flat River and who had frequent dealings with the Cates, Rimmer, Farquhar,

---

[1290] Bertie Co., NC, DB E, p. 129.

[1291] D. B. Gammon, *Abstracts of Wills of Bertie Co., NC, 1722-1774* (Raleigh, 1990), pp. 43-44.

[1292] Bertie Co., NC, Deed Book D, pp. 8, 9.

[1293] Wingo, *Norfolk Co., VA, Tithables, 1730-1750*, pp. 67, 87.

[1294] Ibid., p. 121.

[1295] Bertie Co., NC, DB F, p. 166.

[1296] Bertie Co., NC, DB H, p. 405; Bertie Co., NC, DB I, p. 212; and Bertie Co., NC, DB L-2, p. 86.

[1297] It is believed that Willis Nichols of Person Co., NC, was a son of Willis Nichols of Bertie Co., NC. It is possible, however, since the elder Willis died intestate, that the younger man was a son of Nathaniel Nicholas. The only known guardianship records for Nathaniel Nicholas's estate, however, dating from 1759, indicates that Jonathan Sandly was guardian to William Nicholas and Josiah Nichols, orphans of Nathaniel Nicholas, deceased. If Willis was Nathaniel's son, then he was of age by 1759 and was not named as such in Nathaniel's will. (Bertie Co., NC, Court Minutes, 1759.)

[1298] Wright Nichols in 1790 purchased 130 acres in Bertie County that had been patented by Nathaniel Nichols in 1754. See Bertie Co., NC, DB P, p. 173.

Wells, and related families.[1299] In 1794, Baylor Burch, George Burch, Henry Burch, John Burch, Philip Burch, Richard Burch, Sr., and Richard Burch, Jr., were taxed in Caswell County near the Nichols, Brown, and Cates families.[1300] This group of Burches traces to King and Queen County, Virginia, but, due to the destruction of a substantial portion of King and Queen County records, it is impossible to identify the relationships among these men.

Sarah Burch Nichols had several siblings who lived near her in Caswell and Orange Counties, North Carolina. In 1817, Sarah's brother Nicholas Burch deeded a slave to his niece Jenny Nichols Farquhar and her husband John Farquhar. Wright Nichols witnessed the deed.[1301] Four years later, Nicholas Burch wrote his will in Person County, naming his sister Sarah Nicholas, his "friend Wright Nicholas, Esquire," sister Elizabeth Odonell, brother-in-law Henry Odonell, nephew Elijah Hester, nephew George Burch, niece Jane Broach, and "friend" George Broach. Burch named his brother-in-law Wright Nichols as his executor, along with his nephews Elijah Hester and George Broach.[1302] At the time of the 1790 census,

---

[1299] Pemberton Burch was of age by 2 August 1774 when he appears in Granville Co., NC, at which time he received payment from the estate of George Whitlock (See Gwynn, *Abstracts of Wills and Estate Records of Granville Co., NC, 1746-1808*). He was alive in Caswell County as late as 1801. (Caswell Co., NC, DB M, p. 21.) His estate was inventoried there at January Court 1802 by Daniel Malone. (Caswell Co., NC, Estate Book D, p. 95.) On 29 April 1790, Pemberton Burch of Caswell County sold to Nicholas Burch of the same place 185 acres on South Hico River joining Alexander Cairn. Nicholas paid £80 for the land. Witnesses were John Farrar and William Mitchell. (Caswell Co., NC, DB G, p. 67.) On 15 April 1791, William Gallaugher of Caswell County sold 143 acres on Reedy Branch of Hico River joining Lawrence Vanhook and David Mitchell to Pemberton Burch; John Christenberry and Nicholas Burch were witnesses. (Caswell Co., NC, DB G, pp. 186-7.) On 11 February 1796, Pemberton Burch of Caswell conveyed 330 acres on the South Hico River to William Marshall; the land joined Nicholas Burch and David Mitchell. William Mitchell, Jesse Marshall, and Richard Burch witnessed the deed. (Caswell Co., NC, DB J, p. 306). On 2 December 1799, still of Brunswick County, VA, Marshall deeded eighty-five acres of this tract to Nicholas Burch (Caswell Co., NC, DB M, p. 29). On 18 November 1800, still of Brunswick, he deeded the remaining 250 acres to Henry Burch for £100; the land was described as joining lands of Nicholas Burch and David Mitchell. Witnesses were John Bradsher and Lackey Marshall (Caswell Co., NC, DB N, p. 76). Pemberton Burch purchased land in Caswell County as early as 1784. On 27 February 1788, he purchased 232 acres on Hico River joining McNeil, Mitchell, and Womack from William Bailey; Drury Jones and William Gallaugher witnessed the deed (Caswell Co., NC, DB F, pp. 60-61.)

[1300] Richard Burch (1732-1816) reared a large family with wife Janey, whose maiden name may have been Baylor. They were living in Caswell County by 1779. They were the parents of George Burch (born 18 September 1764); Richard Burch (born 30 December 1767); Janey Burch Crisp (born 18 June 1768); Baylor Burch (born 7 July 1770); Thomas Bowman Burch (born 15 October 1774), husband of Mildred Broach; Edmund Burch (born about 1776); and (probably) Frances Burch Crisp (born about 1781). Some researchers believe that Jennie Burch, wife of George Broach, was a daughter of Richard Burch. This seems doubtful; if so, it would mean that Richard Burch (born 1732) was a brother of Sarah Burch Nichols (born about 1770). See: G. S. Tomlinson, *The Descendants of Richard and Janey Burch of King and Queen County, Virginia, and Person County, North Carolina: A Collaborated Genealogy* (Senatobia, MS, 1994).

Note that a 1782 tax list for King and Queen County shows John Baylor; John Broach; James Burch; Philip Burch; Elizabeth Burch; Henry Burch; and William Burch. Richard Burch and Nicholas Burch were parishioners in Stratton Major Parish, King and Queen County, in 1767. William and John Burch were taxed in King and Queen County as early as 1704, while a Henry Burch was taxed in neighboring King William at that time. Richard Burch appears in Caswell Co., NC, land records as early as 1779.

[1301] Person Co., NC, Records 1815-1819, p. 52-53.

[1302] The estate was divided into five parts, with Elizabeth Odonell and Sarah Burch each receiving one-fifth and one-fifth each to niece and nephews Jane Broach, Elijah Hester, and Jacob Burch. See Person Co., NC, Estate Book 1820-23, pp. 247-49. He also mention's sister Elizabeth Odonell's "son Chisenberry." This suggests that Elizabeth Burch was the same individual who on 24 November 1791 in Caswell Co., NC, married John Chissomberry. Following his death, she probably remarried to Odonnell. Henry Odonell's name also appears as O'Daniel. Note that John Winningham was bondsman for the Burch-Chissomberry marriage, and in 1788 Mary Burch had married John Willingham. Janie Burch, niece of Nicholas Burch, married George Broach on 19 March 1803 in Person County. Jacob Burch married Lucy Gately on 1 July 1809 in Person County. Additional siblings of Nicholas may have been Henry Burch (died childless and testate, 1816); Phillip Burch (died 1819); and Susannah Jones (named as a sister in Henry Burch's will). Elizabeth Burch who married George Whitefield on 25 October 1793 was probably a close relative; George's sister Mary Whitefield Rimmer was the mother of Elizabeth Rimmer Cates. George Whitefield and Wright Nichols both purchased at the estate sale of Henry Burch, as did Phillip Burch. Note that one Henry Burch married Agnes Hester by bond dated 12 April 1781 with Robert Hester bondsman and Reuben Searcy as witness. Robert Hester was taxed in St. Luke's District, Caswell Co., NC, in 1795; his name appears next to that of Henry Burch. See 1795 Caswell Co., NC, Tax List, North Carolina Department of Archives and History, Raleigh, NC.

Caswell County marriages show that one Nancy Burch, widow, married John Lee in 1795 and that Sally Burch married Thomas

Nicholas Burch was living in St. James District, Caswell County, North Carolina. Enumerated in the same district were Willis Nichols, father of Wright Nichols, and George Burch.[1303]

Sally Burch joined Wheeley's Baptist Church in December, 1789. Richard Burch, Sr., had joined before June, 1789, and was elected deacon in July, 1789. Pemberton Burch was also a member by June, 1789. After Sally Burch married Wright Nichols, Nichols later served as a deacon of this same church. Wright Nichols and Baylor Burch appear next door to one another in the 1820 census. Although Sarah's parentage has not been identified, it is clear that -- until the family removed to Mississippi in 1832 -- Sarah lived surrounded by her siblings, cousins, and other Burch kin in Caswell and Person Counties, North Carolina.[1304]

Colonel Drury J. Brown, son of Judith Nichols Brown Cates and Alfred Brown, was reared in Person County, North Carolina. Brown was named for his paternal great-uncle, Drury Jones, son of Jesse Jones and Frances Calthorpe of Southampton County, Virginia, and Caswell County, North Carolina. Drury's father Alfred died when Drury was only a small child, and he was apparently reared by his mother and stepfather, John H. Cates, under the close supervision of his grandparents Wright and Sarah Burch Nichols.[1305] About 1830, shortly before the family moved to Mississippi, Wright Nichols became his grandson's legal guardian, and Drury Brown was apparently enumerated in Wright and Sarah's household in 1830.

About 1832, Drury Brown moved to Mississippi with his mother, stepfather, half-siblings, grandparents, and a host of other relatives from Person County, North Carolina. He was of legal age by 9 January 1834, at which time, as a resident of Hinds County, Mississippi, he sold to John Moore of Person County, North Carolina, 102.5 acres in Person County, land on Double Creek that had been held in trust for Alfred Brown's orphans since Brown's death twenty years earlier.[1306]

On 31 January 1834, Drury J. Brown married Sarah Wells in Hinds County, Mississippi. Like himself a native of Person County, North Carolina, Sarah was a daughter of Stephen Wells and Sarah Farquhar; the couple, in fact, had cousins in common, for Sarah's uncle John Farquhar had married Drury's aunt Nancy Nichols, a marriage that produced the offspring Sarah Burch Nichols had also been concerned to provide for in her Hinds County will. The marriage would last for nearly twenty years, ending with

---

Sharman in 1800 with Jacob Burch as bondsman. Nancy was apparently the widow of William Burch who died in 1794; Caswell County marriages show that as Nancy Dobbins she married William Burch on 10 October 1792. Nancy was a daughter of Thomas and Rachel Dobbins and the mother of John Campbell Burch as per the Caswell Co., NC, will of Rachel Dobbins (Caswell Co., NC, DB C, p. 264). Note that in 1794 James Lea was administrator in right of his wife of the estate of William Burch; he rendered a final account of the estate, showing payments to (among others) Pemberton Burch, John Crisp, John Whitlow, and John Winningham (Caswell Co., NC, Estate Book C, p. 224).

There are several other Burch marriages in Caswell County that cannot presently be identified but which may relate to this family. One John Burch was deceased by 1791 with Jane Burch, probably his widow, as administratrix (Caswell Co., NC, Estate Book B, p. 385). He was deceased by July Court 1790 (Caswell Co., NC, Estate Book B, p. 353) at which time his estate was inventoried.

Caswell Co., NC, Estate Book C, p. 164, shows that John Shearman was deceased by 10 November 1795. Pemberton Burch served as his administrator. Purchasers included John Burch, Willson Jones, and John Christenberry. Other purchasers included Drury Clark, William Wallis, Jeremiah Brooks, William Gallagher, Joseph Neely, and Will Hews. (Note that in 1784, Pemberton Burch, Nicholas Christenberry, and Mary Christanberry were all taxed in St. Luke's District, along with Joshua Cates. Robert Hester was taxed in St. James' District in 1784. See the 1784 Caswell Co., NC, Tax List, North Carolina Department of Archives and History, Raleigh, NC.)

[1303] This George may have been Richard's son George, born in 1764. He was likely the George Burch taxed with 100 acres in St. Luke's District in 1794. At that time, Henry Burch, his neighbor, owned no land. John Burch -- not yet identified -- also owned no land. Phillip Burch (d. 1819) owned 200 acres. Richard Burch, Sr., owned 140 acres, while Richard Burch, Jr., owned no land.

[1304] All of the individuals mentioned in Nicholas Burch's will can be linked directly or indirectly to Pemberton Burch, who was living in Granville County, NC, by 1774. Pemberton was probably either the father of this group or an older brother, perhaps the father of Jacob Burch and/or Jennie Burch Broach.

[1305] Person Co., NC, Guardian Accounts Book A, 1810-19, pp. 174, 178; Book B, pp. 44-45, 73-74, 142, 212. In 1823, as guardian for Alfred Brown's orphans, John Cates paid tax on 102 acres. See also Loose Guardianship Papers, Person Co., NC, NC Department of Archives and History, Raleigh, NC, indicating that by 1830 Wright Nichols was acting as his grandson's guardian.

[1306] Person Co., NC, DB L, pp. 103-5.

Sarah's death in Copiah County about 1853. Drury Brown married second, on 6 January 1857 in Copiah County, Mrs. Elizabeth Grant, a wealthy widow whose family had also come from Person County.

Drury Brown is said to have trained in law, perhaps by reading law in a local law office, as was then the custom. He became a prosperous merchant in Hinds and Copiah Counties and later served as Sheriff of Hinds County and Colonel of "Brown's Fencibles," the regiment in which his son-in-law Anderson Cates served, during the American Civil War. Still a young man, Brown died in 1866 after a successful career.

In August 1835, Drury Brown purchased 160 acres in Hinds County from John and Elizabeth Spencer. His step-father John Cates witnessed the deed.[1307] Brown paid $3,000 for this tract; on the same date, he purchased adjoining acreage from William and Mary Spencer for $2,000.[1308] Drury and Sarah sold a portion of this land back to William Spencer for $3,400 in 1836,[1309] and he and his brother-in-law John Chandler sold two slaves to William Richmond in 1837 for $3,200.[1310]

Brown was enumerated in Hinds County in 1840 and 1850; the 1850 census indicated that he was a Justice of the Peace with real estate valued at $800.[1311] Hinds County deed records indicate that Drury Brown had owned one town lot in Brownsville, which he and Sarah sold for $300 in 1840,[1312] and another in Raymond, at the corner of the Raymond and Vicksburg Roads, which they sold for $500 in 1849.[1313] In late 1849, they purchased another lot in Raymond, probably the location in which they were living at the time of the 1850 census a few months later.[1314]

The 1850s were the most prosperous years of Drury Brown's life. On 1 November 1853, he was elected Sheriff of Hinds County.[1315] During the ensuing years, he was involved in more than fifteen real estate purchases in Hinds County.[1316] At the time of the 1860 census -- by which time Brown had moved to Copiah County -- the total value of his land, slaves, and personal property was $109,000. Living in his household was an overseer controlling property valued at $10,000, which may also have belonged to Brown. The 1850s, the last decade of the Cotton South, had been prosperous ones. Cotton prices rose to all time highs, and the value of land and slaves across the region both soared. Although Brown's property valuation probably reflects this fact, his wealth in that year easily placed him within the top five percent of southern society.[1317]

Months after the 1860 enumeration, Mississippi had left the United States and become a member of the Confederate States of America. Brown served as Commander of the 28th Mississippi Infantry, and the Drury J. Brown Camp, United Confederate Veterans, Hazlehurst, Mississippi, was named in his honor. Brown also was commander of Company K, 36th Mississippi Infantry, where he served as both Captain and Colonel. As Captain, his name appears on a Muster Roll of the Dixie Guards from Copiah County,

---

[1307] Hinds Co., MS, DB 5, pp. 282-83.

[1308] Hinds Co., MS, DB 5, p. 283.

[1309] Hinds Co., MS, DB 6, p. 484.

[1310] Hinds Co., MS, DB 8, p. 531.

[1311] 1850 Hinds Co., MS, Census, p. 227, HH 1644.

[1312] Hinds Co., MS, DB 13, p. 509.

[1313] Hinds Co., MS, DB 20, p. 351.

[1314] Hinds Co., MS, DB 20, p. 170. Drury and Sarah apparently also owned an additional tract in Raymond. In May, 1850, the sold six and three-fourths acres to Lysander and Adeline Wylie. Since they sold this land for only $75, whereas they had in 1849 sold eleven acres for $500, there may have been special circumstances in existence regarding this deed. See Hinds Co., MS, DB 20, pp. 355-56. Drury Brown apparently also had a land claim in Person County, NC, following the death of his grandmother Sarah Jones Brown in 1849 or 1850. On 19 March 1851, John Bradsher of Person Co., NC, Clerk and Master in and for the County of Person and State of North Carolina of the one part, to Joseph Woods of Person Co., for $106, sixty acres, waters of Bushy Fork adjacent lands of James H. Cates and Joseph Wood, "which said land was sold under a petition and decree of the court of equity for the benefit of the heirs at law of Drury Brown and others" (Person Co., NC, Deed Book R, p. 147-48).

[1315] Hinds Co., MS, DB 22, p. 621.

[1316] Hinds Co., MS, DB 23, pp. 528, 608; 24, pp. 149, 601, 712; 25, pp. 23, 366, 421; 26, pp. 79, 159, 193, 426; 28, pp. 664, 665.

[1317] 1860 Copiah Co., MS, Census, p. 917, HH 1008/1617. Brown's sister Malindy Chandler, who apparently had no children, was living with him at the time. She was forty-nine years old.

Mississippi, 24 February 1862. On a muster from 7 March to 30 June 1862, Drury Brown's name appears. He was elected Captain of Company K, 36th Mississippi Volunteers, and then was elected Colonel of the 36th Regiment Mississippi Volunteers on 11 March 1862. He was mustered into the Confederate Service at Meridian Station on 7 March 1862 by Captain Joltson, the mustering officer of the Confederate States of Army. As Colonel Brown, he requested arms and knapsacks for 535 men. Confederate Records for the state of Mississippi indicate that the requisition of the following items for Colonel D. J. Brown's 36th Mississippi Volunteers: 20,000 Enfield Rifle Caps; 7,000 Miscellaneous Caps; 21,000 Enfield Rifle Cartridges; 7,500 Mississippi Rifle Cartridges; 100 Small Powder Flasks; and 650 Knapsacks. A note in Brown's handwriting reads: "I certify that the above requisition is correct; and that the articles are absolutely necessary to arm and equip my equipment." Brown's signature was dated 5 May 1862. In Brown's file is an undated receipt for 155 Enfield Rifles with a note that he lacked sufficient ammunition for all of his men.[1318]

Drury J. Brown survived the American Civil War, dying in Copiah County, Mississippi, between 14 January 1868 and 3 March 1868. His second wife, Elizabeth W. Grant, a widow, had died on 2 May 1867, leaving 800 acres on Bayou Pierre and Foster's Creek.[1319] During the final months of his life, Brown was again active in real estate transactions, purchasing several tracts in Raymond, Hinds County, Mississippi. A deed dated 17 August 1867 reveals that he owned lots 2, 3, and 4, of Square 3, which he had purchased for $3,000.[1320] Brown wrote his will on 14 January 1868. On the surface, the document indicates that Brown had survived the Civil War with both landed and personal estate, although details of its probate reveal that the economic effect of the Civil War and of the abolition of slavery had hit him hard. In his will, Brown made the following provisions for his children and step-children:

First, I direct that all my just debts, funeral and testamentary expenses be paid, by my Executors herein after named, I do hereby subject charge and make liable all of my real and personal estate, all effects of all kinds whatsoever, to the payment of the same, and the legacies herein bequeathed accordingly.

Second, I will and direct that all the meat, flour and provisions of every kind, shall be in my dwelling House at the time of my decease shall be appropriated to the use and support of my stepchildren, Henry C., Hiram B., and Mattie Grant, and Martha Selman, and that no inventory by my Executors or account of shall be taken of the same in the settlement of my estate.

Third, I give and devise to my two sons Edward W. and William W. Brown, A. B. Cates, my son-in-law, and Abbie Doxey Brown all my estate both real and personal viz., One Hundred and Sixty acres of land on which is located the grantors of which is usually known as the Bell Place, said lands conveyed to me by William Shaw and wife and duly recorded, also Three Hundred and twenty acres, entered by me prior to my marriage to my late wife; also one fourth of the sixteenth section, conveyed to me by the school commissioners of Copiah County, formerly owned by William Hartley and D. E. Sheffield, all of which land is situated in the County of Copiah and State of Mississippi.

Fourth, I give and bequeath to my children heretofore named in this will, a certain House and lot, located in the town of Raymond, County of Hinds, State of Mississippi, now occupied by S. B. McCowan and wife as a house of entertainment.

[1318] Mississippi Confederate Muster Lists, Mississippi Department of Archives and History, Jackson, MS.

[1319] Elizabeth left three heirs: Henry E. Grant, Hiram B. Grant, and Martha R. Grant, wife of Benjamin Fairman. See Copiah Co., MS, Probate Files, on microfilm, MS Dept. of Archives and History, Jackson, MS. Buried in the Grant Cemetery, Copiah Co., MS, are: George W. Grant (1789-1854); Drury J. Brown (1813-1868); Elizabeth W. Brown (1818-1867); Sallie Brown (1857-1866); Joel S. Grant (1843-1848); John W. W. Grant (1841-1844); and William M. Grant (1840-1851).

[1320] Hinds Co., MS, DB 30, pp. 507-509.

Fifth, It is my wish that my son William W. Brown shall have two years Education to place him equal with my two other children out of my estate, expenses of clothing Board and tuition not to exceed Five Hundred Dollars, for each year.

Sixth, I do hereby nominate, constitute and appoint my beloved son Edward W. Brown of the County of Claiborne and A. B. Cates of the County of Hinds both of the State aforesaid my Executors to execute and carry out this my last will and testament, hereby giving and granting under them the full, right, control and possession of the premises herein conveyed: granting them the right both being agreed to sell or otherwise dispose of any or all of the premises herein mentioned, without obtaining necessary orders from the Probate Court.

Seventh, I also grant and give to my children aforesaid four mules now on the Bell farm and one chestnut sorrel mare, at my son Edward W. Brown's in Claiborne County.

Eighth, Having full confidence in the honesty and integrity of my Executors herein appointed, it is my wish that no Bond shall be required of them.[1321]

An inventory of Brown's personal estate, undated but probably from 1868, indicates that he owned four mules and one mare valued at $460. The only other inventoried property was furniture, items which give evidence of the prosperous lifestyle the Browns had enjoyed only a few years earlier: a marble topped bureau, a dining table, an armoire, and a wash stand, altogether valued at $45.[1322]

The inventories indicate, however, that Brown died with serious economic obligations. A list of "liabilities" show that he owed fifteen notes valued altogether at $1,067.79, while the sale of his personal effects netted only $414.15 rather than the $505 inventoried. Brown was also owed $1,655 for loans to S. A. Jenkins, C. S. McCloud, Henry Coleman, Robert Lanier, and Skelton B. McCowan.[1323] Edward W. Brown was successful in collecting some of his father's debts, collecting $300 in 1869. After paying taxes, fees, and $300 for his brother's schooling, however, Edward had only $174 on hand belonging to the estate. On 4 July 1871, in recognition of the unpaid debts owed to the estate, however, Edward Brown petitioned the 20th District of Mississippi for relief, indicating that Brown's estate was then "insolvent and wholly insufficient to pay all the put debts of said decedents,"[1324] which amounted to more than $1,120. Had Edward been able to collect the monies owed his father, the estate might have weathered the hard times it faced in 1870 and 1871; but, in the midst of Reconstruction, southern farmers, white as well as black, struggled for a living. Brown's debtors apparently lacked the cash or other tangible resources to satisfy their obligations to him. On 3 April 1871, Edward Brown auctioned off his father's remaining real estate, selling three 160-acre tracts for $544. Also sold were twelve cabins, probably slave residences, for another $240. This sum was applied to the outstanding balance owed by the estate, and Edward Brown gave notice of the estate's insolvency in *The Copiahan* from 29 July 1871 until 29 August 1871. Brown was able to pay off most of his father's obligations, but at a cost of almost total liquidation of Drury Brown's assets.

Drury J. Brown and Sarah Wells Brown were the parents of four children. One son, born between 1835 and 1840, apparently died as a small boy. Captain Edward W. Brown (20 March 1840-) administered his father's estate; he married twice and was living as late as 1899. Abbie Doxey Brown (10 November 1841 - 1 January 1940) married Anderson Bradley Cates (31 July 1834 - 26 April 1884). Both

---

[1321] Copiah Co., MS, Loose Estate Papers, Boxes 374 and 446, Heirs of D. J. Brown, deceased, E. W. Brown, executor.

[1322] Copiah Co., MS, Loose Estate Papers, Boxes 374 and 446, Heirs of D. J. Brown, deceased, E. W. Brown, executor.

[1323] Estate documents indicate that Elizabeth W. Grant Brown brought considerable property to the marriage. On 9 June 1869, the net value of the Grant estate was $5,733.99, which included nearly $2,200 from the sale of cotton and personal property belonging to Elizabeth Brown. Among the payments from the Grant estate was $425 "for tombstones," perhaps purchased for Elizabeth Grant and her first husband (whose name was apparently G. W. Grant). See Copiah Co., MS, Estate Book L, p. 373

[1324] Copiah Co., MS, Loose Estate Papers, Boxes 374 and 446, Heirs of D. J. Brown, deceased, E. W. Brown, executor.

remained in Hinds County, where they were buried in Brownsville Cemetery. William W. Brown, born about 1850, was working as a clerk in Copiah County, Mississippi, in 1870. The insolvency of his father's estate disrupted the education that his father had intended for him and also deprived him of the landed inheritance he had been promised. As a result, William moved west; when last heard of, he was living in Oklahoma City, Oklahoma, in 1899.

D. Sarah Wells.

Sarah Wells Brown was a daughter of Stephen Wells (5 August 1776, North Carolina - 3 July 1835, Hinds Co., MS) and Sarah Farquhar (13 February 1782, Orange County, North Carolina - 24 June 1833, Hinds Co., MS), who married 6 December 1797 in Person County, North Carolina. Stephen and Sarah married shortly after his twenty-first birthday, and a year later Stephen's father Miles Wells deeded him 318.75 acres on Flat Creek. The land was conveyed as a gift and likely followed the birth of Stephen's first child in 1798.[1325]

Stephen Wells was a prosperous farmer in Person County. He conveyed this tract (which joined Joshua Cates' land) to James Wilson for $426 in 1800 and then purchased 220 acres joining James Rimmer on Bushy Fork from Ephraim Hawkins for £130 in 1802. Two years later, he purchased twelve acres on Bushy Fork from John Brown, grandfather of Drury Brown.[1326] This tract joined land owned by James Rimmer, grandfather of Elizabeth Rimmer Cates.[1327] In 1821, Stephen purchased another forty-one and three-fourths acres joining John Brown, one slave, and livestock from Asa Hudgins.[1328]

When Stephen's father-in-law James Farquhar died in 1814, Stephen was one of the executor's of his will. As such, he joined his brother-in-law William Farquhar in deeding 292.5 acres of James Farquhar's land to another brother-in-law, James Farquhar, Jr.[1329] Along with Willis Wells, Miles Wells, John Cates, John Brown, Henry Burch, Baylor Burch, Elijah Hester, and Charles Cates, Stephen Wells was a major purchaser at James Farquhar's August 1814 estate sale.[1330]

At the time of the 1823 Person County Tax List, Stephen owned a total of 232 acres in Person County. Two years later, he purchased another fifty-seven acres on Bushy Fork from John Brown.[1331] In 1828, in three separate deeds, Wells purchased another 137 acres on Bushy Fork from Brown.[1332] In 1830, Stephen conveyed a portion of this land to his sons William and James Wells.[1333] On 29 June 1832, Stephen Wells conveyed the remaining 578 acres on Bushy Fork, joining John Brown and Brown's Spring Branch, to Hugh Woods for $800.[1334] The deed describes Stephen as of Person County, although he must have almost immediately relocated to Hinds County, Mississippi, where he appears on the tax rolls for 1833 and 1834.[1335] Stephen Wells wrote his will in Hinds County on 4 May 1835;[1336] he died two months later, on 3 July 1835. Sarah Farquhar Wells had died two weeks before Stephen, on 24 June 1835. Perhaps the long journey from North Carolina had proved too difficult for them. They were buried in the Stephen Wells Family Cemetery in northern Hinds County.

[1325] Person Co., NC, Deed Book C, pp. 115-6.
[1326] Person Co., NC, Deed Book C, pp. 196, 468-69, 483.
[1327] Person Co., NC, Deed Book E, p. 139.
[1328] Person Co., NC, Deed Book E, pp. 440-42.
[1329] Person Co., NC, DB D, pp. 394-95.
[1330] Person Co., NC, Record Book 6, pp. 227-237.
[1331] Person Co., NC, Deed Book G, pp. 305-6.
[1332] Person Co., NC, Deed Book G, pp. 341-42; I, pp. 166, 219; K, p. 77.
[1333] Person Co., NC, Deed Book K, pp. 103, 146.
[1334] Person Co., NC, Deed Book K, p. 429.
[1335] 1833 Hinds Co., MS, Tax List, p. 64, and 1834 Hinds Co., MS, Tax List, p. 28, Mississippi Department of Archives and History, Jackson, MS.
[1336] C. W. Forrest, ed., *Hinds Co., MS, Will Book I, 1822-57* (Jackson, MS, 1959), p. 9.

Standard Pedigree Tree

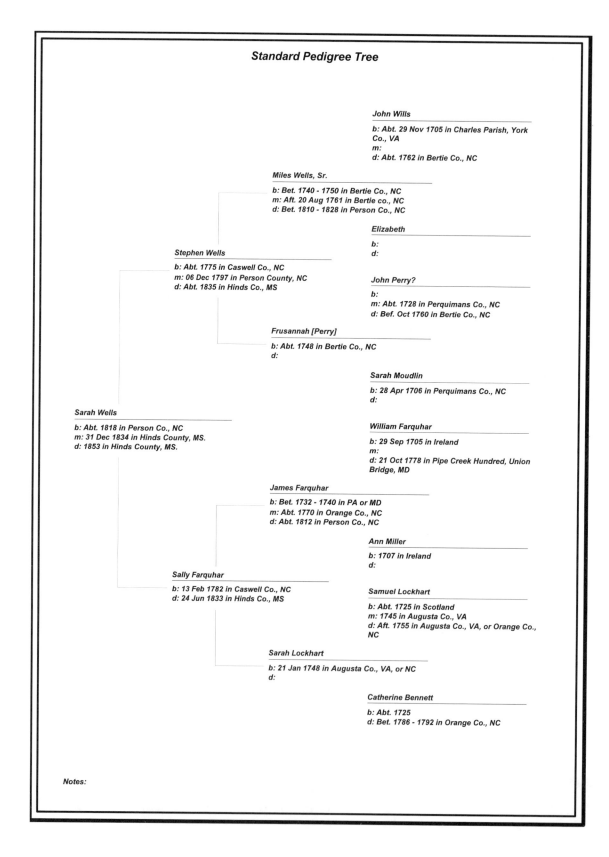

John Wills
b: Abt. 29 Nov 1705 in Charles Parish, York Co., VA
m:
d: Abt. 1762 in Bertie Co., NC

Miles Wells, Sr.
b: Bet. 1740 - 1750 in Bertie Co., NC
m: Aft. 20 Aug 1761 in Bertie co., NC
d: Bet. 1810 - 1828 in Person Co., NC

Elizabeth
b:
d:

Stephen Wells
b: Abt. 1775 in Caswell Co., NC
m: 06 Dec 1797 in Person County, NC
d: Abt. 1835 in Hinds Co., MS

John Perry?
b:
m: Abt. 1728 in Perquimans Co., NC
d: Bef. Oct 1760 in Bertie Co., NC

Frusannah [Perry]
b: Abt. 1748 in Bertie Co., NC
d:

Sarah Moudlin
b: 28 Apr 1706 in Perquimans Co., NC
d:

Sarah Wells
b: Abt. 1818 in Person Co., NC
m: 31 Dec 1834 in Hinds County, MS.
d: 1853 in Hinds County, MS.

William Farquhar
b: 29 Sep 1705 in Ireland
m:
d: 21 Oct 1778 in Pipe Creek Hundred, Union Bridge, MD

James Farquhar
b: Bet. 1732 - 1740 in PA or MD
m: Abt. 1770 in Orange Co., NC
d: Abt. 1812 in Person Co., NC

Ann Miller
b: 1707 in Ireland
d:

Sally Farquhar
b: 13 Feb 1782 in Caswell Co., NC
d: 24 Jun 1833 in Hinds Co., MS

Samuel Lockhart
b: Abt. 1725 in Scotland
m: 1745 in Augusta Co., VA
d: Aft. 1755 in Augusta Co., VA, or Orange Co., NC

Sarah Lockhart
b: 21 Jan 1748 in Augusta Co., VA, or NC
d:

Catherine Bennett
b: Abt. 1725
d: Bet. 1786 - 1792 in Orange Co., NC

Notes:

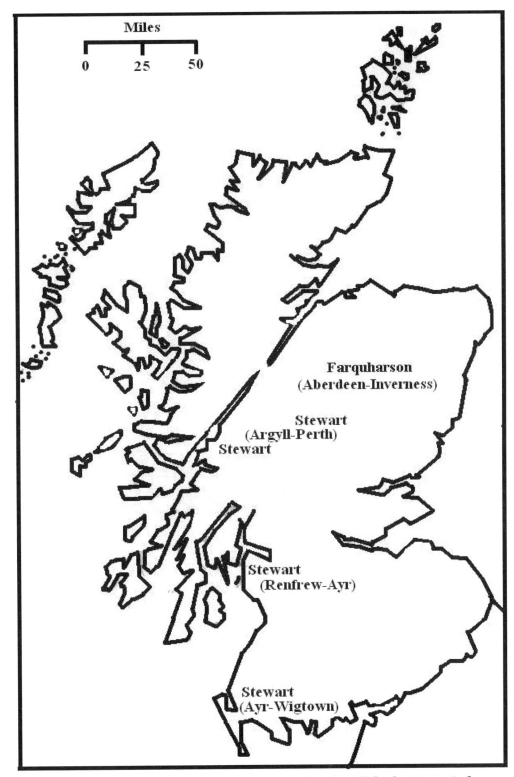

This map shows the areas in which particular Scottish clans exerted power in the past. Shown are the primary places of concentration for the Stewart and Farquharson clans.

There is a strong possibility that Stephen Wells was a descendant of Emanuel Wills of Warwick County, Virginia. Emanuel's mother Elizabeth Wills married four times; her first husband was probably named Emanuel Wills also, and they may be the Emanuel and Elizabeth Wills who baptized a son Emanuel Wills, Jr., on 4 January 1646/7 at St. Olave, Hart Street, London.[1337] Young Emanuel came to the colony with his mother, who married three times after the death of her first husband, to Captain Henry Jackson, Major Edward Griffith, and Thomas Iken, Sheriff of Warwick County. Elizabeth Wills Jackson Griffith married Iken in Warwick County prior to 14 May 1669.

Emanuel married, prior to 11 April 1670 in Virginia, Elizabeth Cary, daughter of Miles Cary and Anne Taylor. According to *Adventurers of Purse and Person in Virginia*,

> Miles Cary, fourth son of John Cary (1583-1661/2), draper of Bristol, England, and his (2) wife Alice Hobson, was baptized 30 January 1622/3 and died 10 June 1657 from wounds received in the attack by the Dutch fleet upon Old Point Comfort. He came to Virginia about 1645, settling in Warwick County at "Windmill Point," and shortly married. He served as commissioner for Warwick, 1654, as major, lieutenant colonel and colonel of the county militia, as collector of tobacco duties for James River, Escheator General, member of the House of Burgesses from Warwick, 1660, 1661-March 1662, and was a member of the Council, 1663-1667. At his death Col. Miles Cary had four separate plantations, "Windmill Point," "The Forest," "Magpie Swamp," and the former Thomas Flint property which "lyeth up Warwick River." these contained at least 2637 acres. He also owned an unseated 3000 acre patent in the Northern Neck and two houses in Bristol, in Ballance Street and St. Nicholas Street, which he directed in his will be sold for the benefit of his three daughters.[1338]

Cary's will, dated 9 June 1667 and proved 21 January 1667/8, identifies his wife as Anne Taylor, daughter of Thomas Taylor. Although they Taylors were Virginians, the couple may have married in England; certainly they had traveled there, for, on 5 October 1654, Cary entered a land claim listing his wife Anne as a headright, indicating that the two had traveled together into the colony. Anne herself may have been a native of Virginia. Her father Thomas Taylor was a mariner who traveled between England and Virginia. He was granted fifty acres of land in what became Elizabeth City before 1625/6, and he was seated at "Windmill Point" in Warwick County where a patent for 350 acres was recorded 23 October 1643. This tract included the fifty acres originally claimed by Thomas Taylor, who was a member of the House of Burgesses in 1646 and a Commissioner of Elizabeth City County from 1647 until at least 1652.[1339]

Of the offspring of Anne Taylor and Miles Cary, Major Thomas Cary became a burgess from Warwick County. He married Anne Milner, daughter of Captain Francis Milner, of Nansemond County. Henry Cary became a merchant and planter in Warwick County. Bridget Cary married Captain William Bassett, Gentleman, of New Kent County, who established a prominent planter family. Miles Cary, Jr., married Mary Milner and then Mary Wilson Roscow, and William Cary married Martha Scasbrook. Miles Cary, III, Elizabeth Wills' nephew, became Secretary of State for Virginia in 1691. Henry Cary, her brother, became a prominent builder, constructing the court house at Yorktown in 1694, the first capitol building at Williamsburg between 1701 and 1703, and the Governor's Palace in Williamsburg between 1705 and 1710. Miles Cary, another brother, was Surveyor General of Virginia from 1699 to 1709, a charter trustee of the College of William and Mary in Virginia in 1693, and Rector of the College from

---

[1337] Dorman, *Adventurers*, p. 604, citing W. B. Bannerman, ed., *The Registers of St. Olave, Hart Street, London, 1563-1700* (Harleian Society, Vol. 96; London, 1916), p. 54.
[1338] Dorman, *Adventurers*, p. 601.
[1339] Ibid., pp. 95, 206, 209, 292, 600-603, 605-606.

1705 to 1706. Lt. Col. William Cary, probably the youngest brother, was county justice, coroner, sheriff, and burgess from Warwick County, serving in the Virginia Assembly from 1691 until 1712.[1340]

Elizabeth Cary Wills and Emanuel Wills were the parents of two documented children, Miles Wills (c. 1670 - after 1721) and Emanuel Wills (c. 1672 - after 1721). Miles Wells held 425 acres in Warwick County in 1704 while his brother Emanuel held 325 acres. Both brothers were living on 11 July 1721 in Warwick County when they sold a tract of land they had purchased together in 1706.[1341] Miles Wills, who married Hannah Scasbrook, daughter of Lt. Col. John Scasbrook and wife Elizabeth, became county justice, coroner, tobacco agent, sheriff, and captain of militia. Miles and Hannah Wills were the parents of John Scasbrook Wills of Warwick County. Elizabeth Cary Wills and Emanuel Wills are thought to have been the parents of a third son, John Wills (c. 1675 - before 1738, York County, Virginia), who married Elizabeth Roberts Harwood, daughter of Thomas Roberts and Ann Noblin of York County. They were the parents of John Wills, Jr., who moved to Bertie County, North Carolina.[1342]

As John Wills of "Norwick Parish, Virginia," John Wills purchased 240 acres on the south side of Morattock River in Bertie County, North Carolina, on 8 November 1725.[1343] He appears regularly in Bertie County deeds for the next three decades, although on 11 May 1742 he claimed rights for bringing wife Elizabeth Wells and Mary Wells, Sarah Wells, and Isaac Spivey into the colony.[1344] John Wells was deceased by 14 October 1762 in Bertie County, when Miles Wells was ordered to "have leave to sell so much of the Perishable part of his Fathers Estate as will Pay all Debts the 25 November Next."[1345] Then, on the second Tuesday of October 1742, a "motion of Miles Wells for administration on the estate of John Wells, deceased, his father," was granted by the Bertie County court.[1346]

Miles Wells, son of John and Elizabeth Wells, was born in or before 1740 as based on a 20 June 1761 deed in which (as "Miles Wills") he purchased 200 acres on Quiakeson Swamp, "where John Wills lived," from James Ward.[1347] Miles Wells probably married Frusannah Perry, daughter of John Perry and Sarah Moudlin Perry, about 1763 in Bertie County.[1348] John Perry was named as an adjacent landowner in the 1761 deed and had been a neighbor of the Wills family for several years. In 1764, as Miles Wells, he conveyed this tract for £35 to John Brittain and apparently moved soon afterwards to Granville County, where he was taxed as early as 1769.[1349] Wells was apparently living in the Grassy Creek area of Granville County when, along with Thomas Willingham, Daniel Wilkerson, and James Hester, he petitioned not to have to pay tax to the Church of England in Granville County.[1350] Miles and Frusannah sold land in Granville County in 1778; they appear simultaneously in Caswell and Granville Counties from 1783 until about 1790. From 1797 onwards, the couple appears exclusively in Person County.

[1340] Ibid., pp. 600-606.

[1341] Ibid., pp. 207, 364, 603-604; York Co., VA, Deeds and Bonds 3, pp. 368-370.

[1342] Some researchers believe instead that John Wills was a son Emanuel Wills, III (c. 1672 - after 1721). No positive documentation has been found to place John Wills, Sr., as a son of Emanuel and Elizabeth Cary, although location and naming patterns suggest a connection with this family. When John Wills does appear in Bertie County about 1725, he is first called "John Wills, Junior," which suggests that his father may have been named John Wills. At the very least, it indicates the presence of a similarly named but older individual somewhere within the immediate environs. Baptisms for some members of this family are found in Bell, *Register of Charles Parish, York Co., VA, 1648-1789.*

[1343] Bertie Co., NC, DB B, pp. 64-66.

[1344] W. P. Haun, *Bertie Co., NC, Court Minutes, 1740-1762* (7 vols., Durham, NC, 1976 -), 2: 357.

[1345] Ibid., 2: 600.

[1346] Haun, *Bertie Co., NC, Court Minutes,* 2: 305.

[1347] Bertie Co., NC, DB K, p. 108.

[1348] Sarah Moudlin was born 28 April 1706 in Perquimans County, a daughter of Ezekiel Moudlin (- 16 March 1706, Perquimans Co., VA) and Hannah [----] Moudlin Charles (- 1752, Perquimans Co., NC).

[1349] Bertie Co., NC, DB K, p. 466.

[1350] Saunders, *Colonial Records of North Carolina,* 9: 95-97.

On 3 February 1783, Wells was part of a group appointed to lay out a road from Sharman's Meeting House in Caswell County to Granville County.[1351] In 1784, he was granted 323 acres on the South Hico River in Caswell County[1352] but is mentioned in 1786 in several court suits in Granville County, where he was enumerated on Tar River at the time of the 1790 census.[1353] As Miles Wells of Granville County, on 2 December 1794 he sold 423 acres on South Hico River on the Orange County line to George Eubanks.[1354] Two weeks later, he purchased 200 acres in Person County but on the Granville County line from James Wells.[1355] Miles, still of Granville County, then sold 186 acres of this tract to James Wells in 1795 before purchasing 353 acres on Aldridge's Creek in Person County from Henry Lyon.[1356] As a resident of Person County, Miles in 1797 sold twenty-six acres to Jane Lyon and six acres to Richard Lyon.[1357] In 1798, Miles joined Wheeley's Meeting House in Person County.[1358] He deeded, for love and affection, 318 acres joining Richard Lyon on Flat River to his son Stephen Wells on 4 December 1798.[1359] He purchased at the estate sale of James Rimmer in 1809 and of James Farquhar in 1814.[1360] He deeded 550 acres in Person County to son Miles Wells, Jr., in 1823 and 425 acres in Person County to William Villiers in 1827.[1361] Miles Wells died about 1829 in Person County, at which time he must have been nearly ninety.

Stephen and Miles Wells (1785-1848) are the only documented offspring of Miles and Frusannah Wells. Miles Wells, Jr. (1785-1848) married Parthena Malone in Person Co., NC, in 1807. She died about 1820, and he remarried Mary Hardee (1786-1855). Miles and Mary moved to Hinds County, Mississippi, with his brother Stephen Wells and are buried there in the New Salem Cemetery. James Wells, who had land dealings with Miles Wells in Granville County, may also have been a son.

Sarah Farquhar, the wife of Stephen Wells, was a daughter of James Farquhar and Sarah Lockhart of Orange, Caswell, and Person Counties, North Carolina. The Farquhar surname is Scottish in origin and a variant of the more common Farquharson. According to the *Scottish Clan and Family Encyclopedia*,[1362] the

> Farquharsons trace their origin back to Farquhar, fourth son of Alexander Cier (Shaw) of Rothiemurcus, who possessed the Braes of Mar near the source of the river Dee in Aberdeenshire. His descendants were called Farquharsons, and his son, Donald, married Isobel Stewart, heiress of Invercauld. Donald's son, Finla Mor, was the real progenitor of the clan. The Gaelic patronymic is MacFionlaigh Mor. He was royal standard bearer at the Battle of Pinkie, where he was killed in 1547. From his lifetime onwards the clan grew in stature, important branches being founded through the nine sons of his two marriages.... In addition to those who bear the name Farquharson and the other variations which clearly denominate the descendants of Farquhar, there are other families which are acknowledged to be septs or dependents, having close affiliation by tradition, and they include the names Hardie, MacCardney, MacCuaigh, Grassick, Riach, Brebner and

---

[1351] T. M. Owen, *History and Genealogies of Old Granville Co., NC, 1746-1800* (Greenville, SC, 1993), p. 131.

[1352] Caswell Co., NC, Deed Book D, p. 815. Aaron Christiansberry was a neighbor.

[1353] Granville Co., NC, Court Minutes, 1786-1787, p. 11; Granville Co., NC, Court Minutes, 1786-1787, p. 42; Granville Co., NC, Court Minutes, 1786-1787, p. 56.

[1354] Person Co., NC, Deed Book A, pp. 262-3.

[1355] Person Co., NC, Deed Book C, p. 477.

[1356] Person Co., NC, Deed Book B, pp. 123-4, 362-3.

[1357] Person Co., NC, Deed Book C, pp. 11-12, 43-44.

[1358] Flat River Primitive Baptist Church Minutes, Vol. 1, 1786-1890, Microfilm, Person Co., NC, Library.

[1359] Person Co., NC, Deed Book C, pp. 115-6.

[1360] Person Co., NC, Record Book 5, p. 128; Person Co., NC, Record Book 6, pp. 227-237.

[1361] Person Co., NC, Deed Book I, pp. 9, 39.

[1362] G. Way, *Scottish Clan and Family Encyclopedia* (Glasgow, 1994), p. 134. Not surprisingly, the name is also found on the Orkney Islands off the northern coast of Scotland, where it is recorded at Warbuster, St. Olave, in 1492. It was often pronounced, and sometimes spelled, Forker and meant "very dear one." Today it is mostly found in the Kirkwall area. See G. Lamb, *Orkney Surnames* (Edinburgh, 1981), p. 24.

Coutts. The Farquharsons were not as numerous as some of their predatory neighbors, and in 1595 they joined the confederation known as Clan Chattan by a bond of manrent to the chief of the Mackintoshes, acknowledging him as their 'natyff cheiff.'

When the Erskines set out to reassert their claim over the ancient Earldom of Mar at the end of the sixteenth century, they were opposed around Braemar by the increasing power and prominence of the Farquharsons. John Erskine, 'de jure' eighteenth Earl of mar, built a castle at Braemar to defend his lands, but this ultimately passed into the hands of the Farquharsons themselves. The clan's fierce reputation led to their being known as the fighting Farquharsons, and they were staunch supporters of the Stuarts. Donald Farquharson of Monaltrie fought with Montrose in 1644, and the family later supported Charles II. John Farquharson of Inverey, known as the Black Colonel, declared for James VII and followed Graham of Claverhouse, the famous 'Bonnie Dundee,' in 1689. He burned Braemar Castle and was a thorn in the flesh of the government until his death in 1698. In the rising of 1715, John Farquharson of Invercauld joined the Clan Chattan regiment of which he was colonel, but was taken prisoner at Preston, later being transferred to London and held in Marshalsea Prison for ten months.

Undaunted, the Farquharsons supported Bonnie Prince Charlie and at Culloden were led by Francis Farquharson of Monaltrie, the Baron Ban who was nephew and commissioner to John. He was taken prisoner and condemned to be executed at the Tower of London, only being reprieved along with two other Highland officers on the very morning set for their execution. However, he remained a prisoner and was later paroled, not being permitted to return to Scotland for over twenty years.[1363]

As indicated, the Farquharsons remained faithful to the Stuarts after 1688 and continued to support the idea of a Stuart restoration to the thrones of Scotland and England into the eighteenth-century. Those who supported the Stuarts at the time of the Glorious Revolution of 1688 as well as in the Rebellions of 1715 and 1745 may have faced repercussions for their allegiance; possibly for this reason the early Farquhars may have left Scotland, settling first in Ireland and eventually in America.[1364]

The earliest known reference to James Farquhar dates from 30 November 1768 in Orange County, North Carolina, when with Ransom Southerland and Darby Henley he witnessed a deed from Vincent Tullock to John Hogan. If he were of legal age, then we may deduce that he was born before 30 November 1747. The deed does not indicate Farquhar's origin, although his appearance with a Scotsman named Southerland may be significant.[1365]

Two theories exist concerning James Farquhar's origin. One is that he was a son of William and Rebecca May Farquhar of Ayr, Scotland, and that the family relocated to America following the 1745 Jacobite uprising aimed at restoring the Stuarts to the Scottish throne. Certainly many Scottish Jacobites settled in North Carolina at mid-century following the massacre at Culloden, where many Scots clans loyal to the Stuarts were at last defeated, and it seems plausible to suspect that James Farquhar's parents may have been among them.[1366]

Another is that James belonged to the Farquhar family of Pipe Creek Hundred, Maryland. Scots-Irish in origin, this family were Quakers by the eighteenth-century, and they had been established in America by Allen Farquhar, a Quaker who emigrated from Ireland to Chester County, Pennsylvania, about 1725. Farquhar soon moved from Pennsylvania to Pipe Creek Township, Frederick County, Maryland, where his family prospered. He wrote his will on 30 November 1738 in Prince George County, Maryland, naming wife Catherine and sons William and Allen as heirs.[1367]

[1363] Ibid. The motto of Clan Farquharson is "By fidelity and fortitude."

[1364] Ibid.

[1365] Orange Co., NC, Deed Book 3, p. 503.

[1366] For a history of the Jacobite movement, see P. K. Monod, *Jacobitism and the English People, 1688-1788* (Cambridge and New York, 1993).

[1367] J. Baldwin, *Maryland Calendar of Wills, 1635-1743* (8 vols., Baltimore, 1904-1928), 8: 4. The name was also spelled Forker and Forquer.

Of these sons, William Farquhar (29 July 1705, Northern Ireland -- 21 September 1778, Pipe Creek Hundred, Frederick County, Maryland) married Ann Miller on 19 April 1733 in Chester County, Pennsylvania. Born in Ireland in 1707, Ann Miller Farquhar was a daughter of James Miller (1682, Ireland - 1749, Pennsylvania) and Katherine Lightfoot (12 December 1682, Ireland - 17 October 1729, Pennsylvania) and a granddaughter of Thomas Lightfoot (1645/46, Cambridgeshire, England - 4 Sept., 1725, Darby, Delaware County, Pennsylvania) and Mary Wyly (1645 - 1716, West Meath, Ireland) and the granddaughter of Thomas Lightfoot (c. 1619 -).[1368]

William and Ann Miller Farquhar settled for a time in Frederick County, Virginia, where his family attended the Hopewell Monthly Meeting. Their membership was transferred, according to Quaker style, on the 31st day of the fifth month, from the New Garden Monthly Meeting in Pennsylvania to Hopewell.[1369] In 1759, William Farquhar helped establish the Pipe Creek Monthly Meeting, which was nearer his home, and meetings were held at his residence before the meeting house was constructed. A tailor by trade, Farquhar made buckskin breeches which he then sold at Annapolis, using the proceeds to fund further land purchases. At one point, he owned nearly 2,000 acres in Maryland and Virginia.[1370]

William and Ann Miller Farquhar became well-known within the Quaker community of northern Virginia and western Maryland. A biographical sketch of William Farquhar, prepared for the edification and inspiration of future generations of Quakers, was written following his death. The sketch merits quoting at length here for the detail it provides, not only of his life and activities but also of his character and spirit:

> He was born in Ireland the 29th of the 7th month, 1705, and came to America about the sixteenth year of his age. He settled in Pennsylvania, where he was convinced of the Truth, and married among Friends. In the year 1735, he removed, and settled at Pipe-creek, where there were very few inhabitants in those parts. Some years afterwards he was concerned that a meeting might be settled, which was allowed to be held at his house at times for several years, still, the number of friends increasing, they concluded to build a meeting house, which our said friend zealously promoted. His house was much resorted to by traveling friends and others, both in that early period and since, to whom he was courteous and kind. Some years after the settlement of a Monthly Meeting at Fairfax, of which he was a member, he was appointed to the station of an elder, which he filled with propriety and reputation; being an example of plainness, and anxiously careful for the education of his children. He was, at times, concerned in meetings, to exhort friends to keep to the testimony of Truth, and particularly the youth, for whom he seemed zealously concerned, that, as they grew in years, they might grow in grace. For some months before his decease, he was in a weak state of body, yet frequently attended meetings, and the last time of his being there was about four days before he died. The night following, being in

---

[1368] As noted above, there was a close connection between the Miller and Jackson families, and Mary Miller Jackson, sister of Ann Miller Farquhar, and wife of Isaac Jackson, moved about 1751 to Orange County, North Carolina. Thomas Lightfoot's first marriage was to wife Mary; among their offspring were Abigail Lightfoot, wife of Joseph Wiley; Katherine Lightfoot, wife of James Miller and mother of Mary Jackson and Ann Farquhar; Michael Lightfoot, husband of Mary Newby; and Margaret Lightfoot, wife of Isaac Starr. There were numerous family connections between the Lightfoots, Millers, Starrs, Newbys, Wileys, and Jacksons. Thomas Lightfoot married (2) Sarah Wiley, a widow, whose children included Mary Wiley (second wife of the immigrant Thomas Jackson, and stepmother of Isaac Jackson who moved to Orange Co., NC, and of Benjamin Jackson who moved to Georgia); Joseph Wiley, husband of Abigail Lightfoot; and John Wiley, husband of Martha Newby, whose sister Mary married Michael Lightfoot. There were at least three Miller families with Lightfoot and Jackson connections: John and Mary Ignew Miller, from Armagh, Ireland, to Pennsylvania in 1709; Gayan and Margaret Henderson Miller from Ireland to Pennsylvania in 1702; and James Miller, Sr., of New Garden Monthly Meeting, who married Katherine Lightfoot in 1700. This family is detailed by J. G. Jackson, *My Search for John Stephen Jackson: His Ancestors and Descendants* (Easley, SC, 2006).

[1369] Hinshaw, *Encyclopedia of American Quaker Genealogy*, 6: 386.

[1370] Hinshaw, *Encyclopedia of American Quaker Genealogy*, 6: 491.

much pain, he several times cried out: 'O Father! mitigate my pain, if it be thy will; and was favoured to keep in the patience and resignation, waiting for his change. The day before he died, his wife leaning over him mourning, he said to her, 'weep not for me, but for thyself and others. The Lord is near.' He departed this life, the 21st of the 9th month, 1778, aged near seventy-three years. P.S. I am willing to communicate a few hints of what has often passed through my mind concerning my dear husband, whose memory, to me, remains precious. He was much concerned for the welfare of the young and rising generation, often cautioning and exhorting friends in their several stations, strictly to examine the great duty and charge committed to their trust; and in a particular manner, his offspring, that they will live in love with each other, and that they might be careful to bring up their children in the nurture and admonition of the Lord. Ann Farquhar.[1371]

Among the offspring of William and Ann Miller Farquhar was James Farquhar, who, according to Quaker records, was born in 1733 in Maryland. No indication is given concerning James's marriage or later life, a sign that he may have left the faith. Other offspring of William and Ann Miller Farquhar included William Farquhar (1735 -), who married Rachel Wright (1737-), a Quaker minister. Allen Farquhar (1737-1798) married Phoebe Hibbard and remained in Pennsylvania. Mary Farquhar (1739-) married Joseph Wright and settled in York County, Pennsylvania. The fate of George Farquhar (1742-) is unknown. Samuel Farquhar (1745-) married Phoebe Yarnall and remained in Frederick County, Maryland. Elizabeth Farquhar (1748-) married Joel Wright and settled in York County, Pennsylvania. Moses Farquhar (1750 -) married Sarah Poultney, and Susannah Farquhar (1753-) married Solomon Shepherd. Both are believed to have remained in Maryland.[1372]

Given the location in which James Farquhar first appears in 1768, either theory concerning his origins seems plausible. Orange County, North Carolina, was a popular Quaker destination, and several religious congregations formed there in the 1740s and 1750s. New Garden Monthly meeting, originally in Orange but later in Guilford County, became one of the best known in the region. Many Quakers came from Chester County, Pennsylvania, to Orange County, North Carolina, and among them were several nieces and nephews of Ann Miller Farquhar. Hence, it is entirely possible that James Farquhar left Maryland and moved to Orange County, North Carolina, with his cousins in the 1760s.[1373]

From his appearance in Orange County in 1768 until his death in Person County about 1814, James Farquhar appears frequently in civic and legal records. James Farquhar and William Lockhart were both debtors to the family of Robert Lytle of Orange County in 1775.[1374] Farquhar was a Captain in the North Carolina troops during the Revolution,[1375] although he was often at home throughout the conflict. On 3 March 1779, he patented 200 acres on Flat River in Caswell County, North Carolina,[1376] and another 250 acres in 1780.[1377] A 1784 deed indicates that this land lay adjacent to land owned by Abraham Brown, Drury Brown's great-grandfather.[1378] By 1786, he was a member of Flat Creek Baptist Church in Caswell

---

[1371] "A Testimony From Pipe-Creek Monthly Meeting, Maryland, Concerning William Farquhar," from *A Collection of Memorials Concerning Divers Deceased Ministers and others of the People called Quakers in Pennsylvania* (3rd ed., Philadelphia, 1824), pp. 304-305.

[1372] Ibid.; Hinshaw, *Encyclopedia of American Quaker Genealogy*, 6: 386, 491.

[1373] See Jackson, *John Stephen Jackson*, pp. 5.1-5.32, 6.1-6.15.

[1374] Inventories, Accounts of Sales, 1758-1785, Orange Co., NC, p. 301.

[1375] NSDAR, *DAR Patriot Index, Centennial Edition* (3 vols., Washington, 1990), 1: 991.

[1376] Caswell Co., NC, Deed Book A, p. 233.

[1377] Caswell Co., NC, Deed Book A, pp. 501-502.

[1378] Caswell Co., NC, Deed Book D, p. 775. By 1797, adjacent landowners included John Brown, Josiah Brown, and James Rimmer. See Person Co., NC, Deed Book C, p. 203.

County (where he was later a deacon),[1379] and his wife Sarah Lockhart Farquhar was received as a member in 1791.[1380]

In 1800, Farquhar -- identified as a millwright -- purchased sixty-two acres on Bushy Fork from Ephraim Hawkins.[1381] On 10 July 1803, again identified as millwright, he sold 232 acres on Bushy Fork to William Farquhar.[1382] The 1805 Person County tax list showed the elder Farquhar taxed with 618 acres, while his son James Farquhar, Jr., paid poll tax only. William Farquhar at that time owned 232 acres, the tract he had purchased from his father.[1383] In 1806, the elder Farquhar deeded to his son John a 233-acre tract on Bushy Fork joining John Brown.[1384] Along with John Brown, Phoebe Rimmer, Baylor Burch, Wright Nichols, and Miles Wells, Sr., James Farquhar on 1 June 1809 purchased items from the estate sale of his neighbor James Rimmer.[1385]

Farquhar did not long survive Rimmer. He wrote his will on 20 September 1812; it was proven in February 1814.[1386] Describing himself as "sick and weak in body but in perfect mind and memory," Farquhar gave his Christian testimony before devising his worldly estate:

> Calling to mind the mortality of my body, and knowing that it is appointed for all men once to die do make and ordain this my last will and testament and as touching my worldly estate wherewith it hath pleased God to bless me with in this life, I give devise and dispose of the same in the following manner (viz.).
>
> First of all, I leave to my beloved wife the plantation whereon I now live, together with the stock of all lands, plantation tools, and the following hands, namely James, Sarah and Dinah, to have and to hold during her natural life or widow Hood.
>
> Then I give unto my son Wm. Farquhar Two hundred and thirty two acres of land lying on the Bushy Fork of Flat River, also the blacksmith tools and, at the death of my wife, my Negro man James, to him his heirs and assigns for Ever.
>
> Item. I give to my son John Farquhar two Hundred and thirty acres of land lying on the Bushy Fork of Flat River and joining Abram Moore and others, also my Negro man Isaac, to him and his heirs for Ever.
>
> Item, my will further is that my son James Farquhar have all my land on the East side of Flat River, together with my Mills and all the utensils thereunto belonging for working the same and at the death of my wife, Dinah to him His heirs and assigns forever.
>
> Item, my will further is that my daughter Sarah Wells have one Hundred and twelve acres of land lying on the Bushy Fork and joining Wm. Farquhar and others and at the death of my wife Sarah, to her and her heirs forever.
>
> Item, my will further is that my daughter Cateran Moore have the following Negro girl Jean, to her and her heirs forever.
>
> Item, my will further is that my daughter Jean Hargis have the following Negro girl, towit, Sinthy to her heirs and assigns forever.
>
> Item. My will further is that my daughter Elizabeth Farquhar have the following property, towit, one Negro girl by the name of Ann, one horse worth at least forty dollars, two cows and calves one head and furniture to her heirs and assigns forever.

[1379] Flat River Primitive Baptist Church Minutes, Vol. 1, 1786-1890, Microfilm, Person Co., NC, Library.

[1380] Flat River Primitive Baptist Church Minutes, Vol. 1, 1786-1890, Microfilm, Person Co., NC, Library.

[1381] Person Co., NC, Deed Book C, p. 197.

[1382] Person Co., NC, Deed Book C, p. 393.

[1383] 1805 Person Co., NC, Tax List, North Carolina Department of Archives and History, Raleigh, NC.

[1384] Person Co., NC, Deed Book C, p. 553.

[1385] Person Co., NC, Record Book 5, p. 128.

[1386] Person Co., NC, Estates, Book 1811-1815, pp. 206-209.

Item. My will further is that at the death or marriage the widow taking a child's part, the whole of the property not already given may be sold and equally divided among my legaties by my executors herein after named, (towit) Sarah Farquhar, Wm. Farquhar and Stn. Wells.

In witness whereof I do hereby acknowledge this and no other to be my last will and testament revoking and annulling all former wills by me made heretofore. In witness hereunto I set my hand and affixed my seal this twentieth day of September one thousand Eight hundred and twelve.

Obediah Pearce and Absolom Johnston witnessed James Farquhar's signature. Soon after completing the original document, Farquhar added a codicil to the document. Therein, he stipulated that the natural increase of his Negro woman Dinah should go "unto the mass of my movable property and household goods" which, following his wife's death, was to be equally divided among his legatees. Farquhar also added that his still was to remain unsold "for the use of my children."[1387]

James Farquhar married Sarah Lockhart, daughter of Samuel and Catherine Bennett Lockhart. Samuel Lockhart was of Scottish or Scots-Irish descent. The first known references to him date from 1745, when he appears among a numerous group of Lockharts in Augusta County, Virginia. These Lockharts, who had come to Pennsylvania from Northern Ireland in the 1720s, may have included Samuel's father; certainly there were Lockharts in the community in which he lived old enough to be his parents, although no legal documents indicating a connection have been found. On 18 March 1746, Samuel Lockhart signed a petition to build a road in Augusta County from "the top of the ridge to John Terald's."[1388] The following month, he and Robert McMahon were charged with illegally killing livestock belonging to William Thompson.[1389] Lockhart traveled seventy miles in 1746 to testify at a court suit in Orange County involving William Frazier,[1390] and in 1752 he succeeded Patrick Frazier as surveyor of highways in Augusta County.[1391]

About 1753, Samuel Lockhart and wife Catherine began making plans to leave Augusta County, probably in order to settle in Orange County, North Carolina. On 22 May 1753, they sold 200 acres on the "North River Shanando" which was part of 400 acres granted to Samuel in 1751.[1392] Five days later, they conveyed a larger tract of 1790 acres, patented in 1747, to Edward Beard.[1393] Samuel was still in Augusta on 22 May 1755, when Andrew Vaught was named his successor as surveyor of highways.[1394] On 20 August 1755, however, he sold the remaining 200 acres of his 400 acre tract to Edward Beard, and, on 24 September 1755, he gave notice at the Augusta Court that he expected "to leave this colony before the next court."[1395]

The Lockharts may have gone directly to Orange County, where there was a substantial loss of eighteenth-century records. No trace of Samuel Lockhart has been discovered after the 1755 statement that he intended to leave the colony, and Catherine's trail is likewise obscure. Yet, from studying their children, it is clear that Catherine must have been in Orange County throughout most of the 1770s,

[1387] Person Co., NC, Estates, Book 1811-1815, pp. 206-209.
[1388] Virginia Transportation Research Council, *Historic Records of Virginia: Augusta County Road Orders, 1745-1769* (Charlottesville, 1998), p. 8.
[1389] L. Chalkley, *Chronicles of the Scotch-Irish Settlement in Virginia: Extracted from the Original Court Records of Augusta County, 1745-1800* (3 vols., repr., Baltimore, 1999), 1: 17, 20.
[1390] Orange Co., VA, Order Book, 1747-1757.
[1391] Virginia Transportation Research Council, *Historic Records of Virginia: Augusta County Road Orders, 1745-1769* (Charlottesville, 1998), p. 37.
[1392] Chalkley, *Scotch-Irish Settlement*, 3: 313.
[1393] Chalkley, *Scotch-Irish Settlement*, 3: 337.
[1394] Virginia Transportation Research Council, *Historic Records of Virginia: Augusta County Road Orders, 1745-1769* (Charlottesville, 1998), p. 63.
[1395] Chalkley, *Scotch-Irish Settlement*, 1: 313.

although she does not appear in surviving records. The next, and final, reference to Catherine Lockhart dates from 24 August 1786, when she wrote her will (proven in November 1792) in Orange County. She stated that she then resided in Hillsborough, the county seat, and devised to her son William Lockhart the house and square where she then lived. She named five married daughters, Catherine Roads, Jean Holt, Sarah Farker, Elizabeth Mucklejohn, and Meary Smith, before appointing her son William Lockhart and her son-in-law "James Farker" to execute her will. John Allison, William Kennedy, and Martin Palmer witnessed the document, which represents the last known reference to Catherine Bennett Lockhart.[1396]

Sarah Lockhart Farquhar survived her husband only by a short while. She did not purchase at the August 1814 estate sale, an indication that she may have then been deceased.[1397] She owned no taxable property at the time of the 1814 Person County tax list, and a membership roster from Flat River Baptist Church dated 1817 reveals that she was "dead" by that date.[1398] John Farquhar married Nancy Nichols, daughter of Wright and Sarah Burch Nichols; they moved to Mississippi with Nancy's family, but they were both deceased by 1833. James Farquhar, Jr., was living in Person County as late as 1820.[1399] Sarah Farquhar married Stephen Wells in 1797 and moved to Mississippi in 1832. Catherine Farquhar married Joseph Moore in 1808; she may have been living in Tennessee as late as 1826.[1400] Jane Farquhar married William Hargis in Person County in 1809; Elizabeth Farquhar was apparently unmarried when her father wrote his will in 1812. Of the offspring of James and Sarah Lockhart Farquhar, William Farquhar died about 1825, leaving four children (including daughter Susannah Farquhar Whitefield).[1401]

Stephen Wells and Sarah Farquhar Wells produced a large family. James Wells (c. 1798, Person County, North Carolina -) married Susan Nichols on 6 January 1822 in Person County. Miles Wells (30 June 1803, Person County, North Carolina - 10 November 1859, Hinds County, Mississippi) married his cousin Dupper Wells, daughter of Miles Wells and Parthena Malone. William M. Wells (2 August 1806, Person County, North Carolina - 18 December 1895, Hinds County, Mississippi) married first Mary Wade (1806-1842) and second Sarah Ann [-----] (c. 1813, Virginia - after 1870, Hinds County, Mississippi). Harriett L. Wells (c. 1810 - c. 1833/35) married George W. Roberts on 9 August 1830 in Person County. Stocks A. Wells (c. 1814, North Carolina - after 1870, Hinds County, Mississippi) married Sarah Stovall on 8 February 1837 in Hinds County. Frusannah Wells (c. 1815, Person County, North Carolina - after 1850, Hinds County, Mississippi) married George W. Roberts on 24 December 1835 in Hinds County. Eliza Wells (c. 1816, Person County, North Carolina – after 1835, Hinds County, Mississippi) was unmarried when her parents died.[1402] Sarah Wells (c. 1818, Person County, North Carolina - c. 1854, Hinds County, Mississippi) married Drury J. Brown on 31 December 1834 in Hinds County. Stephen Wells, Jr. (12 August 1826, Person County, North Carolina - 18 August 1840, Hinds County, Mississippi) died as a teenager. Benjamin Wells was living when his father wrote his will in 1835.

In the two centuries following Emanuel Wills' birth in London, England, in 1647, the family migrated from the Virginia Tidewater into the North Carolina Piedmont and finally into central Mississippi. Retaining their landed wealth across generations, members of the Wells family amplified their holdings in each new location. It was this quest for new, more fertile lands that brought them to Mississippi soon after Indian removal. Stephen and Sarah Farquhar Wells, with their children and a large network of extended relatives, traveled more than 800 miles to settle in central Mississippi in 1833. Neither long survived the journey, but the family they established there still endures.

[1396] Orange Co., NC, Will Book B, p. 194. Some researchers claim that Jean Lockhart married Michael Holt and that Elizabeth married Rev. George Micklejohn, but I have seen no evidence to confirm this belief.

[1397] Person Co., NC, Record Book 6, pp. 227-237.

[1398] Flat River Primitive Baptist Church Minutes, Vol. 1, 1786-1890, Microfilm, Person Co., NC, Library.

[1399] 1820 Person Co., NC, Census, p. 452.

[1400] Person Co., NC, Deed Book G, pp. 341-42.

[1401] Person Co., NC, DB H, p. 101.

[1402] One Eliza Wells married M. J. Standard on 2 June 1836 in Hinds County. Another married Ralph Harvey on 3 October 1839 in Hinds County.

Chapter 25:

Mary Almedia Bankston Hammack of Hinds County, Mississippi

Mary Almedia Bankston Hammack was born 3 April 1894 in Hinds County, Mississippi. She died 9 December 1974 in the same location. Mary was a daughter of John Manly Bankston (2 September 1857, Bibb County, Alabama -- 13 December 1922, Hinds County, Alabama) and of Abi Doxey O'Neal (22 April 1870, Hinds County, Mississippi -- 15 March 1899, Hinds County, Mississippi).

The Bankston ancestry will be treated briefly below through a discussion of the lineage of each of Mary Almedia Bankston's grandparents. Her grandparents Thomas Jefferson Bankston and Martha Adeline Mitchell were natives of Georgia and Tennessee respectively; James Rederick O'Neal and Mary Jane Gary were natives of Georgia and Mississippi, but each had deep roots in Virginia and the Carolinas.

A. Thomas Jefferson Bankston (c. 1830, Coweta County, Georgia -- 1884, Issaquena County, Mississippi).

If the marriage of Louisa Templeton to John T. Hammack added Scots-Irish ancestry to the Hammack gene pool, the family history of Thomas Jefferson Bankston added a mixture of Swedish, Dutch, French, and Italian ancestry, in addition to connections to several prominent Anglo-Virginian families.

The American lineage begins with Andreas Bengtsson, anglicized as Andrew Bankson, who arrived in New Sweden aboard the ship Mercurius in 1656. Believed to have been born in Stockholm, Sweden, in 1640, Bengtsson remained in the colony for more than a decade before he married Gertrude Rambo on 22 November 1668. Gertrude was a daughter of Peter Gunarssen Rambo, who came to New Sweden in 1640 aboard the "Lamar Nychehkel," and Brita Matsdotter, a native of Vasa, Polyjamen, Finland.[1403]

New Sweden capitulated to the Dutch after a brief skirmish in 1655, and much of the area -- including the three lower counties that later came to constitute Delaware -- was added to William Penn's Pennsylvania grant in 1680.[1404] Andrew Bankson served as a justice in Pennsylvania in 1682 and in 1683, 1686, and 1698 sat in the Pennsylvania General Assembly. In 1689, Andrew was a trustee for Gloria Dei, the Swedish church in Philadelphia. Andrew remained in Pennsylvania for the rest of his life; after fifty years in the colony, he accidentally drowned in the Schuylkill River in 1706.[1405]

Born about 1671, Andreas Bengtsson, Jr., was his father's second son. Andreas married Gertrude, daughter of Lars Larsson Boore (1648-1709) and granddaughter of Lars Thomson, a Swedish sailor who entered the colony in 1641. Andreas headed a family of four in 1697, at which time he was living near Gloria Dei in Philadelphia, but, by 1712, he was living in the division of Potquissink, Bucks County, when he joined his siblings to deed the 500-acre family homestead on Schuylkill River to Thomas Oakley.[1406] Andreas died on 20 December 1759 in Chester County, at which time he was nearly ninety years old. He left a large family, including several sons who left Pennsylvania, moving into Maryland and Virginia.

[1403] The best recent treatment of the Bankston family is A. M. Haigler, *Bankston Cousins* (Florissant, MO, 1998). A niece of Mary Almedia Bankston Hammack, Haigler traces the ancestry of Thomas Jefferson Bankston and identifies him as a grandson of Rev. John and Mary Lanier Bankston. In 2004, Mrs. Haigler, then of Birmingham, Alabama, kindly allowed me to examine her Bankston, Stewart, Stephens, and O'Neal family files, which became the basis for much subsequent research on these lines. I have followed Mrs. Haigler's identification of Thomas B. Bankston as a son of John and Mary Lanier Bankston. The maiden name of Thomas' wife Marion has not been determined; based on the identity of associated families in Coweta County, Georgia, it may be that Marion was from the Kettle Creek area of Wilkes County, Georgia, where the family of another Lawrence Bankston also lived.

[1404] See C. E. Hoffecker, R. Waldron, L. E. Williams, and B. E. Benson, *New Sweden in America* (Newark and London, 1995), pp. 65, 174, 177, 194, 201, 292, 339, 355, for information regarding Andrew Bankson and Peter Rambo.

[1405] *Pennsylvania Magazine of History and Biography*, 2 (1878): 227, and Haigler, *Bankston Cousins*, pp. 1-2.

[1406] Philadelphia Deeds E 7, Volume 8, p. 348.

It was the third generation of American Bankstons who made the move from Pennsylvania into the Carolinas. Born about 1704, Lawrence Bankston, son of Andreas and Gertrude, was reared in Philadelphia. He married Rebecca Hendricks, daughter of John Hendricks and Rebecca Wells, in 1725. Rebecca belonged to a Dutch and Swedish family that had converted to the Quaker faith, and many of her relatives continued to reside in Pennsylvania long after her offspring were living along the Southern frontier.

The Hendricks Society identifies Rebecca Hendricks Bankston as a daughter of John Hendricks and Rebecca Groesbeck Wells, widow of Arthur Wells, and mother of Arthur and Thomas Wells. Thomas Wells, Rebecca Bankston's half-brother, was mentioned as an adjacent owner in a 1787 Georgia deed in which the Bankston heirs disposed of their Pennsylvania land. John Hendricks was a son of Albertus Hendrickson (1642 - 1716, Chester County, Pennsylvania) and Aeltje Helchey. Rebecca Groesbeck Wells (1676 -) has been identified by the Hendricks Society as a daughter of Jacob Classen Groesbeck and Annetje Van Der Grift.[1407] Both families were of Swedish and Dutch extraction. Jacob Classen Groesbeck was a son of Nicholas Jacobse Van Rotterdam Groesbeck and wife Elizabeth. Annetje Van Der Grift (1653, New Amsterdam -) was a daughter of Jacob Leendersten Van Der Grift and Rebecca Lubbertszen. Nicholas Jacobse Van Rotterdam Groesbeck (1623, Breda, Netherlands -- 1712, Albany, New York) was a son of Jacob Van Rotterdam, a Dutch trader. Rebecca Lubbertszen is identified as a daughter of Frederick Lubbertszen. Most of these individuals were members of the congregation of the Dutch Reformed Church in New Amsterdam from before 1650 until at least 1700.[1408]

[1407] Many records appear for Jacob Claeszen, first as father (T. G. Evans, ed., *Collections of the New York Genealogical and Biographical Society, Volume II: Baptisms from 1639 to 1730 in the Reformed Dutch Church in New Amsterdam and New York* (New York, 1901), pp. 119, 129, 141, 156, 169) and also as witness (pp. 30, 160). Jacob Claeszen and Annetie Jacobs in 1675 baptized a daughter Rebecca with Jacob Leendersten and Rebecca Jacobs as witnesses (p. 119); Jacob Claeszen and Annetje Vandergrist in 1677 baptized Elisabeth with Claes Jacobszen, Lysbeth Stephens, and Christina Vandergrist as witnesses (p. 129); Jacob Claeszen and Annetie Van der Grist baptized Dina in 1680 with Cornelis Jacobszen Schipper and Maritie Van der Grist as witnesses (p. 141); in 1682 Jacob Claeszen and Annetie Van der Grist baptized Rachel with Leendert Van der Grist and Ytie Roelofs as witnesses (p. 156); and in 1685 Jacob Claeszen and Annetie Van der Grist baptized Johannah with Daniel Veenvos and Christina Van der Grist as witnesses (p. 169).

[1408] Records of the Dutch Church, New York, show that Jacob Claeszen Groesbeck and Anna Jacobs were in 1690 witnesses for the baptism of Rebecca, daughter of Daniel Veenvos and Christina Jacobs. (See Evans, *Dutch Church*, p. 196.) In 1640, one Jan Corn. Van Rotterdam baptized a son Jan. (Ibid., p. 11.) Anna, daughter of Jacob Leenderttszen, was baptized at the Dutch Church in 1653; Paulus Leenderttszen, Jan Pieterszen Van Brug, Janneken Gerrits, and Hillegond Jans witnessed the baptism. In another record in which he served as a witness in 1648, Paulus Leenderttszen Van der grist, Pieter Corneliszen, and Marritje Joris were witnesses for the baptism of Lysbeth, daughter of Joris Rapalje. Paulus Leenderttszen and Jannetje Gerrits baptized a son Johannes in 1655 with Jacob Van der Grist and Rebecca Van der Grist as witnesses. (Ibid., p. 39.) In 1656, Jacob Leenderttszen Van der Grist and wife Rebecca baptized a son Leendert; Paulus Leenderttszen and Jannetje Gerrits were witnesses. (Ibid., p. 40.) In 1658, Jacob Leenderttszen Van der Grist and Rebecca Fredricks baptized a son Nicolaes; Paulus Leenderttszen Van der Grist and Jannetje Gerrits witnessed. (Ibid., p. 49.) On many other occasions Jacob served as witness (Ibid., pp. 46, 49, 166, 169, 182, 201), probably often as a relative. In 1688, he and Rebecca, as Jacob Leendersten Van der Grist and Rebecca Van der Grist, witnessed at the baptism of Rebecca, daughter of Daniel Veenvos and Christina Van der Grist -- perhaps a grandchild? There are many Van der Grist references: Annetje, Christina, Gerrit, Grietie, Grietje, Hendrick, Jacob Leenderttszen, Jannetje Gerrits, Johannes, Leendert, Margareta, Margrietie Leenderts, Maria, Marritie, Nicolaes, Paulus Leenderttszen, Rachel, Rebecca, and Vredrik. As Jacob Leenderttszen, several other records were recorded, including children's births (Ibid., pp. 26, 29, 34, 74, 87): In 1649, the birth of Marritie, daughter of Jacob Leenderttszen, with Paulus Leenderttszen, Olof Stephenszen Van Court, Govert Loockermans, Janneken Gerrits, and Marritie Jacobs as witnesses; in 1651, the baptism of Christina, daughter of Jacob Leenderttszen, with Frederick Lubbertszen en syn hys vr., Borger Joriszen, and Engeltje Mans as witnesses [on the same page Fredrick Lubbertszen en syn hys vr., Jochem Pieterszen, and Pieter Anthony were witnesses for the baptism of Pieter, son of Cors. Pieterszen]; in 1653 the baptism, as cited, of Anna, daughter of Jacob Leenderttszen; in 1664 the baptism of Rachel, daughter of Jacob Leenderttszen and Rebecca Fredricx, with Gerrit Van Tricht and Grietie Paulus as witnesses; and in 1667 the baptism of Johannes, son of Jacob Leenderttszen and Rebecca Fredricks, with Jan Evertszen Bout, Mr. Hans Kierstede, Tryntie Simons, and Jannetie Kierstede as witnesses. Frederick Lubbertszen (Ibid., p. 49) and Tryntje Hendricks baptized a daughter Elsje in 1658 and a daughter Aeltje (Ibid., p. 67) in 1660 with Johannes Pieterszen Van Brug, Jannetie Van Donck, and Susanna Vreught as witnesses, and he served frequently (Ibid., pp. 20, 26, 29, 41, 49, 53) as witness, the earliest occasion being 1646.

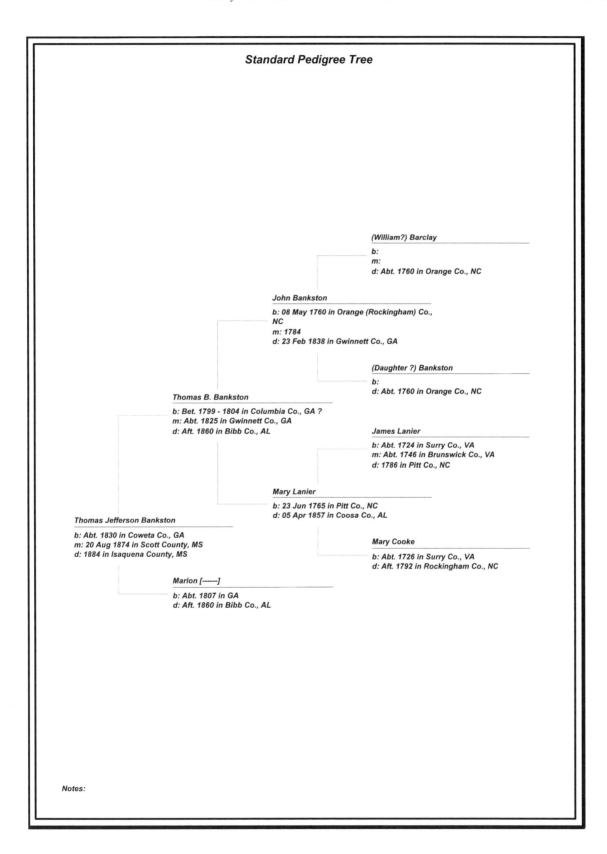

Standard Pedigree Tree

(William?) Barclay

b:
m:
d: Abt. 1760 in Orange Co., NC

John Bankston

b: 08 May 1760 in Orange (Rockingham) Co.,
NC
m: 1784
d: 23 Feb 1838 in Gwinnett Co., GA

(Daughter ?) Bankston

b:
d: Abt. 1760 in Orange Co., NC

Thomas B. Bankston

b: Bet. 1799 - 1804 in Columbia Co., GA ?
m: Abt. 1825 in Gwinnett Co., GA
d: Aft. 1860 in Bibb Co., AL

James Lanier

b: Abt. 1724 in Surry Co., VA
m: Abt. 1746 in Brunswick Co., VA
d: 1786 in Pitt Co., NC

Mary Lanier

b: 23 Jun 1765 in Pitt Co., NC
d: 05 Apr 1857 in Coosa Co., AL

Thomas Jefferson Bankston

b: Abt. 1830 in Coweta Co., GA
m: 20 Aug 1874 in Scott County, MS
d: 1884 in Isaquena County, MS

Mary Cooke

b: Abt. 1726 in Surry Co., VA
d: Aft. 1792 in Rockingham Co., NC

Marion [------]

b: Abt. 1807 in GA
d: Aft. 1860 in Bibb Co., AL

Notes:

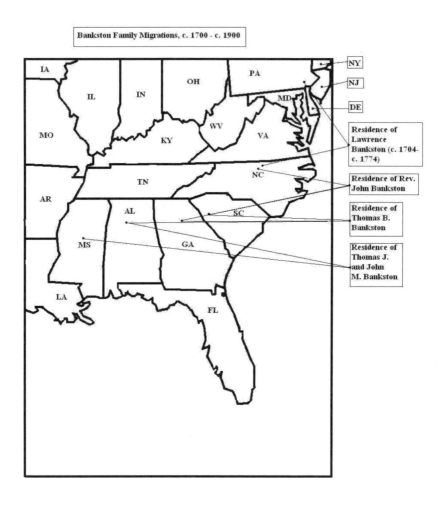

Bankston Family Migrations, c. 1700 - c. 1900

In 1737, John Hendricks and his brother-in-law Lawrence Bankston were jailed in Lancaster County, Pennsylvania, after participating in a riot which destroyed the home of Henry Hendricks in the fall of 1736. Soon after 1737, Lawrence Bankston left Pennsylvania, moving south; family tradition holds that he lived for several years in southern Virginia, but the next documented record of him is from 24 November 1744, when he appeared in Edgecombe County, North Carolina. Lawrence claimed land in Edgecombe at that time on the basis of his recent arrival in the colony; the area in 1746 became a part of Granville County, where Lawrence became a vestryman of St. Matthew's Parish Church.[1409]

On 2 September 1747, "Mr. Bankston" first appeared as a justice in Granville County;[1410] subsequent references identify him as Captain Lawrence Bankston, Justice.[1411] In 1752, when Orange County was organized, Lawrence Bankston became one of the original six justices of the county court; he apparently served as a Granville Justice until the new court was organized in September.[1412] He was living there with five sons at the time of the 1755 Orange County, North Carolina, tax list. Lawrence in April 1757 was named to the commission of roads in Orange County; he was still sitting as a justice at that time. On 23 January 1761, he received a grant for 595 acres in Orange County,[1413] and he is mentioned in Orange County with Lawrence Bankston, Jr., and Andrew Bankston in 1765 and alone in 1772. According to tradition, Lawrence died about 1774 in Orange County.[1414]

Much uncertainty concerns the offspring of Lawrence Bankston. A persistent tradition holds that Rebecca Hendricks Bankston died about 1740 and that Lawrence Bankston married Ann Major soon afterward and began another family. No documentary evidence has been found to support the existence of Ann Major Bankston, although there is nothing to suggest that she did not exist, either. William Lea, who was appointed commissioner of roads after Lawrence Bankston in June 1758,[1415] had married Isabella Major. Some researchers believe that she and Ann were sisters and that the Lea migration to Wilkes County, Georgia, from Caswell County, North Carolina, explains the decision of Lawrence's family to move there in the 1780s. Unfortunately, without firm evidence, these possibilities must remain speculation only.

Lawrence Bankston and Rebecca Hendricks are proven to have been the parents of several children:[1416] Anne Bankston, who married James Lea,[1417] of Kilgore's Branch on the North Hico, about

---

[1409] Haigler, *Bankston Cousins*, pp. 24-28.

[1410] Owen, *History and Genealogies of Old Granville County, North Carolina, 1746-1800*, pp. 115, 234.

[1411] Ibid., pp. 107, 155, 174.

[1412] Orange Co., NC, Records Book 1, 1752-1761, p. 1; Owen, *History and Genealogies of Old Granville County, North Carolina, 1746-1800*, p. 174.

[1413] North Carolina Patent Book 14, p. 343.

[1414] In April 1754, Lawrence Bankston was overseer for the inhabitants of Hico River, to lay out a road across Flat River; the road was to be sixteen feet wide, and John Cate was to be overseer under the inspection of Lawrence Bankston. Interestingly, this is John Cate, ancestor of Sallie Elizabeth Cates Hammack. Significantly, this record suggests that Lawrence Bankston lived in what later became Caswell County, near the modern boundary between Orange, Person, and Caswell Counties. An August, 1755, road order also places Bankston in this neighborhood. See Orange Co., NC, Records Book 1, 1752-1761, p. 151. In September 1755, Bankston was identified as one of the commissioners "from Hico upwards." James Hendricks -- probably his wife's brother who moved to South Carolina -- was also a commissioner. See Orange Co., NC, Records Book 1, 1752-1761, p. 139.

[1415] Orange Co., NC, Records Book 1, 1752-1761, p. 295.

[1416] Wilkes Co., GA, DB BB, p. 114, and AA, p. 127, show that on 4 January 1787, Peter Bankston, Jacob Bankston, and Daniel Bankston, all of Wilkes Co., GA, sold to Matthew Wood of Greene Co., GA, 440 acres, which came to them from their father, Lawrence Bankston, and thirty-seven and one-half acres, located in Philadelphia, Pennsylvania, which was "willed to our mother, Rebecca Hendricks, and is recorded in the State of Pennsylvania, November 27, 1786.' This land was three miles above York on the Great Road leading to Comewato, being the same tract surveyed for "our father Lawrence Bankston" by one Thomas Cresap when the temporary dividing line was run between Pennsylvania and Maryland. Of these sons, Andrew Bankston and Peter Bankston both served as chain carriers in Granville District in July 1751. Daniel Bankston and Jacob Bankston have not been located until later, when they were named to a road commission in Anson County on 12 October 1771. The 1782 tax list for Montgomery Co., NC, shows one Larence Bankston as well as one Ann Bankston. This Ann Bankston was the widow of Andrew Bankston.

[1417] James Lea was a relative of William Lea who married Isabella Major. James Lea stated on 1 January 1797 that "I married a wife out of the family of said Bankson my friend" when asked "Was you ever acquainted with the family of Lawrance Bankson." Lee indicated that Lawrence Bankston "died before the war." He further indicated that Andrew Bankston was Lawrence's oldest son.

1746;[1418] Captain Andrew Bankston, born about 1727, who was deceased by 1783 in Montgomery Co., NC, leaving a son named James Bankston;[1419] Peter Bankston, born about 1729, who died intestate in Clarke County, Georgia, in 1803, leaving a widow named Priscilla;[1420] Lawrence Bankston, Jr., born about 1731, York County, Pennsylvania;[1421] Daniel Bankston, born about 1733 in York County, Pennsylvania, who died in Morgan County, Georgia, in 1811, leaving a widow named Rachel;[1422] Jacob Bankston, born about 1733, who died after 1804 in Clarke County, Georgia.[1423] Laurence Bankston probably also had several daughters whose names have not survived; one may have been a daughter who married William or Thomas Barclay about 1755 in Orange County.[1424]

The next link in the chain connecting the family of Thomas Jefferson Bankston of Mississippi to Lawrence Bankston of North Carolina is a complicated one. The likeliest explanation seems to be that Lawrence Bankston and Rebecca Hendricks had a daughter who married a Barclay -- perhaps William Barclay of Orange County, North Carolina -- about 1755. This daughter and her husband may both have died young, leaving a son -- John Barclay -- who was then reared by his grandfather Lawrence Bankston, Sr., and his uncle, Lawrence Bankston, Jr. John Barclay Bankston grew to manhood in Guilford and Rockingham Counties, North Carolina, moving from there to Spartanburg District, South Carolina, in the 1790s. As Reverend John Bankston (1760-1838), he became a well-known Baptist minister and evangelist, and his biographical details provide several key facts concerning his background.[1425]

According to a biography, Reverend John Bankston was born in 1760 in Rockingham County, North Carolina, where he grew to manhood. After moving to South Carolina, Bankston petitioned the South Carolina Legislature in 1805 to change his name legally. In his petition he indicated that his name "in law" was John Barkley but that he had been known by Bankston for all of his life. The document, found in Assembly Petitions of South Carolina of 1805, No 77, reads:

> The Honorable the Speaker of the House of Representatives and members thereof in General Assembly aforesaid met in the State of South Carolina: *The petition of John Bankston alias Barkley of Spartanburgh District and state aforesaid Humbly sheweth, that your petitioner hath good cause to believe & verily does believe, that in law his name is John Barkley, but he is known by and hath retained the name of Bankston, and for certain good causes he now petitions your Honorable body to take his case into*

When asked "Was not Jacob Bankston the youngest son of the family of said Lawrence Bankson," Lee responded: "Answer yes, for Andrew the oldest son, the next Daniel, the next Lawrence Jnr., and Jacob Bankston was the youngest son of Lawrance Bankson, deceased." See NC State Archives, State Records A, Bankson, Laurance, Orange County, Group: Secretary of State, Office of Granville Proprietary Land Office, Call No. S.108.270-S.108.283, Location MFR, Mars ID 12.12.69.5 (folder). These items were originally located in 2005 by Bess Antes and transmitted by her to other Bankston researchers.

[1418] In 1793, James Lea deposed that "about forty-seven years ago he married in the family of Laurance Banckston senior and he was well acquainted with the proceedings of the family as one might be in that case." Lee indicated that Bankston died in Anson County before the war and that he never knew of a will made by Lawrence Bankston. At this time, Lea stated that "Andrew Bankston was the eldest son of said Laurance, he believes the heir at law and that Peter Bankston was the second son of said Laurance, and that Laurance Bankston was the third son of said Laurance Senr. that Daniel Bankston was the fourth son of said Laurance and Jacob Bankston was the fifth son of said Laurance and the youngest son." Ibid.

[1419] Caswell Co., NC, DB J, pp. 239-40. James is named in both Caswell and Montgomery Counties as "heir at law" of Lawrence Bankston, deceased, suggesting that he was the eldest son of the eldest son. A deposition taken of Henry Williamson, 29 August 1796, indicates that Andrew's eldest son was named Daniel and that he was deceased. This deposition was taken at a court suit concerning a tract of land in Caswell County claimed by Andrew Bankston's heirs; it further indicates that James Bankston was "always understood to be the next eldest to Daniel."

[1420] Peter was the father of John, Lawrence ("Lary", sometimes read as "Levy"); William; Andrew; Judith (wife of Nimrod Taylor); Rhoda (wife of Shadrack Carpenter); and two unknown daughters, who married Thomas Davis and William Browning.

[1421] Lawrence's placement is based on the 1796 testimony of James Lea, who omits Peter Bankston as a son.

[1422] Daniel was the father of Thomas, Abner, Isaac, Spencer, Edith, and Patty Bankston.

[1423] He was the father of John, Jacob, Elijah, and Henry Bankston.

[1424] Barclay will be discussed below.

[1425] Haigler, *Bankston Cousins*, p. 13.

consideration & grant that his name be confirmed & that he be known in law by the name of John Bankston and the name of Bankston shall descend to his posterity - and your Humble petitioners as in duty bound will ever pray....John Bankston, 28ᵗʰ Oct. 1805.[1426]

This document seems to establish that Rev. John Bankston was a Bankston by adoption rather than by birth.

In her study of the Bankston family, Anne Haigler offers the following explanation regarding the parentage of Rev. John Bankston:

This John Bankston certainly must have been the son of a daughter of Lawrence, who died young & John was raised by his Bankston grandparents.[1427]

The known facts seem to fit well with John's having been a grandson of Lawrence Bankston and Rebecca Hendricks. His obituaries identify him as a native of Rockingham or Guilford Counties, North Carolina, and in 1760 both were included within Orange County, where Lawrence Bankston, Sr., lived. Hence, whatever the Bankston connection, it almost certainly was to Lawrence's family. Further, a statement in his biography that he was sent to school by his father could be construed to refer to Lawrence Bankston, Sr., if before 1774 and to Lawrence Bankston, Jr., if after 1774. John's mother may have died at birth or during his infancy, and, if the father wished to remarry, John's mother's family -- the Lawrence Bankstons -- may have reared him. Alternatively, both parents may have died, and as nearest relatives the Bankston grandparents may have taken young John. The likely explanation for the absence of legal records -- wills, deeds, guardianship, court minutes -- is that most Orange County records were lost, and the minority that do survive are incomplete, leading, at best, to fragmentary glimpses of individuals and families. John would have been an adult by the time Guilford and Rockingham Counties were formed. One significant corollary to this discussion is that John and his siblings, if any, may have been considered children of Lawrence Bankston, thus creating the tradition that Lawrence had a second family following Rebecca's death.

John Bankston had a close relationship in North Carolina and South Carolina with Lawrence Bankston, Jr., who was probably his biological uncle (although he may have reared him and have been regarded by him as his father); several deeds, involving Isaac Cantrell and his family, suggest that this Lawrence Bankston married a daughter of Isaac Cantrell. On 16 May 1787, in Guilford County, North Carolina, John Bankston received a warrant for 300 acres in Guilford County. The original warrant had been issued to Lawrence Bankston and sold by him to John Bankston on 2 December 1785; Charles Cantrell witnessed the transfer, and Isaac Cantrell was both an adjacent land owner and a chain carrier for the survey.[1428] In December 1790, John Bankston sold to Lawrence Bankston 300 acres on Wolf Island Creek.[1429] On 16 February 1793, Lawrence Bankston, by then a resident of Spartanburg District, South Carolina, purchased 426 acres on Pacolet River from John Hightower.[1430] John Bankston on 20 December 1796, 5 September 1800, and 6 June 1806 witnessed Spartanburg deeds in which Lawrence sold land[1431]. On 5 February 1807, John Bankston, Lawrence Bankston, and Sally Bankston witnessed a deed from Thomas Burgess to Samuel Gilbert,[1432] and, again, on 8 February 1808, John and Lawrence witnessed a

---

[1426] Ibid.

[1427] Ibid.

[1428] A. B. Pruitt, *Abstracts of Land Warrants of Guilford Co., NC, 1778-1932* (Raleigh, NC, 1989), No. 1520.

[1429] I. B. Webster, *Rockingham Co., NC, Deed Abstracts, 1785-1800* (Madison, NC, 1973), p. 43, citing C: 213.

[1430] Spartanburg Co., SC, DB C , pp. 151-152, in Pruitt, 1: 74.

[1431] Spartanburg Co., SC, DB E, pp. 82-83; Spartanburg Co., SC, DB H, pp. 255-257, in A. B. Pruitt, *Spartanburg County-District, South Carolina, Deed Abstracts, Books A-T, 1785-1827* (Easley, SC, 1988), p. 239; Spartanburg Co., SC, DB N, pp. 156-157, in Pruitt, *Spartanburg*, p. 457.

[1432] Spartanburg Co., SC, DB Q, pp. 24-25, in Pruitt, *Spartanburg*, p. 575.

transaction together.[1433] On 15 July 1809, John Bankston witnessed a transaction in which Mary Garrott bound her son Phillip to serve Lawrence Bankston for twenty years.[1434] When John Bankston sold his Spartanburg lands on 19 July 1821, Lawrence witnessed the deed.[1435]

The Barkley connection is difficult to fathom; as suggested previously, the likeliest explanation is that John Barkley's father died young and that he was reared by his mother's relatives.[1436] Orange County records -- although highly fragmentary -- document the presence of a Thomas Barclay living in Orange, where he was an ordinary keeper, from at least March 1755 until at least December 1757.[1437] There is also a reference to a William Barclay, who on 17 March 1753 was a chain carrier for a survey belonging to Thomas Linville, Senior. William Linville was the second chain carrier; the grant of 200 acres lay on Belew's Creek. The tract lay adjacent another tract of 200 acres on Belew's Creek, below the great meadow, joining one claimed by Thomas Linville, Jr.[1438] This record may be significant because of an indirect linkage to Lawrence Bankston's family. Lawrence's wife, Rebecca Hendricks, was a sister of Henry Hendricks, who had married Ann Linville in Pennsylvania. A daughter of John and Ann Linville of Chester County, Pennsylvania, Ann Linville Hendricks was a sister of Thomas Linville (c. 1706 - c. 1773) who claimed the North Carolina land in 1753.[1439]

Concerning Lawrence Bankston, Jr., much uncertainty exists. The existence of such a son of Lawrence and Rebecca Hendricks Bankston is documented by the testimony of James Lea, son-in-law of Lawrence Bankston, Sr. Lea, who had married Lawrence's daughter, was giving evidence concerning a debt and who, as heir at law of Lawrence, Sr., was legally responsible for it. Otherwise, the existence of even this daughter of Lawrence and Rebecca would be unknown. Lea mentions that he had married a daughter of Lawrence Bankston, Sr., and that this close family relationship gave him intimate knowledge of Lawrence's family. He places Lawrence, Jr., as a son, and his position in the family by Lea in the family birth order suggests that he was born about 1731. Lea gave no information about what became of Lawrence or if he had offspring, but the implication of Lea's testimony is that Lawrence was then, in 1796, alive. If so, the question arises as to where he was? The likeliest scenario is that he was Lawrence Bankston of Guilford and Rockingham Counties, North Carolina, and Spartanburg District, South Carolina. Further corroboration of this identification comes from Lawrence's testimony regarding the will of Isaac Cantrell in South Carolina in 1805. A controversy existed surrounding Isaac Cantrell's will, and friends, neighbors, and relations were subpoenaed to give information concerning its validity.[1440] The testimony, which establishes that Lawrence Bankston had known Cantrell since about 1755, merits quoting at length:

> Court of Ordinary met at Spartanburg Court House to try the protest of Peter Cantrell of Isaac Cantrell's will as requested--the same to be proven in due form of Law.[1441]

[1433] Spartanburg Co., SC, DB L, pp. 304-305, in Pruitt, *Spartanburg*, p. 374.

[1434] Spartanburg Co., S C, DB O, pp. 265-266, in Pruitt, *Spartanburg*, p. 510.

[1435] Spartanburg Co., SC, DB S, pp. 139-140, in Pruitt, *Spartanburg*, p. 684.

[1436] The English surname Berkeley was in the seventeenth and eighteenth centuries pronounced "Barclay" or "Barkley". Hence, research into John Bankston's origins focused on all three spellings.

[1437] Orange Co., NC, Records Book 1, 1752-1761, pp. 104; Shields, *Orange County Minutes*, 66-132.

[1438] Orange Co., NC, Records Book 1, 1752-1761, p. 4.

[1439] Belew's Creek is today in Forsyth County, which joins Guilford County's western boundary. Forsyth was created in 1849 from Stokes County which had been formed in 1789 from Surry. Surry was created in 1770 from Rowan, which was created in 1753 from Anson. The Linville's apparently lived near what is today the boundary between Guilford (formed in 1770 from Rowan and Orange) and Forsyth. Belew's Creek is located in extreme northeastern Forsyth County and flows southeasterly out of Guilford and Stokes Counties.

[1440] 17 February 1806: Isaac Cantrell Estate Papers--File 736, Spartanburg County, S.C.

[1441] Isaac Cantrell was born between about 1729 and 1733 in New Castle Co., DE, a son of Joseph Cantrell and Catherine Heath. He married (1) Talitha Cloud and (2) Mary Linder.

1. James Ezell and John Pirtle deposed that they signed the will of Isaac Cantrell at the testators request in his presence. They did not see him sign the Will nor did they sign at the same time.

2. Lawrence Bankston. He knoweth the testator about fifty years, The dec'd had a very bad pain in his head & he the dec'd told him he thought it made him dull. He was about seventy-two years old. He done little by business but trusted to his wife or generally asked his wife, when any person came to settle, if it was not so and so.

3. Isaac Young deposeth he was not in his right senses in regard to the Church, He never agreed to anything to as to stand to it.

4. Esquire Turner. He knew him for ten years and did not think he was in proper senses. He only knew him in the Church and thought him childish in that respect and that it was common talk in the neighborhood that he was in his dotage, that he lay on a sick bed two years and one month before he died.

5. Capt. J. Turner deposeth he very often saw him and thought he was possessed of as strong a mind as the nature of his infirmament and age would admit. The dec'd asked him to be Executor and he refused because the children were not all equal.

6. John Pirtle, cross examined deposeth that about fourteen years ago he thought was out of his senses but at the time he signed the will he was in his proper senses.

7. James Ezell, cross examined, says he was in his proper mind when he signed as a witness

8. Rev. John Bankston. He had known the dec'd from a boy. He Drew the Will contested. He signed his name as a witness and was named an Executor.. He requested the deceased to take his name out as an Executor. That he did believe that he was of disposing mind and memory, at least it was so to the last he knew and he thinks this to be same.

9. William Garrot. Deposeth he the dec'd was of a right mind and could do his business. That he was an industrious man, never kept an overseer and he thinks he directed his farm and he thinks he was in his proper mind. Some years ago he did not seem submissive to the church and he thought he might not be right.

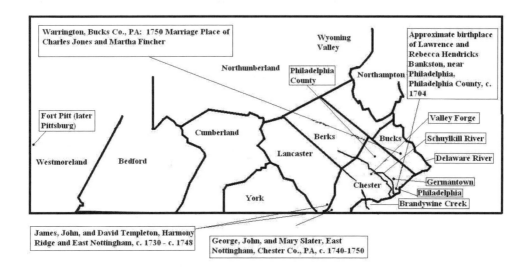

Warrington, Bucks Co., PA: 1750 Marriage Place of Charles Jones and Martha Fincher

Wyoming Valley

Approximate birthplace of Lawrence and Rebecca Hendricks Bankston, near Philadelphia, Philadelphia County, c. 1704

Northumberland

Philadelphia County

Northampton

Fort Pitt (later Pittsburg)

Valley Forge

Cumberland

Berks

Bucks

Schuylkill River

Delaware River

Westmoreland

Bedford

Lancaster

Germantown

York

Chester

Philadelphia

Brandywine Creek

James, John, and David Templeton, Harmony Ridge and East Nottingham, c. 1730 - c. 1748

George, John, and Mary Slater, East Nottingham, Chester Co., PA, c. 1740-1750

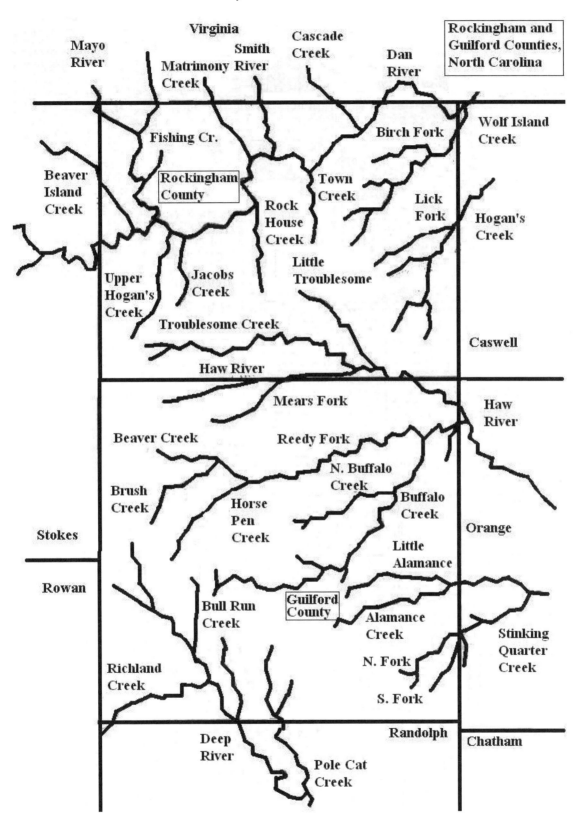

Rockingham and Guilford Counties, North Carolina

Mayo River

Virginia

Matrimony Creek

Smith River

Cascade Creek

Dan River

Fishing Cr.

Birch Fork

Wolf Island Creek

Beaver Island Creek

Rockingham County

Rock House Creek

Town Creek

Lick Fork

Hogan's Creek

Upper Hogan's Creek

Jacobs Creek

Little Troublesome

Troublesome Creek

Haw River

Caswell

Mears Fork

Haw River

Beaver Creek

Reedy Fork

Brush Creek

N. Buffalo Creek

Buffalo Creek

Horse Pen Creek

Orange

Stokes

Little Alamance

Rowan

Bull Run Creek

Guilford County

Alamance Creek

Stinking Quarter Creek

Richland Creek

N. Fork

S. Fork

Randolph

Chatham

Deep River

Pole Cat Creek

Note that he language of the depositions is significant. Lawrence Bankston stated that he had known Cantrell for "about fifty years" while Reverend John Bankston stated that he had known him "from a boy." Born in 1760, John Bankston was forty-five years old in 1805. Since Lawrence, like most of the older deponents, gave the length of his association in years, the implication is that he met Cantrell as an adult and had known him since about 1755. If so, this would place Lawrence's birth as prior to 1734, a placement which agrees perfectly with James Lea's placement of Lawrence Bankston, Jr., in the offspring of Lawrence Bankston and Rebecca Hendricks.[1442] Further, the document ties Reverend John Bankston to Lawrence Bankston and suggests that Lawrence was living in the same neighborhood as John Bankston's parents at the time of Bankston's birth.

Cantrell family researchers posit that Lawrence Bankston married Sarah Cantrell, sister of Isaac Cantrell, and daughter of Joseph and Cathrena Heath Cantrell. The family had moved from Wilmington, Delaware -- where they attended Old Swede's Chapel -- to Orange County, Virginia, and finally to Orange County, North Carolina, settling in the area that later became Rockingham County. It was there that Joseph Cantrell, Sr., died about 1753. If Lawrence Bankston married Sarah Cantrell after reaching adulthood, that marriage probably took place about 1755 -- probably about the time Lawrence Bankston met Isaac Cantrell -- in Orange County, North Carolina.

The first known record of Reverend John Bankston (1760-1838) dates from 1780, when John Bankston and Joseph Linder were chain carriers for a survey of sixty acres granted to Abraham Phillips.[1443] The land lay on Wolf Island Creek, where in 1783 John Bankston and Joseph Linder were chain carriers for John Linder's survey.[1444] Based on the biography of Reverend John Bankston, it seems likely that he was reared "from a boy" by Lawrence and Sarah Cantrell Bankston. As noted, he may have been first reared by his grandfather, Justice Lawrence Bankston of Orange County, but that Lawrence is said to have moved to Anson County, North Carolina, several years before his death in 1774. It may be that Lawrence and Sarah took in young John Barclay after his parents died, and that Barclay always used the Bankston name. Perhaps anticipating the death of Lawrence Bankston -- who would have been about seventy-four in 1805 -- John may have felt it necessary to legally confirm his surname as Bankston. It may even be that the controversy over the Cantrell estate -- the suit was filed the same year Bankston petitioned to have his name changed -- prompted him to take legal action.[1445]

From his appearance in North Carolina in 1780, John Bankston left a clear trail of evidence concerning his life and activities thereafter. On 21 September 1785, Isham Lanier sold him 123 acres on Big Troublesome Creek in Rockingham County for £60; the land joined John Falconer and Henry Brewer.[1446] Two years later, on 16 May 1787, John Bankston received a warrant for 300 acres on Wolf Island Creek. He indicated that the land -- joining Nathaniel Newman, Isaac Cantrell, and Linder's line -- had been sold him on 2 December 1785 by Lawrence Bankston for £60 with Charles Cantrell and John Linder as witnesses.[1447] Bankston's grant for this land was issued by the State of North Carolina on 16 May 1787;[1448] the following year, on 13 February 1788, John Bankston sold 123 acres on Troublesome

---

[1442] The outcome of the case concerning Isaac Cantrell's will was mixed: "Decided: That the Will as far as respects the personal property is valid and sufficiently proved. But it is not sufficient to convey the landed property. This 5th day of March, 1806." Gabriel Bumpap, Ordinary, signed the document.

[1443] Pruitt, *Land Warrants of Guilford Co., NC, 1778-1932*, No. 1390.

[1444] Pruitt, *Land Warrants of Guilford Co., NC, 1778-1932*, No. 1530.

[1445] It is not clear when Lawrence Bankston (c. 1731 - living 1805) died. The eldest son of John and Mary Lanier Bankston, another Lawrence Bankston, was born about 1783 and reached legal age about 1804. Hence, legal records from 1805 onwards could refer to either Lawrence Bankston (born c. 1731) or Lawrence Bankston (born c. 1783). That Spartanburg records do not distinguish the two men through the use of "Sr." and "Jr." suggests that Lawrence (born c. 1731) may have died soon after 1805. It is possible that Lawrence Bankston and Sarah Cantrell had no offspring of their own, since there were no other Bankstons in the area.

[1446] Rockingham Co., NC, DB A: 301, cited in I. B. Webster, *Rockingham Co., NC, Deed Abstracts, 1785-1800* (Madison, NC, 1973), p. 13. Note that Rockingham was formed from Guilford in 1785, that the earliest records are extant, and that certain pages are missing from the record book.

[1447] Pruitt, *Land Warrants of Guilford Co., NC, 1778-1932*, No. 1520.

[1448] Webster, *Rockingham Co., NC, Deed Abstracts*, p. 29, citing C:5.

Creek to Robert Cummings for £50. The land was described as adjoining "James Mulloy (land formerly John Faulkners), Henry Brewer, line of James Lanier, deceased."[1449] On 18 July 1788, John Bankson and John Linder were described as adjacent landowners when Isaac Cantrell was granted 220 acres on Wolf Island Creek.[1450]

Two years later, in December 1790, John Bankston sold to Lawrence Bankston the 300 acres on Wolf Island Creek for £60;[1451] a year later, on 24 December 1791, Isaac Young of Spartanburg County, South Carolina, deeded to John Bankston of the same location 200 acres on Pacolet River for £110 South Carolina money.[1452] As mentioned above, John Bankston enjoyed a close relationship with Lawrence Bankston during these years, often witnessing land transactions with and for him.

During the South Carolina years, John Bankston became increasingly active in the Baptist faith. In 1798 and 1800, he served as messenger from Buck Creek Church in Spartanburg District to the Bethel Association. By 1808, Bankston was pastoring Grove Church in Columbia County, Georgia. Although enumerated in 1810 in Spartanburg County -- where on 24 April 1810 he also purchased 204 acres on the North Tyger River and where on 2 April 1811 he sold 200 acres on the Pacolet River -- Bankston continued to pastor in Georgia, serving as minister for Grove Church in 1811 and 1813. In 1812, however, Bankston was back in South Carolina, a member of Bethlehem Church and a delegate to Bethel Association. He was a member of Mt. Zion Church in South Carolina in 1818, that church being an arm of Bethlehem, and as such he represented Bethlehem as a messenger at the Bethel Association. About this time, he apparently decided to relocate permanently to Georgia; on 19 July 1821 he sold 119.5 acres on Tyger River with Laurence Bankston -- possibly his son -- as witness.[1453]

From 1822 to 1832, Bankston appears to have lived and pastored in Gwinnett County, Georgia. He was a messenger from Redland Church of Gwinnett County to the Yellow River Primitive Baptist Association at Harris Springs Church in Newton County and pastored Sweetwater Church in Gwinnett County in 1825. He and son Joseph were both ministers and deacons at Bethlehem Baptist Church in Gwinnett County. John and sons John and Lawrence were enumerated in Gwinnett in 1830, while sons Joseph and Nathan were both enumerated in Coweta County, on Georgia's western frontier.[1454]

Reverend John Bankston died in Gwinnett County on 23 February 1838. His obituary -- revised in 1886 by the Spartanburg Baptist Association -- provides details of his early life and activities:

> ...being of a serious turn of mind, his father placed him in a school under an eminent Baptist minister, believing him destined for the Gospel ministry.[1455] Under the guidance and instruction of this good man, he acquired knowledge rapidly. He was a close student. He soared above the allurements that too often lure men astray and made books his highest pleasure. His mind was eventually turned to the study of theology, which was the absorbing topic of his thoughts during the last year he was in school. Towards the close of the Revolutionary War, when he attained the military age, he married Miss Mary Lanier of Pitt County, North Carolina, and a few years afterwards moved to the Spartanburg District, South Carolina, near Buck Creek Church on the Pacolet River, where he soon became an influential member and was ordained as a minister of the Gospel (around 1790). He was the pastor of Buck Creek and other churches in the county. He was subsequently a member of the Bethlehem Church and represented that church in the Bethel Association in 1812. The records of that church show that he was

---

[1449] Ibid., p. 39, citing C: 159.
[1450] Ibid., p. 21, citing B: 106.
[1451] Ibid., p. 43, citing C: 213.
[1452] Spartanburg Co., SC, DB C, pp. 94-95, in Pruitt, *Spartanburg*, 1:68.
[1453] Spartanburg Co., SC, DB S, pp. 139-140, in Pruitt, 1: 684.
[1454] Haigler, *Bankston Cousins*, pp. 13-14.
[1455] Perhaps that minister was Reverend Isaac Cantrell, brother of Sarah Bankston?

invited to preach to that church. Later he became a member of the Mount Zion Church, [and]... was by the records the first and only delegate to represent that church at the Association of 1818. His name is prominently mentioned on the old church books of Wolfe Creek and Boiling Spring. In 1822, he removed to Gwinnett County, Georgia, where he labored among the different Baptist churches for ten years[1456] and his plain and successful manner of preaching created for him the name of a 'successful man of God' in his ministerial work. His labors ended on earth on the 23rd of February 1838 when he had reached his seventy-eighth year of age. His wife, Mrs. Mary Bankston, survived him many years and died in her ninetieth year. She was a woman of excellent Christian character and a devoted mother and wife.

Following Reverend John Bankston's death, his widow moved to western Georgia and eastern Alabama with her son Joseph. She died in 1857 in Coosa County, Alabama, at Joseph's home.[1457]

A complete list of the offspring of Reverend John and Mary Lanier Bankston does not survive. Based on the exhaustive research of Anne Martin Haigler, however, it appears that the couple had at least nine children: Lawrence Bankston (c. 1783-1850/60) married Permelia McDowell and Elvira Crowder; he died after 1850 in Chattooga County, Georgia. Based on census records, John Bankston probably had a daughter who was born between 1784 and 1790; her identity and fate are unknown. Joseph Bankston (c. 1792-1863) followed his father into the Baptist ministry. He was living in Gwinnett County in 1828 but in Coweta County by 1829; he was enumerated in Coweta in 1830 and in Heard County, Georgia, in 1840 before settling in Coosa County, Alabama, where he lived from 1850 until at least 1857. He married Agnes Abbott in Spartanburg in 1812. Joseph died in Tallapoosa County, Alabama, in 1863 and Agnes in Jefferson County in 1875. Nathaniel Bankston (1793-1850) married Sarah Light and settled in Chattooga County, Georgia; his widow moved to Tallapoosa County, Alabama, where she died in 1857. Cynthia Bankston (c. 1790 - living 1879) married Joseph Davis and remained in Spartanburg District, South Carolina. John Bankston (1799-1869) married Wiley Johnson and remained in Gwinnett County, Georgia. Thomas B. Bankston (c. 1802 - aft. 1860) settled in Coweta County, Georgia, and Bibb County, Alabama. Lanier Bankston (c. 1803 - aft. 1860) married Priscilla Fling and settled in Cobb County, Georgia. Elizabeth Bankston (1805-1887) married Thomas Lawrence (1798-1873) and settled in Chattooga County, Georgia.[1458]

Before discussing Thomas B. Bankston and his son Thomas Jefferson Bankston, we turn to the family of Mary Lanier, wife of Reverend John Bankston. Mary Lanier Bankston descended from a prominent Southside Virginia family, and the pages that follow address her father's Lanier ancestry as well as her mother's Cooke and Clarke connections.

Mary Lanier Bankston (1767-1857).

Mary Lanier Bankston was born in Pitt County, North Carolina, in 1767, a daughter of James and Mary Cooke Lanier. Her parents, natives of Surry County, Virginia, settled in Pitt County about 1761.[1459] James Lanier served as a Justice there in 1775 and was a member of Pitt County's Committee of Safety during the Revolution. He served as a deputy in the North Carolina Provincial Congress and later served

---

[1456] He is stated with Kinchen Rambo -- a distant cousin -- to have founded the Friendship Baptist Church in Gwinnett County.

[1457] Haigler, *Bankston Cousins*, pp. 13-14. On 4 June 1857, *The South Western Baptist Newspaper* reported Mary's death: "Departed this life on the 5th day of April 1857 at the residence of her son the Rev. Joseph Bankston, in Coosa County, Alabama, Mrs. Mary Bankston, consort of the late Rev. John Bankston of Gwinnett County, Georgia, in the ninetieth year of her age." See M. Kelsey, N. G. Floyd, G. G. Parsons, *Marriages and Death Notices from the "South Western Baptist" Newspaper* (Bowie, MD, 1995), p. 87.

[1458] Haigler, *Bankston Cousins*, pp. 13-14.

[1459] Pitt Co., NC, DB B, 1762-1764, p. 380.

as its Chairman. In 1778, while still living in Pitt County, Lanier began acquiring tracts in Guilford County. Although Lanier died while apparently still living in Pitt County, his Guilford County lands fell into Rockingham County when the new county was created.[1460] It was to Rockingham that the widowed Mary Cooke Lanier relocated with her children -- settling among a group of kin who had recently come there from Brunswick and Surry Counties -- and where her daughter Mary Lanier met and married John Bankston. Later, in the 1790s, when Mary Lanier and John Bankston moved to South Carolina, Mary Cooke Lanier and several of her children relocated to Greene County, Georgia.

Mary Lanier's paternal ancestors originated in France. Nicholas Lanier of Rouen settled in London about 1561. Lanier was brought into England to replace Guilliam de Troches, royal flute player, and held the post for more than half a century. Born about 1523, he died 1 July 1612. Nicholas Lanier married on 13 February 1571 at All Hallow's by the Tower, London, Lucretia Bassano (24 September 1556, Mark Lane, London -- 4 January 1634, St. Alfrege's, Greenwich), daughter of Antonio Bassano and Elena de Nazzi, who married 10 August 1536 in Venice, Italy. Born about 1510, Antonio Bassano was one of the five sons of Jeronimo de Bassano, sackbut player to the Doge of Venice, who were brought to the court of Henry VIII as royal musicians between 1531 and 1539. The brothers Bassano were outstanding wind players and instrument makers, and they may also have composed. Emilia Bassano (1569-1645), a granddaughter of Jeronimo, is believed to have been the "dark lady" who inspired so many of Shakespeare's sonnets.[1461]

During the 1540s, the Bassanos lived at the Charterhouse in London, the former monks' quarters of the dissolved monastery of the Charterhouse. The building still stands. By the time of Antonio's burial on 20 October 1574 at All Hallow's Barking by the Tower, the Bassanos had settled in Mark Lane near the Tower of London.[1462] Of Anthony Bassano's children, Mark Anthony, Arthur, and Andrea were of the "Band of Music to Queen Elizabeth," and Edward and Jeronimo were "of the Presence Chamber to queen Elizabeth." Jeronimo's service extended under James I and Charles I. Lucretia's husband Nicholas Lanier was a court musician, as was Elizabeth's second husband Ambrose Grasso, who was court violinist in 1578.[1463]

Before he married Lucretia Bassano, Nicholas Lanier had been married to a first wife who had not been identified. By this marriage, he fathered three older sons and a daughter; his son John Lanier married Frances Galliardello in 1585, and their son Nicholas Lanier (1588-1666) was Master of the Music to King Charles I, the first person to hold that appointment.[1464] Lucretia Bassano and Nicholas Lanier were the parents of four daughters and three sons. Of these, Clement Lanier (by 1584 -- 1661) was royal sackbut player from 1604 and recorder player from 1629; following the restoration of Charles II to the English throne in 1660, these appointments were reconfirmed by warrant dormant on 26 April 1661, only months before Clement's death.

Clement Lanier married Hannah Collett on 17 April 1628 at St. Martin, Ludgate, in the city of London, just west of the present location of St. Paul's Cathedral. A daughter of John and Ann Collett, Hannah was born about 1608 and was buried 22 December 1653 at St. Alphege's, Greenwich. Her father, John Collett, was an oysterman and innkeeper who was buried in All Hallow's, Lombard Street, in 1630; her mother Ann remarried to a man named Walter Carter and died at St. Alphege's, Greenwich, in 1647. Among the provisions of Ann's will, she did "give graunt and assigne" to "my loveing daughter Hanna

---

[1460] A. B. Pruitt, *Rockingham Co., NC, Land Warrants: 1778-1929* (Raleigh, NC, 2001), Item No. 34.

[1461] Emilia married Alfonso Lanier in 1592. She was mistress, however, to Henry Carey, Lord Hunsdon, first cousin of Elizabeth I and child of William Carey and Mary Boleyn. Her son, the musician Henry Lanier (1592-1633), was Hunsdon's son. See L. Ingersoll, *Lanier: A Genealogy of the family who came to Virginia and their French Ancestors in London* (Washington, D.C., 1965), pp. 1-27, and M. C. Clement, *Lanier: Her Name* (Chatham, VA, 1954), pp. 1-8.

[1462] See B. Harrison, *The Bassanos, Italian Musicians at the English Court, 1531-1664* (La Canada, CA, 1991), pp. 21-27. See also D. Lasocki and R. Prior, *The Bassanos, Venetian Musicians and Instrument Makers in England, 1531-1665* (Aldershot, 1995), pp. 1-15, 27, 43, 88.

[1463] Ibid., pp. 1-15.

[1464] M. I. Wilson, *Nicholas Lanier: Master of the King's Music* (Aldershot, 1994), pp. 1-14.

Lanyer and her husband M[r] Clement Lanyer" a legal title to "the lease of my house in Gration Street London commonly called or knowne by the signe of the Barrell and Oyster." Ann's will, linking her to her first husband's trade as an oysterman, indicates that she was a woman of means; the lease she left daughter Hannah Lanier no doubt amplified the Lanier's assets, especially at a time when the family was facing constrained economic circumstances because of the loss of Clement's royal appointment as a court musician during the English Civil Wars.[1465]

Much older than his wife Hannah, Clement Lanier did not long survive her. He wrote his will 2 February 1659, describing himself as of East Greenwich, Gentleman. The will was proven 3 December 1661 by daughter Hannah Lanier and evidences what was still a comfortable standard of living. Clement provided for his daughter Hannah and then proceeded to consider his other offspring. To his sons Nicholas, John, and Robert Lanier -- who had all left the country -- Clement bequeathed £5 each, if each "in his own person hee shall come to demand the same". Of these three children, Nicholas and Robert are believed to have settled in Barbados, where Robert died in St. Michael's Parish about 1678. John Lanier, our subject, had settled in Virginia.[1466]

Born in 1631 in Lewisham, England, John Lanier was reared during the final years of the reign of Charles I at a time when social, economic, and political affairs in England were becoming increasingly strained. As musicians in the royal court, the Laniers must have felt their positions become precarious as the king came under assault from Parliament. Probably because of the Civil Wars, John Lanier and his brothers decided to seek their fortunes abroad. Although the date of his embarkation is not known, John Lanier was in Charles City County, Virginia, by 25 February 1659, when Howell Price filed a claim for land based on his transportation into the colony. He had probably been in the colony for several months, if not several years, at this time.[1467]

John Lanier may have married three times. His first wife, Lucretia, who accompanied him to Virginia, could have been a relative, for the name Lucretia was common within the Lanier - Bassano - Galliardello family group. Following Lucretia's death, Lanier remarried, although that wife's name is unknown. She was deceased by 1685, when Lanier married Sarah Edmunds, the widow of a Surry County planter named William Edmunds.

A genetic tendency towards longevity favored John Lanier, for he survived six decades in Virginia's harsh climate. His will was proven in Prince George County, Virginia, in 1719, at which time he was nearly ninety years old. During his long residence in the colony, Lanier had amassed a substantial plantation south of the James River in Surry and Prince George Counties. Like many who came to Virginia as indentured servants, however, Lanier rose slowly in the Tidewater. In 1676, he was among those discontented with the colony's ruling regime who sided with the rebel Nathaniel Bacon. John Lanier and John Woodlief[1468] were sent as representatives of the men of Charles City County to confront Governor Berkeley about defending them against the Indians. Berkeley called them "fools" and "loggerheads" and told them to go back home. Bacon then led his men against the Indians without the Governor's permission, ultimately leading to a colonial rebellion. John Lanier was later among the rebels who camped out at Jordan's Point, but there is no further information about his precise role in the rebellion.[1469]

[1465] C. Allen, "Hannah (Collett) Lanier," *The American Genealogist*, Vol. 77, No. 4 (October 2002), p. 300, citing Marriage License Allegation in the Registry of the Bishop of London, vol. 13, 1629-1631, f. 163 [FHL film No. 544,130], located through *A Calendar of the Marriage License Allegations in the Registry of the Bishop of London, 1597 to 1700*, Index Library 62 (London, 1937): 94.

[1466] Prerogative Court of Canterbury, PROB 11/306, q. 210, The National Archives, Kew, Richmond, England, as cited by Allen, "Hannah (Collett) Lanier," p. 300.

[1467] Ingersoll, *Lanier*, pp. 1-27; Clement, *Lanier*, pp. 1-8.

[1468] The Woodlief (Woodley) family has been discussed elsewhere; they were among the ancestors of Martha (Thomas) Moore of Lunenburg Co., VA.

[1469] Ingersoll, *Lanier*, p. 12; for a general account of the conflict, see Morgan, *American Slavery*, esp. pp. 250-271.

Save for this one encounter, John Lanier's decades in Virginia seem to have been peaceful and profitable ones. Eight years after the rebellion, on 14 November 1683, he and Peter Wyche patented 1,482 acres in Charles City County for transporting thirty persons into the colony. Lanier and Wyche apparently split this tract, for at the time of the 1704 Virginia quit rent lists he was taxed with 700 acres in Prince George County, newly formed from Charles City in 1702. The land lay south of Hopewell, near the present town of Garysville.[1470]

John Lanier fathered at least one child by his first marriage, a daughter Katherine Lanier, who smothered as an infant in her crib in 1665. By his second marriage, Lanier fathered three sons -- Robert, John, and Sampson. His third marriage to Sarah Edmunds produced a son and a daughter, Sarah Lanier, who married George Brewer,[1471] and Nicholas Lanier. The purpose of John Lanier's will seems less to have been providing for his older offspring and more to provide for the children of his third marriage, particularly his youngest son Nicholas Lanier. By virtue of the law of primogeniture, Robert Lanier would have inherited the bulk of his father's estate. John Lanier may already have deeded him land before he wrote his will in 1718, for that testament left to sons Robert and John one shilling each and to son Sampson twelve shillings. Such bequests often were used to provide for a child who had already received an inheritance and thus to eliminate the possibility of a legal contest on the ground that one or more children had been omitted from the will. John Lanier's other heirs were all from his third marriage. Sarah Lanier Brewer, John Lanier's only surviving daughter, received a cow or heifer three years old; such a bequest would have provided Sarah with milk, butter, and a potential source for livestock in the future. John Lanier, son of Nicholas Lanier, received a feather bed and bolster, blankets and rugs, "all new and good", a gun, two pewter dishes and basins, a chest with a lock and key, six spoons, an iron pot, pothooks, frying pans, a small pair of stillyards, two combs, a young horse, three years old, and three sheep. For a young man in the early eighteenth-century, such an inheritance -- probably passing along items carefully acquired during the course of a lifetime -- would have been sufficient for him to set up housekeeping and embark on an independent existence. Perhaps the immigrant John, then in his ninth decade, identified with his young namesake as he began to make his own way in the colony. To Nicholas Lanier, John's father, the elder man left all the land which he then lived upon, and land on Otterdams, and all the testator's remaining moveable possessions. Nicholas was also made whole and sole executor.[1472]

Of the sons of John Lanier, Robert Lanier and Sampson Lanier married sisters, Priscilla and Elizabeth Washington. John Washington, grandfather of the sisters, was baptized 14 March 1632 at St. Martin's-in-the-Fields, London. He settled in Surry County, Virginia, prior to 1658 and became a prominent planter there. Less well known than the Westmoreland County Washingtons -- who produced the first American president -- the Surry County Washingtons were nevertheless their cousins, both families being descended from Lawrence Washington (c. 1568-1616) of Sulgrave and Wicken, Northamptonshire. Lawrence married Margaret Butler -- a proven descendant of Edward I, King of England, through her

[1470] Nugent, *Cavaliers and Pioneers*, 2: 271; T. J. Wertenbaker, *The Planters of Colonial Virginia* (Princeton, 1922), pp. 181-249.

[1471] George and Sarah (Lanier) Brewer were the parents of Henry Brewer and the grandparents of Ann Brewer Parker, wife of Major Richard Parker of Chatham Co., NC, and Greene Co., GA. If the analysis that follows is correct, they were the great-grandparents of Martha Parker Stephens and the great-great-grandparents of Mary Stephens O'Neal. See below for a discussion of these families.

[1472] Prince George Co., VA, Deeds, Etc., 1713-1728, pp. 304-305. Nicholas Lanier inherited the same genetic proclivity towards longevity that favored his ancestors; he was probably also in his ninetieth year when he died in Brunswick Co., VA, in 1779 (see Brunswick Co., VA, Order Book 2, p. 169). Nicholas was among the first Brunswick justices in 1736 and later served as Captain of the Company of Militia, Sheriff, and Churchwarden of St. Andrew's Parish. Of his offspring, his youngest son Thomas became a justice in Lunenburg County, Virginia, before moving to Granville County, North Carolina. Thomas Lanier's daughter Rebecca (1757-1832) married Colonel Joseph Williams; their great-grandson was Thomas Lanier "Tennessee" Williams, the noted twentieth century playwright.

paternal grandmother Margaret Sutton Butler; Margaret brought to her husband the right to quarter the royal arms of Plantagenet, a sign of her royal ancestry.[1473]

The Washingtons were a prolific bunch, and Lawrence and Margaret reared a large family. In time, the bulk of their estate passed to their eldest son William, who was living in Packington, Leicestershire, in 1618. As a younger son, Richard Washington (c. 1600 - 1642) became a merchant in London while his younger brother Lawrence (1602-1653) entered the ministry of the Church of England. Two John Washingtons, first cousins, settled in Virginia at mid-century. John Washington, son of Reverend Lawrence, settled along the Potomac River in Westmoreland County; he became the president's great-grandfather. John Washington, son of the merchant Richard, settled along the James River in Surry County; he became James Lanier's great-grandfather.[1474]

In the next generation, Richard Washington, son of John Washington, married Elizabeth Jordan; they were the parents of Priscilla Washington and Elizabeth Washington. By birth, Richard Washington had connections to the Blunt family, well-to-do planters in Surry County, and marriage to Elizabeth Jordan brought him important connections as well. Her uncle George Jordan had come to Virginia from Yorkshire in the middle of the seventeenth-century; he moved rapidly up the social ladder, serving first in the colony's House of Burgesses before becoming a Councillor and then Attorney General of Virginia. George Jordan died without any surviving offspring, and his Surry County will bequeathed the bulk of his assets to his nephews and nieces. Hence, Arthur Jordan profited both politically and economically from his uncle's wealth and status in the colony; marriage to the two Washington sisters thus brought the Laniers significant social, political, and economic ties to the local Virginia establishment south of the James River.[1475]

James Lanier, father of Mary Lanier Bankston, was the youngest son of Sampson Lanier and Elizabeth Washington. Probably born about 1725 in what became Brunswick County, young James was still a minor when his father Sampson -- a county justice and vestryman in Brunswick County -- drafted his will on 8 January 1742/3 in Brunswick County. James was of age, however, by 3 April 1746, when he conveyed to Thomas Whittendon 175 acres in Brunswick County that he had inherited from his father Sampson Lanier in 1743.[1476]

Between 1746 and 1761, James Lanier took part in numerous Brunswick County real estate transactions before selling his home tract there;[1477] at the same time, he began acquiring lands in Pitt County, North Carolina, where he was living by 1 April 1763.[1478] During the next twenty years, Lanier became a leading citizen of Pitt County, serving as county justice, militia officer, and as the county's representative to the colonial assembly. He died there between 13 October 1783 and 18 February 1784, at which time he was nearly sixty years old.[1479]

Lanier married, probably shortly before 22 September 1749, Mary Cooke, daughter of Henry Cooke and Elizabeth Clarke of Brunswick County. On the date referenced, Henry Cooke deeded to James Lanier two 100-acre tracts on Cain Branch in Brunswick County.[1480] Mary's Cooke and Clarke ancestors trace

---

[1473] Ingersoll, *Lanier*, p. 41; D. Faris, *Plantagenet Ancestry of Seventeenth-Century Colonists: The Descent from the Later Plantagenet Kings of England* (Baltimore, 1996), pp. 274-275. The Washington ancestry is treated in detail in the appendix.

[1474] Ibid.

[1475] R. A. Jordan, *Jordan Journal: History of the George and Arthur Jordan Families of Virginia, North Carolina, Indiana from 1634* (Evansville, Indiana, 1996) is the best study to date of the Richard and Arthur Jordan families. See also the wills of George Jordan (C. Torrence, ed., *The Edward Pleasants Valentine Papers: Abstracts of 17th- and 18th-Century Virginia Records Relating to 34 Families* (4 vols., repr., Baltimore, 1979), 2: 686-689) and Arthur Jordan (Torrence, ed., *Valentine Papers*, 2: 692).

[1476] Brunswick Co., VA, DB 3, p. 177.

[1477] Brunswick co., VA, DB 6, p. 528.

[1478] Pitt Co., NC, DB B, 1762-1764, p. 380.

[1479] Pitt Co., NC, Grant Book G, 1779-1784, p. 345-346, and Pruitt, *Rockingham Co., NC, Land Warrants: 1778-1929*, Item No. 34. Perhaps the tendency of the Washingtons and Jordans to die at early ages struck down James Lanier, whose early death seems anomalous when compared with other Laniers.

[1480] Brunswick Co., VA, DB 3, p. 587.

back more than a century into mid-seventeenth-century Isle of Wight, Surry, and Charles City Counties on the south side of the James River. Her grandfather, Joshua Clarke, left Surry County and settled in Brunswick County when it was first opened in the early 1720s; a land speculator and wealthy planter, Joshua Clark partnered with Sterling Clack, for many years the clerk of court in Brunswick County, and the two men operated what amounted to a colonial real estate development corporation. Brunswick, at this point, had been settled for about twenty years and was still attracting many new settlers, among them up and coming planters hoping to prosper on new lands. The Laniers, Cookes, and Clarkes all established themselves as leading figures in Brunswick County, with several of them serving as county court justices and holding other legal offices.[1481]

The Cooke and Clarke longevity may have added significantly to the Lanier-Bankston gene pool. Henry Cooke, married three times and father of eight surviving children, was at least eight-five years old when he died in August 1774; Cooke's own father-in-law, father of Cooke's much younger second life, was nearly the same age when he wrote his Brunswick County will on 27 November 1774, months after his son-in-law's death.[1482]

Following James Lanier's death, Mary Cooke Lanier and her offspring relocated from Pitt County to Rockingham County in the North Carolina Piedmont. John Bankston and Mary Lanier probably married there about 1783; the first known legal instrument involving the two families is a deed dated 13 February 1788 in which Bankston sold to Robert Cummings a tract on Troublesome Creek with Isham Lanier as witness. The land was described as abutting a tract owned by James Lanier, deceased, as well as a tract owned by Henry Brewer, grandson of Sarah Lanier Brewer.[1483]

By about 1790, many members of the Lanier-Bankston clan had begun to leave Rockingham County. John and Mary Lanier Bankston, as well as Lawrence and Sarah Cantrell Bankston, settled in Spartanburg District, South Carolina, about this time, and other members of the Lanier and Brewer families relocated to Greene County, Georgia, then as well. On 6 April 1792, Mary Lanier and Sampson Lanier, along with Sampson's wife Elizabeth, deeded 180 acres on Big Troublesome Creek -- adjoining the tract deeded by John Bankston to Robert Cummings -- to George Lemonds, "this being part of grant to James Lanier, deceased." Sampson Lanier remained in Rockingham County, where he died in 1823; Mary Cooke Lanier may have gone with her son Nathaniel and her cousin Henry Brewer to Greene County, Georgia, about 1792. Of the other siblings of Mary Lanier Bankston, Isham Lanier died in Preble County, Ohio, in 1823, and James Lanier died in Pendleton County, Kentucky, in 1806. Henry Lanier died in Greene County, Georgia, in 1821; his son Reuben moved to western Georgia, where his son LaFayette Lanier (1845-1910) founded West Point Pepperell Manufacturing Company along the Chattahoochee River in Troup County. Cynthia Lanier Philips died in Russell County, Alabama, in 1837, having accompanied her children southward following the death of her husband, Rockingham County surveyor Abram Philips, in 1836. With these migrations into western Georgia and eastern Alabama, it is not surprising that Mary Lanier Bankston and several of her offspring would soon settle in the same region.[1484]

Thomas B. and Marion [------] Bankston.

Born about 1802, probably in Columbia County, Georgia, Thomas B. Bankston was reared in Spartanburg District, South Carolina, Columbia County, Georgia, and Gwinnett County, Georgia. He and wife Marion -- whose maiden name is unknown -- probably married about 1825 in Gwinnett County. By about 1828, Thomas had probably moved west with his brother Joseph, settling in Coweta County, where he lived for many years. Confederate Pension records for Thomas' son Wilson Bankston reveal that Wilson was born in Coweta County in 1842. It seems likely, therefore, that Thomas is the same individual

---

[1481] Brunswick Co., VA, DB 1, p. 304; Brunswick Co., VA, Will Book 4, p. 179.

[1482] Brunswick Co., VA, Will Book 4, Part 1, p. 179.

[1483] Webster, *Rockingham Co., NC, Deed Abstracts, 1785-1800*, p. 39, citing C: 159.

[1484] Ingersoll, *Lanier*, discusses the descendants of James and Mary Lanier in detail.

enumerated in Coweta County in 1840 as Thomas G. Bankston. By September 1849, Thomas and Marion were living about a hundred miles westward, in Bibb County, Alabama. Bibb County legal documents show that Thomas was named administrator for Richard Fancher, an elderly neighbor, in that year.[1485]

At the time of the 1850 census, Thomas B. Bankston headed a household that consisted of himself, wife Marion, and six sons, all born between 1829 and 1848. Only the youngest, Pinckney, was born in Alabama. Thomas and Marion were still living in Bibb County in 1860, when they were enumerated in Centreville on the western side of the Cahaba River. At that time, only three children were living at home; two of these were shown in 1850, while the youngest child, a daughter named Mary, had been born shortly after that census enumeration.[1486]

No record of Thomas and Marion Bankston has been found after 1860. It may be that both died -- possibly in Bibb or Tuscaloosa County, Alabama -- soon after 1860.

Thomas and Marion Bankston were the parents of eight known children. Emeline Bankston, born about 1826, married Willis M. Davis on 25 September 1847 in Bibb County, Alabama. James Wesley Bankston, born 28 May 1828, married Martha J. Mitchell on 25 October 1848 in Bibb County; they moved to Fanning County, Texas, where he died 13 October 1902. Thomas Jefferson Bankston, probably born in 1830 in Coweta County, married Martha Adeline Mitchell on 21 December 1856 in Bibb County, Alabama. Madison Bankston, born about 1833 in Georgia, was living at home in 1850 but has not been located thereafter. Samuel Houston Bankston, born about 1838, probably in Coweta County, Georgia, married Winifred Frances Green on 24 June 1857 in Tuscaloosa County, Alabama; he died in Salisbury, North Carolina, in June of 1864 while serving in the Confederate Army. Winnie survived him for many years, dying 17 April 1913 in Tuscaloosa County, Alabama. Bennett Bankston, born about 1840 in Coweta County, married Amanda Price on 24 September 1857 in Tuscaloosa County, Alabama; he died between 1873 and 1880, probably in Tuscaloosa County, where his family remained. Wilson Lumpkin Bankston, born about 1842 in Coweta County, Georgia, married Elizabeth Moore on 22 August 1861 in Bibb County, Alabama. After the Civil War, he moved to Tennessee, where he died 27 June 1916 in Lumpkin County. Pinckney Monroe Bankston, born about 1848 in Bibb County, Alabama, married three times. He remained in northern Alabama, dying 2 August 1914 in Jefferson County. Mary Bankston, second daughter and youngest child of Thomas and Marion Bankston, was born about 1851 in Bibb County, Alabama. She married John T. Millirons on 17 January 1881 in Tuscaloosa County, Alabama. No record of Mary has been found after their marriage, although Millirons was still living in Bibb County as late as 1907, when he applied for a Confederate pension.[1487]

Thomas Jefferson Bankston, second son of Thomas B. and Marion Bankston, was reared in Coweta County, Georgia, and Bibb County, Alabama. He married Martha Adeline Mitchell in Bibb County on 21 December 1856 and moved to Smith County, Mississippi, about 1860. A native of Tennessee, Martha was born about 1832 and moved to northern central Alabama with her parents as a girl. Martha died, probably in Scott County, Mississippi, as a result of childbirth in February 1871, and, on 2 August 1874, Thomas married Martha J. Jackson in Scott County.[1488]

Thomas and Martha Jackson Bankston were living in Issaquena County, Mississippi, at the time of the 1880 census.[1489] He died there about 1884 and was survived by wife Martha and several children. By his first marriage to Martha Adeline Mitchell, Thomas Jefferson Bankston fathered John Manly Bankston (1857-1922); Eleanora Mourning Bankston (1858-1922), wife of George Daniel Dyer; Joseph Breckinridge Bankston (1860-before 1880); Abraham Lincoln "Link" Bankston (c. 1863-before 1884);

[1485] Tennessee Confederate Pension Applications, Wilson Bankston Application, Tennessee State Library and Archives; 1830 Coweta Co., GA, Census, p. 392; 1840 Coweta Co., GA, Census, p. 346; 1850 Bibb Co., AL, Census, p. 83.

[1486] 1850 Bibb Co., AL, Census, p. 83; 1860 Bibb Co., AL, Census, p. 709.

[1487] Alabama Confederate Pension Applications, Microfilm, Alabama Room, Annie Calhoun Library, Anniston, Alabama. Haigler, *Bankston Cousins*, discusses the descendants of Thomas B. Bankston in detail.

[1488] 1860 Smith Co., MS, Census, p. 304.

[1489] 1880 Issaquena Co., MS, Census, p. 293.

Thomas Jefferson Bankston (c. 1868-1929); and James Wesley Bankston (1870-1963). By his second marriage to Martha Jackson, Thomas J. Bankston fathered Sarah Bankston (c. 1876-before 1884) and Spencer Bankston (c. 1878-before 1884). Of this large family, only four children lived to adulthood.[1490]

John Manly Bankston (2 September 1857-13 December 1922) married Abi Doxey O'Neal (22 Apr., 1870-15 March 1899) on 29 November 1886 in Hinds County. Following Abi Doxey's death, John Manly Bankston married second, on 2 June 1909 in Hinds County, Elizabeth Ludlow (1869 - 1951, Crystal Springs, MS, bur. Old Crystal Springs Cemetery). After leaving Issaquena County, John M. Bankston lived in Clark County, Arkansas, for three years, from 26 January 1887 to 12 December 1889, before settling in Hinds County, Mississippi. He remained there for the rest of his life, dying in 1922 at the age of fifty-five after suffering a stroke. He was buried beside his first wife, Abi Doxey O'Neal Bankston, in the Brownsville Community Cemetery in Hinds County, Mississippi.[1491]

John Manly Bankston and Abi Doxey O'Neal were the parents of seven children: James Rederick Bankston (1887-1934), husband of Leoda Reneaw; Joe Ann (or Joan) Bankston (1889-1982), wife of Andrew Jackson Cates and William Henry Maben; John Malcolm Bankston (1890-1971), husband of Jennie Lea Miller; Thomas Hendrix Bankston (1892-1915), who never married; Mary Almedia Bankston (1894-1974), wife of George Cleveland Hammack; Allie Gertrude Bankston (1896-1986), wife of James Monroe Martin; and Alvin Watts Bankston (1898-1991), husband of Lucile Cook. John Manly Bankston and Elizabeth Ludlow had no offspring.[1492]

B. Martha Adeline Mitchell.

The grandmother of Mary Almedia Bankston Hammack, Martha Adeline Mitchell was a daughter of Hiram and Mourning Mitchell of Bibb County, Alabama. Out of all of the Hammack foreparents, Martha Mitchell's family is the least well documented.

According to census records, Hiram Mitchell was born about 1805 in Tennessee. His family had probably come from western North Carolina into Tennessee during the 1790s and settled in the eastern portion of the state, from which many settlers of northeastern Alabama later migrated.[1493] Hiram and Mourning met and married in Tennessee, where their eldest children were born. No record of the marriage or of its location has been found; family tradition suggests that Mourning's maiden name was Dove and that she was of Cherokee Indian descent.[1494] No confirmation of this tradition has been found. If the tradition is true, however, then the Dove family's history may provide some clue to locating and identifying Hiram's parentage.

[1490] The families of Thomas Jefferson and John Manly Bankston are treated in detail by Haigler in *Bankston Cousins*. For supporting data, see 1900 Hinds Co., MS, Census, p. 167; 1910 Hinds Co., MS, Census, p. 167; 1920 Hinds Co., MS, Census, p. 101.

[1491] Ibid. Mississippi Death Certificate, No. 20334, Mississippi Department of Archives and History, Jackson, MS.

[1492] 1900 Hinds Co., MS, Census, p. 167; 1910 Hinds Co., MS, Census, p. 167; 1920 Hinds Co., MS, Census, p. 101.

[1493] Hiram indicated in the 1880 census enumeration that both of his parents were natives of North Carolina. Many of the North Carolina Mitchells descended from a very early Henry Mitchell (Hiram named his youngest son Henry, a name common in many Mitchell families) who came from Scotland (as per tradition) to Virginia in the middle seventeenth-century. That Henry settled in the area that became Prince George County, and his descendants, accounting for a significant proportion of southern Mitchell families, settled in Henrico, Surry, Prince George, Charles City and other Virginia counties before spreading throughout the South. Genetic DNA evidence, discussed later, suggests, however, that Hiram descended from more recent immigrants who settled in Virginia's Shenandoah Valley or from Mitchells in Virginia's Northern Neck.

[1494] Personal Interview, Anne Martin Haigler, 19 April 2004, Birmingham, AL. Mrs. Haigler began her research in the 1950s and interviewed older relatives, born in the 1880s and 1890s, who recounted this story about Mourning Mitchell. See 1810 Grainger Co., TN, Census, p. 13; 1820 Davidson Co., TN, Census, p. 99.

Standard Pedigree Tree

Hiram Mitchell

b: Abt. 1805 in TN
m: Abt. 1825 in TN
d: Aft. 1880 in Sabine Parish, LA

Martha Adeline Mitchell

b: Abt. 1832 in Tennessee
m: 21 Dec 1856 in Bibb County, AL
d: Feb 1871 in Mississippi

Mourning [Dove?]

b: Abt. 1803 in TN
d: Bet. 1850 - 1854 in Bibb Co., AL

Notes:

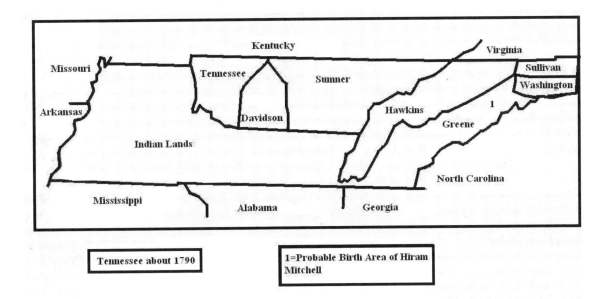

Tennessee about 1790

1=Probable Birth Area of Hiram Mitchell

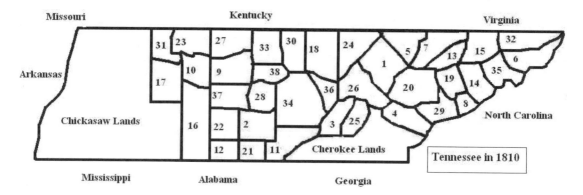

Tennessee in 1810

Tennessee in 1810: Map Key

1. Anderson	20. Knox
2. Bedford	21. Lincoln
3. Bledsoe	22. Maury
4. Blount	23. Montgomery
5. Campbell	24. Overton
6. Carter	25. Rhea
7. Claiborne	26. Roane
8. Cocke	27. Robertson
9. Davidson	28. Rutherford
10. Dickson	29. Sevier
11. Franklin	30. Smith
12. Giles	31. Stewart
13. Grainger	32. Sullivan
14. Greene	33. Sumner
15. Hawkins	34. Warren
16. Hickman	35. Washington
17. Humphreys	36. White
18. Jackson	37. Williamson
19. Jefferson	38. Wilson

The Dove family in Tennessee was a small one. Thomas Dove, aged more than forty-five years, was head of a household in Grainger County, Tennessee, in 1810. At that time he had three daughters and two sons younger than sixteen years of age. A native of Charles County, Maryland, Thomas Dove was born 15 November 1757 and died after 1834 in Knox County, Tennessee. His parents, Joseph and Mary Barker Dove, settled in Pittsylvania County, Virginia, and both died there about 1800. One William Dove, probably Thomas's brother, received a land grant in Davidson County in 1789, and a Dennis Dove was head of household in Davidson County in 1820.[1495] No connection with Mourning Mitchell has been discovered, although she may have been related to Thomas Dove and his family.[1496]

Hiram and Mourning probably married about 1825 in Tennessee and remained there until about 1836, when their son Samuel was born in Alabama. Migrations of single families alone were unusual, and more than likely Hiram and Mourning traveled with kin. Most of their neighbors in Bibb County, Alabama, also came from Tennessee, but no proof of any connection has been found.[1497] By 1840, Hiram and family were living in Shelby County, Alabama, where he was enumerated as "H. Mitchell." Hiram and Mourning were both aged between thirty and forty years; their household consisted of two young sons under five years of age and four daughters under fifteen years of age. Two pages away was a widow, also show as aged between thirty and forty years, listed as "R. Mitchell." She may be the Ruth Mitchell who, like Hiram, was enumerated in Bibb County, Alabama, in 1850 and 1860.[1498]

[1495] Dennis Dove's household contained no offspring. He and his wife were both aged 16-26.

[1496] The Dove surname is Scottish and associated with Clan Buchanan. See: *Scottish Clan and Family Encyclopedia* (Glasgow, 1994), p. 494.

[1497] There was another Hiram Mitchell in Tennessee. This man was a son of Levin and Nancy Mitchell of Rockingham Co., NC, and Tennessee. He was enumerated in Sumner County in 1820, 1830, and 1840. He is named in Nancy Mitchell's 1838 will as a son; other children of Levin and Nancy included Ascenith, wife of Risdon Moore, and Amelia, wife of Lemuel Brashears. These individuals remained in Tennessee and Kentucky. In Bibb Co., AL, the Mitchells lived near the Fancher family, and Thomas Bankston was administrator of Richard Fancher's estate in 1849. The Fanchers had come to Alabama about 1816 from Sevier Co., TN.

[1498] 1840 Shelby Co., AL, Census, p. 69; 1850 Bibb Co., AL, Census, p. 81; 1860 Bibb Co., AL, Census, p. 670. The LDS website, FamilySearch.Org, indicates that the International Genealogical Register contains a record, submitted after 1991, stating that Hiram Mitchell was a son of Ruth Mitchell. No evidence to support this contention has been found, although it may be correct. One John Mitchell married Ruth Henderson on 3 June 1807 in Jefferson Co., TN. One John Mitchell appears there c. 1800-c. 1810 and possibly later. Jefferson County was settled during the Revolution by settlers from NC, VA, and some from SC. The first permanent settlement there dates from 1783. This county contained what later became Cocke, Sevier, and Hamlen Counties. It was legally constituted 11 June 1792 from Greene and Hawkins Counties. In 1793 Sevier County (from which the Fancher family hailed) was created. In 1797 Cocke County was created; in 1870 Hamlen County was created. Dandridge is Jefferson's county seat. *First Families of Tennessee: A Register of Early Settlers and Their Present Day Descendants*, pp. 173-174, lists several Henderson families in Hawkins and Jefferson Counties. Among these was Nathaniel Henderson, a native of Hanover Co., VA, who settled in Hawkins County in 1786 and died there in 1789. One John Mitchell seems to have lived in the Chahata Valley of Jefferson County, where he was a neighbor of John and Thomas Cate, former residents of Orange Co., NC (and kinsmen of John Foster Cates). The 1830 Tennessee census showed Charles Gentry on page 299 of Jefferson County (100001-2001) and John Mitchell (000001-231001) on the same page. On page 301 was Andrew Edgar (000010001-00001001), who married two Henderson wives, and on page 302 appeared Charles Cate (10001-10001). More research should be undertaken on the Jefferson County Mitchell family, for some of its members seem to have been quite wealthy. One Samuel Mitchell was licensed as a lawyer there in 1793, and his son John later became "Supreme Judge in Law." This may be Samuel Mitchell (13 April 1765 -) who married Delilah "Liley" Love, granddaughter of James Logan Colbert (c. 1721, Scotland or NC - 7 January 1784, AL), who was a trader with the Chickasaw Nation as early as 1760. Logan is said to have married three Chickasaw women and to have had five sons and several daughters. Colbert's oldest daughter was Sally Colbert, House of In-cun-no-mar. She married Thomas Love before 1782. A Loyalist during the Revolution, Love also became an Indian trader and later settled in Mississippi. Delilah was the eldest daughter of Sally Colbert and Thomas Love. She married Samuel Mitchell about 1807 in Mississippi. Mitchell, a lawyer by trade, was a son of Joab and Mary Henderson Mitchell of Tennessee and served as agent to the Choctaw and Chickasaw Indians in MS from 1797 to 1806. Much of this information derives from a history of the Samuel Mitchell family (Mitchell Family Records of Hawkins County, Tennessee, by Willie Blount Mitchell) published in 1847. Although the location and the tradition of Indian descent are compelling, there is no evidence of a close connection between Samuel Mitchell and Hiram Mitchell. Delilah Love Mitchell married (2) John B. Moore after 1812 in MS. It is not clear whether Samuel Mitchell died prior to 1812 or whether he and Delilah separated. For an account of the James Logan Colbert family, see http://www.chickasawhistory.com/colbert. Joab Mitchell (11 February 1720/21, Bristol Parish, VA - 1780, Boonesboro, Madison Co., KY) was a son of Thomas and Hannah Mitchell of Prince George Co., VA. Mary Henderson Mitchell (10 January 1734 -)

Although it has not been possible to conclusively identify Hiram Mitchell's parentage, modern technology has proved beneficial in identifying Hiram's ancestry. Through the use of DNA testing, Hiram's male descendants have discovered that Hiram's paternal DNA does not match known Mitchell groupings in eastern Virginia and North Carolina. Yet, the family's DNA matches exactly that of Thomas Mitchell (born about 1780, in Virginia) who was living in Greene County, Tennessee, from about 1820 until after 1860. A second match, although less perfect and with greater mutations (which indicate a more distant connection), proves a link to Mitchell families residing in Pennsylvania during the eighteenth and nineteenth-centuries. The DNA match is sufficient to prove a close connection -- perhaps uncle and nephew -- between Hiram Mitchell and Thomas Mitchell. Since Thomas Mitchell reported that he was born in Virginia, it may be that the family was of Scots-Irish origin, having settled first in Pennsylvania and then having moved through the Virginia backcountry into western North Carolina and eastern Tennessee following the Revolution. The family of Robert and Samuel Mitchell of Pennsylvania, Rowan County, North Carolina, and Tennessee, fits this profile and may suggest a link to Hiram Mitchell's origins. Since many early settlers entered the mountainous region of western North Carolina and eastern Tennessee long before Indian relocation, they sometimes married or formed relationships with Native American women; such an occurrence could have been the source, also, of the family's legend of Indian ancestry.[1499]

At the time of the 1850 census, Hiram Mitchell was living in Household 1102, Ele River District. Nearby were James and Martha Mitchell Bankston in Household 1094, William and Susan Mitchell in Household 1097, Thomas Bankston in Household 1129, and Irwin F. Mitchell -- aged forty-two and a native of South Carolina -- in Household 1144. Whether Hiram and Irwin were related is not known.

Hiram's wife Mourning Mitchell died between 1850 and 1854, when he remarried to Susan Corley. At the time of the 1860 census, Hiram and Susan were enumerated in Household 172, Bibb County, Alabama. Living with them were James Gentry, age twenty-one, a native of Tennessee, and Adeline Russell, age eighteen, a native of Alabama.[1500] By 1870, Hiram, Susan, and several of Susan's Corley relatives had settled in Sabine Parish, Louisiana. Hiram was shown as a farmer and a native of Tennessee; the family was still in Sabine Parish in 1880. Hiram probably remained there for the rest of his life, for his youngest two children were found still in Sabine and Natchitoches Parishes in 1900.[1501]

Hiram Mitchell seems never to have owned land, at least not in Alabama or Tennessee. In 1850, he was working as a collier and owned no taxable property. In 1860, his personal property was valued at $400, but he owned no real estate. In 1870, his personal property was valued at $380. Hiram was still farming in Middle Creek Township in 1880, although the census record does not list his wealth.

Hiram and Mourning Mitchell were the parents of four daughters and two sons. Several daughters married before the 1850 census enumeration, but it is believed that Hiram and Mourning were the parents of the following children: Martha J. Mitchell, born about 1826 in Tennessee, who married James W. Bankston in 1848; Mary Ann Mitchell, born about 1830 in Tennessee, who married Richard Steel in 1849 and moved to Bienville Parish, Louisiana, by 1850 and to Freestone County, Texas, by 1860; Martha

---

married Joab on 14 October 1751 and died 25 August 1803 in Tennessee. She was a daughter of Samuel Henderson and Elizabeth Williams of Virginia. Offspring: Ruth Mitchell Haile (1 August 1753 -); Mark Mitchell (17 January 1756 -); Elizabeth Mitchell Bean (14 March 1758 -); Joab Mitchell (28 May 1760 -); Richard Mitchell (11 September 1762 -); Samuel Mitchell (13 April 1765 -); Thomas Mitchell (19 September 1767 -); Edward Mitchell (3 December 1769 -); Angelia Mitchell Natt (22 December 1771 -); William Mitchell (4 February 1774 -); Polly Mitchell Hall (5 April 1776 -); Susannah Mitchell Dyer (18 November 1779 -). One Ruth Mitchel -- probably the "R. Mitchell" enumerated in Shelby County in 1840 -- was shown in Bibb Co., AL, aged fifty-six, a Tennessee native, in 1850. She was shown as Ruth Mitchell, age seventy, a Tennessee native, in the Bibb Co., AL, census. In terms of age, she might have been the Ruth Henderson who married John Mitchell in Jefferson County in 1807, but there is no corroborating evidence to suggest such a connection.

[1499] The results of Mitchell family DNA tests are posted on-line at: http://www.familytreedna.com/public/Mitchell.

[1500] 1860 Bibb Co., AL, Census, p. 672.

[1501] 1870 Sabine Parish, LA, Census, p. 384; 1880 Sabine Parish, LA, Census, p. 235A; 1900 Sabine Parish, LA, Census, p. 9; 1900 Natchitoches Parish, LA, Census, p. 232.

Adeline Mitchell, born about 1832 in Tennessee, who married Thomas Jefferson Bankston on 17 December 1856 in Bibb County, Alabama; Frances Mitchell, born about 1834 in Tennessee, who married Wesley Parks in Bibb County in 1848 and remained in Bibb County's Cahaba Valley, where she died in 1884; Samuel M. Mitchell, born about 1837 in Alabama, who married Jane McGill in Bibb County in 1859 and died in 1864 during the American Civil War;[1502] Eliza Mitchell, born about 1838 in Alabama, who may have married Ward Wilson on 13 August 1859 in Bibb County; and John Mitchell, born about 1844, in Alabama. The 1840 census indicated that Hiram and Mourning Mitchell had two sons aged under five years; the identity of the second son has not been established. If the age for this son is incorrect, he might be William W. Mitchell, who was living near Hiram Mitchell and James Bankston in 1850. According to the 1850, 1860, and 1870 census, however, that William W. Mitchell was born about 1830 in South Carolina. He was living in Hot Springs County, Arkansas, Clear Creek Township, in 1860 and in Pulaski County, Arkansas, Union Township, in 1870.[1503]

Hiram Mitchell married Susan Corley on 24 August 1854 in Bibb County. Born about 1827 in North Carolina, Susan Corley was probably a daughter of Charles and Nancy Corley who were living in Household 25, Sabine Parish, Louisiana, in 1870.[1504] Hiram and Susan Corley Mitchell were the parents of two children, both born in Bibb County, Alabama, but reared in Sabine Parish, Louisiana. Born about 1855, Henry Doak Mitchell married Patience Jane Russell on 9 April 1874 in Sabine Parish. He was living near his father in Sabine Parish in 1880. Born 25 February 1860, Sarah Louise Mitchell married James Crawford Blunt in Sabine Parish; she died 19 May 1933 in Sabine Parish, Louisiana.

C. James Rederick O'Neal.

James Rederick O'Neal was born 25 July 1847 in Greene County, Georgia, where he spent his early childhood. A son of James Augustus and Georgia Virginia Stewart O'Neal, James Rederick moved first to Tallapoosa County, Alabama, about 1850, and then to Smith County, Mississippi, about 1856. Between 19 July 1861, when James Augustus O'Neal enlisted in the Confederate Army, and 15 November 1862, when Georgia O'Neal gave an affidavit concerning her deceased husband, the family relocated to Brownsville, Hinds County, Mississippi.[1505] The reason for the move is unclear, but James Rederick and family remained in the area. It was there that he met, and on 5 December 1867, married, Mary Jane Gary. James worked as a farm laborer in 1870 and as a farmer in 1880; he remained in Hinds County into the 1890s -- although the 1890 census does not survive -- and died there on 14 January 1893.[1506]

The surname O'Neal indicates Irish ancestry. According to the pre-eminent authority on Irish surnames, O'Neal is "the most famous family of Ulster, from whose arms the famous Red Hand symbol is taken. The name is one of the very few to have retained not only the O' prefix but also (except for the fadas) the Gaelic spelling, O Neill (with the ' above the O and e), 'descendant of Niall'. The name is among the ten most numerous in Ireland and the thirty most numerous in Ulster and is among the first ten in counties Antrim, Derry and Tyrone and the first thirty in County Monaghan."[1507]

In terms of ancestry, the O'Neals claim descent from Conn of the Hundred Battles and Niall of the Nine Hostages. A fifth-century hero, Niall "gave his name to the Cenél Eoghain, of whom the O'Neills were the chief sept, and to Tír Eoghain, a territory comprising not only Tyrone but most of Derry and part of Donegal." The first person known to take O'Neill as his surname was a man named Dormhnall, who

---

[1502] Mitchell served in Company B, 19th Alabama Infantry.

[1503] 1860 Hot Spring Co., AR, Census, p. 1029; 1870 Pulaski Co., AR, Census, p. 412. Ervin Mitchell, a native of South Carolina, was living in Hot Spring County in 1860.

[1504] 1870 Sabine Parish, LA, Census, p. 384.

[1505] Mississippi Confederate Muster Lists, Co. H, 20th Mississippi Infantry, Mississippi Department of Archives and History, Jackson, MS.

[1506] 1860 Smith Co., MS, Census, p. 241; 1870 Hinds Co., MS, Census, p. 676; 1880 Hinds Co., MS, Census, p. 194.

[1507] R. Bell, *The Book of Ulster Surnames* (Belfast, 1988), pp. 209-211. Related names include MacNeill, Neill, and Nelson.

was born about 943. In this case, "Descendant of Niall" referred to his grandfather Niall Glún Dubh, known as "Black Knee", who was a High King of Ireland.[1508]

The O'Neills formed two branches. In the South, the Uí Néill, based in Meath but extending into Cavan in Ulster, became numerous while the northern Uí Néill settled principally in Tyrone. In the fourteenth century, the O'Neills of Tyrone established two branches under Aodh Dubh, 'Black Hugh', King of Ulster, and his brother Niall Ruadh, 'Red Niall', Prince of Tyrone. Bell writes that the "latter branch remained the most powerful, the O'Neills of Tyrone. The former branch, under Aodh Buidhe, 'Yellow Hugh', grandson of Aodh Dubh, won large tracts of land in Antrim and Down from the Normans and these became known as the Clan Aodha Buidhe or Clandeboy O'Nealls." This latter family lived northwest of Antrim at Edenduffcarrig, later known as Shane's Castle. The O'Neills of the Fews in Armagh descend from Aodh, known as Hugh of the Fews, who died in 1475, second son of Eoghan, who was established as chief in 1432. In the sixteenth and seventeenth centuries, the struggles to preserve Gaelic Ireland centered around the O'Neills. According to Bell, "many of them left an indelible imprint on the history of the province of Ulster. These include Conn Bacach O'Neill, 1484-1559, Shane O'Neill, 1530-67, Hugh O'Neill, 1540-1616, Owen Roe O'Neill, 1590-1649, Sir Phelim O'Neill, 1604-53, and Sir Nial O'Neill, 1658-90. Many others distinguished themselves in the armies of Europe."[1509]

The earliest documented member of James Rederick O'Neal's family was a John O'Neal who was living in eastern North Carolina in the early eighteenth-century. There was a family of O'Neals living in far eastern North Carolina in Currituck County and Albemarle Precinct prior to 1700. Whether members of this family moved westward is not yet known. John O'Neal's lineage apparently begins with a John O'Neal who, on 20 February 1733, sold 100 acres on the north side of Pamlico River, near Fishing Creek, to Samuel Horsford for £5. The deed notes that the land joined Thomas Bryant, William Cane, John O'Neal, and Fishing Creek.[1510] Later, on 23 July 1737, John O'Neal deeded 150 acres on Fishing Creek to Arthur Crafford for £8. The land joined lands of Samuel Horsford and was described as "part of a patent to the said O'Neal for 336 acres 1 May 1668."[1511] The 1668 date seems hardly credible for several reasons; John O'Neal would have been nearly ninety by 1737 if the date were correct, and the area conveyed by the deed in 1737 had not yet been surveyed in 1668. Moreover, no record of such a land grant has been located. Barring corroborating evidence, the best that can be deduced is that this land was granted prior to 1733, when John Bryant initiated the first deed found for him in Edgecombe.

In 1738, Captain Thomas Bryant deeded O'Neal a 640-acre tract on the north side of Tar River, along Fishing Creek; O'Neal paid £20 for the tract.[1512] O'Neal is mentioned as an adjacent landowner in deeds from Joseph Bridgers to Jones Stokes (1741), Christopher Guinn to John Yelvington (1741), Benjamin Bridgers to Boaz Kitchings (1742), John Parks to Arthur Crawford (1742), Arthur Crafford to Solomon Thorp (1745), John Yelverton to Jones Stokes (1746), and George and Mary Downing to Thomas Wills (1749). The 19 October 1742 deed from Parks to Crawford described the land as part of a patent to John O'Neal dated 2 August 1727 and named Thomas Bryant and William Cain as adjacent landowners.[1513] The 7 February 1749 deed from Downing to Wills described the land as "part of 327 acres granted to John O'Neal 1 February 1725."[1514] From these deeds we can deduce that John O'Neal was born by 1704 if not earlier; he was likely alive as late as 31 January 1755, when a deed from John Drew to Elias George for land on Fishing Creek describes him as an adjacent landowner.[1515]

[1508] Ibid.

[1509] Ibid.

[1510] M. M. Hoffman, *Abstracts of Deeds, Edgecombe Precinct, N.C., 1732-58* (Weldon, NC, 1969).

[1511] Ibid.

[1512] Ibid.

[1513] Ibid.

[1514] Ibid. This land was part of 327 acres granted to John O'Neal 1 Feb., 1725.

[1515] Ibid.

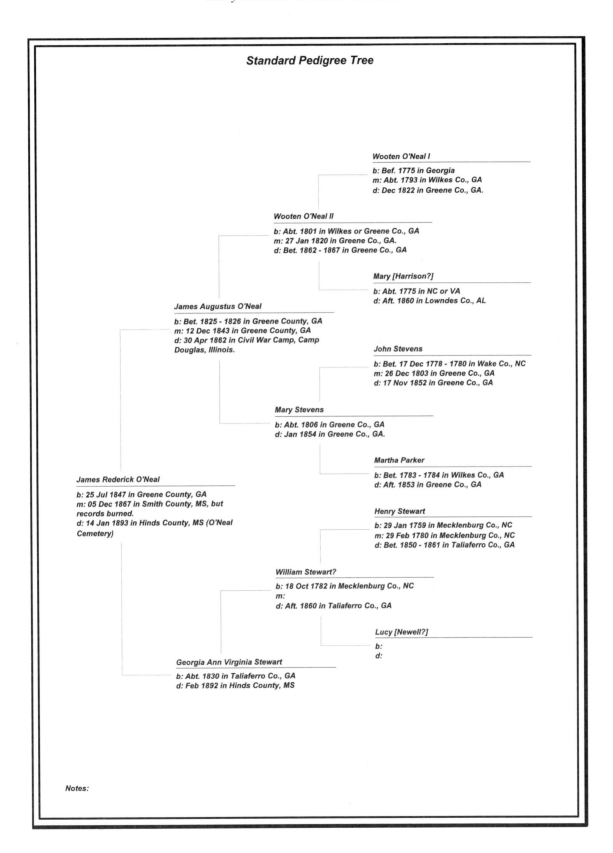

Standard Pedigree Tree

Wooten O'Neal I
b: Bef. 1775 in Georgia
m: Abt. 1793 in Wilkes Co., GA
d: Dec 1822 in Greene Co., GA.

Wooten O'Neal II
b: Abt. 1801 in Wilkes or Greene Co., GA
m: 27 Jan 1820 in Greene Co., GA.
d: Bet. 1862 - 1867 in Greene Co., GA

Mary [Harrison?]
b: Abt. 1775 in NC or VA
d: Aft. 1860 in Lowndes Co., AL

James Augustus O'Neal
b: Bet. 1825 - 1826 in Greene County, GA
m: 12 Dec 1843 in Greene County, GA
d: 30 Apr 1862 in Civil War Camp, Camp
Douglas, Illinois.

John Stevens
b: Bet. 17 Dec 1778 - 1780 in Wake Co., NC
m: 26 Dec 1803 in Greene Co., GA
d: 17 Nov 1852 in Greene Co., GA

Mary Stevens
b: Abt. 1806 in Greene Co., GA
d: Jan 1854 in Greene Co., GA.

Martha Parker
b: Bet. 1783 - 1784 in Wilkes Co., GA
d: Aft. 1853 in Greene Co., GA

James Rederick O'Neal
b: 25 Jul 1847 in Greene County, GA
m: 05 Dec 1867 in Smith County, MS, but
records burned.
d: 14 Jan 1893 in Hinds County, MS (O'Neal
Cemetery)

Henry Stewart
b: 29 Jan 1759 in Mecklenburg Co., NC
m: 29 Feb 1780 in Mecklenburg Co., NC
d: Bet. 1850 - 1861 in Taliaferro Co., GA

William Stewart?
b: 18 Oct 1782 in Mecklenburg Co., NC
m:
d: Aft. 1860 in Taliaferro Co., GA

Lucy [Newell?]
b:
d:

Georgia Ann Virginia Stewart
b: Abt. 1830 in Taliaferro Co., GA
d: Feb 1892 in Hinds County, MS

Notes:

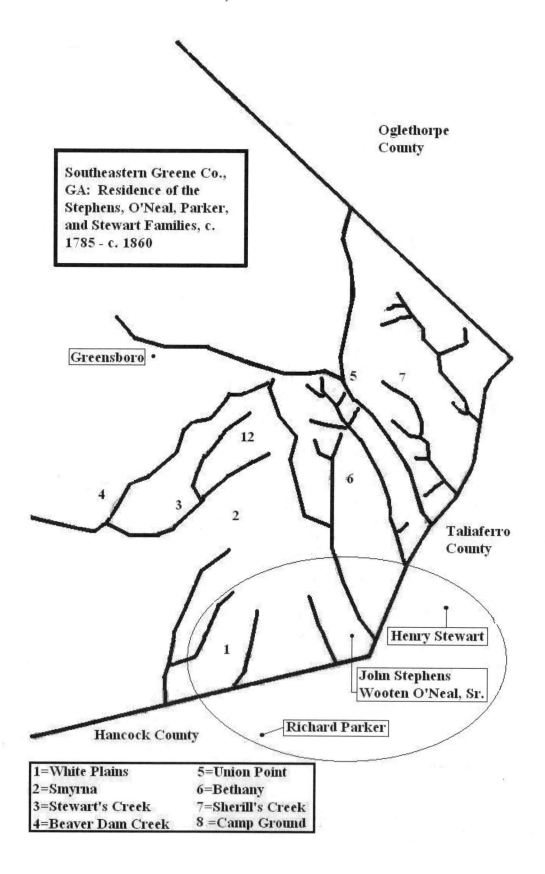

Oglethorpe
County

Southeastern Greene Co.,
GA: Residence of the
Stephens, O'Neal, Parker,
and Stewart Families, c.
1785 - c. 1860

Greensboro •

5   7

12

4

3

2

6

Taliaferro
County

Henry Stewart

1

John Stephens
Wooten O'Neal, Sr.

Richard Parker

Hancock County

1=White Plains	5=Union Point
2=Smyrna	6=Bethany
3=Stewart's Creek	7=Sherill's Creek
4=Beaver Dam Creek	8=Camp Ground

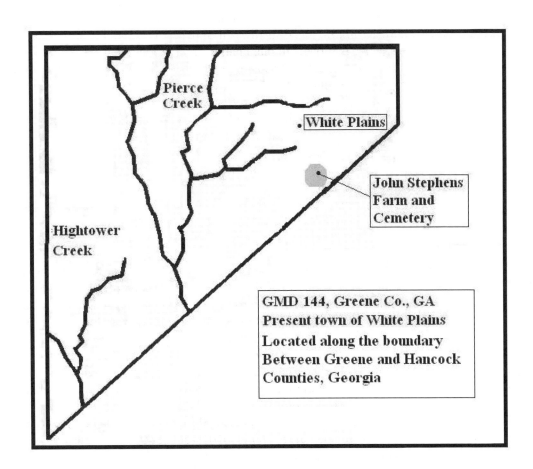

Pierce
Creek

White Plains

John Stephens
Farm and
Cemetery

Hightower
Creek

GMD 144, Greene Co., GA
Present town of White Plains
Located along the boundary
Between Greene and Hancock
Counties, Georgia

Greene County, Georgia: Neighborhood of John Stephens Family

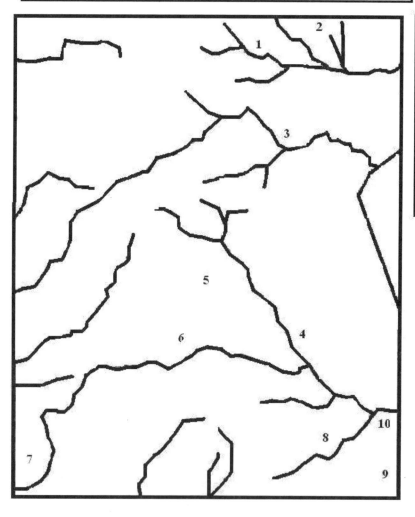

1=Union Point
2=GMD 140
3=Fork of Ogeechee River
4=Fork of Ogeechee River
5=GMD 141
6=Siloam
7=GMD 142
8=Moore's Creek
9=John Stephens Family
Cemetery
10=Thomas Grimes
Cemetery

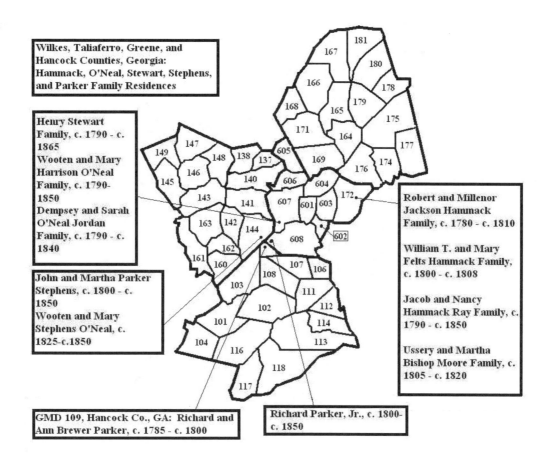

Wilkes, Taliaferro, Greene, and
Hancock Counties, Georgia:
Hammack, O'Neal, Stewart, Stephens,
and Parker Family Residences

Henry Stewart
Family, c. 1790 - c.
1865
Wooten and Mary
Harrison O'Neal
Family, c. 1790-
1850
Dempsey and Sarah
O'Neal Jordan
Family, c. 1790 - c.
1840

John and Martha Parker
Stephens, c. 1800 - c.
1850
Wooten and Mary
Stephens O'Neal, c.
1825-c.1850

Robert and Millenor
Jackson Hammack
Family, c. 1780 - c. 1810

William T. and Mary
Felts Hammack Family,
c. 1800 - c. 1808

Jacob and Nancy
Hammack Ray Family, c.
1790 - c. 1850

Ussery and Martha
Bishop Moore Family, c.
1805 - c. 1820

GMD 109, Hancock Co., GA: Richard and
Ann Brewer Parker, c. 1785 - c. 1800

Richard Parker, Jr., c. 1800-
c. 1850

Note on the formation of Taliaferro County: Before 1826, the southern half of GMD 602, GMD 603, and
GMD 172 was located in Warren County while the northern half was located in Wilkes County. Before
1826, the eastern half of GMD 605, GMD 606, and GMD 607 was located in Wilkes County while the
western half was located in Greene County.

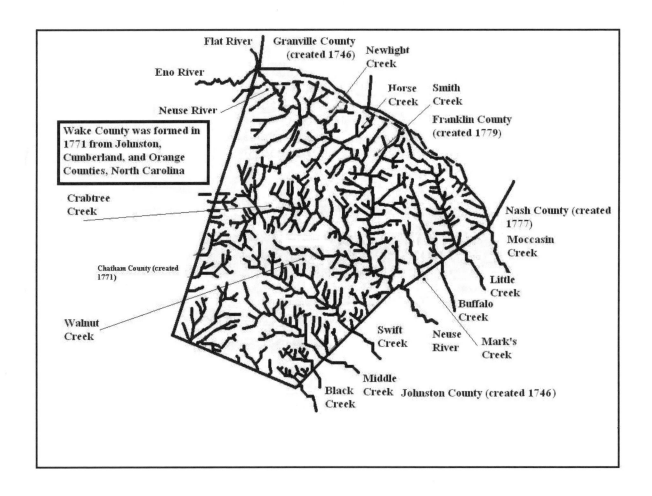

Flat River   Granville County
             (created 1746)   Newlight
                               Creek

Eno River
                          Horse   Smith
                          Creek   Creek

Neuse River
                                   Franklin County
                                   (created 1779)

Wake County was formed in
1771 from Johnston,
Cumberland, and Orange
Counties, North Carolina

Crabtree
Creek   Nash County (created
                                               1777)

                                               Moccasin
                                               Creek

Chatham County (created
1771)   Little
                                               Creek

                                          Buffalo
                                          Creek
Walnut
Creek   Swift   Neuse   Mark's
                              Creek   River   Creek

                         Middle
                  Black   Creek   Johnston County (created 1746)
                  Creek

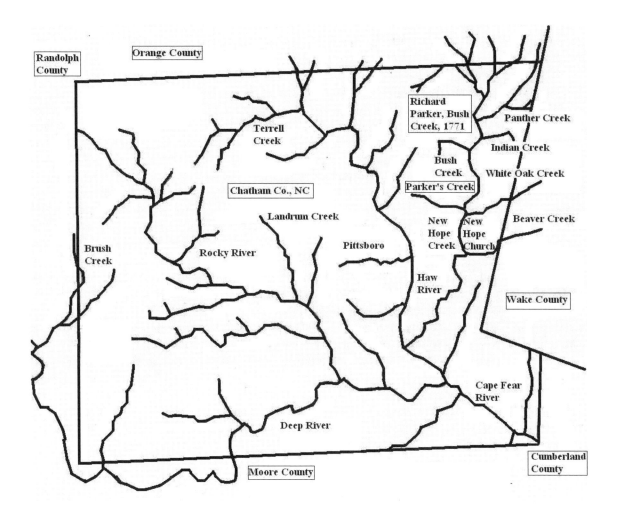

It is believed that this John O'Neal was the father of John O'Neal (by c. 1730 -- c. 1807), who married Sarah Bryant and moved to Wilkes County, Georgia. This John O'Neal as a young man participated in the Regulator incident in central North Carolina in which small farmers attempted to defend their land claims against powerful local elites, who used inflated tax valuations to seize and then auction their farms. In May 1768, Elmer Henley and John O'Neal were accused of treason in Johnston County and arrested.[1516] On 3 October 1768, O'Neal was among those pardoned for his role in the Regulator affair. These men resided in Orange, Anson, Rowan and Johnston Counties and had engaged "in a most riotous and unlawful manner to the disturbance of the publick peace, audaciously attempting to intimidate and deter the Civil Magistrates from doing their duty and committing many Acts of Violence contrary to Law being led on by some evil, wicked and designing men." Governor Tyron wrote: "I do therefore out of compassion to the misguided multitude, being much more inclined to prevent than punish crimes of so high a nature, by and with the unanimous advice and consent of His Majesty's Council, issue this my proclamation, granting unto them His Majesty's most gracious pardon for the several outrageous Acts by them committed at any time before the day of the date hereof".[1517]

Probably because of the Regulator incident, John O'Neal decided to leave North Carolina. Newly opened lands to the south were drawing many North Carolinians to the Georgia frontier, and O'Neal proved no exception. By about 1774, he was living on the north fork of the Ogeechee River in what became Wilkes County, Georgia. He resided on the same tract until at least 1793. He may be the John O'Neal the younger of Johnston County, North Carolina, who, on 13 November 1773, for £45 deeded to Elisha Thomas "land on great Reflector Swamp, it being a track of land granted by Robert Bryant to his daughter Sarah Bryant by will containing 175 acres." Witnesses were John Venson, Drury Venson, and Axum O'Neal.[1518] He may also be the John O'Neal who on 6 June 1775 was sued for non-attendance by the Rowan County court.[1519] O'Neal's reason for non-attendance was likely that he had already removed to Georgia, where between 1774 and 1776 he and his sons Axiom and Theophilus served in Bernard's Rangers.[1520]

Between 1779 and 1782, John O'Neal on several occasions provided beef, pork, and other supplies for the Georgia Continental Line; he may also have actively assisted the patriot cause through military service, as did several of his children and sons-in-law.[1521]

A statement dated 11 February 1837, Taliaferro County, Georgia, and found in the pension application of John O'Neal's son-in-law Dempsey Jordan provides additional details of the family during the Revolutionary conflict. Martha Stevens, apparently a daughter of John O'Neal's neighbor Moses Stevens, gave a statement to support the Jordan couple's claim:

> ....in addition to what she was sworn to on a former occasion respecting the marriage of Dempsey Jordan, late of said county, deceased, with his widow Sarah Jordan, that her reason for saying that said marriage took place in seventeen Hundred and seventy seven or eight is this, that she and said Sarah Jordan were girls together and, in May seventeen Hundred and seventy seven, or sixty years ago, she and said Sarah were together in a fort on the place the said Martha now lives, said fort was called Fort Marbury, that while living there said Fort was attacked by the Indians and she and said Sarah and one Nancy Oneal (the wife of said Sarah's brother) moulded bullets for the men while they were fighting, that afterwards they left said fort in the same year and went to fort Phillips, where Sarah remained but a short time and went down towards Ogeechee River to

---

[1516] *Smithfield (N.C.) Herald*, 21 Sept., 1993.

[1517] Saunders, *Colonial Records of NC*, 7: 851.

[1518] Johnston Co., NC, DB H, p. 121. The will of Robert Bryant is dated 1760.

[1519] Saunders, *Colonial Records of NC*, 10: 8.

[1520] R. S. Davis, Jr., *Georgia Citizens and Soldiers of the American Revolution* (Easley, SC, 1999), pp. 54, 94, 130.

[1521] Ibid.

another fort which she does not recollect, and soon she heard that she was married to Dempsey Jordan -- that she was not at the marriage -- but has always since been acquainted with both said Sarah and Dempsey -- until his death -- that they have raised a family of children -- always since she heard of their marriage they having lived together as man and wife --- nor has she ever heard it contradicted -- or were a doubt suggested about it -- she further says she does not now recollect exactly how long it was after said Sarah left for Philips before she heard of her marriage, but it was not long, and hence she does not know certain whether it was in 1777 or 1778, but she is certain from her distinct recollection of many of the interesting incidents of those times that it was this coming May sixty years ago since she and said Sarah were in the old fort now upon the place where she is now living &c.

Martha Stevens, the writer, stands out as a vigorous and active woman. Apart from what the statement reveals about these two women and their life during the Revolution, it is significant for our discussion of the O'Neal family for several reasons. Not only does it document the family's residence and activity during the Revolutionary conflict, but it also indicates that Sarah and her family remained in the same neighborhood for six decades between 1777 and 1837. Such a lengthy residence was unusual during a period of intense migration, and long-time residents like Sarah Jordan and Martha Stevens would have become guardians of the community's memory.[1522]

Evidence does suggest, however, that John O'Neal may have moved from southwestern Wilkes County across the Ogeechee River into Hancock County in the late 1790s. The community in which the O'Neals and Jordans lived after many boundary changes in 1826 became a new county, Taliaferro, after shifting variously between Wilkes and Greene Counties for half a century. The Ogeechee River had constituted the southern boundary between Wilkes County and its then neighbor Hancock County, and, from about 1793 onwards, records for members of John O'Neal's family are found in both Hancock and Wilkes. O'Neal had received a grant for 500 acres on the Ogeechee River in 1786 following the issuance of a warrant for the land in 1784.[1523] In 1789, he and wife Sarah sold 100 acres of this tract, located on the south fork of the Ogeechee, to Robert Smith.[1524] In 1790, John was taxed with 407 acres in southern Wilkes and in 1791 with 380 acres in Wilkes and 287.5 acres in Franklin County.[1525] John and Sarah sold the Franklin County tract in 1792, and in 1794 they sold an additional thirty-five-acre tract located in Hancock County, "on South Fork of Ogeechee and North Fork of Ogeechee adjoining Alexander and William Whaley."[1526]

From 1794 until his death in 1807, John O'Neal seems to have resided continuously in Hancock County. In 1802, 1803, and 1804, he paid poll tax only; in 1805 he was taxed with one slave but no land. He registered for the 1807 Georgia land lottery as a resident of Captain Barnes' District, where his son Edmund also lived. John was still living on 31 January 1807, when he deeded 150 acres to his son Edmond, it "being all the balance of that tract or parcel of land run by me and granted by the proper authority, which I have not heretofore deeded away out of the said plat or grant, which bears date June 20th, in the year of our Lord one thousand Seven hundred and eighty-four, containing five hundred acres, lying and being formerly in the County of Wilkes but now Hancock...," bounded on the northeastern side by Ogeechee River, on the southwestern side by Glenn, and on all other sides by Samuel Alexander. The deed identifies the grantor as John O'Neal, Sr. Soon afterwards, on 10 March 1807 and in a deed

---

[1522] Revolutionary War Pension Application of Dempsey Jordan, W4462, The National Archives, Washington, D.C., Microfilm Series M805, Roll 483.

[1523] Georgia Land Grant Book HHH, 853.

[1524] Greene Co., GA, DB 1, pp. 214-215.

[1525] These and other referenced Wilkes County tax digests prior to 1806 are as cited above in Hudson, *Wilkes County Tax Records*.

[1526] Wilkes Co., GA, DB PP, p. 335; Wilkes Co., GA, DB RR, p. 286; Wilkes Co., GA, DB VV, p. 264.

reminiscent of the one cited earlier between Ann Morgan Lambert and her son Thomas, John O'Neal deeded his furniture, cattle, and personal property to his son Edmond as well, probably as compensation for caring for him during his final years.[1527]

John may have died about 1807; by 1808, his son Edmund was taxed with 150 acres on the Ogeechee River, six slaves, and 100 acres on Fort Creek. John O'Neal does not appear in the digest for that or any later year.[1528]

No record of John O'Neal's death or of the disposition of his estate has been discovered. A list of his probable offspring has been compiled based on Wilkes, Hancock, and Taliaferro County records. Deeds, wills, estate settlements, and Dempsey Jordan's Revolutionary War pension application provide identification of several of John O'Neal's children. The identification of the others is speculative but based on strong circumstantial evidence. Based on the evidence, it would appear that John O'Neal had the following offspring: Theophilus O'Neal (by c. 1755 - after 1777); Axiom O'Neal (by 1752 - 1793), who was killed by Creek Indians at Burnt Village in western Georgia in 1793; John O'Neal, Jr. (by c. 1755 - c. 1836, Washington County, Georgia); Nathan O'Neal (- c. 1800, Greene County, Georgia); William O'Neal (- c. 1829, Lincoln County, Georgia); Edmund O'Neal (- c. 1831, Putnam County, Georgia); Sarah O'Neal (c. 1760 - c. 1845, Taliaferro County, Georgia), wife of Dempsey Jordan; Wooten O'Neal, Sr. (c. 1770 - c. 1822, Greene County, Georgia); and perhaps James and Jesse O'Neal.[1529]

Born about 1772 in Johnston County, North Carolina, or Wilkes County, Georgia, Wooten O'Neal was probably among the younger offspring of John O'Neal and Sarah Bryant. He seems to have lived all of his life in southwestern Wilkes and southeastern Greene Counties, where he died about 1822. The maiden name of Wooten's wife Mary has not been discovered; based on family naming patterns, many researchers have inferred that she may have been Mary Harrison and that she was perhaps a relative of Thomas Harrison, Vincent Harrison, or Joseph Harrison, all of whom lived in the same neighborhood as Wooten O'Neal. The couple probably married in southern Wilkes County about 1793.[1530]

Wooten O'Neal was a landowner in Greene County prior to 17 July 1801, when Alexander King deeded land bound by Robert Livingston, Wooten O'Neal, Nathaniel Stevens, James Ballard, and Elizabeth Whatley.[1531] Wooten appears infrequently in legal records but was regularly taxed in Greene County until his death in late 1822 or 1823. By the autumn of 1823, Mary O'Neal had been named guardian of her sons William and Thomas, while Harrison O'Neal had been named guardian of his siblings Littleberry and Martha. Shortly afterwards, on 29 December 1833, Clevers A. Nelms, Horatio B. Nunnally, and Martin Woodall made the final distribution of the estate. Wooten owned several slaves with a combined value of $5,750. The eleven heirs were each accorded a share worth $522.72 3/4, although, to reach this sum, certain heirs had to pay small amounts to their siblings. For instance, Quinea O'Neal received a slave named Ezekiel valued at $550; in keeping with his inheritance of $522.72 3/4, he then paid $27.27 1/4 to the estate.[1532]

[1527] 1802 - 1807, 1812-1813 Hancock Co., GA, Tax Digests, Georgia Department of Archives and History, Morrow, GA. See H. and T. Marsh, *Land Deed Genealogy of Hancock County, GA* (Easley, SC, 1997) and Hancock Co., GA, Direct Index to Real Estate Conveyances, Georgia Department of Archives and History, Morrow, GA.

[1528] 1808 Hancock Co., GA, Tax Digest, Georgia Department of Archives and History, Morrow, GA.

[1529] This listing is speculative but based on abundant circumstantial evidence, primary taken from deed books and tax digests in Wilkes, Warren, Greene, Hancock, and Taliaferro Counties, Georgia.

[1530] The late Dudley O'Neal believed that she was a daughter of Thomas Harrison who owned property near Edmund O'Neal in Hancock County in 1807 and who later died in Greene County. My own research suggests that she was perhaps connected with Vincent and Joseph Harrison, who may themselves have come from Caswell Co., NC. At the time of the 1830 census, Mary was living next door to Joseph Harrison, who was shown as being between ten and twenty years her senior. He might have been an older brother or, perhaps, even her father. See Greene Co., GA, Estate Divisions and Annual Returns, 1822-1829, pp. 95, 191, 281, and Wooten O'Neal Estate File, Greene Co., GA, Loose Estate Papers, Greene Co., GA, Probate Court, Greensboro, GA.

[1531] F. P. Turner, *Greene Co., GA, Land Records, Deeds, 1785-1810* (Fernandina Beach, FL, 1997), p. 348, citing DB AA, p. 569.

[1532] Greene Co., GA, Estate Divisions and Annual Returns, 1822-1829, pp. 95, 191, 281, and Wooten O'Neal Estate File, Greene Co., GA, Loose Estate Papers, Greene Co., GA, Probate Court, Greensboro, GA.

For purposes of the estate distribution, Mary O'Neal received a share equivalent to that of her children. The other ten heirs were identified by the distribution record: Quinea O'Neal; Thomas O'Neal; William O'Neal; Jesse O'Neal; Wooten O'Neal; Nathaniel Acree (who married Elizabeth O'Neal); Littleberry O'Neal; Williamson O'Neal; Patsy O'Neal (who later married James Shorter); and Harrison O'Neal.[1533]

Mary O'Neal remained in Greene County until Taliaferro County was created in 1826; she then resided in the new county for more than two decades before heading west. In 1832, she was taxed with five slaves, 200 acres along the Ogeechee River in Taliaferro County, and 202.5 acres, land district 14, land lot 26, Muscogee County, which she had drawn in the 1827 land lottery. In the same year, she sold 100 acres in Taliaferro County, yet the 1834 digest shows that she still owned the 200 acre tract on the Ogeechee River, the Muscogee County tract, and one slave. Possibly the terms of the deed had not yet been satisfied, with the result that a full transfer of the property had not yet taken place.[1534]

Mary paid tax on the 200-acre tract in 1835 and apparently retained ownership until 1839, when she conveyed the entire tract of land (which the deed noted had been granted to her on 2 December 1826); she was still in Taliaferro County on 1 February 1840, when she united with the Crawfordville Baptist Church. When she left the county is unclear.[1535] By 1850, however, she was living in Harris County, Georgia, a county formed from Muscogee County. Her decision to head west may have been influenced by two factors: first the ownership, however brief, of a tract in Muscogee County and, second, the migration concurrently of several members of the O'Neal and Stewart families from Greene and Taliaferro Counties in Georgia to Tallapoosa County in eastern Alabama, only a short distance from Muscogee County. Whatever the reason, Mary in 1850 was living with John Stephens, a relative of her daughter-in-law, Mary Stephens O'Neal. She was listed as seventy-five years old and a native of Virginia.[1536] By 1860, she had moved to Lowndes County, Alabama, where she was enumerated next door to her daughter and son-in-law, Elizabeth (1795-1860) and Nathaniel Acree (1787-1870).[1537]

As noted, Mary and Wooten O'Neal reared a large family, including at least four children who had not yet reached legal age when their father died. Of the offspring, perhaps Quinea O'Neal had the most interesting life. Born about 1794, and apparently the eldest child, Quinea was widowed at an early age and never remarried. As early as 1830, he was a teacher in Taliaferro County, and by 1832 he was treasurer of the Poor School Fund. He apparently held that position until at least 1845. At the same time, Quinea became a Justice of the Inferior Court in Taliaferro and, by 1850, was clerk of that body. At the time of the 1860 census, he was enumerated in the household of Crawfordville lawyer Alexander Hamilton Stephens, who was soon to become Vice-President of the Confederate States of America. Stephens was a forty-eight year old lawyer with an estate valued at $53,000. Quinea O'Neal possessed a far more modest estate -- valued at less than $800 -- and was listed as County Ordinary. George Bristow, another lawyer, and John Stephens, a young law student, lived in the household, as did several orphaned nephews of Alexander Stephens.[1538] Quinea lived until 1884; when Alexander Stephens wrote his will in 1881, he bequeathed to "My friend Quinea O'Neal... a home at 'Liberty Hall' and comfortable support out of my estate as long as he lives." The bond between the two friends must have been a strong one; it

[1533] Greene Co., GA, Estate Divisions and Annual Returns, 1822-1829, pp. 95, 191, 281. Harrison O'Neal married but was deceased by 1831. Thomas and William O'Neal were both deceased without offspring by 1 January 1827. Jesse lived until 1875 and settled in Harris and Muscogee Counties, Georgia. Martha and James Shorter were in Taliaferro County as late as 1831 but may have then moved to Harris County. Littleberry O'Neal died about 1850, probably in Coosa Co., AL. Williamson O'Neal died in 1870.

[1534] As cited previously, all references are from the relevant volume of Taliaferro Co., GA, Tax Digests, Georgia Department of Archives and History, Morrow, GA.

[1535] One Mary, aged 60-70, was enumerated in DeKalb Co., GA, in 1840.

[1536] 1850 Harris Co., GA, Census, p. 85B.

[1537] 1860 Lowndes Co., AL, Census, p. 659.

[1538] 1860 Taliaferro Co., GA, Census, p. 701.

had endured for more than a quarter of a century. Given Stephens' importance for the Confederacy, it gave Quinea O'Neal and his relatives a link with the highest level of the Confederate government.[1539]

Quinea's younger brother Wooten O'Neal, Jr., was the grandfather of James Rederick O'Neal of Mississippi. Born about 1801 in Greene County, Georgia, Wooten married Mary Stephens on 27 January 1820 in Greene County. He was then about eighteen years of age and she about fourteen. The marriage lasted for nearly forty years, ending with Mary's death in 1854. Wooten apparently never remarried and died sometimes between 1862 and 1867 in Greene County, Georgia.[1540]

Like his siblings, Wooten inherited an equal share in his father's estate in 1823. He and his brother Quinea seem to have been well educated, for Wooten also appears in Taliaferro County poor school records as a teacher in 1834 and 1835. At that time, he owned only a modest estate -- fifty acres of land on the Ogeechee River in one tract and ten acres on the Ogeechee in another tract.[1541]

Wooten's land lay along the boundary between Taliaferro and Greene Counties, and he may have owned property in both counties. After 1840, he seems to have shifted the locus of his economic efforts from Taliaferro County to Greene. At the time of the 1850 census, he was enumerated in Household 506, Greene County, a farmer living near several O'Neal and Jordan relatives as well as near his wife's parents, John and Martha Parker Stephens.[1542]

John and Martha Parker Stephens, parents of Mary Stephens O'Neal, married in Greene County, but both belonged to families found earlier in central and eastern North Carolina. According to family records maintained by the descendants of their daughter Martha Stephens Stevens, John Stephens was a son of Edmund and Mary Stephens of Wake and Johnston Counties, North Carolina. No corroborating evidence of that statement has been found, although the connection seems plausible.[1543] John Stephens was born in North Carolina in December 1778. The first known record of him in Georgia dates from 7 March 1800, when he purchased twenty acres in Greene County from William Allen.[1544] From that point onward, he can be documented continuously in Greene County, where he died on 17 November 1852.[1545]

Edmund Stephens, the putative father of John Stephens, can be documented in Johnston County, North Carolina, from 1751 until he died between 1800 and 1802.[1546] He was a son of Edward and Ann Stephens of Tyrell, Craven, and Johnston Counties. Edward Stephens, the grandfather, appeared in

---

[1539] 1850 Taliaferro Co., GA, Census, p. 333, HH 264; 1860 Taliaferro Co., GA, Census, p. 701; V. M. Harris, *Ancient, Curious, and Famous Wills* (Boston, 1911), p. 429.

[1540] Loose Estate Files of John Stephens and Wooten O'Neal, Greene Co., GA, Probate Court, Greene Co., GA, Court House, Greensboro, GA.

[1541] 1834 Taliaferro Co., GA, Poor School Minutes, and 1834 Taliaferro Co., GA, Tax Digest.

[1542] 1850 Greene Co., GA, Census, p. 104.

[1543] M. S. W. Wood, *Stevens-Davis and Allied Families: A Memorial Volume of History, Biography, and Genealogy* (Macon, 1957), pp. 52-53.

[1544] Turner, *Greene Co., GA, Deeds*, p. 357, citing DB AA, 624.

[1545] Stephens's dates of birth and death are as given on his tombstone in the John Stephens Cemetery, near the boundary of Greene, Taliaferro, and Hancock Counties in rural Greene County, Georgia.

[1546] Edmund Stevens, deceased, is mentioned in an 1802 deed from John Stevens, Jr., to William Stevens (W. P. Haun, *Johnston Co., NC, Deeds* (6 vols., Durham, NC, 1980-), Vol. 6, *1799-1803*, No. 745). He witnessed a deed in 1800 (Haun, *Johnston Co., NC, Deeds, 1799-1803*, No. 831). He was of age at least by 13 December 1769 when he witnessed a deed from William Pearsey to John Stephens, Esquire (Haun, *Johnston Co., NC, Deeds, 1759-1771*, Item 422) and possibly as early as 1764 when one "Edwd. Stephens" and Joseph Boon witnessed a deed from John Tiner to Jesse Tiner (Haun, *Johnston Co., NC, Deeds, 1759-1771*, Item 719). There is confusion concerning the marriage of Edmund. There were two contemporary men, Edward and Edmund Stephens, who appear simultaneously in Johnston and Wake Counties. Edward was from Virginia, while Edmund was the son of an earlier Edward who died in 1751. It is clear that Edward was sometimes referred to in legal records as Edmund and vice versa. Edward Stephens, who died about 1792 in Wake County, married Mary Burt of Halifax Co., VA. The identity of the wife of Edmund Stephens is unclear, although descendants of Matilda Stephens Stevens claim that she, too, was named Mary. Others claim that Edmund Stephens married Fereby Whitliff. The will of John Whitliff names single daughters Fereby, Jerusha, Delilah, Nancy, and Honour Whitliff and married daughter Hester Ballard. Also named were sons John Whitliff and Needham Whitliff. The will was proven in 1767. Jerusha is claimed to have married Cary Jernigan. Delilah married Joseph Sessions and died in Washington Co., GA. This connection may have influenced John Stephens's decision to move to Georgia after Edmund Stephens' death.

Craven County as early as September 1735, when he was named as a juror.[1547] On 7 June 1737, he recorded a cattle mark at the county court,[1548] and in September of that year he was sued by James Smith, a neighbor.[1549] He was a juror in Tyrell in 1739 and 1740 before succeeding Charles Barfield as constable in June 1740.[1550] On 3 September 1740, he purchased 160 acres on the north side of Flat Creek from James Conner; two years later, on 18 June 1742, he purchased another 160 acres in the same location from Richard Sparkman.[1551] Edward appears in Tyrell and Craven Counties from 1742 until 1752, selling 160 acres in 1742 and purchasing 370 acres on the Nuse River in 1743.[1552]

Edward Stephens wrote his will 19 February 1751 in Johnston County. He named his brother William as executor and mentioned six children living at home.[1553] To his son Ephraim Stephens, Edward bequeathed 200 acres.[1554] To his son Edmund he bequeathed seventy-five acres of one survey and 220 acres of another. To his wife Anne he left the use of all of his slaves; following his death, Ephraim would inherit two and Edmund would inherit two. To Jacob Stephens and his sisters Edward left cash and slaves. Son Jacob received a slave boy named Jack.[1555] Daughter Sarah received £60, while daughter Mourning received £30 and a young slave.[1556] Daughter Patience received personal property[1557], while all six offspring were to share the remaining estate at wife Anne's death. Arthur Fort, Bennett Blackman, and Rachel Stephens witnessed the will.[1558]

Edward Stephens was certainly born before 1716; he may have been significantly older. He and his brother William have not been identified prior to their appearance in Tyrell and Carven Counties. One possibility is that their family came from southeastern Virginia in the vicinity of Isle of Wight and Nansemond Counties. Arthur Fort and Bennett Blackman -- both witnesses to Edward's will -- originated in Isle of Wight County, as did Phillip and Robert Raiford with whom Edward and his relatives had dealings. At the end of the seventeenth century, there was a substantial migration from Surry and Isle of Wight Counties into eastern North Carolina, one which increased in tempo over the coming decades as more and more new lands were settled and brought into cultivation. Given the migration of associated families from this region of Virginia, it seems reasonable to suspect that the Stephens family's American journey may have begun there as well.[1559]

A persistent tradition among the Stephens families of Eastern North Carolina, however, has been that they descended from early migrants who left New England and settled along the Carolina Coast in the

---

[1547] B. F. Burr, *Tyrell Co., NC, Minutes, Court of Pleas and Quarter Sessions, 1735-1754* (Nacogdoches Co., TX, 1981), p. 7.

[1548] Burr, *Tyrell Co., NC, Court Minutes, 1735-1754*, p. 2

[1549] Burr, *Tyrell Co., NC, Court Minutes, 1735-1754*, p. 7.

[1550] Burr, *Tyrell Co., NC, Court Minutes, 1735-1754*, pp. 64, 75, 80.

[1551] Tyrell Co., NC, DB 1, p. 104, 202.

[1552] Tyrell Co., NC, DB 1, p. 211; A. B. Pruitt, *Craven Co., NC, Deed Books 2, 3, &4 (1708-1765)* (Whitakers, NC, 2004), No. 1679, No. 1682. On 17 December 1743 he purchased 220 acres from William Stephens of Craven County. The land had been granted Stephens on 17 December 1743.

[1553] Craven Co., NC, DB 5, p. 275, cited in Haun, *Craven Co., NC, Deed and Will Abstracts*, p. 154.

[1554] Ephraim was alive in Johnston County as late as 28 August 1770 (Haun, *Johnston Deeds, 1759-1771*, Item 460).

[1555] Jacob married Belinda Jernigan, daughter of Henry and Ann Jernigan, of Johnston County. He died testate in 1783 with a will written in 1780. Belinda then married Abraham Gomillion. Belinda was a sister of Lewis, Joseph, and Cary Jerningan. "Trusty friend Phillip Raiford" was named as Jacob's executor. Born about 1740, Jacob fathered Edward (under eighteen in 1780); Phillip; William (possibly enumerated near Abraham Gomillion in 1790); Henry (probably enumerated near Joseph Jernigan and Edward Stephens in the 1800 Johnston Co., NC, census); John (probably enumerated near Joseph Jernigan in the 1800 Johnston Co., NC, census); and Jacob.

[1556] Descendants of Mourning claim that she married (1) John Stephens, (2) George Kornegay, and (3) Willis Wiggins. Johnston Co., NC, marriages, however, show that Mourning Stephens married Willis Wiggins on 17 December 1779 with Jacob Stevens as bondsman.

[1557] She may be the Pattey Stephens who on 13 September 1778 married James Langden in Johnston County with Richard Whittington as bondsman.

[1558] Craven Co., NC, DB 5, p. 275, cited in Haun, *Craven Co., NC, Deed and Will Abstracts*, p. 154.

[1559] A deed dated 4 March 1744 from Robert Raiford to Andrew Griffin names Edward as a neighbor (Tyrell Co., NC, DB 1, p. 279). The Raiford-Stephens connection continued for several generations in Johnston County.

1680s. Richard Stephens and Mary Lincoln of Deighton, Massachusetts, are claimed by many as ancestors of this family. Their son Nicholas (born 23 February 1668/9) married Remembrance Tisdale. They were the parents of William Stephens, husband of Sarah Durant, whom many researchers claim were the parents of Edward and William Stephens of Craven and Tyrell Counties.[1560]

The accuracy of this claim to New England origins has not been ascertained. Parish registers for Eastern North Carolina do document members of this family living in the vicinity in the early eighteenth century, but the compound of common given names with an equally common surname makes concrete identification difficult, if not impossible. William Stephens married Mrs. Sarah Durant on 1 January 1703/4 in a ceremony performed by Reverend Mr. William Barclift.[1561] The same register, however, shows that one William Stephens, son of Andrew and Grace Stephens of "ould England," was living in the area as early as 25 February 1684, when he married Johannah Williams.[1562] The 1704 marriage indicates that William Stephens was born at last by 1686, if not earlier; thus, he was significantly older than the New England pedigrees claim. The concern over his age alone sheds doubt on his identification as a son of Nicholas Stephens, who was born in 1668/9, although further research would be necessary to determine whether he belongs to this family.[1563]

Whatever his origins, William Stephens was living in Albemarle Precinct by 1704, if not earlier. He appears in 1712 as a tithable in James Morgan's District of Perquimans County with four tithables in his household.[1564] He was taxed in the same district, with the same neighbors, as William Stephenson in 1713 and 1714, but he again appears in 1715 as William Stephens. In each list, the county assessed him with four tithables, as it also did in 1719. The 1720 list shows him as William Stephens, but only with three tithables.[1565]

William Stephens, brother of Edward Stephens, died testate in Beaufort County, North Carolina, in 1750. He had patented land there as early as 1735, and this tract was inherited by his son John Stephens at

---

[1560] See R. D. Tisdale, *Meet the Tisdales: Descendants of John Tisdale of Taunton, Massachusetts, 1634-1980* (Baltimore, 1981) for a general account of the Tisdale origins and migration. The Durant Family Bible, documenting Sarah's death on 16 August 1717, aged forty-eight, was owned by the University of North Carolina at the time it was extracted by J. R. B. Hathaway in *The North Carolina Historical and Genealogical Register*, Vol. 1, No. 1 (1900): 203-204.

[1561] W. P. Haun, *Old Albemarle County, North Carolina, Perquimans Precinct, Births, Marriages, Deaths, and Flesh Marks, 1659-1820*, p. 15. Sarah Durant may have been the daughter Sarah named in George Durant's will on 9 October 1688. His nephew George Durant wrote a will in Albemarle County on 25 May 1730 with John Stephens as witness. John Stephens, son of William Stephens and Sarah Durant, was born 20 December 1704 in Albemarle Precinct. This John Stephens apparently married Parthenia Sutton, daughter of Joseph and Parthenia (Durant) Sutton and granddaughter of George Durant. Hence the wives of William Stephens and John Stephens were aunt and niece.

[1562] Haun, *Ibid.*, p. 13. There is no indication of a connection, but Haun, *Albemarle Surveys*, Item 351, shows: "Albemarle Ss: To ye Surveyor Genrll. or deputy. These are & c. to Survey & lay out for William Stafford 650 acres & c. Due & c. & returne &c. Dat. the 10th day of ~~december~~ October 1695. Benj. Laker, Tho. Pollock, Tho. Harvey, Danl. Akehurst, Ffra. Tomes. Wm. Stafford, Mary his wife, Mary, Wm., John, Jane, Edw. Stafford, Arthur Stephens, Joa¹ his wife, Antho. Wherry, Mary Stephens, Joan Stephens, Jr., Jacob Stephens, ass: by Arthur Stephens." As a result, Stafford was granted 640 acres on the "West side of Majork Creeke in Couratuck prcinct....for important of Wm. Stafford his wife & five children, Arthur Stephens & his wife & 3 children, & Antho. Wherry." William and Johannah sold land in 1686. W. P. Haun, *Perquimans Co., NC, Deed Abstracts, 1681-1729*, p. 8.

[1563] Mrs. Sarah Durant, whom Stephens married, seems to have been the widow of John Durant (born 26 December 1662), who married Sarah Jooke on 9 April 1684. See Hathaway, *Register*, Vol. 1, No. 1 (1900): 268.

[1564] Caleb and Benjamin Stephens were taxed in the county in 1712 and Thomas Stephens in 1701. William's neighbors on the 1712 list -- Nathaniel Sutton, George Sutton, and Richard Whidbee -- strongly suggest that this was the same William who married Sarah Durant. George Durant's 1730 will calls Zebulon Clayton and Richard Whidbee "brothers" and appoints them executors. Joseph Sutton's 1723 will also names "brother Richard Whidbee" as executor. The will of Mrs. Deborah (Astine) Sutton Whidbee, written 8 February 1728/9, Perquimans Co., NC, names grandson Joseph Sutton and son Richard Whidbee as executors. Deborah had first married Nathaniel Sutton about 1668 in Nansemond Co., VA. Following his death, she married John Whidbee, by whom she also left issue. By July 1706, she had married Dennis Macclendon, Esquire, Justice of the Perquimans County Court. The Sutton-Whidbee-Durant-Stephens connection suggests that William Stephens who married Sarah Durant in 1704 is the same man appearing on the 1712 Perquimans tax list, for Richard Whidbee (1686/7 - 1749), son of John and Deborah Whidbee, married Sarah Durant (1695-1728), daughter of John and Sarah Jooke Durant and step-daughter of William Stephens.

[1565] 1712, 1713, 1714, 1715, 1719, and 1720 Perquimans District, NC, Tax Lists, North Carolina Department of Archives and History, Raleigh, N.C.

William's decease. It fell into newly created Pitt County when that county was formed from Beaufort. This John may be the same individual who wrote his will in Johnston County in 1777. That John was apparently quite young, for his oldest child was not yet twenty-one years of age in 1777; hence, we can surmise that John married in or after 1756 and was likely born no earlier than 1735. He appears in Johnston County deeds from 1759 to 1777. He may have had a wife Mary in 1764[1566], but, by 1777, he had married Mourning Stephens, daughter of the Edward Stephens who died in 1751. John's will, dated 17 July 1777 and witnessed by Cary Jernigan, Jacob Stevens, and Joseph Sandefur, names five minor children and a sixth, unborn child: James Stephens (the eldest child); Elizabeth Stephens; John Stephens; Needham Stephens; and Susannah Stephens.[1567]

If the statement made by Mary Stevens Walker, great-granddaughter of John and Martha Parker Stephens, is correct, then John Stephens was a son of Edmund Stephens of Johnston County, North Carolina; a grandson of Edward and Anne Stephens of Tyrell, Craven, and Johnston Counties, North Carolina; and a great-grandson of William Stephens of Perquimans County, Albemarle District, North Carolina, possibly by Mrs. Sarah Jooke Durant Stephens, whom he married in 1704. John Stephens apparently left North Carolina soon after reaching his majority and settled, apparently with means sufficient to purchase a small homestead, in southern Greene County, Georgia.[1568] It was there that John Stephens married Martha Parker on 26 December 1803 in Greene County.

There were several Parker families in the neighborhood in which John and Martha Parker Stephens lived.[1569] Based on a study of Wilkes, Greene, and Hancock County tax, estate, deed, and church records, it would appear that Martha Parker Stephens was a daughter of Major Richard Parker and his wife Ann Brewer Parker, who moved from Chatham County, North Carolina, to Wilkes County, Georgia, about 1784. Richard Parker appears in Chatham County records as early as 7 April 1752, when he obtained a warrant for 300 acres on both sides of New Hope Creek.[1570] He was active in court proceedings for the next two decades, serving as Constable in 1752.[1571] Court proceedings indicate that he was called Mr. Richard Parker, Gentleman, by 1754,[1572] and that he was a justice of the Orange County Court by June 1757 (at which time Lawrence Bankston was also a justice on the same bench).[1573] He was called Captain Richard Parker in 1763, at which time he was still a sitting justice,[1574] and Major Richard Parker afterwards. He seems to have acted as an attorney in Orange County -- although the extent of his formal legal training is unknown. At that time, no formal academies existed to train colonial lawyers, and most

---

[1566] Haun, *Johnston Deeds, 1759-1771*, Item No. 579.

[1567] See Will of John Stevens, Johnston Co., NC, 1777, North Carolina Department of Archives and History, C.R. 050.801.1-11, 1760-1822.

[1568] There were other Stephens and Stevens families in this area. Four principal groups have been identified: (1.) Moses Stephens, who moved from South Carolina to Georgia in the 1780s; (2.) John Stephens and Ann Arnett Stephens, whose family came from Maryland; (3.) Thomas Stephens, who came from Caswell Co., NC; and (4.) Nathaniel and William Duke Stephens, who came from Baltimore Co., MD.

[1569] Each of these Parker families was examined. None revealed evidence of a connection with Martha Parker Stephens. These families included the following: John and Patience Humphrey Parker, whose family is discussed by M. B. Gillis, *Gillis and Other Pioneer Families of Georgia, Second Edition, Ancestral Families of the Author* (Glenview, IL, 2000); John Parker (d. 1793, Greene Co., GA), who came to Georgia from Sussex Co., DE, and Worcester Co., MD, where his offspring were all born; Aaron Parker, who was living in Hancock Co., GA, as early as 1 July 1786, when he was a founding member of Powelton Baptist Church, and who was probably a descendant of Dr. Richard Parker, "Chirurgeon", and whose family was discussed by James M. Wright in a history of Aaron's family based on a 1908 conversation with his son John Parker (1816-1909); William Parker (by 1750 -- c. 1803), of Wilkes Co., GA, who may have been a brother or cousin of Major Richard Parker and whose offspring (Dempsey Parker, Maxey Parker, Jesse Parker, Annis Parker Mulkey, Delilah Parker, Nancy Parker, and Sampson Parker) are identified in Wilkes Co., GA, estate files; and Moses Parker (d. c. 1799, Greene Co., GA), whose wife Susannah and children Moses, James, and Elizabeth survived him. Of this large group, it seems probable that William Parker (d. 1803) and Aaron Parker were relatives of Major Richard Parker.

[1570] Bennett, *Orange Co., NC, Records*, 7: 30.

[1571] W. P. Haun, *Orange Co., NC, Court Minutes, 1752-1761* (Durham, NC, 1991), p. 17.

[1572] Haun, *Orange Co., NC, Court Minutes, 1752-1761*, 77.

[1573] Haun, *Orange Co., NC, Court Minutes, 1752-1761*, p. 224.

[1574] Hoffman, *Granville Proprietary Deeds and Surveys*, p. 787.

attorneys learned their trade by apprenticing with a more experienced lawyer. It may be that Richard Parker had apprenticed in this way, acquiring the skill that allowed him to prosper in colonial Orange County.

Given the high status Richard Parker seems to have occupied in Orange County, the probability is strong that he was the Richard Parker named as a grandson in the 1749 Chowan County, North Carolina, will of an earlier Richard Parker. The father of the younger man is not identified, but he may have been Richard Parker, Jr., who, along with siblings Daniel, Francis, Stephen, Jonathan, Jacob, Peter, Jonas, Elizabeth, Ann, Alice, and Patience, was named in the 1749 will.[1575]

The testator Richard Parker had become a justice of Chowan County in 1731 and thereafter accumulated a large estate, including lands in Nansemond County, Virginia, and more than 2,000 acres in Chowan County.[1576] The testator Richard Parker of 1749 was himself a son of Richard Parker of Nansemond County, Virginia, who was living there in 1714, and a grandson of Thomas Parker (c. 1649 - aft. 1704) of Nansemond County. The great-grandfather, another Richard Parker, noted as "Chirurgeon" for his medical practice, was born about 1629 in Cornwall, England, to an armigerous gentry family. He came to Virginia in the 1640s, following the execution of Charles I, and remained there until his death in 1680. He married twice; the name of his first wife, who was Thomas Parker's mother, is unknown, but he married as his second wife Mary Perkins, whom we have encountered in an earlier section as the widow of Nicholas Perkins of Henrico and Charles City Counties, Virginia (and the ancestor of Sarah Cates Hammack). When Parker died about 1680, he left more than 1,120 acres of land in Nansemond County to be divided among his sons Thomas, Richard, and Francis. These names would recur frequently among the Parkers of eastern North Carolina and Virginia during the following century.[1577]

Richard Parker is believed to have married Anne Brewer, daughter of Henry Brewer of Chatham County, North Carolina, and granddaughter of George and Sarah Lanier Brewer of Brunswick County, Virginia. Sarah's Lanier ancestors had moved from France to England in the sixteenth-century; there they became royal musicians and performed at the courts of Henry VIII, Elizabeth I, James I, and Charles I. Anne's grandfather John Lanier, a native of Greenwich, came to Virginia at mid-century, where he married and left a large family, including her mother Sarah. He, and his ancestry, have been discussed in a previous section dealing with the ancestry of Mary Lanier Bankston, who was a distant cousin of Anne Brewer Parker. Just when Anne Brewer married Richard Parker is a subject of speculation; Henry Brewer was in Orange County by 1755, and the marriage might have taken place soon after that date. Certainly the couple was married when Henry Brewer wrote his will in Chatham County on 2 September 1778, and Anne accompanied Richard on his move to Georgia about 1783. Chatham County, North Carolina, deeds identify Richard's wife as Anne in 1783 and show that he was involved in transactions with Daniel and Stephen Parker in 1783 and with Lewis Parker about the same time. In Georgia, Richard and Anne Parker settled in the region of Wilkes County that later became Greene and Taliaferro Counties. Richard was there by 1784 along with Lewis Parker and Sherrod Hatley, both from Chatham County. (Richard and Ann sold their last Chatham County lands in October 1784.)[1578]

The area where Richard Parker settled lay in southern Wilkes County; in his studies of Wilkes County, Georgia, tax digests, the late Frank Parker Hudson labeled the area District QQ and wrote that

> the district arbitrarily designated as District QQ was commanded by Captain Thompson
> when the tax returns were received in 1785. It was the only complete district in the area

---

[1575] Grimes, *North Carolina Wills*, p. 279.

[1576] W. S. Ray, *Index to Hathaway's Register* (Baltimore, 1956), p. 123. Grimes, *North Carolina Wills*, p. 279. A careful study of Chowan and Gates Co., NC, records suggests that there was a kinship between the Parker and Reddick families that may have influenced later Stephens-O'Neal family naming practices.

[1577] E. D. McSwain, *Some Ancestors and Descendants of Richard Parker, Chirurgeon, Born in Cornwall, 1629, Died in Virginia, Ca. 1680, and Many Other Parker Records* (Macon, GA, 1980), pp. 1-45.

[1578] Richard and Anne appear in Hudson's *Wilkes County Tax Digests*. See also Davidson, *Early Records*, 2: 31.

of Defacto Wilkes County put into Greene County in February 1786. Most of the persons making returns in this district in 1785 in Wilkes County can be found in the following districts of the 1788 Greene County Tax Digest: Captain J. Cain's, Captain Benjamin Gilbert's, and Captain Michael Gilbert's.

In Thompson's District in 1785, Richard Parker was taxed with 200 acres and two slaves. Richard Parker, Jr., paid poll tax only, and Stephen Parker paid poll tax and tax on one slave. Daniel Parker paid tax on 200 acres but owned no slaves. Lewis Parker paid tax on 200 acres but owned no slaves, and Thomas Grimes paid tax on 250 acres (including the twenty acres purchased from him by John Stephens in 1800).[1579]

No estate records for Richard Parker have been located. He was living at least as late as 1798 (and possibly as late as 1812), when he was taxed with 258 acres joining Cain in Richard Royden's District of Greene County. On 1 April 1799, he deeded to son Richard Parker, Jr., slaves and 516 acres of land on Powell's Creek, located partly in Greene County and partly in Hancock County. The land joined the property of John Cain, James Alford, and John Johnston. Although the deed -- which apparently was executed in lieu of a will -- mentions "other children," it does not identify them. [1580]

Richard and Ann Parker were charter members of Powelton Baptist Church in what is now Hancock County, Georgia. The church minutes show that Richard and Anne joined on 1 July 1786 as charter members. Anne Parker, "mother of Daniel," left the church with Daniel Parker and his wife on 5 April 1788. She was finally removed from the church roll on 6 June 1801 while her husband Richard remained a member only until 30 June 1792. Lewis Parker, who had appeared with Richard on the 1784 Wilkes County, Georgia, tax list, joined with wife Sarah on 2 June 1791 "by letter from New Hope Church, Chatham County, North Carolina"; the two remained members until 7 September 1799.[1581] Most of these individuals later appear in the records of Island Creek Baptist Church in Hancock County, where Anne Parker joined in 1802 and where Lewis and Sarah Parker joined in 1800. Since there is no record of Anne Parker's dismissal from that congregation, she probably died while a member.

The identification of Richard Parker and Anne Brewer as parents of Martha Parker Stephens is tentative. Nevertheless, strong circumstantial evidence supports that conclusion. Richard Parker and his sons lived from 1784 onwards on a tract of land adjacent to that purchased by John Stephens in 1800, three years before he married Martha Parker. John Stephens remained in the neighborhood for the rest of his life, and his estate records as well as those of Richard Parker, Jr., evidence a close association between the two families. The conclusion reached is thus that Martha Parker was probably one of the youngest children of Richard and Anne Brewer Parker and that she and her offspring maintained a close connection with her older brother, Richard Parker, Jr.

Based on a study of the Chatham County, North Carolina, Wilkes County, Georgia, Greene County, Georgia, and Hancock County, Georgia, legal records, it appears that Richard and Anne Brewer Parker had at least four sons and two daughters. Lewis Parker (by c. 1756 - c. 1824) reached adulthood before the family left North Carolina; he married wife Sarah there and appears in both deed and church records in Chatham County before the family relocated to Georgia. He wrote his will there on 20 December 1824.[1582] Daniel Parker, a Revolutionary soldier and pensioner, was born by about 1758 in Orange County, North Carolina. He was in Georgia with Richard and Lewis Parker as early as 1785 and remained there for the rest of his life. He appeared in Greene County, Georgia, deed records as late as 1815[1583]

[1579] Hudson, *Wilkes County Tax Digests*, 1: 1-20.

[1580] Greene Co., GA, Deed Book M, p. 533.

[1581] Powelton Baptist Church Records, Membership List, 1786-1852, Hancock Co., GA, Microfilm, Georgia Department of Archives and History, Morrow, GA.

[1582] Hancock Co., GA, Will Book M, 1824-1828.

[1583] Greene Co., GA, DB EE, p. 548. See also Hancock Co., GA, DB F, p. 275, DB H, pp. 97-98, DB I, pp. 158, 277; DB N, p. 252.

before moving to central Georgia, where he died in Upson County after August 1832.[1584] Stephen Parker appeared as a poll in 1784 and was thus born by about 1763; he died after 4 October 1787 but before March 1788 in Greene County, Georgia, with James Alford administrator and George Brewer and Daniel Parker purchasers at his estate sale.[1585] His son Emmanuel Parker remained in Greene County, where in 1850 he was enumerated in Household 439, near Martha Parker Stephens's daughter Saleta Stephens Broome in Household 473. Richard Parker (1761, Orange County, North Carolina - 9 April 1849, Taliaferro County, Georgia) also remained in the same community; his will in Taliaferro County mentioned "land near his father's old house," indicating that Richard Parker's land was then a part of Taliaferro County as well.[1586]

Richard Parker, Jr., appeared regularly in Taliaferro County tax digests; in 1835, he paid tax on the 516-acre tract deeded him by his father as well as on sixteen slaves. Richard's will (written 6 January 1848) named several children, including Bethena Parker Wilson. A widow, Bethena soon remarried to Isaac Moore, whose sister Nancy Moore had married Sarah O'Neal Jordan's son Edmund. When Richard Parker's estate sale was held on 11 December 1849, several members of the Stephens-O'Neal family purchased items. Among these individuals were James O'Neal, Joseph O'Neal, William O'Neal, and Leroy Broome (husband of Saleta Stephens).[1587] Among the daughters of Richard and Anne Brewer Parker, Polly married Charles Simmons in Greene County in 1790 with a voucher signed by Richard Parker. Martha Parker -- who according to census records was probably born about 1783 -- married John Stephens on 26 December 1803.[1588]

As previously noted, John Stephens purchased twenty acres in Greene County on 7 March 1800 from William Allen, a neighbor of Richard Parker as per the 1798 Greene County tax digest.[1589] Later, on 27 August 1801, Stephens paid $250 for 100 acres sold by Thomas Grimes;[1590] as early as 1785, Grimes had appeared adjacent Richard, Lewis, Stephen, and Daniel Parker in that portion of southwestern Wilkes County which in 1786 became Greene County. John Stephens was taxed with 150 acres and three slaves in 1801 and with 120 acres in Captain Day's District in 1802. He purchased another ninety-six acres from William Allen, joining Allen's Branch and Grimes's line, on 4 January 1803,[1591] and another seventy acres from William Stewart on 14 March 1804.[1592] He paid Allen $200 and Stewart $130 for a combined total of 166 acres.

The 1804 Greene County, Georgia, tax digest showed him with 216 acres joining Grimes on the Ogeechee River; he was taxed with the same property in 1805 and with 271 acres joining Grimes on the Ogeechee in 1806. On 14 March 1806, Stephens sold seventy acres on the Ogeechee to Francis Hill for $130.[1593] Greene County's 1807 digest, however, showed him still with 271 acres and no slaves. He owned the same land in 1808, at which time he also paid tax on one slave; Edmund Stevens, who had first appeared as a poll in a neighboring district in 1806 (and who was probably John Stephens' brother), was shown as a poll immediately following John Stephens in this digest. On 24 November 1809, John

---

[1584] Note that the Upson County pension record and the Powelton Church records are significant in identifying Anne Brewer as Daniel's mother. If Daniel was seventy-three in 1832, then Anne Brewer must have married Richard Parker by 1758. See C. W. Nottingham and E. Hannah, *History of Upson County, Georgia* (Macon, GA, 1930), p. 166. See also Hancock Co., GA, DB D, pp. 47, 432.

[1585] Greene Co., GA, Miscellaneous Records, Book A, 1787-1801, pp. 21, 23. See also Greene Co., GA, Wills, 1786-1877, p. 4.

[1586] Inventories, Appraisals, Sales, and Divisions of Estates, Book B, 1834-1850, pp. 481-482, 497-499, 516-519; Taliaferro Co., GA, Will Book A, pp. 201-203. See also Hancock Co., GA, DB I, pp. 421-423, references which could pertain to either Richard, Jr., or Richard, Sr.

[1587] Taliaferro Co., GA, Inventories, Appraisals, Sales, and Divisions of Estates, Book B, 1834-1850, pp. 516-519.

[1588] S. E. Lucas, *Some Georgia County Records* (7 vols., Easley, SC, 1977-), 2: 360-365.

[1589] Turner, *Greene Co., GA, Deeds,* p. 357, citing Greene Co., GA, DB AA, 624.

[1590] Turner, *Greene Co., GA, Deeds,* p. 356, citing Greene Co., GA, DB AA, p. 619.

[1591] Turner, *Greene Co., GA, Deeds,* p. 395, citing Greene Co., GA, DB AA, p. 83.

[1592] Greene Co., GA, DB BB, p. 82.

[1593] Greene Co., GA, DB EE, p. 133.

Stephens purchased fifty-five acres for $125 from Mary Goss, widow of Charles Goss; Edmund Stephens witnessed the deed, and the following year he married the widow Mary Goss.[1594]

On the same day that he purchased land from Mary Goss, John Stephens also purchased 121 acres (for $425) from Thomas Cheves of Greene County.[1595] Adam Hunter's District in the 1810 tax digest showed him with 392 acres on the Ogeechee joining Grimes's land; Stephen Parker's name appears next to that of John Stephens, with Parker being taxed with 120 acres joining James Alford's land. John Stephens still owned 392 acres in 1811 (and no slaves); by 1812, he was shown with the same amount of land but again with one slave. The 1813, 1814, and 1815 digests all showed him with 392 acres and one slave; digests are missing from 1816 to 1821. When the next surviving digest was taken in 1822, John Stephens was taxed still with 392 acres of land, but by this point he owned eleven slaves -- a substantial increase in less than a decade.[1596]

The large number of slaves owned by John Stephens in 1820 indicates that he was on his way to becoming a prosperous planter in Greene County. On 2 August 1823, following the marriage of his eldest daughter Mary to Wooten O'Neal, he deeded to O'Neal, in consideration of $150, a thirty-five acre tract on the South Ogeechee.[1597] On the same day, he also gifted Wooten O'Neal a 100-acre tract on the south fork of the Ogeechee.[1598] Thomas Johnson and Ptolemey Jernigan, whose family also hailed from Johnston County, witnessed the deed.[1599]

From this point onwards, John Stephens made frequent real estate transactions in Greene County. He purchased land from Richard Asbury in 1829, from his son Reddick Stephens in 1834, from Peter C. Johnson in 1838, from Noram and Findley in 1838, and from his son-in-law Henry Stevens in 1841.[1600] In 1837, he conveyed to his daughter Saleta Broom, wife of Leroy Broom, 215 acres on the Ogeechee River,[1601] and in 1841 he conveyed to daughter Matilda Stevens two slaves.[1602] With more than 300 acres purchased and only 215 acres conveyed during these years, Stephens increased his net holdings by more than eighty acres.

John Stephens died in Greene County on 17 November 1852; he was buried in a cemetery on his farm, three miles east of White Plains and across from the present Rock Hill Church. Of at least ten graves in the cemetery, John Stephens's marker is the only legible one:

> John Stephens, late of Greene County, Georgia, who departed this life on the 17th of November 1852 aged 71 years, 11 months.[1603]

John and Martha Parker Stephens had been married for nearly fifty years at this point; months before John's death, his son Jesse Stephens preceded him to the grave. On 21 February 1852, John applied for

---

[1594] Turner, *Greene Co., GA, Deeds*, p. 527, citing Greene Co., GA, DB CC, p. 355.

[1595] Turner, *Greene Co., GA, Deeds*, p. 527, citing Greene Co., GA, DB CC, 354,

[1596] Note that the 1820 census also showed him with eleven slaves. How did he obtain them? Perhaps he inherited them from Richard Parker or a Stephens relative between 1814 and 1820?

[1597] Greene Co., GA, DB HH, pp. 386-387.

[1598] Greene Co., GA, DB HH, p. 387.

[1599] Note that Ptolemy Jernigan had in 1822 bought all of Edmond Stevens's property on the Ogeechee. This association with Ptolemy Jernigan may be significant. Jacob Stephens of Johnston Co., NC, married Belinda Jernigan, a daughter of Henry and Ann Jernigan of Bertie Co., NC, and Johnston Co., NC. Ptolemy Jernigan (born about 1795) was a son of Hardy Jernigan (1766-1836) and a grandson of Needham Jernigan (d. 1814, Hancock Co., GA). Needham Jernigan was a son of Henry and Ann Jernigan. Thus, Ptolemy was a relative of Belinda Jernigan Stephens and of the Johnston Jernigans who appear in many records with the Stephens family there.

[1600] Greene Co., GA, DB KK, p. 298, and DB MM, pp. 12, 257, 320.

[1601] Greene Co., GA, DB MM, p. 129.

[1602] Greene Co., GA, DB NN, p. 176.

[1603] Stephens may have died as a result of an infected tooth. His administrators paid Dr. R. S. Callaway for visits from November 9 to November 16, 1852. Among the charges was one for a tooth extraction on 9 November. See Greene Co., GA, Ordinary Estate Records, Unbound, 1790-1943, James Stewart - Amy Stringfellow.

guardianship of his orphaned grandchildren, John H. and Martha Stephens.[1604] Following John's death, his son-in-law Henry Stevens succeeded him as guardian for Jesse Stephens's minor children[1605] and on 6 December 1852, with Wooten O'Neal, obtained temporary Letters of Administration on the estate of John Stephens.[1606] Later, on 10 January 1853, with Leroy Broome as security, Henry Stevens applied for permanent Letters of Administration on his father-in-law's estate.[1607]

When the Inventory and Appraisement of John Stephens was entered into court two days later, it revealed that Stephens owned twelve slaves valued altogether at $5,625. Stephens also owned horses, hogs, cattle, and other livestock worth $700. The appraisement of his household furnishings reveals that Stephens lived a comfortable existence. His home included a side board, a book case and books, six beds and bed furniture, eight windsor chairs, five other chairs, a desk, a waiter, two looking glasses, a set of china, twelve dozen silver spoons, a pine table, a folding table, a chest, a clock, bed linen, a candle stand, and a number of other household objects. Stephens also owned a quilted saddle worth $12.50 and a pleasure carriage worth $50. His agricultural productivity no doubt benefited from the threshing machine, wheat fan, and two cotton gins he owned, valued altogether at more than $120. Likewise, Stephens's household accounts reveal that, like many wealthy planters, he loaned money to friends, neighbors, and kin. At his death, he held notes on son-in-law Henry Stevens for $425, on son-in-law Leroy Broom for $115, on son John W. Stephens for $350, on Elisha Hunter for $100, and on Isaac Moore (who soon afterwards married Bethena Parker Wilson, daughter of Richard Parker, Jr.) for $8. Stephens' twelve slaves sold for $6,425 on 4 January 1854, and 400 acres of his land sold at the same time for $2,010.[1608]

Martha Parker Stephens was still living on 23 January 1853, when she purchased items worth more than $1400 from her husband's estate sale. She had died by 28 May 1853, however, when John W. and Reddick Stephens advertised the sale of her estate in Greene County.[1609]

John and Martha Parker Stephens reared six children in Greene County, a comparatively small family for the times in which they lived. They were the parents of John W. Stephens (25 February 1820 - 10 November 1861, Nashville, Davidson County, Tennessee, CSA), who married Camilla Ann Hill (1831-1910) in Harris County, Georgia, in 1845 and moved to Smith County, Mississippi, about 1855;[1610] Reddick Stephens (c. 1808 - after 1860, Tallapoosa County, Alabama), who married Olive Acree on 7 February 1827 in Taliaferro County; Mary Stephens, who married Wooten O'Neal; Saleta Stephens (15 January 1815 - 30 April 1889), who married Leroy Broome and moved to Carroll County, Georgia, between 1850 and 1860;[1611] Jesse Stephens (c. 1826 -- c. 1852), who married Mary Irby and predeceased his parents; and Matilda Stephens (27 August 1823 - 9 September 1863), who married Henry Stevens (1813 - 1883) in Greene County in 1839.

The family of Henry Stevens, husband of Matilda Stephens, was unrelated to that of his wife; in fact, given the migration routes which brought most settlers into Georgia, their path of migration differed significantly from those of most other settlers. Henry Stevens, the husband of Matilda Stephens, was born in Duroe, Cornwall, England, in 1813, and came to Georgia with his parents Walter and Elizabeth Libby Stevens and several siblings about 1831. In 1854, Henry purchased a 3,000-acre tract of timber located

---

[1604] T. Evans, *Greene Co., GA, Newspaper Clippings, 1852-1873* (2 vols., Savannah, 1995), 1: 2.

[1605] Evans, *Clippings*, 1: 46.

[1606] See Greene Co., GA, Ordinary Estate Records, Unbound, 1790-1943, James Stewart - Amy Stringfellow.

[1607] See Greene Co., GA, Ordinary Estate Records, Unbound, 1790-1943, James Stewart - Amy Stringfellow.

[1608] Apart from the workings of his plantation, the estate records reveal something of Stephens' religious inclination as well. On 11 March 1853, Isaac A. Williams, Chair of the Building Committee, wrote a receipt to Stephens's estate for $50 donated towards the building of a Methodist Church at Hasting's Camp Ground. See Greene Co., GA, Ordinary Estate Records, Unbound, 1790-1943, James Stewart - Amy Stringfellow.

[1609] Evans, *Clippings*, 1: 73, 82, 93.

[1610] Their daughter Georgia Emma Mariah Stephens (1857-1925) married her cousin William Parks Stevens.

[1611] Leroy Broome was a son of Solomon Broome and Elizabeth Mims. His brother Moses Broome married Loediski Pulaski Harrison (1810-1898), daughter of Revolutionary soldier Joseph Harrison. Anne Broome, another sibling, married William O'Neal. See Carroll County Heritage Book Committee, *The Heritage of Carroll Co., GA, 1826-2001* (Waynesville, NC, 2002), p. 154.

ten miles south of Milledgeville in Baldwin County; there he established a saw mill plant and began work in the lumber business. On the same land was a valuable deposit of fire clay, and, capitalizing on this, he founded the Clay Manufacturing Company, which was later extended by his sons Walter Crawford and John Henry Stevens. During the War Between the States, Stevens-Davis records, the company supplied the Confederate government with many needed items; as a result, Sherman completely destroyed the plant on his march through Georgia to the sea.

After the war, Henry Stevens, "guided by unerring sagacity, with energy and practical business qualifications," rebuilt the mills and potteries and successfully resumed business. He became wealthy and successful, passing to his offspring a legacy of financial stewardship and economic achievement.

Henry Stevens was a devout Methodist and a steward and trustee of the church; near his home, he erected a "Preachers Home" to house itinerant ministers serving the district churches. His personal integrity was well known, and "As honest as Henry Stevens" became a common phrase throughout middle Georgia. Henry Stevens retired from business in 1876, settling the company on his sons Walter Crawford and John Henry, who with their uncle William Stevens later formed Stevens Brothers and Company.

In the series *Memoirs of Georgia*, a lengthy biography of Henry Stevens appeared:[1612]

> Henry Stevens, founder of the great 'pottery' establishment in Baldwin County (about ten miles from Milledgeville), Georgia, was a son of Walter and Elizabeth Stevens, and was born in Cornwall, England, May 21, 1813. Commencing to work in a pottery when quite young, by the time he was eighteen years of age, he had become quite proficient. On reaching that age, he engaged as a sailor on a merchant vessel sailing between Liverpool and New York, and followed a sailor's life five years. When twenty-three years of age, he came to Augusta, Georgia, and accepted a position as foreman of hands at work grading, laying ties, rails, etc., on the Georgia railway, then being built between Augusta and Union Point. When that work was completed, he was appointed a conductor, and continued as such a number of years. He next engaged in the saw-mill business in Greene County, Georgia, and selling and erecting the "page mill," a double circular saw, which being the first introduced into that part of the state, excited no little curiosity and interest. He had very great success both in his saw-milling business and selling and erecting mills throughout middle Georgia, continuing until 1854. That year he bought a large tract of timber land -- virgin forest -- ten miles south of Milledgeville, in Baldwin County, established a saw-mill plant, and launched out extensively in the lumber business. He continued it with phenomenal success until 1871. On the land he had purchased was an extensive and very valuable deposit of fireclay, and Mr. Stevens utilized and profited by his early training by beginning the manufacture of sewer pipe, a great variety of pottery, and stone-ware. This enterprise, like his other ventures, proved to be an extraordinary success from the start. Being the only works of the kind in the south, the output having been excellent at the beginning and improved as experience was gained and facilities added, and the management having been exceptionally able the business has grown to enormous proportions. During the war he supplied the Confederate government with many articles needed by the army, knives, shoe-pegs, and Joe Brown pipes, etc., and as a consequence, when General Sherman was "marching through Georgia," his mills were burned and his works leveled to the ground. After the surrender, he had nothing but his land, an indefinite amount of Confederate currency, and six or seven dollars in gold. He went bravely to work and rebuilt his mills, and as lumber brought good prices, he very

---

[1612] Note that this article also includes an engraving of Henry Stevens. See *Memoirs of Georgia*, 1: 274-275.

rapidly recuperated and placed his vast and varied interests on the road to present prosperity and magnitude. The products of the mills and pottery have attained a wide-spread enviable reputation, and are shipped to all parts of the South. Mr. Stevens was more solid than brilliant. Caution and carefulness were happily combined with energy and enterprise, guided by almost unerring sagacity; and added to these were practical business qualifications which guaranteed the success accomplished. Another thing -- he carried his religion with him into his business, and in his manifold and varied business transactions, with all classes of people, he never lost sight of his Christian obligations and duties. There was always a hearty welcome, a bed in his house, a place and a plate at his table, and money in his palm for the preacher of the gospel of peace. Though remarkably successful in all his worldly pursuits, Christian principle and Christian liberality were a dominant characteristic of his every-day life. An interesting incident which occurred just after the war forcibly illustrates this: A Methodist preacher stopped over night at his house, yet midst the ruins left by Sherman's devastating march. During their conversation the preacher's absolute destitution -- want at his home -- was made apparent to Mr. Stevens. As already stated, all, and the only, good money he had, was six or seven dollars in gold, and this, true to the generous impulses of his heart, and his profound sense of Christian obligation, he freely gave to the preacher. In 1876, he sold out to his sons, and retired to the quiet enjoyment of a home hallowed by Christian practice, faith, and hope.

In discussing the marriage of Henry Stevens, *Memoirs* adds that

> Mr. Stevens was happily married in Greene County, in 1837, to Miss Matilda, daughter of John and Martha Stevens, formerly of North Carolina and descendants of early settlers of that state. Her parents started in life poor, but by hard work, close economy, and good management, accumulated a small fortune. He died about 1850, and his widow died about 1860.

Although it is incorrect concerning the dates, the *Memoirs* article otherwise corresponds well with the known facts about John and Martha Parker Stephens and their families.[1613]

Of the eight children born to Henry and Matilda Stephens Stevens, Walter Crawford Stevens (1845-1916) helped rebuild the Stevens Pottery following the Civil War. Then, in 1876, he joined with his uncle William Stevens and established Stevens Brothers and Company, operating lumbering and farm interests in addition to the manufacture of clay products. He was first president of the Citizens National Bank, Macon, Georgia, and was founder and vice president of H. Stevens Sons' Company in Macon. He founded the Oconee Brick and Tile Company of Milledgeville, Georgia. A staunch Methodist, he and his brother John Henry Stevens built Matilda Chapel Methodist Church in Baldwin County in memory of their mother. Marie Stevens Walker Wood (1883 --), author of *Stevens-Davis and Allied Families*, was his second child and younger daughter. It was in this volume that Mrs. Wood indicated that John Stephens had come to Georgia from Wake County, North Carolina, and that he was a son of Edmund and Mary Stephens of North Carolina.[1614]

At the time of the 1850 Greene County, Georgia, Census, Wooten and Mary Stephens O'Neal were living in Greene County's Household 506, near John and Martha Parker Stephens in Household 334. Leroy and Saleta Broome were in Household 479, and Emanuel and Polly Austin Parker were in Household 439. At the time of the 1850 census, James Augustus O'Neal, son of Wooten and Mary

---

[1613] Ibid.

[1614] See Wood, *Stevens-Davis and Allied Families*, esp. pp. 1-40, for extensive data on the ancestors and descendants of Henry Stevens.

Stephens O'Neal, had already married and was living independently in Household 507. Another son, Wooten, Jr., was living in Household 330, and John O'Neal, the eldest son, was in Household 508. Sarah O'Neal Stevens Stewart and her husband Simeon Henry Stewart were living near her grandparents in Household 328. Unmarried O'Neal children then living at home with Wooten and Mary were Joshua, age sixteen; Martha, age thirteen; Harrison, age twelve; William, age eight; and Albert, age three.[1615]

Wooten and Mary Stephens O'Neal were the parents of: John O'Neal (25 January 1821 - 10 August 1902, Greene County, Georgia), who married Charlotte Hancock (1824-1910); James Augustus O'Neal (1823-1862), who married Georgia Ann Virginia Stewart; Sarah Ann O'Neal (1826-1870), who married first Walter Stevens (1815-1843) and second Simeon Henry Stewart; Elizabeth O'Neal (1829 -), who married George Hancock in Greene County in 1847; Wooten O'Neal, Jr. (c. 1825/30 - after 1870), who married Julia Ellen Stewart (1830 - after 1870) in Tallapoosa County, Alabama, in 1847; Joshua O'Neal (29 July 1834 - 26 September 1927, Fulton County, Georgia), who married Sarah Jane Davis on 14 October 1852 in Greene County, Georgia; Martha O'Neal (1837 -), who married Leroy W. Davis and Abner T. Jones; Horace Harrison O'Neal (1839 - after 7 May 1920, Greene County, Georgia), who married Jane Williams on 9 October 1860 in Greene County, Georgia; William R. O'Neal (1842-1862), who died in the Confederate Army; and Albert Quinea O'Neal (9 May 1847, Greene County, Georgia - 1 June 1911, Greene County, Georgia), who married Emily C. Davis on 3 November 1868 in Greene County.[1616]

In the next generation, James Augustus O'Neal (1823, Greene County, Georgia -- 30 April 1862) was the second son of Wooten O'Neal and Mary Stephens. He married Georgia Ann Virginia Stewart on 12 December 1843 in Greene County, Georgia. The couple lived in Greene County until about 1851, when they relocated to Tallapoosa County, Alabama, where members of the O'Neal, Stewart, and Stephens families were then living. About 1855, they left Alabama, probably with John W. and Camilla Hill Stephens, settling in Smith County, Mississippi, where both families were enumerated at the time of the 1860 census.[1617] At that time, James Augustus O'Neal was working as a farm laborer and owned personal property valued at $175; his uncle John W. Stephens owned land worth $3,200 and slaves and other personal property valued at $10,970. Since Stephens was enumerated in Household 59 and O'Neal in Household 60, it seems likely that James Augustus O'Neal was working as a laborer on his uncle's farm.[1618]

The marriage of James Augustus O'Neal to Georgia Ann Virginia Stewart in 1847 was one of three significant O'Neal-Stewart marriages. Sarah Ann O'Neal Stevens, sister of James, married Simeon Henry Stewart in Taliaferro County on 18 October 1844.[1619] Wooten O'Neal, Jr., brother of James and Sarah, married Judith Ellen Stewart on 11 November 1847 in Tallapoosa County, Alabama. Family tradition indicates that Georgia Ann Virginia Stewart and Simeon Henry Stewart were siblings; Judith Ellen was probably another sister as well.[1620]

It is believed that Georgia Ann Virginia Stewart O'Neal and Simeon Henry Stewart were children of William Stewart (18 October 1782, Wilkes County, Georgia - after 1850, Taliaferro County, Georgia). William may have married Rachel Moore on 19 June 1826 in Warren County, Georgia, just across the Taliaferro County line. William Stewart seems to have left Taliaferro County during the 1820s and not to have returned until the middle 1830s, possibly after the death of his wife. He was not shown in Henry Stewart's household at the time of the 1827 Taliaferro County militia census[1621] and, based on his profile

[1615] 1850 Greene Co., GA, Census, pp. 95-105.

[1616] 1850 Greene Co., GA, Census, pp. 95-105; research notes of Anne Martin Haigler, Birmingham, AL, 2004.

[1617] 1850 Greene Co., GA, Census, p. 105; 1860 Smith Co., MS, Census, p. 241.

[1618] 1860 Smith Co., MS, Census, p. 241.

[1619] Her first husband, Walter Stevens, was a brother of Henry Stevens, who married her aunt Matilda Stephens.

[1620] Anne Martin Haigler recorded this tradition while interviewing family members in Greene and Taliaferro Counties, Georgia, and Mississippi, in the 1950s.

[1621] Although males the right age to be William F. Stewart, Matthew Stewart, and Reuben H. Stewart were shown.

in 1840, he does not fit to have been in Henry's household in 1830. He did not register for the 1832 Gold Lottery in Georgia Militia District 607 along with Henry, Reuben H., and Matthew Stewart, and he does not appear in the 1832, 1833, or 1834 digests for Taliaferro County. He may be the William shown with forty acres in Cherokee County in the 1835 and 1836 digests, although that man could possibly be William F. Stewart. Wherever he was between 1827 and 1834, William Stewart was living in Taliaferro County in 1840, at which time he was head of a household consisting of three teenage children. The family included one male, aged 15-20, and two females, one aged 10-15 and one aged 15-20. These children were the correct age to have been Simeon Henry Stewart, Georgia Ann Virginia Stewart, and Judith Ellen Stewart.[1622]

At the time of the 1850 census, William Stewart gave his age as sixty-two years. His household included Frances Stewart, age twenty-three, and Lucy Ann Stewart, age four. Frances was probably William's second wife. William had apparently died by 1860, when his family appeared in Taliaferro County. Frances was shown as Louisa Stewart, age thirty-seven, and her household included Lucy A., age fourteen; Narcissa, age eight; Matthew, age six; H. J., age four; and Ophelia, age two, all natives of Georgia. If Ophelia were William's youngest child, it would appear that he died between 1857 and 1860.[1623]

William Stewart was a son of Henry Stewart and wife Lucy, who moved from Mecklenburg County, North Carolina, to Greene County, Georgia, following the American Revolution. Born 29 January 1759 in Anson County, Henry Stewart was a son of Matthew Stewart (1720-1808)[1624] and Elizabeth McCall, natives of Scotland and Northern Ireland who immigrated to Pennsylvania in the early eighteenth-century.[1625] About 1783, Henry and Lucy Stewart moved from Mecklenburg County, North Carolina, to Wilkes County, Georgia. They appear in Greene County soon after the new county was created in 1786, being among the first settlers of the Bethany community there.[1626] By 1788, Henry was taxed in Greene

---

[1622] 1840 Taliaferro Co., GA, Census, p. 256.

[1623] 1850 Taliaferro Co., GA, Census, p. 321. Louisa and family were in HH 247, next door to William F., Matthew, and Eleanor in HH 248. See 1860 Taliaferro Co., GA, Census, p. 732.

[1624] Mecklenburg Co., NC, Will Book F, p. 631.

[1625] Elizabeth McCall Stewart is said to have been a sister of James McCall of Ireland, Pennsylvania, and North Carolina, who married Janet Harris. Some early publications claimed, incorrectly, that she was a daughter of James McCall and Janet Harris. K. S. McCall, *A Study of One McCall Family in the Nineteenth Century: Georgia, Mississippi, Louisiana, and Texas* (1979) briefly discusses McCall migration from Ulster to Pennsylvania to North Carolina and into Greene, Jones, and Baldwin Counties, Georgia, but does not include specific mention of Elizabeth McCall Stewart. Of interest is the McCall migration into Mississippi territory between 1790 and 1810, however.

Likewise, E. T. McCall, *McCall-Tidwell and Allied Families* (Atlanta, 1931) discusses this same migration but focuses upon the descendants of Francis McCall of Pennsylvania, Virginia, and North Carolina. McCall states that the family were Scots-Irish Presbyterians who came to America about 1730; she identifies references to Francis McCall in the Cumberland Valley of Pennsylvania between 1737 and 1745, when he was a member of Middle Springs Presbyterian Church. He in 1746 moved to the New River settlement in Southwest Virginia and after Indian raids proceeded to North Carolina, where he settled in that portion of Anson County that became Salisbury District, Mecklenburg County. By 1758 he was obtaining lands in South Carolina but continued to appear in North Carolina until his death there in 1794. Offspring are given as: Charles McCall; George McCall; Francis McCall, Jr.; Thomas McCall, who married Rachel, daughter of James McCall; Joseph McCall; Jean McCall Porter; Elizabeth McCall, wife of Thomas Walker; Mary McCall, wife of John Gibbes; and Iber McCall, wife of Mikel Secrest.

McCall also discusses James Harris, who settled in Pennsylvania but died in Virginia along the New River, allegedly aged 110 years (McCall, *McCall*, p. 585). His daughter Janet married James McCall, and other daughters Martha and Isabelle married James Wylie and Robert Robinson.

By 1756 James McCall and wife Janet (Harris) McCall were in Anson Co., NC. His offspring included James McCall, who married Elizabeth McCall; Hugh McCall; Thomas McCall, who married Jane Harris; Rachel McCall, who married Thomas McCall; Agnes McCall, who married Elias Alexander; William McCall, who married Elizabeth Stewart, daughter of Matthew Stewart; and Jane McCall, who married Robert Harris.

[1626] Williams, *History of Greene Co., GA*, p. 106.

County with 300 acres on Richland Creek, while James Stewart -- probably Henry's brother of the same name -- was taxed with 500 acres on the Ogeechee River.[1627]

Henry Stewart was a modest farmer in Greene and Taliaferro Counties; he never achieved great wealth, but for most of his life he seems to have been self-sufficient and independent. In 1818, he sold 114 acres[1628] but kept the remainder of his tract; when he was taxed in Taliaferro County in 1832, he still owned 250 acres on the Ogeechee River joining the Daniel family and granted to himself. His son Matthew owned 202.5 acres in Houston County, and his son Reuben owned 202.5 acres in Muscogee County, both tracts that had been drawn in Georgia land lotteries. Both men were taxed with the same tracts in 1833, 1834 (although by 1834 Reuben owned only forty acres), 1835, and 1836.[1629] About this time, on 18 July 1836, Henry Stewart of Taliaferro County applied for a federal pension based on his service during the American Revolution. Stewart gave a brief account of his life, military service, and subsequent migrations:

> I entered the War of the Revolution in the early part of the month of August Seventeen Hundred and Seventy six (1776) in the County of Mecklenburg, North Carolina, under Gen. Rutherford -- against the Cherokee Indians my Captain's name was Charles Polk and the name of my Col. was Adam Alexander there was a draft at the time but I volunteered and was in constant service for the time of (3) three months -- there was during the time no general battle but for great skirmishes between our men and the Indians -- We burnt the Tilico Hiwassa & Valley Towns in Tennessee -- These were Indian Towns -- After which we returned home - The service was volunteer - In the year Seventeen Hundred and Eighty (I think it was about I am not so sure of the correctness of this date as the other) I again volunteered under Captain McCurdy for a term of (3) months and continued under him for about two or three weeks and was then transferred with a number of our company to the command of Captain Thomas Ray -- and continued under his command until he with a detachment of his company were defeated by the Tories near Rocky River - which defeat being attributed to the bad conduct of Captain Ray -- he resigned -- and Mathew Stewart my father was made captain in his stead and under whom I completed the term of three months -- this was also volunteer service as before stated -- After which I returned home but at the whole country was in a state of alarm and Cornwallis was then in the neighborhood of Charlotte -- I immediately volunteered again under Captain Wiley for no particular time -- Gen. Davison was then our commanding officer -- we were stationed at the cross roads about fifteen miles below Charlotte -- while Gen. Davison with the main body of the army went in pursuit of Cornwallis - but he made his escape over Catawba River - the place I was garrisoned att was the cross roads where the road from Cheraw to Charlotte & from Camden to Salisbury crossed each other -- After the retreat of Cornwallis Gen. Green with the continental forces came in the vicinity, and we were discharged after being in constant service for one month -- Three or four months after this while Gen. Green was marching towards Camden I again volunteered under Captain Thomas Shelby, and marched to Congaree River to a place called "Fridays [---]" where little Town called Granly where the British were forted -- and laid siege to the fort until Gen. Green sent us Col. Lee with his regiment with a six pounder -- and the British surrender the port -- I think there was about (250) two & fifty British that surrendered at that time with a number of Tories -- Our Col. at this place was named William Polk. Gen. Sumpter was the commanding

---

[1627] 1788 Greene Co., GA, Tax Digest, Georgia Department of Archives and History, Morrow, GA. All subsequent references to taxed property in Greene County are from the relevant digest in the Georgia Department of Archives and History.

[1628] Greene Co., GA, DB HH, p. 19.

[1629] 1833-1836 Taliaferro Co., GA, Tax Digests, Georgia Department of Archives and History, Morrow, GA.

officer. In this service I was engaged at least two months -- which lasted until the Battle of Eutaw Springs -- where we were all discharged -- making in all a term of service of (9) nine months -- I was acquainted with Gen. Green Sumpter, Rutherford, and Davidson -- I have no documentary evidence by which I can establish this service that I know of -- Mr. James Finley was with me during some of the service whose affidavit I here show to that effect -- who now lives in the county of Greene in said state -- and who would have been here to state the same in court had not his great feebleness and inability prevented his attendance -- I do hereby relinquish every claim whatever to a pension or annuity on account of said services, except the present and do declare that my name is not on the pension roll of the Agency of any state -- and in answer to the questions propounded by the court according to the regulations of the War Department -- he says as follows -- to the first -- He says -- I was born in the county of Anson, now Mecklenburg, North Carolina in the year seventeen Hundred & fifty nine -- according to the record of my father -- To the second he says -- I have a record of my age at home in my Bible copied exactly from the record in my fathers Bible - To the third he says - I was living in Mecklenburg County North Carolina -- Since the revolution I moved to Georgia where I now live -- it was then Wilkes County -- afterwards Greene -- and now Taliaferro -- by changes being made in the line of counties and the formation of new counties -- To fourth -- He says all my service was volunteer service under Gen. Rutherford, Gen. Davidson and Gen. Sumpter - And as to the circumstance of his service I refer to the statement above made -- To sixth - I do not Recollect that I ever got a written discharge -- To seventh -- He says I refer to Williamson Bird clergyman & Jonathan Davis Sworn to and Subscribed the day and year aforesaid.[1630]

Williamson Bird, on 16 January 1837, gave a statement that

for as I ever knew or heard he has been an orderly and worthy member of the Presbyterian Church -- that his character is unimpeachable -- and he is and has always been considered in the sphere of his acquaintance as having been a Revolutionary soldier -- and that I should not feel the slightest hesitancy in giving the fullest belief to whatever the old gentleman (who now indeed seems very old and decrepit) should or might solemnly swear or affirm.[1631]

On 7 February 1837, Stewart was awarded a pension at a rate of $30 per year. Although "very old and decrepit," as Reverend Bird noted, Henry would live another twenty years, dying at nearly one hundred years of age.[1632]

Henry Stewart was head of household in Taliaferro County in 1830, 1840, and 1850, at which time he was ninety-one years of age and living with his grandson, William F. Stewart, and his daughter Ellen Stewart.[1633]

Henry Stewart married Lucy, whose maiden name may have been Lucy Newell. They were the parents of four sons and one daughter:[1634] William Stewart (18 October 1782 - after 1850, Taliaferro County, Georgia); Ellen Stewart (1784 - after 1860, Taliaferro County, Georgia); Matthew Stewart (20 September 1786, Greene County, Georgia -- after 1860, Taliaferro County, Georgia); John Stewart (14

[1630] Revolutionary War Pension Application of Henry Stewart, S31,982, The National Archives, Washington, D.C., Microfilm Series 805, Roll 772.

[1631] Ibid.

[1632] Ibid.

[1633] 1830 Taliaferro Co., GA, Census, p. 363; 1840 Taliaferro Co., GA, Census, p. 256; 1850 Taliaferro Co., GA, Census, p. 332.

[1634] Stewart's offspring are identified in *Stewart Clan Magazine*, F (1949); 227.

June 1791 --); James Stewart (25 December 1795, Greene County, Georgia -- c. 1826, Greene County, Georgia), who married Margaret Nelson; Samuel Stewart (c. 1797, Greene County, Georgia --), who is said to have died young; and Reuben H. Stewart (3 September 1804 -- 1887, Greene County, Georgia), who married Polly Derby and Penelope Brantley.[1635]

Ties between the Stewart and O'Neal families extended back in time at least a generation before Georgia Ann Virginia Stewart married James Augustus O'Neal. As early as 1826, Henry Stewart, Wooten O'Neal, and Matthew Stewart entered together into a bond when Henry Stewart was appointed administrator of the estate of his son James Stewart.[1636] There was no known kinship between the two families at that point, but Stewart and O'Neal were neighbors and continued to be so for several years. Taliaferro County digests throughout the 1830s show that Wooten O'Neal and Henry Stewart both owned

---

[1635] Descendants of Simeon H. Stewart claim that he was a son of James C. Stewart and Margaret Nelson Stewart. Other descendants of James C. Stewart claim that he married Margaret Seawright Corry (18 April 1796, Washington or Greene Co., GA -- 9 January 1890, Carroll Co., GA), daughter of Robert Corry and Jane Seawright, on 18 April 1816 in Greene Co., GA. No proof that Simeon was James and Margaret's son has been discovered. James Stewart died about 1826 in Greene County with Henry Stewart as administrator. His widow Margaret Nelson Stewart apparently married (2) 27 April 1836, Hancock Co., GA, *another* James Stewart. She was enumerated as Margaret Stewart in Heard Co., GA, in 1840 (where another James and Margaret Stewart had also settled), and she was enumerated in Carroll Co., GA, 1850-1870, with her daughter Eliza Brown. She is buried in the Brown family cemetery in Carroll County.

Alexander Corry lived near Margaret Stewart in Heard Co., GA, in 1840, and William A. Corry was mentioned in James Stewart's estate records. Estate records of James Stewart reveal that he had three children who were in school by 1827. A receipt dated 28 December 1827 identifies Robert, James, and Eliza as James's offspring (James Stewart Loose Estate File, Greene Co., GA). James's widow Margaret Stuart was living in Greene County in 1830, near Wooten O'Neal. Her household consisted of one male aged 5-10, 2 males aged 10-15, one female aged 0-5, and one female aged 10-15. In 1832, the orphans of James Stewart of Greene County drew LL 97, LD 10, 3rd Section, in what is today Murray County. Margaret was head of household in Heard County in 1840 with one male aged 15-20, two males aged 20-30, and two females aged 15-20. The 1850 and 1860 census reports indicate that her daughter Eliza Stewart Brown was born about 1820/21. Of the five children indicated by the 1830 and 1840 census reports, four are identified: Robert Stewart (born 1816/20); James Stewart (born 1816/20); Eliza Stewart Brown (born about 1821); Mary Angeline Stewart Brown (born about 1821); and a son born between 1820 and 1825.

Stewart Clan Magazine, F (1949): 227, identifies Simeon Henry Stewart as a son of James and Margaret Stewart but cites no source. Simeon Henry Stewart married 18 October 1844 in Taliaferro County to Mrs. Sarah O'Neal Stevens. Although it is possible that he was the son of James and Margaret Stewart, if so, he returned to Taliaferro County, leaving his mother and siblings in Heard County. Further, if he was a son of James and Margaret, it does not seem possible that he was a brother of Georgia Ann Virginia Stewart O'Neal, as family lore alleges. (Anne Martin Haigler indicated in April 2004 that Georgia Ann Virginia Stewart O'Neal had one known sibling, Simeon Henry Stewart. While living in South Carolina, Haigler was able to visit Greene and Taliaferro Counties, to research in the county records there, and to interview and correspond with older members of the Stewart and O'Neal families living in Georgia and Mississippi. Older relatives living in the 1950s and 1960s had indicated that Simeon Henry and Georgia Ann Virginia were siblings, but no documentary evidence to conclusively prove the connection has been located (Personal Interview with Anne Martin Haigler, 19 April 2004, Birmingham, AL).

Of the other sons of Henry Stewart, Samuel, John, Matthew, William, and Reuben thus remain viable possibilities. It seems unlikely that Reuben Stewart was the father of Simeon, Georgia, and Judith Ellen inasmuch as he was head of a household in 1840 consisting only of himself, his wife (aged 20-30, and two males and one female aged 0-5. Of these males, James C. Stewart (born about 1835) married Cornelia O'Neal, a niece of James Augustus O'Neal. Samuel Stewart, son of Henry, is said to have died young and without issue. John Stewart likewise is either said to have died young or to have left the area. The only two remaining sons of Henry Stewart who might have been the father of the three Stewarts who married into the O'Neal family were thus Matthew and William. Matthew appeared in the Greene-Taliaferro area from about 1820 until his death (although he was not a head of household in 1830 or 1840). Matthew may have been the male aged 30-40 in Henry's household in 1830 and the male aged 50-60 in Henry's household in 1840; his correct age would have been forty-two and fifty-two at the time of these enumerations. Likewise, William F. Stewart -- probably Matthew's son -- may have been the male aged 20-30 living with Henry in 1830. Matthew registered for the 1832 Gold Lottery as a resident of GMD 607, Taliaferro County, along with Henry and Reuben H. Stewart, and he was taxed there from 1832 until at least 1836 (the last digest examined). Matthew seems never to have remarried and to have lived the rest of his life with his father Henry, his sister Eleanor, and his son William F. At the time of the 1860 census, William F., Matthew, and Eleanor were enumerated in the same household.

Thus the conclusion was reached that, of the sons of Henry Stewart, the one most likely to have been the father of Georgia Ann, Simeon Henry, and Judith Ellen was William Stewart. He was the only son with a family profile matching that of the man who had fathered these children, and there are strong grounds to eliminate each of the other sons of Henry and Lucy Stewart.

[1636] Greene Co., GA, Ordinary Estate Records, Unbound, 1790-1943, James Stewart - Amy Stringfellow.

land adjoining the farm of James Daniel. At some time during the 1840s, Wooten O'Neal moved across the line into Greene County, but his family maintained property and family ties in Taliaferro County as well.

About 1851, James Augustus O'Neal and family moved to Tallapoosa County, Alabama; from there they relocated about 1855 to Scott County, Mississippi. James apparently worked as a farm laborer there for the remainder of his life. Following the outbreak of hostilities between the North and the South, on 19 July 1861, he enlisted in Company H, 20th MS Infantry, Confederate States Army, at Iuka, Mississippi. He was captured at Fort Donelson on 16 February 1862 and transferred to prison at Camp Douglas, where he contracted pneumonia. He died at Camp Douglas on 30 April 1862, when he was about thirty-nine years old. On 25 October 1862, Captain Joseph H. Barber confirmed that "there is due him by pay rolls made out and returned, Eighty Eight ($88) dollars which does not include Bounty or Commutation money. And that he owes Ten Dollars for Clothing to Confederate States Government." O'Neal had not received payment for his service at the time of his death, and on 15 November 1862 Georgia Stewart O'Neal entered a claim for the payment due his heirs.[1637] After two years of petitioning, Georgia was finally awarded her husband's pay on 27 January 1864; a month later, on 23 February 1864, a certificate for $150 was issued to the heirs of James A. O'Neal for compensation due him.[1638]

Georgia Ann Virginia Stewart O'Neal was only about thirty-six years old when she was left a widow with a large family to support; moreover, she found herself in eastern Mississippi, hundreds of miles from her native region and from her biological kin. The nearest relatives she and her offspring had was the family of her husband's uncle, John Stephens, who also died during the American Civil War. How Georgia survived, and managed to hold together her family, are matters of conjecture, but, lacking any substantial amount of real estate or personal property, she and the children must have combined efforts to support themselves until receiving compensation for James's military service.

The next record we have of the family dates from 1867, a personal document written from Wooten O'Neal, Jr. (husband of Judith Ellen Stewart) to his nephew John Henry O'Neal. The letter indicates that the Mississippi O'Neals retained contact, if irregularly, with their relatives in Georgia and Alabama. Further, this particular letter plays an important role in supporting the identification of Georgia Ann Virginia Stewart O'Neal's parentage.

> Union Point, GA May 12 1867: Dear Nephew: I seat my self this evening to rite you A few lines which leaves Me & family well & I hope this may find you & all the relaition well also all of our relation as far as I know I received your letter of the 29th of April & was more than hapy to hear from you all & to hear that all was well. I give you A list of the Deaths that has ocured in the Oneal & Stewart familys as I Dont know whether you have heard of any or not since you left Alabama your two granfathers are dead[1639] & Brother Billy was Kiled in the Army & Brother Johns son in law frank Akins & his own son Bud also his Daughter Pete was killed by lightning she left one child which is a fine looking little girl about 6 years old Brother John had the child adopted & its name changed from Akins to Oneal none of the young Oneals is not married John lost his three oldest children bud & pete & tete Sim Stewarts oldest daughter Married H. Hancock he

---

[1637] Note that there are several examples of the signature of Georgia O'Neal in this file. On one occasion she signed as "G. A. V. O'Neal" and another as "Georgiann V. O'Neal."

[1638] Mississippi Confederate Muster Lists, Company H, 20th Mississippi Infantry, Mississippi Department of Archives and History, Jackson, MS.

[1639] This is a very significant statement. Wooten O'Neal died between 1862 and 1867. The elder Wooten and John Stephens were both dead long before the family left Greene County. Hence the second grandfather must refer to the Stewart side. This tells us that Georgia's father (or grandfather) apparently died during the Civil War years. This fits the profile of Henry Stewart, who was alive in 1860 but deceased by 1870. It further suggests that Georgia's father died before his father Henry (i.e., it was not necessary to explain which grandfathers. Wooten wrote only "your two grandfathers are dead," indicating that there were no more than two grandfathers at that time.

has 3 more ready to mary John has 6 children living 4 Boys and 2 girls I have 8 children 4 boys 4 girls all living & grown Alf & Sook I am living at Union Point working at my trade Buggy & waggon & cabinet work I am doing as well as could be expected Alfred works with me in the shop & has ever since the war he can do very fine work I have bought me a lot & build me a house on it you would not know Union Point if you was to see it is a great business place now we have two stores & a church Blacksmith shop two wood shops & two steam mills & shoe shop drugs & groceries & the best school that I ever saw they have nearly a hundred schollars & four teachers they teach music embroidery & all languages that is taught in America I am sending three children & they cost me nearly 200 dollars a year I have changed my mode of life and am trying to live a pious life I have atached my self to the Methodist Episcopal Church. At this place & so is my oldest daughter we have sabath scool & preaching & singing evry Sabbath. Union Point is noted for its Piety the people are very kind to me & family they help us along by patronizing us in work also gifing Elen and the girls work to do sewing & c. times are generally very hard here provisions are very scarce & so is money henry you never told me any thing about your wife nor how you was geting on in the world nor about George Anns husband nor how they were geting on nor about Jesse & his wife nor how they were geting on You neer said a word about Jimmie nor Kate nor Webster nor gally do take time & rite me a long letter give me a full history of the hole family & all the canexian that is out there Brother albert is living with Sim Stewart near Woodstock on Ab Janes River plantation they are farming and geting on very well I believe tell all the children to rite to me tell George Ann to rite she need not forget us because she is married for I am glad she is married if she has a good & kind husband Elen is glad she is married again provided Goergeann is satisfied she sees she had rather her be happy than any lady on earth she wants her to rite to us & give her a history of her life generaly henry I don't understand the way you asign your name you asign it J. T. Oneal I thought it was John henry Oneal. I must close for this line for year I tire your patience with my scribling so nothing more at present but subscribe myself as ever your affection uncle and friend and well wisher til death. Wooten O'Neal.

Dear Unkle i seat myself answer your kind letter which gave me Great stfaction to hear from you and family this me & Family well and hope this may Find you and Family Well all of our Relation is well so far as know.[1640]

Family tradition holds that Georgia O'Neal married second to a man name Lindsay; the marriage, apparently, was a brief one. Wooten O'Neal references it in his 1867 letter, but no record of the marriage has been found. Further, by 1870, Georgia was enumerated once again as Georgia O'Neal, the name she continued to use for the remainder of her life. Cumulatively, this evidence suggests that Georgia's second husband died between 1867 and 1870 or that they separated or divorced between those dates.[1641]

By 1870, Georgia and her offspring were living in Brownsville, Hinds County, Mississippi. She was keeping house and owned property valued altogether at $700. Living with her were her three unmarried children, Catherine, Joseph, and Mary, while her married sons Jesse and James were living with their families in adjacent households.[1642] The family was still in Brownsville in 1880, at which time Georgia was living in the household of her son Jesse O'Neal.[1643]

[1640] This transcription was made from the handwritten letter in possession of Anne Martin Haigler in May 2004, during a visit with her in Birmingham, AL.

[1641] 1870 Hinds Co., MS, Census, Brownsville P.O., Township 7, p. 676.

[1642] 1870 Hinds Co., MS, Census, Brownsville P.O., Township 7, p. 676.

[1643] 1880 Hinds Co., MS, Census, p. 194.

Georgia Stewart O'Neal spent the remainder of her life in Hinds County, Mississippi, where she died in February 1892, at which time she was probably in her middle sixties. Family tradition indicates that she was crippled for life after being thrown from a horse and that she walked with crutches during her later years. These injuries may have contributed, along with the strains placed on her by the death of her husband and the challenges of rearing her children alone, to a relatively short lifespan, given that of other members of her family.

Georgia and James O'Neal had six surviving children. John Henry O'Neal (1844-1909) married Mary Bailey and died in Smith County, Mississippi. Jesse Wooten O'Neal (1845-1915) married Mary Bunyard (1852-1902) and Anna Howard (1857-1927). He died in Brownsville, Mississippi, and was buried in the Brownsville Cemetery. Catherine Luticia O'Neal (1851-1925) married William Joshua Gary (1846-1937); both died in Madison County, Mississippi, where they were buried in the Old Jackson Cemetery. Joseph Webster O'Neal (1852-1926) married Betty Lorance (1856-1940); Betty was a daughter of John Lorance and Elizabeth Cates and a niece of Anderson Bradley Cates, father-in-law of William Simms Hammack. Joseph Webster and Betty are buried in the Flora Cemetery, Madison County, Mississippi.[1644] Mary Frances O'Neal (1854-1910), called "Gally," married William Franklin Campbell (1851-1921). Both were buried in Lula Baptist Church Cemetery.

Of the offspring of James and Georgia, James Rederick O'Neal (25 July, 1847, Greene County, Georgia - 14 Jan., 1893, Hinds County, Mississippi) was named for his uncle Reddick Stephens and his father James O'Neal. The given name Reddick traces to Parker connections in northeastern North Carolina in the mid-eighteenth-century and is probably indicative of an early family connection.

James Rederick O'Neal moved with his parents to Tallapoosa County, Alabama; when he was about eight, the family relocated to Scott County, Mississippi. James was only fourteen when his father died in April 1862; too young for the Confederate service, he probably assumed a heavy burden in assisting his mother and younger siblings during and immediately following the American Civil War.

On 5 December 1867, when he was twenty, James R. O'Neal married Mary Jane Gary. Like James, Mary had lost her father in the Confederate Army, and she was left with a widowed mother and several siblings. The marriage of James and Mary Jane lasted for thirteen years, ending on 11 June 1881 when Mary died following childbirth. James soon remarried to a woman named Lula Harvey; that marriage, however, was a brief one, ending with James's death in 1893.

James Rederick O'Neal fathered seven children by each marriage. He and Mary Jane Gary were the parents of the following: Mary Virginia O'Neal (1869-1890), who married James R. Ratliff; Abi Doxey O'Neal (1870-1899), who married John Manly Bankston (1857-1922); Frances E. O'Neal (1872-1876); Ellen Rebecca O'Neal (1873-1948), who married R. R. "Noah" Roberts; Mittie Catherine O'Neal (1876-1877); William Henry O'Neal (1881-1881); and Joshua Pinckney O'Neal (1881-1881). James Rederick O'Neal and Lula Harvey were the parents of the following: Katherine Elizabeth O'Neal (1882-), who married John Peter Smith and K. O. Bryant; Viola Constance O'Neal (1885-1964), who married John Crawford; Frances Louise O'Neal (1887-); Olivia O'Neal (1889-1970), who married William LaFayette Hawkins; James Augustus O'Neal (1891-1892); James Rederick O'Neal (1892-1951), who married Nell Knox Jackson; and Ella O'Neal (1892-), who married L. R. Krumm.

Abi Doxey O'Neal (1870-1899) married John Manly Bankston (1857-1922). They were the parents of Mary Almedia Bankston Hammack.

D. Mary Jane Gary.

The daughter of Starling Tucker Gary and Mary Ann Stringer, Mary Jane Gary was born 28 August 1850, probably in Lauderdale or Scott County, Mississippi. She died 11 June 1881 in Hinds County. She and James Rederick O'Neal were married 5 December 1867 in Smith County, Mississippi.

[1644] H. W. O'Neal, son of Joseph Webster, married Ethel Hammack.

The Gary family traces to Charles City County, Virginia, in the late seventeenth-century. The family's immigrant ancestor is said to have arrived in the colony as a soldier following Bacon's Rebellion in 1676 and to have remained in Virginia after the disorder ended. No confirmation of this tradition has been found, but the earliest documented ancestor seems to have been William Gary who died about 1716 in Westover Parish, Charles City County, Virginia. Most colonial records for Charles City County and its offspring, Prince George County, were destroyed during the nineteenth-century, although a small number of contemporary documents exist. Among these is the will of William Gary. Gary names several offspring, including Sarah, Elizabeth, Mary, John, and Richard. It seems likely that he was also the father or grandfather of the Thomas Gary who moved to Edgecombe County, North Carolina. Thomas might have been the eldest son of William Gary; if so, the laws of primogeniture in Virginia held that he would automatically inherit significant properties from his father without being included in his will. On the other hand, he might have been a son of one of Thomas's sons, perhaps John Gary.[1645]

Based on his life in South Carolina, one can project that Thomas Gary was probably born by at least 1705 and perhaps as early as 1695. Thomas Gary was an adult head of household with young children when he appeared in Edgecombe County, North Carolina, in 1738.[1646] He patented 600 acres in North Carolina, suggesting that he was head of a household which -- including servants and slaves -- may have included as many as twelve individuals. A February 1738 inventory of Col. James Milliken of Bertie County lists bonds held "against Thomas Garrie and Henry West".[1647] Gary patented 200 acres in Edgecombe County on 27 June 1738; later, on 23 September 1741, he proved his rights to land based on twelve individuals in his household.[1648] On 25 September 1741, he was granted 400 acres in Edgecombe County; coupled together, the 1738 and 1741 grants totaled 600 acres, the amount due an individual with twelve individuals in his household.[1649]

Thomas Gary was involved in several Edgecombe County land transactions, some of them involving William West of Bertie and Edgecombe Counties. The connection is significant, for Gary's son Charles later married a daughter of Captain William West, a former neighbor and associate in Edgecombe County. The two families had apparently been neighbors since the 1730s, if not earlier, and had moved to South Carolina together in the early 1750s.

When Thomas and Mary Gary sold portions of their Edgecombe properties to Benjamin Lane in 1742, William West witnessed the deed.[1650] Gary sold an additional tract of 128 acres to Lane in 1744, and another 156 acres to John Haywood two weeks later; West was not directly involved in either transaction, although the location -- the south side of Conocoanry Swamp, on Marsh Branch and Conerree Branch -- indicates that the land lay near that of William West.[1651] On 13 March 1746, Gary sold another 100 acres on Conocoanry Swamp, this tract joining the tract sold to Haywood earlier, to Thomas Maples. John Lane witnessed the deed.[1652]

[1645] See Ethel S. Updike, *Gary Family of England to Virginia to South Carolina* (Salt Lake City, UT, 1976), pp. 1-10. The speculation about Thomas's placement within the Virginia Gary family is my own, not Updike's.

[1646] Updike, *Gary*, p. 10.

[1647] Note that Beale Brown and Henry West moved to Bertie Co., NC, from Isle of Wight Co., VA, by way of Bertie's parent county, Chowan. Beale Brown's name appears eight lines after that of Henry West. See Gammon, *Records of Estates, Bertie Co., NC, 1728-1744, 1762-1790*, p. 10

[1648] Updike, *Gary*, p. 10.

[1649] Ibid.

[1650] William and Henry West also had transactions with Joseph Lane, who was from Surry Co., VA, and whose wife Ann Drew belonged to a family with ties connecting them to the Wests and Braswells of Isle of Wight County.

[1651] Updike, p. 10, citing Edgecombe Co., NC, DB 5, pp. 375-376.

[1652] Edgecombe Co., NC, DB 5, p. 491. Note that there seems to have been a connection between Thomas Gary and James Gary, who was in Edgecombe by 1739, when he applied for a brand. In 1747, James Gary gave a power of attorney to John Lane, Jr., of Edgecombe, to confirm a patent to Gary for 100 acres joining William Taylor. Solomon Hawkins and John Haywood witnessed (Edgecombe Co., NC, DB 3, pp. 153-54).

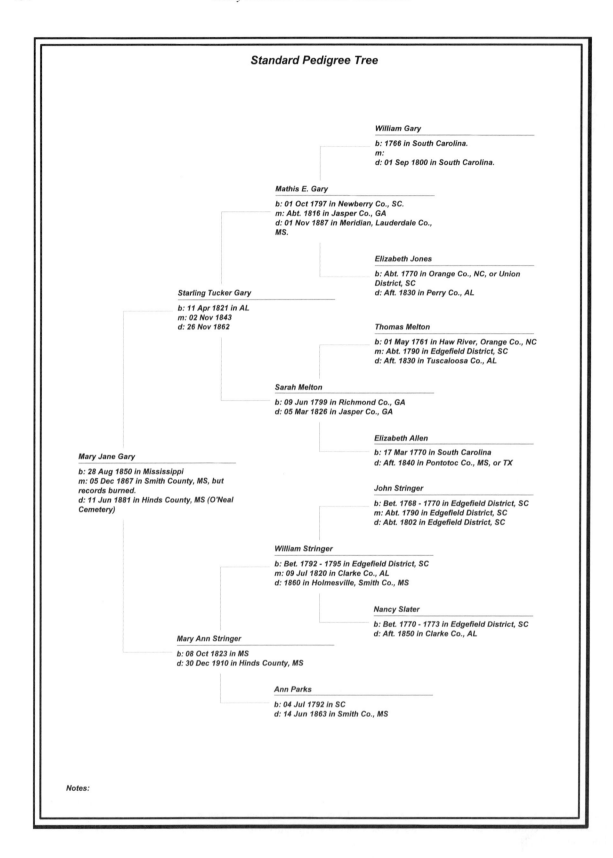

Standard Pedigree Tree

William Gary

b: 1766 in South Carolina.
m:
d: 01 Sep 1800 in South Carolina.

Mathis E. Gary

b: 01 Oct 1797 in Newberry Co., SC.
m: Abt. 1816 in Jasper Co., GA
d: 01 Nov 1887 in Meridian, Lauderdale Co.,
MS.

Elizabeth Jones

b: Abt. 1770 in Orange Co., NC, or Union
District, SC
d: Aft. 1830 in Perry Co., AL

Starling Tucker Gary

b: 11 Apr 1821 in AL
m: 02 Nov 1843
d: 26 Nov 1862

Thomas Melton

b: 01 May 1761 in Haw River, Orange Co., NC
m: Abt. 1790 in Edgefield District, SC
d: Aft. 1830 in Tuscaloosa Co., AL

Sarah Melton

b: 09 Jun 1799 in Richmond Co., GA
d: 05 Mar 1826 in Jasper Co., GA

Elizabeth Allen

b: 17 Mar 1770 in South Carolina
d: Aft. 1840 in Pontotoc Co., MS, or TX

Mary Jane Gary

b: 28 Aug 1850 in Mississippi
m: 05 Dec 1867 in Smith County, MS, but
records burned.
d: 11 Jun 1881 in Hinds County, MS (O'Neal
Cemetery)

John Stringer

b: Bet. 1768 - 1770 in Edgefield District, SC
m: Abt. 1790 in Edgefield District, SC
d: Abt. 1802 in Edgefield District, SC

William Stringer

b: Bet. 1792 - 1795 in Edgefield District, SC
m: 09 Jul 1820 in Clarke Co., AL
d: 1860 in Holmesville, Smith Co., MS

Nancy Slater

b: Bet. 1770 - 1773 in Edgefield District, SC
d: Aft. 1850 in Clarke Co., AL

Mary Ann Stringer

b: 08 Oct 1823 in MS
d: 30 Dec 1910 in Hinds County, MS

Ann Parks

b: 04 Jul 1792 in SC
d: 14 Jun 1863 in Smith Co., MS

Notes:

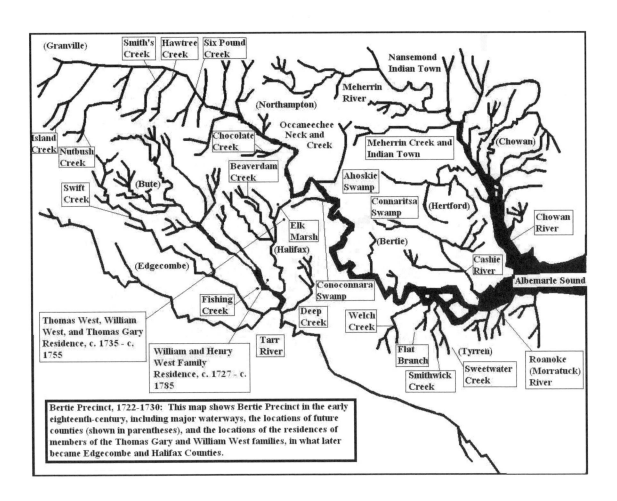

Bertie Precinct, 1722-1730: This map shows Bertie Precinct in the early eighteenth-century, including major waterways, the locations of future counties (shown in parentheses), and the locations of the residences of members of the Thomas Gary and William West families, in what later became Edgecombe and Halifax Counties.

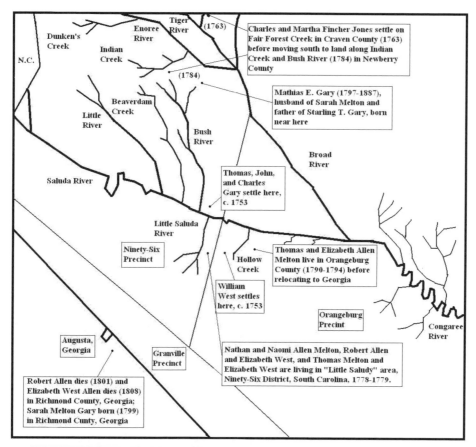

Dunken's Creek

Enoree River

Tiger River

(1763)

Indian Creek

N.C.

(1784)

Charles and Martha Fincher Jones settle on Fair Forest Creek in Craven County (1763) before moving south to land along Indian Creek and Bush River (1784) in Newberry County

Mathias E. Gary (1797-1887), husband of Sarah Melton and father of Starling T. Gary, born near here

Beaverdam Creek

Little River

Bush River

Broad River

Saluda River

Thomas, John, and Charles Gary settle here, c. 1753

Little Saluda River

Ninety-Six Precinct

Hollow Creek

Thomas and Elizabeth Allen Melton live in Orangeburg County (1790-1794) before relocating to Georgia

William West settles here, c. 1753

Orangeburg Precint

Congaree River

Augusta, Georgia

Granville Precinct

Nathan and Naomi Allen Melton, Robert Allen and Elizabeth West, and Thomas Melton and Elizabeth West are living in "Little Saludy" area, Ninety-Six District, South Carolina, 1778-1779.

Robert Allen dies (1801) and Elizabeth West Allen dies (1808) in Richmond County, Georgia; Sarah Melton Gary born (1799) in Richmond Cunty, Georgia

South Carolina Homesites of Thomas Gary, William West, Charles Jones, Nathan Melton, and Robert Allen (c. 1753 - c. 1800), ancestors of Mathias E. Gary (1797-1887) and Sarah Melton Gary (1799-1826).

Shortly after this date, Thomas Gary relocated to South Carolina. On 27 and 28 December 1754, by lease and release, Gary purchased 200 acres on the east side of Bush River from John Pitts; the deed describes him as "of Saludy" at the time of purchase. In 1755 Charles and Thomas Gary were among the petitioners for relief from Indian depredations. Their neighbor Thomas Johnson also signed the petition, which represented inhabitants of Saludy, Enoree, and "parts adjacent," praying for a "Troop of Rangers to protect them from the Indians." The petition alleged that "In short they have burned and destroyed all up Bush River, except Jacob Brooks, where there are some people gathered together to stand in their own defense." Thomas and Charles Gary lived near the line between Laurens and Newberry Counties, and documents appear in both localities.[1653]

On 6 June 1758, Thomas Gary received a warrant for 100 acres on Saludy River and Bush Fork; shortly thereafter, on 7 November, he received a warrant for 200 acres in Berkeley County and for another eighty-eight acres in the same location. The eighty-eight-acre tract, granted on 4 July 1769, was described as bound by William Gary, Thomas Johnson, and Thomas Gearry.[1654]

About this time, Thomas Gary wrote his will in Ninety-Sixth District, South Carolina; the will was probated before 1779, but the original document and the recorded copy have not survived.[1655]

Based on land records in what became Newberry County, it appears that Thomas Gary had at least four sons:[1656] John Gary (by 1732 - 1804, Newberry District, South Carolina); Charles Gary (by 1733 - 1808, Newberry District, South Carolina); William Gary (by 1735 - 1773/79, Newberry District, South Carolina); Thomas Gary (by 1738 - 1797, Newberry District, South Carolina). There were likely several daughters whose names have not survived. The descendants of these four siblings became prolific, creating a complicated extended cousinage of Gary kinsmen in Newberry District, South Carolina. Details of these descendants have been set out in extended form by Ethel Updike in her history of the Newberry County Gary family. Of the children of Thomas Gary, John married a woman named Elizabeth, whose maiden name has not survived. Charles married Patience West, daughter of William West. William married Millie Brooks, daughter of Jacob Brooks and Rosanna Sheppard. Thomas married Uriah Newman, daughter of Reverend Samuel Newman, formerly of Maryland, who was a pioneer minister at Bush River Baptist Church in Newberry District.[1657]

Charles Gary, great-grandfather of Starling Tucker Gary, was born about 1735, probably in Edgecombe or Bertie County, North Carolina. Growing up in Edgecombe County, his family lived on a farm near that of Captain William West. About 1755, the Garys and Wests moved to what became Newberry and Edgefield Districts, South Carolina. Charles Gary first appears in legal records on 6 December 1755, when he joined other residents of Saluda River District in a petition to request assistance against Indians who were raiding their farms along Bush River.[1658]

It was probably soon after this that Charles Gary married Patience West. Certainly Charles was married before 2 December 1765, when he received a grant for 150 acres on "on a fork between Broad and Saluda Rivers near Bush Creek bound by Thomas Gary and vacant lands." A year later, on 2 December 1766, he received another 200 acres on Saluda River joining the property of Reverend Samuel Newman. On 1 February 1768, these two grants were reconfirmed, and, in 1784, Gary received an additional 150 acres joining the earlier tracts. Gary sold this tract to Nathan Williams in 1787,[1659] but he apparently retained the bulk of his other holdings until his death.[1660]

[1653] Updike, *Gary*, pp. 11-12.

[1654] Ibid.

[1655] The surviving record indicates that the will was filed in Bundle H, Package 26, Charleston.

[1656] Updike, *Gary*, pp. 10-12.

[1657] Ibid. The remainder of Updike's work traces the descendants of the sons of Thomas Gary.

[1658] Ibid., p. 19.

[1659] Newberry Co., SC, DB A, pp. 314-316.

[1660] Updike, *Gary*, pp. 19-20.

During the American Revolution, Charles Gary, his siblings, and nephews all supported the patriot cause. Rather than active military service, Charles seems to have supplied material assistance to support the continental troops. In 1781 and 1782, he supplied provisions for the local military, and, in 1785, he received compensation, nearly £10, for supplies he had furnished during the Revolution.[1661]

Charles and Patience Gary were early members of Bush River Baptist Church along Bush River in Newberry District. This historic Baptist Church and its members spawned many other congregations in Georgia, Alabama, and Mississippi during the decades after 1800, and two of its early ministers -- Samuel Newman and John Cole -- are remembered as pioneers of the faith in the Carolina backcountry.[1662]

Patience West Gary died on 17 June 1798, and Charles Gary on 18 July 1808. Both were buried at Bush River Baptist Church. Almost exactly two years before his death, on 17 July 1808, Charles Gary wrote his will in Newberry County. He named five heirs: Thomas Gary (1764-1818, Butler County, Alabama); John Gary (1765-1848, Carroll County, Mississippi); Sarah Gary Gary Jones McGraw, wife of Thomas Gary, Jr., Joshua Jones, and Stephen McGraw; Polly Williams, wife of John Williams; and Captain West Gary (1774-1814, Newberry District, South Carolina). William Gary, a sixth child, had predeceased his father, although his heirs were also entitled to a share of the estate. Witnesses to Charles Gary's will included William's wife's relatives, Charles Jones and Joshua Jones.[1663]

William Gary, the son who predeceased Charles Gary, was the grandfather of Starling Tucker Gary. Born about 1766, he married Elizabeth Jones, daughter of Charles and Martha Fincher Jones of Newberry County. Charles and Martha had married in Pennsylvania, where both were born, before moving into Orange County, North Carolina, with Martha's parents and siblings.[1664] In the late 1760s, they relocated to South Carolina, where they remained for more than three decades. In the 1790s, several of Charles's sons, and perhaps Charles and Martha themselves, moved to Christian County, Kentucky, where Charles's descendants lived for several generations.[1665]

A Quaker by birth, Martha Fincher Jones belonged to a well-known Anglo-American Quaker family from the west of England. Her great-grandfather, Francis Fincher, had been a Quaker in England and suffered imprisonment and the loss of his estates there because of his faith. He, his wife Mary Achelly Fincher, and their children emigrated from Worcester, England, to Philadelphia on the *Bristol Comfort* in 1683.[1666] In Pennsylvania, he became a prosperous farmer and reared a large family. Francis's son John, born about 1679 in England, married as his first wife Martha Taylor, daughter of Robert Taylor (7 December, 1633, Little Leigh, Cheshire, England - 14 April 1695, Spring Township, Chester County, Pennsylvania) and Mary Hayes (1642, Clatterwhitch, Cheshire, England -- 11 February, 1728, Chester

[1661] Ibid.

[1662] Bush River Baptist Church Records, 1771-1921, Southern Baptist Historical Library and Archives, Nashville, TN.

[1663] Updike, *Gary*, pp. 19-20.

[1664] The marriage took place in the vicinity of Warrington Monthly Meeting prior to 18 June 1750, when Martha was dismissed for marrying out of unity. Charles Jones, apparently, was not a Quaker by birth or conversion. See Warrington, PA, Monthly Meeting, Department of Records, Yearly Meeting of Religious Society of Friends, Philadelphia, PA.

[1665] See E. D. Fincher and A. W. Fincher, *Fincher in the USA, 1683-1900* (Greenville, SC, 1981), p. 319. For land and legal records relating to Charles Jones between 1763 and 1800, see the following: B. H. Holcomb, *Petitions for Land from South Carolina Council Journals* (7 vols., Columbia, SC, 1998), 5: 119, 269; 6: 227, 273; 7: 142, 205, 287, 291; South Carolina Department of Archives and History, Series S213184, 17: 328-329; SCDAH Series S213019, 29: 68; SCDAH Series S111001, 12: 268, Item 1; SCDAH Series S111001, 12: 356, Item 4; Series S213019, 33: 436; SCDAH Series S111001, 13: 425, Item 2; SCDAH Series S108092, Reel 80, Frame 223; G. C. Hendrix, *The Jury Lists of SC, 1778-1779* (Baltimore, 1975), p. 101; SCDAH Series S213190, 5: 406; Union Co., SC, DB A, pp. 279-284, 315-316, pp. 449-450, 545-546; Union Co., SC, DB B, pp. 353-354, ; SCDAH Series S213190, Volume 9, p. 317, Item 3; SCDAH Series S213190, Volume 9, p. 318, Item 1; SCDAH Series S213190, Volume 16, p. 361, Item 1; SCDAH Series S213190, Volume 17, p. 18; Laurens Co., SC, DB B, p. 217; Laurens Co., SC, DB D, p. 116; Laurens Co., SC, DB F, p. 92; Laurens Co., SC, DB G, pp. 7, 313, 679; Laurens Co., SC, DB H, p. 172; Newberry Co., SC, DB A, pp. 356-357; Newberry Co., SC, DB D, pp. 62-64, 642-643; Newberry Co., SC, DB E, pp. 354-355; Newberry Co., SC, DB F, pp. 249-250; Newberry Co., SC, DB G, pp. 188-189, 195-196; Newberry Co., SC, DB H, pp. 344-345.

[1666] Fincher and Fincher, *Fincher*, pp. 1-30, discusses the origins, background, and experiences of Francis Fincher and his offspring.

County, Pennsylvania) of Little Leigh, Cheshire, who emigrated to Pennsylvania in 1682[1667]. Deed records refer to John Fincher as cordwainer (shoemaker) and yeoman; he was the first supervisor of London Grove Township in 1723, and he remained in New Garden and London Grove Townships of Chester County until he died in 1747. At that time, John Fincher owned 300 acres of land an estate valued at £278, of which bonds, bills, promissory notes, and book debts constituted £228.[1668]

Beginning in the 1740s, several of the children of John and Martha Taylor Fincher left Chester County, heading south and west. Jonathan Fincher settled in Orange County, North Carolina -- the same county where we have encountered such diverse characters as Justice Lawrence Bankston, John Cates, James Farquhar, Samuel Lockhart, Major Richard Parker, and Henry Brewer -- before 1755, dying there in 1757. Elizabeth Fincher Cocks, daughter of John and Martha Taylor Fincher, died about 1730 in Pennsylvania, but her husband Thomas Cocks, his second wife Mary Cooke Cocks, and the children of Thomas and Elizabeth moved to Orange County, North Carolina, about 1757.

Francis Fincher, born about 1710 and one of the two youngest sons of John and Martha Taylor Fincher, married Hannah Shewin on 4 September 1731 in Chester County, Pennsylvania. Hannah was a daughter of William Shewin and Sarah Martin of Kennett, Chester County, Pennsylvania, whose family had originated in Bedwin Magna, Wiltshire.[1669] Although born into the Quaker faith, Francis Fincher's adherence seems to have been erratic. On 21 August 1746, the Sudbury Friends Meeting in Pennsylvania recorded complaints against Francis Fincher for quarrelling and drinking alcohol; later, on 18 June 1750, Francis was formally dismissed from the Society of Friends for his errant ways. Francis's wife and children, however, remained members in good standing, and, in 1758, Hannah Shewin Fincher requested a certificate to New Garden Monthly Meeting in Orange County, North Carolina. The family seems to have remained in Orange County from about 1758 until 1765, when Francis Fincher received a grant for 150 acres in Craven District, South Carolina.[1670] Francis and Hannah, their married children Armel Fincher and Martha Fincher Jones, and their families all settled along Fairforest Creek in 1765 and lived there until moving westward; Charles and Martha settled next along Bush River in Newberry District, while Francis and Hannah settled in Ninety-Sixth District, where they were living in Union County as late as 1790.[1671]

[1667] Robert Taylor was son of Thomas Taylor (18 Feb., 1594, Little Leigh, Cheshire, England -- January 1669, Clatterwick, Cheshire, England), who m. 21 Sept., 1630, Mary Barrow of Davenham, Cheshire. Thomas Taylor was a son of John Taylor (1550-1627) and Ellen Massey (1565-1611) of Little Leigh, Cheshire, England. Martha Hayes Taylor was a daughter of Jonathan Hayes (1616, Clatterwitch, Cheshire, England --) and Margaret Merrick, who married 1 August 1640, Clatterwitch, Cheshire, England.

[1668] Fincher and Fincher, *Fincher*, pp. 10-30.

[1669] J. S. Futhey and G. Cope, *The History of Chester Co., PA* (Philadelphia, 1881), p. 652: "Thomas Martin with wife Margery Mendenhall came from Bedwin Magna, in Wiltshire, in 1685, bringing children -- Mary, Sarah, Hannah, and Rachel. They settled in Middletown, where their son Moses, and probably other children, were born. We find George and Elinor Martin, for whom we can assign no other parentage. These children married as follows: Mary to James Whitaker, 1690; Sarah to William Shewin; Rachel to Thomas Woodward, 1704; Moses to Margaret Battin, 1714; George to Lydia Buffington; Elinor to John Scarlet, 1715." Thomas Martin, father of Sarah Martin Shewin, was born 4 March 1649/50 at Bedwin Magna, Wiltshire, England, and married 30 January 1675/76 at Lambourne, Wiltshire, Margery Mendenhall (Dec., 1655, Marridge Hill, Ramsbury, Wiltshire -- 1742, Chester Co., PA), daughter of Thomas Mendenhall (1630 - 1682) and Joane Strode of Marridge Hill, Ramsbury, Wiltshire. Thomas Mendenhall and Joane Strode married 12 August 1649 at Marridge Hill. Grandparents of Margery were: Thomas Mildenhall, Jr. (24 Dec., 1609, Ramsbury, Wiltshire -- 7 Nov., 1673, Beeson, Little Bedwin, Wiltshire) and Anne [----] (died 22 Nov., 1640, Ramsbury, Wiltshire) and William Strode (of Shepton Mallet, Somerset, who died 20 Dec., 1666, at Beminister, Dorset) and Joanne Barnard (1607, Downside, Shepton Mallet, Somerset -- 23 August 1649, Barrington, Somerset). Thomas Mildenhall, Jr., was a son of Thomas Mildenhall (1580-1639) and a grandson of John Mildenhall (c. 1560 - 1614) and Elizabeth Bates (c. 1560 - 1602). Joanne Barnard Strode was a daughter of Edward Barnard (1585-1641) and Jane Smythers (1590-1658) of Shepton, Somerset, and a granddaughter of Edward Barnard (c. 1555 - 1623) and Christian Whitcombe (c. 1560 - bef. 1622) of Shepton, Somerset, and of John Smythes (1551-1621) and Joan Bickombe (c. 1570-1639) of Dorrington, Somerset. The Smythes line traces to Willus Smythes (c. 1470 --) of Wrington, Somerset, and the Barnard line traces to Edward Barnard (c. 1500 --) of Downside, Shepton Mallet, Somerset, England.

[1670] Index to Land Survey Plats to 1776, South Carolina Department of Archives and History, Columbia, SC.

[1671] According to Fincher and Fincher, *Fincher*, pp. 319-324, Martha's siblings included Armel Fincher of Union Co., SC; Moses Fincher; Aaron Fincher of Union Co., SC; Jesse Fincher of Newberry District, SC, a Loyalist who was living in Spanish Florida by 1783; John Fincher, of Newberry and Union Districts, SC; Rebecca Fincher Martingale; Sarah Fincher, wife of William Gist, a

William Gary and Elizabeth Jones, daughter of Charles and Martha Fincher Jones, were married about 1785 in Newberry District. William died there 1 September 1800, and Elizabeth remarried to George Whitmore, who died childless in 1810. Twice widowed, Elizabeth never again married, moving in her middle age with her son Matthias to Jasper County, Georgia, and finally to Perry and Sumter Counties, Alabama, where she probably died.

William Gary appears frequently as a witness on legal documents in Newberry District between 1785 and 1800; he is probably the William Gary who purchased forty acres from Philip Phagan on 28 February 1790.[1672] He may be the William Gary who purchased 100 acres from Daniel Williams in 1794[1673] and 162 acres on Indian Creek from William Cannon in 1795.[1674] He seems to have been the William Gary who, on 15 October 1786, purchased 100 acres on Bush River and Indian Creek from John and Jenny Gary; the land had been granted to William Gary's father-in-law Charles Jones on 5 June 1786.[1675]

On 14 August 1802, two years after William Gary died, Thomas Gary and Elizabeth Gary, administrators of William Gary, purchased thirty-eight acres of land from Walter West, for £10.[1676] The following year, Elizabeth instituted an act of partition against Thomas Gary as William's administrator, stating that William owned 1,470 acres at the time of his death. Her husband had died in 1800, "leaving your petitioner and six minor children, namely: Isaac, David, William, Henry, Mathias and Patience Gary. The said William Gary, deceased, left sundry tracts of land in the county, towit: 150 acres purchased from Thomas Johnson, forty acres from Phillip Fagin, 100 acres from Clement Davis, 110 acres from Marmaduke Maples, 100 acres from John Gary, 100 acres from Daniel Williams, 32 acres from Robert Harp, 100 acres from John Fletcher, 200 acres given to William Gary from his father Charles Gary, 200 acres and 150 acres grants to himself, making the whole 1,470 acres." The lands, however, remained under Thomas Gary's control, and, in 1815, when William Gary, Jr., came of age, he filed suit against his mother, Elizabeth Jones Gary Whitmore, and his uncle, Thomas Gary, for a division of the estate. By this time, Isaac Gary, Henry Gary, and Patience Gary had all died unmarried and without issue. David Gary had died a decade earlier, leaving two small children, and, of William Gary's six children, only Matthias and William were then living.[1677]

About this time, Elizabeth Gary Whitmore and her two living sons removed to Georgia, where they settled in Jasper County. At the time of the 1820 Georgia federal census, Elizabeth Whitmore was enumerated as being more than forty-five years of age. Living next door to her were sons William Gary, with four sons and two daughters under age twenty, and Matthias Gary, with two sons aged under ten years.[1678] By 1830, the family was living in Perry County, Alabama, where Elizabeth was enumerated as being 70-80 years of age; she was then residing in the household of her son, Matthias E. Gary.[1679] Elizabeth apparently died between 1830 and 1840, probably in Perry County, Alabama.

Of the two surviving sons of William and Elizabeth Jones Gary, Matthias was the father of Starling Tucker Gary. William Gary (1790-1856) married Ruth Teague (1791-1868) and moved ultimately to Bosque County, Texas, after migrating from Perry County, Alabama, to Newton County, Mississippi, and from there to Rusk County, Texas. From Rusk County, the Garys settled in McLennan County, where they resided when Bosque County was created. William and Ruth were buried in a family cemetery on

---

Loyalist merchant from 96th District, SC; and Hannah Fincher, wife of Major Edward Musgrove, a lawyer, merchant, and miller, of Union and Laurens Counties.

[1672] Newberry Co., SC, DB A, p. 950, cited in B. H. Holcomb, *Newberry Co., SC, Deed Abstracts, 1785-1806* (3 vols., Columbia, SC, 1999-2000), 1: 72.

[1673] Newberry Co., SC, DB E, pp. 467-469, cited in Holcomb, *Newberry Deeds*, 3: 59.

[1674] Newberry Co., SC, DB E, pp. 477-478, in Holcomb, *Newberry Deeds*, 3: 60.

[1675] Newberry Co., SC, DB E, pp. 466-67, cited in Holcomb, *Newberry Deeds*, 3: 59.

[1676] Newberry Co., SC, DB E, p. 469, cited in Holcomb, *Newberry Deeds*, 3: 59.

[1677] See William Gary Loose Estate File, Newberry Co., SC, Probate Court, Newberry, SC.

[1678] 1820 Jasper Co., GA, Census, p. 125.

[1679] 1830 Perry Co., AL, Census, p. 70.

their property; in 1996, more than a century later, the Texas Highway Department erected a historical marker near the site:

> South Carolina natives William and Rutha Gary migrated west with their family, and by 1852 settled in this area, then part of McLennan County. In 1854, when Bosque County was formed, William Gary was chosen as one of five county commissioners. Five Gary family members were among the voters in the first county election. William Gary died in 1855, followed by Rutha in 1868. Their graves formed the nucleus of this cemetery that grew slowly over the next sixty years. About thirty-five graves are marked; twenty-five more stones are not inscribed. The last burial occurred in 1932.

The area where William and Rutha Gary settled became known as the Gary Creek Valley. Gary Creek Valley, Gary Creek Road, and the Gary Cemetery survive today to mark the significance of this early family to that area.[1680]

Matthias E. Gary (1 October 1797, Newberry District, South Carolina - 1 November 1887, Lauderdale County, Mississippi), the other surviving son of William and Elizabeth Jones Gary, left South Carolina about 1815. He and his brother William lived briefly in Jones County, Georgia, where, as residents of that county, they began acquiring tracts of land in western Alabama.[1681] In 1817, Matthias E. Gary and William Gary of Jones County claimed a tract in Alabama's Cahaba Land District.[1682] Although already speculating in Alabama property, Matthias remained in Georgia until at least 1820. He was living in Jasper County by 1818, when he sold 188 acres on Bush River in Newberry County, South Carolina, to Mary Pitts, widow of James Pitts, and Nancy Pitts, daughter of James Pitts; the land had been granted Thomas Johnston and included 38 acres granted to Henry Wilson in 1799.[1683]

While living in Jasper County, Matthias Gary married Sarah Melton (9 June 1799, Greene County, Georgia - 5 March 1826, Jasper County, Georgia, or Perry County, Alabama), daughter of Thomas and Elizabeth Melton. Matthias and Sarah had two children before the 1820 census; they had several others born prior to her death in 1826. Probably because of Sarah's death, Matthias's mother Elizabeth moved into Matthias's household; she likely played a significant role in rearing his and Sarah's offspring, for Matthias did not marry again until 18 December 1841, when he took Amanda White as his wife in Sumter County, Alabama. This marriage, too, was a brief one, for Matthias married once more, on 13 August 1847, to Rachel J. Seale Elliott Anderson (1803-1880), an Irish immigrant and widow.[1684]

All five children fathered by Matthias Gary were born from his marriage to Sarah Melton. Sarah's parents had moved to Georgia from Edgefield District, South Carolina, where both families had lived since the 1760s. In fact, a complicated set of family relationships united Sarah's parents. Thomas Melton (1 May 1761, Haw River, Orange County, North Carolina - after 1830, Tuscaloosa County, Alabama) married Elizabeth Allen (17 March 1770, Edgefield District, South Carolina - after 1840, Pontotoc County, Mississippi, or Texas) about 1790 in Edgefield District, South Carolina. Thomas Melton's father

---

[1680] Bosque County Historical Markers (http://www.forttours.com/pages/hmbosque.asp).

[1681] Alabama Department of Archives and History, Montgomery, AL, Card File Index to Early Alabama Residents, Gary.

[1682] See US Land Records, Receiver's Office, Milledgeville, 4 August 1817 - November 1818, and Cahaba, AL, December 1818, pp. 151, 249, cited in Alabama Department of Archives and History, Montgomery, AL, Card File Index to Early Alabama Residents, Gary.

[1683] This land was mentioned in William Gary's listing of properties filed for the court suits concerning his estate. See Updike, *Gary*, p. 61. Updike notes that the Alabama Garys claim a kinship with the Pitts family but states that no documentation has been found. Note that this purchaser was Mary Pitts, later wife of Richard S. Cannon, who was widow of James Pitts, son of Caleb and Frances (Cole) Pitts. Frances Cole's sister Catherine Cole married Stephen Williams, and their daughter Catherine (c. 1797, Newberry Co., SC - aft. 1870, Tishomingo Co., MS) married Thomas Joshua Gary, son of William Gary and Sarah Teague. At the time of this transaction -- 1818 -- Catherine Williams and Thomas Joshua Gary were likely already married. This would mean that the descendants of Thomas Joshua Gary were cousins of the descendants of Caleb and Frances Cole Pitts.

[1684] Updike, *Gary*, pp. 60-62.

Nathan Melton belonged to a family that had settled in Tidewater Virginia in the late seventeenth-century. Richard Melton died about 1730 in New Kent County, Virginia. He appears to have fathered Robert Melton, who moved from New Kent County to Orange County, North Carolina, before 1740. Robert Melton died there testate about 1759, leaving several sons. Among these was Nathan Melton (1735/40 - about October 1806), who settled in Edgefield District, South Carolina, after leaving Orange County in the 1760s. Nathan Melton married in Orange County; deed and estate records indicate that his wife was named Nancy, and a persistent tradition among his descendants holds that she was Nancy Allen, daughter of William Allen (1709-1786) and Mary Owen and granddaughter of Robert Allen (c. 1675 - c. 1758) and Elizabeth Walker (c. 1685 - after 1734) of New Kent and Henrico Counties, Virginia.[1685]

If this relationship is correct, Thomas Melton and his wife Elizabeth Allen Melton were cousins. Elizabeth's father, grandfather, and great-grandfather were all named Robert Allen. The first Robert Allen (c. 1675 - c. 1758) married Elizabeth Walker, daughter of William Walker and Elizabeth Warren of New Kent County, Virginia. Robert Allen, Jr. (c. 1704 - 1782/84) moved from New Kent County to Caswell County, North Carolina; he married Elizabeth, perhaps a Young before her marriage, and they were the parents of Robert Allen (c. 1735, Hanover County, Virginia - c. August 1801, Richmond County, Georgia), who married Elizabeth West. Robert Allen and Elizabeth West Allen were the parents of Elizabeth Allen Melton. Robert and Elizabeth West Allen reared their family in Edgefield District before moving across the state line into Richmond County, Georgia; it was there that Robert Allen died testate about August 1801, with his widow Elizabeth surviving him until 1808.[1686]

As noted, Thomas Melton and Elizabeth Allen Melton may have been second cousins, each being a great-grandchild of Robert Allen and Elizabeth Walker. Such marriages among distant kin were not uncommon in the colonial South. Indeed, common intermarriage into the West family on the part of Charles Gary and Robert Allen indicates that Matthias E. Gary and his wife Sarah Melton Gary were also second cousins. William Melton's mother Patience West Gary was a daughter of Captain William West of Edgefield County, who moved from Edgecombe County, North Carolina, to Saluda River, South Carolina, about 1754. Captain William West died testate in Edgefield County in 1780. Another daughter of Captain William West was Elizabeth West, wife of Robert Allen, III, and mother of Elizabeth Allen Melton.[1687]

Captain William West was one of the first settlers of what became Newberry and Edgefield Counties, South Carolina. A petition from 1754 indicates that his was the only white family living in the Saluda River area. West became a wealthy landowner in South Carolina; he was one of three William Wests, all contemporaries and all kin, who lived in Edgecombe County, North Carolina, before 1750. All three men had been born in Isle of Wight County, Virginia. Captain William West (1715/20 - 1780) was a son of Thomas West (before 1695 - after 1738), of Isle of Wight County, Virginia, and Edgecombe County, North Carolina. William West (1674/1678, Isle of Wight County, Virginia - after 1720, Isle of Wight County, Virginia) was a son of William West (before 1646, Isle of Wight County, Virginia - c. 1709, Isle of Wight County, Virginia) and Rebecca Braswell (c. 1646, Isle of Wight County, Virginia - after 1694, Isle of Wight County, Virginia) and a grandson of Henry West (c. 1610, England - c. 1644, Isle of Wight County, Virginia) and of Rev. Mr. Robert Bracewell (1613, London, England - between February and March 1668, Isle of Wight County, Virginia).[1688]

[1685] Background data on the West, Allen, and Melton families is found in the following sources: D. A. Avant, *Some Southern Colonial Families* (Tallahassee, FL, 1982), pp. 47-120, 304-317; P. Freeman and E. P. Harper, *Twenty-One Southern Families: Notes and Genealogies* (Atlanta, 1985), pp. 116-129; N. C. and G. L. Miller, *Allens of the South States* (Baltimore, 1989), pp. 1-37, 109-118.

[1686] Miller and Miller, *Allens*, pp. 1-37; Avant, *Families*, pp. 105-121.

[1687] Ibid., pp. 105-121.

[1688] Ibid. Identification of the earlier West lineage is based on my study of Bertie and Edgecombe Co., NC, land deeds and the Isle of Wight Co., VA, Wills of William and Robert West.

Henry West, progenitor of the family, may have died in the 1644 Powhattan attack on the settlements of eastern Virginia. The Powhattans had struck once before, in 1622, and rallied in 1644 in a final effort to rid Virginia of the English presence. Henry West's two sons, William and another Henry, were left orphaned. William West would have been an infant at that time. Nothing further is known of his early years except that he was married before 15 February 1667 to Rebecca Braswell, daughter of the local minister, in Isle of Wight County. The names William, Henry, Robert, and Thomas were repeated in each generation of the West family, making it difficult to distinguish one family member from another.[1689] Fortunately, William West, Sr., and William West, Jr., both died testate, with wills proving the family connection. William West, Jr., left a will identifying his son Thomas, who can be traced to North Carolina by virtue of a deed dated 24 August 1723, in which Thomas West, yeoman, and wife Sarah, of North Carolina, sold 600 acres in Isle of Wight County to Richard Beatman. The tract was described as "in the lower parish on the main Blackwater Swamp and Kingsale Swamp and is bounded by James Bryan, being land granted to Henry Applewhaite on 15 October 1696 who deserted it and then it was granted to William West on 17 April 1705, who devised it to his son, the said Thomas West."[1690]

Shortly after the Isle of Wight deed, on 11 November 1724, Thomas West purchased 150 acres on Morratacky River from William and Grace Boddie.[1691] Thomas and Sarah West sold land to William and Grace Boddie in 1729;[1692] they purchased another tract from the Boddies in 1735.[1693] Also in 1729, John and Mourning Pope sold 240 acres joining John Pope and Thomas West to William Bennett.[1694] In 1730, the Popes sold 240 acres to Thomas West with Benjamin Lane (who in 1741 purchased land from Thomas and Mary Gary) and Joseph Watts as witnesses.[1695] On 31 January 1739, Thomas West of Edgecombe County purchased 300 acres on the south side of Swift Creek from John Speir; the land bordered that of Beal Brown, and John Holland, William West, and William Stuart witnessed the deed.[1696] Thomas and Sarah West sold 300 acres on the south side of Swift Creek in Edgecombe County to Captain William Kinchen of Northampton County on 12 December 1741; Thomas West, Jr., probably a son, witnessed the deed.[1697] Thomas and Sarah remained for several years in Edgecombe County, although they may have eventually relocated to South Carolina with their son William West and his family in the 1750s.[1698]

Connections through the West family suggest that Matthias Gary and Sarah Melton likely knew one another well before the time of their marriage in 1818; while Matthias was growing up in Newberry County, members of the Melton family still lived a short distance away in Edgefield and Orangeburg Districts. The family connection, in fact, may have been what prompted Matthias and his mother Elizabeth Jones Gary Whitmore to move from Jones County, Georgia, to Jasper County, Georgia, where they had West and Melton kin residing.

About 1826, around the time that Sarah Melton Gary died, Matthias Gary moved to western Alabama; it is unclear whether Sarah died before or after the move. By 1830, Matthias was living in Perry County, Alabama, probably on the land he had claimed as early as 1817. When he left Perry is not clear;

[1689] See J. B. Boddie, *Seventeenth-Century Isle of Wight* (Chicago, 1938), p. 263.

[1690] Isle of Wight Co., VA, Deeds, Wills, Etc., Great Book, 1715-1726, p. 565.

[1691] Bell, *Bertie Deeds, A-H, 1720-1757*, p. 13, citing Book A, p. 292.

[1692] Bell, *Bertie Deeds, A-H, 1720-1757*, 75, citing Book C, p. 183.

[1693] Hoffman, *Edgecombe Deeds, 1732-1758*, p. 29.

[1694] Bell, *Bertie Deeds, A-H, 1720-1757*, p. 71, citing Book C, p. 136.

[1695] Bell, *Bertie Deeds, A-H, 1720-1757*, p. 81, Book C, p. 253.

[1696] Hoffman, *Edgecombe Deeds, 1732-1758*, p. 33.

[1697] Hoffman, *Edgecombe Deeds, 1732-1758*, p. 172.

[1698] Note that one Thomas West is shown with a plat for 150 acres in Granville Co., SC, Three Runs Creek, Savannah River, on 25 March 1754; a plat for 500 acres in Craven County, Pee Dee River, on 25 June 1757; a grant for 500 acres in Craven County on 20 February 1760; a memorial for 500 acres in Craven County, Pee Dee River, on 1 May 1761; a land grant for 150 acres in Granville County on 7 May 1762; and a memorial for 150 acres on Three Runs Creek, Savannah River, in Granville County on 8 October 1763. These references can be accessed through the on-line records index at the South Carolina Department of Archives and History, Columbia, SC.

he has not been located in the 1840 census, but by 1850 he was living in Sumter County, Alabama, near the boundary between Alabama and Mississippi. At that time he was a farmer with property valued at $1,500; he was living next to his adult son, John Gary, also a farmer, but with property valued at $3,000.[1699] Matthias was taxed in Smith County, Mississippi, in 1853 and in 1857, being shown in the latter roll with his son Starling Tucker Gary.[1700] Matthias was enumerated in Smith County, Mississippi, in 1860, but about this time he purchased a tract of land in Lauderdale County, where he remained for the rest of his life.[1701] At the time of the 1880 census, Matthias was enumerated as aged 82, a native of South Carolina and a boarder in the household of his son, John H. Gary, a cotton broker in Meridian, Mississippi.[1702]

Matthias Gary died on 1 November 1887 at the age of ninety. The *Meridian Messenger* carried news of his death:

> Died yesterday at eleven o'clock, Mr. Mathias E. Gary, the venerable father of Col. John H. Gary, Sr. He departed this life at his son's residence. He was one of the eldest men of this part of the Southern Country, having first seen the light in Newberry District, South Carolina. From there he moved first to Georgia, from there he moved to Sumter County, Alabama. In 1853, he removed to Smith County, Mississippi, living there for twelve years, and from there he moved to this County, where he has since lived continuously with the exception of a few years again spent in Sumter. Where ever this good man dwelt, he had the respect and esteem of all who knew him, retaining to the last his devotion to principle and his faith in the Christian religion. Few men have lived so long and so blamelessly and, though for a long time sightless here, he saw the mercies allotted by God to the faithful on earth and walked close to his God, for very many years of his life.[1703]

Descendants of Starling Tucker Gary recalled visits from Starling's father Matthias, who at advanced age traveled alone by horseback to visit his grandchildren.[1704]

Matthias Gary and Sarah Melton were parents of five children.[1705] West Melton Gary (22 February 1819 - about 1841) died unmarried. Colonel John Henry Gary (16 May 1820, Jasper County, Georgia - c. 1892, Meridian, Lauderdale County, Mississippi) married Elizabeth Monett; he was Sheriff of Sumter County, Alabama, from 1860 to 1865 and built a grand ante-bellum home in Meridian, Mississippi, where his father died in 1887. Starling Tucker Gary -- named for Edgefield District, South Carolina, Senator Starling Tucker -- was born 11 April 1821 in Jasper County, Georgia, or Perry County, Alabama. He died in November 1862 while a Confederate soldier in Scott County, Mississippi.[1706] Thomas Gary (6 May 1823 - abt. 1841) also died unmarried. Pernecia Gary (7 June 1825-27 August 1887, Navarro County, Texas) married David Maggard (1817-1903) in 1842.

[1699] 1850 Sumter Co., AL, Census, p. 259.

[1700] 1853 and 1857 Smith Co., MS, Tax Rolls, Mississippi Department of Archives and History, Jackson, MS.

[1701] Lauderdale Co., MS, DB Z, p. 464; 1860 Smith Co., MS, Census, p. 277.

[1702] 1880 Census, Lauderdale, Meridian Co., MS, p. 26, HH 448/531.

[1703] Updike, *Gary Family*, p. 62, citing *Meridian Messenger*, 2 November, 1887, and Maggard Family Bible.

[1704] This story was related to me on 19 April 2004 by Anne Martin Haigler, Birmingham, AL.

[1705] See Updike, *Gary*, pp. 60-62.

[1706] Anne Martin Haigler indicated in a personal interview, 19 April 2004, Birmingham, AL, that family tradition indicated that Starling Tucker Gary was a son of Mathias and Sarah Melton Gary and that other Gary researchers had also maintained this. Unfortunately, proof of all of the children of Matthias and Sarah has not been located. Anne Martin Haigler was able to establish Starling's parentage sufficiently for membership in the National Society Daughters of the American Revolution. A. A. Gary -- a grandson of Starling Tucker Gary -- in the 1950s identified Matthias as Starling's father. Family tradition holds that Mathias rode a horse from Meridian to be with the family of Starling Tucker Gary when news arrived of Starling's death.

The third son of Matthias E. and Sarah Melton Gary, Starling Tucker Gary was reared in Perry and Sumter Counties, Alabama. He married Mary Ann Stringer (8 October, 1823, Mississippi - 30 December, 1910, Madison County, Mississippi) on 2 November 1843 in Meridian.[1707] Rev. Isaac Gary, Starling's cousin and a Baptist minister in western Alabama and eastern Mississippi, may have played a role in introducing the couple; at the time of the 1850 Lauderdale County, Mississippi, census, Isaac was living in Household 727 while the Stringers were living nearby in Household 758.[1708]

Starling Gary has not been located in the 1850 census; he was taxed in Lauderdale County in 1848, when he paid poll tax only, and in Smith County, Mississippi, in 1857 with his father Matthias Gary.[1709] On 9 September 1858, as Starling T. Gary of Smith County, he purchased the W1/2 of SW 1/4 of Section 31, Township 5, Range 6 East -- what is today southern Scott County -- for $800. Starling was taxed in Scott County in 1859, but he has not been located in the 1860 census, although both Matthias Gary and William Stringer and their families were found in neighboring Smith County at that time.[1710]

Starling T. Gary enlisted in the Confederate army on 5 July 1862 in Scott County, Mississippi, serving in Company D, 1st Battalion, Mississippi State Troops. The decision would prove to have momentous consequences for Starling's family. He was present as late as 31 October 1862, and his name appears on a roster for November and December 1862, with the notation that he died on 27 November at his home in Scott County.[1711] Later records indicate that Starling died "sick while home on leave."[1712]

Although widowed at a young age, Mary Ann Stringer Gary was surrounded by her own biological kin in Smith and Scott Counties as well as by many of her husband's relatives in western Alabama and eastern Mississippi. She remained in Scott County into the 1870s, having been enumerated at Morton Post Office at the time of the 1870 census.[1713] By 1880, the Garys had relocated to Tinnin School Precinct, Hinds County, Mississippi,[1714] where Mary headed a household that included her two youngest children She was still living with these two children at Flora in Madison County in 1900, at which time she was seventy-six years of age.[1715]

While living in Madison County, on 29 August 1907, Mary initiated a claim for a Confederate widow's pension based on the service of her husband Starling T. Gary. Mary stated that she was "nearly eighty-four" and that she had been a widow for forty-five years. She deposed that her husband was sent home because of illness on 24 November 1862 and died at home two days later; she had never remarried and applied in 1907 because she was then unable to work and earn a living for herself. At the time of her

---

[1707] Gary Family History, p. 227. HUNTING FORBEARs shows this marriage 27 October 1843 in Lauderdale Co., MS, with the surname recorded as Garey. Also married there was John M. Stringer to Martha J. Miller on 1 January 1856; Lydye Gary to Curtis J. Smith, 31 January 1887; and of T. P. Gary to Sadie Overby, 9 June 1890.

[1708] 1850 Lauderdale Co., MS, Census, pp. 377-379.

[1709] 1848 Lauderdale Co., MS, Tax Roll; 1857 Smith Co., MS, Tax Roll, Mississippi Department of Archives and History, Jackson, MS.

[1710] 1860 Scott Co., MS, Census, p. 116. The only Gary family shown in Scott County was living at Morton Post Office, HH 775/775, 24 August 1860, and appeared as follows: James Gary, 40, SC; Mary, 35, SC; Martha, 18, AL; William, 12, AL; Pinkney, 10, AL; Mary, 8, AL; and Emaly, 6, AL. This James is not found before 1860 or afterwards. He could be the James Gary claimed as a brother of Martha Gary Clay, Benjamin Gary, and John Gary. It is possible, however, that this census is mistaken and that this man is actually Starling Tucker Gary. Starling's family should have been enumerated in this way: Starling Tucker Gary, 39, GA; Mary, 36, AL; Martha, 15, MS; William, 13, MS; Mary, 10, MS; Emily, 8, MS; Pinkney, 5, MS. Many census takers recorded information from neighbors without visiting every household. It is striking that the names of the children shown are the same names as the then living children of Starling and Mary Ann, and in the same birth order, except for Pinkney. A possible explanation there -- especially if the census taker relied on second hand information -- is that Allen Gary (1848 - 1860) had died less than two months before the enumeration. The person supplying the census data may have confused the ages of the boy who died with the one who survived.

[1711] Mississippi Confederate Military Rosters, Mississippi Department of Archives and History, Jackson, MS.

[1712] Mississippi Confederate Widow's Pension Application of Mary Gary, Madison Co., MS, Mississippi Department of Archives and History, Jackson, MS.

[1713] 1870 Scott Co., MS, Census, Morton P.O., Beat No. 3, p. 22.

[1714] 1880 Hinds Co., MS, Census, Beat No. 1, Tinnin School Precinct, p. 123, HH 662/692.

[1715] 1900 Madison Co., MS, Census, p. 147.

application, she had two sons and two daughters living and was residing with her unmarried son S. M. Gary.[1716] Aged eighty-six, Mary Ann Stringer Gary was still living in Flora with her son Starling and daughter Emily at the time of the 1910 federal census; she died on 30 December 1910 at the age of eighty-seven, having outlived her husband by nearly half a century.[1717]

Mary Ann Stringer Gary was a daughter of William Stringer (c. 1792, Edgefield District, South Carolina - 1860, Holmesville, Smith County, Mississippi) and Ann Parks (4 July 1792, South Carolina -- 14 June 1863, Smith County, Mississippi), who married in Clark County, Alabama, on 9 July 1820. Both William and Ann were natives of South Carolina; William's family had come from Edgefield District, although nothing definite has been learned about Ann's parentage.[1718] William Stringer's family traces to a group of Stringers living in southern Virginia and eastern North Carolina in the early eighteenth century. Dr. Francis Stringer, a prominent physician and justice in Craven County, North Carolina, wrote a will on 8 January 1749 in which he names his wife, offspring, mother, and several other relatives. After providing for his wife Hannah and daughter Elizabeth, Stringer wrote:

> Second, I give and bequeath unto my dear Mother, Mary Stringer, if Living and claiming by herself or any person for her within the term and space of ten years ensuing the date hereof; one of my best feather Good Rugs, One good pair of Blankets, One good pair of muslin sheets, One good feather bolster and pillow, One good pillow case, One Bedstead, two middle sized Iron Pots, Twelve new pewter plates, two new pewter dishes, one good case of knives and forks, to be bought by my Executors out of my personal estate and delivered by them to her. Likeways, I give and bequeath unto my said mother Mary Stringer, if living and should come into this said province or claim as above said my stock of hoggs that are upon a plantation or belonging thereto, which I formerly bought of Henry Summerlin, ten cows and calves, I further will desire that my said mother when in this province, shall live upon said plantation on Contentoe, which I bought of said Henry Summerlin, and have the whole profits of said Plantation and the use and labor of two Negroes, towit, of one Negro man called Bigg Ceesar and of one Negro woman said Ceesar's wife called Rose during my said Mother's natural life and after her, my said Mother's decease, I devise and bequeath said plantation and land containing three hundred acres unto my half-brother Ralph Stringer, his heirs and assigns forever, provided he or his representative claims the said land within ten years after my said mother's decease. And the above said two Negroes after my said Mother's decease I give to my daughter Elizabeth Stringer. And in case my said Mother should not come into this

---

[1716] Mississippi Confederate Widow's Pension Application of Mary Gary, Madison Co., MS, Mississippi Department of Archives and History, Jackson, MS.

[1717] 1910 Madison Co., MS, Census, p. 197.

[1718] There was a large Parker family in Clarke Co., AL. Researching this family is complicated by the fact that another William Stringer married Ann Parker, daughter of Jesse and Charlotte Parker, about the same time that this William Stringer married Ann Parks. It is possible that Ann's maiden name was Parks instead of Parker, but the two recorded versions of the name spell it as Parks and Parke. Further, there are only three other marriage records for individuals named Parks in Clarke County before 1850. These were the marriages of "Mary Parks" to John Purvis on 14 December 1819; of "Sarah Parks" to William Nelson on 5 December 1819; and of "Lucy Parks" to Charles Lane in 17 May 1828. The marriage of Sarah Parks to William Nelson spells the name as both Parks and Parker. William Nelson and William Stringer were neighbors in Copiah County, MS, by 1830; William Nelson remained in Copiah County as late as 1840. Sarah apparently died, however, and William Nelson returned to Clarke Co., AL, before 1850, where he may have married Winifred Traywick as his second wife. John Purvis was in Rankin Co., MS, by 1840; he remained there in 1850 and 1860, both times shown with wife Mary, born about 1796 in South Carolina. Charles and Lucy Lane were living in Clarke Co., MS, in 1850; Lucy was aged 42 and born in South Carolina. Note that all four of the Parks women marrying in Clarke County, Alabama, between 1818 and 1828 were born in South Carolina between 1792 and 1808. Charner Parks and John Parks were living in Rankin Co., MS, by 1830; they may have been relatives of these four women, who were likely sisters. Since Parks was sometimes written as Parker in Clarke County, it is difficult to distinguish between the two names. The surname Parks does not appear on the 1816 Clarke County tax list, although deed records do contain a reference to one John Parks.

Province, & claim by herself or Others any part or parcell of any bequest or legacy left her before in this my will, it is then my will and desire that my Executors herein after mentioned shall make sale of my land in Adam's Creek and out of the money arising from such sale pay unto my said Mother if living and claiming by herself or others one hundred pistoles.[1719]

In addition to his mother, Stringer identified several other relatives, giving clues to the maiden identity of his wife as well as to his own family connections in North Carolina and beyond. To his "Brother-in-law John Shine",[1720] who had apparently married a sister of Francis Stringer's wife, Stringer bequeathed the one half of a tract of land I bought of Durham Handcock, lying on the East side of Stoney Town Creek in Craven County, and to his heirs and assigns forever. I further order and direct after said land shall be divided he shall have his Choice of which part he will except. I give and bequeath unto my said Brother-in-law John Shine the sums of money he is indebted to me at the date hereof, my silver mounted cutter, and all my Family Books.[1721]

To another brother-in-law, Daniel Shine, Stringer left land on Upper Falling Creek in Johnston County. The bequests to his own kin are more complicated. Francis Stringer attempted to provide not only for his siblings but also for more distant cousins as well:

Fifthly. I give, devise and bequeath unto my brother William Stringer, to him his heirs and assigns forever, all my Lotts in Newbern Town, provided he or any person for him Claims in ten years, and until such claim is made I give the rents and profits of said lotts in Newbern unto my Daughter Elizabeth Stringer.

....I give and bequeath unto John Stringer, a crippled Boy, son of George Stringer, of Core Creek in this County, One hundred forty-three pounds eleven shillings old Bill Money which his Father George Stringer is indebted to me, which said sum of one hundred forty-three pounds eleven shillings I desire my Executors to buy cows and calves with and take up a piece of land for said John in a good place for cattle and put the cattle out on said land for the use of the said John Stringer.

....I give and bequeath unto my Nephew Thomas Stringer, Jun'r Son of my said Brother Ralph Stringer, and unto my Illegitimate Brother Thomas Stringer, Equally, to them their heirs and assigns forever, provided they, or any person for them, claim in ten years, my land commonly called Dover, containing more or less two hundred and fifty acres, and if any one of them or any person empowered by them should claim before the other, then it is my desire that my Executors should lay off to him so claiming the full one half of my said land called Dover.

....I given and bequeath unto my said daughter Elizabeth Stringer all my real estate I am now possessed with, except such part as this will is otherwise given or bequeathed, to her and her heirs lawfully begotten...and in case my said Daughter should die before she arrives at age or has lawful issue...unto the before mentioned William Stringer, my

---

[1719] Original Will of Francis Stringer, Craven Co., NC, NC Department of Archives and History, Raleigh, NC.

[1720] J. W. Shine, *Shine Family in Europe and America* (Sault St. Marie, MI, 1917) indicates that three brothers -- Daniel, Francis, and John Shine, came from Dublin, Ireland, to America, about 1710. They settled around Newbern and Duplin, North Carolina. Daniel married Elizabeth Greene, and had a large family. His eldest child Hannah was born 16 July 1718. He had a grandson Francis Stringer Shine born 24 March 1761.

[1721] Original Will of Francis Stringer, Craven Co., NC, NC Department of Archives and History, Raleigh, NC.

Brother[1722], and to his heirs lawfully begotten of his body forever, and for want of such heirs I then devise and bequeath the whole that I have given to my said Daughter to be equally divided between my before mentioned Nephew Thomas Stringer, my half-brother Ralph Stringer, and my illegitimate brother Thomas Stringer, and their heirs lawfully begotten forever, and for want to such heirs I then desire my Executors may deliver up my said daughters estate unto the churchwardens of Christ Church Parish in this county aforesaid for the time being and do hereby give my said daughter's estate unto the poor of said Christ Church Parish...the money arising...to be applied in putting out poor people's children to School in said parish in perpetium the principal untouched.[1723]

Unfortunately, the details that led to Francis Stringer's complicated family structure remain unclear. His father, apparently, had married twice, producing a "half-brother" Ralph Stringer as well as Francis and his "brother" William Stringer, who must have been sons of the Mary Stringer identified by Francis in his will as his mother. Since Francis's mother was still living, Ralph Stringer must have been older than Francis. In addition to these three sons, the unidentified father of Francis Stringer -- who had certainly lived in another colony, if not in Ireland or England -- must have produced a son Thomas by an illicit relationship. Yet, for good or ill, Francis and his siblings seem to have been aware of this illegitimate brother, for Francis took it upon himself to include him a residual heir for the real estate bequeathed to his daughter Elizabeth Stringer.[1724]

Francis Stringer was apparently attempting to cast himself in the style of the English gentry, to whom he may in fact have belonged. An ancient Stringer family -- using the given names Francis, William, Thomas, Ralph, and George -- is found in Overthrope and Thornhill, Yorkshire, and can be traced to the thirteenth-century. Armigerous and well-connected, these Stringers were lords of the manor and minor officials in rural Yorkshire. The bequest to the poor of Christ Church Parish indicates that Francis was following the gentry custom of leaving a small sum to those less fortunate; unlike many colonials, though, Francis' claim to gentry status may have been authentic.[1725]

The remainder of Francis' will concerned his wife and daughter. Francis attempted to secure his real property and to ensure that both would be handsomely maintained by his estate:

Item. It is my desire that my wife, Hannah Stringer, shall have the use and profits of my Plantation on Stony Town Creek whereon I now live during the course of her natural life, provided she claims nor takes any dower out of my lands, but if she claims or takes any Dower of my said lands then my will is She shall have no part of any of my personal Estate Except forty pounds sterling which I desire my Executors may pay her, and in case my said wife Hannah Remains unmarried after my deceased I desire she may Keep my said Daughter with her and Educate and maintain her handsomely untill my said Daughter shall arrive at the age of Twenty-one years, or the Day of marriage which shall first happen, and that my said wife for and towards such educating and maintaining my said Daughter shall have keep to her own use the profits of the lands and Negroes by this Will given to my said Daughter, but in case my said wife marries before my said Daughter arrives to age or is married as aforesaid then and in such case, I hereby order

---

[1722] Boddie, *Seventeenth Century Isle of Wight*, p. 556, discusses a deed for land assigned to William Stringer on 2 March 1639 and from William Stringer to Samuel Davis, deceased, on 15 June 1642. Also, Boddie, *Seventeenth Century Isle of Wight*, p. 555, mentions William Stringer, attorney for Mary Markes, of Barbados, on 9 February 1668. William Stringer apparently was in Isle of Wight at this time.

[1723] Original Will of Francis Stringer, Craven Co., NC, NC Department of Archives and History, Raleigh, NC.

[1724] Ibid.

[1725] See the pedigree of Stringer of Sharleton in J. W. Clay, ed., *Dugdale's Visitation of Yorkshire, 1665-1666, With Additions* (3 vols., Exeter, 1917).

and direct that my Executors hereafter named shall take into their hands all the estate hereby given to my said Daughter and apply it in the best manner for the use of my said Daughter so that they nor any of them make sale thereof in case my wife marries before my Daughter comes of age or is married then I appoint my Executors Guardians to my Daughter.

....In case my Mother should choose in full for all legacies left her in this Will to be paid said hundred pistoles, then and in such case I empower hereby my Executors to sell and convey my land that I bought of Humphrey Smith and John Smith which lies in Adams Creek down Nuse River and out of the product of such sale to pay unto my said Mother or her order the said One hundred pistoles and in case any of the said --- should be left after my said Mother is paid of said hundred pistoles I desire my Executors divide it equally between my said wife and my said daughter. But in case my Mother or her heirs should not choose to take the said hundred pistoles, I then desire my Executors to in no manner or way whatever to sell or convey any part of my real estate.

....I give and bequeath unto my loving wife, Hannah Stringer, eight Negroes to wit.....the one half part of my household goods and stocks of cattle, horses, and hogs, except what is heretofore given, also one half of all my outstanding debts, goods, wares, and merchandize of any denomination whatever.

....I give and bequeath unto my Daughter Elizabeth Stringer, eight slaves....the full one half of all my household goods stocks of cattle, horses, and hogs, except what is before given to my mother, Mary Stringer, also the one half of all my outstanding debts, goods, wares, and merchandize, of any denomination whatever.[1726]

Having provided for his wife and only child, Francis appointed "friends" Daniel Shine, James Greene, and Thomas Grave to execute his will. Again, in gentry custom, he left each executor "one Mourning...Each ring to be in value one Guinea."[1727]

Stringer's will, which was dated 8 January 1749 and proven 30 March 1753, is significant for several reasons. First, it indicates that William had close relatives still residing in England or Ireland, suggesting that he and his siblings were likely all born there. Second, it evidences a family connection between William and a second family of Stringers living in Craven County headed by George and John Stringer. Third, it indicates that William's father -- whose name is unknown -- had both legitimate and illegitimate offspring, a fact that was well known to Francis and his siblings.

Dr. Francis Stringer was a man of considerable importance in eighteenth century North Carolina. In addition to being a prominent physician and justice in Craven County, Stringer served in the North Carolina Assembly from 1745 to 1754. He married Elizabeth Ann Mackilwean, daughter of James and Eleanor Mackilwean of Craven County. James Mackilwean was Surveyor General of North Carolina and an elected member of the colony's legislature. Mackilwean's other daughters, sisters of Hannah Stringer, married Major General Richard Caswell (1729-1789), later Governor of North Carolina; John Shine (1725-1783), named as a brother-in-law in Francis Stringer's will; General Samuel McClure; and General Samuel Simpson. Caswell, who rose to prominence during the American struggle against Great Britain,

[1726] Original Will of Francis Stringer, Craven Co., NC, NC Department of Archives and History, Raleigh, NC.

[1727] Original Will of Francis Stringer, Craven Co., NC, NC Department of Archives and History, Raleigh, NC. For an abstract, see Grimes, *North Carolina Wills*, pp. 363-364.

became the first Governor of the independent state of North Carolina and was the only governor ever to serve for six one year terms.[1728]

The relationship, if any, between Dr. Francis Stringer and William Stringer's ancestor John Stringer of Chowan County, North Carolina, is unclear. Dr. Francis Stringer's will named George Stringer as his cousin; many records identify George Stringer of Chowan County, documenting his residence there as early as 1732 and perhaps well before.[1729] George Stringer owned several tracts of land in Craven and Chowan Counties and appears in deed and court records with both Dr. Francis Stringer and Daniel Shine, brother of John Shine. In September 1749, George Stringer gave a statement that he was then "upwards of sixty-six years of age" and alleged that he had "grown very infirm."[1730] This record requested that George be exempted from the county levy because of disability and further requested "that John Stringer his son being Born a Cripple and not able to work might be Discharged from all Duties and Paying Taxes Granted."[1731] From this record, we learn that John Stringer was thus born by 1731 at the latest, and possibly well before that date. George Stringer in 1756 deeded 150 acres of land in Craven to John Stringer;[1732] George apparently died in 1764, at which time George Stringer, Jr., served as administrator of George and Mary Stringer.[1733] These records cumulatively suggest that George Stringer (by 1683 -- 1764) fathered at least two children, John Stringer and George Stringer, Jr.

There is no clear indication of the age of the crippled John Stringer of Chowan County. On 2 August 1742, one John Stringer -- perhaps this man -- purchased 200 acres on Fort Run in Craven County from Abraham Odum.[1734] The deed was proven in September 1743 before Captain Francis Stringer, Justice of Craven County.[1735] John Stringer purchased another 100 acres in Craven in 1748[1736] and was apparently still in Craven County when George Stringer deeded him land in 1756.

The relationship between George Stringer of Craven and John Stringer of Chowan is uncertain. George Stringer was far less prominent than his cousin Francis Stringer, although he was apparently a respected landowner and planter. It may be that John Stringer of Chowan and George Stringer of Craven were brothers. Certainly, John Stringer of Chowan County had died long before Dr. Francis Stringer wrote his will in 1749. The death date of this John Stringer is unclear; what is clear, however, is that he predeceased his wife, that she had been previously married, and that she had several children and even adult grandchildren by 1748. These facts suggest that she had been a second wife of John Stringer, probably one whom he married late in life, and that any children he fathered would have been by an earlier marriage. Further, it should be emphasized that this Mary Stringer was not Mary Stringer, mother of Francis Stringer of Craven, whom he mentioned in his will several years later. While the evidence is not yet conclusive, it seems likely that the adult John Stringer who appears in Chowan from at least about 1745 until 1750 was John Stringer, Jr., a son of John Stringer, Sr. This would suggest that John Stringer, Jr., was born at least by about 1724 and that John Stringer, Sr., was born by about 1700.[1737]

The earliest known reference to the younger John Stringer of Chowan dates from the "3rd Tuesday in October 1745," when he was impaneled to serve on a jury in Chowan.[1738] Months earlier, on 27 April

---

[1728] "The Story of Governor Richard Caswell of Lenoir," in Lenoir County Heritage Commission, *The Heritage of Lenoir County, North Carolina* (Kinston, NC, 1981); see also W. K. Sparrow and C. B. Alexander, *"First of Patriots and the Best of Men": Richard Caswell in Public Life* (Kinston, NC, 2007).

[1729] Haun, *Craven Precinct, North Carolina, Precinct County Court Minutes*, 2: 65.

[1730] Ibid., 2: 15.

[1731] Ibid., 2: 15.

[1732] Ibid., 2: 334.

[1733] S. A. Bradley, *Craven Co., NC, Wills, Deeds, Inventories* (2 vols., Lawrenceville, VA, 2001), 2: 273.

[1734] Ibid., 2: 44.

[1735] Haun, *Craven Precinct, North Carolina, Precinct County Court Minutes*, 3: 375.

[1736] North Carolina Land Patent Book 5, p. 234.

[1737] Grimes, *North Carolina Wills*, p. 364.

[1738] W. P. Haun, *Chowan Co., NC, County Court Minutes Pleas & Quarter Sessions, 1730-1754* (3 vols., Durham, NC, 1983), 1: 242.

1744, Mary Stringer, "widow of John Stringer, deceased, of the county of Chowan in the Province of North Carolina" wrote her will. Mary names no children by John Stringer but does identify her sons John Sanders and Francis Sanders, along with several daughters and grandchildren. Although the evidence is circumstantial, the Chowan records suggest that John Stringer had been married before he married Mary Sanders Stringer and that the younger John Stringer of Chowan may have been his son. The younger man, born at least by 1724, gave evidence in a court suit in 1748[1739] and served as a juror in 1749.[1740] Although the actual deed has not been located, Chowan Court Minutes indicate that he sold his lands in Chowan prior to April 1750, when a deed from John and Martha Stringer to Robert Powell was proved on oath of Henry Smith.[1741]

This John Stringer vanished from North Carolina records after 1750; the timing is ideal for him to have been identical with the John Stringer who appears soon thereafter in South Carolina, where he petitioned the South Carolina Governor's Council for a grant of land on 3 December 1751:

> The petition of John Stringer humbly setting forth that the petitioner has lately come from the northward with an intent to settle in this province, and has fixed on some land which he has begun to plant, but the Indians have entirely ruined his crop your petitioner is *desirous of settling himself on Stephens Creek, where he has begun to Improve some land proper for the benefit of his family, that he has a wife and four children and never had any land granted him for said family*: he prays to lay out to your petitioner 300 acres of land on the Stephens Creek as aforesaid and that he may have a grant for the same.[1742]

The Council granted Stringer's petition. Note that Stringer received fifty acres for himself, fifty acres for his wife, and then fifty acres for each child under age sixteen. The record indicates that John and his wife had four children born prior to 1751; if the children were born in 1750, 1748, 1746, and 1744, then the parents were likely born in the early 1720s -- dates fitting well with the projected birth date of John Stringer of Chowan.

John Stringer remained in western South Carolina for the rest of his life; the date of his death is uncertain. He may have been one of the John Stringers living in Edgefield District during the American Revolution, and he might even be the John Stringer enumerated in Abbeville District, aged more than forty-five years, in 1800. Unfortunately, records do not permit a positive identification.

It is believed that John and Martha Stringer were the parents of four younger men who later appear in Edgefield and Abbeville Districts: Francis Stringer, who began claiming South Carolina lands in 1762;[1743] William Stringer, who began claiming South Carolina lands in 1771; George Stringer, who was serving as a Revolutionary soldier in 96th District as early as 1778 and who was killed about 1781 in an ambush by Tories;[1744] and John Stringer, Jr., mentioned in George Stringer's 1783 estate accounts and probably the man who in 1781 furnished beef and supplies to the Continental Army.

William Stringer of Edgefield County, South Carolina, was apparently one of the four children of John Stringer mentioned in the 1751 land petition. On 1 January 1771, he petitioned for 150 acres in South Carolina, suggesting that he was married and that he may already have had one child at that

---

[1739] Ibid., 2: 203.

[1740] Ibid., 3: 17.

[1741] Ibid., 3: 39.

[1742] Holcomb, *Petitions for Land from South Carolina Council Journals*, Volume 3, 3 December 1751.

[1743] Francis probably left South Carolina after 1765; he fits to be the Francis Stringer in St. Paul's Parish, Georgia, between 1765 and 1774. He may be ancestor of many of the Stringers of eastern Georgia and South Alabama, probably also including the other Stringer families of Clarke Co., AL. He may be the Francis Stringer who settled in Washington Co., Mississippi Territory (later Alabama), about 1796.

[1744] Leonardo Andrea, The Leonardo Andrea Genealogical Collection for South Carolina, South Caroliniana Library, The University of South Carolina, Stringer File, Item 25.

date.[1745] On 12 July 1771, William was granted 150 acres on Stephens' Creek in what was then Granville County but later Edgefield District, South Carolina.[1746] Between 1780 and 1782, William served as a private in the South Carolina militia under Col. Robert Anderson, in Abbeville County.[1747] Although not shown as a head of household in 1790, William was granted 500 acres on the Saluda River in 1792[1748] and still owned land in Edgefield in 1798.[1749] In 1799, he received plats for 426 acres on Beaverdam in Washington District and for 333 acres on Fall Creek in the Saluda Mountains.[1750] One William Stringer was enumerated in Greenville District in 1800 (although the census indicates that he was born later than 1755). The William Stringer who patented land in 1771, however, died in Edgefield about 1801, leaving a wife and administratrix named Elizabeth Stringer.[1751] The clearest evidence of a connection with John Stringer of the 1751 petition is a posthumous one recounted in a deed from Benjamin Mock to John Morange of Abbeville County in 1819, wherein Mock conveyed two tracts on the Savannah River, "one granted John Stringer 13 December 1752 and conveyed by William Stringer to John Scott 26 February 1769 and from him to George Mock 7 July 1769; the other tract granted George Mock 21 February 1772."[1752] This last record is especially significant, for it indicates that William Stringer was of legal age before 7 July 1769 and thus born prior to 7 July 1748; one likely interpretation is that John Stringer had deeded the tract to his son William when he came of age in the 1760s.

William Stringer seems to have married two, if not three, times. The identity of his first wife is unknown. His second wife, who lived from about 1764 to about 1788, was a daughter of Michael Burkhalter (1725, Luetzelflueh, Berne, Switzerland - 1807, Edgefield District, South Carolina) and Anna Dentzler (c. 1726, Ilnau Parish, Zurich, Switzerland -), and a granddaughter of Michael Burkhalter (6 April 1694, Luetzelflueh, Berne, Switzerland -) and Adelheit Kobel (18 December 1696, Luetzelflueh, Switzerland -) and Conrad Dentzler (4 March 1702/3, Ilnau Parish, Zurich, Switzerland -) and Anna Wetzstein (c. 1702, Ilnau, Zurich, Switzerland -).[1753] William Stringer probably married for a third time following the death of his second wife to a woman named Elizabeth, who survived him.

Circumstantial evidence in Edgefield County indicates that William Stringer fathered at least three children by a first marriage: John Stringer (c. 1767 - c. 1802); Jeremiah Stringer (c. 1772 - aft. 1800); and Eli Stringer (c. 1775 - after 1850). John Stringer will be discussed below. Jeremiah Stringer purchased a tract of land joining William Stringer on 5 April 1797 from John Slater, Sr.[1754] John Stringer and William Stringer witnessed the transaction, and, in 1800, Jeremiah was enumerated near the Slater family as aged 26-45. Eli Stringer, born about 1775 and called brother in the will of John Stringer, married Peggy Henderson and moved from South Carolina to Indiana, where he was living as late as 1850.

William Stringer was married by about 1784 to a daughter of Michael Burkhalter; Burkhalter's estate settlement names only Jonathan and Willis Stringer as heirs, suggesting, but not establishing, that his daughter was not the mother of the three older children.[1755] Jonathan Stringer, born about 1784, died 2 May 1826 in Edgefield County; he married Martha Williams, who moved with his large family to Harris County, Georgia, and then Russell County, Alabama. Willis Stringer, born about 1787, lived in Coweta

---

[1745] Holcombe, *Petitions for land from the SC Council Journals*, Volume 7, 1 January 1771.

[1746] Andrea, Stringer File, Item 14.

[1747] Andrea, Stringer File, Item 26.

[1748] Andrea, Stringer File, Item 16. He received a plat for this land in 1797. See Andrea, Stringer File, Item 22.

[1749] Edgefield Co., SC, DB 16, pp. 6-8.

[1750] Andrea, Stringer File, Items 22a, 16.

[1751] William Stringer Loose Estate File, Edgefield Co., SC, Probate Court Files, Edgefield, SC.

[1752] C. Wells, *Edgefield Co., SC, Deed Books 36-38* (Baltimore, 2007), p. 41.

[1753] The Burkhalters immigrated to Georgia about 1735 as part of the Salzburger Colony. Michael married Anna Denzler 18 May 1745 in Georgia. They moved to South Carolina about 1755. Michael Burkhalter, Sr., died in 1762 at Vernonburg in Georgia. See P. R. Gnann, A. G. LeBey, M. L. Lassiter, et. al., *Georgia Salzburgers and Allied Families* (4 vols., Greenville, SC, 1956-2003), 1: 32.

[1754] Edgefield Co., SC, DB 14, pp. 443-445.

[1755] Michael Burkhalter Loose Estate File, Edgefield Co., SC, Probate Court, Edgefield, SC.

County, Georgia, from before 1830 to after 1840; by 1850, he had settled in Ouachita County, Arkansas, where he and wife Lenora were enumerated at the time of the 1850 census.

John Stringer, probably born about 1767, is believed to have been the eldest son of William Stringer.[1756] There is no indication that his mother was Michael Burkhalter's daughter, although such a relationship is not impossible.

The earliest known reference to John Stringer dates from 5 February 1788, when he bought 100 acres in Edgefield County on the south side of Stephens's Creek, joining land owned by William Stringer.[1757] This land was located in the same neighborhood where John Stringer had petitioned for land in 1751. John was enumerated in Edgefield County in 1790, head of a household that consisted only of himself, his wife, and an infant son. He had probably married recently to Nancy Slater, born about 1775, daughter of John Slater, who lived a few households away. On 11 September 1791, John Stringer received a plat for 406 acres in Edgefield County, located on Stephens' Creek of the Savannah River and joining lands owned by the said John Stringer and John Slater.[1758] On 30 August 1796, John and Ann Stringer sold 300 of these acres to Joel Grizzel with John Slater as witness; adjacent landowners were John Stringer, William Stringer, and Col. John Purvis.[1759] John and William Stringer were witnesses in 1797 when his father-in-law John Slater deeded land to Jeremiah Stringer[1760]. On 1 December 1798, John Stringer purchased 150 acres from Samuel Melton of Columbia County, Georgia, with his brother Eli Stringer as witness.[1761] He and William Stringer were witnesses in February 1799 when Evan Morgan sold land on Stephens' Creek,[1762] and, on 2 November 1799, John and Ann Stringer sold 125 acres joining William Stringer on Stephens Creek, again with William and Eli Stringer as witnesses.[1763]

At the time of the 1800 census, John Stringer and wife Ann were both aged twenty-six to forty-five, hence born between 1755 and 1774. Their household included two sons and a daughter under age ten and a slightly older female.[1764] Soon after the census, on 9 May 1801, Jonathan Dawson and Davis Williams sold 280 acres off Stephens Creek of the Savannah River to John Stringer; the land had originally been granted to Jefferson Williams, and Eli Stringer and William Stringer witnessed the deed.[1765] On the same day, Jonathan Dawson sold John Stringer's brother Eli 169 acres adjoining the tract he had deeded to John Stringer.[1766] On 17 July 1801, John Stringer witnessed a deed in which Luke Gardner purchased land near his own tracts, and, on 19 March 1802, he witnessed a deed in which Jeremiah Burkhalter sold land to George Horn.[1767]

[1756] ***Establishing John Stringer as a son of William Stringer:*** Note that this relationship is not proven but seems the most likely one from the available evidence. John Stringer (grandfather of Mary Ann Gary) identifies Eli Stringer as his brother in his will. Descendants of Eli Stringer in Indiana (where Eli died after 1855) identify from family tradition William Stringer of Edgefield as Eli's father. Edgefield deeds establish that John Stringer, Eli Stringer, and William Stringer were adjacent landowners. Moreover, records of the Michael Burkhalter estate establish that William had married a daughter of Michael Burkhalter, by whom he had at least two children, Jonathan Stringer (born 1784) and Willis Stringer (born about 1787). The deeds below establish that John Stringer (grandfather of Mary Ann Gary) had a close relationship with Jonathan Stringer and with Davis Williams, Jonathan Stringer's father-in-law. Hence it would appear that John Stringer was a son of William Stringer, a brother of Eli, Jonathan, Willis, and (probably) Jeremiah, and a grandson of John Stringer who moved from Chowan Co., NC, to South Carolina about 1749. Note also that the eldest sons of both Eli Stringer and John Stringer were named William. Moreover, Jonathan Stringer and William Stringer (son of John and Nancy Slater) both had sons named Williamson Stringer.

[1757] Edgefield Co., SC, DB 13, pp. 177-180.

[1758] Andrea, Stringer File, Item 20.

[1759] Edgefield Co., SC, DB 13, pp. 639-641.

[1760] Edgefield Co., SC, DB 14, pp. 443-445.

[1761] Edgefield Co., SC, DB 16, pp. 576-578.

[1762] Edgefield Co., SC, DB 16, pp. 566-571.

[1763] Edgefield Co., SC, DB 22, pp. 423-424.

[1764] 1800 Edgefield Co., SC, Census, p. 164.

[1765] Edgefield Co., SC, DB 21, pp. 15-18.

[1766] Edgefield Co., SC, DB 21, pp. 21-22. NOTE that these two deeds -- dated the same day -- seem significant. Davis Williams was likely father-in-law of William Stringer's son Jonathan. Eli Stringer was another son of William, as probably was John Stringer.

[1767] Edgefield Co., SC, DB 20, pp. 428-430, and DB 21, pp. 299-301.

Soon afterwards, on 10 April 1802, Stringer wrote his will in Edgefield District. Describing himself as "very sick and weak," he mentions his mill, lands, estate, debts, and other property. He names three surviving children, William, George, and Martha Stringer, as well as his brother, Eli Stringer. Eli Stringer, John's wife Ann, and Ann's brother Grove were to be guardians; witnesses were Jonathan Stringer and Frances Dawson.[1768]

Of the offspring of John and Ann Slater Stringer, George died single and childless about 1814 in Clarke County, Alabama. Martha Stringer (c. 1799 - after 1882) married Stephen Pace, whom she survived by almost half a century. She moved to Mississippi in her youth with her older brother William and members of the Pace family but returned to Clarke County, Alabama, where she remained for the rest of her life, after her husband's death.

Nancy Slater Stringer was only about thirty years old when her husband John Stringer died in 1802; soon afterwards, she married William L. Thornton and moved to Clarke County, Alabama, with her husband and her own Slater relatives. Located along the Tombigbee River in southwestern Alabama, Clarke County had originally been a part of Washington County and a Spanish province until shortly before the Stringers and Slaters settled there. These rich, fertile lands had begun to attract cotton planters from the Carolinas and Georgia, and the Stringers were among the region's early settlers. Nancy Slater Stringer Thornton was still living at the time of the 1850 census, aged seventy-seven, and a native of South Carolina.[1769]

William L. and Nancy Slater Stringer Thornton were the parents of two sons. John W. Thornton (c. 1805-after 1880), the older son, married Sarah Fluker and lived in Clarke County, Alabama, until his death. He became a well-known farmer and reared a large family in Clarke County, Alabama. Eli S. Thornton (c. 1808-after 1880) married first Margaret Earle Scruggs Turner and second Sallie Pace. Eli S. Thornton farmed as well but had a long career in public service. Reverend Ball, in his *History of Clarke County*, describes Thornton's earliest years:

> Hon. Eli S. Thornton, who was born in South Carolina, but whose earliest recollections are connected with the Tombigbee River scenery, has been thoroughly identified with the whole life and growth of Clarke County. Passing in boyhood through the Indian troubles, he saw the commencement of county, territorial, and state life. With the leading men of St. Stephens and the old Washington County he was well acquainted.... The first offices held by E. S. Thornton were those of county surveyor and deputy United States surveyor. While proceeding to Nashville in 1833, on business connected with the latter office, he was for a time the guest of General Coffee at his home near Florence. In 1832, he had been retracing lines in Sumter County, and, in 1842, he was engaged in the same work in Greene. For the most part, he has given his attention to the care of a large river plantation, in the mean time attending to public and official duties. Among these may be named the guardianship of James M. Scruggs, closed in 1847; of Gross Scruggs and Jesse Scruggs, closed in 1850; and representing the county in the state legislature in 1853 and 1854. In 1876, he was elected state senator for four years. Senator Thornton is very mild, refined in feeling, and genial in social life; he is an earnest, intelligent Christian, active in his church and in the Bethel Association; and his attractive and pleasant home is well supplied with comforts for physical and the appliances for intellectual life. Few men so truly excellent can be found in any community.[1770]

[1768] J. E. and V. Wooley, *Edgefield Co., SC, Wills, 1787-1836* (Greenville, SC, 1991), p. 171.

[1769] Nancy was enumerated in the household of her son, Eli S. Thornton. See 1850 Clarke Co., AL, Census, p. 221.

[1770] T. W. Ball, *A Glance Into The Great South-East or Clarke County, Alabama, and Its Surroundings, From 1540 to 1877* (Grove Hill, AL, 1882), pp. 517-518

Thornton became a wealthy planter in Clarke County, owning fifty slaves at the time of the 1860 census. Senator Thornton married late in life and reared ten children, establishing the Thornton family as one of Clarke County's most prominent.[1771]

Nancy Slater Stringer Thornton, mother of William Stringer, George Stringer, Martha Stringer Pace, John W. Thornton, and Eli S. Thornton, was a daughter of John Slater, Jr., and Susannah Gardner of Edgefield District, South Carolina, and a granddaughter of John Slater, Sr., and of Samuel Gardner. Both men and their origins are obscure. John Slater of Edgefield seems to have come there from Chester County, Pennsylvania, by way of a residence in Orange County, North Carolina. These Slaters had Quaker ties, and many members of the family belonged to Quaker Monthly Meetings in Pennsylvania and North Carolina. One John Slater was a son of George Slater who wrote his will in 1756 and died about 1763 in Chester County, while another John Slater was a son of Mary Slater Shepheard Stafford, who moved from Chester County, Pennsylvania, to Orange County, North Carolina, where she died in 1761.[1772] Orange County records from the eighteenth-century are fragmentary at best; what is clear, however, is that by the early 1760s the Slaters and their kin had begun to leave Orange County. One John Slater, along with members of the Jackson, Money, and Dennis families, who had moved with the Slaters from Rhode Island into Pennsylvania and North Carolina, settled in the Quaker village of Wrightsboro on the Georgia frontier. He received a land grant there in 1770. Wrightsboro was located about twenty miles west of Stephens' Creek in Edgefield District, where John Slater and John Stringer both lived. It is not clear from surviving records whether John Slater moved from Wrightsboro to Edgefield after 1770 or whether there were two John Stringers, one a son of Mary Slater Shepheard Stafford and another a son of George Slater, who lived in these two nearby communities. If the latter scenario should prove correct, then one man may have moved to Wrightsboro while his cousin settled twenty miles away in Edgefield.[1773]

John Slater, Sr., of Edgefield County, was apparently living in South Carolina by 30 October 1775, when he served in the Colleton County militia under Captain Andrew Cummins.[1774] Beginning 11 July 1779, he served 180 days in the South Carolina militia under one Captain Morris, finally receiving compensation for his service in 1787.[1775] John Slaiter, Sr., John Slaiter, Jr., Levi Slaiter, and George Slaiter were all granted land in Ninety-Six District in 1784.[1776] In 1790, one John Slater -- a single man with no family -- was enumerated in Edgefield District, while another John Slater was living nearby in Orangeburg District. It is believed that John in Edgefield was John Slater, Sr., while John Slater, Jr., and his family were living in Orangeburg.[1777]

John Slater, Jr., born about 1750, married Susannah Gardner. He was probably living in Orangeburg District, South Carolina, in 1790, and he may have moved with his children to Washington County, Alabama, about 1808. John and Susannah were the parents of several children, including Nancy Slater

[1771] 1860 Clarke Co., AL, Census, p. 553.

[1772] Several references to John Slater appear in Shields, *Orange Co., NC, Court Minutes*. The will of Mary Shepherd is found in Orange Co., NC, Will Book A, p. 17. The will of George Slater is found in Chester Co., PA, Will Book D, p. 399. Several of the individuals associated with Mary Shepherd and John Slater in Orange Co., NC, were clearly from Chester Co., PA, including Samuel Money and John Dennis. These individuals appear in the records of Nottingham Monthly Meeting, Chester Co., PA.

[1773] See Georgia Land Grant Book I, pp. 154, 624. For additional information see R. S. Davis, *Quaker Records in Georgia: Wrightsborough 1772-1793, Friendsborough, 1776-1777* (Augusta, GA, 1986).

[1774] B. G. Moss, *Roster of South Carolina Patriots in the American Revolution* (Baltimore, 1983), p. 870.

[1775] Accounts Audited of Claims Growing Out of the American Revolution, File No. 7076, SCDAH Series S108092, Reel 135, Frame 269: "Slaiter, John. Claim No. 7076."

[1776] SCDAH, Series S2313190, Volume 7, p. 226; SCDAH, Series S213190, Volume 14, p. 318; SCDAH, Series S213190, Volume 12, p. 253; SCDAH, Series S213190, Volume 14, p. 318.

[1777] Based on Edgefield District, SC, records, it appears that John Slater, Sr., was father of: John Slater, Jr., born about 1750; William Slater, a soldier in South Carolina in 1776, and born by about 1755; George Slater, a soldier in South Carolina in 1778, and probably born about 1757, who was living in Edgefield as late as 1803; Levi Slater, a soldier in South Carolina in 1779, and probably born about 1758, who was living in Edgefield District in 1784; and Mary Ann Slater, who married, as his second wife, Samuel Gardner, Sr. See 1790 Edgefield Co., SC, Census, p. 509; 1790 Orangeburg Co., SC, Census.

Stringer, born about 1773; John D. Slater, born about 1775, who married Sarah Bowman and moved to Washington County, Alabama, about 1808; George Slater, born about 1777, who moved to Washington County, Alabama, about 1808 and died, unmarried and childless, about 1835 in Mobile, Alabama. No record of John Slater have been found after about 1808, when his family began relocating to Alabama.[1778]

William Stringer, father of Mary Ann Stringer Gary, was thus born about 1792 in Edgefield District, South Carolina, a son of John Stringer and Ann Slater and a grandson of William Stringer and John Slater, Jr. Losing his father when he was about ten years old, he was reared by his mother, stepfather William L. Thornton, and his mother's Slater relatives. About 1808, the entire group moved together from South Carolina, settling on the Tombigbee River in what was then Washington County but soon became Clarke County. He married Ann Parks there in 1820, and soon afterwards moved with his brother-in-law Stephen Pace and several of his wife's Parks relatives to Copiah County, Mississippi, where he was taxed from 1825 to at least 1832. Stringer was also enumerated there in 1830, near his brothers-in-law William Nelson and Stephen Pace.[1779]

William Stringer settled in Lauderdale County, Mississippi, as early as 1838. He paid poll tax in Lauderdale County from 1838 to 1850 and seems to have lived there as late as 1853, when he appeared as a Lauderdale resident in the state census.[1780] By 1857, William and Ann were described as "of Smith County" when they sold 160 acres of Section 5, Township 7, Range 15 East, in Lauderdale County.[1781] William and Ann were enumerated in Smith County in 1860; William died there in Holmesville in 1860, and Ann died there three years later, on 14 June 1863.[1782]

In both the 1850 and 1860 enumerations, William Stringer was working as a farmer. His estate was valued at $1,250 in 1850 and $2,800 in 1860. An estate of this size suggests that the Stringers were prosperous and comfortable but hardly rich, better off than the many landless laborers living in the community but a notch below the truly wealthy cotton planters scattered throughout the area.

William and Ann Parks Stringer were the parents of a large family. George Washington Stringer (1821-1899, Toro, Sabine Parish, Louisiana) married Jane Godwin (1837-1877); his family was living in Sabine Parish as late as 1920. Mary Ann Stringer (c. 1823 -) married Starling Tucker Gary. Martha Emily Stringer (c. 1825 -) either died or married prior to 1850; no record of her after that date has been found. William Williamson Stringer (c. 1827-1891, Bosque County, Texas) married Nancy Womack Prine. Joseph M. Stringer (6 September 1829-17 September 1898, Toro, Sabine Parish, Louisiana) was unmarried as late as 1880. James Madison Stringer (24 September 1831- 29 January 1898, Sabine Parish, Louisiana) married Sarah I. Brewster (13 March 1842-23 May 1941) in Sabine Parish after 1860; Sarah was living with her children in Sabine Parish as late as 1920. Nancy Caroline Stringer (12 January 1837-17 September 1898, Toro, Sabine Parish, Louisiana) was living with her brother Joseph Stringer at the time of the 1880 census; she never married. Thomas Jefferson Stringer (1846-1912) married twice, first to Mrs. Louisa Walters and second to Lorena Curtis; he outlived both wives and was enumerated as a widower at the time of the 1910 Sabine Parish, Louisiana, census.[1783]

[1778] Ball, *Clarke County*, p. 521; J. S. Graham, *A History of Clarke County* (Birmingham, 1923), p. 112.

[1779] 1830 Copiah Co., MS, Census, pp. 107, 111.

[1780] 1838-1850 Lauderdale Co., MS, Tax Lists, Mississippi Department of Archives and History, Jackson, MS.

[1781] Lauderdale Co., MS, DB I/J, p. 172.

[1782] 1850 Lauderdale Co., MS, Census, pp. 377-379; 1860 Smith Co., MS, Census, p. 326.

[1783] 1910 Sabine Parish, LA, Census, p. 35.

Chapter 26:

Conclusion

Discussing the family of William and Ann Parks Stringer brings us to the conclusion of this family history, spanning four centuries, nearly every British American colony, many European countries, and every one of the United States. Let us briefly review the ground we have covered.

Probably a member of the family of John Hammack of Ermington, Devonshire, William Hammack arrived as an indentured laborer in Virginia no later than 1656. The Hammack surname had probably evolved in the century or so before William arrived in Virginia, possibly taking its origins from Hammet, an English surname that could either be a diminutive for the given name Hamo or a derivation of a place name indicating a meadow alongside a stream. The English Hammacks -- whose name was spelled variously as Hammock, Hammick, Hameak, and Hammot -- appear to have been prosperous yeomen. Almost without exception, the name in the earliest years was confined to the southern half of England, and it is found most often along the southern coast, from Cornwall in the west to Essex and Middlesex in the east. The greatest single concentration of the name appears to have been in southern Devonshire, where the family of John Hammack settled.

The English Hammacks were never numerous. By the time of the 1841 and 1851 census returns, there were only about one hundred individuals in the British Isles bearing this surname in *any* form. But, William Hammack's progeny prospered, biologically as well as financially, in the new American environment. Two centuries after he arrived in Virginia, there were more than a thousand Hammacks and Hammocks living in the southern United States; if one considers the descendants of Hammack women as well as Hammack men, William's progeny could be considered numerous indeed.

Given the rate of biological increase, the question of financial stability arises. The English custom of primogeniture had favored the concentration of whatever wealth a family possessed into the hands of the eldest male offspring and his descendants. The Americans, especially following the Revolution, but in many cases before it as well, rejected the English system of primogeniture for the more equitable, perhaps even democratic, system of partible inheritance. In the latter form, an individual's wealth was shared among all of her or his heirs, with daughters sometimes receiving substantial amounts of real as well as personal property. When wealth was limited, however, this often meant that a substantial tract, which might have been more than sufficient to support a single family, had to be divided among several heirs. For instance, a six hundred acre tract might well support a single family while providing products for commercial marketing as well, ultimately increasing that family's economic productivity and financial standing. Over time, that family might rise in status, whereas those without such a tract might falter. By contrast, were the tract divided among ten different sets of heirs, it might provide sustenance for all but prosperity for none.[1784]

How, then, did William's progeny fare financially? For the first century and a half of its American saga, the family was confined entirely to the slave-holding region of the American South, where first tobacco and then later wheat, indigo, sugar, and, finally, cotton were cultivated for commercial production. Not until the 1830s -- as Hammacks moved finally into Indiana, Illinois, Wisconsin, and lands that would later include Iowa, Kansas, and Nebraska -- did the Hammacks leave the South.

Like most of their peers, many of the early Hammacks were slaveholders. As noted, several of them -- especially those living in Georgia, Alabama, Mississippi, and Louisiana between about 1780 and 1860 -- could even have been considered planters, individuals owning twenty or more slaves and hundreds of acres of cotton-producing land. Despite the system of partible inheritance, they profited from the liberal land policies of the colonies and later states in which they settled. In Georgia, they acquired bounty lands

---

[1784] See H. Brewer, "Entailing Aristocracy in Colonial Virginia: 'Ancient Feudal Restraints' and Revolutionary Reform," *William and Mary Quarterly*, 3rd Ser., Vol. 54, No. 2 (April 1997), pp. 307-346.

following the American Revolution, and they continued to augment those tracts with lands drawn in the 1805, 1807, 1820, 1821, 1827, and 1832 land lotteries. In Alabama, Mississippi, Louisiana, and other states, they homesteaded and then later purchased these tracts from the state governments. The availability of vast tracts of land -- made possible by the Indian cessions of the 1780s and 1790s, by Jefferson's Louisiana Purchase in 1803, by John Quincy Adams's Transcontinental Treaty in 1819, by Andrew Jackson's Indian Removal Act of 1830, by James K. Polk's Annexation of Texas, and by the Treaty of Guadalupe-Hidalgo following the conclusion of the Mexican War in 1848 -- fueled westward migration and provided always the possibility of economic success through land acquisition and agricultural production. Following Eli Whitney's invention of an engine for separating the seeds from cotton fiber in 1793, it became possible to "'gin" mechanically far more cotton -- fifty times as much, in fact -- in one day than a slave could separate by hand. This mechanical feat removed any upward limit that had existed on the amount of cotton one person could grow and process in a single season. It drove expansion, providing impetus for much of the land acquisition that took place between 1793 and 1860.[1785]

Thus it was that the Hammacks of central Georgia -- Jones and Crawford Counties, for instance -- and their offspring became upwardly mobile during this period, profiting from the investments begun by Robert and Millenor Jackson Hammack in the Virginia Southside in the 1760s and along the Georgia frontier in the 1770s. The descendants of Benedict Hammack of Wilkes County, Georgia, and those of John Hammack of Lincoln County, Georgia, followed similar paths, spreading across the lower South from Georgia to Texas by the 1840s. Although not all became wealthy planters, few were landless laborers, either; most owned land enough to be self-sufficient farmers, while a few clearly outranked their brethren in terms of wealth and social status.

Beginning in the 1790s, Hammacks began to move into Tennessee and Kentucky: in many regards, their fate would differ from that of their more southerly relatives. Many of these individuals would be small farmers, and few would own slaves at all. William Hammack, a Revolutionary veteran, left Wilkes County, Georgia, and moved to Christian County, Kentucky, in the 1790s. Daniel and Mary Martin Hammack, who lived briefly in South Carolina, would do the same thing by the end of the decade, settling in Smith County, Tennessee, rather than Kentucky. Four of the sons of Richard and Mary Witcher Hammack of Pittsylvania County, Virginia, would cross the Appalachians at the end of the 1790s -- just two decades after Daniel Boone had discovered a route through the mountains -- to settle in Madison County, Kentucky. The sons and daughters of these men and women would die in such distant, and in the 1790s -- when George Washington and John Adams were Presidents -- largely unheard of, locations as Indiana, Iowa, Kansas, Nebraska, California, and Oregon. Moving north of the Ohio River, into Indiana and Illinois in the 1830s, these Hammacks followed a path through land designated by the Northwest Ordinance of 1787 as forever free from the taint of slavery. When the "Mountain Men" began to report the lures of the Northwest in the 1830s, and when Gold Fever Struck in California in 1849, it was these Hammacks who followed rather than their southern cousins.

When the nation divided in the 1840s and 1850s, the American Hammacks would divide as well. Perhaps those who felt the tensions most acutely were those who had remained in the eastern hill country of Tennessee and Kentucky and the mountainous region of western Virginia. After Virginia withdrew from the federal union to join the Confederate States of America in 1861, the descendants of Martin Hammack, another Revolutionary soldier, would, without moving an inch, find themselves residents of Kanawha and Roane Counties, West Virginia, where their families live to this day. In Overton County, Tennessee, rival "gangs" would fight out their differences and administer frontier justice of their own sort. On 17 February 1864, the "Hammock Gang" and the "Tinker Dave Beatty Gang" clashed at the Battle of Raven Cliff. According to family lore, nine young Hammocks fought off more than seventy of the Beatty clan, but not without losses. Franklin Hammock, just twenty-five, and with three young

---

[1785] Howe, *What God Hath Wrought*, pp. 2, 16, 23, 54, 108-111, 152, 154, 204, 258, 592, 659, 670, 684, 797.

children to support, died on that day, as did several of his kindred. A year earlier, on 3 July 1863, in another clash between the Hammocks and Beattys, his cousin John C. Hammock had also died.[1786]

While these Hammocks fought their own Civil War, another one raged throughout the region. A day after John C. Hammock died in Overton County, the long Siege of Vicksburg, Mississippi, ended. The Confederate defenses collapsed, and forces led by Union General Ulysses S. Grant took the city. Six weeks earlier, on 22 May 1863, Zebedee Hammack -- a soldier from the 81st Illinois Infantry -- had died while taking part in the Siege. Twenty-six when he died, the Illinois native had trained as a lawyer before the war. Zebedee's grandfather Lewis Hammack had settled in Madison County, Kentucky; Lewis's son Benjamin moved the family to Perry County, Illinois, where he worked as a wheelwright and furniture maker while also serving as County Commissioner, County Assessor, Justice of the Peace, and County Treasurer. Zebedee's brother, Judge Lewis Hammack, survived the war, living a long and prosperous life in Pinckneyville, Illinois.[1787]

The same month that Zebedee Hammock died, a distant cousin Mansel W. Hammack, a soldier in Company F, 42nd Georgia Infantry, was ill at Vicksburg. Captured at the city's fall, he died in hospital at Fort Delaware in July 1863, leaving a widow and three children back home in Georgia.[1788] Another cousin, Virginia-born John Henry Hammack, who had grown up in Northumberland County before moving to Amite County in the Mississippi Delta about 1850, was at Vicksburg, too. A soldier in Company K, 17th Louisiana Infantry, Hammack survived the war, dying in Natchez, Mississippi, at the age of eighty in 1917. Although six children survived him, John Henry Hammack had lost another three in 1866 and 1868, during the Reconstruction, as the South struggled to adjust to its changed economic, social, and political reality.[1789]

Life for the descendants of the immigrant William Hammack differed significantly following the American Civil War. William Hammack at that time had no known descendants living northeast of Washington, D. C., and Baltimore, Maryland, in the most heavily industrialized region of the nation. Most of his descendants resided in what had briefly been the Confederate nation, although a significant number also farmed the midwestern plains or lived in Oregon and California. The descendants of Martin Hammack of Missouri, who had settled in Lake County, California, in the early 1850s, became prosperous ranchers there; decade by decade, a stream of Hammacks from the east joined them in California -- some of them refugees from the hardships of war -- so that by the turn of the century there were several dozen Hammack families in California. Also, from 1850 onwards, Hammacks from Indiana and Missouri made the six month long, 2000-mile journey to Oregon, where they farmed, mined, and later worked the timber mills. In Kansas, Nebraska, Iowa, Indiana, and Illinois, Hammacks continued to farm their small tracts throughout the second half of the nineteenth-century, although a host of agricultural misfortunes -- very hot summers, bitterly cold winters, mortgages and other debts -- fueled popular discontent throughout the region. As organizations like the Grange, or Patrons of Husbandry, as it was properly known, formed to agitate for improving the lot of the nation's farmers, many farmers chose to head west rather than face a bleak future on the plains. This widespread despair probably propelled

[1786] For an account of the battle, see Report of Col. John M. Hughs, Twenty-fifth Tennessee Infantry, C.S.A., 28 April 1864, in U.S. War Department, *The War of the Rebellion: A Compilation of the Official Records of the Union and Confederate Armies* (53 vols., Washington, D.C., 1880-1901), Series 1, 32: 1. See also L. D. Bryant, "Tinker Dave Beatty," in Fentress County Historical Society, *History of Fentress Co., Tennessee* (Dallas, 1987), pp. 80-82; J. A. Brents, *The Patriots and Guerillas of East Tennessee and Kentucky...including Sketches of Noted Guerillas and Distinguished Patriots* (New York, 1863), pp. 110-115; and D. Welch, "Tinker Dale Beaty tells why he rose up against Champ Ferguson," Cookeville, TN, *Herald-Citizen*, 22 May 1998, B-1.

[1787] Vicksburg National Military Park Commission, *Indiana at Vicksburg* (Vicksburg, 1911), p. 53.

[1788] Georgia Confederate Service Records, Company F, 42nd Georgia Infantry, Newton Co., GA, Newton Rifles or Newton Rangers, Georgia Department of Archives and History, Morrow, GA.

[1789] Louisiana Confederate Service Records, Company K, 17th Louisiana Infantry, Louisiana State Archives, Baton Rouge, LA.

many of the Hammacks westward during this period, explaining the flux of migrants to the Pacific realm during these decades.[1790]

Hammacks across the Deep South faced the aftermath of Confederate defeat in a variety of ways. The decades between 1865 and 1900 also witnessed a significant westward migration throughout the region, although it was primarily to Texas that Southern migrants moved, rather than Oregon and California. The American Civil War had settled the issue of slavery's westward expansion, and, in the decades after the war ended, the Indians of the western plains were vanquished and placed on reservations. The best known of these conflicts -- Custer's defeat at the hands of Crazy Horse and Sitting Bull along the Little Bighorn River in Montana in 1876 -- was part of a series of clashes between native peoples and white Americans in the late nineteenth-century, culminating with the Wounded Knee massacre in South Dakota in 1890.[1791] In the South, the U. S. Army -- including African American cavalrymen known as "buffalo soldiers" -- fought against the Kiowa and Comanche who were rampaging the Texas Panhandle.[1792] The defeat of these peoples in the Red River War of 1874-1875 marked the end of warfare with native peoples in the Southwest and removed a significant barrier to migration into parts of Texas that had hitherto witnessed little migration from the southeastern states.[1793] Hammacks from all of the southern states began to move into these areas. Migration trails across the Deep South -- through Georgia, Alabama, Mississippi, and Arkansas into Texas -- and those across the Upper South -- through Virginia, West Virginia, Kentucky, Tennessee, Missouri, and Arkansas into Texas -- meant that Hammacks who had not encountered one another in a century or more again mixed along the Texas frontier. Brice Wiseman Hammack, who reared a family in Lincoln Co., Missouri -- became a Judge in Coryell County, Texas, in the 1860s, while Thomas Hammock of Chambers County, Alabama, James Hammack of Lee County, Alabama, and Edward Hammock of Muscogee County, Georgia -- all of whose families had been prosperous cotton planters before the war -- joined him in Fanning, Cooke, and Bell Counties in the 1870s and 1880s.

Although the general theme of the Hammack response across the South to the deprivations of war was resilience -- the willingness to rebuild their farms with free labor following the war, or the readiness to pick up and move to Texas -- many families faced hardships as well. The tense racial climate of the 1860s and 1870s, as former slaves sought to give meaning to the freedom promised them through emancipation, prompted widespread violence throughout the region.[1794] Voters were terrorized to keep them away from the polls as "redeemers" sought to return southern government to the hands of the old planter elites who had controlled them before the war, and politicians -- white as well as black -- were assassinated when their platforms and agendas brought them into open conflict with those who were trying to reclaim southern white governments. Racist organizations -- the Ku Klux Klan, organized in Tennessee in 1866 -- spread throughout the region; in Louisiana, the group was known as the Knights of the White Camellia, while in Texas called them Knights of the Rising Sun. Operating against blacks who sought to realize their freedom, or southern scalawags or northern carpetbaggers who assisted them, these groups played a significant role in restoring white authority throughout the region. With the actions of the "Redeemers" in the original state governments, they together defeated Republican reconstruction and

---

[1790] See M. Hild, *Greenbackers, Knights of Labor, and Populists: Farmer-Labor Insurgency in the Late Nineteenth-Century South* (Athens and London, 2007), pp. 1-12. For background, see L. Goodwyn, *The Populist Moment: A Short History of the Agrarian Revolt* (Oxford, 1978).

[1791] D. Brown, *Bury My Heart at Wounded Knee: An Indian History of the American West* (New York, 1970; repr., 2001), pp. 439-451.

[1792] See J. B. Cruse, *Battles of the Red River War* (College Station, 2008), pp. 27-32, and J. L. Haley, *The Buffalo War: The History of the Red River Indian Uprising of 1874* (Austin, 1998), pp. 1-5.

[1793] Ibid.

[1794] See L. Litwack, *Been in the Storm So Long: The Aftermath of Slavery* (New York, 1979) and E. Foner, *Reconstruction: American's Unfinished Revolution, 1863-1877* (New York, 1988).

restored Democratic control of the region before the Compromise of 1877 formally ended military occupation throughout the South.[1795]

In addition to the specter of violence, there were hardships of another sort. As former planters experimented with new labor relations throughout the region, they first tried hiring back their former slaves with annual contracts. These contracts often proved extortionate and little more than slavery in another form; for their part, whites complained that blacks violated them by moving away before harvesting the crops or otherwise completing their contracted obligations. In addition, the fact that the region was cash poor -- most of its financial resources had been consumed by fighting the war if not by the war itself -- represented a problem when it came to southern whites honoring their side of the agreements.[1796]

Gradually, then, a system of tenancy -- amounting ultimately to little more than peonage -- developed. Large tracts were subdivided, and the landless -- white as well as black -- rented and farmed them. Those with means might rent a tract outright, but, lacking financial resources, many rented the land in exchange for a portion of its profits. Hence was the system known as sharecropping born. A family might rent a tract of land in exchange for a quarter of the crop's profits when it was sold the following autumn; to facilitate production, seeds, tools, and other necessities were advanced, also against the coming profits when the crop was sold. Drought, a poor harvest, infestation by insects -- all of these could act to reduce whatever profits a farmer might realize. Before long, he or she was enmeshed in debt, often with little prospect of repayment. Families found themselves with debts so great that often they remained on the land for generations, working for a bare survival.[1797]

In the 1880s and 1890s, an economic crisis hit the nation as a whole. Crop prices fell, meaning that tenants had difficulty meeting their obligations. Those who owned their own lands often borrowed also against the coming crop. What prices fell from $2 per bushel in 1866 to $1.30 in 1880 to less than thirty cents in 1893, while the price of cotton fell from more than $10 per pound in 1880 to below $5 per pound in 1893. The price of corn, less a regional staple than mid-western wheat or southern cotton, fell from sixty-three cents a bushel in 1881 to twenty-eight cents per bushel in 1890. Landowners who had mortgaged their land to pay for supplies often found themselves unable to meet their obligations; thousands lost their farms, and their livelihoods, between 1880 and 1900. Among these were many of the Hammacks who chose to move west into Texas, where the prospect of a new farm in the Panhandle, or of a cattle ranch deep in the heart of Texas, or of adventure on the western frontier -- offered them a new start.[1798]

But in the years after the close of the American Civil War, many southern Hammacks faced hardship of another sort. It is one thing to speak abstractly of declining prices for staple crops, of alternative labor arrangements, or of liberal land policies such as the Homestead Act -- but these do not measure the human dimension of war and its aftermath. No single quantitative instrument can adequately measure the impact of the conflict which raged from 1861 to 1865. More than 600,000 young Americans died during those years. The South, with its smaller population, faced a loss that was proportionally greater. A generation of southern youths was in its grave, and families across the region had lost sons, husbands, brothers, and fathers.[1799]

The latter portion of our study focuses on the family of Simeon Hammack and his wife Elizabeth Jane Moore; hence, an example from their family is appropriate. Simeon's grandparents had settled along the eastern Georgia frontier during the Revolution. His grandfather and father both amassed land and slaves,

---

[1795] Foner, *Reconstruction*, pp. 412-444, 512-589. See also C. V. Woodward, *Origins of the New South, 1877-1913* (Baton Rouge, 1951); E. L. Ayers, *The Promise of the New South: Life After Reconstruction* (Oxford, 1993); C. V. Woodward, *Reunion and Reaction: The Compromise of 1877 and the End of Reconstruction* (Oxford, 1991).

[1796] Foner, *Reconstruction*, pp. 412-444, 512-589.

[1797] Ayers, *New South*, pp. 81-104, 132-160, 187-214.

[1798] Ibid., pp. 81-104, 249-283.

[1799] See D. G. Faust, *Republic of Suffering: Death and the American Civil War* (New York, 2009).

each dying with substantial property. At his death, Simeon's father William would have been considered a "planter," as would William's older brother Lewis. Both men owned twenty or so slaves and several hundred acres of cotton lands in central Georgia. Simeon himself owned six or seven slaves by the time he was in his forties, but a dispute with one of his brothers prompted him to sell his prosperous farm and to move away from the rest of his family in Hammack's District of Crawford County.

Simeon's older children began moving to Mississippi in the 1840s, and Simeon, Elizabeth Jane, and the younger children followed them in the early 1850s, settling in Choctaw County. The 1860 agricultural schedule for Choctaw County indicated that Simeon and his son John T. Hammack were both prosperous farmers whose prosperity might have increased steadily had not war intervened; another son, William T. H. Hammack, had settled in southern central Mississippi, near Canton in Madison County, where he was overseer for one of the region's large plantations and led a comfortable existence.

When the Civil War began in 1861, all of Simeon's sons, except William, who was then forty, joined the Confederate forces, as did all of Simeon's grandsons of military age. A year into the conflict, Simeon and Elizabeth Jane had buried two of their youngest sons, and within another year Simeon himself was dead. The final two years of the war and its immediate aftermath were filled with disruption. Simeon's widow Elizabeth and the younger children were in Choctaw County in 1863, in Madison County in central Mississippi the following year, back in Choctaw County in 1866, and then in Madison County thereafter. Whatever land Simeon's estate had owned had apparently been lost or sold by 1870, and Elizabeth herself seems to have died soon after the war ended.

John T. Hammack, Simeon's third son, was taken ill during the war and discharged. His health never recovered, and he died in 1870. John left behind him a young widow and six children. Within a decade, she, too, was dead, as apparently were the two youngest children and the family's only other daughter. Whatever land John T. Hammack had farmed in 1860 and 1870 had also by this point been lost; in 1870, the agricultural schedule indicated that John's eldest son William Simms Hammack was responsible for the family's 100-acre farm.

Of the three Hammack children still surviving in 1880, William Simms Hammack was living in Madison County near his uncle William T. H. Hammack. Felix Wilburn Hammack and John Robert Hammack, aged twenty-two and twenty-one, were living with James Criss, a neighboring farmer. All three men were working as farm laborers, although the 1880 agricultural schedule, which shows Felix and John renting "for a share of products," suggests that they were really sharecropping. Felix was responsible for eighteen acres, while John was responsible for thirteen acres. Soon after 1880, the two brothers parted company; both left Choctaw and Calhoun Counties, where they had been reared. Although their mother had come from a well-to-do family in Georgia, both of her parents and all of her known siblings were deceased by 1880. Three of Simeon Hammack's sons were still farming in Calhoun County in the 1880s, but Felix W. Hammack followed his brother William to Madison County in central Mississippi.

For these three brothers, then, the years immediately following the war were ones of loss. Two of their youngest uncles, not much older than the boys themselves, died during the war, and by the time the boys reached adulthood they had lost both Hammack grandparents, both of their own parents, and three of their siblings. Whether through forfeiture or sale, the family farm had also been lost, and the young men, all working as laborers in 1880, apparently possessed no substantial property of their own. With nothing to tie them to Calhoun County, they drifted away. John Robert Hammack, the youngest surviving sibling, headed west, ranching for thirty years in the Dakotas. William Simms Hammack married the daughter of prosperous Hinds County, Mississippi, farmer, produced a large family, and died in 1899 at the age of forty-seven. Felix W. Hammack never married and died in the 1930s when he was more than eighty years old; through careful management over the course of a long life, he acquired several tracts of land in Hinds County and operated a mercantile business until near his death.

The subject of the marriage of William S. Hammack to Sallie Elizabeth Cates raises the issue of bilateral kinship connections and their importance to the family's development. Sallie's family had come from North Carolina to Mississippi in 1833, and her father, an only surviving child, had inherited property from his parents and grandfather. Sallie's grandmother, and ultimately her parents as well, left her property, including the family homestead, and this provided the physical setting in which Sallie and William reared and supported their children. The Cates heritage proved crucial economically to the family of William and Sallie Hammack and played a significant role in their ability to rear and educate their children, especially following William's death, when Sallie was left to rear nine children alone.

More than an economic legacy, crucial though it was, the Cates family also bequeathed a genetic and cultural one to its Hammack descendants. Sallie's mother Abbie Doxey Brown Cates (1841-1940) died in her ninety-ninth year; born soon after Andrew Jackson's presidency, when the family had settled on Indian lands along the Mississippi frontier, she lived until after Hitler's invasion of Poland and the outbreak of World War II. In the course of a long and eventful life, Abbie survived her husband, who died in 1884, by nearly sixty years and her son-in-law, who died in 1899, by more than four decades. Her impact on her Hammack grandchildren and great-grandchildren was great.

Abbie's ancestors had settled in Virginia in its earliest days. Her ancestor Christopher Calthorpe belonged to an armigerous family from Norfolk, England, that can be traced to the Norman Conquest and includes among its ancestors a direct lineal tie to Edward III, King of England. The Calthorpes became burgesses, justices, vestrymen, and churchwardens in Virginia and were one of the leading families in York County. Frances Calthorpe Jones moved with her husband Jesse to Caswell County, North Carolina, and their sons became planters and officials there. Frances's great-grandson, Colonel Drury J. Brown, named for Frances's son Drury Jones, became a Colonel in the Confederate Army and was a lawyer, justice, and Sheriff in Hinds and Copiah Counties, Mississippi. Abbi Doxey Brown Cates came of age in the heyday of the "Old South," and her father belonged to the class of wealthy southern planters who typify the popular image of that period. Although he died just after the war ended, Colonel Drury J. Brown passed to his daughter Abi a cultural, and perhaps a genetic, legacy of achievement and service that she in turn transmitted to future generations of her offspring.

Just as Sallie Cates Hammack and her mother Abbie Doxey Brown Cates passed to their offspring important economic, cultural, and genetic legacies that have impacted them, so, too, have each of the Hammack foremothers since Joan Sparkwell and John Hammack married at Ermington, Devonshire, in 1608. In Virginia, the first William Hammack married a woman called Grace, who was herself probably also an indentured servant. Their son William married Christian Middleton, whose prosperous planter family became a fixture in Northern Neck political and cultural development for the next century. The first Robert Hammack, whose long life spanned the transition from colonial British to independent American government and society, married Ann Lambert, who had a pedigree deeply rooted in the Northern Neck. Her ancestor James Claughton had settled in Maryland in the 1630s and in Virginia in the 1640s; her Welsh Morgan and Lewis ancestors had settled in Rappahannock County before Richmond County was formed. At the time, Indians still lived along Totuskey Creek, which would become the site of so much significant Hammack activity later. Ann's Claughton connections gave her a link to leading Northumberland County families, just as Christian Hammack's Middleton connections did the same in Westmoreland County. By the middle eighteenth-century, the Hammacks had become a substantial middle-tier planter family with alliances that linked them to the most substantial planters in the area.

Robert and Ann Lambert Hammack produced a large family; several of their children chose to leave the Northern Neck, where land supplies were limited and tobacco cultivation was in crisis. Among these was Robert Hammack, Jr., who accompanied his grandparents Hugh and Ann Morgan Lambert into the Southside. There he met and married Millenor Jackson, whose family had deep roots south of the James River. William Jackson had lived in Surry County since the 1680s; his son John Jackson acquired several thousand acres of land in Brunswick and Amelia Counties, although he and his wife Mary Worrell Jackson remained in Surry and Sussex Counties for the duration of their lives. William's grandson Edward Jackson married Lucy Parrish and settled on his father's lands in Brunswick and Amelia Counties, where his family first encountered that of Hugh Lambert. Robert Hammack and Millenor Jackson married about 1764, and a deed of gift from Robert's father-in-law Edward Jackson provided the first tract of land the young man ever owned. A slave bequeathed him by his grandfather Hugh Lambert augmented the labor force; little more than a decade after marriage, Robert and Millenor liquidated their Virginia resources and settled on the Georgia frontier.

The Georgia frontier brought the Hammacks into a new cultural milieu. Their neighbors included related families they had known in Virginia as well as immigrants from New England, Pennsylvania, and the Carolinas. Of the offspring of Robert and Millenor Jackson Hammack, several married into families they had known in Virginia, but others allied themselves with frontier families who had hailed from other areas. The wife of John Hammack was a Pennsylvania native, while William T. Hammack married a North Carolinian named Mary Felts. Mary's family came from Surry County, south of the James River, but, unlike Millenor's Jackson relatives, they had headed south into the sparsely settled Carolina country rather than westward into the Virginia Southside. As early as 1714, several of the sons of Humphrey Felts had settled along the Albemarle Sound in eastern North Carolina, and Mary's father John Felts had joined his kin there in the 1760s. The post-Revolutionary economic crisis that gripped much of the new nation had repercussions for him; John was forced to sell off his property to satisfy financial obligations and moved to the Georgia frontier, where he rented tracts for more than a decade before drawing a "fortunate grant" in the 1807 land lottery. Moving from Wilkes County to Putnam County, John established a family that had crucial interactions with the Hammacks for the next century.

In the next generation, Simeon Hammack married Elizabeth Jane Moore, whose roots extended deep into Virginia soil. If tentative links to the Ussery, Blackwell, and Croshaw families are correct, then Elizabeth was a direct descendant of Captain Rawleigh Croshaw, Gentleman, who arrived at Jamestown in the Second Supply in September 1608. A member of the House of Burgesses in 1623, Croshaw died at Elizabeth City in 1625. The family moved in subsequent generations into New Kent County, where Joseph Croshaw died about 1672.[1800] When Lunenburg County was established in 1746, a group of related Blackwells, Usserys, and Moores settled there. The first Robert Moore became owner of several thousand acres in Lunenburg. In a subsequent generation, Ussery Moore married Martha Bishop; her ancestor Captain John Bishop, who had come to Virginia in 1638, served as a member of the House of Burgesses on three occasions before he died in 1656. Ussery Moore and his large family left the Southside about 1804, settling among kin and friends in Wilkes County, Georgia. Among these was the family of Robert Hammack, into which group Ussery's sons James Wilburn Moore and Matthew Moore along with his grandchildren Martha Moore Bentley and Elizabeth Jane Moore Hammack would marry.

In central Georgia, Simeon and Elizabeth Jane Moore crossed paths with the family of Milton and Martha Fuller Templeton. Martha Fuller's family, like the Felts and Jackson families, traces to southeastern Virginia, where Ezekiel Fuller married Deborah Spivey in Nansemond County and died in neighboring Isle of Wight. The family moved next to Orange County, North Carolina, and then, in the 1750s, into the western South Carolina frontier. During the 1780s, they migrated across the Savannah River into Georgia, settling in what became Columbia County. John Fuller's family became neighbors of the family of Thomas Templeton, of Scots-Irish descent, whose family had settled in Pennsylvania in the 1720s and in the 1740s were among the very first settlers in southwestern North Carolina. Thomas moved to Georgia in the 1790s; although Milton and Martha did not marry until 1817 in Morgan County, the two families had known each other since before the births of either spouse. Milton Templeton prospered and died a wealthy man in Macon County, Georgia, about 1850; estate records indicate that Louisa Templeton Hammack grew up in comfortable circumstances and brought to her marriage with John T. Hammack a small tract of land and a modest financial inheritance that no doubt significantly amplified his financial resources.

The marriages of William T. Hammack and Mary Felts, of Simeon Hammack and Elizabeth Jane Moore, and of John T. Hammack and Louisa Templeton all occurred in Georgia. Those of William S. Hammack and Sallie Cates and George C. Hammack and Mary Almedia Bankston would both take place

---

[1800] Dorman, *Adventurers*, pp. 217-223.

in Hinds County, Mississippi, three hundred miles westward. In Mississippi, the early Hammacks encountered families whose histories differed in significant ways from their own. As previously noted, the Cates heritage provided important economic and cultural legacies for the Hammack descendants. In the next generation, Mary Almedia Bankston Hammack, a daughter of John Manly Bankston and Abi Doxey O'Neal, provided her offspring with a rich heritage. Among her ancestors were names as diverse as Andreas Bengttson, Peter Gunarrson Rambo, Jacob Claeszen Groesbeck, Jacob Leenertszen Van Der Grift, John O'Neal, Matthew Stewart, Elizabeth McCall, Richard Parker, Lawrence Washington, Amphyllis Twigden, Hiram Mitchell, Mourning Dove, Antonio Bassano, Elena de Nazzi, Nicholas Lanier, Mathis Gary, Thomas Melton, Robert Allen, Henry West, John Stringer, Francis Fincher, and William Shewin. Swedish, Dutch, Finnish, German, Scottish, English, Italian, and French foreparents provided links to Swedish Delaware, Dutch New York, and much of northern Europe. Lawrence Washington and Amphyllis Twigden provide links to half a dozen English gentry families with significant connections in Tudor and Stuart England. Antonio Bassano and Elena de Nazzi came from Venice, Italy, to serve as musicians for the court of Henry VIII, as did their son-in-law, the Frenchman Nicholas Lanier. Hiram Mitchell and wife Mourning Dove, parents of Martha Mitchell Bankston, provided Scots-Irish and Native American heritage. Francis Fincher, a Worcestershire Quaker, was among the early settlers of Pennsylvania; he died at Philadelphia in 1688, but his grandchildren carried the Quaker faith into the southern backcountry in the 1740s and 1750s. William West, another of Mary Almedia Bankston's ancestors, died in Isle of Wight County, Virginia, in 1709. His father Henry West is believed to have been killed during the 1644 Powhattan uprising in Virginia, while William West's father-in-law, an Oxford-trained Anglican cleric called Robert Bracewell, ministered in Isle of Wight County until his death in 1668.

Although the Hammack lineage itself extends from the Northern Neck of Virginia to eastern Georgia and then central Mississippi, these bilateral kinship connections enrich the family heritage by providing links to ethnic, cultural, and religious groups as well as to physical locations outside the sphere of direct Hammack connections. Together they complete the family circle, forming a web linking the descendants of George Cleveland Hammack and Mary Almedia Bankston to a rich and diverse heritage. They also testify to the ability of these early immigrants from a variety of cultural background to overcome the limitations of time and place and create a legacy that has endured for more than three centuries.

Appendix 1:

Glossary

Except when quoting from original documents, modern spelling, punctuation, and English phrasing have been employed in the text. When quoting legal documents such as wills and deeds or personal letters and newspaper articles, the original spelling, punctuation, and phrasing have generally been retained. Likewise, some legal and religious terminology relating to the original documents and events appears in the text. In most instances, it will not be familiar to readers. Therefore, the following glossary is offered to assist readers who might have questions about these terms.

Banns:

Entering into a marriage in England and early America could be a complicated affair.

Until 1754 in England, there were several different ways of entering into marriage. If individuals owned property, several distinct steps were required. Initially a written contract had to be negotiated between parents of the intended couple stipulating particular financial arrangements concerning the marriage (i.e., the payment of dowry from the bride's family as well as any particular properties the groom would bring to the marriage). Second, spousals were required; this step, also called a contract, involved a formal oral exchange of promises between the bride and groom, usually with witnesses present.

Third, the couple had to issue a public proclamation of banns in church. Banns were issued three times with the intention of allowing prior claims of contract to be heard. At this point, if an intended bride or groom had negotiated a still valid contract with another individual, that individual could make her or his claims publicly known. Although in England by the seventeenth-century most well-to-do families avoided this step by acquiring a legal marriage license, this step continued in the American colonies into the late eighteenth-century. If no prior claims came to light as a result of the publication of banns, the intended couple could then proceed to the fourth, a church wedding in which both parties verified their mutual consent through the exchange of vows.

As part of the fourth step, the couple received the formal blessing of the church. The fifth, and final, step came next: sexual consummation of the union.

In England, according to ecclesiastical law, the spousals "was as legally binding a contract as the church wedding, although to many laity it was no more than a conditional contract." Legally, any witnessed exchange of promises followed by cohabitation constituted a valid marriage, and in remote areas, especially among the poor, a betrothal ceremony was regarded as all that was necessary for a binding marriage without the blessing of the church.[1801]

Marriage Bonds:

In early America, individuals wishing to marry often perform four legal actions: posting a marriage bond, acquiring a marriage license, returning evidence that the marriage had taken place, and registering the marriage. Couples who wished to marry took to court evidence that they met legal qualifications for marriage -- usually evidence that they were of legal age to marry or, if not, that they had the permission of their parents to do so. They then "bonded" the proof of their eligibility by posting a sum of money, usually with the assistance of a male relative identified in the marriage bond as a bondsman. (This relative was usually a brother or uncle of the bride.) After posting the bond, the couple received a marriage

---

[1801] Lawrence Stone, *The Family, Sex, and Marriage in England, 1500-1800* (London, 1977; abridged edition, reprint, 1990), p. 34.

license from the clerk. They then took this license to the minister whom they had selected to marry them. Once the marriage had taken place, the minister signed a "return", which the couple then took to court to verify that the marriage had taken place on a particular date and in a particular location. Upon receipt of this document, the marriage was legally registered at the county level.

If all legal records had survived, researchers would thus have four separate items to document the marriage of an individual. In some instances, couples posted a marriage bond and acquired a marriage license but never married. In others, poor records keeping or the loss of records has meant that marriage bonds survive but that the registration of the actual marriage does not. One reason for this is that sometimes documents were stored in separate locations. During the colonial and early national periods, clerks often filed these documents without recording them in bound record books. In some locations, clerks filed bonds and licenses but recorded the actual marriage returns in the bound record books. In some instances, certain records were retained at the state level, while others were kept at the county level. Hence, a copy of a marriage bond might survive in the state records office, while the marriage registration and original bond might be lost in a local clerk's office.

In North Carolina, a collection of marriage bonds unparalleled elsewhere in the South has survived. So long as the Anglican Church remained established in the South, marriages were recorded by ministers in their parish registers. Often these registers have been destroyed, but where they survive -- as in the case of North Farnham Parish, Richmond County, Virginia, for instance -- they provide excellent documentation of family relationships. Once the Anglican Church was disestablished, county clerks gradually took over responsibility for recording marriages, but this was an irregular process, different from state to state. In Georgia, for instance, marriages were not required to be recorded until the early nineteenth-century, and South Carolina clerks did not register marriages until the middle nineteenth-century.

In North Carolina and Virginia, marriage bonds often exist, while the registration of the marriage may have been lost. From other sources, it can be inferred that a marriage actually took place, but the date is unknown. Hence, when the phrase "married, by bond dated" occurs in the text, it means that the couple acquired a marriage bond on a particular date but that the date of the actual marriage is unknown. Often couples married within a day or two of acquiring the bond.

Inheritance:

Individuals owning property in early America had several possible options for providing for their offspring. Many colonial Americans of British origin practiced the English traditions of primogeniture and entail. The bulk of an individual's landed wealth passed automatically to his eldest son. While many wills specified adherence to this system, some wills failed even to note the existence of an eldest son because his inheritance was regarded as automatic. A will, then, might include bequests only to younger sons and daughters who would not inherit property through primogeniture. Many fathers, especially in England and among wealthy colonial southern planters, also entailed their lands. By entail, fathers stipulated that lands, and in some instances even slaves and their offspring, could never be sold by a son or his descendants but must pass unaltered (except, in the instance of the slaves, by natural increase and death) to their male descendants.

Over time, many American families came to favor a system of partible inheritance, where lands and other properties were divided among all offspring. Often an elder son would receive a more substantial portion, but, in many instances, younger sons and even daughters received land, slaves, and other personal property.

Rather than leaving a will, some parents provided for their offspring through deeds of gift. As evidenced in the text, Edward Jackson provided for his daughter Millenor Jackson Hammack and her husband Robert in this way by deeding them a tract of land soon after they married. Although Jackson later wrote a will, also naming Millenor as an heir, for many parents a deed of gift was the only method of specifically providing for their offspring. For example, Millenor Jackson Hammack herself in Jones County, Georgia, issued multiple deeds of gift to her children and grandchildren for slaves and personal property she had inherited from her husband Robert. She left no will.

If an individual died intestate (without a will), an administrator was appointed by the court. An inventory and appraisement of one's property was then taken, and the personal possessions were often sold at a public auction, usually with family members and close neighbors being the primary purchasers. The resulting money was then used to pay off outstanding debts and legal fees.

In the event that an individual left minor children, a final division could not occur until the eldest child came of age. Hence, estates sometimes remained in probate for one or two decades. In such cases, the administrator filed annual returns which document credits received (for instance, money from the estate sale or from hiring out slaves and renting out tracts of land) as well as payments made by the estate (for instance, boarding and educating the minor children).

In many instances, preliminary divisions took place soon after the bulk of outstanding debts had been paid. Usually the final division took place once all debts had been paid or when the minor children came of age. As noted, in colonial America, the bulk of an individual's possessions automatically passed to the eldest son. Younger offspring might receive nothing, although this practiced differed regionally and changed over time. By the early nineteenth-century, once debts and legal fees had been paid, intestate estates were divided equally among the heirs. Usually widows received a "dowry" for life or until remarriage of control of one-third of the land. The remaining land was either divided equally among the offspring or sold and the proceeds divided equally among the offspring. Likewise, the value of the sold personal property was equally divided among the offspring.

Prior to the American Civil War, slaves would have been inventoried separately. If an individual owned slaves valued at $12,000 and left ten heirs, each heir would receive slaves to the value of $1,200. Sometimes slaves were sold and the money paid the heirs, but, more often, slaves were separated in an effort to even out the payments. For instance, in this scenario, one heir might receive an adult male slave valued at $1,200, while another heir might receive two adult women valued at $500 each and one child valued at $200. Often values could not be matched precisely to the amounts due each heir. In such a scenario, one individual might receive slaves valued at $1,450 but be required to pay $250 to another heir who had received slaves valued at only $950. In addition to the complications arising from the necessity to match appraised values with the value of each distributive share, some historians have argued that these complex inheritance patterns evidence efforts on the part of some owners to keep slave families together rather than to separate parents and children unnecessarily.

In instances where a widow inherited a portion of the land and never remarried, she remained in control of the property for her natural life. If she owned the land in her own right (say, through an original gift from her father, or if acquired after widowhood), she could bequeath it to whomever she chose, and she was free also to write a will bequeathing any personal possessions she owned. The dowry that came to her from her husband's estate, or its monetary value after its sale, would normally be equally divided among her surviving offspring at the time of her death.

Processioning:

Processioning is a term that signifies the method of determining legal boundaries between tracts of land.[1802]

In colonial America, land boundaries were usually processioned annually. Prior to the disestablishment of the Anglican Church in Virginia during the American Revolution, the processioning of lands fell to officials of the Church of England. Each year, the parish vestry would identify a number of

---

[1802] John Bouvier, *A Law Dictionary Adapted to the Constitution and Laws of the United States of America and of the Several States of the American Union* (Revised Edition, 1856).

individuals who were responsible for processioning lands in any given parish. Usually they were divided by precinct, and often individuals were responsible for only one neighborhood in a larger precinct. Usually three individuals measured the boundary line, one being a neutral individual and the other two being in some way connected with the land on one or the other side of the land. Processioners noted changes in ownership as well as changes in geographical features – such as a fallen tree or a meandering creek – which had once been identified as markers determining land boundaries. The process became less necessary with the development of the Township and Range system, which across much of America replaced the more traditional "meets and bounds" system.

Relict:

Legally, relict is used in the same manner as the word widow, referring to a woman who has survived her husband. Occasionally the word was also used to refer to a man who has survived his wife.

Religious Affiliations:

Several terms considered here derive from the structure of the Anglican Church and the relationship between law and religion as they shaped government and society in England during the early modern period. For that reason, a brief discussion of religion is in order.

Prior to the Protestant Reformation initiated in England during the reign of Henry VIII, England, like the rest of western Europe before that period, had been a Catholic nation. Henry VIII removed England from papal control, created the Church of England, and established himself, as reigning monarch, as head of the English church. The Church of England, or Anglican Church, continues to be the dominant religious institution in England today.

With the exception of the Catholic colonists who settled in Maryland under Lord Baltimore, most other Chesapeake colonists settling in Maryland and Virginia belonged to the Church of England when they arrived in America. In Virginia, the Church of England remained the established church, meaning that it was publicly supported and that attendance was legally mandated, until the beginning of the American Revolution. Most of the early Hammacks and Hammocks considered in this study were members of the Church of England at least until the 1750s and 1760s, when the Revolutionary crisis began. They baptized their offspring at North Farnham Parish Church in Richmond County, Virginia, and those records provide a key source in determining early Hammack family relationships. Many Hammacks and Hammocks remaining in Richmond County in fact continued as members of the Episcopal Church (formed after the formal link with the Church of England was severed during the American Revolution) and worshipped at the North Farnham Church into the nineteenth-century.

Beginning in the 1730s and 1740s, a powerful religious movement swept through Virginia that lured colonists, especially those living in frontier regions, away from the established Church of England into dissenting Baptist, Methodist, and Presbyterian churches. These churches were more egalitarian and less hierarchical than the Church of England and appealed more to small farmers and their families living in rural regions than did the Church of England. Lunenburg County, Virginia, was a prime location in this evangelical movement, and most of the early Hammacks and Hammocks settling in that region probably left the Church of England for dissenting congregations in the period between 1740 and 1780. Those who settled in Georgia seem to have adhered to the Baptist faith, although others later joined Methodist and, in some cases, Presbyterian congregations.

This movement intensified in the nineteenth-century during what historians refer to as the "Second Great Awakening" from about 1800 to 1830, when thousands of new converts joined Baptist and Methodist churches. After the American Civil War, in the 1870s and 1880s, another wave of revivalism swept the south, increasing church attendance and adding to the region's reputation as a center of religious activity. Most of the families considered in this study lived in the southern United States from the American Revolutionary era until the twentieth-century, and these religious developments shaped part of their cultural heritage.

In New England and the mid-Atlantic colonies (referred to by historians as the "Middle Colonies"), religious life differed significantly. Most settlers in New England followed the teachings of John Calvin, a critical figure in the Protestant Reformation, and practiced an extreme form of Protestant faith known as Puritanism, which held that all traces of Catholicism needed to be removed from religious life and which focused more closely than the Church of England on literacy and Bible study among the ordinary population. Some researchers believe that the Stephens family, considered near the end of this study as ancestors of Abi Doxey O'Neal Bankston, originated in Massachusetts, where they were members of the Puritan (later known as Congregationalist) church.

While the followers of John Calvin in England were known as Puritans, Calvin had numerous followers in Continental Europe and Scotland as well. John Knox, regarded as the father of the Scottish Presbyterian Church, drew heavily from Calvin's teachings. When Scots began settling in Northern Ireland, they brought their Presbyterian faith with them. Several families considered in this study, including the Stewarts and Templetons and, more than likely, the O'Neals, were members of the Presbyterian Church when they arrived in America.

Martin Luther's teachings played a crucial role in the development of the Protestant faith in Germany and northern Europe, and many of Luther's followers later came to America, settling in Pennsylvania. Founded by William Penn, a member of the Society of Friends (also called Quakers), Pennsylvania became a haven for religious dissenters whose beliefs conflicted with those of the Church of England or the orthodox Puritans in New England. It attracted colonists from New York and Delaware, among them descendants of the Dutch and Swedish settlers in those regions, whose beliefs drew from both Calvin and Luther. The Dutch Reformed Church was heavily Calvinist in nature, while the Church of Sweden had formally been of the Lutheran faith since the Uppsala Synod in 1593. The family of Lawrence and Rebecca Hendricks Bankston, who moved from Pennsylvania to Virginia and North Carolina, drew from both faiths, with ancestors among the first colonists of New Sweden as well as early Dutch settlers in New Amsterdam.

In Pennsylvania, William Penn's venture attracted thousands of Quakers like himself. Founded by George Fox as the Society of Friends, the Friends practiced an extreme form of protestant faith that focused on "Divine communion" with God. Because they trembled (or quaked) when in a state of "Divine communion," the early Friends were pejoratively called "Quakers," although the term gradually lost its negative connotation over time. The early Friends believed in equality between men and women as well as between different racial and ethnic groups; they thus became distinguished for their comparatively benign treatment of Native Americans and African Americans during the colonial period when compared with the Puritans further north in New England or the Chesapeake colonists to the South. Several generations of the Fincher family, ancestors of Mary Jane Gary O'Neal, belonged to the Society of Friends and practiced their faith in Pennsylvania and North Carolina.

As families like the Bankstons, Finchers, Hammacks, Stephenses, and Templetons moved further south into the Carolinas and Georgia, they converted from the original faiths they had brought with them to America to other denominations, chiefly the Baptist and Methodist churches which proliferated throughout the region in the nineteenth-century. Also with the American Revolution, older customs – such as the system of tithables, land processioning, and the elaborate procedures required for marriage – became simplified under new American law that was divested from much of its ecclesiastical heritage.

Tithable:

In colonial America, the word tithable "referred to a person who paid (or for whom someone else paid) one of the taxes imposed by the General Assembly for the support of civil government in the colony. In colonial Virginia, a poll tax or capitation tax was assessed on free white males, African

American slaves, and Native American servants (both male and female), age sixteen or older." Tithables do not list any individual younger than sixteen years of age, and they do not list adult white women who were not heads of households.[1803]

During the eighteenth-century, the age at which the payment of tithables for white males was required remained sixteen years, although there were several redefinitions of tithable requirements for slaves, mulattoes, Indians, and free blacks. Generally, when an individual appears for the first time on a tithable list in the household of another individual with the same surname, he had turned sixteen years old within the preceding year. When an individual appears as a tithable in his own right for the first time, he had usually, but not always, turned twenty-one years old within the preceding year.

On the whole, tithable lists record the taxable work force; they do not, therefore, list all of an individual's slaves or servants, and many white men were exempted because of age or debility. In Virginia, the personal property tax was established in 1782, and tithables continued to be a taxable category. In some instances, tithable lists exist after 1782 independent of personal property tax lists, although they were often combined. When implemented in 1782, the law required that all white male tithables over the age of twenty-one be listed by name, while those between the ages of sixteen and twenty-one were enumerated but not named.

[1803] J. Christian Kolbe, *The Library of Virginia, Research Notes Number 17: Colonial Tithables* (Richmond, 2001), pp. 1-4; Minor T. Weisiger, *The Library of Virginia, Research Notes Number 3: Using Personal Property Tax Records in the Archives at the Library of Virginia* (Richmond, 2001), pp. 1-4.

Appendix 2:

Notable Lineages

The lineages that follow trace the family histories of individuals mentioned in the earlier text back to British and European monarchs or to nobles involved with the creation of the Magna Carta in 1215. There are several excellent works that expand upon earlier generations of these lineages and provide comprehensive coverage of the British royal and noble families. For the lay reader, I recommend Alison Weir, *Britain's Royal Families: The Complete Genealogy* (London, 1996), a concise and readable account of the Saxon, Danish, Norman, Plantagenet, Tudor, and Stuart monarchies. I refer the serious scholar to D. Richardson and K. G. Everingham, eds., *Magna Carta Ancestry: A Study in Colonial and Medieval Ancestry* (Baltimore, 2005) and D. Richardson and K. G. Everingham, eds., *Plantagenet Ancestry: A Study in Colonial and Medieval Families* (Baltimore, 2004), themselves revisions of pioneering works by the late Frederick L. Weis, Walter L. Sheppard, and David Farris. These well documented works provide references to authoritative sources for establishing and expanding these pedigrees. Another useful work is *The Royal Descent of 500 Immigrants to the American Colonies* (Baltimore, 1993) by Gary Boyd Roberts.

A. Calthorpe: Magna Carta Lineage[1804]

I. Richard de Clare (1153-1217), Knight, Earl of Hertford, Magna Carta Surety, 1215, m. Amice of Gloucester, daughter of William Fitz Robert, Earl of Gloucester, by Hawise de Beaumont. He was present at the coronation of Kings Richard I and John in 1189 and 1199 respectively, but he later sided with the barons against King John and subsequently played a leading role in the negotiations for the Magna Carta. Richard de Clare was a descendant of Richard Fitz Gilbert, Lord of Clare, Bienfaite, Orbec, and Tonbridge, a Norman lord who participated in the Norman conquest of 1066 with William the Conqueror.

II. Maud de Clare, m. William de Brewes, of Bramber, Sussex, son of William de Braose, 7th Baron Abergavenny and 4th Lord of Bramber, who was once a favorite of King John. Braose, who had been responsible for the Abergavenny Massacre of 1175, wherein he lured three Welsh princes and other Welsh leaders to their deaths, fell out of favor with the king about 1208. Braose spent the next three years in exile and flight, dying in Corbeil, France, in 1211. William de Brewes, husband of Maude de Clare, was starved to death in 1210 upon orders from the king. He and Maude were already parents of four sons, who were imprisoned until 1218. John de Brewes, eldest son, acquired the baronetcies of both Gower and Bramber from his uncle, Reginald de Braose.

III. John de Brewes (-1232), of Bramber, Sussex, Lord of Gower, m. 1220, Margaret of Wales (- 1263), daughter of Llewellyn ap Iorwerth, Prince of Wales.

IV. Richard de Brewes (-bef. 18 June 1292), Knight, Lord of Stinton, m. bef. 9 September 1265, Alice le Rus, widow of Richard Longespee, daughter of William le Rus and Agatha, daughter of Roger de Clere.

V. Giles de Brewes, Knight, m. (2) by 1303, Joan de Beaumont, daughter of Richard de Beaumont.

VI. John de Brewes, Knight, m. Eve de Ufford, daughter of Robert de Ufford, 1st Lord Ufford, and Cecily de Valoines.

[1804] This lineage is as presented in D. Richardson and K. G. Everingham, eds., *Magna Carta Ancestry: A Study in Colonial and Medieval Ancestry* (Baltimore, 2005), pp. 165-168.

VII. John Brewes, Knight, Sheriff of Norfolk and Suffolk, Keeper of Norwich Castle, m. bef. 1 April 1376, Agnes [-----], widow of Richard de Freville.

VIII. Robert Brewes, Knight, m. Ela Stapleton, daughter of Miles Stapleton, Knight, and Ela de Ufford, of Bedale, Yorkshire, and Ingham, Norfolk.

IX. Margaret Brewes, m. John Shelton, Esq., of Shelton, Great Snoring, Thetford, and Hindringham, Norfolk.

X. Ralph Shelton, Knight, Sheriff of Norfolk and Suffolk, m. (2) Margaret Clere, daughter of Robert Clere, Esq., of Ormesby, Norfolk, and Elizabeth Uvedale.

XI. Ralph Shelton, Esq., of Broome and Norwich, Norfolk, m. Mary Brome, widow of John Jenny, Esq., and daughter of Gilbert Brome, of Broome, Norfolk.

XII. Ralph Shelton, Esq., of Broome, Norfolk, m. (1) 1545, Prudence Calthorpe, daughter of Edward Calthorpe, Esq., of Kirby Cane, Norfolk, and Thomasine Gavell.

XIII. Grace Shelton, m. 29 April 1582, Broome, Norfolk, John Thurton, Gent., of Broome, Norfolk.

XIV. Maud Thurton, m. 8 Sept., 1602, Broome, Norfolk, Christopher Calthorpe, Esq., of Cockthorpe and East Barsham, Norfolk, son of James Calthorpe, Knight, of Cockthorpe and Blakeney, and Barbara Bacon, daughter of John Bacon, Esq., of Hessett, Suffolk.

XV. Col Christopher Calthorpe (bapt. 22 April 1605, Ditchingham, Norfolk -- bef. 24 April 1662, North Carolina), m. Anne [-----] (-- bur. 9 December 1667, Charles Parish, York Co., VA). Calthorpe arrived in Virginia on the Furtherance in 1622. He served in the Virginia House of Burgesses in 1644-46, 1652-53, and 1660.

XVI. James Calthorpe (Bet. 1640-1650, York Co., VA -- 3 Aug., 1689, Charles Parish, York Co., VA), m. Elizabeth [-----].

XVII. Elestrange Calthorpe (4 September 1680, Charles Parish, York Co., VA -- 4 Oct., 1726, Charles Parish, York Co., VA), m. abt. 1705, Charles Parish, York Co., VA, Mary Butts (4 September 1684, Charles Parish, York Co., VA -- 24 October 1718, Charles Parish, York Co., VA), daughter of Anthony Butts and Mary Rookesby.

XVIII. Charles Calthorpe (8 Oct., 1709, Charles Parish, York Co., VA -- bef. 14 April 1763, Southampton Co., VA), m. bef. Dec., 1731, Charles Parish, York Co., VA, Eleanor Clifton (13 March 1714, Charles Parish, York Co., VA -- bet. 1772-1775, Southampton Co., VA), daughter of Benjamin Clifton and Sarah Hay.

XIX. Frances Calthorpe (6 September 1737, Charles Parish, York Co., VA -- abt. 1814, Person Co., NC), m. bef. 8 November 1756, Southampton Co., VA, Jesse Jones (bef. 1735, Isle of Wight Co., VA -- abt. 1780, Caswell Co., NC), son of William Jones and Elizabeth [-----].

XX. Sarah Jones (abt. 1766, Southampton Co., VA -- abt. 1846, Person Co., NC), m. 29 Dec., 1786, Caswell Co., NC, John Brown (abt. 1765, Mecklenburg Co., VA -- abt. 1837, Person Co., NC), son of Abraham Brown and Frances [------].

XXI. Alfred Brown (abt. 1787, Caswell Co., NC -- abt. 1816, Person Co., NC), m. abt. 16 February 1812, Person Co., NC, Judith Nichols (abt. 1794, Person Co., NC -- aft. 1870, Hinds Co., MS), daughter of Wright Nichols and Sarah Burch. She m. (2) John H. Cates, Sr.

XXII. Col. Drury J. Brown (abt. 1813, Person Co., NC -- 1866, Copiah Co., MS), m. 31 Dec., 1834, Hinds Co., MS, Sarah Wells (abt. 1818, Person Co., NC -- 1853, Hinds Co., MS), daughter of Stephen Wells and Sally Farquhar.

XXIII. Abbie Doxey Brown (10 Nov., 1841, Hinds Co., MS -- 1 January 1940, Hinds Co., MS), m. 19 September 1860, Raymond, Hinds Co., MS, Anderson Bradley Cates (31 July 1834, Hinds Co., MS -- 26 April 1884, Hinds Co., MS), son of John Foster Cates and Elizabeth Rimmer.

XXIV. Sallie Elizabeth Cates (14 January 1863, Hinds Co., MS -- 30 April 1951, Hinds Co., MS), m. 20 December 1883, Hinds Co., MS, William S. Hammack (14 April 1852, Macon Co., GA -- 25 December 1899, Hinds Co., MS).

XXV. George Cleveland Hammack (26 Oct., 1884, Hinds Co., MS -- 17 Nov., 1963, Hinds Co., MS), m. 19 February 1911, Hinds Co., MS, Mary Almedia Bankston (3 April 1894, Hinds Co., MS -- 9 December 1974, Hinds Co., MS).

B. Calthorpe: Plantagenet Lineage[1805].

I. Edward I, King of England, m. Eleanor of Castile.

II. Joan of England, m. Gilbert de Clare, Knight, Earl of Gloucester and Hertford.

III. Elizabeth de Clare, m. Roger Damory, Knight, Lord Damory.

IV. Elizabeth Damory, m. bef. 25 December 1327, John Bardolf, Knight, 3rd Lord Bardolf, of Wormegay, Cantley, and Caistor, Norfolk, son of Thomas Bardolf, Knight, 2nd Lord Bardolf, and Agnes de Grandison.

V. William Bardolf, Knight, 4th Lord Bardolf, m. aft. 10 February 1365/6, Agnes Poynings, daughter of Michael de Poynings, Knight, 1st Lord Poynings, and Joan Rokesley, Knight.

VI. Cecily Bardolf, m. Brian Stapleton, Knight, de jure Lord Ingham, of Ingham, Norfolk, Bedale, Yorkshire, and North Moreton, Berkshire, Sheriff of Norfolk and Suffolk, son of Miles Stapleton and Ela de Ufford.

VII. Miles Stapleton, Knight, de jure Lord Ingham, m. (2) 1438, Katherine Pole, daughter of Thomas de la Pole and Anne Cheyne.

VIII. Elizabeth Stapleton, m. (1) bef. 7 March 1463/4, William Calthorpe, Knight, of Burnham Thorpe, Norfolk, Sheriff of Norfolk and Suffolk, son of John Calthorpe, Knight, and Anne Wythe, m. (2) John Fortescue, Knight, of Ponsbourne, Herefordshire, Chief Butler of England, m. (3) Edward Howard, Knight, K.G., Lord High Admiral.

[1805] This lineage is as presented in D. Richardson and K. G. Everingham, eds., *Plantagenet Ancestry: A Study in Colonial and Medieval Families* (Baltimore, 2004), pp. 56-59.

IX. Edward Calthorpe, m. Anne Cromer.

X. Edward Calthorpe, Esq., of Kirby Cane, Norfolk, m. 1525, Thomasine Gavell, widow of Leonard Copledike, of Horsham, Suffolk, and daughter of Thomas Gavell, Esq., and Olive Everard, Esq.

XI. Prudence Calthorpe, m. Ralph Shelton.

XII. Grace Shelton, m. 29 April 1582, Broome, Norfolk, John Thurton, Gent., of Broome, Norfolk.

XIII. Maud Thurton, m. 8 Sept., 1602, Broome, Norfolk, Christopher Calthorpe, Esq., of Cockthorpe and East Barsham, Norfolk, son of James Calthorpe, Knight, of Cockthorpe and Blakeney, and Barbara Bacon, daughter of John Bacon, Esq., of Hessett, Suffolk.

XIV. Col Christopher Calthorpe (bapt. 22 April 1605, Ditchingham, Norfolk -- bef. 24 April 1662, North Carolina), m. Anne [-----] (-- bur. 9 December 1667, Charles Parish, York Co., VA). Calthorpe arrived in Virginia on the Furtherance in 1622. He served in the Virginia House of Burgesses in 1644-46, 1652-53, and 1660.

XV. James Calthorpe (Bet. 1640-1650, York Co., VA -- 3 Aug., 1689, Charles Parish, York Co., VA), m. Elizabeth [-----].

XVI. Elestrange Calthorpe (4 September 1680, Charles Parish, York Co., VA -- 4 Oct., 1726, Charles Parish, York Co., VA), m. abt. 1705, Charles Parish, York Co., VA, Mary Butts (4 September 1684, Charles Parish, York Co., VA -- 24 October 1718, Charles Parish, York Co., VA), daughter of Anthony Butts and Mary Rookesby.

XVII. Charles Calthorpe (8 Oct., 1709, Charles Parish, York Co., VA -- bef. 14 April 1763, Southampton Co., VA), m. bef. Dec., 1731, Charles Parish, York Co., VA, Eleanor Clifton (13 March 1714, Charles Parish, York Co., VA -- bet. 1772-1775, Southampton Co., VA), daughter of Benjamin Clifton and Sarah Hay.

XVIII. Frances Calthorpe (6 September 1737, Charles Parish, York Co., VA -- abt. 1814, Person Co., NC), m. bef. 8 November 1756, Southampton Co., VA, Jesse Jones (bef. 1735, Isle of Wight Co., VA -- abt. 1780, Caswell Co., NC), son of William Jones and Elizabeth [-----].

XIX. Sarah Jones (abt. 1766, Southampton Co., VA -- abt. 1846, Person Co., NC), m. 29 Dec., 1786, Caswell Co., NC, John Brown (abt. 1765, Mecklenburg Co., VA -- abt. 1837, Person Co., NC), son of Abraham Brown and Frances [------].

XX. Alfred Brown (abt. 1787, Caswell Co., NC -- abt. 1816, Person Co., NC), m. abt. 16 February 1812, Person Co., NC, Judith Nichols (abt. 1794, Person Co., NC -- aft. 1870, Hinds Co., MS), daughter of Wright Nichols and Sarah Burch. She m. (2) John H. Cates, Sr.

XXI. Col. Drury J. Brown (abt. 1813, Person Co., NC -- 1866, Copiah Co., MS), m. 31 Dec., 1834, Hinds Co., MS, Sarah Wells (abt. 1818, Person Co., NC -- 1853, Hinds Co., MS), daughter of Stephen Wells and Sally Farquhar.

XXII. Abbie Doxey Brown (10 Nov., 1841, Hinds Co., MS -- 1 January 1940, Hinds Co., MS), m. 19 September 1860, Raymond, Hinds Co., MS, Anderson Bradley Cates (31 July 1834, Hinds Co., MS -- 26 April 1884, Hinds Co., MS), son of John Foster Cates and Elizabeth Rimmer.

XXIII. Sallie Elizabeth Cates (14 January 1863, Hinds Co., MS -- 30 April 1951, Hinds Co., MS), m. 20 December 1883, Hinds Co., MS, William S. Hammack (14 April 1852, Macon Co., GA -- 25 December 1899, Hinds Co., MS).

XXIV. George Cleveland Hammack (26 Oct., 1884, Hinds Co., MS -- 17 Nov., 1963, Hinds Co., MS), m. 19 February 1911, Hinds Co., MS, Mary Almedia Bankston (3 April 1894, Hinds Co., MS -- 9 December 1974, Hinds Co., MS).

C. Parker: Magna Carta Lineage[1806].

I. Robert de Vere (1164-1221), Earl of Oxford, Magna Carta Surety, m. Isabel de Bolebec.

II. Hugh de Vere, Earl of Oxford, m. Hawise de Quincy.

III. Isabel de Vere, m. (1) John de Courtenay, Knight, son of Robert de Courtenay, Knight, and Mary de Vernon, m. (2) Oliver de Dinham, Knight, Keeper of Lundy Isle, who was summoned to attend the king at Shrewsbury 28 June 1283 and to Parliament from 24 June 1295 to 26 August 1296. John de Courtenay served in Gascony in 1243 and in Wales in 1257 and 1258.

IV. Hugh de Courtenay, Knight, m. Eleanor le Despenser, daughter of Hugh le Despenser and Aline Basset. Hugh de Courtenay served in the Army of West Wales by 1282 and was summoned to attend the King at Shrewsbury on 28 June 1283.

V. Hugh de Courtenay, Knight, m. 1292, Agnes de Saint John, daughter of John de Saint John, Knight, and Alice Fitz Peter, Knight. Hugh de Courtenay was summoned to Parliament in 1298/9. He served in the Scottish wars and fought at the Siege of Caerlaverock Castle in 1300. He was chosen one of the Lords Ordainers in 1313 and served on the King's Council from 9 August 1318. He was declared Earl of Devon on 22 February 1334/5.

VI. Hugh de Courtenay, Knight of the Garter, 10th Earl of Devon, Lord Courtenay, lord of Oakhampton, Devon, Joint Warden of Devon and Cornwall, Chief Warden of Devon, m. 11 August 1325, Margaret de Bohun, daughter of Humphrey de Bohun, Knight, Earl of Hereford and Essex, and Elizabeth, daughter of Edward I, King of England. Hugh de Courtenay was summoned to Parliament 23 April 1337. He became Earl of Devon following his father's death in 1340. He helped repel the French attack on Cornwall in 1339 and in 1347 was one of the Knights' of the King's Chamber. He was in 1348 a Founder Knight of the Order of the Garter.

VII. Edward de Courtenay, Knight, m. Emeline Dauney, daughter of John Dauney, Knight, and Sibyl de Treverbyn, of Treverbyn, Cornwall.

VIII. Hugh de Courtenay, Knight, m. (4) by license dated 16 October 1417, Maud Beaumont, daughter of William Beaumont, Knight, and Isabel Willington, of Heanton Punchardon, Devon.

[1806] This lineage is as presented in Richardson and Everingham, eds., *Magna Carta Ancestry*, pp. 234-241.

IX. Hugh Courtenay, Knight, m. Margaret Carminow, daughter of Thomas Carminow and Joan Hill.

X. Elizabeth Courtenay, m. bef. 1477, John Tretherff, Esq., son of Reynold Tretherff, Esq., and Margaret St. Aubyn.

XI. Thomas Tretherff, Esq., m. Maud Trevisa, of Trevisa, Cornwall.

XII. Margaret Tretherff, m. (1) John Boscawen, of Tregothnan, Cornwall, son of John Boscawen and Elizabeth Lower, m. (2) bef. 1536, Edward Courtenay, m. (3) bef. 1546, Richard Buller, Esq., of Shillingham and Tregarrick, Cornwall, son of Alexander Buller and Elizabeth Horsey, Knight.

XIII. Francis Buller, Esq., m. Thomasine Williams, daughter of Thomas Williams and Emlyn Crewse.

XIV. Richard Buller, Esq., of Shillingham, Cornwall, Sheriff of Cornwall, m. bef. 1603, Alice Hayward, daughter of Rowland Hayward, Knight, and Katherine Smythe.

XV. Catherine Buller, m. 31 December 1616, St. Stephen-juxta-Saltash, Cornwall, James Parker, Gent., of Trengoff and Blisland, Cornwall, son of Rev. William Parker (-- bur. 25 May 1631, Warleggan, Cornwall), Rector of Blisland, Cornwall, 1601, and Archdeacon of Cornwall, 1616, and Joan Panchard. Rev. William Parker was the third son of Robert Parker (-- 1591, Browsholme, Yorkshire), Bowbearer of the Forest of Bowland, and Elizabeth Chadderton, daughter of Edmund Chadderton, of Nuthurst, Lancashire, who were married 8 January 1544/5 in Whalley, Lancashire.[1807] Robert Parker was the third son of Edmund Parker (1481-1547), of Browsholme, Yorkshire, and Jennet Redmayne, daughter of John Redmayne, of Thornton, Yorkshire, and Elizabeth Parker, daughter of Robert Parker of Browsholme.[1808] Edmund Parker in 1507 received a lease for lands at Browsholme, Yorkshire, and then erected Browsholme Hall, which is today the oldest family-owned home in Lancashire, England.[1809] Edmund Parker was a direct lineal descendant of Peter de Alcancotes, holder of the Manor of Alkincoats in Colne in the middle thirteenth-century. Adam de Alcancotes , Peter's son, was living at Alkincoats in 1311. His younger son, Richard le Parker of Trawden, succeeded him, and the Parker lands then passed to his son Edmund Parker, park-keeper of Radholme Laund, near Browsholme. In 1393, Edmund's two sons Richard and John were deputy parkers of Radholme, but from 1380 they possessed a lease of the pastures at Browsholme, a lease which was renewed in 1400. Richard probably built the original house at Nether Browsholme; he received a pension in 1411 and was succeeded by his son Edmund Parker of Foulscales and Nether Browsholme. This Edmund was the father of Giles Parker of Horrocksford, tenant of Nether Browsholme in 1482, who was buried in Waddington Church. This Giles was the father of Edmund Parker, who in 1507 obtained a new lease for Browsholme and erected the house that still stands there.

XVI. Richard Parker, Chirurgeon (bapt. 29 November 1630, Warleggon, Cornwall -- aft. 1669, Henrico Co., VA), m. bef. 5 September 1656, Charles City Co., VA, Mary [----], widow of Nicholas Perkins.[1810]

[1807] See "Parker of Brousholme," in Clay, ed., *Dugdale's Visitation of Yorkshire*, pp. 379-385. It has been supplemented by "The Parkers of Browsholme," at the Browsholme Hall website (*http://www.browsholme.co.uk*). There was a strong clerical tradition in the Parker family. Giles Parker of Horrockford was the father of Giles Parker, Incumbent of Waddington, 1523-1577, and grandfather of Giles Parker, a chantry priest. Robert Parker and Elizabeth Chadderton were the parents of William Parker, Bishop of Chester (1579-1595) and Bishop of Lincoln (1595-1608). Robert's younger son, Roger, served as Dean of Lincoln from 1613 to 1629.

[1808] Robert of Browsholme was the great-uncle of Jennet's husband Edmund Parker and a brother of Edmund Parker of Foulscales and Nether Browsholme. Robert Parker was parker of Radholme in 1434.

[1809] Through redistricting, this land in 1975 became a part of Lancashire rather than Yorkshire.

[1810] Nicholas and Mary Perkins were the parents of Nicholas Perkins (abt. 1647, Henrico Co., VA -- 1712, Henrico Co., VA), who married Sarah Childers, daughter of Abrah Childers. This Nicholas Perkins was the father of Philemon Perkins (who married Obedience Cox), the grandfather of John Perkins (who married Rachel Ferguson), great-grandfather of Nancy Perkins (who married

XVI. Richard Parker (Abt. 1656, Charles City Co., VA -- aft. 1714, Nansemond Co., VA).

XVII. Richard Parker (Abt. 1676-1680, Nansemond Co., VA -- bet. September 1749-April 1752, Chowan Co., NC).[1811]

XVIII. Unknown Son.[1812]

XIX. Major Richard Parker (Abt. 1731, Chowan Co., NC -- Aft. 1812, Hancock Co., GA), named as grandson in 1749 will of Richard Parker, m. bef. 20 January 1775, Orange or Chatham Co., NC, Ann Brewer (bet. 1740-1750, Brunswick Co., VA -- aft. 6 June 1801, Greene or Hancock Co., GA), daughter of Henry Brewer and Mary [------].

XX. Martha Parker (abt. 1783-1784, Wilkes Co., GA -- aft. 1853, Greene Co., GA), m. 26 December 1803, Greene Co., GA, John Stephens (abt. 17 Dec., 1778, Wake Co., NC -- 17 Nov., 1852, Greene Co., GA), son of Edmund Stephens and Mary [------].[1813]

XXI. Mary Stephens (abt. 1806, Greene Co., GA -- Jan., 1854, Greene Co., GA), m. 27 January 1820, Greene Co., GA, Wooten O'Neal, II (abt. 1801, Wilkes Co., GA -- bet. 1862-1867, Greene Co., GA), son of Wooten O'Neal, I, and Mary [Harrison?].

XXII. James Augustus O'Neal (c. 1825-1826, Greene Co., GA -- 30 April 1862, Camp Douglas, IL), m. 12 Dec., 1843, Greene Co., GA, Georgia Ann Virginia Stewart (abt. 1830, Taliaferro Co., GA -- Feb., 1892, Hinds Co., MS), prob. daughter of William Stewart and granddaughter of Henry and Lucy Stewart.

XXIII. James Rederick O'Neal (25 July 1847, Greene Co., GA -- 14 January 1893, Hinds Co., MS), m. 5 December 1867, Smith Co., MS, Mary Jane Gary (28 Aug., 1850, MS -- 11 June 1881, Hinds Co., MS), daughter of Starling Tucker Gary and Mary Ann Stringer.

XXIV. Abi Doxey O'Neal (22 April 1870, Hinds Co., MS -- 15 March 1899, Hinds Co., MS), m. 29 November 1886, Bolton, Hinds Co., MS, John Manly Bankston (2 September 1857, Bibb Co., AL -- 13 December 1922, Hinds Co., MS), son of Thomas Jefferson Bankston and Martha Adeline Mitchell.

XXV. Mary Almedia Bankston (3 April 1894, Hinds Co., MS -- 9 December 1974, Hinds Co., MS), m. 19 February 1911, Hinds Co., MS, George Cleveland Hammack (26 October 1884, Hinds Co., MS -- 17 November 1963, Hinds Co., MS).

D. Parker: Plantagenet Lineage[1814].

I. Geoffrey Plantagenet, Count of Anjou.

John Foster), great-great-grandfather of Elizabeth Foster (who married John H. Cates), and great-great-great-grandfather of John Foster Cates. It is unclear whether Richard Parker and Nicholas Perkins were half-brothers of step-brothers. Perkins researchers believe that Mary [----] Perkins Parker's maiden name was Burton, while some Parker genealogists believe that Richard Parker had previously been married to a woman called Mary Beauchamp before he married Mary Perkins.

[1811] Grimes, *North Carolina Wills*, p. 279, abstracts Richard Parker's 1749 Chowan County, N.C., will that names his grandson Richard Parker as an heir.

[1812] Richard Parker's will names a grandson Richard Parker but does not specify the grandson's paternity.

[1813] As noted in the text, Martha is believed to have been a daughter of Richard and Anne Brewer Parker based on family association between 1800 and 1850 and the proximity between the residences of John Stephens and Richard Parker, Sr., and Richard Parker, Jr.

[1814] This lineage is as presented in Richardson and Everingham, eds., *Plantagenet Ancestry*, pp. 238-243.

II. Hamelin, 5th Earl of Surrey, m. Isabel de Warenne.

III. Maude de Warenne, m. Henry of Eu, Count of Eu.

IV. Alice of Eu, Countess of Eu, m. Raoul D'Exoudun, Count of Eu.

V. Maud of Eu, m. Humphrey de Bohun, Knight, Earl of Hereford and Essex.

VI. Humphrey de Bohun, Knight, of Kimbolton, Huntingdonshire, m. Eleanor de Brewes.

VII. Humphrey de Bohun, Earl of Hereford and Essex, m. Maud de Fiennes.

VIII. Humphrey de Bohun, Knight, Earl of Hereford, m. Elizabeth of England.

IX. Margaret de Bohun, m. 11 August 1325, Hugh de Courtenay, Knight of the Garter, 10th Earl of Devon, Lord Courtenay, lord of Oakhampton, Devon, Joint Warden of Devon and Cornwall, Chief Warden of Devon, son of Hugh de Courtenay, 9th Earl of Devon, Lord Courtenay, Baron of Okehampton, Devon, and Agnes St. John.

X. Edward de Courtenay, Knight, m. Emeline Dauney.

XI. Hugh Courtenay, Knight, m. Maud Beaumont.

XII. Hugh Courtenay, Knight, m. Margaret Carminow.

XIII. Elizabeth Courtenay, m. John Tretherff, Esq.

XIV. Thomas Tretherff, Esq., m. Maud Trevisa.

XV. Margaret Tretherff, m. (1) John Boscawen, m. (2) Edward Courtenay, m. (3) Richard Buller.

XVI. Francis Buller, Esq., m. Thomasine Williams.

XVII. Richard Buller, Knight, m. Alice Hayward.

XVIII. Catherine Buller, m. James Parker.

XIX. Richard Parker, m. Mary [----], widow of Nicholas Perkins.

XX. Richard Parker (Abt. 1656, Charles City Co., VA -- aft. 1714, Nansemond Co., VA).

XXI. Richard Parker (Abt. 1676-1680, Nansemond Co., VA -- bet. September 1749-April 1752, Chowan Co., NC).

XXII. Unknown Son.

XXIII. Major Richard Parker (Abt. 1731, Chowan Co., NC -- Aft. 1812, Hancock Co., GA), named as grandson in 1749 will of Richard Parker, m. bef. 20 January 1775, Orange or Chatham Co., NC, Ann

Brewer (bet. 1740-1750, Brunswick Co., VA -- aft. 6 June 1801, Greene or Hancock Co., GA), daughter of Henry Brewer and Mary [------].

XXIV. Martha Parker (abt. 1783-1784, Wilkes Co., GA -- aft. 1853, Greene Co., GA), m. 26 December 1803, Greene Co., GA, John Stephens (abt. 17 Dec., 1778, Wake Co., NC -- 17 Nov., 1852, Greene Co., GA), son of Edmund Stephens and Mary [------].

XXV. Mary Stephens (abt. 1806, Greene Co., GA -- Jan., 1854, Greene Co., GA), m. 27 January 1820, Greene Co., GA, Wooten O'Neal, II (abt. 1801, Wilkes Co., GA -- bet. 1862-1867, Greene Co., GA), son of Wooten O'Neal, I, and Mary [Harrison?].

XXVI. James Augustus O'Neal (c. 1825-1826, Greene Co., GA -- 30 April 1862, Camp Douglas, IL), m. 12 Dec., 1843, Greene Co., GA, Georgia Ann Virginia Stewart (abt. 1830, Taliaferro Co., GA -- Feb., 1892, Hinds Co., MS), prob. daughter of William Stewart and granddaughter of Henry and Lucy Stewart.

XXVII. James Rederick O'Neal (25 July 1847, Greene Co., GA -- 14 January 1893, Hinds Co., MS), m. 5 December 1867, Smith Co., MS, Mary Jane Gary (28 Aug., 1850, MS -- 11 June 1881, Hinds Co., MS), daughter of Starling Tucker Gary and Mary Ann Stringer.

XXVIII. Abi Doxey O'Neal (22 April 1870, Hinds Co., MS -- 15 March 1899, Hinds Co., MS), m. 29 November 1886, Bolton, Hinds Co., MS, John Manly Bankston (2 September 1857, Bibb Co., AL -- 13 December 1922, Hinds Co., MS), son of Thomas Jefferson Bankston and Martha Adeline Mitchell.

XXIX. Mary Almedia Bankston (3 April 1894, Hinds Co., MS -- 9 December 1974, Hinds Co., MS), m. 19 February 1911, Hinds Co., MS, George Cleveland Hammack (26 October 1884, Hinds Co., MS -- 17 November 1963, Hinds Co., MS).

E. Washington Lineage.[1815]

I. John Washington, Esquire, of Tuwhitfield, Lancashire.

II. Robert Washington, Gentleman, of Warton, Lancashire.

III. John Washington, Gentleman, of Warton, m. Margaret Kitson, daughter of Robert Kitson of Warton.

IV. Lawrence Washington, of Sulgrave, m. (2) Amy Pargiter, daughter of Robert Pargiter, Gentleman, of Greatworth, Northampton, and Anne Knight, daughter of John Knight of Carlton, Northampton.[1816]

[1815] The first six generations here are as given in W. C. Metcalfe, *The Visitation of Northamptonshire, 1564, 1618-19* (London, 1887). See also J. B. Boddie, *Historical Southern Families* (23 vols., Redwood City, CA, 1957-), 4: 149-174; D. Faris, *Plantagenet Ancestry of Seventeenth-Century Colonists* (Baltimore, 1996), pp. 91-95, 274-277; G. S. H. L. Washington, *The Earliest Washingtons and Their Anglo-Scottish Connections* (Cambridge, 1964), pp. 1-11, 23, and Tables 1 and 2.

[1816] Metcalfe, *Northamptonshire, 1564*, p. 40, states:

Richard Pargiter of Greatworth, co. Northampton, married *Anne, daughter of Richard Coles of Preston* in the said county, and had issue: Robert.

Robert Pargiter of Greatworth, Northamptonshire, Gent., eldest son and heir to Richard, married *Anne, daughter of John Knight of Carlton, Northamptonshire*, and by her had issue: William, eldest son; Anthony, second son; George, third son; Edward fourth son; Mary, married William Mowle; Anne, married John Blencowe; *Amey, married Lawrence Washington of Sulgrave, Northamptonshire, Gentleman*; Cicely, married Edward Manly of Northamptonshire.

V. Robert Washington[1817], of Sulgrave, m. (1) Elizabeth, daughter of Walter Light of Radway Grange, Warwickshire. Robert was living and head of the family at the time of the Northamptonshire Visitation of 1618-19.

VI. Lawrence Washington (c. 1568 -- 13 December 1616, Wickamon, Northampton, bur. St. Michael's Brington, Northampton), Gent., of Sulgrave and Wicken, m. 3 August 1588, Aston-le-Walls, Northamptonshire, Margaret Butler (c. 1570 -- 16 March 1651/2, bur. East Haddon, Northamptonshire), eldest daughter of William Butler and Margaret Greeke, and granddaughter of John Butler and Margaret Sutton (descendant of Edward I) and of Thomas Greeke and Jane Thomson. Margaret Butler Washington brought to her husband the right to quarter the royal arms of the Plantagenet family with those of the Washingtons.

VII. Rev. Lawrence Washington (1602, Sulgrave Manor, Northampton -- bur. 21 January 1652/3, Maldon) who married Amphylis Twigden, daughter of John Twigden of Little Creaton, Northampton, and Anne Dickens. Reverend Lawrence Washington was educated at Brasenose College, Oxford, where he took his B.A. in 1623. He was Fellow (1624), M.A. (1626), Lector (1627-1631), and Proctor (1634).

VIII. Col. John Washington (c. 1634 - 1677), m. Ann Pope. Col. Washington emigrated to Westmoreland Co., VA, from which he became a delegate to the Virginia House of Burgesses.

IX. Lawrence Washington (1659 - 1698), m. Mildred Warner.

X. Captain Augustine Washington (1694-1743), m. (2) Mary Ball, daughter of Joseph Ball and Mrs. Mary (Bennett) Johnson Ball.

XI. General George Washington (1731-1799), First President of the United States of America, m. 1758, Mrs. Martha (Dandridge) Custis.

F. Washington - Lanier - Bankston Lineage.

VII. Richard Washington[1818] (abt. 1605, Sulgrave, Northampton -- bur. 8 January 1641/2, St. Martin in the Fields, London), m. 17 April 1627, St. Martin in the Fields, Frances Browne.[1819] Frances (Browne) Washington m. (2) 17 January 1642/3, London, Ralph Hall.

VIII. John Washington (bapt. 14 March 1631/2, St. Martin in the Fields, London --), m. bef. 31 January 1662/3, Surry Co., VA, m. c. 1658, Mary [-----] Blunt Ford (-- c. 1678), widow of Richard Blunt (1616 - 1656) and Charles Ford ("ffoord") (-- 1657). After John Washington's death, Mary m. (4) Henry Briggs (1635 -- 1686).[1820]

IX. Richard Washington (c. 1659, Surry Co., VA - 1724, Surry Co., VA), m. Elizabeth Jordan, daughter of Arthur Jordan and Mrs. Elizabeth [-----] Bavin Jordan, of Surry Co., VA.[1821]

[1817] Metcalfe, *Northamptonshire, 1564*, pp. 53, 152.

[1818] Richard was a brother of Reverend Lawrence Washington, shown above.

[1819] Ingersoll, *Lanier*, p. 41, was among the first to discuss this possibility.

[1820] Dorman, *Adventurers*, p. 291. See also *Virginia Genealogical Society Quarterly*, Volume II, pp. 28-29.

[1821] Ingersoll, *Lanier*, p. 41, gives the date as 5 September 1660. Robert A. Jordan, *Jordan Journal: History of the George and Arthur Jordan Families of Virginia, North Carolina, Indiana from 1634* (Evansville, Indiana, 1996) is the best study to date of the Richard and Arthur Jordan families. See also the wills of George Jordan (Torrence, *Valentine*, 2: 686-689) and Arthur Jordan (Torrence, *Valentine*, 2: 692).

X. Elizabeth Washington (c. 1690, Surry Co., VA --), m. by 1706, Surry Co., VA, Sampson Lanier (c. 1682, Charles City Co., VA -- c. 1742/3, Brunswick Co., VA), son of John Lanier (October 1631, Lewisham, England -- 1717/1719, Prince George Co., VA) and grandson of Clement Lanier, Court Musician to English Kings Charles I and Charles II, and Hannah Collett, of Greenwich, England.

XI. James Lanier (after 11 November 1724, Brunswick Co., VA -- 1786, Pitt Co., NC), m. c. 1746, Brunswick Co., VA, Mary Cooke (c. 1726, Brunswick Co., VA -- aft. 1792, Rockingham Co., NC, or Greene Co., GA), daughter of Henry Cooke and Mary Clark, of Surry and Brunswick Counties, VA.

XII. Mary Lanier (23 June 1765, Pitt Co., NC -- 5 April 1857, Coosa Co., AL), m. abt. 1784, Rockingham Co., NC, Rev. John Bankston (8 May 1760, Orange Co., NC -- 23 Feb., 1838, Gwinnett Co., GA).

XIII. Thomas B. Bankston (c. 1799, prob. Columbia Co., GA -- aft. 1860, Bibb Co., AL), m. abt. 1825, prob. Gwinnett Co., GA, Marion [------] (abt. 1807, GA -- aft. 1860, Bibb Co., AL).

XIV. Thomas Jefferson Bankston (c. 1830, prob. Heard Co., GA -- 1884, Issaquena Co., MS), m. 21 Dec., 1856, Bibb Co., GA, Martha Adeline Mitchell (c. 1832, TN -- Feb., 1871, MS), daughter of Hiram Mitchell and Mourning [Dove?] Mitchell.

XV. John Manly Bankston (2 Sept., 1857, Bibb Co., AL -- 13 Dec., 1922, Hinds Co., MS), m. 29 Nov., 1886, Bolton, Hinds Co., MS, Abi Doxey O'Neal (22 Apr., 1870, Hinds Co., MS -- 15 Mar., 1899, Hinds Co., MS), daughter of James Rederick O'Neal and Mary Jane Gary.

XVI. Mary Almedia Bankston (3 April 1894, Hinds Co., MS -- 9 Dec., 1974, Hinds Co., MS), m. 19 Feb., 1911, Hinds Co., MS, George Cleveland Hammack (26 Oct., 1884, Hinds Co., MS -- 17 Nov., 1963, Hinds Co., MS).

G. Plantagenet - Clare- Audley - Stafford - Sutton - Butler Lineage.

I. Edward I, King of England, m. Alianore de Castille.[1822]

II. Joan of Acre, m. Gilbert de Clarke, Earl of Gloucester, son of Richard de Clare (of Magna Charta Surety descent and descendant of Charlemagne) by Maud, daughter of John de Lacy, Earl of Lincoln, Magna Charta Surety (and descendant of Charlemagne).

III. Margaret de Clare, m. (2) 28 April 1317, Windsor, Hugh de Audley, 8th Earl of Stafford, second son of Hugh Audley, of Stratton Audley, Oxfordshire (descendant of Charlemagne) by Isolt, daughter of Edmund de Mortimer, Knight, Baron of Wigmore, Herefordshire (descendant of Charlemagne).

IV. Margaret de Audley, m. bef. 6 July 1336, Ralph de Stafford, Baron of Stafford, Staffordshire, 2nd Lord Stafford, son and heir of Edmund Stafford, Baron of Stafford, Staffordshire, by Margaret, daughter of Ralph Basset, Lord Basset of Drayton, Staffordshire (descendant of Charlemagne).

V. Katharine de Stafford, m., as his first wife, John de Sutton, Baron of Dudley, Worcestershire, son and heir of John de Sutton, Baron of Dudley (descendant of Charlemagne) by Isabel, daughter of John de Charleton, Lord of Powis. John de Sutton was born in or before November 1338, as he was of age in 1359. Katherine de Stafford died, probably aged about fourteen years, before 25 December 1361,

---

[1822] This line is discussed in David Faris, *Plantagenet Ancestry of Seventeenth-Century Colonists* (Boston, 1999), pp. 274-275.

probably in the childbirth of her only child on 6 December. John de Sutton served in the army in France and died aged about thirty-one, probably in France, in 1369 or early 1370.[1823]

VI. John de Sutton, Baron of Dudley, m. Joan [----].

John de Sutton was son and heir by his father's first marriage and was born at Coleshill in Arden, Warwickshire, on 6 December 1361, his mother probably dying at his birth. His birth occurred at Coleshill probably because "it was the home of his father's nearest cousin, Joan (later his father's second wife), while Dudley Castle was occupied by his father's widowed mother and (since November 1359) her second husband, Richard le Fisher, with whom John de Sutton was in frequent litigation. After the death of his father about 1369 his wardship and marriage were granted to Richard FitzAlan, Earl of Arundel. During this period he was married to Joan, whose maiden name is unknown. He served in the King's Fleet under the Earl of Arundel after he came of age and died on 10 March 1395/6. His widow died in April 1408.

VII. John Sutton, Baron of Dudley (-- 28 August 1406), m. Constance Blount, childless widow of Hugh Hastings, of Elsing, Norfolk, 7th Lord Hastings (died 2 November 1396 without issue), and daughter of Walter Blount, Knight, of Barton Blount, co. Derby, by Sancha de Ayala, daughter of Diego Gomez de Toledo, *alcalde maior* de Toledo.

VIII. John Sutton, Knight (25 December 1400 --), m. aft. 14 March 1420/1, Elizabeth Berkeley, childless widow of Edward Cherleton, 5th Lord Cherleton (died 14 March 1420/1), and daughter of John Berkeley, Knight, of Beverstone, Gloucestershire (descendant of Charlemagne) by Elizabeth, daughter of John Betteshoren, Knight, of Bisterne, Hampshire.

IX. Edmund Sutton, Knight, m. (1) Joyce Tibetot, third and youngest daughter of John Tiptoft, Lord Tiptoft, by his second wife, Joyce (descendant of King Edward I), younger daughter and co-heiress of Edward Cherleton, Lord Cherleton (see Charleton 10). She was sister of John, Earl of Worcester

X. John Sutton, Knight, of Dudley, of Aston le Walls, Northampton, m. [-----] Charroll. "Descent of Sutton and Butler (of Aston-le-Walls) and Washington," by F. W. Ragg and filed at the Society of Genealogists Library, London, states that he was "Sir John Sutton, of Dudley, owner of Aston-le-Walls, by gift of his brother, living 1541."

XI. Margaret Sutton, m. John Butler, Gentleman, of Aston Le Walls, Northampton, second son of Ralph Butler of Sawbridgeworth, Hertford. "Descent of Sutton and Butler" indicates that he was buried at Aston-le-Walls 14 October 1558 and that Margaret was buried at Aston 17 April 1563.

XII. William Butler, of Tyes Hall, Cuckfield, Sussex, third son, m. Margaret Greeke, daughter of Thomas Greeke, Gentleman, of Palsters, Lancashire, by Jane, daughter of George Thomson.

XIII. Margaret Butler, m. 3 August 1588, Lawrence Washington, Gentleman.

XIV. Richard Washington (c. 1605, Sulgrave -- bur. 8 Jan., 1641/2, St. Martin in the Fields, London), fourth son, apprenticed to Clothworker's Company, London, 7 July 1614, m. 17 April 1627, St. Martin's in the Fields, London, Frances Browne. He seems to have gone to Virginia about 1637-38 but to have returned to England, where he died and is buried at St. Martin's in the Field, Middlesex.

[1823] Faris, *Plantagenet Ancestry*, p. 90.

XV. John Washington (bapt. 14 March 1631/2, St. Martin's in the Fields -- by 31 January 1662/3, Surry Co., VA.

H. Clare - Audley - Stafford - Cherleton – Tiptoft.[1824]

I. Edward I, King of England, m. Alianore de Castille.

II. Joan of Acre (abt. 1272, Acre, the Holy Land -- 23 April 1307, bur. Austin Friars', Clare, Suffolk), m. (1) 30 April 1290, Westminster Abbey, Gilbert de Clare (2 September 1243, Christ Church, Hampshire -- 7 Dec., 1295, Monmouth Castle, bur. Tewkesbury), the Red, Knight, Baron of Clare, Suffolk, 9th Earl of Clare, 3rd Earl of Gloucester, 6th Earl of Hertford, m. (2), secretly, and to her father's great displeasure, about 1297, Ralph de Monthermer (-- 10 May 1325), a member of the late Earl's household.

Gilbert de Clare was son and heir of Richard de Clare (descendant of both Magna Charta Sureties and the Emperor Charlemagne) and Maude de Lacy, daughter of John de Lacy, Earl of Lincoln, Magna Charta Surety and descendant of Charlemagne.[1825] Gilbert de Clare had first married in the spring of 1253 to Alice de Lusignan, daughter of Hughes XI de Lusignan le Brun, Combe de la Marche et de Angouleme, and uterine brother of King Henry III. Gilbert and Alice had two daughters and were divorced. Following the death of King Henry III on 16 November 1272, the earl took the lead in swearing loyalty to Edward I, then in Sicily returning from the Crusade. Gilbert de Clare was Joint Guardian of England during the King's absence. Proposals for his marriage to the King's daughter were made as early as May 1283.[1826]

III. Margaret de Clare (prob. Oct., 1292, Caerphilly Castle -- 9 April 1342), m. (1) Nov., 1307, Peter de Gaveston (abt. 1284, Gascony -- beheaded, 19 June 1312), Earl of Cornwall, probable son of Sir Ernaud de Gaveston by Clarmunda de Marsau et de Louvigny, m. (2) 28 April 1317, Windsor, Hugh de Audley (abt. 1289 -- 10 Nov., 1347, bur. Tonbridge Priory), 8th Earl of Gloucester, second son of Hugh Audley, of Stratton Audley, Oxfordshire, a descendant of Charlemagne, by Isolt, daughter of Edmund de Mortimer, Knight, Baron of Wigmore, Hertfordshire, and also descendant of Charlemagne. Audley was summoned to Parliament on 30 November 1317 by writ directed Hugoni Daudele juniori whereby he may be held to have become Lord Audley. In right of his wife he was created Earl of Gloucester on 1 March 1336/7.[1827]

IV. Margaret de Audley (c. 1325 -- 16 Sept., 1348, bur. Tonbridge, Kent), Baroness Audley, m. bef. 6 July 1336, Ralph de Stafford (24 Sept., 1301 -- 31 Aug., 1372, bur. Tonbridge, Kent), Baron of Stafford, Staffordshire, 2nd Lord Stafford, son and heir of Edmund Stafford, Baron of Stafford, and Margaret, daughter of Ralph Basset, Lord Basset of Drayton, Staffordshire, himself a descendant of Charlemagne.

Ralph de Stafford had been previously married about 1326/7 to Katherine de Hastang, daughter of John de Hastang, Knight, of Chebsey, Staffordshire, by his wife Eve. They had one daughter. Ralph's first wife, Katherine, died prior to 6 July 1336 on which date a commission was appointed to enquire into a complaint by Hugh de Audley, Lord Audley, soon to be created Earl of Gloucester, that Ralph de Stafford and others broke his close at Thaxted, Essex, carried away his goods, abducted Margaret his daughter and heiress, and married her against her will. Margaret was then aged about twelve. King Edward III intervened to protect Ralph, and, after making his peace, Ralph and Margaret were given the reversion to a large part of the Gloucester inheritance. They had two sons and five daughters.

[1824] Faris, *Plantagenet Ancestry*, p. 60.
[1825] Faris, *Plantagenet Ancestry*, p. 60.
[1826] Faris, *Plantagenet Ancestry*, p. 61.
[1827] Faris, *Plantagenet Ancestry*, p. 5.

Ralph was summoned to Parliament from 29 November 1336 as Radulpho Baroni de Stafford, and was a Founder Knight of the Order of the Garter on 23 April 1349. He was created Earl of Stafford on 5 March 1350/1. Ralph de Stafford, Earl of Stafford, was buried at Tonbridge, with his second wife, at the feet of Margaret's parents."[1828]

Children of Ralph de Stafford, by Margaret de Audley, included Elizabeth de Stafford, wife of John de Ferrers; Beatrice de Stafford, wife of Thomas de Ros; Joan de Stafford, wife of John de Cherleton; Hugh de Stafford, Knight, husband of Philippe de Beauchamp; Katherine de Stafford, wife of John de Sutton.

V. Joan de Stafford, m. John Cherleton, 3rd Lord Cherleton, feudal Lord of Powis, Montgomeryshire, son and heir of John Cherleton, 2nd Lord Cherleton, feudal Lord of Powis, by Maud, daughter of Roger de Mortimer, 1st Earl of March, Baron of Wigmore, Herefordshire (of Magna Charta Surety descent and descendant of Charlemagne).

VI. Edward Cherleton (c. 1371 --), 5th Lord Cherleton, feudal lord of Powis, K. G., m. (1) June 1399, Alianor de Holand, widow of Roger de Mortimer, Earl of March and Ulster, Lord Mortimer (died 1398), and fourth daughter of Thomas de Holand, Knight (descendant of Edward I), 2nd Earl of Kent, by Alice (descendant of King Henry III), daughter of Richard FitzAlan, Earl of Arundel. Edward Cherleton m. (2) Elizabeth Berkeley (-- bef. 8 Dec., 1478), daughter of John Berkeley, Knight, of Beverstone, Gloucestershire, by Elizabeth, daughter of John Betteshorne, Knight. They had no issue. She then m. (2) John Sutton, Lord Dudley.

VII. Joyce Cherleton (c. 1403 --), m. by license dated 28 February 1421/2, John Tiptoft, Knight, Member of Parliament for Huntingdonshire and Somerset, Speaker of the House of Commons, son and heir of Payne Tiptoft, Knight, of Burwell, Cambridgeshire (of Magna Charta Surety descent) by Agnes, daughter of John Wroth, Knight, of Enfield, Middlesex.

VIII. Joyce Tiptoft, m. Edmund Sutton, Knight.

I. Plantagenet - Kent - Holand - Tiptoft – Sutton.[1829]

I. Edward I, King of England, m. Marguerite de France.

II. Edmund of Kent (5 August 1301, Woodstock, England --), m. Margaret Wake, widow of John Comyn, of Badenoch, and daughter of John Wake, 1st Lord Wake, by Joan, daughter of William de Fiennes.

III. Joan of Kent (29 Sept., 1328 --), Countess of Kent, Baroness Wake, called "the Fair Maid of Kent", m. (1) c. 1339, Thomas de Holand, Knight, of Broughton, Buckinghamshire, Earl of Kent, younger son of Robert de Holand, Knight, 1st Lord Holand, of Upholland, Lancashire, by Maud, daughter of Alan la Zouche, Baron Zouche of Ashby (of Magna Charta Surety descent and descendant of Charlemagne).

IV. Thomas de Holand (abt. 1350 -- 25 April 1397, bur. Bourne Abbey, Lincolnshire), Knight, K. G., 2nd Earl of Kent, Lord Holand, Lord Wake, Lord Woodstock, m. shortly after 10 April 1364, Alice Fitz Alan (-- 17 March 1415/6), daughter of Richard FitzAlan, Knight, Earl of Arundel and Warenne, by Alianor, daughter of Henry, Earl of Lancaster (grandson of Henry III).

[1828] Faris, *Plantagenet Ancestry*, p. 6.
[1829] Faris, *Plantagenet Ancestry*, pp. 139-140.

V. Alianor de Holand, m. (2) Edward Cherleton.

J. Plantagenet - Lancaster - FitzAlan - Holand – Sutton.[1830]

I. Henry III of England, King of England (1 October 1207, Winchester Castle -- 16 November 1272, Bury St. Edmunds, Suffolk, bur. Westminster Abbey), m. Éléonore de Provence (1217, Aix-en-Provence -- 24 June 1291, Amesbury, Wiltshire), daughter of Raymond Berengar V, Comte de Provence (descendant of Charlemagne) by Beatrix, daughter of Thomas I, Comte de Savoie (descendant of Charlemagne).

II. Edmund of Lancaster (16 January 1244/5, London -- 5 June 1296, Bayonne, bur. Westminster Abbey), Earl of Lancaster, called "Crouchback", m. bet. 27 July and 29 October 1276, Paris, Blanche D'Artois (-- 2 May 1302, Paris), widow of Henri de France, Roi de Navarre (died 22 July 1276), and daughter of Robert, Comte d'Artois (descendant of Charlemagne) by Matilde, daughter of Heinrich II, Herzog von Brabant (descendant of Charlemagne).

III. Henry of Lancaster (c. 1281, Grosmont Castle -- 22 September 1345, bur. Newark Abbey, Leicester), m. (1) by 2 March 1296/7, Maude de Chaworth (1282 - bet. 19 February 1317 and 3 December 1322, bur. Mottisfont Priory), daughter of Patrick de Chaworth, Knight, of Kidwelly and Ogmore, Carmarthenshire (of baronial descent) by Isabel (of Magna Charta Surety descent), daughter of William de Beauchamp, 1st Earl of Warwick (descendant of Charlemagne).

IV. Alianor of Lancaster (-- 11 January 1371/2, Arundel), m. (1) bef. June 1337, John Beaumont (-- May 1342), Earl of Buchan, 2nd Lord Beaumont, m. (2) 5 February 1344/5, Ditton, in the presence of King Edward III, Richard Fitz Alan (abt. 1306 -- 24 Jan., 1375/6, bur. Lewes), 3rd Earl of Arundel and 4th Earl of Surrey, called "Copped Hat", son of Edmund FitzAlan, 8th Earl of Arundel, Baron of Oswetry, Baron of Clun, Shropshire (descendant of Charlemagne) by Alice, daughter of William de Warenne (descendant of Charlemagne).

V. Alice Fitz Alan, m. Thomas de Holand, Knight, Earl of Kent.

K. Barack Obama Kinship.[1831]

I. Nicholas Perkins (c. 1614, England -- by 31 July 1656, Charles City Co., VA), m. Mary [-----], who m. (2) abt. 31 July 1656, Charles City Co., VA, Dr. Richard Parker.

II. Nicholas Perkins (c. 1647, Charles City Co., VA -- c. 1712, Henrico Co., VA), m. Sarah Childers.

III. Constantine Perkins (c. 1682, Henrico Co., VA -- 18 December 1770, Goochland Co., VA), m. Anne [Pollard?] (c. 1684, VA -- aft. 1754, Goochland Co., VA).[1832]

IV. Stephen Perkins (c. 1717, Henrico Co., VA -- abt. July 1772, Goochland Co., VA), m. Mary Hughes.

[1830] Faris, *Plantagenet Ancestry*, pp. 6, 139-140.

[1831] Obama's ancestry has been researched by William Addams Reitwiesner. A summary of the Perkins connection may be found on-line (*http://www.wargs.com/political.obama.html*). Generations 1-6 and 7-12 have been verified by my own research, but I have relied on Reitwiesner for the link between David Jesse Bowles and Harriet Bowles Payne. Jones, *Douglas Register*, p. 160, documents the parentage of David Jesse Bowles, and sources for earlier generations have already been cited.

[1832] Constantine Perkins was a brother of Philemon Perkins, who married Obedience Cox, and uncle of John Perkins, who married Rachel Ferguson. Philemon Perkins was direct ancestor of Sallie Elizabeth Cates Hammack.

V. Hannah Perkins (c. 1756, Goochland Co., VA --), m. 3 March 1770, Goochland Co., VA, Jesse Bowles (c. 1750, Goochland Co., VA -- abt. 1820, Bourbon Co., KY).

VI. David Jesse Bowles (26 February 1776, Goochland Co., VA -- 23 November 1823, Bourbon Co., KY), m. 23 December 1797, Woodford Co., KY, Elizabeth Thomas Martin (28 February 1774, Goochland Co., VA -- aft. 1823, Marion Co., MO), daughter of Thomas Martin and Susannah Walker.

VII. Harriet Bowles (11 April 1806, Bourbon Co., KY -- 27 May 1857, Marion Co., MO), m. 2 January 1822, Bourbon Co., KY, Francis Thomas Payne (19 August 1794, Monongahela Co., VA -- 28 November 1867, near Hannibal, MO).

VIII. Benjamin F. Payne (30 April 1839, MO -- 15 April 1878, Knox Co., MO), m. Eliza Black (3 April 1837, Quincy, Adams Co., IL -- 1921, Kansas City, MO).

IX. Charles T. Payne (June 1861, MO -- aft. 1920, KA), m. 14 January 1889, Johnson, KA, Della Wolfley (May, 1863, OH -- 1900/1910, KA).

X. Rolla Charles Payne (23 August 1892, Olathe, KA -- October 1968, KA), m. 1922, KA, Leona McCurry (May 1897, KA -- aft. 1930, KA).

XI. Madelyn Lee Payne (26 October 1922, Peru, KA -- 2 November 2008, Honolulu, HI), m. 5 May 1940, KA, Stanley Armour Dunham (23 March 1918, KA -- 8 February 1992, Honolulu, HI).

XII. Stanley Ann Dunham (29 November 1942, Wichita, KA -- 7 November 1995, Honolulu, HI), m. 2 Feb., 1961, Maui, HI (div. 1964), Barack Hussein Obama, Ph.D. (1936, Alego, Kenya -- 1982, Alego, Kenya).

XIII. Barack Hussein Obama, II (4 August 1961, Honolulu, HI --), m. 18 October 1992, Chicago, IL, Michelle LaVaughn Robinson (17 January 1964, Chicago, IL --).

L. Perkins - Foster - Cates - Hammack Lineage.

NOTE: Philemon Perkins, Generation III, below, was brother of Constantine Perkins, Generation III, above.

III. Philemon Perkins (1680/1690, Henrico Co., VA -- c. 1769, Goochland Co., VA), m. Obedience Cox (1700/1710, Henrico Co., VA -- 1771, Goochland Co., VA), daughter of Richard Cox (c. 1683 - c. 1735) and Mary Trent (c. 1684 - c. 1736). Obedience Cox Perkins was great-granddaughter of William Coxe (c. 1598 - c. 1656), Ancient Planter, who arrived on 10 June 1610, aged 12 years, aboard the Godspeed, with the party of Thomas West, 3rd Lord De La Warr. Obedience Cox Perkins was also a great-granddaughter of Henry Sherman (c. 1630 - 1695) and Mrs. Cicely [Farrar?] Hutchins (c. 1625 - 1704). Mrs. Cicely Sherman is believed to have been the eldest daughter of William Farrar and Mrs. Cicely [----] Baley Jordan Farrar. William Farrar, a native of Croxton, Lincolnshire, England, was a cousin of Nicholas Ferrar (1544-1620), a merchant and leading member of the Virginia Company of London. William Farrar left London 16 March 1617/18 aboard the Neptune with Lord De La Warr; the party arrived in Virginia in August 1618. William Farrar was appointed to the Virginia Council on 14 March, 1625/6, and served for the rest of his life. According to the 1623/4 Census of Virginia, William Farrar and his wife Cicely were living at Jordan's Journey, named for Cicley's deceased second husband, Samuel Jordan. Cicely indicated that she had arrived in Virginia in 1610, aged ten years, aboard the Swan. William Coxe, William Farrar, and Cicely [-----] Baley Jordan Farrar are called Ancient Planters because they arrived in Virginia -- first colonized at Jamestown in 1607 -- prior to 1624, when the charter issued to the Virginia Company of London was revoked and Virginia became a royal colony. William Coxe and Cicely [-----] Baley Jordan Farrar arrived in Virginia just following the end of the "Starving Time," the disastrous winter of 1609-1610. Between October 1609 and March 1160, the population of the struggling colony fell from five hundred to only about sixty people; at least some of the colonists were reduced to cannibalism. This period of suffering was so great that when spring arrived, the band of surviving colonists decided to abandon the settlement and return to England. "Only the timely arrival of the governor, Thomas, Lord Delaware, and new colonists" -- among them William Coxe -- "saved the colony from collapse."[1833]

IV. John Perkins (c. 1735, Goochland Co., VA -- 1787/1791, Caswell Co., NC), m. 6 Sept., 1757, Goochland Co., VA, Rachel Ferguson (c. 1737/1740, Goochland Co., VA -- c. 1787, Caswell Co., NC), who is believed to have been his second cousin and a granddaughter of James Ferguson (1680/1700, Henrico Co., VA - c. 1741, Goochland Co., VA) and Martha Cox (c. 1702, Henrico Co., VA -- aft. 1726, Henrico Co., VA).

V. Nancy ("Ann") Perkins (c. 1765, Goochland Co., VA -- aft. 1811, Caswell Co., NC), m. 22 Dec., 1783, Caswell Co., NC, John Foster (c. 1762, VA or NC -- c. 1810, Caswell Co., NC), probably son of Thomas Foster (living, Caswell Co., NC, 1780).

VI. Elizabeth Foster (c. 1783/85, Caswell Co., NC -- 1811/1817, Person Co., NC), m. c. 1804, Caswell Co., NC, John H. Cates (c. 1780, Caswell Co., NC -- c. 1832, Hinds Co., MS), son of Joshua Cates (c. 1740/1750, VA or NC -- c. 1834, Person Co., NC) and Jane Holleman (c. 1750, NC -- aft. 1830, Person Co., NC). John H. Cates m. (2) Mrs. Judith (Nichols) Brown (c. 1794, Caswell Co., NC - aft. 1870, Hinds Co., MS), daughter of Wright Nichols (c. 1770, NC -- 1832/1834, Hinds Co., MS) and Sarah Burch (c. 1770, NC - c. 1833, Hinds Co., MS). Mrs. Judith (Nichols) Brown was the widow of Alfred Brown (c. 1787, Caswell Co., NC - c. 1816, Person Co., NC), son of John Brown (c. 1765, Mecklenburg Co., VA - c. 1837, Person Co., NC) and Sarah Jones (c. 1766, Southampton Co., VA - c. 1846, Person Co., NC), whom she married on or about 16 February 1812, Person Co., NC.

VII. John Foster Cates (22 Dec., 1809, Person Co., NC -- 24 Sept., 1869, Hinds Co., MS), m. bef. 1833, Person Co., NC, Elizabeth Rimmer (4 Nov., 1805, Person Co., NC - 5 March 1885, Brownsville, Hinds Co., MS), daughter of John Rimmer (c. 1778, Caswell Co., NC - aft. 1830, Sullivan Co., TN) and Mary ("Polly") Whitfield (30 May 1782, Goochland Co., VA - aft. 1850, LaClede Co., MO), who married 21 June 1800, Orange Co., NC.

VIII. Anderson Bradley Cates (31 July 1834, Hinds Co., MS -- 26 April 1884, Hinds Co., MS), m. 19 Sept., 1860, Raymond, Hinds Co., MS, Abi Doxey Brown (10 Nov., 1841, Hinds Co., MS - 1 Jan., 1940, Hinds Co., MS), daughter of Col. Drury J. Brown (c. 1813, Person Co., NC - 1866, Copiah Co., MS) and Sarah Wells (c. 1818, Person Co., NC - 1853, Hinds Co., MS), who married 31 Dec., 1834, Hinds Co., MS. Abi Doxey Brown Cates was granddaughter of Judith (Nichols) Brown Cates, wife of (1) Alfred Brown and (2) John H. Cates.

IX. Sallie Elizabeth Cates (14 January 1863, Hinds Co., MS -- 30 April 1951, Hinds Co., MS), m. 20 December 1883, Hinds Co., MS, William S. Hammack (14 April 1852, Macon Co., GA -- 25 December 1899, Hinds Co., MS).

[1833] Billings, *The Old Dominion in the Seventeenth-Century* (Chapel Hill and Williamsburg, 1975), p. 6. See also Dorman, *Adventurers*, pp. 137-138, 212-213, 275, 558.

X. George Cleveland Hammack (26 Oct., 1884, Hinds Co., MS -- 17 Nov., 1963, Hinds Co., MS), m. 19 February 1911, Hinds Co., MS, Mary Almedia Bankston (3 April 1894, Hinds Co., MS -- 9 December 1974, Hinds Co., MS).

M. Abraham Lincoln Connection.

I. William Hanks (1 Feb., 1655, -- by 7 Feb., 1704, Richmond Co., VA), m. Sarah Woodbridge (c. 1653 --).[1834] Sarah remarried to Richard White.

II. William Hanks (7 Feb., 1679, Richmond Co., VA - prob. 1 May, 1732, Richmond Co., VA), m. Hester Mills (c. 1690, Richmond Co., VA --).

III. Richard Hanks (14 Aug., 1723, Richmond Co., VA -- 1788/89, Rowan Co., NC), m. Mary Hinds (c. 1725 --). Richard Hanks sired a large family, including Thomas Hanks (m. 6 August 1791, Lunenburg Co., VA, Nancy Hammack, and Katy Hanks, m. John Hammack). Thomas Hanks, age 80, and John Hammack (c. 1767, Lunenburg Co., VA -- 1 April 1856, Lunenburg Co., VA), age 83, were still neighbors at the time of the 1850 Lunenburg Co., VA, census. John Hammack would have been Lincoln's great-great-uncle.[1835]

IV. Abraham Hanks (c. 1744, Richmond Co., VA -- 1793, Piper's Gap, Carroll Co., VA), m. c. 1764, Fauquier Co., VA, Sally Harper (-- 1792, Piper's Gap, Carroll Co., VA), daughter of George Harper and Elizabeth Shipley.[1836]

V. Nancy Hanks (5 February 1784, Carroll Co., VA -- 5 October 1818, Spencer Co., IN), m. 12 June 1806, Washington Co., KY, Thomas Lincoln (6 January 1778, Rockingham Co., VA -- 17 January 1851, Coles Co., IL), son of Abraham Lincoln and Bathsheba Herring.

VI. Abraham Lincoln (12 February 1809 - 15 April 1865), m. Mary Todd.

N. Thomas Jefferson Connection.[1837]

I. Lionel Branch (18 Aug., 1566, Abingdon, Berkshire, England -- c. 1605, St. Martin, Ludgate, London), m. Valentia Sparkes.

II. Christopher Branch (c. 1602/3, Henrico Co., VA – 1681/82, Henrico Co., VA), m. 1619, St. Peter's Westcheap, London, Mary Addie of Darton, Yorkshire.

[1834] The chronology of the Hanks family is taken from the LDS Ancestral File, August, 1993, version. It may contain inaccuracies. Generations II and III are as found in the North Farnham Parish Register.

[1835] John Hammack was a son of William Hammack (27 September 1742, North Farnham Parish, Richmond Co., VA - bef. 10 November 1785, Lunenburg Co., VA), grandson of John Hammack (14 December 1718, Richmond Co., VA - abt. 1781, Lunenburg Co., VA) and Mildred Lambert, great-grandson of William Hammack the Younger (15 March 1688, North Farnham Parish, Richmond Co., VA - aft. 1739, Richmond Co., VA) and wife Eleanor and of Hugh Lambert and Anne Morgan, and great-great-grandson of William "O" Hammack, the immigrant, and wife Alice [-----] and of William Lambert, Anne Claughton Lambert, William Morgan, and Anne [Lewis?] Morgan. William Lambert (b. 1742) and Robert Hammack, Jr. (husband of Millenor Jackson) were first cousins, and John Hammack (m. Katy Hanks) and William T. Hammack (husband of Mary Felts) were second cousins.

[1836] Some researchers believe that Abraham Hanks was a son of Luke Hanks and a nephew of William Hanks who married Hester Mills. I have followed the lineage as presented in Adin Baber, *Nancy Hanks of "Undistinguished families, second families"* (Bloomington, IN, 1959); Adin Banks, *Nancy Hanks, The Destined Mother of a President* (Glendale, CA, 1963); William E. Barton, *The Lineage of Lincoln*, p. 230; and David A. Sturgill, *Who Was Nancy Hanks Lincoln* (Piney Creek, NC, 1995). Other possibilities are discussed in Gary Boyd Roberts, *Ancestors of American Presidents* (Santa Clarita, CA, 1995), pp. 33-36.

[1837] Adapted from G. B. Roberts, *Ancestors of American Presidents* (Santa Clarita, CA, 1995), pp. 7-10.

III. Christopher Branch, Jr., of Henrico Co., VA (c. 1627, Henrico Co., VA -- c. 1665, Charles City Co., VA). The name of Christopher's spouse is unknown.

IV. Mary Branch, m. (1) c. 1678/79, Thomas Jefferson (d. bef. 7 Dec., 1696, Henrico Co., VA), m. (2) Joseph Mattox.[1838]

V. Thomas Jefferson, Jr. (c. 1679, Henrico Co., VA -- c. 1730/31, Henrico Co., VA), m. 20 Nov., 1697, Mary Field (3 Feb., 1679/80, Henrico Co., VA -- c. 13 Aug., 1715, Henrico Co., VA), daughter of Peter Field (c. 1647 - 1707) and Judith Soane (c. 1646 - c. 1703), who was the widow of Peter Randolph, Jr.

VI. Peter Jefferson (29 Feb., 1707/8, Henrico Co., VA -- 17 Aug., 1757, Goochland Co., VA), m. 1739, Jane Randolph (20 Feb., 1720 - 31 March, 1776), daughter of Isham Randolph (1685-1742) and Jane Rogers (c. 1695/1700 - 1760/61).

VII. Thomas Jefferson (1743-1826), m. 1772, Mrs. Martha Wayles Skelton (1748-1782), widow of Bathurst Skelton.

Now on the National Register of Historic Places, the John Foster Cates home in Hinds County, Mississippi, was built prior to 1850 and has served as home to several generations of the Cates and Hammack families. It remains within the Hammack family today.

[1838] Mary's brother Christopher Branch, III (c. 1659 -- 1727/28, m. Anne Sherman, daughter of Henry Sherman and Cicely, and widow of John Crowley who died in 1687. Anne Sherman Crowley Branch's sister Elizabeth married Henry Trent and was the mother of Mary Trent Cox and the grandmother of Obedience Cox Perkins. Obedience Cox Perkins was the direct lineal ancestor of Sallie Elizabeth Cates Hammack. Christopher Branch, III, and Anne Sherman were thus great-aunt and great-uncle of Peter Jefferson (father of the President) and Obedience Cox Perkins.

Confederate Colonel Drury J. Brown (1813 – 1868), commander of Brown's Fencibles, Hinds County, Mississippi, descended from England's royal Plantagenet family and several signers of the Magna Carta through his ancestor Christopher Calthorpe of Virginia. Brown was born in Person County, North Carolina, and became a wealthy planter in Mississippi. He was a merchant, land speculator, and judge in Hinds and Copiah Counties, where he also served as Sheriff. Shown below are his daughter Abbie Doxey Brown (1841-1940) and her husband Anderson Bradley Cates (1834-1884). A soldier in Company K, 36th Regiment, Mississippi Volunteer Infantry, Cates was captured by Union forces on July 4, 1863, following the Siege of Vicksburg. He and Abbie, who married in 1860, lived in the John Foster Cates home (shown on the preceding page). Their daughter Sallie Elizabeth Cates (1863-1951) and her husband William Simms Hammack (1852-1899) later lived in the house, where their son George Cleveland Hammack (1884-1963) was born and died.

Descendants of John Hammot
(Hammack, Hammock, Hammick, Hammat)
Of Ermington Parish, Devonshire, England

Due to space constraints, this book attempts here to follow the American descendants of the immigrant William Hammack only to about 1850, except for the family of Simeon and Elizabeth Jane Moore Hammack, whose descendants are discussed in greater detail. The author has extensive materials on later generations of Hammacks and Hammocks extending into the twentieth-century and in many instances to the present day, however. This compilation should serve as a guide for identifying particular family groups and placing them within the overall context of Hammack and Hammock kinship and migration. Following this report is a section examining Hammacks and Hammocks whom it has proved difficult to place. Most of them are descendants of the immigrant William, but records discovered thus far do not conclusively identify to which branches of the family those individuals belong. In some cases, in the report below, the author has speculated about the identity of particular individuals; where information was too sketchy even to posit an identity, those individuals have been placed in the section detailing unidentified Hammacks and Hammocks.

Generation No. 1

1. ? JOHN[1] HAMMOT was born Abt. 1550 in Cornwall, and probably died Aft. 1600 in Devonshire. His wife's identity is unknown.
Children of ? JOHN HAMMOT are:
2.   i.   JOHN[2] HAMMOCKE, b. Abt. 1585, Ermington, Devonshire.
3.   ii.   RICHARD HAMMICKE, b. Abt. 1590, Ermington, Devonshire.
Key Sources: Ermington Parish Register. See Chapter 1 of the text for a discussion of the early Devonshire Hammacks. The existence of this John Hammot in Devonshire and his identity as father of John and Richard is conjectural; such a man did exist in eastern Cornwall, where he appears on the 1569 muster roll, and might have moved eastward into Devonshire after that date, where one "John Hammat" (later Hammick) married Joane Sparkwill in 1607. The surname is spelled variously in both locations as Hammot, Hammat, Hammick, Hammock, Hammack, Hameak, and many other variants.

Generation No. 2

2. JOHN[2] HAMMOCKE *(? JOHN[1] HAMMOT)* was born Abt. 1585 in Ermington, Devonshire. He married JOANE SPARKWILL. She was born Abt. 1587 in Ermington, Devonshire.
Children of JOHN HAMMOCKE and JOANE SPARKWILL are:
     i.   JOHANE[3] HAMMECKE, b. Abt. 05 Oct 1608, Ermington, Devonshire; m. WILLIAM BENNETT, 22 Feb 1625, Ermington, Devonshire.
4.   ii.   HENRYE HAMICKE, b. Abt. 20 Mar 1610, Ermington, Devonshire.
     iii.   THOMAS HAMICK, b. Abt. 1612, Ermington, Devonshire; d. 1636, Ermington, Devonshire.
5.   iv.   ? LEONARD HAMICK, b. Abt. 1614, Ermington, Devonshire.
6.   v.   JOHN HAMICK, b. Abt. 06 Feb 1619, Ermington, Devonshire.
7.   vi.   WILLIAM "O" HAMMACK, b. Abt. 11 Jul 1623, Ermington, Devonshire; d. Abt. 1701, Virginia.
Key Source: Ermington Parish Register.

3. RICHARD² HAMMICKE *(? JOHN¹ HAMMOT)* was born Abt. 1590 in Ermington, Devonshire. He married ALICE MORRISH 18 Nov 1611 in Ermington, Devonshire. She was born Abt. 1592 in Ermington, Devonshire.

Children of RICHARD HAMMICKE and ALICE MORRISH are:
	i.	RICHARD³ HAMMICK, b. Abt. 02 Dec 1614, Ermington, Devonshire.
8.	ii.	ARTHUR HAMECKE, b. Abt. 27 Jul 1616, Ermington, Devonshire.
	iii.	JOHN HAMMECK, b. Abt. 23 May 1619, Ermington, Devonshire.
	iv.	SARA HAMICK, b. Abt. 12 Aug 1621, Ermington, Devonshire.
	v.	JOAN HAMICK, b. Abt. 16 Apr 1624, Ermington, Devonshire.
	vi.	? ELIZABETH HAMICK, b. Abt. 1626, Ermington, Devonshire; m. JOHN QUICK, 02 Apr 1646, Ermington, Devonshire.

Key Source: Ermington Parish Register.

Generation No. 3

4. HENRYE³ HAMICKE *(JOHN² HAMMOCKE, ? JOHN¹ HAMMOT)* was born Abt. 20 Mar 1610 in Ermington, Devonshire. He married (1) PHILLIPA BLASE 17 May 1636 in Ermington, Devonshire. She was born Abt. 1610 in Devonshire, and died Bet. 1642 - 1645 in Ermington, Devonshire. He married (2) DORCAS PHILLIPS 27 May 1645 in Ermington, Devonshire. She was born Abt. 1625 in Ermington, Devonshire, and died Aft. 1645 in Ermington, Devonshire.

Children of HENRYE HAMICKE and PHILLIPA BLASE are:
	i.	JOAN⁴ HAMICK, b. Abt. 29 Mar 1637, Ermington, Devonshire; m. THOMAS ELWILL, 18 Nov 1657, Yealmpton, Devonshire.
	ii.	DORRYTYE HAMICK, b. Abt. 01 Jan 1639, Ermington, Devonshire; m. DANIEL BALL, 01 Oct 1675, Ermington, Devonshire.
9.	iii.	THOMAS HAMICK, b. Abt. 22 Apr 1642, Ermington, Devonshire.

Children of HENRYE HAMICKE and DORCAS PHILLIPS are:
	iv.	PENTICOST⁴ HAMMICK, b. Abt. 02 Apr 1646, Ermington, Devonshire.
10.	v.	JOHN HAMICK, b. Abt. 22 May 1648, Ermington, Devonshire.
	vi.	DORCAS HAMICK, b. Abt. 04 Feb 1650, Ermington, Devonshire; m. JOHN GUNNETT, 29 Nov 1672, Ermington, Devonshire.
11.	vii.	HENRIE HAMICKE, b. Abt. 09 Aug 1653, Ermington, Devonshire; d. Abt. 1693, Ermington, Devonshire.
12.	viii.	ARTHUR HAMICK, b. Abt. 08 Nov 1655, Ermington, Devonshire.
	ix.	SAMUEL HAMICK, b. Abt. 19 Mar 1657, Ermington, Devonshire.
13.	x.	MICHAEL HAMMICK, b. Abt. 02 Jan 1661, Ermington, Devonshire.

Key Source: Ermington Parish Register.

5. LEONARD³ HAMICK *(JOHN² HAMMOCKE, ? JOHN¹ HAMMOT)* was born Abt. 1614 in Ermington, Devonshire.

Children of LEONARD HAMICK are:
	i.	ALICE⁴ HAMICK, b. Abt. 02 Mar 1644, Ermington, Devonshire.
	ii.	REMOND HAMICK, b. Abt. 08 Feb 1645, Ermington, Devonshire.
	iii.	ANNE HAMICK, b. Abt. 28 Mar 1647, Ermington, Devonshire; m. JOHN FEASANT, Abt. 05 May 1668, Ermington, Devonshire.
	iv.	MARY HAMICKE, b. Abt. 16 Oct 1649, Ermington, Devonshire; m. SAMUEL WAKEHAM, 24 Oct 1676, Ermington, Devonshire.
	v.	SAMUEL HAMICKE, b. Abt. 23 Jul 1652, Ermington, Devonshire.

vi. ISETT HAMMICKE, b. Abt. 05 May 1655, Ermington, Devonshire.
Key Source: Ermington Parish Register.

6. JOHN[3] HAMICK *(JOHN[2] HAMMOCKE, ? JOHN[1] HAMMOT)* was born Abt. 06 Feb 1619 in Ermington, Devonshire. He married MARTHA CREESE 25 Nov 1645 in Ermington, Devonshire. She was born 28 Feb 1620 in Ermington, Devonshire.

Children of JOHN HAMICK and MARTHA CREESE are:

   i. JOHN[4] HAMICKE, b. 1646, Ermington, Devonshire; d. 1646, Ermington, Devonshire.
   ii. SARAH HAMICKE, b. Abt. 10 Dec 1647, Ermington, Devonshire; m. BARTHOLOMEW FOX, 20 Oct 1674, Ermington, Devonshire.
   iii. MARYE HAMICKE, b. Abt. 31 Dec 1650, Ermington, Devonshire.
14. iv. CHRISTOPHER HAMICK, b. Abt. 29 Apr 1653, Ermington, Devonshire.
   v. ELIZABETH HAMICKE, b. Abt. 31 Jul 1655, Ermington, Devonshire; m. JOHN ELLIS, 13 Apr 1681, Ermington, Devonshire.
15. vi. THOMAS HAMICK, b. 02 Oct 1657, Ermington, Devonshire.
16. vii. JOHN HAMICKE, b. Abt. 29 Jul 1662, Ermington, Devonshire.
Key Source: Ermington Parish Register.

7. WILLIAM "O"[3] HAMMACK *(JOHN[2] HAMMOCKE, ? JOHN[1] HAMMOT)* was born Abt. 11 Jul 1623 in Ermington, Devonshire, and died Abt. 1701 in Virginia. He married (1) GRACE ? Bef. 1668. He married (2) ALICE ? Bef. 1688. He married (3) MARGARET ? MASSEY Aft. 1690.
Children of WILLIAM HAMMACK and GRACE ? are:
17. i. WILLIAM "THE ELDER"[4] HAMMACK, b. Abt. 1670, Rappahannock Co., VA; d. 07 Jul 1730, N. Farnham Parish, Richmond Co., VA.
18. ii. RICHARD HAMMACK, b. 04 May 1674, North Farnham Parish, Richmond Co., VA; d. Abt. 1750, Albermarle, Louisa County, VA.
19. iii. JOHN HAMMACK, b. Aft. 1674, Rappahannock Co., VA; d. Bef. 15 Feb 1708, Richmond Co., VA.
Children of WILLIAM HAMMACK and ALICE ? are:
20. iv. WILLIAM "THE YOUNGER"[4] HAMMACK, b. 15 Mar 1688, North Farnham Parish, Richmond Co., VA; d. Aft. 1739, Richmond Co., VA.
   v. ELIZABETH HAMMACK, b. Abt. 1690, Richmond Co., VA; d. Aft. 1702, Richmond Co., VA.
Key Sources: Ermington Parish Register; North Farnham Parish Register, Richmond Co., VA; R. Headley, *Wills of Richmond Co., VA* (Baltimore, MD, 1983), p. 7.

8. ARTHUR[3] HAMECKE *(RICHARD[2] HAMMICKE, ? JOHN[1] HAMMOT)* was born Abt. 27 Jul 1616 in Ermington, Devonshire.
Children of ARTHUR HAMECKE are:
   i. RICHARD[4] HAMMECK, b. Abt. 23 Sep 1648, Ashburton, Devonshire.
   ii. EDWARD HAMECKE, b. Abt. 04 Oct 1654, Ashburton, Devonshire.
21. iii. ? WILLIAM HAMMECK, b. Abt. 1656, Ashburton, Devonshire.
Key Source: Ashburton Parish Register.

Generation No. 4

9. THOMAS[4] HAMICK *(HENRYE[3] HAMICKE, JOHN[2] HAMMOCKE, ? JOHN[1] HAMMOT)* was born Abt. 22 Apr 1642 in Ermington, Devonshire. He married AGNES RECKWOOD 15 May 1671 in Ermington, Devonshire.
Children of THOMAS HAMICK and AGNES RECKWOOD are:
- i. PHILLIPA[5] HAMMICK, b. Abt. 08 Mar 1672, Ermington, Devonshire; m. JOHN HUTCHINS, 07 May 1700, Ermington, Devonshire.
- ii. SARAH HAMMICK, b. Abt. 22 Jun 1675, Ermington, Devonshire.
- iii. THOMAS HAMMICK, b. Abt. 28 Jan 1679, Ermington, Devonshire.
- 22. iv. MICHAEL HAMMICK, b. Abt. 25 Dec 1684, Ermington, Devonshire.
- v. CHRISTOPHER HAMMICK, b. Abt. 25 Dec 1684, Ermington, Devonshire.
- vi. ELIZABETH HAMMICK, b. Abt. 25 Dec 1684, Ermington, Devonshire.
- vii. ANN HAMMICK, b. Abt. 18 May 1688, Ermington, Devonshire.
Key Source: Ermington Parish Register.

10. JOHN[4] HAMICK *(HENRYE[3] HAMICKE, JOHN[2] HAMMOCKE, ? JOHN[1] HAMMOT)* was born Abt. 22 May 1648 in Ermington, Devonshire. He married ELIZABETH SLEVELL 02 Feb 1669 in Ermington, Devonshire.
Children of JOHN HAMICK and ELIZABETH SLEVELL are:
- i. HENRY[5] HAMMICK, b. Abt. 05 Nov 1670, Ermington, Devonshire.
- 23. ii. JOHN HAMMICK, b. Abt. 13 Jun 1673, Ermington, Devonshire.
- 24. iii. STEPHEN HAMMICK, b. Abt. 10 Jun 1677, Ermington, Devonshire.
Key Source: Ermington Parish Register.

11. HENRIE[4] HAMICKE *(HENRYE[3], JOHN[2] HAMMOCKE, ? JOHN[1] HAMMOT)* was born Abt. 09 Aug 1653 in Ermington, Devonshire, and died Abt. 1693 in Ermington, Devonshire.
Child of HENRIE HAMICKE is:
- i. HENRY[5] HAMMICK, b. 24 May 1683, Totnes, Devonshire.
Key Source: Totnes Parish Register.

12. ARTHUR[4] HAMICK *(HENRYE[3] HAMICKE, JOHN[2] HAMMOCKE, ? JOHN[1] HAMMOT)* was born Abt. 08 Nov 1655 in Ermington, Devonshire.
Children of ARTHUR HAMICK are:
- i. AGNES[5] HAMOCKE, b. Abt. 28 Aug 1683, Totnes, Devonshire.
- 25. ii. ARTHUR HAMMACKE, b. Abt. 19 Aug 1685, Totnes, Devonshire.
- iii. WILLIAM HAMICKE, b. Abt. 20 Apr 1692, Totnes, Devonshire.
Key Source: Totnes Parish Register.

13. MICHAEL[4] HAMMICK *(HENRYE[3] HAMICKE, JOHN[2] HAMMOCKE, ? JOHN[1] HAMMOT)* was born Abt. 02 Jan 1661 in Ermington, Devonshire. He married SUSANNAH GODFREE 01 Jan 1683 in Ermington, Devonshire. She was born Abt. 1660 in Ermington, Devonshire.
Child of MICHAEL HAMMICK and SUSANNAH GODFREE is:
- 26. i. RICHARD[5] HAMICK, b. Abt. 05 Sep 1684, Ermington, Devonshire.
Key Source: Ermington Parish Register.

14. CHRISTOPHER[4] HAMICK *(JOHN[3], JOHN[2] HAMMOCKE, ? JOHN[1] HAMMOT)* was born Abt. 29 Apr 1653 in Ermington, Devonshire. He married (1) MARY LAMBERT Abt. 05 May 1679 in Ermington, Devonshire. He married (2) MARY REVELL 30 Jan 1680 in Ermington, Devonshire.
Children of CHRISTOPHER HAMICK and MARY REVELL are:
- i. MARTHA[5] HAMMICK, b. Abt. 30 Jan 1680, Ermington, Devonshire.

ii. HANNAH HAMICK, b. Abt. 30 May 1682, Ermington, Devonshire; d. 1751, Modbury, Devonshire; m. ABRAHAM LETHBRIDGE, 18 Mar 1704, Modbury, Devonshire; b. 26 Dec 1682, Modbury, Devonshire.

iii. JOHN HAMMICK, b. Abt. 10 Feb 1687, Ermington, Devonshire.

Key Sources: Ermington Parish Register; Modbury Parish Register.

15. THOMAS[4] HAMICK *(JOHN[3], JOHN[2] HAMMOCKE, ? JOHN[1] HAMMOT)* was born 02 Oct 1657 in Ermington, Devonshire. He married MARY [------] Abt. 1677 in Ermington, Devonshire.

Children of THOMAS HAMICK and MARY [------] are:

i. MARY[5] HAMMICK, b. Abt. 23 Mar 1679, Ermington, Devonshire.

ii. ROBERT HAMICK, b. Abt. 17 Jan 1681, Ermington, Devonshire.

iii. MATTHEW HAMICK, b. Abt. 08 Apr 1683, Ermington, Devonshire.

Key Source: Ermington Parish Register.

16. JOHN[4] HAMICKE *(JOHN[3] HAMICK, JOHN[2] HAMMOCKE, ? JOHN[1] HAMMOT)* was born Abt. 29 Jul 1662 in Ermington, Devonshire. He married (1) MARY STEVENS 1680 in Ermington, Devonshire. He married (2) ? THOMAZIN [------] Abt. 1697 in Ermington, Devonshire.

Child of JOHN HAMICKE and MARY STEVENS is:

i. RICHARD[5] HAMICK, b. 18 May 1683, Ermington, Devonshire; d. 1742, Ermington, Devonshire.

Children of JOHN HAMICKE and ? [------] are:

ii. HENERY[5] HAMICKE, b. Abt. 10 Nov 1699, Ermington, Devonshire.

iii. JOHN HAMICKE, b. Abt. 11 Mar 1701, Ermington, Devonshire.

iv. MARY HAMICKE, b. Abt. 11 Nov 1703, Ermington, Devonshire.

27.   v. CHARLES HAMICKE, b. Abt. 10 Apr 1706, Ermington, Devonshire.

vi. THOMAZIN HAMMACK, b. Abt. 09 Apr 1708, Ermington, Devonshire.

vii. GEORGE HAMMACK, b. Abt. 28 Jan 1709, Ermington, Devonshire.

Key Source: Ermington Parish Register.

17. WILLIAM "THE ELDER"[4] HAMMACK *(WILLIAM "O"[3], JOHN[2] HAMMOCKE, ? JOHN[1] HAMMOT)* was born Abt. 1670 in Rappahannock Co., VA, and died 07 Jul 1730 in N. Farnham Parish, Richmond Co., VA. He married CHRISTIAN MIDDLETON Bef. 29 Nov 1693 in UNKNOWN, daughter of ROBERT MIDDLETON and MARY ?. She was born Abt. 1675 in Westmoreland Co., VA, and died Aft. 1730 in Richmond Co., VA.

Children of WILLIAM HAMMACK and CHRISTIAN MIDDLETON are:

28.   i. WILLIAM[5] HAMMACK, b. Abt. 1690, Richmond Co., VA; d. Bef. 16 Oct 1724, Westmoreland Co., VA.

29.   ii. BENEDICT HAMMACK, b. Bet. 1696 - 1702, Richmond Co., VA; d. Aft. 30 Nov 1766, Amelia Co., VA.

30.   iii. ROBERT HAMMACK SR., b. Abt. 1704, Richmond Co., VA; d. Abt. 02 Oct 1786, Richmond County, VA.

31.   iv. MARY HAMMACK, b. Abt. 1705, Richmond Co., VA; d. Bet. 1748 - 1753, Richmond Co., VA.

32.   v. JANE HAMMACK, b. 23 Jan 1711, Richmond Co., VA; d. Abt. 1728, Richmond Co., VA.

33.   vi. ELIZABETH HAMMACK, b. 15 Sep 1714, Richmond Co., VA.

Key Sources: Key Sources: North Farnham Parish Register, Richmond Co., VA; Richmond Co., VA, Will Book 5, 1725-1753, pp. 155-160.

18. RICHARD[4] HAMMACK *(WILLIAM "O"[3], JOHN[2] HAMMOCKE, ? JOHN[1] HAMMOT)* was born 04 May 1674 in North Farnham Parish, Richmond Co., VA, and died Abt. 1750 in Albermarle, Louisa County, VA. He married MRS. ELIZABETH [------] BAKER Bet. 1695 - 1703 in Westmoreland. She was born Abt. 1675 in Virginia, and died Bet. 1708 - 1710 in Westmoreland.
Children of RICHARD HAMMACK and MRS. BAKER are:
34.   i.   WILLIAM[5] HAMMACK, b. Bet. 1698 - 1700, Westmoreland Co., VA; d. Aft. 1779, Albemarle Co., VA.
35.   ii. RICHARD HAMMACK, JR., b. Abt. 1700, Westmoreland Co., VA; d. Aft. 1771, Pittsylvania Co., VA.
Key Sources: Westmoreland Co., VA, Order Book 1698-1705, p. 260; Westmoreland Co., VA, Deed and Will Book 1723-1738, pp. 212-212a; Richmond Co., VA, Order Book 1732-1739, p. 585; Louisa Co., VA, Will Book A, p. 23.

19. JOHN[4] HAMMACK *(WILLIAM "O"[3], JOHN[2] HAMMOCKE, ? JOHN[1] HAMMOT)* was born Aft. 1674 in Rappahannock Co., VA, and died Bef. 15 Feb 1708 in Richmond Co., VA.
Child of JOHN HAMMACK is:
       i.   WILLIAM[5] HAMMACK, b. Abt. 1695, Richmond Co., VA; d. Aft. 1708, Richmond Co., VA.
Key Source: R. Headley, *Wills of Richmond Co., VA* (Baltimore, MD, 1983), pp. 7, 12.

20. WILLIAM "THE YOUNGER"[4] HAMMACK *(WILLIAM "O"[3], JOHN[2] HAMMOCKE, ? JOHN[1] HAMMOT)* was born 15 Mar 1688 in North Farnham Parish, Richmond Co., VA, and died Aft. 1739 in Richmond Co., VA. He married ELEANOR [------] Abt. 1714 in Richmond Co., VA. She was born Abt. 1694 in Virginia, and died Aft. 1739 in Richmond Co., VA.
Children of WILLIAM HAMMACK and ELEANOR [------] are:
       i.   ALICE[5] HAMMACK, b. 04 Mar 1715, Richmond Co., VA; d. Abt. 1715, Richmond Co., VA.
36.   ii. JOHN HAMMACK, b. 14 Dec 1718, Richmond Co., VA; d. Abt. 1784, Lunenburg Co., VA.
      iii. WILLIAM HAMMACK, b. 10 May 1720, Richmond Co., VA; d. Aft. 1720, Richmond Co., VA.
      iv. ALICE HAMMACK, b. 22 Mar 1724, Richmond Co., VA; d. 23 Feb 1725, Richmond Co., VA.
      v. ? DAVID HAMMACK, b. Abt. 1732, Richmond Co., VA; d. Aft. 1760, Richmond Co., VA.
      vi. ELIZABETH HAMMACK, b. 14 Apr 1734, Richmond Co., VA; d. Aft. 1734, Richmond Co., VA.
      vii. CATY HAMMACK, b. 08 Nov 1735, Richmond Co., VA; d. Aft. 1735, Richmond Co., VA.
     viii. ELEANOR HAMMACK, b. 07 Oct 1739, Richmond Co., VA; d. Aft. 1739, Richmond Co., VA.
Key Source: North Farnham Parish Register, Richmond Co., VA.

21. WILLIAM[4] HAMMECK *(ARTHUR[3] HAMECKE, RICHARD[2] HAMMICKE, ? JOHN[1] HAMMOT)* was born Abt. 1656 in Ashburton, Devonshire.
Child of WILLIAM HAMMECK is:
       i.   JANE[5] HAMMECK, b. Abt. 30 Sep 1677, Ashburton, Devonshire.
Key Source: Ashburton Parish Register.

Generation No. 5

22. MICHAEL⁵ HAMMICK *(THOMAS⁴ HAMICK, HENRYE³ HAMICKE, JOHN² HAMMOCKE, ? JOHN¹ HAMMOT)* was born Abt. 25 Dec 1684 in Ermington, Devonshire.
Children of MICHAEL HAMMICK are:
      i.   AGNIS⁶ HAMMICK, b. Abt. 24 Jun 1709, Yealmpton, Devonshire.
37.   ii. MICHAEL HAMMICK, b. Abt. 02 Apr 1713, Yealmpton, Devonshire.
Key Source: Yealmpton Parish Register.

23. JOHN⁵ HAMMICK *(JOHN⁴ HAMICK, HENRYE³ HAMICKE, JOHN² HAMMOCKE, ? JOHN¹ HAMMOT)* was born Abt. 13 Jun 1673 in Ermington, Devonshire.
Child of JOHN HAMMICK is:
      i.   JOHN⁶ HAMMOCK, b. Abt. 28 Apr 1692, Ashburton, Devonshire.
Key Source: Ashburton Parish Register.

24. STEPHEN⁵ HAMMICK *(JOHN⁴ HAMICK, HENRYE³ HAMICKE, JOHN² HAMMOCKE, ? JOHN¹ HAMMOT)* was born Abt. 10 Jun 1677 in Ermington, Devonshire. He married JANE Abt. 1710 in Ermington, Devonshire.
Children of STEPHEN HAMMICK and JANE are:
      i.   JOHANNAH⁶ HAMMICK, b. Abt. 12 Aug 1711, Ermington, Devonshire.
38.   ii. STEPHEN HAMMICK, b. Abt. 27 Apr 1714, Ermington, Devonshire.
     iii. WILLIAM HAMMICK, b. Abt. 19 Oct 1716, Ermington, Devonshire.
     iv. JANE HAMMICK, b. Abt. 07 Aug 1719, Ermington, Devonshire.
      v. JOAN HAMMICK, b. Abt. 30 May 1722, Ermington, Devonshire.
     vi. AMY HAMMICK, b. Abt. 09 Jan 1724, Ermington, Devonshire.
Key Source: Ermington Parish Register.

25. ARTHUR⁵ HAMMACKE *(ARTHUR⁴ HAMICK, HENRYE³ HAMICKE, JOHN² HAMMOCKE, ? JOHN¹ HAMMOT)* was born Abt. 19 Aug 1685 in Totnes, Devonshire.
Children of ARTHUR HAMMACKE are:
      i.   ARTHUR⁶ HAMMICK, b. Abt. 27 Sep 1723, Marldon, Devonshire.
     ii. NICHOLAS HAMMICK, b. Abt. 04 Mar 1726, Marldon, Devonshire.
    iii. JOHN HAMMICK, b. Abt. 26 Apr 1728, Marldon, Devonshire.
    iv. CHARITY HAMMICK, b. Abt. 26 Feb 1731, Marldon, Devonshire.
     v. WILLIAM HAMMICK, b. Abt. 11 Dec 1733, Marldon, Devonshire.
    vi. SAMUEL HAMMICK, b. Abt. 13 Apr 1736, Marldon, Devonshire.
39.   vii. HONIWELL HAMMICK, b. Abt. 15 Mar 1739, Marldon, Devonshire.
   viii. THOMAS HAMMICK, b. Abt. 30 Jan 1742, Marldon, Devonshire.
Key Source: Marldon Parish Register.

26. RICHARD⁵ HAMICK *(MICHAEL⁴ HAMMICK, HENRYE³ HAMICKE, JOHN² HAMMOCKE, ? JOHN¹ HAMMOT)* was born Abt. 05 Sep 1684 in Ermington, Devonshire. He married AGNES [------].
Children of RICHARD HAMICK and AGNES [------] are:
      i.   MARY⁶ HAMMICK, b. Abt. 03 Jan 1717, Ermington, Devonshire.
     ii. TOMASIN HAMMICK, b. Abt. 08 Mar 1722, Ermington, Devonshire.
    iii. JOHN HAMMICK, b. Abt. 07 Oct 1726, Ermington, Devonshire.
Key Source: Ermington Parish Register.

27. CHARLES⁵ HAMICKE *(JOHN⁴, JOHN³ HAMICK, JOHN² HAMMOCKE, ? JOHN¹ HAMMOT)* was born Abt. 10 Apr 1706 in Ermington, Devonshire. He married MARY [------] Abt. 1737 in Stoke Damerel, Devonshire.

Children of CHARLES HAMICKE and MARY [------] are:

40.   i.   JOHN[6] HAMILK, b. Abt. 20 May 1739, Stoke Damerel, Devonshire.
       ii.   MARY HAMICK, b. Abt. 25 Jan 1740, Stoke Damerel, Devonshire.
       iii. CHARLES HAMICK, b. Abt. 02 Nov 1743, Stoke Damerel, Devonshire.
       iv.   CATHERINE HAMMICK, b. Abt. 11 Jun 1749, Stoke Damerel, Devonshire.
Key Source: Stoke Damerel Parish Register.

28. WILLIAM[5] HAMMACK *(WILLIAM "THE ELDER"[4], WILLIAM "O"[3], JOHN[2] HAMMOCKE, ? JOHN[1] HAMMOT)* was born Abt. 1690 in Richmond Co., VA, and died Bef. 16 Oct 1724 in Westmoreland Co., VA. He married MARGARET [------]. She was born Abt. 1698 in Virginia, and died Aft. 1724 in Richmond Co., VA.
Children of WILLIAM HAMMACK and MARGARET [------] are:

       i.   MARY[6] HAMMACK, b. Abt. 1720, Westmoreland; m. FRANCIS ELMORE, 23 Feb 1738, North Farnham Parish, Richmond Co., VA.
41.   ii.   JOHN HAMMACK, b. Abt. 1722, Westmoreland Co., VA; d. Abt. 1776, Granville Co., NC.
       iii. WILLIAM HAMMACK, b. 14 Dec 1724, Richmond Co., VA.
Key Source: Richmond Co., VA, Will Book 5, 1725-1753, p. 155.

29. BENEDICT[5] HAMMACK *(WILLIAM "THE ELDER"[4], WILLIAM "O"[3], JOHN[2] HAMMOCKE, ? JOHN[1] HAMMOT)* was born Bet. 1696 - 1702 in Richmond Co., VA, and died Aft. 30 Nov 1766 in Amelia Co., VA. He married ELIZABETH [LEWIS?] Abt. 1720 in Richmond Co., GA. She was born Bet. 1700 - 1702 in Richmond Co., VA, and died Aft. 30 Nov 1766 in Amelia Co., VA.
Children of BENEDICT HAMMACK and ELIZABETH [LEWIS?] are:

42.   i.   CHRISTIAN[6] HAMMOCK, b. 28 May 1723, North Farnham Parish, Richmond Co., VA; d. Aft. 1775, Onslow Co., NC.
       ii.   LEWIS HAMMOCK, b. Bet. 1724 - 1728, Richmond Co., VA; d. Abt. 1744, Amelia Co., VA.
43.   iii. WILLIAM HAMMOCK, b. Bet. 1726 - 1730, Richmond Co., VA; d. Abt. 1808, Wilkes County, GA.
44.   iv.   BENEDICT HAMMOCK II, b. 28 Aug 1732, North Farnham Parish, Richmond Co., VA; d. Bef. 31 Jul 1787, Wilkes County, GA.
45.   v.   JOHN HAMMOCK, b. 17 Aug 1736, North Farnham Parish, Richmond Co., VA; d. Aft. 1776, Edgecombe Co., NC, or Georgia.
46.   vi.   ABIGAIL HAMMOCK, b. 29 Jun 1739, North Farnham Parish, Richmond Co., VA; d. Aft. 27 Nov 1775, Lunenburg Co., VA.
Key Sources: North Farnham Parish Register; Amelia Co., VA, Deed Book 5, p. 464; Amelia Co., VA, Deed Book 6, pp. 142, 204, 241, 246.

30. ROBERT HAMMACK[5] SR. *(WILLIAM "THE ELDER"[4] HAMMACK, WILLIAM "O"[3], JOHN[2] HAMMOCKE, ? JOHN[1] HAMMOT)* was born Abt. 1704 in Richmond Co., VA, and died Abt. 02 Oct 1786 in Richmond County, VA. He married ANNE LAMBERT Abt. 1725, daughter of HUGH LAMBERT and ANNE MORGAN. She was born Abt. 1710, and died Aft. 1787 in Farnham Parish, Richmond Co., VA.
Children of ROBERT SR. and ANNE LAMBERT are:

       i.   WILLIAM[6] HAMMACK, b. 10 Sep 1726, Richmond Co., VA; d. Abt. 1726, Richmond Co., VA.
       ii.   JOHN HAMMACK, b. 03 Aug 1730, Richmond Co., VA; d. Abt. 1730, Richmond Co., VA.
       iii. HUGH HAMMACK, b. 30 Oct 1732, Richmond Co., VA; d. Abt. 1783, Wilkes County, GA.

47.   iv.   NANCY HAMMACK, b. Abt. 1735, Richmond Co., VA; d. Aft. 02 Oct 1786, Richmond Co., VA.

48.   v.   ROBERT HAMMACK JR., b. 17 Oct 1737, Richmond Co., VA; d. Bef. 24 Feb 1800, Wilkes Co., GA.

49.   vi.   BENEDICT HAMMACK, b. 04 Apr 1740, Richmond Co., VA; d. Abt. 1815, Richmond Co., VA.

50.   vii.   CHRISTIAN HAMMACK, b. Abt. 1742, Richmond Co., VA; d. Bet. 1786 - 1790, Richmond Co., VA.

   viii.   LAMBERT HAMMACK, b. 06 Sep 1744, Richmond Co., VA; d. Abt. 1744, Richmond Co., VA.

   ix.   MARY HAMMACK, b. 10 Nov 1746, Richmond Co., VA; d. Aft. 1792, Richmond Co., VA; m. [DANIEL?] CRAWLEY, Abt. 1766, Richmond Co., VA; b. Abt. 1742, Richmond Co., VA; d. Abt. 1789, Richmond Co., VA.

51.   x.   LEWIS HAMMACK, b. 17 Jun 1749, Richmond Co., VA; d. Aft. 1820, Warren Co., TN.

52.   xi.   REYNE HAMMACK, b. Abt. 1760, Richmond Co., VA; d. Aft. 02 Oct 1786, Richmond Co., VA.

53.   xii.   MILLY HAMMACK, b. 11 Jan 1757, Richmond Co., VA; d. Aft. 14 Jun 1814, Lunenburg Co., VA.

Key Sources: North Farnham Parish Register, Richmond Co., VA; Richmond Co., VA, Will Book 8, 1787-1794, pp. 9-11.

31. MARY[5] HAMMACK *(WILLIAM "THE ELDER"[4], WILLIAM "O"[3], JOHN[2] HAMMOCKE, ? JOHN[1] HAMMOT)* was born Abt. 1705 in Richmond Co., VA, and died Bet. 1748 - 1753 in Richmond Co., VA. She married CHARLES JONES 22 Aug 1727 in North Farnham Parish, Richmond Co., VA, son of EDWARD JONES and MRS. LUNN. He was born Abt. 28 Aug 1697 in Richmond Co., VA, and died Bet. Dec 1768 - Mar 1769 in Richmond Co., VA.

Children of MARY HAMMACK and CHARLES JONES are:

   i.   SAMFORD[6] JONES, b. Abt. 27 Dec 1728, Richmond Co., VA; d. Abt. 1728, Richmond Co., VA.

54.   ii.   ALICIA JONES, b. Abt. 14 Jun 1731, Richmond Co., VA; d. Aft. 1794, Richmond Co., VA.

55.   iii.   MARY JONES, b. Abt. 1735, Richmond Co., VA; d. Aft. 1771, Richmond Co., VA.

   iv.   NANNY JONES, b. Abt. 29 Apr 1738, Richmond Co., VA; d. Abt. 1738, Richmond Co., VA.

   v.   SAMFORD JONES, b. Abt. 30 Dec 1740, Richmond Co., VA; d. Abt. 1800, Richmond Co., VA; m. (1) CHRISTIAN HAMMACK; m. (2) ELIZABETH STEPHENS.

   vi.   BETTY JONES, b. Abt. 26 Mar 1743, Richmond Co., VA; d. Abt. 1743, Richmond Co., VA.

   vii.   EDWARD JONES, b. Abt. 16 May 1748, Richmond Co., VA; d. Abt. 1748, Richmond Co., VA.

   viii.   ? ANNE JONES, b. Abt. 1750, Richmond Co., VA; d. Aft. 1771, Richmond Co., VA; m. WILLIAM WILDEN/WILDEY, Bet. 1769 - 1771, Richmond Co., VA.

Key Sources: North Farnham Parish Register, Richmond Co., VA; Richmond Co., VA, Account Book, pp. 589-90.

32. JANE[5] HAMMACK *(WILLIAM "THE ELDER"[4], WILLIAM "O"[3], JOHN[2] HAMMOCKE, ? JOHN[1] HAMMOT)* was born 23 Jan 1711 in Richmond Co., VA, and died Abt. 1728 in Richmond Co., VA. She married JOHN SEAMONS 02 Sep 1727 in North Farnham Parish, Richmond Co., VA. He was born Bef. 1706 in Richmond Co., VA, and died Aft. 1728 in Richmond Co., VA.

Child of JANE HAMMACK and JOHN SEAMONS is:

      i.   WILLIAM[6] SEAMONS, b. 14 Sep 1728, Richmond Co., VA.
Key Source: North Farnham Parish Register, Richmond Co., VA.

33. ELIZABETH[5] HAMMACK *(WILLIAM "THE ELDER"*[4]*, WILLIAM "O"*[3]*, JOHN*[2] *HAMMOCKE, ? JOHN*[1] *HAMMOT)* was born 15 Sep 1714 in Richmond Co., VA. She married JOHN MORGAN 21 Aug 1729 in North Farnham Parish, Richmond Co., VA.
Children of ELIZABETH HAMMACK and JOHN MORGAN are:
      i.   WILLIAM[6] MORGAN, b. 10 Dec 1730, Richmond Co., VA.
     ii.   JOHN MORGAN, b. 13 Nov 1732, Richmond Co., VA.
    iii.   NANNY MORGAN, b. 11 Sep 1735, Richmond Co., VA.
Key Source: North Farnham Parish Register, Richmond Co., VA.

34. WILLIAM[5] HAMMACK *(RICHARD*[4]*, WILLIAM "O"*[3]*, JOHN*[2] *HAMMOCKE, ? JOHN*[1] *HAMMOT)* was born Bet. 1698 - 1700 in Westmoreland Co., VA, and died Aft. 1779 in Albemarle Co., VA. He married (1) ANN ROCHESTER Abt. 1719 in Westmoreland Co., VA. She was born Abt. 1700 in Westmoreland Co., VA, and died Bef. 1736 in Westmoreland Co., VA. He married (2) JANE WILLIAMS Abt. 1736 in Richmond Co., VA, daughter of DAVID WILLIAMS and MARY. She was born 19 Aug 1709 in Richmond Co., VA, and died Aft. 1776 in Albemarle Co., VA.
Child of WILLIAM HAMMACK and JANE WILLIAMS is:
56.   i.   DANIEL[6] HAMMACK, b. Abt. 1737, Westmoreland Co., VA; d. Aft. 1786, Campbell Co., VA.
Key Source: Albemarle Co., VA, Deed Book 2, 1758-61, pp. 1-2; Albemarle Co., VA, Deed Book 3, pp. 244-45, 387-89. This relationship is circumstantial, not proven.

35. RICHARD[5] HAMMACK, JR. *(RICHARD*[4]*, WILLIAM "O"*[3]*, JOHN*[2] *HAMMOCKE, ? JOHN*[1] *HAMMOT)* was born Abt. 1700 in Westmoreland Co., VA, and died Aft. 1771 in Pittsylvania Co., VA. He married FRANCES Bef. 1722 in Richmond Co., VA.
Children of RICHARD HAMMACK and FRANCES are:
57.   i.   JOHN[6] HAMMACK, b. 20 Sep 1722, Richmond Co., VA; d. Abt. 1770, Albemarle Co., VA.
58.   ii.   RICHARD HAMMACK, b. Bet. 1723 - 1735, Westmoreland Co., VA; d. Bet. 1795 - 1796, Pittsylvania Co., VA.
Key Sources: North Farnham Parish Register, Richmond Co., VA. The placement of Richard Hammack as son of Richard, Jr., is circumstantial and unproven.

36. JOHN[5] HAMMACK *(WILLIAM "THE YOUNGER"*[4]*, WILLIAM "O"*[3]*, JOHN*[2] *HAMMOCKE, ? JOHN*[1] *HAMMOT)* was born 14 Dec 1718 in Richmond Co., VA, and died Abt. 1784 in Lunenburg Co., VA. He married MILDRED LAMBERT 26 Aug 1741 in Richmond Co., VA. She was born Abt. 1720 in Richmond Co., VA.
Children of JOHN HAMMACK and MILDRED LAMBERT are:
59.   i.   WILLIAM[6] HAMMACK, b. 27 Sep 1742, Richmond Co., VA; d. 1785, Lunenburg Co., VA.
     ii.   ANN HAMMACK, b. 13 Mar 1745, Richmond Co., VA; d. Aft. 1745, Richmond Co., VA.
    iii.   JOHN HAMMACK, b. Abt. 1748, Lunenburg Co., VA; d. Bet. 1776 - 1781, Lunenburg Co., VA.
60.   iv.   HUGH HAMMACK, b. Abt. 1753, Lunenburg Co., VA; d. 1804, Lunenburg Co., VA.
Key Sources: North Farnham Parish Register, Richmond Co., VA; 1764, 1769, 1772, 1774, 1775, and 1776 Lunenburg Co., VA, Tithable Lists.

Generation No. 6

37. MICHAEL⁶ HAMMICK *(MICHAEL⁵, THOMAS⁴ HAMICK, HENRYE³ HAMICKE, JOHN² HAMMOCKE, ? JOHN¹ HAMMOT)* was born Abt. 02 Apr 1713 in Yealmpton, Devonshire. He married ELIZABETH [------].
Children of MICHAEL HAMMICK and ELIZABETH [------] are:
      i.   AGNES⁷ HAMMICK, b. Abt. 08 Mar 1733, Yealmpton, Devonshire.
61.   ii. MICHAEL HAMICK, b. Abt. 26 Apr 1736, Yealmpton, Devonshire.
     iii. JOHN HAMICK, b. Abt. 07 Sep 1740, Yealmpton, Devonshire.
Key Source: Yealmpton Parish Register.

38. STEPHEN⁶ HAMMICK *(STEPHEN⁵, JOHN⁴ HAMICK, HENRYE³ HAMICKE, JOHN² HAMMOCKE, ? JOHN¹ HAMMOT)* was born Abt. 27 Apr 1714 in Ermington, Devonshire. He married PRUDENCE [------] Abt. 1742 in Ermington, Devonshire.
Child of STEPHEN HAMMICK and PRUDENCE [------] is:
      i.   STEPHEN⁷ HAMMICK, b. Abt. 31 Aug 1744, Ermington, Devonshire.
Key Source: Ermington Parish Register.

39. HONIWELL⁶ HAMMICK *(ARTHUR⁵ HAMMACKE, ARTHUR⁴ HAMICK, HENRYE³ HAMICKE, JOHN² HAMMOCKE, ? JOHN¹ HAMMOT)* was born Abt. 15 Mar 1739 in Marldon, Devonshire. He married ELIZABETH Abt. 1770 in Devonshire.
Child of HONIWELL HAMMICK and ELIZABETH is:
62.   i.   SAMUEL⁷ HAMMACK, b. Abt. 14 Feb 1772, Brixham, Devonshire.
Key Source: Brixham Parish Register.

40. JOHN⁶ HAMILK *(CHARLES⁵ HAMICKE, JOHN⁴, JOHN³ HAMICK, JOHN² HAMMOCKE, ? JOHN¹ HAMMOT)* was born Abt. 20 May 1739 in Stoke Damerel, Devonshire. He married GRACE [---] Abt. 1761 in Stoke Damerel, Devonshire.
Children of JOHN HAMILK and GRACE [---] are:
      i.   ELIZABETH⁷ HAMMICK, b. Abt. 11 May 1763, Stoke Damerel, Devonshire.
     ii. JOHN HAMMICK, b. Abt. 06 Oct 1764, Stoke Damerel, Devonshire.
    iii. JOHN HAMMICK, b. Abt. 07 Oct 1765, Plymouth, Devonshire.
    iv. ELIZABETH HAMMICK, b. Abt. 07 Dec 1767, Plymouth, Devonshire.
     v. WILLIAM HAMMICK, b. Abt. 27 Mar 1770, Plymouth, Devonshire.
    vi. JOHN HAMMICK, b. Abt. 11 Apr 1774, Plymouth, Devonshire.
Key Source: Stoke Damerel and Plymouth Parish Registers.

41. JOHN⁶ HAMMACK *(WILLIAM⁵, WILLIAM "THE ELDER"⁴, WILLIAM "O"³, JOHN² HAMMOCKE, ? JOHN¹ HAMMOT)* was born Abt. 1722 in Westmoreland Co., VA, and died Abt. 1776 in Granville Co., NC. He married (1) SUSANNAH [------] Abt. 1743 in Richmond Co., VA. She was born Abt. 1724 in Virginia, and died Bet. 1753 - 1755 in Richmond Co., VA. He married (2) MARY ANN [LEWIS?] Abt. 1755 in Richmond Co., VA, possible daughter of THOMAS LEWIS of Richmond Co., VA. She was born Abt. 1733 in Richmond Co., VA, and died Bet. 1802 - 1805 in Wilkes Co., GA.
Children of JOHN HAMMACK and SUSANNAH [------] are:
63.   i.   CHARLES⁷ HAMMACK, b. 29 Jan 1744, Richmond Co., VA; d. 1796, Warren Co., NC.
     ii. WILLIAM HAMMACK, b. 06 Jul 1747, Richmond Co., VA; d. Abt. 1747, Richmond Co., VA.
64.   iii. DAVID HAMMACK, b. Bet. 1748 - 1753, Richmond Co., VA; d. Aft. 1788, Warren Co., NC.
65.   iv. MARY HAMMACK, b. 13 Jun 1753, Richmond Co., VA; d. 14 Jan 1837, Wilkes Co., GA.

    v. CATY HAMMACK, b. Abt. 1755, Richmond Co., VA; d. Bet. 1849 - 1850, Crawford Co.,
        GA; m. WILLIAM SIMMONS, Bet. 1811 - 1812, Jones Co., GA; b. Abt. 1759, North
        Carolina; d. Abt. 1828, Jasper Co., GA.
Children of JOHN HAMMACK and MARY ANN [LEWIS?] are:
66.   vi. JOHN[7] HAMMACK, b. Abt. 19 Apr 1756, Richmond Co., VA; d. Abt. 1832, Lincoln Co.,
        GA.
      vii. ANN HAMMACK, b. Abt. 01 Apr 1758, Richmond Co., VA.
     viii. DAUGHTER HAMMACK, b. Abt. 1760, Richmond Co., VA.
       ix. ? ELLIDA HAMMACK, b. Abt. 1762, Richmond Co., VA; m. WILLIAM CUNNINGHAM,
        11 Mar 1782, Warren Co., NC.
        x. DAUGHTER HAMMACK, b. Abt. 1764, Richmond Co., VA.
67.   xi. THOMAS HAMMACK, b. Abt. 1766, Granville Co., NC; d. Bet. 1806 - 1814, Wilkes Co.,
        GA.
68.   xii. WILLOUGHBY HAMMACK, b. Abt. 1768, Granville Co., NC; d. Abt. 1824, Newton Co.,
        GA.
69. xiii. ELIZABETH HAMMACK, b. Abt. 1770, Granville Co., NC; d. Aft. 1830, Upson Co., GA.
70.   xiv. LEWIS HAMMACK, b. Abt. 1772, Granville Co., NC; d. Aft. 1830, Bibb Co., GA.
71.   xv. WILLIAM HAMMACK, b. Abt. 1774, Granville Co., NC; d. Aft. 1830, Ware Co., GA.
72.   xvi. JAMES HAMMACK, b. Abt. 1776, Granville Co., NC; d. Aft. 1835, Bibb Co., GA.
Key Sources: North Farnham Parish Register, Richmond Co., VA; 1787-1790 Pittsylvania Co., VA,
Personal Property Tax Lists; Z. H. Gwynn, *Abstracts of Wills and Estate Records of Granville Co., NC,
1746-1808* (Rocky Mount, NC, 1973), p. 148; 1785 Pittsylvania Co., VA, Tax List; 1797, 1799, 1800,
1801, 1802, 1804, and 1805 Wilkes Co., GA, Tax Digests. Evidence is strong to link Thomas Hammock
as a son of John and Mary Ann; Willoughby's identity is more speculative. See the concluding section for
a discussion of Robert Hammack, who was an associate of Willoughby in Clarke Co., GA.

42. CHRISTIAN[6] HAMMOCK *(BENEDICT[5] HAMMACK, WILLIAM "THE ELDER"[4], WILLIAM "O"[3],
JOHN[2] HAMMOCKE, ? JOHN[1] HAMMOT)* was born 28 May 1723 in North Farnham Parish, Richmond
Co., VA, and died Aft. 1775 in Onslow Co., NC. She married JOHN BENTLEY Bef. 09 Jan 1756 in
Amelia Co., VA, son of DANIEL BENTLEY and ANN [------]. He was born Abt. 1715 in Richmond Co.,
VA, and died Abt. 1797 in Lincoln Co., GA.
Children of CHRISTIAN HAMMOCK and JOHN BENTLEY are:
        i. JAMES[7] BENTLEY, b. Bef. 1753, Amelia Co., VA; d. Aft. 1786, Brunswick Co., VA.
73.   ii. WILLIAM BENTLEY, b. Bef. 1753, Amelia Co., VA; d. Bet. 1791 - 1792, Wilkes Co., GA.
74.   iii. ? BALAAM BENTLEY, b. Aft. 1765, Onslow Co., NC; d. Abt. 1816, Lincoln Co., GA.
       iv. ? CHLOE BENTLEY, b. Bef. 1755, Virginia; d. Aft. 1802, Wilkes Co., GA; m. JOHN
        HOLMES, Bef. 1775, North Carolina; b. Bef. 1755, Virginia; d. Abt. 1802, Wilkes Co., GA.
Key Sources: Onslow Co., NC, Deed Books F, p. 67; H, p. 8; I, p. 78-79; 1769 and 1770 Onslow Co.,
NC, Tax Lists; 1786-1796 Wilkes Co., GA, Tax Digests.

43. WILLIAM[6] HAMMOCK *(BENEDICT[5] HAMMACK, WILLIAM "THE ELDER"[4], WILLIAM "O"[3],
JOHN[2] HAMMOCKE, ? JOHN[1] HAMMOT)* was born Bet. 1726 - 1730 in Richmond Co., VA, and died
Abt. 1808 in Wilkes County, GA. He married BETTY ANN HAMES Bef. 1760 in Amelia Co., VA,
daughter of JOHN HAMES and RUTH ?. She was born Abt. 1735 in Virginia, and died Aft. 10 Mar 1806
in Wilkes Co., GA.
Children of WILLIAM HAMMOCK and BETTY HAMES are:
75.   i. WILLIAM[7] HAMMOCK, b. 15 Jun 1760, Amelia Co., VA; d. 03 Jan 1849, Union Co., KY.
       ii. BENEDICT HAMMOCK, b. Abt. 1762, Amelia Co., VA.
      iii. RUTH HAMMOCK, b. Abt. 1765, Amelia Co., VA; d. Aft. 1824, Wilkes Co., GA.

76. iv. CHARITY HAMMOCK, b. Abt. 1763, Amelia Co., VA; d. Aft. 31 Mar 1846, Vermillion Co., IN.

Key Sources: 1769 and 1770 Onslow Co., NC, Tax Lists; Wilkes Co., GA, Deed Book WW, p. 61; Revolutionary War Pension Applications of William Hammock, Union Co., KY, and Abraham Hamman, Vermillion Co., IN. The placement of Benedict Hammock and Ruth Hammock as children of William is speculative.

44. BENEDICT[6] HAMMOCK II *(BENEDICT[5] HAMMACK, WILLIAM "THE ELDER"[4], WILLIAM "O"[3], JOHN[2] HAMMOCKE, ? JOHN[1] HAMMOT)* was born 28 Aug 1732 in North Farnham Parish, Richmond Co., VA, and died Bef. 31 Jul 1787 in Wilkes County, GA. He married MARY [COMBS?] Abt. 1757 in Amelia Co., VA. She was born Abt. 1738 in Virginia, and died Abt. 1811 in Greene Co., GA.
Children of BENEDICT HAMMOCK and MARY [COMBS?] are:

77. i. PATSY[7] HAMMOCK, b. Abt. 1758, Amelia Co., VA; d. Aft. 1807, Lincoln Co., GA.
78. ii. JOHN C. HAMMOCK, b. Bet. 1760 - 1770, Onslow Co., NC; d. Bef. 07 Jan 1813, Greene Co., GA.
79. iii. ROBERT HAMMOCK, b. Bet. 1760 - 1770, Onslow Co., NC; d. Aft. 1823, Wilkes Co., GA.
     iv. WILLIAM HAMMOCK, b. Abt. 1771, Onslow Co., NC; d. Aft. 1775, Wilkes Co., GA.
80. v. BENJAMIN HAMMOCK, b. Abt. 1773, Wilkes Co., GA; d. Aft. 1850, Jasper Co., GA.
81. vi. BENEDICT HAMMOCK III, b. Bef. 1775, Onslow Co., NC; d. Bet. 1825 - 1826, Jones Co., GA.
82. vii. ELIZABETH COMBS HAMMOCK, b. Abt. 1778, Wilkes Co., GA; d. Aft. 1822, Wilkes Co., GA.

Key Sources: A. E. Wynne, *Southern Lineages: Records of Thirteen Families* (Aberdeen, MS, 1940), esp. pp. 84-89; 1769 and 1770 Onslow Co., NC, Tax Lists; G. G. Davidson, *Early Records of Georgia, Wilkes County* (2 vols., Macon, GA, 1932), 1: 27, 46, 236, 241, and 2: 235; Wilkes Co., GA, Deed Book NN, fos. 70-72; Greene Co., GA, Executions and Adminstrations, Book G.

45. JOHN[6] HAMMOCK *(BENEDICT[5] HAMMACK, WILLIAM "THE ELDER"[4], WILLIAM "O"[3], JOHN[2] HAMMOCKE, ? JOHN[1] HAMMOT)* was born 17 Aug 1736 in North Farnham Parish, Richmond Co., VA, and died Aft. 1776 in Edgecombe Co., NC, or Georgia. He married SARAH [------] Abt. 1756 in Amelia Co., VA. She was born Bet. 1736 - 1740 in Virginia, and died Aft. 1765 in Amelia Co., VA.
Children of JOHN HAMMOCK and SARAH [------] are:

83. i. ? JOHN[7] HAMMOCK, b. Abt. 1760, Amelia Co., VA; d. Aft. 1819, Monroe Co., AL.
84. ii. ? SAMUEL HAMMOCK, b. Bet. 1760 - 1764, Amelia Co., VA; d. Aft. 1825, Laurens Co., GA.
85. iii. ? JESSE HAMMOCK, b. Bef. 1775, Edgecombe Co., NC; d. Aft. 1820, Tennessee or Alabama.
     iv. ? WILLIAM HAMMOCK, b. Bef. 1774, Edgecombe Co., NC; d. Aft. 1795, Burke Co., GA.
86. v. ? EMANUEL HAMMOCK, b. Bet. 1780 - 1783, Edgecombe Co., NC; d. Bet. 1850 - 1860, Tattnall Co., GA.

Key Sources: Edgecombe Co., NC, Deed Books C, p. 376; 3, pp. 84, 86; 4, p. 349; 1799-1805 Jefferson Co., GA, Tax Digests; 1805 and 1807 Georgia Land Lottery Registrants and Fortunate Draws; A. Thomas, *Laurens Co., GA, Legal Records, 1807-1857* (2 vols., Roswell, GA, 1991), 1: 340-341; 1820 Bedford Co., TN, Census. Based on similarity in names and common associations in Granville Co., NC, and Jefferson, Laurens, and Washington Counties, Georgia, and Conecuh and Monroe Counties, Alabama, I have theorized that John Hammack was the common ancestor of these Hammack, Hammock, and Hammac families. This conclusion is speculative and not proven.

46. ABIGAIL[6] HAMMOCK *(BENEDICT[5] HAMMACK, WILLIAM "THE ELDER"[4], WILLIAM "O"[3], JOHN[2] HAMMOCKE, ? JOHN[1] HAMMOT)* was born 29 Jun 1739 in North Farnham Parish, Richmond Co., VA, and died Aft. 27 Nov 1775 in Lunenburg Co., VA. She married PHILLIP COMBS Bet. 1760 - 1762 in Amelia Co., VA. He was born Abt. 1739 in Virginia, and died Bet. 1822 - 1838 in Wilkes Co., GA.

Children of ABIGAIL HAMMOCK and PHILLIP COMBS are:

87.	i.	JOHN[7] COMBS, b. 07 Sep 1764, Amelia Co., VA; d. Bet. 1849 - 1850, Cobb Co., GA.
	ii.	NANCY COMBS, b. Bet. 1766 - 1770, Amelia Co., VA; d. Bet. 1820 - 1838, Wilkes Co., GA; m. ROBERT HAMMACK.
88.	iii.	STERLING COMBS, b. Bet. 1768 - 1769, Amelia Co., VA; d. 15 Jun 1847, Richmond Co., GA.
89.	iv.	JAMES COMBS, b. Abt. 1770, Lunenburg Co., VA; d. Bet. 1817 - 1818, Wilkes Co., GA.
90.	v.	PHILLIP COMBS, b. Abt. 1771, Lunenburg Co., VA; d. Aft. 1830, Wilkes Co., GA.
91.	vi.	MARTHA COMBS, b. Bef. 1775, Lunenburg Co., VA; d. Aft. 1838, Georgia.
92.	vii.	ENOCH COMBS, b. 03 Feb 1782, Wilkes Co., GA; d. Aft. 1822, Wilkes Co., GA.
	viii.	DAUGHTER COMBS, b. Bet. 1775 - 1783, Wilkes Co., GA; d. Aft. 1820, Wilkes Co., GA; m. JAMES WOODRUFF, Bef. 1802, Wilkes Co., GA; b. Bet. 1775 - 1783, Wilkes Co., GA; d. Aft. 1838, Wilkes Co., GA.
93.	ix.	THOMAS COMBS, b. Bet. 1787 - 1790, Wilkes Co., GA; d. Bef. 1832, Wilkes Co., GA.

Key Sources: North Farnham Parish Register, Richmond Co., VA; 1762 Amelia Co., VA, Tithable List; Lunenburg Co., VA, Deed Book 12, p. 479; 1791-1804 Wilkes Co., GA, Tax Digests; Wilkes Co., GA, Deed Book YY, p. 307; G. G. Davidson, *Early Records of Georgia, Wilkes County* (2 vols., Macon, GA, 1932), 1: 330, and 2: 210; 1820 Wilkes Co., GA, Census.

47. NANCY[6] HAMMACK *(ROBERT HAMMACK[5] SR., WILLIAM "THE ELDER"[4] HAMMACK, WILLIAM "O"[3], JOHN[2] HAMMOCKE, ? JOHN[1] HAMMOT)* was born Abt. 1735 in Richmond Co., VA, and died Aft. 02 Oct 1786 in Richmond Co., VA. She married THOMAS JESPER Abt. 1755 in Richmond Co., VA, son of THOMAS JESPER and ELIZABETH HAMMOND. He was born 14 Apr 1735 in Richmond Co., VA, and died Bet. 1786 - 1797 in Richmond Co., VA.

Children of NANCY HAMMACK and THOMAS JESPER are:

i.	ELIZABETH[7] JESPER, b. 03 Oct 1757, Richmond Co., VA; d. Aft. 1786, Richmond Co., VA.
ii.	ROBERT JESPER, b. 06 Feb 1760, Richmond Co., VA; d. Aft. 14 Dec 1799, Richmond Co., VA; m. BETTY B. HARFORD, Abt. 15 Jan 1781, Richmond Co., VA.
iii.	ANN JESPER, b. 27 Sep 1762, Richmond Co., VA; d. Aft. 1786, Richmond Co., VA.
iv.	WILLIAM JESPER, b. 14 Apr 1765, Richmond Co., VA; d. Aft. 1786, Richmond Co., VA.
v.	SARAH JESPER, b. 29 Jul 1767, Richmond Co., VA; d. Aft. 1786, Richmond Co., VA.
vi.	MILLY JESPER, b. 06 Apr 1769, Richmond Co., VA; d. Bef. 1786, Richmond Co., VA.
vii.	JOHN JESPER, b. 07 Mar 1771, Richmond Co., VA; d. Aft. 1786, Richmond Co., VA.
viii.	RANEY JESPER, b. Bet. 1771 - 1776, Richmond Co., VA; d. Aft. 1796, Richmond Co., VA.
ix.	MARY ANN JESPER, b. 24 Aug 1776, Richmond Co., VA; d. Aft. 1786, Richmond Co., VA.
x.	THOMAS JESPER, b. 14 Apr 1777, Richmond Co., VA; d. Bef. 1786, Richmond Co., VA.
xi.	ELANDER JESPER, b. Abt. 1780, Richmond Co., VA; d. Aft. 1800, Richmond Co., VA; m. MARK STEPHENS, Abt. 28 Jan 1800, Richmond Co., VA; b. Abt. 1780, Richmond Co., VA; d. Bef. 06 Aug 1810, Richmond Co., VA.
xii.	FANNY JESPER, b. 01 Apr 1782, Richmond Co., VA; d. Bef. 1786, Richmond Co., VA.

Key Sources: North Farnham Parish Register, Richmond Co., VA; Richmond Co., VA, Will Book, 1795-1822, pp. 86-87.

48. ROBERT HAMMACK[6] JR. *(ROBERT HAMMACK[5] SR., WILLIAM "THE ELDER"[4] HAMMACK, WILLIAM "O"[3], JOHN[2] HAMMOCKE, ? JOHN[1] HAMMOT)* was born 17 Oct 1737 in Richmond Co., VA, and died Bef. 24 Feb 1800 in Wilkes Co., GA. He married MILLENOR JACKSON Abt. 1758 in Amelia Co., VA, daughter of EDWARD JACKSON and LUCY PARRISH. She was born Abt. 1740 in Brunswick Co., VA, and died Aft. 1830 in Jones County, GA.

Children of ROBERT JR. and MILLENOR JACKSON are:

94.   i.   LEWIS[7] HAMMACK, b. Bet. 1765 - 1766, Amelia Co., VA; d. Abt. 1845, Jones County, GA.

95.   ii.   ROBERT HAMMACK, b. Bet. 1766 - 1767, Amelia Co., VA; d. 1862, Warren County, GA.

96.   iii.   JOSHUA HAMMACK, b. Bet. 1769 - 1770, Amelia Co., VA; d. Aft. 1864, Newton Co., GA.

97.   iv.   JOHN HAMMACK, b. Bet. 1771 - 1772, Amelia Co., VA; d. Bet. Aug - Sep 1843, Talbot Co., GA.

98.   v.   NANCY (ANNA) HAMMACK, b. Abt. 1773, Wilkes Co., GA; d. Aft. 1850, Taliaferro Co., GA.

       vi.   BETSY HAMMACK, b. Abt. 1775, Wilkes Co., GA; d. Abt. 1825, Wilkes Co., GA; m. JOSIAH MONCRIEF; b. Abt. 1740, Currituck Co., NC; d. Abt. 1824, Wilkes Co., GA.

99.   vii.   WILLIAM T. HAMMACK, b. Abt. 1775, Wilkes Co., GA; d. Apr 1828, Crawford County, GA.

       viii.   LUCY HAMMACK, b. Abt. 1778, Wilkes Co., GA; d. Bet. 1820 - 1827, Bibb Co., GA; m. JAMES HAMMACK.

100.   ix.   MARY "POLLY" HAMMACK, b. Bet. 1780 - 1784, Wilkes Co., GA; d. 1842, Jones Co., GA.

       x.   EDWARD HAMMACK, b. Abt. 1784, Wilkes Co., GA; d. Bet. 1841 - 1842, Jones Co., GA; m. CHARLOTTE FELTS GRIFFIN, Bet. 1820 - 1825, Jones Co., GA; b. Abt. 1790, North Carolina; d. Abt. 1856, Jones Co., GA.

       xi.   LURINA HAMMACK, b. Abt. 1786, Wilkes Co., GA; d. Aft. 1800, Wilkes Co., GA; m. JAMES BRYANT, 01 Jun 1806, Clarke Co., GA.

101.   xii.   CATHERINE HAMMACK, b. 1792, Wilkes Co., GA; d. Aft. 1860, Russell Co., AL.

Key Sources: Amelia Co., VA, Deed Book 11, p. 125; Revolutionary War Pension Application of John C. Jackson; Robert Hammack Estate File, Wilkes Co., GA, Loose Papers, Georgia Department of Archives and History, Morrow, GA.

49. BENEDICT[6] HAMMACK *(ROBERT HAMMACK[5] SR., WILLIAM "THE ELDER"[4] HAMMACK, WILLIAM "O"[3], JOHN[2] HAMMOCKE, ? JOHN[1] HAMMOT)* was born 04 Apr 1740 in Richmond Co., VA, and died Abt. 1815 in Richmond Co., VA. He married SARAH [------] Abt. 1765 in Richmond Co., VA. She was born Abt. 1745 in Richmond Co., VA, and died Abt. 1835 in Richmond Co., VA.

Children of BENEDICT HAMMACK and SARAH [------] are:

102.   i.   BENJAMIN[7] HAMMACK, b. Abt. 1766, Richmond Co., VA; d. Abt. 1801, Richmond Co., VA.

       ii.   SARAH HAMMACK, b. 06 Nov 1771, Richmond Co., VA; d. Abt. 1771, Richmond Co., VA.

       iii.   MOLLY HAMMACK, b. 22 Jan 1777, Richmond Co., VA; m. CHARLES HABRON, Abt. 20 Dec 1797, Richmond Co., VA; d. Aft. 1830, Richmond Co., VA.

103.   iv.   JOHN HAMMACK, b. Abt. 1776, Richmond Co., VA; d. Aft. 1830, Richmond Co., VA.

      v.   SARAH HAMMACK, b. Abt. 25 May 1783, Richmond Co., VA; d. Aft. 1820, Northumberland Co., VA; m. JOHN HUGHES, Abt. 28 Aug 1805, Richmond Co., VA; b. Abt. 1783, Richmond Co., VA; d. Aft. 1810, Northumberland Co., VA.

     vi.   WILLIAM HAMMACK, b. Abt. 1792, Richmond Co., VA; d. Bet. 1805 - 1815, Richmond Co., VA.

    vii.   ELIZABETH HAMMACK, b. Abt. 1787, Richmond Co., VA; d. Bef. 1815, Richmond Co., VA; m. GEORGE D. TUNE, Abt. 01 Feb 1808, Richmond Co., VA; d. Abt. 1823, Richmond Co., VA.

104. viii.   LEWIS HAMMACK, b. Bef. 1792, Richmond Co., VA; d. Abt. 1824, Richmond Co., VA.

     ix.   LUCY HAMMACK, b. Abt. 1794, Richmond Co., VA; d. Aft. 1815, Richmond Co., VA; m. THOMAS TUCKER, Abt. 13 Sep 1815, Richmond Co., VA.

     x.   ? FRANCES HAMMACK, m. SAMUEL WROE, Abt. 10 Dec 1823, Richmond Co., VA.

Key Sources: North Farnham Parish Register, Richmond Co., VA; 1789-1835 Richmond Co., VA, Personal Property Tax Lists; 1820 Richmond Co., VA, Census, p. 226A; 1830 Richmond Co., VA, Census, p. 89; Richmond Co., VA, Will Book 1794-1822, p. 463; Richmond Co., VA, Will Book 11, 1846-1879, p. 332; G. H. S. King, *Marriages of Richmond Co., VA, 1668-1853* (Fredericksburg, VA, 1964).

50. CHRISTIAN[6] HAMMACK *(ROBERT HAMMACK[5] SR., WILLIAM "THE ELDER"[4] HAMMACK, WILLIAM "O"[3], JOHN[2] HAMMOCKE, ? JOHN[1] HAMMOT)* was born Abt. 1742 in Richmond Co., VA, and died Bet. 1786 - 1790 in Richmond Co., VA. She married (2) SAMFORD JONES Abt. 1760 in Richmond Co., VA, son of CHARLES JONES and MARY HAMMACK. He was born 30 Dec 1740 in Richmond Co., VA, and died Abt. 1800 in Richmond Co., VA.

Child of CHRISTIAN HAMMACK is:

105.   i.   WILLIAM[7] HAMMACK, b. Abt. 09 Feb 1761, Richmond Co., VA; d. Abt. 1815, Richmond Co., VA.

Children of CHRISTIAN HAMMACK and SAMFORD JONES are:

     ii.   CHARLES[7] JONES, b. 03 Jun 1771, Richmond Co., VA; d. Bef. 1800, Richmond Co., VA.

    iii.   LAMBARD HAMMACK JONES, b. 17 Nov 1776, Richmond Co., VA; d. Bef. 1800, Richmond Co., VA.

    iv.   MELINDA JONES, b. Abt. 1778, Richmond Co., VA; d. Bef. 1814, Richmond Co., VA.

     v.   MOLLY JONES, b. Abt. 1780, Richmond Co., VA; d. Aft. 1814, Richmond Co., VA.

106.   vi.   SAMFORD JONES, b. Abt. 1778, Richmond Co., VA; d. Bet. 1814 - 1820, Richmond Co., VA.

Key Sources: North Farnham Parish Register, Richmond Co., VA; G. H. S. King, *Marriages of Richmond Co., VA, 1668-1853* (Fredericksburg, VA, 1964); 1789-1799 Richmond Co., VA, Personal Property Tax Lists; Richmond Co., VA, Account Book 3, 1798-1821, p. 189.

51. LEWIS[6] HAMMACK *(ROBERT HAMMACK[5] SR., WILLIAM "THE ELDER"[4] HAMMACK, WILLIAM "O"[3], JOHN[2] HAMMOCKE, ? JOHN[1] HAMMOT)* was born 17 Jun 1749 in Richmond Co., VA, and died Aft. 1820 in Warren Co., TN. He married BETTY [------] Abt. 1775 in Richmond Co., VA. She was born Abt. 1752 in Richmond Co., VA, and died Aft. 1800 in Charlotte Co., VA.

Children of LEWIS HAMMACK and BETTY [------] are:

107.   i.   ? LEWIS[7] HAMMACK, b. Abt. 1774, Charlotte Co., VA; d. Bet. 1834 - 1835, Washington Co., AR.

108.   ii.   ? THOMAS HAMMACK, b. Abt. 1776, Charlotte Co., VA; d. Aft. 1850, Bedford Co., VA.

    iii.   BENJAMIN HAMMACK, b. Abt. 1781, Charlotte Co., VA; d. Aft. 1803, Charlotte Co., VA.

109.   iv.   ? JOSIAH HAMMACK, b. Abt. 1783, Charlotte Co., VA; d. Aft. 1840, Pulaski Co., KY.

110.   v.   ? WINNEY HAMMACK, b. 17 Dec 1787, Charlotte Co., VA; d. Dec 1851, Carroll Co., TN. Key Sources: 1782 and 1787 Charlotte Co., VA, Tax Lists; Charlotte Co., VA, Deed Books 6, p. 19; 7, p. 206; 8, p. 218; 9, p. 238-39; 1790-1801 Charlotte Co., VA, Personal Property Tax Lists; 1805-1807, 1809-1810, 1811-1812 Franklin Co., VA, Personal Property Tax Lists; 1810 Franklin Co., VA, Census, pp. 296, 310-11; Franklin Co., VA, Deed Book 6, p. 166; 1820 Warren Co., TN, Census, pp. 9, 14, 20. Identification of offspring of Lewis Hammack is speculative, based on common associations, common migration, and nomenclature.

52. REYNE[6] HAMMACK *(ROBERT HAMMACK[5] SR., WILLIAM "THE ELDER"[4] HAMMACK, WILLIAM "O"[3], JOHN[2] HAMMOCKE, ? JOHN[1] HAMMOT)* was born Abt. 1760 in Richmond Co., VA, and died Aft. 02 Oct 1786 in Richmond Co., VA. She married JAMES SAMFORD Abt. 04 Apr 1782 in Richmond Co., VA, son of JAMES SAMFORD. He was born Abt. 1760 in Richmond Co., VA, and died Aft. 1810 in Richmond Co., VA.
Child of REYNE HAMMACK and JAMES SAMFORD is:
         i.   WILLIAM[7] SAMFORD, b. 01 Oct 1785, Richmond Co., VA; m. MARY RUICKS, Abt. 29 Jul 1806, Richmond Co., VA.
Key Sources: North Farnham Parish Register, Richmond Co., VA; G. H. S. King, *Marriages of Richmond Co., VA, 1668-1853* (Fredericksburg, VA, 1964).

53. MILLY[6] HAMMACK *(ROBERT HAMMACK[5] SR., WILLIAM "THE ELDER"[4] HAMMACK, WILLIAM "O"[3], JOHN[2] HAMMOCKE, ? JOHN[1] HAMMOT)* was born 11 Jan 1757 in Richmond Co., VA, and died Aft. 14 Jun 1814 in Lunenburg Co., VA. She married DANIEL BENTLEY Abt. 1780 in Richmond Co., VA, son of SAMUEL BENTLEY and MARY [------]. He was born Abt. 1755 in Virginia, and died Bef. 1804 in Lunenburg Co., VA.
Children of MILLY HAMMACK and DANIEL BENTLEY are:
111.   i.   JOHN H.[7] BENTLEY, b. Abt. 1785, Lunenburg Co., VA; d. Abt. 1858, Crawford Co., GA.
112.   ii.   ANNY BENTLEY, b. Aft. 1787, Lunenburg Co., VA; d. 03 Feb 1843, Hancock Co., GA.
113.   iii. ROBERT H. BENTLEY, b. Aft. 1786, Nottoway Co., VA; d. Aft. 1860, Charlotte Co., VA.
Key Sources: Lunenburg Co., VA, Guardians' Accounts, 1791-1810, pp. 85, 94, 98, 106, 122, 128, 144; Wilkes Co., GA, Deed Books CCC, pp. 42-48.

54. ALICIA[6] JONES *(MARY[5] HAMMACK, WILLIAM "THE ELDER"[4], WILLIAM "O"[3], JOHN[2] HAMMOCKE, ? JOHN[1] HAMMOT)* was born Abt. 14 Jun 1731 in Richmond Co., VA, and died Aft. 1794 in Richmond Co., VA. She married ALEXANDER BRYANT Bef. 13 Dec 1768 in Richmond Co., VA. He was born Bef. 1722 in Richmond Co., VA, and died Abt. 1785 in Richmond Co., VA.
Children of ALICIA JONES and ALEXANDER BRYANT are:
         i.   MARY[7] BRYANT, b. 13 Jan 1771, Richmond Co., VA; m. ? GEORGE DAMERON, 10 Mar 1797, Richmond Co., VA.
         ii.   ANN E. BRYANT, b. Abt. 1773, Richmond Co., VA; d. Aft. 1794, Richmond Co., VA; m. EZEKIEL FOSTER, Abt. 20 Oct 1794, Richmond Co., VA.
Key Sources: North Farnham Parish Register, Richmond Co., VA; G. H. S. King, *Marriages of Richmond Co., VA, 1668-1853* (Fredericksburg, VA, 1964).

55. MARY[6] JONES *(MARY[5] HAMMACK, WILLIAM "THE ELDER"[4], WILLIAM "O"[3], JOHN[2] HAMMOCKE, ? JOHN[1] HAMMOT)* was born Abt. 1735 in Richmond Co., VA, and died Aft. 1771 in Richmond Co., VA. She married ANTHONY DOWTEN Bet. 1761 - 1768 in Richmond Co., VA. He was born Abt. 28 Jun 1727 in Richmond Co., VA, and died 1771 in Richmond Co., VA.
Child of MARY JONES and ANTHONY DOWTEN is:

   i. BETTY JONES[7] DOWTEN, b. 19 Jul 1770, Richmond Co., VA; d. Abt. 1770, Richmond Co., VA.

Key Sources: North Farnham Parish Register, Richmond Co., VA; G. H. S. King, *Marriages of Richmond Co., VA, 1668-1853* (Fredericksburg, VA, 1964).

56. DANIEL[6] HAMMACK *(WILLIAM[5], RICHARD[4], WILLIAM "O"[3], JOHN[2] HAMMOCKE, ? JOHN[1] HAMMOT)* was born Abt. 1737 in Westmoreland Co., VA, and died Aft. 1786 in Campbell Co., VA. He married ANN RUST Abt. 1760 in Albemarle Co., VA, daughter of GEORGE RUST. She was born Abt. 1740 in Virginia, and died Unknown.

Children of DANIEL HAMMACK and ANN RUST are:

114. i. ? WILLIAM[7] HAMMACK, b. Bet. 1760 - 1765, Albemarle Co., VA; d. Aft. 1840, Chatham Co., NC.

115. ii. ? JOHN HAMMACK, b. Bet. 1770 - 1775, Bedford Co., VA; d. Aft. 1840, Overton Co., TN.

Key Sources: Albemarle Co., VA, Deed Book 2, 1758-61, pp. 1-2; Bedford Co., VA, Will Book 1, 1763-87, p. 238; Campbell Co., VA, Deed Book 1, 1782-84, p. 38, 253; Campbell Co., VA, Deed Book 2, 1784-90, p. 155. There is no clear record of Daniel Hammack after he sells land in Campbell County, Virginia, in 1784. I have speculated that he might be the father of William and John Hammack of Chatham Co., NC, because of its nearness to Campbell County, because of the use of common family names, and because John Hammack's family moved to Tennessee with other descendants of Richard Hammack.

57. JOHN[6] HAMMACK *(RICHARD[5], RICHARD[4], WILLIAM "O"[3], JOHN[2] HAMMOCKE, ? JOHN[1] HAMMOT)* was born 20 Sep 1722 in Richmond Co., VA, and died Abt. 1770 in Albemarle Co., VA. He married MARY MARTIN Abt. 1745 in Louisa Co., VA, daughter of JOSEPH MARTIN and SUSANNAH CHILDS. She was born Abt. 1722, and died Aft. 1770 in Albemarle Co., VA.

Children of JOHN HAMMACK and MARY MARTIN are:

116. i. ? ROBERT[7] HAMMACK, b. Abt. 1745, Louisa Co., VA; d. Abt. 1822, Surry Co., NC.

   ii. SUSANNAH CHILES HAMMACK, b. Bet. 1745 - 1755, Louisa Co., VA; d. Aft. 1850, Monroe Co., WV; m. REV. JAMES SEYMORE SWEENEY, Abt. 1770, Albemarle Co., VA; b. Abt. 1750, Ireland; d. 1835, Monroe Co., WV.

117. iii. WILLIAM HAMMACK, b. Bet. 1749 - 1752, Louisa Co., VA; d. Aft. 1782, Campbell Co., VA.

118. iv. JOHN HAMMACK, b. Abt. 1755, Albemarle Co., VA; d. Bet. 1840 - 1850, Grainger Co., TN.

119. v. MARTIN HAMMACK, b. Abt. 1760, Albemarle Co., VA; d. Aft. 1838, Kanawha Co., VA.

120. vi. DANIEL HAMMACK, b. Abt. 1762, Albemarle Co., VA; d. 16 Jul 1829, Smith Co., TN.

   vii. MILLY HAMMACK, b. Bet. 1750 - 1760, Albemarle Co., VA; d. Aft. 1770, Albemarle Co., VA.

   viii. PATTY HAMMACK, b. Bet. 1750 - 1760, Albemarle Co., VA; d. Aft. 1770, Albemarle Co., VA.

Key Sources: Louisa Co., VA, Deed Book A, pp. 210-11, 229-30, 406-7, 454-55; Louisa Co., VA, Deed Book B, pp. 63-64, 269-70, 303-4, 332-35; Albemarle Co., VA, Deed Book 2, pp. 1-2; Albemarle Co., VA, Deed Book 3, pp. 128-30; Albemarle Co., VA, Deed Book 5, pp. 211-12; Albemarle Co., VA, Deed Book 6, pp. 329-31; Harold B. Gill, Jr., *Apprentices of Virginia, 1623-1800* (Salt Lake City, 1989), p. 108.

58. RICHARD[6] HAMMACK *(RICHARD[5], RICHARD[4], WILLIAM "O"[3], JOHN[2] HAMMOCKE, ? JOHN[1] HAMMOT)* was born Bet. 1723 - 1735 in Westmoreland Co., VA, and died Bet. 1795 - 1796 in

Pittsylvania Co., VA. He married MARY WITCHER Abt. 1758 in Albemarle Co., VA. She was born Abt. 1740 in Virginia, and died Aft. 1802 in Pittsylvania Co., VA.

Children of RICHARD HAMMACK and MARY WITCHER are:

	i.	JEMIMA[7] HAMMACK, b. Abt. 1760, Albemarle Co., VA; d. Aft. 1840, Union Co., TN; m. THOMAS BOLTON, Abt. 1777, Pittsylvania Co., VA; b. Abt. 1746, Halifax Co., VA; d. 1826, Grainger Co., TN.
121.	ii.	JOHN HAMMACK, b. Bet. 1760 - 1763, Albemarle Co., VA; d. Abt. 1844, Pittsylvania Co., VA.
	iii.	MARY HAMMACK, b. 04 Feb 1762, Albemarle Co., VA; m. MICHAEL BRANSON, 19 Oct 1790, Pittsylvania Co., VA; b. 15 Sep 1766, Pittsylvania Co., VA; d. 1829, Claiborne Co., TN.
122.	iv.	PETER HAMMACK, b. Abt. 1764, Albemarle Co., VA; d. Aft. 1830, Giles Co., TN.
123.	v.	DANIEL HAMMACK, b. Bet. 1765 - 1770, Pittsylvania Co., VA; d. Bet. 1818 - 1820, Knox Co., KY.
	vi.	GEORGE HAMMACK, b. Abt. 1775, Pittsylvania Co., VA.
124.	vii.	EPHRAIM HAMMACK, b. Abt. 1776, Pittsylvania Co., VA; d. Aft. 1830, Madison Co., KY.
125.	viii.	JAMES HAMMACK, b. Bef. 1776, Pittsylvania Co., VA; d. Bet. 1808 - 1810, Grainger Co., TN.
126.	ix.	WILLIAM HAMMACK, b. Bet. 1775 - 1781, Pittsylvania Co., VA; d. Bet. 1813 - 1814, Madison Co., KY.
127.	x.	LEWIS HAMMACK, b. Abt. 1780, Pittsylvania Co., VA; d. Aft. 1816, Madison Co., KY.
	xi.	? SUSANNAH HAMMACK, b. Abt. 1785, Pittsylvania Co., VA; d. Bef. 1820, Grainger Co., TN; m. EDMUND MAPLES, 07 Dec 1805, Grainger Co., TN; b. Abt. 1785, South Carolina.

Key Sources: Pittsylvania Co., VA, Deed Book 1, p. 492; Pittsylvania Co., VA, Order Book 1, p. 323; Pittsylvania Co., VA, Deed Book 6, p. 2; 1787 Franklin Co., VA, Personal Property Tax List; 1788-1809 Pittsylvania Co., VA, Personal Property Tax Lists; Pittsylvania Co., VA, Deed Book 9, p. 534; Pittsylvania Co., VA, Deed Book 15, p. 53. The identification of the offspring of Richard and Mary Hammack is speculative, based on tax lists, common association, common migration, and nomenclature.

59. WILLIAM[6] HAMMACK *(JOHN[5], WILLIAM "THE YOUNGER"[4], WILLIAM "O"[3], JOHN[2] HAMMOCKE, ? JOHN[1] HAMMOT)* was born 27 Sep 1742 in Richmond Co., VA, and died 1785 in Lunenburg Co., VA. He married ELIZABETH [------] Abt. 1765 in Lunenburg Co., VA. She was born Abt. 1745 in Virginia, and died Aft. 1790 in Lunenburg Co., VA.

Children of WILLIAM HAMMACK and ELIZABETH [------] are:

	i.	JOHN[7] HAMMACK, b. Abt. 1764, Lunenburg Co., VA; d. 01 Apr 1856, Lunenburg Co., VA; m. (1) KATY HANKS, 06 Aug 1791, Lunenburg Co., VA; m. (2) ELIZABETH AMOS, 25 Mar 1815, Lunenburg Co., VA; b. Bef. 1775, Lunenburg Co., VA; d. Bet. 1825 - 1840, Lunenburg Co., VA; m. (3) MARY [------], Bef. 1840, Lunenburg Co., VA; b. Abt. 1782, Virginia; d. Aft. 1850, Lunenburg Co., VA.
	ii.	? MARY HAMMACK, b. Abt. 1768, Lunenburg Co., VA; d. Aft. 1789, Lunenburg Co., VA; m. DAVID MOSELEY, 29 May 1789, Lunenburg Co., VA.
	iii.	NANCY HAMMACK, b. Abt. 1770, Lunenburg Co., VA; d. Aft. 1791, Lunenburg Co., VA; m. THOMAS HANKS, 31 Mar 1791, Lunenburg Co., VA; b. Abt. 1770, Virginia; d. Aft. 1850, Lunenburg Co., VA.
	iv.	? ELIZABETH HAMMACK, b. Abt. 1775, Lunenburg Co., VA; d. Aft. 1796, Nottoway Co., VA; m. SAMUEL MEANLEY, 06 May 1796, Nottoway Co., VA.
128.	v.	JAMES HAMMACK, b. Abt. 1778, Lunenburg Co., VA; d. Abt. 1835, Lunenburg Co., VA.

vi.   WILLIAM HAMMACK, b. Abt. 1785, Lunenburg Co., VA; d. 1824, Lunenburg Co., VA.
Key Source: Lunenburg Co., VA, Will Book 3, p. 235.

60. HUGH⁶ HAMMACK *(JOHN⁵, WILLIAM "THE YOUNGER"⁴, WILLIAM "O"³, JOHN² HAMMOCKE, ? JOHN¹ HAMMOT)* was born Abt. 1753 in Lunenburg Co., VA, and died 1804 in Lunenburg Co., VA. He married ANNA [------] Abt. 1781 in Lunenburg Co., VA. She was born Abt. 1760 in Virginia, and died Aft. 1830 in Lunenburg Co., VA.
Children of HUGH HAMMACK and ANNA [------] are:
      i.   ROBERT⁷ HAMMACK, b. Aft. 1783, Lunenburg Co., VA.
      ii. LEWIS HAMMACK, b. Abt. 1782, Lunenburg Co., VA; d. Bet. 1853 - 1862, Lunenburg Co., VA.
129. iii. HUGH HAMMACK, b. Abt. 1799, Lunenburg Co., VA; d. 05 Apr 1860, Lunenburg Co., VA.
      iv. MILLEY HAMMACK, b. Bef. 1804, Lunenburg Co., VA; d. Aft. 1830, Lunenburg Co., VA.
      v.   CATHERINE HAMMACK, b. Bet. 1790 - 1800, Lunenburg Co., VA; d. Bet. 1830 - 1852, Lunenburg Co., VA.
      vi. ANN HAMMACK, b. Abt. 1796, Lunenburg Co., VA; d. Abt. 1852, Lunenburg Co., VA.
Key Source: Lunenburg Co., VA, Will Book 6, p. 93.

Generation No. 7

61. MICHAEL⁷ HAMICK *(MICHAEL⁶ HAMMICK, MICHAEL⁵, THOMAS⁴ HAMICK, HENRYE³ HAMICKE, JOHN² HAMMOCKE, ? JOHN¹ HAMMOT)* was born Abt. 26 Apr 1736 in Yealmpton, Devonshire. He married MARY [------].
Children of MICHAEL HAMICK and MARY [------] are:
130. i.   MICHAEL⁸ HAMMICK, b. Abt. 27 Dec 1765, Yealmpton, Devonshire.
      ii. MARY HAMMICK, b. Abt. 22 Jan 1768, Yealmpton, Devonshire.
Key Source: Yealmpton Parish Register.

62. SAMUEL⁷ HAMMACK *(HONIWELL⁶ HAMMICK, ARTHUR⁵ HAMMACKE, ARTHUR⁴ HAMICK, HENRYE³ HAMICKE, JOHN² HAMMOCKE, ? JOHN¹ HAMMOT)* was born Abt. 14 Feb 1772 in Brixham, Devonshire. He married ELIZABETH [------] Abt. 1805 in Devonshire.
Children of SAMUEL HAMMACK and ELIZABETH [------] are:
      i.   ELIZABETH⁸ HAMMICK, b. Abt. 25 Sep 1806, Brixham, Devonshire.
      ii.   SAMUEL HAMMACK, b. Abt. 20 Aug 1809, Brixham, Devonshire.
      iii. ANN HAMMACK, b. Abt. 09 Jun 1811, Brixham, Devonshire.
      iv.   HORATIO HONNIWILL HAMMICK, b. Abt. 14 Mar 1816, Brixham, Devonshire.
      v.   ANNA MARY HAMMICK, b. Abt. 24 Jul 1817, Brixham, Devonshire.
      vi.   ELIZA ELIZABETH HAMMICK, b. Abt. 04 Feb 1819, Brixham, Devonshire.
      vii. JOHN WOTTON HAMMICK, b. Abt. 07 Dec 1820, Brixham, Devonshire.
Key Source: Brixham Parish Register.

63. CHARLES⁷ HAMMACK *(JOHN⁶, WILLIAM⁵, WILLIAM "THE ELDER"⁴, WILLIAM "O"³, JOHN² HAMMOCKE, ? JOHN¹ HAMMOT)* was born 29 Jan 1744 in Richmond Co., VA, and died 1796 in Warren Co., NC.
Children of CHARLES HAMMACK are:
      i.   DAUGHTER⁸ HAMMACK, b. Bef. 1790, Warren Co., NC.
      ii. DAUGHTER HAMMACK, b. Bef. 1790, Warren Co., NC.

Key Source: 1771 Granville Co., NC, Tax List; 1784 Granville Co., NC, State Census; 1785 Granville Co., NC, Tax List; 1787-1790 Warren Co., NC, Tax Lists; 1790 Warren Co., NC, Census; 1800 Warren Co., NC, Census.

64. DAVID⁷ HAMMACK *(JOHN⁶, WILLIAM⁵, WILLIAM "THE ELDER"⁴, WILLIAM "O"³, JOHN² HAMMOCKE, ? JOHN¹ HAMMOT)* was born Bet. 1748 - 1753 in Richmond Co., VA, and died Aft. 1788 in Warren Co., NC. He married ? BETTY [------] Abt. 1775 in Warren Co., NC. She died Aft. 1800 in Warren Co., NC.
Children of DAVID HAMMACK and ? [------] are:
  i. DAUGHTER⁸ HAMMACK, b. Abt. 1780, Warren Co., NC.
  ii. SON HAMMACK, b. Abt. 1782, Warren Co., NC.
  iii. SON HAMMACK, b. Abt. 1784, Warren Co., NC.
Key Source: 1771 Granville Co., NC, Tax List; 1784 Granville Co., NC, State Census; 1785 Granville Co., NC, Tax List; 1787-1790 Warren Co., NC, Tax Lists; 1790 Warren Co., NC, Census.

65. MARY⁷ HAMMACK *(JOHN⁶, WILLIAM⁵, WILLIAM "THE ELDER"⁴, WILLIAM "O"³, JOHN² HAMMOCKE, ? JOHN¹ HAMMOT)* was born 13 Jun 1753 in Richmond Co., VA, and died 14 Jan 1837 in Wilkes Co., GA. She married WILLIAM PASCHAL Bef. 1776 in Granville Co., NC. He was born 15 Apr 1753 in Granville Co., NC, and died Mar 1807 in Wilkes Co., GA.
Children of MARY HAMMACK and WILLIAM PASCHAL are:
  i. WILLIAM⁸ PASCHAL, b. 15 Mar 1776, Granville Co., NC; d. 25 Jun 1853, Lincoln Co., GA; m. ELIZABETH ELLIOTT, 22 Jul 1802, Wilkes Co., GA.
  ii. THOMAS PASCHAL, b. 20 Apr 1779, Granville Co., NC; d. 24 Nov 1848, Lincoln Co., GA; m. (1) ANNIE LEVERETT, 05 Aug 1806, Lincoln Co., GA; b. 14 Jan 1789, Georgia; d. 21 May 1845, Lincoln Co., GA; m. (2) MRS. JANE COLE, 15 Apr 1846, Lincoln Co., GA.
  iii. SUSANNA PASCHAL, b. 06 Aug 1782, Granville Co., NC; d. Bef. 1812, Wilkes Co., GA; m. JOHN GRESHAM, 11 Oct 1799, Wilkes Co., GA.
  iv. MARGARET PASCHAL, b. 18 Jun 1783, Granville Co., NC; d. Bef. 1813, Wilkes Co., GA; m. KAUFMAN GRESHAM.
  v. SAMUEL PASCHAL, b. 07 May 1788, Wilkes Co., GA; d. Abt. 1854, Wilkes Co., GA; m. FANNY GRESHAM, 15 Feb 1810, Wilkes Co., GA.
  vi. POLLY PASCHAL, b. 06 Jun 1791, Wilkes Co., GA; m. [-----] REVIER.
  vii. ISAIAH PASCHAL, b. 14 Jul 1793, Wilkes Co., GA; m. PATIENCE ASHMORE.
  viii. JEREMIAH PASCHAL, b. 14 Jul 1793, Wilkes Co., GA.
  ix. DENNIS PASCHAL, b. 18 May 1796, Wilkes Co., GA; m. DICEY GRESHAM; b. 16 Feb 1802, Wilkes Co., GA; d. 1868, Georgia.
Key Sources: G. G. Davidson, *Early Records of Georgia, Wilkes County* (2 vols., Macon, GA, 1932), 1: 354.

66. JOHN⁷ HAMMACK *(JOHN⁶, WILLIAM⁵, WILLIAM "THE ELDER"⁴, WILLIAM "O"³, JOHN² HAMMOCKE, ? JOHN¹ HAMMOT)* was born Abt. 19 Apr 1756 in Richmond Co., VA, and died Abt. 1832 in Lincoln Co., GA. He married (1) MRS. SARAH [------] THORNTON. He married (2) RELIANCE PASCHALL Bet. 1773 - 1774 in Granville Co., NC. She was born 08 Feb 1749 in North Carolina, and died Bef. 1786 in North Carolina. He married (3) PHOEBE [------] Bef. 23 Jan 1786 in Wilkes Co., GA. She was born Abt. 1760, and died Abt. 1808 in Wilkes Co., GA.
Children of JOHN HAMMACK and RELIANCE PASCHALL are:
131. i. SAMUEL⁸ HAMMACK, b. Abt. 1775, Granville Co., NC; d. Bef. 1803, Edgefield District, SC.

132.   ii.   WILLIAM HAMMACK, b. Abt. 1776, Granville Co., NC; d. Aft. 1840, Chambers Co., AL.

133.   iii.   JOHN HAMMACK, b. 04 Mar 1776, Granville Co., NC; d. 05 Jan 1824, Newton Co., GA.

        iv.   FERIBY HAMMACK, b. Abt. 1778, Granville Co., NC; d. Aft. 1850, Lincoln Co., GA; m. ROBERT MUNFORD; b. Abt. 1776, Virginia; d. Abt. 1850, Lincoln Co., GA.

134.   v.   ELIJAH HAMMACK, b. Abt. 1779, Warren Co., NC; d. Aft. 1840, Early Co., GA.

135.   vi.   PASCHAL HAMMACK, b. Jun 1782, Warren Co., NC; d. Jul 1865, Randolph Co., GA.

Children of JOHN HAMMACK and PHOEBE [------] are:

        vii.   MARGARET "PEGGY"[8] HAMMACK, b. Abt. 1788, Wilkes Co., GA; d. Aft. 1860, Jasper Co., GA; m. GEORGE GREEN, 28 Aug 1808, Wilkes Co., GA.

136.   viii.   CHARLES HAMMACK, b. Abt. 1789, Wilkes Co., GA; d. Aft. 1850, Houston Co., GA.

137.   ix.   THOMAS HAMMACK, b. Abt. 1796, Wilkes Co., GA; d. Aft. 1860, Barbour Co., AL.

138.   x.   DAVID HAMMACK, b. Bet. 1798 - 1800, Wilkes Co., GA; d. Bet. 1840 - 1850, Houston Co., GA.

        xi.   ELIZABETH HAMMACK, b. Abt. 1804, Wilkes Co., GA; m. (1) [--------] ROWLAND; d. Bef. 1832, Lincoln Co., GA; m. (2) RICHARD POWELL, 22 Feb 1832, Lincoln Co., GA.

        xii.   RELIANCE HAMMACK, b. Abt. 1806, Wilkes Co., GA; m. JOHN STEADHAM, 23 Nov 1828, Lincoln Co., GA.

Key Sources: Abbeville District Wills and Bonds, Estate Box 73, Pack 1782, Samuel Paschall Estate File; Lincoln Co., GA, Will Book D, p. 250; 1830 Lincoln Co., GA, Census; Lincoln Co., GA, Inventories and Appraisements, pp. 38, 89; Lincoln Co., GA, Annual Returns Book Z, p. 171.

67. THOMAS[7] HAMMOCK *(JOHN[6], WILLIAM[5], WILLIAM "THE ELDER"[4], WILLIAM "O"[3], JOHN[2] HAMMOCKE, ? JOHN[1] HAMMOT)* was born Abt. 1766 in Granville Co., NC, and died Bet. 1806 - 1814 in Wilkes Co., GA. He married MARGARET [SMITH?] Abt. 1796 in Wilkes Co., GA. She was born Abt. 1774 in Georgia, and died Bet. 1840 - 1841 in Wilkes Co., GA.

Children of THOMAS HAMMOCK and MARGARET [SMITH?] are:

139.   i.   GRANVILLE[8] HAMMOCK, b. Abt. 1800, Wilkes Co., GA; d. 11 Jul 1879, Gadsden, AL.

140.   ii.   STEPHEN WALKER HAMMOCK, b. 01 Jan 1806, Wilkes Co., GA; d. Aft. 1870, Kemper Co., MS.

141.   iii.   JOHN P. HAMMOCK, b. Bet. 1809 - 1811, Wilkes Co., GA; d. Aft. 1880, Polk Co., GA.

142.   iv.   JAMES L. HAMMOCK, b. Abt. 1798, Wilkes Co., GA; d. Aft. 1850, Upson Co., GA.

        v.   MARY HAMMOCK, b. Abt. 1796, Wilkes Co., GA; d. Aft. 1831, Wilkes Co., GA.

        vi.   LUCY HAMMOCK, b. Abt. 1810, Wilkes Co., GA; d. Aft. 1831, Wilkes Co., GA; m. THOMAS JOHNSON, 02 Dec 1842, Wilkes Co., GA.

143.   vii.   ELIZABETH HAMMOCK, b. Abt. 1812, Wilkes Co., GA; d. Aft. 1872, Wilkes Co., GA.

Key Source: Thomas Hammock Estate File, Wilkes Co., GA, Loose Estate Files, Georgia Department of Archives and History, Morrow, GA.

68. WILLOUGHBY[7] HAMMOCK *(JOHN[6], WILLIAM[5], WILLIAM "THE ELDER"[4], WILLIAM "O"[3], JOHN[2] HAMMOCKE, ? JOHN[1] HAMMOT)* was born Abt. 1768 in Granville Co., NC, and died Abt. 1824 in Newton Co., GA. He married LEVISY NELSON. She was born Abt. 1770 in North Carolina, and died 01 Jul 1848 in DeKalb Co., AL.

Children of WILLOUGHBY HAMMOCK and LEVISY NELSON are:

        i.   LOUISIANA[8] HAMMOCK, b. Abt. 1798, Jackson Co., GA; d. Aft. 1850, Louisiana; m. BENJAMIN HODNETT, 14 Aug 1817, Jasper Co., GA; b. Abt. 1798, Virginia; d. Bet. 1860 - 1870, Rapides Parish, LA.

        ii.   ELIZABETH HAMMOCK, b. 27 Jul 1801, Clarke Co., GA; d. 06 Feb 1852, Heard Co., GA; m. JOHN BARNES GARRETT, 12 Oct 1816, Jasper Co., GA; b. 11 Jul 1793, Georgia; d. 22 Apr 1840, Heard Co., GA.

144.   iii.   THOMAS HAMMOCK, b. 04 Sep 1808, Clarke Co., GA; d. 01 Dec 1881, DeKalb Co., AL.

      iv.   SARAH HAMMOCK, b. 22 Feb 1805, Clarke Co., GA; d. 02 Feb 1882, DeKalb Co., AL; m. THOMAS GARRETT, 21 Dec 1819, Jasper Co., GA; b. Abt. 1800, Georgia; d. 21 Nov 1853, DeKalb Co., AL.

      v.   MATILDA HAMMOCK, b. Abt. 1808, Clarke Co., GA; d. Aft. 1831, Georgia; m. WILLIAMSON F. MUNNY.

145.   vi.   AARON G. HAMMOCK, b. Abt. 1810, Clarke Co., GA; d. Abt. 1867, DeKalb Co., AL.

146.   vii.   WILLOUGHBY HAMMOCK, b. 1811, Clarke Co., GA; d. 1887, DeKalb Co., AL.

      viii.   JACKSON HAMMOCK, b. Abt. 1814, Clarke Co., GA; d. Aft. 1835, Crawford Co., GA.

      ix.   LEVISY HAMMOCK, b. Abt. 1814, Jasper Co., GA; d. Abt. 1835, Harris Co., GA; m. THOMAS THORNTON.

Key Sources: 1790 Wilkes Co., GA, Tax Digest; Warren Co., GA, Deed Book B, pp. 43, 53; 1799 Jackson Co., GA, Tax Digest; 1802 Clarke Co., GA, Deed Book A, pp. 60, 88; Clarke Co., GA, Deed Book C, p. 305; Clarke Co., GA, Deed Book I, p. 124; 1802-1807 Clarke Co., GA, Tax Digests; Newton Co., GA, Estate Book 1, p. 56; Willoughby Hammock Estate File, Newton Co., GA. As noted above, the author has speculated that Willoughby Hammock might have been a son of John and Mary Ann Hammock based on his age and location of residence when he first appears in Georgia; the late Henry Franklin Hammack speculated that he was a son of Hugh Hammack (c. 1732 – c. 1783), but there is no conclusive evidence that Hugh left offspring. See the note in the concluding section regarding Robert Hammock, who appeared near Willoughby in Clarke County, Georgia.

69. ELIZABETH[7] HAMMACK *(JOHN[6], WILLIAM[5], WILLIAM "THE ELDER"[4], WILLIAM "O"[3], JOHN[2] HAMMOCKE, ? JOHN[1] HAMMOT)* was born Abt. 1770 in Granville Co., NC, and died Aft. 1830 in Upson Co., GA. She married WILLIAM BROWN Abt. 1795 in Wilkes Co., GA. He was born Abt. 1773 in Caswell Co., NC, and died Aft. 1812 in Tennessee.
Children of ELIZABETH HAMMACK and WILLIAM BROWN are:

      i.   ALFRED[8] BROWN, b. Abt. 1797, Wilkes Co., GA; d. Aft. 1861, Talbot Co., GA; m. AMY PYE.

      ii.   BASWELL BROWN, b. Abt. 1801, Hancock Co., GA; d. Aft. 1860, Upson Co., GA; m. LUCY DELOACH.

      iii.   FRANKLIN BROWN, b. Abt. 1803, Hancock Co., GA; d. 1877, Upson Co., GA; m. MARTHA DELOACH.

Key Source: 1807 Georgia Land Lottery Fortunate Draw of Catharine Hammock, Young's District, Wilkes Co., GA; 1811- 1825 Jones Co., GA, Tax Digests; Jones Co., GA, Deed Book D, p. 81; Jones Co., GA, Deed Book E, p. 232. Elizabeth Hammack Brown was the ancestor of Thomas Daniel Knight.

70. LEWIS[7] HAMMACK *(JOHN[6], WILLIAM[5], WILLIAM "THE ELDER"[4], WILLIAM "O"[3], JOHN[2] HAMMOCKE, ? JOHN[1] HAMMOT)* was born Abt. 1772 in Granville Co., NC, and died Aft. 1830 in Bibb Co., GA. He married ELIZABETH [------] Abt. 1797 in Wilkes Co., GA. She was born Bet. 1778 - 1780 in Georgia, and died Aft. 1840 in Marion Co., GA.
Children of LEWIS HAMMACK and ELIZABETH [------] are:

147.   i.   HARRISON[8] HAMMACK, b. Abt. 1798, Wilkes Co., GA; d. Aft. 1850, LaFayette Co., MS.

      ii.   DAUGHTER HAMMACK, b. Abt. 1800, Wilkes Co., GA; d. Aft. 1820, Jones Co., GA.

      iii.   ? JEREMIAH HAMMACK, b. Abt. 1804, Wilkes Co., GA; d. Aft. 1840, Marion Co., GA.

      iv.   ? JOHNSTON HAMMACK, b. Abt. 1803, Wilkes Co., GA; d. Aft. 1850, Coosa Co., AL; m. (1) ESTHER CHESSER, 27 Aug 1822, Jasper Co., GA; m. (2) SUSANNAH HAMMACK STRINGFIELD, Abt. 1830, Alabama.

      v.   DAUGHTER HAMMACK, b. Bet. 1806 - 1810, Wilkes Co., GA; d. Aft. 1820, Jones Co., GA.

vi. DAUGHTER HAMMACK, b. Bet. 1806 - 1810, Wilkes Co., GA; d. Aft. 1820, Jones Co., GA.

vii. DAUGHTER HAMMACK, b. Abt. 1812, Wilkes Co., GA; d. Aft. 1830, Bibb Co., GA.

viii. SON HAMMACK, b. Abt. 1815, Wilkes Co., GA; d. Aft. 1830, Bibb Co., GA.

ix. DAUGHTER HAMMACK, b. Abt. 1817, Wilkes Co., GA; d. Aft. 1830, Bibb Co., GA.

x. DAUGHTER HAMMACK, b. Abt. 1819, Jones Co., GA; d. Aft. 1840, Marion Co., GA.

xi. SON HAMMACK, b. Bet. 1820 - 1825, Jones Co., GA; d. Aft. 1840, Marion Co., GA.

xii. DAUGHTER HAMMACK, b. Bet. 1825 - 1830, Jones Co., GA; d. Aft. 1840, Marion Co., GA.

Key Sources: Bibb Co., GA, Deed Book A, pp. 163, 281; 1830 Bibb Co., GA, Census, p. 70; 1840 Marion Co., GA, Census, p. 75. The identity of Lewis Hammack's offspring is speculative. Lewis Hammack and his brothers William and James were probably the fathers of the several unidentified Hammack men born between about 1800 and 1825 who appear as adults in western Georgia and eastern Alabama in the 1840s and 1850s. Because they cannot be clearly identified, those men and their families are discussed in the section dealing with unidentified Hammack families.

71. WILLIAM[7] HAMMACK *(JOHN[6], WILLIAM[5], WILLIAM "THE ELDER"[4], WILLIAM "O"[3], JOHN[2] HAMMOCKE, ? JOHN[1] HAMMOT)* was born Abt. 1774 in Granville Co., NC, and died Aft. 1830 in Ware Co., GA. He married UNKNOWN Abt. 1800 in Wilkes Co., GA. She was born Bet. 1770 - 1780, and died Aft. 1830 in Ware Co., GA.

Children of WILLIAM HAMMACK and UNKNOWN are:

i. SON[8] HAMMACK, b. Abt. 1800, Wilkes Co., GA; d. Aft. 1820, Wilkes Co., GA.

ii. DAUGHTER HAMMACK, b. Abt. 1810, Wilkes Co., GA; d. Aft. 1820, Wilkes Co., GA.

Key Source: 1820 Wilkes Co., GA, Census, p. 164; 1820 Georgia Land Lottery Fortunate Draws; 1830 Ware Co., GA, Census, p. 217.

72. JAMES[7] HAMMACK *(JOHN[6], WILLIAM[5], WILLIAM "THE ELDER"[4], WILLIAM "O"[3], JOHN[2] HAMMOCKE, ? JOHN[1] HAMMOT)* was born Abt. 1776 in Granville Co., NC, and died Aft. 1835 in Bibb Co., GA. He married (1) LUCY HAMMACK Bet. 1797 - 1800 in Wilkes Co., GA. She was born Bet. 1775 - 1780 in Wilkes Co., GA, and died Bet. 1820 - 1827 in Bibb Co., GA. He married (2) MARY POLLARD 02 Aug 1827 in Bibb Co., GA. She was born Abt. 1805 in Georgia, and died Aft. 1830 in Bibb Co., GA.

Children of JAMES HAMMACK and LUCY HAMMACK are:

i. ABEL[8] HAMMACK, b. Abt. 1800, Wilkes Co., GA; d. Aft. 1830, Fayette Co., GA.

ii. ELZEY HAMMACK, b. Abt. 1802, Wilkes Co., GA; d. Aft. 1824, Jones Co., GA.

148.   iii. CELIA HAMMACK, b. Bet. 1802 - 1803, Wilkes Co., GA; d. Aft. 1860, Columbia Co., AR.

iv. SON HAMMACK, b. Abt. 1805, Wilkes Co., GA; d. Aft. 1820, Jones Co., GA.

v. SON HAMMACK, b. Abt. 1807, Wilkes Co., GA; d. Aft. 1820, Jones Co., GA.

vi. CATHERINE HAMMACK, b. Abt. 1809, Jones Co., GA; d. Aft. 1830, Jones Co., GA; m. JOHN W. GRIFFIN, 02 May 1830, Bibb Co., GA.

vii. DAUGHTER HAMMACK, b. Bet. 1810 - 1820, Jones Co., GA; d. Aft. 1820, Jones Co., GA.

viii. SON HAMMACK, b. Bet. 1815 - 1820, Jones Co., GA; d. Aft. 1830, Bibb Co., GA.

ix. SON HAMMACK, b. Bet. 1815 - 1820, Jones Co., GA; d. Aft. 1830, Bibb Co., GA.

x. DAUGHTER HAMMACK, b. Bet. 1820 - 1825, Jones Co., GA; d. Aft. 1830, Bibb Co., GA.

xi. SON HAMMACK, b. Bet. 1820 - 1825, Jones Co., GA; d. Aft. 1830, Bibb Co., GA.

xii. SON HAMMACK, b. Abt. 1826, Bibb Co., GA; d. Aft. 1830, Bibb Co., GA.

Children of JAMES HAMMACK and MARY POLLARD are:

xiii. DAUGHTER[8] HAMMACK, b. Abt. 1828, Bibb Co., GA; d. Aft. 1830, Bibb Co., GA.

xiv. SON HAMMACK, b. Abt. 1830, Bibb Co., GA; d. Aft. 1830, Bibb Co., GA.

xv. CHILD HAMMACK, b. Abt. 1832, Bibb Co., GA; d. Aft. 1832, Bibb Co., GA.

xvi. CHILD HAMMACK, b. Abt. 1834, Pike Co., GA; d. Aft. 1834, Pike Co., GA.

xvii. ELIZA HAMMACK, b. Bet. 1831 - 1836, Pike Co., GA; d. Aft. 1880, Muscogee Co., GA; m. ABRAHAM GAMMELL, Abt. 1855, Muscogee Co., GA; b. 1819, Georgia; d. 1902, Muscogee Co., GA.

Key Sources: 1801 and 1805 Wilkes Co., GA, Tax Digests; 1807 Georgia Land Lottery Fortunate Draws; 1811-1820 Jones Co., GA, Tax Digests; Wilkes Co., GA, Deed Book FFF, p. 151; Jones Co., GA, Deed Book E, pp. 224, 232; Jones Co., GA, Deed Book J, pp. 44, 257; Jones Co., GA, Deed Book K, p. 131; Jones Co., GA, Deed Book L, pp. 265, 316, 435; Bibb Co., GA, Deed Book A, pp. 11, 13, 73, 163, 172, 281; Bibb Co., GA, Deed Book B, p.165; 1827 Georgia Land Lottery Fortunate Draws; 1830 Bibb Co., GA, Census; 1831 Pike Co., GA, Tax Digest.

73. WILLIAM[7] BENTLEY (*CHRISTIAN[6] HAMMOCK, BENEDICT[5] HAMMACK, WILLIAM "THE ELDER"[4], WILLIAM "O"[3], JOHN[2] HAMMOCKE, ? JOHN[1] HAMMOT*) was born Bef. 1753 in Amelia Co., VA, and died Bet. 1791 - 1792 in Wilkes Co., GA. He married JANE HAMMOND 08 Oct 1774 in Onslow Co., NC. She was born Abt. 1755 in Virginia, and died Aft. 1792 in Wilkes Co., GA.

Children of WILLIAM BENTLEY and JANE HAMMOND are:

i. SUSANNAH[8] BENTLEY, b. Abt. 1776, North Carolina; d. Aft. 1798, Wilkes Co., GA; m. DAVID (OR DANIEL) TOMLINSON.

ii. LEWIS BENTLEY, b. Abt. 1777, North Carolina; d. Aft. 1805, Wilkes Co., GA.

iii. JOHN BENTLEY, b. Abt. 1783, Wilkes Co., GA; d. Aft. 1804, Wilkes Co., GA.

iv. JAMES BENTLEY, b. Abt. 1783, Wilkes Co., GA; d. Aft. 1804, Wilkes Co., GA.

v. CATHERINE BENTLEY, b. Abt. 1785, Wilkes Co., GA.

Key Sources: G. G. Davidson, *Early Records of Georgia, Wilkes County* (2 vols., Macon, GA, 1932), 1: 27, 52, and 2: 203.

74. BALAAM[7] BENTLEY (*CHRISTIAN[6] HAMMOCK, BENEDICT[5] HAMMACK, WILLIAM "THE ELDER"[4], WILLIAM "O"[3], JOHN[2] HAMMOCKE, ? JOHN[1] HAMMOT*) was born Aft. 1765 in Onslow Co., NC, and died Abt. 1816 in Lincoln Co., GA. He married NANCY [------]. She died Aft. 1816 in Lincoln Co., GA.

Children of BALAAM BENTLEY and NANCY [------] are:

i. JOHN[8] BENTLEY, m. NANCY PASCHALL, 21 Feb 1822, Lincoln Co., GA.

ii. BENJAMIN BENTLEY, m. MARY PASCHALL, 1829, Lincoln Co., GA.

iii. VINCEY BENTLEY, m. ELI GARRETT.

iv. KEZIAH BENTLEY.

Key Source: Lincoln Co., GA, Will Book B, 1807-1832, p. 55.

75. WILLIAM[7] HAMMOCK (*WILLIAM[6], BENEDICT[5] HAMMACK, WILLIAM "THE ELDER"[4], WILLIAM "O"[3], JOHN[2] HAMMOCKE, ? JOHN[1] HAMMOT*) was born 15 Jun 1760 in Amelia Co., VA, and died 03 Jan 1849 in Union Co., KY. He married NANCY BROWN Abt. 1790 in Georgia. She was born Abt. 1770 in North Carolina, and died 16 Aug 1843 in Union Co., KY.

Children of WILLIAM HAMMOCK and NANCY BROWN are:

149. i. ? BENJAMIN[8] HAMMOCK, b. Abt. 1791, Wilkes Co., GA; d. Aft. 1870, Saline Co., IL.

ii. RUTH HAMMOCK, b. Abt. 1793, Georgia or Kentucky; d. Aft. 1810, Caldwell Co., KY; m. CHARLES SULLIVANT, 09 Jan 1810, Kentucky.

iii. WINNIE HAMMOCK, b. Abt. 1795, Georgia or Kentucky; d. Aft. 1812, Caldwell Co., KY; m. JOSEPH GREGORY.

iv.   NANCY HAMMOCK, b. Abt. 1800, Christian Co., KY; d. Aft. 1817, Caldwell Co., KY; m. WILLIAM ANDERSON.
150. v.   WILLIAM B. HAMMOCK, b. Abt. 1801, Christian Co., KY; d. 1836, Union Co., KY.
151. vi.   MORGAN BROWN HAMMOCK, b. 1804, Christian Co., KY; d. 1870, Union Co., KY.
152. vii. DANIEL B. HAMMOCK, b. 1808, Caldwell Co., KY; d. 1877, Union Co., KY.
153. viii. JEREMIAH HAMMOCK, b. 1811, Caldwell Co., KY; d. 1865, Union Co., KY.
      ix.   ISAIAH HAMMOCK, b. 1813, Caldwell Co., KY; d. 1840, Union Co., KY.

Key Source: Revolutionary War Pension Application of William Hammock, Union Co., KY; 1810 Caldwell Co., KY, Census; 1820 Union Co., KY, Census, p. 149; 1830 Union Co., KY, Census, pp. 41-43; Henry Franklin Hammack (afterwards, HFH), 1: 160-161, 2: 225, 311.

76. CHARITY[7] HAMMOCK *(WILLIAM[6], BENEDICT[5] HAMMACK, WILLIAM "THE ELDER"[4], WILLIAM "O"[3], JOHN[2] HAMMOCKE, ? JOHN[1] HAMMOT)* was born Abt. 1763 in Amelia Co., VA, and died Aft. 31 Mar 1846 in Vermillion Co., IN. She married ABRAHAM HAMMAN Bet. 03 Mar 1783 - 1784 in Wilkes Co., GA. He was born Bet. 1753 - 1754 in New Jersey, and died 02 Mar 1844 in Vermillion Co., IN.
Children of CHARITY HAMMOCK and ABRAHAM HAMMAN are:
      i.   ANNE[8] HAMMAN, b. 08 Jun 1787, Wilkes Co., GA; m. NICHOLAS CARTER.
      ii.   RUTH HAMMAN, m. GEORGE PHENICE.
      iii. NANCY HAMMAN.
      iv.   EVE HAMMAN.
      v.   JOHN HAMMAN.
      vi.   WILLIAM HAMMAN.
      vii. JEREMIAH HAMMAN.
      viii. ABRAHAM HAMMAN.
      ix.   GEORGE HAMMAN.
      x.   ISAAC HAMMAN.
Key Source: Abraham Hamman Revolutionary War Pension Application, Vermillion Co., IL.

77. PATSY[7] HAMMACK *(BENEDICT[6] HAMMOCK II, BENEDICT[5] HAMMACK, WILLIAM "THE ELDER"[4], WILLIAM "O"[3], JOHN[2] HAMMOCKE, ? JOHN[1] HAMMOT)* was born Abt. 1758 in Amelia Co., VA, and died Aft. 1807 in Lincoln Co., GA. She married ROBERT LEVERETT Abt. 1780 in Wilkes Co., GA. He was born Bef. 1758 in Lunenburg Co., VA, and died Abt. 1807 in Lincoln Co., GA.
Children of PATSY HAMMACK and ROBERT LEVERETT are:
      i.   NANCY[8] LEVERETT, b. Abt. 1782, Wilkes Co., GA; d. Aft. 1806, Lincoln Co., GA; m. JOHN MCELROY, Bef. 1806, Lincoln Co., GA.
      ii.   PEGGY LEVERETT, b. Abt. 1784, Wilkes Co., GA; d. Aft. 1806, Lincoln Co., GA; m. [---------] HAMMACK OR HAMRICK, Bef. 1806, Lincoln Co., GA.
      iii. PATSY LEVERETT, b. 08 Jul 1787, Wilkes Co., GA; d. 30 Oct 1857, Macon Co., AL; m. TRAVIS MCKINNEY, 13 Dec 1808, Lincoln Co., GA; b. 17 Mar 1787, Georgia; d. Aft. 1850, Macon Co., AL.
      iv.   JORDAN LEVERETT, b. Abt. 1795, Lincoln Co., GA; d. Bef. 1827, Lincoln Co., GA; m. DELILAH JORDAN, 30 May 1817, Lincoln Co., GA.
      v.   POLLY LEVERETT, b. Abt. 1797, Lincoln Co., GA; d. Aft. 1819, Lincoln Co., GA; m. ZACHARIAS MCKINNEY, 25 Feb 1819, Lincoln Co., GA.
      vi.   ROBERT LEVERETT, b. Abt. 1797, Lincoln Co., GA; d. Aft. 1806, Lincoln Co., GA.
      vii. BETSEY LEVERETT, b. Abt. 1799, Lincoln Co., GA; d. Aft. 1820, Lincoln Co., GA; m. JOHN BLALOCK, 13 Jul 1820, Lincoln Co., GA.
      viii. SALLY LEVERETT, b. Abt. 1801, Lincoln Co., GA; d. Aft. 1806, Lincoln Co., GA.

ix. HARDY LEVERETT, b. Abt. 1803, Lincoln Co., GA; d. Aft. 1841, Lincoln Co., GA; m. (1) MARY A. RAMSEY, 14 Mar 1827, Lincoln Co., GA; m. (2) ELIZABETH JENNINGS, 10 Aug 1841, Lincoln Co., GA.

x. ABSALOM LEVERETT, b. Abt. 1805, Lincoln Co., GA; d. Aft. 1828, Lincoln Co., GA; m. ANN E. CAVER, 01 Jun 1828, Lincoln Co., GA.

xi. JINCY LEVERETT, b. Abt. 1805; m. GEORGE ZELLNER, 16 May 1822, Lincoln Co., GA.

Key Source: Lincoln Co., GA, Will Book A, pp. 66-70.

78. JOHN C.[7] HAMMACK *(BENEDICT[6] HAMMOCK II, BENEDICT[5] HAMMACK, WILLIAM "THE ELDER"[4], WILLIAM "O"[3], JOHN[2] HAMMOCKE, ? JOHN[1] HAMMOT)* was born Bet. 1760 - 1770 in Onslow Co., NC, and died Bef. 07 Jan 1813 in Greene Co., GA. He married (1) ANNA MCKENNEY Abt. 1791 in Wilkes Co., GA. She was born Abt. 1773 in Virginia, and died Aft. 19 Dec 1808 in Greene Co., GA. He may have married (2) CATHERINE [------] Aft. 1808 in Greene Co., GA. She died Aft. 1820 in Walton Co., GA.

Children of JOHN HAMMACK and ANNA MCKENNEY are:

154. i. BENJAMIN[8] HAMMACK, b. Abt. 1793, Wilkes Co., GA; d. Bef. 03 Nov 1845, Walton Co., GA.

155. ii. TRAVIS HAMMACK, b. Abt. 1794, Lincoln Co., GA; d. Abt. 1832, Walton Co., GA.

156. iii. JOHN M. HAMMACK, b. Bet. 1793 - 1799, Lincoln Co., GA; d. Aft. 1870, Chambers Co., AL.

iv. ANNA HAMMACK, b. Bet. 1793 - 1799, Lincoln Co., GA; d. Aft. 1814, Greene Co., GA.

v. WILLIAM HAMMACK, b. Aft. 1800, Lincoln Co., GA; d. Aft. 1816, Greene Co., GA.

vi. WINNIE HAMMACK, b. Aft. 1800, Lincoln Co., GA; d. Aft. 1816, Greene Co., GA.

vii. COLUMBUS HAMMACK, b. Bet. 1800 - 1814, Lincoln Co., GA; d. Aft. 1814, Greene Co., GA.

157. viii. ASA A. HAMMACK, b. 25 Sep 1807, Greene Co., GA; d. 14 Dec 1873, Gwinnett Co., GA.

Key Sources: Wilkes Co., GA, Deed Book OO, p. 2; Lincoln Co., GA, Will Book A, pp. 39-40; Wilkes Co., GA, Deed Book SS, p. 63; Greene Co., GA, Deed Book 1821-1824, p. 451; 1805 Georgia Land Lottery Registrants, Lincoln Co., GA; Greene Co., GA, Deed Book 4, p. 495; Greene Co., GA, Deed Book HH, p. 450; Greene Co., GA, Returns Book H, p. 71; 1820 Walton Co., GA, Census, pp. 123, 135. Caty Hammock (aged 45+) appears in the 1820 Walton Co., GA, Census with a son aged 0-10 and a son aged 16-18. I have theorized that she may have been John C. Hammack's second wife.

79. ROBERT[7] HAMMACK *(BENEDICT[6] HAMMOCK II, BENEDICT[5] HAMMACK, WILLIAM "THE ELDER"[4], WILLIAM "O"[3], JOHN[2] HAMMOCKE, ? JOHN[1] HAMMOT)* was born Bet. 1760 - 1770 in Onslow Co., NC, and died Aft. 1823 in Wilkes Co., GA. He married NANCY COMBS Abt. 1795 in Wilkes Co., GA. She was born Aft. 1775 in Fairfield District, SC, and died Bet. 1820 - 1838 in Wilkes Co., GA.

Children of ROBERT HAMMACK and NANCY COMBS are:

158. i. SEABORN[8] HAMMACK, b. Abt. 1796, Wilkes Co., GA; d. Bet. 1850 - 1860, Coweta Co., GA.

ii. WILLIAM HAMMACK, b. Abt. 1807, Wilkes Co., GA; d. Aft. 1860, Coweta Co., GA.

159. iii. MARTHA HAMMACK, b. Abt. 1793, Wilkes Co., GA; d. Aft. 1860, Coweta Co., GA.

iv. JANE HAMMACK, b. Abt. 1800, Wilkes Co., GA; d. Aft. 1860, Coweta Co., GA.

v. NANCY HAMMACK, b. Abt. 1813, Wilkes Co., GA; d. Aft. 1860, Coweta Co., GA.

Key Source: G. G. Davidson, *Early Records of Georgia, Wilkes County* (2 vols., Macon, GA, 1932), 2: 210.

80. BENJAMIN[7] HAMMACK *(BENEDICT[6] HAMMOCK II, BENEDICT[5] HAMMACK, WILLIAM "THE ELDER"[4], WILLIAM "O"[3], JOHN[2] HAMMOCKE, ? JOHN[1] HAMMOT)* was born Abt. 1773 in Wilkes Co., GA, and died Aft. 1850 in Jasper Co., GA. He married UNKNOWN Abt. 1800 in Wilkes Co., GA. She was born Bet. 1775 - 1780 in Georgia, and died Bet. 1830 - 1840 in Jasper Co., GA.

Children of BENJAMIN HAMMACK and UNKNOWN are:

160.   i.   ? THOMAS JEFFERSON[8] HAMMACK, b. Abt. 1800, Lincoln Co., GA.

       ii.   SON HAMMACK, b. Bet. 1804 - 1810, Lincoln Co., GA; d. Aft. 1830, Morgan Co., GA.

      iii.   NANCY HAMMACK, b. Abt. 1805, Lincoln Co., GA; d. Aft. 1850, Claiborne Parish, LA; m. JOHN A. MALONE, 24 Jan 1828, Claiborne Parish, LA; b. 29 Aug 1805, Wilkes Co., GA; d. 09 Mar 1887, Claiborne Parish, LA.

      iv.   SON HAMMACK, b. Bet. 1810 - 1815, Greene Co., GA; d. Aft. 1830, Morgan Co., GA.

       v.   SON HAMMACK, b. Bet. 1810 - 1815, Greene Co., GA; d. Aft. 1820, Morgan Co., GA.

      vi.   DAUGHTER HAMMACK, b. Bet. 1810 - 1820, Greene or Morgan Co., GA; d. Aft. 1820, Morgan Co., GA.

161.   vii.   JEPTHA J. HAMMACK, b. Abt. 1820, Morgan Co., GA; d. Aft. 1850, Jasper Co., GA.

Key Sources: 1801, 1805 Lincoln Co., GA, Tax Digests; 1807 Georgia Land Lottery Fortunate Draws; 1809 Greene Co., GA, Tax Digest; A. E. Wynne, Southern Lineages, pp. 100-104; 1815 Greene Co., GA, Tax Digest; 1817 Morgan Co., GA, Tax Digest; 1820 Morgan Co., GA, Census, p. 80; Morgan Co., GA, Deed Book E, p. 203; Morgan Co., GA, Deed Book F, p. 267; Greene Co., GA, Annual Returns and Divisions, 1816-1829, p. 1; Morgan Co., GA, Deed Book I, p. 448; 1830 Jasper Co., GA, Census, p. 381; 1840 Jasper Co., GA, Census, p. 73; 1850 Jasper Co., GA, Census, p. 87.

81. BENEDICT[7] HAMMACK III *(BENEDICT[6] HAMMOCK II, BENEDICT[5] HAMMACK, WILLIAM "THE ELDER"[4], WILLIAM "O"[3], JOHN[2] HAMMOCKE, ? JOHN[1] HAMMOT)* was born Bef. 1775 in Onslow Co., NC, and died Bet. 1825 - 1826 in Jones Co., GA. He married SARAH [------]. She was born Abt. 1775, and died Aft. 29 Nov 1826 in Jones Co., GA.

Children of BENEDICT HAMMACK and SARAH [------] are:

       i.   REBECCA[8] HAMMACK, b. Abt. 1795, Wilkes Co., GA; d. Aft. 1850, Harris Co., GA; m. JOEL CULPEPER, 26 Aug 1819, Jones Co., GA.

      ii.   SARAH HAMMACK, b. Abt. 1792, Wilkes Co., GA; d. Aft. 1826, Jones Co., GA; m. ? [------] LEE, Bef. 1826, Jones Co., GA.

      iii.   DAUGHTER HAMMACK, b. Abt. 1800, Wilkes Co., GA; d. Aft. 1820, Jones Co., GA.

Key Sources: Wilkes Co., GA, Deed Book RR, 1798-1805, p. 407; G. G. Davidson, *Early Records of Georgia, Wilkes County* (2 vols., Macon, GA, 1932), 1: 147, 175; 1805 and 1806 Wilkes Co., GA, Tax Digests; 1807 Georgia Land Lottery Fortunate Draws; 1811 Jones Co., GA, Tax Digest; 1820 Jones Co., GA, Census, p. 130; Jones Co., GA, Deed Book O, p. 367; Jones Co., GA, Will Book A.

82. ELIZABETH COMBS[7] HAMMACK *(BENEDICT[6] HAMMOCK II, BENEDICT[5] HAMMACK, WILLIAM "THE ELDER"[4], WILLIAM "O"[3], JOHN[2] HAMMOCKE, ? JOHN[1] HAMMOT)* was born Abt. 1778 in Wilkes Co., GA, and died Aft. 1822 in Wilkes Co., GA. She married WILLIAM EVANS Abt. 1795 in Wilkes Co., GA. He was born 23 Dec 1776 in Pittsylvania Co., VA, and died 14 Oct 1822 in Wilkes Co., GA.

Children of ELIZABETH HAMMACK and WILLIAM EVANS are:

       i.   MARTHA ANN[8] EVANS, b. Abt. 1796, Wilkes Co., GA; d. Sep 1871, Morgan Co., GA; m. JAMES CHENOWITH PETEET, 23 Mar 1815, Wilkes Co., GA; b. Abt. 1795, Wilkes Co., GA; d. 1845, Wilkes Co., GA.

      ii.   POLLY EVANS, b. 08 Feb 1798, Wilkes Co., GA; d. 04 Jul 1868, Monroe Co., MS; m. (1) CALEB MALONE, 09 Apr 1812, Wilkes Co., GA; d. Bef. 1818, Wilkes Co., GA; m. (2)

JAMES ARDEN EVANS, 08 Nov 1818, Wilkes Co., GA; b. 1800, Wilkes Co., GA; d. 1855, Monroe Co., MS.

iii. WILLIAM GILBERT EVANS, b. 1800, Wilkes Co., GA; d. 1885, Monroe Co., MS; m. ADALINE E. HEARD, 26 May 1830, Morgan Co., GA; b. 1809, Wilkes Co., GA; d. 1849, Monroe Co., MS.

iv. SUSANNAH C. EVANS, b. Bet. 1802 - 1807, Wilkes Co., GA; d. Abt. 1847, Morgan Co., GA; m. (1) JAMES CUNNINGHAM, 03 Jun 1820, Wilkes Co., GA; b. Abt. 1800, Wilkes Co., GA; d. Bef. 15 Mar 1823, Wilkes Co., GA; m. (2) JOSEPH N. EVANS, 10 Dec 1824, Wilkes Co., GA; b. Abt. 1800, Georgia; d. 1847, Clay Co., MS.

v. NANCY EVANS, b. Bet. 1805 - 1808, Wilkes Co., GA; d. Aft. 1828, Wilkes Co., GA; m. DANIEL LEE, 20 Apr 1826, Wilkes Co., GA.

vi. ELIZABETH EVANS, b. Abt. 1812, Wilkes Co., GA; d. Bet. 1888 - 1891, Wilkes Co., GA; m. JOHN SWANSON, 21 May 1829, Wilkes Co., GA.

vii. AMANDA CAROLINE EVANS, b. Bet. 1810 - 1814, Wilkes Co., GA; d. Aft. 1831, Morgan Co., GA; m. JAMES L. HORN, 05 Jan 1831, Morgan Co., GA.

viii. EMILY EVANS, b. Abt. 1816, Wilkes Co., GA; d. Abt. 1822, Wilkes Co., GA.

Key Source: Wynne, *Southern Lineages*, pp. 1-32, 100-106.

83. JOHN[7] HAMMOCK (*JOHN[6], BENEDICT[5] HAMMACK, WILLIAM "THE ELDER"[4], WILLIAM "O"[3], JOHN[2] HAMMOCKE, ? JOHN[1] HAMMOT*) was born Abt. 1760 in Amelia Co., VA, and died Aft. 1819 in Monroe Co., AL.
Child of JOHN HAMMOCK is:

i. ? JOHN[8] HAMMOCK, b. Abt. 1805, Georgia; d. Aft. 1860, Escambia Co., FL.

Key Sources: 1796, 1799, 1802, 1804, and 1810 Jefferson Co., GA, Tax Digests; M. D. Hahn, Old Cahaba Land Office Records & Military Warrants, 1817-1853 (Easley, SC, 1981), pp. 29, 81; M. D. Hahn, Old Sparta & Elba Land Office Records, Military Warrants, 1822-1860 (Easley, SC, 1983), pp. 21, 27, 31, 65. I have speculated that this John Hammock was the father of John Hammock of Escambia Co., FL, based on location and nomenclature.

84. SAMUEL[7] HAMMOCK (*JOHN[6], BENEDICT[5] HAMMACK, WILLIAM "THE ELDER"[4], WILLIAM "O"[3], JOHN[2] HAMMOCKE, ? JOHN[1] HAMMOT*) was born Bet. 1760 - 1764 in Amelia Co., VA, and died Aft. 1825 in Laurens Co., GA. He married UNKNOWN Bet. 1780 - 1790 in North Carolina.
Children of SAMUEL HAMMOCK and UNKNOWN are:

i. ? SARAH[8] HAMMOCK, b. Abt. 1790, NC or GA; m. BRITTAIN SANFORD, 05 Aug 1812, Laurens Co., GA.

162. ii. ? JOHN HAMMOCK, b. Abt. 1796, Jefferson Co., GA; d. Bef. 1820, Jefferson Co., GA.

iii. ? REDDICK P. HAMMOCK, b. Abt. 1800, Jefferson Co., GA; d. Bet. 1843 - 1850, Laurens Co., GA; m. SARAH [------].

163. iv. ? JACKSON HAMMOCK, b. Abt. 1800, Jefferson Co., GA; d. Aft. 1850, Benton Co., FL.

164. v. ? GEORGE HAMMOCK, b. Abt. 1818, Georgia; d. Aft. 1860, Madison Co., FL.

Key Sources: Edgecombe Co., NC, Deed Bok 4, p. 363; Edgecombe Co., NC, Court Minutes, 1775-1785, p. 349; Daughters of the American Revolution, *Roster of Soldiers from North Carolina in the American Revolution* (Baltimore, MD, 1984); 1799, 1802, and 1805 Jefferson Co., GA, Tax Digests; 1807 Georgia Land Lottery Fortunate Draws; A. Thomas, Thomas, *Laurens Co., GA, Legal Records, 1807-1857* (2 vols., Roswell, GA, 1991), 1: 340-341. I have speculated that Samuel was the father of these individuals who appear in Laurens Co., GA, in the period from 1820 to 1850. Many researchers identify Jackson and George Hammack as sons of Paschall Hammack, son of John Hammack of Lincoln County, but I am unaware of any documented evidence that links them to Paschall. I have assigned them to Samuel based on age, location, and nomenclature. It appears that this group of Hammacks moved from Granville Co.,

NC, to Jefferson and Laurens Counties, GA, to Monroe and Conecuh Counties, AL, and various counties in northern Florida.

85. JESSE[7] HAMMOCK *(JOHN[6], BENEDICT[5] HAMMACK, WILLIAM "THE ELDER"[4], WILLIAM "O"[3], JOHN[2] HAMMOCKE, ? JOHN[1] HAMMOT)* was born Bef. 1775 in Edgecombe Co., NC, and died Aft. 1820 in Tennessee or Alabama. He married ELIZABETH [------] Abt. 1798 in Jefferson Co., GA. She was born Bet. 1780 - 1790 in Georgia, and died Aft. 1840 in Conecuh Co., AL.
Children of JESSE HAMMOCK and ELIZABETH [------] are:

	i.	DAUGHTER[8] HAMMOCK, b. Abt. 1802, Jefferson Co., GA.
	ii.	? WILLOUGHBY HAMMOCK, b. Abt. 1805, Jefferson Co., GA; d. Aft. 1860, Kentucky.
165.	iii.	? JOSHUA S. HAMMAC, b. 25 Sep 1805, Jefferson Co., GA; d. 05 Dec 1890, Escambia Co., FL.
	iv.	? MARY HAMMAC, b. Bet. 1804 - 1810, Jefferson Co., GA; m. (1) ELI KENT; d. Aft. 1830, Clay Co., GA; m. (2) NATHAN TOWNSEND; d. Aft. 1830, Santa Rosa Co., FL.
166.	v.	? ROBERT HAMMAC, b. Abt. 1810, Georgia; d. Bet. 1840 - 1850, Conecuh Co., AL.
167.	vi.	? GEORGE W. HAMMAC, b. Abt. 1812, Tennessee; d. Aft. 1860, Conecuh Co., AL.
	vii.	SON HAMMOCK, b. Bet. 1810 - 1820, Tennessee or Alabama; d. Aft. 1840, Conecuh Co., AL.
	viii.	DAUGHTER HAMMOCK, b. Bet. 1810 - 1820, Tennessee; d. Aft. 1820, Bedford Co., TN.
	ix.	DAUGHTER HAMMOCK, b. Bet. 1810 - 1820, Tennessee; d. Aft. 1820, Bedford Co., TN.
	x.	DAUGHTER HAMMOCK, b. Bet. 1810 - 1820, Tennessee; d. Aft. 1820, Bedford Co., TN.
	xi.	SON HAMMOCK, b. Abt. 1828, Alabama; d. Aft. 1840, Conecuh Co., AL.

Key Sources: 1799, 1802, and 1805 Jefferson Co., GA, Tax Digests; 1807 Georgia Land Lottery Fortunate Draws; 1820 Bedford Co., TN, Census; 1830 Monroe Co., AL, Census, 1840 Conecuh Co., AL, Census, p. 262, 263, 267. This family group needs more research. Jesse Hammack was part of the group who moved from Granville Co., NC, to Laurens and Jefferson Counties, GA, and then to Monroe and Conecuh Counties, AL, with families such as the Godwins, with whom they intermarried. Given later census records that place South Alabama Hammacs and Hammacks with births in Tennessee, I have speculated that Jesse Hammack moved from Jefferson Co., GA, to Bedford Co., TN, before his family settled in Alabama. These relationships are speculative and not proven. More research is needed. See previous note.

86. EMANUEL[7] HAMMOCK *(JOHN[6], BENEDICT[5] HAMMACK, WILLIAM "THE ELDER"[4], WILLIAM "O"[3], JOHN[2] HAMMOCKE, ? JOHN[1] HAMMOT)* was born Bet. 1780 - 1783 in Edgecombe Co., NC, and died Bet. 1850 - 1860 in Tattnall Co., GA. He married ZILPHA [------] Abt. 1804 in Jefferson Co., GA. She was born Abt. 1780 in North Carolina, and died Aft. 1860 in Tattnall Co., GA.
Children of EMANUEL HAMMOCK and ZILPHA [------] are:

	i.	DAUGHTER[8] HAMMOCK, b. Abt. 1806, Jefferson Co., GA; d. Aft. 1820, Tattnall Co., GA.
168.	ii.	LITTLETON HAMMOCK, b. 03 Feb 1808, Jefferson Co., GA; d. 16 May 1877, Tattnall Co., GA.
	iii.	DAUGHTER HAMMOCK, b. Abt. 1810, Jefferson Co., GA; d. Aft. 1820, Tattnall Co., GA.
	iv.	DAUGHTER HAMMOCK, b. Abt. 1812, Jefferson Co., GA; d. Aft. 1820, Tattnall Co., GA.
	v.	ELIZA HAMMOCK, b. Abt. 1814, Jefferson Co., GA; d. Aft. 1850, Tattnall Co., GA.
	vi.	KIZZIAH HAMMOCK, b. 1816, Jefferson Co., GA; d. 11 Jun 1869, Tattnall Co., GA.
169.	vii.	MOSES HAMMOCK, b. Abt. 1818, Tattnall Co., GA; d. Aft. 1870, Tattnall Co., GA.
	viii.	ELIZABETH HAMMOCK, b. Abt. 1822, Tattnall Co., GA; d. Aft. 1850, Tattnall Co., GA.
170.	ix.	JOHN E. HAMMOCK, b. Apr 1824, Jefferson Co., GA; d. 1912, Tattnall Co., GA.

    x.   NANCY ANN HAMMOCK, b. 25 Apr 1825, Tattnall Co., GA; d. 06 Sep 1906, Tattnall Co., GA; m. SILAS TOOTLE, Bef. 1848, Tattnall Co., GA; b. 28 Jan 1810, Georgia; d. 04 Nov 1877, Tattnall Co., GA.

   xi.   SON HAMMOCK, b. Abt. 1827, Tattnall Co., GA; d. Aft. 1840, Tattnall Co., GA.

  xii.   SARAH HAMMOCK, b. Abt. 1827, Tallapoosa Co., AL; d. Aft. 1850, Tattnall Co., GA.

 xiii.   CAROLINE HAMMOCK, b. Abt. 1830, Tattnall Co., GA; d. Aft. 1850, Tattnall Co., GA.

Key Sources: 1804, 1810, 1812, 1814, and 1816 Jefferson Co., GA, Tax Digests; 1807 Georgia Land Lottery Fortunate Draws; 1817 Tattnall Co., GA, Tax Digest; 1820 Tattnall Co., GA, Census, p. 117; 1830 Tattnall Co., GA, Census, p. 376; 1840 Tattnall Co., GA, Census, pp. 266, 272; 1850 Tattnall Co., GA, Census, p. 365; 1860 Tattnall Co., GA, Census, pp. 571, 768, 769.

87. JOHN[7] COMBS *(ABIGAIL[6] HAMMOCK, BENEDICT[5] HAMMACK, WILLIAM "THE ELDER"[4], WILLIAM "O"[3], JOHN[2] HAMMOCKE, ? JOHN[1] HAMMOT)* was born 07 Sep 1764 in Amelia Co., VA, and died Bet. 1849 - 1850 in Cobb Co., GA. He married (1) HANNAH [------] Bef. 09 Apr 1790 in Wilkes Co., GA. She died Bet. 1790 - 1797 in Wilkes Co., GA. He married (2) MILDRED RUSSELL Bef. 04 Sep 1797 in Wilkes Co., GA. She was born Bef. 1777, and died Aft. 1816 in Wilkes Co., GA.

Children of JOHN COMBS and HANNAH [------] are:

    i.   PHILLIP[8] COMBS, b. Bet. 1789 - 1790, Wilkes Co., GA; d. Aft. 1850, Cobb Co., GA; m. (1) LUCY SMALLWOOD, 10 Sep 1815, Wilkes Co., GA; m. (2) SUSANNAH WALKER MOORE, 11 Jul 1832, Wilkes Co., GA; b. Abt. 1799, Virginia; d. Aft. 1850, Cobb Co., GA.

171.   ii.   JOHN COMBS, b. Abt. 1791, Wilkes Co., GA; d. Bet. 1825 - 1830, Wilkes Co., GA.

   iii.   SON COMBS, b. Abt. 1792, Wilkes Co., GA.

   iv.   ? WILLIAM COMBS, b. 29 Jul 1794, Wilkes Co., GA; d. 1868, Chambers Co., AL; m. SARAH EVANS SLAYDEN, 24 Oct 1823, Wilkes Co., GA; b. 1793, Wilkes Co., GA; d. 1868, Chambers Co., AL.

Children of JOHN COMBS and MILDRED RUSSELL are:

    v.   DAUGHTER[8] COMBS, b. Abt. 1800, Wilkes Co., GA; d. Aft. 1820, Wilkes Co., GA.

   vi.   ? ZACHARIAH COMBS, b. Abt. 1801, Wilkes Co., GA; d. Bef. 1831, Wilkes Co., GA; m. MARY ROSE, 19 Dec 1819, Wilkes Co., GA.

  vii.   DAUGHTER COMBS, b. Bet. 1804 - 1810, Wilkes Co., GA; d. Aft. 1820, Wilkes Co., GA.

 viii.   SON COMBS, b. Bet. 1810 - 1820, Wilkes Co., GA; d. Aft. 1820, Wilkes Co., GA.

   ix.   SON COMBS, b. Bet. 1810 - 1820, Wilkes Co., GA; d. Aft. 1820, Wilkes Co., GA.

Key Sources: Wilkes Co., GA, Deed Book NN, p. 75; Wilkes Co., GA, Deed Book QQ, p. 528; Wilkes Co., GA, Deed Book, OO, p. 11; Wilkes Co., GA, Deed Book RR, p. 121; S. E. Lucas, *Some Georgia County Records* (9 vols., Easley, SC, 1977 -), 2: 231, 313-314; 1820 Wilkes Co., GA, Census, p. 189; 1830 Wilkes Co., GA, Census, GMD 175; 1840 Wilkes Co., GA, Census, p. 251; Revolutionary War Pension Application of John Combs, Wilkes Co., GA. The names of the offspring of John Combs are speculative and are based on a study of Combs families in Wilkes County between 1800 and 1850. Philip Combs is specifically identified as a son of John in his registration for the 1820 Georgia Land Lottery.

88. STERLING[7] COMBS *(ABIGAIL[6] HAMMOCK, BENEDICT[5] HAMMACK, WILLIAM "THE ELDER"[4], WILLIAM "O"[3], JOHN[2] HAMMOCKE, ? JOHN[1] HAMMOT)* was born Bet. 1768 - 1769 in Amelia Co., VA, and died 15 Jun 1847 in Richmond Co., GA. He married (1) MARY MCKINNEY Abt. 06 Jan 1792 in Wilkes Co., GA. She died Abt. 1806 in Wilkes Co., GA. He married (2) MILDRED WINGFIELD SIMS Bef. 04 Mar 1806 in Wilkes Co., GA. She was born Bef. 1775 in Virginia, and died Abt. 1839 in Jackson Co., GA.

Children of STERLING COMBS and MARY MCKINNEY are:

    i.   MARY[8] COMBS, b. Abt. 1798, Wilkes Co., GA; m. JOHN WESLEY PENTECOST, 1818, Jackson Co., GA.

  ii. NANCY COMBS, b. Abt. 1800, Wilkes Co., GA.

Children of STERLING COMBS and MILDRED SIMS are:
  iii. SARAH GARLAND[8] COMBS, b. 06 Jun 1811, Jackson Co., GA; d. 04 Mar 1876, Richmond Co., GA; m. DR. JOSEPH A. EVE.
  iv. ? ELIZABETH TERRELL COMBS, b. Abt. 1809, Wilkes Co., GA; d. Aft. 1820, Jackson Co., GA.
  v. ? GEORGE B. COMBS, b. Abt. 1813, Jackson Co., GA; d. Aft. 1820, Jackson Co., GA.
  vi. ? STERLING THOMAS COMBS, b. Abt. 1807, Wilkes Co., GA; d. Aft. 1820, Jackson Co., GA.
  vii. ? SUSAN COMBS, b. 1810, Wilkes Co., GA; d. 1810, Wilkes Co., GA.
  viii. ? MILDRED COMBS, b. 1812, Wilkes Co., GA; d. 1812, Wilkes Co., GA.
  ix. ? SUSAN COMBS, b. 1816, Wilkes Co., GA.
  x. ? FRANCIS COMBS, b. 1818, Jackson Co., GA.
  xi. ? MILDRED COMBS, b. 1819, Jackson Co., GA.

Key Sources: Wilkes Co., GA, Deed Book RR, p. 530; Wilkes Co., GA, Deed Book TT, p. 121; Wilkes Co., GA, Deed Book SS, p. 149; Wilkes Co., GA, Deed Book RR, p. 515; G. G. Davidson, Early Records of Georgia, Wilkes County (2 vols., Macon, GA, 1932), 1: 150, 172; 1820 Jackson Co., GA, Census, p. 239; Obituary of Sarah Combs Garland Eve, *Southern Christian Advocate*, 4 March 1876.

89. JAMES[7] COMBS (*ABIGAIL[6] HAMMOCK, BENEDICT[5] HAMMACK, WILLIAM "THE ELDER"[4], WILLIAM "O"[3], JOHN[2] HAMMOCKE, ? JOHN[1] HAMMOT*) was born Abt. 1770 in Lunenburg Co., VA, and died Bet. 1817 - 1818 in Wilkes Co., GA. He married PAMELIA "MILLY" [------] Abt. 1795 in Wilkes Co., GA. She was born Bet. 1770 - 1775 in Georgia, and died Abt. 1843 in Putnam Co., GA.
Children of JAMES COMBS and PAMELIA [------] are:
  i. THOMAS R.[8] COMBS, b. Abt. 1796, Wilkes Co., GA; d. Bef. 1832, Wilkes Co., GA; m. MRS. MARGARET EUDAILY, 06 May 1828, Wilkes Co., GA.
  ii. FRANCIS COMBS, b. Aft. 1796, Wilkes Co., GA; d. Aft. 1817, Wilkes Co., GA.
  iii. JAMES COMBS, b. Aft. 1796, Wilkes Co., GA; d. Aft. 1817, Wilkes Co., GA.
  iv. WILLIAM COMBS, b. Aft. 1796, Wilkes Co., GA; d. Aft. 1817, Wilkes Co., GA.
  v. JOHN COMBS, b. Bet. 1798 - 1800, Wilkes Co., GA; d. Aft. 1819, Wilkes Co., GA.
  vi. JANE COMBS, b. Abt. 1799, Wilkes Co., GA; d. Aft. 1819, Wilkes Co., GA; m. ANDERSON BATES, 04 Jul 1819, Wilkes Co., GA.
  vii. MARY ANN COMBS, b. Abt. 1802, Wilkes Co., GA; d. Aft. 1823, Wilkes Co., GA; m. ? THOMAS MARLER, 27 Nov 1823, Wilkes Co., GA.

Key Sources: G. G. Davidson, *Early Records of Georgia, Wilkes County* (2 vols., Macon, GA, 1932), 1: 93, 210, 243, 303, 332, and 2: 326, 347; 1820 Wilkes Co., GA, Census, p. 182; Wilkes Co., GA, Deed Book GGG, p. 176.

90. PHILLIP[7] COMBS (*ABIGAIL[6] HAMMOCK, BENEDICT[5] HAMMACK, WILLIAM "THE ELDER"[4], WILLIAM "O"[3], JOHN[2] HAMMOCKE, ? JOHN[1] HAMMOT*) was born Abt. 1771 in Lunenburg Co., VA, and died Aft. 1830 in Wilkes Co., GA. He married ELIZABETH EIDSON Abt. 1796 in Wilkes Co., GA, daughter of THOMAS EIDSON. She was born Abt. 1778 in Georgia, and died Bet. 1850 - 1860 in Wilkes Co., GA.
Children of PHILLIP COMBS and ELIZABETH EIDSON are:
  i. ? SARAH[8] COMBS, b. Abt. 1800, Wilkes Co., GA; d. Aft. 1860, Wilkes Co., GA; m. [------] MARLER.
  ii. DAUGHTER COMBS, b. Abt. 1802, Wilkes Co., GA; d. Aft. 1830, Wilkes Co., GA.
  iii. JEREMIAH R. COMBS, b. Abt. 1806, Wilkes Co., GA; d. Aft. 1864, Wilkes Co., GA.

iv. DAUGHTER COMBS, b. Abt. 1808, Wilkes Co., GA; d. Aft. 1830, Wilkes Co., GA.

v. REV. PHILLIP FOWLER COMBS, b. Abt. 1810, Wilkes Co., GA; d. 11 Jun 1895, Wilkes Co., GA; m. SARAH ANN GARRARD, 13 Sep 1832, Wilkes Co., GA; b. 10 Apr 1813, Wilkes Co., GA; d. 02 Mar 1892, Wilkes Co., GA.

vi. DAUGHTER COMBS, b. Abt. 1812, Wilkes Co., GA; d. Aft. 1820, Wilkes Co., GA.

vii. DAUGHTER COMBS, b. Abt. 1814, Wilkes Co., GA; d. Aft. 1820, Wilkes Co., GA.

viii. SON COMBS, b. Abt. 1816, Wilkes Co., GA; d. Aft. 1820, Wilkes Co., GA.

ix. DAUGHTER COMBS, b. Abt. 1818, Wilkes Co., GA; d. Aft. 1820, Wilkes Co., GA.

x. NANCY COMBS, b. Abt. 1827, Wilkes Co., GA; d. Aft. 1860, Wilkes Co., GA.

Key Sources: Wilkes Co., GA, Deed Book YY, p. 367; 1820 Wilkes Co., GA, Census, p. 186, 190, 194; 1830 Wilkes Co., GA, Census; 1840 Wilkes Co., GA, Census, p. 264; Sarah Quinn Smith, *Early Georgia Wills and Settlements of Estates: Wilkes County* (Washington, GA, 1959), p. 33; 1850 Wilkes Co., GA, Census, HH 86/86, 87/87, 309/309, 310/310; 1860 Wilkes Co., GA, Census, HH 311/311.

91. MARTHA[7] COMBS *(ABIGAIL[6] HAMMOCK, BENEDICT[5] HAMMACK, WILLIAM "THE ELDER"[4], WILLIAM "O"[3], JOHN[2] HAMMOCKE, ? JOHN[1] HAMMOT)* was born Bef. 1775 in Lunenburg Co., VA, and died Aft. 1838 in Georgia. She married ROBERT JACKSON Abt. 1800 in Wilkes Co., GA. He was born Abt. 1770 in Virginia, and died Aft. 1815 in Wilkes Co., GA.
Child of MARTHA COMBS and ROBERT JACKSON is:
i. DANIEL C.[8] JACKSON.
Key Source: G. G. Davidson, *Early Records of Georgia, Wilkes County* (2 vols., Macon, GA, 1932), 2: 210.

92. ENOCH[7] COMBS *(ABIGAIL[6] HAMMOCK, BENEDICT[5] HAMMACK, WILLIAM "THE ELDER"[4], WILLIAM "O"[3], JOHN[2] HAMMOCKE, ? JOHN[1] HAMMOT)* was born 03 Feb 1782 in Wilkes Co., GA, and died Aft. 1822 in Wilkes Co., GA. He married UNKNOWN Abt. 1804 in Wilkes Co., GA. She was born Bet. 1780 - 1790 in Wilkes Co., GA, and died Aft. 1830 in Wilkes Co., GA.
Children of ENOCH COMBS and UNKNOWN are:
i. DAUGHTER[8] COMBS, b. Abt. 1800, Wilkes Co., GA; d. Aft. 1820, Wilkes Co., GA.

ii. DAUGHTER COMBS, b. Abt. 1802, Wilkes Co., GA; d. Aft. 1820, Wilkes Co., GA.

iii. DAUGHTER COMBS, b. Abt. 1807, Wilkes Co., GA; d. Aft. 1830, Wilkes Co., GA.

iv. DAUGHTER COMBS, b. Abt. 1806, Wilkes Co., GA; d. Aft. 1830, Wilkes Co., GA.

v. DAUGHTER COMBS, b. Abt. 1808, Wilkes Co., GA; d. Aft. 1830, Wilkes Co., GA.

vi. SON COMBS, b. Abt. 1804, Wilkes Co., GA; d. Aft. 1820, Wilkes Co., GA.

vii. SON COMBS, b. Abt. 1810, Wilkes Co., GA; d. Aft. 1820, Wilkes Co., GA.

viii. ABIGAIL COMBS, b. Abt. 1820, Wilkes Co., GA; d. Aft. 1831, Wilkes Co., GA.

ix. SON COMBS, b. Bet. 1825 - 1830, Wilkes Co., GA; d. Aft. 1830, Wilkes Co., GA.

Key Sources: 1820 Wilkes Co., GA, Census, p. 190; 1830 Wilkes Co., GA, Census; Wilkes Co., GA, Deed Book YY, p. 367; Wilkes Co., GA, Deed Book KKK, p. 39; 1831 Wilkes Co., GA, Poor School List.

93. THOMAS[7] COMBS *(ABIGAIL[6] HAMMOCK, BENEDICT[5] HAMMACK, WILLIAM "THE ELDER"[4], WILLIAM "O"[3], JOHN[2] HAMMOCKE, ? JOHN[1] HAMMOT)* was born Bet. 1787 - 1790 in Wilkes Co., GA, and died Bef. 1832 in Wilkes Co., GA. He married (1) JUDY JOHNSON 26 Jun 1808 in Wilkes Co., GA. She was born Abt. 1790 in Wilkes Co., GA, and died Bef. 04 Mar 1816 in Wilkes Co., GA. He married (2) MARY JOHNSON 04 Mar 1816 in Wilkes Co., GA. She was born Abt. 1790 in Georgia, and died Aft. 1850 in Wilkes Co., GA.
Children of THOMAS COMBS and JUDY JOHNSON are:
i. DAUGHTER[8] COMBS, b. Abt. 1810, Wilkes Co., GA; d. Aft. 1820, Wilkes Co., GA.

    ii. DAUGHTER COMBS, b. Abt. 1812, Wilkes Co., GA; d. Aft. 1830, Wilkes Co., GA.

    iii. SON COMBS, b. Abt. 1814, Wilkes Co., GA; d. Aft. 1830, Wilkes Co., GA.

Child of THOMAS COMBS and MARY JOHNSON is:

    iv. ELIZABETH[8] COMBS, b. Abt. 1822, Wilkes Co., GA; d. 1912, Sumter Co., AL; m. WILLIS R. DORROUGH, 1836, Oglethorpe Co., GA; b. Abt. 1812, Georgia; d. Aft. 1850, Wilkes Co., GA.

Key Sources: 1812 Wilkes Co., GA, Militia Roster; 1820 Wilkes Co., GA, Census, p. 189; 1830 Wilkes Co., GA, Census; G. G. Davidson, *Early Records of Georgia, Wilkes County* (2 vols., Macon, GA, 1932), 1: 352-353; 1850 Wilkes Co., GA, Census, HH 213/213.

94. LEWIS[7] HAMMACK *(ROBERT HAMMACK[6] JR., ROBERT HAMMACK[5] SR., WILLIAM "THE ELDER"[4] HAMMACK, WILLIAM "O"[3], JOHN[2] HAMMOCKE, ? JOHN[1] HAMMOT)* was born Bet. 1765 - 1766 in Amelia Co., VA, and died Abt. 1845 in Jones County, GA. He married (1) ELIZABETH (RAY?) Abt. 1792 in Wilkes Co., GA. She was born Bet. 1774 - 1780 in Georgia, and died Bet. 1840 - 1841 in Jones Co., GA. He married (2) NANCY MILLER 30 Dec 1841 in Jones Co., GA.

Children of LEWIS HAMMACK and ELIZABETH (RAY?) are:

172.   i. JACOB[8] HAMMACK, b. Abt. 1797, Wilkes Co., GA; d. Aft. 1850, Perry Co., AL.

173.   ii. MILLY HAMMACK, b. Abt. 1792, Wilkes Co., GA; d. Aft. 1870, Upson Co., GA.

    iii. CHRISTIANNA HAMMACK, b. 01 Nov 1794, Wilkes Co., GA; d. 20 Mar 1868, Jones Co., GA; m. (1) SAMUEL M. MOORE; b. Abt. 1800, Lunenburg Co., VA; d. Abt. 1831, Jones Co., GA; m. (2) BEAUFORD STALLSWORTH, 31 Jul 1834, Jones Co., GA; b. 10 Jan 1810, South Carolina; d. 20 Jun 1868, Jones Co., GA.

174.   iv. JOHN M. HAMMACK, b. Bet. 1800 - 1802, Wilkes Co., GA; d. Bet. 1844 - 1846, Jones Co., GA.

175.   v. MARY HAMMACK, b. Abt. 1808, Wilkes Co., GA; d. Aft. 1850, Crawford Co., GA.

Key Sources: 1790-1811 Wilkes Co., GA, Tax Digests; Jones Co., GA, Deed Book F, p. 15; 1820 Jones Co., GA, Census; 1830 Jones Co., GA, Census; 1840 Jones Co., GA, Census; 1825-1844 Jones Co., GA, Tax Digests; Jones Co., GA, Deed Book O, p. 43; Jones Co., GA, Deed Book P, p. 254; Jones Co., GA, Annual Returns, 1842-1847, pp. 461, 493, 527; Jones Co., GA, Annual Returns, 1847-1850, pp. 32, 129.

95. ROBERT[7] HAMMACK *(ROBERT HAMMACK[6] JR., ROBERT HAMMACK[5] SR., WILLIAM "THE ELDER"[4] HAMMACK, WILLIAM "O"[3], JOHN[2] HAMMOCKE, ? JOHN[1] HAMMOT)* was born Bet. 1766 - 1767 in Amelia Co., VA, and died 1862 in Warren County, GA. He married NANCY [------] Abt. 1790 in Wilkes Co., GA. She was born Bet. 1766 - 1770 in Georgia, and died Aft. 1840 in Taliaferro Co., GA.

Children of ROBERT HAMMACK and NANCY [------] are:

176.   i. JOHN[8] HAMMACK, b. 1792, Georgia; d. 1872, Taliaferro Co., GA.

177.   ii. MARTHA HAMMACK, b. 1794, Wilkes Co., GA; d. Aft. 1894, Greene Co., GA.

    iii. DAUGHTER HAMMACK, b. Bef. 1794, Wilkes Co., GA; d. Aft. 1820, Warren Co., GA.

    iv. SARAH HAMMACK, b. 1796, Wilkes Co., GA; d. Aft. 1823, Warren Co., GA; m. RICHARD RHODES, 07 Feb 1823, Warren Co., GA.

178.   v. GUSTAVUS STARLING HAMMACK, b. 1811, Wilkes Co., GA; d. Abt. 1895, Warren Co., GA.

    vi. DR. T. B. HAMMACK, b. Bef. 1811, Wilkes Co., GA; d. Aft. 1838, Taliaferro Co., GA.

Key Sources: Wynne, *Southern Lineages*, pp. 96-106; 1790, 1793 Wilkes Co., GA, Tax Digests; 1820 Warren Co., GA, Census; 1830 Taliaferro Co., GA, Census, p. 360; 1834-1836 Taliaferro Co., GA, Tax Digests; Taliaferro Co., GA, Deed Book 1, p. 197; 1840 Taliaferro Co., GA, Census, p. 247; 1850 Warren Co., GA, Census, p. 148; 1860 Warren Co., GA, Census, p. 19.

96. JOSHUA[7] HAMMACK *(ROBERT HAMMACK[6] JR., ROBERT HAMMACK[5] SR., WILLIAM "THE ELDER"[4] HAMMACK, WILLIAM "O"[3], JOHN[2] HAMMOCKE, ? JOHN[1] HAMMOT)* was born Bet. 1769 - 1770 in Amelia Co., VA, and died Aft. 1864 in Newton Co., GA. He married UNKNOWN Abt. 1790 in Wilkes Co., GA. She was born Bet. 1770 - 1780 in Georgia, and died Bet. 1840 - 1850 in Newton Co., GA.

Children of JOSHUA HAMMACK and UNKNOWN are:

      i.   ? RANEY[8] HAMMACK, b. Abt. 1791, Wilkes Co., GA; d. Aft. 1808, Clarke Co., GA; m. JAMES BRYANT, 01 Jan 1805, Clarke Co., GA.

179.   ii.   JESSE HAMMOCK, b. Abt. 1793, Wilkes Co., GA; d. Aft. 1849, Cobb Co., GA.

180.   iii.   JOSHUA HAMMOCK, b. Abt. 1798, Wilkes Co., GA; d. Aft. 1870, Carroll Co., GA.

181.   iv.   JOHN HAMMOCK, b. Abt. 1801, Hancock Co., GA; d. Bet. 1880 - 1883, Newton Co., GA.

182.   v.   SUSANNAH HAMMOCK, b. Abt. 1806, Clarke Co., GA; d. Aft. 1850, Newton Co., GA.

Key Sources: 1793 Wilkes Co., GA, Tax Digest; Hancock Co., GA, Deed Book E, p. 184; Clarke Co., GA, Deed Book C, p. 253; 1804-1818 Clarke Co., GA, Tax Digests; 1820 Walton Co., GA, Census, p. 518; 1830 Newton Co., GA, Census, pp. 17, 41-42; Newton Co., GA, Deed Book D, p. 117; 1840 Newton Co., GA, Census, pp. 14, 29, 44; 1850 Newton Co., GA, Census, p. 433; 1860 Newton Co., GA, Census, p. 509.

97. JOHN[7] HAMMACK *(ROBERT HAMMACK[6] JR., ROBERT HAMMACK[5] SR., WILLIAM "THE ELDER"[4] HAMMACK, WILLIAM "O"[3], JOHN[2] HAMMOCKE, ? JOHN[1] HAMMOT)* was born Bet. 1771 - 1772 in Amelia Co., VA, and died Bet. Aug - Sep 1843 in Talbot Co., GA. He married RACHEL [-----] Abt. 1790 in Wilkes Co., GA. She was born Abt. 1767 in Pennsylvania, and died Aft. 1850 in Talbot Co., GA.

Children of JOHN HAMMACK and RACHEL [------] are:

183.   i.   ROBERT BERRY[8] HAMMACK, b. Abt. 1794, Wilkes Co., GA; d. Aft. 1850, Carroll Co., GA.

184.   ii.   WILLIAM B. HAMMACK, b. Abt. 1795, Wilkes Co., GA; d. May 1848, Talbot Co., GA.

     iii.   MARY HAMMACK, b. Abt. 1797, Wilkes Co., GA; m. LEMUEL POSEY.

185.   iv.   REBECCA HAMMACK, b. 20 Aug 1799, Wilkes Co., GA; d. 12 Aug 1883, Talbot Co., GA.

186.   v.   JOHN P. HAMMACK, b. Abt. 1800, Wilkes Co., GA; d. Aft. 1850, Tallapoosa Co., AL.

187.   vi.   JACKSON HAMMACK, b. 01 Jul 1801, Hancock Co., GA; d. 03 Dec 1883, Chambers Co., AL.

188.   vii.   ELIZABETH HAMMACK, b. Abt. 1803, Hancock Co., GA; d. 27 Aug 1895, Hunt Co., TX.

189. viii.   LEWIS W. HAMMACK, b. Abt. 1805, Hancock Co., GA; d. Aft. 1870, Muscogee Co., GA.

190.   ix.   HOPE HULL HAMMACK, b. Abt. 1806, Hancock Co., GA; d. Aft. 1870, Talbot Co., GA.

191.   x.   NANCY HAMMACK, b. Abt. 1806, Hancock Co., GA; d. Aft. 1850, Schley Co., GA.

Key Sources: Jones Co., GA, Deed Book B, p. 470; Jones Co., GA, Deed Book C, p. 106; Jones Co., GA, Deed Book B, p. 326; 1811, 1813-1814, 1825 Jones Co., GA, Tax Digests; 1820 Jones Co., GA, Census; 1830 Talbot Co., GA, Census, pp. 334-336; 1840 Talbot Co., GA, Census, pp. 223-224, 226, 229; Talbot Co., GA, Will Book A, pp. 135-138.

98. NANCY (ANNA)[7] HAMMACK *(ROBERT HAMMACK[6] JR., ROBERT HAMMACK[5] SR., WILLIAM "THE ELDER"[4] HAMMACK, WILLIAM "O"[3], JOHN[2] HAMMOCKE, ? JOHN[1] HAMMOT)* was born Abt. 1773 in Wilkes Co., GA, and died Aft. 1850 in Taliaferro Co., GA. She married JACOB RAY Bet. 1790 - 1792 in Wilkes Co., GA, son of SANDERS RAY and CHRISTIANNA [------]. He was born Abt. 1770 in Lunenburg Co., VA, and died Abt. 1847 in Taliaferro Co., GA.

Children of NANCY HAMMACK and JACOB RAY are:

192.   i.   MARY[8] RAY, b. Abt. 1792, Georgia; d. Aft. 1850, Jones Co., GA.

     ii. ELIZABETH RAY, b. Abt. 1794, Wilkes Co., GA; d. Aft. 1850, Pike Co., GA; m. MARTIN PITTS, 22 Dec 1812, Wilkes Co., GA; d. 1843, Pike Co., GA.

     iii. SON RAY, b. Bet. 1794 - 1804, Wilkes Co., GA; d. Aft. 1820, Wilkes Co., GA.

193.   iv. MARTHA RAY, b. Abt. 1796, Wilkes Co., GA; d. Abt. 15 Mar 1866, Jones Co., GA.

     v. ? LUSANAH RAY, b. Abt. 1801, Wilkes Co., GA; d. Aft. 1850, Taliaferro Co., GA; m. THOMAS TROUTON, 21 Mar 1821, Wilkes Co., GA; b. Abt. 1795, Ireland; d. Aft. 1860, Coweta Co., GA.

194.   vi. JANE RAY, b. Abt. 1802, Wilkes Co., GA; d. Aft. 1850, Taliaferro Co., GA.

     vii. LUCY RAY, b. Abt. 1808, Wilkes Co., GA; d. Bet. 1826 - 1836, Taliaferro Co., GA; m. CHESLEY RAY, 26 Dec 1826, Taliaferro Co., GA; b. Abt. 1807, Wilkes Co., GA; d. Aft. 1850, Greene Co., GA.

     viii. DAUGHTER RAY, b. Bet. 1810 - 1815, Wilkes Co., GA; d. Aft. 1830, Taliaferro Co., GA.

Key Sources: Warren Co., GA, Deed Book C, pp. 45-46; Washington Co., AL, Deed Book A, p. 203; Williams Creek Baptist Church Records, 1787-1840; Wilkes Co., GA, Inferior Court Minutes, Book B, 1811-1817, p. 130; Taliaferro Co., GA, Deed Book B, p. 516; 1820 Wilkes Co., GA, Census, p. 212; 1830 Wilkes Co., GA, Census, p. 293; Taliaferro Co., GA, Deed Book A, p. 232; 1836 Taliaferro Co., GA, Tax Digest; 1840 Taliaferro Co., GA, Census, p. 242; Taliaferro Co., GA, Deed Book C, p. 392; Taliaferro Co., GA, Inventories, Appraisals, Sales, and Divisions of Estates, Book B, 1834-1850, pp. 477-78; Taliaferro Co., GA, Deed Book D, pp. 323, 387; 1850 Taliaferro Co., GA, Census, HH 234.

99. WILLIAM T.[7] HAMMACK *(ROBERT HAMMACK*[6] *JR., ROBERT HAMMACK*[5] *SR., WILLIAM "THE ELDER"*[4] *HAMMACK, WILLIAM "O"*[3]*, JOHN*[2] *HAMMOCKE, ? JOHN*[1] *HAMMOT)* was born Abt. 1775 in Wilkes Co., GA, and died Apr 1828 in Crawford County, GA. He married MARY FELTS Abt. 1797 in Wilkes Co., GA, daughter of JOHN FELTS. She was born Abt. 1780 in Warren Co., NC, and died 04 Sep 1843 in Crawford County, GA.

Children of WILLIAM HAMMACK and MARY FELTS are:

195.   i. SIMEON J.[8] HAMMACK, b. Abt. 1798, Wilkes Co., GA; d. Abt. 1863, Calhoun Co., MS.

     ii. WILBURN J. HAMMACK, b. Abt. 1800, Wilkes Co., GA; d. Bet. 1832 - 1833, Crawford County, GA.

196.   iii. LEWIS M. HAMMOCK, b. Abt. 1801, Wilkes Co., GA; d. Bef. 02 Sep 1867, Sumter County, GA.

197.   iv. TALBOT DAVIDSON HAMMACK, b. 02 Oct 1802, Wilkes County, GA; d. 08 Mar 1873, Crawford County, GA.

     v. CAPTAIN FELIX L. HAMMACK, b. Bet. 1803 - 1804, Wilkes Co., GA; d. Abt. 1830, Crawford Co., GA.

198.   vi. SARAH C. HAMMACK, b. 1804, Wilkes Co., GA; d. 1878, Taliaferro Co., GA.

199.   vii. MANSEL W. HAMMACK, b. Abt. 1805, Wilkes Co., GA; d. Abt. 1860, Crawford County, GA.

200.   viii. ELIZABETH HAMMACK, b. Abt. 04 May 1809, Jones Co., GA; d. 11 Sep 1871, Jones Co., GA.

201.   ix. JANE C. HAMMACK, b. Abt. 1814, Jones Co., GA; d. 1889, Crawford Co., GA.

202.   x. KATHERINE HAMMACK, b. 08 May 1817, Jones Co., GA; d. 08 Oct 1886, Coffee Co., AL.

203.   xi. MARTHA ANN HAMMACK, b. Abt. 1822, Jones Co., GA; d. Aft. 1850, Crawford Co., GA.

Key Sources: 1805 Wilkes Co., GA, Tax Digest; 1807-1827 Jones Co., GA, Tax Digests; Jones Co., GA, Deed Book M, pp. 103, 385; Crawford Co., GA, Deed Book B, p. 421; 1830 Crawford Co., GA, Census; Crawford Co., GA, Annual Returns, Book C, pp. 135, 240, 309; Crawford Co., GA, Annual Returns,

Book D, pp. 182, 313-314; Crawford Co., GA, Annual Returns, Book E, pp. 44, 123-124; 1840 Crawford Co., GA, Census; Crawford Co., GA, Will Book A, p. 48.

100. MARY "POLLY"[7] HAMMACK *(ROBERT HAMMACK[6] JR., ROBERT HAMMACK[5] SR., WILLIAM "THE ELDER"[4] HAMMACK, WILLIAM "O"[3], JOHN[2] HAMMOCKE, ? JOHN[1] HAMMOT)* was born Bet. 1780 - 1784 in Wilkes Co., GA, and died 1842 in Jones Co., GA. She married JOHN JACKSON I 12 Aug 1800 in Wilkes County, GA. He was born Abt. 1785 in Culpepper Co., VA, and died Abt. 1859 in Barnesville, Monroe Co., GA.
Children of MARY HAMMACK and JOHN JACKSON are:
204.   i.   WILLIAM P.[8] JACKSON, b. 1803, Wilkes Co., GA; d. Aft. 1870, Jones Co., GA.
205.   ii.   THOMPSON JACKSON, b. 1805, Wilkes Co., GA; d. Aft. 1870, Jones Co., GA.
        iii. EDWARD JACKSON, b. 08 Nov 1808, Wilkes Co., GA; d. 02 Jul 1894, Jones Co., GA.
206.   iv.   LUCY JACKSON, b. Abt. 1810, Wilkes Co., GA; d. Aft. 1850, Jones Co., GA.
207.   v.   WILKINS JACKSON, b. Abt. 1812, Wilkes Co., GA; d. Aft. 1850, Jones Co., GA.
208.   vi.   JOHN JACKSON II, b. 03 Jan 1815, Wilkes County, GA; d. 11 Feb 1868, Macon Co., GA.
        vii. ANDREW JACKSON, b. 08 Dec 1816, Wilkes Co., GA; d. 24 Nov 1903, Jones Co., GA.
209.   viii. LEWIS JACKSON, b. 1820, Jones Co., GA; d. Bef. 14 Mar 1865, Jones Co., GA.
Key Sources: C. W. Williams, *History of Jones Co., GA, 1807-1907* (Macon, GA, 1967), pp. 631-633.

101. CATHERINE[7] HAMMACK *(ROBERT HAMMACK[6] JR., ROBERT HAMMACK[5] SR., WILLIAM "THE ELDER"[4] HAMMACK, WILLIAM "O"[3], JOHN[2] HAMMOCKE, ? JOHN[1] HAMMOT)* was born 1792 in Wilkes Co., GA, and died Aft. 1860 in Russell Co., AL. She married (1) JOHN GUNN 05 Aug 1810 in Wilkes Co., GA, son of WILLIAM GUNN. He was born Abt. 1785 in Wilkes Co., GA, and died Bef. 06 May 1816 in Wilkes Co., GA. She married (2) DAVID POOLE Abt. 1828 in Taliaferro Co., GA. He was born Abt. 1800 in Georgia, and died Bef. 1840 in Talbot Co., GA.
Children of CATHERINE HAMMACK and JOHN GUNN are:
210.   i.   SICILY CATHERINE[8] GUNN, b. Abt. 1811, Wilkes Co., GA; d. Aft. 1870, Russell Co., AL.
211.   ii.   GEORGE GUNN, b. Abt. 1814, Wilkes Co., GA; d. Aft. 1880, Calhoun/Talladega Co., AL.
Children of CATHERINE HAMMACK and DAVID POOLE are:
        iii. DAUGHTER[8] POOLE, b. Abt. 1824, Taliaferro Co., GA; d. Aft. 1830, Taliaferro Co., GA.
        iv.   ROBERT J. POOLE, b. Abt. 1826, Taliaferro Co., GA; d. Aft. 1820, Taliaferro Co., GA.
212.   v.   JOHN J. POOLE, b. Abt. 1828, Taliaferro Co., GA; d. Abt. 1908, Rusk Co., TX.
        vi.   DAUGHTER POOLE, b. Abt. 1830, Taliaferro Co., GA; d. Aft. 1830, Taliaferro Co., GA.
213.   vii. WILLIAM POOLE, b. Abt. 1832, Taliaferro Co., GA; d. Aft. 1860, Russell Co., AL.
214.   viii. DAVID POOLE, b. Abt. 1834, Taliaferro Co., GA; d. Aft. 1880, Lee Co., AL.
Key Sources: 1840 Talbot Co., GA, Census, p. 224; 1850 Russell Co., AL, Census, HH 497/497; 1860 Russell Co., AL, Census, HH 595/593; G. G. Davidson, *Early Records of Georgia, Wilkes County* (2 vols., Macon, GA, 1932), 1: 209, and 2: 179, 229.

102. BENJAMIN[7] HAMMACK *(BENEDICT[6], ROBERT HAMMACK[5] SR., WILLIAM "THE ELDER"[4] HAMMACK, WILLIAM "O"[3], JOHN[2] HAMMOCKE, ? JOHN[1] HAMMOT)* was born Abt. 1766 in Richmond Co., VA, and died Abt. 1801 in Richmond Co., VA. He married (1) MOLLY SCUTT Abt. 18 Dec 1786 in Richmond Co., VA. She was born Abt. 1766 in Virginia, and died Bef. 31 Jan 1792 in Richmond Co., VA. He married (2) PATTY SCUTT Abt. 31 Jan 1792 in Westmoreland Co., VA.
Child of BENJAMIN HAMMACK and MOLLY SCUTT is:
215.   i.   CHARLES[8] HAMMACK, b. Bef. 31 Jan 1792, Richmond Co., VA; d. Bet. 1830 - 1840, Richmond Co., VA.
Children of BENJAMIN HAMMACK and PATTY SCUTT are:

ii.   ROBERT[8] HAMMACK, b. Abt. 1795, Richmond Co., VA; m. ANN BEALE RUICK, Abt. 08 Aug 1816, Richmond Co., VA.

iii. JANE HAMMACK, b. Abt. 1797, Richmond Co., VA; d. Bef. 31 Jul 1824, Northumberland Co., VA; m. HENRY LEWIS, Abt. 02 Jan 1818, Richmond Co., VA; b. Abt. 1795, Virginia; d. Aft. 1830, Northumberland Co., VA.

216. iv.   WILLIAM HAMMACK, b. Abt. 1795, Richmond Co., VA; d. Bet. 1844 - 1845, Northumberland Co., VA.

Key Sources: G. S. S. King, *Marriages of Richmond Co., VA, 1668-1853* (Fredericksburg, VA, 1964); 1789-1801, 1816 Richmond Co., VA, Personal Property Tax Lists. The 1816 tax list establishes Benjamin as the father of Charles. The identification of the other three children is speculative but based on tax, census, and land records as well as nomenclature.

103. JOHN[7] HAMMACK *(BENEDICT[6], ROBERT HAMMACK[5] SR., WILLIAM "THE ELDER"[4] HAMMACK, WILLIAM "O"[3], JOHN[2] HAMMOCKE, ? JOHN[1] HAMMOT)* was born Abt. 1776 in Richmond Co., VA, and died Aft. 1830 in Richmond Co., VA. He married ANNA BEALE Abt. 26 Jun 1799 in Richmond Co., VA, daughter of SAMUEL BEALE. She was born Bef. 1775 in Virginia, and died Bet. 1820 - 1830 in Richmond Co., VA.

Children of JOHN HAMMACK and ANNA BEALE are:

i.   DAUGHTER[8] HAMMACK, b. Bet. 1794 - 1804, Richmond Co., VA; d. Aft. 1810, Richmond Co., VA.

ii.   DAUGHTER HAMMACK, b. Bet. 1794 - 1804, Richmond Co., VA; d. Aft. 1810, Richmond Co., VA.

iii. DAUGHTER HAMMACK, b. Bet. 1794 - 1804, Richmond Co., VA; d. Aft. 1810, Richmond Co., VA.

iv.   DAUGHTER HAMMACK, b. Bet. 1804 - 1810, Richmond Co., VA; d. Aft. 1820, Richmond Co., VA.

v.   JOHN S. HAMMACK, b. Abt. 1815, Richmond Co., VA; d. Aft. 1842, Northumberland Co., VA.

vi.   DAUGHTER HAMMACK, b. Bet. 1810 - 1815, Richmond Co., VA; d. Aft. 1820, Richmond Co., VA.

vii. DAUGHTER HAMMACK, b. Bet. 1810 - 1815, Richmond Co., VA; d. Aft. 1820, Richmond Co., VA.

viii. DAUGHTER HAMMACK, b. Bet. 1815 - 1820, Richmond Co., VA; d. Aft. 1820, Richmond Co., VA.

Key Sources: 1797-1833 Richmond Co., VA, Personal Property Tax Lists; 1820 Richmond Co., VA, Census, p. 226A; 1830 Richmond Co., VA, Census, p. 92. The 1831 tax list establishes John as the father of John S. Hammack.

104. LEWIS[7] HAMMACK *(BENEDICT[6], ROBERT HAMMACK[5] SR., WILLIAM "THE ELDER"[4] HAMMACK, WILLIAM "O"[3], JOHN[2] HAMMOCKE, ? JOHN[1] HAMMOT)* was born Bef. 1792 in Richmond Co., VA, and died Abt. 1824 in Richmond Co., VA. He married LUCY CLARKE Abt. 26 Dec 1811 in Richmond Co., VA. She was born Abt. 1792 in Richmond Co., VA, and died Aft. 1842 in Richmond Co., VA.

Children of LEWIS HAMMACK and LUCY CLARKE are:

i.   LEWIS[8] HAMMACK, b. Abt. 1812, Richmond Co., VA; d. Bef. 06 Jun 1850, Richmond Co., VA; m. ELIZABETH LITTRELL LEADER, Abt. 18 Dec 1844, Richmond Co., VA.

217. ii.   BENEDICT HAMMACK, b. 10 Dec 1814, Richmond Co., VA; d. 17 May 1895, Richmond Co., VA.

218.   iii.   RODHAM CLARKE HAMMACK, b. Abt. 1817, Richmond Co., VA; d. 20 Sep 1874, Richmond Co., VA.

iv.   DAUGHTER HAMMACK, b. Bet. 1810 - 1820, Richmond Co., VA; d. Aft. 1820, Richmond Co., VA.

Key Sources: G. S. S. King, *Marriages of Richmond Co., VA, 1668-1853* (Fredericksburg, VA, 1964); 1813-1840 Richmond Co., VA, Personal Property Tax Lists; 1820 Richmond Co., VA, Census, p. 225A; 1830 Richmond Co., VA, Census, p. 89; Richmond Co.,VA, Deed Book 23, p. 532.

105. WILLIAM[7] HAMMACK (*CHRISTIAN[6], ROBERT HAMMACK[5] SR., WILLIAM "THE ELDER"[4] HAMMACK, WILLIAM "O"[3], JOHN[2] HAMMOCKE, ? JOHN[1] HAMMOT*) was born Abt. 09 Feb 1761 in Richmond Co., VA, and died Abt. 1815 in Richmond Co., VA. He married (1) SARAH "SALLY" [------] Abt. 1780 in Richmond Co., VA. She died Bef. 1797 in Richmond Co., VA. He married (2) ELIZABETH PURSLEY Abt. 13 Nov 1797 in Westmoreland Co., VA. She was born Abt. 1775 in Westmoreland Co., VA, and died Aft. 1815 in Richmond Co., VA.
Children of WILLIAM HAMMACK and SARAH [------] are:

i.   SON[8] HAMMACK, b. Abt. 1788, Richmond Co., VA; d. Bet. 1810 - 1816, Richmond Co., VA.

219.   ii.   JOHN W. HAMMACK, b. Abt. 1792, Richmond Co., VA; d. Bet. 1829 - 1830, Richmond Co., VA.

iii.   NANCY HAMMACK, b. Abt. 1784, Richmond Co., VA; d. Aft. 1815, Northumberland Co., VA; m. (1) WILLIAM EFFORD, Abt. 26 Jan 1802, Richmond Co., VA; m. (2) CHAPMAN AUSTIN, Abt. 26 Nov 1815, Northumberland Co., VA; d. Aft. 1820, Northumberland Co., VA.

220.   iv.   SALLY HAMMACK, b. 12 Jun 1790, Richmond Co., VA; d. Bet. 1810 - 1815, Richmond Co., VA.

v.   POLLY HAMMACK, b. 15 Dec 1794, Richmond Co., VA; d. Bet. 1794 - 1802, Richmond Co., VA.

Children of WILLIAM HAMMACK and ELIZABETH PURSLEY are:

vi.   MARY P.[8] HAMMACK, b. Aft. 1801, Richmond Co., VA; d. Aft. 1827, Richmond Co., VA; m. JAMES BERRICK, Abt. 05 Mar 1827, Richmond Co., VA.

vii.   MARIA HAMMACK, b. Abt. 1802, Richmond Co., VA; d. Bef. 1836, Richmond Co., VA; m. TURNER HANKS, Abt. 04 Dec 1823, Richmond Co., VA.

viii.   WILLIAM J. HAMMACK, b. Aft. 1802, Richmond Co., VA; d. Aft. 1823, Richmond Co., VA.

ix.   SOPHIA HAMMACK, b. Abt. 1810, Richmond Co., VA; d. Aft. 1850, Northumberland Co., VA; m. JOHN D. RUICK, Abt. 22 Mar 1841, Richmond Co., GA.

Key Sources: 1789-1815 Richmond Co., VA, Personal Property Tax Lists; Richmond Co., VA, Account Book 3, 1798-1821, p. 79; Richmond Co., VA, Deed Book 18, p. 112; 1810 Richmond Co., VA, Census, p. 338; Richmond Co., VA, Deed Book 19, p. 104; Richmond Co., VA, Order Book 24, 1816-1820, pp. 6, 43; Richmond Co., VA, Chancery Court Orders, 1815-1828, pp. 41-46; Richmond Co., VA, Order Book, 1816-1820, p. 231; 1819-1820 Richmond Co., VA, Personal Property Tax Lists; Richmond Co., VA, Order Book 1820-1822, pp. 26, 47, 306; Richmond Co., VA, Order Book, 1822-1826, p. 60; Richmond Co., VA, Order Book, 1832-1837, p. 204.

106. SAMFORD[7] JONES (*CHRISTIAN[6] HAMMACK, ROBERT HAMMACK[5] SR., WILLIAM "THE ELDER"[4] HAMMACK, WILLIAM "O"[3], JOHN[2] HAMMOCKE, ? JOHN[1] HAMMOT*) was born Abt. 1778 in Richmond Co., VA, and died Bet. 1814 - 1820 in Richmond Co., VA. He married REBECCA BEACHAM SELF Abt. 15 Aug 1798 in Richmond Co., VA, daughter of JEREMIAH SELF and

HANNAH [------]. She was born Abt. 1770 in Richmond Co., VA, and died Aft. 1829 in Richmond Co., VA.

Children of SAMFORD JONES and REBECCA SELF are:

        i.   DAUGHTER[8] JONES, b. Abt. 1800, Richmond Co., VA; d. Aft. 1810, Richmond Co., VA.

       ii.   DAUGHTER JONES, b. Abt. 1802, Richmond Co., VA; d. Aft. 1810, Richmond Co., VA.

     iii.   DAUGHTER JONES, b. Abt. 1805, Richmond Co., VA; d. Aft. 1810, Richmond Co., VA.

221.   iv.   MATILDA JONES, b. 01 Jan 1807, Richmond Co., VA; d. Aft. 1849, Richmond Co., VA.

Key Sources: G. S. S. King, *Marriages of Richmond Co., VA, 1668-1853* (Fredericksburg, VA, 1964); Richmond Co., VA, Deed Book 23, pp. 149-151; 1820 Richmond Co., VA, Census, p. 228; Richmond Co., VA, Deed Book 19, p. 331; Richmond Co., VA, Accounts Book 3, 1798-1821, p. 315.

107. LEWIS[7] HAMMACK (*LEWIS[6], ROBERT HAMMACK[5] SR., WILLIAM "THE ELDER"[4] HAMMACK, WILLIAM "O"[3], JOHN[2] HAMMOCKE, ? JOHN[1] HAMMOT*) was born Abt. 1774 in Charlotte Co., VA, and died Bet. 1834 - 1835 in Washington Co., AR. He married (1) BETSY HARVEY 20 Dec 1796 in Campbell Co., VA. She was born Abt. 1776 in Virginia, and died Bef. 1830 in Warren or Carroll Co., TN. He married (2) MARY [------] STOCKARD Abt. 1829 in Carroll Co., TN. She died Aft. 1834 in Carroll Co., TN.

Children of LEWIS HAMMACK and BETSY HARVEY are:

        i.   SARAH P.[8] HAMMACK, b. Abt. 1798, Charlotte Co., VA; d. Aft. 1828, Tennessee; m. AMAZIAH JONES, Abt. 1828, Tennessee; b. Abt. 1798, North Carolina.

       ii.   ELIZABETH F. HAMMACK, b. 08 Feb 1800, Charlotte Co., VA; d. Aft. 1827, Kentucky; m. HAYMOND B. CULVER, Abt. 1822, Tennessee; b. Abt. 1801, Tennessee.

     iii.   MARY HAMMACK, b. 25 Aug 1801, Charlotte Co., VA; d. Aft. 1840, Hunt Co., TX; m. SAMUEL GRENADE CULVER, Abt. 1822, Tennessee; b. 19 Jul 1802, North Carolina.

     iv.   NANCY HAMMACK, b. 06 Mar 1803, Charlotte Co., VA; m. JOSEPH BAXTER.

222.   v.   WILLIAM MORGAN HAMMACK, b. 09 Nov 1804, Franklin Co., VA; d. 13 Jun 1859, Benton Co., AR.

     vi.   WINNEFRED HAMMACK, b. Abt. 1807, Franklin Co., VA; d. Aft. 1830, Tennessee; m. JOHN LOUIS BAILEY.

    vii.   MARTHA A. HAMMACK, b. Abt. 1810, Franklin Co., VA; d. Aft. 1840, Benton Co., AR; m. JOHN P. MAXWELL.

223. viii.   JOHN H. HAMMACK, b. 25 Dec 1811, Warren Co., TN; d. 01 Mar 1880, Hunt Co., TX.

224.   ix.   THOMAS HAMMACK, b. Abt. 1814, Warren Co., TN; d. Aft. 1850, Arkansas.

     x.   ANNA W. HAMMACK, b. 12 Jul 1815, Warren Co., TN; d. Aft. 1835, Carroll Co., TN; m. JAMES W. MAXWELL, Abt. 1835, Carroll Co., TN.

     xi.   MARGARET FIELDS HAMMACK, b. 18 Feb 1816, Warren Co., TN; d. 1894, Benton Co., AR; m. DAVID WILLIAMS, Abt. 1835, Carroll Co., TN; b. 28 Sep 1816, Overton Co., TN.

225.   xii.   JESSE HARVEY HAMMACK, b. 06 Dec 1817, Warren Co., TN; d. 16 May 1896, Hunt Co., TX.

Key Sources: HFH, 2: 196; Washington Co., AR, Probate Book A-B, 1829-1887, p. 74. Lewis's will and probate records filed in Washington and Benton Counties, AR, document all twelve offspring.

108. THOMAS[7] HAMMACK (*LEWIS[6], ROBERT HAMMACK[5] SR., WILLIAM "THE ELDER"[4] HAMMACK, WILLIAM "O"[3], JOHN[2] HAMMOCKE, ? JOHN[1] HAMMOT*) was born Abt. 1776 in Charlotte Co., VA, and died Aft. 1850 in Bedford Co., VA. He married KATEY HAZELWOOD 08 Feb 1798 in Charlotte Co., VA. She was born Abt. 1778 in Virginia.

Children of THOMAS HAMMACK and KATEY HAZELWOOD are:

226.   i.   JOHN[8] HAMMACK, b. Abt. 1802, Virginia; d. Aft. 1870, Roanoke Co., VA.

     ii.   ? MARGARET HAMMACK, b. Abt. 1805, Virginia; d. Aft. 1850, Bedford Co., VA.

    iii. NANCY HAMMACK, b. Abt. 1815, Virginia; d. Aft. 1850, Bedford Co., VA.

    iv. ELIZABETH HAMMACK, b. Abt. 1817, Virginia; d. Aft. 1850, Bedford Co., VA.

Key Sources: 1799-1801 Charlotte Co., VA, Personal Property Tax Lists; Charlotte Co., VA, Deed Book 9, pp. 48, 238-239; Franklin Co., VA, Deed Book 6; 1820 Bedford Co., VA, Census, p. 13; 1830 Bedford Co., VA, Census, p. 195; 1840 Bedford Co., VA, Census, p. 261; 1850 Bedford Co., VA, Census, p. 296. Thomas was taxed adjacent Lewis Hammack in Charlotte County from 1799 to 1801; both men had close dealings with members of the Hazelwood family.

109. JOSIAH[7] HAMMACK *(LEWIS[6], ROBERT HAMMACK[5] SR., WILLIAM "THE ELDER"[4] HAMMACK, WILLIAM "O"[3], JOHN[2] HAMMOCKE, ? JOHN[1] HAMMOT)* was born Abt. 1783 in Charlotte Co., VA, and died Aft. 1840 in Pulaski Co., KY.

Children of JOSIAH HAMMACK are:

    i. SON[8] HAMMACK, b. Bet. 1802 - 1804; d. Aft. 1820, Warren Co., TN.

    ii. DAUGHTER HAMMACK, b. Bet. 1802 - 1804; d. Aft. 1820, Warren Co., TN.

    iii. SON HAMMACK, b. Bet. 1804 - 1810; d. Aft. 1820, Warren Co., TN.

    iv. DAUGHTER HAMMACK, b. Bet. 1804 - 1810; d. Aft. 1820, Warren Co., TN.

    v. DAUGHTER HAMMACK, b. Bet. 1804 - 1810; d. Aft. 1820, Warren Co., TN.

    vi. SON HAMMACK, b. Bet. 1810 - 1820; d. Aft. 1820, Warren Co., TN.

    vii. ? ANDREW J. HAMMACK, b. Abt. 1818, Tennessee; d. Aft. 1870, Polk Co., MO.

    viii. DAUGHTER HAMMACK, b. Bet. 1810 - 1820, Tennessee; d. Aft. 1820, Warren Co., TN.

Key Sources: 1820 Warren Co., TN, Census, p. 9. Josiah is tentatively placed with Lewis Hammack, partially because of location. He also witnessed a deed in Lunenburg County in 1799 but appears in few records otherwise. See Lunenburg Co., VA, Deed Book 18, p. 142. The land conveyed in the deed lay in northern Lunenburg County, along the road from Lunenburg Court House to Hungry Town, and was a short distance from Charlotte County, another reason for tentatively placing Josiah Hammack with Lewis's family. The placement of Andrew J. Hammack as Josiah's son is based primarily on location and is speculative, not proven.

110. WINNEY[7] HAMMACK *(LEWIS[6], ROBERT HAMMACK[5] SR., WILLIAM "THE ELDER"[4] HAMMACK, WILLIAM "O"[3], JOHN[2] HAMMOCKE, ? JOHN[1] HAMMOT)* was born 17 Dec 1787 in Charlotte Co., VA, and died Dec 1851 in Carroll Co., TN. She married (1) SAMUEL SWINNEY 11 Mar 1811 in Franklin Co., VA. He was born 24 Sep 1786 in Virginia, and died Dec 1821 in Warren Co., TN. She married (2) JAMES CRAWFORD Bet. 1827 - 1832 in Carroll Co., TN. He died Bef. 12 Sep 1850 in Carroll Co., TN.

Children of WINNEY HAMMACK and SAMUEL SWINNEY are:

    i. JOSEPH[8] SWINNEY, b. 01 May 1812, Warren Co., TN; d. Aft. 1837, Carroll Co., TN; m. SARAH BURNS, 29 Mar 1837, Tennessee.

    ii. LEWIS SWINNEY, b. 19 Sep 1813, Warren Co., TN; d. Dec 1856, Tennessee; m. MARY [------].

    iii. ELIZABETH JANE SWINNEY, b. 07 Apr 1815, Warren Co., TN; d. 01 May 1903, Gentry Co., MO; m. JOHN SULLINGER RAINEY, 1832, Carroll Co., TN; b. 20 Jan 1797, Orange Co., NC.

    iv. JANE SWINNEY, b. 23 Jul 1817, Warren Co., TN; d. Aft. 1832, Carroll Co., TN; m. THOMAS E. CREWS, Abt. 1838, Tennessee; b. Abt. 1815, Virginia.

    v. POLLY SWINNEY, b. 25 Apr 1820, Warren Co., TN; d. Jul 1826, Warren Co., TN.

Key Sources: 1820 Warren Co., TN, Census; 1850 Carroll Co., TN, Census. Winney's identification is speculative and is based on the common connection with Franklin Co., VA, and Warren Co., TN. It is possible, however, that she belongs to the family of Richard Hammack and Mary Witcher.

111. JOHN H.[7] BENTLEY *(MILLY[6] HAMMACK, ROBERT HAMMACK[5] SR., WILLIAM "THE ELDER"[4] HAMMACK, WILLIAM "O"[3], JOHN[2] HAMMOCKE, ? JOHN[1] HAMMOT)* was born Abt. 1785 in Lunenburg Co., VA, and died Abt. 1858 in Crawford Co., GA. He married MARTHA MOORE Abt. 1810 in Wilkes Co., GA, daughter of ROBERT MOORE. She was born Abt. 1792 in Lunenburg Co., VA, and died Aft. 1860 in Crawford Co., GA.

Children of JOHN BENTLEY and MARTHA MOORE are:

    i.   WILLIAM WILLIAMSON[8] BENTLEY, b. Abt. 1813, Wilkes Co., GA; d. Abt. 1873, Crawford Co., GA; m. EVALINE CLEMENTS, 08 Sep 1833, Jones Co., GA; b. Abt. 1815, Georgia; d. Aft. 1850, Crawford Co., GA.

227.   ii.   MILLY ANN BENTLEY, b. Abt. 1815, Wilkes Co., GA; d. Bef. 1841, Crawford Co., GA.

    iii.   SAMUEL BENTLEY, b. 07 Jun 1816, Jones Co., GA; d. 19 May 1887, Upson Co., GA; m. SARAH CARTER, 02 Dec 1838, Crawford Co., GA; b. Abt. 1814, Georgia; d. Aft. 1880, Upson Co., GA.

    iv.   DANIEL W. BENTLEY, b. Abt. 1827, Jones Co., GA; d. Bet. 1853 - 1858, Crawford Co., GA; m. FLORIDA E. ROBERTSON; b. 23 Feb 1830, Georgia; d. 11 Dec 1907, Crawford Co., GA.

    v.   ELIZABETH BENTLEY, b. Abt. 1828, Jones Co., GA; d. Aft. 1860, Crawford Co., GA; m. ISHAM E. MILLER.

    vi.   DAUGHTER BENTLEY, b. Bet. 1810 - 1815, Wilkes Co., GA; d. Aft. 1820, Wilkes Co., GA.

Key Sources: Arthur Curtis Carter, *Carter and Kinsmen* (Montgomery, AL, 1990); 1850 Crawford Co., GA, Census, HH 156; Crawford Co., GA, Annual Returns, Book I, p. 101; Crawford Co., GA, Annual Returns, Book J, p. 51; 1860 Crawford Co., GA, Census, HH 575/565.

112. ANNY[7] BENTLEY *(MILLY[6] HAMMACK, ROBERT HAMMACK[5] SR., WILLIAM "THE ELDER"[4] HAMMACK, WILLIAM "O"[3], JOHN[2] HAMMOCKE, ? JOHN[1] HAMMOT)* was born Aft. 1787 in Lunenburg Co., VA, and died 03 Feb 1843 in Hancock Co., GA. She married GEORGE AMOS 08 Oct 1807 in Lunenburg Co., VA, son of JAMES AMOS and LENA BRADFORD. He was born Abt. 1785 in Lunenburg Co., VA, and died Aft. 1840 in Hancock Co., GA.

Children of ANNY BENTLEY and GEORGE AMOS are:

    i.   DANIEL J.[8] AMOS, b. 26 Sep 1808, Hancock Co., GA; d. Aft. 1830, Hancock Co., GA; m. CAROLINE J. HARPER, 30 Sep 1829, Hancock Co., GA.

    ii.   MARTHA ANN AMOS, b. 12 Apr 1810, Hancock Co., GA; d. Aft. 1860, Crawford Co., GA; m. MANCEL W. HAMMACK, 07 Nov 1826, Hancock Co., GA.

    iii.   GEORGE WASHINGTON AMOS, b. 09 Feb 1813, Hancock Co., GA; m. KATHERINE HAMMACK, 24 Aug 1831, Hancock Co., GA.

    iv.   HENRY D. AMOS, b. 15 Dec 1813, Hancock Co., GA; d. Aft. 1841, Hancock Co., GA; m. MARY A. WALKER, 09 Sep 1841, Hancock Co., GA.

    v.   BEVERLY C. AMOS, b. 05 Jul 1815, Hancock Co., GA; d. Aft. 1837, Hancock Co., GA; m. MARY E. BUTTS, 27 Dec 1837, Hancock Co., GA.

    vi.   JOHN W. AMOS, b. 15 Feb 1817, Hancock Co., GA; d. Aft. 1845, Hancock Co., GA; m. ELIZABETH C. HARPER, 17 May 1845, Hancock Co., GA.

    vii.   WILLIAM AMOS, b. 10 Jan 1819, Hancock Co., GA; d. Aft. 1845, Hancock Co., GA; m. REBECCA B. LATTIMER, 25 Feb 1845, Hancock Co., GA.

    viii.   WYATT AMOS, b. 19 Sep 1820, Hancock Co., GA; d. Aft. 1830, Hancock Co., GA.

    ix.   MILLYANN AMOS, b. 30 Aug 1822, Hancock Co., GA; d. Aft. 1830, Hancock Co., GA.

    x.   JAMES M. AMOS, b. 05 Sep 1824, Hancock Co., GA; d. Aft. 1830, Hancock Co., GA.

xi. CAROLINE F. AMOS, b. 07 Jan 1826, Hancock Co., GA; d. Aft. 1870, Baldwin Co., GA; m. ORRICK JEFFERSON MURRAY, 22 Aug 1843, Hancock Co., GA; b. Abt. 1821, GA; d. Aft. 1880, Baldwin Co., GA.

xii. MARY J. AMOS, b. 03 Jun 1828, Hancock Co., GA; d. Aft. 1830, Hancock Co., GA.

xiii. SUSAN C. AMOS, b. 04 May 1830, Hancock Co., GA; d. Aft. 1830, Hancock Co., GA.

Key Sources: Amos Family File, Fort Smith Public Library, Fort Smith, AR; 1820 Hancock Co., GA, Census.

113. ROBERT H.[7] BENTLEY *(MILLY[6] HAMMACK, ROBERT HAMMACK[5] SR., WILLIAM "THE ELDER"[4] HAMMACK, WILLIAM "O"[3], JOHN[2] HAMMOCKE, ? JOHN[1] HAMMOT)* was born Aft. 1786 in Nottoway Co., VA, and died Aft. 1860 in Charlotte Co., VA. He married CATHERINE INGE Abt. 1808 in Lunenburg Co., VA. She was born 03 Feb 1777 in Dinwiddie Co., VA, and died Aft. 1860 in Charlotte Co., VA.

Children of ROBERT BENTLEY and CATHERINE INGE are:

i. DANIEL VINCENT[8] BENTLEY, b. 12 Feb 1809, Lunenburg Co., VA; d. Aft. 1860, Lunenburg Co., VA; m. MACCA ANN SATTERFIELD, 18 Dec 1834, Lunenburg Co., VA.

ii. JOHN J. BENTLEY, b. 24 Jul 1811, Lunenburg Co., VA; d. Aft. 1840, Charlotte Co., VA.

iii. MILLEY HANNAH BENTLEY, b. 12 Nov 1813, Lunenburg Co., VA; d. Aft. 1880, Lunenburg Co., VA.

iv. ROBERT HAMMACK BENTLEY, b. 18 Mar 1816, Lunenburg Co., VA; d. Aft. 1860, Lunenburg Co., VA; m. CLARISSA BARNES, 09 Jan 1842, Lunenburg Co., VA.

v. MARTHA SMITH BENTLEY, b. 28 Jun 1818, Lunenburg Co., VA; d. Aft. 1880, Lunenburg Co., VA.

vi. MARKY ANN ELIZABETH BENTLEY, b. 22 Nov 1821, Charlotte Co., VA; d. Aft. 1830, Charlotte Co., VA.

Key Sources: 1810 Lunenburg Co., VA, Census; 1820-1860 Charlotte Co., VA, Census.

114. WILLIAM[7] HAMMACK *(DANIEL[6], WILLIAM[5], RICHARD[4], WILLIAM "O"[3], JOHN[2] HAMMOCKE, ? JOHN[1] HAMMOT)* was born Bet. 1760 - 1765 in Albemarle Co., VA, and died Aft. 1840 in Chatham Co., NC. He married UNKNOWN Abt. 1795 in Chatham Co., NC. She was born Bet. 1770 - 1775, and died Bet. 1830 - 1840 in Chatham Co., NC.

Children of WILLIAM HAMMACK and UNKNOWN are:

i. DAUGHTER[8] HAMMACK, b. Abt. 1796, Chatham Co., NC; d. Aft. 1810, Chatham Co., NC.

ii. DAUGHTER HAMMACK, b. Abt. 1798, Chatham Co., NC; d. Aft. 1810, Chatham Co., NC.

iii. DAUGHTER HAMMACK, b. Bet. 1799 - 1805, Chatham Co., NC; d. Aft. 1820, Chatham Co., NC.

228. iv. ? JOHN HAMMACK, b. Abt. 1802, Chatham Co., NC; d. Aft. 1860, Chatham Co., NC.

v. DAUGHTER HAMMACK, b. Bet. 1810 - 1820, Chatham Co., NC; d. Aft. 1840, Chatham Co., NC.

Key Sources: 1800 Chatham Co., NC, Census, p. 203; 1810 Chatham Co., NC, Census, p. 191; 1820 Chatham Co., NC, Census, p. 31; 1830 Chatham Co., NC, Census, p. 440; 1840 Chatham Co., NC, Census, pp. 170, 193; 1850 Chatham Co., NC, Census, p. 460; 1860 Chatham Co., NC, Census, p. 17. Geography, nomenclature, and migration suggest that William and John were members of the Richard Hammack family. The most likely candidates to have been their father seem to have been Daniel and Ann Rust Hammack of Campbell Co., VA, or William Hammack, son of John and Mary Martin Hammack, who was last found in Campbell Co., VA, about 1782.

115. JOHN[7] HAMMOCK *(DANIEL[6], WILLIAM[5], RICHARD[4], WILLIAM "O"[3], JOHN[2] HAMMOCKE, ? JOHN[1] HAMMOT)* was born Bet. 1770 - 1775 in Bedford Co., VA, and died Aft. 1840 in Overton Co., TN. He married RACHEL SELLARS Abt. 1795 in Chatham Co., NC. She was born Abt. 1775 in NC, and died Aft. 1850 in Overton Co., TN.
Children of JOHN HAMMOCK and RACHEL SELLARS are:
229.   i.   WILLIAM[8] HAMMOCK, b. Abt. 1796, Chatham Co., NC; d. Abt. 1855, Overton Co., TN.
230.   ii.   LAIRD HAMMOCK, b. Abt. 1799, Chatham Co., NC; d. Aft. 1860, Overton Co., TN.
         iii. JAMES HAMMOCK, b. Abt. 1799, Chatham Co., NC; d. Aft. 1860, Overton Co., TN.
         iv.   DAUGHTER HAMMOCK, b. Bet. 1790 - 1800, Chatham Co., NC.
231.   v.   JOHN HAMMOCK, b. Abt. 1806, Chatham Co., NC; d. Aft. 1850, Overton Co., TN.
         vi.   ANN HAMMOCK, b. Abt. 1806, Chatham Co., NC; d. Aft. 1880, Overton Co., TN.
         vii. ELIZABETH HAMMOCK, b. 10 Jun 1809, Overton Co., TN; d. 20 Jun 1890, Madison Co., AR; m. REUBEN PHILLIPS; b. 15 May 1810, NC; d. 05 Apr 1883, Madison Co., AR.
         viii. DAVID HAMMOCK, b. Abt. 1811, TN; d. 19 Sep 1880, Overton Co., TN; m. MARY; b. Abt. 1806, TN; d. Aft. 1860, Overton Co., TN.
         ix.   SON HAMMOCK, b. Bet. 1815 - 1820, TN; d. Aft. 1830, Overton Co., TN.
         x.   DAUGHTER HAMMOCK, b. Bet. 1815 - 1820, TN; d. Aft. 1830, Overton Co., TN.
         xi.   RACHEL HAMMOCK, b. Abt. 1817, TN; d. Aft. 1880, Overton Co., TN.
Key Sources: 1800 Chatham Co., NC, Census, p. 203; Overton Co., TN, Deed Book P, p. 573; 1830 Overton Co., TN, Census, pp. 212-213; 1840 Overton Co., TN, Census, pp. 3, 17, 33; 1850 Overton Co., TN, Census, HH 607/608. Laird Hammock was likely named for Laird Sellars.

116. ROBERT[7] HAMMACK *(JOHN[6], RICHARD[5], RICHARD[4], WILLIAM "O"[3], JOHN[2] HAMMOCKE, ? JOHN[1] HAMMOT)* was born Abt. 1745 in Louisa Co., VA, and died Abt. 1822 in Surry Co., NC. He married ELIZABETH Bef. 1779 in Albemarle Co., VA.
Children of ROBERT HAMMACK and ELIZABETH are:
         i.   BARTLETT[8] HAMMACK, b. Abt. 1796, Surry Co., NC; d. Abt. 1822, Surry Co., NC.
         ii.   RUTH HAMMACK, b. Abt. 1785, Surry Co., NC; d. Aft. 1850, Surry Co., NC.
         iii. POLLY HAMMACK, b. Abt. 1779, Albemarle Co., VA; d. Aft. 1850, Surry Co., NC; m. WILLIAM FORD FLEMING; b. 1769, Carroll Co., VA; d. 1859, Surry Co., NC.
         iv.   CATURY HAMMACK, d. Aft. 1822, Surry Co., NC; m. [-------] BURRUS.
232.   v.   WILLIAM HAMMOCK, b. Bef. 1784, Albemarle Co., VA; d. Aft. 1850, Overton Co., TN.
Key Sources: Albemarle Co., VA, Deed Book 7, pp. 2991, 297, 462; 1785 Albemarle Co., VA, Tax List; 1786 Surry Co., NC, State Census; 1790 Surry Co., NC, Census; Surry Co., NC, Will Book 3, p. 13; 1800 Surry Co., NC, Census, p. 661; 1810 Surry Co., NC, Census, p. 630; 1817 Surry Co., NC, Tax List; Original Will of Robert Hammock, 22 January 1823, Surry Co., NC; 1830 Surry Co., NC, Census, p. 136; 1840 Surry Co., NC, Census, p. 33; 1850 Surry Co., NC, Census, p. 299. While the probability is strong that this Robert is the Robert who is the son of John and Mary Martin Hammack of Virginia, he has not been conclusively proven to be the same individual. Likewise, the identification of his son William as William Hammock of Overton Co., TN, is speculative.

117. WILLIAM[7] HAMMACK *(JOHN[6], RICHARD[5], RICHARD[4], WILLIAM "O"[3], JOHN[2] HAMMOCKE, ? JOHN[1] HAMMOT)* was born Bet. 1749 - 1752 in Louisa Co., VA, and died Aft. 1782 in Campbell Co., VA.
Child of WILLIAM HAMMACK is:
233.   i.   ? WILLIAM[8] HAMMACK, b. Bet. 1790 - 1800; d. Abt. 1828, Lincoln Co., MO.
Key Sources: Albemarle Co., VA, Deeds, 1772-1776, pp. 251-52, 332-33; 1782 Albemarle Co., VA, Public Service Claims. There is no clear record of this man after 1782. I have speculated that he might be

the father of William Hammack who died in Lincoln Co., MO, or of John and William Hammack of Chatham Co., NC.

118. JOHN[7] HAMMACK *(JOHN[6], RICHARD[5], RICHARD[4], WILLIAM "O"[3], JOHN[2] HAMMOCKE, ? JOHN[1] HAMMOT)* was born Abt. 1755 in Albemarle Co., VA, and died Bet. 1840 - 1850 in Grainger Co., TN. He married NANCY MAPLES Abt. 1780 in Pittsylvania Co., VA, daughter of WILLIAM MAPLES, SR.. She was born Abt. 1760 in Virginia.

Children of JOHN HAMMACK and NANCY MAPLES are:

234.　i.　JOHN[8] HAMMACK, b. Abt. 1775, Pittsylvania Co., VA; d. Aft. 1850, Grainger Co., TN.

235.　ii.　WILLIAM HAMMACK, b. Abt. 1779, Pittsylvania Co., VA; d. Bet. 1830 - 1840, Grainger Co., TN.

　　iii.　SUSANNAH HAMMACK, b. 01 Jul 1789, VA; d. 20 Oct 1859, Washington Co., IN; m. SAMUEL WAGGONER, 19 May 1807, Grainger Co., TN; b. 01 Jul 1784, NC; d. Abt. 1850, Whitley Co.,KY.

　　iv.　ELIZABETH JANE HAMMACK, b. 10 Sep 1787, Pittsylvania Co., VA; d. Bef. 1860, Campbell Co., VA; m. JOHN BOLTON, 21 Aug 1805, Grainger Co., TN; b. 15 Jan 1781, VA; d. 1855, Campbell Co., VA.

236.　v.　MARTIN HAMMACK, b. Abt. 1784, Pittsylvania Co., VA; d. Abt. 1839, Claiborne Co., TN.

237.　vi.　DANIEL HAMMACK, b. Abt. 1795, Greenbriar Co., VA; d. Aft. 1870, Union Co., TN.

238.　vii.　EPHRAIM HAMMACK, b. Abt. 1799, Greenbriar Co., VA; d. Abt. 1855, IN.

　　viii.　? SARAH HAMMACK, b. Abt. 1790, Pittsylvania Co., VA; d. Aft. 1833, Laurel Co., KY; m. REV. JEHU BANNER BROCK; b. Abt. 1787; d. Aft. 1833, Laurel Co., KY.

　　ix.　? MARY HAMMACK, b. Abt. 1790, Pittsylvania Co., VA; m. WILLIAM GRAY, 28 Feb 1810, Grainger Co., TN.

Key Sources: Revolutionary War Pension Application of John Hammack, Grainger Co., TN; 1830 Grainger Co., TN, Census, p. 363; 1840 Grainger Co., TN, Census, pp. 138, 140.

119. MARTIN[7] HAMMOCK *(JOHN[6], RICHARD[5], RICHARD[4], WILLIAM "O"[3], JOHN[2] HAMMOCKE, ? JOHN[1] HAMMOT)* was born Abt. 1760 in Albemarle Co., VA, and died Aft. 1838 in Kanawha Co., VA. He married SUSANNE ELLISON 21 Mar 1793 in Kanawha Co., WV, daughter of JAMES ELLISON and ANNE ENGLISH. She was born Abt. 1775 in Virginia.

Children of MARTIN HAMMOCK and SUSANNE ELLISON are:

　　i.　CYNTHIA[8] HAMMOCK, b. Abt. 1790, Kanawha Co., VA; d. Aft. 1835, Kanawha Co., VA; m. PRESLEY VINEYARD; b. Abt. 1790, Virginia; d. Aft. 1860, Roane Co., WV.

239.　ii.　WILLIAM HAMMOCK, b. Abt. 1796, Kanawha Co., VA; d. Abt. 1876, Roane Co., WV.

240.　iii.　JOHN HAMMOCK, b. Abt. 1798, Kanawha Co., VA; d. Aft. 1870, Kanawha Co., VA.

241.　iv.　DELANA HAMMOCK, b. Abt. 1802, Kanawha Co., VA; d. Bet. 1850 - 1860, Kanawha Co., VA.

　　v.　ELIJAH HAMMOCK, b. Abt. 1799, Kanawha Co., VA; d. Aft. 1860, Taylor Co., VA.

242.　vi.　JAMES HAMMOCK, b. Abt. 1805, Kanawha Co., VA; d. Aft. 1850, Kanawha Co., VA.

　　vii.　MARY J. HAMMOCK, b. Abt. 1806, Kanawha Co., VA.

　　viii.　SUSANNAH HAMMOCK, b. 13 Apr 1807, Kanawha Co., VA; d. 15 Dec 1885.

243.　ix.　MARTIN HAMMOCK, b. Abt. 1807, Kanawha Co., VA; d. 02 May 1862, CSA, Virginia Volunteers.

　　x.　ELIZABETH HAMMOCK, b. Abt. 1814, Kanawha Co., VA.

　　xi.　RACHEL HAMMOCK, b. Abt. 1816, Kanawha Co., VA; m. NATHAN JUDY.

244.　xii.　ANDREW HAMMOCK, b. Abt. 1817, Kanawha Co., VA; d. 08 Aug 1855, Kanawha Co., VA.

Key Sources: Revolutionary War Pension Application of Martin Hammock, Kanawha Co., VA; 1800 Kanawha Co., VA, Personal Property Tax List; 1820 Kanawha Co., VA, Census, p. 5A; 1830 Kanawha Co., VA, Census, p. 196; Virginia Land Grants Book 90, p. 467; 1840 Kanawha Co., VA, Census, pp. 53, 60, 61.

120. DANIEL[7] HAMMACK *(JOHN[6], RICHARD[5], RICHARD[4], WILLIAM "O"[3], JOHN[2] HAMMOCKE, ? JOHN[1] HAMMOT)* was born Abt. 1762 in Albemarle Co., VA, and died 16 Jul 1829 in Smith Co., TN. He married MARY MARTIN Abt. 1789 in Henry Co., VA. She was born Bet. 1767 - 1773 in Pittsylvania Co., VA, and died 21 Aug 1852 in Smith Co., TN.
Children of DANIEL HAMMACK and MARY MARTIN are:

	i.	MARTHA[8] HAMMACK, b. 1790, VA; d. Aft. 1832, Carroll Co., MS; m. ARCHIBALD D. YOUNG.
245.	ii.	MARTIN HAMMACK, b. 1791, South Carolina; d. 31 Aug 1873, Lake Co., CA.
246.	iii.	BRICE WISEMAN HAMMACK, b. 1796, Georgia; d. Abt. 05 Jan 1867, Coryell Co., TX.
247.	iv.	WILLIAM H. HAMMACK, b. 1799, Smith Co., TN; d. 1881, Lincoln Co., MO.
248.	v.	JAMES DANIEL HAMMACK, b. 1800, Smith Co., TN; d. Aft. 1880, Madison Co., MO.
	vi.	SARAH HAMMACK, b. 1806, Smith Co., TN; d. Aft. 1832, Wayne Co., MO.
	vii.	JOSEPH HAMMACK, b. 1808, Smith Co., TN; d. Aft. 1829, Tennessee.
	viii.	LEMUEL AUSTIN HAMMACK, b. 10 Feb 1810, Smith Co., TN; d. 20 Aug 1859, Smith Co., TN; m. MARY J. GAMMON; b. 14 Apr 1822, Tennessee; d. 02 Oct 1857, Smith Co., TN.
	ix.	ELIJAH H. HAMMACK, b. 1813, Smith Co., TN; d. Bef. Sep 1846, Smith Co., TN.

Key Source: G. P. Omohundro, *Ancestors and Descendants of Brice Wiseman Hammack* (Santa Ana, CA, 1986); 1790 Greenville Co., SC, Census; Franklin Co., GA, Deed Book KK, pp. 9-10; 1820 Smith Co., TN, Census, p. 61; 1820 Lincoln Co., MO, Census; 1830 Smith Co., TN, Census, p. 44; 1830 Lincoln Co., MO, Census, pp. 13-14; 1840 Smith Co., TN, Census, p. 259; 1840 Lincoln Co., MO, Census, pp. 207-208, 218; 1850 Smith Co., TN, Census, HH 1047/572.

121. JOHN[7] HAMMACK *(RICHARD[6], RICHARD[5], RICHARD[4], WILLIAM "O"[3], JOHN[2] HAMMOCKE, ? JOHN[1] HAMMOT)* was born Bet. 1760 - 1763 in Albemarle Co., VA, and died Abt. 1844 in Pittsylvania Co., VA. He married MARTHA GOAD May 1784 in Pittsylvania Co., VA. She was born Abt. 1760 in Pittsylvania Co., VA, and died Jul 1855 in Pittsylvania Co., VA.
Children of JOHN HAMMACK and MARTHA GOAD are:

249.	i.	SPENCER[8] HAMMACK, b. Abt. 1785, Pittsylvania Co., VA; d. Aft. 1870, Pittsylvania Co., VA.
250.	ii.	TALIAFERRO HAMMACK, b. Abt. 1787, Pittsylvania Co., VA; d. Aft. 1850, Macon Co., TN.
251.	iii.	COLEMAN HAMMACK, b. Abt. 1793, Pittsylvania Co., VA; d. Aft. 1850, Westmoreland Co., TN.
252.	iv.	JOHN T. HAMMACK, b. Bet. 1794 - 1800, Pittsylvania Co., VA; d. Aft. 1842, Pittsylvania Co., VA.
	v.	ELIZABETH HAMMACK, b. Abt. 1805, Pittsylvania Co., VA; m. JOHN JACOBS, Abt. 26 May 1825, Pittsylvania Co., VA.
	vi.	MILDRED HAMMACK, b. Abt. 1795, Pittsylvania Co., VA; m. ABRAHAM MEESE, Abt. 05 Oct 1813, Pittsylvania Co., VA.

Key Sources: 1782 Pittsylvania Co., VA, Tax List; Pittsylvania Co., VA, Deed Book 8, p. 524; Pittsylvania Co., VA, Deed Book 10, p. 130; Pittsylvania Co., VA, Deed Book 13, p. 216; 1785 Pittsylvania Co., VA, Tax List; Pittsylvania Co., VA, Order Book 1783-1787, p. 220; 1787-1810 Pittsylvania Co., VA, Personal Property Tax Lists; Pittsylvania Co., VA, Order Book 17, p. 88; 1820

Pittsylvania Co., VA, Census, pp. 51, 69; Pittsylvania Co., VA, Deed Book 28, p. 443; 1830 Pittsylvania Co., VA, Census, pp. 313, 318, 320; Pittsylvania Co., VA, Order Bok 33, p. 303; 1840 Pittsylvania Co., VA, Census, pp. 80, 89, 114; Pittsylvania Co., VA, Deed Book 48, p. 38; Pittsylvania Co., VA, Deed Book 47, p. 377; Pittsylvania Co., VA, Order Book 38, pp. 193-194; Pittsylvania Co., VA, Estate Book 16, p. 19; Pittsylvania Co., VA, Order Book 39, pp. 111, 237; 1850 Pittsylvania Co., VA, Census, p. 256; Pittsylvania Co., VA, Register of Deaths.

122. PETER[7] HAMMACK *(RICHARD[6], RICHARD[5], RICHARD[4], WILLIAM "O"[3], JOHN[2] HAMMOCKE, ? JOHN[1] HAMMOT)* was born Abt. 1764 in Albemarle Co., VA, and died Aft. 1830 in Giles Co., TN. He married NANCY PRUNTY 26 Jan 1788 in Franklin Co., VA. She was born Abt. 1770 in Virginia, and died Aft. 1830 in Giles Co., TN.

Children of PETER HAMMACK and NANCY PRUNTY are:

    i. ELIZABETH[8] HAMMACK, b. Bet. 1789 - 1790, Franklin Co., VA; d. Aft. 1820, Grainger Co., TN; m. JONATHAN BRANSON, 10 May 1807, Grainger Co., TN.

    ii. MARY HAMMACK, b. Bet. 1790 - 1792, Franklin Co., VA; d. Aft. 1810, Grainger Co., TN; m. GEORGE H. BEELER, JR., 30 Jan 1810, Grainger Co., TN.

    iii. ? WILLIAM HAMMACK, b. Bet. 1790 - 1794, Pittsylvania Co., VA; d. Aft. 1810, Grainger Co., TN.

    iv. SON HAMMACK, b. Bet. 1794 - 1802, Pittsylvania Co., VA; d. Aft. 1820, Giles Co., TN.

    v. DAUGHTER HAMMACK, b. Bet. 1795 - 1800, Pittsylvania Co., VA; d. Aft. 1820, Giles Co., TN.

    vi. DAUGHTER HAMMACK, b. Bet. 1800 - 1804, Tennessee; d. Aft. 1830, Giles Co., TN.

    vii. SON HAMMACK, b. Bet. 1804 - 1810, Tennessee; d. Aft. 1820, Giles Co., TN.

    viii. DAUGHTER HAMMACK, b. Bet. 1804 - 1810, Tennessee; d. Aft. 1830, Giles Co., TN.

Key Sources: 1787-1790 Pittsylvania Co., VA, Personal Property Tax Lists; Pittsylvania Co., VA, Deed Book 8, p. 386; Pittsylvania Co., VA, Deed Book 9, p. 534; Pittsylvania Co., VA, Deed Book 10, p. 148; Grainger Co., TN, Minutes of the Court of Pleas, 1802-1812, p. 20; 1804, 1805, 1809 Grainger Co., TN, Tax Lists; 1812 Knox Co., TN, Tax List; 1820 Giles Co., TN, Census, p. 12; 1830 Giles Co., TN, Census, p. 167. The names of the offspring of Peter Hammack and of his male siblings are largely speculative and are based on common associations, nomenclature, and migration.

123. DANIEL[7] HAMMACK *(RICHARD[6], RICHARD[5], RICHARD[4], WILLIAM "O"[3], JOHN[2] HAMMOCKE, ? JOHN[1] HAMMOT)* was born Bet. 1765 - 1770 in Pittsylvania Co., VA, and died Bet. 1818 - 1820 in Knox Co., KY. He married AGGY PREWETT 26 Jan 1788 in Pittsylvania Co., VA. She was born Bet. 1765 - 1770 in Virginia, and died Bet. 1830 - 1840 in Perry Co., IN.

Children of DANIEL HAMMACK and AGGY PREWETT are:

253.   i. JOHN[8] HAMMACK, b. 11 Mar 1791, Pittsylvania Co., VA; d. Aft. 1840, Posey Co., IN.

    ii. NANCY HAMMACK, b. 12 Jun 1793, Pittsylvania Co., VA.

    iii. MARY HAMMACK, b. 24 Jan 1796, Pittsylvania Co., VA; d. Aft. 19 Sep 1850, Marion Co., MO; m. NICHOLAS FOX, 10 Nov 1814, Knox Co., KY; b. Abt. 1794; d. Aft. 1840, Knox Co., KY.

254.   iv. EPHRAIM HAMMACK, b. 26 Feb 1798, Pittsylvania Co., VA; d. 18 Apr 1855, Perry Co., IN.

255.   v. DANIEL HAMMACK, b. 06 Jul 1800, Pittsylvania Co., VA; d. 18 May 1855, Mercer Co., IL.

256.   vi. ISAIAH HAMMACK, b. 07 Aug 1804, Pittsylvania Co., VA; d. Aft. 1830, Knox Co., KY.

257.   vii. JAMES MARION HAMMACK, b. Abt. 1814, Madison Co., KY; d. 22 Apr 1890, Union Co., OR.

viii. ? FRANCES HAMMACK, b. Abt. 1795, Pittsylvania Co., VA; d. 11 Oct 1851, Perry Co., IN; m. JONATHAN DAVID ESRAY, 07 Jan 1844, Perry Co., IN; b. 29 Sep 1783, Louisville, KY.

Key Sources: 1791-1803 Pittsylvania Co., VA, Personal Property Tax Lists; 1810 Madison Co., KY, Census, p. 215; 1814 Madison Co., KY, Tax List; 1816-1818 Knox Co., KY, Tax Lists; 1820 Knox Co., KY, Census, p. 278.

124. EPHRAIM[7] HAMMACK *(RICHARD[6], RICHARD[5], RICHARD[4], WILLIAM "O"[3], JOHN[2] HAMMOCKE, ? JOHN[1] HAMMOT)* was born Abt. 1776 in Pittsylvania Co., VA, and died Aft. 1830 in Madison Co., KY. He married UNKNOWN. She was born Abt. 1775 in Virginia, and died Aft. 1830 in Kentucky.
Children of EPHRAIM HAMMACK and UNKNOWN are:
　　　i. SON[8] HAMMACK, b. Abt. 1794, Pittsylvania Co., VA; d. Aft. 1810, Madison Co., KY.
258.　ii. WILLIAM HAMMACK, b. 25 Jul 1798, Pittsylvania Co., VA; d. 11 Jun 1873, Franklin Co., MO.
　　　iii. DAUGHTER HAMMACK, b. Abt. 1804, Kentucky; d. Aft. 1820, Kentucky.
259.　iv. MARTIN HAMMACK, b. Abt. 1807, Kentucky; d. 30 Dec 1857, Parke Co., IN.
260.　v. JAMES HAMMACK, b. Abt. 1810, Madison Co., KY; d. 28 Oct 1845, Franklin Co., MO.
　　　vi. DAUGHTER HAMMACK, b. Abt. 1806, Madison Co., KY; d. Aft. 1820, Madison Co., KY.
　　　vii. ELIZABETH HAMMACK, b. 10 Apr 1810, Madison Co., KY; d. 23 Jan 1877, Pettis Co., MO; m. WILLIAM WALKER GLENN, 01 Apr 1830, Madison Co., MO; b. 07 Aug 1803, Madison Co., KY; d. 23 Jul 1874, Pettis Co., MO.
261.　viii. GEORGE WASHINGTON HAMMACK, b. 10 Sep 1817, Madison Co., KY; d. 11 Jan 1859, Garrard Co., KY.
　　　ix. ? ANDREW J. HAMMACK, b. Abt. 1818, Madison Co., KY; d. Aft. 1840, Lincoln Co., KY.

Key Sources: 1797-1804 Pittsylvania Co., VA, Personal Property Tax Lists; Pittsylvania Co., VA, Deed Book 13, p. 443; Pittsylvania Co., VA, Deed Book 15, p. 322; 1810 Madison Co., KY, Census, p. 216; 1820 Madison Co., KY, Census, pp. 136, 168; 1830 Garrard Co., KY, Census, p. 299; HFH, 2: 233-234.

125. JAMES[7] HAMMACK *(RICHARD[6], RICHARD[5], RICHARD[4], WILLIAM "O"[3], JOHN[2] HAMMOCKE, ? JOHN[1] HAMMOT)* was born Bef. 1776 in Pittsylvania Co., VA, and died Bet. 1808 - 1810 in Grainger Co., TN. He married ELIZABETH BROCK Bet. 1795 - 1798 in Pittsylvania Co., VA.
Children of JAMES HAMMACK and ELIZABETH BROCK are:
262.　i. WILLIAM[8] HAMMACK, b. 12 Jun 1800, Pittsylvania Co., VA; d. 05 Oct 1858, Hamilton Co., IN.
263.　ii. JOHN BROCK HAMMACK, b. Abt. 1806, Tennessee; d. Aft. 1880, Miles Co., IA.
　　　iii. DAUGHTER HAMMACK, b. Bet. 1800 - 1810, Tennessee; d. Aft. 1810, Tennessee.
　　　iv. DAUGHTER HAMMACK, b. Bet. 1800 - 1810, Tennessee; d. Aft. 1810, Tennessee.
　　　v. DAUGHTER HAMMACK, b. Bet. 1800 - 1810, Tennessee; d. Aft. 1810, Tennessee.

Key Sources: 1797-1803 Pittsylvania Co., VA, Personal Property Tax Lists; Pittsylvania Co., VA, Order Book 9, p. 475; Grainger Co., TN, Minutes of the Court of Pleas, 1802-1812, p. 20.

126. WILLIAM[7] HAMMACK *(RICHARD[6], RICHARD[5], RICHARD[4], WILLIAM "O"[3], JOHN[2] HAMMOCKE, ? JOHN[1] HAMMOT)* was born Bet. 1775 - 1781 in Pittsylvania Co., VA, and died Bet. 1813 - 1814 in Madison Co., KY. He married JANE LONG 20 Dec 1800 in Pittsylvania Co., VA. She was born Bet. 1780 - 1784 in Pittsylvania Co., VA, and died Aft. 1820 in Madison Co., KY.
Children of WILLIAM HAMMACK and JANE LONG are:

264.   i.   JAMES L.⁸ HAMMACK, b. 05 Aug 1801, Pittsylvania Co., VA; d. 03 May 1862, Mercer Co., MO.

       ii.   ELIZABETH HAMMACK, b. 11 Feb 1803, Pittsylvania Co., VA; d. 08 Jun 1843, Garrard Co., KY; m. JAMES MURPHY, 21 Aug 1822, Garrard Co., KY; b. 25 Dec 1799, Garrard Co., KY; d. 04 Apr 1883, Garrard Co., KY.

265.   iii.   GEORGE HAMMACK, b. Abt. 1806, Tennesseee; d. Bet. 1880 - 1882, Vigo Co., IN.

266.   iv.   DANIEL HAMMACK, b. 08 Mar 1811, Madison Co., KY; d. 30 Apr 1888, Anderson Co., KY.

       v.   FANNY HAMMACK, b. Abt. 1814, Madison Co., KY; d. Aft. 1831, Garrard Co., KY; m. WILLIAM MURPHY, 11 Apr 1831, Garrard Co., KY; b. Bet. 1812 - 1814, Garrard Co., KY; d. Bef. 1870, Kentucky.

Key Sources: 1797-1803 Pittsylvania Co., VA, Personal Property Tax Lists; Pittsylvania Co., VA, Order Book 9, p. 475; 1810 Madison Co., KY, Census, p. 215; 1820 Madison Co., KY, Census, p. 168.

127. LEWIS⁷ HAMMACK *(RICHARD⁶, RICHARD⁵, RICHARD⁴, WILLIAM "O"³, JOHN² HAMMOCKE, ? JOHN¹ HAMMOT)* was born Abt. 1780 in Pittsylvania Co., VA, and died Aft. 1816 in Madison Co., KY. He married KEZIAH DANIEL 15 Mar 1802 in Pittsylvania Co., VA. She was born Bet. 1765 - 1775 in Virginia.
Children of LEWIS HAMMACK and KEZIAH DANIEL are:

267.   i.   COLEMAN⁸ HAMMACK, b. Abt. 1802, Pittsylvania Co., VA; d. Bef. 04 Jan 1843, Monroe Co., MO.

268.   ii.   BENJAMIN HAMMACK, b. Abt. 1804, Pittsylvania Co., VA; d. 1875, Marion Co., IL.

       iii.   DAUGHTER HAMMACK, b. Abt. 1806, Kentucky.

       iv.   DAUGHTER HAMMACK, b. Abt. 1808.

Key Sources: 1801-1803 Pittsylvania Co., VA, Personal Property Tax Lists; 1810 Madison Co., KY, Census, p. 215; 1813 and 1816 Madison Co., KY, Census.

128. JAMES⁷ HAMMACK *(WILLIAM⁶, JOHN⁵, WILLIAM "THE YOUNGER"⁴, WILLIAM "O"³, JOHN² HAMMOCKE, ? JOHN¹ HAMMOT)* was born Abt. 1778 in Lunenburg Co., VA, and died Abt. 1835 in Lunenburg Co., VA. He married ELIZABETH AMOS 20 Jun 1805 in Lunenburg Co., VA. She was born Abt. 1784 in Lunenburg Co., VA, and died Aft. 1850 in Lunenburg Co., VA.
Children of JAMES HAMMACK and ELIZABETH AMOS are:

       i.   JOHN⁸ HAMMACK, b. Abt. 1808, Lunenburg Co., VA; d. Aft. 1835, Lunenburg Co., VA.

       ii.   GEORGE HAMMACK, b. Abt. 1811, Lunenburg Co., VA; d. Aft. 1880, Lunenburg Co., VA.

       iii.   JAMES HAMMACK, b. Abt. 1813, Lunenburg Co., VA; d. Aft. 1835, Lunenburg Co., VA.

       iv.   LEWIS LAMBERT HAMMACK, b. Abt. 1814, Lunenburg Co., VA; d. May 1865, Point Lookout, VA; m. ELIZABETH S. FREEMAN, 04 Oct 1852, Lunenburg Co., VA.

       v.   ANN ELIZABETH H. HAMMACK, b. Abt. 1823, Lunenburg Co., VA; d. Aft. 1850, Lunenburg Co., VA; m. ? THOMAS J. LAMBERT, 20 Dec 1853, Lunenburg Co., VA.

269.   vi.   HUGH M. HAMMACK, b. Abt. 1824, Lunenburg Co., VA; d. Aft. 1870, Lunenburg Co., VA.

       vii.   SAMUEL P. HAMMACK, b. Abt. 1827, Lunenburg Co., VA; d. Aft. 1881, Lunenburg Co., VA; m. LOUISA B. [------], Abt. 1851, Lunenburg Co., VA; b. Abt. 1830, Lunenburg Co., VA; d. Aft. 1881, Lunenburg Co., VA.

Key Sources: 1800-1807 Lunenburg Co., VA, Personal Property Tax Lists; Lunenburg Co., VA, Will Book 6, p. 174; 1810 Lunenburg Co., VA, Census, p. 8; 1820 Lunenburg Co., VA, Census, p. 169; 1820 Lunenburg Co., VA, Land Tax List; Lunenburg Co., VA, Deed Book 27, p. 60; 1830 Lunenburg Co., VA, Census; Lunenburg Co., VA, Will Book 11, p. 53A; Lunenburg Co., VA, Deed Book 30, p. 381;

1840 Lunenburg Co., VA, Census; Lunenburg Co., VA, Deed Book 31, p. 403; 1850 Lunenburg Co., VA, Census, HH 79, HH 80; Lunenburg Co., VA, Deed Book 35, p. 576; Lunenburg Co., VA, Deed Book 35, p. 589; Lunenburg Co., VA, Deed Bok 37, p. 26; Lunenburg Co., VA, Deed Book 37, p. 27; 1870 Lunenburg Co., VA, Census, p. 507; Lunenburg Co., VA, Deed Book 40, pp. 598-599.

129. HUGH[7] HAMMACK *(HUGH[6], JOHN[5], WILLIAM "THE YOUNGER"[4], WILLIAM "O"[3], JOHN[2] HAMMOCKE, ? JOHN[1] HAMMOT)* was born Abt. 1799 in Lunenburg Co., VA, and died 05 Apr 1860 in Lunenburg Co., VA. He married LUCY M. PEACE Abt. 14 Nov 1825 in Lunenburg Co., VA. She was born Abt. 1805 in Lunenburg Co., VA, and died Aft. 1870 in Lunenburg Co., VA.

Children of HUGH HAMMACK and LUCY PEACE are:

   i.   PERMELIA[8] HAMMACK, b. Abt. 1826, Lunenburg Co., VA; d. Aft. 1850, Lunenburg Co., VA; m. (1) SPENCER INGE, 11 Aug 1845, Lunenburg Co., VA; b. Abt. 1821, Lunenburg Co., VA; d. Bet. 1850 - 1860, Lunenburg Co., VA; m. (2) RICHARD J. MORGAN, Bef. 1860, Lunenburg Co., VA.

   ii. MARY C. HAMMACK, b. Abt. 1828, Lunenburg Co., VA; d. Aft. 1850, Lunenburg Co., VA; m. WILLIAM W. KIRK.

   iii. JOHN L. HAMMACK, b. Abt. 1830, Lunenburg Co., VA; d. Aft. 1870, Brunswick Co., VA.

   iv. EMMA JANE HAMMACK, b. Abt. 1831, Lunenburg Co., VA; d. Bet. 1850 - 1860, Lunenburg Co., VA; m. RICHARD J. MORGAN, 08 Nov 1852, Lunenburg Co., VA.

   v.   JAMES R. HAMMACK, b. Abt. 1833, Lunenburg Co., VA; d. Abt. Oct 1855, Lunenburg Co., VA.

   vi. WILLIAM C. HAMMACK, b. Abt. 1835, Lunenburg Co., VA; d. Aft. 1850, Lunenburg Co., VA.

   vii. JOCEPHUS HAMMACK, b. Abt. 1841, Lunenburg Co., VA; d. Bet. 01 May 1862 - 1863, Lunenburg Co., VA.

   viii. LUCY E. HAMMACK, b. Abt. 1844, Lunenburg Co., VA; d. Aft. 1871, Lunenburg Co., VA.

Key Sources: Lunenburg Co., VA, Deed Book 28, pp. 65-66; 1850 Lunenburg Co., VA, Census, HH 383, HH 388; Lunenburg Co., VA, Estates Book F-2, pp. 257, 260, 401-402, 559-560; Lunenburg Co., VA, Estates Book F-3, pp. 161, 209, 211, 275, 468; Lunenburg Co., VA, Estates Book F-4, p. 181; Lunenburg Co., VA, Register of Deaths.

Generation No. 8

130. MICHAEL[8] HAMMICK *(MICHAEL[7] HAMICK, MICHAEL[6] HAMMICK, MICHAEL[5], THOMAS[4] HAMICK, HENRYE[3] HAMICKE, JOHN[2] HAMMOCKE, ? JOHN[1] HAMMOT)* was born Abt. 27 Dec 1765 in Yealmpton, Devonshire. He married (1) FRANCES [------]. He married (2) ANN [------] Abt. 1795 in St. Petrox, Devonshire.

Children of MICHAEL HAMMICK and FRANCES [------] are:

270.   i.   JOHN[9] HAMMICK, b. Abt. 23 Sep 1788, Yealmpton, Devonshire.

       ii. MARY HAMMICK, b. Abt. 19 Oct 1790, Yealmpton, Devonshire.

Children of MICHAEL HAMMICK and ANN [------] are:

      iii. MARY ANN[9] HAMMICK, b. Abt. 22 Jan 1797, St. Petrox, Dartmouth, Devonshire.

      iv.   AGNESS HAMMICK, b. Abt. 14 Apr 1799, St. Petrox, Dartmouth, Devonshire.

      v.   MICHAEL HAMMICK, b. Abt. 21 Jun 1801, St. Petrox, Dartmouth, Devonshire.

      vi.   ELIZABETH HAMMICK, b. Abt. 21 Oct 1804, St. Petrox, Dartmouth, Devonshire.

      vii. ROBERT PATERSON HAMMICK, b. Abt. 11 Jan 1807, St. Petrox, Dartmouth, Devonshire.

Key Sources: Yealmpton Parish Register; St. Petrox Parish Register.

131. SAMUEL[8] HAMMACK *(JOHN[7], JOHN[6], WILLIAM[5], WILLIAM "THE ELDER"[4], WILLIAM "O"[3], JOHN[2] HAMMOCKE, ? JOHN[1] HAMMOT)* was born Abt. 1775 in Granville Co., NC, and died Bef. 1803 in Edgefield District, SC. He married ELIZABETH [------] Abt. 1796 in Wilkes Co., GA. She was born Abt. 1775, and died Aft. 1806 in Lincoln Co., GA.

Children of SAMUEL HAMMACK and ELIZABETH [------] are:

271.   i.   THOMAS B.[9] HAMMACK, b. Abt. 1797, Lincoln Co., GA; d. Abt. 1844, Chambers Co., AL.

272.   ii.   JOHN B. HAMMACK, b. Abt. 1799, Lincoln Co., GA; d. Aft. 1850, Wilkes Co., GA.

       iii.   SUSANNAH HAMMACK, b. Abt. 1800, Lincoln Co., GA; d. Aft. 1870, Brazoria Co., TX; m. (1) [--------] HUGHES; m. (2) ELISHA STRINGFIELD, 18 Aug 1817, Richmond Co., GA; m. (3) JOHNSTON HAMMACK, 19 Oct 1830, Alabama.

Key Sources: Lincoln Co., GA, Will Book A, p. 49; Lincoln Co., GA, Will Book B, p. 250; Lincoln Co., GA, Deed Book A, pp. 156-157, 158-159, 159-160, 160-161; 1805, 1806, 1810 Lincoln Co., GA, Tax Digests.

132. WILLIAM[8] HAMMACK *(JOHN[7], JOHN[6], WILLIAM[5], WILLIAM "THE ELDER"[4], WILLIAM "O"[3], JOHN[2] HAMMOCKE, ? JOHN[1] HAMMOT)* was born Abt. 1776 in Granville Co., NC, and died Aft. 1840 in Chambers Co., AL. He married RUTHA [------] Abt. Jan 1797 in Lincoln Co., GA. She was born Abt. 1775 in Georgia, and died Aft. 1850 in Chambers Co., AL.

Children of WILLIAM HAMMACK and RUTHA [------] are:

       i.   WILLIAM[9] HAMMACK, b. 09 Dec 1797, Lincoln Co., GA; d. Bef. 1815, Pulaski Co., GA.

273.   ii.   JOHN S. HAMMACK, b. 09 Mar 1800, Lincoln Co., GA; d. Aft. 1870, Yell Co., AR.

       iii.   SAMUEL HAMMACK, b. 25 Aug 1803, Lincoln Co., GA; d. Aft. 1803, Lincoln Co., GA.

274.   iv.   PASCHAL HAMMACK, b. 25 Jan 1806, Lincoln Co., GA; d. 21 Oct 1890, Newton Co., MS.

       v.   POLLY HAMMACK, b. 02 Dec 1808, Lincoln Co., GA; d. Aft. 1808, Lincoln Co., GA.

275.   vi.   ALFRED D. HAMMACK, b. 27 Nov 1811, Pulaski Co., GA; d. 11 Mar 1891, Smith Co., MS.

       vii.   ELIJAH HAMMACK, b. 28 Oct 1813, Pulaski Co., GA; d. Aft. 1830, Autauga Co., AL.

276.   viii.   WILLIAM B. HAMMACK, b. 30 Sep 1815, Pulaski Co., GA; d. Aft. 1880, Lee Co., AL.

       ix.   EPHRAIM B. HAMMACK, b. 17 Sep 1818, Pulaski Co., GA; d. 28 May 1863, Vicksburg, MS; m. MARYANN SMITH, 13 Jan 1853, Chambers Co., AL; b. 25 Nov 1833, Georgia; d. 20 Mar 1903, Chambers Co., AL.

Key Source: "William Hammack Family Bible," *Tap Roots*, Vol. 24 (1987).

133. JOHN[8] HAMMACK *(JOHN[7], JOHN[6], WILLIAM[5], WILLIAM "THE ELDER"[4], WILLIAM "O"[3], JOHN[2] HAMMOCKE, ? JOHN[1] HAMMOT)* was born 04 Mar 1776 in Granville Co., NC, and died 05 Jan 1824 in Newton Co., GA. He married ELIZABETH [------] Abt. 1802 in Lincoln Co., GA. She was born Abt. 1780, and died Aft. 1832 in Newton Co., GA.

Children of JOHN HAMMACK and ELIZABETH [------] are:

       i.   WILLIAM G.[9] HAMMACK, b. Abt. 1803, Lincoln Co., GA; d. Aft. 1880, Lee Co., AL.

277.   ii.   JEREMIAH HAMMACK, b. 09 Jan 1806, Lincoln Co., GA; d. 22 Nov 1888, Lee Co., AL.

278.   iii.   JOHN G. HAMMACK, b. Abt. 1809, Lincoln Co., GA; d. Aft. 1870, Murray Co., GA.

279.   iv.   SIMEON HAMMACK, b. 29 Nov 1811, Wilkes Co., GA; d. Aft. 1880, Lee Co., AL.

       v.   ELIZA HAMMACK, b. 29 Nov 1811, Wilkes Co., GA; d. Aft. 1870, Ware Co., GA; m. (1) WILILAM MONCRIEF, 16 Sep 1833, Lincoln Co., GA; b. Abt. 1810, Lincoln Co., GA; d. Abt. 1845, Lincoln Co., GA; m. (2) MAHLON BEDELL, Abt. 1856, Ware Co., GA; d. Bet. 1860 - 1870, Ware Co., GA.

Key Sources: "Jeremiah Hammack Family Bible," *Tap Roots*, Vol. 7 (1970); Wilkes Co., GA, Deed Book HHH, p. 403; Newton Co., GA, Annual Returns, 1822-1827, pp. 106-118; Newton Co., GA, Deed Book D, p. 471; Newton Co., GA, Deed Book D, pp. 473, 572.

134. ELIJAH[8] HAMMACK *(JOHN[7], JOHN[6], WILLIAM[5], WILLIAM "THE ELDER"[4], WILLIAM "O"[3], JOHN[2] HAMMOCKE, ? JOHN[1] HAMMOT)* was born Abt. 1779 in Warren Co., NC, and died Aft. 1840 in Early Co., GA. He married (1) ANNIE CHAPMAN 01 Jan 1800 in Wilkes Co., GA. She was born Abt. 1780 in Georgia, and died Bet. 1807 - 1808 in Wilkinson Co., GA. He married (2) ALCY [------] Bef. 1809 in Wilkinson Co., GA. She was born Bet. 1790 - 1800 in Georgia, and died 24 Jan 1844 in Wilkinson Co., GA.

Children of ELIJAH HAMMACK and MARY CHAPMAN are:

     i.   CHILD[9] HAMMACK, b. Abt. 1801, Lincoln Co., GA.

    ii.   CHILD HAMMACK, b. Abt. 1803, Lincoln Co., GA.

   iii.   CHILD HAMMACK, b. Abt. 1805, Lincoln Co., GA.

280.   iv.   JAMES HAMMACK, b. Abt. 1807, Lincoln Co., GA; d. Aft. 1870, Twiggs Co., GA.

Children of ELIJAH HAMMACK and ALCY [------] are:

281.   v.   JOSEPH[9] HAMMACK, b. Abt. 1810, Wilkinson Co., GA; d. Aft. 1850, Muscogee Co., GA.

   vi.   SON HAMMACK, b. Bet. 1815 - 1820, Wilkinson Co., GA; d. Aft. 1840, Early Co., GA.

  vii.   DAUGHTER HAMMACK, b. Bet. 1815 - 1820, Wilkinson Co., GA; d. Aft. 1840, Early Co., GA.

 viii.   SON HAMMACK, b. Bet. 1825 - 1830, Wilkinson Co., GA; d. Aft. 1840, Early Co., GA.

Key Sources: 1818 Twiggs Co., GA, Census; 1830 Wilkinson Co., GA, Census; 1840 Early Co., GA, Census, p. 122; Records of Big Sandy Church, Wilkinson Co., GA; Records of New Providence Church, Twiggs Co., GA; Records of Richland Baptist Church, Twiggs Co., GA. Many false claims have been made regarding the offspring of Elijah Hammack, stemming primarily from speculation in Henry Franklin Hammack's *Wandering Back*. The identification of James and Joseph Hammack as offspring of Elijah is speculative and is based on location and nomenclature. Elijah had at least two sons whose identity is unknown; they are probably among the adult Hammack males in western Georgia and eastern Alabama in the 1840s and 1850s who cannot be conclusively placed.

135. PASCHAL[8] HAMMACK *(JOHN[7], JOHN[6], WILLIAM[5], WILLIAM "THE ELDER"[4], WILLIAM "O"[3], JOHN[2] HAMMOCKE, ? JOHN[1] HAMMOT)* was born Jun 1782 in Warren Co., NC, and died Jul 1865 in Randolph Co., GA. He married (1) ZILPHA GREEN Abt. 1812 in Wilkes Co., GA. She was born Abt. 1790 in Georgia, and died Abt. 1830 in Randolph Co., GA. He married (2) UNKNOWN Abt. 1831 in Twiggs Co., GA. She was born Bet. 1800 - 1810 in Georgia, and died Bet. 1840 - 1850 in Randolph Co., GA.

Children of PASCHAL HAMMACK and ZILPHA GREEN are:

282.   i.   WILLIAM HARRISON[9] HAMMOCK, b. 02 Feb 1814, Twiggs Co., GA; d. 03 Apr 1863, Randolph Co., GA.

    ii.   SON HAMMACK, b. Abt. 1816, Twiggs Co., GA; d. Aft. 1830, Twiggs Co., GA.

283.   iii.   ELIJAH HAMMACK, b. Abt. 1818, Twiggs Co., GA; d. Aft. 1862, Dothan, Alabama.

   iv.   DAUGHTER HAMMACK, b. Abt. 1820, Twiggs Co., GA; d. Aft. 1830, Twiggs Co., GA.

    v.   ZYLPHA HAMMACK, b. Abt. 1822, Twiggs Co., GA; d. Aft. 1830, Twiggs Co., GA.

284.   vi.   VINCENT OSCAR HAMMACK, b. Abt. 1824, Twiggs Co., GA; d. 08 May 1887, Randolph Co., GA.

  vii.   DAUGHTER HAMMACK, b. Abt. 1826, Twiggs Co., GA; d. Aft. 1830, Twiggs Co., GA.

Children of PASCHAL HAMMACK and UNKNOWN are:

 viii.   DAUGHTER[9] HAMMACK, b. Abt. 1833, Twiggs Co., GA.

   ix.   SON HAMMACK, b. Abt. 1835, Twiggs Co., GA.

x. DAUGHTER HAMMACK, b. Abt. 1837, Twiggs Co., GA.
xi. DAUGHTER HAMMACK, b. Abt. 1839, Twiggs Co., GA.

Key Sources: 1810 Pulaski Co., GA, Tax Digest; 1818 Twiggs Co., GA, Tax Digest; 1826 Twiggs Co., GA, Tax Digest; 1830 Twiggs Co., GA, Census, p. 68; 1840 Twiggs Co., GA, Census, p. 377; 1850 Randolph Co., GA, Census, p. 376; 1860 Randolph Co., GA, Census, p. 704; *Memoirs of Georgia*, 2: 752. Paschall also had at least one unidentified son by his first marriage. Descendants of George and Jackson Hammack of Pulaski and Laurens County claim that Paschall was their father, but I am unaware of any primary evidence which connects them to Paschall. Based on location, I have theorized that they were descendants of John Hammack of Granville County, NC (see above). Note that one John Hammack, presently unidentified, appears adjacent Paschall Hammack in the 1826 Twiggs Co., GA, Tax Digest Typescript, microfilm, Washington Memorial Library, Macon, GA. In 1830, Paschal was taxed as agent for John Hammock in Captain Oliver's District, Twiggs County.

136. CHARLES[8] HAMMACK *(JOHN[7], JOHN[6], WILLIAM[5], WILLIAM "THE ELDER"[4], WILLIAM "O"[3], JOHN[2] HAMMOCKE, ? JOHN[1] HAMMOT)* was born Abt. 1789 in Wilkes Co., GA, and died Aft. 1850 in Houston Co., GA. He married (1) MARY [------] Abt. 1810 in Lincoln Co., GA. She was born Bet. 1780 - 1790 in Georgia, and died Bet. 1840 - 1850 in Houston Co., GA. He married (2) ELIZABETH [------] Abt. 1847 in Houston Co., GA. She was born Abt. 1810 in Georgia, and died Aft. 1850 in Houston Co., GA.

Children of CHARLES HAMMACK and MARY [------] are:
285. i. JOHN A.[9] HAMMACK, b. Abt. 1815, Lincoln Co., GA; d. Aft. 1860, Baldwin Co., AL.
ii. MARGARET HAMMACK, b. Abt. 1810, Lincoln Co., GA; d. Aft. 1838, Houston Co., GA; m. [-------] MCCONNOR.

Child of CHARLES HAMMACK and ELIZABETH [------] is:
iii. CHARLES[9] HAMMACK, b. Abt. 1848, Houston Co., GA.

Key Sources: 1810 Lincoln Co., GA, Tax Digest; 1826 Twiggs Co., GA, Tax Digest; 1830 Houston Co., GA, Census, p. 274; Houston Co., GA, Deed Book G, p. 462; 1840 Houston Co., GA, Census, p. 373; 1850 Houston Co., GA, Census, p. 376.

137. THOMAS[8] HAMMACK *(JOHN[7], JOHN[6], WILLIAM[5], WILLIAM "THE ELDER"[4], WILLIAM "O"[3], JOHN[2] HAMMOCKE, ? JOHN[1] HAMMOT)* was born Abt. 1796 in Wilkes Co., GA, and died Aft. 1860 in Barbour Co., AL. He married MARY [------] Abt. 1816 in Lincoln Co., GA. She was born Abt. 1800 in North Carolina, and died Aft. 1880 in Dale Co., AL.

Children of THOMAS HAMMACK and MARY [------] are:
286. i. ? JAMES URIAH[9] HAMMACK, b. Abt. 1818, Lincoln Co., GA; d. Aft. 1870, Columbia Co., GA.
ii. DAUGHTER HAMMACK, b. Bet. 1820 - 1825, Lincoln Co., GA; d. Aft. 1840, Barbour Co., AL.
iii. ? ROSS HAMMACK, b. Abt. 1826, Lincoln Co., GA; d. Aft. 1850, Barbour Co., AL.
iv. SARAH HAMMACK, b. Abt. 1828, Lincoln Co., GA; d. Aft. 1850, Barbour Co., AL.
287. v. JESSE THOMAS HAMMACK, b. 05 Oct 1835, Dooly Co., GA; d. 27 Dec 1911, Early Co., GA.
vi. DAUGHTER HAMMACK, b. Bet. 1835 - 1840, Dooly Co., GA; d. Aft. 1840, Barbour Co., AL.

Key Sources: 1818 Twiggs Co., GA, Tax Digest; 1826 Twiggs Co., GA, Tax Digest; 1830 Dooly Co., GA, Census, p. 82; 1840 Barbour Co., AL, Census, p. 84; 1850 Barbour Co., AL, Census, p. 147; 1860 Barbour Co., AL, Census, p. 425. I have speculated that James Uriah and Ross Hammack were Thomas's sons based on their appearance in Barbour County in 1850 and Thomas's having had sons their age in the 1830 and 1840 census reports. I have also identified Thomas's son Thomas as Jesse Thomas Hammack.

In the 1880 Dale Co., AL, Census, he was shown with Thomas's widow Mary Hammack in his household.

138. DAVID[8] HAMMACK *(JOHN[7], JOHN[6], WILLIAM[5], WILLIAM "THE ELDER"[4], WILLIAM "O"[3], JOHN[2] HAMMOCKE, ? JOHN[1] HAMMOT)* was born Bet. 1798 - 1800 in Wilkes Co., GA, and died Bet. 1840 - 1850 in Houston Co., GA. He married SARAH SIKES 02 Jan 1822 in Lincoln Co., GA. She was born 20 Dec 1799 in Georgia, and died 29 Aug 1874 in Henry Co., AL.

Children of DAVID HAMMACK and SARAH SIKES are:

	i.	PHOEBE JANE[9] HAMMACK, b. 10 Dec 1822, Lincoln Co., GA; d. 01 Oct 1898, Henry Co., AL; m. RICHARD I. HARDY, 14 Apr 1842, Houston Co., GA; b. 07 Jan 1817, North Carolina; d. 03 Oct 1891, Henry Co., AL.
	ii.	DAUGHTER HAMMACK, b. Abt. 1824, Lincoln Co., GA; d. Aft. 1830, Wilkes Co., GA.
	iii.	MARGARET HAMMACK, b. Abt. 1828, Wilkes Co., GA; d. Aft. 1850, Randolph Co., GA.
288.	iv.	ISAIAH PASCHAL HAMMACK, b. Abt. 1825, Wilkes Co., GA; d. Bet. 1860 - 1870, Randolph Co., GA.
289.	v.	DANIEL HAMMACK, b. Abt. 1827, Wilkes Co., GA; d. Aft. 1860, Randolph Co., GA.
290.	vi.	WILLIAM G. HAMMACK, b. Abt. 1833, Wilkes Co., GA; d. Bet. 1860 - 1870, Clay Co., GA.
	vii.	DAUGHTER? HAMMACK, b. Abt. 1835, Wilkes Co., GA; d. Aft. 1840, Houston Co., GA.

Key Sources: 1830 Wilkes Co., GA, Census, p. 305; 1840 Houston Co., GA, Census, p. 377; 1850 Randolph Co., GA, Census, p. 430; 1870 Henry Co., AL, Census, p. 329.

139. GRANVILLE[8] HAMMOCK *(THOMAS[7], JOHN[6], WILLIAM[5], WILLIAM "THE ELDER"[4], WILLIAM "O"[3], JOHN[2] HAMMOCKE, ? JOHN[1] HAMMOT)* was born Abt. 1800 in Wilkes Co., GA, and died 11 Jul 1879 in Gadsden, AL. He married PRISCILLA WHEATLEY 03 Jan 1825 in Wilkes Co., GA. She was born Abt. 1810 in Georgia, and died Aft. 1850 in Jefferson Co., AL.

Children of GRANVILLE HAMMOCK and PRISCILLA WHEATLEY are:

i.	? SALLY[9] HAMMOCK, b. Abt. 1826, Jefferson Co., AL; d. Aft. 1846, Jefferson Co., AL; m. CALVIN M. FRANSHER, 12 Jan 1846, Jefferson Co., GA.
ii.	DAUGHTER HAMMOCK, b. Bet. 1825 - 1830, Jefferson Co., AL; d. Aft. 1840, Jefferson Co., AL.
iii.	MARTHA HAMMOCK, b. Abt. 1835, Jefferson Co., AL; d. Aft. 1850, Jefferson Co., AL.
iv.	WILLIAM HAMMOCK, b. Abt. 1838, Jefferson Co., AL; d. Aft. 1860, Texas.
v.	JESSE BRAZIL HAMMOCK, b. 08 Feb 1842, Jefferson Co., AL; d. 29 Aug 1911, Murray Co., GA; m. EMMA MAY LEBKESHER; b. 10 May 1853, Georgia.
vi.	ELIZABETH HAMMOCK, b. Abt. 1844, Jefferson Co., AL; d. Aft. 1850, Jefferson Co., AL.
vii.	MARINDA F. HAMMOCK, b. Abt. 1848, Jefferson Co., AL; d. Aft. 1850, Jefferson Co., AL.
viii.	ARMINDA F. HAMMOCK, b. Abt. 1848, Jefferson Co., AL; d. Aft. 1850, Jefferson Co., AL.

Key Sources: 1830 Jefferson Co., AL, Census, p. 169; 1840 Jefferson Co., AL, Census, p. 199; 1850 Jefferson Co., AL, Census, p. 204; 1860 St. Clair Co., AL, Census, p. 157.

140. STEPHEN WALKER[8] HAMMOCK *(THOMAS[7], JOHN[6], WILLIAM[5], WILLIAM "THE ELDER"[4], WILLIAM "O"[3], JOHN[2] HAMMOCKE, ? JOHN[1] HAMMOT)* was born 01 Jan 1806 in Wilkes Co., GA, and died Aft. 1870 in Kemper Co., MS. He married RHODA BERRY Abt. 1826 in Wilkes Co., GA. She was born Abt. 1800 in Georgia, and died Aft. 1860 in Kemper Co., MS.

Children of STEPHEN HAMMOCK and RHODA BERRY are:

      i.   DAUGHTER[9] HAMMOCK, b. Bet. 1825 - 1830, Georgia; d. Aft. 1830, Georgia.

     ii.   DIALTHA HAMMOCK, b. Abt. 1830, Georgia; d. Aft. 1870, Kemper Co., MS; m. HENRY BAILEY.

291.   iii.   AUGUSTUS C. HAMMOCK, b. Dec 1830, Newton Co., GA; d. 1911, Kemper Co., MS.

292.   iv.   JOHN CULPEPPER HAMMOCK, b. Abt. 1834, Newton Co., GA; d. 1899, Young Co., TX.

     v.   AMANDA HAMMOCK, b. Abt. 1835, Newton Co., GA; d. 1925, Kemper Co., MS; m. JOHN H. BETHANY.

293.   vi.   STEPHEN T. HAMMOCK, b. Abt. 1839, Newton Co., GA; d. 11 May 1862, Corinth, MS.

294.   vii.   WILLIAM ISHAM HAMMOCK, b. Aug 1843, Newton Co., GA; d. 16 Jan 1923, Kemper Co., MS.

Key Sources: Wilkes Co., GA, Deed Book LLL, p. 216; 1830 Newton Co., GA, Census, p. 16; 1850 Kemper Co., MS, Census, p. 182; 1860 Kemper Co., MS, Census, p. 841; 1870 Kemper Co., MS, Census, p. 387.

141. JOHN P.[8] HAMMOCK (*THOMAS[7], JOHN[6], WILLIAM[5], WILLIAM "THE ELDER"[4], WILLIAM "O"[3], JOHN[2] HAMMOCKE, ? JOHN[1] HAMMOT*) was born Bet. 1809 - 1811 in Wilkes Co., GA, and died Aft. 1880 in Polk Co., GA. He married EMELINE C. MOORE 22 Dec 1835 in Wilkes Co., GA, daughter of JOHN MOORE and SARAH [------]. She was born Abt. 1813 in Wilkes Co., GA, and died Aft. 1880 in Polk Co., GA.

Children of JOHN HAMMOCK and EMELINE MOORE are:

      i.   JOHN T.[9] HAMMOCK, b. Abt. 1836, Wilkes Co., GA; d. 19 Sep 1864, Ft. Harrison, VA.

     ii.   JAMES W. HAMMOCK, b. Abt. 1838, Wilkes Co., GA; d. Aft. 1870, Polk Co., GA; m. JULIA ANN TALBOT, 03 Nov 1866, Polk Co., GA; b. Abt. 1845, Georgia; d. Aft. 1870, Polk Co., GA.

    iii.   JULIUS F. HAMMOCK, b. Abt. 1840, Wilkes Co., GA; d. Aft. 1850, Polk Co., GA.

    iv.   STEPHEN LEWIS HAMMOCK, b. 12 Mar 1844, Paulding Co., GA; d. Bef. 1911, Lamar Co., AL; m. (1) FANNY A. CAMBRON, 27 Dec 1866, Polk Co., GA; b. 1851, Georgia; d. 1883, Lamar Co., AL; m. (2) MARY VIRGINIA ADAMS MARKHAM, 31 Aug 1892, Lamar Co., AL; d. Aft. 1920, Lamar Co., AL.

     v.   MARTHA M. HAMMOCK, b. Abt. 1844, Paulding Co., GA; d. Aft. 1860, Polk Co., GA.

    vi.   MEREDITH STANTON HAMMOCK, b. 24 Sep 1849, Paulding Co., GA; d. 09 Apr 1916, Cullman Co., AL; m. ELIZA CAROLINE PATTERSON, 23 Jan 1873, Polk Co., GA; b. 18 Jan 1848, Georgia; d. 03 Dec 1916, Cullman Co., AL.

   vii.   SARAH V. HAMMOCK, b. Abt. 1852, Paulding Co., GA; d. Aft. 1860, Polk Co., GA; m. [-------] HENSON.

  viii.   SIMEON WILEY. HAMMOCK, b. 06 Jan 1855, Paulding Co., GA; d. 04 Dec 1926, Choctaw Co., OK; m. (1) SARAH ANN PRICHETT, 03 Dec 1875, Polk Co., GA; b. Abt. 1855, Georgia; d. Sep 1880, Polk Co., GA; m. (2) EMMA LODASKI SHIFLET, 27 Feb 1881, Polk Co., GA; b. 18 Jul 1862, Hart Co., GA; d. 09 Jan 1938, Fannin Co., TX.

Key Sources: Wilkes Co., GA, Deed Book NNN, p. 336; Wilkes Co., GA, Deed Book MMM, p. 145; Wilkes Co., GA, Deed Book OOO, p. 291; Wilkes Co., GA, Deed Book QQQ, p. 415; 1850 Paulding Co., GA, Census, p. 74; 1860 Polk Co., GA, Census, p. 233; 1870 Polk Co., GA, Census, p. 303; 1880 Polk Co., GA, Census, pp. 185, 194.

142. JAMES L.[8] HAMMOCK (*THOMAS[7], JOHN[6], WILLIAM[5], WILLIAM "THE ELDER"[4], WILLIAM "O"[3], JOHN[2] HAMMOCKE, ? JOHN[1] HAMMOT*) was born Abt. 1798 in Wilkes Co., GA, and died Aft. 1850 in UPson Co., GA. He married MARTHA [------] Abt. 1820 in Wilkes Co., GA. She was born Abt. 1802 in Wilkes Co., GA, and died Aft. 1870 in Pike Co., GA.

Children of JAMES HAMMOCK and MARTHA [------] are:

    i.   ARMENIA CAROLINE[9] HAMMOCK, b. Abt. 1824, Wilkes Co., GA; d. Aft. 1870, Pike Co., GA; m. BIGGERS DANIEL; b. Abt. 1824, South Carolina; d. Aft. 1870, Pike Co., GA.

    ii. SON HAMMOCK, b. Abt. 1826, Wilkes Co., GA; d. Aft. 1840, Talbot Co., GA.

   iii. RICHARD HAMMOCK, b. Abt. 1828, Wilkes Co., GA; d. Aft. 1880, Upson Co., GA; m. ELIZABETH MCCLUNG, Abt. 1851, Upson Co., GA; b. Abt. 1830, Georgia; d. Aft. 1880, Upson Co., GA.

   iv. RHOENA HAMMOCK, b. 04 May 1830, Wilkes Co., GA; d. 05 Jul 1915, Upson Co., GA; m. NOAH DANIEL, 02 Aug 1849, Upson Co., GA; b. 17 Jun 1815, South Carolina; d. 05 Apr 1892, Upson Co., GA.

    v. THOMAS HAMMOCK, b. Abt. 1832, Wilkes Co., GA; d. Abt. 1863, Confederate States Army; m. NANCY MCCLUNG; b. Abt. 1830, Georgia; d. Aft. 1861, Upson Co., GA.

   vi. JAMES B. HAMMOCK, b. Abt. 1834, Wilkes Co., GA; d. Bef. 1860, Upson Co., GA; m. EMELINE TALLEY, 05 May 1854, Upson Co., GA; b. Abt. 1832, Georgia; d. Aft. 1857, Upson Co., GA.

   vii. GEORGE W. HAMMOCK, b. Abt. 1836, Talbot Co., GA; d. Aft. 1880, Upson Co., GA; m. SARAH DANIEL, Abt. 1867, Upson Co., GA; b. Abt. 1847, Georgia; d. Aft. 1880, Upson Co., GA.

  viii. STEPHEN HAMMOCK, b. Abt. 1837, Talbot Co., GA; d. Aft. 1860, Upson Co., GA; m. MARGARET DANIEL, 26 Dec 1860, Upson Co., GA.

   ix. F. HAMMOCK, b. Abt. 1842, Talbot Co., GA; d. Aft. 1860, Upson Co., GA.

Key Sources: 1830 Wilkes Co., GA, Census, p. 313; Wilkes Co., GA, Deed Book MMM, p. 200; 1840 Talbot Co., GA, Census, p. 196; Wilkes Co., GA, Deed Book III, p. 357; 1860 Upson Co., GA, Census, p. 583.

143. ELIZABETH[8] HAMMOCK (*THOMAS[7], JOHN[6], WILLIAM[5], WILLIAM "THE ELDER"[4], WILLIAM "O"[3], JOHN[2] HAMMOCKE, ? JOHN[1] HAMMOT*) was born Abt. 1812 in Wilkes Co., GA, and died Aft. 1872 in Wilkes Co., GA.
Children of ELIZABETH HAMMACK are:

    i.   JOHN THOMAS[9] HAMMOCK, b. 19 Mar 1849, Wilkes Co., GA; d. 26 Jun 1932, Wilkes Co., GA; m. MARY L. HANSFORD, 04 Feb 1875, Taliaferro Co., GA; b. 18 Feb 1841, Elbert Co., GA; d. 17 Sep 1927, Wilkes Co., GA.

295.   ii. GRANVILLE HAMMOCK, b. Abt. 1829, Wilkes Co., GA; d. Aft. 1860, Wilkes Co., GA.

Key Sources: 1850 Wilkes Co., GA, Census, p. 304; 1860 Wilkes Co., GA, Census, p. 828.

144. THOMAS[8] HAMMOCK (*WILLOUGHBY[7], JOHN[6], WILLIAM[5], WILLIAM "THE ELDER"[4], WILLIAM "O"[3], JOHN[2] HAMMOCKE, ? JOHN[1] HAMMOT*) was born 04 Sep 1808 in Clarke Co., GA, and died 01 Dec 1881 in DeKalb Co., AL. He married (1) ELIZABETH NELSON 03 Jan 1826 in Fayette Co., GA. She was born Abt. 1810 in Georgia, and died Aft. 1850 in DeKalb Co., AL. He married (2) HARRIETT JACK SPANGLER 15 Jun 1858 in DeKalb Co., AL. She was born 14 Sep 1821 in Georgia, and died 26 Jun 1889 in DeKalb Co., AL.
Children of THOMAS HAMMOCK and ELIZABETH NELSON are:

    i.   WILLIAM NELSON[9] HAMMOCK, b. 02 May 1827, Fayette Co., GA; d. 04 Mar 1891, Etowah Co., AL; m. (1) NANCY KATHERINE COLLINS, 28 Feb 1860, DeKalb Co., AL; b. Abt. 1834, Georgia; d. Aft. 1860, DeKalb Co., AL; m. (2) WINNIE EVELYN GARRETT, Oct 1864, Etowah Co., AL; b. 16 Sep 1833, Alabama; d. 29 Jul 1890, Etowah Co., AL.

    ii. SON HAMMOCK, b. Abt. 1829, Fayette Co., GA; d. Aft. 1830, Fayette Co., GA.

   iii. ? DAUGHTER HAMMOCK, b. Abt. 1831, Fayette Co., GA; d. Aft. 1831, Fayette Co., GA.

   iv. JAMES M. HAMMOCK, b. Abt. 1834, Fayette Co., GA; d. Aft. 1850, DeKalb Co., AL.

v. WILLOUGHBY HAMMOCK, b. Abt. 1836, DeKalb Co., AL; d. Aft. 1900, Washington Co., OK.

vi. AARON H. HAMMOCK, b. Abt. 1838, DeKalb Co., AL; d. Aft. 1850, DeKalb Co., AL.

vii. ELIZABETH J. HAMMOCK, b. Abt. 1840, DeKalb Co., AL; m. THOMAS B. GARRETT.

viii. JOHN M. HAMMOCK, b. Abt. 1842, DeKalb Co., AL; d. Aft. 1870, Texas.

ix. ANN H. J. HAMMOCK, b. Abt. 1844, DeKalb Co., AL; d. Aft. 1870, Lamar Co., TX; m. R. B. LANGFORD.

x. MARY P. HAMMOCK, b. Abt. 1846, DeKalb Co., AL; d. Aft. 1860, DeKalb Co., AL.

xi. EMILY C. HAMMOCK, b. Abt. 1848, DeKalb Co., AL; d. Aft. 1860, DeKalb Co., AL.

Children of THOMAS HAMMOCK and HARRIETT SPANGLER are:

xii. THOMAS JEFFERSON[9] HAMMOCK, b. Abt. 1858, DeKalb Co., AL; d. 1921, Honey Grove, TX; m. HELEN COLLINS.

xiii. HUGH JACK HAMMOCK, b. 20 Jul 1859, DeKalb Co., AL; d. 07 Dec 1932, DeKalb Co., AL; m. MARY LYONS, Abt. 1886, DeKalb Co., AL; b. 13 Oct 1862, Alabama; d. 23 Jan 1944, DeKalb Co., AL.

xiv. KATIE S. HAMMOCK, b. Abt. 1861, DeKalb Co., AL; d. Aft. 1880, DeKalb Co., AL; m. [------] EVANS.

xv. SARAH ELLEN HAMMOCK, b. Abt. 1863, DeKalb Co., AL; d. Aft. 1880, DeKalb Co., AL; m. [--------] BALDWIN.

Key Sources: 1830 Fayette Co., GA, Census, p. 199; 1850 DeKalb Co., AL, Census, p. 377; 1860 DeKalb Co., AL, Census, p. 58; Obituary of Thomas Hammock, *The Alabama Baptist*, 1 December 1881; Obituary of Mary Hammock, *The Gadsden Times*, 12 May 1887. See also Henry Franklin Hammack, 2: 192, 271.

145. AARON G.[8] HAMMOCK *(WILLOUGHBY[7], JOHN[6], WILLIAM[5], WILLIAM "THE ELDER"[4], WILLIAM "O"[3], JOHN[2] HAMMOCKE, ? JOHN[1] HAMMOT)* was born Abt. 1810 in Clarke Co., GA, and died Abt. 1867 in DeKalb Co., AL. He married (1) MARY CARROLL 07 Jan 1830 in Fayette Co., GA. She was born Abt. 1810 in Georgia, and died Aft. 1850 in Fayette Co., GA. He married (2) CLARISSA [------] Bet. 1850 - 1860 in DeKalb Co., AL. She was born Abt. 1800 in North Carolina, and died Aft. 1860 in DeKalb Co., AL.

Child of AARON HAMMOCK and MARY CARROLL is:

i. MARY ANN[9] HAMMOCK, b. Abt. 1833, Fayette Co., GA; m. BENJAMIN LEWIS.

Key Sources: Fayette Co., GA, Will Book A, pp. 38-42; 1830 Coweta Co., GA, Census, p. 381; 1840 Coweta Co., GA, Census, p. 360; 1850 Fayette Co., GA, Census, p. 4; 1860 DeKalb Co., AL, Census, p. 59.

146. WILLOUGHBY[8] HAMMOCK *(WILLOUGHBY[7], JOHN[6], WILLIAM[5], WILLIAM "THE ELDER"[4], WILLIAM "O"[3], JOHN[2] HAMMOCKE, ? JOHN[1] HAMMOT)* was born 1811 in Clarke Co., GA, and died 1887 in DeKalb Co., AL. He married NANCY POYTHRESS Abt. 1839 in Harris Co., GA. She was born 1812 in Georgia, and died 1886 in DeKalb Co., AL.

Children of WILLOUGHBY HAMMOCK and NANCY POYTHRESS are:

i. SARAH ANN R.[9] HAMMOCK, b. Abt. 1840, DeKalb Co., AL; d. Aft. 1850, DeKalb Co., AL.

ii. JAMES J. HAMMOCK, b. Abt. 1843, DeKalb Co., AL; d. Aft. 1870, Cooke Co., TX; m. AMANDA [------], Abt. 1869, Cooke Co., TX; b. Abt. 1840, Mississippi; d. Aft. 1870, Cooke Co., TX.

iii. ELIZA EMILY HAMMOCK, b. Abt. 1847, DeKalb Co., AL; d. Aft. 1860, DeKalb Co., AL.

iv. NANCY LEVICY HAMMOCK, b. Abt. 1849, DeKalb Co., AL; d. Aft. 1860, DeKalb Co., AL; m. WILLIAM S. A. LYONS, 1868, DeKalb Co., AL.

v.   WALLACE M. HAMMOCK, b. Abt. 1852, DeKalb Co., AL; d. 1925, Oregon; m. MAGGIE [------], Abt. 1880, Montague Co., TX; b. Abt. 1860, Missouri; d. Aft. 1900, Cooke Co., OR.
Key Sources: 1850 DeKalb Co., AL, Census, p. 377; 1860 DeKalb Co., AL, Census, p. 45.

147. HARRISON[8] HAMMACK *(LEWIS[7], JOHN[6], WILLIAM[5], WILLIAM "THE ELDER"[4], WILLIAM "O"[3], JOHN[2] HAMMOCKE, ? JOHN[1] HAMMOT)* was born Abt. 1798 in Wilkes Co., GA, and died Aft. 1850 in LaFayette Co., MS. He married CELIA HAMMACK 01 Dec 1817 in Jones Co., GA, daughter of JAMES HAMMACK and LUCY HAMMACK. She was born Bet. 1802 - 1803 in Wilkes Co., GA, and died Aft. 1860 in Columbia Co., AR.
Children of HARRISON HAMMACK and CELIA HAMMACK are:

      i.   ELIZA[9] HAMMACK, b. Abt. 1818, Jones Co., GA; d. Aft. 1840, Bibb Co., GA.
296. ii.   WILLIAM HAMMACK, b. Abt. 1820, Jones Co., GA; d. Aft. 1862, Stateline, AR.
     iii. DAUGHTER HAMMACK, b. Bet. 1820 - 1825, Jones Co., GA; d. Aft. 1840, Russell Co., AR.
     iv.   LUCY HAMMACK, b. Abt. 1827, Marion Co., GA; d. Aft. 1850, Alabama.
     v.   SON HAMMACK, b. Bet. 1830 - 1835, Marion Co., GA; d. Aft. 1840, Russell Co., AR.
     vi.   ELIZABETH S. HAMMACK, b. Abt. 1835, Marion Co., GA; d. Aft. 1870, Columbia Co., AR; m. HENRY B. WALLIS, Bet. 1850 - 1860, Claiborne Parish, LA; b. Abt. 1832, Tennessee; d. Aft. 1900, Columbia Co., AR.
297. vii. JAMES LEWIS HAMMACK, b. Abt. 1837, Marion Co., GA; d. Aft. 1865, Columbia Co., AR.
    viii. NANCY HAMMACK, b. Abt. 1842, Russell Co., AR; d. Aft. 1890, Columbia Co., AR; m. JOHN CASEY.
Key Sources: 1820 Jones Co., GA, Census; 1830 Marion Co., GA, Census, p. 139; 1840 Russell Co., AL, Census, p. 27; 1850 LaFayette Co., MS, Census, p. 241; 1860 Columbia Co., AR, Census, p. 334. See also Henry Franklin Hammack, 1: 37, 44, 300-305.

148. CELIA[8] HAMMACK *(JAMES[7], JOHN[6], WILLIAM[5], WILLIAM "THE ELDER"[4], WILLIAM "O"[3], JOHN[2] HAMMOCKE, ? JOHN[1] HAMMOT)* was born Bet. 1802 - 1803 in Wilkes Co., GA, and died Aft. 1860 in Columbia Co., AR. She married HARRISON HAMMACK 01 Dec 1817 in Jones Co., GA, son of LEWIS HAMMACK and ELIZABETH [------]. He was born Abt. 1798 in Wilkes Co., GA, and died Aft. 1850 in LaFayette Co., MS.
Children are listed above under (147) Harrison Hammack.

149. BENJAMIN[8] HAMMOCK *(WILLIAM[7], WILLIAM[6], BENEDICT[5] HAMMACK, WILLIAM "THE ELDER"[4], WILLIAM "O"[3], JOHN[2] HAMMOCKE, ? JOHN[1] HAMMOT)* was born Abt. 1791 in Wilkes Co., GA, and died Aft. 1870 in Saline Co., IL. He married (1) UNKNOWN. She was born Abt. 1790. He married (2) ANNICE MURPHY 11 Jul 1824 in Hamilton Co., IL. She was born Abt. 1804 in North Carolina, and died Aft. 1870 in Saline Co., IL.
Children of BENJAMIN HAMMOCK and UNKNOWN are:

      i.   SON[9] HAMMOCK, b. Abt. 1807, Kentucky; d. Aft. 1830, Gallatin Co., IL.
298. ii.   JEPTHA HAMMOCK, b. Abt. 1809, Kentucky; d. Aft. 1880, Jefferson Co., MO.
     iii. DAUGHTER HAMMOCK, b. Bet. 1815 - 1820, Kentucky; d. Aft. 1830, Illinois.
     iv.   DAUGHTER HAMMOCK, b. Bet. 1815 - 1820, Kentucky; d. Aft. 1830, Illlinois.
     v.   DAUGHTER HAMMOCK, b. Bet. 1820 - 1825, Kentucky; d. Aft. 1830, Illlinois.
299. vi.   ? WILLIAM HAMMOCK, b. Abt. 1820, Kentucky; d. Aft. 1887, Arkansas or Oklahoma.
Children of BENJAMIN HAMMOCK and ANNICE MURPHY are:

     vii. DAUGHTER[9] HAMMOCK, b. Bet. 1825 - 1830, Illinois.

viii. ? JAMES HAMMOCK, b. Abt. 1827, Illinois; d. Aft. 1870, Saline Co., IL; m. MARY
 CAROLINE [------], Abt. 1850, Lawrence Co., AR; b. Abt. 1827, Tennessee or Illinois; d.
 Aft. 1870, Saline Co., IL.
ix. MARK HAMMOCK, b. Abt. 1829, Illlinois.
x. NANCY HAMMOCK, b. Abt. 1831, Illlinois.
xi. FRANCES HAMMOCK, b. Abt. 1833, Saline Co., IL.
xii. ELIZA A. HAMMOCK, b. Abt. 1835, Saline Co., IL.
xiii. RUTH J. HAMMOCK, b. Abt. 1837, Saline Co., IL.
xiv. BENJAMIN HAMMOCK, b. 18 Nov 1842, Illinois; d. 04 Sep 1898, Saline Co., IL; m.
 MARTHA RHINE.
xv. ANNISE HAMMOCK, b. Abt. 1844, Illinois; d. Aft. 1850, Saline Co., IL.

Key Sources: 1820 Union Co., KY, Census, p. 149; 1830 Gallatin Co., IL, Census, p. 291; 1850 Saline Co., IL, Census, p. 43; 1860 Saline Co., IL, Census, p. 803; 1870 Saline Co., IL, Census, p. 409; 1880 Saline Co., IL, Census, p. 76. See the notation regarding James and William Hammock in the section on unidentified Hammocks. Although Henry Franklin Hammock links them to an Ephraim Hammock, it may be that James and William Hammock of Arkansas and Oklahoma were sons of Benjamin. James Hammock, although found in Arkansas in 1850, returned to Saline County, where he was enumerated near Benjamin in 1860 and 1870.

150. WILLIAM B.[8] HAMMOCK *(WILLIAM[7], WILLIAM[6], BENEDICT[5] HAMMACK, WILLIAM "THE ELDER"[4], WILLIAM "O"[3], JOHN[2] HAMMOCKE, ? JOHN[1] HAMMOT)* was born Abt. 1801 in Christian Co., KY, and died 1836 in Union Co., KY. He married MARTHA MOBLEY 23 Mar 1823 in Kentucky. She was born 1808 in Kentucky, and died Aft. 1850 in Union Co., KY.
Children of WILLIAM HAMMOCK and MARTHA MOBLEY are:
i. PAULINA[9] HAMMOCK, b. Abt. 1827, Kentucky; m. TERRY O'LACY.
ii. CAPT. THORNTON MOBLEY HAMMOCK, b. 1829, Kentucky; d. 1912, Kentucky; m.
 (1) NANCY CROMWELL; b. Abt. 1830, Kentucky; d. 1872, Kentucky; m. (2) BETTIE
 CROMWELL; m. (3) ANNIE JONES.
iii. JOHN WILLIAM HAMMOCK, b. 13 May 1831, Union Co., KY; d. 1914, Union Co., KY;
 m. MARY E. WRIGHT.
iv. CHARLES W. HAMMOCK, b. Abt. 1834, Union Co., KY; d. Aft. 1860, Union Co., KY; m.
 LUCINDA [------].

Key Sources: 1850 Union Co., KY, Census, p. 480. Later generations of this family are discussed extensively by Henry Franklin Hammack, 1: 158-161, and 2: 311.

151. MORGAN BROWN[8] HAMMOCK *(WILLIAM[7], WILLIAM[6], BENEDICT[5] HAMMACK, WILLIAM "THE ELDER"[4], WILLIAM "O"[3], JOHN[2] HAMMOCKE, ? JOHN[1] HAMMOT)* was born 1804 in Christian Co., KY, and died 1870 in Union Co., KY. He married MARGARET BISHOP 27 Mar 1823 in Union Co., KY. She was born 1807 in Maryland, and died Aft. 1850 in Kentucky.
Children of MORGAN HAMMOCK and MARGARET BISHOP are:
i. SARAH[9] HAMMOCK, b. Abt. 1827, Union Co., KY; d. Aft. 1850, Union Co., KY; m.
 EDWARD WILLIAMS.
ii. NANCY HAMMOCK, b. Abt. 1825, Union Co., KY; d. Aft. 1850, Union Co., KY; m.
 STEPHEN SULLIVANT.
iii. THOMAS HAMMOCK, b. Abt. 1829, Union Co., KY; d. Aft. 1850, Union Co., KY; m.
 ELIZABETH MONTGOMERY, 1852, Union Co., KY.
iv. DANIEL HAMMOCK, b. Abt. 1841, Union Co., KY; d. Aft. 1850, Union Co., KY; m.
 ALICE DAVIS.

   v. HENRY HAMMOCK, b. Abt. 1839, Union Co., KY; d. Aft. 1860, Union Co., KY; m.
       ELIZABETH R. CROMWELL.
  vi. JEREMIAH HAMMOCK, b. Abt. 1834, Union Co., KY; d. Aft. 1850, Union Co., KY; m.
       SALLY DIAL.
 vii. WILLIAM HAMMOCK, b. Abt. 1837, Union Co., KY; d. Aft. 1870, Union Co., KY; m.
       MOLLIE PRIDE.
Key Sources: 1850 Union Co., KY, Census, p. 485. See also Henry Franklin Hammack, 1: 158-161, and
2: 225.

152. DANIEL B.[8] HAMMOCK *(WILLIAM[7], WILLIAM[6], BENEDICT[5] HAMMACK, WILLIAM "THE
ELDER"[4], WILLIAM "O"[3], JOHN[2] HAMMOCKE, ? JOHN[1] HAMMOT)* was born 1808 in Caldwell Co.,
KY, and died 1877 in Union Co., KY. He married (1) ANN GILMORE. She was born 1812 in Kentucky,
and died 1870 in Kentucky. He married (2) REBECCA GREGORY Abt. 1830 in Union Co., KY.
Children of DANIEL HAMMOCK and REBECCA GREGORY are:
    i. ELIZABETH[9] HAMMOCK, b. 1833, Union Co., KY; m. WYNN DIXON, 04 Nov 1852,
        Union Co., KY.
   ii. SARAH HAMMOCK, b. 1835, Union Co., KY; m. EDWIN R. MOORE, 05 Aug 1856,
        Union Co., KY.
  iii. NANCY HAMMOCK, b. 1837, Union Co., KY; m. EDWIN R. MOORE, 22 Jan 1856,
        Union Co., KY.
   iv. STEPHEN HAMMOCK, b. 1841, Union Co., KY; d. Bet. 1861 - 1865, Kentucky.
    v. MARTHA HAMMOCK, b. 1845, Union Co., KY; m. JAMES F. GILMORE, 06 Feb 1867,
        Union Co., KY.
   vi. KITTURAH HAMMOCK, b. 1851, Union Co., KY; m. W. N. N. NOTT, 06 Jan 1869,
        Union Co., KY.
Key Sources: 1840 Union Co., KY, Census, p. 22, and Henry Franklin Hammack, 1: 158-161.

153. JEREMIAH[8] HAMMOCK *(WILLIAM[7], WILLIAM[6], BENEDICT[5] HAMMACK, WILLIAM "THE
ELDER"[4], WILLIAM "O"[3], JOHN[2] HAMMOCKE, ? JOHN[1] HAMMOT)* was born 1811 in Caldwell Co.,
KY, and died 1865 in Union Co., KY. He married (1) MRS. SYRENA WITHERS. He married (2)
POLLY SULLIVANT 18 Jan 1831 in Union Co., KY.
Children of JEREMIAH HAMMOCK and POLLY SULLIVANT are:
    i. MORGAN[9] HAMMOCK, b. 1834, Union Co., KY; d. 1915, Union Co., KY; m. (1) NANCY
        E. MAGILL; b. 1837, Union Co., KY; d. 1871, Union Co., KY; m. (2) LUCY MAGILL.
   ii. RUTH HAMMOCK, b. 1838, Union Co., KY; d. Aft. 1850, Union Co., KY.
  iii. MARTHA HAMMOCK, b. 1840, Union Co., KY; d. Aft. 1850, Union Co., KY; m. G. M.
        CLARK.
   iv. NANCY HAMMOCK, b. 1842, Union Co., KY; d. Aft. 1850, Union Co., KY; m. [------]
        FREER.
    v. CLAYBOURN C. HAMMOCK, b. Abt. 1843, Union Co., KY; m. ELLEN V. DOHRER.
   vi. WILLIAM HAMMOCK, b. Abt. 1846, Union Co., KY; m. HELEN A. V. MOORE.
  vii. PENELOPE JANE HAMMOCK, b. 1850, Union Co., KY; d. 1944, Union Co., KY; m. I.
        W. MOORE; b. 1844, Union Co., KY; d. 1899, Union Co., KY.
 viii. SARAH DOROTHY HAMMOCK, b. 1854, Union Co., KY; d. Aft. 1872, Union Co., KY;
        m. THOMAS BLACKWELL, 08 Oct 1872, Union Co., KY.
Key Sources: 1850 Union Co., KY, Census, pp. 464-465, and Henry Franklin Hammack, 1: 158-161.

154. BENJAMIN[8] HAMMOCK *(JOHN C.[7], BENEDICT[6] HAMMOCK II, BENEDICT[5] HAMMACK,
WILLIAM "THE ELDER"[4], WILLIAM "O"[3], JOHN[2] HAMMOCKE, ? JOHN[1] HAMMOT)* was born Abt.

1793 in Wilkes Co., GA, and died Bef. 03 Nov 1845 in Walton Co., GA. He married UNKNOWN Abt. 1813 in Morgan Co., GA.

Children of BENJAMIN HAMMOCK and UNKNOWN are:

	i.	SON[9] HAMMOCK, b. Bet. 1815 - 1820, Morgan Co., GA.
300.	ii.	BENJAMIN F. HAMMOCK, b. Abt. 1820, Morgan Co., GA; d. Aft. 1870, Tallapoosa Co., AL.
301.	iii.	? CICERO C. HAMMOCK, b. 1823, Walton Co., GA; d. Aft. 1890, Fulton Co., GA.
	iv.	DAUGHTER HAMMOCK, b. Bet. 1820 - 1825, Walton Co., GA; d. Aft. 1830, Walton Co., GA.
	v.	SON HAMMOCK, b. Bet. 1825 - 1830, Walton Co., GA; d. Aft. 1830, Walton Co., GA.
	vi.	DAUGHTER HAMMOCK, b. Bet. 1825 - 1830, Walton Co., GA; d. Aft. 1830, Walton Co., GA.
	vii.	? FRANCES HAMMOCK, b. Abt. 1828, Walton Co., GA; d. Aft. 1850, Jackson Co., GA; m. JOHN P. H. BRISCOE, 12 Dec 1847, Walton Co., GA; b. Abt. 1819, Georgia; d. Aft. 1850, Jackson Co., GA.
	viii.	? MARTHA HAMMOCK, b. Abt. 1832, Walton Co., GA; d. Aft. 1850, Jackson Co., GA.

Key Sources: Morgan Co., GA, Deed Book E, p. 338; Morgan Co., GA, Deed Book F, pp. 404, 479; Morgan Co., GA, Deed Book B, p. 479; Morgan Co., GA, Deed Book G, p. 180; Wynne, *Southern Lineages*, p. 102-103; 1820 Walton Co., GA, Census, p. 123; Morgan Co., GA, Deed Book H, p. 343; Morgan Co., GA, Deed Book I, p. 448; Walton Co., GA, Applications Docket,1820-1852, p. 38; Walton Co., GA, Deed Book G, pp. 150-51; 1830 Walton Co., GA, Census, p. 125; Walton Co., GA, Applications Docket, 1820-1852, p. 131; 1840 Walton Co., GA, Census, pp. 96-97; Walton Co., GA, Minutes of Court of Ordinary, p. 114.

155. TRAVIS[8] HAMMOCK *(JOHN C.[7], BENEDICT[6] HAMMOCK II, BENEDICT[5] HAMMACK, WILLIAM "THE ELDER"[4], WILLIAM "O"[3], JOHN[2] HAMMOCKE, ? JOHN[1] HAMMOT)* was born Abt. 1794 in Lincoln Co., GA, and died Abt. 1832 in Walton Co., GA. He married MAHALA TURMAN 20 May 1824 in Walton Co., GA. She was born Abt. 1802 in Georgia, and died Aft. 1832 in Georgia.

Children of TRAVIS HAMMOCK and MAHALA TURMAN are:

	i.	JOHN T.[9] HAMMOCK, b. Bet. 1824 - 1830, Walton Co., GA; d. Aft. 1850, Walton Co., GA.
	ii.	LUCIAN T. HAMMOCK, b. Bet. 1824 - 1832, Walton Co., GA; d. Aft. 1840, Walton Co., GA.

Key Sources: Wynne, *Southern Lineages*, pp. 102-103; 1850 Walton Co., GA, Census, p. 13.

156. JOHN M.[8] HAMMOCK *(JOHN C.[7], BENEDICT[6] HAMMOCK II, BENEDICT[5] HAMMACK, WILLIAM "THE ELDER"[4], WILLIAM "O"[3], JOHN[2] HAMMOCKE, ? JOHN[1] HAMMOT)* was born Bet. 1793 - 1799 in Lincoln Co., GA, and died Aft. 1870 in Chambers Co., AL. He married MARTHA CLEMENTS 16 Oct 1823 in Jones Co., GA. She was born Abt. 1801 in Georgia, and died Aft. 1870 in Chambers Co., AL.

Children of JOHN HAMMOCK and MARTHA CLEMENTS are:

	i.	CHILD[9] HAMMOCK, b. Abt. 1825, Georgia; d. Aft. 1825, Georgia.
	ii.	ROBERTUS HAMMOCK, b. Abt. 1827, Georgia; d. Aft. 1864, Chambers Co., AL.
	iii.	EMILY C. HAMMOCK, b. Abt. 1830, Georgia; d. Aft. 1850, Chambers Co., AL; m. J. J. MUSICK, 11 Aug 1850, Chambers Co., AL.
	iv.	MARTHA A. HAMMOCK, b. Abt. 1832, Georgia; d. Aft. 1870, Chambers Co., AL; m. G. W. BAILEY, 25 Jun 1850, Chambers Co., AL.
	v.	WILLIAM L. HAMMOCK, b. Abt. 1836, Georgia; d. Bet. 1860 - 1870, Chambers Co., AL; m. ELIZA [------]; b. Abt. 1835, Georgia; d. Aft. 1870, Chambers Co., AL.

vi. JACKSON H. HAMMOCK, b. Abt. 1840, Georgia; d. Bet. 1860 - 1870, Chambers Co., AL; m. MARY F. JARRELL, 05 Dec 1861, Chambers Co., AL; b. Abt. 1833, Chambers Co., AL; d. Aft. 1870, Chambers Co., AL.

vii. BENJAMIN HAMPTON HAMMOCK, b. Abt. 1843, Georgia; d. 13 Jan 1901, Tallapoosa Co., AL; m. LUCY JANE SMITH, 06 Sep 1863, Chambers Co., AL; b. Abt. 1845, Alabama; d. Aft. 1901, Chambers Co., AL.

Key Sources: 1850 Chambers Co., AL, Census, p. 303; 1860 Chambers Co., AL, Census, p. 786; 1870 Chambers Co., AL, Census, p. 48.

157. ASA A.[8] HAMMOCK *(JOHN C.[7], BENEDICT[6] HAMMOCK II, BENEDICT[5] HAMMACK, WILLIAM "THE ELDER"[4], WILLIAM "O"[3], JOHN[2] HAMMOCKE, ? JOHN[1] HAMMOT)* was born 25 Sep 1807 in Greene Co., GA, and died 14 Dec 1873 in Gwinnett Co., GA. He married (1) SARAH E. FLYNT 30 Sep 1832 in Walton Co., GA. He married (2) MARY LUCRETIA MOON 30 Dec 1857 in Walton Co., GA. She was born Abt. 1830 in Georgia, and died Aft. 1870 in Walton Co., GA.
Child of ASA HAMMACK and SARAH FLYNT is:

i. HILLMAN W.[9] HAMMOCK, b. Abt. 1836, Walton Co., GA; d. Aft. 1870, Walton Co., GA; m. JOANNA BAKER, 09 Jan 1866, Walton Co., GA.

Key Sources: 1840 Walton Co., GA, Census, p. 96; 1860 Walton Co., GA, Census, p. 954.

158. SEABORN[8] HAMMOCK *(ROBERT[7], BENEDICT[6] HAMMOCK II, BENEDICT[5] HAMMACK, WILLIAM "THE ELDER"[4], WILLIAM "O"[3], JOHN[2] HAMMOCKE, ? JOHN[1] HAMMOT)* was born Abt. 1796 in Wilkes Co., GA, and died Bet. 1850 - 1860 in Coweta Co., GA. He married (2) MARY LACEY 21 Dec 1822 in Wilkes Co., GA. She was born Bet. 1795 - 1797 in Wilkes Co., GA, and died Aft. 1860 in Coweta Co., GA.
Children of SEABORN HAMMACK are:

302. i. JAMES T.[9] HAMMOCK, b. Abt. 1820, Wilkes Co., GA; d. 08 Jun 1877, Tallapoosa Co., AL.

303. ii. JOSEPH T. HAMMOCK, b. Abt. 1821, Wilkes Co., GA; d. Aft. 1870, Sevier Co., AR.

Children of SEABORN HAMMOCK and MARY LACEY are:

iii. ALETHIA ANN EUNICY[9] HAMMOCK, b. 24 Aug 1824, Wilkes Co., GA; d. 17 Jul 1897, Louisiana; m. JOSEPH DOOLITTLE LAND, 15 Apr 1845, Coweta Co., GA; b. 18 Feb 1816, Georgia; d. 30 Dec 1901, Louisiana.

iv. DAUGHTER HAMMOCK, b. Bet. 1825 - 1830, Wilkes Co., GA; d. Aft. 1830, Wilkes Co., GA.

v. SON HAMMOCK, b. Bet. 1825 - 1830, Wilkes Co., GA; d. Aft. 1830, Wilkes Co., GA.

304. vi. WILLIAM HAMMOCK, b. Abt. 1827, Wilkes Co., GA; d. Aft. 1868, Coweta Co., GA.

vii. MARY HAMMOCK, b. Bet. 1830 - 1834, Wilkes Co., GA; d. Aft. 1860, Coweta Co., GA; m. ROBERT THOMAS JOHNSON, Abt. 1850, Coweta Co., GA; b. Abt. 1820, Georgia; d. Bet. 1850 - 1860, Coweta Co., GA.

Key Sources: 1829 Wilkes Co., GA, Poor School List, GMD 171; 1830 Wilkes Co., GA, Census, p. 313; 1840 Coweta Co., GA, Census, p. 346; 1850 Coweta Co., GA, Census, p. 340.

159. MARTHA[8] HAMMACK *(ROBERT[7], BENEDICT[6] HAMMOCK II, BENEDICT[5] HAMMACK, WILLIAM "THE ELDER"[4], WILLIAM "O"[3], JOHN[2] HAMMOCKE, ? JOHN[1] HAMMOT)* was born Abt. 1793 in Wilkes Co., GA, and died Aft. 1860 in Coweta Co., GA. She married JOHN COMBS 31 Dec 1811 in Wilkes Co., GA. He was born Abt. 1790 in Wilkes Co., GA, and died Aft. 1820 in Wilkes Co., GA.
Child of MARTHA HAMMACK and JOHN COMBS is:

i. ENOCH[9] COMBS, b. Bet. 1813 - 1814, Wilkes Co., GA; d. Aft. 1829, Wilkes Co., GA.

ii. DAUGHTER COMBS, b. Bet. 1812 - 1815, Wilkes Co., GA; d. Aft. 1830, Wilkes Co., GA.
iii. ASA COMBS, b. Bet. 1818 - 1819, Wilkes Co., GA; d. Aft. 1829, Wilkes Co., GA.
iv. EMILY COMBS (c. 1817, Wilkes Co., GA – aft. 1860, Tallapoosa Co., AL), m. (1) 18 April 1831, Wilkes Co., GA, WILKINSON SMALLWOOD, m. (2) 3 December 1848, Meriwether Co., GA, JAMES RUNNELLS (c. 1809, Wilkes Co., GA – aft. 1860, Tallapoosa Co., AL).
v. DAUGHTER COMBS, b. Bet. 1825 - 1830, Wilkes Co., GA; d. Aft. 1830, Wilkes Co., GA.
Key Sources: 1850 Coweta Co., GA, Census, pp. 313-314.

160. THOMAS JEFFERSON[8] HAMMOCK *(BENJAMIN[7], BENEDICT[6] HAMMOCK II, BENEDICT[5] HAMMACK, WILLIAM "THE ELDER"[4], WILLIAM "O"[3], JOHN[2] HAMMOCKE, ? JOHN[1] HAMMOT)* was born Abt. 1800 in Lincoln Co., GA. He married RHODA [------].
Children of THOMAS JEFFERSON HAMMOCK and RHODA [------] are:
305. i. COLUMBUS W.[9] HAMMOCK, b. Bet. 1825 - 1830, Georgia; d. Aft. 1880, Sabine Co., TX.
ii. GEORGE HAMMOCK.
iii. THOMAS HAMMOCK.
iv. MARSHA HAMMOCK.
v. SUSAN HAMMOCK.
vi. EUGENIA HAMMOCK.
Key Sources: 1860 Jasper Co., TX, Census, p. 397; 1870 Jasper Co.,TX, Census, p. 484; 1880 Sabine Co., TX, Census, p. 237. This generation is speculative but is claimed as such by the descendants of Columbus W. Hammock. I have not located evidence to prove that Thomas Jefferson Hammock was the father of Columbus W. Hammock or that he was the son of Benjamin Hammock.

161. JEPTHA J.[8] HAMMOCK *(BENJAMIN[7], BENEDICT[6] HAMMOCK II, BENEDICT[5] HAMMACK, WILLIAM "THE ELDER"[4], WILLIAM "O"[3], JOHN[2] HAMMOCKE, ? JOHN[1] HAMMOT)* was born Abt. 1820 in Morgan Co., GA, and died Aft. 1850 in Jasper Co., GA. He married BARBARA LUNCEFORD 24 Apr 1839 in Walton Co., GA. She was born Abt. 1822 in Georgia, and died Aft. 1880 in Spalding Co., GA.
Children of JEPTHA HAMMOCK and BARBARA LUNCEFORD are:
i. MARY[9] HAMMOCK, b. Abt. 1840, Walton Co., GA; d. Aft. 1860, Spalding Co., GA.
ii. NANCY HAMMOCK, b. Abt. 1842, Jasper Co., GA; d. Aft. 1860, Spalding Co., GA.
iii. BENJAMIN HAMMOCK, b. 08 Jul 1844, Butts Co., GA; d. 27 Aug 1862, Bristol Station, VA.
iv. WILLIAM HAMMOCK, b. Abt. 1846, Jasper Co., GA; d. Aft. 1870, Spalding Co., GA.
v. AMANDA HAMMOCK, b. Abt. 1847, Jasper Co., GA; d. Aft. 1860, Spalding Co., GA.
vi. MISSOURI "DINK" HAMMOCK, b. Abt. 1849, Jasper Co., GA; d. Aft. 1870, Spalding Co., GA.
vii. JEPTHA HAMMOCK, b. Abt. 1851, Spaldingr Co., GA; d. Aft. 1870, Spalding Co., GA.
viii. CHARLIE HAMMOCK, b. Abt. 1853, Spalding Co., GA; d. Aft. 1870, Spalding Co., GA.
ix. SARAH HAMMOCK, b. Abt. 1855, Spalding Co., GA; d. Aft. 1870, Spalding Co., GA.
x. THOMAS D. HAMMOCK, b. Abt. 1860, Spalding Co., GA; d. Aft. 1880, Spalding Co., GA.
xi. ALEXANDER H. S. HAMMOCK, b. 22 Aug 1862, Spalding Co., GA; d. 24 May 1910, Henry Co., GA; m. MARY FRANCES COMBS.
Key Sources: 1850 Jasper Co., GA, Census, p. 87; 1860 Spalding Co., GA, Census, p. 224; 1870 Spalding Co., GA, Census, p. 391; 1880 Spalding Co., GA, Census, p. 320.

162. JOHN[8] HAMMOCK *(? SAMUEL[7], JOHN[6], BENEDICT[5] HAMMACK, WILLIAM "THE ELDER"[4], WILLIAM "O"[3], JOHN[2] HAMMOCKE, ? JOHN[1] HAMMOT)* was born Abt. 1796 in Jefferson Co., GA, and died Bef. 1820 in Jefferson Co., GA. He married NANCY WILLIAMS 12 Jun 1817 in Laurens Co., GA.

Child of JOHN HAMMOCK and NANCY WILLIAMS is:

306.   i.   GEORGE W.[9] HAMMOCK, b. Abt. 1817, Laurens Co., GA; d. Aft. 1880, Johnson Co., GA.

Key Sources: A. Thomas, *Laurens Co., GA, Legal Records, 1807-1857* (2 vols., Roswell, GA, 1991), 1: 340-41; 1821 Georgia Land Lottery Fortunate Draws; 1822 Jefferson Co., GA, Tax Digest; Henry Co., GA, Deed Book B, p. 149; Washington Co., GA, Division of Estates, Book A, 1829-1871, Estate of Samuel Smith.

163. JACKSON[8] HAMMOCK *(? SAMUEL[7], JOHN[6], BENEDICT[5] HAMMACK, WILLIAM "THE ELDER"[4], WILLIAM "O"[3], JOHN[2] HAMMOCKE, ? JOHN[1] HAMMOT)* was born Abt. 1800 in Jefferson Co., GA, and died Aft. 1850 in Benton Co., FL. He married (1) LYDIA PASSMORE 25 Oct 1827 in Pulaski Co., GA. She was born Abt. 1805 in Georgia, and died Bef. 1850 in Benton Co., FL. He married (2) SARAH [------] Abt. 1850 in Florida. She was born Abt. 1818 in Georgia, and died Aft. 1860 in Madison Co., FL.

Children of JACKSON HAMMOCK and LYDIA PASSMORE are:

    i.   ELIZA[9] HAMMOCK, b. Abt. 1828, Georgia; d. Aft. 1850, Benton Co., FL.

    ii.   NANCY HAMMOCK, b. Abt. 1830, Georgia; d. Aft. 1850, Benton Co., FL.

    iii. BECKY HAMMOCK, b. Abt. 1832, Georgia; d. Aft. 1850, Benton Co., FL.

    iv.   SAMUEL HAMMOCK, b. Abt. 1834, Georgia; d. Aft. 1880, Madison Co., FL; m. MARY FRANCES HADDEN, 20 Nov 1862, Madison Co., FL.

    v.   GEORGE HAMMOCK, b. Abt. 1836, Alabama; d. Aft. 1850, Benton Co., FL.

    vi.   SUSAN HAMMOCK, b. Abt. 1838, Alabama; d. Aft. 1850, Benton Co., FL.

    vii. JACKSON HAMMOCK, b. Abt. 1840, Alabama; d. Aft. 1850, Benton Co., FL.

    viii. PHOEBE HAMMOCK, b. Abt. 1842, Alabama; d. Aft. 1850, Benton Co., FL.

Child of JACKSON HAMMOCK and SARAH [------] is:

    ix.   MARY A.[9] HAMMOCK, b. Abt. 1854, Florida; d. Aft. 1860, Madison Co., FL.

Sources: 1850 Benton Co., FL, Census, p. 25; 1860 Madison Co., FL, Census, pp. 206, 207, 220; 1870 Hamilton Co., FL, Census, p. 1. Descendants claim that Jackson and George Hammock were brothers and sons of Paschall Hammack. It is possible that they were sons of Paschall, but I have speculated that they were sons or grandsons of Samuel Hammock instead. At the time that Jackson Hammock married, Pulaski County joined both Twiggs (where Paschall and Elijah lived) and Laurens County (where the Samuel Hammock family lived). Without better evidence, it is possible that Jackson and George belonged to any of these Hammock families.

164. GEORGE[8] HAMMOCK *(? SAMUEL[7], JOHN[6], BENEDICT[5] HAMMACK, WILLIAM "THE ELDER"[4], WILLIAM "O"[3], JOHN[2] HAMMOCKE, ? JOHN[1] HAMMOT)* was born Abt. 1818 in Georgia, and died Aft. 1860 in Madison Co., FL. He married (1) MARY [------]. She was born Abt. 1830 in Florida, and died Aft. 1870 in Madison Co., FL. He married (2) SARAH J. P. WESSON 25 Nov 1847 in Madison Co., FL. She was born 11 Jul 1817 in Laurens Co., GA, and died Aft. 1850 in Madison Co., FL. He married (3) CHRISTIAN ELIZABETH MCCALL Abt. 1850 in Madison Co., FL. She was born 14 Oct 1825 in Bulloch Co., GA, and died Aft. 1860 in Madison Co., FL.

Children of GEORGE HAMMOCK and CHRISTIAN MCCALL are:

    i.   GEORGE WESSON[9] HAMMOCK, b. Abt. 1851, Madison Co., FL; d. 02 May 1934, Pinellas Co., FL; m. MARY LEVICY WHITEHURST.

    ii.   HENRY HAMMOCK, b. Abt. 1855, Madison Co., FL; d. Aft. 1860, Madison Co., FL.

    iii. SUSAN HAMMOCK, b. Abt. 1857, Madison Co., FL; d. Aft. 1870, Madison Co., FL.

    iv.   GEORGIA A. HAMMOCK, b. Abt. 1858, Madison Co., FL; d. Aft. 1870, Madison Co., FL; m. RUFUS FAIN MCMULLEN.

v.   CIMODOCIA CAROLYN HAMMOCK, b. Abt. 1860, Madison Co., FL; d. Aft. 1870, Madison Co., FL; m. JOHN GIDEON BLITCH.

vi.   LAURA PINK HAMMOCK, b. Abt. 1863, Madison Co., FL; d. Aft. 1870, Madison Co., FL.

vii.   BARBARA ELLEN HAMMOCK, b. 05 Jan 1865, Madison Co., FL; d. 28 Oct 1939, Madison Co., FL; m. JOHN THOMAS MCMULLEN.

Key Sources: 1850 Madison Co., FL, Census, p. 114; 1860 Madison Co., FL, Census, pp. 206, 207, 220; 1870 Hillsborough Co., FL, Census, p. 145. See previous note.

165. JOSHUA S.[8] HAMMAC *(? JESSE[7] HAMMOCK, JOHN[6], BENEDICT[5] HAMMACK, WILLIAM "THE ELDER"[4], WILLIAM "O"[3], JOHN[2] HAMMOCKE, ? JOHN[1] HAMMOT)* was born 25 Sep 1805 in Jefferson Co., GA, and died 05 Dec 1890 in Escambia Co., FL. He married (1) NANCY BURROWS Abt. 1822 in Alabama. He married (2) AMANDA KENT TRAWICK Abt. 1830 in Alabama. She was born Abt. 1812 in Alabama, and died Bef. 1882 in Escambia Co., FL. He married (3) SALLIE ADAMS 03 Dec 1882 in Escambia Co., AL.

Children of JOSHUA HAMMAC and NANCY BURROWS are:

307.   i.   ? THOMAS[9] HAMMAC, b. 1824, Alabama; d. 1863, Alabama.

308.   ii.   JOSHUA S. HAMMAC, b. 06 Nov 1832, Alabama; d. 28 May 1904, Escambia Co., AL.

iii.   GEORGE W. HAMMAC, b. 1834, Alabama; d. 1899, Butler Co., AL.

309.   iv.   WILLOBY HAMMAC, b. 23 Dec 1838, Conecuh Co., AL; d. 1862, Tennessee.

v.   ELLINDER HAMMAC, b. 1842, Conecuh Co., AL; d. Aft. 1860, Conecuh Co., AL; m. CHARLES BEAL.

vi.   HENRY E. HAMMAC, b. 1842, Conecuh Co., AL; d. Aft. 1860, Conecuh Co., AL; m. MARY J. [------].

310.   vii.   ? JESSE HAMMAC, b. Abt. 1830, Conecuh Co., AL; d. Aft. 1860, Conecuh Co., AL.

Children of JOSHUA HAMMAC and AMANDA TRAWICK are:

viii.   ROBERT[9] HAMMAC, b. Abt. 1849, Conecuh Co., AL; d. Bef. 1860, Conecuh Co., AL.

ix.   LOUISA E. HAMMAC, b. Abt. 1851, Conecuh Co., AL; d. Jun 1914, Escambia Co., AL; m. GEORGE COLUMBUS EVANS.

x.   LEVINIA HAMMAC, b. Abt. 1857, Conecuh Co., AL; d. 1936, Crenshaw Co., AL; m. WILLIAM HORTON, 30 Aug 1887, Escambia Co., AL.

xi.   W. B. HAMMAC, b. Abt. 1860, Conecuh Co., AL; d. Aft. 1900, Jackson Co., MS; m. SARAH CAROLINE DOWNING, 12 Jan 1882, Escambia Co., AL; b. Abt. 1867, Alabama; d. Aft. 1900, Jackson Co., MS.

Key Sources: M. D. Hahn, *Old Sparta and Elba Land Office Records and Military Warrants, 1822-1860* (Easley, SC, 1983), pp. 21, 27, 31, 65; 1850 Conecuh Co., AL, Census, pp. 351, 363, 364, 371; 1860 Conecuh Co., AL, Census, pp. 1071, 1075, 1078, 1082, 1084. Note that this family group has consistently used the spelling Hammac since settling in South Alabama in the early nineteenth-century.

166. ROBERT[8] HAMMAC *(? JESSE[7] HAMMOCK, JOHN[6], BENEDICT[5] HAMMACK, WILLIAM "THE ELDER"[4], WILLIAM "O"[3], JOHN[2] HAMMOCKE, ? JOHN[1] HAMMOT)* was born Abt. 1810 in Georgia, and died Bet. 1840 - 1850 in Conecuh Co., AL. He married EADY GODWIN Abt. 1822 in Alabama. She was born Bet. 1800 - 1810 in Jefferson Co., GA, and died Aft. 1850 in Conecuh Co., AL.

Children of ROBERT HAMMAC and EADY GODWIN are:

i.   DAUGHTER[9] HAMMAC, b. Abt. 1825, Alabama; d. Aft. 1830, Monroe Co., AL.

ii.   DAUGHTER HAMMAC, b. Bet. 1825 - 1830.

iii.   SON HAMMAC, b. Bet. 1825 - 1830, Alabama; d. Aft. 1830, Monroe Co., AL.

iv.   STEPHEN HAMMAC, b. Abt. 1830, Conecuh Co., AL; d. Aft. 1850, Conecuh Co., AL.

v.   SARAH HAMMAC, b. Abt. 1834, Conecuh Co., AL; d. Aft. 1850, Conecuh Co., AL.

vi. LOUVICIA M. HAMMAC, b. 05 Oct 1836, Conecuh Co., AL; d. 30 Jan 1870, Franklin Co., TX; m. GEORGE W. TITTLE, 20 Mar 1856, Titus Co., TX.

vii. JOSEPHINE HAMMAC, b. Abt. 1841, Conecuh Co., AL; d. Aft. 1850, Conecuh Co., AL.

viii. CAROLINE HAMMAC, b. Abt. 1842, Conecuh Co., AL; d. Aft. 1850, Conecuh Co., AL.

Key Sources: 1830 Monroe Co., AL, Census, p. 44; 1850 Conecuh Co., AL, Census, p. 363.

167. GEORGE W.[8] HAMMAC (*? JESSE[7] HAMMOCK, JOHN[6], BENEDICT[5] HAMMACK, WILLIAM "THE ELDER"[4], WILLIAM "O"[3], JOHN[2] HAMMOCKE, ? JOHN[1] HAMMOT*) was born Abt. 1812 in Tennessee, and died Aft. 1860 in Conecuh Co., AL. He married MARY A. BAGGETT. She was born Abt. 1815 in Jefferson Co., GA, and died 1890 in Escambia Co., AL.

Children of GEORGE HAMMAC and MARY BAGGETT are:

i. JOHN ROY THOMAS[9] HAMMAC, b. 08 Apr 1836, Conecuh Co., AL; d. 13 May 1903, Escambia Co., AL; m. MARY ELIZABETH WHITE; b. Abt. 1843, Alabama; d. Aft. 1860, Conecuh Co., AL.

ii. MAZELLA HAMMAC, b. 22 Jun 1839, Conecuh Co., Alabama; d. 19 May 1908, Escambia Co., AL; m. F. M. MILES.

iii. GEORGE WASHINGTON HAMMAC, b. 22 Feb 1841, Conecuh Co., AL; d. 09 May 1899, Conecuh Co., AL; m. JANE HOLLAND.

iv. JESSE HAMMAC, b. Abt. 1843, Alabama.

v. SOLOMON WADKINS HAMMAC, b. 09 Feb 1845, Conecuh Co., AL; d. 13 Apr 1917, Escambia Co., AL; m. CAROLINE MANNING.

vi. ROBERT HAMMAC, b. Abt. 1847, Alabama; d. Aft. 1870, Escambia Co., AL; m. (1) ELLEN DAVIS; m. (2) FRANCES SIMMONS, Abt. 1870, Escambia Co., AL.

vii. MARY ELIZABETH HAMMAC, b. 13 May 1851, Conecuh Co., AL; d. 13 Oct 1935, Escambia Co., AL; m. B. B. BELL.

viii. MARTHA ANN HAMMAC, b. Abt. 1852, Alabama; d. 08 Apr 1920, Escambia Co., AL; m. C. L. WIGGINS.

Key Sources: 1850 Conecuh Co., AL, Census, p. 371; 1860 Conecuh Co., AL, Census, p. 1075.

168. LITTLETON[8] HAMMOCK (*? EMANUEL[7], JOHN[6], BENEDICT[5] HAMMACK, WILLIAM "THE ELDER"[4], WILLIAM "O"[3], JOHN[2] HAMMOCKE, ? JOHN[1] HAMMOT*) was born 03 Feb 1808 in Jefferson Co., GA, and died 16 May 1877 in Tattnall Co., GA. He married ELIZABETH RIGGS Abt. 1838 in Tattnall Co., GA. She was born Abt. 1818 in Bulloch Co., GA, and died Aft. 1850 in Tattnall Co., GA.

Children of LITTLETON HAMMOCK and ELIZABETH RIGGS are:

i. EMANUEL[9] HAMMOCK, b. Abt. 1840, Tattnall Co., GA; d. Aft. 1850, Tattnall Co., GA.

ii. ABRAHAM HAMMOCK, b. Abt. 1847, Tattnall Co., GA; d. Aft. 1850, Tattnall Co., GA.

Key Source: 1850 Tattnall Co., GA, Census, p. 365.

169. MOSES[8] HAMMOCK (*? EMANUEL[7], JOHN[6], BENEDICT[5] HAMMACK, WILLIAM "THE ELDER"[4], WILLIAM "O"[3], JOHN[2] HAMMOCKE, ? JOHN[1] HAMMOT*) was born Abt. 1818 in Tattnall Co., GA, and died Aft. 1870 in Tattnall Co., GA. He married ELIZABETH SMITH 02 Jul 1843 in Tattnall Co., GA. She was born Abt. 1818 in Tattnall Co., GA, and died Aft. 1850 in Tattnall Co., GA.

Children of MOSES HAMMOCK and ELIZABETH SMITH are:

i. MARYANN[9] HAMMOCK, b. Abt. 1846, Tattnall Co., GA; d. Aft. 1850, Tattnall Co., GA.

ii. MARTHA HAMMOCK, b. Abt. 1847, Tattnall Co., GA; d. Aft. 1850, Tattnall Co., GA.

iii. ELIZABETH HAMMOCK, b. Abt. 1849, Tattnall Co., GA; d. Aft. 1850, Tattnall Co., GA.

Key Source: 1850 Tattnall Co., GA, Census, p. 344.

170. JOHN E.[8] HAMMOCK *(? EMANUEL[7], JOHN[6], BENEDICT[5] HAMMACK, WILLIAM "THE ELDER"[4], WILLIAM "O"[3], JOHN[2] HAMMOCKE, ? JOHN[1] HAMMOT)* was born Apr 1824 in Jefferson Co., GA, and died 1912 in Tattnall Co., GA. He married NANCY MCCALL Abt. 1846 in Tattnall Co., GA, daughter of FRANCIS MCCALL and SARAH PEARCE. She was born 08 Dec 1822 in Bulloch Co., GA, and died 08 Jun 1889 in Tattnall Co., GA.
Children of JOHN HAMMOCK and NANCY MCCALL are:
     i.   CHARLES[9] HAMMOCK, b. Abt. 1847, Tattnall Co., GA; d. Aft. 1850, Tattnall Co., GA.
    ii.   HANNAH HAMMOCK, b. Abt. 1849, Tattnall Co., GA; d. Aft. 1580, Tattnall Co., GA.
Key Source: 1850 Tattnall Co., GA, Census, p. 345.

171. JOHN[8] COMBS *(JOHN[7], ABIGAIL[6] HAMMOCK, BENEDICT[5] HAMMACK, WILLIAM "THE ELDER"[4], WILLIAM "O"[3], JOHN[2] HAMMOCKE, ? JOHN[1] HAMMOT)* was born Abt. 1791 in Wilkes Co., GA, and died Bet. 1825 - 1830 in Wilkes Co., GA. He married MARTHA HAMMOCK 31 Dec 1811 in Wilkes Co., GA. She was born Abt. 1792 in Wilkes Co., GA, and died Aft. 1860 in Coweta Co., GA.
Children of JOHN COMBS and MARTHA HAMMOCK are:
     i.   ENOCH[9] COMBS, b. Bet. 1813 - 1814, Wilkes Co., GA; d. Aft. 1829, Wilkes Co., GA.
    ii.   DAUGHTER COMBS, b. Bet. 1812 - 1815, Wilkes Co., GA; d. Aft. 1830, Wilkes Co., GA.
   iii.   ASA COMBS, b. Bet. 1818 - 1819, Wilkes Co., GA; d. Aft. 1829, Wilkes Co., GA.
   iv.   Emily Combs (c. 1817, Wilkes Co., GA – aft. 1860, Tallapoosa Co., AL), m. (1) 18 April 1831, Wilkes Co., GA, Wilkinson Smallwood, m. (2) 3 December 1848, Meriwether Co., GA, James Runnells (c. 1809, Wilkes Co., GA – aft. 1860, Tallapoosa Co., AL).
    v.   DAUGHTER COMBS, b. Bet. 1825 - 1830, Wilkes Co., GA; d. Aft. 1830, Wilkes Co., GA.
Key Sources: 1830 Wilkes Co., GA, Census, p. 315; G. G. Davidson, *Early Records of Georgia, Wilkes County* (2 vols., Macon, GA, 1932), 1: 352-353; 1829 Wilkes Co., GA, Poor School List, GMD 171; 1850 Coweta Co., GA, Census, p. 313-314.

172. JACOB[8] HAMMACK *(LEWIS[7], ROBERT HAMMACK[6] JR., ROBERT HAMMACK[5] SR., WILLIAM "THE ELDER"[4] HAMMACK, WILLIAM "O"[3], JOHN[2] HAMMOCKE, ? JOHN[1] HAMMOT)* was born Abt. 1797 in Wilkes Co., GA, and died Aft. 1850 in Perry Co., AL. He married HANNAH JONES 28 Jan 1817 in Jones Co., GA. She was born Abt. 1798 in GA, and died Aft. 1860 in Mississippi.
Children of JACOB HAMMACK and HANNAH JONES are:
     i.   JANE[9] HAMMACK, b. Abt. 1819, Jones Co., GA; d. Aft. 1856, Dallas Co., AL; m. EZEKIEL HOLLINSHEAD.
311.   ii.   KEZIAH HAMMACK, b. Abt. 1820, Jones Co., GA; d. Aft. 1870, Crawford Co., GA.
312.   iii.   JOHN W. HAMMACK, b. Nov 1823, Jones Co., GA; d. Aft. 1900, Cleburne Co., AR.
   iv.   LEWIS J. HAMMACK, b. Abt. 1822, Jones Co., GA; d. Aft. 1860, Lauderdale Co., MS.
313.   v.   WILLIAM/WILSON H. HAMMACK, b. Bet. 1826 - 1828, Jones Co., GA, or Alabama; d. Aft. 1910, Hinds Co., MS.
314.   vi.   CATHERINE HAMMACK, b. Abt. 1833, Dallas Co., AL; d. Aft. 1880, Lauderdale Co., MS.
   vii.   JACOB W. HAMMACK, b. Abt. 1839, Dallas Co., AL; d. Aft. 1861, Yazoo Co., MS.
  viii.   MARTHA HAMMACK, b. Abt. 1841, Dallas Co., AL; d. Aft. 1856, Dallas Co., AL.
Key Sources: 1820 Jones Co., GA, Census; 1825-1827 Jones Co., GA, Tax Digests; 1840 Dallas Co., AL, Census, p. 52; Jones Co., GA, Returns Book T, p. 329; 1850 Perry Co., AL, Census, p. 363; Crawford Co., GA, Annual Returns, Book H, pp. 69, 208, 494, 504; 1860 Lauderdale Co., MS, Census, p. 289.

173. MILLY[8] HAMMACK *(LEWIS[7], ROBERT HAMMACK[6] JR., ROBERT HAMMACK[5] SR., WILLIAM "THE ELDER"[4] HAMMACK, WILLIAM "O"[3], JOHN[2] HAMMOCKE, ? JOHN[1] HAMMOT)* was born Abt. 1792 in Wilkes Co., GA, and died Aft. 1870 in Upson Co., GA. She married (1) JEREMIAH POOLE

Abt. 1808 in Wilkes Co., GA. He was born Abt. 1790 in Georgia, and died Bef. 1834 in Jones Co., GA. She married (2) TALBOT DAVIDSON 1833 in Jones Co., GA. He was born Abt. 1800 in Georgia, and died Abt. 1875 in Upson Co., GA.

Child of MILLY HAMMACK and JEREMIAH POOLE is:

315.   i.   ELIZA[9] POOLE, b. Abt. 1809, Wilkes Co., GA; d. Bef. 1844, Jones Co., GA.

Key Sources: Jones Co., GA, Annual Returns, 1842-1847, p. 93; 1850 Upson Co., GA, Census.

174. JOHN M.[8] HAMMACK *(LEWIS[7], ROBERT HAMMACK[6] JR., ROBERT HAMMACK[5] SR., WILLIAM "THE ELDER"[4] HAMMACK, WILLIAM "O"[3], JOHN[2] HAMMOCKE, ? JOHN[1] HAMMOT)* was born Bet. 1800 - 1802 in Wilkes Co., GA, and died Bet. 1844 - 1846 in Jones Co., GA. He married (1) MATILDA TOLLS 02 Jan 1823 in Jones Co., GA. She was born Abt. 1802 in Georgia, and died Bef. 1841 in Jones Co., GA. He married (2) LIVELY ADAMS 03 Aug 1841 in Jones Co., GA.

Children of JOHN HAMMACK and MATILDA TOLLS are:

316.   i.   JACKSON LEWIS[9] HAMMACK, b. Abt. 1824, Jones Co., GA; d. Abt. 1847, Jones Co., GA.

          ii.   HENRY S. HAMMACK, b. Abt. 1826, Jones Co., GA; d. Aft. 1850, Jones Co., GA.

317.   iii.   JAMES M. HAMMACK, b. Abt. 1828, Jones Co., GA; d. Abt. 1863, Confederate States Army.

318.   iv.   JOHN ALEXANDER HAMMACK, b. 20 Feb 1830, Jones Co., GA; d. 17 May 1895, Houston Co., GA.

          v.   WILLIAM L. N. HAMMACK, b. Abt. 1832, Jones Co., GA; d. Aft. 1858, Jones Co., GA; m. CATHERINE HAMMACK, 1854, Crawford Co., GA.

          vi.   ISAAC W. HAMMACK, b. Abt. 1836, Jones Co., GA; d. Aft. 1850, Jones Co., GA.

          vii.   BENJAMIN F. HAMMACK, b. Abt. 1837, Jones Co., GA; d. Aft. 1850, Jones Co., GA.

          viii.   CHRISTIAN "KITTY" HAMMACK, b. Abt. 1837, Jones Co., GA; d. Aft. 1871, Jones Co., GA; m. SAMUEL MORGAN, SR., 26 Dec 1871, Jones Co., GA.

          ix.   ELIZABETH HAMMACK, b. Abt. 1840, Jones Co., GA; d. Aft. 1858, Jones Co., GA; m. ? WILLIAM O. WHITE, 18 Sep 1879, Jones Co., GA.

          x.   MATILDA HAMMACK, b. Abt. 1840, Jones Co., GA; d. Aft. 1860, Jones Co., GA; m. JOSEPH T. LEONARD, Bef. 1856, Jones Co., GA.

Key Sources: 1826-1827 Jones Co., GA, Tax Digests; 1830 Jones Co., GA, Census, p. 451; Jones Co., GA, Deed Book O, p. 403; Jones Co., GA, Deed Book P, p. 254; 1840 Jones Co., GA, Census, p. 135; 1840-1844 Jones Co., GA, Tax Digests; Jones Co., GA, Annual Returns, 1842-1847, pp. 452, 459, 489; Jones Co., GA, Annual Returns, Book M, pp. 162-163, 175, 181, 202, 297; 1850 Jones Co., GA, Census, p. 205; Jones Co., GA, Annual Returns Book N, 1851-1853, pp. 155, 585; Jones Co., GA, Annual Returns, Book T, pp. 275, 319-320, 379.

175. MARY[8] HAMMACK *(LEWIS[7], ROBERT HAMMACK[6] JR., ROBERT HAMMACK[5] SR., WILLIAM "THE ELDER"[4] HAMMACK, WILLIAM "O"[3], JOHN[2] HAMMOCKE, ? JOHN[1] HAMMOT)* was born Abt. 1808 in Wilkes Co., GA, and died Aft. 1850 in Crawford Co., GA. She married MASON MILLER 05 May 1823 in Jones Co., GA. He was born Abt. 1804 in Georgia, and died Aft. 1850 in Crawford Co., GA.

Children of MARY HAMMACK and MASON MILLER are:

          i.   DAUGHTER[9] MILLER, b. Bet. 1825 - 1830, Jones Co., GA; d. Aft. 1830, Jones Co., GA.

          ii.   SUSAN EVELINE MILLER, b. Abt. 1826, Jones Co., GA; d. 1892, Crawford Co., GA; m. CULLEN DAVISON, 10 Dec 1844, Jones Co., GA; b. Abt. 1825, Georgia; d. Aft. 1860, Crawford Co., GA.

          iii.   J. C. MILLER, b. Abt. 1831, Jones Co., GA; d. Aft. 1850, Crawford Co., GA.

          iv.   ELIZABETH MILLER, b. Abt. 1834, Jones Co., GA; d. Aft. 1850, Crawford Co., GA.

          v.   J. W. MILLER, b. Abt. 1837, Jones Co., GA; d. Aft. 1850, Crawford Co., GA.

    vi.   M. J. MILLER, b. Abt. 1840, Jones Co., GA; d. Aft. 1850, Crawford Co., GA.

   vii.   WILLIAM MILLER, b. Abt. 1842, Jones Co., GA; d. Aft. 1850, Crawford Co., GA.

  viii.   M. A. MILLER, b. Abt. 1846, Jones Co., GA; d. Aft. 1850, Crawford Co., GA.

Key Sources: 1830 Jones Co., GA, Census, p. 146; 1850 Crawford Co., GA, Census, p. 406.

176. JOHN[8] HAMMACK *(ROBERT[7], ROBERT HAMMACK[6] JR., ROBERT HAMMACK[5] SR., WILLIAM "THE ELDER"[4] HAMMACK, WILLIAM "O"[3], JOHN[2] HAMMOCKE, ? JOHN[1] HAMMOT)* was born 1792 in Georgia, and died 1872 in Taliaferro Co., GA. He married LUCINDA CRENSHAW 29 Jun 1821 in Warren Co., GA. She was born 1804 in Georgia, and died 1880 in Taliaferro Co., GA.

Children of JOHN HAMMACK and LUCINDA CRENSHAW are:

           i.   JOSEPHINE ELIZA[9] HAMMACK, b. 1818, Wilkes Co., GA; d. 1823, Wilkes Co., GA.

319.   ii.   JOSEPH DAVIS HAMMACK, b. 1822, Wilkes Co., GA; d. 1899, Taliaferro Co., GA.

320.   iii.   HENRY T. HAMMACK, b. 1824, Wilkes Co., GA; d. 1891, Taliaferro Co., GA.

          iv.   JULIA ANN HAMMACK, b. 1826, Taliaferro Co., GA; d. 1882, Taliaferro Co., GA.

           v.   JAMES M. HAMMACK, b. Abt. 1833, Taliaferro Co., GA; d. Abt. 1868, Taliaferro Co., GA.

          vi.   NANCY C. HAMMACK, b. Abt. 1836, Taliaferro Co., GA; d. Aft. 1872, Taliaferro Co., GA; m. A. J. CHENEY, 08 Feb 1866, Taliaferro Co., GA.

         vii.   WILILAM H. HAMMACK, b. Abt. 1842, Taliaferro Co., GA; d. Bef. 1872, Taliaferro Co., GA.

Key Sources: 1816 Wilkes Co., GA, Tax Digest; 1830 Taliaferro Co., GA, Poor School List, GMD 602; 1832-1835 Taliaferro Co., GA, Tax Digest; 1840 Wilkes Co., GA, Census, p. 257; 1850 Taliaferro Co., GA, Census, pp. 1, 50; 1860 Taliaferro Co., GA, Census, pp. 1-5; Obituary of John Hammack, *Columbus (GA) Enquirer*, 3 September 1872; Taliaferro Co., GA, Will Book B, p. 55.

177. MARTHA[8] HAMMACK *(ROBERT[7], ROBERT HAMMACK[6] JR., ROBERT HAMMACK[5] SR., WILLIAM "THE ELDER"[4] HAMMACK, WILLIAM "O"[3], JOHN[2] HAMMOCKE, ? JOHN[1] HAMMOT)* was born 1794 in Wilkes Co., GA, and died Aft. 1894 in Greene Co., GA. She married WILLIAM FRANK 19 May 1811 in Wilkes Co., GA. He was born Abt. 1794 in Georgia, and died Bef. 1832 in Taliaferro Co., GA.

Children of MARTHA HAMMACK and WILLIAM FRANK are:

           i.   ? JOHN[9] FRANK, b. Abt. 1814, Wilkes Co., GA; d. Aft. 1836, Taliaferro Co., GA.

          ii.   ? ELIZABETH FRANK, b. Abt. 1818, Wilkes Co., GA; d. Aft. 1830, Taliaferro Co., GA; m. MICHAEL SWINDERMAN, 26 Jan 1841, Taliaferro Co., GA.

        iii.   ? NANCY FRANK, b. Abt. 1821, Wilkes Co., GA; d. Aft. 1830, Taliaferro Co., GA.

         iv.   ? ROBERT FRANK, b. Abt. 1822, Wilkes Co., GA; d. Aft. 1840, Taliaferro Co., GA.

          v.   MARY ELLEN FRANK, b. Abt. 1823, Wilkes Co., GA; d. Aft. 1850, Greene Co., GA; m. JOHN WINTER; b. Abt. 1810, Germany; d. Aft. 1850, Greene Co., GA.

Key Sources: Taliaferro Co., GA, Deed Book A, p. 410; Taliaferro Co., GA, Deed Book B, p. 40; "An Interesting Family Reunion," *Washington (GA) Chronicle*, 23 July 1894, detailing 100th birthday of Martha Hammack Frank.

178. GUSTAVUS STARLING[8] HAMMACK *(ROBERT[7], ROBERT HAMMACK[6] JR., ROBERT HAMMACK[5] SR., WILLIAM "THE ELDER"[4] HAMMACK, WILLIAM "O"[3], JOHN[2] HAMMOCKE, ? JOHN[1] HAMMOT)* was born 1811 in Wilkes Co., GA, and died Abt. 1895 in Warren Co., GA. He married PARTHENA HUNDLEY 02 Aug 1830 in Taliaferro Co., GA. She was born Abt. 1811 in Georgia, and died Aft. 1870 in Warren Co., GA.

Children of GUSTAVUS HAMMACK and PARTHENA HUNDLEY are:

    i.   ELIZABETH[9] HAMMACK, b. Abt. 1832, Taliaferro Co., GA; d. Aft. 1850, Warren Co., GA.

    ii.   ? VIRGINIA HAMMACK, b. Abt. 1830, Taliaferro Co., GA; m. JOHN C. HUMPHREY; b. Abt. 1814, Georgia.

    iii.   DR. WILLIAM T. HAMMACK, b. Abt. 1839, Taliaferro Co., GA; d. Aft. 1860, Warren Co., GA.

    iv.   GEORGE R. HAMMACK, b. Abt. 1842, Taliaferro Co., GA; d. Aft. 1860, Warren Co., GA.

    v.   NANCY HAMMACK, b. Abt. 1844, Taliaferro Co., GA; d. Aft. 1870, Warren Co., GA.

    vi.   BENJAMIN RICHARD HAMMACK, b. Abt. 1847, Taliaferro Co., GA; d. Aft. 1870, Warren Co., GA; m. LENA ANN WALDEN.

    vii.   ALBERT HAMMACK, b. Abt. 1849, Warren Co., GA; d. Aft. 1870, Warren Co., GA.

    viii.   COLUMBUS HAMMACK b. Abt. 1852, Warren Co., GA; d. Aft. 1870, Warren Co., GA.

    xi.   MISSOURI HAMMACK, b. Abt. 1857, Warren Co., GA; d. Aft. 1860, Warren Co., GA.

    x.   THOMAS HAMMACK, b. Abt. 1857, Warren Co., GA; d. Aft. 1870, Warren Co., GA.

Key Sources: Wynne, *Southern Lineages*, pp. 100-106; 1840 Taliaferro Co., GA, Census, p. 247; 1850 Warren Co., GA, Census, p. 148; 1860 Warren Co., GA, Census, p. 19; 1870 Warren Co., GA, Census, p. 56.

179. JESSE[8] HAMMOCK *(JOSHUA[7], ROBERT HAMMACK[6] JR., ROBERT HAMMACK[5] SR., WILLIAM "THE ELDER"[4] HAMMACK, WILLIAM "O"[3], JOHN[2] HAMMOCKE, ? JOHN[1] HAMMOT)* was born Abt. 1793 in Wilkes Co., GA, and died Aft. 1849 in Cobb Co., GA. He married POLLY JONES 01 Nov 1813 in Clarke Co., GA. She was born Abt. 1793 in Georgia, and died Bet. 1830 - 1832 in Clarke Co., GA.
Children of JESSE HAMMOCK and POLLY JONES are:

    i.   ? REBECCA[9] HAMMOCK, b. Abt. 1814, Clarke Co., GA; d. Aft. 1860, Jefferson Co., AL; m. TIMOTHY HICKSON, 05 Jan 1845, Newton Co., GA; b. Abt. 1794, Georgia; d. Aft. 1860, Jefferson Co., AL.

321.   ii.   ? ROBERT HAMMOCK, b. Abt. 1816, Clarke Co., GA; d. Aft. 1880, Talladega Co., AL.

    iii.   SON HAMMOCK, b. Bet. 1815 - 1820, Clarke Co., GA; d. Aft. 1840, Newton Co., GA.

    iv.   DAUGHTER HAMMOCK, b. Bet. 1815 - 1820, Clarke Co., GA; d. Aft. 1840, Newton Co., GA.

    v.   DAUGHTER HAMMOCK, b. Bet. 1825 - 1830, Newton Co., GA; d. Aft. 1840, Newton Co., GA.

    vi.   DAUGHTER HAMMOCK, b. Bet. 1825 - 1830, Newton Co., GA; d. Aft. 1840, Newton Co., GA.

Key Sources: 1830 Newton Co., GA, Census, p. 41; 1840 Newton Co., GA, Census, p. 29; Newton Co., GA, Deed Book I, p. 519. Identification of Rebecca and Robert as offspring of Jesse is speculative and based on location and common association with the Hickson family.

180. JOSHUA[8] HAMMOCK *(JOSHUA[7], ROBERT HAMMACK[6] JR., ROBERT HAMMACK[5] SR., WILLIAM "THE ELDER"[4] HAMMACK, WILLIAM "O"[3], JOHN[2] HAMMOCKE, ? JOHN[1] HAMMOT)* was born Abt. 1798 in Wilkes Co., GA, and died Aft. 1870 in Carroll Co., GA. He married (1) NANCY BURROWS Abt. 1820 in Walton Co., GA, daughter of PHILLIP BURROWS, SR.. She was born Abt. 1803 in South Carolina, and died Bet. 1860 - 1870 in Carroll Co., GA. He married (2) DORCUS [------].
She was born Abt. 1820 in North Carolina, and died Aft. 1870 in Carroll Co., GA.
Children of JOSHUA HAMMOCK and NANCY BURROWS are:

    i.   RACHEL C.[9] HAMMOCK, b. 22 Dec 1821, Walton Co., GA; d. 28 Jul 1853, Carroll Co., GA; m. REMES C. DAVENPORT.

    ii.   MELINDA PERNELIPA HAMMOCK, b. May 1823, Walton Co., GA; d. Apr 1905; m. WESLEY C. WILLIAMS.

322. iii. GEORGE BARTLETT WILLIAM HAMMOCK, b. 1825, Newton Co., GA; d. 13 Dec 1862, Fredericksburg, VA.

323. iv. JOHN THOMAS HAMMOCK, b. 1828, Newton Co., GA; d. Aft. 1860, Carroll Co., GA.

v. WILLIAM HAMMOCK, b. 1830, Newton Co., GA; d. Aft. 1850, Carroll Co., GA.

324. vi. ABNER MASTIN W. HAMMOCK, b. 1832, Newton Co., GA; d. Aft. 1870, Haralson Co., GA.

vii. SARAH ALLINDA HAMMOCK, b. 1835, Newton Co., GA; d. Aft. 1860, Carroll Co., GA; m. DANIEL BRACKNELL, 29 Oct 1857, Carroll Co., GA; b. Abt. 1831, South Carolina; d. Aft. 1860, Carroll Co., GA.

viii. JOSHUA MARION HAMMOCK, b. 1837, Newton Co., GA; d. Aft. 1860, Carroll Co., GA; m. NANCY SERCY.

ix. THOMAS NEWTON HAMMOCK, b. 1840, Newton Co., GA; d. Aft. 1870, Newton Co., GA; m. SUSANNAH HAMMOCK; b. Abt. 1834, Georgia; d. Aft. 1870, Newton Co., GA.

x. JOSEPH BEATON HAMMOCK, b. 1842, Newton Co., GA; d. Aft. 1860, Carroll Co., GA.

xi. JAMES WESLEY C. HAMMOCK, b. Abt. 1846, Newton Co., GA; d. Aft. 1920, Marshall Co., AL; m. SARAH A. [------], Bet. 1870 - 1880, Gwinnett Co., GA; b. Abt. 1850, Georgia; d. Aft. 1920, Marshall Co., AL.

Key Sources: 1820 Georgia Land Lottery Fortunate Drawers; 1830 Newton Co., GA, Census, p. 42; Newton Co., GA, Deed Book I, p. 85; 1850 Carroll Co., GA, Census; 1860 Carroll Co., GA, Census, p. 561; 1870 Carroll Co., GA, Census, p. 154; W. F. Nuss, *My Hammock Family, 1656-: A History of the Ancestors and Descendants of George Bartlett William Hammock (1825-1862)* (Cullman, AL, 1997).

181. JOHN[8] HAMMOCK *(JOSHUA[7], ROBERT HAMMACK[6] JR., ROBERT HAMMACK[5] SR., WILLIAM "THE ELDER"[4] HAMMACK, WILLIAM "O"[3], JOHN[2] HAMMOCKE, ? JOHN[1] HAMMOT)* was born Abt. 1801 in Hancock Co., GA, and died Bet. 1880 - 1883 in Newton Co., GA. He married (1) PIETY DAY 07 Nov 1822 in Newton Co., GA. She was born Abt. 1795 in Georgia, and died Aft. 1860 in Newton Co., GA. He married (2) HARRIETT ADELINE ODUM 31 Mar 1864 in Newton Co., GA.

Children of JOHN HAMMOCK and PIETY DAY are:

i. ELIZABETH[9] HAMMOCK, b. Abt. 1822, Newton Co., GA; d. Aft. 1860, Newton Co., GA; m. LEVI L. JARRELL, 16 Nov 1863, Newton Co., GA.

ii. ALEXANDER F. HAMMOCK, b. Abt. 1824, Newton Co., GA; d. 05 Apr 1863, Canton, MS.

325. iii. JAMES M. HAMMOCK, b. Abt. 1827, Newton Co., GA; d. Bet. 1860 - 1870, Confederate States Army.

326. iv. MANSEL W. HAMMOCK, b. Abt. 1831, Newton Co., GA; d. 08 Jul 1863, Fort Delaware, DE.

v. SUSAN E. HAMMOCK, b. Abt. 1834, Newton Co., GA; d. Aft. 1870, Newton Co., GA; m. THOMAS N. HAMMOCK; b. Abt. 1840, Newton Co., GA; d. Aft. 1870, Newton Co., GA.

Children of JOHN HAMMOCK and HARRIETT ODUM are:

vi. JOHN A.[9] HAMMOCK, b. Abt. 1865, Newton Co., GA; d. Bef. 1880, Rockdale Co., GA.

vii. ROBERT SCOTT HAMMOCK, b. 29 Sep 1866, Newton Co., GA; d. Aft. 1900, Gwinnett Co., GA; m. INDIA [------]; b. 01 Apr 1872, Georgia; d. 07 Feb 1936, DeKalb Co., GA.

viii. ALBERT T. HAMMOCK, b. Abt. 1868, Newton Co., GA; d. Aft. 1880, Rockdale Co., GA.

ix. EMMA HAMMOCK, b. Abt. 1870, Newton Co., GA; d. Aft. 1880, Rockdale Co., GA.

Key Sources: Newton Co., GA, Deed Book A, p. 589; 1840 Newton Co., GA, Census, p. 44; Newton Co., GA, Deed Book I, pp. 127, 519; 1850 Newton Co., GA, Census, p. 433; 1860 Newton Co., GA, Census, p. 509; Newton Co., GA, Deed Book N, pp. 36, 222; 1870 Newton Co., GA, Census, p. 176; 1880 Rockdale Co., GA, Census, p. 68C.

182. SUSANNAH[8] HAMMACK *(JOSHUA[7], ROBERT HAMMACK[6] JR., ROBERT HAMMACK[5] SR., WILLIAM "THE ELDER"[4] HAMMACK, WILLIAM "O"[3], JOHN[2] HAMMOCKE, ? JOHN[1] HAMMOT)* was born Abt. 1806 in Clarke Co., GA, and died Aft. 1850 in Newton Co., GA. She married JOHN DAY 10 Oct 1823 in Newton Co., GA. He was born Abt. 1793 in Georgia, and died Aft. 1850 in Newton Co., GA. Children of SUSANNAH HAMMACK and JOHN DAY are:

    i.   PENELOPE[9] DAY, b. Abt. 1826, Georgia; d. Aft. 1850, Newton Co., GA.

    ii.   JOHN DAY, b. Abt. 1829, Georgia; d. Aft. 1850, Newton Co., GA.

    iii.   MATILDA DAY, b. Abt. 1831, Georgia; d. Aft. 1850, Newton Co., GA.

    iv.   FRANKLIN DAY, b. Abt. 1832, Georgia; d. Aft. 1850, Newton Co., GA.

    v.   MARTHA DAY, b. Abt. 1835, Georgia; d. Aft. 1850, Newton Co., GA.

    vi.   JESSE C. DAY, b. Abt. 1838, Georgia; d. Aft. 1850, Newton Co., GA.

    vii.   HARRIS DAY, b. Abt. 1841, Georgia; d. Aft. 1850, Newton Co., GA.

    viii.   ELIZABETH DAY, b. Abt. 1842, Georgia; d. Aft. 1850, Newton Co., GA.

    ix.   GEORGE W. DAY, b. Abt. 1845, Georgia; d. Aft. 1850, Newton Co., GA.

    x.   ANDREW DAY, b. Abt. 1845, Georgia; d. Aft. 1850, Newton Co., GA.

    xi.   JAMES DAY, b. Abt. 1847, Georgia; d. Aft. 1850, Newton Co., GA.

    xii.   SUSAN DAY, b. Abt. 1849, Georgia; d. Aft. 1850, Newton Co., GA.

Key Source: 1850 Newton Co., GA, Census, p. 434-435.

183. ROBERT BERRY[8] HAMMOCK *(JOHN[7], ROBERT HAMMACK[6] JR., ROBERT HAMMACK[5] SR., WILLIAM "THE ELDER"[4] HAMMACK, WILLIAM "O"[3], JOHN[2] HAMMOCKE, ? JOHN[1] HAMMOT)* was born Abt. 1794 in Wilkes Co., GA, and died Aft. 1850 in Carroll Co., GA. He married NANCY [WHATLEY?] Bef. Sep 1814 in Jones Co., GA. She was born Bef. 1794 in Georgia, and died Aft. 1840 in Coweta Co., GA.

Children of ROBERT HAMMOCK and NANCY [WHATLEY?] are:

    i.   GREEN BERRY[9] HAMMOCK, b. Abt. 1814, Jones Co., GA; d. Aft. 1870, Carroll Co., GA; m. SUSAN ANN PARKER, 20 Mar 1834, Pike Co., GA; b. Abt. 1816, Georgia; d. Aft. 1870, Carroll Co., GA.

327.   ii.   MARY HAMMOCK, b. Abt. 1815, Jones Co., GA; d. Aft. 1870, Carroll Co., GA.

    iii.   RACHEL HAMMOCK, b. Abt. 1817, Jones Co., GA; m. JAMES DAVENPORT, 05 Sep 1838, Coweta Co., GA.

    iv.   MARTHA HAMMOCK, b. Abt. 1818, Jones Co., GA; d. Aft. 1850, Henry Co., AL; m. (1) PENDLETON GEORGE, 20 Sep 1838, Coweta Co., GA; b. Abt. 1815, Georgia; d. 1841, Carroll Co., GA; m. (2) ABSALOM HASTY, 04 Nov 1841, Coweta Co., GA; d. Aft. 1850, Henry Co., AL.

    v.   DAUGHTER HAMMOCK, b. Bet. 1814 - 1820, Jones Co., GA.

    vi.   DAUGHTER HAMMOCK, b. Bet. 1825 - 1830, Jones Co., GA.

    vii.   CHRISTOPHER C. HAMMOCK, b. Abt. 1835, Jones Co., GA; m. MARY F. HARRIS, 17 Dec 1857, Carroll Co., GA.

Key Sources: Georgia Journal, 7 September 1814 and 12 October 1814; Jones Co., GA, Deed Book K, pp. 17, 27; Jones Co., GA, Deed Book L, p. 176; 1820 Jones Co., GA, Census; Pike Co., GA, Deed Book E, p. 303; Jones Co., GA, Deed Book P, p. 301; 1840 Jones Co., GA, Census, p. 137; 1840 Coweta Co., GA, Census, p. 334; Pike Co., GA, Deed Book F, p. 686; 1850 Carroll Co., GA, Census, p. 33; 1860 Carroll Co., GA, Census, p. 584. Robert and Nancy apparently separated but continued to live in the same area. Identification of children is speculative but is based on close association in Pike, Coweta, and Carroll Counties.

184. WILLIAM B.[8] HAMMOCK *(JOHN[7], ROBERT HAMMACK[6] JR., ROBERT HAMMACK[5] SR., WILLIAM "THE ELDER"[4] HAMMACK, WILLIAM "O"[3], JOHN[2] HAMMOCKE, ? JOHN[1] HAMMOT)* was born Abt. 1795 in Wilkes Co., GA, and died May 1848 in Talbot Co., GA. He married POLLY TUCKER 27 Dec 1816 in Jasper Co., GA. She was born Abt. 1800 in Georgia, and died Aft. 1840 in Talbot Co., GA.

Children of WILLIAM HAMMOCK and POLLY TUCKER are:

      i.   ? MICHAEL S.[9] HAMMOCK, b. Abt. 1818, Georgia; d. Aft. 1836, Talbot Co., GA; m. SARAH WILLIAMS, 22 Sep 1836, Talbot Co., GA.

328.   ii. JOHN PINKNEY HAMMOCK, b. 20 Aug 1820, Jones Co., GA; d. 11 Oct 1889, Marion Co., GA.

     iii. SON HAMMOCK, b. Bet. 1820 - 1825, Jones Co., GA; d. Aft. 1840, Talbot Co., GA.

     iv. DAUGHTER HAMMOCK, b. Bet. 1825 - 1830, Jones Co., GA; d. Aft. 1840, Talbot Co., GA.

     v. DAUGHTER HAMMOCK, b. Bet. 1825 - 1830, Jones Co., GA; d. Aft. 1840, Talbot Co., GA.

     vi. SON HAMMOCK, b. Bet. 1825 - 1830, Jones Co., GA; d. Aft. 1840, Talbot Co., GA.

     vii. HOPE HULL HAMMOCK, b. Abt. 1827, Jones Co., GA; d. Aft. 1840, Talbot Co., GA.

     viii. SON HAMMOCK, b. Bet. 1830 - 1835, Talbot Co., GA; d. Aft. 1840, Talbot Co., GA.

     ix. DAUGHTER HAMMOCK, b. Bet. 1835 - 1840, Talbot Co., GA; d. Aft. 1840, Talbot Co., GA.

Key Sources: 1820 Jones Co., GA, Census, p. 117; 1830 Talbot Co., GA, Census, p. 334; 1840 Talbot Co., GA, Census, p. 229. Like James, Elijah, and Lewis Hammack, William B. Hammock had several unidentified sons who probably include some of the unidentified Hammock and Hammack males in western Georgia and eastern Alabama between 1840 and 1860. There is a possibility that Michael S. Hammock was a son of William's first cousin, Jesse Hammock of Cobb Co., GA.

185. REBECCA[8] HAMMOCK *(JOHN[7], ROBERT HAMMACK[6] JR., ROBERT HAMMACK[5] SR., WILLIAM "THE ELDER"[4] HAMMACK, WILLIAM "O"[3], JOHN[2] HAMMOCKE, ? JOHN[1] HAMMOT)* was born 20 Aug 1799 in Wilkes Co., GA, and died 12 Aug 1883 in Talbot Co., GA. She married RANSOM MCBRIDE 15 May 1817 in Jones Co., GA. He was born 11 Feb 1797 in Georgia, and died 04 Jul 1860 in Talbot Co., GA.

Children of REBECCA HAMMOCK and RANSOM MCBRIDE are:

     i. JOHN T.[9] MCBRIDE, b. 02 May 1819, Georgia; d. Feb 1896, Talbot Co., GA; m. GRACY E. DURDEN, 04 Mar 1851, Talbot Co., GA.

     ii. WILLIAM J. MCBRIDE, b. 09 May 1820, Georgia; d. 22 Sep 1895, Talbot Co., GA; m. SARAH T. BOYNTON, 19 Jun 1849, Talbot Co., GA.

     iii. MANCEL THEODORE B. MCBRIDE, b. 07 Jul 1821, Georgia; d. 02 Nov 1896, Bell Co., TX; m. JANE W. GORE, 08 Sep 1844, Talbot Co., GA.

     iv. RACHEL MCBRIDE, b. 02 Apr 1824, Georgia; d. 26 Apr 1894, Georgia; m. [------] GLOVER.

     v. LEWIS P. MCBRIDE, b. 1825, Georgia; m. MARY ANN CHILDERS, 26 Nov 1843, Talbot Co., GA.

     vi. ADALINE ARIADNE MCBRIDE, b. 25 May 1829, Georgia; d. 25 Nov 1895, Talbot Co., GA; m. GEORGE W. AMOS, 03 Jul 1846, Talbot Co., GA.

     vii. GEORGIA ANN MCBRIDE, b. 08 Nov 1832, Georgia; d. 27 Sep 1909, Talbot Co., GA; m. JOHN W. ROSE.

     viii. DIANA MCBRIDE, b. 01 Apr 1833, Talbot Co., GA; d. 06 Jul 1869, Talbot Co., GA; m. JOSIAH T. COLLEY.

     ix. CICERO MCBRIDE, b. 24 Feb 1836, Talbot Co., GA; d. 15 Jun 1882, Talbot Co., GA; m. DOROTHEA [------].

   x.   NANCY A. MCBRIDE, b. Abt. 1839, Talbot Co., GA; m. FRANCIS M. MCFARLAND, 15 Mar 1860, Talbot Co., GA.

Key Sources: 1850 Talbot Co., GA, Census, p. 227; 1860 Talbot Co., GA, Census, p. 570; 1870 Talbot Co., GA, Census, p. 111.

186. JOHN P.[8] HAMMOCK *(JOHN[7], ROBERT HAMMACK[6] JR., ROBERT HAMMACK[5] SR., WILLIAM "THE ELDER"[4] HAMMACK, WILLIAM "O"[3], JOHN[2] HAMMOCKE, ? JOHN[1] HAMMOT)* was born Abt. 1800 in Wilkes Co., GA, and died Aft. 1850 in Tallapoosa Co., AL. He married (1) UNKNOWN Abt. 1820 in Jones Co., GA. He married (2) SARAH USSERY 27 May 1829 in Jones Co., GA. She was born Abt. 1800 in Jones Co., GA, and died Aft. 1870 in Jones Co., GA.
Children of JOHN HAMMOCK and UNKNOWN are:
   i.   SON[9] HAMMOCK, b. Bet. 1820 - 1825, Jones Co., GA; d. Aft. 1840, Talbot Co., GA.
   ii. DAUGHTER HAMMOCK, b. Bet. 1825 - 1830, Jones Co., GA.
   iii. MARY HAMMOCK, b. Abt. 1840, Talbot Co., GA; d. Aft. 1850, Tallapoosa Co., AL.

Key Sources: 1820 Georgia Land Lottery Fortunate Draws; Bibb Co., GA, Deed Book K, p. 106; 1825 Jones Co., GA, Tax Digest; 1830 Jones Co., GA, Census, p. 428; 1850 Tallapoosa Co., AL, Census, p. 55; 1870 Jones Co., GA, Census, p. 265.

187. JACKSON[8] HAMMOCK *(JOHN[7], ROBERT HAMMACK[6] JR., ROBERT HAMMACK[5] SR., WILLIAM "THE ELDER"[4] HAMMACK, WILLIAM "O"[3], JOHN[2] HAMMOCKE, ? JOHN[1] HAMMOT)* was born 01 Jul 1801 in Hancock Co., GA, and died 03 Dec 1883 in Chambers Co., AL. He married REBECCA HARDAWAY 17 Oct 1821 in Jones Co., GA. She was born 24 Jun 1797 in Georgia, and died 13 Oct 1874 in Chambers Co., AL.
Children of JACKSON HAMMOCK and REBECCA HARDAWAY are:
   i.   SON[9] HAMMOCK, b. Bet. 1821 - 1825, Jones Co., GA.
   ii.   ? EMALINE HAMMOCK, b. Abt. 1822, Jones Co., GA; d. Aft. 1836, Jones Co., GA; m. GREEN MERRITT, 12 Nov 1836, Jones Co., GA.
   iii. ? BETSY HAMMOCK, b. Abt. 1824, Jones Co., GA; d. Aft. 1839, Talbot Co., GA; m. RICHARD C. CROSBY, 29 Dec 1839, Talbot Co., GA.
   iv.   ? MARY HAMMOCK, b. Abt. 1829, Jones Co., GA; d. Aft. 1850, Tallapoosa Co., AL; m. WILLIAM DOWNS/DOSSEY; b. Abt. 1828, Georgia; d. Aft. 1850, Tallapoosa Co., AL.
   v.   ? JANE HAMMOCK, b. Abt. 1832, Talbot Co., GA; d. Aft. 1850, Tallapoosa Co., AL; m. JAMES M. DOWNS, 27 Sep 1849, Tallapoosa Co., AL.
   vi.   NANCY HAMMOCK, b. Abt. 1836, Talbot Co., GA; d. Aft. 1850, Tallapoosa Co., AL; m. HAMILTON F. SMITH, 03 Dec 1857, Tallapoosa Co., AL.
329.   vii. GILLEY ANN HAMMOCK, b. 19 Sep 1837, Talbot Co., GA; d. Aft. 1860, Tallapoosa Co., AL.
   viii. COLUMBUS GREEN HAMMOCK, b. Abt. 1844, Tallapoosa Co., AL; d. Aft. 1850, Tallapoosa Co., AL.

Key Sources: 1825 Jones Co., GA, Tax Digest; 1840 Talbot Co., GA, Tax Digest, p. 224; 1850 Tallapoosa Co., AL, Census, p. 61; 1855 Tallapoosa Co., AL, State Census; 1860 Tallapoosa Co., AL, Census, p. 73; 1870 Tallapoosa Co., AL, Census, p. 196. The identities of Jackson's older offspring are speculative. Note that William and Mary Dossey were living adjacent Jackson Hammock in 1850.

188. ELIZABETH[8] HAMMOCK *(JOHN[7], ROBERT HAMMACK[6] JR., ROBERT HAMMACK[5] SR., WILLIAM "THE ELDER"[4] HAMMACK, WILLIAM "O"[3], JOHN[2] HAMMOCKE, ? JOHN[1] HAMMOT)* was born Abt. 1803 in Hancock Co., GA, and died 27 Aug 1895 in Hunt Co., TX. She married CALEB ADAMS 25 Jun 1825 in Jones Co., GA. He was born Abt. 1803 in Clarke Co., GA, and died 12 Aug 1844 in Chambers Co., AL.

Children of ELIZABETH HAMMOCK and CALEB ADAMS are:

    i.   ELIZABETH ANNA[9] ADAMS, b. 02 Nov 1826, Monroe Co., GA; d. 03 Aug 1908, Naples Co., TX; m. BENJAMIN JAMES LUCAS POWELL, 04 Mar 1840, Chambers Co., AL; b. 14 Jun 1814, South Carolina.

    ii.   EMELINE ADAMS, b. Abt. 1828, Monroe Co., GA; d. Aft. 1849, Tallapoosa Co., AL; m. WILLIAM A. HIGGINS, 17 Oct 1849, Tallapoosa Co., AL.

    iii.   AUGUSTUS ADAMS, b. Abt. 1829, Monroe Co., GA; d. Aft. 1829, Monroe Co., GA.

    iv.   NIPPER ADAMS, b. 24 May 1831, Talbot Co., GA; d. Aft. 1831, Talbot Co., GA.

    v.   MARY ANN ADAMS, b. 14 Sep 1833, Stewart Co., GA; d. Aft. 1850, Chambers Co., AL; m. GREEN LEE GRIFFIN, 26 Dec 1850, Chambers Co., AL.

    vi.   JOHN W. ADAMS, b. Abt. 1834, Stewart Co., GA; d. Aft. 1865, Tallapoosa Co., AL; m. NETTIE ROGERS, 1865, Tallapoosa Co., AL.

    vii.   MARTHA ADAMS, b. Abt. 1836, Chambers Co., AL; d. Aft. 1850, Chambers Co., AL; m. CHRISTOPHER SPRAGGINS.

    viii.   WILLIAM ADAMS, b. Abt. 1837, Chambers Co., AL; d. Aft. 1850, Chambers Co., AL.

    ix.   JOSHUA ADAMS, b. Abt. 1838, Chambers Co., AL; d. Aft. 1850, Chambers Co., AL.

    x.   SARAH JANE ADAMS, b. Abt. 1840, Chambers Co., AL; d. 11 Sep 1911, Alabama; m. (1) JOHN G. BENTON; m. (2) JAMES HENRY BEARD.

Key Source: 1850 Tallapoosa Co., AL, Census, p. 55.

189. LEWIS W.[8] HAMMACK *(JOHN[7], ROBERT HAMMACK[6] JR., ROBERT HAMMACK[5] SR., WILLIAM "THE ELDER"[4] HAMMACK, WILLIAM "O"[3], JOHN[2] HAMMOCKE, ? JOHN[1] HAMMOT)* was born Abt. 1805 in Hancock Co., GA, and died Aft. 1870 in Muscogee Co., GA. He married AMANDA DAVENPORT 09 Jul 1829 in Jones Co., GA, daughter of RAYMOND DAVENPORT. She was born Abt. 1814 in South Carolina, and died Bef. 1860 in Muscogee Co., GA.

Children of LEWIS HAMMACK and AMANDA DAVENPORT are:

    i.   A. M. T.[9] HAMMACK, b. Abt. 1832, Marion Co., GA; d. Aft. 1850, Muscogee Co., GA.

    ii.   JOHN HAMMACK, b. Abt. 1832, Muscogee Co., GA; d. Aft. 1850, Muscogee Co., GA; m. ? REBECCA DANIEL, Abt. 1858, Talbot Co., GA; b. Abt. 1838, Georgia; d. Aft. 1860, Talbot Co., GA.

    iii.   MARY E. R. W. HAMMACK, b. Abt. 1833, Georgia; d. 13 Apr 1851, Muscogee Co., GA.

    iv.   ROBERT HAMMACK, b. Abt. 1835, Georgia; d. Aft. 1860, Taylor Co., GA.

    v.   WILLIAM CHARLES T. B. HAMMOCK, b. 04 Dec 1838, Marion Co., GA; d. 22 Mar 1914, Spalding Co., GA; m. MARY CAROLINE DODD, 14 May 1865, Bartow Co., GA; b. 16 Sep 1838, Union Co., SC; d. 28 Apr 1910, Spalding Co., GA.

    vi.   SUSAN MARTHA ANN HAMMACK, b. Abt. 1840, Marion Co., GA; d. Aft. 1858, Muscogee Co., GA; m. JOSIAH ASBURY BOLAND, 30 Sep 1858, Muscogee Co., GA; b. Abt. 1839, Fayette Co., GA; d. Aft. 1858, Muscogee Co., GA.

    vii.   GEORGE HAMMACK, b. Abt. 1841, Marion Co., GA; d. 30 Nov 1864, Franklin, TN.

330.   viii.   EDMUND HARPER WORRELL HAMMACK, b. 18 Sep 1843, Muscogee Co., GA; d. 03 Jan 1933, Bell Co., TX.

    ix.   FRANCES HAMMACK, b. Abt. 1847, Muscogee Co., GA; d. Aft. 1860, Muscogee Co., GA; m. RICHARD IVY MORRIS, 26 Aug 1865, Muscogee Co., GA.

    x.   MATILDA ARTEMESIA HAMMACK, b. 18 Apr 1848, Muscogee Co., GA; d. 21 Feb 1930, Jones Co., TX; m. [----] KERNS.

Key Sources: 1825 Jones Co., GA, Tax Digest; 1830 Jones Co., GA, Census, p. 428; 1840 Marion Co., GA, Census; 1850 Muscogee Co., GA, Census, p. 316; 1860 Muscogee Co., GA, Census, p. 350; 1870 Muscogee Co., GA, Census, p. 772. Note that this family used both spellings. On William C. T. B.

Hammock's tombstone, the name is spelled Hammock; on Edmund H. W. Hammack's tombstone, it is spelled Hammack.

190. HOPE HULL[8] HAMMOCK *(JOHN[7], ROBERT HAMMACK[6] JR., ROBERT HAMMACK[5] SR., WILLIAM "THE ELDER"[4] HAMMACK, WILLIAM "O"[3], JOHN[2] HAMMOCKE, ? JOHN[1] HAMMOT)* was born Abt. 1806 in Hancock Co., GA, and died Aft. 1870 in Talbot Co., GA. He married MARTHA A. MCCRARY 30 Oct 1830 in Talbot Co., GA, daughter of WILLIAM MCCRARY and MARY [------]. She was born Abt. 1812 in Georgia, and died 21 Apr 1887 in Talbot Co., GA.
Children of HOPE HAMMOCK and MARTHA MCCRARY are:

      i.   MARY ELIZABETH[9] HAMMOCK, b. 28 Aug 1831, Talbot Co., GA; d. 20 Dec 1851, Taylor Co., GA; m. JORDAN WILCHER, 03 Aug 1851, Marion Co., GA.

331.   ii.   WILLIAM J. HAMMOCK, b. 21 May 1834, Talbot Co., GA; d. 27 Sep 1890, Talbot Co., GA.

     iii.   ULESIS HAMMOCK, b. Abt. 1836, Talbot Co., GA; d. 12 Jul 1862, Cold Harbor, VA.

     iv.   CATHERINE MELISSA HAMMOCK, b. 17 Aug 1838, Talbot Co., GA; d. 23 May 1920, Falls Co., TX; m. BENJAMIN F. ELLISTON, 27 Oct 1859, Talbot Co., GA; b. Abt. 1833, Talbot Co., GA; d. Abt. 1895, Falls Co., TX.

     v.   VIRGINIA ANN HAMMOCK, b. 14 Jan 1841, Talbot Co., GA; d. 10 Oct 1880, Bell Co., TX; m. (1) JORDAN WILCHER, 10 Sep 1865, Taylor Co., GA; m. (2) JOHN WESLEY SMITH, 10 Dec 1870, Bell Co., TX; b. 18 Feb 1834, Tennessee.

     vi.   FRANCES M. HAMMOCK, b. Abt. 1843, Talbot Co., GA; d. Aft. 1870, Taylor Co., GA; m. SAMUEL L. DUKE, 09 Feb 1870, Talbot Co., GA.

     vii.   WELBORN HAMMOCK, b. Abt. 1845, Talbot Co., GA; d. Aft. 1870, Talbot Co., GA; m. ELDORADO "ELDORA" MCFARLAND, 20 Feb 1870, Talbot Co., GA.

   viii.   JULIUS FELIX HAMMOCK, b. Jun 1847, Talbot Co., GA; d. 1901, Texas; m. ESBY MCCRARY, 23 Dec 1866, Talbot Co., GA; b. Nov 1843, Dale Co., AL; d. 1906, Texas.

     ix.   JONATHAN S. HAMMOCK, b. Oct 1849, Talbot Co., GA; d. Aft. 1870, Talbot Co., GA.

     x.   ZORALDA RUTH HAMMOCK, b. 12 Jun 1852, Talbot Co., GA; d. Aft. 1871, Talbot Co., GA; m. JOHN THOMAS MCFARLAND; b. 04 Oct 1845, Georgia; d. 07 Jan 1915, Taylor Co., GA.

Key Sources: Upson Co., GA, Deed Book B, p. 514; 1850 Talbot Co., GA, Census, pp. 223-226; 1860 Talbot Co., GA, Census, p. 571; 1870 Talbot Co., GA, Census, p. 108.

191. NANCY[8] HAMMOCK *(JOHN[7], ROBERT HAMMACK[6] JR., ROBERT HAMMACK[5] SR., WILLIAM "THE ELDER"[4] HAMMACK, WILLIAM "O"[3], JOHN[2] HAMMOCKE, ? JOHN[1] HAMMOT)* was born Abt. 1806 in Hancock Co., GA, and died Aft. 1850 in Schley Co., GA. She married JOHN CHILDERS 17 Jan 1821 in Jones Co., GA. He was born Abt. 1800 in Georgia, and died Aft. 1853 in Schley Co., GA.
Children of NANCY HAMMOCK and JOHN CHILDERS are:

      i.   ? EDMUND[9] CHILDERS, b. Abt. 1822, Jones Co., GA.

     ii.   ? PRUDENCE CHILDERS, b. Abt. 1824, Jones Co., GA; d. 21 May 1895, Muscogee Co., GA; m. BENJAMIN W. GREEN, 26 Oct 1843, Talbot Co., GA.

     iii.   ? JANE CHILDERS, b. Abt. 1826, Jones Co., GA; d. Aft. 1842, Talbot Co., GA; m. WILLIAM M. WILLIAMS, 15 Dec 1842, Talbot Co., GA.

     iv.   HOPE CHILDERS, b. Abt. 1828, Jones Co., GA.

     v.   JACKSON CHILDERS, b. Abt. 1830, Jones Co., GA.

     vi.   NANCY CHILDERS, b. Abt. 1833, Talbot Co., GA; m. WILLIAM LUMPKIN.

     vii.   ZACHARIAH CHILDERS, b. Abt. 1835, Talbot Co., GA.

   viii.   MARTHA CHILDERS, b. Abt. 1837, Talbot Co., GA.

     ix.   WILLIAM WINFREY CHILDERS, b. Abt. 1840, Talbot Co., GA.

x. REBECCA FRANCES CHILDERS, b. Abt. 1842, Talbot Co., GA; m. GEORGE WASHINGTON TISON.

xi. HONOR CHILDERS, b. Abt. 1844, Talbot Co., GA.

xii. LUCINDA CHILDERS, b. Abt. 1846, Talbot Co., GA.

xiii. SARAH CHILDERS, b. Abt. 1848, Talbot Co., GA.

xiv. ELMIRA Z. CHILDERS, b. Abt. 1852, Schley Co., GA.

Key Source: 1850 Talbot Co., GA, Census, p. 227.

192. MARY[8] RAY *(NANCY (ANNA)[7] HAMMACK, ROBERT HAMMACK[6] JR., ROBERT HAMMACK[5] SR., WILLIAM "THE ELDER"[4] HAMMACK, WILLIAM "O"[3], JOHN[2] HAMMOCKE, ? JOHN[1] HAMMOT)* was born Abt. 1792 in Georgia, and died Aft. 1850 in Jones Co., GA. She married MATTHEW MOORE Abt. 1810 in Wilkes Co., GA, son of USSERY MOORE and MARTHA BISHOP. He was born Abt. 1789 in Lunenburg Co., VA, and died Abt. 1852 in Jones Co., GA.

Children of MARY RAY and MATTHEW MOORE are:

i. CHESLEY B.[9] MOORE, b. Abt. 1812, Wilkes Co., GA; d. Aft. 1880, Fayette Co., TX; m. ABINA SHAW, 1832, Jones Co., GA; b. Abt. 1815, Jones Co., GA; d. Aft. 1850, Muscogee Co., GA.

ii. JACOB MOORE, b. Abt. 1814, Wilkes Co., GA; d. Aft. 1850, Jones Co., GA; m. ANTIMA FREEMAN, 26 May 1844, Jones Co., GA; b. Abt. 1815, Georgia; d. Aft. 1850, Jones Co., GA.

iii. JAMES MOORE, b. Abt. 1816, Wilkes Co., GA; d. Aft. 1854, Macon Co., GA; m. ELIZABETH GRAY, 03 Jan 1837, Jones Co., GA; b. Abt. 1819, Putnam Co., GA; d. Aft. 1850, Muscogee Co., GA.

iv. NANCY MOORE, b. Abt. 1821, Wilkes Co., GA; d. Aft. 1860, Jones Co., GA.

v. WILLIAM F. MOORE, b. Abt. 1823, Wilkes Co., GA; d. Aft. 08 Mar 1852, Jones Co., GA.

vi. THOMAS MOORE, b. Abt. 1825, Jones Co., GA; d. Aft. 08 Mar 1852, Jones Co., GA.

vii. ABSALOM MOORE, b. Abt. 1830, Jones Co., GA; d. Aft. 08 Mar 1852, Jones Co., GA.

viii. WILBURN MOORE, b. 15 Jul 1833, Jones Co., GA; d. Aft. 04 Jun 1912, Ouachita Co., AR; m. HARRIETT N. SCROGGINS; b. 19 Mar 1831, Henry Co., GA.

Key Sources: 1809-1823 Wilkes Co., GA, Tax Digests; 1820 Wilkes Co., GA, Census, p. 273; 1825-1851 Jones Co., GA, Tax Digests; Records of Williams Creek Baptist Church, Warren Co., GA; 1830 Jones Co., GA, Census, p. 452; 1840 Jones Co., GA, Census, p. 135; 1850 Jones Co., GA, Census, pp. 184-187, 191-195; Jones Co., GA, Will Book C; 1860 Jones Co., GA, Census, p. 542.

193. MARTHA[8] RAY *(NANCY (ANNA)[7] HAMMACK, ROBERT HAMMACK[6] JR., ROBERT HAMMACK[5] SR., WILLIAM "THE ELDER"[4] HAMMACK, WILLIAM "O"[3], JOHN[2] HAMMOCKE, ? JOHN[1] HAMMOT)* was born Abt. 1796 in Wilkes Co., GA, and died Abt. 15 Mar 1866 in Jones Co., GA. She married SIMEON FELTS 08 May 1823 in Jones Co., GA. He was born Abt. 1790 in Warren Co., NC, and died Abt. 1844 in Putnam Co., GA.

Children of MARTHA RAY and SIMEON FELTS are:

i. WILLIAM A.[9] FELTS, b. 1824, Jones Co., GA; d. 1856, Jones Co., GA; m. MARGARET W. TAYLOR; b. Abt. 1825, Georgia; d. Aft. 1860, Jones Co., GA.

ii. NANCY J. FELTS, b. Abt. 1826, Jones Co., GA; d. Aft. 1850, Jones Co., GA.

iii. LOUISA CATHERINE FELTS, b. Abt. 1836, Jones Co., GA; d. Aft. 1866, Jones Co., GA; m. JOHN F. LOVE.

iv. MARTHA C. FELTS, b. Abt. 1837, Jones Co., GA; m. GABRIEL PITTS.

v. SIMEON J. FELTS, b. 1839, Jones Co., GA; d. 1863, Richmond, VA.

vi. ROBERT LEWIS FELTS, b. 26 Aug 1841, Jones Co., GA; d. 28 Nov 1898, Jones Co., GA; m. MARY SAMANTHA HUDSON; b. 12 Mar 1845, Jones Co., GA; d. 02 Jul 1905, Jones Co., GA.

Key Sources: Putnam Co., GA, Will Book Q, p. 102; 1860 Jones Co., GA, Census, p. 560.

194. JANE[8] RAY *(NANCY (ANNA)[7] HAMMACK, ROBERT HAMMACK[6] JR., ROBERT HAMMACK[5] SR., WILLIAM "THE ELDER"[4] HAMMACK, WILLIAM "O"[3], JOHN[2] HAMMOCKE, ? JOHN[1] HAMMOT)* was born Abt. 1802 in Wilkes Co., GA, and died Aft. 1850 in Taliaferro Co., GA. She married EDMUND MCLAUGHLIN 07 Oct 1821 in Wilkes Co., GA. He was born Abt. 1794 in Maryland, and died Aft. 1850 in Taliaferro Co., GA.
Child of JANE RAY and EDMUND MCLAUGHLIN is:
> i.   ELIZABETH[9] MCLAUGHLIN, b. Abt. 1822, Wilkes Co., GA; m. WILLIAM G. MOODY, 08 Jan 1843, Taliaferro Co., GA.

Key Source: 1850 Taliaferro Co., GA, Census, p. 337.

195. SIMEON J.[8] HAMMACK *(WILLIAM T.[7], ROBERT HAMMACK[6] JR., ROBERT HAMMACK[5] SR., WILLIAM "THE ELDER"[4] HAMMACK, WILLIAM "O"[3], JOHN[2] HAMMOCKE, ? JOHN[1] HAMMOT)* was born Abt. 1798 in Wilkes Co., GA, and died Abt. 1863 in Calhoun Co., MS. He married ELIZABETH JANE MOORE 19 Jan 1820 in Wilkes County, GA, daughter of ROBERT MOORE. She was born Abt. 1804 in Wilkes Co., GA, and died Aft. 1866 in Mississippi?.
Children of SIMEON HAMMACK and ELIZABETH MOORE are:
332.	i.	WILLIAM T. H.[9] HAMMACK, b. Abt. 1821, Jones Co., GA; d. Mar 1880, Madison County, MS.
333.	ii.	MARY JANE HAMMACK, b. Abt. 1826, Jones Co., GA; d. Abt. 1880, Navarro Co., TX.
334.	iii.	CHARLES M. HAMMACK, b. Abt. 1823, Jones County, GA; d. Bef. 01 Apr 1879, Calhoun County, MS.
335.	iv.	SARAH ANN E. HAMMACK, b. Abt. 1826, Jones Co., GA; d. Aft. 1870, Madison Co., MS..
336.	v.	JOHN T. HAMMACK, b. Abt. 1830, Crawford Co., GA; d. Jan 1870, Calhoun County, MS.
337.	vi.	FELIX WILBORN HAMMACK, b. Abt. 1834, Crawford Co., GA; d. Abt. 1903, Sabougla, Calhoun County, MS..
338.	vii.	ALFRED WASHINGTON "DOCK" HAMMACK, b. 17 Jun 1838, Crawford Co., GA; d. 18 Jul 1898, Ashley County, AR.
	viii.	CLAYTON M. HAMMACK, b. Abt. 1840, Crawford Co., GA; d. Bet. 1861 - 1865, Confederate States Army.
	ix.	FRANKLIN F. HAMMACK, b. Abt. 1843, Crawford Co., GA; d. 08 Oct 1862, Graysville, GA.
339.	x.	MARTHA HAMMACK, b. Apr 1845, Crawford Co., GA; d. Aft. 1900, Madison Co., MS.
340.	xi.	GEORGE W. T. HAMMACK, b. 06 Oct 1847, Crawford County, GA; d. 24 Dec 1893, Calhoun Co., MS.

Key Sources: 1820 Jones Co., GA, Census, p. 134; 1830 Crawford Co., GA, Census, p. 410; 1840 Crawford Co., GA, Census, p. 371; 1850 Macon Co., GA, Census, p. 124; 1860 Choctaw Co., MS, Census, p. 421.

196. LEWIS M.[8] HAMMOCK *(WILLIAM T.[7] HAMMACK, ROBERT HAMMACK[6] JR., ROBERT HAMMACK[5] SR., WILLIAM "THE ELDER"[4] HAMMACK, WILLIAM "O"[3], JOHN[2] HAMMOCKE, ? JOHN[1] HAMMOT)* was born Abt. 1801 in Wilkes Co., GA, and died Bef. 02 Sep 1867 in Sumter County, GA. He married NANCY FEAGIN 03 Aug 1820 in Jones County, GA. She was born Abt. 1801 in South Carolina, and died Bef. 10 Sep 1870 in Sumter County, GA.
Children of LEWIS HAMMOCK and NANCY FEAGIN are:
| 341. | i. | JULIA ANN[9] HAMMACK, b. Abt. 1821, Jones Co., GA; d. Aft. 1830, Jones Co., GA. |
| 342. | ii. | W. H. HAMMACK, b. Abt. 1823, Jones Co., GA; d. Aft. 1860, Sumter Co., GA. |

343. iii. WILLIAM H. HAMMACK, b. Abt. 1825, Jones Co., GA; d. Aft. 1860, Crawford Co., GA.

344. iv. FELIX L. HAMMACK, b. Abt. 1827, Jones Co., GA; d. Bet. 1863 - 1870, Crawford County, GA.

    v. MARY HAMMACK, b. Abt. Mar 1829, Jones Co., GA; d. Aft. 1900, Sumter Co., GA.

    vi. MILLIE ANN HAMMACK, b. Abt. 1831, Jones Co., GA; d. Abt. 1892, Sumter Co., GA; m. JOSHUA G. DAVIDSON, Abt. 1846, Sumter Co., GA; b. Abt. 1830, Georgia; d. Aft. 1850, Georgia.

345. vii. GEORGIE ANN VIRGINIA HAMMACK, b. Apr 1833, Jones Co., GA; d. 27 Oct 1904, Sumter Co., GA.

    viii. CAMILLA HAMMACK, b. Abt. 1835, Jones Co., GA; d. Aft. 1850, Sumter Co., GA.

    ix. LEONIDAS HAMMACK, b. Abt. 1837, Jones Co., GA; d. Aft. 1850, Sumter Co., GA.

    x. MICHAEL HAMMACK, b. Abt. 1839, Jones Co., GA; d. Aft. 1850, Sumter Co., GA.

    xi. JOHN HAMMACK, b. Abt. 1843, Jones Co., GA; d. Aft. 1850, Sumter Co., GA.

Key Sources: 1830 Jones Co., GA, Census, pp. 428, 451; 1840 Jones Co., GA, Census, p. 135; 1850 Sumter Co., GA, Census, p. 198.

197. TALBOT DAVIDSON[8] HAMMACK *(WILLIAM T.[7], ROBERT HAMMACK[6] JR., ROBERT HAMMACK[5] SR., WILLIAM "THE ELDER"[4] HAMMACK, WILLIAM "O"[3], JOHN[2] HAMMOCKE, ? JOHN[1] HAMMOT)* was born 02 Oct 1802 in Wilkes County, GA, and died 08 Mar 1873 in Crawford County, GA. He married REBECCA HARRELL 1829, daughter of HARDY HARRELL and SUSAN. She was born 21 Sep 1809 in Georgia, and died 24 May 1886 in Crawford County, GA.

Children of TALBOT HAMMACK and REBECCA HARRELL are:

346. i. SUSAN MATILDA[9] HAMMACK, b. 26 Oct 1829, Crawford Co., GA; d. 11 Apr 1907, Montezuma, Macon County, GA.

347. ii. WILLIAM WELBORN HAMMACK, b. 03 Jan 1831, Crawford Co., GA; d. 08 Oct 1857, Crawford County, GA.

348. iii. MARY JANE HAMMACK, b. 09 Sep 1832, Crawford Co., GA; d. 14 Nov 1914, Crawford County, GA.

349. iv. MALINDA CAROLINE (LYNN) HAMMACK, b. 30 May 1834, Crawford Co., GA; d. 16 Aug 1899, Macon Co., GA.

    v. RACHAEL AMANDA BELLE (PUSS) HAMMACK, b. 12 Oct 1836, Crawford Co., GA; d. 16 Mar 1905, Bibb Co., GA; m. JOHN ROBERTS, Aft. 1860, Crawford Co., GA.

    vi. TALBOT DAVIDSON HAMMACK, JR., b. Abt. 1839, Crawford Co., GA; d. 16 May 1864, Drewry's Bluff, Virginia.

    vii. MARTHA ANN ELIZABETH (LIZZIE) HAMMACK, b. 19 Dec 1840, Crawford Co., GA; d. 07 May 1899, Crawford County, GA.

    viii. EMALINE REBECCA LOUISA (MITTIE) HAMMACK, b. 09 Jul 1842, Crawford Co., GA; d. 19 Oct 1921, Crawford County, GA; m. CHARLIE C. GRADDICK, 08 Apr 1897, Crawford Co., GA.

350. ix. SARAH CATHERINE BAYNE HAMMACK, b. Abt. 1843, Crawford Co., GA; d. Aft. 1880, Pike Co., GA.

    x. ARIAN CAMILLA ANTOINETTE (NETTIE) HAMMACK, b. 12 Apr 1848, Crawford Co., GA; d. 22 Oct 1891, Crawford Co., GA; m. CHARLIE C. GRADDICK, 17 Feb 1885, Crawford Co., GA.

    xi. ROXANA CALDONIA EUGENIA (ROXIE) HAMMACK, b. 06 Nov 1850, Crawford Co., GA; d. 07 May 1899, Crawford County, GA.

Key Sources: 1830 Crawford Co., GA, Census, Records of Mt. Carmel Primitive Baptist Church, Crawford Co., GA; 1840 Crawford Co., GA, Census, p. 372; 1850 Crawford Co., GA, Census, p. 32;

1860 Crawford Co., GA, Census, p. 941; 1870 Crawford Co., GA, Census, p. 452; Crawford Co., GA, Will Book B, pp. 66, 174.

198. SARAH C.[8] HAMMACK *(WILLIAM T.[7], ROBERT HAMMACK[6] JR., ROBERT HAMMACK[5] SR., WILLIAM "THE ELDER"[4] HAMMACK, WILLIAM "O"[3], JOHN[2] HAMMOCKE, ? JOHN[1] HAMMOT)* was born 1804 in Wilkes Co., GA, and died 1878 in Taliaferro Co., GA. She married JAMES WILBURN MOORE 04 Dec 1823 in Jones Co., GA, son of USSERY MOORE and MARTHA BISHOP. He was born 1787 in Lunenburg Co., VA, and died 1856 in Taliaferro Co., GA.
Children of SARAH HAMMACK and JAMES MOORE are:
351.   i.   FELIX C.[9] MOORE, b. Abt. 1825, Wilkes Co., GA; d. Bef. 1895, Quitman Co., GA.
352.   ii.   WILLIAM M. MOORE, b. Abt. 1824, Wilkes Co., GA; d. Aft. 1895, Taliaferro Co., GA.
353.   iii.   JAMES WILBURN MOORE, b. 02 Feb 1827, Taliaferro Co., GA; d. 09 Mar 1907, Hancock Co., GA.
         iv.   DAUGHTER MOORE, b. Bet. 1825 - 1830, Taliaferro Co., GA; d. Aft. 1830, Taliaferro Co., GA.
354.   v.   THOMAS R. MOORE, b. Bet. 1830 - 1832, Taliaferro Co., GA; d. Aft. 1895, Hancock Co., GA.
         vi.   ? SARAH MOORE, b. Abt. 1832, Taliaferro Co., GA; d. Bef. 20 Sep 1849, Taliaferro Co., GA; m. DAVID E. DARDEN, 07 Sep 1846, Taliaferro Co., GA; b. 1815, Wilkes Co., GA; d. 1878, Taliaferro Co., GA.
        vii.   GEORGE W. MOORE, b. Abt. 1834, Taliaferro Co., GA; d. Bet. 1861 - 1865, Confederate States Army.
       viii.   LEWIS MOORE, b. Abt. 1836, Taliaferro Co., GA; d. Bef. 1895, Taliaferro Co., GA.
         ix.   DAUGHTER MOORE, b. Abt. 1838, Taliaferro Co., GA; d. Bet. 1840 - 1850, Taliaferro Co., GA.
355.   x.   OWEN D. MOORE, b. 1839, Taliaferro Co., GA; d. 1910, Taliaferro Co., GA.
         xi.   LUCIUS A. MOORE, b. 1842, Taliaferro Co., GA; d. 1921, Taliaferro Co., GA; m. MATILDA A. [------]; b. Abt. 1848, Georgia.
356.   xii.   RICHARD H. MOORE, b. Aug 1844, Taliaferro Co., GA; d. Aft. 1895, Hancock Co., GA.
Key Sources: 1830 Wilkes Co., GA, Census, GMD 172; 1840 Taliaferro Co., GA, Census, GMD 172; 1850 Taliaferro Co., GA, Census, p. 340; Taliaferro Co., GA, Annual Returns, 1857, pp. 150, 196-197, 207; Taliaferro Co., GA, Deed Book E, p. 460; Taliaferro Co., GA, Deed Book H, p. 137; 1860 Taliaferro Co., GA, Census, p. 713.

199. MANSEL W.[8] HAMMACK *(WILLIAM T.[7], ROBERT HAMMACK[6] JR., ROBERT HAMMACK[5] SR., WILLIAM "THE ELDER"[4] HAMMACK, WILLIAM "O"[3], JOHN[2] HAMMOCKE, ? JOHN[1] HAMMOT)* was born Abt. 1805 in Wilkes Co., GA, and died Abt. 1860 in Crawford County, GA. He married MARTHA ANN AMOS 07 Nov 1826 in Hancock County, GA. She died Aft. 1870 in Knoxville, Crawford County, GA.
Children of MANSEL HAMMACK and MARTHA AMOS are:
          i.   M. A.[9] HAMMACK, b. Abt. 1829, Hancock Co., GA; d. Aft. 1850, Crawford Co., GA.
         ii.   WILLIAM N. HAMMACK, b. Abt. 1832, Crawford Co., GA; d. Aft. 1860, Mississippi; m. CATHERINE HAMMACK, 19 Jan 1854, Crawford Co., GA.
357.   iii.   FELIX WILBORN HAMMACK, b. Abt. 1835, Crawford Co., GA; d. Abt. 1862, Confederate States Army.
358.   iv.   AURELIUS HARRISON HAMMACK, b. Abt. 1838, Crawford Co., GA; d. Aft. 1880, Houston Co., Ga.
359.   v.   JAMES MANSEL HAMMACK, b. 02 Jul 1838, Crawford Co., GA; d. 10 Apr 1930, Crawford Co., GA.

vi.   A. HAMMACK, b. Abt. 1840, Crawford Co., GA; d. Aft. 1850, Crawford Co., GA.

vii. MARTHA HAMMACK, b. Abt. 1845, Crawford Co., GA; d. Aft. 1860, Crawford Co., GA.

360. viii. CAROLINE R. HAMMACK, b. 02 Dec 1847, Crawford Co., GA; d. 09 Jan 1913, Bibb Co., GA.

361. ix. JOHN WILBUR HAMMACK, b. Abt. 1851, Crawford Co., GA; d. Abt. 1937, Crawford Co., GA.

x.   ROBERT W. HAMMACK, b. Abt. 1853, Crawford Co., GA; d. Aft. 1860, Crawford Co., GA.

Key Sources: Jones Co., GA, Deed Book O, p. 158; 1830 Hancock Co., GA, Census, p. 155; Records of Mt. Carmel Primitive Baptist Church, Crawford Co., GA; 1840 Crawford Co., GA, Census, p. 371; 1850 Crawford Co., GA, Census, p. 299; 1860 Crawford Co., GA, Census, p. 935; 1870 Crawford Co., GA, Census, p. 443.

200. ELIZABETH[8] HAMMACK *(WILLIAM T.[7], ROBERT HAMMACK[6] JR., ROBERT HAMMACK[5] SR., WILLIAM "THE ELDER"[4] HAMMACK, WILLIAM "O"[3], JOHN[2] HAMMOCKE, ? JOHN[1] HAMMOT)* was born Abt. 04 May 1809 in Jones Co., GA, and died 11 Sep 1871 in Jones Co., GA. She married JOHN BRYANT 02 Apr 1829 in Crawford Co., GA. He was born Abt. 1794 in Georgia, and died 08 Oct 1858 in Jones Co., GA.
Children of ELIZABETH HAMMACK and JOHN BRYANT are:

i.   MARTHA C.[9] BRYANT, b. 18 Sep 1835, Jones Co., GA; d. 05 Oct 1866, Jones Co., GA; m. JOHN ROBERTS, 17 Jan 1850, Jones Co., GA.

ii. WILLIAM T. BRYANT, b. Abt. 1830, Jones Co., GA; d. 23 Jul 1862, Danville, Virginia.

iii. JAMES W. BRYANT, b. Abt. 1832, Jones Co., GA; d. 29 Mar 1865, Richmond, Virginia.

362. iv. CORNELIUS L. BRYANT, b. Abt. 1834, Jones Co., GA; d. Aft. 1875, Jones Co., GA.

v.   JULIUS/JULIA C. BRYANT, b. Abt. 1837, Jones Co., GA; d. Aft. 1860, Jones Co., GA.

vi. MARY BRYANT, b. 1839, Jones Co., GA; d. 1906, Taliaferro Co., GA; m. OWEN D. MOORE, 28 Nov 1859, Jones Co., GA.

363. vii. FELIX THEODORE BRYANT, b. 09 Jun 1840, Jones Co., GA; d. 11 Oct 1915, Jones Co., GA.

viii. LOUISANA BRYANT, b. Abt. 1842, Jones Co., GA; d. Bef. 1875, Jones Co., GA.

ix. JOSEPHINE BRYANT, b. Abt. 1845, Jones Co., GA; d. Aft. 1867, Jones Co., GA; m. ? GREEN C. SMITH, 23 Jul 1867, Jones Co., GA.

364. x.   MELISSA G. BRYANT, b. 26 Sep 1847, Jones Co., GA; d. 12 Nov 1899, Jones Co., GA.

Key Sources: Jones Co., GA, Deed Book P, p. 418; 1840 Jones Co., GA, Census, p. 136; 1850 Jones Co., GA, Census, p. Jones Co., GA, Deed Book S, p. 72; 1860 Jones Co., GA, Census, pp. 189, 191, 192, 198, 204; 1860 Jones Co., GA, Census, p. 560; 1870 Jones Co., GA, Census, p. 225.

201. JANE C.[8] HAMMACK *(WILLIAM T.[7], ROBERT HAMMACK[6] JR., ROBERT HAMMACK[5] SR., WILLIAM "THE ELDER"[4] HAMMACK, WILLIAM "O"[3], JOHN[2] HAMMOCKE, ? JOHN[1] HAMMOT)* was born Abt. 1814 in Jones Co., GA, and died 1889 in Crawford Co., GA. She married JOHN N. TANNER 29 Jan 1837 in Crawford Co., GA. He was born Abt. 1812 in Georgia, and died Bef. 17 Nov 1840 in Crawford Co., GA.
Children of JANE HAMMACK and JOHN TANNER are:

i.   MARY E.[9] TANNER, b. Abt. 1838, Crawford Co., GA; d. Bet. 1859 - 1861, Crawford Co., GA; m. DR. GEORGE MONROE BAZEMORE, 17 Nov 1859, Crawford Co., GA; b. 19 Feb 1834, Houston Co., Ga; d. 10 Mar 1910, Hamilton Co., TN.

ii. SARAH TANNER, b. Abt. 1840, Crawford Co., GA; d. Bet. 1850 - 1860, Crawford Co., GA.

Key Sources: Jones Co., GA, Deed Book P, p. 418; 1850 Crawford Co., GA, Census, p. 489; 1865 Crawford Co., GA, Census, p. 930; Crawford Co., GA, Deed Book G, p. 612; Records of Mt. Carmel Primitive Baptist Church, Crawford Co., GA.

202. KATHERINE[8] HAMMACK *(WILLIAM T.[7], ROBERT HAMMACK[6] JR., ROBERT HAMMACK[5] SR., WILLIAM "THE ELDER"[4] HAMMACK, WILLIAM "O"[3], JOHN[2] HAMMOCKE, ? JOHN[1] HAMMOT)* was born 08 May 1817 in Jones Co., GA, and died 08 Oct 1886 in Coffee Co., AL. She married GEORGE WASHINGTON AMOS 24 Aug 1831 in Hancock Co., GA, son of GEORGE AMOS and ANNIE BENTLEY. He was born 09 Feb 1812 in Hancock Co., GA, and died 01 Apr 1889 in Coffee Co., AL.
Children of KATHERINE HAMMACK and GEORGE AMOS are:

      i.   MARY ANN[9] AMOS, b. 19 Feb 1832, Talbot Co., GA; d. Aft. 1850, Talbot Co., GA; m. THOMAS BRYANT ALLEN.

365.   ii. WILLIAM WELBORN AMOS, b. 25 Jan 1834, Talbot Co., GA; d. 12 Sep 1863, Confederate States Army.

     iii. SARAH T. AMOS, b. 24 Jun 1835, Talbot Co., GA; d. Aft. 1850, Talbot Co., GA; m. JOHN HESTON.

     iv. JANE AMOS, b. Abt. 1836, Talbot Co., GA; d. Aft. 1850, Talbot Co., GA.

366.   v. HENRY WASHINGTON AMOS, b. 08 Apr 1837, Talbot Co., GA; d. 01 Dec 1889, Coffee Co., AL.

     vi. BEVERLY AMOS, b. 1839, Talbot Co., GA; d. 29 Jun 1863, Confederate States Army; m. MARY J. ROSEBURY, 08 May 1861, Coffee Co., AL.

     vii. SUSAN C. AMOS, b. 05 Oct 1840, Talbot Co., GA; d. 20 Sep 1841, Talbot Co., GA.

367. viii. WILLIAM GREENBURY AMOS, b. 25 Aug 1842, Talbot Co., GA; d. 23 Apr 1916, Coffee Co., AL.

368.   ix. GEORGE WASHINGTON AMOS, b. 28 Feb 1845, Talbot Co., GA; d. 20 Feb 1915, Sebastian Co., AR.

369.   x. MARTHA ELIZABETH "MAT" AMOS, b. 05 Dec 1846, Talbot Co., GA; d. 27 Jul 1915, Coffee Co., AL.

370.   xi. JOHN ZACHARIAH "ZACHARY" AMOS, b. 06 Oct 1848, Talbot Co., GA; d. 18 Aug 1909, Pike Co., AL.

371.   xii. REBECCA CAROLINE AMOS, b. 28 Sep 1852, Talbot Co., GA; d. 12 May 1902, Escambia Co., AL.

372. xiii. ISAAC LAFAYETTE AMOS, b. 09 May 1854, Pike Co., AL; d. 07 Feb 1917, Coffee Co., AL.

     xiv. MARY ANN RETINCY AMOS, b. 31 Oct 1856, Pike Co., AL; d. Aft. 1860, Pike Co., AL.

     xv. ELIZABETH AMOS, b. Abt. 1858, Pike Co., AL; d. Abt. 1858, Pike Co., AL.

Key Sources: 1850 Talbot Co., GA, Census, p. 68; 1860 Pike Co., AL, Census, p. 297; 1870 Pike Co., AL, Census, p. 378; 1880 Pike Co., AL, Census, p. 154; Amos Family File, Fort Smith Public Library, Fort Smith, AR.

203. MARTHA ANN[8] HAMMACK *(WILLIAM T.[7], ROBERT HAMMACK[6] JR., ROBERT HAMMACK[5] SR., WILLIAM "THE ELDER"[4] HAMMACK, WILLIAM "O"[3], JOHN[2] HAMMOCKE, ? JOHN[1] HAMMOT)* was born Abt. 1822 in Jones Co., GA, and died Aft. 1850 in Crawford Co., GA. She married (1) WILLIAM P. WRIGHT 24 Nov 1836 in Crawford Co., GA, son of ROBERT WRIGHT and NANCY [--------]. He was born Bet. 1815 - 1820 in Georgia, and died Bef. 04 Jan 1842 in Crawford Co., GA. She married (2) JOHN ALEXANDER SUMPTER 31 Aug 1843 in Crawford Co., GA. He was born Abt. 1816 in North Carolina, and died Aft. 1850 in Crawford Co., GA.
Children of MARTHA HAMMACK and WILLIAM WRIGHT are:

      i.   MARY ANN[9] WRIGHT, b. Abt. 1838, Georgia; d. Aft. 1850, Crawford Co., GA.

ii. ADALINE JANE MASURIAH WRIGHT, b. Abt. 1840, Georgia; d. Aft. 1850, Crawford Co., GA.

373. iii. WILLIAM P. ROBERT SIMEON WRIGHT, b. Abt. 1842, Georgia; d. Aft. 1880, Pike Co., GA.

Children of MARTHA HAMMACK and JOHN SUMPTER are:

iv. SARAH[9] SUMPTER, b. Abt. 1844, Georgia; d. Aft. 1850, Crawford Co., GA.

v. JOHN SUMPTER, b. Abt. 1850, Georgia; d. Aft. 1850, Crawford Co., GA.

Key Sources: Crawford Co., GA, Will Book A, p. 40; Crawford Co., GA, Deed Book E, p. 696; 1850 Crawford Co., GA, Census, p. 396.

204. WILLIAM P.[8] JACKSON *(MARY "POLLY"[7] HAMMACK, ROBERT HAMMACK[6] JR., ROBERT HAMMACK[5] SR., WILLIAM "THE ELDER"[4] HAMMACK, WILLIAM "O"[3], JOHN[2] HAMMOCKE, ? JOHN[1] HAMMOT)* was born 1803 in Wilkes Co., GA, and died Aft. 1870 in Jones Co., GA. He married (1) FRANKY MURPHY 20 Mar 1825 in Jones Co., GA. She was born Abt. 1805 in Georgia, and died Bef. 21 Dec 1843 in Jones Co., GA. He married (2) TEMPERANCE LANE 21 Dec 1843 in Jones Co., GA. She was born Abt. 1809 in North Carolina, and died Aft. 1870 in Jones Co., GA.

Children of WILLIAM JACKSON and FRANKY MURPHY are:

i. JOHN[9] JACKSON, b. Abt. 1831, Jones Co., GA; m. SOPHIA VESTOR, 03 Apr 1857, Jones Co., GA.

ii. WILLIAM H. JACKSON, b. Abt. 1833, Jones Co., GA; m. FRANCES MCGEHEE, 13 Feb 1859, Jones Co., GA.

iii. REUBEN JACKSON, b. Abt. 1835, Jones Co., GA; d. Aft. 1870, Jones Co., GA; m. LUCY MAYNARD, 18 Dec 1866, Jones Co., GA; b. Abt. 1843, Jones Co., GA; d. Aft. 1870, Jones Co., GA.

iv. MARY JACKSON, b. Abt. 1836, Jones Co., GA; d. Aft. 1850, Jones Co., GA.

v. ROBERT JACKSON, b. Abt. 1839, Jones Co., GA; d. Aft. 1850, Jones Co., GA.

374. vi. ALLEN GREEN JACKSON, b. Abt. 1832, Jones Co., GA; d. Bet. 1862 - 1870, Jones Co., GA.

Children of WILLIAM JACKSON and TEMPERANCE LANE are:

vii. LUCY[9] JACKSON, b. Abt. 1846, Jones Co., GA; d. Aft. 1868, Jones Co., GA; m. WILEY J. WILLIAMS, 20 Feb 1868, Jones Co., GA.

viii. GEORGE W. JACKSON, b. Abt. 1847, Jones Co., GA; d. Aft. 1850, Jones Co., GA.

ix. TEMPERANCE JACKSON, b. Abt. 1850, Jones Co., GA; d. 27 Jun 1931, Jones Co., GA.

x. NANCY "NANNIE" JACKSON, b. 13 Apr 1852, Jones Co., GA; d. 21 Apr 1919, Jones Co., GA; m. Z. T. GORDON, 12 Apr 1874, Jones Co., GA; b. 05 Jan 1849, Jones Co., GA; d. 25 Aug 1924, Jones Co., GA.

Key Sources: 1850 Jones Co., GA, Census, p. 223; 1860 Jones Co., GA, Census, p. 519; 1870 Jones Co., GA, Census, p. 266.

205. THOMPSON[8] JACKSON *(MARY "POLLY"[7] HAMMACK, ROBERT HAMMACK[6] JR., ROBERT HAMMACK[5] SR., WILLIAM "THE ELDER"[4] HAMMACK, WILLIAM "O"[3], JOHN[2] HAMMOCKE, ? JOHN[1] HAMMOT)* was born 1805 in Wilkes Co., GA, and died Aft. 1870 in Jones Co., GA. He married MARY A. M. LANE 24 Nov 1850 in Jones Co., GA. She was born Abt. 1832 in Jones Co., GA, and died Aft. 1850 in Jones Co., GA.

Children of THOMPSON JACKSON and MARY LANE are:

i. JAMES[9] JACKSON, b. Abt. 1852, Jones Co., GA; d. Aft. 1870, Jones Co., GA.

ii. SAMUEL JACKSON, b. Abt. 1856, Jones Co., GA; d. Aft. 1870, Jones Co., GA; m. MARY E. GORDON, 03 Oct 1878, Jones Co., GA.

    iii.   GREEN THOMPSON JACKSON, b. 12 Sep 1857, Jones Co., GA; d. 28 Aug 1931, Jones Co., GA; m. LUCY J. HATTAWAY, 25 Jan 1882, Jones Co., GA; b. 28 Aug 1861, Jones Co., GA; d. 23 Mar 1939, Jones Co., GA.

Key Sources: 1850 Jones Co., GA, Census, p. 227; 1860 Jones Co., GA, Census, p. 512; 1870 Jones Co., GA, Census, p. 266.

206. LUCY[8] JACKSON *(MARY "POLLY"[7] HAMMACK, ROBERT HAMMACK[6] JR., ROBERT HAMMACK[5] SR., WILLIAM "THE ELDER"[4] HAMMACK, WILLIAM "O"[3], JOHN[2] HAMMOCKE, ? JOHN[1] HAMMOT)* was born Abt. 1810 in Wilkes Co., GA, and died Aft. 1850 in Jones Co., GA. She may be the Lucy Jackson who married SAMUEL MORGAN 02 Mar 1834 in Jones Co., GA. He was born Abt. 1809 in Georgia, and died Aft. 1870 in Jones Co., GA. Samuel Morgan later married (2) Kittie Hammack, granddaughter of Lewis Hammack.
Children of LUCY JACKSON and SAMUEL MORGAN are:
    i.   AMANDA M.[9] MORGAN, b. Abt. 1839, Jones Co., GA; d. Aft. 1850, Jones Co., GA.
    ii.   JOHN T. MORGAN, b. Abt. 1841, Jones Co., GA; d. Aft. 1850, Jones Co., GA.
    iii.   SAMUEL T. MORGAN, b. Abt. 1848, Jones Co., GA; d. Aft. 1850, Jones Co., GA.
Key Source: 1850 Jones Co., GA, Census, p. 2.

207. WILKINS[8] JACKSON *(MARY "POLLY"[7] HAMMACK, ROBERT HAMMACK[6] JR., ROBERT HAMMACK[5] SR., WILLIAM "THE ELDER"[4] HAMMACK, WILLIAM "O"[3], JOHN[2] HAMMOCKE, ? JOHN[1] HAMMOT)* was born Abt. 1812 in Wilkes Co., GA, and died Aft. 1850 in Jones Co., GA. He married (1) SABRINA GREENE 01 Jun 1834 in Jones Co., GA. She was born Abt. 1812 in Georgia, and died Abt. 1845 in Georgia. He married (2) LIVELY ADAMS HAMMACK 28 Jan 1846 in Jones Co., GA. She was born Abt. 1816 in Jones Co., GA, and died Aft. 1850 in Jasper Co., GA.
Children of WILKINS JACKSON and SABRINA GREENE are:
    i.   JOHN[9] JACKSON, b. Abt. 1835, Jones Co., GA; d. Aft. 1850, Jasper Co., GA.
    ii.   THOMAS JACKSON, b. Abt. 1837, Jones Co., GA; d. Aft. 1850, Jasper Co., GA.
    iii.   MARY JACKSON, b. Abt. 1839, Jones Co., GA; d. Aft. 1850, Jasper Co., GA.
    iv.   FELIX JACKSON, b. Abt. 1841, Jones Co., GA; d. Aft. 1850, Jasper Co., GA.
    v.   CELIA JACKSON, b. Abt. 1843, Jones Co., GA; d. Aft. 1850, Jasper Co., GA.
    vi.   CHRISTIANA JACKSON, b. Abt. 1843, Jones Co., GA; d. Aft. 1850, Jasper Co., GA.
    vii.   ELIZABETH JACKSON, b. Abt. 1844, Jones Co., GA; d. Aft. 1850, Jasper Co., GA.
Children of WILKINS JACKSON and LIVELY HAMMACK are:
    viii.   LUCH[9] JACKSON, b. Abt. 1848, Jasper Co., GA; d. Aft. 1850, Jasper Co., GA.
    ix.   MARION JACKSON, b. Abt. 1849, Jasper Co., GA; d. Aft. 1850, Jasper Co., GA.
Key Source: 1850 Jasper Co., GA, Census.

208. JOHN[8] JACKSON II *(MARY "POLLY"[7] HAMMACK, ROBERT HAMMACK[6] JR., ROBERT HAMMACK[5] SR., WILLIAM "THE ELDER"[4] HAMMACK, WILLIAM "O"[3], JOHN[2] HAMMOCKE, ? JOHN[1] HAMMOT)* was born 03 Jan 1815 in Wilkes County, GA, and died 11 Feb 1868 in Macon Co., GA. He married MALITIA "LITTIE" ROWE 1839 in Jones Co., GA. She was born 08 Mar 1820 in Georgia, and died 24 Sep 1886 in Jones Co., GA.
Children of JOHN JACKSON and MALITIA ROWE are:
    i.   JOSHUA[9] JACKSON, b. 05 Oct 1840, Jones Co., GA; d. 08 May 1862, McDowell, VA.
    ii.   MARY JACKSON, b. 05 Dec 1841, Jones Co., GA; d. 04 Jun 1917, Jones Co., GA; m. ELDER J. H. GRESHAM; b. 02 Jan 1847, Jones Co., GA; d. 28 Dec 1929, Jones Co., GA.
    iii.   AMANDA E. JACKSON, b. 05 Jun 1843, Jones Co., GA; d. 04 Oct 1905, Jones Co., GA; m. SAMUEL W. GREENE, 20 Dec 1860, Jones Co., GA; b. 30 Jan 1839, Georgia; d. Aft. 1860, Jones Co., GA.

      iv. LUCY JACKSON, b. 01 Nov 1844, Jones Co., GA; d. Aft. 1870, Jones Co., GA; m. JOHN F. GREEN, 12 Dec 1867, Jones Co., GA.

375.   v. JOHN JACKSON III, b. 19 Dec 1845, Jones Co., GA; d. 1927, Texas.

376.   vi. WILLIAM JACKSON, b. 21 Jul 1847, Jones Co., GA; d. 20 Mar 1926, Jones Co., GA.

     vii. THOMAS JACKSON, b. 02 Dec 1849, Jones Co., GA; d. Aft. 1880, Texas.

377. viii. DANIEL JACKSON, b. 20 Sep 1850, Jones Co., GA; d. 29 Dec 1930, Jones Co., GA.

     ix. JOEL WILKINS JACKSON, b. 15 May 1852, Jones Co., GA; d. Aft. 1880, Texas; m. SUSAN GOOLSBY, 13 Dec 1872, Jones Co., GA.

     x. PERRY JACKSON, b. 22 May 1854, Jones Co., GA; d. Aft. 1880, Texas; m. ELLA JOYCE.

    xi. DOCTOR FRANKLIN JACKSON, b. 27 May 1856, Jones Co., GA; d. 16 Dec 1928, Jones Co., GA; m. SALLIE E. CHILDS; b. 20 Jan 1865, Jones Co., GA; d. 12 Jun 1920, Jones Co., GA.

378.   xii. GEORGE W. JACKSON, b. 03 May 1859, Jones Co., GA; d. 20 Jan 1940, Jones Co., GA.

   xiii. JOSHUA G. JACKSON, b. Abt. 1862, Jones Co., GA; d. Aft. 1880, Jones Co., GA; m. BELLE ROBY.

Key Sources: 1850 Jones Co., GA, Census, p. 212; 1860 Jones Co., GA, Census, p. 511-512.

209. LEWIS[8] JACKSON *(MARY "POLLY"[7] HAMMACK, ROBERT HAMMACK[6] JR., ROBERT HAMMACK[5] SR., WILLIAM "THE ELDER"[4] HAMMACK, WILLIAM "O"[3], JOHN[2] HAMMOCKE, ? JOHN[1] HAMMOT)* was born 1820 in Jones Co., GA, and died Bef. 14 Mar 1865 in Jones Co., GA. He married MARGERY ANN CARMICHAEL 14 Apr 1846 in Jones Co., GA. She was born 27 Feb 1822 in Jones Co., GA, and died 26 Jul 1871 in Jones Co., GA.

Children of LEWIS JACKSON and MARGERY CARMICHAEL are:

      i. JULIA ANN[9] JACKSON, b. Abt. 1847, Jones Co., GA; d. 20 Feb 1932, Jones Co., GA.

     ii. MARY ANN ELIZABETH JACKSON, b. Abt. 1849, Jones Co., GA; d. Aft. 1904, Jones Co., GA.

    iii. MARGERY CATHERINE JACKSON, b. Abt. 1855, Jones Co., GA; d. 09 Jan 1934, Jones Co., GA.

    iv. LUCY ANN T. JACKSON, b. Abt. 1852, Jones Co., GA; d. 04 Dec 1933, Jones Co., GA.

     v. SARAH AMANDA JACKSON, b. 23 Aug 1857, Jones Co., GA; d. 25 Nov 1916, Jones Co., GA.

    vi. CYNTHIA JACKSON, b. Abt. 1859, Jones Co., GA; d. Aft. 1904, Jones Co., GA.

   vii. J. L. JACKSON, b. 06 Jul 1863, Jones Co., GA; d. 19 Jul 1863, Jones Co., GA.

Key Sources: 1850 Jones Co., GA, Census, p. 226; 1860 Jones Co., GA, Census, p. 566; 1880 Jones Co., GA, Census, p. 471.

210. SICILY CATHERINE[8] GUNN *(CATHERINE[7] HAMMACK, ROBERT HAMMACK[6] JR., ROBERT HAMMACK[5] SR., WILLIAM "THE ELDER"[4] HAMMACK, WILLIAM "O"[3], JOHN[2] HAMMOCKE, ? JOHN[1] HAMMOT)* was born Abt. 1811 in Wilkes Co., GA, and died Aft. 1870 in Russell Co., AL. She married JOHN WYNNE 09 Jul 1826 in Taliaferro Co., GA. He was born Abt. 1810 in Georgia, and died Aft. 1870 in Russell Co., AL.

Children of SICILY GUNN and JOHN WYNNE are:

379.   i. ELIZABETH[9] WYNNE, b. Abt. 1828, Taliaferro Co., GA; d. Aft. 1880, Russell Co., AL.

     ii. JOHN WYNNE, b. Abt. 1832, Taliaferro Co., GA; d. Aft. 1860, Russell Co., AL.

    iii. MARY CATHERINE WYNNE, b. Abt. 1835, Talbot Co., GA; d. Aft. 1870, Russell Co., AL.

    iv. MARTHA WYNNE, b. Abt. 1839, Talbot Co., GA; d. Aft. 1860, Russell Co., AL.

     v. SAMANTHA ELLEN WYNNE, b. Abt. 1842, Talbot Co., GA; d. Aft. 1870, Russell Co., AL.

    vi.   SARAH WYNNE, b. Abt. 1846, Talbot Co., GA; d. Aft. 1860, Russell Co., AL.
   vii.   ELIZA LOUISE WYNNE, b. Abt. 1849, Talbot Co., GA; d. Aft. 1870, Russell Co., AL.
  viii.   WILLIAM H. WYNNE, b. Abt. 1852, Russell Co., AL; d. Aft. 1880, Russell Co., AL.

Key Sources: 1850 Russell Co., AL, Census, p. 57; 1860 Russell Co., AL, Census, p. 949; 1870 Russell Co., AL, Census, p. 216.

211. GEORGE[8] GUNN *(CATHERINE[7] HAMMACK, ROBERT HAMMACK[6] JR., ROBERT HAMMACK[5] SR., WILLIAM "THE ELDER"[4] HAMMACK, WILLIAM "O"[3], JOHN[2] HAMMOCKE, ? JOHN[1] HAMMOT)* was born Abt. 1814 in Wilkes Co., GA, and died Aft. 1880 in Calhoun/Talladega Co., AL. He married NANCY R. DOSTER 22 May 1831 in Taliaferro Co., GA. She was born Abt. 1812 in Georgia, and died Aft. 1860 in Russell Co., AL.
Child of GEORGE GUNN and NANCY DOSTER is:
    i.   F. E.[9] GUNN, b. Abt. 1840, Georgia; d. Aft. 1860, Russell Co., AL.
Key Sources: 1860 Russell Co., AL, Census, p. 1104; 1880 Calhoun Co., AL, Census, p. 621A.

212. JOHN J.[8] POOLE *(CATHERINE[7] HAMMACK, ROBERT HAMMACK[6] JR., ROBERT HAMMACK[5] SR., WILLIAM "THE ELDER"[4] HAMMACK, WILLIAM "O"[3], JOHN[2] HAMMOCKE, ? JOHN[1] HAMMOT)* was born Abt. 1828 in Taliaferro Co., GA, and died Abt. 1908 in Rusk Co., TX. He married (1) LYDIA BALLOU Abt. 1849 in Alabama. She was born Abt. 1825 in Georgia, and died Bet. 1870 - 1874 in Alabama. He married (2) MARY MCWHORTER Abt. 1873 in Alabama. She was born 1855 in Alabama, and died 1883 in Texas.
Children of JOHN POOLE and LYDIA BALLOU are:
    i.   JOSEPH W. POOLE, b. 1847, Alabama; d. AFT. 1880, Rusk Co., Texas.
   ii.   W. THOMAS POOLE, b. 1849, Alabama; d. AFT. 1880, Rusk Co., Texas.
  iii.   GEORGE FRANK[9] POOLE, b. 1850, Alabama; d. 1940, Texas; m. INDIANA BURTON.
  iv.   MARY CATHERINE POOLE, b. 1852, Alabama; d. Aft. 1870, Rusk Co., Texas.
   v.   JOHN DAVID POOLE, b. Abt. 1855, Alabama; d. Aft. 1870, Rusk Co., Texas.
  vi.   ROBERT SAMUEL POOLE, b. 1853, Alabama; d. 1918, Texas; m. MOLLIE SILVEY.
  vi.   FELIX WILBURN POOLE, b. 1861, Alabama; d. 1953, Texas; m. NANCY CATHERINE GREENE.
  vii.   PHILLIP H. POOLE, b. 1866, Alabama; d. 1942, Texas; m. GEORGIA A. GARY.
Children of JOHN POOLE and MARY MCWHORTER are:
  viii.   LEWIS[9] POOLE, b. Abt. 1875, Alabama; d. Aft. 1880, Texas.
  ix.   MARION POOLE, b. Abt. 1877, Alabama; d. Aft. 1880, Texas.
   x.   OLA POOLE, b. Abt. 1878, Alabama; d. Aft. 1900, Texas; m. WALTER PINNELL.
  xi.   MATTIE POOLE, b. Abt. 1881, Alabama; d. Aft. 1881, Texas.
  xii.   MARSHALL COLQUITT POOLE, b. Abt. 1883, Alabama; d. 1954, Texas.
Key Sources: 1850 Russell Co., AL, Census, pp. 33, 36, 76; 1860 Coosa Co., AL, Census, p. 90; 1870 Rusk Co., TX, p. 456; 1880 Rusk Co., TX, pp. 105-106, 205-207.

213. WILLIAM[8] POOLE *(CATHERINE[7] HAMMACK, ROBERT HAMMACK[6] JR., ROBERT HAMMACK[5] SR., WILLIAM "THE ELDER"[4] HAMMACK, WILLIAM "O"[3], JOHN[2] HAMMOCKE, ? JOHN[1] HAMMOT)* was born Abt. 1832 in Taliaferro Co., GA, and died Aft. 1860 in Russell Co., AL. He married N. E. [------] Abt. 1856 in Russell Co., AL. She was born Abt. 1830 in Alabama, and died Aft. 1860 in Russell Co., AL.
Children of WILLIAM POOLE and N. [------] are:
    i.   S. J.[9] POOLE, b. Abt. 1857, Alabama; d. Aft. 1860, Russell Co., AL.
   ii.   L. L. POOLE, b. Abt. 1859, Alabama; d. Aft. 1860, Russell Co., AL.
Key Source: 1860 Russell Co., AL, Census, p. 1058.

214. DAVID[8] POOLE *(CATHERINE[7] HAMMACK, ROBERT HAMMACK[6] JR., ROBERT HAMMACK[5] SR., WILLIAM "THE ELDER"[4] HAMMACK, WILLIAM "O"[3], JOHN[2] HAMMOCKE, ? JOHN[1] HAMMOT)* was born Abt. 1834 in Taliaferro Co., GA, and died Aft. 1880 in Lee Co., AL. He married FRANCIS CONWAY 04 Sep 1853 in Russell Co., AL. She was born Abt. 1835 in South Carolina, and died Aft. 1880 in Lee Co., AL.

Children of DAVID POOLE and FRANCIS CONWAY are:

     i.   M.[9] POOLE, b. Abt. 1856, Alabama; d. Aft. 1860, Russell Co., AL.

     ii.   GEORGIA ANN E. POOLE, b. Abt. 1858, Alabama; d. Aft. 1860, Russell Co., AL.

     iii.   CHARLIE POOLE, b. Abt. 1862, Alabama; d. Aft. 1880, Lee Co., AL.

     iv.   WILLIE POOLE, b. Abt. 1868, Alabama; d. Aft. 1880, Lee Co., AL.

     v.   WALTON POOLE, b. Abt. 1872, Alabama; d. Aft. 1880, Lee Co., AL.

     vi.   ZEBULON POOLE, b. Abt. 1875, Alabama; d. Aft. 1880, Lee Co., AL.

Key Source: 1860 Russell Co., AL, Census, p. 1058; 1880 Lee Co., AL, Census, p. 191D.

215. CHARLES[8] HAMMACK *(BENJAMIN[7], BENEDICT[6], ROBERT HAMMACK[5] SR., WILLIAM "THE ELDER"[4] HAMMACK, WILLIAM "O"[3], JOHN[2] HAMMOCKE, ? JOHN[1] HAMMOT)* was born Bef. 31 Jan 1792 in Richmond Co., VA, and died Bet. 1830 - 1840 in Richmond Co., VA. He married (1) ALICE G. DAVIS Abt. 31 May 1816 in Richmond Co., VA. She was born Abt. 1791 in Richmond Co., VA, and died Bef. 1830 in Richmond Co., VA. He married (2) MRS. CHARLOTTE P. TARPLEY DEATLEY Abt. 16 Aug 1830 in Richmond Co., VA. She was born Abt. 1812 in Richmond Co., VA, and died Aft. 1850 in Richmond Co., VA.

Children of CHARLES HAMMACK and ALICE DAVIS are:

380.   i.   ROBERT[9] HAMMACK, b. Bet. 1817 - 1824, Richmond Co., VA; d. 15 Feb 1859, Northumberland Co., VA.

381.   ii.   SARAH HAMMACK, b. Abt. 1827, Richmond Co., VA; d. 15 Sep 1862, Northumberland Co., VA.

     iii.   ANN C. HAMMACK, b. Abt. 1818, Richmond Co., VA; m. GEORGE JONES, Abt. 20 Oct 1838, Northumberland Co., VA.

     iv.   SON HAMMACK, b. Bet. 1820 - 1825, Richmond Co., VA.

     v.   DAUGHTER HAMMACK, b. Bet. 1825 - 1830, Richmond Co., VA.

     vi.   DAUGHTER HAMMACK, b. Bet. 1825 - 1830, Richmond Co., VA.

Children of CHARLES HAMMACK and MRS. DEATLEY are:

     vii.   SON[9] HAMMACK, b. Bet. 1830 - 1835, Richmond Co., VA.

     viii.   FRANCES E. HAMMACK, b. Abt. 1837, Richmond Co., VA.

Key Sources: 1816-1830 Richmond Co., VA, Personal Property Tax Lists; 1817 Northumberland Co., VA, Personal Property Tax List; 1820 Richmond Co., VA, Census, p. 226A; 1830 Richmond Co., VA, Census, p. 91; 1840 Richmond Co., VA, Census, p. 91; 1850 Richmond Co., VA, Census, p. 191; Richmond Co., VA, Deed Book 20, p. 695; Richmond Co., VA, Order Book 25, 1820-1822, p. 40; G. H. S. King, King, *Marriages of Richmond Co., VA, 1668-1853* (Fredericksburg, VA, 1964). Identification of Robert as son of Charles Hammack is speculative.

216. WILLIAM[8] HAMMACK *(BENJAMIN[7], BENEDICT[6], ROBERT HAMMACK[5] SR., WILLIAM "THE ELDER"[4] HAMMACK, WILLIAM "O"[3], JOHN[2] HAMMOCKE, ? JOHN[1] HAMMOT)* was born Abt. 1795 in Richmond Co., VA, and died Bet. 1844 - 1845 in Northumberland Co., VA. He married (1) JUDITH CLARKE SYDNOR Abt. 20 Dec 1815 in Richmond Co., VA. He married (2) MARIA ELMORE Abt. 17 Dec 1834 in Northumberland Co., VA.

Children of WILLIAM HAMMACK and JUDITH SYDNOR are:

382.   i.   BENJAMIN[9] HAMMACK, b. Abt. 1819, Richmond Co., VA; d. Aft. 1880, Washington, D. C.

383.   ii. WILLIAM CLARKE HAMMACK, b. Abt. 1820, Richmond Co., VA; d. Bet. 1870 - 1880, Franklin Co., MS.

        iii. ELIZABETH J. HAMMACK, b. Abt. 1831, Richmond Co., VA; d. Bet. 1860 - 1870, Caldwell Parish, LA; m. DAVID DUNN, 21 Dec 1852, Amite Co., MS.

384.   iv. JOHN HENRY HAMMACK, b. Bet. 1830 - 1833, Northumberland Co., VA; d. 1917, Adams Co., MS.

        v. SON HAMMACK, b. Abt. 1817, Richmond Co., VA; d. Aft. 1830, Richmond Co., VA.

        vi. DAUGHTER HAMMACK, b. Bet. 1825 - 1830, Richmond Co., VA; d. Aft. 1830, Northumberland Co., VA.

Key Sources: G. H. S. King, *Marriages of Richmond Co., VA, 1668-1853* (Fredericksburg, VA, 1964); 1816-1828, 1844 Richmond Co., VA, Personal Property Tax Lists; 1828-1844 Northumberland Co., VA, Personal Property Tax Lists; Richmond Co., VA, Deed Book 20, p. 439; 1820 Richmond Co., VA, Census, p. 226A; 1830 Northumberland Co., VA, Census, p. 208; Richmond Co., VA, Order Book 27, 1825-1832, p. 418. Offspring of William Hammack is speculative. A common association of William and John Henry Hammack of Mississippi with Griffin P. Claughton, neighbor of William Hammack in Northumberland County, links these Hammacks with William Hammack of Northumberland. The residence of and marriage of John Henry Hammack in Alexandria, Virginia, also links him with Benjamin Hammack of Washington, D.C.

217. BENEDICT[8] HAMMACK (*LEWIS[7], BENEDICT[6], ROBERT HAMMACK[5] SR., WILLIAM "THE ELDER"[4] HAMMACK, WILLIAM "O"[3], JOHN[2] HAMMOCKE, ? JOHN[1] HAMMOT*) was born 10 Dec 1814 in Richmond Co., VA, and died 17 May 1895 in Richmond Co., VA. He married (1) ELLEN BALL POLK Abt. 23 Dec 1834 in Richmond Co., VA, daughter of CHARLES POLK and ELLEN DOWNMAN. She was born 14 Feb 1818 in Richmond Co., VA, and died 20 Sep 1855 in Fredericksburg, VA. He married (2) JANE E. ASKINS MUIRE 22 Feb 1860 in Richmond Co., VA. She was born Abt. 1820 in Richmond Co., VA, and died 20 Mar 1898 in Richmond Co., VA.

Children of BENEDICT HAMMACK and ELLEN POLK are:

        i. LAVINIA ANN[9] HAMMACK, b. 30 Apr 1836, Richmond Co., VA; d. 26 Nov 1849, Richmond Co., VA.

        ii. LUCY CORNELIA HAMMACK, b. 16 Dec 1838, Richmond Co., VA; d. Aft. 1860, Richmond Co., VA.

        iii. CHARLES PEALE HAMMACK, b. 06 Jan 1840, Richmond Co., VA; d. 22 Oct 1846, Richmond Co., VA.

        iv. MARIA ELLOR HAMMACK, b. 21 Dec 1843, Richmond Co., VA; d. Aft. 1860, Richmond Co., VA; m. (1) MARTIN L. PUGH, 27 Dec 1860, Richmond Co., VA; m. (2) JAMES L. HAMMACK, 24 Dec 1868, Richmond Co., VA.

        v. MARY CAROLINE HAMMACK, b. Abt. 1845, Richmond Co., VA; d. 07 Aug 1849, Richmond Co., VA.

        vi. BENEDICT HAMMACK, b. 18 May 1848, Richmond Co., VA; d. 27 Jul 1861, Richmond Co., VA.

        vii. EMELINE JUDSON HAMMACK, b. 20 May 1851, Richmond Co., VA; d. Aft. 1860, Richmond Co., VA.

385.   viii. CHARLES POLK HAMMACK, b. 18 Jan 1854, Richmond Co., VA; d. 08 Mar 1932, Richmond Co., VA.

Child of BENEDICT HAMMACK and JANE MUIRE is:

        ix. ALVERTA LEE[9] HAMMACK, b. 03 May 1863, Richmond Co., VA; d. 20 Jun 1943, Richmond Co., VA; m. W. ANDREW JONES.

Key Sources: Benedict Hammack Family Bible, The Library of Virginia, Richmond, VA; 1832-1843 Richmond Co., VA, Personal Property Tax Lists; G. H. S. King, *Marriages of Richmond Co., VA, 1668-*

1853 (Fredericksburg, VA, 1964); 1840 Richmond Co., VA, Census, p. 50; 1850 Richmond Co., VA, Census, p. 158.

218. RODHAM CLARKE[8] HAMMACK *(LEWIS[7], BENEDICT[6], ROBERT HAMMACK[5] SR., WILLIAM "THE ELDER"[4] HAMMACK, WILLIAM "O"[3], JOHN[2] HAMMOCKE, ? JOHN[1] HAMMOT)* was born Abt. 1817 in Richmond Co., VA, and died 20 Sep 1874 in Richmond Co., VA. He married (1) FANNIE [----]. She died Aft. 1874 in Richmond Co., VA. He married (2) CAROLINE M. YEATMAN Abt. 08 Dec 1838 in Westmoreland, daughter of JAMES YEATMAN and ANN WELDON.
Children of RODHAM HAMMACK and CAROLINE YEATMAN are:

    i.   ISABELLA[9] HAMMACK, b. Abt. 1839, Richmond Co., VA; m. JOHN R. DAVIS, 27 Jan 1857, Richmond Co., VA; b. Abt. 1830, Richmond Co., VA.

    ii.   FRANCIS HAMMACK, b. Abt. 1842, Richmond Co., VA.

    iii.   JAMES HAMMACK, b. Abt. 1845, Richmond Co., VA; d. Aft. 1900, Richmond Co., VA; m. MARIA HAMMACK PUGH, 24 Dec 1868, Richmond Co., VA; d. Aft. 1900, Richmond Co., VA.

    iv.   EDWIN R. HAMMACK, b. Abt. 1849, Richmond Co., VA.

    v.   THOMAS F. HAMMACK, b. Abt. 1851, Richmond Co., VA; d. Aft. 1884, Richmond Co., VA; m. SARAH A. L. WINSTEAD, 29 Apr 1877, Richmond Co., VA; b. Abt. 1852, Richmond Co., VA; d. Aft. 1884, Richmond Co., VA.

Key Sources: 1838-1850 Richmond Co., VA, Personal Property Tax Lists; Westmoreland Co., VA, Marriage Bonds; 1840 Richmond Co., VA, Census, p. 51; 1850 Richmond Co., VA, Census, p. 158; 1860 Richmond Co., VA, Census, p. 327; 1870 Richmond Co., VA, Census, p. 272; Richmond Co., VA, Will Book 1846-1879, p. 710. Note that James and Maria Hammack were the parents of Marvin Benjamin Hammack (1880-1973), who married Margaret Anne Cralle. Their family was one of several Hammack families to remain in Richmond County, Virginia, where Russell Cralle Hammack, son of Marvin and Margaret, and his family were members of the Northern Neck of Virginia Historical Society.

219. JOHN W.[8] HAMMACK *(WILLIAM[7], CHRISTIAN[6], ROBERT HAMMACK[5] SR., WILLIAM "THE ELDER"[4] HAMMACK, WILLIAM "O"[3], JOHN[2] HAMMOCKE, ? JOHN[1] HAMMOT)* was born Abt. 1792 in Richmond Co., VA, and died Bet. 1829 - 1830 in Richmond Co., VA. He married WINEFRED DEMERETT Abt. 10 Jul 1815 in Richmond Co., VA, daughter of MOLLY [------]. She was born Abt. 1795 in Northumberland Co., VA, and died Aft. 1870 in Washington, D. C.
Children of JOHN HAMMACK and WINEFRED DEMERETT are:

    i.   AUGUSTA M.[9] HAMMACK, b. Bet. 1820 - 1822, Richmond Co., VA; d. Aft. 1870, Washington, D. C.; m. JOHN ROBINSON, Abt. 02 May 1842, Richmond Co., VA.

    ii.   NAPOLEAN B. HAMMACK, b. Bet. 1816 - 1817, Richmond Co., VA; d. Aft. 1847, Northumberland Co., VA.

386.   iii.   WILLIAM GUSTAVUS HAMMACK, b. Abt. 1825, Richmond Co., VA; d. Aft. 1852, Baltimore, MD.

    iv.   JOHN DEMERETT HAMMACK, b. Abt. 1828, Richmond Co., VA; d. Aft. 1860, Washington, D. C.; m. SYNTHIA A. [------], Abt. 1850, Washington, D. C.; b. Abt. 1828, South Carolina; d. Aft. 1860, Washington, D. C..

Key Sources: G. H. S. King, *Marriages of Richmond Co., VA, 1668-1853* (Fredericksburg, VA, 1964); 1811-1836 Richmond Co., VA, Personal Property Tax Lists; Richmond Co., VA, Order Book 24, 1816-1820, pp. 128, 174, 256, 285, 342; 1820 Richmond Co., VA, Census, p. 226A; Richmond Co., VA, Order Book 27, 1825-1832, p. 323; 1830 Richmond Co., VA, Census, p. 96; Richmond Co., VA, Order Book 1837-1844, pp. 22, 47, 105, 296, 315, 317, 348, 374; 1860 Washington, D.C., Census, p. 784; 1870 Washington, D.C., Census, p. 285.

220. SALLY[8] HAMMACK *(WILLIAM[7], CHRISTIAN[6], ROBERT HAMMACK[5] SR., WILLIAM "THE ELDER"[4] HAMMACK, WILLIAM "O"[3], JOHN[2] HAMMOCKE, ? JOHN[1] HAMMOT)* was born 12 Jun 1790 in Richmond Co., VA, and died Bet. 1810 - 1815 in Richmond Co., VA. She married CHAPMAN AUSTIN Abt. 11 Feb 1808 in Richmond Co., VA.

Children of SALLY HAMMACK and CHAPMAN AUSTIN are:

    i.   JOHN[9] AUSTIN, b. Bet. 1809 - 1815, Northumberland Co., VA; m. LUCY THRIFT, Abt. 15 Sep 1847, Richmond Co., VA.

    ii. THOMAS AUSTIN, b. Bet. 1809 - 1815, Northumberland Co., VA.

    iii. BETSEY AUSTIN, b. Bet. 1809 - 1815, Northumberland Co., VA; m. JOSEPH HAZARD, Abt. 28 Feb 1833, Richmond Co., VA.

Key Source: G. H. S. King, *Marriages of Richmond Co., VA, 1668-1853* (Fredericksburg, VA, 1964).

221. MATILDA[8] JONES *(SAMFORD[7], CHRISTIAN[6] HAMMACK, ROBERT HAMMACK[5] SR., WILLIAM "THE ELDER"[4] HAMMACK, WILLIAM "O"[3], JOHN[2] HAMMOCKE, ? JOHN[1] HAMMOT)* was born 01 Jan 1807 in Richmond Co., VA, and died Aft. 1849 in Richmond Co., VA. She married SAMUEL MEALY Abt. 07 Nov 1828 in Richmond Co., VA. He was born 14 Sep 1806 in Richmond Co., VA, and died Aft. 1849 in Richmond Co., VA.

Children of MATILDA JONES and SAMUEL MEALY are:

    i.   JOHN S.[9] MEALY, b. Abt. 03 Oct 1839, Richmond Co., VA.

    ii. ELIAS MEALY, b. Abt. 30 Oct 1841, Richmond Co., VA.

    iii. FRANCES MEALY, b. Abt. 1844, Richmond Co., VA; d. Aft. 1884, Clay Co., NE; m. HIRAM JACOB PENSE; b. 24 Oct 1822, Licking Co., OH; d. Aft. 1884, Clay Co., NE.

    iv. DANIEL LAMPKIN MEALY, b. 30 May 1849, Richmond Co., VA; m. MARY ANN PENSE; b. 1853, Ohio.

Key Sources: G. H. S. King, *Marriages of Richmond Co., VA, 1668-1853* (Fredericksburg, VA, 1964); 1860 McLean Co., IL, Census, p. 260.

222. WILLIAM MORGAN[8] HAMMACK *(? LEWIS[7], LEWIS[6], ROBERT HAMMACK[5] SR., WILLIAM "THE ELDER"[4] HAMMACK, WILLIAM "O"[3], JOHN[2] HAMMOCKE, ? JOHN[1] HAMMOT)* was born 09 Nov 1804 in Franklin Co., VA, and died 13 Jun 1859 in Benton Co., AR. He married NANCY WOOD 19 Mar 1829 in Carroll Co., TN, daughter of SAMUEL WOOD and ANNE PURVIANCE. She was born 08 Sep 1808 in Preble Co., OH, and died 04 Mar 1859 in Benton Co., AR.

Children of WILLIAM HAMMACK and NANCY WOOD are:

    i.   LEWIS[9] HAMMACK, b. Abt. 1830, Carroll Co., TN; d. Bef. 1850, Benton Co., AR.

    ii. MARTHA A. HAMMACK, b. Abt. 1833, Carroll Co., TN; d. Aft. 1850, Benton Co., AR; m. M. C. WALKER.

    iii. MARY J. HAMMACK, b. 10 Oct 1835, Washington Co., AR; d. Abt. 1876, Benton Co., AR; m. ROBERT A. WALKER, 10 Aug 1852, Benton Co., AR; b. Abt. 1832, Tennessee; d. Aft. 1860, Benton Co., AR.

    iv. CYNTHIA CYRENE HAMMACK, b. Abt. 1836, Washington Co., AR; d. 1876, Benton Co., AR; m. ROBERT MANN, Abt. 1855, Benton Co., AR; b. 27 Aug 1827, Hawkins Co., TN.

    v. JOHN WESLEY HAMMACK, b. 21 Aug 1837, Benton Co., AR; d. Aft. 1860, Benton Co., AR.

    vi. ELIZABETH PENELOPE HAMMACK, b. 10 May 1839, Benton Co., AR; d. Bef. 1850, Benton Co., AR.

    vii. ARTIMISSA ELIZA HAMMACK, b. 04 Jan 1841, Benton Co., AR; d. 07 Jul 1916, Benton Co., AR; m. (1) JACOB MITCHELL HARDY, 30 Aug 1866, Benton Co., AR; m. (2) ALEX

GILLESPIE GAMBLE, Abt. 1876, Benton Co., AR; b. 08 Dec 1819, Rhea Co., TN; d. Aft. 1876, Benton Co., AR.

   viii. SARAH ELLEN HAMMACK, b. Abt. 1843, Benton Co., AR; d. Aft. 1868, Benton Co., AR; m. GEORGE BRAITHWAITE, 09 Jan 1868, Benton Co., AR.

   ix. NANCY VIRGINIA HAMMACK, b. Abt. 1848, Benton Co., AR; d. 1901, Benton Co., AR; m. DAVID VANCE WALKER, 09 Feb 1868, Benton Co., AR.

   x. WILLIAM AZER MACLIN HAMMACK, b. 08 Mar 1851, Benton Co., AR; d. 12 Oct 1936, Benton Co., AR; m. (1) SUSAN F. PATTERSON, 13 Aug 1871, Benton Co., AR; b. 27 Feb 1854, Benton Co., AR; d. 28 Feb 1887, Missouri; m. (2) MARTHA J. WILLIAMS VANDERGRIFF, Abt. 1888, Missouri; b. 27 Sep 1857, Benton Co., AR; d. 20 May 1924, Benton Co., AR.

Key Sources: Henry Franklin Hammack, 2: 186; 1840 Benton Co., AR, Census, p. 17; 1850 Benton Co., AR, Census, p. 69.

223. JOHN H.[8] HAMMACK *(? LEWIS[7], LEWIS[6], ROBERT HAMMACK[5] SR., WILLIAM "THE ELDER"[4] HAMMACK, WILLIAM "O"[3], JOHN[2] HAMMOCKE, ? JOHN[1] HAMMOT)* was born 25 Dec 1811 in Warren Co., TN, and died 01 Mar 1880 in Hunt Co., TX. He married JANE P. MAXWELL Abt. 1832 in Carroll Co., TN. She was born Abt. 1812 in Tennessee, and died Aft. 1870 in Hunt Co., TX.

Children of JOHN HAMMACK and JANE MAXWELL are:

   i. JOSEPH P.[9] HAMMACK, b. Abt. 1834, Arkansas; d. Aft. 1850, Pulaski Co., AR.

   ii. THOMAS P. HAMMACK, b. Abt. 1836, Arkansas; d. Aft. 1860, Benton Co., AR.

   iii. NANCY E. HAMMACK, b. Abt. 1838, Arkansas; d. Aft. 1850, Pulaski Co., AR.

   iv. WILLIAM R. HAMMACK, b. Abt. 1842, Arkansas; d. Aft. 1860, Benton Co., AR.

   v. JOHN JAMES HAMMACK, b. Abt. 1844, Arkansas; d. Aft. 1880, Hunt Co., TX.

   vi. MARTHA J. HAMMACK, b. Abt. 1847, Arkansas; d. Aft. 1860, Benton Co., AR.

   vii. BENJAMIN F. HAMMACK, b. Abt. 1853, Arkansas; d. Aft. 1880, Hunt Co., TX; m. ELIZABETH [------]; b. Abt. 1857, Illinois; d. Aft. 1880, Hunt Co., TX.

   viii. JOSEPHINE HAMMACK, b. Aft. 1856, Arkansas; d. Aft. 1880, Hunt Co., TX; m. WILLIAM J. HIGHTOWER.

   ix. ROBERT H. HAMMACK, b. Abt. 1858, Arkansas; d. Aft. 1880, Hunt Co., TX.

   x. JOHN T. HAMMACK, b. Abt. 1860, Arkansas; d. Aft. 1860, Benton Co., AR.

Key Sources: 1840 Benton Co., AR, Census, p. 16; 1850 Pulaski Co., AR, Census, p. 394; 1860 Benton Co., AR, Census, p. 230; 1870 Hood Co., TX, Census, p. 339; 1880 Hunt Co., TX, Census, pp. 461, 478.

224. THOMAS[8] HAMMACK *(? LEWIS[7], LEWIS[6], ROBERT HAMMACK[5] SR., WILLIAM "THE ELDER"[4] HAMMACK, WILLIAM "O"[3], JOHN[2] HAMMOCKE, ? JOHN[1] HAMMOT)* was born Abt. 1814 in Warren Co., TN, and died Aft. 1850 in Arkansas. He married MARGARET WILLIAMS 28 Apr 1838 in Gibson Co., TN. She was born Abt. 1818 in North Carolina.

Children of THOMAS HAMMACK and MARGARET WILLIAMS are:

   i. SARAH E.[9] HAMMACK, b. Abt. 1839, Tennessee; d. Aft. 1860, Benton Co., AR.

   ii. MARTHA J. HAMMACK, b. Abt. 1841, Tennessee; d. Aft. 1860, Benton Co., AR.

   iii. LEWIS E. HAMMACK, b. Abt. 1844, Missouri; d. Aft. 1860, Benton Co., AR.

   iv. NANCY HAMMACK, b. Abt. 1848, Missouri; d. Aft. 1860, Benton Co., AR.

   v. WILLIAM THOMAS HAMMACK, b. Abt. 1849, Arkansas; d. Aft. 1860, Benton Co., AR.

   vi. MARGARET ANN PALESTINE HAMMACK, b. 10 Apr 1854, Benton Co., AR; d. 23 Nov 1931, Crawford Co., AR; m. (1) ISAAC G. HOBBS, 29 Apr 1872, Carroll Co., AR; m. (2) ROBERT HOWARD YOUNG, 02 May 1882, Carroll Co., AR.

Key Source: Henry Franklin Hammack, 2: 186.

225. JESSE HARVEY[8] HAMMACK *(? LEWIS[7], LEWIS[6], ROBERT HAMMACK[5] SR., WILLIAM "THE ELDER"[4] HAMMACK, WILLIAM "O"[3], JOHN[2] HAMMOCKE, ? JOHN[1] HAMMOT)* was born 06 Dec 1817 in Warren Co., TN, and died 16 May 1896 in Hunt Co., TX. He married MARY JANE WALKER Abt. 1845 in Benton Co., AR. She was born Bet. 1823 - 1833 in Tennessee, and died Aft. 1860 in Benton Co., AR.

Children of JESSE HAMMACK and MARY WALKER are:

    i.   SAMUEL[9] HAMMACK, b. Abt. 1848, Benton Co., AR; d. Aft. 1870, Hunt Co., TX; m. SARAH J. [------], Abt. 1870, Hunt Co., TX; b. Abt. 1850, Arkansas; d. Aft. 1870, Hunt Co., TX.

    ii.   JOHN WILLIAM HAMMACK, b. Abt. 1853, Benton Co., AR; d. Aft. 1911, Hunt Co., TX; m. (1) MARY KATHERINE HAVENS; b. Abt. 1856, Texas; d. Bef. 1888, Texas; m. (2) LOUVENIA HAVENS; b. 22 Jan 1869, Hopkins Co., TX; d. Aft. Aug 1911, Hunt Co., TX.

    iii.   SARAH J. HAMMACK, b. Abt. 1856, Benton Co., AR; d. Aft. 1870, Hunt Co., TX.

    iv.   MARTHA E. HAMMACK, b. Abt. 1857, Benton Co., AR; d. Aft. 1870, Hunt Co., TX.

    v.   ROBERT FRANKLIN HAMMACK, b. 17 Jan 1859, Benton Co., AR; d. Aft. 1880, Hunt Co., TX; m. ELLA OLIVIA THOMAS; b. 27 Jan 1862, Texas.

    vi.   SYNTHA E. HAMMACK, b. Abt. 1861, Benton Co., AR; d. Aft. 1880, Hunt Co., TX.

    vii.   MARY V. HAMMACK, b. Abt. 1865, Benton Co., AR; d. Aft. 1880, Hunt Co., TX.

    viii.   NANNIE C. HAMMACK, b. Abt. 1868, Benton Co., AR; d. Aft. 1880, Hunt Co., TX.

    ix.   THOMAS J. HAMMACK, b. Abt. 1872, Hunt Co., TX; d. Aft. 1880, Hunt Co., TX.

    x.   PRETTY HAMMACK, b. Abt. 1878, Hunt Co., TX; d. Aft. 1880, Hunt Co., TX.

Key Sources: 1850 El Dorado Co., CA, Census, p. 405; 1860 Benton Co., AR, Census, p. 236; 1870 Hunt Co., TX, Census, p. 337; 1880 Hunt Co., TX, Census, p. 448.

226. JOHN[8] HAMMACK *(? THOMAS[7], LEWIS[6], ROBERT HAMMACK[5] SR., WILLIAM "THE ELDER"[4] HAMMACK, WILLIAM "O"[3], JOHN[2] HAMMOCKE, ? JOHN[1] HAMMOT)* was born Abt. 1802 in Virginia, and died Aft. 1870 in Roanoke Co., VA. He married SARAH [------] Abt. 1824 in Virginia. She was born Abt. 1808 in Virginia, and died Aft. 1870 in Roanoke Co., VA.

Children of JOHN HAMMACK and SARAH [------] are:

387.   i.   WILLIAM[9] HAMMACK, b. Abt. 1825, Virginia; d. Aft. 1850, Bedford Co., VA.

    ii.   ELIZABETH HAMMACK, b. Abt. 1828, Virginia; d. Aft. 1850, Bedford Co., VA.

    iii.   JACOB HAMMACK, b. Abt. 1831, Virginia; d. Aft. 1850, Bedford Co., VA.

    iv.   MARY C. HAMMACK, b. Abt. 1833, Virginia; d. Aft. 1850, Bedford Co., VA.

    v.   NANCY J. HAMMACK, b. Abt. 1835, Virginia; d. Aft. 1860, Bedford Co., VA.

    vi.   MATILDA A. HAMMACK, b. Abt. 1837, Virginia; d. Aft. 1870, Roanoke Co., VA.

    vii.   ALICE HAMMACK, b. Abt. 1839, Virginia; d. Aft. 1850, Bedford Co., VA.

    viii.   SARAH HAMMACK, b. Abt. 1841, Virginia; d. Aft. 1860, Bedford Co., VA.

    ix.   MALINDA HAMMACK, b. Abt. 1842, Virginia; d. Aft. 1870, Roanoke Co., VA.

    x.   NICHOLAS THOMAS V. HAMMACK, b. Abt. 1844, Virginia; d. Aft. 1870, Bedford Co., VA.

    xi.   MATTHEW JOHN HAMMACK, b. Abt. 1847, Virginia; d. Aft. 1870, Roanoke Co., VA.

Key Sources: 1840 Bedford Co., VA, p. 261; 1850 Bedford Co., VA, Census, p. 296; 1860 Bedford Co., VA, Census, p. 501; 1870 Roanoke Co., VA, Census, p. 294.

227. MILLY ANN[8] BENTLEY *(JOHN H.[7], MILLY[6] HAMMACK, ROBERT HAMMACK[5] SR., WILLIAM "THE ELDER"[4] HAMMACK, WILLIAM "O"[3], JOHN[2] HAMMOCKE, ? JOHN[1] HAMMOT)* was born Abt. 1815 in Wilkes Co., GA, and died Bef. 1841 in Crawford Co., GA. She married JOEL CARTER 08 Jan 1835 in Jones Co., GA.

Children of MILLY BENTLEY and JOEL CARTER are:

> i. SARAH[9] CARTER, m. JOHN M. KENDRICK, Bef. 1858, Crawford Co., GA.
>
> ii. MARTHA A. V. CARTER, m. ALEXANDER C. SANDERS.

Key Source: Arthur C. Carter, *Carter and Kinsmen: Folmar - Rodgers - Sanders - Bryan* (Montgomery, AL, 1990).

228. JOHN[8] HAMMACK *(? WILLIAM[7], DANIEL[6], WILLIAM[5], RICHARD[4], WILLIAM "O"[3], JOHN[2] HAMMOCKE, ? JOHN[1] HAMMOT)* was born Abt. 1802 in Chatham Co., NC, and died Aft. 1860 in Chatham Co., NC. He married JANE [------] Abt. 1825 in Chatham Co., NC. She was born Abt. 1803 in NC, and died Aft. 1860 in Chatham Co., NC.

Children of JOHN HAMMACK and JANE [------] are:

> i. MARTHA FRANCIS[9] HAMMACK, b. Abt. 1826, Chatham Co., NC; d. Aft. 1860, Chatham Co., NC.
>
> ii. JOHN A. HAMMACK, b. Abt. 1828, Chatham Co., NC; d. Aft. 1870, Chatham Co., NC; m. SOPHIA [------]; b. Abt. 1832, Chatham Co., NC; d. Aft. 1870, Chatham Co., NC.
>
> iii. DAVID HAMMACK, b. Abt. 1833, Chatham Co., NC; d. Aft. 1870, Chatham Co., NC; m. ELIZA [------]; b. Abt. 1844, Chatham Co., NC; d. Aft. 1870, Chatham Co., NC.
>
> iv. JANE HAMMACK, b. Abt. 1834, Chatham Co., NC; d. Aft. 1860, Chatham Co., NC.
>
> v. GEORGE SIDNEY HAMMACK, b. Abt. 1839, Chatham Co., NC; d. Aft. 1870, Chatham Co., NC; m. FRANCIS [------]; b. Abt. 1832, Chatham Co., NC; d. Aft. 1870, Chatham Co., NC.
>
> vi. JULIA HAMMACK, b. Abt. 1843, Chatham Co., NC; d. Aft. 1870, Chatham Co., NC.

Key Sources: 1840 Chatham Co., NC, Census, p. 193; 1850 Chatham Co., NC, Census, p. 460; 1860 Chatham Co., NC, Census, p. 17.

229. WILLIAM[8] HAMMOCK *(? JOHN[7], DANIEL[6], WILLIAM[5], RICHARD[4], WILLIAM "O"[3], JOHN[2] HAMMOCKE, ? JOHN[1] HAMMOT)* was born Abt. 1796 in Chatham Co., NC, and died Abt. 1855 in Overton Co., TN. He married (1) UNKNOWN BILBREY, daughter of JOHN BILBREY and HOLLY. She was born Abt. 1796 in Chatham Co., NC, and died Bef. 1845 in Chatham Co., NC. He married (2) EMALINE Abt. 1845 in TN. She was born Abt. 1824 in TN, and died Abt. 1906 in TN.

Children of WILLIAM HAMMOCK and UNKNOWN BILBREY are:

> i. MELINDA[9] HAMMOCK, b. Abt. 1816; m. JOHN HARRIS.
>
> ii. CANDACE HAMMOCK, m. AMOS HARRIS.
>
> iii. DICEY HAMMOCK, b. Abt. 1815; d. 1899, Adams Co., IL; m. JAMES COOK.
>
> iv. FRANCES HAMMOCK, b. Abt. 1812; d. 1898; m. ISAAC JEFFERSON SWALLOWS.
>
> v. LUCINDA TENNESSEE HAMMOCK, b. 22 Apr 1826, TN; d. 01 Sep 1900, Overton Co., TN; m. THOMPSON G. COPELAND.

Children of WILLIAM HAMMOCK and EMALINE are:

> vi. POLLY[9] HAMMOCK, b. Abt. 1846, Overton Co., TN.
>
> vii. MARTHA HAMMOCK, b. Abt. 1848, Overton Co., TN.
>
> viii. NANCY HAMMOCK, b. Abt. 1849, Overton Co., TN.
>
> ix. WILLIAM CARROLL HAMMOCK, b. 06 Jan 1852, Overton Co., TN; d. 11 Feb 1929, Overton Co., TN.
>
> x. DAVID S. HAMMOCK, b. Abt. 1854, Overton Co., TN.

Key Sources: 1850 Overton Co., TN, Census, p. 45; Overton Co., TN, County Court Minutes, 1855, p. 160; 1860 Overton Co., TN, Census, p. 196.

230. LAIRD[8] HAMMOCK *(? JOHN[7], DANIEL[6], WILLIAM[5], RICHARD[4], WILLIAM "O"[3], JOHN[2] HAMMOCKE, ? JOHN[1] HAMMOT)* was born Abt. 1799 in Chatham Co., NC, and died Aft. 1860 in

Overton Co., TN. He married POLLY [PHILLIPS?]. She was born Abt. 1802 in NC, and died 1879 in Overton Co., TN.

Children of LAIRD HAMMOCK and POLLY [PHILLIPS?] are:

388.   i.   DANIEL⁹ HAMMOCK, b. 18 May 1819, Overton Co., TN; d. 11 Jan 1886, Overton Co., TN.

389.   ii.   WILLIAM HAMMOCK, b. Abt. 1826, Overton Co., TN; d. Aft. 1880, Overton Co., TN.

        iii.   JAMES HAMMOCK, b. 10 Apr 1828, Overton Co., TN; d. 12 Apr 1907, Overton Co., TN; m. MARY PHILLIPS; b. 10 Nov 1835, Overton Co., TN; d. 20 Mar 1907, Overton Co., TN.

        iv.   EDITH HAMMOCK, b. Abt. 1832, Overton Co., TN; d. Aft. 1910, Overton Co., TN.

        v.   JOHN HAMMOCK, b. Abt. 1833, Overton Co., TN; d. Aft. 1870, Jackson Co., TN; m. PARTHENA ANN RAY; b. Abt. 1833, Overton Co., TN.

        vi.   ROANNA HAMMOCK, b. Abt. 1835, Overton Co., TN; d. Aft. 1910, Overton Co., TN; m. LABORN PHILLIPS, 11 Sep 1869, Overton Co., TN; b. Abt. 1845, Overton Co., TN.

        vii.   LAIRD HAMMOCK, b. 10 Dec 1840, Overton Co., TN; d. 01 Dec 1912, Overton Co., TN; m. NANCY J. COPELAND; b. Abt. 1840, TN.

        viii.   FRANKLIN HAMMOCK, b. Abt. 1838, Overton Co., TN; d. 17 Feb 1864, Overton Co., TN; m. MARY MAXWELL; b. Abt. 1840, Overton Co., TN.

        ix.   POLLY HAMMOCK, b. Abt. 1841, Overton Co., TN; m. WILLIAM AUSTIN.

        x.   LOUISA HAMMOCK, b. Abt. 1842, Overton Co., TN; d. Bef. 1920, Putnam Co., TN; m. SPENCER PHILLIPS; b. Mar 1825, Overton Co., TN; d. 1913, Putnam Co., TN.

        xi.   LEVI HAMMOCK, b. Abt. 1846, Overton Co., TN.

Key Sources: 1850 Overton Co., TN, Census, p. 50 ; 1860 Overton Co., TN, Census, p. 215.

231. JOHN⁸ HAMMOCK *(? JOHN⁷, DANIEL⁶, WILLIAM⁵, RICHARD⁴, WILLIAM "O"³, JOHN² HAMMOCKE, ? JOHN¹ HAMMOT)* was born Abt. 1806 in Chatham Co., NC, and died Aft. 1850 in Overton Co., TN. He married RUTH [PHILLIPS?] Abt. 1830 in Overton Co., TN. She was born Abt. 1806 in NC, and died Aft. 1850 in Overton Co., TN.

Children of JOHN HAMMOCK and RUTH [PHILLIPS?] are:

        i.   MILLIE⁹ HAMMOCK, b. Abt. 1832, Overton Co., TN; d. Aft. 1870, Jackson Co., TN; m. MOSES NETHERTON; b. Abt. 1826, TN.

        ii.   JAMES HAMMOCK, b. Abt. 1836, Overton Co., TN; d. Aft. 1850, Overton Co., TN.

        iii.   JULIA CATHERINE HAMMOCK, b. Abt. 1837, Overton Co., TN; m. GEORGE W. GULLETT; b. 23 Apr 1835, TN; d. 07 Jan 1916, Putnam Co., TN.

        iv.   SARAH HAMMOCK, b. Abt. 1838, Overton Co., TN; d. Aft. 1860, Overton Co., TN; m. JOHN SWALLOWS; b. Bet. 1831 - 1839, TN.

        v.   LUCINDA HAMMOCK, b. Abt. 1839, Overton Co., TN; d. Aft. 1870, Jackson Co., TN; m. JOHN NETHERTON; b. Abt. 1835, TN; d. Aft. 1870, Jackson Co., TN.

        vi.   FLETCHER HAMMOCK, b. Abt. 1840, Overton Co., TN; d. Aft. 1850, Overton Co., TN.

        vii.   ELIZABETH HAMMOCK, b. Abt. 1841, Overton Co., TN; d. Aft. 1850, Overton Co., TN.

Key Source: 1850 Overton Co., TN, Census, p. 6.

232. WILLIAM⁸ HAMMOCK *(? ROBERT⁷, JOHN⁶, RICHARD⁵, RICHARD⁴, WILLIAM "O"³, JOHN² HAMMOCKE, ? JOHN¹ HAMMOT)* was born Bef. 1784 in Albemarle Co., VA, and died Aft. 1850 in Overton Co., TN. He married (1) UNKNOWN. She was born Bet. 1784 - 1794, and died Aft. 1820. He married (2) MILLY QUARLES OAKLEY. She was born Abt. 1800 in Henry Co., VA, and died Aft. 1850 in Overton Co., TN.

Children of WILLIAM HAMMOCK and UNKNOWN are:

        i.   DAUGHTER⁹ HAMMOCK, b. Bet. 1810 - 1820.

        ii.   DAUGHTER HAMMOCK, b. Bet. 1810 - 1820.

iii. DAUGHTER HAMMOCK, b. Bet. 1810 - 1820.
iv. DAUGHTER HAMMOCK, b. Bet. 1810 - 1820.
v. THOMAS HAMMOCK, b. Abt. 1824, Tennessee.
vi. MARY HAMMOCK, b. Abt. 1828, Tennessee.
vii. SUSAN HAMMOCK, b. Abt. 1830, Tennessee.

Key Sources: 1820 Overton Co., TN, Census, p. 14; 1840 Overton Co., TN, Census, p. 17; 1850 Overton Co., TN, Census, p. 45.

233. WILLIAM[8] HAMMOCK *(WILLIAM[7], JOHN[6], RICHARD[5], RICHARD[4], WILLIAM "O"[3], JOHN[2] HAMMOCKE, ? JOHN[1] HAMMOT)* was born Bet. 1790 - 1800, and died Abt. 1828 in Lincoln Co., MO. He married MARY BURRUS Abt. 1815 in Smith Co., TN. She was born Abt. 1793 in Tennessee, and died Aft. 1860 in Warren Co., MO.

Children of WILLIAM HAMMOCK and MARY BURRUS are:
390.   i. JAMES M.[9] HAMMOCK, b. Abt. 1819, Missouri; d. Bet. 1860 - 1870, Lincoln Co., MO.
391.   ii. BRICE MARTIN HAMMOCK, b. 1820, Missouri; d. 1911, Howell Co., MO.
        iii. ELIZABETH HAMMOCK, b. Abt. 1822, Missouri; d. Aft. 1860, Warren Co., MO.
        iv. JANE HAMMOCK, b. Abt. 1823, Missouri; d. Aft. 1850, Lincoln Co., MO.
392.   v. ANDREW HAMMOCK, b. Abt. 1824, Missouri; d. Aft. 1880, Lincoln Co., MO.
        vi. DAVIS HAMMOCK, b. Abt. 1826, Missouri; d. Aft. 1860, Touloumne Co., CA.
393.   vii. GEORGE HAMMOCK, b. Abt. 1826, Missouri; d. Aft. 1900, Alameda Co., CA.

Key Sources: G. P. Omohundro, *Ancestors and Descendants of Brice Wiseman Hammack* (Santa Ana, CA, 1986); 1850 Lincoln Co., MO, Census, p. 444. This identification is speculative. Another William Hammack (c. 1799-1881) married Caroline Matilda Burrus and lived in Lincoln Co., MO, as well. He was a son of Daniel and Mary Martin Hammack and a brother of Brice Wiseman Hammack. Robert Hammack of Surry Co., NC, also had ties to the Burrus family. Mary Burrus, wife of William Hammack, and Caroline Matilda Burrus, wife of William M. Hammack, were daughters of Jacob and Susannah Martin Burrus.

234. JOHN[8] HAMMACK *(JOHN[7], JOHN[6], RICHARD[5], RICHARD[4], WILLIAM "O"[3], JOHN[2] HAMMOCKE, ? JOHN[1] HAMMOT)* was born Abt. 1775 in Pittsylvania Co., VA, and died Aft. 1850 in Grainger Co., TN. He married (1) UNKNOWN Abt. 1793 in Virginia. He married (2) SALLEY HARVEY 23 Sep 1807 in Grainger Co., TN. He married (3) SALLY SHARP 21 Feb 1820 in Grainger Co., TN. He married (4) NANCY MAPLES Abt. 1848 in Grainger Co., TN.

Children of JOHN HAMMACK and UNKNOWN are:
394.   i. JOHN[9] HAMMACK, b. Abt. 1795, VA; d. Aft. 1860, Grainger Co., TN.
        ii. ELIZABETH HAMMACK, b. Abt. 1795, VA; d. Bef. 1860, Grainger Co., TN.
        iii. WILLIAM HAMMACK, b. Bet. 1800 - 1810, TN; d. Aft. 1830, Grainger Co., TN.

Child of JOHN HAMMACK and SALLEY HARVEY is:
        iv. ? REBECCA[9] HAMMACK, b. Abt. 1815, Grainger Co., TN; d. Aft. 1832, Grainger Co., TN; m. WILLIAM HILL.

Children of JOHN HAMMACK and SALLY SHARP are:
        v. DAUGHTER[9] HAMMACK, b. Bet. 1820 - 1825, Grainger Co., TN; d. Aft. 1840, Grainger Co., TN.
        vi. ? MARY HAMMACK, b. Abt. 1825, Grainger Co., TN; d. Aft. 1842, Grainger Co., TN; m. ALFRED DOFFSON, 05 Jan 1842, Grainger Co., TN.

Key Sources: 1830 Grainger Co., TN, Census, p. 363; 1840 Grainger Co., TN, Census, p. 138; 1850 Grainger Co., TN, Census, p. 115; 1860 Grainger Co., TN, Census, p. 229; 1870 Union Co., TN, Census, p. 227. I have speculated that this is the John Hammack who married Sarah Harvey and Sally Sharp based on circumstantial evidence, but further research is needed.

235. WILLIAM[8] HAMMACK *(JOHN[7], JOHN[6], RICHARD[5], RICHARD[4], WILLIAM "O"[3], JOHN[2] HAMMOCKE, ? JOHN[1] HAMMOT)* was born Abt. 1779 in Pittsylvania Co., VA, and died Bet. 1830 - 1840 in Grainger Co., TN. He married SARA BROCK 10 Aug 1801 in Grainger Co., TN, daughter of MOSES BROCK and SUSANNAH DYER. She was born Abt. 1780 in Virginia.
Children of WILLIAM HAMMACK and SARA BROCK are:
395.   i.   PLEASANT[9] HAMMACK, b. Abt. 1802, Grainger Co., TN; d. Aft. 1860, Union Co., TN.
        ii.   ? MARY HAMMACK, b. Abt. 1804, Grainger Co., TN; m. JESSE COATS, 17 Dec 1825, Grainger Co., TN.
396.   iii.   NOAH HAMMACK, b. Abt. 1806, Grainger Co., TN; d. Aft. 1860, Woodford Co., IL.
        iv.   JOHN BROCK HAMMACK, b. Abt. 1809, Grainger Co., TN.
397.   v.   WILLIAM HAMMACK, b. Abt. 1815, Grainger Co., TN; d. Bet. 1860 - 1870, Laurel Co., KY.
        vi.   SUSAN HAMMACK, b. Abt. 1818, Grainger Co., TN; m. H. C. RIDENOR, 15 Oct 1852, Laurel Co., KY.
        vii.   SON HAMMACK, b. Bet. 1810 - 1820, Grainger Co., TN.
        viii.   SON HAMMACK, b. Bet. 1810 - 1820, Grainger Co., TN.
398.   ix.   STERLING HAMMACK, b. Bet. 1820 - 1823, Union Co., TN; d. 1908, Grainger Co., TN.
        x.   LEVI HAMMACK, b. 14 Dec 1826, Grainger Co., TN; d. 17 Dec 1893, Laurel Co., KY; m. (1) MARGARET BROCK, 26 Aug 1848, Laurel Co., KY; b. 31 Oct 1833, Tennessee; d. 30 Jan 1870, Laurel Co., KY; m. (2) SARAH SMITH, 30 Sep 1872, Laurel Co., KY; b. Abt. 1830, Tennessee.
399.   xi.   ELI HAMMACK, b. 14 Dec 1826, Grainger Co., TN; d. Aft. 1870, Laurel Co., KY.
Key Sources: 1830 Grainger Co., TN, Census, p. 363; 1840 Grainger Co., TN, Census, p. 140. Evidence about William's offspring is largely speculative and is based on location, association, and nomenclature.

236. MARTIN[8] HAMMACK *(JOHN[7], JOHN[6], RICHARD[5], RICHARD[4], WILLIAM "O"[3], JOHN[2] HAMMOCKE, ? JOHN[1] HAMMOT)* was born Abt. 1784 in Pittsylvania Co., VA, and died Abt. 1839 in Claiborne Co., TN. He married SARAH JANEWAY 24 Apr 1812 in Knox Co., TN. She was born Abt. 1795 in Virginia, and died Aft. 1860 in Marion Co., TN.
Children of MARTIN HAMMACK and SARAH JANEWAY are:
        i.   WILLIAM[9] HAMMACK, b. 12 Dec 1812, Claiborne Co., TN.
        ii.   GARRETT MARTIN HAMMACK, b. 22 May 1814, Claiborne Co., TN; d. 1860, Union Co., TN; m. NANCY.
400.   iii.   SAMUEL HAMMACK, b. 30 Aug 1818, Claiborne Co., TN; d. 10 Dec 1867, Marion Co., TN.
        iv.   JOHN HAMMACK, b. 09 Jun 1821, Claiborne Co., TN; d. 07 May 1907, Dade Co., GA.
401.   v.   JOSEPH HAMMACK, b. 17 Jan 1825, Claiborne Co., TN; d. 23 Feb 1904, Sulphur Springs, GA.
402.   vi.   SINTHY HAMMACK, b. 27 Aug 1826, Claiborne Co., TN; d. Aft. 1851, Rhea Co., TN.
        vii.   DAVID HAMMACK, b. 05 Jun 1828, Claiborne Co., TN; d. 08 Jul 1868, Marion Co., TN.
        viii.   NANCY JANE HAMMACK, b. 15 Sep 1831, Claiborne Co., TN; d. 18 Dec 1875, Tennessee.
        ix.   MARTIN HAMMACK, b. 08 Oct 1835, Claiborne Co., TN; d. Abt. 1880, Marion Co., OH.
        x.   JAMES HAMMACK, b. 25 Dec 1837, Claiborne Co., TN; d. 04 Dec 1897, Tennessee.
Key Sources: 1830 Claiborne Co., TN, Census, p. 126; 1840 Claiborne Co., TN, Census, p. 210; 1850 Claiborne Co., TN, Census, p. 339; 1860 Marion Co., TN, Census, p. 264; 1880 Marion Co., TN, Census, p. 238.

237. DANIEL[8] HAMMACK *(JOHN[7], JOHN[6], RICHARD[5], RICHARD[4], WILLIAM "O"[3], JOHN[2] HAMMOCKE, ? JOHN[1] HAMMOT)* was born Abt. 1795 in Greenbriar Co., VA, and died Aft. 1870 in Union Co., TN. He married ELIZABETH SPIRES 18 Aug 1818 in Grainger Co., TN. She was born Abt. 1799 in North Carolina, and died Bet. 1850 - 1870 in Union Co., TN.

Children of DANIEL HAMMACK and ELIZABETH SPIRES are:

403.   i.   MARSHALL[9] HAMMACK, b. Abt. 1819, Tennessee; d. Aft. 1880, Grainger Co., TN.
404.   ii.   MARY HAMMACK, b. Abt. 1823, Tennessee; d. Aft. 1880, Laurel Co., KY.
       iii.   NANCY HAMMACK, b. Abt. 1825, Tennessee; d. Aft. 1850, Union Co., TN.
       iv.   RUTH HAMMACK, b. Abt. 1827, Tennessee; d. Aft. 1850, Union Co., TN; m. JOSEPH PAUL, 05 Jun 1854, Grainger Co., TN.
       v.   BETSY HAMMACK, b. Abt. 1829, Tennessee; d. Aft. 1850, Union Co., TN.
405.   vi.   DANIEL HAMMACK, b. Abt. 1831, Tennessee; d. Aft. 1870, Grainger Co., TN.
       vii.   WILLIAM HAMMACK, b. Abt. 1833, Tennessee; d. Aft. 1850, Grainger Co., TN.
       viii.   JOHN HAMMACK, b. Abt. 1836, Tennessee; d. Aft. 1860, Grainger Co., TN; m. SALLY ANN [------]; b. Abt. 1840, Tennessee; d. Aft. 1870, Grainger Co., TN.

Key Sources: S.L. Butler, *Virginia Soldiers in the United States Army, 1800-1815* (Athens, GA, 1986); 1850 Grainger Co., TN, Census, p. 363; 1870 Union Co., TN, Census, p. 221.

238. EPHRAIM[8] HAMMACK *(JOHN[7], JOHN[6], RICHARD[5], RICHARD[4], WILLIAM "O"[3], JOHN[2] HAMMOCKE, ? JOHN[1] HAMMOT)* was born Abt. 1799 in Greenbriar Co., VA, and died Abt. 1855 in IN. He married JANE LONG 02 Sep 1820 in Grainger Co., TN, daughter of ISAAC LONG and NANCY BOLTON. She was born Abt. 1800 in Franklin Co., VA, and died Aft. 1880 in Fentress Co., TN.

Children of EPHRAIM HAMMACK and JANE LONG are:

406.   i.   ? ISAAC[9] HAMMACK, b. Abt. 1823, Knox Co., TN; d. Aft. 1860, Anderson Co., TN.
       ii.   NANCY HAMMACK, b. 12 Jan 1823, Knox Co., TN; d. Aft. 1850, Benton Co., AR; m. GARLAND TAYLOR, 04 Aug 1841, Knox Co., TN.
       iii.   ELIZABETH HAMMACK, b. 09 Jun 1824, Knox Co., TN; d. 29 Jun 1883, Fentress Co., TN.
       iv.   SON HAMMACK, b. Bet. 1825 - 1830, Knox Co., TN; d. Aft. 1830, Knox Co., TN.
       v.   SON HAMMACK, b. Bet. 1825 - 1830, Knox Co., TN; d. Aft. 1830, Knox Co., TN.
       vi.   ANNA HAMMACK, b. Abt. 1828, Knox Co., TN; m. WILLIAM THOMAS.
       vii.   DANIEL HAMMOCK, b. Abt. 1831, Knox Co., TN; d. Aft. 1880, Mason Co., IL; m. AMANDA [------], Abt. 1855, Anderson Co., TN; b. Abt. 1830, Tennessee; d. Bet. 1870 - 1880, Mason Co., IL.
       viii.   ? WILLIAM WESLEY HAMMACK, b. 22 Oct 1832, Knox Co., TN; d. 08 Apr 1893, Grainger Co., TN; m. SUSANNAH LONG, 18 Feb 1851, Grainger Co., TN; b. 15 Apr 1827, Tennessee; d. 07 Nov 1911, Grainger Co., TN.
       ix.   AGNES EMERINE HAMMACK, b. Abt. 1832, Knox Co., TN.
       x.   JEMIMA HAMMACK, b. Abt. 1835, Knox Co., TN; d. 24 Mar 1915, Scott Co., TN.
       xi.   JOHN W. HAMMACK, b. Abt. 1837, Knox Co., TN; d. Aft. 1910, Benton Co., AR; m. CLARA HURST.
       xii.   MARY J. HAMMACK, b. Abt. 1839, Anderson Co., TN; m. ARMSTED DEW, 12 Jul 1873, Anderson Co., Tn.
       xiii.   LUCINDA HAMMACK, b. 20 Feb 1841, Anderson Co., TN; d. Aft. 1860, Scott Co., TN.
       xiv.   GEORGE HAMMACK, b. Abt. 1845, Anderson Co., TN; d. Aft. 1860, Scott Co., TN; m. SARAH J. CLARK, 10 Aug 1867, Anderson Co., TN.

Key Sources: 1830 Knox Co., TN, Census, p. 370; 1840 Anderson Co., TN, Census, p. 12; 1850 Anderson Co., TN, Census, p. 45; 1860 Scott Co., TN, Census, p. 200; 1870 Fentress Co., TN, Census, p. 553; 1880 Fentress Co., TN, Census, p. 526.

239. WILLIAM[8] HAMMACK *(MARTIN[7], JOHN[6], RICHARD[5], RICHARD[4], WILLIAM "O"[3], JOHN[2] HAMMOCKE, ? JOHN[1] HAMMOT)* was born Abt. 1796 in Kanawha Co., VA, and died Abt. 1876 in Roane Co., WV. He married SARAH ASHLEY Abt. 1822 in Kanawha Co., WV. She was born Abt. 1800 in NC, and died Abt. 1886 in Roane Co., WV.

Children of WILLIAM HAMMACK and SARAH ASHLEY are:

407.   i.   ST. CLAIR "SINK"[9] HAMMACK, b. Abt. 1822, Kanawha Co., VA; d. Aft. 1880, Roane Co., WV.

    ii.   POLLY HAMMACK, b. 13 Feb 1824, Kanawha Co., VA; d. 14 Jan 1888, Marion Co., OH; m. JACOB CYRUS HELPER; b. Abt. 1823, Virginia; d. Aft. 1870, Roane Co., WV.

408.   iii. SUSAN HAMMACK, b. Abt. 1828, Kanawha Co., VA; d. Aft. 1880, Roane Co., WV.

    iv.   MARTIN HAMMACK, b. Abt. 1829, Kanawha Co., VA; d. Aft. 1890, Roane Co., WV; m. ANNA ELIZA GIVEN, Abt. 1863, Roane Co., WV; b. Abt. 1840, WV; d. Aft. 1880, Roane Co., WV.

    v.   CYNTHIA HAMMACK, b. Abt. 1830, Kanawha Co., VA.

    vi.   JOHN HAMMACK, b. Abt. 1832, Kanawha Co., VA; d. Aft. 1870, Roane Co., WV; m. ANN J. [------], Abt. 1858, Roane Co., WV; b. Abt. 1843, Virginia; d. Aft. 1870, WV.

    vii. SYLVESTER HAMMACK, b. 15 Oct 1832, Kanawha Co., VA; d. 03 Oct 1892, Kanawaha Co., WV; m. JANE SUMMERS, Abt. 1854, Kanawha Co., WV; b. Abt. 1835, Virginia; d. Aft. 1880, Kanawha Co., VA.

    viii. CATHERINE "KATY" HAMMACK, b. Abt. 1836, Kanawha Co., VA; m. (1) JAMES K. KERNS; m. (2) WILLIAM J. BOND.

    ix.   ANDREW J. HAMMACK, b. 09 Jan 1840, Kanawha Co., VA; d. 13 Mar 1902, Kanawha Co., VA; m. EDITH SMITH; b. 23 Feb 1840, Virginia; d. 08 Oct 1920, Kanawha Co., VA.

    x.   BARBARA HAMMACK, b. Abt. 1842, Kanawha Co., VA; d. Aft. 1862, Kanawha Co., VA; m. JOHN SUMMERS, 27 Dec 1862, Kanawha Co., WV.

    xi.   REBECCA HAMMACK, b. Abt. 1844, Kanawha Co., VA.

Key Sources: 1850 Kanawha Co., VA, Census, p. 98; William H. Bishop, History of Roane Co., WV (Spencer, WV, 1927), pp. 536-37; 1860 Roane Co., VA, Census, p. 573; 1870 Roane Co., VA, Census, p. 83. Members of this family buried in the Baxter Cemetery, Kanawha Co., WV, used the Hammack spelling.

240. JOHN[8] HAMMOCK *(MARTIN[7], JOHN[6], RICHARD[5], RICHARD[4], WILLIAM "O"[3], JOHN[2] HAMMOCKE, ? JOHN[1] HAMMOT)* was born Abt. 1798 in Kanawha Co., VA, and died Aft. 1870 in Kanawha Co., VA. He married JANE CLECK 13 Jan 1826 in Kanawha Co., WV. She was born Abt. 1805 in Virginia, and died Aft. 1870 in Kanawha Co., VA.

Children of JOHN HAMMOCK and JANE CLECK are:

    i.   LEWIS A.[9] HAMMOCK, b. 18 May 1832, Kanawha Co., VA; d. Aft. 1900, Kanawha Co., VA; m. ROXALANO ACES, 16 Aug 1859, Kanawha Co., WV; b. Abt. 1842, Virginia; d. Bet. 1880 - 1900, Kanawha Co., VA.

    ii.   JOHN C. HAMMOCK, b. Abt. 1835, Kanawha Co., VA; d. Aft. 1860, Kanawha Co., VA.

    iii. DELANA HAMMOCK, b. Abt. 1838, Kanawha Co., VA; d. Aft. 1880, Kanawha Co., VA; m. MELISSA [------], Abt. 1867, Kanawha Co., WV; b. Abt. 1846, Kanawha Co., VA; d. Aft. 1900, Kanawha Co., VA.

    iv.   PERRY HAMMOCK, b. Abt. 1840, Kanawha Co., VA; d. Aft. 1860, Kanawha Co., VA.

    v.   JANE HAMMOCK, b. Abt. 1843, Kanawha Co., VA; d. Abt. 1874, Kanawha Co., VA; m. ADAM BUCHANAN PAULEY.

    vi.   HENRY HAMMOCK, b. Abt. 1845, Kanawha Co., VA; d. Aft. 1870, Kanawha Co., VA.

Key Sources: Virginia Land Grant Book 90, p. 468; Virginia Land Grant Book 89, p. 728; Virginia Land Grant Book 102, p. 683; 1850 Kanawha Co., VA, Census, p. 120; 1860 Kanawha Co., VA, Census, p. 195; 1870 Kanawha Co., WV, Census, p. 110.

241. DELANA[8] HAMMACK *(MARTIN[7], JOHN[6], RICHARD[5], RICHARD[4], WILLIAM "O"[3], JOHN[2] HAMMOCKE, ? JOHN[1] HAMMOT)* was born Abt. 1802 in Kanawha Co., VA, and died Bet. 1850 - 1860 in Kanawha Co., VA. He married BARBARA CLECK Abt. 1825 in Kanawha Co., WV. She was born 04 Aug 1811 in Kanawha Co., VA, and died 14 Mar 1883 in Roane Co., WV.
Children of DELANA HAMMACK and BARBARA CLECK are:

- i. PETER[9] HAMMACK, b. Abt. 1826, Kanawha Co., VA; d. Aft. 1880, Roane Co., WV; m. CATHERINE HAMMACK.
- ii. ANDREW JACKSON HAMMACK, b. Abt. 1829, Kanawha Co., VA; m. MELISSA DIAS AULTZ, 15 Dec 1854, Kanawha Co., WV; b. Abt. 1835, Kanawha Co., VA.
- iii. JANE HAMMACK, b. 27 Jan 1831, Kanawha Co., VA; d. 30 May 1899, Roane Co., WV; m. HENRY SUMMERS, 15 Nov 1850, Kanawha Co., WV.
- iv. PRESLEY HAMMACK, b. Abt. 1833, Kanawha Co., VA; d. Aft. 1850, Kanawha Co., VA.
- v. MARTIN HAMMACK, b. Abt. 1836, Kanawha Co., VA; d. Aft. 1850, Kanawha Co., VA.
- vi. MARY HAMMACK, b. Abt. 1841, Kanawha Co., VA; d. Aft. 1850, Kanawha Co., VA.
- vii. CAROLINE HAMMACK, b. Abt. 1845, Kanawha Co., VA; d. Aft. 1850, Kanawha Co., VA.
- viii. ANN HAMMACK, b. Abt. 1848, Kanawha Co., VA; d. Aft. 1850, Kanawha Co., VA.

Key Sources: Virginia Land Grant Book 80, p. 689; 1850 Kanawha Co., VA, Census, p. 98; 1860 Kanawha Co., VA, Census, p. 191; 1870 Roane Co., WV, Census, p. 81; 1880 Roane Co., WV, Census, p. 129D.

242. JAMES[8] HAMMACK *(MARTIN[7], JOHN[6], RICHARD[5], RICHARD[4], WILLIAM "O"[3], JOHN[2] HAMMOCKE, ? JOHN[1] HAMMOT)* was born Abt. 1805 in Kanawha Co., VA, and died Aft. 1850 in Kanawha Co., VA. He married NANCY GREEN 22 Jan 1848 in Kanawha Co., WV. She was born Abt. 1826 in Kanawha Co., VA, and died Aft. 1870 in Kanawha Co., VA.
Children of JAMES HAMMACK and NANCY GREEN are:

- i. ANDREW[9] HAMMACK, b. Abt. 1847, Kanawha Co., VA; d. Aft. 1900, Roane Co., WV; m. MARTHA [------]; b. Abt. 1871, WV; d. Aft. 1900, Roane Co., WV.
- ii. MARIA HAMMACK, b. Abt. 1848, Kanawha Co., VA; d. Aft. 1870, Kanawha Co., VA.
- iii. NANCY HAMMACK, b. Abt. 1852, Kanawha Co., VA; d. Aft. 1870, Kanawha Co., VA.
- iv. ELIZA A. HAMMACK, b. Abt. 1853, Kanawha Co., VA; d. Aft. 1870, Kanawha Co., VA.
- v. JAMES M. HAMMACK, b. Abt. 1855, Kanawha Co., VA; d. Aft. 1870, Kanawha Co., VA.
- vi. SARA E. HAMMACK, b. 05 Oct 1858, Kanawha Co., VA.
- vii. MARY M. HAMMACK, b. 28 Jan 1859, Kanawha Co., VA; d. Aft. 1870, Kanawha Co., VA.
- viii. MAHALA HAMMACK, b. Abt. 1863, Kanawha Co., VA; d. Aft. 1870, Kanawha Co., VA.

Key Sources: 1850 Kanawha Co., VA, Census, p. 120; 1870 Kanawha Co., WV, Census, p. 122.

243. MARTIN[8] HAMMACK *(MARTIN[7], JOHN[6], RICHARD[5], RICHARD[4], WILLIAM "O"[3], JOHN[2] HAMMOCKE, ? JOHN[1] HAMMOT)* was born Abt. 1807 in Kanawha Co., VA, and died 02 May 1862 in CSA, Virginia Volunteers. He married (1) ELIZABETH SUMMERS 20 Sep 1827 in Kanawha Co., WV. She was born Abt. 1807 in VA, and died Bef. 1856 in Kanawha Co., VA. He married (2) MELIVINA MCDANIELS 05 Sep 1856 in Kanawha Co., WV. She was born Abt. 1832 in Kanawha Co., VA, and died Aft. 1860 in Kanawha Co., VA.
Children of MARTIN HAMMACK and ELIZABETH SUMMERS are:

    i. ELIZABETH S.[9] HAMMACK, b. Abt. 1834, Kanawha Co., VA; d. Aft. 1850, Kanawha Co., VA.

   ii. GRANVILLE HAMMACK, b. Abt. 1850, Kanawha Co., VA; d. Aft. 1900, Kanawha Co., VA; m. ANNA [------]; b. Abt. 1876, Kanawha Co., VA; d. Aft. 1900, Kanawha Co., VA.

Key Sources: 1850 Kanawha Co., VA, Census, p. 120; 1860 Kanawha Co., VA, Census, p. 221; 1870 Kanawha Co., VA, Census, p. 106; 1880 Kanawha Co., WV, Census, p. 303A.

244. ANDREW[8] HAMMACK (*MARTIN[7], JOHN[6], RICHARD[5], RICHARD[4], WILLIAM "O"[3], JOHN[2] HAMMOCKE, ? JOHN[1] HAMMOT*) was born Abt. 1817 in Kanawha Co., VA, and died 08 Aug 1855 in Kanawha Co., VA. He married MARY GREEN 13 Jan 1843 in Kanawha Co., WV.

Children of ANDREW HAMMACK and MARY GREEN are:

    i. MARTIN[9] HAMMACK, b. Abt. 1844, Kanawha Co., VA; d. 23 Jul 1864, CSA, Virginia Volunteers.

   ii. Rev. JOHN HAMMACK, b. Abt. 1845, Kanawha Co., VA; d. 1933, Kanawha Co.,WV; m. MARTHA MINNER, Abt. 1875, Kanawha Co., WV; b. 05 Jan 1857, Kanawha Co., VA; d. 30 Jan 1928, Kanawha Co., WV.

   iii. SUSAN HAMMACK, b. Abt. 1848, Kanawha Co., VA; d. Aft. 1850, Kanawha Co., VA.

   iv. ANDREW HAMMACK, b. 15 Mar 1855, Kanawha Co., VA; d. Aft. 1880, Kanawha Co., WV.

Key Sources: 1850 Kanawha Co., VA, Census, p. 121; 1880 Kanawha Co., WV, Census, p. 236D.

245. MARTIN[8] HAMMACK (*DANIEL[7], JOHN[6], RICHARD[5], RICHARD[4], WILLIAM "O"[3], JOHN[2] HAMMOCKE, ? JOHN[1] HAMMOT*) was born 1791 in South Carolina, and died 31 Aug 1873 in Lake Co., CA. He married ELEANOR ANN MCNAIR 22 Feb 1822 in Lincoln Co., MO. She was born 09 Mar 1803.

Children of MARTIN HAMMACK and ELEANOR MCNAIR are:

    i. JOHN[9] HAMMACK, b. 1828, Missouri; d. Aft. 1854, Lincoln Co., MO.

   ii. BRICE MARTIN HAMMACK, b. 23 Jan 1831, Missouri; d. 1865, Lake Co., CA; m. ELIZAETH ANN GREY, 25 Dec 1852, St. Charles Co., MO; b. 08 Mar 1836, Missouri; d. Aft. 1900, Lake Co., CA.

   iii. MARY JANE HAMMACK, b. Abt. 1829, Missouri; m. EBENEAZER BOLE.

   iv. MARTHA HAMMACK, b. Abt. 1837, Missouri; m. JONAS INGRAM.

   v. MARGARET ANN HAMMACK, b. Abt. 1831, Missouri; m. WOODS CRAWFORD.

   vi. WILLIAM H. HAMMACK, b. Abt. 1837, Missouri; d. Aft. 1920, Mendocino Co., CA.

   vii. ROBERT JASPER HAMMACK, b. Abt. 1842, Missouri; d. Aft. 1920, Lake Co., CA.

   viii. SARAH ELEANOR HAMMACK, b. Abt. 1848, Missouri; m. WILLIAM MONROE WOODS.

Key Sources: G. P. Omohundro, *Ancestors and Descendants of Brice Wiseman Hammack* (Santa Ana, CA, 1986); 1850 Lincoln Co., MO, Census, p. 444; 1860 Napa Co., CA, Census, p. 122.

246. BRICE WISEMAN[8] HAMMACK (*DANIEL[7], JOHN[6], RICHARD[5], RICHARD[4], WILLIAM "O"[3], JOHN[2] HAMMOCKE, ? JOHN[1] HAMMOT*) was born 1796 in Georgia, and died Abt. 05 Jan 1867 in Coryell Co., TX. He married JANE WOMACK 1817 in Dixon Springs, Smith Co., Tennessee, daughter of WILLIAM WOMACK and CATHERINE STREETMAN. She was born Abt. 21 Dec 1800 in Tennessee, and died 27 Mar 1848 in Lincoln Co., MO.

Children of BRICE HAMMACK and JANE WOMACK are:

409.   i. LEANDER MARTIN[9] HAMMACK, b. 16 Jan 1818, Smith Co., TN; d. Aft. 1870, Lincoln Co., MO.

410. ii. WILLIAM WESLEY HAMMACK, b. 25 Aug 1820, Lincoln Co., MO; d. 17 Feb 1893, Coryell Co., TX.

411. iii. DANIEL ALEXANDER HAMMACK, b. 22 Nov 1822, Lincoln Co., MO; d. 09 May 1909, Coryell Co., TX.

412. iv. SENECA WATTS HAMMACK, b. 19 Feb 1825, Lincoln Co., MO; d. 30 Jan 1893, Montgomery Co., MO.

413. v. JAMES TYRA HAMMACK, b. 31 Mar 1827, Lincoln Co., MO; d. 04 Jun 1877, Lincoln Co., MO.

vi. MARY AMANDA HAMMACK, b. 19 Nov 1829, Lincoln Co., MO; d. 30 Oct 1911, St. Louis, MO; m. MORDICAI RICHARD WATTS, 03 Dec 1847, Lincoln Co., MO; b. 05 Oct 1823, Missouri; d. 05 Jul 1885, Missouri.

vii. HORACE CLAY HAMMACK, b. 09 Sep 1832, Lincoln Co., MO; d. 1877, Coryell Co., TX.

viii. SARAH JANE HAMMACK, b. 21 Jan 1835, Lincoln Co., MO; d. Aft. 1907, Coryell Co., TX; m. (1) GEORGE F. ADAMS; b. 01 Feb 1827, South Carolina; d. 14 May 1871, Coryell Co., TX; m. (2) G. W. WILSON, 07 Jan 1879, Coryell Co., TX.

ix. MARTHA CATHERINE HAMMACK, b. 20 Nov 1837, Lincoln Co., MO; d. Jan 1860, Coryell Co., TX; m. JOE HAYNES.

x. LOUISA ANN HAMMACK, b. 10 Aug 1840, Lincoln Co., MO; d. Aft. 1872, Oklahoma; m. LAFAYETTE HAYNES; b. Abt. 1832, Tennessee; d. Aft. 1880, Texas.

Key Sources: G. P. Omohundro, *Ancestors and Descendants of Brice Wiseman Hammack* (Santa Ana, CA, 1986); Henry Franklin Hammack, 1: 168; 1850 Lincoln Co., MO, Census, p. 471; 1860 Coryell Co., TX, Census, p. 268.

247. WILLIAM H.[8] HAMMOCK *(DANIEL[7], JOHN[6], RICHARD[5], RICHARD[4], WILLIAM "O"[3], JOHN[2] HAMMOCKE, ? JOHN[1] HAMMOT)* was born 1799 in Smith Co., TN, and died 1881 in Lincoln Co., MO. He married CAROLINE MATILDA BURRIS Bet. 1825 - 1829 in Smith Co., TN. She was born Abt. 1805 in Tennessee, and died Aft. 1880 in Lincoln Co., MO.
Children of WILLIAM HAMMOCK and CAROLINE BURRIS are:

i. BRICE M.[9] HAMMOCK, b. 1829, Tennessee; d. Aft. 1880, Montgomery Co., IL; m. (1) MARTHA A. [------], Abt. 1850, Missouri; b. Abt. 1830, Tennessee; d. Bet. 1850 - 1860, Wayne Co., MO; m. (2) LUCY A. [------], Abt. 1858, Montgomery Co., IL; b. Abt. 1837, Tennessee; d. Aft. 1880, Montgomery Co., IL.

ii. ELIZABETH HAMMOCK, b. 1831, Lincoln Co., MO; d. Aft. 1850, Lincoln Co., MO.

iii. VIRGIL S. HAMMOCK, b. Abt. 1837, Lincoln Co., MO; d. Aft. 1880, Lincoln Co., MO; m. SARAH [------], Abt. 1862, Lincoln Co., MO; b. Abt. 1843, Lincoln Co., MO; d. Aft. 1880, Lincoln Co., MO.

iv. GEORGE S. HAMMOCK, b. Abt. 1839, Lincoln Co., MO; d. Aft. 1860, Lincoln Co., MO.

Key Sources: G. P. Omohundro, *Ancestors and Descendants of Brice Wiseman Hammack* (Santa Ana, CA, 1986); 1850 Lincoln Co., MO, Census, p. 444; 1860 Lincoln Co., MO, Census, p. 473; 1870 Lincoln Co., MO, Census, p. 84; 1880 Lincoln Co., MO, Census, p. 220.

248. JAMES DANIEL[8] HAMMACK *(DANIEL[7], JOHN[6], RICHARD[5], RICHARD[4], WILLIAM "O"[3], JOHN[2] HAMMOCKE, ? JOHN[1] HAMMOT)* was born 1800 in Smith Co., TN, and died Aft. 1880 in Madison Co., MO. He married MARTHA LOUISA RICHARDSON Abt. 1824 in Tennessee. She was born Abt. 1805 in Tennessee, and died Aft. 02 Aug 1872 in Madison Co., MO.
Children of JAMES HAMMACK and MARTHA RICHARDSON are:

i. AMANDA ELIZABETH[9] HAMMACK, b. Abt. 1826, Tennessee; m. WILLIAM E. MILLER, 16 Sep 1849, Madison Co., MO.

ii. SARAH ANN HAMMACK, b. Abt. 1828, Tennessee; m. DANIEL H. DUGLESS, 23 Sep 1853, Madison Co., MO.

iii. HARRISON DANIEL HAMMACK, b. Abt. 1832, Smith Co., TN; d. 1898, LeFlore Co., OK; m. (1) MARY C. BESS, 04 Feb 1858, Madison Co., MO; m. (2) JENNIE PARALEE HURST, 22 Apr 1885, Madison Co., AR.

iv. JAMES HAMMACK, b. Abt. 1834, Smith Co., TN.

v. BALEY P. HAMMACK, b. Abt. 1844, Smith Co., TN; d. Aft. 1880, Madison Co., MO; m. SARAH C. WELCH, 04 Oct 1868, Madison Co., MO.

vi. WILLIAM B. C. HAMMACK, b. Abt. 1848, Smith Co., TN; d. Aft. 1860, Madison Co., MO.

Key Sources: G. P. Omohundro, *Ancestors and Descendants of Brice Wiseman Hammack* (Santa Ana, CA, 1986); *Goodspeed's History of Northwest Arkansas* (Chicago, IL, 1889), p. 1150; 1860 Madison Co., MO, Census, p. 500; 1880 Madison Co., MO, Census, p. 76.

249. SPENCER[8] HAMMACK *(JOHN[7], RICHARD[6], RICHARD[5], RICHARD[4], WILLIAM "O"[3], JOHN[2] HAMMOCKE, ? JOHN[1] HAMMOT)* was born Abt. 1785 in Pittsylvania Co., VA, and died Aft. 1870 in Pittsylvania Co., VA. He married SARAH MEESE Abt. 17 Jan 1810 in Pittsylvania Co., VA. She was born Abt. 1787 in Pittsylvania Co., VA, and died 12 Dec 1853 in Pittsylvania Co., VA.

Children of SPENCER HAMMACK and SARAH MEESE are:

414.   i. JOHN ALFRED[9] HAMMACK, b. Abt. 1813, Pittsylvania Co., VA; d. Abt. 1866, Pittsylvania Co., VA.

ii. SON HAMMACK, b. Bet. 1810 - 1820, Pittsylvania Co., VA; d. Bef. 1830, Pittsylvania Co., VA.

415.   iii. WILLIAM HAMMACK, b. Abt. 1816, Pittsylvania Co., VA; d. Aft. 1860, Henry Co., IN.

416.   iv. TALIAFERRO HAMMACK, b. Abt. 1818, Pittsylvania Co., VA; d. Aft. 1870, Pittsylvania Co., VA.

417.   v. OLIVER HAMMACK, b. Abt. 1820, Pittsylvania Co., VA; d. Aft. 1880, Hancock Co., IN.

418.   vi. LEWIS HAMMACK, b. Abt. 1823, Pittsylvania Co., VA; d. Aft. 1860, Roanoke Co., VA.

vii. SON HAMMACK, b. Bet. 1820 - 1825, Pittsylvania Co., VA; d. Aft. 1830, Pittsylvania Co., VA.

419.   viii. SPENCER HAMMACK, b. Abt. 1827, Pittsylvania Co., VA; d. Aft. 1860, Henry Co., IN.

ix. SARAH HAMMACK, b. Abt. 1831, Pittsylvania Co., VA; d. Aft. 1850, Pittsylvania Co., VA.

x. MARTHA HAMMACK, b. Abt. 1834, Pittsylvania Co., VA; d. Aft. 1850, Pittsylvania Co., VA.

xi. MARY HAMMACK, b. Abt. 1839, Pittsylvania Co., VA; d. Aft. 1850, Pittsylvania Co., VA.

xii. SON HAMMACK, b. Bet. 1835 - 1840, Pittsylvania Co., VA; d. Aft. 1840, Pittsylvania Co., VA.

Key Sources: Pittsylvania Co., VA, Order Book 17, p. 88; Pittsylvania Co., VA, Order Book 20, p. 209; Pittsylvania Co., VA, Order Book 21, p. 90; 1820 Pittsylvania Co., VA, Census, p. 69A; Pittsylvania Co., VA, Order Book 22, p. 277; Pittsylvania Co., VA, Order Book 24, pp. 148, 288, 365; Pittsylvania Co., VA, Order Book 26, p. 245; 1830 Pittsylvania Co., VA, Census, p. 318; Pittsylvania Co., VA, Order Book 30, p. 159; Pittsylvania Co., VA, Register of Deaths; 1840 Pittsylvania Co., VA, Census, p. 80; Pittsylvania Co., VA, Deed Book 49, p. 454; Pittsylvania Co., VA, Deed Book 51, pp. 50, 104; 1850 Pittsylvania Co., VA, Census, p. 256; Pittsylvania Co., VA, Order Bok 40, pp. 375, 410; Pittsylvania Co., VA, Order Book 41, pp. 11, 152; Pittsylvania Co., VA, Deed Book 54, p. 544; Pittsylvania Co., VA, Deed Book 47, p. 377; Pittsylvania Co., VA, Deed Book 54, p. 321; Pittsylvania Co., VA, Order Book 43, pp. 289, 369; Pittsylvania Co., VA, Deed Book 56, p. 413; 1860 Pittsylvania Co., VA, Census, pp. 161, 168-170; 1870 Pittsylvania Co., VA, Census, pp. 353-355.

250. TALIAFERRO[8] HAMMACK *(JOHN[7], RICHARD[6], RICHARD[5], RICHARD[4], WILLIAM "O"[3], JOHN[2] HAMMOCKE, ? JOHN[1] HAMMOT)* was born Abt. 1787 in Pittsylvania Co., VA, and died Aft. 1850 in Macon Co., TN. He married ELIZABETH VANCE Abt. 10 Feb 1810 in Pittsylvania Co., VA. She was born Abt. 1783 in Pittsylvania Co., VA, and died Aft. 1850 in Macon Co., TN.
Children of TALIAFERRO HAMMACK and ELIZABETH VANCE are:

      i.   DAUGHTER[9] HAMMACK, b. Bet. 1810 - 1815, Pittsylvania Co., VA; d. Aft. 1830, Smith Co., TN.

420.   ii.   LACE J. HAMMACK, b. Abt. 1819, Pittsylvania Co., VA; d. Aft. 1880, Wayne Co., IL.

      iii.   DAUGHTER HAMMACK, b. Bet. 1815 - 1820, Pittsylvania Co., VA; d. Aft. 1830, Smith Co., TN.

421.   iv.   JOHN D. HAMMACK, b. Abt. 1822, Smith Co., TN; d. Aft. 1860, Newton Co., MO.

      v.   DAUGHTER HAMMACK, b. Bet. 1825 - 1830, Smith Co., TN; d. Aft. 1830, Smith Co., TN.

Key Sources: 1820 Pittsylvania Co., VA, Census, p. 51; Smith Co., TN, Deed Book I, p. 525; 1830 Smith Co., TN, Census, p. 67; 1840 Smith Co., TN, Census, p. 289; 1850 Macon Co., TN, Census, p. 157.

251. COLEMAN[8] HAMMACK *(JOHN[7], RICHARD[6], RICHARD[5], RICHARD[4], WILLIAM "O"[3], JOHN[2] HAMMOCKE, ? JOHN[1] HAMMOT)* was born Abt. 1793 in Pittsylvania Co., VA, and died Aft. 1850 in Westmoreland Co., TN. He married FRANCES JACOBS Abt. 1820 in Pittsylvania Co., VA. She was born Abt. 1799 in Pittsylvania Co., VA, and died Aft. 1850 in Westmoreland Co., TN.
Children of COLEMAN HAMMACK and FRANCES JACOBS are:

      i.   SON[9] HAMMACK, b. Bet. 1820 - 1825, Pittsylvania Co., VA; d. Aft. 1840, Pittsylvania Co., VA.

      ii.   SON HAMMACK, b. Bet. 1820 - 1825, Pittsylvania Co., VA; d. Aft. 1840, Pittsylvania Co., VA.

      iii.   MARTHA F. HAMMACK, b. Abt. 1821, Pittsylvania Co., VA; d. Aft. 1850, Pittsylvania Co., VA.

      iv.   MARY C. HAMMACK, b. Abt. 1827, Pittsylvania Co., VA; d. Aft. 1850, Pittsylvania Co., VA.

422.   v.   COLEMAN A. HAMMACK, b. Abt. 1828, Pittsylvania Co., VA; d. Aft. 1872, Westmoreland Co., TN.

      vi.   NANCY A. HAMMACK, b. Abt. 1832, Pittsylvania Co., VA; d. Aft. 1850, Pittsylvania Co., VA; m. JEHU STINSON.

      vii.   DANIEL R. HAMMACK, b. Abt. 1834, Pittsylvania Co., VA; d. Aft. 1850, Texas.

      viii.   TALIAFERRO ALLEN HAMMACK, b. 11 Nov 1836, Pittsylvania Co., VA; d. 22 Sep 1906, Pope Co., IL; m. (1) MILLY C. [------]; b. Abt. 1841, Kentucky; d. Bet. 1860 - 1862, Pope Co., IL; m. (2) MARY [------] JACOBS, Abt. 1862, Pope Co., IL; b. Abt. 1833, Tennessee; d. Aft. 1880, Pope Co., IL.

      ix.   ELIZA J. HAMMACK, b. Abt. 1837, Pittsylvania Co., VA; d. Aft. 1850, Pittsylvania Co., VA.

      x.   GILLY HARRIET HAMMACK, b. Abt. 1839, Pittsylvania Co., VA; d. Aft. 1860, Macon Co., TN; m. CALVIN GREEN SIMMONS.

      xi.   WILLIAM HAMMACK, b. Abt. 1841, Pittsylvania Co., VA; d. Aft. 1850, Tennessee.

      xii.   BETSY HAMMACK, b. Abt. 1843, Pittsylvania Co., VA; d. Aft. 1850, Pike Co., MO.

Key Sources: 1830 Franklin Co., VA, Census, p. 68; Pittsylvania Co., VA, Deed Book 41, p. 395; 1840 Pittsylvania Co., VA, Census, p. 114; 1850 Pittsylvania Co., VA, Census, p. 90.

252. JOHN T.[8] HAMMACK (*JOHN[7], RICHARD[6], RICHARD[5], RICHARD[4], WILLIAM "O"[3], JOHN[2] HAMMOCKE, ? JOHN[1] HAMMOT*) was born Bet. 1794 - 1800 in Pittsylvania Co., VA, and died Aft. 1842 in Pittsylvania Co., VA. He married UNKNOWN Abt. 1820 in Pittsylvania Co., VA. She was born Abt. 1800 in Virginia, and died Aft. 1830 in Pittsylvania Co., VA.
Children of JOHN HAMMACK and UNKNOWN are:

    i.   DAUGHTER[9] HAMMACK, b. Bet. 1820 - 1825, Pittsylvania Co., VA; d. Aft. 1830, Pittsylvania Co., VA.

    ii.   DAUGHTER HAMMACK, b. Bet. 1820 - 1825, Pittsylvania Co., VA; d. Aft. 1830, Pittsylvania Co., VA.

    iii.   SON HAMMACK, b. Bet. 1825 - 1830, Pittsylvania Co., VA; d. Aft. 1830, Pittsylvania Co., VA.

    iv.   DAUGHTER HAMMACK, b. Bet. 1825 - 1830, Pittsylvania Co., VA; d. Aft. 1830, Pittsylvania Co., VA.

    v.   DAUGHTER HAMMACK, b. Bet. 1825 - 1830, Pittsylvania Co., VA; d. Aft. 1830, Pittsylvania Co., VA.

Key Sources: 1820 Pittsylvania Co., VA, Census, p. 69A; 1830 Pittsylvania Co., VA, Census, p. 313; Pittsylvania Co., VA, Order Book 30, p. 159; Pittsylvania Co., VA, Order Book 37, p. 27.

253. JOHN[8] HAMMACK (*DANIEL[7], RICHARD[6], RICHARD[5], RICHARD[4], WILLIAM "O"[3], JOHN[2] HAMMOCKE, ? JOHN[1] HAMMOT*) was born 11 Mar 1791 in Pittsylvania Co., VA, and died Aft. 1840 in Posey Co., IN. He married FRANCES HUMPHREYS 22 Dec 1812 in Pulaski Co., KY. She was born Abt. 1796 in South Carolina, and died Aft. 1850 in Posey Co., IN.
Children of JOHN HAMMACK and FRANCES HUMPHREYS are:

    i.   MAHALA A.[9] HAMMACK, b. 13 Oct 1813, Knox Co., KY; d. 29 Dec 1888, Washington Co., IN; m. JOHN HENRY MILLER, Bet. 1832 - 1833, Vigo Co., IN; b. 04 Jul 1807, Kentucky.

423.   ii.   DANIEL HAMMACK, b. Abt. 1814, Kentucky; d. 29 Aug 1887, Marion Co., OR.

424.   iii.   GEORGE HAMMACK, b. 10 Sep 1817, Kentucky; d. 28 Apr 1904, Wayne Co., IA.

Key Sources: 1820 Pulaski Co., KY, Census, p. 39; 1830 Vigo Co., IL, Census, p. 95.

254. EPHRAIM[8] HAMMACK (*DANIEL[7], RICHARD[6], RICHARD[5], RICHARD[4], WILLIAM "O"[3], JOHN[2] HAMMOCKE, ? JOHN[1] HAMMOT*) was born 26 Feb 1798 in Pittsylvania Co., VA, and died 18 Apr 1855 in Perry Co., IN. He married CYNTHIA HELEN HIX 10 Apr 1828 in Perry Co., IN. She was born 28 Jan 1804 in South Carolina, and died 12 Apr 1895 in Indiana.
Children of EPHRAIM HAMMACK and CYNTHIA HIX are:

    i.   ELIZABETH[9] HAMMACK, b. 03 Feb 1829, Perry Co., IN.

    ii.   DANIEL HAMMACK, b. Abt. 1830, Perry Co., IN; d. Bef. 1860, Appanoose Co., IA; m. LUCRETIA CRIST, 21 Feb 1850, Perry Co., IN; b. Abt. 1830, Indiana; d. Aft. 1860, Appanoose Co., IA.

    iii.   AGNES EMERINE HAMMACK, b. 11 Jan 1832, Perry Co., IN; d. Aft. 1851, Perry Co., IN; m. JAMES HILEY, 31 May 1851, Perry Co., IN.

    iv.   WILLIAM WESLEY HAMMACK, b. Abt. 1834, Perry Co., IN; d. Aft. 1860, Iowa; m. REBECCA [------].

    v.   MARY ANN MALINDA HAMMACK, b. 12 Feb 1835, Perry Co., IN; d. Aft. 1880, Hamilton Co., IL; m. CHRISTOPHER LOWERY HAYES, 17 Jan 1861, Indiana; b. 18 Aug 1831, Pike Co., IN; d. Bef. 1880, Hamilton Co., IL.

    vi.   JAMES HAMMACK, b. 22 Oct 1836, Perry Co., IN; d. Aft. 1860, Perry Co., IN; m. MARY A. [------]; b. Abt. 1837, Perry Co., IN; d. Aft. 1860, Perry Co., IN.

vii. NANCY HAMMACK, b. 26 Mar 1838, Perry Co., IN; d. Aft. 1864, Perry Co., IN; m. ENOCH T. RUSSELL.

viii. HENRY HARRISON HAMMACK, b. 03 Nov 1839, Perry Co., IN; d. 1919, Indiana; m. NANCY PARKS, 21 Nov 1865, Perry Co., IN; b. 29 Mar 1843, Perry Co., IN; d. Aft. 1880, Perry Co., IN.

ix. EPHRAIM THOMAS HAMMACK, b. Abt. 1841, Perry Co., IN; d. Aft. 1860, Perry Co., IN.

x. BENJAMIN FRANKLIN HAMMACK, b. Abt. 1843, Perry Co., IN; d. Aft. 1880, Hamilton Co., IL; m. ZILPHA [------]; b. Abt. 1850, Ohio; d. Aft. 1880, Hamilton Co., IL.

xi. BAXTER HAMMACK, b. 08 Dec 1845, Perry Co., IN; d. 17 Feb 1920, White Co., IL; m. NANCY JACKSON, 25 Dec 1868, Perry Co., IN; b. 14 Jan 1849, Perry Co., IN; d. Aft. 1880, Perry Co., IN.

Key Sources: 1830 Perry Co., IN, Census, p. 302; 1860 Perry Co., IN, Census, p. 1071; 1880 Hamilton Co., IL, Census, p. 507.

255. DANIEL[8] HAMMACK *(DANIEL[7], RICHARD[6], RICHARD[5], RICHARD[4], WILLIAM "O"[3], JOHN[2] HAMMOCKE, ? JOHN[1] HAMMOT)* was born 06 Jul 1800 in Pittsylvania Co., VA, and died 18 May 1855 in Mercer Co., IL. He married MARY DODSON 02 Sep 1824 in Perry Co., IN. She was born 16 Apr 1807 in Wayne Co., KY, and died Aft. 1870 in Henderson Co., IL.

Children of DANIEL HAMMACK and MARY DODSON are:

425. i. EPHRAIM[9] HAMMACK, b. 13 Aug 1825, Perry Co., IN; d. 22 Sep 1901, Audobon Co., IA.

ii. ABISHA HAMMACK, b. Abt. 1828, Perry Co., IN; d. Aft. 1900, Illinois; m. MINERVA JANE WALKER, 24 Mar 1851, Mercer Co., IL; b. Abt. 1830, Indiana; d. Aft. 1851, Mercer Co., IL.

Key Sources: 1830 Perry Co., IN, Census, p. 302; 1850 Mercer Co., IL, Census, pp. 352-353; 1870 Henderson Co., IL, Census, p. 212; Henry Franklin Hammack, 2: 231.

256. ISAIAH[8] HAMMACK *(DANIEL[7], RICHARD[6], RICHARD[5], RICHARD[4], WILLIAM "O"[3], JOHN[2] HAMMOCKE, ? JOHN[1] HAMMOT)* was born 07 Aug 1804 in Pittsylvania Co., VA, and died Aft. 1830 in Knox Co., KY. He married SARAH SMOCK 12 Jun 1841 in Perry Co., IN. She was born Abt. 1817 in Kentucky, and died 10 Jul 1894 in Sullivan Co., IN.

Children of ISAIAH HAMMACK and SARAH SMOCK are:

i. LEVINA[9] HAMMACK, b. Jul 1843, Indiana; d. Aft. 1900, Indiana.

ii. ANNA HAMMACK, b. Abt. 1844, Indiana.

iii. DANIEL HAMMACK, b. Abt. 1847, Indiana; d. Aft. 1920, Okmulgee Co., OK; m. (1) MARY [------]; m. (2) LOTTIE [------].

iv. MARY ELIZABETH HAMMACK, b. Sep 1850, Indiana; d. 03 Dec 1915, Sullivan Co., IN; m. A. J. EWING, 04 Jan 1872, Sullivan Co., IN.

v. CAROLINE HAMMACK, b. Abt. 1852, Indiana; d. Aft. 1872, Sullivan Co., IN; m. WILLIAM S. JEWELL, 06 Jul 1872, Sullivan Co., IN.

vi. JAMES J. HAMMACK, b. Mar 1856, Sullivan Co., IN; d. Aft. 1900, Indiana.

Key Sources: 1860 Sullivan Co., IN, Census, p. 1071; 1880 Sullivan Co., IN, Census, p. 446.

257. JAMES MARION[8] HAMMOCK *(DANIEL[7], RICHARD[6], RICHARD[5], RICHARD[4], WILLIAM "O"[3], JOHN[2] HAMMOCKE, ? JOHN[1] HAMMOT)* was born Abt. 1814 in Madison Co., KY, and died 22 Apr 1890 in Union Co., OR. He married ELIZABETH MOORE 20 Nov 1834 in Knox Co., KY. She was born 05 Jan 1816 in Knox Co., KY, and died 17 Dec 1903 in Union Co., OR.

Children of JAMES HAMMOCK and ELIZABETH MOORE are:

i. THOMAS MARTIN[9] HAMMOCK, b. 02 Sep 1835, Knox Co., KY; d. 14 Nov 1893, Union Co., OR; m. ALMEDIA NIDA, 12 Jul 1856, Wayne Co., IA; b. Abt. 1840, Kentucky; d. Aft. 1900, Union Co., OR.

    ii.   JAMES WESLEY HAMMOCK, b. 02 Apr 1838, Knox Co., KY; d. 15 Oct 1912, Wallowa Co., OR; m. SARAH ANN MILLER, 10 Oct 1857, Wayne Co., IA; b. 17 Oct 1842, Perry Co., IN; d. 03 Jun 1927, Wallowa Co., OR.

    iii.   DANIEL MARION HAMMOCK, b. Jun 1841, Knox Co., KY; d. 23 Apr 1908, Wallowa Co., OR.

    iv.   EPHRAIM P. HAMMOCK, b. Dec 1843, Missouri; d. 10 Jan 1907, Union Co., OR; m. SUSANNA PROW, Abt. 1862, Union Co., OR; b. Abt. 1840, Willamette Valley, OR; d. 18 Nov 1895, Union Co., OR.

    v.   NANCY ANN HAMMOCK, b. 22 Dec 1845, Missouri; d. 26 Oct 1913, Union Co., OR; m. BENJAMIN FRANKLIN SEE, 23 Apr 1865, Page Co., IA; b. 26 Nov 1845, Estill Co., KY; d. Aft. 1880, Union Co., OR.

    vi.   AMANDA J. HAMMOCK, b. 26 Apr 1848, Wayne Co., IA; d. 09 May 1916, Union Co., OR; m. (1) GEORGE WASHINGTON SEE, 20 Oct 1865, Union Co., OR; m. (2) C. C. ANDERSON, 20 Sep 1875, Union Co., OR; m. (3) JOSEPH WEATHERS, 20 Jan 1894, Union Co., OR; m. (4) WILLIAM THOMAS GRIDER, 06 Sep 1903, Umatilla Co., OR; m. (5) L. T. BRYANT, Abt. 1910, Union Co., OR.

    vii.   SUSAN MARY HAMMOCK, b. Abt. 1851, Wayne Co., IA; d. 1892, Union Co., OR; m. JOHN PROW, 03 Dec 1871, Union Co., OR.

    viii.   ELLEN HAMMOCK, b. Abt. 1854, Wayne Co., IA; d. Aft. 1860, Wayne Co., IA.

    ix.   WILLIAM A. HAMMOCK, b. May 1857, Wayne Co., IA; d. Aft. 1900, Umatilla Co., OR.

Key Sources: 1850 Wayne Co., IA, Census, p. 578; 1860 Wayne Co., IA, Census, p. 460; 1870 Union Co., OR, Census, p. 392; 1880 Union Co., OR, Census, p. 135.

258. WILLIAM[8] HAMMACK *(EPHRAIM[7], RICHARD[6], RICHARD[5], RICHARD[4], WILLIAM "O"[3], JOHN[2] HAMMOCKE, ? JOHN[1] HAMMOT)* was born 25 Jul 1798 in Pittsylvania Co., VA, and died 11 Jun 1873 in Franklin Co., MO. He married DAMARIS RICHARDSON 21 Mar 1819 in Franklin Co., MO. She was born Abt. 1804 in Kentucky, and died Aft. 1870 in Franklin Co., MO.
Children of WILLIAM HAMMACK and DAMARIS RICHARDSON are:

    i.   ELIJAH B.[9] HAMMACK, b. 10 Oct 1826, Franklin Co., MO; d. 19 Nov 1888, Grant Co., OR; m. (1) RACHEL HIATT, 12 Mar 1846, Franklin Co., MO; b. Abt. 1824, Missouri; d. Aft. 1850, Missouri; m. (2) MARY [------], Abt. 1870, Texas; b. Abt. 1847, Tennesseee; d. Aft. 1880, Comanche Co., TX.

    ii.   MARGARET HAMMACK, b. Abt. 1827, Madison Co., MO; d. Aft. 1842, Franklin Co., MO; m. ROBERT PHILLIPS, 16 Feb 1842, Franklin Co., MO.

    iii.   ? ANDREW HAMMACK, b. Abt. 1824, Franklin Co., MO; d. Aft. 1860, Franklin Co., MO.

Key Sources: 1850 Franklin Co., MO, Census, p. 114; 1860 Franklin Co., MO, Census, p. 18; 1870 Franklin Co., MO, Census, p. 226; 1880 Franklin Co., MO, Census, p. 144.

259. MARTIN[8] HAMMACK *(EPHRAIM[7], RICHARD[6], RICHARD[5], RICHARD[4], WILLIAM "O"[3], JOHN[2] HAMMOCKE, ? JOHN[1] HAMMOT)* was born Abt. 1807 in Kentucky, and died 30 Dec 1857 in Parke Co., IN. He married JEMIMA MOORE Abt. 1830 in Parke Co., IN. She was born Abt. 1804 in Tennesseee, and died Aft. 1860 in Parke Co., IN.
Children of MARTIN HAMMACK and JEMIMA MOORE are:

    i.   GILLEYANN[9] HAMMACK, b. 19 Sep 1831, Parke Co., IN; d. 14 May 1885, Parke Co., IN; m. THOMAS M. MOORE, 18 May 1851, Parke Co., IN.

    ii.   MAHALA HAMMACK, b. Abt. 1833, Parke Co., IN; d. 06 Sep 1852, Parke Co., IN.

    iii.   JOAB HAMMACK, b. Abt. 1835, Parke Co., IN; d. Aft. 1860, Parke Co., IN; m. NANCY ELLEN JONES, 05 Aug 1857, Parke Co., IN.

    iv.   MARY ANN HAMMACK, b. Abt. 1836, Parke Co., IN; d. 25 Feb 1858, Parke Co., IN.

    v.   MARGARET HAMMACK, b. Abt. 1841, Parke Co., IN; d. Bef. 1857, Parke Co., IN.

    vi. HENRY C. HAMMACK, b. Abt. 1842, Parke Co., IN; d. Aft. 1870, Parke Co., IN; m. SERILDA J. BRAMBLETT, 02 May 1861, Parke Co., IN.

    vii. COLEMAN HAMMACK, b. Abt. 1844, Parke Co., IN; d. Aft. 1860, Parke Co., IN; m. ELIZABETH DAVIS.

    viii. MATILDA HAMMACK, b. Abt. 1846, Parke Co., IN; d. 06 May 1890, Parke Co., IN; m. ISAAC MILLER, 17 Mar 1860, Parke Co., IN.

    ix. JAMES HAMMACK, b. Abt. 1848, Parke Co., IN; d. Aft. 1850, Parke Co., IN.

Key Sources: 1850 Parke Co., IN, Census, p. 157; 1860 Parke Co., IN, Census, p. 151.

260. JAMES[8] HAMMACK *(EPHRAIM[7], RICHARD[6], RICHARD[5], RICHARD[4], WILLIAM "O"[3], JOHN[2] HAMMOCKE, ? JOHN[1] HAMMOT)* was born Abt. 1810 in Madison Co., KY, and died 28 Oct 1845 in Franklin Co., MO. He married MARGARET GLENN 24 Apr 1827 in Madison Co., KY. She was born Abt. 1794 in Kentucky, and died Aft. 1850 in Franklin Co., MO.

Children of JAMES HAMMACK and MARGARET GLENN are:

    i.   WILLIAM[9] HAMMACK, b. Abt. 1827, Madison Co., KY; d. 1881, Franklin Co., MO; m. ELLENDER BRAY, 24 Jan 1850, Franklin Co., MO; b. 30 Nov 1827, Missouri; d. Aft. 1870, Franklin Co., MO.

    ii. ALEXANDER DUDGEON HAMMACK, b. 16 Mar 1830, Madison Co., KY; d. 16 Jan 1892, Franklin Co., MO; m. (1) ELIZA ANN BRAY, 18 Mar 1866, Madison Co., MO; b. Abt. 1844, Missouri; d. 05 Oct 1887, Madison Co., MO; m. (2) VIRGINIA C. TRAIL, 31 Dec 1889, Franklin Co., MO; b. 17 Dec 1852, Missouri; d. 05 Oct 1919, Franklin Co., MO.

    iii. NANCY MARGARET HAMMACK, b. 22 Feb 1836, Franklin Co., MO; d. 1917, Franklin Co., MO; m. WILLIAM ADOLPH PHILLIPS, 12 Aug 1856, Franklin Co., MO; b. Nov 1831, Missouri; d. 08 Jan 1905, Franklin Co., MO.

Key Sources: 1850 Franklin Co., MO, Census, p. 114; 1860 Franklin Co., MO, Census, p. 14.

261. GEORGE WASHINGTON[8] HAMMACK *(EPHRAIM[7], RICHARD[6], RICHARD[5], RICHARD[4], WILLIAM "O"[3], JOHN[2] HAMMOCKE, ? JOHN[1] HAMMOT)* was born 10 Sep 1817 in Madison Co., KY, and died 11 Jan 1859 in Garrard Co., KY. He married ELIZABETH JOSLIN 01 Jan 1834 in Garrard Co., KY. She was born 16 Oct 1807 in Garrard Co., KY, and died 19 Apr 1870 in Garrard Co., KY.

Children of GEORGE HAMMACK and ELIZABETH JOSLIN are:

    i.   EPHRAIM[9] HAMMACK, b. 21 Apr 1835, Garrard Co., KY; d. 22 Nov 1888, Garrard Co., KY; m. (1) SARAH CLOYD; b. 28 Nov 1838, Kentucky; d. 05 Dec 1883, Garrard Co., KY; m. (2) RACHEL A. REID, 28 Dec 1858, Garrard Co., KY; b. 22 Dec 1837, Garrard Co., KY; d. 02 Sep 1864, Garrard Co., KY.

    ii. REBECCA J. HAMMACK, b. 03 Feb 1838, Garrard Co., KY; d. 24 Jan 1881, Garrard Co., KY; m. THOMAS AUSTIN, 02 Apr 1854, Garrard Co., KY.

    iii. SARAH ELIZABETH HAMMACK, b. 03 Feb 1840, Garrard Co., KY; d. 20 Jun 1921, Garrard Co., KY; m. ISAAC HOLMES, 30 Aug 1858, Garrard Co., KY.

    iv. ANDREW J. HAMMACK, b. 18 Aug 1842, Garrard Co., KY; d. 21 Apr 1912, Garrard Co., KY; m. MARY W. BRADY, 29 Sep 1869, Garrard Co., KY; b. 29 Sep 1844, Lincoln Co., KY; d. 22 Jan 1916, Garrard Co., KY.

    v.   JAMES M. HAMMACK, b. Abt. 1844, Garrard Co., KY; d. Abt. 1864, Andersonville Prison, GA.

Key Sources: 1850 Garrard Co., KY, Census, p. 217; Henry Franklin Hammack, 2: 227-228, 262-263.

262. WILLIAM[8] HAMMACK *(JAMES[7], RICHARD[6], RICHARD[5], RICHARD[4], WILLIAM "O"[3], JOHN[2] HAMMOCKE, ? JOHN[1] HAMMOT)* was born 12 Jun 1800 in Pittsylvania Co., VA, and died 05 Oct 1858 in Hamilton Co., IN. He married ELIZABETH KOFFMAN Abt. 1825 in Grainger Co., TN. She was born 06 Sep 1803 in Tennesseee, and died 26 Aug 1870 in Hamilton Co., IN.

Children of WILLIAM HAMMACK and ELIZABETH KOFFMAN are:

    i. POLLY ANN⁹ HAMMACK, b. Abt. 1826, Tennesseee; d. Aft. 1845, Hamilton Co., IN; m. SAMUEL MONDAY, 13 Mar 1845, Hamilton Co., IN.

    ii. EPHRAIM W. HAMMACK, b. Abt. 1830, Hamilton Co., IN; d. Aft. 1870, Hamilton Co., IN; m. MARY CHEW, 21 Oct 1852, Hamilton Co., IN; b. Abt. 1830, Ohio; d. Aft. 1880, Boone Co., IN.

    iii. LOUISA JANE HAMMACK, b. Abt. 1833, Hamilton Co., IN; d. Abt. 1883, Hamilton Co., IN; m. JOEL JOSEPH CASH, 25 Sep 1856, Hamilton Co., IN.

    iv. WILLIAM MARION HAMMACK, b. Abt. 1837, Hamilton Co., IN; d. Aft. 1880, Hamilton Co., IN; m. NANCY ELLEN PARR, 24 Mar 1858, Hamilton Co., IN; b. Abt. 1836, Tennesseee; d. Aft. 1880, Hamilton Co., IN.

    v. ISAAC N. HAMMACK, b. Abt. 1839, Hamilton Co., IN; d. Aft. 1870, Hamilton Co., IN.

    vi. SARAH E. HAMMACK, b. 04 Jan 1842, Hamilton Co., IN; d. 28 Apr 1887, Clinton Co., IN; m. PETER M. WILES, 31 Mar 1878, Hamilton Co., IN; b. 31 Jul 1840, Hamilton Co., IN.

    vii. ELIZA E. HAMMACK, b. Abt. 1843, Hamilton Co., IN; d. Aft. 1850, Hamilton Co., IN.

Key Sources: 1840 Hamilton Co., IN, Census, p. 151; 1850 Hamilton Co., IN, Census, p. 23; 1860 Hamilton Co., IN, Census, p. 351; 1870 Hamilton Co., IN, Census, p. 202.

263. JOHN BROCK⁸ HAMMACK (*JAMES⁷, RICHARD⁶, RICHARD⁵, RICHARD⁴, WILLIAM "O"³, JOHN² HAMMOCKE, ? JOHN¹ HAMMOT*) was born Abt. 1806 in Tennessee, and died Aft. 1880 in Miles Co., IA. He married SARAH [------] Abt. 1830 in Tennessee. She was born Abt. 1808 in Tennessee, and died Bet. 1860 - 1870 in Jasper Co., IA.

Children of JOHN HAMMACK and SARAH [------] are:

    i. CALVIN⁹ HAMMACK, b. Abt. 1832, Tennesseee; d. Aft. 1870, Amador Co., CA; m. ANN WHITE, 16 Nov 1851, Jasper Co., IA.

    ii. ANN HAMMACK, b. Abt. 1834, Tennesseee; d. Aft. 1855, Jasper Co., IA; m. C. W. HOLWELL, 15 Mar 1855, Jasper Co., IA.

    iii. CALLAWAY HAMMACK, b. Abt. 1836, Indiana; d. Aft. 1910, Harrison Co., IA; m. TELITHA A. VOWELL, 06 Dec 1855, Jasper Co., IA; b. Abt. 1837, Indiana; d. Aft. 1880, Mills Co., IA.

    iv. ELIZABETH HAMMACK, b. Abt. 1838, Indiana; d. Aft. 1854, Jasper Co., IA; m. LEONARD LIKENS, 01 Feb 1854, Jasper Co., IA.

    v. SARAH HAMMACK, b. Abt. 1840, Indiana; d. Aft. 1856, Jasper Co., IA; m. HARDING VANDERPOOL, 25 Mar 1856, Jasper Co., IA.

    vi. JOHN HAMMACK, b. Abt. 1842, Tennesseee; d. Aft. 1861, Jasper Co., IA; m. AMANDA PARKER, 09 Jun 1861, Jasper Co., IA.

    vii. LOUISA HAMMACK, b. Abt. 1844, Indiana; d. Aft. 1863, Jasper Co., IA; m. SAMUEL HUNTER, 17 Sep 1863, Jasper Co., IA.

    viii. ANDREW HAMMACK, b. Abt. 1846, Indiana; d. Aft. 1860, Jasper Co., IA.

    ix. MATILDA HAMMACK, b. Abt. 1848, Indiana; d. Aft. 1863, Jasper Co., IA; m. JAMES DENSMORE, 28 Jun 1863, Jasper Co., IA.

    x. JACOB HAMMACK, b. Abt. 1849, Iowa; d. Aft. 1860, Jasper Co., IA.

    xi. LAFAYETTE HAMMACK, b. Abt. 1852, Iowa; d. Aft. 1860, Jasper Co., IA.

Key Sources: 1850 Jasper Co., IA, Census, p. 374B; 1860 Jasper Co., IA, Census, p. 929; 1870 Jasper Co., IA, Census, p. 462; 1880 Mills Co., IA, Census, p. 404.

264. JAMES L.[8] HAMMACK *(WILLIAM[7], RICHARD[6], RICHARD[5], RICHARD[4], WILLIAM "O"[3], JOHN[2] HAMMOCKE, ? JOHN[1] HAMMOT)* was born 05 Aug 1801 in Pittsylvania Co., VA, and died 03 May 1862 in Mercer Co., MO. He married SARAH ANN "SALLY" LANE 30 Dec 1823 in Garrard Co., KY. She was born 06 Jun 1806 in Kentucky, and died 01 Sep 1891 in Harrison Co., MO.

Children of JAMES HAMMACK and SARAH LANE are:

    i.   WILLIAM[9] HAMMACK, b. 27 Nov 1824, Kentucky.

    ii. JANE HAMMACK, b. 11 Mar 1826, Indiana; d. 24 Jul 1857, Harrison Co., MO; m. WILLIAM REEDER; b. 07 Apr 1825, Indiana; d. 11 Feb 1892, Harrison Co., MO.

    iii. SAMUEL HAMMACK, b. 15 Apr 1828, Indiana; d. 23 Jan 1898, Harrison Co., MO; m. (1) ELIZABETH [------], Abt. 1851, Indiana; b. Abt. 1832, Indiana; d. Abt. 1873, Missouri; m. (2) NANCY [------], Abt. 1875, Harrison Co., MO; b. Abt. 1830, Virginia; d. Aft. 1880, Harrison Co., MO.

    iv. SARAH HAMMACK, b. 06 Jun 1830, Indiana; d. Aft. 1850, Morgan Co., IN; m. GREENBERRY HARRISON BUIS; b. Abt. 1819; d. 23 Sep 1872, Indiana.

    v.   ELIZABETH HAMMACK, b. 07 Jun 1832, Indiana.

    vi. JAMES LANE HAMMACK, b. 30 May 1834, Morgan Co., IN; d. 06 Dec 1903, Pottawatomie Co., OK; m. (1) MARTHA J. BRIDGES, Abt. 1859, Indiana; b. Abt. 1838; d. Bef. 1882; m. (2) SARAH E. HUDSON, 02 Jul 1883, Carroll Co., AR; b. 1866, Missouri; d. 26 Aug 1893, Carroll Co., AR; m. (3) MARY LOUELDA CHRISTIAN, 25 Jun 1894, Carroll Co., AR; m. (4) CYNTHIA A. THURMAN, 21 Sep 1900, Carroll Co., AR.

    vii. ANNA HAMMACK, b. 10 Jun 1836, Putnam Co., IN; d. 13 Jun 1921, Harrison Co., MO; m. JAMES P. BUIS.

    viii. FANNY HAMMACK, b. 28 Apr 1838, Putnam Co., IN; d. 30 Aug 1913, Missouri.

    ix. GEORGE M. HAMMACK, b. 01 Sep 1840, Hendricks Co., IN; d. 21 Sep 1913, Putnam Co., MO; m. MARIETTA E. LUELLEN, 20 Jul 1864, Harrison Co., MO; b. 05 Feb 1848, Iowa; d. 25 May 1933, Putnam Co., MO.

    x.   JOHN WILSON HAMMACK, b. 27 Mar 1843, Hendricks Co., IN; d. Aft. 1894, Missouri; m. HELLEN H. WELLER, 25 Mar 1894, Bates Co., MO; b. 28 Apr 1876, Vernon Co., MO; d. Aft. 1894, Bates Co., MO.

    xi. LORINDA HAMMACK, b. Abt. 1845, Hendricks Co., IN; d. Aft. 1860, Harrison Co., MO.

    xii. ISAIAH HAMMACK, b. 18 May 1847, Morgan Co., IN; d. 1916, Harrison Co., MO; m. ELIZABETH JOSEPHINE CHAMBERS, Abt. 1890, Harrison Co., MO; b. 15 Sep 1857, Missouri; d. 04 Jan 1919, Harrison Co., MO.

Key Sources: 1850 Morgan Co., IN, Census, p. 169; 1860 Harrison Co., MO, Census, p. 690; 1870 Harrison Co., MO, Census, pp. 11, 151.

265. GEORGE[8] HAMMACK *(WILLIAM[7], RICHARD[6], RICHARD[5], RICHARD[4], WILLIAM "O"[3], JOHN[2] HAMMOCKE, ? JOHN[1] HAMMOT)* was born Abt. 1806 in Tennessee, and died Bet. 1880 - 1882 in Vigo Co., IN. He married MARY A. [------] Abt. 1835 in Sullivan Co., IN. She was born 24 Dec 1809 in Kentucky, and died 25 Mar 1882 in Vigo Co., IN.

Children of GEORGE HAMMACK and MARY [------] are:

    i.   SARAH ANN[9] HAMMACK, b. 22 Jul 1836, Illinois; d. Aft. 1850, Putnam Co., IN; m. JOAB CAVINESS.

    ii. ASENITH FRANCES HAMMACK, b. Abt. 1841, Vigo Co., IN; d. Aft. 1860, Morgan Co., IN.

    iii. MARY THELMA HAMMACK, b. 14 Mar 1846, Putnam Co., IN; d. Aft. 1860, Morgan Co., IN.

    iv. GEORGE W. HAMMACK, b. Abt. 1849, Putnam Co., IN; d. Aft. 1870, Morgan Co., IN.

    v.   DANIEL B. HAMMACK, b. Abt. 1854, Morgan Co., IN.

Key Sources: 1840 Vigo Co., IN, Census, p. 426; 1850 Putnam Co., IN, Census, p. 473; 1860 Morgan Co., IN, Census, p. 748; 1870 Morgan Co., IN, Census, p. 377.

266. DANIEL[8] HAMMACK *(WILLIAM[7], RICHARD[6], RICHARD[5], RICHARD[4], WILLIAM "O"[3], JOHN[2] HAMMOCKE, ? JOHN[1] HAMMOT)* was born 08 Mar 1811 in Madison Co., KY, and died 30 Apr 1888 in Anderson Co., KY. He married (1) SARAH GOODMAN 05 Mar 1832 in Madison Co., KY. She was born 15 Jan 1815 in Kentucky, and died 14 Feb 1839 in Anderson Co., KY. He married (2) FRANCES GOODMAN 15 Jul 1839 in Madison Co., KY. She was born 18 Aug 1823 in Kentucky, and died 01 Mar 1901 in Anderson Co., KY.
Children of DANIEL HAMMACK and SARAH GOODMAN are:

      i. GEORGE[9] HAMMACK, b. Abt. 1834, Anderson Co., KY; d. Bet. 1862 - 1870, Anderson Co., KY; m. ESTHER [------], Abt. 1853, Anderson Co., KY; b. Abt. 1832, Kentucky; d. Aft. 1860, Anderson Co., KY.

      ii. MARY HAMMACK, b. 15 May 1835, Kentucky; d. Aft. 1850, Washington Co., KY; m. ZACHARIAH KING.

      iii. WILLIAM HAMMACK, b. 12 Mar 1837, Anderson Co., KY; d. Aft. 1880, Jasper Co., IA; m. EMILY WEIS; b. 26 Aug 1841, Kentucky.

Key Sources: 1850 Washington Co., KY, Census, p. 163; 1860 Anderson Co., KY, Census, p. 528; 1880 Anderson Co., KY, Census, p. 359.

267. COLEMAN[8] HAMMACK *(LEWIS[7], RICHARD[6], RICHARD[5], RICHARD[4], WILLIAM "O"[3], JOHN[2] HAMMOCKE, ? JOHN[1] HAMMOT)* was born Abt. 1802 in Pittsylvania Co., VA, and died Bef. 04 Jan 1843 in Monroe Co., MO. He married NANCY SCOTT 16 May 1822 in Madison Co., MO. She was born Abt. 1800 in Virginia, and died Aft. 1880 in Pulaski Co., MO.
Children of COLEMAN HAMMACK and NANCY SCOTT are:

      i. SARAH ANN[9] HAMMACK, b. 06 Jan 1823, Madison Co., KY; d. 21 Aug 1859, Pulaski Co., MO; m. PLESANT GROVE TURNER, 16 Sep 1841, Monroe Co., MO.

426.   ii. WILLIAM HENRY HAMMACK, b. 15 Sep 1824, Madison Co., KY; d. 18 Oct 1890, Pulaski Co., MO.

427.   iii. ANDREW H. HAMMACK, b. Abt. 1826, Madison Co., KY; d. 07 Jan 1884, Osage Co., MO.

      iv. HENRY HAMMACK, b. Abt. 1828, Madison Co., KY; d. Aft. 1848, Franklin Co., MO; m. ELIZABETH J. WEEDEN, 29 May 1848, Franklin Co., MO.

428.   v. ASA HAMMACK, b. Abt. 1832, Floyd Co., KY; d. 28 Feb 1900, Sebastian Co., AR.

      vi. REBECCA HAMMACK, b. Abt. 1834, Kentucky; d. May 1883, Pulaski Co., MO; m. CALVIN KANATZER, 11 Jan 1855, Franklin Co., MO.

      vii. NANCY JANE HAMMACK, b. Abt. 1837, Missouri; d. Aft. 1880, Pulaski Co., MO; m. JOSEPH HENRY PICKERING, 17 Oct 1861, Pulaski Co., KY.

      viii. JOSHUA HAMMACK, b. Abt. 1838, Missouri; d. 14 Nov 1867, Pulaski Co., MO.

429.   ix. JAMES G. HAMMACK, b. Abt. 1840, Missouri; d. 14 Nov 1867, Pulaski Co., MO.

Key Sources: 1830 Madison Co., KY, Census, p. 157; 1840 Howard Co., MO, Census, p. 32; 1850 Franklin Co., MO, Census, pp. 67, 109, 114; 1880 Pulaski Co., MO, Census, p. 408.

268. BENJAMIN[8] HAMMACK *(LEWIS[7], RICHARD[6], RICHARD[5], RICHARD[4], WILLIAM "O"[3], JOHN[2] HAMMOCKE, ? JOHN[1] HAMMOT)* was born Abt. 1804 in Pittsylvania Co., VA, and died 1875 in Marion Co., IL. He married SARAH HULL Abt. 1823 in Madison Co., KY. She was born Abt. 1808 in Kentucky, and died Aft. 1880 in Marion Co., IL.
Children of BENJAMIN HAMMACK and SARAH HULL are:

      i. ELIZABETH[9] HAMMACK, b. Abt. 1824, Tennessee; d. Aft. 1880, Marion Co., IL.

    ii.   JUDGE LEWIS HAMMACK, b. 25 Jun 1825, Warren Co., TN; d. Aft. 1894, Perry Co., IL; m. (1) CORDELIA EDWARDS, Abt. 1855, Perry Co., IL; b. Abt. 1832, Tennessee; d. Bet. 1870 - 1880, Perry Co., IL; m. (2) MARIE J. RIGG GUTHRIE, Bef. 1880, Perry Co., IL; b. Abt. 1842, Tennessee; d. Aft. 1880, Perry Co., IL.

430.   iii.   AMANDA E. HAMMACK, b. Abt. 1827, Missouri; d. Aft. 1870, Perry Co., IL.

    iv.   WILLIAM HAMMACK, b. Abt. 1829, Perry Co., IL; d. Aft. 1894, Illinois; m. LIZZIE ORABELL THREFFTZS, 15 Sep 1885, Perry Co., IL.

    v.   RICHARD HAMMACK, b. 1831, Perry Co., IL; d. Abt. 1849, California.

    vi.   ZEBEDEE HAMMACK, b. 06 Jan 1837, Perry Co., IL; d. 22 May 1863, Vicksburg, MS.

    vii.   NANCY J. HAMMACK, b. Abt. 1840, Perry Co., IL; d. Aft. 1860, Perry Co., IL.

   viii.   THOMAS H. HAMMACK, b. Abt. 1843, Perry Co., IL; d. Aft. 1894, Illinois.

    ix.   BENJAMIN F. HAMMACK, b. Abt. 1849, Perry Co., IL; d. Aft. 1894, Perry Co., IL; m. NANCY LAUGHTON; b. Abt. 1852, Illinois; d. Aft. 1880, Perry Co., IL.

Key Sources: 1850 Perry Co., IL, Census, pp. 338, 383, 388; 1860 Perry Co., IL, Census, p. 2; 1870 Perry Co., IL, Census, p. 102; 1880 Marion Co., IL, Census, p. 233; Henry Franklin Hammack, 2: 130.

269. HUGH M.[8] HAMMACK *(JAMES[7], WILLIAM[6], JOHN[5], WILLIAM "THE YOUNGER"[4], WILLIAM "O"[3], JOHN[2] HAMMOCKE, ? JOHN[1] HAMMOT)* was born Abt. 1824 in Lunenburg Co., VA, and died Aft. 1870 in Lunenburg Co., VA. He married MARTHA R. [------] Abt. 1844 in Lunenburg Co., VA. She was born Abt. 1827 in Brunswick Co., VA, and died 10 Apr 1857 in Lunenburg Co., VA.
Children of HUGH HAMMACK and MARTHA [------] are:

    i.   JOSEPH[9] HAMMACK, b. Abt. 1845, Lunenburg Co., VA; d. Aft. 1850, Lunenburg Co., VA.

    ii.   ELIZABETH HAMMACK, b. Abt. 1846, Lunenburg Co., VA; d. Aft. 1850, Lunenburg Co., VA.

   iii.   GEORGE HAMMACK, b. Abt. 1849, Lunenburg Co., VA; d. Aft. 1850, Lunenburg Co., VA.

Key Sources: Lunenburg Co., VA, Deed Book 35, pp. 622-23; 1870 Lunenburg Co., VA, Census, p. 495.

Generation No. 9

270. JOHN[9] HAMMICK *(MICHAEL[8], MICHAEL[7] HAMICK, MICHAEL[6] HAMMICK, MICHAEL[5], THOMAS[4] HAMICK, HENRYE[3] HAMICKE, JOHN[2] HAMMOCKE, ? JOHN[1] HAMMOT)* was born Abt. 23 Sep 1788 in Yealmpton, Devonshire. He married MARY [------].
Children of JOHN HAMMICK and MARY [------] are:

431.   i.   JOHN[10] HEMMICK, b. 20 May 1814, Yealmpton, Devonshire.

    ii.   MICHAEL HAMMICK, b. Abt. 27 Oct 1816, Yealmpton, Devonshire.

   iii.   BETSEY HAMICK, b. Abt. 13 Sep 1818, St. Columb Minor, Cornwall.

    iv.   MARY ANN HAMMICK, b. Abt. 05 Nov 1820, Brixton and Yealmpton, Devonshire.

    v.   RICHARD HAMMICK, b. Abt. 17 Aug 1823, Brixton and Yealmpton, Devonshire.

Key Sources: Yealmpton Parish Register; St. Columb Minor Parish Register.

271. THOMAS B.[9] HAMMOCK *(SAMUEL[8], JOHN[7], JOHN[6], WILLIAM[5], WILLIAM "THE ELDER"[4], WILLIAM "O"[3], JOHN[2] HAMMOCKE, ? JOHN[1] HAMMOT)* was born Abt. 1797 in Lincoln Co., GA, and died Abt. 1844 in Chambers Co., AL. He married MATILDA SUDDITH Abt. 1820 in Lincoln Co., GA. She was born Abt. 1802 in Lincoln Co., GA, and died Aft. 1850 in Chambers Co., AL.
Children of THOMAS HAMMOCK and MATILDA SUDDITH are:

    i.   ELIZA G.[10] HAMMOCK, b. Abt. 1820, Lincoln Co., GA; d. Aft. 1850, Chambers Co., AL.

    ii.   SUSANNAH HAMMOCK, b. Abt. 1822, Lincoln Co., GA; d. Aft. 1839, Lincoln Co., GA.

432.   iii.   JEREMIAH G. HAMMOCK, b. 10 Aug 1823, Lincoln Co., GA; d. 14 Feb 1899, Upshur Co., TX.
433.   iv.   JOHN A. HAMMOCK, b. Oct 1825, Lincoln Co., GA; d. 22 Jan 1900, Union Parish, LA.
        v.   MARIAH HAMMOCK, b. Abt. 1828, Lincoln Co., GA; d. Aft. 1839, Chambers Co., AL.
       vi.   FRANCES HAMMOCK, b. Abt. 1832, Lincoln Co., GA; d. Aft. 1860, Union Parish, LA; m. THOMAS GRAY, 09 Nov 1852, Chambers Co., AL; b. Abt. 1835, Georgia; d. Bet. 1860 - 1870, Union Parish, LA.
      vii.   THOMAS J. HAMMOCK, b. Abt. 1834, Lincoln Co., GA; d. Aft. 1880, Upshur Co., TX; m. ELIZABETH MATHIS, 12 Aug 1882, Upshur Co., TX.
     viii.   MARY ANN HAMMOCK, b. 23 Jun 1835, Lincoln Co., GA; d. 15 Nov 1916, Union Parish, LA; m. (1) RICHARD S. SHERRER, 25 Jan 1855, Chambers Co., AL; m. (2) RICHMOND C. HOWELL, 22 May 1862, Union Parish, LA; d. 26 Jun 1864, Confederate States Army; m. (3) QUINCY ADAMS BYRAM, 27 Sep 1866, Union Parish, LA; d. 24 Apr 1911, Union Parish, LA.
       ix.   MARTHA HAMMOCK, b. Abt. 1838, Lincoln Co., GA; d. Aft. 1850, Chambers Co., AL; m. [-------] DICKSON.
        x.   LUCINDA HAMMOCK, b. Abt. 1840, Chambers Co., AL; d. Aft. 1857, Union Parish, LA; m. VIRGIL CRANFORD, Abt. 1857, Union Parish, LA.

Key Sources: 1820 Lincoln Co., GA, Census, p. 161; 1830 Lincoln Co., GA, Census, p. 74; J. H. Austin, *Georgia Intestate Records* (Baltimore, MD, 1985), p. 133; Chambers Co., AL, Will Book 1, p. 148; 1840 Chambers Co., AL, Census, p. 229; 1850 Chambers Co., AL, Census, p. 315.

272. JOHN B.[9] HAMMOCK *(SAMUEL[8], JOHN[7], JOHN[6], WILLIAM[5], WILLIAM "THE ELDER"[4], WILLIAM "O"[3], JOHN[2] HAMMOCKE, ? JOHN[1] HAMMOT)* was born Abt. 1799 in Lincoln Co., GA, and died Aft. 1850 in Wilkes Co., GA. He married LOUISA MOREMAN Bef. 1835 in Wilkes Co., GA, daughter of THOMAS MOREMAN and RACHEL SIMMONS.
Children of JOHN HAMMOCK and LOUISA MOREMAN are:
        i.   SON[10] HAMMOCK, b. Bet. 1820 - 1825, Wilkes Co., GA; d. Aft. 1830, Lincoln Co., GA.
434.   ii.   SAMUEL MOREMAN HAMMOCK, b. 28 Sep 1836, Wilkes Co., GA; d. 01 Nov 1877, Harris Co., TX.
       iii.   STERN HAMMOCK, b. Abt. 1838, Wilkes Co., GA; d. Aft. 1850, Lincoln Co., GA.
       iv.   ANALYZA HAMMOCK, b. Abt. 1840, Wilkes Co., GA; d. Aft. 1850, Lincoln Co., GA.

Key Sources: 1840 Lincoln Co., GA, Census, p. 211; 1850 Wilkes Co., GA, Census, p. 317; 1850 Meriwether Co., GA, Census, p. 368; 1860 Wilkes Co., GA, Census, p. 775.

273. JOHN S.[9] HAMMACK *(WILLIAM[8], JOHN[7], JOHN[6], WILLIAM[5], WILLIAM "THE ELDER"[4], WILLIAM "O"[3], JOHN[2] HAMMOCKE, ? JOHN[1] HAMMOT)* was born 09 Mar 1800 in Lincoln Co., GA, and died Aft. 1870 in Yell Co., AR. He married FRANCIS [------] Abt. 1829 in Alabama. She was born Abt. 1814 in Georgia, and died Bet. 1860 - 1870 in Louisiana.
Children of JOHN HAMMACK and FRANCIS [------] are:
435.   i.   WILLIAM P.[10] HAMMACK, b. Abt. 1830, Alabama; d. Aft. 1880, Yell Co., AR.
        ii.   GEORGE HAMMACK, b. Abt. 1833, Alabama; d. Aft. 1850, Chambers Co., AL.
       iii.   ROBERT HAMMACK, b. Abt. 1835, Alabama; d. Aft. 1856, Union Parish, LA; m. JANE HARRIS, 13 Nov 1856, Union Parish, LA.
       iv.   ELIZABETH HAMMACK, b. Abt. 1838, Alabama; d. Aft. 1850, Chambers Co., AL.
        v.   JOHN W. HAMMACK, b. Abt. 1841, Alabama; d. Aft. 1860, Union Parish, LA.
       vi.   EPHRAIM B. HAMMACK, b. Abt. 1843, Alabama; d. Aft. 1880, Yell Co., AR.

vii. FRANCIS M. HAMMACK, b. Abt. 1846, Alabama; d. Aft. 1900, Yell Co., AR; m. MARTHA [------], Abt. 1870, Yell Co., AR; b. Abt. 1851, Arkansas; d. Aft. 1900, Yell Co., AR.

viii. MARTIN HAMMACK, b. Abt. 1848, Alabama; d. Aft. 1850, Chambers Co., AL.

Key Sources: 1840 Chambers Co., AL, Census, p. 229; 1850 Chambers Co., AL, Census, p. 309; 1860 Union Parish, LA, p. 527; 1870 Yell Co., AR, Census, p. 575.

274. PASCHAL⁹ HAMMACK *(WILLIAM⁸, JOHN⁷, JOHN⁶, WILLIAM⁵, WILLIAM "THE ELDER"⁴, WILLIAM "O"³, JOHN² HAMMOCKE, ? JOHN¹ HAMMOT)* was born 25 Jan 1806 in Lincoln Co., GA, and died 21 Oct 1890 in Newton Co., MS. He married CHARLOTTE VINCENT 27 Aug 1841 in Chambers Co., AL. She was born Abt. 1822 in Georgia, and died Aug 1879 in Newton Co., GA.
Children of PASCHAL HAMMACK and CHARLOTTE VINCENT are:

i. WILLIAM JACKSON¹⁰ HAMMACK, b. Abt. 1842, Alabama; d. Aft. 1860, Newton Co., MS.

ii. LETITIA COLISTA HAMMACK, b. Abt. 1854, Alabama; d. Aft. 1870, Newton Co., MS.

Key Sources: 1850 Coosa Co., AL, Census, p. 73; 1860 Newton Co., MS, Census, p. 754; 1870 Newton Co., MS, Census, p. 492; 1880 Newton Co., MS, Mortality Schedule, p. 54; Newton Co., MS, Masonic Records, 1890.

275. ALFRED D.⁹ HAMMACK *(WILLIAM⁸, JOHN⁷, JOHN⁶, WILLIAM⁵, WILLIAM "THE ELDER"⁴, WILLIAM "O"³, JOHN² HAMMOCKE, ? JOHN¹ HAMMOT)* was born 27 Nov 1811 in Pulaski Co., GA, and died 11 Mar 1891 in Smith Co., MS. He married MARTHA ANN WEATHERS Abt. 1840 in Chambers Co., AL. She was born 1822 in Alabama, and died Jun 1887 in Smith Co., MS.
Children of ALFRED HAMMACK and MARTHA WEATHERS are:

i. CLARINDA S.¹⁰ HAMMACK, b. Abt. 1842, Alabama; d. Aft. 1860, Tallapoosa Co., AL; m. JASPER M. BAILEY, 12 Dec 1865, Tallapoosa Co., AL.

ii. LUCINDA URSULA HAMMACK, b. 29 Nov 1843, Alabama; d. 22 Nov 1907, Smith Co., MS; m. WILLIAM HARRISON WILKERSON; b. 04 Sep 1836, Alabama.

iii. HENRIETTA C. HAMMACK, b. Abt. 1846, Alabama; d. Aft. 1865, Tallapoosa Co., AL; m. WESLEY F. BAILEY, 12 Dec 1865, Tallapoosa Co., AL.

iv. COLISTA RENTHIA HAMMACK, b. Abt. 1847, Alabama; d. 02 Apr 1898, Smith Co., MS; m. ALFRED MOORE ANDERSON.

v. ALABAMA C. HAMMACK, b. Abt. 1850, Alabama; d. 1915, Smith Co., MS; m. DAVID W. CHARLES.

vi. RUTHY B. HAMMACK, b. Abt. 1853, Alabama; d. Aft. 1870, Smith Co., MS.

vii. WILLIAM M. HAMMACK, b. Abt. 1855, Alabama; d. Aft. 1880, Smith Co., MS.

viii. MARTHA A. HAMMACK, b. Abt. 1857, Alabama; d. Aft. 1870, Smith Co., MS.

ix. MARION W. HAMMACK, b. Abt. 1858, Alabama; d. Aft. 1880, Smith Co., MS.

x. MARY HAMMACK, b. Abt. 1861, Alabama; d. Aft. 1880, Smith Co., MS.

xi. CHARLES HAMMACK, b. Abt. 1867, Alabama; d. Bef. 1880, Smith Co., MS.

Key Sources: 1850 Tallapoosa Co., AL, Census, p. 19; 1855 Tallapoosa Co., AL, State Census; 1870 Scott Co., MS, Census, p. 165; 1880 Smith Co., MS, Census, p. 348.

276. WILLIAM B.⁹ HAMMACK *(WILLIAM⁸, JOHN⁷, JOHN⁶, WILLIAM⁵, WILLIAM "THE ELDER"⁴, WILLIAM "O"³, JOHN² HAMMOCKE, ? JOHN¹ HAMMOT)* was born 30 Sep 1815 in Pulaski Co., GA, and died Aft. 1880 in Lee Co., AL. He married SUSANNAH LIGON 13 Apr 1848 in Chambers Co., AL. She was born Abt. 1825 in GA, and died Aft. 1880 in Lee Co., AL.
Children of WILLIAM HAMMACK and SUSANNAH LIGON are:

i.   EUGENIA[10] HAMMACK, b. Abt. 1852, Russell Co., AL; d. Aft. 1870, Muscogee Co., GA; m. ROBERT SHORT.

436. ii. WILLIAM DAVID HAMMACK, b. 15 Feb 1853, Russell Co., AL; d. 24 Sep 1915, Kaufman Co., TX.

iii. PASCHALL H. HAMMACK, b. Abt. 1855, Russell Co., AL; d. Aft. 1870, Abilene, TX.

iv. JOHN D. HAMMACK, b. Abt. 1858, Russell Co., AL; d. Aft. 1915, Lee Co., AL.

v.   WESLEY W. HAMMACK, b. Abt. 1860, Russell Co., AL; d. Bet. 1880 - 1915, Kaufman Co., TX.

vi. ROBERT E. LEE HAMMACK, b. Abt. 1863, Russell Co., AL; d. Aft. 1915, Muscogee Co., GA.

vii. JOSEPH HAMMACK, b. Abt. 1865, Russell Co., AL; d. Bef. 1915, Abilene, TX.

viii. INEZ HAMMACK, b. Abt. 1868, Russell Co., AL; d. Aft. 1915, Young Co., TX; m. ROBERT MCKINNEY.

Key Sources: F. W. Johnson and E. W. Winkler, *A History of Texas and Texans* (5 vols., New York, NY, and Chicago, IL, 1914); 1880 Lee Co., AL, Census, p. 121.

277. JEREMIAH[9] HAMMACK (*JOHN[8], JOHN[7], JOHN[6], WILLIAM[5], WILLIAM "THE ELDER"[4], WILLIAM "O"[3], JOHN[2] HAMMOCKE, ? JOHN[1] HAMMOT*) was born 09 Jan 1806 in Lincoln Co., GA, and died 22 Nov 1888 in Lee Co., AL. He married MARTHA MCKINNEY 07 Sep 1831 in Lincoln Co., GA, daughter of TRAVIS MCKINNEY and PATSY LEVERETT. She was born 06 Jul 1814 in Lincoln Co., GA, and died 21 Mar 1882 in Lee Co., AL.
Children of JEREMIAH HAMMACK and MARTHA MCKINNEY are:

i.   JOHN M.[10] HAMMACK, b. 04 Aug 1832, Lincoln Co., GA; d. 10 Jun 1905, Fannin Co., TX.

ii. JOSEPH H. HAMMACK, b. 18 Jun 1834, Lincoln Co., GA; d. 18 Nov 1899, Dallas Co., TX; m. MARY E. GUICE, 08 Jan 1858, Tallapoosa Co., AL; b. 18 Apr 1840, Georgia; d. 12 Jul 1912, Dallas Co., TX.

iii. EMILY L. HAMMACK, b. 26 Sep 1836, Lincoln Co., GA; d. Aft. 1854, Chambers Co., AL; m. EZEKIAL W. GILHAM, 07 Dec 1854, Chambers Co., AL.

iv. ROBERT SIMEON HAMMACK, b. 18 Nov 1838, Lincoln Co., GA; d. Aft. 1900, Lee Co., AL; m. (1) ELVA JANE MORRIS, 08 Dec 1859, Tallapoosa Co., AL; b. Abt. 1844, Georgia; d. 30 Aug 1885, Lee Co., AL; m. (2) LOULA WRIGHT, 09 Apr 1887, Tallapoosa Co., AL; b. Oct 1842, Georgia; d. Aft. 1900, Lee Co., AL.

v.   TRAVIS G. HAMMACK, b. 20 Nov 1840, Lincoln Co., GA; d. 13 Sep 1898, Denton Co., TX; m. LAURA A. YARBROUGH, 27 Feb 1866, Chambers Co., AL; b. 06 Feb 1848, Alabama; d. 30 Jun 1898, Denton Co., TX.

vi. WILLIAM HAMMACK, b. Abt. 1844, Lincoln Co., GA; d. Aft. 1865, Lee Co., AL.

437. vii. ALFONZO J. "FONEY" HAMMACK, b. 23 Jun 1849, Macon Co., AL; d. 25 Jun 1893, Williamson Co., TX.

Key Sources: 1850 Macon Co., AL, Census, p. 255; 1860 Chambers Co., AL, Census, p. 951; 1870 Lee Co., AL, Census, p.381; "Jeremiah Hammack Family Bible," *Tap Roots*, Vol. 7, No. 3 (1970): 123-125.

278. JOHN G.[9] HAMMOCK (*JOHN[8], JOHN[7], JOHN[6], WILLIAM[5], WILLIAM "THE ELDER"[4], WILLIAM "O"[3], JOHN[2] HAMMOCKE, ? JOHN[1] HAMMOT*) was born Abt. 1809 in Lincoln Co., GA, and died Aft. 1870 in Murray Co., GA. He married ELIZABETH MEALOR 16 Sep 1833 in Oglethorpe Co., GA. She was born Abt. 1808 in Oglethorpe Co., GA, and died Aft. 1870 in Murray Co., GA.
Children of JOHN HAMMOCK and ELIZABETH MEALOR are:

i.   MARTHA A. E.[10] HAMMOCK, b. Abt. 1836, Oglethorpe Co., GA; d. Aft. 1860, Murray Co., GA.

ii. MARY E. HAMMOCK, b. Abt. 1838, Oglethorpe Co., GA; d. Aft. 1870, Murray Co., GA; m. JOHN T. CHRISTIAN, 26 Jul 1854, Murray Co., GA.

iii. ISHAM B. HAMMOCK, b. Abt. 1839, Oglethorpe Co., GA; d. Aft. 1850, Murray Co., GA.

iv. SARAH E. HAMMOCK, b. Abt. 1842, Oglethorpe Co., GA; d. Aft. 1860, Murray Co., GA; m. JOHN H. MOORE, 23 Feb 1865, Murray Co., GA.

v. JAMES W. HAMMOCK, b. Abt. 1844, Oglethorpe Co., GA; d. Aft. 1880, Murray Co., GA; m. NANCY ELLROD, Abt. 1872, Murray Co., GA; b. Abt. 1850, Georgia; d. Aft. 1880, Murray Co., GA.

Key Sources: 1840 Oglethorpe Co., GA, Census, p. 91; 1850 Murray Co., GA, Census, p. 268; 1860 Murray Co., GA, Census, p. 47; 1870 Murray Co., GA, Census, p. 524.

279. SIMEON[9] HAMMACK *(JOHN[8], JOHN[7], JOHN[6], WILLIAM[5], WILLIAM "THE ELDER"[4], WILLIAM "O"[3], JOHN[2] HAMMOCKE, ? JOHN[1] HAMMOT)* was born 29 Nov 1811 in Wilkes Co., GA, and died Aft. 1880 in Lee Co., AL. He married (1) UNKNOWN Abt. 1835 in Georgia. He married (2) JANE C. Hammack Abt. 1847 in Alabama. She was born Abt. 1824 in Alabama, and died Aft. 1880 in Lee Co., AL.

Child of SIMEON HAMMACK and UNKNOWN is:

i. ANGELINA[10] HAMMACK, b. Abt. 1836, Georgia.

Children of SIMEON HAMMACK and JANE Hammack are:

ii. MARY A.[10] HAMMACK, b. Jan 1848, Barbour Co., AL; d. Aft. 1900, Lee Co., AL.

iii. JEREMIAH HAMMACK, b. Abt. 1849, Barbour Co., AL; d. Bet. 1850 - 1860, Alabama.

iv. JOHN T. HAMMACK, b. Jan 1850, Barbour Co., AL; d. Aft. 1900, Lee Co., AL; m. EMMA [------]; b. May 1865, Alabama; d. Aft. 1900, Lee Co., AL.

v. SARAH HAMMACK, b. Abt. 1851, Barbour Co., AL; d. Aft. 1870, Lee Co., AL.

Key Sources: Henry Co., GA, Deed Book F, p. 409; Troup Co., GA, Deed Book D, p. 341; Newton Co., GA, Annual Returns, 1827-1837, p. 457; 1850 Barbour Co., AL, Census, p. 215; 1860 Barbour Co., AL, Census, p. 313; 1870 Barbour Co., AL, Census, p. 29; 1880 Lee Co., AL, Census, p. 106; Simeon Hammack, Indian War Pension Application, SC-1454 Alabama, 9 September 1892, Florida War. Some researchers maintain that Simeon Hammack married Jane Caroline HAMMACK on 15 October 1843 in Barbour Co., AL. She may have been a daughter of Thomas and Mary Hammack and thus Simeon's first cousin.

280. JAMES[9] HAMMOCK *(ELIJAH[8], JOHN[7], JOHN[6], WILLIAM[5], WILLIAM "THE ELDER"[4], WILLIAM "O"[3], JOHN[2] HAMMOCKE, ? JOHN[1] HAMMOT)* was born Abt. 1807 in Lincoln Co., GA, and died Aft. 1870 in Twiggs Co., GA. He married (1) MARY CRANFORD Abt. 1830 in Twiggs Co., GA. She was born Abt. 1810 in Twiggs Co., GA, and died Abt. 1849 in Twiggs Co., GA. He married (2) ANN JANE CRANFORD Abt. 1850 in Twiggs Co., GA. She was born Abt. 1827 in Twiggs Co., GA, and died Aft. 1860 in Twiggs Co., GA.

Children of JAMES HAMMOCK and MARY CRANFORD are:

i. AMANDA[10] HAMMOCK, b. Abt. 1832, Twiggs Co., GA; d. Aft. 1850, Twiggs Co., GA.

ii. LOUISA HAMMOCK, b. Abt. 1833, Twiggs Co., GA; d. Aft. 1850, Twiggs Co., GA.

438. iii. WILLIAM J. HAMMOCK, b. Abt. 1835, Twiggs Co., GA; d. 25 Jun 1862, King's School House, VA.

iv. JANE HAMMOCK, b. Abt. 1837, Twiggs Co., GA; d. Aft. 1850, Twiggs Co., GA.

v. JAMES M. HAMMOCK, b. Abt. 1839, Twiggs Co., GA; d. Aft. 1850, Twiggs Co., GA.

vi. MISSOURI HAMMOCK, b. Abt. 1841, Twiggs Co., GA; d. Aft. 1860, Twiggs Co., GA; m. NEWMAN NELSON, Abt. 1858, Twiggs Co., GA; b. Abt. 1840, Georgia; d. Aft. 1860, Twiggs Co., GA.

   vii.   JOHN A. HAMMOCK, b. Abt. 1844, Twiggs Co., GA; d. 10 May 1864, Spotsylvania Co.,
        VA.
  viii.   ALBERT J. HAMMOCK, b. Abt. 1846, Twiggs Co., GA; d. 10 May 1864, Spotsylvania
        Co., VA.
    ix.   HENRY J. HAMMOCK, b. Abt. 1848, Twiggs Co., GA; d. Aft. 1850, Twiggs Co., GA.
     x.   ELIJAH F. HAMMOCK, b. Abt. 1849, Twiggs Co., GA; d. Aft. 1850, Twiggs Co., GA.

Children of JAMES HAMMOCK and ANN CRANFORD are:
    xi.   ELIZABETH[10] HAMMOCK, b. Abt. 1852, Twiggs Co., GA; d. Aft. 1860, Twiggs Co., GA.
   xii.   NANCY HAMMOCK, b. Abt. 1854, Twiggs Co., GA; d. Aft. 1860, Twiggs Co., GA.
  xiii.   MARY A. HAMMOCK, b. Abt. 1856, Twiggs Co., GA; d. Aft. 1860, Twiggs Co., GA.
  xiv.   ROXIE HAMMOCK, b. 11 Oct 1856, Twiggs Co., GA; d. Aft. 1873, Twiggs Co., GA; m.
        JOHN HOLLAND, 18 Dec 1873, Twiggs Co., GA.
   xv.   JULIA A. HAMMOCK, b. Abt. 1859, Twiggs Co., GA; d. Aft. 1860, Twiggs Co., GA.
  xvi.   LAURA HAMMOCK, b. 10 Oct 1863, Twiggs Co., GA.
  xvii.   MARTHA HAMMOCK, b. 01 Nov 1867, Twiggs Co., GA.
 xviii.   ANNA HAMMOCK, b. 03 Jul 1869, Twiggs Co., GA.

Key Sources: 1830 Twiggs Co., GA, Census, p. 73; 1840 Twiggs Co., GA, Census, p. 389; 1850 Twiggs Co., GA, Census, p. 164; 1853 Twiggs Co., GA, Tax Digest; 1860 Twiggs Co., GA, Census, p. 404. He was called James Hammack, Gentleman and Esquire, as early as 1833 in Twiggs County. He was taxed in 1830 in Twiggs County in Bostick's District near John and William Cranford; a defaulter in the same district was Henry Hammock, possibly the man who moved to Texas. He was taxed in the same district in 1833.

281. JOSEPH[9] HAMMACK *(ELIJAH[8], JOHN[7], JOHN[6], WILLIAM[5], WILLIAM "THE ELDER"[4], WILLIAM "O"[3], JOHN[2] HAMMOCKE, ? JOHN[1] HAMMOT)* was born Abt. 1810 in Wilkinson Co., GA, and died Aft. 1850 in Muscogee Co., GA. He married SARAH [------] Bef. 1838 in Georgia. She was born Abt. 1797 in Columbia Co., GA, and died Aft. 1850 in Muscogee Co., GA.
Child of JOSEPH HAMMACK and SARAH [------] is:
     i.   WILLIAM[10] HAMMACK, b. Abt. 1838, Baker Co., GA; d. Aft. 1850, Muscogee Co., GA.
Key Sources: 1840 Muscogee Co., GA, Census, p. 301; 1850 Muscogee Co., GA, Census, p. 415; 1860 Muscogee Co., GA, Census, p. 359.

282. WILLIAM HARRISON[9] HAMMOCK *(PASCHAL[8], JOHN[7], JOHN[6], WILLIAM[5], WILLIAM "THE ELDER"[4], WILLIAM "O"[3], JOHN[2] HAMMOCKE, ? JOHN[1] HAMMOT)* was born 02 Feb 1814 in Twiggs Co., GA, and died 03 Apr 1863 in Randolph Co., GA. He married BARBARA OLIVER WOOLEY Abt. 1833 in Randolph Co., GA. She was born 03 Aug 1814 in South Carolina, and died 02 Feb 1894 in Randolph Co., GA.
Children of WILLIAM HAMMOCK and BARBARA WOOLEY are:
439.   i.   CATHERINE[10] HAMMOCK, b. Abt. 1835, Georgia; d. Aft. 1850, Randolph Co., GA.
440.   ii.   JAMES PASCHAL HAMMOCK, b. Abt. 1838, Georgia; d. Bet. 1861 - 1865, Confederate
        States Army.
   iii.   ZILPHY HAMMOCK, b. 31 Aug 1840, Randolph Co., Georgia; d. Aft. 1874, Randolph Co.,
        GA; m. SAMPSON EUGENE DAVIS; b. 01 Jan 1846, Georgia; d. 24 Jan 1902, Randolph
        Co., GA.
441.   iv.   WILILAM DAVID HAMMOCK, b. 13 Apr 1842, Randolph Co., Georgia; d. 19 Mar 1936,
        Randolph Co., GA.
442.   v.   JOHN GILBERT HAMMOCK, b. 29 Oct 1844, Randolph Co., Georgia; d. 1929, Randolph
        Co., GA.
   vi.   M. W. HAMMOCK, b. Abt. 1847, Georgia; d. Aft. 1860, Randolph Co., GA.

443.   vii.   DANIEL WARREN HAMMOCK, b. 19 Feb 1850, Georgia; d. 02 Jul 1928, New Mexico.

       viii.   RILLA F. HAMMOCK, b. 1852, Randolph Co., Georgia; d. 1952, Randolph Co., GA; m. H. W. MOORE.

       ix.   JOSEPH JACKSON HAMMOCK, b. 08 Oct 1856, Randolph Co., GA; d. 12 Aug 1909, Randolph Co., GA; m. KATE LORAINE SUTTON; b. Abt. 1865, Georgia; d. 20 May 1945, Randolph Co., GA.

Key Sources: 1850 Randolph Co., GA, Census, p. 377; 1860 Randolph Co., GA, Census, p. 704.

283. ELIJAH[9] HAMMACK *(PASCHAL[8], JOHN[7], JOHN[6], WILLIAM[5], WILLIAM "THE ELDER"[4], WILLIAM "O"[3], JOHN[2] HAMMOCKE, ? JOHN[1] HAMMOT)* was born Abt. 1818 in Twiggs Co., GA, and died Aft. 1880 in Quitman Co., GA. He married ELIZABETH [------] Abt. 1845 in Georgia. She was born Bet. 1820 - 1827 in Georgia, and died Aft. 1860 in Quitman Co., GA.

Children of ELIJAH HAMMACK and ELIZABETH [------] are:

       i.   SARAH CATHERINE[10] HAMMACK, b. Abt. 1846, Randolph Co., GA; d. Aft. 1870, Quitman Co., GA.

       ii.   WILLIAM P. HAMMACK, b. Abt. 1848, Randolph Co., GA; d. Aft. 1870, Quitman Co., GA.

       iii.   JOHN J. HAMMACK, b. Abt. 1850, Randolph Co., GA; d. Aft. 1870, Quitman Co., GA.

       iv.   ROBERT E. HAMMACK, b. Abt. 1851, Randolph Co., GA; d. Aft. 1870, Quitman Co., GA.

       v.   CHARITY A. HAMMACK, b. Abt. 1855, Randolph Co., GA; d. Aft. 1860, Quitman Co., GA.

       vi.   MARTHA A. HAMMACK, b. Abt. 1858, Randolph Co., GA; d. Aft. 1870, Quitman Co., GA.

       vii.   ANDREW J. HAMMACK, b. Abt. 1862, Alabama; d. 16 Mar 1927, Dale Co., AL; m. WINNIE [------].

Key Sources: 1838 Laurens Co., GA, State Census, p. 8; 1850 Randolph Co., GA, Census, p. 1; 1860 Quitman Co., GA, Census, p. 448; 1870 Quitman Co., GA, Census, p. 148. Note that there is some confusion regarding Elijah Hammacks. Andrew J. Hammack (1862-1927)'s children identified Elijah Hammack as his father, but Andrew does not appear in this Elijah's household in 1870 or 1880. Andrew J. Hammack died 16 March 1927 in Dale Co., AL and was survived by his wife Winnie Dykes. See also Henry Franklin Hammack, 1: 6. Andrew was living in Early Co., GA, in 1900 and in Dale Co., AL, in 1910.

284. VINCENT OSCAR[9] HAMMACK *(PASCHAL[8], JOHN[7], JOHN[6], WILLIAM[5], WILLIAM "THE ELDER"[4], WILLIAM "O"[3], JOHN[2] HAMMOCKE, ? JOHN[1] HAMMOT)* was born Abt. 1824 in Twiggs Co., GA, and died 08 May 1887 in Randolph Co., GA. He married AMANDA C. POWELL 19 Nov 1855 in Randolph Co., GA. She was born Abt. 1838 in Georgia, and died Aft. 1870 in Randolph Co., GA.

Children of VINCENT HAMMACK and AMANDA POWELL are:

       i.   BENJAMIN F.[10] HAMMACK, b. Abt. 1857, Randolph Co., GA; d. 1880, Randolph Co., GA.

       ii.   JOSEPH OSCAR HAMMACK, b. Abt. 1858, Randolph Co., GA; d. 03 Jan 1929, Randolph Co., GA; m. MATTIE L. GOODE, 25 Jan 1883, Randolph Co., GA; d. 19 Feb 1938, Randolph Co., GA.

       iii.   ALONZO V. HAMMACK, b. Abt. 1860, Randolph Co., GA; d. Aft. 1880, Randolph Co., GA; m. MOLLIE J. WOODMAN, 05 Jan 1886, Randolph Co., GA.

       iv.   ALBERT DEWITT HAMMACK, b. Abt. 1863, Randolph Co., GA; d. 17 Nov 1892, Randolph Co., GA; m. BLACKIE COCKERELL, 1889, Randolph Co., GA.

       v.   JAMES HAMMACK, b. Abt. 1866, Randolph Co., GA; d. Aft. 1870, Randolph Co., GA.

       vi.   CHARLES HAMMACK, b. Abt. 1868, Randolph Co., GA; d. Aft. 1870, Randolph Co., GA.

vii. MARY HAMMACK, b. Abt. 1870, Randolph Co., GA; d. Aft. 1898, Randolph Co., GA; m. V. G. REDDICK, Nov 1898, Randolph Co., GA.

Key Sources: 1850 Randolph Co., GA, Census, p. 423; 1860 Randolph Co., GA, Census, p. 649; 1870 Randolph Co., GA, Census, p. 316.

285. JOHN A.[9] HAMMACK (*CHARLES[8], JOHN[7], JOHN[6], WILLIAM[5], WILLIAM "THE ELDER"[4], WILLIAM "O"[3], JOHN[2] HAMMOCKE, ? JOHN[1] HAMMOT*) was born Abt. 1815 in Lincoln Co., GA, and died Aft. 1860 in Baldwin Co., AL. He married PRUDENCE [------] Abt. 1838 in Baldwin Co., AL. She was born Abt. 1817 in Mississippi, and died Aft. 1860 in Mobile Co., AL.
Children of JOHN HAMMACK and PRUDENCE [------] are:
   i. GEORGIANNA[10] HAMMACK, b. Abt. 1838, Baldwin Co., AL; d. Aft. 1860, Mobile Co., AL.
   ii. RESCILLA HAMMACK, b. Abt. 1842, Baldwin Co., AL; d. Aft. 1860, Mobile Co., AL.
   iii. PALMER HAMMACK, b. Abt. 1845, Baldwin Co., AL; d. Aft. 1860, Mobile Co., AL.

Key Sources: 1840 Baldwin Co., AL, Census, p. 88; 1850 Baldwin Co., AL, Census, p. 93; 1860 Mobile Co., AL, Census, p. 654; 1860 Baldwin Co., AL, Census, p. 262.

286. JAMES URIAH[9] HAMMACK (*THOMAS[8], JOHN[7], JOHN[6], WILLIAM[5], WILLIAM "THE ELDER"[4], WILLIAM "O"[3], JOHN[2] HAMMOCKE, ? JOHN[1] HAMMOT*) was born Abt. 1818 in Lincoln Co., GA, and died Aft. 1870 in Columbia Co., GA. He married ARTEMISHA E. TYE 13 Apr 1853 in Barbour Co., AL. She was born Abt. 1835 in Georgia, and died Aft. 1870 in Columbia Co., GA.
Children of JAMES URIAH HAMMACK and ARTEMISHA TYE are:
   i. JOHN T.[10] HAMMACK, b. Abt. 1854, Alabama; d. Aft. 1900, Columbia Co., AR; m. JANE OGLESBY, 10 Sep 1879, Columbia Co., AR.
444. ii. JAMES WISE HAMMACK, b. Abt. 1857, Alabama; d. Aft. 1875, Columbia Co., AR.
   iii. MARY F. HAMMACK, b. Abt. 1858, Alabama; d. Aft. 1870, Columbia Co., AR.
   iv. DELILA L. HAMMACK, b. Abt. 1859, Columbia Co., AR; d. Aft. 1880, Columbia Co., AR; m. JAMES S. BISHOP, 12 May 1881, Columbia Co., AR.
   v. SARAH HENRIETTA HAMMACK, b. Abt. 1864, Columbia Co., AR; d. Aft. 1880, Columbia Co., AR; m. H. R. POWERS, 05 Sep 1888, Columbia Co., AR.
   vi. ADDA FRANCES HAMMACK, b. 08 Aug 1869, Columbia Co., AR; d. 03 Aug 1959, Columbia Co., AR; m. E. S. GOOCH, 26 Jan 1890, Columbia Co., AR.
   vii. ELLA J. HAMMACK, b. Abt. 1870, Columbia Co., AR; d. Aft. 1880, Columbia Co., AR; m. T. N. GOODSON.
   viii. MARTHA ANN HAMMACK, b. Abt. 1872, Columbia Co., AR; d. Aft. 1880, Columbia Co., AR; m. D. W. A. BANION, Dec 1890, Columbia Co., AR.

Key Sources: 1850 Barbour Co., AL, Census, p. 432; 1860 Columbia Co., AR, Census, p. 426; 1880 Columbia Co., AR, Census, p. 190; Henry Franklin Hammack, 2: 326.

287. JESSE THOMAS[9] HAMMACK (*THOMAS[8], JOHN[7], JOHN[6], WILLIAM[5], WILLIAM "THE ELDER"[4], WILLIAM "O"[3], JOHN[2] HAMMOCKE, ? JOHN[1] HAMMOT*) was born 05 Oct 1835 in Dooly Co., GA, and died 27 Dec 1911 in Early Co., GA. He married MARY ANN CORBITT 27 Dec 1855 in Henry Co., AL. She was born 09 Mar 1837 in Alabama, and died 28 Feb 1926 in Early Co., GA.
Children of JESSE HAMMACK and MARY CORBITT are:
   i. WILLIAM THOMAS[10] HAMMACK, b. Abt. 1857, Henry Co., AL; d. Aft. 1904, Texas.
   ii. HENRY EDGAR HAMMACK, b. Abt. 1865, Dale Co., AL; d. Aft. 1900, Early Co., GA.
   iii. MARY JANE HAMMACK, b. Abt. 1864, Alabama; d. Aft. 1880, Dale Co., AL.
   iv. ROBERT LAMAR HAMMACK, b. Abt. 1867, Alabama; d. Aft. 1880, Dale Co., AL.
   v. LESLEY U. HAMMACK, b. Abt. 1869, Alabama; d. Aft. 1880, Dale Co., AL.

vi. LILLIE WINONA HAMMACK, b. Abt. 1872, Alabama; d. Aft. 1880, Dale Co., AL.

vii. ANNIE GERTRUDE HAMMACK, b. Abt. 1874, Alabama; d. Aft. 1880, Dale Co., AL.

viii. CORAL ANN HAMMACK, b. Abt. 1878, Alabama; d. Aft. 1880, Dale Co., AL.

Key Sources: 1870 Dale Co., AL, Census, p. 240; 1880 Dale Co., AL, Census, p. 665.

288. ISAIAH PASCHAL[9] HAMMACK *(DAVID[8], JOHN[7], JOHN[6], WILLIAM[5], WILLIAM "THE ELDER"[4], WILLIAM "O"[3], JOHN[2] HAMMOCKE, ? JOHN[1] HAMMOT)* was born Abt. 1825 in Wilkes Co., GA, and died Bet. 1860 - 1870 in Randolph Co., GA. He married EMILY BRITT Abt. 1852 in Randolph Co., GA. She was born Abt. 1835 in Georgia, and died Aft. 1870 in Randolph Co., GA.

Children of ISAIAH HAMMACK and EMILY BRITT are:

i. MARY E.[10] HAMMACK, b. 28 Dec 1852, Randolph Co., GA; d. 20 Mar 1942, Dale Co., AL; m. W. H. MULLINS.

ii. JULIA A. HAMMACK, b. Abt. 1855, Randolph Co., GA; d. Aft. 1870, Randolph Co., GA.

iii. MARTHA J. HAMMACK, b. Abt. 1857, Randolph Co., GA; d. Aft. 1870, Randolph Co., GA.

iv. SARAH E. HAMMACK, b. Abt. 1859, Randolph Co., GA; d. 20 Dec 1930, Dale Co., AL; m. C. M. DOWLING.

v. JOHN HAMMACK, b. Abt. 1861, Randolph Co., GA; d. Aft. 1870, Randolph Co., GA.

vi. VATULA HAMMACK, b. Abt. 1864, Randolph Co., GA; d. Aft. 1870, Randolph Co., GA.

Key Sources: 1860 Randolph Co., GA, Census, p. 679; 1870 Randolph Co., GA, Census, p. 307.

289. DANIEL[9] HAMMACK *(DAVID[8], JOHN[7], JOHN[6], WILLIAM[5], WILLIAM "THE ELDER"[4], WILLIAM "O"[3], JOHN[2] HAMMOCKE, ? JOHN[1] HAMMOT)* was born Abt. 1827 in Wilkes Co., GA, and died Aft. 1860 in Randolph Co., GA. He married NANCY JACKSON 20 Nov 1856 in Clay Co., GA. She was born Abt. 1834 in Georgia, and died Aft. 1860 in Randolph Co., GA.

Children of DANIEL HAMMACK and NANCY JACKSON are:

i. THOMAS J.[10] HAMMACK, b. Abt. 1858, Randolph Co., GA; d. Aft. 1870, Clay Co., GA.

ii. MARTHA ANNA HAMMACK, b. Abt. 1860, Randolph Co., GA; d. Aft. 1870, Clay Co., GA.

Key Source: 1860 Randolph Co., GA, Census, p. 701.

290. WILLIAM G.[9] HAMMACK *(DAVID[8], JOHN[7], JOHN[6], WILLIAM[5], WILLIAM "THE ELDER"[4], WILLIAM "O"[3], JOHN[2] HAMMOCKE, ? JOHN[1] HAMMOT)* was born Abt. 1833 in Wilkes Co., GA, and died Bet. 1860 - 1870 in Clay Co., GA. He married MARTHA J. JACKSON 28 Dec 1856 in Clay Co., GA. She was born Abt. 1831 in Georgia, and died Aft. 1870 in Clay Co., GA.

Children of WILLIAM HAMMACK and MARTHA JACKSON are:

i. MARY E.[10] HAMMACK, b. Abt. 1858, Randolph Co., GA; d. Aft. 1870, Clay Co., GA.

ii. JOHN H. L. HAMMACK, b. Abt. 1859, Randolph Co., GA; d. Aft. 1870, Clay Co., GA.

iii. ADELINE HAMMACK, b. Abt. 1860, Randolph Co., GA; d. Aft. 1870, Clay Co., GA.

iv. WILLIAM HAMMACK, b. Abt. 1862, Randolph Co., GA; d. Aft. 1870, Clay Co., GA.

Key Sources: 1860 Randolph Co., GA, Census, p. 701; 1870 Clay Co., GA, Census, p. 45-46.

291. AUGUSTUS C.[9] HAMMOCK *(STEPHEN WALKER[8], THOMAS[7], JOHN[6], WILLIAM[5], WILLIAM "THE ELDER"[4], WILLIAM "O"[3], JOHN[2] HAMMOCKE, ? JOHN[1] HAMMOT)* was born Dec 1830 in Newton Co., GA, and died 1911 in Kemper Co., MS. He married MARTHA POWELL COBB Abt. 1858 in Kemper Co., MS. She was born Feb 1841 in Mississippi, and died Aft. 1900 in Kemper Co., MS.

Children of AUGUSTUS HAMMOCK and MARTHA COBB are:

i. HENRY POWELL[10] HAMMOCK, b. 1858, Mississippi; d. 1893, Kemper Co., MS.

    ii.   ALBERT AUGUSTUS HAMMOCK, b. Sep 1861, Mississippi; d. 1937, Kemper Co., MS; m. PEARL M. HARDIN, Abt. 1894, Kemper Co., MS; b. Sep 1873, Mississippi; d. Aft. 1956, Kemper Co., MS.

    iii. LELA JANE HAMMOCK, b. 1864, Kemper Co., MS; d. 1940, Kemper Co., MS; m. HENRY SAVAGE.

    iv. EMMA JANE HAMMOCK, b. 1867, Kemper Co., MS; d. 1910, Kemper Co., MS; m. GEORGE TIPTON HUNNICUTT.

    v.   MATTIE HAMMOCK, b. May 1870, Kemper Co., MS; d. 1953, Kemper Co., MS; m. STEPHEN BETHANY.

    vi. REBECCA BELL HAMMOCK, b. 1873, Kemper Co., MS; d. 1875, Kemper Co., MS.

    vii. ANNIE MAY HAMMOCK, b. May 1876, Kemper Co., MS; d. 1938, Kemper Co., MS; m. WALTER BETHANY.

    viii. ALICE HAMMOCK, b. Jul 1879, Kemper Co., MS; d. 1917, Dime Box, TX; m. DR. [------] STEWART.

    ix. VERNON C. HAMMOCK, b. May 1887, Kemper Co., MS; d. Aft. 1900, Kemper Co., MS.

Key Sources: 1860 Kemper Co., MS, Census, p. 841; 1870 Kemper Co., MS, Census, p. 385; 1880 Kemper Co., MS, Census, p. 124.

292. JOHN CULPEPPER[9] HAMMOCK *(STEPHEN WALKER[8], THOMAS[7], JOHN[6], WILLIAM[5], WILLIAM "THE ELDER"[4], WILLIAM "O"[3], JOHN[2] HAMMOCKE, ? JOHN[1] HAMMOT)* was born Abt. 1834 in Newton Co., GA, and died 1899 in Young Co., TX. He married MARY ELIZA BETHANY Abt. 1856 in Mississippi. She was born Abt. 1838 in Mississippi, and died Aft. 1880 in Kemper Co., MS.
Children of JOHN HAMMOCK and MARY BETHANY are:

    i.   DR. JOHN A.[10] HAMMOCK, b. 1864; d. 1957, Texas.

    ii. ROBERT A. HAMMOCK, b. Oct 1857, Kemper Co., MS; d. Aft. 1920, Kemper Co., MS; m. ELIZABETH [------], Abt. 1881, Kemper Co., MS; b. Dec 1860, Mississippi; d. Aft. 1920, Kemper Co., MS.

    iii. ANN E. HAMMOCK, b. Abt. 1859, Kemper Co., MS; d. Aft. 1860, Kemper Co., MS.

    iv. JAMES W. HAMMOCK, b. Abt. 1862, Kemper Co., MS; d. Aft. 1883, Kemper Co., MS; m. LOVEDY EMMA GULLY, 20 Dec 1883, Neshoba Co., MS; b. Aug 1860, Mississippi; d. Aft. 1920, Lamar Co., MS.

    v.   LENORA HAMMOCK, b. Abt. 1866, Kemper Co., MS; d. Aft. 1880, Kemper Co., MS.

    vi. STEPHEN T. HAMMOCK, b. Abt. 1869, Kemper Co., MS; d. Aft. 1920, Noxubee Co., MS; m. GERTRUDE LIPSCOMB, 29 Nov 1893, Noxubee Co., MS; b. Nov 1874, Mississippi; d. Aft. 1920, Noxubee Co., MS.

    vii. LAVATA HAMMOCK, b. Abt. 1874, Kemper Co., MS; d. Aft. 1880, Kemper Co., MS.

    viii. ANDERSON HAMMOCK, b. Abt. 1877, Kemper Co., MS; d. Aft. 1880, Kemper Co., MS.

    ix. AUBREY HAMMOCK, b. Abt. 1879, Kemper Co., MS; d. Aft. 1880, Kemper Co., MS.

Key Sources: 1860 Kemper Co., MS, Census, pp. 584, 841; 1880 Kemper Co., MS, Census, p. 161; Henry Franklin Hammack, 2: 127.

293. STEPHEN T.[9] HAMMOCK *(STEPHEN WALKER[8], THOMAS[7], JOHN[6], WILLIAM[5], WILLIAM "THE ELDER"[4], WILLIAM "O"[3], JOHN[2] HAMMOCKE, ? JOHN[1] HAMMOT)* was born Abt. 1839 in Newton Co., GA, and died 11 May 1862 in Corinth, MS. He married JULIA HOPPER Abt. 1860 in Kemper Co., MS. She was born Abt. 1840 in Alabama, and died Aft. 1870 in Kemper Co., MS.
Child of STEPHEN HAMMOCK and JULIA HOPPER is:

    i.   JENNY DRUSILLA[10] HAMMOCK, b. Jul 1862, Kemper Co., MS; d. Aft. 1900, Kemper Co., MS; m. GEORGE TARA HASKINS.

Key Sources: 1860 Kemper Co., MS, Census, p. 841; 1870 Kemper Co., MS, Census, p. 378; 1880 Kemper Co., MS, Census, p. 147.

294. WILLIAM ISHAM[9] HAMMOCK *(STEPHEN WALKER[8], THOMAS[7], JOHN[6], WILLIAM[5], WILLIAM "THE ELDER"[4], WILLIAM "O"[3], JOHN[2] HAMMOCKE, ? JOHN[1] HAMMOT)* was born Aug 1843 in Newton Co., GA, and died 16 Jan 1923 in Kemper Co., MS. He married LOUISA E. F. COBB Abt. 1865 in Kemper Co., MS. She was born 18 Aug 1846 in Alabama, and died 30 Mar 1925 in Kemper Co., MS.

Children of WILLIAM HAMMOCK and LOUISA COBB are:

  i.   DORA REBECCA[10] HAMMOCK, b. 30 Mar 1866, Mississippi; m. WILLIAM A. THOMAS.
  ii. SARAH MARGARET HAMMOCK, b. 22 Nov 1867, Mississippi; m. [-------] WALKER.
  iii. FLORENCE LOUETTA HAMMOCK, b. 23 Jun 1870, Mississippi; d. 04 Jan 1896, Mississippi.
  iv. ALBERT CURTIS HAMMOCK, b. 04 Oct 1872, Mississippi; d. 1938, Perry Co., MS; m. (1) LILLIE MILLS; m. (2) EUNIE MAE RICHARDSON, 24 Jan 1895, Sumter Co., AL.
  v.   WILLIAM HENRY HAMMOCK, b. 18 Jun 1875, Kemper Co., MS; d. 05 Aug 1954, DeKalb Co., AL; m. LENORA GOFF, 16 Jun 1909, Mississippi.
  vi. STEPHEN CLIFFORD HAMMOCK, b. 22 Jan 1880, Kemper Co., MS; d. 16 Apr 1951, Mississippi; m. ELLA EAKINS.
  vii. LAURA AMANDA HAMMOCK, b. Apr 1882, Kemper Co., MS; d. 1903, Kemper Co., MS; m. MORGAN E. MOORE.
  viii. MARTHA IDA HAMMOCK, b. 10 Aug 1885, Kemper Co., MS; m. (1) RICHARD H. COOPER; m. (2) HARVEY C. POOL, 04 Sep 1904, Kemper Co., MS.
  ix. CORA I. C. HAMMOCK, b. 17 Mar 1883, Kemper Co., MS; d. Abt. 1885, Kemper Co., MS.

Key Sources: 1860 Kemper Co., MS, Census, p. 841; 1880 Kemper Co., MS, Census, p. 25; W. I. Hammack, Confederate Pension Application, Kemper Co., MS.

295. GRANVILLE[9] HAMMOCK *(ELIZABETH[8], THOMAS[7], JOHN[6], WILLIAM[5], WILLIAM "THE ELDER"[4], WILLIAM "O"[3], JOHN[2] HAMMOCKE, ? JOHN[1] HAMMOT)* was born Abt. 1829 in Wilkes Co., GA, and died Aft. 1860 in Wilkes Co., GA. He married ELIZABETH [------] Abt. 1851 in Wilkes Co., GA. She was born Abt. 1825 in Wilkes Co., GA, and died Aft. 1860 in Wilkes Co., GA.

Children of GRANVILLE HAMMACK and ELIZABETH [------] are:

  i.   LUCY ANN[10] HAMMOCK, b. Abt. 1852, Wilkes Co., GA; d. Aft. 1860, Wilkes Co., GA.
  ii. LEWIS D. HAMMOCK, b. Abt. 1853, Wilkes Co., GA; d. Aft. 1860, Wilkes Co., GA.
  iii. ELLEN R. HAMMOCK, b. Abt. 1855, Wilkes Co., GA; d. Aft. 1860, Wilkes Co., GA.
  iv. JESSE E. HAMMOCK, b. Abt. 1857, Wilkes Co., GA; d. Aft. 1860, Wilkes Co., GA.
  v.   HENRY T. HAMMOCK, b. Abt. 1859, Wilkes Co., GA; d. Aft. 1860, Wilkes Co., GA.

Key Source: 1860 Wilkes Co., GA, Census, p. 826.

296. WILLIAM[9] HAMMACK *(HARRISON[8], LEWIS[7], JOHN[6], WILLIAM[5], WILLIAM "THE ELDER"[4], WILLIAM "O"[3], JOHN[2] HAMMOCKE, ? JOHN[1] HAMMOT)* was born Abt. 1820 in Jones Co., GA, and died Aft. 1862 in Stateline, AR. He married ELIZABETH HUNTER HOUSE 10 Sep 1839 in Russell Co., AL. She was born Abt. 1820 in Georgia, and died Aft. 1850 in Claiborne Parish, LA.

Children of WILLIAM HAMMACK and ELIZABETH HOUSE are:

  i.   CATHERINE[10] HAMMACK, b. 18 Mar 1841, Russell Co., AR; d. 14 Feb 1908, Arkansas; m. WILLIAM JOEL RUSHTON, 22 Jan 1857, Columbia Co., AR; b. 16 Aug 1837, Alabama; d. 22 Jun 1901, Arkansas.

    ii.   LOUISA HAMMACK, b. Abt. 1842, Arkansas; d. Aft. 1850, Claiborne Parish, LA; m. [--------] CRABTREE.

   iii.   ELIZABETH HAMMACK, b. Abt. 1845, Arkansas; d. Aft. 1850, Claiborne Parish, LA; m. (1) [-------] LANIER; m. (2) JAMES SIMS.

   iv.   REBECCCA HAMMACK, b. Abt. 1849, Claiborne Parish, LA; d. Aft. 1850, Claiborne Parish, LA.

Key Source: 1850 Claiborne Parish, LA, Census, p. 115; 1860 Columbia Co., AR, Census, p. 263.

297. JAMES LEWIS[9] HAMMACK *(HARRISON[8], LEWIS[7], JOHN[6], WILLIAM[5], WILLIAM "THE ELDER"[4], WILLIAM "O"[3], JOHN[2] HAMMOCKE, ? JOHN[1] HAMMOT)* was born Abt. 1837 in Marion Co., GA, and died Aft. 1865 in Columbia Co., AR.
Children of JAMES LEWIS HAMMACK are:

    i.   SON[10] HAMMACK, b. Aft. 1857, Arkansas.

    ii.   SON HAMMACK, b. Aft. 1857, Arkansas.

   iii.   SON HAMMACK, b. Aft. 1857, Arkansas.

   iv.   DAUGHTER HAMMACK, b. Aft. 1857, Arkansas.

    v.   DAUGHTER HAMMACK, b. Aft. 1857, Arkansas.

   vi.   DAUGHTER HAMMACK, b. Aft. 1857, Arkansas.

Key Source: Henry Franklin Hammack, 1: 37, 44, 300.

298. JEPTHA[9] HAMMOCK *(? BENJAMIN[8], WILLIAM[7], WILLIAM[6], BENEDICT[5] HAMMACK, WILLIAM "THE ELDER"[4], WILLIAM "O"[3], JOHN[2] HAMMOCKE, ? JOHN[1] HAMMOT)* was born Abt. 1809 in Kentucky, and died Aft. 1880 in Jefferson Co., MO. He married POLLY OLDHAM 30 Jan 1834 in Gallatin Co., IL. She was born Abt. 1814 in Tennessee, and died Bet. 1860 - 1870 in Jefferson Co., MO.
Children of JEPTHA HAMMOCK and POLLY OLDHAM are:

    i.   HENRIETTA[10] HAMMOCK, b. Abt. 1840, Gallatin Co., IL; d. Aft. 1880, Jefferson Co., MO.

    ii.   EMALINE HAMMOCK, b. Abt. 1842, Gallatin Co., IL; d. Aft. 1860, Madison Co., MO.

   iii.   GEORGE HAMMOCK, b. Abt. 1846, Madison Co., MO; d. Aft. 1880, Jefferson Co., MO.

   iv.   THOMAS HAMMOCK, b. Abt. 1850, Madison Co., MO; d. Aft. 1860, Madison Co., MO.

    v.   JEPTHA HAMMOCK, b. Abt. 1854, Madison Co., MO; d. Aft. 1880, Jefferson Co., MO.

   vi.   SUSAN HAMMOCK, b. Abt. 1855, Madison Co., MO; d. Aft. 1860, Madison Co., MO.

Key Sources: 1840 Gallatin Co., IL, Census, p. 31; 1860 Madison Co., MO, Census, p. 486; 1880 Jefferson Co., MO, Census, p. 34.

299. WILLIAM[9] HAMMOCK *(? BENJAMIN[8], WILLIAM[7], WILLIAM[6], BENEDICT[5] HAMMACK, WILLIAM "THE ELDER"[4], WILLIAM "O"[3], JOHN[2] HAMMOCKE, ? JOHN[1] HAMMOT)* was born Abt. 1820 in Kentucky, and died Aft. 1887 in Arkansas or Oklahoma. He married (1) ARMINDA COOPER. She was born 24 Aug 1843 in Alabama, and died 08 May 1928 in Wagoner Co., OK. He married (2) MARY ANN BUSH Aug 1844 in Arkansas. She was born 19 Jan 1827 in Tennessee, and died 23 Oct 1870 in Marion Co., AR.
Children of WILLIAM HAMMOCK and ARMINDA COOPER are:

    i.   IRENA CATHERINE[10] HAMMOCK, b. 30 May 1872; m. ROMEY DEATHERAGE.

    ii.   MARTHA JANE HAMMOCK, b. 30 Nov 1873; m. ABNER JOHNSON DEATHERAGE; b. 1874; d. 1958.

   iii.   ROBERT HENRY HAMMOCK, b. 27 Feb 1877, Arkansas; d. 02 Oct 1946, Oklahoma; m. LEANER KASINGER.

iv. NANCY JANETTE HAMMOCK, b. 24 Mar 1879, Arkansas; d. 24 May 1958, Oklahoma; m. GEORGE ROBERT DEATHERAGE; b. 16 Feb 1875, Arkansas; d. 22 Apr 1941, Oklahoma.

v. GEORGE WASHINGTON HAMMOCK, b. 13 Jan 1883, Arkansas; d. 11 Jan 1913, Oklahoma; m. MAGGIE WILLIAMS.

vi. ALBERT MARION HAMMOCK, b. 21 Aug 1883, Arkansas; d. 14 Jun 1940, Oklahoma; m. DAISY HART.

Children of WILLIAM HAMMOCK and MARY BUSH are:

vii. WILLIAM BENJAMIN[10] HAMMOCK, b. 1847, Arkansas; d. 1866, Lawrence Co., AR.

viii. JAMES MONROE HAMMOCK, b. 1848, Arkansas; d. Aft. 1880, Baxter Co., AR.

ix. JOHN DEPHTHAH HAMMOCK, b. 1850, Arkansas; d. 1851, Lawrence Co., AR.

x. STEPHEN MALACHI HAMMOCK, b. 1852, Arkansas; d. 1852, Lawrence Co., AR.

xi. EMILY FRANCIS HAMMOCK, b. 1853, Arkansas; d. 1865, Lawrence Co., AR.

xii. SARAH ELIZABETH HAMMOCK, b. 1856, Arkansas; d. 1865, Lawrence Co., AR.

xiii. MARY EMELINE HAMMOCK, b. 1858, Arkansas; d. 1886, Baxter Co., AR.

xiv. LOUISE ANGELINE HAMMOCK, b. 1858, Arkansas; d. 1884, Baxter Co., AR.

xv. JASPER NEWTON HAMMOCK, b. 1860, Arkansas; d. Aft. 1860, Lawrence Co., AR.

xvi. MARGARET ANN HAMMOCK, b. 1862, Arkansas; d. 1925, Baxter Co., AR.

xvii. THOMAS EDWARD HAMMOCK, b. 1864, Arkansas; d. 1956, Oklahoma.

xviii. HENRIETTA HAMMOCK, b. 1866, Arkansas; d. 1930, Arkansas.

Key Sources: 1850 Lawrence Co., AR, Census, p. 214; 1860 Lawrence Co., AR, Census, p. 129; 1870 Marion Co., AR, Census; 1880 Baxter Co., AR, Census, p. 254; Henry Franklin Hammack, 2: 28.

300. BENJAMIN F.[9] HAMMOCK (*BENJAMIN*[8], *JOHN C.*[7], *BENEDICT*[6] *HAMMOCK II, BENEDICT*[5] *HAMMACK, WILLIAM "THE ELDER"*[4], *WILLIAM "O"*[3], *JOHN*[2] *HAMMOCKE, ? JOHN*[1] *HAMMOT*) was born Abt. 1820 in Morgan Co., GA, and died Aft. 1870 in Tallapoosa Co., AL. He married (1) FRANCES M. SHEPHERD 28 Apr 1842 in Walton Co., GA. She was born Abt. 1827 in Walton Co., GA, and died Aft. 1860 in Tallapoosa Co., AL. He married (2) BETHANY E. BLYTHE 27 Jan 1869 in Tallapoosa Co., AL.

Children of BENJAMIN HAMMOCK and FRANCES SHEPHERD are:

i. GEORGE W.[10] HAMMOCK, b. Abt. 1847, Walton Co., GA; d. Aft. 1860, Tallapoosa Co., AL.

ii. ANN ELIZABETH HAMMOCK, b. Abt. 1848, Chambers Co., AL; d. Aft. 1860, Tallapoosa Co., AL; m. STEVEN A. TURNER, 01 Nov 1865, Tallapoosa Co., AL.

Key Sources: 1850 Chambers Co., AL, Census, p. 393; 1860 Tallapoosa Co., AL, Census, p. 104.

301. CICERO C.[9] HAMMOCK (*BENJAMIN*[8], *JOHN C.*[7], *BENEDICT*[6] *HAMMOCK II, BENEDICT*[5] *HAMMACK, WILLIAM "THE ELDER"*[4], *WILLIAM "O"*[3], *JOHN*[2] *HAMMOCKE, ? JOHN*[1] *HAMMOT*) was born 1823 in Walton Co., GA, and died Aft. 1890 in Fulton Co., GA. He married MARY LETICIA JANE BUTLER 1853 in Oglethorpe Co., GA. She was born Abt. 1836 in Georgia, and died Aft. 1870 in Fulton Co., GA.

Child of CICERO HAMMOCK and MARY BUTLER is:

i. SARAH POPE[10] HAMMOCK, b. Abt. 1858, Oglethorpe Co., GA; m. ALEXANDER CREAGH BRISCOE.

Key Sources: 1850 Madison Co., GA, Census, p. 195; 1860 Oglethorpe Co., GA, Census, p. 88; 1870 Fulton Co., GA, Census, p. 219. Cicero C. Hammock served as mayor of Atlanta, Georgia.

302. JAMES T.[9] HAMMOCK (*SEABORN*[8], *ROBERT*[7], *BENEDICT*[6] *HAMMOCK II, BENEDICT*[5] *HAMMACK, WILLIAM "THE ELDER"*[4], *WILLIAM "O"*[3], *JOHN*[2] *HAMMOCKE, ? JOHN*[1] *HAMMOT*) was born Abt. 1820 in Wilkes Co., GA, and died 08 Jun 1877 in Tallapoosa Co., AL. He married REBECCA JOHNSON.

Children of JAMES HAMMOCK and REBECCA JOHNSON are:

    i.   MARY ELIZABETH[10] HAMMOCK, b. Abt. 1848, Coweta Co., GA.

    ii.   WILLIAM R. HAMMOCK, b. Abt. 1850, Coweta Co., GA; d. Aft. 1870, Tallapoosa Co., AL.

    iii.   JOHN C. HAMMOCK, b. Abt. 1852, Coweta Co., GA; d. 1909, Tallapoosa Co., AL; m. MARTHA JANE ADAMS, 05 Jun 1881, Tallapoosa Co., AL; b. 1860, Alabama; d. 1922, Alabama.

    iv.   GEORGE WASHINGTON HAMMOCK, b. Abt. 1854, Coweta Co., GA; m. MARTHA ELIZABETH BERRY.

    v.   JAMES FRANKLIN HAMMOCK, b. Abt. 1857, Coweta Co., GA; m. ISABELLA BARNHART.

    vi.   NANCY I. VICTORIA HAMMOCK, b. Abt. 1860, Chambers Co., AL; m. PINKNEY K. COUCH, 14 Dec 1876, Tallapoosa Co., AL.

    vii.   SEABORN HAMMOCK, b. Abt. 1862, Chambers Co., AL.

    viii.   ENOCH JACKSON HAMMOCK, b. Abt. 1865, Tallapoosa Co., AL.

    ix.   IDA T. HAMMOCK, b. Abt. 1868, Tallapoosa Co., AL; d. Aft. 1883, Tallapoosa Co., AL; m. HENRY BERRY, 08 Mar 1883, Tallapoosa Co., AL.

Key Sources: 1850 Coweta Co., GA, Census, p. 313; 1860 Chambers Co., AL, Census, pp. 786-787; 1870 Tallapoosa Co., AL, Census, p. 81; James T. Hammack Estate File, Tallapoosa Co., AL.

303. JOSEPH T.[9] HAMMOCK (*SEABORN*[8], *ROBERT*[7], *BENEDICT*[6] *HAMMOCK II, BENEDICT*[5] *HAMMACK, WILLIAM "THE ELDER"*[4], *WILLIAM "O"*[3], *JOHN*[2] *HAMMOCKE, ? JOHN*[1] *HAMMOT*) was born Abt. 1821 in Wilkes Co., GA, and died Aft. 1870 in Sevier Co., AR. He married MARY JANE LAND 06 Jan 1845 in Coweta Co., GA.

Children of JOSEPH HAMMOCK and MARY LAND are:

    i.   ELIZABETH[10] HAMMOCK, b. Abt. 1846, Coweta Co., GA; d. Aft. 1850, Coweta Co., GA.

    ii.   CEPHAS HAMMOCK, b. Abt. 1848, Coweta Co., GA; d. Aft. 1870, Sevier Co., AR.

    iii.   CLEOPHAS HAMMOCK, b. Abt. 1849, Coweta Co., GA; d. 09 Jul 1931, Cass Co., TX.

    iv.   MARY HAMMOCK, b. 1851, Coweta Co., GA; d. Aft. 1870, Sevier Co., AR.

    v.   LUCINDA HAMMOCK, b. Abt. 1853, Coweta Co., GA; d. Aft. 1880, Sevier Co., AR.

    vi.   FLAVIOUS HAMMOCK, b. Abt. 1856, Sevier Co., AR; d. Aft. 1880, Cass Co., TX.

    vii.   PAULINE HAMMOCK, b. Abt. 1860, Sevier Co., AR; d. Aft. 1880, Sevier Co., AR; m. JOE E. BLACKSTOCK, 20 Oct 1884, Sevier Co., AR.

    viii.   ROSANNA HAMMOCK, b. Abt. 1864, Sevier Co., AR; d. Aft. 1880, Sevier Co., AR.

    ix.   VICTORIA HAMMOCK, b. Abt. 1867, Sevier Co., AR; d. Aft. 1880, Sevier Co., AR.

    x.   JOHN HAMMOCK, b. Abt. 1870, Sevier Co., AR; d. Aft. 1880, Sevier Co., AR.

    xi.   ALLA HAMMOCK, b. Abt. 1872, Sevier Co., AR; d. Aft. 1880, Sevier Co., AR.

Key Sources: 1850 Coweta Co., GA, Census, p. 346; 1860 Sevier Co., AR, Census, p. 112; 1870 Sevier Co., AR, Census, p. 271; 1880 Howard Co., AR, Census, p. 18.

304. WILLIAM[9] HAMMOCK (*SEABORN*[8], *ROBERT*[7], *BENEDICT*[6] *HAMMOCK II, BENEDICT*[5] *HAMMACK, WILLIAM "THE ELDER"*[4], *WILLIAM "O"*[3], *JOHN*[2] *HAMMOCKE, ? JOHN*[1] *HAMMOT*) was born Abt. 1827 in Wilkes Co., GA, and died Aft. 1868 in Coweta Co., GA. He married MILLIE ANN HAYNES 05 Nov 1852 in Coweta Co., GA. She was born Abt. 1836 in Georgia, and died Aft. 1860 in Coweta Co., GA.

Children of WILLIAM HAMMOCK and MILLIE HAYNES are:

    i.   NANCY[10] HAMMOCK, b. Abt. 1858, Coweta Co., GA; d. Aft. 1860, Coweta Co., GA.

    ii. ENOCH ROBERT HAMMOCK, b. 15 Jun 1863, Coweta Co., GA; d. 14 Oct 1912, Palo Pinto Co., TX; m. (1) MARY ANN REYNOLDS, 16 Jan 1881, Coweta Co., GA; m. (2) AMANDA GEORGIANNA ROGERS, 08 Sep 1887, Limestone Co., TX.

    iii. JOHN C. HAMMOCK, b. 10 Sep 1866, Coweta Co., GA; d. Aft. 1886, Coweta Co., GA; m. LULA SMITH, 21 Oct 1886, Coweta Co., GA.

    iv. MARY FRANCES HAMMOCK, b. 23 Aug 1859, Coweta Co., GA; d. 03 Aug 1913, Coweta Co., GA; m. WILLIAM T. MORGAN.

Key Sources: 1860 Coweta Co., GA, Census, p. 701; 1870 Coweta Co., GA, Census, p. 358.

305. COLUMBUS W.[9] HAMMOCK *(? THOMAS JEFFERSON[8], BENJAMIN[7], BENEDICT[6] HAMMOCK II, BENEDICT[5] HAMMACK, WILLIAM "THE ELDER"[4], WILLIAM "O"[3], JOHN[2] HAMMOCKE, ? JOHN[1] HAMMOT)* was born Bet. 1825 - 1830 in Georgia, and died Aft. 1880 in Sabine Co., TX. He married (1) ZIMALAR CALDWELL Abt. 1845 in Alabama. She was born Abt. 1830 in Georgia, and died Bet. 1859 - 1860 in Arkansas or Texas. He married (2) AMANDA B. HOARD Abt. 1860 in Jasper Co., GA. She was born Abt. 1839 in Georgia, and died Aft. 1880 in Sabine Co., TX.

Children of COLUMBUS HAMMOCK and ZIMALAR CALDWELL are:

    i. MARY FRANCES[10] HAMMOCK, b. Abt. 1846, Alabama.

    ii. JOHN CHARLES HAMMOCK, b. Abt. 1848, Alabama.

    iii. MARTHA ANN HAMMOCK, b. Abt. 1851, Alabama.

    iv. BENJAMIN FRANKLIN HAMMOCK, b. Abt. 1854, Arkansas; d. Aft. 1880, Nacogdoches Co., TX.

    v. JOSEPH EUGENE HAMMOCK, b. Abt. 1859, Arkansas.

Children of COLUMBUS HAMMOCK and AMANDA HOARD are:

    vi. ELLEN J.[10] HAMMOCK, b. Abt. 1863, Jasper Co., TX; d. Aft. 1880, Sabine Co., TX.

    vii. MORGAN M. HAMMOCK, b. Abt. 1864, Jasper Co., TX; d. Aft. 1880, Sabine Co., TX.

    viii. LEWIS D. HAMMOCK, b. Abt. 1866, Jasper Co., TX; d. Aft. 1880, Sabine Co., TX.

    ix. OSCAR HAMMOCK, b. Abt. 1869, Jasper Co., TX; d. Aft. 1880, Sabine Co., TX.

    x. FLOYD HAMMOCK, b. Abt. 1870, Jasper Co., TX; d. Aft. 1880, Sabine Co., TX.

    xi. VALENTINE HAMMOCK, b. Abt. 1872, Jasper Co., TX; d. Aft. 1880, Sabine Co., TX.

    xii. COLUMBUS HAMMOCK, b. Abt. 1874, Jasper Co., TX; d. Aft. 1880, Sabine Co., TX.

    xiii. SALLIE H. HAMMOCK, b. Abt. 1876, Jasper Co., TX; d. Aft. 1880, Sabine Co., TX.

    xiv. AMANDA B. HAMMOCK, b. Abt. 1878, Sabine Co., TX; d. Aft. 1880, Sabine Co., TX.

Key Sources: 1860 Jasper Co., TX, Census, p. 397; 1870 Jasper Co., TX, Census, p. 484; 1880 Sabine Co., TX, Census, p. 237.

306. GEORGE W.[9] HAMMOCK *(? JOHN[8], ? SAMUEL[7], JOHN[6], BENEDICT[5] HAMMACK, WILLIAM "THE ELDER"[4], WILLIAM "O"[3], JOHN[2] HAMMOCKE, ? JOHN[1] HAMMOT)* was born Abt. 1817 in Laurens Co., GA, and died Aft. 1880 in Johnson Co., GA. He married (1) SARAH ANN SMITH 24 Jan 1841 in Washington Co., GA. She was born Abt. 1820 in Georgia. He married (2) ABNEA [------] Abt. 1860 in Johnson Co., GA. She was born Abt. 1837 in Georgia, and died Aft. 1880 in Washington Co., GA.

Children of GEORGE HAMMOCK and SARAH SMITH are:

    i. SAMUEL J.[10] HAMMOCK, b. Abt. 1843, Washington Co., GA; d. Aft. 1880, Montgomery Co., GA; m. VIANNA R. HIGHTOWER, 17 Dec 1865, Johnson Co., GA.

    ii. JAMES ADDISON HAMMOCK, b. Abt. 1845, Washington Co., GA; d. Aft. 1890, Washington Co., GA; m. MARIA D. PAGE, 22 Jan 1868, Washington Co., GA.

    iii. NANCY HAMMOCK, b. Abt. 1847, Washington Co., GA.

    iv. CHILD HAMMOCK, b. Abt. 1850, Washington Co., GA.

    v. CHILD HAMMOCK, b. Abt. 1852, Washington Co., GA.

   vi.   CHILD HAMMOCK, b. Abt. 1854, Washington Co., GA.

   vii.   CHILD HAMMOCK, b. Abt. 1856, Washington Co., GA.

   viii.   CHILD HAMMOCK, b. Abt. 1858, Washington Co., GA.

Children of GEORGE HAMMOCK and ABNEA [------] are:

   ix.   JACKSON M.[10] HAMMOCK, b. Abt. 1860, Johnson Co., GA.

   x.   ANN HAMMOCK, b. Abt. 1863, Johnson Co., GA.

   xi.   GEORGIANN HAMMOCK, b. Abt. 1864, Johnson Co., GA.

   xii.   MARTIN HAMMOCK, b. Abt. 1866, Johnson Co., GA; d. Aft. 1890, Washington Co., GA.

   xiii.   CHILD HAMMOCK, b. Abt. 1868, Johnson Co., GA.

   xiv.   BENJAMIN HAMMOCK, b. Abt. 1871, Washington Co., GA.

   xv.   LOUANN L. HAMMOCK, b. Abt. 1872, Washington Co., GA.

   xvi.   JOHN HAMMOCK, b. Abt. 1876, Washington Co., GA.

   xvii.   MARY A. HAMMOCK, b. Abt. 1878, Washington Co., GA.

Key Sources: 1850 Washington Co., GA, Census, p. 250; 1870 Washington Co., GA, Census, p. 176; 1880 Washington Co., GA, Census, p. 198.

307. THOMAS[9] HAMMAC *(JOSHUA S.[8], ? JESSE[7] HAMMOCK, JOHN[6], BENEDICT[5] HAMMACK, WILLIAM "THE ELDER"[4], WILLIAM "O"[3], JOHN[2] HAMMOCKE, ? JOHN[1] HAMMOT)* was born 1824 in Alabama, and died 1863 in Alabama. He married ELIZABETH A. STEELE Abt. 1841 in Conecuh Co., AL. She was born Abt. 1824 in Alabama, and died Aft. 1850 in Conecuh Co., AL.

Children of THOMAS HAMMAC and ELIZABETH STEELE are:

   i.   LUCINDA[10] HAMMAC, b. Dec 1842, Conecuh Co., AL; d. 24 Apr 1911, Escambia Co., AL; m. JAMES A. SIMMONS.

   ii.   MARY JANE HAMMAC, b. 16 Oct 1843, Conecuh Co., AL; d. Aft. 1850, Conecuh Co., AL.

   iii.   JOHN HAMMAC, b. 28 Dec 1845, Conecuh Co., AL; d. Bef. 1850, Conecuh Co., AL.

   iv.   SARA E. HAMMAC, b. 26 Jan 1845, Conecuh Co., AL; d. Aft. 1850, Conecuh Co., AL.

   v.   MALISSA HAMMAC, b. 11 Feb 1849, Conecuh Co., AL; d. Aft. 1850, Conecuh Co., AL.

   vi.   CADER ZACHERIAH HAMMAC, b. 03 May 1851, Conecuh Co., AL.

   vii.   EDMOND HAMMAC, b. 23 Apr 1857, Conecuh Co., AL; m. (1) MARTHA [------]; m. (2) MARY TRAWICK.

   viii.   WILLIAM J. HAMMAC, b. 16 Jan 1861, Conecuh Co., AL.

Key Sources: 1850 Conecuh Co., AL, Census, p. 364; 1860 Conecuh Co., AL, Census, p. 1071.

308. JOSHUA S.[9] HAMMAC *(JOSHUA S.[8], ? JESSE[7] HAMMOCK, JOHN[6], BENEDICT[5] HAMMACK, WILLIAM "THE ELDER"[4], WILLIAM "O"[3], JOHN[2] HAMMOCKE, ? JOHN[1] HAMMOT)* was born 06 Nov 1832 in Alabama, and died 28 May 1904 in Escambia Co., AL. He married MARGARET JANE MERRITT Abt. 1857 in Conecuh Co., AL. She was born Abt. 1838 in Alabama.

Children of JOSHUA HAMMAC and MARGARET MERRITT are:

   i.   MARY[10] HAMMAC, b. 1859, Conecuh Co., AL; d. Bef. Jul 1904, Escambia Co., AL; m. JAMES RILEY MANNING.

   ii.   MARTHA ELIZABETH HAMMAC, b. 1862, Conecuh Co., AL; d. Bef. Jul 1904, Escambia Co., AL; m. J. C. WHITE, 12 Jan 1880, Escambia Co., AL.

   iii.   JOSHUA S. HAMMAC, b. 29 Jan 1863, Conecuh Co., AL; m. MARY CAROLINE TIPPINS.

   iv.   SUSANNA A. HAMMAC, b. Sep 1865, Conecuh Co., AL; d. Bef. Dec 1932, Florida; m. WILLIAM J. MILLIGAN.

   v.   JESSE MANUEL HAMMAC, b. 22 Nov 1867, Conecuh Co., AL; d. 18 Nov 1933, Escambia Co., AL; m. HARRIETT LOUISE HAWKINS.

vi. GEORGE W. HAMMAC, b. Jan 1869, Conecuh Co., AL.

vii. JOHN H. HAMMAC, b. 1872, Escambia Co., AL; m. CAROLINE WARD.

viii. HENRY J. HAMMAC, b. 1874, Escambia Co., AL; m. ANNIE JORDAN.

ix. ELLEN S. HAMMAC, b. 28 Sep 1876, Conecuh Co., AL; d. 19 Feb 1917, Escambia Co., AL; m. W. M. HAWKINS.

x. M. J. HAMMAC, b. 25 Aug 1879, Escambia Co., AL; d. 20 May 1957, Escambia Co., AL.

Key Source: 1860 Conecuh Co., AL, Census, p. 1082; 1870 Escambia Co., AL, Census, p. 230; 1880 Escambia Co., AL, Census, pp. 225-226.

309. WILLOBY[9] HAMMAC *(JOSHUA S.[8], ? JESSE[7] HAMMOCK, JOHN[6], BENEDICT[5] HAMMACK, WILLIAM "THE ELDER"[4], WILLIAM "O"[3], JOHN[2] HAMMOCKE, ? JOHN[1] HAMMOT)* was born 23 Dec 1838 in Conecuh Co., AL, and died 1862 in Tennessee. He married ISABELLA GODWIN 09 Jan 1859 in Conecuh Co., AL. She was born Abt. 1841 in Alabama, and died Aft. 1860 in Conecuh Co., AL.

Child of WILLOBY HAMMAC and ISABELLA GODWIN is:

i. ELIZABETH[10] HAMMAC, b. Abt. 1860, Conecuh Co., AL.

Key Source: 1860 Conecuh Co., AL, Census, p. 1071.

310. JESSE[9] HAMMAC *(JOSHUA S.[8], ? JESSE[7] HAMMOCK, JOHN[6], BENEDICT[5] HAMMACK, WILLIAM "THE ELDER"[4], WILLIAM "O"[3], JOHN[2] HAMMOCKE, ? JOHN[1] HAMMOT)* was born Abt. 1830 in Conecuh Co., AL, and died Aft. 1860 in Conecuh Co., AL. He married MARY [------] Abt. 1852 in Conecuh Co., AL. She was born Abt. 1833 in Alabama, and died Aft. 1860 in Conecuh Co., AL.

Children of JESSE HAMMAC and MARY [------] are:

i. JANE[10] HAMMAC, b. Abt. 1852, Conecuh Co., AL; d. Aft. 1860, Conecuh Co., AL.

ii. MARY M. HAMMAC, b. Abt. 1860, Conecuh Co., AL; d. Aft. 1860, Conecuh Co., AL.

Key Source: 1860 Conecuh Co., AL, Census, p. 1084.

311. KEZIAH[9] HAMMACK *(JACOB[8], LEWIS[7], ROBERT HAMMACK[6] JR., ROBERT HAMMACK[5] SR., WILLIAM "THE ELDER"[4] HAMMACK, WILLIAM "O"[3], JOHN[2] HAMMOCKE, ? JOHN[1] HAMMOT)* was born Abt. 1820 in Jones Co., GA, and died Aft. 1870 in Crawford Co., GA. She married JACOB LOWE Abt. 1840 in Crawford Co., GA. He was born Abt. 1825 in Georgia, and died Aft. 1870 in Crawford Co., GA.

Children of KEZIAH HAMMACK and JACOB LOWE are:

i. ELIZABETH[10] LOWE, b. Abt. 1850, Georgia; d. Aft. 1870, Crawford Co., GA.

ii. JOHN W. LOWE, b. Abt. 1853, Georgia; d. Aft. 1870, Crawford Co., GA.

Key Source: 1870 Crawford Co., GA, Census, p. 426.

312. JOHN WESLEY[9] HAMMOCK *(JACOB[8], LEWIS[7], ROBERT HAMMACK[6] JR., ROBERT HAMMACK[5] SR., WILLIAM "THE ELDER"[4] HAMMACK, WILLIAM "O"[3], JOHN[2] HAMMOCKE, ? JOHN[1] HAMMOT)* was born Nov 1823 in Jones Co., GA, and died Aft. 1900 in Cleburne Co., AR. He married JULIA ANN SMITH Abt. 1845 in Alabama, daughter of WILLIAM SMITH. She was born 23 August 1827 in Georgia, and died 1882 in Arkansas.

Children of JOHN HAMMACK and JULIA SMITH are:

445. i. GEORGE W.[10] HAMMOCK, b. 1847, Perry Co., AL; d. 1925, Faulkner Co., AR.

446. ii. CRAWFORD MILTON HAMMOCK, b. 27 Sep 1848, Perry Co., AL; d. 1929, White Co., AR.

iii. MARGARET C. HAMMOCK, b. Abt. 1850, Perry Co., AL; d. Aft. 1860, Calhoun Co., MS.

iv. JOHN D. HAMMOCK, b. Abt. 1852, Perry Co., AL; d. Aft. 1860, Calhoun Co., MS.

v. BENJAMIN FRANKLIN HAMMOCK, b. 1854, Perry Co.,AL; d. 1894, Faulkner Co., AR.

vi. WILLIAM MURL HAMMOCK, b. 1858, Perry Co., AL; d. 1900, Faulkner Co., AR.

    vii. JAMES G. HAMMOCK, b. 1861, Calhoun Co., MS; d. 1923, AR.

   viii. JULIA HAMMOCK, b. 1863, Calhoun Co., MS; d. 1899, Cleburne Co., AR; m. JOHN JULIUS CONNELL.

    ix. WALTER HAMMOCK, b. Abt. 1868, Calhoun Co., MS; d. Aft. 1900, Sebastian Co., AR; m. OLLIE [------]; b. Abt. 1880, Mississippi; d. Aft. 1920, Sebastian Co., AR.

     x. MARY HAMMOCK, b. Abt. 1871, Calhoun Co., MS; d. Aft. 1880, Arkansas.

Key Sources: 1870 Calhoun Co., MS, Census, p. 430; 1880 Faulkner Co., AR, Census, p. 660; 1900 Cleburne Co., AR, Census, p. 214.

313. WILLIAM/WILSON H.[9] HAMMACK (*JACOB*[8], *LEWIS*[7], *ROBERT HAMMACK*[6] *JR., ROBERT HAMMACK*[5] *SR., WILLIAM "THE ELDER"*[4] *HAMMACK, WILLIAM "O"*[3], *JOHN*[2] *HAMMOCKE, ? JOHN*[1] *HAMMOT)* was born Bet. 1826 - 1828 in Jones Co., GA, or Alabama, and died Aft. 1910 in Hinds Co., MS. He married MARTHA J. BAKER 19 Dec 1872 in Madison Co., MS. She was born 05 Dec 1846 in Mississippi, and died 26 May 1901 in Hinds Co., MS.
Children of WILLIAM/WILSON HAMMACK and MARTHA BAKER are:

     i. JOHN S.[10] HAMMACK, b. Feb 1877, Hinds Co., MS; d. Aft. 1910, Hinds Co., MS; m. LENA M. HAMMACK, 17 Jan 1910, Hinds Co., MS; b. Feb 1876, Madison Co., MS; d. Aft. 1910, Madison Co., MS.

447.   ii. JAMES A. HAMMACK, b. Mar 1880, Hinds Co., MS; d. Aft. 1910, Hinds Co., MS.

Key Sources: 1880 Hinds Co., MS, Census, p. 118; 1900 Hinds Co., MS, Census, p. 29. Crawford Co., GA, Returns Book H, p. 494, indicates that Jacob Hammack had a son William Hammack and a son-in-law W. N. Hammack (who was married to Jacob's daughter Catherine). William Hammack has not been conclusively identified. He was not enumerated in his father's household in 1850. I have speculated that he was identical with Wilson H. Hammack, who entered the Confederate Service in Alabama and later appears in Hinds Co., MS, about 1876. This identification is speculative, but Wilson H. Hammack had a close association with other descendants of Robert and Millenor Hammack in Mississippi.

314. CATHERINE[9] HAMMACK (*JACOB*[8], *LEWIS*[7], *ROBERT HAMMACK*[6] *JR., ROBERT HAMMACK*[5] *SR., WILLIAM "THE ELDER"*[4] *HAMMACK, WILLIAM "O"*[3], *JOHN*[2] *HAMMOCKE, ? JOHN*[1] *HAMMOT)* was born Abt. 1833 in Dallas Co., AL, and died Aft. 1880 in Lauderdale Co., MS. She married WILLIAM N. HAMMACK 19 Jan 1854 in Crawford Co., GA. He was born Bet. 1830 - 1837 in Georgia, and died Aft. 1880 in Lauderdale Co., MS.
Children of CATHERINE HAMMACK and WILLIAM HAMMACK are:

     i. JACOB W.[10] HAMMACK, b. Abt. 1857, Mississippi; d. Aft. 1900, Forrest Co., MS; m. EMMA [------]; b. Dec 1861, Mississippi; d. Aft. 1920, Forrest Co., MS.

    ii. WILLIAM H. HAMMACK, b. Abt. 1862, Mississippi; d. Aft. 1880, Lauderdale Co., MS.

   iii. CHARLEY HAMMACK, b. Abt. 1866, Mississippi; d. Aft. 1880, Lauderdale Co., MS.

Key Sources: 1860 Lauderdale Co., MS, Census, p. 289; 1880 Lauderdale Co., TN, Census, p. 59.

315. ELIZA[9] POOLE (*MILLY*[8] *HAMMACK, LEWIS*[7], *ROBERT HAMMACK*[6] *JR., ROBERT HAMMACK*[5] *SR., WILLIAM "THE ELDER"*[4] *HAMMACK, WILLIAM "O"*[3], *JOHN*[2] *HAMMOCKE, ? JOHN*[1] *HAMMOT)* was born Abt. 1809 in Wilkes Co., GA, and died Bef. 1844 in Jones Co., GA. She married ELIJAH SMALLWOOD 02 Nov 1826 in Jones Co., GA. He was born Bet. 1780 - 1790 in Wilkes Co., GA, and died Aft. 1844 in Jones Co., GA.
Children of ELIZA POOLE and ELIJAH SMALLWOOD are:

448.   i. LEWIS SHEPPARD[10] SMALLWOOD, b. 1827, Jones Co., GA; d. Aft. 1852, Mississippi.

449.   ii. MILLY ANN SMALLWOOD, b. 1829, Jones Co., GA; d. Aft. 1880, Crawford Co., GA.

   iii. JACOB W. SMALLWOOD, b. 1832, Jones Co., GA; d. 19 Oct 1864, Confederate States Army; m. CATHERINE WOOD.

Key Sources: 1830 Jones Co., GA, Census; 1850 Wilkinson Co., GA, Census, p. 346; 1860 Jones Co., GA, Census, p. 573; 1870 Jones Co., GA, Census, p. 215; 1880 Jones Co., GA, Census, p. 360.

316. JACKSON LEWIS[9] HAMMACK *(JOHN M.[8], LEWIS[7], ROBERT HAMMACK[6] JR., ROBERT HAMMACK[5] SR., WILLIAM "THE ELDER"[4] HAMMACK, WILLIAM "O"[3], JOHN[2] HAMMOCKE, ? JOHN[1] HAMMOT)* was born Abt. 1824 in Jones Co., GA, and died Abt. 1847 in Jones Co., GA. He married MARY GREENE 19 Jan 1845 in Jones Co., GA. She was born Abt. 1819 in Georgia, and died Abt. 1918 in Jones Co., GA.
Children of JACKSON HAMMACK and MARY GREENE are:
450.   i.   MARTHA A.[10] HAMMACK, b. 25 Oct 1845, Jones Co., GA; d. 23 Apr 1906, Jones Co., GA.
       ii.   SARAH A. L. HAMMACK, b. Abt. 1847, Jones Co., GA; d. Aft. 1866, Jones Co., GA; m. JOHN JACKSON, JR., 13 Nov 1866, Jones Co., GA.
Key Sources: Jones Co., GA, Returns, Book M, 1847-1850, pp. 70, 121, 153, 229, 273, 341, 375; Jones Co., GA, Annual Returns, Book N, p. 266; Jones Co., GA, Annual Returns, Book W, 1862-1863, p. 123; 1850 Jones Co., GA, Census, p. 222.

317. JAMES M.[9] HAMMACK *(JOHN M.[8], LEWIS[7], ROBERT HAMMACK[6] JR., ROBERT HAMMACK[5] SR., WILLIAM "THE ELDER"[4] HAMMACK, WILLIAM "O"[3], JOHN[2] HAMMOCKE, ? JOHN[1] HAMMOT)* was born Abt. 1828 in Jones Co., GA, and died Abt. 1863 in Confederate States Army. He married MARTHA EMMERSON 1848 in Jones Co., GA. She was born Abt. 1828 in Jones Co., GA, and died 01 May 1894 in Bibb Co., GA.
Children of JAMES HAMMACK and MARTHA EMMERSON are:
       i.   JOHN LEWIS[10] HAMMACK, b. 1849, Jones Co., GA; d. Aft. 1870, Houston Co., GA, or Texas.
       ii.   REBECCA HAMMACK, b. Abt. 1852, Jones Co., GA; d. Aft. 1870, Houston Co., GA.
       iii.   MARY THOMAS HAMMACK, b. Abt. 1854, Jones Co., GA; d. 1926, Bibb Co., GA; m. WILEY LEVERETT.
       iv.   JAMES B. HAMMACK, b. 14 Oct 1856, Jones Co., GA; d. 23 Nov 1923, Bibb Co., GA.
       v.   SUSAN E. HAMMACK, b. Abt. 1860, Jones Co., GA; d. Aft. 1870, Houston Co., GA.
Key Sources: 1850 Jones Co., GA, Census, p. 189; 1870 Houston Co., GA, Census, p. 60; 1880 Houston Co., GA, Census, p. 408.

318. JOHN ALEXANDER[9] HAMMACK *(JOHN M.[8], LEWIS[7], ROBERT HAMMACK[6] JR., ROBERT HAMMACK[5] SR., WILLIAM "THE ELDER"[4] HAMMACK, WILLIAM "O"[3], JOHN[2] HAMMOCKE, ? JOHN[1] HAMMOT)* was born 20 Feb 1830 in Jones Co., GA, and died 17 May 1895 in Houston Co., GA. He married SARAH J. EMMERSON 24 Feb 1853 in Jones Co., GA. She was born Apr 1833 in Jones Co., GA, and died Dec 1909 in Houston Co., GA.
Children of JOHN HAMMACK and SARAH EMMERSON are:
       i.   CYNTHIA[10] HAMMACK, b. Abt. 1854, Jones Co., GA; d. Aft. 1880, Houston Co., GA.
       ii.   SHARRON HAMMACK, b. Abt. 1858, Jones Co., GA; d. Bef. 1870, Houston Co., GA.
Key Sources: 1860 Houston Co., GA, Census, p. 1070; 1870 Houston Co., GA, Census, p. 60; 1880 Houston Co., GA, Census, p. 408.

319. JOSEPH DAVIS[9] HAMMACK *(JOHN[8], ROBERT[7], ROBERT HAMMACK[6] JR., ROBERT HAMMACK[5] SR., WILLIAM "THE ELDER"[4] HAMMACK, WILLIAM "O"[3], JOHN[2] HAMMOCKE, ? JOHN[1] HAMMOT)* was born 1822 in Wilkes Co., GA, and died 1899 in Taliaferro Co., GA. He married (1) MARY E. WILSON 30 Sep 1846 in Taliaferro Co., GA, daughter of CHARLES H. WILSON. She was born Abt. 1826 in Georgia, and died 05 Dec 1855 in Taliaferro Co., GA. He married (2) JULIA A.

HARRIS 03 Feb 1859 in Taliaferro Co., GA, daughter of SINGLETON HARRIS. She was born 1829 in Georgia, and died 1900 in Taliaferro Co., GA.

Children of JOSEPH HAMMACK and MARY WILSON are:

     i.   ELLA C.[10] HAMMACK, b. Abt. 1848, Taliaferro Co., GA; m. JOHN L. HOLZENDORF, 09 May 1870, Taliaferro Co., GA.

    ii.   SUSAN F. HAMMACK, b. Abt. 1850, Taliaferro Co., GA.

451.   iii. SALLY S. HAMMACK, b. Abt. 1852, Taliaferro Co., GA; d. Bef. 1880, Taliaferro Co., GA.

Children of JOSEPH HAMMACK and JULIA HARRIS are:

    iv. DR. WILLIAM F.[10] HAMMACK, b. 25 Mar 1865, Taliaferro Co., GA.

    v.   KATIE HAMMACK, b. Abt. 1868, Taliaferro Co., GA; m. WILLIE W. BIRD, 13 May 1883, Taliaferro Co., GA.

    vi. MAMIE HAMMACK, b. Abt. 1870, Taliaferro Co., GA.

Key Sources: *Biographical Souvenir of the States of Georgia and Florida* (Chicago, IL, 1889), pp. 363-364; 1870 Taliaferro Co., GA, Census, p. 157; 1880 Taliaferro Co., GA, Census, p. 344.

320. HENRY T.[9] HAMMACK *(JOHN[8], ROBERT[7], ROBERT HAMMACK[6] JR., ROBERT HAMMACK[5] SR., WILLIAM "THE ELDER"[4] HAMMACK, WILLIAM "O"[3], JOHN[2] HAMMOCKE, ? JOHN[1] HAMMOT)* was born 1824 in Wilkes Co., GA, and died 1891 in Taliaferro Co., GA. He married SARAH JANE CRAWFORD. She was born 1822 in Georgia, and died 1898 in Taliaferro Co., GA.

Child of HENRY HAMMACK and SARAH CRAWFORD is:

452.   i.   LUCINDA FRANCES[10] HAMMACK, b. 1849, Taliaferro Co., GA; d. 1945, Taliaferro Co., GA.

    ii.   JOSEPHINE HAMMACK, b. 1848, Columbia Co., GA; d. aft. 1850, Columbia Co., GA.

Key Sources: 1850 Columbia Co., GA, Census, p. 240; 1860 Taliaferro Co., GA, Census, p. 702; 1870 Taliaferro Co., GA, Census, p. 157; 1880 Taliaferro Co., GA, Census, p. 344. Henry's wife in 1850 was shown as Ann, age 26, GA.

321. ROBERT[9] HAMMACK *(JESSE[8], JOSHUA[7], ROBERT HAMMACK[6] JR., ROBERT HAMMACK[5] SR., WILLIAM "THE ELDER"[4] HAMMACK, WILLIAM "O"[3], JOHN[2] HAMMOCKE, ? JOHN[1] HAMMOT)* was born Abt. 1816 in Clarke Co., GA, and died Aft. 1880 in Talladega Co., AL. He married LODUSKY S. J. HIXSON 30 Dec 1840 in Newton Co., GA. She was born Abt. 1817 in Georgia, and died Aft. 1880 in Talladega Co., AL.

Children of ROBERT HAMMACK and LODUSKY HIXSON are:

    i.   ELIZABETH A.[10] HAMMACK, b. Abt. 1841, Newton Co., GA; d. Aft. 1880, Talladega Co., AL.

    ii.   ROBERT R. HAMMACK, b. Abt. 1843, Newton Co., GA; d. Aft. 1860, Newton Co., GA.

   iii. WILLIAM R. HAMMACK, b. Abt. 1845, Newton Co., GA; d. Bef. 1860, Newton Co., GA.

    iv. MARY A. C. HAMMACK, b. Abt. 1848, Newton Co., GA; d. Bef. 1860, Newton Co., GA.

    v.   LODUSKA A. J. HAMMACK, b. Abt. 1855, Newton Co., GA; d. Aft. 1880, Talladega Co., AL.

    vi. NANCY M. HAMMACK, b. Abt. 1858, Newton Co., GA; d. Aft. 1880, Talladega Co., AL.

Key Sources: 1850 Newton Co., GA, Census, p. 182; 1860 Newton Co., GA, Census, p. 484; 1870 Clay Co., AL, Census, p. 207; 1880 Talladega Co., AL, Census, p. 238.

322. GEORGE BARTLETT WILLIAM[9] HAMMOCK *(JOSHUA[8], JOSHUA[7], ROBERT HAMMACK[6] JR., ROBERT HAMMACK[5] SR., WILLIAM "THE ELDER"[4] HAMMACK, WILLIAM "O"[3], JOHN[2] HAMMOCKE, ? JOHN[1] HAMMOT)* was born 1825 in Newton Co., GA, and died 13 Dec 1862 in Fredericksburg, VA. He married (1) DELPHA LOVORN 17 Feb 1842 in Newton Co., GA. She was born

Abt. 1825 in Georgia, and died 1858 in Newton Co., GA. He married (2) MARY FALKS RICKS 18 Dec 1859 in Carroll Co., GA. She was born Abt. 1833 in Georgia, and died Aft. 1916 in Fannin Co., TX.

Children of GEORGE HAMMOCK and DELPHA LOVORN are:

   i.   JAMES MARION[10] HAMMOCK, b. 14 Jul 1848, Georgia; d. 21 Sep 1921, Cullman Co., AL; m. MARGY NAOMI JANE WILLIAMS GRAY, 24 Jul 1881, Alabama; b. 14 Aug 1851, Georgia; d. 1945, Cullman Co., AL.
   ii. DELILA A. HAMMOCK, b. 10 Oct 1850, Newton Co., GA; d. 01 Jan 1913, Carroll Co., GA; m. JOHN R. DANIELL, 08 Mar 1868, Newton Co., GA; b. 26 Jun 1848, Georgia; d. 14 Aug 1917, Carroll Co., GA.
   iii. CORDELIA HAMMOCK, b. 24 Mar 1854, Georgia; d. 18 May 1933, Cullman Co., AL; m. LEONARD T. DAVIS.
   iv. SARAH ANALIZA HAMMOCK, b. 17 Sep 1855, Georgia; d. 20 Mar 1938, Rockdale Co., GA; m. JOHN WESLEY WILLIAMS, 21 Aug 1879, Georgia.
   v.   JOHN W. HAMMOCK, b. Abt. 1858, Georgia; d. Abt. 1892, Newton Co., GA; m. MOLLY MANN.

Child of GEORGE HAMMOCK and MARY RICKS is:

   vi. EMILY[10] HAMMOCK, b. Abt. 1860, Newton Co., GA; d. Aft. 1900, Rockwall Co., TX.

Key Source: W. E. Nuss, *My Hammock Family, 1656-: A History of the Ancestors and Descendants of George Bartlett William Hammock (1825-1862)* (Cullman, AL, 1997).

323. JOHN THOMAS[9] HAMMOCK *(JOSHUA[8], JOSHUA[7], ROBERT HAMMACK[6] JR., ROBERT HAMMACK[5] SR., WILLIAM "THE ELDER"[4] HAMMACK, WILLIAM "O"[3], JOHN[2] HAMMOCKE, ? JOHN[1] HAMMOT)* was born 1828 in Newton Co., GA, and died Aft. 1860 in Carroll Co., GA. He married BETSY MCDOWELL. She was born Abt. 1831 in Georgia, and died Aft. 1860 in Carroll Co., GA.

Children of JOHN HAMMOCK and BETSY MCDOWELL are:

   i.   MISSOURI[10] HAMMOCK, b. Abt. 1850, Georgia.
   ii. NANCY E. HAMMOCK, b. Abt. 1859, Georgia.

Key Source: 1860 Carroll Co., GA, Census, p. 364.

324. ABNER MASTIN W.[9] HAMMOCK *(JOSHUA[8], JOSHUA[7], ROBERT HAMMACK[6] JR., ROBERT HAMMACK[5] SR., WILLIAM "THE ELDER"[4] HAMMACK, WILLIAM "O"[3], JOHN[2] HAMMOCKE, ? JOHN[1] HAMMOT)* was born 1832 in Newton Co., GA, and died Aft. 1870 in Haralson Co., GA. He married MARY WASHINGTON 15 Dec 1859 in Carroll Co., GA. She was born Abt. 1845 in Georgia, and died Aft. 1880 in Randolph Co., AL.

Children of ABNER HAMMOCK and MARY WASHINGTON are:

   i.   NANCY[10] HAMMOCK, b. Abt. 1862, Georgia; d. Aft. 1870, Haralson Co., GA.
   ii.   MALINDA P. HAMMOCK, b. Abt. 1866, Georgia; d. Aft. 1880, Randolph Co., AL.
   iii. FRANCES C. HAMMOCK, b. Abt. 1868, Georgia; d. Aft. 1880, Randolph Co., AL.
453. iv.   THOMAS N. HAMMOCK, b. Abt. 1870, Georgia; d. Aft. 1900, Cleburne Co., AL.
   v.   JOSEPHINE M. HAMMOCK, b. Abt. 1873, Alabama; d. Aft. 1880, Randolph Co., AL.

Key Sources: 1860 Carroll Co., GA, Census, p. 570; 1870 Carroll Co., GA, Census, p. 49; 1880 Randolph Co., AL, Census, p. 261.

325. JAMES M.[9] HAMMOCK *(JOHN[8], JOSHUA[7], ROBERT HAMMACK[6] JR., ROBERT HAMMACK[5] SR., WILLIAM "THE ELDER"[4] HAMMACK, WILLIAM "O"[3], JOHN[2] HAMMOCKE, ? JOHN[1] HAMMOT)* was born Abt. 1827 in Newton Co., GA, and died Bet. 1860 - 1870 in Confederate States Army. He married CATHERINE [------] Abt. 1860 in Newton Co., GA. She was born Abt. 1830 in Newton Co., GA, and died Aft. 1870 in Newton Co., GA.

Child of JAMES HAMMOCK and CATHERINE [------] is:
>   i.   SUSAN E. J.[10] HAMMOCK, b. Abt. 1863, Newton Co., GA; d. Aft. 1870, Newton Co., GA.

Key Source: 1870 Newton Co., GA, Census, p. 176.

326. MANSEL W.[9] HAMMOCK (*JOHN*[8], *JOSHUA*[7], *ROBERT HAMMACK*[6] *JR., ROBERT HAMMACK*[5] *SR., WILLIAM "THE ELDER"*[4] *HAMMACK, WILLIAM "O"*[3], *JOHN*[2] *HAMMOCKE, ? JOHN*[1] *HAMMOT*) was born Abt. 1831 in Newton Co., GA, and died 08 Jul 1863 in Fort Delaware, DE. He married MARY ELIZABETH SNEAD Abt. 1857 in Newton Co., GA. She was born Abt. 1838 in Georgia, and died Aft. 1860 in Newton Co., GA.

Children of MANSEL HAMMOCK and MARY SNEAD are:
>   i.   MARY P.[10] HAMMOCK, b. Abt. 1858, Newton Co., GA; d. Aft. 1875, DeKalb Co., GA.
>   ii.   JOHN H. HAMMOCK, b. Abt. 1859, Newton Co., GA; d. Aft. 1875, DeKalb Co., GA.
>   iii. CAROLINE JULIA HAMMOCK, b. 13 Mar 1860, Newton Co., GA; d. 04 May 1942, Johnson Co., TX; m. LEVI SUMMERLIN.
>   iv.   WILLIAM D. D. HAMMOCK, b. Abt. 1861, Newton Co., GA; d. Aft. 1875, DeKalb Co., GA.

Key Source: 1860 Newton Co., GA, Census, p. 508.

327. MARY[9] HAMMACK (*ROBERT BERRY*[8], *JOHN*[7], *ROBERT HAMMACK*[6] *JR., ROBERT HAMMACK*[5] *SR., WILLIAM "THE ELDER"*[4] *HAMMACK, WILLIAM "O"*[3], *JOHN*[2] *HAMMOCKE, ? JOHN*[1] *HAMMOT*) was born Abt. 1815 in Jones Co., GA, and died Aft. 1870 in Carroll Co., GA. She married JAMES PARKER 06 Apr 1834 in Pike Co., GA. He was born Abt. 1814 in Georgia, and died Bet. 1861 - 1865 in Confederate States Army.

Children of MARY HAMMACK and JAMES PARKER are:
>   i.   JAMES C.[10] PARKER, b. Abt. 1837, GA, d. Aft. 1860, Carroll Co., GA.
>   ii.   ELIZABETH PARKER, b. Abt. 1844, GA, d. Aft. 1850, GA.
>   iii. SARAH PARKER, b. Abt. 1847, GA, d. Aft. 1860, Carroll Co., GA.
>   iv.   NANCY J. PARKER, b. Abt. 1854, GA, d. Aft. 1860, Carroll Co., GA.

Key Sources: 1850 Carroll Co., GA, Census, p. 28; 1860 Carroll Co., GA, Census, p. 583.

328. JOHN PINKNEY[9] HAMMOCK (*WILLIAM B.*[8], *JOHN*[7], *ROBERT HAMMACK*[6] *JR., ROBERT HAMMACK*[5] *SR., WILLIAM "THE ELDER"*[4] *HAMMACK, WILLIAM "O"*[3], *JOHN*[2] *HAMMOCKE, ? JOHN*[1] *HAMMOT*) was born 20 Aug 1820 in Jones Co., GA, and died 11 Oct 1889 in Marion Co., GA. He married (1) MARTHA ANN WHATLEY Abt. 1843 in Talbot Co., GA. She was born Abt. 1822 in Georgia, and died Bet. 1850 - 1860 in Talbot Co., GA. He married (2) GRACIE [------] Abt. 1864 in Talbot Co., GA. She was born 2 Nov 1846 in Georgia, and died 8 Jan 1911 in Marion Co., GA.

Children of JOHN HAMMOCK and MARTHA WHATLEY are:
>   i.   ELIZA J.[10] HAMMOCK, b. Abt. 1844, Talbot Co., GA; d. Aft. 1860, Talbot Co., GA.
>   ii.   MARTHA A. V. HAMMOCK, b. Abt. 1847, Talbot Co., GA; d. Aft. 1860, Talbot Co., GA.
>   iii. MARY FRANCES HAMMOCK, b. 20 Nov 1848, Talbot Co., GA; d. 18 Dec 1906, Talbot Co., GA.

Children of JOHN HAMMOCK and GRACIE [------] are:
>   iv.   QUINCY F.[10] HAMMOCK, b. Abt. 1864, Georgia; d. Aft. 1870, Marion Co., GA.
>   v.   ADALINE E. HAMMOCK, b. Abt. 1867, Georgia; d. Aft. 1870, Marion Co., GA; m. JAMES BAKER.
>   vi.   JOHN WILLIAM HAMMOCK, b. 22 Mar 1869, Georgia; d. 04 Jul 1941, Taylor Co., GA.
>   vii. HOPE HULL HAMMOCK, b. Abt. 1872, Marion Co., GA; m. EMMA J. MCCRARY, 11 Oct 1891, Taylor Co., GA.
>   viii. JAMES L. HAMMOCK, b. Abt. 1876, Marion Co., GA; m. NINA SMITH.

ix. NAPOLOEN BONAPARTE HAMMOCK, b. Mar 1879, Marion Co., GA; m. (1) GEORGIA ALENE MARTIN; m. (2) LULA BAILEY.

x. ROBERT HARRIS HAMMOCK, b. 09 Nov 1881, Marion Co., GA; d. 28 Sep 1953, Taylor Co., GA; m. GLENNIE MARTIN.

xi. GEORGIA HAMMOCK, b. Feb 1884, Marion Co., GA; d. Aft. 1900, Taylor Co., GA; m. BUFORD MCCRARY; b. May 1875, Georgia; d. Aft. 1900, Taylor Co., GA.

xii. CHARLIE CLEVELAND HAMMOCK, b. 16 May 1886, Marion Co., GA; d. 19 Nov 1954, Taylor Co., GA.

Key Sources: Bibb Co., GA, Deed Book K, p. 106; 1850 Talbot Co., GA, Census, p. 226; 1860 Talbot Co., GA, Census, p. 572; 1870 Marion Co., GA, Census, p. 144; 1880 Marion Co., GA, Census, p. 178.

329. GILLEY ANN[9] HAMMACK *(JACKSON[8], JOHN[7], ROBERT HAMMACK[6] JR., ROBERT HAMMACK[5] SR., WILLIAM "THE ELDER"[4] HAMMACK, WILLIAM "O"[3], JOHN[2] HAMMOCKE, ? JOHN[1] HAMMOT)* was born 19 Sep 1837 in Talbot Co., GA, and died Aft. 1860 in Tallapoosa Co., AL. She married HENRY H. HOWARD 10 May 1854 in Tallapoosa Co., AL.

Children of GILLEY HAMMACK and HENRY HOWARD are:

i. REBECCA J.[10] HOWARD, b. Abt. 1865, Tallapoosa Co., AL; d. Aft. 1870, Tallapoosa Co., AL.

ii. ASA B. HOWARD, b. Abt. 1868, Tallapoosa Co., AL; d. Aft. 1870, Tallapoosa Co., AL.

iii. HENRY HAWKINS HOWARD, b. 1862, Tallapoosa Co., AL; d. 04 Dec 1934, Talladega Co., AL; m. OLA MOODY.

Key Source: 1860 Tallapoosa Co., AL, Census, p. 73.

330. EDMUND HARPER WORRELL[9] HAMMACK *(LEWIS W.[8], JOHN[7], ROBERT HAMMACK[6] JR., ROBERT HAMMACK[5] SR., WILLIAM "THE ELDER"[4] HAMMACK, WILLIAM "O"[3], JOHN[2] HAMMOCKE, ? JOHN[1] HAMMOT)* was born 18 Sep 1843 in Muscogee Co., GA, and died 03 Jan 1933 in Bell Co., TX. He married MARGARET VELVET BOLAND 22 Jun 1866 in Waco, McLennan Co., TX. She was born 13 Nov 1850 in Robertson Co., TX, and died 18 Jul 1911 in Burnett Co., TX.

Children of EDMUND HAMMACK and MARGARET BOLAND are:

i. GEORGE LEWIS[10] HAMMACK, b. 25 Mar 1867, Texas; d. Aft. 1880, Bell Co., TX.

ii. SARAH ANN E. HAMMACK, b. 01 Feb 1869, Texas; d. Aft. 1880, Bell Co., TX.

iii. HENRY L. HAMMACK, b. 20 Mar 1871, Texas; d. Aft. 1880, Bell Co., TX.

iv. ALICE HAMMACK, b. 11 Jan 1873, Texas; d. Aft. 1880, Bell Co., TX.

v. ELLA HAMMACK, b. 08 Apr 1875, Texas; d. Aft. 1880, Bell Co., TX.

vi. MARY HAMMACK, b. 19 Apr 1877, Texas; d. Aft. 1880, Bell Co., TX.

vii. FRANKLIN HAMMACK, b. 13 Feb 1879, Texas; d. Aft. 1880, Bell Co., TX.

viii. JANNIE HAMMACK, b. 05 Jan 1881, Texas; d. Aft. 1881, Bell Co., TX.

ix. EMMA HAMMACK, b. 03 Dec 1883, Texas; d. Aft. 1883, Bell Co., TX.

x. ANNIE HAMMACK, b. 09 Sep 1885, Texas; d. Aft. 1885, Bell Co., TX.

xi. ARA HAMMACK, b. 22 Jul 1889, Texas; d. Aft. 1889, Bell Co., TX.

Key Source: 1880 Bell Co., TX, Census, p. 456.

331. WILLIAM J.[9] HAMMOCK *(HOPE HULL[8] HAMMACK, JOHN[7], ROBERT HAMMACK[6] JR., ROBERT HAMMACK[5] SR., WILLIAM "THE ELDER"[4] HAMMACK, WILLIAM "O"[3], JOHN[2] HAMMOCKE, ? JOHN[1] HAMMOT)* was born 21 May 1834 in Talbot Co., GA, and died 27 Sep 1890 in Talbot Co., GA. He married ROXANNA VIRGINIA HOLLIS 25 Jun 1853 in Talbot Co., GA, daughter of JOSEPH HOLLIS and RHODA ALLUMS. She was born Abt. 1837 in Georgia, and died Aft. 1900 in Taylor Co., GA.

Children of WILLIAM HAMMOCK and ROXANNA HOLLIS are:

    i.   TIMOLIA CICERO[10] HAMMOCK, b. Abt. 1858, Georgia; d. Aft. 1870, Taylor Co., GA.

    ii.   LOUISEANA E. HAMMOCK, b. Abt. 1860, Georgia; d. Aft. 1870, Taylor Co., GA; m. ALONZO WALL.

    iii.   WILLIAM HAMMOCK, b. Abt. 1862, Taylor Co., GA; d. Aft. 1880, Taylor Co., GA.

    iv.   ROXANNA HAMMOCK, b. Abt. 1864, Taylor Co., GA; d. Aft. 1880, Taylor Co., GA; m. ALONZO WALL.

    v.   HOPE HULL HAMMOCK, b. Abt. 1866, Taylor Co., GA; d. Aft. 1880, Taylor Co., GA.

    vi.   MARY F. HAMMOCK, b. Abt. 1868, Taylor Co., GA; d. Aft. 1880, Taylor Co., GA.

    vii.   JOSEPH H. HAMMOCK, b. Abt. 1870, Taylor Co., GA; d. Aft. 1880, Taylor Co., GA.

    viii.   NATHAN BUSSEY HAMMOCK, b. Abt. 1872, Taylor Co., GA; d. Aft. 1900, Taylor Co., GA; m. ADA FOUNTAIN.

    ix.   RHODA A. HAMMOCK, b. Abt. 1874, Taylor Co., GA; d. Aft. 1880, Taylor Co., GA.

    x.   HOMER OSCAR HAMMOCK, b. Abt. 1876, Taylor Co., GA; d. Aft. 1880, Taylor Co., GA.

Key Sources: 1860 Talbot Co., GA, Census, p. 571; 1870 Taylor Co., GA, Census, p. 349; 1880 Taylor Co., GA, Census, p. 35.

332. WILLIAM T. H.[9] HAMMACK *(SIMEON J.[8], WILLIAM T.[7], ROBERT HAMMACK[6] JR., ROBERT HAMMACK[5] SR., WILLIAM "THE ELDER"[4] HAMMACK, WILLIAM "O"[3], JOHN[2] HAMMOCKE, ? JOHN[1] HAMMOT)* was born Abt. 1821 in Jones Co., GA, and died Mar 1880 in Madison County, MS. He married (1) GEORGIA ELIZABETH JOLLY 16 Jan 1842 in Crawford County, GA. She was born Abt. 1825 in Georgia, and died 23 Jun 1855 in Yazoo County, MS. He married (2) MARY MARTIN 29 Oct 1859 in Crawford County, GA. She was born Abt. 1827 in Georgia, and died Aft. 1880 in Madison County, MS.

Children of WILLIAM HAMMACK and GEORGIA JOLLY are:

454.   i.   JAMES WILBURN[10] HAMMACK, b. 02 Jan 1843, Crawford Co., GA; d. 07 Jan 1917, Flora, Madison County, MS.

    ii.   CHARLES J. HAMMACK, b. Abt. 1845, Crawford Co., GA; d. Aft. Nov 1864, Madison Co., MS.

455.   iii.   MARY A. E. HAMMACK, b. Abt. 1846, Crawford Co., GA; d. Aft. 1880, Madison Co., MS.

456.   iv.   JOHN ASA HAMMACK, b. 13 Nov 1847, Crawford Co., GA; d. 24 May 1897, Madison County, MS.

    v.   SIMEON HAMMACK, b. Abt. 1849, Crawford Co., GA; d. Aft. 1850, Crawford Co., GA.

    vi.   WILLIAM M. HAMMACK, b. Aug 1851, Crawford Co., GA; d. Aft. 1910, Flora, Madison County, MS; m. MARY FAUST ?, 10 Mar 1875, Yazoo Co., MS.

Children of WILLIAM HAMMACK and MARY MARTIN are:

457.   vii.   GEORGE THOMAS[10] HAMMACK, b. 21 Sep 1860, Madison Co., MS; d. 15 Oct 1931, Madison Co., MS.

    viii.   LAURA A. HAMMACK, b. Abt. 1862, Madison Co., MS; d. Aft. 1881, Madison Co., MS; m. G. W. SANDERFORD, 24 Dec 1881, Madison County, MS.

    ix.   MARGARET "MAGGIE" HAMMACK, b. Abt. 1864, Madison Co., MS; d. Aft. 1882, Madison Co., MS; m. T. E. LORANCE, 18 Dec 1882, Madison County, MS.

458.   x.   JOSEPHINE HAMMACK, b. 10 Feb 1869, Madison Co., MS; d. 04 Apr 1930, Harrison Co., MS.

    xi.   INFANT DAUGHTER HAMMACK, b. 12 Oct 1873, Madison Co., MS; d. 12 Oct 1873, Madison Co., MS.

    xii.   WILLIE C. HAMMACK, b. 25 Oct 1874, Madison Co., MS; d. 03 Jul 1876, Madison Co., MS.

Key Sources: 1850 Crawford Co., GA, Census, p. 299; 1860 Madison Co., MS, Census, p. 823; 1861 and 1868 Madison Co., MS, Personal Property Tax Lists; 1870 Madison Co., MS, Census, p. 95; Madison Co., MS, Deed Book EE, p. 569; Madison Co., MS, Deed Book II, pp. 174, 199, 406, 409; 1880 Madison Co., MS, Census, p. 117; 1880 Madison Co., MS, Mortality Schedule.

333. MARY JANE[9] HAMMACK *(SIMEON J.[8], WILLIAM T.[7], ROBERT HAMMACK[6] JR., ROBERT HAMMACK[5] SR., WILLIAM "THE ELDER"[4] HAMMACK, WILLIAM "O"[3], JOHN[2] HAMMOCKE, ? JOHN[1] HAMMOT)* was born Abt. 1826 in Jones Co., GA, and died Abt. 1880 in Navarro Co., TX. She married MILLEDGEVILLE COLLUM 14 Apr 1842 in Crawford Co., GA, son of JOHN COLLUM and CATHERENA [------]. He was born Abt. 1822 in Edgefield District, South Carolina, and died Aft. 1900 in Navarro Co., TX.
Children of MARY HAMMACK and MILLEDGEVILLE COLLUM are:

      i.   MARY E.[10] COLLUM, b. Abt. 1843, Crawford Co., GA; d. Aft. 1850, Yazoo Co., MS.
459.   ii.   JOHN SIMEON COLLUM, b. Abt. 1844, Yazoo Co., MS; d. Aft. 1880, Navarro Co., TX.
      iii. WILLIAM J. COLLUM, b. Abt. 1846, Yazoo Co., MS; d. Aft. 1880, Navarro Co., TX.
      iv. MILLEDGEVILLE CLAYTON COLLUM, b. Abt. 1848, Yazoo Co., MS; d. Aft. 1880, Navarro Co., TX; m. MARY ELLA LANE, 08 Jan 1878, Madison Co., MS; b. 23 Oct 1853, Mississippi; d. 28 Apr 1888, Hinds Co., MS.
460.   v.   SIMON CICERO COLLUM, b. Abt. 1851, Yazoo Co., MS; d. 24 Jul 1907, Navarro Co., TX.
461.   vi. ALFRED EUGENE COLLUM, b. 27 Dec 1853, Yazoo Co., MS; d. 05 Apr 1920, Navarro Co., TX.

Key Sources: 1850 Yazoo Co., MS, Census, p. 50; 1860 Madison Co., MS, Census, p. 822; 1870 Holmes Co., MS, Census; 1880 Navarro Co., TX, Census, p. 504.

334. CHARLES M.[9] HAMMACK *(SIMEON J.[8], WILLIAM T.[7], ROBERT HAMMACK[6] JR., ROBERT HAMMACK[5] SR., WILLIAM "THE ELDER"[4] HAMMACK, WILLIAM "O"[3], JOHN[2] HAMMOCKE, ? JOHN[1] HAMMOT)* was born Abt. 1823 in Jones County, GA, and died Bef. 01 Apr 1879 in Calhoun County, MS. He married (1) SARAH JANE CURTIS 15 Dec 1844 in Crawford County, GA, daughter of THOMAS CURTIS and SAREPTA ?. She was born Abt. 1826 in Georgia., and died 06 Apr 1861 in Calhoun Co., MS. He married (2) ANGELINE RANDOLPH BROWN Abt. 1866. She was born Abt. 1838 in Kentucky, and died Bef. 1880 in Calhoun Co., MS.
Children of CHARLES HAMMACK and SARAH CURTIS are:

462.   i.   SAREPTA ANN ELIZABETH[10] HAMMACK, b. 01 Feb 1846, Crawford Co., GA; d. 25 Apr 1919, Calhoun Co., MS.
      ii.   MARY JANE HAMMACK, b. Apr 1850, Choctaw Co., MS; d. Aft. 1864, Choctaw Co., MS.
463.   iii. ISABELLA HAMMACK, b. 10 Oct 1852, Choctaw Co., MS; d. 07 Jul 1884, Calhoun Co., MS.

Children of CHARLES HAMMACK and ANGELINE BROWN are:

464.   iv. CHARLES[10] HAMMACK, b. Abt. 1867, Calhoun Co., MS; d. Bet. 1898 - 1900, Calhoun Co., MS.
      v.   ORPHIE HAMMACK, b. Abt. 1869, Calhoun Co., MS; d. Aft. 1891, Calhoun Co., MS.
465.   vi. NAOMI HAMMACK, b. 20 Jun 1875, Calhoun Co., MS; d. Abt. Sep 1897, Sunflower Co., MS.

Key Sources: 1850 Choctaw Co., MS, Census, pp. 4-5; Calhoun Co., MS, Land Abstract Book 1 East; Bethel Baptist Church Minutes, Calhoun Co., MS; 1860 Calhoun Co., MS, Personal Property Tax Roll; 1860 Calhoun Co., MS, Census, p. 40; 1870 Calhoun Co., MS, Census, p. 445; 1880 Calhoun Co., MS, Census, p. 607.

335. SARAH ANN E.[9] HAMMACK *(SIMEON J.[8], WILLIAM T.[7], ROBERT HAMMACK[6] JR., ROBERT HAMMACK[5] SR., WILLIAM "THE ELDER"[4] HAMMACK, WILLIAM "O"[3], JOHN[2] HAMMOCKE, ? JOHN[1] HAMMOT)* was born Abt. 1826 in Jones Co., GA, and died Aft. 1870 in Madison Co., MS.. She married DANIEL D. TAYLOR 24 Dec 1844 in Crawford Co., GA. He was born Abt. 1806 in Georgia, and died Bet. 1867 - 1870 in Madison Co., MS.

Children of SARAH HAMMACK and DANIEL TAYLOR are:

       i.   MARY A.[10] TAYLOR, b. Abt. 1846, Crawford Co., GA; d. Aft. 1860, Choctaw Co., MS.

466.   ii. JOHN S. TAYLOR, b. Abt. 1849, Crawford Co., GA; d. Aft. 1880, Madison Co., MS.

467.   iii. AMANDA V. TAYLOR, b. Abt. 1851, Crawford Co., GA; d. Aft. 1900, Henderson Co., TX.

468.   iv. SARAH TAYLOR, b. Jun 1854, Choctaw Co., MS; d. Aft. 1900, Madison Co., MS.

469.   v. DANIEL W. TAYLOR, b. Abt. 1859, Choctaw Co., MS; d. Aft. 1920, Madison Co., MS.

      vi. LAURA TAYLOR, b. Abt. 1861, Choctaw Co., MS; d. Aft. 1880, Madison Co., MS.

    vii. MARCUS TAYLOR, b. Abt. 1867, Madison Co., MS; d. Aft. 1870, Madison Co., MS.

Key Sources: 1850 Sumter Co., GA, Census, p. 148; 1860 Choctaw Co., MS, Census, p. 421; 1863 Choctaw Co., MS, Personal Property Tax Roll; Philadelphia Baptist Church Minutes, Calhoun Co., MS; 1870 Madison Co., MS, Census, p. 93; 1880 Madison Co., MS, Census, p. 97.

336. JOHN T.[9] HAMMACK *(SIMEON J.[8], WILLIAM T.[7], ROBERT HAMMACK[6] JR., ROBERT HAMMACK[5] SR., WILLIAM "THE ELDER"[4] HAMMACK, WILLIAM "O"[3], JOHN[2] HAMMOCKE, ? JOHN[1] HAMMOT)* was born Abt. 1830 in Crawford Co., GA, and died Jan 1870 in Calhoun County, MS. He married LOUISA TEMPLETON Abt. 1851 in Macon Co., GA, daughter of MILTON TEMPLETON and MARTHA FULLER. She was born Abt. 1833 in Morgan Co., GA, and died Bet. 1870 - 1880 in Calhoun Co., Mississippi.

Children of JOHN HAMMACK and LOUISA TEMPLETON are:

470.   i. WILLIAM SIMMS[10] HAMMACK, b. 14 Apr 1852, Macon Co., GA; d. 25 Dec 1899, Hinds County, MS.

      ii. MARTHA E. HAMMACK, b. Abt. 1854, Choctaw Co., MS; d. Bet. 1870 - 1880, Calhoun Co., MS.

   iii. FELIX W. HAMMACK, b. 29 Jul 1856, Macon Co., GA, or MS; d. 15 Jan 1938, Flora, Madison County, Mississippi.

471.   iv. JOHN ROBERT HAMMACK, b. 13 May 1858, Macon Co., GA; d. 11 Feb 1919, Stanton, ND.

      v. JAMES HAMMACK, b. Abt. 1864, Calhoun Co., MS; d. Bet. 1870 - 1880, Calhoun Co., MS.

    vi. EUDIE HAMMACK, b. Abt. 1867, Calhoun Co., MS; d. Bet. 1870 - 1880, Calhoun Co., MS.

Key Sources: 1852 Macon Co., GA, Tax Digest; Macon Co., GA, Deed Book A, p. 571; 1860 Choctaw Co., MS, Census, p. 421; 1870 Mississippi Mortality Schedule, Calhoun County; 1870 Calhoun Co., MS, Census, p. 445.

337. FELIX WILBORN[9] HAMMACK *(SIMEON J.[8], WILLIAM T.[7], ROBERT HAMMACK[6] JR., ROBERT HAMMACK[5] SR., WILLIAM "THE ELDER"[4] HAMMACK, WILLIAM "O"[3], JOHN[2] HAMMOCKE, ? JOHN[1] HAMMOT)* was born Abt. 1834 in Crawford Co., GA, and died Abt. 1903 in Sabougla, Calhoun County, MS. He married MARY LEE "POLLY" DOOLITTLE Bet. Sep - Nov 1866 in Calhoun Co., MS, daughter of STERLING DOOLITTLE and ELIZABETH FLOWERS. She was born 04 Jan 1840 in Slate Springs, Calhoun Co., MS, and died Abt. 1900 in Sabougla, Calhoun Co., MS.

Children of FELIX HAMMACK and MARY DOOLITTLE are:

472.   i.   GERTRUDE A.[10] HAMMACK, b. 09 Nov 1867, Calhoun Co., MS; d. 24 Jun 1945, Morristown, MO.

       ii.   SIMEON S. HAMMACK, b. 03 May 1870, Calhoun Co., MS; d. 26 Sep 1887, Calhoun Co., MS.

473.   iii.   BETSY ANN HAMMACK, b. 09 Aug 1872, Calhoun Co., MS; d. 14 Jul 1941, Calhoun Co., MS.

474.   iv.   SIDNEY W. HAMMACK, b. 30 Jul 1875, Calhoun Co., MS; d. 23 Aug 1943, Oklahoma City., OK.

475.   v.   MARY LEE ELIZABETH HAMMACK, b. Abt. 1877, Calhoun Co., MS; d. 1945, Boone Co., Arkansas.

476.   vi.   MARTHA VIRGINIA HAMMACK, b. 16 Nov 1882, Calhoun Co., MS; d. 07 Nov 1959, Custer Co., OK.

Key Sources: Calhoun Co., MS, Land Abstract Book 2 East, p. 184; Calhoun Co., MS, Land Abstract Book 1 East, pp. 184-185; Calhoun Co., MS, Land Abstract Book 3 East, p. 184; 1870 Calhoun Co., MS, Census, p. 446; 1880 Calhoun Co., MS, Census, p. 632; 1900 Calhoun Co., MS, Census, p. 245; W. F. Doolittle, *The Doolittle Family in America* (Cleveland, OH, 1901).

338. ALFRED WASHINGTON "DOCK"[9] HAMMOCK *(SIMEON J.[8], WILLIAM T.[7], ROBERT HAMMACK[6] JR., ROBERT HAMMACK[5] SR., WILLIAM "THE ELDER"[4] HAMMACK, WILLIAM "O"[3], JOHN[2] HAMMOCKE, ? JOHN[1] HAMMOT)* was born 17 Jun 1838 in Crawford Co., GA, and died 18 Jul 1898 in Ashley County, AR. He married NANCY ELIZA EZELL 12 Aug 1869 in Webster County, MS. She was born 03 May 1852 in Pickens County, AL, and died 27 Nov 1941 in Ashley County, AR.

Children of ALFRED HAMMOCK and NANCY EZELL are:

477.   i.   FELIX A.[10] HAMMOCK, b. 02 Dec 1870, Calhoun Co., MS; d. 15 Aug 1946, Ashley County, AR.

478.   ii.   BETTIE HAMMOCK, b. 06 May 1872, Calhoun Co., MS; d. 06 Mar 1891, Ashley County, AR.

479.   iii.   JEFFIE JANE HAMMOCK, b. 08 Oct 1875, Calhoun Co., MS; d. 07 Oct 1937, Ashley County, AR.

       iv.   WILLIAM HAMMOCK, b. 1876, Calhoun Co., MS; d. 1882, Ashley County, AR.

       v.   AMBROSE HAMMOCK, b. 1879, Calhoun Co., MS; d. 1891, Ashley County, AR.

       vi.   WILLIE HAMMOCK, b. 1882, Calhoun Co., MS; d. 1896, Ashley County, AR.

       vii.   AUSTIN HAMMOCK, b. 1884, Calhoun Co., MS; d. 09 Mar 1891, Ashley County, AR.

480.   viii.   VIRGINIA MARGARET "JENNY" HAMMOCK, b. 19 Feb 1886, Ashley County, AR; d. 23 Feb 1917, Ashley County, AR.

       ix.   GROVER LEE HAMMOCK, b. Abt. 1888, Ashley Co., AR; d. 15 Aug 1892, Ashley Co., AR.

Key Sources: Lois Hagood, *The Elusive Ancestor* (Crossett, AR, 1992); Bethel Baptist Church Minutes, Calhoun Co., MS; 1870 Calhoun Co., MS, Census, p. 445; 1880 Calhoun Co., MS, Census, p. 632; 1884, 1885, 1887, 1889, and 1892 Calhoun Co., MS, Personal Property Tax Lists; 1900 Ashley Co., AR, Census, p. 338B; 1910 Ashley Co., AR, Census, p. 276; 1920 Ashley Co., AR, Census, p. 150.

339. MARTHA[9] HAMMACK *(SIMEON J.[8], WILLIAM T.[7], ROBERT HAMMACK[6] JR., ROBERT HAMMACK[5] SR., WILLIAM "THE ELDER"[4] HAMMACK, WILLIAM "O"[3], JOHN[2] HAMMOCKE, ? JOHN[1] HAMMOT)* was born Apr 1845 in Crawford Co., GA, and died Aft. 1900 in Madison Co., MS. She married STEPHEN D. SMITH 23 Jul 1868 in Madison Co., MS. He was born Oct 1849 in Madison Co., MS, and died Aft. 1900 in Madison Co., MS.

Children of MARTHA HAMMACK and STEPHEN SMITH are:

481.   i.   LOUANNA[10] SMITH, b. Abt. 1869, Madison Co., MS; d. Aft. 1910, Yazoo Co., Mississippi.

ii.   MARY SMITH, b. Bet. Mar 1872 - 1875, Madison Co., MS; d. Aft. 1900, Madison Co., MS.

iii. LULA SMITH, b. Abt. 1873, Madison Co., MS; d. Aft. 1880, Madison Co., MS.

iv.   JOSEPHINE SMITH, b. Dec 1876, Madison Co., MS; d. Aft. 1900, Madison Co., MS.

v.   LIDA SMITH, b. Abt. 1878, Madison Co., MS; d. Aft. 1900, Madison Co., MS.

vi.   ESTIS SMITH, b. Abt. Dec 1879, Madison Co., MS; d. Aft. 1900, Madison Co., MS.

vii. BELLE SMITH, b. Jan 1885, Madison Co., MS; d. Aft. 1900, Madison Co., MS.

Key Sources: Philadelphia Baptist Church Minutes, Calhoun Co., MS; 1870 Madison Co., MS, Census, p. 90; 1880 Madison Co., MS, Census, p. 105; 1900 Madison Co., MS, Census, p. 147.

340. GEORGE W. T.[9] HAMMACK *(SIMEON J.[8], WILLIAM T.[7], ROBERT HAMMACK[6] JR., ROBERT HAMMACK[5] SR., WILLIAM "THE ELDER"[4] HAMMACK, WILLIAM "O"[3], JOHN[2] HAMMOCKE, ? JOHN[1] HAMMOT)* was born 06 Oct 1847 in Crawford County, GA, and died 24 Dec 1893 in Calhoun Co., MS. He married SARAH JANE LAY Abt. 1870 in Calhoun Co., MS, daughter of JESSE LAY and BARBARA COOK. She was born 16 Dec 1848 in Choctaw Co., MS, and died 16 Sep 1931 in Tutwiler, Tallahatchie County, MS.

Children of GEORGE HAMMACK and SARAH LAY are:

482.   i.   LESLIE L.[10] HAMMACK, b. Nov 1871, Calhoun Co., MS; d. Bet. 1931 - 1961, Calhoun Co., MS.

483.   ii.   BARBARA HAMMACK, b. 16 Sep 1874, Calhoun Co., MS; d. 20 Sep 1961, Calhoun Co., MS.

       iii. WALTER HAMMACK, b. 03 Sep 1876, Calhoun Co., MS; d. 16 Jan 1901, Calhoun Co., MS.

484.   iv.   ELLA ELIZABETH HAMMACK, b. 07 Jul 1878, Calhoun Co., MS; d. 13 Mar 1947, Tallahatchie Co., MS.

485.   v.   SARA HAMMACK, b. 11 Aug 1880, Calhoun Co., MS; d. 24 Apr 1973, Hillsborough Co., FL.

486.   vi.   JESSE G. HAMMACK, b. 10 Jun 1882, Calhoun Co., MS; d. 08 May 1959, Calhoun Co., MS.

487.   vii. MARY CLEVIE HAMMACK, b. 23 Nov 1885, Calhoun Co., MS; d. 07 Mar 1939, Calhoun Co., MS.

       viii. OLA HICKS HAMMACK, b. 03 Feb 1887, Calhoun Co., MS; d. 22 Aug 1889, Calhoun Co., MS.

488.   ix.   FRANCIS FOLSOM HAMMACK, b. 15 Aug 1890, Calhoun Co., MS; d. 16 Dec 1968, Tallahatchie Co., MS.

       x.   VENE HAMMACK, b. 19 Oct 1893, Calhoun Co., MS; d. 26 Oct 1893, Calhoun Co., MS.

Key Sources: Bethel Baptist Church Minutes, Calhoun Co., MS; Calhoun Co., MS, Land Abstract Book 1 East, p. 175; 1880 Calhoun Co., MS, Census, p. 608; 1883 Calhoun Co., MS, Land Roll; 1884, 1885, 1887, 1889, 1892 Calhoun Co., MS, Personal Property Tax Rolls; 1900 Calhoun Co., MS, Census, p. 243; *Calhoun Monitor*, September 1931.

341. JULIA ANN[9] HAMMACK *(LEWIS M.[8] HAMMOCK, WILLIAM T.[7] HAMMACK, ROBERT HAMMACK[6] JR., ROBERT HAMMACK[5] SR., WILLIAM "THE ELDER"[4] HAMMACK, WILLIAM "O"[3], JOHN[2] HAMMOCKE, ? JOHN[1] HAMMOT)* was born Abt. 1821 in Jones Co., GA, and died Aft. 1840 in Jones Co., GA. She married JOHN MCNEIL 03 Nov 1839 in Jones Co., GA.

Child of JULIA HAMMACK and JOHN MCNEIL is:

       i.   SAMUEL[10] MCNEIL, b. Abt. 1852, Sumter Co., GA; d. Aft. 1870, Sumter Co., GA.

Key Source: 1870 Sumter Co., GA, Census, p. 282. Julia is believed to have been a daughter of Lewis because Samuel McNeil was living with his family in the 1870 census.

342. W. H.[9] HAMMACK *(LEWIS M.[8] HAMMOCK, WILLIAM T.[7] HAMMACK, ROBERT HAMMACK[6] JR., ROBERT HAMMACK[5] SR., WILLIAM "THE ELDER"[4] HAMMACK, WILLIAM "O"[3], JOHN[2] HAMMOCKE, ? JOHN[1] HAMMOT)* was born Abt. 1823 in Jones Co., GA, and died Aft. 1860 in Sumter Co., GA. He married MATILDA MATTHEWS 11 Nov 1852 in Georgia. She was born Abt. 1825 in Georgia, and died Aft. 1860 in Sumter Co., GA.

Children of W. HAMMACK and MATILDA MATTHEWS are:

- i. MARION[10] HAMMACK, b. Abt. 1858, Sumter Co., GA; d. Aft. 1870, Sumter Co., GA.
- ii. MARY V. HAMMACK, b. Abt. 1860, Sumter Co., GA; d. Aft. 1880, Sumter Co., GA.
- iii. HENRY HAMMACK, b. Abt. 1862, Sumter Co., GA; d. Aft. 1870, Sumter Co., GA.
- iv. SILAS HAMMACK, b. Abt. 1864, Sumter Co., GA; d. Aft. 1880, Sumter Co., GA.

Key Source: 1860 Sumter Co., GA, Census, p. 487; 1870 Sumter Co., GA, Census, p. 282. These children were living with their grandmother in 1870, at which time neither parent was listed. What became of W. H. Hammack has not been determined. There is some possibility that he is Wilson H. Hammack of Hinds Co., MS, whom I have speculated above might also have been a son of Jacob and Hannah Hammack.

343. WILLIAM H.[9] HAMMACK *(LEWIS M.[8] HAMMOCK, WILLIAM T.[7] HAMMACK, ROBERT HAMMACK[6] JR., ROBERT HAMMACK[5] SR., WILLIAM "THE ELDER"[4] HAMMACK, WILLIAM "O"[3], JOHN[2] HAMMOCKE, ? JOHN[1] HAMMOT)* was born Abt. 1825 in Jones Co., GA, and died Aft. 1860 in Crawford Co., GA. He married (1) MATILDA MATTHEWS. He married (2) MILLIE SMALLWOOD 15 May 1845 in Jones Co., GA. She was born Bet. 1825 - 1830 in Jones Co., GA, and died Aft. 1880 in Crawford Co., GA.

Children of WILLIAM HAMMACK and MILLIE SMALLWOOD are:

- i. MARY[10] HAMMACK, b. Abt. 1848, Jones Co., GA; d. Aft. 1880, Crawford Co., GA.
- ii. HENRY B. HAMMACK, b. Abt. 1853, Jones Co., GA; d. Aft. 1860, Crawford Co., GA.
- iii. JOSEPHINE HAMMACK, b. Abt. 1858, Crawford Co., GA; d. Aft. 1880, Crawford Co., GA.

Key Sources: 1850 Dallas Co., AL, Census, p. 323; 1860 Crawford Co., GA, Census, p. 911; 1870 Crawford Co., GA, Census, p. 451; 1880 Crawford Co., GA, Census, p. 714.

344. FELIX L.[9] HAMMACK *(LEWIS M.[8] HAMMOCK, WILLIAM T.[7] HAMMACK, ROBERT HAMMACK[6] JR., ROBERT HAMMACK[5] SR., WILLIAM "THE ELDER"[4] HAMMACK, WILLIAM "O"[3], JOHN[2] HAMMOCKE, ? JOHN[1] HAMMOT)* was born Abt. 1827 in Jones Co., GA, and died Bet. 1863 - 1870 in Crawford County, GA. He married LOUVENIA MORTON 13 Apr 1846 in Jones County, GA, daughter of OLIVER MORTON and CATHERINE HARRIS. She was born 06 Jul 1827 in Jones Co., GA, and died Aft. 1862 in Jones Co., GA.

Children of FELIX HAMMACK and LOUVENIA MORTON are:

- i. ROXY M.[10] HAMMACK, b. Abt. 1848, Jones Co., GA; d. Aft. 1860, Jones Co., GA; m. NATHAN CASTLEBERRY COURSEY, 06 Oct 1868, Jones Co., GA; b. 16 Nov 1846, Henry Co., GA; d. Aft. 1868, Jones Co., GA.
- ii. CATHERINE HAMMACK, b. Abt. 1849, Jones Co., GA; d. Aft. 1860, Jones Co., GA.
- iii. IDA HAMMACK, b. Abt. 1856, Jones Co., GA; d. Aft. 1860, Jones Co., GA.
- iv. WILLIAM JUDSON HAMMACK, b. Abt. 1858, Jones Co., GA; d. Aft. 1880, Jones Co., GA.
- 489. v. THOMAS COLUMBUS HAMMACK, b. 16 Dec 1860, Jones Co., GA; d. 18 Dec 1936, Jones Co., GA.
- vi. SARAH HAMMACK, b. Abt. 1862, Jones Co., GA; d. Aft. 1870, Jones Co., GA.

Key Sources: 1850 Sumter Co., GA, Census, p. 110; 1860 Jones Co., GA, Census, p. 552; 1870 Jones Co., GA, Census, p. 305; 1880 Jones Co., GA, Census, p. 388.

345. GEORGIE ANN VIRGINIA⁹ HAMMACK *(LEWIS M.⁸ HAMMOCK, WILLIAM T.⁷ HAMMACK, ROBERT HAMMACK⁶ JR., ROBERT HAMMACK⁵ SR., WILLIAM "THE ELDER"⁴ HAMMACK, WILLIAM "O"³, JOHN² HAMMOCKE, ? JOHN¹ HAMMOT)* was born Apr 1833 in Jones Co., GA, and died 27 Oct 1904 in Sumter Co., GA. She married BENJAMIN WEAVER 31 Jan 1850 in Sumter Co., GA, son of JAMES WEAVER and DELPHIA ?. He was born 22 Mar 1831 in North Carolina, and died 17 Jan 1884 in Sumter Co., GA.

Children of GEORGIE HAMMACK and BENJAMIN WEAVER are:

  i.   HENRIETTA JOSEPHINE¹⁰ WEAVER, b. 23 Nov 1850, Sumter Co., GA; d. Aft. 1871, Sumter Co., GA; m. THOMAS C. TYNER, 09 Feb 1871, Sumter Co., GA.

  ii. MARY SAVANNAH WEAVER, b. 01 May 1852, Sumter Co., GA; d. 21 Apr 1930, Sumter Co., GA; m. WILLIAM FRANKLIN EASTERLIN, 10 Nov 1872, Sumter Co., GA; b. 07 Nov 1849, Sumter Co., GA; d. 06 May 1893, Sumter Co., GA.

  iii. JAMES LEWIS WEAVER, b. Nov 1854, Sumter Co., GA; d. 14 Aug 1920, Colquitt Co., GA; m. (1) FLORENCE LAW; m. (2) LAURA AYCOCK.

  iv. WILLIAM BENTON WEAVER, b. 10 Oct 1855, Sumter Co., GA; d. 19 Jul 1928, Dooly Co., GA; m. FLORA MORGAN.

  v.   DELPHIA WEAVER, b. Abt. 1856, Sumter Co., GA; d. 27 Apr 1874, Sumter Co., GA.

  vi. BUNYON WEAVER, b. Abt. 1858, Sumter Co., GA; d. 1893, Sumter Co., GA; m. ELLA SPIVEY.

  vii. GEORGE B. WEAVER, b. Abt. 1860, Sumter Co., GA; d. 09 Aug 1912, Baldwin Co., GA.

 viii. JULIA ANN WEAVER, b. Abt. 1862, Sumter Co., GA; d. 16 Aug 1874, Sumter Co., GA.

  ix. JESSE JACKSON WEAVER, b. Jul 1864, Sumter Co., GA; d. 08 Aug 1912, Baldwin Co., GA; m. LOUANNA ROUSE.

  x.   EMORY LEONIDAS WEAVER, b. 01 Jun 1867, Sumter Co., GA; d. Abt. 1950, Sumter Co., GA; m. PEARLIE DAVIDSON.

  xi. THOMAS WEAVER, b. Abt. 1868, Sumter Co., GA; d. Aft. 1894, Sumter Co., GA; m. MYRTLE RIVERS, 14 Jan 1894, Sumter Co., GA.

  xii. EMILY WEAVER, b. 29 Dec 1871, Sumter Co., GA; d. 22 Dec 1938, Macon Co., GA; m. DAVIS A. MCBRIDE.

 xiii. NANCY WEAVER, b. 08 Dec 1873, Sumter Co., GA; d. Aft. 1893, Sumter Co., GA; m. JOHN H. RODGERS.

  xiv. BENJAMIN P. WEAVER, b. Oct 1874, Sumter Co., GA; d. 15 Oct 1874, Sumter Co., GA.

Key Sources: 1850 Sumter Co., GA, Census, p. 110; 1870 Sumter Co., GA, Census, p. 354; 1880 Sumter Co., GA, Census, p. 7; 1900 Sumter Co., GA, Census, p. 270.

346. SUSAN MATILDA⁹ HAMMACK *(TALBOT DAVIDSON⁸, WILLIAM T.⁷, ROBERT HAMMACK⁶ JR., ROBERT HAMMACK⁵ SR., WILLIAM "THE ELDER"⁴ HAMMACK, WILLIAM "O"³, JOHN² HAMMOCKE, ? JOHN¹ HAMMOT)* was born 26 Oct 1829 in Crawford Co., GA, and died 11 Apr 1907 in Montezuma, Macon County, GA. She married JOHN BLACKSTONE FOWLER 08 Oct 1850 in Crawford County, GA.

Children of SUSAN HAMMACK and JOHN FOWLER are:

  i.   NATHAN T.¹⁰ FOWLER, b. Abt. 1851, Taylor Co., GA; d. 28 Nov 1924, Macon Co., GA; m. ISABEL LAYFIELD.

  ii. WILLIAM W. Z. FOWLER, b. 08 Jan 1853, Taylor Co., GA; d. 31 Mar 1855, Taylor Co., GA.

  iii. JOHN BLACKSTONE FOWLER, JR., b. 01 Sep 1854, Taylor Co., GA; d. 03 Apr 1940, Macon Co., GA; m. (1) MARY SOLOMON WINDHAM; m. (2) NANCY A. SHEPHERD.

  iv. JAMES WILBORN FOWLER, b. 16 Nov 1856, Taylor Co., GA; d. 30 Dec 1932, Macon Co., GA.

v. ELBERT MALVOLA FOWLER, b. 31 Jan 1862, Taylor Co., GA; d. 26 Sep 1863, Taylor Co., GA.

vi. PAULINE FOWLER, b. Abt. 1865, Taylor Co., GA.

vii. CHARLIE FOWLER, b. 16 Feb 1867, Taylor Co., GA; d. 1868, Taylor Co., GA.

Key Sources: 1860 Crawford Co., GA, Census, p. 918; 1870 Taylor Co., GA, Census, p. 311; 1880 Taylor Co., GA, Census, p. 3.

347. WILLIAM WELBORN[9] HAMMACK *(TALBOT DAVIDSON[8], WILLIAM T.[7], ROBERT HAMMACK[6] JR., ROBERT HAMMACK[5] SR., WILLIAM "THE ELDER"[4] HAMMACK, WILLIAM "O"[3], JOHN[2] HAMMOCKE, ? JOHN[1] HAMMOT)* was born 03 Jan 1831 in Crawford Co., GA, and died 08 Oct 1857 in Crawford County, GA. He married ELIZABETH (BETTY) PARHAM 19 Dec 1853 in Crawford County, GA. She was born Abt. 1836 in Crawford Co., GA, and died Aft. 1870 in Crawford Co., GA. ELIZABETH PARHAM HAMMACK married as her second husband LEONIDAS BLEWSTER. He was born Abt. 1825 in Georgia and died Aft. 1870 in Crawford Co., GA.

Children of WILLIAM HAMMACK and ELIZABETH PARHAM are:

i. NANCY REBECCA[10] HAMMACK, b. Abt. 1855, Crawford Co., GA; d. Aft. 1870, Crawford Co., GA.

ii. MARION HAMMACK, b. Abt. 1856, Crawford Co., GA; d. Aft. 1870, Crawford Co., GA.

Key Sources: *Crawford Co., GA: Families on the Fall Line* (Roberta, GA, 2006), p. 44; 1860 Crawford Co., GA, Census, p. 948; 1870 Crawford Co., GA, Census, p. 432; Crawford Co., GA, Deed Book F, p. 429.

348. MARY JANE[9] HAMMACK *(TALBOT DAVIDSON[8], WILLIAM T.[7], ROBERT HAMMACK[6] JR., ROBERT HAMMACK[5] SR., WILLIAM "THE ELDER"[4] HAMMACK, WILLIAM "O"[3], JOHN[2] HAMMOCKE, ? JOHN[1] HAMMOT)* was born 09 Sep 1832 in Crawford Co., GA, and died 14 Nov 1914 in Crawford County, GA. She married ROBERT C. PARHAM 16 Jan 1851 in Crawford County, GA. He was born 24 Aug 1827 in Georgia, and died 28 Sep 1882 in Crawford Co., GA.

Children of MARY HAMMACK and ROBERT PARHAM are:

i. WILLIAM NAPOLEON[10] PARHAM, b. Abt. 1854, Crawford Co., GA; d. Aft. 1870, Crawford Co., GA.

ii. SUSAN R. PARHAM, b. Abt. 1856, Crawford Co., GA; d. Aft. 1870, Crawford Co., GA.

iii. HENRY T. PARHAM, b. Abt. 1858, Crawford Co., GA; d. Aft. 1870, Crawford Co., GA.

iv. ELVIN PARHAM, b. Abt. 1859, Crawford Co., GA; d. Aft. 1870, Crawford Co., GA.

v. LEONIDAS E. PARHAM, b. Abt. 1860, Crawford Co., GA; d. Aft. 1880, Crawford Co., GA.

vi. SARAH E. PARHAM, b. Abt. 1865, Crawford Co., GA; d. Aft. 1880, Crawford Co., GA.

vii. MARY PARHAM, b. Abt. 1868, Crawford Co., GA; d. Aft. 1880, Crawford Co., GA.

viii. JOHN R. PARHAM, b. Abt. 1871, Crawford Co., GA; d. Aft. 1880, Crawford Co., GA.

ix. RAYMOND PARHAM, b. Abt. 1874, Crawford Co., GA; d. Aft. 1880, Crawford Co., GA.

Key Sources: Crawford Co., GA, Deed Book F, p. 429; 1860 Crawford Co., GA, Census, p. 942; 1870 Crawford Co., GA, Census, p. 462; 1880 Crawford Co., GA, Census, p. 631.

349. MALINDA CAROLINE (LYNN)[9] HAMMACK *(TALBOT DAVIDSON[8], WILLIAM T.[7], ROBERT HAMMACK[6] JR., ROBERT HAMMACK[5] SR., WILLIAM "THE ELDER"[4] HAMMACK, WILLIAM "O"[3], JOHN[2] HAMMOCKE, ? JOHN[1] HAMMOT)* was born 30 May 1834 in Crawford Co., GA, and died 16 Aug 1899 in Macon Co., GA. She married H. T. PARHAM Abt. 1859 in Crawford Co., GA. He was born Abt. 1831 in Georgia, and died 1863 in Confederate States Army.

Child of MALINDA HAMMACK and H. PARHAM is:

i. ISADORA[10] PARHAM, b. Abt. 1861, Crawford Co., GA; d. Aft. 1880, Crawford Co., GA.

Key Sources: 1860 Crawford Co., GA, Census, p. 943; 1880 Crawford Co., GA, Census, p. 635.

350. SARAH CATHERINE BAYNE[9] HAMMACK *(TALBOT DAVIDSON[8], WILLIAM T.[7], ROBERT HAMMACK[6] JR., ROBERT HAMMACK[5] SR., WILLIAM "THE ELDER"[4] HAMMACK, WILLIAM "O"[3], JOHN[2] HAMMOCKE, ? JOHN[1] HAMMOT)* was born Abt. 1843 in Crawford Co., GA, and died Aft. 1880 in Pike Co., GA. She married WILLIAM P. ROBERT SIMEON WRIGHT Abt. 1865 in Crawford Co., GA, son of WILLIAM WRIGHT and MARTHA HAMMACK. He was born Abt. 1842 in Georgia, and died Aft. 1880 in Pike Co., GA.
Children of SARAH HAMMACK and WILLIAM WRIGHT are:
    i.   TALLIE H.[10] WRIGHT, b. Abt. 1866, Crawford Co., GA; d. Aft. 1880, Pike Co., GA.
    ii. ALICE F. WRIGHT, b. Abt. 1870, Crawford Co., GA; d. Aft. 1870, Crawford Co., GA.
    iii. ADDIE WRIGHT, b. Abt. 1874, Crawford Co., GA; d. Aft. 1880, Pike Co., GA.
    iv. WILLIE WRIGHT, b. Abt. 1876, Crawford Co., GA; d. Aft. 1880, Pike Co., GA.
    v. CLAUDE WRIGHT, b. Abt. 1879, Crawford Co., GA; d. Aft. 1880, Pike Co., GA.
Key Sources: 1870 Crawford Co., GA, Census, p. 453; 1880 Pike Co., GA, Census, p. 111.

351. FELIX C.[9] MOORE *(SARAH C.[8] HAMMACK, WILLIAM T.[7], ROBERT HAMMACK[6] JR., ROBERT HAMMACK[5] SR., WILLIAM "THE ELDER"[4] HAMMACK, WILLIAM "O"[3], JOHN[2] HAMMOCKE, ? JOHN[1] HAMMOT)* was born Abt. 1825 in Wilkes Co., GA, and died Bef. 1895 in Quitman Co., GA. He married CELIA CORNELIA REESE 05 Apr 1853 in Taliaferro Co., Georgia. She was born Abt. 1834 in Georgia, and died Aft. 1880 in Quitman Co., GA.
Children of FELIX MOORE and CELIA REESE are:
    i.   MIRZA H.[10] MOORE, b. Abt. 1855, Schley Co., GA; d. Aft. 1880, Quitman Co., GA.
    ii. CORNELIA MOORE, b. Abt. 1856, Schley Co., GA; d. Aft. 1880, Quitman Co., GA.
    iii. MARCIA MOORE, b. Abt. 1859, Schley Co., GA; d. Aft. 1870, Schley Co., GA.
    iv. A. P. MOORE, b. Abt. 1860, Schley Co., GA; d. Aft. 1880, Quitman Co., GA.
    v. JOHN H. MOORE, b. Abt. 1865, Schley Co., GA; d. Aft. 1880, Quitman Co., GA.
    vi. FELIX E. MOORE, b. Abt. 1868, Schley Co., GA; d. Aft. 1880, Quitman Co., GA.
    vii. MARCELLUS A. MOORE, b. Abt. 1870, Schley Co., GA; d. Aft. 1880, Quitman Co., GA.
   viii. WILLIAM J. MOORE, b. Abt. 1871, Schley Co., GA; d. Aft. 1880, Quitman Co., GA.
    ix. SARAH P. MOORE, b. Abt. 1872, Schley Co., GA; d. Aft. 1880, Quitman Co., GA.
    x. LOFTON L. MOORE, b. Abt. 1878, Schley Co., GA; d. Aft. 1880, Quitman Co., GA.
Key Sources: 1850 Taliaferro Co., GA, Census, p. 4; 1860 Schley Co., GA, Census, p. 10; 1870 Schley Co., GA, Census, p. 236; 1880 Quitman Co., GA, Census, p. 24; Taliaferro Co., GA, Deed Book C, p. 365. Felix was working as a teacher in Taliaferro County as early as 1845 and was an attorney as early as 1870. He served as administrator of the estate of Tilman Moore in 1844 when he conveyed land to John J. and Henry D. Moore. I have speculated that Felix was the oldest son of James Moore by his marriage to Sarah Hammack; the connection has not been proven. Note that Felix was listed as being 63 years of age in 1880, 53 in 1870, 42 in 1860, and 29 in 1850. If the birthdate about 1817 is correct, then he cannot have been Sarah Hammack Moore's son.

352. WILLIAM M.[9] MOORE *(SARAH C.[8] HAMMACK, WILLIAM T.[7], ROBERT HAMMACK[6] JR., ROBERT HAMMACK[5] SR., WILLIAM "THE ELDER"[4] HAMMACK, WILLIAM "O"[3], JOHN[2] HAMMOCKE, ? JOHN[1] HAMMOT)* was born Abt. 1824 in Wilkes Co., GA, and died Aft. 1895 in Taliaferro Co., GA. He married NANCY DARDEN 19 May 1847 in Taliaferro Co., GA. She was born Abt. 1829 in Taliaferro Co., GA, and died Aft. 1850 in Taliaferro Co., GA.
Children of WILLIAM MOORE and NANCY DARDEN are:
    i.   STEPHEN T.[10] MOORE, b. Abt. 1848, Taliaferro Co., GA; d. Aft. 1850, Taliaferro Co., GA.
    ii. SARAH E. MOORE, b. Abt. 1850, Taliaferro Co., GA; d. Aft. 1850, Taliaferro Co., GA.

Key Sources: 1850 Taliaferro Co., GA, Census, p. 42; Southern Historical Association, *Memoirs of Georgia* (2 vols., Atlanta, GA, 1895).

353. JAMES WILBURN[9] MOORE *(SARAH C.[8] HAMMACK, WILLIAM T.[7], ROBERT HAMMACK[6] JR., ROBERT HAMMACK[5] SR., WILLIAM "THE ELDER"[4] HAMMACK, WILLIAM "O"[3], JOHN[2] HAMMOCKE, ? JOHN[1] HAMMOT)* was born 02 Feb 1827 in Taliaferro Co., GA, and died 09 Mar 1907 in Hancock Co., GA. He married (1) FRANCES CHANDLER 31 Aug 1848 in Taliaferro Co., GA. She was born Abt. 1828 in Georgia, and died Apr 1849 in Taliaferro Co., GA. He married (2) MARY JOSEPHINE CULVER 14 Oct 1852 in Hancock Co., GA. She was born 02 Jun 1834 in Georgia, and died 31 Mar 1906 in Hancock Co., GA.

Children of JAMES MOORE and MARY CULVER are:
  i. WILLIAM R.[10] MOORE, b. Abt. 1853, Hancock Co., GA; d. Bef. 1895, Hancock Co., GA; m. WILLIE PEARSON, 25 Jan 1876, Hancock Co., GA; b. 1857, Georgia; d. Aft. 1880, Hancock Co., GA.
  ii. AMAZON "AMMIE" ELIZABETH MOORE, b. 01 Mar 1860, Hancock Co., GA; d. 10 Mar 1952, Hancock Co., GA; m. ROBERT LEWIS, 11 Dec 1881, Hancock Co., GA.
  iii. TOMMIE LOUISIANA MOORE, b. Abt. 1862, Hancock Co., GA; d. Aft. 1887, Hancock Co., GA; m. H. FLETCHER WALLER, 28 Oct 1880, Hancock Co., GA.
  iv. LEWIS EDWARD MOORE, b. 1865, Hancock Co., GA; d. 12 Dec 1922, Hancock Co., GA; m. MAMMIE DE BEAUGINE; b. 10 Jun 1869, Georgia; d. 21 Aug 1950, Hancock Co., GA.
  v. JAMES GORDON MOORE, b. Abt. 1868, Hancock Co., GA; d. Aft. 1890, Hancock Co., GA; m. MARY E. JONES, 15 May 1889, Hancock Co., GA.
  vi. JUDGE RICHARD WELLBORN MOORE, b. 03 Sep 1873, Hancock Co., GA; d. Bet. 1919 - 1925, Hancock Co., GA; m. (1) MARY TREADWELL, 16 Dec 1896, Hancock Co., GA; b. Abt. 1875, Hancock Co., GA; d. Bef. 1908, Hancock Co., GA; m. (2) EFFIE BROWN, 1908, Hancock Co., GA; b. Abt. 1886, Georgia; d. Aft. 1908, Hancock Co., GA.
  vii. SARAH CLAIRE "SALLIE" MOORE, b. 06 Jul 1875, Hancock Co., GA; d. Aft. 1902, Hancock Co., GA; m. ROBERT CHAPMAN, 24 Aug 1893, Hancock Co., GA; b. 23 Dec 1860, Hancock Co., GA; d. 22 Nov 1951, Wilkes Co., GA.
  viii. MARY JOSEPHINE MOORE, b. 1877, Hancock Co., GA; d. Aft. 1900, Hancock Co., GA; m. DAVID LEROY BROWN, 26 Dec 1893, Hancock Co., GA.

Key Sources: 1860 Hancock Co., GA, Census, p. 276; Southern Historical Association, *Memoirs of Georgia* (2 vols., Atlanta, GA, 1895), 1: 1040. James became a prominent planter in Hancock County and operated a plantation of more than 1,500 acres. He operated several businesses, represented the county in the state legislature, and served as sheriff and tax collector for Hancock County.

354. THOMAS R.[9] MOORE *(SARAH C.[8] HAMMACK, WILLIAM T.[7], ROBERT HAMMACK[6] JR., ROBERT HAMMACK[5] SR., WILLIAM "THE ELDER"[4] HAMMACK, WILLIAM "O"[3], JOHN[2] HAMMOCKE, ? JOHN[1] HAMMOT)* was born Bet. 1830 - 1832 in Taliaferro Co., GA, and died Aft. 1895 in Hancock Co., GA. He married MARY E. [------] Abt. 1862 in Hancock Co., GA. She was born Abt. 1844 in Georgia, and died Aft. 1880 in Hancock Co., GA.

Children of THOMAS MOORE and MARY [------] are:
  i. SARAH[10] MOORE, b. Abt. 1864, Hancock Co., GA; d. Aft. 1880, Hancock Co., GA.
  ii. MARY J. MOORE, b. Abt. 1866, Hancock Co., GA; d. Aft. 1880, Hancock Co., GA.
  iii. FELIX T. MOORE, b. Abt. 1869, Hancock Co., GA; d. Aft. 1880, Hancock Co., GA.
  iv. WILLIE E. MOORE, b. Abt. 1871, Hancock Co., GA; d. Aft. 1880, Hancock Co., GA.
  v. BURTHA B. MOORE, b. Abt. 1877, Hancock Co., GA; d. Aft. 1880, Hancock Co., GA.

Key Sources: 1880 Hancock Co., GA, Census, p. 232; Southern Historical Association, *Memoirs of Georgia* (2 vols., Atlanta, GA, 1895), 1: 1040.

355. OWEN D.⁹ MOORE *(SARAH C.⁸ HAMMACK, WILLIAM T.⁷, ROBERT HAMMACK⁶ JR., ROBERT HAMMACK⁵ SR., WILLIAM "THE ELDER"⁴ HAMMACK, WILLIAM "O"³, JOHN² HAMMOCKE, ? JOHN¹ HAMMOT)* was born 1839 in Taliaferro Co., GA, and died 1910 in Taliaferro Co., GA. He married MARY E. BRYANT 28 Nov 1859 in Jones Co., GA. She was born 1839 in Taliaferro Co., GA, and died 1906 in Taliaferro Co., GA.

Children of OWEN MOORE and MARY BRYANT are:

    i.   EULIOUS¹⁰ MOORE, b. 1860, Taliaferro Co., GA; d. 1891, Taliaferro Co., GA.
    ii. MARY L. MOORE, b. 1862, Taliaferro Co., GA; d. 1864, Taliaferro Co., GA.
    iii. OWEN D. MOORE, b. 1864, Taliaferro Co., GA; d. 1865, Taliaferro Co., GA.
    iv. JAMES L. MOORE, b. Abt. 1866, Taliaferro Co., GA; d. Aft. 1907, Taliaferro Co., GA.
    v.   SARAH E. "TOMMIE" MOORE, b. 1868, Taliaferro Co., GA; d. 1893, Taliaferro Co., GA; m. W. D. BARNETT.
    vi. WILLIAM R. MOORE, b. Abt. 1874, Taliaferro Co., GA; d. Aft. 1907, Taliaferro Co., GA.
    vii. IDA DELLA MOORE, b. Abt. 1876, Taliaferro Co., GA; d. Aft. 1907, Taliaferro Co., GA; m. [--------] BARNETT.
    viii. JOHNNIE MOORE, b. 1879, Taliaferro Co., GA; d. 1888, Taliaferro Co., GA.

Key Sources: 1870 Taliaferro Co., GA, Census, p. 163; 1880 Taliaferro Co., GA, Census, p. 397; Jones Co., GA, Deed Book T, pp. 396-397; Taliaferro Co., GA, Deed Book J, p. 238; Southern Historical Association, *Memoirs of Georgia* (2 vols., Atlanta, GA, 1895), 1: 1040.

356. RICHARD H.⁹ MOORE *(SARAH C.⁸ HAMMACK, WILLIAM T.⁷, ROBERT HAMMACK⁶ JR., ROBERT HAMMACK⁵ SR., WILLIAM "THE ELDER"⁴ HAMMACK, WILLIAM "O"³, JOHN² HAMMOCKE, ? JOHN¹ HAMMOT)* was born Aug 1844 in Taliaferro Co., GA, and died Aft. 1895 in Hancock Co., GA. He married (1) MARY MISSOURI CULVER Abt. 1869 in Hancock Co., GA, daughter of JOHN CULVER and MARY CHEELY. She was born Aug 1852 in Hancock Co., GA, and died Aft. 1880 in Hancock Co., GA. He married (2) IDA REAMS.

Children of RICHARD MOORE and MARY CULVER are:

    i.   HENRY E.¹⁰ MOORE, b. Jul 1870, Hancock Co., GA; m. MARY HOLIDAY.
    ii. JOHN D. MOORE, b. 1877, Hancock Co., GA; m. MAY TURNER.
    iii. ROBERT MOORE.
    iv. PIERCE MOORE, m. LOUISE CORNELL.
    v.   MASOUVAR MOORE.
    vi. MARY CORNELIA MOORE.
    vii. ANNA LOU MOORE.

Children of RICHARD MOORE and IDA REAMS are:

    viii. REAMS¹⁰ MOORE.
    ix. LYNN MOORE.
    x.   PERCY MOORE.
    xi. TERRELL MOORE, m. VIRGINIA HARTSFIELD.

Key Sources: *Men of Mark in Georgia* (Atlanta, GA, 1912); Southern Historical Association, *Memoirs of Georgia* (2 vols., Atlanta, GA, 1895), 1: 1040; Forrest Shivers, *The Land Between: A History of Hancock County, Georgia, to 1940* (Spartanburg, SC, 1990), 2: 114. Richard Moore became a prominent businessman and politician in Hancock Co., GA, and his son became Mayor of Sparta and Judge of the Sparta City Court. Moore's son Dr. Terrell Moore was educated at Johns Hopkins University and taught history at Columbia University in New York for many years.

357. FELIX WILBORN⁹ HAMMACK *(MANSEL W.⁸, WILLIAM T.⁷, ROBERT HAMMACK⁶ JR., ROBERT HAMMACK⁵ SR., WILLIAM "THE ELDER"⁴ HAMMACK, WILLIAM "O"³, JOHN²*

HAMMOCKE, ? JOHN[1] HAMMOT) was born Abt. 1835 in Crawford Co., GA, and died Abt. 1862 in Confederate States Army. He married NANCY ELLEN JOHNSON 08 Nov 1855 in Crawford Co., GA. She was born Abt. 1838 in Crawford Co., GA, and died Aft. 1870 in Crawford Co., GA.

Children of FELIX HAMMACK and NANCY JOHNSON are:

      i.   MARY CATHERINE E.[10] HAMMACK, b. Abt. 1856, Crawford Co., GA; d. Aft. 1875, Crawford Co., GA.

     ii.   WILLIAM H. HAMMACK, b. Abt. 1858, Crawford Co., GA; d. Aft. 1880, Crawford Co., GA.

490.   iii.   FELIX WILBORN HAMMACK, JR., b. 09 Apr 1862, Crawford Co., GA; d. 24 Apr 1940, Monroe Co., GA.

Key Sources: 1860 Crawford Co., GA, Census, p. 946; 1870 Crawford Co., GA, Census, p. 448; Crawford Co., GA, Guardians Bonds, 1874-1906, p. 9.

358. AURELIUS HARRISON[9] HAMMACK *(MANSEL W.[8], WILLIAM T.[7], ROBERT HAMMACK[6] JR., ROBERT HAMMACK[5] SR., WILLIAM "THE ELDER"[4] HAMMACK, WILLIAM "O"[3], JOHN[2] HAMMOCKE, ? JOHN[1] HAMMOT)* was born Abt. 1838 in Crawford Co., GA, and died Aft. 1880 in Houston Co., Ga. He married LOUISA M. SIMPSON 18 Dec 1866 in Crawford Co., GA. She was born Abt. 1841 in Georgia, and died Aft. 1880 in Houston Co., Ga.

Children of AURELIUS HAMMACK and LOUISA SIMPSON are:

      i.   MARTHA[10] HAMMACK, b. Abt. 1867, Crawford Co., GA; d. Aft. 1880, Houston Co., Ga.

     ii.   HENRY HAMMACK, b. Abt. 1870, Crawford Co., GA; d. Aft. 1880, Houston Co., Ga.

    iii.   BENJAMIN HAMMACK, b. Abt. 1873, Crawford Co., GA; d. Aft. 1880, Houston Co., Ga.

    iv.   HILLIARD HAMMACK, b. Abt. 1877, Crawford Co., GA; d. Aft. 1880, Houston Co., Ga.

Key Sources: 1870 Crawford Co., GA, Census, p. 443; 1880 Crawford Co., GA, Census, p. 281.

359. JAMES MANSEL[9] HAMMACK *(MANSEL W.[8], WILLIAM T.[7], ROBERT HAMMACK[6] JR., ROBERT HAMMACK[5] SR., WILLIAM "THE ELDER"[4] HAMMACK, WILLIAM "O"[3], JOHN[2] HAMMOCKE, ? JOHN[1] HAMMOT)* was born 02 Jul 1838 in Crawford Co., GA, and died 10 Apr 1930 in Crawford Co., GA. He married SAMANTHA WHITE 29 Oct 1865 in Crawford Co., GA. She was born 17 Jan 1848 in Crawford Co., GA, and died 04 Mar 1917 in Crawford Co., GA.

Children of JAMES HAMMACK and SAMANTHA WHITE are:

491.   i.   WILLIAM[10] HAMMACK, b. Abt. 1867, Crawford Co., GA; d. Bet. 1880 - 1895, Crawford Co., GA.

     ii.   MARTHA A. HAMMACK, b. Abt. 1869, Crawford Co., GA; d. Aft. 1880, Crawford Co., GA.

    iii.   JAMES TALBOT HAMMACK, b. Abt. 1872, Crawford Co., GA; d. Aft. 1900, Crawford Co., GA.

    iv.   ORLENA H. HAMMACK, b. Jul 1877, Crawford Co., GA; d. Aft. 1900, Crawford Co., GA.

     v.   CHARLES HAMMACK, b. Mar 1880, Crawford Co., GA; d. Aft. 1880, Crawford Co., GA.

Key Sources: 1870 Crawford Co., GA, Census, p. 443; Mt. Carmel Primitive Baptist Church Minutes, Crawford Co., GA; 1880 Crawford Co., GA, Census, p. 719; 1900 Crawford Co., GA, Census, p. 136.

360. CAROLINE R.[9] HAMMACK *(MANSEL W.[8], WILLIAM T.[7], ROBERT HAMMACK[6] JR., ROBERT HAMMACK[5] SR., WILLIAM "THE ELDER"[4] HAMMACK, WILLIAM "O"[3], JOHN[2] HAMMOCKE, ? JOHN[1] HAMMOT)* was born 02 Dec 1847 in Crawford Co., GA, and died 09 Jan 1913 in Bibb Co., GA. She married WILLIAM T. HAMRICK 20 Feb 1868 in Crawford Co., GA. He was born 1842 in Upson Co., GA, and died Bef. 1880 in Crawford Co., GA.

Children of CAROLINE HAMMACK and WILLIAM HAMRICK are:

> i.   WILLIAM WRIGHT[10] HAMRICK, b. 15 Mar 1872, Crawford Co., GA; d. Aft. 1880, Crawford Co., GA.
> ii. HORACE CLIFFORD HAMRICK, b. Abt. 1874, Crawford Co., GA; d. Aft. 1900, Bibb Co., GA.
> iii. JAMES HARRISON HAMRICK, b. Abt. 1877, Crawford Co., GA; d. Aft. 1880, Crawford Co., GA.

Key Source: 1880 Crawford Co., GA, Census, p. 717.

361. JOHN WILBUR[9] HAMMACK *(MANSEL W.[8], WILLIAM T.[7], ROBERT HAMMACK[6] JR., ROBERT HAMMACK[5] SR., WILLIAM "THE ELDER"[4] HAMMACK, WILLIAM "O"[3], JOHN[2] HAMMOCKE, ? JOHN[1] HAMMOT)* was born Abt. 1851 in Crawford Co., GA, and died Abt. 1937 in Crawford Co., GA. He married LOUISA ELIZABETH COCHRAN Abt. 1870 in Crawford Co., GA. She was born 23 Feb 1850 in Crawford Co., GA, and died 12 May 1904 in Crawford Co., GA.

Children of JOHN HAMMACK and LOUISA COCHRAN are:

> i.   LULA F.[10] HAMMACK, b. Abt. 1871, Crawford Co., GA; d. Aft. 1918, Crawford Co., GA; m. H. J. RIGDON, 29 Dec 1892, Crawford Co., GA.
> ii.   THOMAS HAMMACK, b. Jun 1872, Crawford Co., GA; d. Aft. 1918, Crawford Co., GA.
> iii. ADA AURELIA HAMMACK, b. Dec 1875, Crawford Co., GA; d. Aft. 1918, Crawford Co., GA.
> iv.   JOHN HAMMACK, b. Jan 1877, Crawford Co., GA; d. Aft. 1918, Crawford Co., GA.
> v.   CHARLEY E. HAMMACK, b. Mar 1879, Crawford Co., GA; d. Aft. 1918, Crawford Co., GA.
> vi.   CARRIE HAMMACK, b. Aug 1883, Crawford Co., GA; d. Aft. 1900, Crawford Co., GA.
> vii. MATTIE EUGENIA HAMMACK, b. Apr 1886, Crawford Co., GA; d. Aft. 1918, Crawford Co., GA.
> viii. EMMA HAMMACK, b. May 1888, Crawford Co., GA; d. Aft. 1918, Crawford Co., GA; m. [-------] VISAGE.
> ix.   BLANNIE SELMA HAMMACK, b. Aug 1892, Crawford Co., GA; d. Aft. 1918, Crawford Co., GA.
> x.   JAMES C. HAMMACK, b. Aug 1895, Crawford Co., GA; d. Aft. 1918, Crawford Co., GA.

Key Sources: *Crawford County, Georgia: Families on the Fall Line* (Roberta, GA, 2006), p. 48; 1880 Crawford Co., GA, Census, p. 717; 1900 Crawford Co., GA, Census, p. 136; Crawford Co., GA, Will Book C, p. 184.

362. CORNELIUS L.[9] BRYANT *(ELIZABETH[8] HAMMACK, WILLIAM T.[7], ROBERT HAMMACK[6] JR., ROBERT HAMMACK[5] SR., WILLIAM "THE ELDER"[4] HAMMACK, WILLIAM "O"[3], JOHN[2] HAMMOCKE, ? JOHN[1] HAMMOT)* was born Abt. 1834 in Jones Co., GA, and died Aft. 1875 in Jones Co., GA. He married ELVIRA [------] Abt. 1866 in Jones Co., GA. She was born Abt. 1845 in Georgia, and died Aft. 1870 in Jones Co., GA.

Children of CORNELIUS BRYANT and ELVIRA [------] are:

> i.   GEORGE[10] BRYANT, b. Abt. 1867, Jones Co., GA; d. Aft. 1870, Jones Co., GA.
> ii. MARY BRYANT, b. Abt. 1869, Jones Co., GA; d. Aft. 1870, Jones Co., GA.

Key Sources: 1870 Jones Co., GA, Census, p. 308; Jones Co., GA, Deed Book T, pp. 396-397.

363. FELIX THEODORE[9] BRYANT *(ELIZABETH[8] HAMMACK, WILLIAM T.[7], ROBERT HAMMACK[6] JR., ROBERT HAMMACK[5] SR., WILLIAM "THE ELDER"[4] HAMMACK, WILLIAM "O"[3], JOHN[2] HAMMOCKE, ? JOHN[1] HAMMOT)* was born 09 Jun 1840 in Jones Co., GA, and died 11 Oct 1915 in Jones Co., GA. He married MARTHA EILZABETH FELTS 14 Jan 1875 in Jones Co., GA, daughter of

WILLIAM FELTS and MARTHA/MARGARET TAYLOR. She was born 18 Mar 1847 in Jones Co., GA, and died 12 Aug 1891 in Jones Co., GA.

Children of FELIX BRYANT and MARTHA FELTS are:

  i. JAMES[10] BRYANT, b. Abt. 1866, Jones Co., GA; d. Aft. 1880, Jones Co., GA.
  ii. SARAH BRYANT, b. Abt. 1868, Jones Co., GA; d. Aft. 1880, Jones Co., GA.
  iii. JOHN BRYANT, b. Abt. 1870, Jones Co., GA; d. Aft. 1880, Jones Co., GA.
  iv. MAUDE BRYANT, b. Abt. 1871, Jones Co., GA; d. Aft. 1880, Jones Co., GA.
  v. NORA BRYANT, b. Abt. 1875, Jones Co., GA; d. Aft. 1880, Jones Co., GA.
  vi. MINNIE BRYANT, b. Abt. 1877, Jones Co., GA; d. Aft. 1880, Jones Co., GA.
  vii. MARY FLOYD BRYANT, b. 1879, Jones Co., GA; d. Aft. 1900, Jones Co., GA; m. EUGENE EVERIDGE.
  viii. CLIFFORD BRYANT, b. 1883, Jones Co., GA; d. Aft. 1900, Jones Co., GA.
  ix. CLAUDE OWEN BRYANT, b. 22 Feb 1885, Jones Co., GA; d. 19 Apr 1936, Jones Co., GA; m. SUSIE MAE BROWN; b. 14 May 1894, Jones Co., GA; d. 25 Jun 1961, Jones Co., GA.
  x. MATTIE TORA BRYANT, b. Abt. 1887, Jones Co., GA; d. Aft. 1887, Jones Co., GA.
  xi. MAGGIE BELLE BRYANT, b. 17 May 1887, Jones Co., GA; d. 17 May 1888, Jones Co., GA.

Key Source: 1870 Jones Co., GA, Census, pp. 224-225; 1880 Jones Co., GA, Census, p. 399. Although they are listed as Bryants in the 1880 census, it seems probable that James, Sarah, John, and Maude Bryant may actually have been surnamed Felts and children of Martha Felts born prior to her marriage to Theodore Bryant. Note that James and Sallie Felts appear in the household of Margaret Felts in 1870.

364. MELISSA G.[9] BRYANT (*ELIZABETH[8] HAMMACK, WILLIAM T.[7], ROBERT HAMMACK[6] JR., ROBERT HAMMACK[5] SR., WILLIAM "THE ELDER"[4] HAMMACK, WILLIAM "O"[3], JOHN[2] HAMMOCKE, ? JOHN[1] HAMMOT*) was born 26 Sep 1847 in Jones Co., GA, and died 12 Nov 1899 in Jones Co., GA. She married JAMES W. SLOCUMB 26 Sep 1867 in Jones Co., GA. He was born Abt. 1846 in Georgia, and died Aft. 1880 in Jones Co., GA.

Children of MELISSA BRYANT and JAMES SLOCUMB are:

  i. CHARLES[10] SLOCUMB, b. Abt. 1868, Jones Co., GA; d. Aft. 1880, Jones Co., GA.
  ii. WILLIAM SLOCUMB, b. Abt. 1870, Jones Co., GA; d. Aft. 1880, Jones Co., GA.
  iii. JOHN SLOCUMB, b. Abt. 1872, Jones Co., GA; d. Aft. 1880, Jones Co., GA.
  iv. ALICE E. SLOCUMB, b. 30 Jun 1873, Jones Co., GA; d. 20 Feb 1874, Jones Co., GA.
  v. PERRY L. SLOCUMB, b. 30 Jul 1874, Jones Co., GA; d. 25 Sep 1875, Jones Co., GA.

Key Source: 1880 Jones Co., GA, Census, p. 398.

365. WILLIAM WELBORN[9] AMOS (*KATHERINE[8] HAMMACK, WILLIAM T.[7], ROBERT HAMMACK[6] JR., ROBERT HAMMACK[5] SR., WILLIAM "THE ELDER"[4] HAMMACK, WILLIAM "O"[3], JOHN[2] HAMMOCKE, ? JOHN[1] HAMMOT*) was born 25 Jan 1834 in Talbot Co., GA, and died 12 Sep 1863 in Confederate States Army. He married ? ORPHY FLOWERS Abt. 1861 in Alabama. She was born Abt. 1832 in Alabama, and died Aft. 1870 in Pike Co., AL.

Children of WILLIAM AMOS and ? FLOWERS are:

  i. ? WILBORN[10] AMOS, b. Abt. 1862, Pike Co., AL; d. Aft. 1870, Pike Co., AL.
  ii. ? CATHERINE AMOS, b. Abt. 1864, Pike Co., AL; d. Aft. 1870, Pike Co., AL.

Key Source: Amos Family File, Fort Smith Public Library, Fort Smith, AR.

366. HENRY WASHINGTON[9] AMOS (*KATHERINE[8] HAMMACK, WILLIAM T.[7], ROBERT HAMMACK[6] JR., ROBERT HAMMACK[5] SR., WILLIAM "THE ELDER"[4] HAMMACK, WILLIAM "O"[3], JOHN[2] HAMMOCKE, ? JOHN[1] HAMMOT*) was born 08 Apr 1837 in Talbot Co., GA, and died 01 Dec

1889 in Coffee Co., AL. He married (1) EMELINE MILES 22 Oct 1857 in Pike Co., GA. She was born Abt. 1838 in Alabama, and died Abt. 1868 in Coffee Co., AL. He married (2) MARTHA JANE AINSWORTH 30 Aug 1870 in Pike Co., GA.

Children of HENRY AMOS and EMELINE MILES are:

    i.   DAVID W.[10] AMOS, b. Sep 1858, Pike Co., AL; d. Aft. 1900, Gilmer Co., TX; m. RACHEL ARP.

    ii.   DONIE AMOS, b. Abt. 1860, Pike Co., AL; d. Aft. 1900, Gilmer Co., TX; m. WILLIAM LONGSHORE.

    iii.   LULA AMOS, b. 03 Nov 1862, Pike Co., AL; d. 04 Aug 1934, Coffee Co., AL; m. (1) R. M. HUGHES; b. 28 Jan 1853, Alabama; d. 20 Dec 1923, Coffee Co., AL; m. (2) J. N. WALKER, 25 Aug 1881, Pike Co., GA.

    iv.   MARTHA F. AMOS, b. Abt. 1866, Pike Co., AL; m. FRAIGHT SMITH.

Children of HENRY AMOS and MARTHA AINSWORTH are:

    v.   ADA E.[10] AMOS, b. 26 Apr 1871, Coffee Co., AL; d. 22 Feb 1894, Coffee Co., AL; m. R. M. HUGHES, 1888, Coffee Co., AL.

    vi.   SARAH BEVERLY AMOS, b. 19 Jun 1872, Coffee Co., AL; d. 06 Jan 1942, Pike Co., AL; m. SOLOMON G. GRIMES, 08 Jan 1891, Pike Co., GA; b. 24 Aug 1869, Pike Co., AL; d. 25 Apr 1943, Pike Co., AL.

    vii.   ELIZABETH JANE AMOS, b. 30 Nov 1874, Coffee Co., AL; d. Aft. 1880, Coffee Co., AL; m. GEORGE W. HUGHES, 15 Feb 1894, Pike Co., GA.

    viii.   REBECCA CARY AMOS, b. 30 Sep 1875, Coffee Co., AL; d. 03 May 1932, Coffee Co., AL; m. J. T. STANTON, 1889, Pike Co., GA.

    ix.   SUSANNAH AMOS, b. 10 Mar 1878, Coffee Co., AL; d. Aug 1945, Coffee Co., AL; m. J. M. MATTHEWS, 07 Feb 1893, Pike Co., GA.

    x.   JULIA A. E. AMOS, b. Abt. 1880, Coffee Co., AL; d. Aft. 1880, Coffee Co., AL; m. T. H. BUNDY, 1907, Coffee Co., AL.

    xi.   CELESTE AMOS, b. Abt. 1881, Coffee Co., AL; d. 01 Apr 1973, Coffee Co., AL; m. J. H. PEACOCK, 1897, Coffee Co., AL.

Key Source: Amos Family File, Fort Smith Public Library, Fort Smith, AR.

367. WILLIAM GREENBURY[9] AMOS (*KATHERINE*[8] *HAMMACK, WILLIAM T.*[7]*, ROBERT HAMMACK*[6] *JR., ROBERT HAMMACK*[5] *SR., WILLIAM "THE ELDER"*[4] *HAMMACK, WILLIAM "O"*[3]*, JOHN*[2] *HAMMOCKE, ? JOHN*[1] *HAMMOT*) was born 25 Aug 1842 in Talbot Co., GA, and died 23 Apr 1916 in Coffee Co., AL. He married LAURINE R. WYNN ROBERTSON 04 Jan 1866 in Pike Co., GA. She was born 02 Aug 1838 in Monroe Co., GA, and died 31 Oct 1909 in Coffee Co., AL.

Children of WILLIAM AMOS and LAURINE ROBERTSON are:

    i.   FRANCES ELIZABETH CATHERINE[10] AMOS, b. 29 Nov 1866, Coffee Co., AL; d. 13 Feb 1889, Coffee Co., AL; m. THOMAS EDMUND HEAD, 25 Nov 1886, Coffee Co., AL; b. 30 Aug 1866, Coffee Co., AL; d. 19 Apr 1939, Coffee Co., AL.

    ii.   SARAH MILLANDA AMOS, b. 07 Feb 1868, Coffee Co., AL; d. 09 Nov 1918, Coffee Co., AL; m. THOMAS EDMUND HEAD, 05 Oct 1889, Coffee Co., AL.

    iii.   IDA E. AMOS, b. 28 Aug 1870, Coffee Co., AL; d. 14 Aug 1945, Coffee Co., AL; m. J. W. WILLIAMSON, 1895, Coffee Co., AL.

    iv.   JAMES W. BEVERLY AMOS, b. 31 Oct 1872, Coffee Co., AL; d. 17 Jan 1930, Pike Co., AL; m. IDA REVILL.

    v.   MATTIE R. AMOS, b. 29 Sep 1874, Coffee Co., AL; d. 02 Sep 1929, Coffee Co., AL; m. GEORGE SELLARS, 1889, Coffee Co., AL.

    vi.   NANCY VICTORIA AMOS, b. 17 Jun 1876, Coffee Co., AL; d. 07 Jan 1929, Coffee Co., AL; m. W. C. "WILL" CLARK, 1898, Coffee Co., AL.

vii. MARY DELLA AMOS, b. 18 Jul 1878, Coffee Co., AL; d. 04 Nov 1911, Coffee Co., AL; m. D. M. MARLER, 1908, Coffee Co., AL.

viii. ALA "ALER" EMELINE AMOS, b. 04 Mar 1882, Coffee Co., AL; d. 16 Feb 1952, Coffee Co., AL; m. JAMES R. CLARK, 1903, Coffee Co., AL.

Key Source: Amos Family File, Fort Smith Public Library, Fort Smith, AR.

368. GEORGE WASHINGTON[9] AMOS *(KATHERINE[8] HAMMACK, WILLIAM T.[7], ROBERT HAMMACK[6] JR., ROBERT HAMMACK[5] SR., WILLIAM "THE ELDER"[4] HAMMACK, WILLIAM "O"[3], JOHN[2] HAMMOCKE, ? JOHN[1] HAMMOT)* was born 28 Feb 1845 in Talbot Co., GA, and died 20 Feb 1915 in Sebastian Co., AR. He married (1) SARAH RAMBO. She was born Abt. 1850 in Arkansas, and died 14 Sep 1922 in Sebastian Co., AR. He married (2) MARY JANE CARTER 30 Aug 1866 in Pike Co., GA. She was born 29 Sep 1842 in Pike Co., AL, and died 16 Mar 1895 in Sebastian Co., AR. He married (3) MRS. M. A. CARTER 18 Sep 1899 in Sebastian Co., AR.

Children of GEORGE AMOS and MARY CARTER are:

i. WILLIAM WILBURN[10] AMOS, b. 18 Jul 1867, Pike Co., AL; d. 17 Feb 1931, Sebastian Co., AR; m. ARSULA JANE CALHOUN, 27 Dec 1890, Sebastian Co., AR.

ii. SEABORN WASHINGTON AMOS, b. Abt. 1869, Pike Co., AL; d. 20 Mar 1908, Sebastian Co., AR; m. NANCY FORGE, 16 Mar 1886, Sebastian Co., AR; b. Abt. 1871, Arkansas; d. 17 Feb 1938, Sebastian Co., AR.

iii. JOHN HENRY AMOS, b. 02 Feb 1871, Pike Co., AL; d. 26 Aug 1935, Washington Co., AR; m. (1) MARY ANN ELIZABETH FRYE, 13 Dec 1890, Sebastian Co., AR; b. 03 Jul 1871, Sebastian Co., AR; d. 09 Jan 1954, Sebastian Co., AR; m. (2) LINNIE B. HOPKINS, Abt. 1915, Sebastian Co., AR.

iv. JAMES BEVERLY AMOS, b. 12 Jan 1873, Sebastian Co., AR; d. 20 Jun 1964, Sebastian Co., AR; m. (1) SARAH HASSIE JAMERSON; m. (2) AMY ARCHINA OLDHAM, 19 Oct 1893, Sebastian Co., AR.

v. MARY CATHERINE AMOS, b. 14 Apr 1876, Sebastian Co., AR; d. Abt. 1952, Sebastian Co., AR; m. HENRY JOHNSON, 09 Nov 1891, Sebastian Co., AR.

vi. MARTHA MATILDA AMOS, b. 16 Jun 1877, Sebastian Co., AR; d. 01 Jan 1968, Sebastian Co., AR; m. GENERAL PRICE CROSSLAND, 17 Oct 1897, Sebastian Co., AR; b. 10 Dec 1873, Arkansas; d. 26 Feb 1956, Sebastian Co., AR.

vii. ALEXANDER ZACHARIAH AMOS, b. 06 Jan 1879, Sebastian Co., AR; d. Feb 1973, Sebastian Co., AR; m. (1) MARY TALKINGTON; m. (2) CORA HALEY, 20 Aug 1899, Sebastian Co., AR.

viii. ADA LEE AMOS, b. 22 Aug 1882, Sebastian Co., AR; d. 22 May 1973, Sebastian Co., AR; m. MARVIN CROSSLAND, 14 Oct 1894, Sebastian Co., AR; b. 21 May 1880, Sebastian Co., AR; d. 26 Mar 1966, Sebastian Co., AR.

ix. NETTIE AMOS, b. 03 Apr 1886, Sebastian Co., AR; d. 14 Jan 1942, Sebastian Co., AR; m. HERBERT MCFALL.

Key Source: Amos Family File, Fort Smith Public Library, Fort Smith, AR.

369. MARTHA ELIZABETH "MAT"[9] AMOS *(KATHERINE[8] HAMMACK, WILLIAM T.[7], ROBERT HAMMACK[6] JR., ROBERT HAMMACK[5] SR., WILLIAM "THE ELDER"[4] HAMMACK, WILLIAM "O"[3], JOHN[2] HAMMOCKE, ? JOHN[1] HAMMOT)* was born 05 Dec 1846 in Talbot Co., GA, and died 27 Jul 1915 in Coffee Co., AL. She married WILLIAM BRYCE PAUL 16 Jul 1866 in Coffee Co., AL. He was born 1846 in Alabama.

Children of MARTHA AMOS and WILLIAM PAUL are:

i. ELIZABETH VICTORIA[10] PAUL, b. 13 Jan 1868, Coffee Co., AL; d. 16 Feb 1955, Coffee Co., AL; m. SAMUEL PICKENS WILSON.

ii.   GEORGE FREEMAN PAUL, b. Abt. 1870, Coffee Co., AL; d. Aft. 1880, Pike Co., AL; m. ROXY WILKINS.

iii. WALLACE PAUL, b. 20 May 1875, Coffee Co., AL; d. 30 Mar 1931, Coffee Co., AL; m. VICKEY SANDERS.

iv.   N. LAFAYETTE PAUL, b. 19 Jan 1877, Coffee Co., AL; d. 21 Nov 1946, Coffee Co., AL; m. JULIA WILKINS.

v.   BRYCE PAUL, m. ADDIE GIBSON.

vi.   LELA PAUL, b. 1869, Coffee Co., AL; d. 13 Sep 1953, Coffee Co., AL; m. PERRY FLOWERS.

vii. KATIE SARAH PAUL, b. 1880, Coffee Co., AL; d. Aft. 1900, Coffee Co., AL; m. ASA LOWERY.

Key Source: Amos Family File, Fort Smith Public Library, Fort Smith, AR.

370. JOHN ZACHARIAH "ZACHARY"[9] AMOS *(KATHERINE[8] HAMMACK, WILLIAM T.[7], ROBERT HAMMACK[6] JR., ROBERT HAMMACK[5] SR., WILLIAM "THE ELDER"[4] HAMMACK, WILLIAM "O"[3], JOHN[2] HAMMOCKE, ? JOHN[1] HAMMOT)* was born 06 Oct 1848 in Talbot Co., GA, and died 18 Aug 1909 in Pike Co., AL. He married FRANCES MARY "MOLLIE" MOORE 22 Mar 1866 in Pike Co., GA. She was born Abt. 1843 in Alabama, and died Aft. 1882 in Pike Co., AL.
Children of JOHN AMOS and FRANCES MOORE are:

i.   ELLA L.[10] AMOS, b. 01 Jan 1867, Pike Co., AL; d. Bef. 1870, Pike Co., AL.

ii.   JOSEPHINE T. AMOS, b. 21 Nov 1867, Pike Co., AL; d. Aft. 1880, Pike Co., AL.

iii. EUGENIA AUGUSTA AMOS, b. 01 Oct 1869, Pike Co., AL; d. Aft. 1880, Pike Co., AL.

iv.   MARIETTA AMOS, b. 17 Mar 1871, Pike Co., AL; d. Aft. 1880, Pike Co., AL.

v.   JOHN L. AMOS, b. 12 Feb 1873, Pike Co., AL; d. Bef. 1880, Pike Co., AL.

vi.   CATHERINE ELIZABETH AMOS, b. 11 Nov 1874, Pike Co., AL; d. Aft. 1880, Pike Co., AL.

vii. OLIVE A. AMOS, b. 18 Feb 1876, Pike Co., AL; d. Aft. 1880, Pike Co., AL.

viii. WALTER HOOD AMOS, b. 16 Sep 1878, Pike Co., AL; d. Aft. 1880, Pike Co., AL.

ix.   GEORGE BURKETT AMOS, b. 24 Apr 1882, Pike Co., AL.

Key Source: Amos Family File, Fort Smith Public Library, Fort Smith, AR.

371. REBECCA CAROLINE[9] AMOS *(KATHERINE[8] HAMMACK, WILLIAM T.[7], ROBERT HAMMACK[6] JR., ROBERT HAMMACK[5] SR., WILLIAM "THE ELDER"[4] HAMMACK, WILLIAM "O"[3], JOHN[2] HAMMOCKE, ? JOHN[1] HAMMOT)* was born 28 Sep 1852 in Talbot Co., GA, and died 12 May 1902 in Escambia Co., AL. She married BUCHANNON WISE 04 Sep 1875 in Pike Co., GA. He was born 14 Nov 1856 in Coffee Co., AL, and died 29 Aug 1928 in Escambia Co., AL.
Children of REBECCA AMOS and BUCHANNON WISE are:

i.   JAMES DANIEL[10] WISE, b. Jul 1878, Coffee Co., AL; d. Aft. 1900, Escambia Co., AL.

ii.   SARAH CATHERINE WISE, b. Oct 1876, Coffee Co., AL; d. Aft. 1900, Escambia Co., AL; m. ANDEW DRISCOL, Abt. 1898, Coffee Co., AL.

iii. WALTER WILLIAM WISE, b. Nov 1887, Coffee Co., AL; d. 1952, Escambia Co., AL; m. IDA BELL HALL.

iv.   FREEMAN WISE, b. May 1890, Coffee Co., AL; d. Aft. 1900, Escambia Co., AL.

v.   OLA PEARL WISE, b. Jan 1896, Coffee Co., AL; d. Aft. 1900, Escambia Co., AL.

vi.   EXA J. WISE, b. Jul 1897, Coffee Co., AL; d. Aft. 1900, Escambia Co., AL.

Key Source: Amos Family File, Fort Smith Public Library, Fort Smith, AR.

372. ISAAC LAFAYETTE[9] AMOS *(KATHERINE[8] HAMMACK, WILLIAM T.[7], ROBERT HAMMACK[6] JR., ROBERT HAMMACK[5] SR., WILLIAM "THE ELDER"[4] HAMMACK, WILLIAM "O"[3], JOHN[2]*

HAMMOCKE, ? JOHN[1] HAMMOT) was born 09 May 1854 in Pike Co., AL, and died 07 Feb 1917 in Coffee Co., AL. He married TEMPERANCE ELIZABETH SMART 10 Jan 1878 in Coffee Co., AL. She was born 11 Aug 1862 in Alabama, and died Aft. 1893 in Coffee Co., AL.

Children of ISAAC AMOS and TEMPERANCE SMART are:

    i.   JAMES BEVERLY[10] AMOS, b. 10 Feb 1879, Coffee Co., AL; d. 23 Jul 1940, Coffee Co., AL; m. LURLENE TOWNSEND.

    ii.   SELMA AMOS, b. 21 Dec 1881, Coffee Co., AL; d. 06 Nov 1962, Coffee Co., AL; m. JAMES BAKER LEE.

    iii.   KITTY CLYDE AMOS, b. 03 Apr 1883, Coffee Co., AL; d. 08 Nov 1953, Coffee Co., AL; m. RICHARD FITZHUGH LEE.

    iv.   MARY VERNON AMOS, b. 16 Sep 1886, Coffee Co., AL; d. Aft. 1900, Coffee Co., AL; m. CHARLES TINDALL.

    v.   MAUDE MAE AMOS, b. 16 Dec 1890, Coffee Co., AL; d. Aft. 1900, Coffee Co., AL; m. DAVID DIXON MITCHELL.

    vi.   JOHN SHELBY AMOS, b. 18 Oct 1893, Coffee Co., AL; d. Aft. 1900, Coffee Co., AL; m. HELEN MULLINS.

Key Source: Amos Family File, Fort Smith Public Library, Fort Smith, AR.

373. WILLIAM P. ROBERT SIMEON[9] WRIGHT *(MARTHA ANN[8] HAMMACK, WILLIAM T.[7], ROBERT HAMMACK[6] JR., ROBERT HAMMACK[5] SR., WILLIAM "THE ELDER"[4] HAMMACK, WILLIAM "O"[3], JOHN[2] HAMMOCKE, ? JOHN[1] HAMMOT)* was born Abt. 1842 in Georgia, and died Aft. 1880 in Pike Co., GA. He married SARAH CATHERINE BAYNE HAMMACK Abt. 1865 in Crawford Co., GA, daughter of TALBOT HAMMACK and REBECCA HARRELL. She was born Abt. 1843 in Crawford Co., GA, and died Aft. 1880 in Pike Co., GA.

Children are listed above under (350) Sarah Catherine Bayne Hammack.

Key Sources: 1870 Crawford Co., GA, Census, p. 453; 1880 Pike Co., GA, Census, p. 111.

374. ALLEN GREEN[9] JACKSON *(WILLIAM P.[8], MARY "POLLY"[7] HAMMACK, ROBERT HAMMACK[6] JR., ROBERT HAMMACK[5] SR., WILLIAM "THE ELDER"[4] HAMMACK, WILLIAM "O"[3], JOHN[2] HAMMOCKE, ? JOHN[1] HAMMOT)* was born Abt. 1832 in Jones Co., GA, and died Bet. 1862 - 1870 in Jones Co., GA. He married CAROLINE M. LESLIE 04 Dec 1852 in Jones Co., GA. She was born Abt. 1834 in Jones Co., GA, and died Aft. 1870 in Jones Co., GA.

Children of ALLEN JACKSON and CAROLINE LESLIE are:

    i.   MARY ELIZABETH[10] JACKSON, b. 17 Sep 1853, Jones Co., GA; d. Aft. 1877, Jones Co., GA; m. WILEY HENRY WILLIAMS, 19 Feb 1877, Jones Co., GA.

    ii.   WILLIAM MONROE JACKSON, b. 11 Nov 1854, Jones Co., GA; d. 09 Jan 1939, Monroe Co., GA; m. ELLA SAMANTHA JAMES, Abt. 1878, Jones Co., GA; b. 19 Sep 1858, Jones Co., GA; d. 29 Nov 1937, Jones Co., GA.

    iii.   JULIA ANN JACKSON, b. Abt. 1856, Jones Co., GA; d. Aft. 1870, Jones Co., GA; m. WILLIAM T. SMITH.

    iv.   CHRISTOPHER COLUMBUS JACKSON, b. Abt. 1858, Jones Co., GA; d. Aft. 1860, Jones Co., GA.

    v.   SARAH J. JACKSON, b. Abt. 1861, Jones Co., GA; d. Aft. 1880, Jones Co., GA; m. WILLIAM WALDON.

Key Sources: 1860 Jones Co., GA, Census, p. 516; 1870 Jones Co., GA, Census, p. 283; 1880 Jones Co., GA, Census, p. 445.

375. JOHN[9] JACKSON III *(JOHN[8], MARY "POLLY"[7] HAMMACK, ROBERT HAMMACK[6] JR., ROBERT HAMMACK[5] SR., WILLIAM "THE ELDER"[4] HAMMACK, WILLIAM "O"[3], JOHN[2] HAMMOCKE, ?*

JOHN¹ HAMMOT) was born 19 Dec 1845 in Jones Co., GA, and died 1927 in Texas. He married SALLIE HAMMOCK 22 Nov 1866 in Jones Co., GA.
Children of JOHN JACKSON and SALLIE HAMMOCK are:

    i.   JOHN¹⁰ JACKSON, b. Abt. 1867, Jones Co., GA; d. Aft. 1870, Jones Co., GA.
    ii.   FLORENCE JACKSON, b. Abt. 1869, Jones Co., GA; d. Aft. 1870, Jones Co., GA.
Key Source: 1870 Jones Co., GA, Census, p. 266.

376. WILLIAM⁹ JACKSON *(JOHN⁸, MARY "POLLY"⁷ HAMMACK, ROBERT HAMMACK⁶ JR., ROBERT HAMMACK⁵ SR., WILLIAM "THE ELDER"⁴ HAMMACK, WILLIAM "O"³, JOHN² HAMMOCKE, ? JOHN¹ HAMMOT)* was born 21 Jul 1847 in Jones Co., GA, and died 20 Mar 1926 in Jones Co., GA. He married MARTHA A. HAMMACK 15 Nov 1866 in Jones Co., GA, daughter of JACKSON HAMMACK and MARY GREENE. She was born 25 Oct 1845 in Jones Co., GA, and died 23 Apr 1906 in Jones Co., GA.
Children of WILLIAM JACKSON and MARTHA HAMMACK are:

    i.   MANDA E.¹⁰ JACKSON, b. Abt. 1868, Jones Co., GA; d. Aft. 1870, Jones Co., GA.
    ii.   WILLIAM JACKSON, b. Abt. 1869, Jones Co., GA; d. Aft. 1870, Jones Co., GA.
    iii.   JUDGE JOSEPH BENJAMIN JACKSON, b. 03 Aug 1876, Jones Co., GA; d. 09 Nov 1956, Jones Co., GA; m. LILLIE PEARL JACKSON MOBLEY, 10 Jan 1915, Jones Co., GA; b. 31 Jan 1885, Jones Co., GA; d. 22 Aug 1964, Jones Co., GA.
Key Sources: 1870 Jones Co., GA, Census, p. 266; 1880 Jones Co., GA, Census, p. 439.

377. DANIEL⁹ JACKSON *(JOHN⁸, MARY "POLLY"⁷ HAMMACK, ROBERT HAMMACK⁶ JR., ROBERT HAMMACK⁵ SR., WILLIAM "THE ELDER"⁴ HAMMACK, WILLIAM "O"³, JOHN² HAMMOCKE, ? JOHN¹ HAMMOT)* was born 20 Sep 1850 in Jones Co., GA, and died 29 Dec 1930 in Jones Co., GA. He married ALMIRAH CHILDS 13 Jan 1874 in Jones Co., GA, daughter of JOHN CHILDS and SARAH BARKER. She was born 30 Mar 1854 in Jones Co., GA, and died 23 Jun 1931 in Jones Co., GA.
Children of DANIEL JACKSON and ALMIRAH CHILDS are:

    i.   LULA¹⁰ JACKSON, b. 08 May 1884, Jones Co., GA; d. 03 Jun 1885, Jones Co., GA.
    ii.   KITTIE B. JACKSON, b. 01 Sep 1885, Jones Co., GA; d. 07 Dec 1885, Jones Co., GA.
    iii.   THOMAS C. JACKSON, b. 24 Oct 1886, Jones Co., GA; d. 20 Jun 1887, Jones Co., GA.
    iv.   OTIS M. JACKSON, b. 30 Jan 1894, Jones Co., GA; d. Jun 1894, Jones Co., GA.
    v.   INFANT JACKSON, b. Dec 1896, Jones Co., GA; d. Dec 1896, Jones Co., GA.
Key Source: 1900 Jones Co., GA, Census, p. 42.

378. GEORGE W.⁹ JACKSON *(JOHN⁸, MARY "POLLY"⁷ HAMMACK, ROBERT HAMMACK⁶ JR., ROBERT HAMMACK⁵ SR., WILLIAM "THE ELDER"⁴ HAMMACK, WILLIAM "O"³, JOHN² HAMMOCKE, ? JOHN¹ HAMMOT)* was born 03 May 1859 in Jones Co., GA, and died 20 Jan 1940 in Jones Co., GA. He married DOLLIE KING JACKSON. She was born 18 May 1865 in Jones Co., GA, and died 25 Jan 1946 in Jones Co., GA.
Children of GEORGE JACKSON and DOLLIE JACKSON are:

    i.   PEARL¹⁰ JACKSON, b. Abt. 1885, Jones Co., GA; d. Aft. 1900, Jones Co., GA.
    ii.   JOHN W. JACKSON, b. Abt. 1887, Jones Co., GA; d. Aft. 1900, Jones Co., GA.
    iii.   GEORGE JACKSON, b. Abt. 1889, Jones Co., GA; d. Aft. 1900, Jones Co., GA.
    iv.   HATTIE JACKSON, b. Abt. 1891, Jones Co., GA; d. Aft. 1900, Jones Co., GA.
    v.   HENRY JACKSON, b. Abt. 1893, Jones Co., GA; d. Aft. 1900, Jones Co., GA.
    vi.   EUNICE JACKSON, b. Abt. 1895, Jones Co., GA; d. Aft. 1900, Jones Co., GA.
    vii. GLADYS JACKSON, b. Abt. 1896, Jones Co., GA; d. Aft. 1900, Jones Co., GA.
    viii. EDWARD ERNEST JACKSON, b. Abt. 1899, Jones Co., GA; d. Aft. 1900, Jones Co., GA.
    ix.   DOUGLAS JACKSON, b. Abt. 1900, Jones Co., GA; d. Aft. 1900, Jones Co., GA.

Key Source: 1900 Jones Co., GA, Census, p. 42.

379. ELIZABETH[9] WYNNE *(SICILY CATHERINE[8] GUNN, CATHERINE[7] HAMMACK, ROBERT HAMMACK[6] JR., ROBERT HAMMACK[5] SR., WILLIAM "THE ELDER"[4] HAMMACK, WILLIAM "O"[3], JOHN[2] HAMMOCKE, ? JOHN[1] HAMMOT)* was born Abt. 1828 in Taliaferro Co., GA, and died Aft. 1880 in Russell Co., AL. She married GEORGE W. STRINGER.

Children of ELIZABETH WYNNE and GEORGE STRINGER are:

i.   JOHN[10] STRINGER, b. 10 Jul 1847, Russell Co., AL; d. 22 Sep 1924, Russell Co., AL.

ii.   GEORGIA ELIZABETH STRINGER, b. Abt. 1849, Russell Co., AL; d. 1920, Lee Co., AL; m. L. E. CORBETT.

Key Sources: 1860 Russell Co., AL, Census, p. 920; 1870 Russell Co., AL, Census, p. 216.

380. ROBERT[9] HAMMACK *(CHARLES[8], BENJAMIN[7], BENEDICT[6], ROBERT HAMMACK[5] SR., WILLIAM "THE ELDER"[4] HAMMACK, WILLIAM "O"[3], JOHN[2] HAMMOCKE, ? JOHN[1] HAMMOT)* was born Bet. 1817 - 1824 in Richmond Co., VA, and died 15 Feb 1859 in Northumberland Co., VA. He married SARAH CAMPBELL Abt. 04 Jan 1841 in Northumberland Co., VA. She was born Abt. 1822 in Virginia, and died Aft. 11 Oct 1869 in Northumberland Co., VA.

Children of ROBERT HAMMACK and SARAH CAMPBELL are:

i.   CHARLES P.[10] HAMMACK, b. Abt. 1842, Northumberland Co., VA; d. 11 Oct 1869, Northumberland Co., VA; m. FRANCES [------].

ii.   WILLIAM R. HAMMACK, b. Abt. 1845, Northumberland Co., VA; d. Aft. 1900, Northumberland Co., VA; m. B. ELIZA [------].

iii. GEORGE A. HAMMACK, b. Abt. 1851, Northumberland Co., VA; d. 06 Jun 1874, Northumberland Co., VA.

iv.   BENJAMIN F. HAMMACK, b. Abt. 1857, Northumberland Co., VA; d. Aft. 1900, Northumberland Co., VA; m. MARY [------], Abt. 1877, Northumberland Co., VA.

Key Sources: 1844-1848 Northumberland Co., VA, Personal Property Tax Lists; 1850 Northumberland Co., VA, Census, p. 342; Northumberland Co., VA, Will Book A, p. 87; 1900 Northumberland Co., VA, Census, p. 725.

381. SARAH[9] HAMMACK *(CHARLES[8], BENJAMIN[7], BENEDICT[6], ROBERT HAMMACK[5] SR., WILLIAM "THE ELDER"[4] HAMMACK, WILLIAM "O"[3], JOHN[2] HAMMOCKE, ? JOHN[1] HAMMOT)* was born Abt. 1827 in Richmond Co., VA, and died 15 Sep 1862 in Northumberland Co., VA. She married JOSEPH DAMERON Abt. 10 Aug 1841 in Northumberland Co., VA, son of WILLIAM DAMERON and MILLY [------]. He was born Abt. 1820 in Richmond Co., VA, and died Aft. 1860 in Northumberland Co., VA.

Children of SARAH HAMMACK and JOSEPH DAMERON are:

i.   ALICE J.[10] DAMERON, b. Abt. 1842, Northumberland Co., VA; m. WILLIAM S. OBEIR, Abt. 18 May 1865, Northumberland Co., VA; b. Abt. 1842, Northumberland Co., VA.

ii.   LETITICIA ANN DAMERON, b. Abt. 1844, Northumberland Co., VA; m. FREDERICK TYSON, Abt. 22 Dec 1872, Northumberland Co., VA; b. Abt. 1842, Northumberland Co., VA.

iii. BARZILLA JAMES DAMERON, b. Abt. 1847, Northumberland Co., VA; m. ISABELLA EDWARDS, Abt. 1867, Northumberland Co., VA.

iv.   MARY FRANCES DAMERON, b. Abt. 1850, Northumberland Co., VA; m. HENRY TAYLOR, Abt. 07 Mar 1872, Northumberland Co., VA; b. Abt. 1841, Northumberland Co., VA.

  v. ANDREW FRANKLIN JACKSON DAMERON, b. Abt. 1854, Northumberland Co., VA; m. ELIZABETH H. RICHARDSON, Abt. 20 Apr 1881, Northumberland Co., VA; b. Abt. 1859, Northumberland Co., VA.

  vi. CHARLES STEPTOE DAMERON, b. Abt. 1858, Northumberland Co., VA; m. MARY ADELINE ANDERSON, 10 Jan 1880, Northumberland Co., VA; b. Abt. 1864, Northumberland Co., VA.

  vii. FERDINAND JEFFERSON DAMERON, b. 05 Mar 1860, Northumberland Co., VA.

  viii. JOSEPHINE K. DAMERON, b. 26 Apr 1862, Northumberland Co., VA.

Key Sources: 1850 Northumberland Co., VA, Census, p. 321; 1860 Northumberland Co., VA, Census, p. 859; Northumberland Co., VA, Register of Deaths; Northumberland Co., VA, Register of Marriages, 1853-1917; *The Dameron-Damron Genealogy, the descendants of Lawrence Dameron* (Madison, CN, 1953), pp. 61-j, 61-k, 61-l.

382. BENJAMIN[9] HAMMACK *(WILLIAM[8], BENJAMIN[7], BENEDICT[6], ROBERT HAMMACK[5] SR., WILLIAM "THE ELDER"[4] HAMMACK, WILLIAM "O"[3], JOHN[2] HAMMOCKE, ? JOHN[1] HAMMOT)* was born Abt. 1819 in Richmond Co., VA, and died Aft. 1880 in Washington, D. C. He married (1) SUSAN PIDDITT 08 May 1839 in Alexandria, VA. She was born Abt. 1819 in Virginia, and died Bef. 19 Dec 1855 in Alexandria, VA. He married (2) MARY ANN HARPER 19 Dec 1855 in Alexandria, VA. She was born Abt. 1828 in Massachusetts, and died Aft. 1900 in Washington, D. C..
Children of BENJAMIN HAMMACK and MARY HARPER are:

  i. WILLIAM L.[10] HAMMACK, b. Abt. 1857, Virginia; d. Aft. 1870, Washington, D. C.

  ii. FRANCIS A. HAMMACK, b. Abt. 1860, Virginia; d. Aft. 1870, Washington, D. C.

Key Sources: 1840 Washington, D.C., Census, p. 203; 1870 Washington, D.C., Census, p. 330; 1880 Washington, D.C., Census, p. 163.

383. WILLIAM CLARKE[9] HAMMACK *(WILLIAM[8], BENJAMIN[7], BENEDICT[6], ROBERT HAMMACK[5] SR., WILLIAM "THE ELDER"[4] HAMMACK, WILLIAM "O"[3], JOHN[2] HAMMOCKE, ? JOHN[1] HAMMOT)* was born Abt. 1820 in Richmond Co., VA, and died Bet. 1870 - 1880 in Franklin Co., MS. He married NANCY FAUST 20 Jan 1842 in Amite Co., MS. She was born Abt. 1826 in Amite Co., MS, and died Aft. 1880 in Amite Co., MS.
Children of WILLIAM HAMMACK and NANCY FAUST are:

  i. GEORGE HENRY M.[10] HAMMACK, b. Abt. 1843, Amite Co., MS; d. Mar 1862, Jackson, TN.

  ii. ALMEDA J. HAMMACK, b. 20 Oct 1844, Amite Co., MS; d. 06 Apr 1936, Franklin Co., MS; m. PASCHAL SEALES, 26 Jul 1869, Franklin Co., MS; b. 01 Jun 1844, Franklin Co., MS; d. 12 Dec 1913, Franklin Co., MS.

  iii. VIRGINIA L. HAMMACK, b. Abt. 1846, Amite Co., MS; d. Aft. 1850, Amite Co., MS.

  iv. THOMAS GRUNDY HAMMACK, b. Abt. 1848, Amite Co., MS; d. Bet. 1920 - 1928, Franklin Co., MS; m. LAURA A. BOWLIN, 28 Nov 1868, Franklin Co., MS; b. 06 Dec 1852, Mississippi; d. 11 Sep 1933, Franklin Co., MS.

  v. GRIFFIN P. HAMMACK, b. Abt. 1849, Amite Co., MS; d. Aft. 1860, Amite Co., MS.

  vi. CHRISTOPHER HAMMACK, b. Abt. 1852, Amite Co., MS; d. Aft. 1860, Amite Co., MS.

  vii. L. PENN HAMMACK, b. Abt. 1854, Amite Co., MS; d. Bet. 1890 - 1900, Franklin Co., MS; m. ELIZABETH VIRGINIA LONG, 23 Dec 1875, Franklin Co., MS; b. Jun 1852, Mississippi; d. Aft. 1920, Franklin Co., MS.

  viii. SEABORN T. HAMMACK, b. Abt. 1855, Amite Co., MS; d. Bet. 1880 - 1883, Franklin Co., MS; m. ANNA CASTON, 10 Jun 1875, Franklin Co., MS.

  ix. MATTHEW DARIUS HAMMACK, b. Abt. 1856, Amite Co., MS; d. Aft. 1860, Amite Co., MS.

x. RICHARD ROAN HAMMACK, b. 30 Jan 1859, Amite Co., MS; d. 18 Feb 1941, Franklin Co., MS; m. LOUISA A. CORBAN; b. 05 Sep 1864, Mississippi; d. 27 Feb 1953, Franklin Co., MS.

xi. MARGARET LORRETA HAMMACK, b. 31 Mar 1861, Franklin Co., MS; d. 31 Dec 1956, Franklin Co., MS; m. ELBERT E. LEGGETT, 14 Apr 1881, Franklin Co., MS; b. 26 Sep 1856, Mississippi; d. 17 Apr 1915, Franklin Co., MS.

xii. CYNTHIA HAMMACK, b. Abt. 1864, Franklin Co., MS; m. SILAS BOLIN, 27 May 1877, Franklin Co., MS.

Key Sources: Amite Co., MS, Deed Book 7, p. 507; Amite Co., MS, Deed Book 10, p. 340; Franklin Co., MS, Deed Book G, p. 477; 1850 Amite Co., MS, Census, p. 79; 1860 Amite Co., MS, Census, p. 233; 1870 Franklin Co., MS, Census, p. 74.

384. JOHN HENRY⁹ HAMMACK *(WILLIAM⁸, BENJAMIN⁷, BENEDICT⁶, ROBERT HAMMACK⁵ SR., WILLIAM "THE ELDER"⁴ HAMMACK, WILLIAM "O"³, JOHN² HAMMOCKE, ? JOHN¹ HAMMOT)* was born Bet. 1830 - 1833 in Northumberland Co., VA, and died 1917 in Adams Co., MS. He married ELIZABETH ANN SINCLAIR Abt. 1858 in Alexandria, VA, daughter of GEORGE SINCLAIR. She was born 1835 in Alexandria, VA, and died 06 May 1913 in Natchez, MS.
Children of JOHN HAMMACK and ELIZABETH SINCLAIR are:

i. B. F.¹⁰ HAMMACK, b. 11 Jun 1857, Franklin Co., MS; d. 22 Jun 1866, Adams Co., MS.

ii. ALICE VIVIAN HAMMACK, b. 05 May 1859, Franklin Co., MS; d. 07 Jul 1866, Adams Co., MS.

iii. LAURA ELLA HAMMACK, b. 04 Apr 1862, Franklin Co., MS; d. 02 Dec 1938, Gregg Co., TX; m. JAMES F. STROUD, 22 Feb 1888, Adams Co., MS; b. 28 Dec 1855, Simpson Co., MS; d. 02 Jul 1933, Adams Co., MS.

iv. WILLIAM HARDING HAMMACK, b. 25 May 1864, Franklin Co., MS; d. 1943, Adams Co., MS; m. KATHERINE REBECCA MYERS, 04 Oct 1887, Tensas Parish, LA; b. 30 Apr 1862, Mississippi; d. 1935, Adams Co., MS.

v. RUFUS LEARNED HAMMACK, b. 31 Oct 1866, Franklin Co., MS; d. 11 Oct 1868, Adams Co., MS.

vi. HATTIE MAE HAMMACK, b. 05 Feb 1870, Franklin Co., MS; d. Nov 1946, Adams Co., MS; m. (1) ARCHIBALD MCD. SEAMAN; b. Jun 1861, Mississippi; d. Aft. 1900, Adams Co., MS; m. (2) JACK LEGRAND.

vii. CARRIE LEE HAMMACK, b. 24 Mar 1871, Adams Co., MS; d. 11 Jul 1957, Adams Co., MS; m. (1) JOHN C. SMITH, 19 Nov 1890, Adams Co., MS; d. 1897, Adams Co., MS; m. (2) JAMES ROBERT MARLOW, 1900, Adams Co., MS; b. 28 Feb 1863, Independence, MO; d. 11 Sep 1933, Adams Co., MS.

viii. GEORGE SINCLAIR HAMMACK, b. 23 Dec 1873, Adams Co., MS; d. 02 Aug 1919, Adams Co., MS; m. ANNIE KOERBER POINDEXTER, 19 Feb 1896, Adams Co., MS; b. Abt. 1878, Mississippi; d. 1930, Adams Co., MS.

ix. IDA GERTRUDE HAMMACK, b. 24 Nov 1878, Adams Co., MS; d. Aft. 1880, Adams Co., MS; m. DUNCAN JOSEPH EIDT, 16 Dec 1896, Adams Co., MS; b. 1877, Mississippi; d. 1949, Adams Co., MS.

Key Sources: 1860 Franklin Co., MS, Census, p. 258; 1870 Adams Co., MS, Census, p. 85; 1880 Adams Co., MS, Census, p. 50.

385. CHARLES POLK⁹ HAMMACK *(BENEDICT⁸, LEWIS⁷, BENEDICT⁶, ROBERT HAMMACK⁵ SR., WILLIAM "THE ELDER"⁴ HAMMACK, WILLIAM "O"³, JOHN² HAMMOCKE, ? JOHN¹ HAMMOT)* was born 18 Jan 1854 in Richmond Co., VA, and died 08 Mar 1932 in Richmond Co., VA. He married (1) NELLIE B. [------]. She died 10 Feb 1924 in Richmond Co., VA. He married (2) FLORENCE

ELIZABETH EVANS 18 Apr 1880 in Richmond Co., VA. She was born Abt. 1860 in Richmond Co., VA, and died 03 Aug 1894 in Northumberland Co., VA.
Children of CHARLES HAMMACK and FLORENCE EVANS are:

- i.   LAURENS CAREY[10] HAMMACK, b. 10 Feb 1881, Richmond Co., VA; d. 27 Mar 1925, Cook Co., IL; m. MADGE P. STONE; d. 06 Sep 1949, Cook Co., IL.
- ii. CHARLES ORVILLE HAMMACK, b. 05 Nov 1883, Richmond Co., VA; d. 17 Jul 1964; m. EVELYN NELSON, 28 Jan 1914, Omaha, NE; d. 30 Oct 1971.
- iii. ALVIN MITCHELL HAMMACK, b. 15 Mar 1888, Richmond Co., VA; d. 16 Jan 1925, Richmond Co., VA; m. MAMIE WILLIAMS, 17 Nov 1909, Richmond Co., VA.
- iv. TENNYSON EVANS HAMMACK, b. 24 Feb 1890, Richmond Co., VA; d. Abt. 1988, Reedville, VA.

Key Source: Benedict Hammack Family Bible, 1816-1971, The Library of Virginia, Richmond, VA.

386. WILLIAM GUSTAVUS[9] HAMMACK *(JOHN W.[8], WILLIAM[7], CHRISTIAN[6], ROBERT HAMMACK[5] SR., WILLIAM "THE ELDER"[4] HAMMACK, WILLIAM "O"[3], JOHN[2] HAMMOCKE, ? JOHN[1] HAMMOT)* was born Abt. 1825 in Richmond Co., VA, and died Aft. 1852 in Baltimore, MD. He married EMMA LOUISE WRIGHT Abt. 1850 in Washington, D. C.. She was born Abt. 1830 in Maryland, and died Aft. 1852 in Baltimore, MD.
Child of WILLIAM HAMMACK and EMMA WRIGHT is:

- i.   WILLIAM GUSTAVUS[10] HAMMACK, b. 23 May 1851, Baltimore Co., MD; d. 18 Oct 1931, Richmond, VA; m. ROBERTA CATHERINE CRABBIN, 08 Jun 1887, Virginia.

Key Sources: Henry Franklin Hammack, 1: 272-3, 315-18; Richmond Co., VA, Order Book 27, 1825-1832, p. 237.

387. WILLIAM[9] HAMMACK *(JOHN[8], ? THOMAS[7], LEWIS[6], ROBERT HAMMACK[5] SR., WILLIAM "THE ELDER"[4] HAMMACK, WILLIAM "O"[3], JOHN[2] HAMMOCKE, ? JOHN[1] HAMMOT)* was born Abt. 1825 in Virginia, and died Aft. 1850 in Bedford Co., VA. He married SUSAN [------] Abt. 1849 in Bedford Co., VA.
Child of WILLIAM HAMMACK and SUSAN [------] is:

- i.   SARAH N.[10] HAMMACK, b. Abt. 1850, Bedford Co., VA.

Key Source: 1850 Bedford Co., VA, Census, p. 296.

388. DANIEL[9] HAMMOCK *(LAIRD[8], ? JOHN[7], DANIEL[6], WILLIAM[5], RICHARD[4], WILLIAM "O"[3], JOHN[2] HAMMOCKE, ? JOHN[1] HAMMOT)* was born 18 May 1819 in Overton Co., TN, and died 11 Jan 1886 in Overton Co., TN. He married ELIZABETH. She was born 1823 in TN, and died 19 Mar 1893 in Overton Co., TN.
Children of DANIEL HAMMOCK and ELIZABETH are:

- i.   MATILDA[10] HAMMOCK, b. 13 Sep 1841, Overton Co., TN; d. 09 Jun 1908, Overton Co., TN.
- ii. WILLIAM M. HAMMOCK, b. 01 Dec 1844, Overton Co., TN; d. 17 Feb 1864, Overton Co., TN.
- iii. JOHN C. HAMMOCK, b. 11 Feb 1847, Overton Co., TN; d. 03 Jul 1863, Overton Co., TN.
- iv. JAMES CARROLL HAMMOCK, b. 22 Nov 1848, Overton Co., TN; d. 05 Apr 1924, Overton Co., TN; m. MARTHA RAMSEY, 27 Jan 1870, Overton Co., TN; b. Abt. 1846, Overton Co., TN; d. Aft. 1900, Overton Co., TN.
- v.   ANDREW J. HAMMOCK, b. 27 Oct 1850, Overton Co., TN; d. 12 Dec 1924, Overton Co., TN; m. MARY N. HARRIS; b. May 1863, Overton Co., TN; d. Aft. 1900, Overton Co., TN.
- vi. NANCY E. HAMMOCK, b. May 1853, Overton Co., TN; m. MILES JEFFERSON "JEFF" HAMMACK, 02 Feb 1869, Overton Co., TN.

    vii.   RACHEL HAMMOCK, b. 01 Jun 1859, Overton Co., TN; d. 12 Apr 1893, Overton Co., TN.

   viii.   MAHALA ANN HAMMOCK, b. 17 Aug 1860, Overton Co., TN; d. 02 Jul 1915, Overton Co., TN; m. GEROGE F. HAMMOCK, 19 Jan 1898, Overton Co., TN.

    ix.   HORACE A. HAMMOCK, b. Abt. 1860, Overton Co., TN; d. Aft. 1900, Overton Co., TN; m. SARAH E. [------]; b. Jun 1863, TN; d. Aft. 1900, TN.

Key Sources: 1850 Overton Co., TN, Census, p. 89; 1860 Overton Co., TN, Census, p. 258; 1880 Overton Co., TN, Census, p. 342.

389. WILLIAM[9] HAMMOCK (*LAIRD[8], ? JOHN[7], DANIEL[6], WILLIAM[5], RICHARD[4], WILLIAM "O"[3], JOHN[2] HAMMOCKE, ? JOHN[1] HAMMOT*) was born Abt. 1826 in Overton Co., TN, and died Aft. 1880 in Overton Co., TN. He married POLLY DISHMAN. She was born 10 Nov 1835 in TN, and died 20 Mar 1907 in TN.

Children of WILLIAM HAMMOCK and POLLY DISHMAN are:

     i.   NANCY[10] HAMMOCK, b. Abt. 1850, Overton Co., TN; d. Aft. 1880, Overton Co., TN.

    ii.   LAIRD HAMMOCK, b. Abt. 1854, Overton Co., TN; d. Aft. 1870, Overton Co., TN.

   iii.   MILES JEFFERSON HAMMOCK, b. Abt. 1855, Overton Co., TN; d. Aft. 1900, Overton Co., TN; m. NANCY E. HAMMOCK.

   iv.   BENJAMIN MACK HAMMOCK, b. 03 Jul 1855, Overton Co., TN; d. 26 Aug 1909, Overton Co., TN; m. MARTHA E. POSTON, 25 May 1879, Overton Co., TN; b. 13 Apr 1865, TN; d. 02 Oct 1948, Overton Co., TN.

    v.   MARTELIA ELIZABETH HAMMOCK, b. Abt. 1859, Overton Co., TN; d. Aft. 1877, Overton Co., TN; m. A. C. TAYES, 19 Aug 1877, Overton Co., TN.

   vi.   MARTHA HAMMOCK, b. Abt. 1863, Overton Co., TN; d. Aft. 1877, Overton Co., TN; m. STEPHEN HAMMACK, 02 Aug 1877, Overton Co., TN.

   vii.   MARION HAMMOCK, b. Abt. 1865, Overton Co., TN; d. Aft. 1880, Overton Co., TN.

   viii.   AMELIA C. HAMMOCK, b. Abt. 1866, Overton Co., TN; d. Aft. 1880, Overton Co., TN.

    ix.   MITCHELL W. HAMMOCK, b. Abt. 1869, Overton Co., TN; d. Aft. 1880, Overton Co., TN.

Key Sources: 1860 Overton Co., TN, Census, p. 214; 1870 Overton Co., TN, Census, p. 361; 1880 Overton Co., TN, Census, p. 343.

390. JAMES M.[9] HAMMOCK (*? WILLIAM[8], WILLIAM[7], JOHN[6], RICHARD[5], RICHARD[4], WILLIAM "O"[3], JOHN[2] HAMMOCKE, ? JOHN[1] HAMMOT*) was born Abt. 1819 in Missouri, and died Bet. 1860 - 1870 in Lincoln Co., MO. He married CATHERINE Abt. 1844 in Lincoln Co., MO. She was born Abt. 1823 in Missouri, and died Aft. 1870 in Lincoln Co., MO.

Children of JAMES HAMMOCK and CATHERINE are:

     i.   NANCY[10] HAMMOCK, b. Abt. 1845, Lincoln Co., MO; d. Aft. 1860, Lincoln Co., MO.

    ii.   MARTIN LEWIS HAMMOCK, b. Abt. 1847, Lincoln Co., MO; d. Aft. 1870, Lincoln Co., MO; m. SARAH [------], Abt. 1869, Lincoln Co., MO; b. Abt. 1850, Missouri; d. Aft. 1870, Lincoln Co., MO.

   iii.   THOMAS HAMMOCK, b. Abt. 1848, Lincoln Co., MO; d. Aft. 1850, Lincoln Co., MO.

   iv.   JAMES A. HAMMOCK, b. Abt. 1849, Lincoln Co., MO; d. Aft. 1870, Lincoln Co., MO.

    v.   HENRY W. HAMMOCK, b. Abt. 1851, Lincoln Co., MO; d. Aft. 1870, Lincoln Co., MO.

   vi.   MARY R. HAMMOCK, b. Abt. 1854, Lincoln Co., MO; d. Aft. 1870, Lincoln Co., MO.

   vii.   SARAH E. HAMMOCK, b. Abt. 1857, Lincoln Co., MO; d. Aft. 1870, Lincoln Co., MO.

   viii.   MATILDA HAMMOCK, b. Abt. 1861, Lincoln Co., MO; d. Aft. 1870, Lincoln Co., MO.

    ix.   RHODA HAMMOCK, b. Abt. 1864, Lincoln Co., MO; d. Aft. 1870, Lincoln Co., MO.

Key Sources: 1860 Lincoln Co., MO, Census, p. 463; 1870 Lincoln Co., MO, Census, p. 57.

391. BRICE MARTIN[9] HAMMOCK *(? WILLIAM[8], WILLIAM[7], JOHN[6], RICHARD[5], RICHARD[4], WILLIAM "O"[3], JOHN[2] HAMMOCKE, ? JOHN[1] HAMMOT)* was born Abt. 1820 in Missouri, and died Aft. 1900 in Howell Co., MO. He married ELECTA M. [------] Abt. 1851 in Warren Co., MO. She was born Abt. 1820 in Missouri, and died Aft. 1880 in Warren Co., MO.
Children of BRICE HAMMOCK and ELECTA [------] are:

    i.   MARY E.[10] HAMMOCK, b. Abt. 1852, Warren Co., MO; d. Aft. 1880, Warren Co., MO.
    ii. ENOS M. HAMMOCK, b. Abt. 1854, Warren Co., MO; d. Aft. 1860, Warren Co., MO.
    iii. MARGARET E. HAMMOCK, b. Abt. 1858, Warren Co., MO; d. Aft. 1880, Warren Co., MO.
    iv. EMMA J. HAMMOCK, b. Abt. 1860, Warren Co., MO; d. Aft. 1900, Howell Co., MO.
    v.   GEORGE B. HAMMOCK, b. Abt. 1862, Warren Co., MO; d. Aft. 1880, Warren Co., MO.

Key Sources: 1860 Warren Co., MO, Census, p. 214; 1880 Warren Co., MO, Census, p. 727.

392. ANDREW[9] HAMMOCK *(? WILLIAM[8], WILLIAM[7], JOHN[6], RICHARD[5], RICHARD[4], WILLIAM "O"[3], JOHN[2] HAMMOCKE, ? JOHN[1] HAMMOT)* was born Abt. 1824 in Missouri, and died Aft. 1880 in Lincoln Co., MO. He married RACHEL [------] Abt. 1840 in Lincoln Co., MO. She was born Abt. 1819 in Missouri, and died Aft. 1880 in Lincoln Co., MO.
Children of ANDREW HAMMOCK and RACHEL [------] are:

    i.   GEORGE[10] HAMMOCK, b. Abt. 1842, Missouri; d. Aft. 1880, Lincoln Co., MO.
    ii. MARY J. HAMMOCK, b. Abt. 1845, Missouri; d. Aft. 1870, Lincoln Co., MO.
    iii. ELLA ELIZABETH HAMMOCK, b. Abt. 1847, Missouri; d. Aft. 1870, Lincoln Co., MO.

Key Sources: 1860 Lincoln Co., MO, Census, p. 460; 1870 Lincoln Co., MO, Census, p. 101.

393. GEORGE[9] HAMMOCK *(? WILLIAM[8], WILLIAM[7], JOHN[6], RICHARD[5], RICHARD[4], WILLIAM "O"[3], JOHN[2] HAMMOCKE, ? JOHN[1] HAMMOT)* was born Abt. 1826 in Missouri, and died Aft. 1900 in Alameda Co., CA. He married SARAH [------] Abt. 1860 in California. She was born Abt. 1832 in Missouri, and died Aft. 1880 in Stanislaus Co., CA.
Children of GEORGE HAMMOCK and SARAH [------] are:

    i.   CHARLES R.[10] HAMMOCK, b. Abt. 1860, California; d. Aft. 1900, Alameda Co., CA.
    ii. JOEL D. HAMMOCK, b. Abt. 1865, California; d. Aft. 1900, Alameda Co., CA.
    iii. WILLIAM M. HAMMOCK, b. Abt. 1870, California; d. Aft. 1880, Stanislaus Co., CA.
    iv. GEORGE F. HAMMOCK, b. Abt. 1873, California; d. Aft. 1900, Alameda Co., CA.
    v.   MAJOR LAFAYETTE HAMMOCK, b. Abt. 1875, California; d. Aft. 1900, Alameda Co., CA.

Key Sources: 1860 Touloume Co., CA, Census, p. 437; 1880 Stanislaus Co., CA, Census, p. 370. I have speculated that George was a son of William and Mary Burrus Hammock; this connection has not been proven.

394. JOHN[9] HAMMACK *(JOHN[8], JOHN[7], JOHN[6], RICHARD[5], RICHARD[4], WILLIAM "O"[3], JOHN[2] HAMMOCKE, ? JOHN[1] HAMMOT)* was born Abt. 1795 in VA, and died Aft. 1860 in Grainger Co., TN. He married (1) UNKNOWN Abt. 1813 in Grainger Co., TN. She was born Abt. 1795 in Ireland, and died Bef. 1820 in Grainger Co., TN. He married (2) LEVICEY (VICEY) SAVAGE 21 Jan 1820 in Grainger Co., TN, daughter of ? SAVAGE and MARGARET [------]. She was born Abt. 1795 in Virginia, and died Aft. 1860 in Grainger Co., TN.
Children of JOHN HAMMACK and UNKNOWN are:

492.   i.   JESSE[10] HAMMACK, b. Abt. 1814, Grainger Co., TN; d. Aft. 1880, Union Co., TN.
493.   ii. MARTIN HAMMACK, b. Abt. 1817, Grainger Co., TN; d. Aft. 1880, Grainger Co., TN.

Key Sources: 1830 Grainger Co., TN, Census, p. 363; 1850 Grainger Co., TN, Census, p. 268; 1860 Union Co., TN, Census, p. 440; 1880 Grainger Co., TN, p. 241. I have speculated that John was the father of Jesse and Martin due to location, associations, and nomenclature. John's wife in 1850 was identified as Levicy; hence he must have had an earlier wife who was the mother of his sons, both of whom indicated in 1880 that their mother was born in Ireland.

395. PLEASANT[9] HAMMACK *(WILLIAM[8], JOHN[7], JOHN[6], RICHARD[5], RICHARD[4], WILLIAM "O"[3], JOHN[2] HAMMOCKE, ? JOHN[1] HAMMOT)* was born Abt. 1802 in Grainger Co., TN, and died Aft. 1860 in Union Co., TN. He married MARY MURPHY 12 Nov 1826 in Jefferson Co., TN. She was born Abt. 1809 in SC, and died Aft. 1880 in Unicoi Co., TN.
Children of PLEASANT HAMMACK and MARY MURPHY are:
     i.   JONATHAN[10] HAMMACK, b. Abt. 1828, Grainger Co., TN; d. Aft. 1880, Logan Co., KY; m. (1) GEMMA CABBAGE, 12 Oct 1852, Grainger Co., TN; m. (2) MARY WYRICK, 13 Mar 1853, Grainger Co., TN.
    ii.   JOSHUA HAMMACK, b. Abt. 1829, Grainger Co., TN; d. Aft. 1870, Union Co., TN; m. (1) REBECCA COATES, 18 Feb 1851, Grainger Co., TN; m. (2) ALCY SMITH, 29 Oct 1853, Grainger Co., TN.
    iii.   SARAH HAMMACK, b. Abt. 1834, Grainger Co., TN; d. Aft. 1860, Union Co., TN; m. ROBERT CARTER, 18 Apr 1859, Union Co., TN.
    iv.   JAMES HAMMACK, b. Abt. 1838, Grainger Co., TN; d. Aft. 1860, Union Co., TN.
    v.   ISAAC HAMMACK, b. Abt. 1841, Grainger Co., TN; d. Aft. 1860, Union Co., TN.
    vi.   MARY HAMMACK, b. Abt. 1844, Grainger Co., TN; d. Abt. 1914, Oklahoma; m. WILLIAM CARTER, 04 Jul 1864, Union Co., TN.
    vii.   LEVI HAMMACK, b. 21 Jun 1845, Union Co., TN; d. 15 Dec 1916, Grainger Co., TN; m. ELIZA V. THOMAS, 01 Aug 1869, Union Co., TN; b. 28 Dec 1846, Grainger Co., TN.
    viii.   JOHN HAMMACK, b. 11 Nov 1848, Grainger Co., TN; d. 30 May 1925, Grainger Co., TN; m. ELIZABETH JANE CARTER, 23 Jul 1869, Grainger Co., TN.
    ix.   ELIZABETH HAMMACK, b. Abt. 1851, Grainger Co., TN; m. JEREMIAH MUNCEY, 14 Mar 1874, Grainger Co., TN.
Key Sources: 1830 Jefferson Co., TN, Census, p. 314; 1850 Grainger Co., TN, Census, p. 224; 1860 Union Co., TN, Census, p. 436; 1870 Grainger Co., TN, Census, p. 149; 1880 Unicoi Co., TN, Census, p. 148.

396. NOAH[9] HAMMACK *(WILLIAM[8], JOHN[7], JOHN[6], RICHARD[5], RICHARD[4], WILLIAM "O"[3], JOHN[2] HAMMOCKE, ? JOHN[1] HAMMOT)* was born Abt. 1806 in Grainger Co., TN, and died Aft. 1860 in Woodford Co., IL. He married ELIZABETH [------] Abt. 1830 in Grainger Co., TN. She was born Abt. 1803 in East Tennessee, and died Aft. 1860 in McLean Co., IL.
Children of NOAH HAMMACK and ELIZABETH [------] are:
    i.   JANE[10] HAMMACK, b. Abt. 1832, East Tennessee.
494.   ii.   PETER HAMMACK, b. Abt. 1840, Indiana; d. Aft. 1880, LaClede Co., MO.
    iii.   MARTHA HAMMACK, b. Abt. 1849, Illinois.
Key Sources: 1850 McLean Co., IL, Census, p. 32; 1860 Woodford Co., IL, Census, p. 836; 1860 McLean Co., IL, Census, p. 661.

397. WILLIAM[9] HAMMOCK *(WILLIAM[8], JOHN[7], JOHN[6], RICHARD[5], RICHARD[4], WILLIAM "O"[3], JOHN[2] HAMMOCKE, ? JOHN[1] HAMMOT)* was born Abt. 1815 in Grainger Co., TN, and died Bet. 1860 - 1870 in Laurel Co., KY. He married RACHEL MURPHY 26 Jan 1837 in Grainger Co., TN. She was born 26 Sep 1816 in Tennessee, and died 03 Apr 1881 in Laurel Co., KY.
Children of WILLIAM HAMMOCK and RACHEL MURPHY are:
    i.   ISHAM[10] HAMMOCK, b. 24 Mar 1839, Grainger Co., TN; d. 18 Oct 1880, Laurel Co., KY; m. REBECCA HARTHEAD, 09 Jan 1876, Grainger Co., TN.

     ii.   NOAH HAMMOCK, b. Abt. 1841, Grainger Co., TN; d. Aft. 1880, Laurel Co., KY; m. NANCY DECKER, 28 Mar 1866, Laurel Co., KY.

    iii. ROBERT HAMMOCK, b. 18 May 1845, Grainger Co., TN; d. 07 Dec 1926, Fulton Co., AR; m. MARGARET C. SHERMAN, 27 Aug 1866, Laurel Co., KY; b. 17 Aug 1845, KY; d. 11 Nov 1923, Fulton Co., AR.

    iv. LEVI HAMMOCK, b. 17 Feb 1848, Grainger Co., TN.

     v. NEWTON EVANS HAMMOCK, b. 02 Aug 1850, Laurel Co., KY; d. 31 Jul 1929, Wallowa Co., OR; m. MARY ANN WEAVER, 23 Oct 1869, Laurel Co., KY.

    vi. JOHN B. HAMMOCK, b. 20 Sep 1853, Laurel Co., KY; d. Aft. 1900, Laurel Co., KY.

   vii. MARY JANE HAMMOCK, b. 25 Sep 1856, Laurel Co., KY; m. JOHN RILEY EATON, Abt. 1871, Laurel Co., KY.

Key Sources: 1850 Laurel Co., KY, Census, pp. 18, 23; 1870 Laurel Co., KY, Census, p. 120; 1880 Laurel Co., KY, Census, p. 269.

398. STERLING[9] HAMMACK *(WILLIAM[8], JOHN[7], JOHN[6], RICHARD[5], RICHARD[4], WILLIAM "O"[3], JOHN[2] HAMMOCKE, ? JOHN[1] HAMMOT)* was born Bet. 1820 - 1823 in Union Co., TN, and died 1908 in Grainger Co., TN. He married POLLY JORDAN 26 Oct 1843 in Claiborne Co., TN. She was born Abt. 1829 in Tennessee, and died Aft. 1880 in Grainger Co., TN.

Children of STERLING HAMMACK and POLLY JORDAN are:

     i. ALICE[10] HAMMACK, b. Abt. 1845, Grainger Co., TN; d. Aft. 1870, Grainger Co., TN.

     ii. EMELINE HAMMACK, b. Abt. 1848, Grainger Co., TN; d. Aft. 1870, Grainger Co., TN.

    iii. ELI HAMMACK, b. Abt. 1848, Grainger Co., TN; d. 21 Apr 1928, Harlan Co., KY; m. (1) MARY COLLINS, Abt. 1865, Lee Co., VA; m. (2) MATILDA CATHERINE COLLINS, 12 Jul 1887, Lee Co., VA; m. (3) LAURA JENNINGS, 1915, Lee Co., VA.

    iv. JONATHAN HAMMACK, b. Abt. 1851, Grainger Co., TN; d. Aft. 1866, Grainger Co., TN; m. LUCINDA BRYANT, 22 Sep 1866, Laurel Co., KY.

     v. MINERVA HAMMACK, b. Abt. 1854, Grainger Co., TN; d. Aft. 1870, Grainger Co., TN.

    vi. HENRY HAMMACK, b. Abt. 1856, Grainger Co., TN; d. Aft. 1910, Laurel Co., KY; m. REBECCA BRYANT; b. Abt. 1847, KY; d. Aft. 1910, Laurel Co., KY.

   vii. MATILDA HAMMACK, b. Abt. 1858, Grainger Co., TN; d. Aft. 1870, Grainger Co., TN.

  viii. LOUISA HAMMACK, b. Abt. 1865, Grainger Co., TN; d. Aft. 1870, Grainger Co., TN.

    ix. WILLIAM HAMMACK, b. Abt. 1865, Grainger Co., TN; d. Aft. 1870, Grainger Co., TN.

Key Sources: 1850 Grainger Co., TN, Census, p. 225; 1860 Grainger Co., TN, Census, p. 524; 1870 Grainger Co., TN, Census, p. 157; 1880 Grainger Co., TN, Census, p. 515.

399. ELI[9] HAMMOCK *(WILLIAM[8], JOHN[7], JOHN[6], RICHARD[5], RICHARD[4], WILLIAM "O"[3], JOHN[2] HAMMOCKE, ? JOHN[1] HAMMOT)* was born 14 Dec 1826 in Grainger Co., TN, and died Aft. 1870 in Laurel Co., KY. He married (1) SUSAN NICELY 12 Dec 1845 in Grainger Co., TN. She was born Abt. 1824 in Tennessee, and died Aft. 1870 in Laurel Co., KY. He married (2) MARY ORTON 15 Nov 1894 in Rockcastle Co., KY.

Children of ELI HAMMOCK and SUSAN NICELY are:

     i. S. A.[10] HAMMOCK, b. Abt. 1845, Grainger Co., TN; d. Aft. 1850, Grainger Co., TN.

     ii. LUCINDA HAMMOCK, b. Abt. 1848, Grainger Co., TN; d. Aft. 1850, Laurel Co., KY.

    iii. STERLING HAMMOCK, b. Abt. 1850, Laurel Co., KY; d. Aft. 1850, Laurel Co., KY.

    iv. ABIGAIL HAMMOCK, b. Abt. 1853, Laurel Co., KY; d. Aft. 1860, Laurel Co., KY.

     v. GEORGE HAMMOCK, b. Abt. 1859, Laurel Co., KY; m. SARAH TANNER, 01 Aug 1875, Rockcastle Co., KY.

    vi. WILLIAM S. HAMMOCK, b. Abt. 1860, Laurel Co., KY.

vii. ENOCH HAMMOCK, b. Abt. 1863, Rockcastle Co., KY; d. Aft. 1886, Rockcastle Co., KY; m. MARTHA ELLEN PITTMAN, 22 Dec 1881, Rockcastle Co., KY; b. 09 Oct 1865, Rockcastle Co., KY; d. 24 Aug 1928, Rockcastle Co., KY.

Key Sources: 1850 Laurel Co., KY, Census, pp. 18, 23; 1860 Laurel Co., KY, Census, p. 380; 1870 Laurel Co., KY, Census, p. 139.

400. SAMUEL[9] HAMMOCK *(MARTIN[8], JOHN[7], JOHN[6], RICHARD[5], RICHARD[4], WILLIAM "O"[3], JOHN[2] HAMMOCKE, ? JOHN[1] HAMMOT)* was born 30 Aug 1818 in Claiborne Co., TN, and died 10 Dec 1867 in Marion Co., TN. He married THERESA QUARLES Abt. 1842 in TN. She was born Abt. 1817 in South Carolina, and died Aft. 1860 in Marion Co., TN.
Children of SAMUEL HAMMOCK and THERESA QUARLES are:
   i. HUBBARD[10] HAMMOCK, b. Abt. 1843, Tennessee; d. Aft. 1920, Pawnee Co., OK.
   ii. LOUISA HAMMOCK, b. Abt. 1846, Alabama; d. Aft. 1860, Marion Co., TN.
   iii. ISHAM HAMMOCK, b. Abt. 1849, Alabama; d. Aft. 1860, Marion Co., TN.
   iv. AMERICA HAMMOCK, b. Abt. 1852, Alabama; d. Aft. 1870, Marion Co., OH.
   v. ELIZABETH HAMMOCK, b. Abt. 1854, Alabama; d. Aft. 1860, Marion Co., OH.
   vi. JOHN HAMMOCK, b. Abt. 1857, Alabama; d. Aft. 1860, Marion Co., OH.
Key Sources: 1850 Claiborne Co., TN, Census, p. 209; 1860 Marion Co., TN, Census, p. 262; 1880 Saline Co., MO, Census, p. 566.

401. JOSEPH[9] HAMMOCK *(MARTIN[8], JOHN[7], JOHN[6], RICHARD[5], RICHARD[4], WILLIAM "O"[3], JOHN[2] HAMMOCKE, ? JOHN[1] HAMMOT)* was born 17 Jan 1825 in Claiborne Co., TN, and died 23 Feb 1904 in Sulphur Springs, GA. He married MARY ANN SANDRIDGE Abt. 1851 in Madison Co., AL. She was born 19 Apr 1823 in Alabama, and died 08 Jul 1899 in Sulphur Springs, GA.
Children of JOSEPH HAMMOCK and MARY SANDRIDGE are:
   i. WILLIAM[10] HAMMOCK, b. Abt. 1852, Madison Co., AL; d. Aft. 1860, Dade Co., GA.
   ii. JOHN HAMMOCK, b. Abt. 1853, Madison Co., AL; d. Aft. 1860, Dade Co., GA.
   iii. MARY J. HAMMOCK, b. Abt. 1856, Madison Co., AL; d. Aft. 1860, Dade Co., GA.
   iv. SARAH HAMMOCK, b. Abt. 1859, Tennessee; d. Aft. 1860, Tennessee.
   v. NATHAN HAMMOCK, b. 1860, Dade Co., GA; d. Aft. 1860, Dade Co., GA.
Key Sources: 1850 Madison Co., AL, Census, p. 404; 1860 Dade Co., GA, Census, p. 969.

402. SINTHY[9] HAMMACK *(MARTIN[8], JOHN[7], JOHN[6], RICHARD[5], RICHARD[4], WILLIAM "O"[3], JOHN[2] HAMMOCKE, ? JOHN[1] HAMMOT)* was born 27 Aug 1826 in Claiborne Co., TN, and died Aft. 1851 in Rhea Co., TN. She married JESSE RICHARDSON QUARLES 29 Dec 1847 in Marion Co., TN. He was born 1829 in Georgia, and died 1891 in Marion Co., TN.
Children of SINTHY HAMMACK and JESSE QUARLES are:
   i. MARGARET[10] QUARLES, b. Abt. 1849, Rhea Co., TN.
   ii. PRUDENCE QUARLES, b. Abt. 1851, Rhea Co., TN.
Key Source: 1860 Marion Co., TN, Census, p. 246.

403. MARSHALL[9] HAMMACK *(DANIEL[8], JOHN[7], JOHN[6], RICHARD[5], RICHARD[4], WILLIAM "O"[3], JOHN[2] HAMMOCKE, ? JOHN[1] HAMMOT)* was born Abt. 1819 in Tennessee, and died Aft. 1880 in Grainger Co., TN. He married (1) UNKNOWN. He married (2) LOUISA J. GRIST 17 Dec 1838 in Grainger Co., TN. She was born Abt. 1820 in Tennessee, and died Aft. 1850 in Grainger Co., TN. He married (3) MALINDA DAVIS 07 Oct 1879 in Grainger Co., TN. She was born Abt. 1835 in Tennessee, and died Aft. 1880 in Grainger Co., TN.
Children of MARSHALL HAMMACK and UNKNOWN are:

      i.   MARSHALL[10] HAMMACK, b. Abt. 1869, Tennessee; d. Aft. 1900, Marshall Co., IA; m. ELIZA YOUNG.
     ii.   MARION WESLEY HAMMACK, b. Abt. 1872, Tennessee; d. Aft. 1910, Anderson Co., TN.
   iii.   JAMES H. HAMMACK, b. Abt. 1875, Tennessee; d. Aft. 1910, Pulaski Co., Ky.
   iv.   NANCY J. HAMMACK, b. Abt. 1879, Tennessee.

Children of MARSHALL HAMMACK and LOUISA GRIST are:
     v.   MALINDA[10] HAMMACK, b. Abt. 1839, Tennessee.
   vi.   DELANEY HAMMACK, b. Abt. 1841, Tennessee.
  vii.   MALER HAMMACK, b. Abt. 1843, Tennessee.
 viii.   LOUISA J. HAMMACK, b. Abt. 1845, Tennessee.
   ix.   SARAH ANN HAMMACK, b. Abt. 1847, Tennessee.
    x.   DANIEL R. HAMMACK, b. Abt. 1849, Tennessee; d. Aft. 1910, Scott Co., TN; m. ELIZABETH ANN THOMPSON.
   xi.   EPHRAIM G. W. HAMMACK, b. Abt. 1851, Tennessee.

Key Sources: 1850 Grainger Co., TN, Census, p. 223; 1860 Wayne Co., KY, Census, p. 403; 1880 Grainger Co., TN, Census, p. 498.

404. MARY[9] HAMMACK *(DANIEL[8], JOHN[7], JOHN[6], RICHARD[5], RICHARD[4], WILLIAM "O"[3], JOHN[2] HAMMOCKE, ? JOHN[1] HAMMOT)* was born Abt. 1823 in Tennessee, and died Aft. 1880 in Laurel Co., KY.
Children of MARY HAMMACK are:
     i.   HENRY[10] HAMMACK, b. Abt. 1853, Tennessee; d. Aft. 1870, Union Co., TN.
     ii.   GREEN HAMMACK, b. Abt. 1856, Tennessee; d. Aft. 1870, Union Co., TN.
   iii.   REBECCA HAMMACK, b. Abt. 1862, Tennessee.

Key Source: 1870 Union Co., TN, Census, pp. 222, 226. I have speculated that Mary may have been the daughter of Daniel Hammack and that she was the mother of these three children.

405. DANIEL[9] HAMMACK *(DANIEL[8], JOHN[7], JOHN[6], RICHARD[5], RICHARD[4], WILLIAM "O"[3], JOHN[2] HAMMOCKE, ? JOHN[1] HAMMOT)* was born Abt. 1831 in Tennessee, and died Aft. 1870 in Grainger Co., TN. He married SUSAN [------] Abt. 1854 in Grainger Co., TN. She was born Abt. 1825 in Tennessee, and died Aft. 1880 in Grainger Co., TN.
Children of DANIEL HAMMACK and SUSAN [------] are:
     i.   SARAH[10] HAMMACK, b. Abt. 1855, Tennessee.
     ii.   LIZA HAMMACK, b. Abt. 1858, Tennessee.

Key Sources: 1860 Grainger Co., TN, Census, p. 523; 1870 Grainger Co., TN, Census, p. 148; 1880 Grainger Co., TN, Census, p. 498.

406. ISAAC[9] HAMMACK *(EPHRAIM[8], JOHN[7], JOHN[6], RICHARD[5], RICHARD[4], WILLIAM "O"[3], JOHN[2] HAMMOCKE, ? JOHN[1] HAMMOT)* was born Abt. 1823 in Knox Co., TN, and died Aft. 1860 in Anderson Co., TN. He married FRANCES RUCKER 11 Jun 1846 in Tennessee. She was born Abt. 1814 in Tennessee, and died Aft. 1860 in Anderson Co., TN.
Children of ISAAC HAMMACK and FRANCES RUCKER are:
     i.   EPHRAIM ELVIS[10] HAMMACK, b. 24 May 1847, Anderson Co., TN; d. Aft. 1920, Spokane Co., WA.
     ii.   ELIZA J. HAMMACK, b. Abt. 1849, Anderson Co., TN; d. Aft. 1860, Anderson Co., TN.
   iii.   NANCY HAMMACK, b. Abt. 1852, Anderson Co., TN; d. Aft. 1860, Anderson Co., TN.
   iv.   JAMES W. HAMMACK, b. Abt. 1855, Anderson Co., TN; d. Aft. 1860, Anderson Co., TN.

Key Source: 1860 Anderson Co., TN, Census, p. 70. I have speculated that Isaac might have been a son of Ephraim; the connection has not been established.

407. ST. CLAIR "SINK"[9] HAMMACK *(WILLIAM[8], MARTIN[7], JOHN[6], RICHARD[5], RICHARD[4], WILLIAM "O"[3], JOHN[2] HAMMOCKE, ? JOHN[1] HAMMOT)* was born Abt. 1822 in Kanawha Co., VA, and died Aft. 1880 in Roane Co., WV. He married CATHERINE PHILLIPS 24 Nov 1840 in Kanawha Co., WV. She was born Abt. 1820 in Virginia, and died Aft. 1880 in Roane Co., WV.

Children of ST. HAMMACK and CATHERINE PHILLIPS are:

    i. MEREDITH[10] HAMMACK, b. Abt. 1843, Kanawha Co., VA; d. Aft. 1880, Roane Co., WV; m. MARTHA J. WALKER.

    ii. SALLY HAMMACK, b. Abt. 1847, Kanawha Co., VA; d. Aft. 1860, Roane Co., WV; m. GRANVILLE LANCE.

    iii. SUSAN HAMMACK, b. Abt. 1849, Kanawha Co., VA; d. Aft. 1880, Roane Co., WV.

    iv. MARTIN HAMMACK, b. Abt. 1852, Kanawha Co., VA; d. Aft. 1880, Putnam Co., WV; m. NANCY COTTERRELL.

    v. VIRGINIA HAMMACK, b. 29 Jun 1852, Kanawha Co., VA; d. 16 May 1915, Roane Co., WV; m. JOHN A. CAMP.

    vi. WILLIAM WILEY HAMMACK, b. 28 May 1854, Roane Co., WV; d. Aft. 1900, Roane Co., WV; m. DICY PAXTON.

    vii. LEWIS HAMMACK, b. Abt. 1857, Roane Co., WV; d. Aft. 1860, Roane Co., WV.

    viii. SOPHIA HAMMACK, b. Abt. 1860, Roane Co., WV; d. Aft. 1880, Roane Co., WV.

Key Sources: 1860 Roane Co., VA, Census, p. 613; 1870 Roane Co., VA, Census, p. 46; 1880 Roane Co., WV, Census, p. 71C.

408. SUSAN[9] HAMMACK *(WILLIAM[8], MARTIN[7], JOHN[6], RICHARD[5], RICHARD[4], WILLIAM "O"[3], JOHN[2] HAMMOCKE, ? JOHN[1] HAMMOT)* was born Abt. 1828 in Kanawha Co., VA, and died Aft. 1880 in Roane Co., WV. She married PETER HAMMACK Abt. 1850 in Kanawha Co., WV. He was born Abt. 1825 in Kanawha Co., VA, and died Aft. 1880 in Roane Co., WV.

Children of SUSAN HAMMACK and PETER HAMMACK are:

    i. CHRISTOPHER[10] HAMMACK, b. Abt. 1852, Kanawha Co., VA; d. Bet. 1880 - 1900, Roane Co., WV; m. MARY; b. Abt. 1859, Roane Co., WV.

    ii. SARAH J. HAMMACK, b. Abt. 1854, Kanawha Co., VA; d. Aft. 1870, Roane Co., WV.

    iii. MARY E. HAMMACK, b. Abt. 1856, Kanawha Co., VA; d. Aft. 1870, Roane Co., WV.

    iv. JOHN H. HAMMACK, b. Abt. 1857, Kanawha Co., VA; d. Aft. 1880, Roane Co., WV.

    v. LYLE HAMMACK, b. Abt. 1859, Roane Co., WV; d. Aft. 1870, Roane Co., WV.

    vi. PERRY HAMMACK, b. Abt. 1866, Roane Co., WV; d. Aft. 1880, Roane Co., WV.

    vii. ANN H. HAMMACK, b. Abt. 1873, Roane Co., WV; d. Aft. 1880, Roane Co., WV.

Key Sources: 1860 Roane Co., VA, Census, p. 613; 1870 Roane Co., WV, Census, p. 55; 1880 Roane Co., WV, Census, p. 64B.

409. LEANDER MARTIN[9] HAMMACK *(BRICE WISEMAN[8], DANIEL[7], JOHN[6], RICHARD[5], RICHARD[4], WILLIAM "O"[3], JOHN[2] HAMMOCKE, ? JOHN[1] HAMMOT)* was born 16 Jan 1818 in Smith Co., TN, and died Aft. 1870 in Lincoln Co., MO. He married VIRDILLA WATTS 18 Mar 1840 in Lincoln Co., MO. She was born Abt. 1820 in Virginia, and died 20 Feb 1860 in Lincoln Co., MO.

Child of LEANDER HAMMACK and VIRDILLA WATTS is:

    i. WESLEY WASHINGTON[10] HAMMACK, b. 30 Dec 1841, Lincoln Co., MO; d. 06 Jan 1882, Lincoln Co., MO; m. ARTEMECIA GIBSON, 09 Oct 1862, Lincoln Co., MO; b. 15 Oct 1845, Lincoln Co., MO; d. 03 Jul 1883, Lincoln Co., MO.

Key Source: G. P. Omohundro, *Ancestors and Descendants of Brice Wiseman Hammack* (Santa Ana, CA, 1986).

410. WILLIAM WESLEY[9] HAMMACK *(BRICE WISEMAN[8], DANIEL[7], JOHN[6], RICHARD[5], RICHARD[4], WILLIAM "O"[3], JOHN[2] HAMMOCKE, ? JOHN[1] HAMMOT)* was born 25 Aug 1820 in Lincoln Co., MO, and died 17 Feb 1893 in Coryell Co., TX. He married ELIZABETH THOMPSON Abt. 1845 in Madison Co., AL. She was born 28 Jul 1824 in Bourbon Co., KY, and died 15 Jan 1874 in Coryell Co., TX.

Children of WILLIAM HAMMACK and ELIZABETH THOMPSON are:

   i.   JOHN WESLEY[10] HAMMACK, b. 1844, Madison Co., AL; d. 02 Nov 1924, Coryell Co., TX; m. HETTY C. MCCARTY, 01 Feb 1866, Coryell Co., TX; b. 03 Oct 1851, Mississippi; d. 12 May 1946, Coryell Co., TX.

   ii.   DANIEL LEROY HAMMACK, b. 23 Dec 1845, Wisconsin; d. 08 Feb 1909, Texas; m. LAURIE BATEMAN, 05 May 1866, Coryell Co., TX; b. 14 Jun 1848, Texas; d. 09 Oct 1896, Hamilton Co., TX.

   iii. WILLIAM TAYLOR HAMMACK, b. 18 Nov 1848, Missouri; d. 19 Feb 1923, McLennan Co., TX; m. EMMA BOONE LOVEJOY, 14 Mar 1872, Coryell Co., TX; b. 05 Jun 1854, Alabama; d. 25 Nov 1913, Lampassas Co., TX.

   iv. MARTHA J. HAMMACK, b. 1853, Missouri; d. Aft. 1880, Texas; m. (1) JAMES A. ALLEN; m. (2) WILLIAM HOLMES LOVEJOY.

   v.   MATILDA L. HAMMACK, b. 1856, Texas; d. Bef. 1870, Coryell Co., TX.

Key Source: G. P. Omohundro, *Ancestors and Descendants of Brice Wiseman Hammack* (Santa Ana, CA, 1986).

411. DANIEL ALEXANDER[9] HAMMACK *(BRICE WISEMAN[8], DANIEL[7], JOHN[6], RICHARD[5], RICHARD[4], WILLIAM "O"[3], JOHN[2] HAMMOCKE, ? JOHN[1] HAMMOT)* was born 22 Nov 1822 in Lincoln Co., MO, and died 09 May 1909 in Coryell Co., TX. He married SUSAN NORRIS 22 Dec 1859 in Coryell Co., TX. She was born 13 May 1843 in Texas, and died 27 Apr 1892 in Coryell Co., TX.

Children of DANIEL HAMMACK and SUSAN NORRIS are:

   i.   WILLIAM WISEMAN[10] HAMMACK, b. 07 Sep 1860, Coryell Co., TX; d. 27 Aug 1913, Coryell Co., TX; m. MATTIE AMELIA TUCKER, 15 Sep 1881, Coryell Co., TX.

   ii.   SUSAN HAMMACK, b. 1867, Coryell Co., TX; d. Bef. 1880, Coryell Co., TX.

   iii. EMILY J. HAMMACK, b. 1870, Coryell Co., TX; d. Aft. 1909, Coryell Co., TX; m. [-----] MCKINZIE.

   iv. EUNICE HAMMACK, b. 16 Apr 1871, Coryell Co., TX; d. 07 May 1872, Coryell Co., TX.

Key Source: G. P. Omohundro, *Ancestors and Descendants of Brice Wiseman Hammack* (Santa Ana, CA, 1986).

412. SENECA WATTS[9] HAMMACK *(BRICE WISEMAN[8], DANIEL[7], JOHN[6], RICHARD[5], RICHARD[4], WILLIAM "O"[3], JOHN[2] HAMMOCKE, ? JOHN[1] HAMMOT)* was born 19 Feb 1825 in Lincoln Co., MO, and died 30 Jan 1893 in Montgomery Co., MO. He married (1) MARTHA C. HAMILTON. She was born 06 Jun 1836 in Warren Co., MO, and died 18 Aug 1918 in Montgomery Co., MO. He married (2) ELIZABETH MARY HAMILTON 06 Aug 1846 in Lincoln Co., MO. She was born 21 Dec 1829 in Augusta Co., VA, and died 16 May 1865 in Lincoln Co., MO.

Children of SENECA HAMMACK and MARTHA HAMILTON are:

   i.   EUGENIA VIANNE[10] HAMMACK, b. 16 Jan 1868, Montgomery Co., MO; d. 08 Aug 1945, Mexico, MO; m. FRANK S. WAGNER; b. 16 Aug 1861; d. 09 Jul 1940.

   ii.   DELOS WEBSTER HAMMACK, b. 01 Mar 1871, Montgomery Co., MO; d. 06 Jul 1871, Montgomery Co., MO.

iii. WILILAM WARREN HAMMACK, b. 11 Apr 1874, Montgomery Co., MO; d. 04 Jun 1952, Montgomery Co., MO.

Children of SENECA HAMMACK and ELIZABETH HAMILTON are:

iv. LAURA JANE[10] HAMMACK, b. 02 Feb 1848, Lincoln Co., MO; d. 07 Feb 1927, San Bernadino Co., CA; m. P. D. HOCKADAY.

v. ALEXANDER WISEMAN HAMMACK, b. 16 Oct 1851, Lincoln Co., MO; d. 11 Apr 1919, Middleton, MO.

vi. MARGARET DIANNA HAMMACK, b. 21 Nov 1853, Lincoln Co., MO; d. 30 Dec 1938, St. Louis, MO; m. P. H. ULRICH.

vii. NAPOLEAN B. HAMMACK, b. 18 Aug 1856, Montgomery Co., MO; d. 23 Sep 1857, Montgomery Co., MO.

viii. EUDORA IMOGENE HAMMACK, b. 29 Aug 1858, Montgomery Co., MO; d. 25 Feb 1952, San Bernadino Co., CA.

ix. GEORGE WASHINGTON HAMMACK, b. 21 Feb 1861, Montgomery Co., MO; d. 01 May 1934, San Bernadino Co., CA.

x. ELIZABETH MARY HAMMACK, b. 12 May 1865, Montgomery Co., MO; d. 31 May 1865, Montgomery Co., MO.

Key Source: G. P. Omohundro, *Ancestors and Descendants of Brice Wiseman Hammack* (Santa Ana, CA, 1986).

413. JAMES TYRA[9] HAMMACK *(BRICE WISEMAN[8], DANIEL[7], JOHN[6], RICHARD[5], RICHARD[4], WILLIAM "O"[3], JOHN[2] HAMMOCKE, ? JOHN[1] HAMMOT)* was born 31 Mar 1827 in Lincoln Co., MO, and died 04 Jun 1877 in Lincoln Co., MO. He married (1) MARY ELIZABETH ELSBERRY 02 Dec 1847 in Lincoln Co., MO. She was born 23 Apr 1829 in Bourbon Co., KY, and died 13 Jun 1863 in Lincoln Co., MO. He married (2) ELIZABETH A. GALLOWAY 08 Aug 1864 in Lincoln Co., MO. She was born 10 Mar 1833 in Missouri, and died 10 Apr 1900 in Lincoln Co., MO.

Children of JAMES HAMMACK and MARY ELSBERRY are:

i. SARAH ANN[10] HAMMACK, b. 03 Mar 1849, Lincoln Co., MO; d. 19 Mar 1929, Lincoln Co., MO; m. WILLIAM ALPHEUS TAYLOR, 20 Feb 1868, New Hope, MO.

ii. LYDIA JANE HAMMACK, b. 16 May 1851, Lincoln Co., MO; d. 27 Aug 1937, Lincoln Co., MO; m. GEORGE J. DRYDEN; b. 29 May 1836, Missouri; d. 06 Aug 1902, Lincoln Co., MO.

iii. WILLIAM WISEMAN HAMMACK, b. 07 Jan 1855, Lincoln Co., MO; d. 16 Nov 1932, Lincoln Co., MO; m. (1) LYDIA ELSBERRY, 11 Mar 1875, Lincoln Co., MO; m. (2) ALICE R. ELSBERRY, 07 May 1887, Lincoln Co., MO; m. (3) SUSAN HATFIELD, 11 Jan 1891, Lincoln Co., MO.

iv. JAMES FRANKLIN HAMMACK, b. 16 Mar 1856, Lincoln Co., MO; d. 23 Feb 1882, Lincoln Co., MO.

v. MARY LEE HAMMACK, b. 31 Aug 1861, Lincoln Co., MO; d. 06 May 1878, Lincoln Co., MO.

Children of JAMES HAMMACK and ELIZABETH GALLOWAY are:

vi. GEORGE MORGAN[10] HAMMACK, b. 1866, Lincoln Co., MO; d. Aft. 1880, Pike Co., MO.

vii. ALBERT SIDNEY HAMMACK, b. 1868, Lincoln Co., MO; d. Aft. 1880, Pike Co., MO.

viii. EUGENE HAMMACK, b. 1869, Lincoln Co., MO; d. Aft. 1880, Pike Co., MO.

Key Source: G. P. Omohundro, *Ancestors and Descendants of Brice Wiseman Hammack* (Santa Ana, CA, 1986).

414. JOHN ALFRED[9] HAMMACK *(SPENCER[8], JOHN[7], RICHARD[6], RICHARD[5], RICHARD[4], WILLIAM "O"[3], JOHN[2] HAMMOCKE, ? JOHN[1] HAMMOT)* was born Abt. 1813 in Pittsylvania Co., VA, and died Abt. 1866 in Pittsylvania Co., VA. He married MATILDA CLEMENT Abt. 1835 in Pittsylvania Co., VA. She was born Abt. 1814 in Pittsylvania Co., VA, and died Aft. 1860 in Pittsylvania Co., VA.

Children of JOHN HAMMACK and MATILDA CLEMENT are:

    i.   LUCY[10] HAMMACK, b. Abt. 1837, Pittsylvania Co., VA; d. Aft. 1860, Pittsylvania Co., VA.

    ii.   NANCY HAMMACK, b. Abt. 1843, Pittsylvania Co., VA; d. Aft. 1860, Pittsylvania Co., VA.

    iii.   MARION HAMMACK, b. Abt. 1845, Pittsylvania Co., VA; d. Aft. 1860, Pittsylvania Co., VA.

    iv.   EMILY HAMMACK, b. Abt. 1848, Pittsylvania Co., VA; d. Aft. 1850, Pittsylvania Co., VA.

    v.   JAMES M. HAMMACK, b. Abt. 1850, Pittsylvania Co., VA; m. D. A. TOWLER, 31 Oct 1872, Pittsylvania Co., VA.

    vi.   WILLIAM SPENCER HAMMACK, b. Abt. 1855, Pittsylvania Co., VA; m. LIVELY JAMES ARTHUR, 1888, Pittsylvania Co., VA.

    vii.   MARY HAMMACK, b. Abt. 1859, Pittsylvania Co., VA; d. February, 1861, Pittsylvania Co., VA.

Key Sources: 1840 Pittsylvania Co., VA, Census, p. 80; 1850 Pittsylvania Co., VA, Census, p. 255; 1860 Pittsylvania Co., VA, Census, p. 161; 1870 Pittsylvania Co., VA, Census, p. 353; Pittsylvania Co., VA, Register of Deaths.

415. WILLIAM[9] HAMMACK *(SPENCER[8], JOHN[7], RICHARD[6], RICHARD[5], RICHARD[4], WILLIAM "O"[3], JOHN[2] HAMMOCKE, ? JOHN[1] HAMMOT)* was born Abt. 1816 in Pittsylvania Co., VA, and died Aft. 1860 in Henry Co., IN. He married ROSEY ANN HEDRICK 24 Oct 1838 in Pittsylvania Co., VA. She was born Abt. 1811 in Pittsylvania Co., VA, and died 1888 in Henry Co., IN.

Children of WILLIAM HAMMACK and ROSEY HEDRICK are:

    i.   MARY[10] HAMMACK, b. Abt. 1840, Pittsylvania Co., VA; d. Aft. 1870, Madison Co., IN.

    ii.   JOHN HAMMACK, b. Abt. 1848, Pittsylvania Co., VA; d. Aft. 1860, Henry Co., IN.

Key Sources: 1840 Pittsylvania Co., VA, Census, p. 89; 1850 Pittsylvania Co., VA, Census, p. 256; 1860 Henry Co., IN, Census, p. 405; 1870 Madison Co., IN, Census, p. 14; 1880 Henry Co., IN, Census, p. 97.

416. TALIAFERRO[9] HAMMACK *(SPENCER[8], JOHN[7], RICHARD[6], RICHARD[5], RICHARD[4], WILLIAM "O"[3], JOHN[2] HAMMOCKE, ? JOHN[1] HAMMOT)* was born Abt. 1818 in Pittsylvania Co., VA, and died Aft. 1870 in Pittsylvania Co., VA. He married MARY HEDRICK Abt. 1838 in Pittsylvania Co., VA. She was born Abt. 1819 in Pittsylvania Co., VA, and died Aft. 1850 in Pittsylvania Co., VA.

Children of TALIAFERRO HAMMACK and MARY HEDRICK are:

    i.   ABRAHAM[10] HAMMACK, b. Abt. 1840, Pittsylvania Co., VA; d. 1862, Fredericksburg, VA; m. MARY [------].

    ii.   BOOKER HAMMACK, b. Abt. 1845, Pittsylvania Co., VA; d. Aft. 1850, Pittsylvania Co., VA.

    iii.   MILDRED HAMMACK, b. Abt. 1848, Pittsylvania Co., VA; d. Aft. 1870, Pittsylvania Co., VA.

    iv.   NATHANIEL HAMMACK, b. Abt. 1849, Pittsylvania Co., VA; d. Aft. 1850, Pittsylvania Co., VA.

    v.   RAWLEY HAMMACK, b. Abt. 1849, Pittsylvania Co., VA; d. Aft. 1870, Pittsylvania Co., VA.

vi.   SALLIE HAMMACK, b. Abt. 1853, Pittsylvania Co., VA; d. Aft. 1870, Pittsylvania Co., VA.

vii.   LOTTY HAMMACK, b. Abt. 1855, Pittsylvania Co., VA; d. Aft. 1870, Pittsylvania Co., VA.

Key Sources: 1850 Pittsylvania Co., VA, Census, p. 252; 1870 Pittsylvania Co., VA, Census, p. 355; Pittsylvania Co., VA, Register of Deaths.

417. OLIVER[9] HAMMACK *(SPENCER[8], JOHN[7], RICHARD[6], RICHARD[5], RICHARD[4], WILLIAM "O"[3], JOHN[2] HAMMOCKE, ? JOHN[1] HAMMOT)* was born Abt. 1820 in Pittsylvania Co., VA, and died Aft. 1880 in Hancock Co., IN. He married ANNA GOAD 30 Jan 1844 in Bedford Co., VA. She was born 17 Dec 1821 in Pittsylvania Co., VA, and died Aft. 1880 in Hancock Co., IN.

Children of OLIVER HAMMACK and ANNA GOAD are:

i.   RUBIN[10] HAMMACK, b. Abt. 1847, Pittsylvania Co., VA.

ii.   MARY HAMMACK, b. Abt. 1848, Pittsylvania Co., VA; d. Aft. 1870, Madison Co., IN; m. WILLIAM ANDERSON HUNT.

iii.   JAMES J. HAMMACK, b. Abt. 1850, Pittsylvania Co., VA; d. Aft. 1870, Madison Co., IN.

iv.   DALIE A. HAMMACK, b. Abt. 1851, Pittsylvania Co., VA; d. Aft. 1870, Madison Co., IN.

v.   VIRGINIA E. HAMMACK, b. 23 Oct 1854, Pittsylvania Co., VA; d. Aft. 1870, Madison Co., AL.

vi.   SUSAN K. HAMMACK, b. 1854, Pittsylvania Co., VA; d. 06 Oct 1860, Pittsylvania Co., VA.

vii.   FANNIE HAMMACK, b. 1860, Pittsylvania Co., VA; d. 18 May 1860, Pittsylvania Co., VA.

viii.   MARY HAMMACK, b. 1856, Pittsylvania Co., VA; d. 10 Jan 1860, Pittsylvania Co., VA.

ix.   JOHNSON HAMMACK, d. Oct 1862, Pittsylvania Co., VA.

x.   SUSAN K. HAMMACK, b. 1863, Pittsylvania Co., VA; d. Aft. 1880, Hancock Co., IN.

Key Sources: 1850 Pittsylvania Co., VA, Census, p. 221; 1870 Madison Co., IN, Census, p. 16; 1880 Hancock Co., IN, Census, p. 4; Pittsylvania Co., VA, Register of Deaths.

418. LEWIS[9] HAMMACK *(SPENCER[8], JOHN[7], RICHARD[6], RICHARD[5], RICHARD[4], WILLIAM "O"[3], JOHN[2] HAMMOCKE, ? JOHN[1] HAMMOT)* was born Abt. 1823 in Pittsylvania Co., VA, and died Aft. 1860 in Roanoke Co., VA. He married MARTHA ANN YOUNG 19 Jun 1848 in Pittsylvania Co., VA. She was born Abt. 1825 in Virginia, and died Aft. 1860 in Roanoke Co., VA.

Children of LEWIS HAMMACK and MARTHA YOUNG are:

i.   PAULINA[10] HAMMACK, b. Abt. 1849, Pittsylvania Co., VA; d. Aft. 1850, Pittsylvania Co., VA.

ii.   NANCY HAMMACK, b. Abt. 1851, Pittsylvania Co., VA; d. Aft. 1860, Roanoke Co., VA.

iii.   CASS HAMMACK, b. Abt. 1853, Pittsylvania Co., VA; d. Aft. 1860, Roanoke Co., VA.

iv.   MARY HAMMACK, b. Abt. 1855, Pittsylvania Co., VA; d. Aft. 1860, Roanoke Co., VA.

v.   MICHAEL HAMMACK, b. Abt. 1859, Pittsylvania Co., VA; d. Aft. 1860, Roanoke Co., VA.

Key Sources: 1850 Pittsylvania Co., VA, Census, p. 256; 1860 Roanoke Co., VA, Census, p. 736. I have not conclusively established that Lewis and Martha Hammack of Pittsylvania Co., VA, are the Lewis and Martha Hammack living in Roanoke Co., VA, in 1860.

419. SPENCER[9] HAMMACK *(SPENCER[8], JOHN[7], RICHARD[6], RICHARD[5], RICHARD[4], WILLIAM "O"[3], JOHN[2] HAMMOCKE, ? JOHN[1] HAMMOT)* was born Abt. 1827 in Pittsylvania Co., VA, and died Aft. 1860 in Henry Co., IN. He married CHARLOTTE [------] Abt. 1856 in Henry Co., IN. She was born Abt. 1838 in Indiana, and died Aft. 1860 in Henry Co., IN.

Children of SPENCER HAMMACK and CHARLOTTE [------] are:
>   i.   MARY[10] HAMMACK, b. Abt. 1857, Henry Co., IN; d. Aft. 1860, Henry Co., IN.
>   ii. WILLIAM HAMMACK, b. Abt. 1859, Henry Co., IN; d. Aft. 1860, Henry Co., IN.

Key Source: 1860 Henry Co., IN, Census, p. 400.

420. LACE J.[9] HAMMACK *(TALIAFERRO[8], JOHN[7], RICHARD[6], RICHARD[5], RICHARD[4], WILLIAM "O"[3], JOHN[2] HAMMOCKE, ? JOHN[1] HAMMOT)* was born Abt. 1819 in Pittsylvania Co., VA, and died Aft. 1880 in Wayne Co., IL. He married ELIZABETH [------] Abt. 1840 in Smith Co., TN. She was born Abt. 1820 in Tennessee, and died Aft. 1860 in Wayne Co., IL.

Children of LACE HAMMACK and ELIZABETH [------] are:
>   i.   JAMES L.[10] HAMMACK, b. Abt. 1840, Smith Co., TN; d. Aft. 1860, Wayne Co., IL.
>   ii. MELVINA HAMMACK, b. Abt. 1844, Smith Co., TN; d. Aft. 1870, Wayne Co., IL.
>   iii. JOHN L. HAMMACK, b. Abt. 1848, Macon Co., TN; d. Aft. 1870, Wayne Co., IL.
> 495. iv. WYATT H. HAMMACK, b. Abt. 1851, Wayne Co., IL; d. Aft. 1880, Wayne Co., IL.
>   v.   DAVID HAMMACK, b. Abt. 1853, Wayne Co., IL; d. Aft. 1880, Wayne Co., IL.

Key Sources: 1850 Macon Co., TN, Census, p. 30; 1860 Wayne Co., IL, Census, p. 91; 1870 Wayne Co., IL, Census, p. 105; 1880 Wayne Co., IL, Census, p. 11.

421. JOHN D.[9] HAMMACK *(TALIAFERRO[8], JOHN[7], RICHARD[6], RICHARD[5], RICHARD[4], WILLIAM "O"[3], JOHN[2] HAMMOCKE, ? JOHN[1] HAMMOT)* was born Abt. 1822 in Smith Co., TN, and died Aft. 1860 in Newton Co., MO. He married ORRA [------] Abt. 1846 in Macon Co., TN. She was born Abt. 1816 in Tennessee, and died Aft. 1860 in Newton Co., MO.

Children of JOHN HAMMACK and ORRA [------] are:
>   i.   AMANDA[10] HAMMACK, b. Abt. 1848, Macon Co., TN; d. Aft. 1860, Newton Co., MO.
>   ii. JAMES M. HAMMACK, b. Abt. 1849, Macon Co., TN; d. Aft. 1860, Newton Co., MO.

Key Sources: 1850 Macon Co., TN, Census, p. 30; 1860 Jackson Co., MO, Census, p. 960.

422. COLEMAN A.[9] HAMMACK *(COLEMAN[8], JOHN[7], RICHARD[6], RICHARD[5], RICHARD[4], WILLIAM "O"[3], JOHN[2] HAMMOCKE, ? JOHN[1] HAMMOT)* was born Abt. 1828 in Pittsylvania Co., VA, and died Aft. 1872 in Westmoreland Co., TN. He married ADELINE EMILY VANCE.

Children of COLEMAN HAMMACK and ADELINE VANCE are:
>   i.   ELLA S.[10] HAMMACK, b. Abt. 1855, Westmoreland Co., TN.
>   ii.   FRANCES JANE HAMMACK, b. Abt. 1856, Westmoreland Co., TN.
>   iii. JACOB E. HAMMACK, b. Abt. 1860, Westmoreland Co., TN.
>   iv.   DAVID VANCE HAMMACK, b. Abt. 1862, Westmoreland Co., TN; m. MAHALA JANE TEMPLETON.
>   v.   ELIZABETH C. HAMMACK, b. Abt. 1866, Westmoreland Co., TN.
>   vi.   MARTHA A. HAMMACK, b. Abt. 1870, Westmoreland Co., TN.
>   vii. JOHN HAMMACK, b. Abt. 1870, Westmoreland Co., TN.
>   viii. THOMAS WILLIAM HAMMACK, b. Abt. 1872, Westmoreland Co., TN.

Key Source: Henry Franklin Hammack, 1: 139-140.

423. DANIEL[9] HAMMACK *(JOHN[8], DANIEL[7], RICHARD[6], RICHARD[5], RICHARD[4], WILLIAM "O"[3], JOHN[2] HAMMOCKE, ? JOHN[1] HAMMOT)* was born Abt. 1814 in Kentucky, and died 29 Aug 1887 in Marion Co., OR. He married JANE FRAKES 04 Mar 1839 in Perry Co., IN. She was born 22 Jan 1822 in Indiana, and died 31 Aug 1887 in Marion Co., OR.

Children of DANIEL HAMMACK and JANE FRAKES are:
>   i.   ELIZABETH[10] HAMMACK, b. Abt. 1839, Indiana; m. SOLOMON MORRIS, Abt. 1858, Wayne Co., IN.

ii. JOHN F. HAMMACK, b. Abt. 1841, Marion Co., IL; d. 21 Oct 1908, Marion Co., OR.

iii. GEORGE HAMMACK, b. Abt. 1844, Marion Co., IL; d. Aft. 1887, Marion Co., OR; m. NANCY [------], Abt. 1875, Oregon; b. Abt. 1841, Ohio; d. Aft. 1880, Marion Co., OR.

iv. GRAYSON HAMMACK, b. Abt. 1847, Marion Co., IL; d. 02 Jul 1911, Washington Co., OR; m. MARTHA [------]; b. Oct 1861, Oregon; d. Aft. 1900, Washington Co., IN.

v. FREDERICK HAMMACK, b. 22 Oct 1849, Wayne Co., Iowa; d. 09 Dec 1930, Marion Co., OR; m. MARY FRANCENA CHRISTY, 08 Aug 1878, Yamhill Co., OR; b. Jul 1860, Iowa; d. Aft. 1900, Marion Co., OR.

vi. NANCY JANE HAMMACK, b. Mar 1852, Wayne Co., Iowa; d. Aft. 1887, Marion Co., OR; m. WILLIAM A. DAVIS; b. Abt. 1843, Indiana.

vii. MAHALAH A. HAMMACK, b. Abt. 1857, Willamette Valley, OR; d. 27 Jul 1939, Marion Co., OR; m. (1) DELMER GROSLINE; b. Abt. 1857, New York; d. Aft. 1931, Washington; m. (2) WILLIAM JACOB CABBAGE, 18 Jan 1877, Marion Co., TN; b. 21 Apr 1854, Illinois; d. 15 Oct 1931, Waverly, WA.

viii. MARY JANE HAMMACK, b. Abt. 1859, Willamette Valley, OR; m. [-------] MACKINNON.

ix. FRANCIS SANFORD HAMMACK, b. Abt. 1862, Willamette Valley, OR; d. 14 Jun 1912, Washington Co., OR.

x. MARTHA F. HAMMACK, b. Abt. 1870, Oregon; d. Aft. 1880, Oregon.

Key Source: 1860 Wayne Co., IA, Census, p. 464; 1870 Marion Co., OR, Census, p. 38; 1880 Marion Co., OR, Census, p. 62.

424. GEORGE[9] HAMMACK *(JOHN[8], DANIEL[7], RICHARD[6], RICHARD[5], RICHARD[4], WILLIAM "O"[3], JOHN[2] HAMMOCKE, ? JOHN[1] HAMMOT)* was born 10 Sep 1817 in Kentucky, and died 28 Apr 1904 in Wayne Co., IA. He married (1) ELIZABETH MILLER 12 Nov 1837 in Perry Co., IN. She was born Sep 1818 in Kentucky, and died Bef. 1885 in Iowa. He married (2) CAROLINE HARPER 09 May 1885 in Appanoose Co., IA. She was born May 1846.

Children of GEORGE HAMMACK and ELIZABETH MILLER are:

i. FRANCES[10] HAMMACK, b. Abt. 1838, Indiana; d. Aft. 1850, Perry Co., IN.

ii. JOHN HAMMACK, b. Abt. 1840, Indiana; d. Aft. 1860, Wayne Co., IA.

iii. PHILLIP HAMMACK, b. Abt. 1842, Illinois; d. Aft. 1860, Wayne Co., IA.

496. iv. DANIEL HAMMACK, b. Abt. 1843, Indiana; d. Aft. 1870, Washington Co., NE.

v. LEWIS HAMMACK, b. Abt. 1845, Indiana; d. Aft. 1920, Boulder Co., CO; m. HANNA FRANCINA DEAN, 1866, Iowa; b. Abt. 1849, Ohio; d. Aft. 1910, Kansas.

vi. TAYLOR HAMMACK, b. Abt. 1848, Indiana; d. Aft. 1850, Perry Co., IN.

vii. SARAH HAMMACK, b. Abt. 1851, Indiana; d. Aft. 1860, Wayne Co., IA.

viii. MAHALAH HAMMACK, b. Abt. 1853, Indiana; d. Aft. 1870, Wayne Co., IA.

ix. ELIZABETH HAMMACK, b. Abt. 1855, Illinois; d. Aft. 1870, Wayne Co., IA.

x. WILLIAM HAMMACK, b. Abt. 1857, Iowa; d. Aft. 1870, Wayne Co., IA; m. STELLA [------]; b. Abt. 1860, Iowa; d. Aft. 1880, Wayne Co., IA.

xi. JAMES M. HAMMACK, b. 1859, Wayne Co., IA; d. Aft. 1880, Wayne Co., IA.

xii. MARION HAMMACK, b. Abt. 1861, Wayne Co., IA; d. Aft. 1880, Wayne Co., IA.

xiii. VIOLA HAMMACK, b. Abt. 1864, Wayne Co., IA; d. Aft. 1880, Wayne Co., IA.

Key Sources: 1850 Perry Co., IN, Census, p. 418; 1860 Wayne Co., IN, Census, p. 463; 1870 Wayne Co., IN, Census, p. 249; 1880 Wayne Co., IN, Census, p. 281; 1900 Harrison Co., IA, Census, p. 15.

425. EPHRAIM[9] HAMMACK *(DANIEL[8], DANIEL[7], RICHARD[6], RICHARD[5], RICHARD[4], WILLIAM "O"[3], JOHN[2] HAMMOCKE, ? JOHN[1] HAMMOT)* was born 13 Aug 1825 in Perry Co., IN, and died 22

Sep 1901 in Audobon Co., IA. He married MARANDA ELLEN MOSELEY 25 Mar 1847 in Mercer Co., IL. She was born Sep 1829 in Tazewell Co., IL, and died Aft. 1920 in Henry Co., IA.

Children of EPHRAIM HAMMACK and MARANDA MOSELEY are:

    i.   DANIEL M.[10] HAMMACK, b. Abt. 1847, Illinois; d. Aft. 1910, Los Angeles Co., CA; m. ISABELLA [------], Abt. 1874, Iowa; b. Abt. 1850, Illinois; d. Aft. 1910, Los Angeles Co., CA.

    ii.   WILLIAM HENRY HAMMACK, b. Abt. 1849, Illinois; d. Aft. 1920, San Bernardino Co., CA; m. RHUHAMA J. [------]; b. Abt. 1850, Indiana; d. Aft. 1900, Harlan Co., NE.

    iii.   EPHRAIM PAYNE HAMMACK, b. 18 Nov 1850, Mercer Co., Illinois; d. 12 Oct 1937, San Diego Co., CA; m. ADDIE LOUISA TOLAND, 05 Mar 1869, Iowa.

    iv.   SAMUEL ABISHA HAMMACK, b. Abt. 1853, Illinois; d. Aft. 1880, Henderson Co., IL; m. SUSAN [------]; b. Abt. 1858, Illinois; d. Aft. 1880, Henderson Co., IL.

    v.   MARY AMANDA HAMMACK, b. 15 Mar 1854, Henderson Co., IL; d. 11 Apr 1946, Los Angeles Co., CA.

    vi.   NOTTLEY SCOTT HAMMACK, b. 03 Sep 1855, Henderson Co., IL; d. Aft. 1920, San Diego Co., CA; m. MARY JANE BRAMHALL, 29 Sep 1881, Iowa.

    vii.   NANCY HAMMACK, b. Abt. 1858, Henderson Co., IL; d. Aft. 1870, Mercer Co., IL.

    viii.   FRANCES ANNE HAMMACK, b. Nov 1859, Henderson Co., IL; d. Aft. 1880, Desmoines Co., IA; m. WILLIAM DREWER.

    ix.   ELMIRA ADELLA HAMMACK, b. 10 Sep 1863, Henderson Co., IL; d. Aft. 1880, Desmoines Co., IA.

    x.   ALICE MYRTLE HAMMACK, b. 21 Apr 1865, Henderson Co., Illinois; d. 18 Dec 1951, Los Angeles Co., CA.

    xi.   LYDIA ELLEN HAMMACK, b. 27 Aug 1866, Mercer Co., IL; d. Aft. 1880, Desmoines Co., IA.

    xii.   JOHN MOSELEY HAMMACK, b. 22 Apr 1868, Mercer Co., IL; d. Aft. 1910, Burleigh Co., ND; m. FRANCES [------]; b. Abt. 1874, Iowa; d. Aft. 1910, Burleigh Co., ND.

    xiii.   THOMAS HILLARY HAMMACK, b. 06 Apr 1857, Henderson Co., IL; d. Bef. 1870, Henderson Co., IL.

Key Sources: 1850 Mercer Co., IL, Census, pp. 352-353; 1870 Mercer Co., IL, Census, p. 299; 1880 Des Moines Co., IA, Census, p. 86; 1910 Burleigh Co., ND, Census, p. 174; 1920 Henry Co., IA, Census, p. 88; Henry Franklin Hammack, 2: 231.

426. WILLIAM HENRY[9] HAMMACK *(COLEMAN[8], LEWIS[7], RICHARD[6], RICHARD[5], RICHARD[4], WILLIAM "O"[3], JOHN[2] HAMMOCKE, ? JOHN[1] HAMMOT)* was born 15 Sep 1824 in Madison Co., KY, and died 18 Oct 1890 in Pulaski Co., MO. He married SAMANTHA JANE KANTZLER 05 Feb 1846 in Franklin Co., MO. She was born Oct 1828 in Sullivan Co., IN.

Children of WILLIAM HAMMACK and SAMANTHA KANTZLER are:

    i.   DAMARIS[10] HAMMACK, b. 13 Nov 1846, Franklin Co., MO.

497.   ii.   WILLIAM THOMAS HAMMACK, b. Abt. 1848, Franklin Co., MO; d. Aft. 1892, Baxter Co., AR.

    iii.   MELISSA HAMMACK, b. Abt. 1856, Pulaski Co., MO; d. Aft. 1860, Pulaski Co., MO.

Key Sources: 1860 Pulaski Co., MO, Census, p. 331; 1880 Pulaski Co., MO, Census, p. 393; 1900 Pulaski Co., MO, Census, p. 239.

427. ANDREW H.[9] HAMMACK *(COLEMAN[8], LEWIS[7], RICHARD[6], RICHARD[5], RICHARD[4], WILLIAM "O"[3], JOHN[2] HAMMOCKE, ? JOHN[1] HAMMOT)* was born Abt. 1826 in Madison Co., KY, and died 07 Jan 1884 in Osage Co., MO. He married (1) SARAH WEEDEN 06 Sep 1849 in Franklin Co., MO. He

married (2) JULIA ANN GREENSTREET 08 Sep 1862 in Franklin Co., MO. She was born Abt. 1831 in Missouri, and died Aft. 1870 in Osage Co., MO.
Children of ANDREW HAMMACK and SARAH WEEDEN are:
    i.   ALEXANDER[10] HAMMACK, b. Abt. 1850, Franklin Co., MO.
    ii. WALLACE HAMMACK, b. Abt. 1852, Franklin Co., MO; d. Aft. 1880, Franklin Co., MO.

Children of ANDREW HAMMACK and JULIA GREENSTREET are:
    iii. ROBERT FRANKLIN[10] HAMMACK, b. 25 Jan 1865, Franklin Co., MO.
    iv. JOHN BENJAMIN HAMMACK, b. 15 Jun 1867, Osage Co., MO.
    v. GEORGE HAMMACK, b. 1870, Osage Co., MO.
Key Sources: 1870 Osage Co., MO, Census, p. 136; Henry Franklin Hammack, 2: 133.

428. ASA[9] HAMMACK *(COLEMAN[8], LEWIS[7], RICHARD[6], RICHARD[5], RICHARD[4], WILLIAM "O"[3], JOHN[2] HAMMOCKE, ? JOHN[1] HAMMOT)* was born Abt. 1832 in Floyd Co., KY, and died 28 Feb 1900 in Sebastian Co., AR. He married RUTH SUTES LASSITER 01 Aug 1865 in Pulaski Co., MO. She was born Abt. 1838 in Missouri, and died 10 Feb 1892 in Lawrence Co., AR.
Children of ASA HAMMACK and RUTH LASSITER are:
    i.   NANCY[10] HAMMACK, b. Abt. 1865, Missouri; d. Aft. 1880, Camden Co., MO; m. JOHN W. MCKAY.
    ii. MARY HAMMACK, b. Abt. 1865, Missouri; d. Aft. 1880, Camden Co., MO; m. WILLIAM HARRINGTON.
    iii. PERMELIA HAMMACK, b. Abt. 1868, Missouri; d. Aft. 1880, Camden Co., MO.
    iv. ELLEN HAMMACK, b. Abt. 1870, Missouri; d. Aft. 1880, Camden Co., MO.
    v. EMMA JANE HAMMACK, b. 11 Jan 1871, Missouri; d. Aft. 1880, Camden Co., MO; m. ALEXANDER LAWRENCE MORRIS.
    vi. JOHN FRANKLIN HAMMACK, b. 28 Sep 1874, Pulaski Co., MO; d. 04 Feb 1963, Henry Co., IL; m. EVIE SNODGRASS.
    vii. BARBARA HAMMACK, b. Abt. 1876, Missouri; d. Aft. 1880, Camden Co., MO; m. [-----] THATCHER.
    viii. MARTHA ANN CLEMENTINE HAMMACK, b. 11 Apr 1876, Pulaski Co., MO; d. Aft. 1880, Camden Co., MO.
    ix. CYNDA HAMMACK, b. Abt. 1880, Pulaski Co., MO.
Key Source: 1880 Camden Co., MO, Census, p. 12.

429. JAMES G.[9] HAMMACK *(COLEMAN[8], LEWIS[7], RICHARD[6], RICHARD[5], RICHARD[4], WILLIAM "O"[3], JOHN[2] HAMMOCKE, ? JOHN[1] HAMMOT)* was born Abt. 1840 in Missouri, and died 14 Nov 1867 in Pulaski Co., MO. He married SOPHIA JANE BRAY 08 Apr 1859 in Gasconade Co., MO. She was born Abt. 1839 in Missouri, and died Aft. 1880 in Pulaski Co., MO.
Children of JAMES HAMMACK and SOPHIA BRAY are:
    i.   MARY E.[10] HAMMACK, b. 28 Feb 1859, Pulaski Co., MO.
    ii. JOHN F. HAMMACK, b. 20 May 1862, Pulaski Co., MO; d. Aft. 1880, Pulaski Co., MO.
    iii. JAMES C. HAMMACK, b. 07 Nov 1864, Pulaski Co., MO; d. Aft. 1880, Pulaski Co., MO.
    iv. NANCY R. HAMMACK, b. 11 Oct 1866, Pulaski Co., MO; d. Aft. 1880, Pulaski Co., MO.
Key Source: 1880 Pulaski Co., MO, Census, p. 407.

430. AMANDA E.[9] HAMMACK *(BENJAMIN[8], LEWIS[7], RICHARD[6], RICHARD[5], RICHARD[4], WILLIAM "O"[3], JOHN[2] HAMMOCKE, ? JOHN[1] HAMMOT)* was born Abt. 1827 in Missouri, and died Aft. 1870 in Perry Co., IL.
Child of AMANDA E. HAMMACK is:

  i.   JAMES LEWIS[10] HAMMACK, b. Abt. 1854, Perry Co., IL; d. Aft. 1860, Perry Co., IL.
Key Sources: 1850 Perry Co., IL, Census, pp. 338, 383, 388; 1860 Perry Co., IL, Census, p. 2; 1870 Perry Co., IL, Census, p. 116; Henry Franklin Hammack, 2: 132.

Generation No. 10

431. JOHN[10] HEMMICK *(JOHN[9] HAMMICK, MICHAEL[8], MICHAEL[7] HAMICK, MICHAEL[6] HAMMICK, MICHAEL[5], THOMAS[4] HAMICK, HENRYE[3] HAMICKE, JOHN[2] HAMMOCKE, ? JOHN[1] HAMMOT)* was born 20 May 1814 in Yealmpton, Devonshire. He married MARY [------].
Children of JOHN HEMMICK and MARY [------] are:
  i.   MARY JULIA ANN[11] HAMACH, b. Abt. 22 Apr 1854, St. Columb Minor, Cornwall.
  ii. JULIA HAMACK, b. Abt. 02 Jul 1857, St. Columb Minor, Cornwall.
Key Source: St. Columb Minor Parish Register.

432. JEREMIAH G.[10] HAMMOCK *(THOMAS B.[9], SAMUEL[8], JOHN[7], JOHN[6], WILLIAM[5], WILLIAM "THE ELDER"[4], WILLIAM "O"[3], JOHN[2] HAMMOCKE, ? JOHN[1] HAMMOT)* was born 10 Aug 1823 in Lincoln Co., GA, and died 14 Feb 1899 in Upshur Co., TX. He married MARTHA ANN UTZEMAN 12 Oct 1858 in Rusk Co., TX. She was born 29 Aug 1834 in Rhea Co., TN, and died Aft. 1870 in Upshur Co., TX.
Children of JEREMIAH HAMMACK and MARTHA UTZEMAN are:
    i.   FRANCES AFIA[11] HAMMOCK, b. 28 Jul 1859, Rusk Co., TX; d. Aft. 1870, Upshur Co., TX.
    ii. FRANCIS MARION HAMMOCK, b. 08 Oct 1861, Rusk Co., TX; d. 11 Oct 1937, Upshur Co., TX; m. NANNIE [------].
    iii. JOHN FRANKLIN HAMMOCK, b. 21 Dec 1866, Upshur Co., TX; d. Aft. 1870, Upshur Co., TX.
Key Sources: 1860 Rusk Co., TX, Census, p. 274; 1870 Upshur Co., TX, Census, p. 53.

433. JOHN A.[10] HAMMOCK *(THOMAS B.[9], SAMUEL[8], JOHN[7], JOHN[6], WILLIAM[5], WILLIAM "THE ELDER"[4], WILLIAM "O"[3], JOHN[2] HAMMOCKE, ? JOHN[1] HAMMOT)* was born Oct 1825 in Lincoln Co., GA, and died 22 Jan 1900 in Union Parish, LA. He married MARY ANN T. COGGIN 04 Sep 1844 in Chambers Co., AL. She was born Abt. 1828 in Florida, and died Aft. 1870 in Union Parish, LA.
Children of JOHN HAMMOCK and MARY COGGIN are:
    i.   LOUISA L.[11] HAMMOCK, b. Abt. 1845, Chambers Co., AL; d. Aft. 1860, Union Parish, LA.
    ii. EDWIN M. HAMMOCK, b. Abt. 1847, Chambers Co., AL; d. Aft. 1860, Union Parish, LA.
    iii. WILLIAM THOMAS HAMMOCK, b. Abt. 1850, Chambers Co., AL; d. Aft. 1882, Union Parish, LA; m. PAMELA ANTOINETTE PORTER.
    iv. JOHN A. J. HAMMOCK, b. Abt. 1855, Chambers Co., AL; d. Aft. 1870, Union Parish, LA.
    v.   E. E. HAMMOCK, b. Abt. 1859, Union Parish, LA; d. Aft. 1860, Union Parish, LA.
Key Sources: Chambers Co., AL, Marriages Book 3, No. 110; 1850 Chambers Co., AL, Census, p. 273; 1860 Union Co., LA, Census, p. 506; 1870 Union Parish, LA, Census, p. 73; Eula Green Johnson, *Hammacks and Hammocks in Our Family* (1988). This man was previously incorrectly identified as a son of John Seaborne Hammock of Coweta Co., GA. His mother Matilda Hammock gave permission for him to marry in 1844.

434. SAMUEL MOREMAN[10] HAMMACK *(JOHN B.[9], SAMUEL[8], JOHN[7], JOHN[6], WILLIAM[5], WILLIAM "THE ELDER"[4], WILLIAM "O"[3], JOHN[2] HAMMOCKE, ? JOHN[1] HAMMOT)* was born 28 Sep

1836 in Wilkes Co., GA, and died 01 Nov 1877 in Harris Co., TX. He married JANE ELIZABETH POWELL Abt. 1870 in Texas. She was born Abt. 1844 in Alabama, and died Aft. 1880 in Harris Co., TX.
Children of SAMUEL HAMMACK and JANE POWELL are:
    i.   SAMUEL L.[11] HAMMACK, b. Abt. 1869, Texas; d. Aft. 1880, Harris Co., TX.
    ii.   JOHN D. HAMMACK, b. Abt. 1870, Texas; d. Aft. 1880, Harris Co., TX.
    iii.   ARABELLA HAMMACK, b. Abt. 1871, Texas; d. Aft. 1880, Harris Co., TX.
    iv.   LUELLA HAMMACK, b. Abt. 1872, Texas; d. Aft. 1880, Harris Co., TX.
    v.   JAMES HAMMACK, b. Abt. 1875, Texas; d. Aft. 1880, Harris Co., TX.
    vi.   EMMA HAMMACK, b. Abt. 1877, Texas; d. Aft. 1880, Harris Co., TX.
    vii.   WILILE P. HAMMACK, b. Abt. 1878, Texas; d. Aft. 1880, Harris Co., TX.
Key Sources: 1850 Wilkes Co., GA, Census, p. 305; 1860 Leake Co., MO, Census, p. 579; 1880 Harris Co., TX, Census, p. 141.

435. WILLIAM P.[10] HAMMACK *(JOHN S.[9], WILLIAM[8], JOHN[7], JOHN[6], WILLIAM[5], WILLIAM "THE ELDER"[4], WILLIAM "O"[3], JOHN[2] HAMMOCKE, ? JOHN[1] HAMMOT)* was born Abt. 1830 in Alabama, and died Aft. 1880 in Yell Co., AR. He married HARRIETT E. [------] Abt. 1860 in Louisiana. She was born Abt. 1841 in Alabama, and died Aft. 1880 in Yell Co., AR.
Children of WILLIAM HAMMACK and HARRIETT [------] are:
    i.   JOHN A.[11] HAMMACK, b. Abt. 1860, Louisiana.
    ii.   WILLIAM FRANKLIN HAMMACK, b. Abt. 1862, Louisiana.
    iii.   JAMES W. HAMMACK, b. Abt. 1865, Louisiana.
    iv.   GEORGE W. HAMMACK, b. Abt. 1868, Arkansas.
    v.   ANNA F. HAMMACK, b. Abt. 1870, Arkansas.
    vi.   PERRY HAMMACK, b. Abt. 1873, Arkansas.
Key Sources: 1870 Yell Co., AR, Census, p. 575; 1880 Yell Co., AR, Census, p. 139.

436. WILLIAM DAVID[10] HAMMACK *(WILLIAM B.[9], WILLIAM[8], JOHN[7], JOHN[6], WILLIAM[5], WILLIAM "THE ELDER"[4], WILLIAM "O"[3], JOHN[2] HAMMOCKE, ? JOHN[1] HAMMOT)* was born 15 Feb 1853 in Russell Co., AL, and died 24 Sep 1915 in Kaufman Co., TX. He married (1) MARY ROGERS. She was born 1854 in Mississippi, and died 1892 in Kaufman Co., TX. He married (2) RUTH SEABERRY YATES 04 Jan 1893 in Kaufman Co., TX.
Children of WILLIAM HAMMACK and MARY ROGERS are:
    i.   RUSSELL P.[11] HAMMACK, b. 29 Jun 1873, Kaufman Co., TX; d. 05 Aug 1962, Tarrant Co., TX; m. MAGGIE MCSHANE.
    ii.   MARTHA HAMMACK, b. 18 Nov 1874, Kaufman Co., TX; d. 16 Nov 1943, Clay Co., TX; m. J. W. WEBB.
    iii.   HENRY MARSAILES HAMMACK, b. 11 Jan 1876, Kaufman Co., TX; d. 07 Jan 1944, Kaufman Co., TX.
    iv.   JOHN D. HAMMACK, b. 28 Mar 1883, Kaufman Co., TX; d. 03 Jan 1927, Cherokee Co., TX; m. LULA TYRA.
Key Sources: F. W. Johnson and E. W. Winkler, *A History of Texas and Texans* (5 vols., New York, NY, and Chicago, IL, 1914); 1880 Kaufman Co., TX, Census, p. 70.

437. ALFONZO J. "FONEY"[10] HAMMACK *(JEREMIAH[9], JOHN[8], JOHN[7], JOHN[6], WILLIAM[5], WILLIAM "THE ELDER"[4], WILLIAM "O"[3], JOHN[2] HAMMOCKE, ? JOHN[1] HAMMOT)* was born 23 Jun 1849 in Macon Co., AL, and died 25 Jun 1893 in Williamson Co., TX. He married GEORGIA ANN MADDOX. She was born 05 Mar 1850 in Alabama, and died 28 Feb 1940 in Williamson Co., TX.
Children of ALFONZO HAMMACK and GEORGIA MADDOX are:

     i.   MINNIE LOU[11] HAMMACK, b. 27 Oct 1872, White Co., AR; d. 31 Jan 1939, Jones Co., TX; m. J. W. TEMPLE.
     ii.   MATTIE HAMMACK, b. Abt. 1874, White Co., AR; d. Aft. 1880, White Co., AR.
     iii.   ROBERT EARL HAMMACK, b. 17 Jan 1878, White Co., AR; d. 08 Dec 1910, Williamson Co., TX.
     iv.   LINDSEY BROWN HAMMACK, b. 23 Jun 1880, White Co., AR; d. 20 Aug 1959, Jones Co., TX.
     v.   VIRGINIA RUTH HAMMACK, b. 01 Jul 1882, White Co., AR; d. 27 Dec 1964, Tom Green Co., TX; m. W. M. VAN NESS.
     vi.   JESSIE HAMMACK, b. Sep 1890, Texas; d. Aft. 1900, Bell Co., TX.

Key Sources: Henry Franklin Hammack, 2: 56; 1870 White Co., AR, Census, p. 391; 1880 White Co., AR, Census, p. 184; 1900 Bell Co., TX, Census, p. 88; Texas Death Certificates for Georgia Maddox Hammack, Minnie Hammack Temple, Robert Earl Hammack, Lindsey Brown Hammack, and Virginia Hammack Van Ness.

438. WILLIAM J.[10] HAMMOCK *(JAMES[9], ELIJAH[8], JOHN[7], JOHN[6], WILLIAM[5], WILLIAM "THE ELDER"[4], WILLIAM "O"[3], JOHN[2] HAMMOCKE, ? JOHN[1] HAMMOT)* was born Abt. 1835 in Twiggs Co., GA, and died 25 Jun 1862 in King's School House, VA. He married WYLANTA CATHERINE WOODALL Abt. 1858 in Twiggs Co., GA. She was born Abt. 1835 in Bibb Co., GA, and died Aft. 1880 in Cass Co., TX.
Children of WILLIAM HAMMOCK and WYLANTA WOODALL are:
     i.   ROXIE A. ELIZABETH[11] HAMMOCK, b. Abt. 1855, Twiggs Co., GA; d. 10 Jan 1920, Cass Co., TX; m. JAMES SAMUEL FLETCHER; b. 1844, Georgia; d. 1917, Texas.
     ii.   MARY A. M. HAMMOCK, b. Abt. 1858, Twiggs Co., GA; d. Aft. 1870, Davis Co., TX.
     iii.   JAMES WILLIAM S. HAMMOCK, b. Abt. 1860, Twiggs Co., GA; d. 1940, Shreveport, Caddo Parish, LA; m. HELEN SUMMERS; b. Abt. 1869, Texas; d. 1939, Caddo Parish, LA.
     iv.   JOHN J. D. HAMMOCK, b. 28 Dec 1861, Twiggs Co., GA; d. 29 Jan 1936, Camp Co., TX; m. SALLIE HODGE; b. 1862, Mississippi; d. 27 Jan 1948, Upshur Co., TX.

Key Sources: 1860 Twiggs Co., GA, Census, pp. 404-405; 1870 Davis Co., TX, Census, p. 33; 1880 Cass Co., TX, Census, p. 113; Texas Death Certificates of Roxie Hammock Fletcher and John J. D. Hammock; Louisiana Death Certificates of James William and Helen Summers Hammock. Note that the identity of James William Hammock as James W. S. Hammock is not positive.

439. CATHERINE[10] HAMMACK *(WILLIAM HARRISON[9], PASCHAL[8], JOHN[7], JOHN[6], WILLIAM[5], WILLIAM "THE ELDER"[4], WILLIAM "O"[3], JOHN[2] HAMMOCKE, ? JOHN[1] HAMMOT)* was born Abt. 1835 in Georgia, and died Aft. 1850 in Randolph Co., GA. She married (2) JACK GASSETT.
Children of CATHERINE HAMMACK are:
     i.   VIRGINIA[11] HAMMACK, b. Abt. 1855, Randolph Co., GA; d. Aft. 1860, Randolph Co., GA.
     ii.   URIAH HAMMACK, b. Abt. 1857, Randolph Co., GA; d. Aft. 1860, Randolph Co., GA.
Key Source: 1860 Randolph Co., GA, Census, p. 704.

440. JAMES PASCHAL[10] HAMMACK *(WILLIAM HARRISON[9], PASCHAL[8], JOHN[7], JOHN[6], WILLIAM[5], WILLIAM "THE ELDER"[4], WILLIAM "O"[3], JOHN[2] HAMMOCKE, ? JOHN[1] HAMMOT)* was born Abt. 1838 in Georgia, and died Bet. 1861 - 1865 in Confederate States Army. He married ADELINE BEVERLY 08 Jan 1861 in Dooly Co., GA. She was born 26 Dec 1836 in Georgia, and died 26 Jul 1912 in Macon Co., GA.
Child of JAMES HAMMACK and ADELINE BEVERLY is:
     i.   LULA[11] HAMMACK, b. Abt. 1862, Georgia; d. 15 Jun 1876, Randolph Co., GA.

Key Sources: 1870 Macon Co., GA, Census, p. 577; Georgia Division, *United Daughters of the Confederacy, Ancestor Roster*, Volume 4.

441. WILILAM DAVID[10] HAMMACK *(WILLIAM HARRISON[9], PASCHAL[8], JOHN[7], JOHN[6], WILLIAM[5], WILLIAM "THE ELDER"[4], WILLIAM "O"[3], JOHN[2] HAMMOCKE, ? JOHN[1] HAMMOT)* was born 13 Apr 1842 in Randolph Co., Georgia, and died 19 Mar 1936 in Randolph Co., GA. He married (1) VICTORIA VEAZY Abt. 1872 in Randolph Co., GA. She was born Abt. 1844 in Georgia, and died Bef. 1886 in Randolph Co., GA. He married (2) JULIA JENKINS 08 Aug 1888 in Randolph Co., GA. She was born 10 Jun 1866 in Georgia, and died 01 Aug 1936 in Randolph Co., GA.
Child of WILILAM HAMMACK and VICTORIA VEAZY is:
  i.   EVA L.[11] HAMMACK, b. Abt. 1873, Randolph Co., GA; d. Aft. 1880, Randolph Co., GA.
Key Sources: Georgia Division, *United Daughters of the Confederacy, Ancestor Roster*; 1870 Randolph Co., GA, Census, p. 267; 1880 Randolph Co., GA, Census, p. 153.

442. JOHN GILBERT[10] HAMMACK *(WILLIAM HARRISON[9], PASCHAL[8], JOHN[7], JOHN[6], WILLIAM[5], WILLIAM "THE ELDER"[4], WILLIAM "O"[3], JOHN[2] HAMMOCKE, ? JOHN[1] HAMMOT)* was born 29 Oct 1844 in Randolph Co., Georgia, and died 1929 in Randolph Co., GA. He married HULDAH MANGHAM Abt. 1866 in Randolph Co., GA. She was born Abt. 1846 in Georgia, and died Aft. 1880 in Randolph Co., GA.
Children of JOHN HAMMACK and HULDAH MANGHAM are:
  i.   HERSCHEL ADOLPHUS[11] HAMMACK, b. 31 Aug 1868, Randolph Co., GA; d. Aft. 1880, Randolph Co., GA.
  ii.   EARNEST MALSCHUM HAMMACK, b. 06 Mar 1871, Randolph Co., GA; d. Aft. 1880, Randolph Co., GA.
  iii.   ALICE EVELYN HAMMACK, b. 06 Feb 1873, Randolph Co., GA; d. Aft. 1880, Randolph Co., GA.
  iv.   HUGH VIRGIL HAMMACK, b. 09 Apr 1875, Randolph Co., GA; d. Aft. 1880, Randolph Co., GA.
  v.   MARY LAURA HAMMACK, b. 30 Apr 1876, Randolph Co., GA; d. Aft. 1880, Randolph Co., GA.
  vi.   JOHN BERNARD HAMMACK, b. 03 Mar 1878, Randolph Co., GA; d. Aft. 1920, Dougherty Co., GA.
  vii.   GUY LAWRENCE HAMMACK, b. 28 Dec 1879, Randolph Co., GA; d. Aft. 1880, Randolph Co., GA.
  viii. WILLOUGHBY HERBERT HAMMACK, b. 02 Dec 1884, Randolph Co., GA; d. Aft. 1950, Lake City, FL.
Key Sources: 1880 Randolph Co., GA, Census, p. 143B; Henry Franklin Hammack, 2: 237.

443. DANIEL WARREN[10] HAMMACK *(WILLIAM HARRISON[9], PASCHAL[8], JOHN[7], JOHN[6], WILLIAM[5], WILLIAM "THE ELDER"[4], WILLIAM "O"[3], JOHN[2] HAMMOCKE, ? JOHN[1] HAMMOT)* was born 19 Feb 1850 in Georgia, and died 02 Jul 1928 in New Mexico. He married EMMA GRANT Abt. 1873 in Randolph Co., GA. She was born 20 Jan 1850 in Georgia, and died 02 Aug 1944 in New Mexico.
Children of DANIEL HAMMACK and EMMA GRANT are:
  i.   HOMER EUGENE[11] HAMMACK, b. 16 Apr 1875, Randolph Co., GA; d. 02 Aug 1944.
  ii.   NANCY BARBARA HAMMACK, b. 02 Feb 1878, Randolph Co., GA; d. 21 Nov 1938.
  iii.   RUSSELL GRANT HAMMACK, b. 23 Jul 1880, Randolph Co., GA.
  iv.   EMMA PEARL HAMMACK, b. 15 Nov 1882, Randolph Co., GA; m. LEE O. GAY.
  v.   AVIS EARLINE HAMMACK, b. 03 May 1885, Randolph Co., GA.
  vi.   EMMA MELL HAMMACK, b. 23 Sep 1889, Randolph Co., GA.

vii. THOMAS MUSE HAMMACK, b. 19 Feb 1896, Randolph Co., GA; d. 10 Oct 1920, Grant Co., New Mexico.

Key Source: Henry Franklin Hammack, 2: 194, 237.

444. JAMES WISE[10] HAMMACK *(? JAMES URIAH[9], THOMAS[8], JOHN[7], JOHN[6], WILLIAM[5], WILLIAM "THE ELDER"[4], WILLIAM "O"[3], JOHN[2] HAMMOCKE, ? JOHN[1] HAMMOT)* was born Abt. 1857 in Alabama, and died Aft. 1875 in Columbia Co., AR. He married MARY FRANCES RUSH 09 Dec 1875 in Columbia Co., AR. She died 26 May 1928.

Children of JAMES HAMMACK and MARY RUSH are:

i. BENJAMIN FRANKLIN[11] HAMMACK, m. SRAH ELMIRA LOWE.

ii. EUNICE A. HAMMACK, m. ELBERT WRAY.

iii. ANNA HAMMACK.

iv. CHARLES HENRY HAMMACK, b. 1887, Columbia Co., AR; d. 1923, Columbia Co., AR; m. BERTHA BURRIS; b. 1888, Arkansas; d. 1959, Arkansas.

Key Source: Henry Franklin Hammack, 2: 92, 111, 278, 306-308.

445. GEORGE W.[10] HAMMOCK *(JOHN W.[9], JACOB[8], LEWIS[7], ROBERT HAMMACK[6] JR., ROBERT HAMMACK[5] SR., WILLIAM "THE ELDER"[4] HAMMACK, WILLIAM "O"[3], JOHN[2] HAMMOCKE, ? JOHN[1] HAMMOT)* was born 5 February 1847 in Perry Co., AL, and died 12 January 1925 in Faulkner Co., AR. He married MARY JANE SIBLEY Abt. 1865 in Calhoun Co., MS. She was born 28 January 1850 in Mississippi, and died 25 February 1930 in Mississippi.

Children of GEORGE HAMMACK and MARY SIBLEY are:

i. WILLIAM THOMAS[11] HAMMOCK, b. 24 Dec 1866, Calhoun Co., MS; d. Aft. 1927, Pulaski Co., AR; m. MARGARET HENRIETTA JENKINS; b. Abt. Jan 1874, Arkansas; d. Aft. 1927, Arkansas.

ii. GEORGIA ANN HAMMOCK, b. Abt. 1871, Calhoun Co., MS; d. Aft. 1880, Arkansas.

iii. JOHN W. HAMMOCK, b. Abt. 1873, Arkansas; d. Aft. 1880, Faulkner Co., AR.

iv. JAMES R. HAMMOCK, b. Abt. 1875, Arkansas; d. Aft. 1880, Arkansas.

v. EDWARD C. HAMMOCK, b. Abt. 1876, Arkansas; d. Aft. 1880, Arkansas.

vi. LUTHER HAMMOCK, b. Abt. 1878, Arkansas; d. Aft. 1900, Faulkner Co., AR.

vii. ISAAC HAMMOCK, b. Abt. 1880, Arkansas; d. Aft. 1880, Faulkner Co., AR.

viii. SALLIE HAMMOCK, b. Abt. 1881, Arkansas; d. Aft. 1900, Faulkner Co., AR.

ix. GLENN HAMMOCK, b. Abt. 1884, Arkansas; d. Aft. 1900, Faulkner Co., AR.

x. MYRTLE HAMMOCK, b. Abt. 1886, Arkansas; d. Aft. 1900, Faulkner Co., AR.

xi. GERALDINE HAMMOCK, b. Abt. 1894, Arkansas; d. Aft. 1900, Faulkner Co., AR.

Key Sources: 1860 Choctaw Co., MS, Census, p. 422; 1870 Calhoun Co., MS, Census, p. 435; 1880 Washington Co., AR, Census, p. 223; 1900 Faulkner Co., AR, Census, p. 130. William Thomas Hammock served as state senator from 1899 to 1903 and Arkansas State Tax Commissioner in 1927. He was twice mayor of Quitman, Arkansas, and served there for many years as county judge.

446. CRAWFORD MILTON[10] HAMMOCK *(JOHN W.[9], JACOB[8], LEWIS[7], ROBERT HAMMACK[6] JR., ROBERT HAMMACK[5] SR., WILLIAM "THE ELDER"[4] HAMMACK, WILLIAM "O"[3], JOHN[2] HAMMOCKE, ? JOHN[1] HAMMOT)* was born 27 Sep 1848 in Perry Co., AL, and died Aft. 1900 in White Co., AR. He married (1) PERMELIA TAPLEY 12 Jun 1867 in Calhoun Co., MS. She was born Abt. 1849 in Mississippi, and died Aft. 1870 in Calhoun Co., MS. He married (2) MOLLY [------] Abt. 1875 in Arkansas. She was born Jan 1849 in Alabama, and died Aft. 1900 in White Co., AR.

Children of CRAWFORD HAMMOCK and PERMELIA TAPLEY are:

i. FANNIE[11] HAMMOCK, b. Abt. 1870, Arkansas; m. JOHN SMITH.

ii. CAMILLA HAMMOCK, b. Abt. 1872, Arkansas; m. NAPOLEON BICKLE.

Children of CRAWFORD HAMMOCK and MOLLY [------] are:

    iii. ADDIE[11] HAMMOCK, b. Mar 1877, Arkansas; d. Aft. 1900, White Co., AR; m. GEORGE BENNETT.

    iv. BASCUM HAMMOCK, b. Sep 1884, Arkansas; d. Aft. 1900, White Co., AR.

    v. ELICK HAMMOCK, b. Nov 1887, Arkansas; d. Aft. 1900, White Co., AR.

    vi. CLARANCE HAMMOCK, b. Oct 1889, Arkansas; d. Aft. 1900, White Co., AR.

    vii. CLEMENT HAMMOCK, b. Aug 1891, Arkansas; d. Aft. 1900, White Co., AR.

    viii. WARREN HAMMOCK, b. Jan 1900, Arkansas; d. Aft. 1900, White Co., AR.

Key Sources: 1870 Calhoun Co., MS, Census, p. 428; 1900 White Co., AR, Census, p. 213.

447. JAMES A.[10] HAMMACK *(WILLIAM/WILSON H.[9], JACOB[8], LEWIS[7], ROBERT HAMMACK[6] JR., ROBERT HAMMACK[5] SR., WILLIAM "THE ELDER"[4] HAMMACK, WILLIAM "O"[3], JOHN[2] HAMMOCKE, ? JOHN[1] HAMMOT)* was born Mar 1880 in Hinds Co., MS, and died Aft. 1910 in Hinds Co., MS. He married MAMIE [------] Abt. 1908 in Hinds Co., MS. She was born Abt. 1879 in Mississippi, and died Aft. 1910 in Hinds Co., MS.

Child of JAMES HAMMACK and MAMIE [------] is:

    i. JAMES A.[11] HAMMACK, b. 1909, Hinds Co., MS; d. Aft. 1910, Hinds Co., MS.

Key Source: 1910 Hinds Co., MS, Census, p. 26.

448. LEWIS SHEPPARD[10] SMALLWOOD *(ELIZA[9] POOLE, MILLY[8] HAMMACK, LEWIS[7], ROBERT HAMMACK[6] JR., ROBERT HAMMACK[5] SR., WILLIAM "THE ELDER"[4] HAMMACK, WILLIAM "O"[3], JOHN[2] HAMMOCKE, ? JOHN[1] HAMMOT)* was born 1827 in Jones Co., GA, and died Aft. 1852 in Mississippi. He married MARY A. MCLEROY 23 Dec 1844 in Jones Co., GA.

Children of LEWIS SMALLWOOD and MARY MCLEROY are:

    i. AARON AUGUSTUS[11] SMALLWOOD, b. 25 Jan 1847, Jones Co., GA; d. 17 Jul 1918, Rankin Co., MS; m. JOSEPHINE PEARSON; b. 26 Oct 1861, Marion Co., MS; d. 1948, Rankin Co., MS.

    ii. JOHN T. SMALLWOOD, b. 08 Apr 1852, Houston Co., GA; d. 06 Sep 1938, Jones Co., GA.

Key Sources: 1860 Simpson Co., MS, Census, p. 196; 1880 Hinds Co., MS, Census, p. 369; 1880 Rankin Co., MS, Census, p. 315.

449. MILLY ANN[10] SMALLWOOD *(ELIZA[9] POOLE, MILLY[8] HAMMACK, LEWIS[7], ROBERT HAMMACK[6] JR., ROBERT HAMMACK[5] SR., WILLIAM "THE ELDER"[4] HAMMACK, WILLIAM "O"[3], JOHN[2] HAMMOCKE, ? JOHN[1] HAMMOT)* was born 1829 in Jones Co., GA, and died Aft. 1880 in Crawford Co., GA. She married WILLIAM HENRY CLIFTON HAMMACK 15 May 1845 in Jones Co., GA.

Children of MILLY SMALLWOOD and WILLIAM HAMMACK are:

    i. MARY[11] HAMMACK, b. Abt. 1848, Jones Co., GA.

    ii. HENRY B. HAMMACK.

    iii. JOSEPHINE HAMMACK, b. Abt. 1850, Jones Co., GA.

Key Sources: 1870 Crawford Co., GA, Census, p. 451; 1800 Crawford Co., GA, Census, p. 714.

450. MARTHA A.[10] HAMMACK *(JACKSON LEWIS[9], JOHN M.[8], LEWIS[7], ROBERT HAMMACK[6] JR., ROBERT HAMMACK[5] SR., WILLIAM "THE ELDER"[4] HAMMACK, WILLIAM "O"[3], JOHN[2] HAMMOCKE, ? JOHN[1] HAMMOT)* was born 25 Oct 1845 in Jones Co., GA, and died 23 Apr 1906 in Jones Co., GA. She married WILLIAM JACKSON 15 Nov 1866 in Jones Co., GA, son of JOHN JACKSON and MALITIA ROWE. He was born 21 Jul 1847 in Jones Co., GA, and died 20 Mar 1926 in Jones Co., GA.

Children are listed above under (376) William Jackson.

451. SALLY S.[10] HAMMACK *(JOSEPH DAVIS*[9], *JOHN*[8], *ROBERT*[7], *ROBERT HAMMACK*[6] *JR., ROBERT HAMMACK*[5] *SR., WILLIAM "THE ELDER"*[4] *HAMMACK, WILLIAM "O"*[3], *JOHN*[2] *HAMMOCKE, ? JOHN*[1] *HAMMOT)* was born Abt. 1852 in Taliaferro Co., GA, and died Bef. 1880 in Taliaferro Co., GA. She married THOMAS E. BRISTOW 28 May 1872 in Taliaferro Co., GA.
Children of SALLY HAMMACK and THOMAS BRISTOW are:

    i. PAULINE[11] BRISTOW, b. Abt. 1874, Taliaferro Co., GA; d. Aft. 1880, Taliaferro Co., GA.
    ii. CLAUDIE BRISTOW, b. Abt. 1876, Taliaferro Co., GA; d. Aft. 1880, Taliaferro Co., GA.
Key Source: 1880 Taliaferro Co., GA, Census, p. 344.

452. LUCINDA FRANCES[10] HAMMACK *(HENRY T.*[9], *JOHN*[8], *ROBERT*[7], *ROBERT HAMMACK*[6] *JR., ROBERT HAMMACK*[5] *SR., WILLIAM "THE ELDER"*[4] *HAMMACK, WILLIAM "O"*[3], *JOHN*[2] *HAMMOCKE, ? JOHN*[1] *HAMMOT)* was born 1849 in Taliaferro Co., GA, and died 1945 in Taliaferro Co., GA. She married DR. LINTON ALEXANDER STEPHENS 11 Dec 1867 in Taliaferro Co., GA. He was born 14 Feb 1845 in Taliaferro Co., GA, and died 17 Jun 1894 in Taliaferro Co., GA.
Children of LUCINDA HAMMACK and DR. STEPHENS are:

    i. JOHN HENRY[11] STEPHENS, b. 27 Mar 1869, Taliaferro Co., GA; d. 29 Nov 1893, Taliaferro Co., GA; m. LEILA ANDERSON.
    ii. MARY JANE STEPHENS, b. 05 Jan 1871, Taliaferro Co., GA; m. J. EDWARD WHITE.
    iii. SARA IRENE STEPHENS, b. 01 Oct 1874, Taliaferro Co., GA; d. 13 Jul 1956, Taliaferro Co., GA; m. HENRY F. WHITE; b. Abt. 1874, Taliaferro Co., GA; d. 24 Jan 1953, Taliaferro Co., GA.
    iv. MAUDE A. STEPHENS, b. Abt. 1876, Taliaferro Co., GA; m. ROBERT LEE HADAWAY.
Key Source: 1880 Taliaferro Co., GA, Census, p. 346. Linton Alexander Stephens was a nephew of Confederate Vice-President Alexander H. Stephens.

453. THOMAS N.[10] HAMMOCK *(ABNER MASTIN W.*[9], *JOSHUA*[8], *JOSHUA*[7], *ROBERT HAMMACK*[6] *JR., ROBERT HAMMACK*[5] *SR., WILLIAM "THE ELDER"*[4] *HAMMACK, WILLIAM "O"*[3], *JOHN*[2] *HAMMOCKE, ? JOHN*[1] *HAMMOT)* was born Abt. 1870 in Georgia, and died Aft. 1900 in Cleburne Co., AL. He married EMILY HAND Abt. 1892 in Cleburne Co., AL. She was born May 1870 in Cleburne Co., AL, and died Aft. 1900 in Cleburne Co., AL.
Children of THOMAS HAMMOCK and EMILY HAND are:

    i. GEORGE WESLEY[11] HAMMOCK, b. 30 Jul 1894, Alabama; d. 11 Apr 1972, Cleburne Co., AL; m. DOVIE L. SHEPPARD; b. 05 Nov 1894, Randolph Co., AL; d. 18 May 1959, Cleburne Co., AR.
    ii. GIHURBERT HAMMOCK, b. Mar 1897, Alabama.
    iii. MARY J. HAMMOCK, b. Oct 1899, Alabama.
    iv. ISAIAH HAMMOCK, b. 1892, Alabama; d. 1938, Cleburne Co., AL.
Key Source: 1900 Cleburne Co., AL, Census, p. 290.

454. JAMES WILBURN[10] HAMMACK *(WILLIAM T. H.*[9], *SIMEON J.*[8], *WILLIAM T.*[7], *ROBERT HAMMACK*[6] *JR., ROBERT HAMMACK*[5] *SR., WILLIAM "THE ELDER"*[4] *HAMMACK, WILLIAM "O"*[3], *JOHN*[2] *HAMMOCKE, ? JOHN*[1] *HAMMOT)* was born 02 Jan 1843 in Crawford Co., GA, and died 07 Jan 1917 in Flora, Madison County, MS. He married JEFFERSONIA A. E. COLLUM 02 Sep 1865 in Madison County, MS, daughter of JOHN COLLUM and MARY [--------]. She was born 17 Aug 1836 in Crawford Co., GA, and died 14 Jan 1915 in Vernon, Madison County, MS.
Children of JAMES HAMMACK and JEFFERSONIA COLLUM are:

      i. GEORGIA[11] HAMMACK, b. Abt. 1866, Madison Co., MS; d. Aft. 1886, Madison Co., MS; m. W. B. NOBLES, 24 Dec 1886, Madison Co., MS.

      ii. JAMES WILLIAM HAMMACK, JR., b. Dec 1869, Madison Co., MS; d. Aft. 1900, Madison Co., MS, or Louisiana; m. SUSIE LEAVELL, 27 May 1897, Hinds County, MS; b. Abt. 1877, Mississippi; d. Bef. 1900, Madison Co., MS.

498.   iii. MINNIE E. HAMMACK, b. 27 Sep 1871, Madison Co., MS; d. 16 Sep 1952, Hinds Co., MS.

499.   iv. FREDERICK WILLIAM HAMMACK, b. 24 Jan 1874, Madison Co., MS; d. 18 Nov 1924, Flora, Madison County, MS.

500.   v. LENA M. HAMMACK, b. Feb 1876, Madison Co., MS; d. Aft. 1910, Madison Co., MS.

501.   vi. CHARLES CLIFTON HAMMACK, b. Abt. 1878, Madison Co., MS; d. Aft. 1920, Madison Co., MS.

Key Sources: 1870 Madison Co., MS, Census, p. 93; 1880 Madison Co., MS, Census, p. 117; 1900 Madison Co., MS, Census, p. 115; 1910 Madison Co., MS, Census, p. 201.

455. MARY A. E.[10] HAMMACK *(WILLIAM T. H.[9], SIMEON J.[8], WILLIAM T.[7], ROBERT HAMMACK[6] JR., ROBERT HAMMACK[5] SR., WILLIAM "THE ELDER"[4] HAMMACK, WILLIAM "O"[3], JOHN[2] HAMMOCKE, ? JOHN[1] HAMMOT)* was born Abt. 1846 in Crawford Co., GA, and died Aft. 1880 in Madison Co., MS. She married JOHN M. WARD 02 Dec 1867 in Madison County, MS, son of DAVID WARD and NANCY TEMPLETON. He was born Abt. 1833 in Georgia, and died Aft. 1880 in Madison Co., MS.

Children of MARY HAMMACK and JOHN WARD are:

      i. DAVID[11] WARD, b. Abt. 1872, Madison Co., MS; d. Aft. 1880, Madison Co., MS.

      ii. G. E. WARD, b. Abt. 1874, Madison Co., MS; d. Aft. 1880, Madison Co., MS.

      iii. JAMES W. WARD, b. Abt. 1876, Madison Co., MS; d. Aft. 1880, Madison Co., MS.

Key Source: 1880 Madison Co., MS, Census, p. 105.

456. JOHN ASA[10] HAMMACK *(WILLIAM T. H.[9], SIMEON J.[8], WILLIAM T.[7], ROBERT HAMMACK[6] JR., ROBERT HAMMACK[5] SR., WILLIAM "THE ELDER"[4] HAMMACK, WILLIAM "O"[3], JOHN[2] HAMMOCKE, ? JOHN[1] HAMMOT)* was born 13 Nov 1847 in Crawford Co., GA, and died 24 May 1897 in Madison County, MS. He married CORA A. BRIGGS 20 Dec 1876 in Madison County, MS, daughter of ARTHUR BRIGGS and JEFFERSONIA COLLUM. She was born 10 Oct 1855 in Mississippi, and died 24 May 1897 in Madison County, MS.

Children of JOHN HAMMACK and CORA BRIGGS are:

502.   i. ETHEL[11] HAMMACK, b. 12 Jul 1878, Madison Co., MS; d. Aug 1966, Madison Co., MS.

503.   ii. IMOGENE HAMMACK, b. Oct 1879, Madison Co., MS; d. 1951, Madison Co., MS.

      iii. WILBURN EUGENE HAMMACK, b. 23 Sep 1882, Madison Co., MS; d. 07 Feb 1952, Madison Co., MS.

      iv. MYRTLE HAMMACK, b. Mar 1884, Madison Co., MS; d. Bef. 1980, Madison Co., MS; m. [------] CHILDRESS.

      v. JEFFIE A. HAMMACK, b. 31 Mar 1886, Madison Co., MS; d. 12 Apr 1913, Madison Co., MS; m. W. W. HOPSON.

      vi. ASA HAMMACK, b. Mar 1888, Madison Co., MS; d. Bef. 1980, Madison Co., MS.

      vii. CORA HAMMACK, b. 12 Nov 1889, Madison Co., MS; d. 19 Jul 1932, Madison Co., MS; m. FRANCIS E. DAVIS, Aft. 1920, Madison Co., MS; b. 1883, Mississippi; d. 1953, Madison Co., MS.

      viii. LUCY HAMMACK, b. Feb 1892, Madison Co., MS; d. Bef. 1990, Madison Co., MS; m. [------] LYNES.

ix. RUBY HAMMACK, b. Sep 1894, Madison Co., MS; d. Bef. 1990, Madison Co., MS; m. [------] BRIEN.

Key Sources: 1880 Madison Co., MS, Census, p. 117; 1900 Madison Co., MS, Census, p. 115.

457. GEORGE THOMAS[10] HAMMACK *(WILLIAM T. H.[9], SIMEON J.[8], WILLIAM T.[7], ROBERT HAMMACK[6] JR., ROBERT HAMMACK[5] SR., WILLIAM "THE ELDER"[4] HAMMACK, WILLIAM "O"[3], JOHN[2] HAMMOCKE, ? JOHN[1] HAMMOT)* was born 21 Sep 1860 in Madison Co., MS, and died 15 Oct 1931 in Madison Co., MS. He married VIOLA JANE SANDERFORD 12 Jan 1882 in Madison County, MS, daughter of GEORGE SANDERFORD. She was born 23 Jan 1866 in Madison Co., MS, and died 04 Jan 1944 in Copiah County, MS.

Children of GEORGE HAMMACK and VIOLA SANDERFORD are:

504.   i. WILLIAM HOWARD[11] HAMMACK, b. 12 Oct 1882, Madison County, MS; d. 13 Sep 1937, Madison County, MS.

505.   ii. LILLIAN G. HAMMACK, b. 15 Feb 1885, Hinds County, MS; d. Aft. 1930, Copiah County, MS.

506.   iii. MABEL E. HAMMACK, b. 06 Jul 1889, Hinds County, MS; d. Aft. 1930, Hinds County, MS.

     iv. INFANT SON HAMMACK, b. 25 Jul 1890, Hinds Co., MS; d. 25 Jul 1890, Hinds Co., MS.

507.   v. MARION CLAIBORNE HAMMACK, b. 01 Jul 1891, Texas; d. 01 Jul 1967, Gatesville, Copiah County, MS.

508.   vi. THOMAS CLIVE HAMMACK, b. 01 Jul 1891, Texas; d. Aft. 1910, Copiah County, MS.

     vii. ALMA G. HAMMACK, b. 09 Jul 1894, Hinds County, MS; d. Aft. 1910, Copiah County, MS; m. T. Y. WILLARD, 23 Jun 1912, Copiah Co., MS.

509.   viii. IVA VIOLA HAMMACK, b. 14 Feb 1898, Hinds County, MS; d. Aft. 1930, Hinds County, MS.

510.   ix. EMOGENE HAMMACK, b. 20 Sep 1900, Mississippi; d. 28 Aug 1937, Copiah County, MS.

511.   x. ALBERT E. "PRINCE" HAMMACK, b. 05 May 1903, Mississippi; d. Aft. 1920, Copiah County, MS.

512.   xi. AUDREY ELAINE HAMMACK, b. 02 Apr 1906, Mississippi; d. Aft. 1940, Copiah County, MS.

     xii. EFFIE MILDRED HAMMACK, b. 18 May 1909, Copiah Co., MS; d. 11 Jul 1911, Copiah County, MS.

     xiii. MARGARET N. HAMMACK, b. 14 Feb 1912, Copiah Co., MS; d. 11 Sep 1912, Copiah County, MS.

Key Sources: 1900 Hinds Co., MS, Census, p. 38; 1910 Copiah Co., MS, Census, p. 83; 1920 Copiah Co., MS, Census, p. 247.

458. JOSEPHINE[10] HAMMACK *(WILLIAM T. H.[9], SIMEON J.[8], WILLIAM T.[7], ROBERT HAMMACK[6] JR., ROBERT HAMMACK[5] SR., WILLIAM "THE ELDER"[4] HAMMACK, WILLIAM "O"[3], JOHN[2] HAMMOCKE, ? JOHN[1] HAMMOT)* was born 10 Feb 1869 in Madison Co., MS, and died 04 Apr 1930 in Harrison Co., MS. She married BENJAMIN FRANKLIN COLLUM 20 Dec 1888 in Madison County, MS, son of JOHN COLLUM and HESTER ASHLEY. He was born 06 Feb 1865 in Rankin Co., MS, and died 01 Mar 1941 in Jackson Co., MS.

Children of JOSEPHINE HAMMACK and BENJAMIN COLLUM are:

     i. FRANKLIN HAMMACK[11] COLLUM, b. 16 Oct 1889, Mississippi; d. 02 Nov 1912, Harrison Co., MS.

     ii. MARY CLAIR COLLUM, b. 31 May 1891, Mississippi; d. 11 Nov 1891, Harrison Co., MS.

   iii. HAZELL ARZELL COLLUM, b. 07 Feb 1893, Mississippi; d. Aft. 1925, Harrison Co., MS; m. FERDINAND F. FOSTER, 27 Jul 1913, Harrison Co., MS.
   iv. MAGGIE DELL COLLUM, b. 11 Apr 1895, Mississippi; d. 10 Oct 1917, Mississippi; m. HORACE SWITZER, 29 Aug 1915, Harrison Co., MS.
   v. CLARENCE CECIL COLLUM, b. 04 Jun 1896, Hinds Co., MS; d. 29 Dec 1987, Mobile Co., AL; m. (1) DAISY ARDEE BARRON, 12 May 1920, Harrison Co., MS; b. 16 Oct 1901, Escambia Co., AL; d. 05 Feb 1950, Mobile Co., AL; m. (2) JOHNNIE ELIZABETH ALLDAY, 28 Oct 1950, Harrison Co., MS; b. 13 Aug 1921, Mississippi.
   vi. THELMA COLLUM, b. 07 Mar 1898, Hinds Co., MS; d. Aft. 1920, Hinds Co., MS; m. BILL MASON.
   vii. JOHN WILLIAM COLLUM, b. 01 Oct 1901, Hinds Co., MS; d. Aft. 1920, Harrison Co., MS; m. ELOISE YOUNG.
   viii. JOSEPH CLEO COLLUM, b. 12 Apr 1906, Harrison Co., MS; d. Aft. 1940, Harrison Co., MS; m. (1) LUCILLE ENTRIKEN, 09 Aug 1923, Harrison Co., MS; m. (2) EUNICE SCHMITT, 22 Jun 1935, Harrison Co., MS.
   ix. CORA FREDONIA COLLUM, b. 22 Aug 1907, Harrison Co., MS; d. 19 Apr 1908, Harrison Co., MS.
   x. ROSALIND EUGENIA COLLUM, b. 23 Jun 1909, Harrison Co., MS; m. D. D. HARPER, 15 Dec 1924, Harrison Co., MS.
   xi. ACY BOWEN COLLUM, b. 06 Oct 1912, Harrison Co., MS; m. HELEN RIVERS SCHMITZ, 17 Jul 1951, Harrison Co., MS; b. 1925, Mississippi; d. 1994, Mississippi.
Key Sources: 1900 Hinds Co., MS, Census, p. 50; 1910 Harrison Co., MS, Census, p. 8.

459. JOHN SIMEON[10] COLLUM (*MARY JANE[9] HAMMACK, SIMEON J.[8], WILLIAM T.[7], ROBERT HAMMACK[6] JR., ROBERT HAMMACK[5] SR., WILLIAM "THE ELDER"[4] HAMMACK, WILLIAM "O"[3], JOHN[2] HAMMOCKE, ? JOHN[1] HAMMOT*) was born Abt. 1844 in Yazoo Co., MS, and died Aft. 1880 in Navarro Co., TX. He married NETTIE [------] Abt. 1872 in Mississippi. She was born Abt. 1862 in Illinois, and died Aft. 1880 in Navarro Co., TX.
Children of JOHN COLLUM and NETTIE [------] are:
   i. EUGENIA[11] COLLUM, b. Abt. 1876, Mississippi; d. Aft. 1880, Navarro Co., TX.
   ii. INFANT COLLUM, b. Apr 1880, Mississippi; d. Aft. 1880, Navarro Co., TX.
Key Source: 1880 Navarro Co., TX, Census, p. 504.

460. SIMON CICERO[10] COLLUM (*MARY JANE[9] HAMMACK, SIMEON J.[8], WILLIAM T.[7], ROBERT HAMMACK[6] JR., ROBERT HAMMACK[5] SR., WILLIAM "THE ELDER"[4] HAMMACK, WILLIAM "O"[3], JOHN[2] HAMMOCKE, ? JOHN[1] HAMMOT*) was born Abt. 1851 in Yazoo Co., MS, and died 24 Jul 1907 in Navarro Co., TX. He married PAULINE KELLEY Abt. 1876 in Mississippi or Texas, daughter of WILLIAM KELLEY and MARY WILLIAMS. She was born 07 Jun 1858 in Holmes Co., Mississippi, and died 09 May 1932 in Navarro Co., TX.
Children of SIMON COLLUM and PAULINE KELLEY are:
513.   i. KATIE M.[11] COLLUM, b. 09 Mar 1878, Navarro Co., TX; d. 06 Apr 1952, Bell Co., TX.
   ii. LAWRENCE WILLIAM COLLUM, b. 01 Feb 1879, Navarro Co., TX; d. 03 Aug 1966, McLennan Co., TX.
514.   iii. DAISEY COLLUM, b. 12 Apr 1881, Navarro Co., TX; d. 14 Dec 1936, Navarro Co., TX.
   iv. THAD COLLUM, b. Abt. 1898, Navarro Co., TX; d. Aft. 1920, Navarro Co., TX.
Key Sources: 1880 Navarro Co., TX, Census, p. 501; 1910 Narvarro Co., TX, Census, p. 145; Texas Death Certificates of Simon Cicero Collum, Pauline Kelley Collum, Katie Collum, Lawrence Collum, and Daisey Collum Story.

461. ALFRED EUGENE[10] COLLUM *(MARY JANE[9] HAMMACK, SIMEON J.[8], WILLIAM T.[7], ROBERT HAMMACK[6] JR., ROBERT HAMMACK[5] SR., WILLIAM "THE ELDER"[4] HAMMACK, WILLIAM "O"[3], JOHN[2] HAMMOCKE, ? JOHN[1] HAMMOT)* was born 27 Dec 1853 in Yazoo Co., MS, and died 05 Apr 1920 in Navarro Co., TX. He married ROSE ANNA KELLY Abt. 1876 in Mississippi, daughter of WILLIAM KELLY and MARY WILLIAMS. She was born Abt. 1856 in Holmes Co., Mississippi, and died Aft. 1930 in Navarro Co., TX.

Child of ALFRED COLLUM and ROSE KELLY is:

515.   i.   MARY (MAYME)[11] COLLUM, b. 21 Sep 1877, Mississippi; d. 22 Oct 1942, Hardeman Co., TX.

Key Sources: 1880 Navarro Co., TX, Census, p. 504; 1910 Navarro Co., TX, Census, p. 157; Texas Death Certificates of Alfred Eugene Collum and Mayme Collum Johnston.

462. SAREPTA ANN ELIZABETH[10] HAMMACK *(CHARLES M.[9], SIMEON J.[8], WILLIAM T.[7], ROBERT HAMMACK[6] JR., ROBERT HAMMACK[5] SR., WILLIAM "THE ELDER"[4] HAMMACK, WILLIAM "O"[3], JOHN[2] HAMMOCKE, ? JOHN[1] HAMMOT)* was born 01 Feb 1846 in Crawford Co., GA, and died 25 Apr 1919 in Calhoun Co., MS. She married SAMUEL MEEK DOOLITTLE 1865 in Calhoun Co., MS, son of STERLING DOOLITTLE and ELIZABETH FLOWERS. He was born Jan 1846 in Mississippi, and died 21 Jan 1914 in Slate Springs, Calhoun Co., MS.

Children of SAREPTA HAMMACK and SAMUEL DOOLITTLE are:

         i.   LAURA[11] DOOLITTLE, b. 04 Feb 1866, Calhoun Co., MS; d. 22 Mar 1910, Webster Co., MS; m. JOHN WILLIAM BRITTAIN EMBRY, 06 Nov 1884, Calhoun Co., MS; b. 22 Dec 1862, Mississippi; d. 16 Apr 1941, Webster Co., MS.

         ii.   SAMUEL CLAYTON DOOLITTLE, b. 26 Nov 1867, Calhoun Co., MS; d. 19 Oct 1886, Calhoun Co., MS.

516.   iii.   THOMAS EATMON DOOLITTLE, b. 10 May 1869, Calhoun Co., MS; d. 04 Sep 1954, Slate Springs, Calhoun Co., MS.

517.   iv.   JAMES WILLIAM DOOLITTLE, b. 21 Jun 1871, Calhoun Co., MS; d. 06 Mar 1949, Calhoun Co., MS.

         v.   SARAH ELIZABETH DOOLITTLE, b. 1874, Calhoun Co., MS; d. 06 Oct 1880, Slate Springs, Calhoun Co., MS.

518.   vi.   CALVIN CHARLES DOOLITTLE, b. 1876, Calhoun Co., MS; d. Aft. 1949, Rogers, AR.

519.   vii.   MAYBELLE DOOLITTLE, b. 17 Feb 1880, Calhoun Co., MS; d. 20 Oct 1967, Calhoun Co., MS.

520.   viii. GEORGIA ANN DOOLITTLE, b. 1884, Calhoun Co., MS; d. 1950, Vardaman, MS.

         ix.   LUCINDA DOOLITTLE, b. 22 Mar 1886, Calhoun Co., MS; d. 12 Jul 1891, Calhoun Co., MS.

Key Sources: W. F. Doolittle, *The Doolittle Family in America* (Cleveland, OH, 1901); 1880 Calhoun Co., MS, Census, p. 629; 1900 Calhoun Co., MS, Census, p. 236; 1910 Calhoun Co., MS, Census, p. 111; "Death of Grandmother Doolittle," *Calhoun Monitor*, 1 May 1913.

463. ISABELLA[10] HAMMACK *(CHARLES M.[9], SIMEON J.[8], WILLIAM T.[7], ROBERT HAMMACK[6] JR., ROBERT HAMMACK[5] SR., WILLIAM "THE ELDER"[4] HAMMACK, WILLIAM "O"[3], JOHN[2] HAMMOCKE, ? JOHN[1] HAMMOT)* was born 10 Oct 1852 in Choctaw Co., MS, and died 07 Jul 1884 in Calhoun Co., MS. She married WILLIAM H. STODDARD Abt. 1875 in Calhoun Co., MS. He was born 18 Apr 1857 in Mississippi, and died 16 Jul 1886 in Calhoun Co., MS.

Child of ISABELLA HAMMACK and WILLIAM STODDARD is:

         i.   WILLIAM[11] STODDARD, b. Abt. Oct., 1878, Calhoun Co., MS; d. Aft. 1900, Calhoun Co., MS.

Key Source: 1880 Calhoun Co., MS, Census, p. 629; 1900 Calhoun Co., MS, Census, p. 236.

464. CHARLES[10] HAMMACK *(CHARLES M.[9], SIMEON J.[8], WILLIAM T.[7], ROBERT HAMMACK[6] JR., ROBERT HAMMACK[5] SR., WILLIAM "THE ELDER"[4] HAMMACK, WILLIAM "O"[3], JOHN[2] HAMMOCKE, ? JOHN[1] HAMMOT)* was born Abt. 1867 in Calhoun Co., MS, and died Bet. 1898 - 1900 in Calhoun Co., MS. He married SALLIE E. [--------] Abt. 1890 in Calhoun Co., MS. She was born Sep 1869 in Mississippi, and died Aft. 1910 in Calhoun Co., MS.
Children of CHARLES HAMMACK and SALLIE [--------] are:
521.   i.   LESTER[11] HAMMACK, b. Apr 1891, Calhoun Co., MS; d. Aft. 1920, Sunflower Co., MS.
        ii.   ANNIE HAMMACK, b. Nov 1895, Calhoun Co., MS; d. Aft. 1900, Calhoun Co., MS.
        iii.   JOSEPH HAMMACK, b. Aug 1898, Calhoun Co., MS; d. Aft. 1900, Calhoun Co., MS.
Key Sources: 1900 Calhoun Co., MS, Census, p. 236; 1920 Sunflower Co., MS, Census, p. 280.

465. NAOMI[10] HAMMACK *(CHARLES M.[9], SIMEON J.[8], WILLIAM T.[7], ROBERT HAMMACK[6] JR., ROBERT HAMMACK[5] SR., WILLIAM "THE ELDER"[4] HAMMACK, WILLIAM "O"[3], JOHN[2] HAMMOCKE, ? JOHN[1] HAMMOT)* was born 20 Jun 1875 in Calhoun Co., MS, and died Abt. Sep 1897 in Sunflower Co., MS. She married JOHN ALEXANDER WASSON 14 May 1891 in Sunflower Co., MS. He was born 14 May 1868 in Attala Co., MS, and died 13 Jul 1946 in Sunflower Co., MS.
Children of NAOMI HAMMACK and JOHN WASSON are:
        i.   RUTH[11] WASSON, b. 01 Apr 1892, Sunflower Co., MS; d. Aft. 1910, Sunflower Co., MS; m. JOHN FRANK WISE.
522.   ii.   CHARLES RANDOLPH WASSON, b. 04 Jul 1895, Sunflower Co., MS; d. 30 Dec 1960, Greenville, MS.
        iii.   KATE WASSON, b. 08 Sep 1897, Sunflower Co., MS; d. Abt. Sep 1897, Sunflower Co., MS.
Key Sources: 1900 Sunflower Co., MS, Census, p. 217; 1910 Sunflower Co., MS, Census, p. 130; 1920 Sunflower Co., MS, Census, p. 94; S. F. Brewster, *Data on Wasson Families and Allied Lines* (unpublished, 1973), pp. 138-140, housed in Eudora Welty Library, Jackson, MS.

466. JOHN S.[10] TAYLOR *(SARAH ANN E.[9] HAMMACK, SIMEON J.[8], WILLIAM T.[7], ROBERT HAMMACK[6] JR., ROBERT HAMMACK[5] SR., WILLIAM "THE ELDER"[4] HAMMACK, WILLIAM "O"[3], JOHN[2] HAMMOCKE, ? JOHN[1] HAMMOT)* was born Abt. 1849 in Crawford Co., GA, and died Aft. 1880 in Madison Co., MS. He married F. J. LAIRD 14 Feb 1873 in Madison Co., MS. She was born Abt. 1854 in Mississippi, and died Aft. 1880 in Madison Co., MS.
Children of JOHN TAYLOR and F. LAIRD are:
        i.   POLLY[11] TAYLOR, b. Abt. 1876, Madison Co., MS; d. Aft. 1880, Madison Co., MS.
        ii.   FRANK TAYLOR, b. Abt. 1878, Madison Co., MS; d. Aft. 1880, Madison Co., MS.
Key Source: 1880 Madison Co., MS, Census, p. 97.

467. AMANDA V.[10] TAYLOR *(SARAH ANN E.[9] HAMMACK, SIMEON J.[8], WILLIAM T.[7], ROBERT HAMMACK[6] JR., ROBERT HAMMACK[5] SR., WILLIAM "THE ELDER"[4] HAMMACK, WILLIAM "O"[3], JOHN[2] HAMMOCKE, ? JOHN[1] HAMMOT)* was born Abt. 1851 in Crawford Co., GA, and died Aft. 1900 in Henderson Co., TX. She married WILLIAM SANDERFORD 27 Jan 1869 in Madison Co., MS. He was born Abt. 1846 in Mississippi, and died Bef. 1900 in Henderson Co., TX.
Children of AMANDA TAYLOR and WILLIAM SANDERFORD are:
        i.   WILLIAM P.[11] SANDERFORD, b. Feb 1870, Madison Co., MS; d. Aft. 1880, Madison Co., MS.
        ii.   S. L. SANDERFORD, b. Abt. 1871, Madison Co., MS; d. Aft. 1880, Madison Co., MS.
523.   iii.   CHARLIE FRANKLIN SANDERFORD, b. 16 Mar 1873, Madison Co., MS; d. 05 Dec 1922, Henderson Co., TX.
524.   iv.   ROBERT M. SANDERFORD, b. Apr 1875, Madison Co., MS; d. Aft. 1920, Ellis Co., TX.

v. D. KEMP SANDERFORD, b. Dec 1878, Madison Co., MS; d. Aft. 1900, Henderson Co., TX.

vi. JENNIE V. SANDERFORD, b. 01 Jun 1881, Madison Co., MS; d. 01 Sep 1949, Dallas Co., TX; m. ELBERT PICKLE.

vii. JOHN S. SANDERFORD, b. Aug 1884, Texas; d. Aft. 1900, Henderson Co., TX.

viii. ANDREW J. SANDERFORD, b. Apr 1890, Texas; d. Aft. 1900, Henderson Co., TX.

Key Sources: 1870 Madison Co., MS, Census, p. 94; 1880 Madison Co., MS, Census, p. 105; 1900 Henderson Co., TX, Census, p. 80; 1910 Henderson Co., TX, Census, p. 125; 1910 Jack Co., TX, Census, p. 124.

468. SARAH[10] TAYLOR *(SARAH ANN E.[9] HAMMACK, SIMEON J.[8], WILLIAM T.[7], ROBERT HAMMACK[6] JR., ROBERT HAMMACK[5] SR., WILLIAM "THE ELDER"[4] HAMMACK, WILLIAM "O"[3], JOHN[2] HAMMOCKE, ? JOHN[1] HAMMOT)* was born Jun 1854 in Choctaw Co., MS, and died Aft. 1900 in Madison Co., MS. She married [--------] DILLARD Abt. 1875 in Madison Co., MS.
Children of SARAH TAYLOR and [--------] DILLARD are:

i. JOHN D.[11] DILLARD, b. Aug 1878, Madison Co., MS; d. Aft. 1900, Madison Co., MS.

ii. EUGENE A. DILLARD, b. Jun 1884, Madison Co., MS; d. Aft. 1900, Madison Co., MS.

iii. ALICE M. DILLARD, b. Jun 1886, Madison Co., MS; d. Aft. 1900, Madison Co., MS.

iv. ROBERT NEAL DILLARD, b. Feb 1892, Madison Co., MS; d. 1947, Madison Co., MS; m. MILDED E. [------], Abt. 1915, Madison Co., MS; b. 1891, Mississippi; d. 1958, Madison Co., MS.

Key Sources: 1900 Madison Co., MS, Census, p. 114; 1910 Madison Co., MS, Census, p. 185.

469. DANIEL W.[10] TAYLOR *(SARAH ANN E.[9] HAMMACK, SIMEON J.[8], WILLIAM T.[7], ROBERT HAMMACK[6] JR., ROBERT HAMMACK[5] SR., WILLIAM "THE ELDER"[4] HAMMACK, WILLIAM "O"[3], JOHN[2] HAMMOCKE, ? JOHN[1] HAMMOT)* was born Abt. 1859 in Choctaw Co., MS, and died Aft. 1920 in Madison Co., MS. He married MARTHA M. "PATSY" SANDERFORD 29 Jan 1881 in Madison Co., MS. She was born Mar 1860 in Mississippi, and died Aft. 1900 in Madison Co., MS.
Children of DANIEL TAYLOR and MARTHA SANDERFORD are:

i. LOUELLA[11] TAYLOR, b. Oct 1881, Madison Co., MS; d. Aft. 1900, Madison Co., MS.

ii. MARY J. TAYLOR, b. Aug 1884, Madison Co., MS; d. Aft. 1900, Madison Co., MS.

iii. HAL WILBURN TAYLOR, b. 20 Dec 1886, Madison Co., MS; d. 14 May 1948, Madison Co., MS; m. ANNE BLACK, Abt. 1907, Madison Co., MS; b. 29 Feb 1888, Mississippi; d. 13 May 1977, Madison Co., MS.

iv. MINTA TAYLOR, b. Sep 1888, Madison Co., MS; d. Aft. 1910, Madison Co., MS.

v. LORENE TAYLOR, b. Mar 1893, Madison Co., MS; d. Aft. 1910, Madison Co., MS.

vi. LELA TAYLOR, b. Jul 1895, Madison Co., MS; d. Aft. 1910, Madison Co., MS.

vii. WILLIE TAYLOR, b. Feb 1898, Madison Co., MS; d. Aft. 1910, Madison Co., MS.

Key Sources: 1880 Madison Co., MS, Census, p. 105; 1900 Madison Co., MS, Census, p. 115; 1910 Madison Co., MS, Census, p. 185; 1920 Madison Co., MS, Census, p. 110.

470. WILLIAM SIMMS[10] HAMMACK *(JOHN T.[9], SIMEON J.[8], WILLIAM T.[7], ROBERT HAMMACK[6] JR., ROBERT HAMMACK[5] SR., WILLIAM "THE ELDER"[4] HAMMACK, WILLIAM "O"[3], JOHN[2] HAMMOCKE, ? JOHN[1] HAMMOT)* was born 14 Apr 1852 in Macon Co., GA, and died 25 Dec 1899 in Hinds County, MS. He married SALLIE ELIZABETH CATES 20 Dec 1883 in Hinds County, MS, daughter of ANDERSON CATES and ABBIE BROWN. She was born 14 Jan 1863 in Hinds County, MS, and died 30 Apr 1951 in Hinds County, MS.
Children of WILLIAM HAMMACK and SALLIE CATES are:

525.   i.   GEORGE CLEVELAND[11] HAMMACK, b. 26 Oct 1884, Hinds County, Mississippi; d. 17 Nov 1963, Hinds County, Mississippi.

526.   ii. ROBERT FELIX HAMMACK, b. 15 Oct 1885, Hinds County, MS; d. 02 Apr 1949.

         iii. LITTLE DOLLIE HAMMACK, b. 05 Nov 1886, Hinds County, MS; d. 31 Dec 1886, Hinds County, MS.

         iv. ALICE WILLIAMS HAMMACK, b. 08 Nov 1887, Hinds County, MS; d. 08 Oct 1949, West Monroe, LA; m. E. L. LEHMAN, 12 Jan 1920.

527.   v.   DRURY BROWN "DOOLEY" HAMMACK, b. 11 Sep 1889, Hinds County, MS; d. 23 Apr 1962, Hinds County, MS.

528.   vi. CLARA BELLE HAMMACK, b. 10 Apr 1892, Hinds County, MS; d. 27 Apr 1989, Hinds County, MS near Brownsville.

529.   vii. DOLLIE CLIFFORD HAMMACK, b. 01 Mar 1894, Hinds County, MS near Brownsville; d. 09 Oct 1977, Hinds County, MS near Brownsville.

         viii. MATTIE ELIZABETH HAMMACK, b. 11 Oct 1895, Hinds County, MS; d. 27 Sep 1907, Hinds County, MS.

530.   ix. EDD BROWN HAMMACK, b. 24 Dec 1897, Hinds County, MS; d. May 1981, Jackson, MS.

         x.   JOHN WILLIAM WATTS HAMMACK, b. 18 Nov 1899, Hinds County, MS; d. 19 Dec 1912, Hinds County, MS.

Key Sources: 1880 Madison Co., MS, Census, p. 21; 1900 Hinds Co., MS, Census, p. 166; 1910 Hinds Co., MS, Census, p. 167; 1920 Hinds Co., MS, Census, p. 102; Family records of Felix Maben Hammack, Bend, OR.

471. JOHN ROBERT[10] HAMMACK *(JOHN T.[9], SIMEON J.[8], WILLIAM T.[7], ROBERT HAMMACK[6] JR., ROBERT HAMMACK[5] SR., WILLIAM "THE ELDER"[4] HAMMACK, WILLIAM "O"[3], JOHN[2] HAMMOCKE, ? JOHN[1] HAMMOT)* was born 13 May 1858 in Macon Co., GA, and died 11 Feb 1919 in Stanton, ND. He married EMMA CHRISTIANE BEAL Abt. 1893 in Stanton, ND. She was born Abt. 1874 in Sweden, and died 08 Jun 1920 in Bismarck, ND.
Children of JOHN HAMMACK and EMMA BEAL are:

         i.   LAVALLE[11] HAMMACK, b. 20 Nov 1894, ND; d. Jan 1970; m. ? SALISBURY.

531.   ii. MYRTLE LOUISE HAMMACK, b. 15 Nov 1896, Bismarck, ND; d. 08 Sep 1978, Bengough, Sask.

532.   iii. ROMEY HAMMACK, b. 11 Aug 1898, ND; d. 01 Oct 1976, Minot, ND.

533.   iv. HARRY HERBERT HAMMACK, b. 28 Aug 1900, Bismarck, ND; d. 02 Nov 1936, Kenmare, Ward County, ND.

         v.   WILLIE HAMMACK, b. 27 Apr 1904, ND; d. 19 Feb 1907, Stanton, ND.

534.   vi. EUGENE HAMMACK, b. 25 Jul 1905, Stanton, ND; d. 26 Feb 1986, Stanley, ND.

535.   vii. WILBON HAMMACK, b. 28 Sep 1907, Ruso, McLean County, ND; d. 1987, Portland, OR.

         viii. IRENE LOTTIE HAMMACK, b. 25 Oct 1910, Turtle Lake, McLean County, ND; d. Sep 1990, Houston, TX; m. (1) ? CASSIDAY; m. (2) ? BRANTON.

536.   ix. JONAS ALAN HAMMACK, b. 02 Oct 1914, Big Bend, Mercer County, ND.

Key Sources: 1900 McLean Co., ND, Census, p. 31; 1910 McLean Co., ND, Census, p. 162; 1920 Mercer Co., ND, Census, p. 264; Family records of Felix Maben Hammack, Bend, OR; Family records of Jonas Hammack, Bend, OR.

472. GERTRUDE A.[10] HAMMACK *(FELIX WILBORN[9], SIMEON J.[8], WILLIAM T.[7], ROBERT HAMMACK[6] JR., ROBERT HAMMACK[5] SR., WILLIAM "THE ELDER"[4] HAMMACK, WILLIAM "O"[3], JOHN[2] HAMMOCKE, ? JOHN[1] HAMMOT)* was born 09 Nov 1867 in Calhoun Co., MS, and died 24 Jun

1945 in Morristown, MO. She married WILLIAM M. NOLAN Abt. 1889 in Calhoun Co., MS. He was born 20 Sep 1864 in Mississippi, and died 28 Dec 1900 in Calhoun Co., MS.

Children of GERTRUDE HAMMACK and WILLIAM NOLAN are:

	i.	SHERMAN[11] NOLAN, b. Nov 1889, Calhoun Co., MS; d. Aft. 1910, Calhoun Co., MS.
537.	ii.	GRANVILLE NOLAN, b. Apr 1891, Calhoun Co., MS; d. Aft. 1930, Webster Co., MS.
	iii.	WILLIAM LEE NOLAN, b. 20 Mar 1893, Calhoun Co., MS; d. 20 Apr 1905, Calhoun Co., MS.
	iv.	BESSIE A. NOLAN, b. Jan 1895, Calhoun Co., MS; d. Aft. 1910, Calhoun Co., MS; m. THAD TINDALL.
	v.	MARY A. NOLAN, b. Oct 1897, Calhoun Co., MS; d. Aft. 1910, Calhoun Co., MS.
	vi.	STERLING J. NOLAN, b. Apr 1900, Calhoun Co., MS; d. Aft. 1910, Calhoun Co., MS.

Key Sources: 1900 Calhoun Co., MS, Census, p. 237; 1910 Calhoun Co., MS, Census, p. 137; W. F. Doolittle, *The Doolittle Family in America* (Cleveland, OH, 1901).

473. BETSY ANN[10] HAMMACK *(FELIX WILBORN[9], SIMEON J.[8], WILLIAM T.[7], ROBERT HAMMACK[6] JR., ROBERT HAMMACK[5] SR., WILLIAM "THE ELDER"[4] HAMMACK, WILLIAM "O"[3], JOHN[2] HAMMOCKE, ? JOHN[1] HAMMOT)* was born 09 Aug 1872 in Calhoun Co., MS, and died 14 Jul 1941 in Calhoun Co., MS. She married JAMES LAY DAVIS 29 Aug 1892 in Sabougla, Calhoun Co., MS, son of JOHN DAVIS and MARY LAY. He was born 03 Aug 1873 in Calhoun Co., MS, and died 13 Apr 1931 in Calhoun Co., MS.

Children of BETSY HAMMACK and JAMES DAVIS are:

538.	i.	WILLIAM ROSCOE[11] DAVIS, b. 13 Jul 1893, Calhoun Co., MS; d. 04 Aug 1959, Calhoun Co., MS.
	ii.	RUBY IRENE DAVIS, b. 04 Feb 1895, Calhoun Co., MS; d. 03 Mar 1963, Noxubee Co., MS; m. (1) L. E. ESTES; m. (2) CHARLES D. FULTON, Abt. 1915, Mississippi; b. 02 Mar 1885, Mississippi; d. 18 Oct 1952, Calhoun Co., MS.
	iii.	SIMEON ROY DAVIS, b. 30 Nov 1896, Calhoun Co., MS; d. 02 Aug 1950, Calhoun Co., MS; m. MARGARET ALEXANDER.
	iv.	JAMES RUSSELL DAVIS, b. 03 Feb 1899, Calhoun Co., MS; d. 27 Jul 1935, Calhoun Co., MS; m. ETHEL VANCE; b. 1897, Calhoun Co., MS; d. 1937, Calhoun Co., MS.
	v.	ROBERT SIDNEY DAVIS, b. Sep 1902, Calhoun Co., MS; d. 27 Dec 1957, Calhoun Co., MS; m. OLIVE FLANAGAN.
	vi.	RALPH SISSON DAVIS, b. 29 Sep 1908, Calhoun Co., MS; d. 19 May 1976, Grenada Co., MS; m. LORENE LOWERY.
	vii.	JESSE RAY DAVIS, b. 28 Feb 1914, Calhoun Co., MS; d. 12 Jun 1979, Calhoun Co., MS; m. DELORES CLANTON.

Key Sources: W. F. Doolittle, *The Doolittle Family in America* (Cleveland, OH, 1901); 1920 Calhoun Co., MS, Census, p. 211; "Mrs. Lay Davis Dies," *Calhoun Monitor-Herald*, 17 July 1941; Personal Interview with William Roscoe Davis, Jr., July 1996, Grenada, MS.

474. SIDNEY W.[10] HAMMACK *(FELIX WILBORN[9], SIMEON J.[8], WILLIAM T.[7], ROBERT HAMMACK[6] JR., ROBERT HAMMACK[5] SR., WILLIAM "THE ELDER"[4] HAMMACK, WILLIAM "O"[3], JOHN[2] HAMMOCKE, ? JOHN[1] HAMMOT)* was born 30 Jul 1875 in Calhoun Co., MS, and died 23 Aug 1943 in Oklahoma City, OK. He married GRACE FOX Abt. 1898 in Calhoun Co., MS, daughter of SAMUEL FOX and VIRGINIA COOKE. She was born 06 Mar 1882 in Calhoun Co., MS, and died 24 Feb 1900 in Calhoun Co., MS.

Child of SIDNEY HAMMACK and GRACE FOX is:

	i.	GRACE[11] HAMMACK, b. 30 Nov 1899, Calhoun Co., MS; d. 17 Jul 1900, Calhoun Co., MS.

Key Source: 1900 Calhoun Co., MS, Census, p. 243; 1910 Washita Co., OK, Census, p. 210; 1920 Custer Co., OK, Census, p. 70.

475. MARY LEE ELIZABETH[10] HAMMACK *(FELIX WILBORN[9], SIMEON J.[8], WILLIAM T.[7], ROBERT HAMMACK[6] JR., ROBERT HAMMACK[5] SR., WILLIAM "THE ELDER"[4] HAMMACK, WILLIAM "O"[3], JOHN[2] HAMMOCKE, ? JOHN[1] HAMMOT)* was born Abt. 1877 in Calhoun Co., MS, and died 1945 in Boone Co., Arkansas. She married SAMUEL R. YEAGER Aft. 1900 in Calhoun Co., MS. He was born Abt. 1872 in Mississippi, and died Aft. 1930 in Poinsett Co., AR.

Children of MARY HAMMACK and SAMUEL YEAGER are:

    i.   ADDIE[11] YEAGER, b. Abt. 1901, Calhoun Co., MS; d. Aft. 1910, Calhoun Co., MS.

    ii.   JAMES S. YEAGER, b. Abt. 1904, Calhoun Co., MS; d. Aft. 1920, Grenada Co., MS.

    iii.   SAM R. YEAGER, b. 09 Nov 1906, Calhoun Co., MS; d. Feb 1976, Harrison Co., Arkansas.

    iv.   WILILAM R. YEAGER, b. Abt. 1908, Calhoun Co., MS; d. Aft. 1930, Poinsett Co., AR.

    v.   ESSIE M. YEAGER, b. Abt. 1910, Calhoun Co., MS; d. Aft. 1930, Poinsett Co., AR.

    vi.   SIDNEY HAMMACK YEAGER, b. 17 Jan 1911, Calhoun Co., MS; d. Feb 1977, Poinsett Co., AR.

    vii.   WOODROW W. YEAGER, b. 18 Mar 1913, Calhoun Co., MS; d. 29 Apr 1989, Washington Co., AR.

    viii.   LOUIS B. YEAGER, b. Abt. 1915, Grenada Co., MS; d. Aft. 1930, Poinsett Co., AR.

Key Sources: 1910 Calhoun Co., MS, Census, p. 139; 1920 Grenada Co., MS, Census; 1930 Poinsett Co., AR, Census.

476. MARTHA VIRGINIA[10] HAMMACK *(FELIX WILBORN[9], SIMEON J.[8], WILLIAM T.[7], ROBERT HAMMACK[6] JR., ROBERT HAMMACK[5] SR., WILLIAM "THE ELDER"[4] HAMMACK, WILLIAM "O"[3], JOHN[2] HAMMOCKE, ? JOHN[1] HAMMOT)* was born 16 Nov 1882 in Calhoun Co., MS, and died 07 Nov 1959 in Custer Co., OK. She married JAMES ELLIS RILEY Abt. 1900 in Calhoun Co., MS. He was born 17 Oct 1880 in Mississippi, and died 26 Jul 1954 in Custer Co., OK.

Children of MARTHA HAMMACK and JAMES RILEY are:

    i.   JAMES SIDNEY[11] RILEY, b. Abt. 1906, Mississippi; d. Aft. 1920, Custer Co., OK.

    ii.   LIZZIE ODEAN RILEY, b. 09 Nov 1907, Calhoun Co., MS; d. 05 Jan 1916, Custer Co., OK.

    iii.   CLAUDE RILEY, b. Abt. 1912, Custer Co., OK; d. Aft. 1920, Custer Co., OK.

    iv.   CARL RILEY, b. 19 Oct 1914, Custer Co., OK; d. 02 May 1980, Canadian Co., OK.

    v.   JAMES ELLIS RILEY, JR., b. 27 Nov 1917, Custer Co., OK; d. 07 Oct 1989, Canadian Co., OK.

Key Sources: 1910 Torrance Co., NM, Census, p. 258; 1920 Custer Co., OK, Census, p. 55.

477. FELIX A.[10] HAMMOCK *(ALFRED WASHINGTON "DOCK"[9] HAMMACK, SIMEON J.[8], WILLIAM T.[7], ROBERT HAMMACK[6] JR., ROBERT HAMMACK[5] SR., WILLIAM "THE ELDER"[4] HAMMACK, WILLIAM "O"[3], JOHN[2] HAMMOCKE, ? JOHN[1] HAMMOT)* was born 02 Dec 1870 in Calhoun Co., MS, and died 15 Aug 1946 in Ashley County, AR. He married ANNIE J. CARMAN Abt. 1893 in Ashley County, AR. She was born 20 Sep 1874 in Louisiana, and died 18 May 1939 in Ashley County, AR.

Children of FELIX HAMMOCK and ANNIE CARMAN are:

539.   i.   ERNEST F.[11] HAMMOCK, b. 1900, Ashley County, AR; d. Aft. 1920, Ashley County, AR.

540.   ii.   WILLIE B. HAMMOCK, b. 1902, Ashley Co., AR; d. Aft. 1920, Ashley Co., AR.

    iii.   CLIFTON HAMMOCK, b. 1903, Ashley Co., AR; d. Aft. 1920, Ashley Co., AR.

541.   iv.   JAMES PELL HAMMOCK, b. 31 Jul 1907, Ashley Co., AR; d. 02 Jan 1981, Monticello, AR.

Key Source: Lois Hagood, *The Elusive Ancestor* (Crossett, AR, 1992); 1900 Ashley Co., AR, Census, p. 338B; 1910 Ashley Co., AR, Census, p.276; 1920 Ashley Co., AR, Census, p. 147.

478. BETTIE[10] HAMMOCK *(ALFRED WASHINGTON "DOCK"[9] HAMMACK, SIMEON J.[8], WILLIAM T.[7], ROBERT HAMMACK[6] JR., ROBERT HAMMACK[5] SR., WILLIAM "THE ELDER"[4] HAMMACK, WILLIAM "O"[3], JOHN[2] HAMMOCKE, ? JOHN[1] HAMMOT)* was born 06 May 1872 in Calhoun Co., MS, and died 06 Mar 1891 in Ashley County, AR. She married BEN MORMON.
Child of BETTIE HAMMOCK and BEN MORMON is:
542.   i.   GERTRUDE[11] MORMON, b. 18 Sep 1888, Ashley Co., AR; d. 09 Dec 1975, Ashley Co., AR.

Key Source: Lois Hagood, *The Elusive Ancestor* (Crossett, AR, 1992).

479. JEFFIE JANE[10] HAMMOCK *(ALFRED WASHINGTON "DOCK"[9] HAMMACK, SIMEON J.[8], WILLIAM T.[7], ROBERT HAMMACK[6] JR., ROBERT HAMMACK[5] SR., WILLIAM "THE ELDER"[4] HAMMACK, WILLIAM "O"[3], JOHN[2] HAMMOCKE, ? JOHN[1] HAMMOT)* was born 08 Oct 1875 in Calhoun Co., MS, and died 07 Oct 1937 in Ashley County, AR. She married CHARLES WESLEY ROBERTS 20 Aug 1893 in Ashley Co., AR. He was born 16 Jun 1864 in Arkansas, and died 22 Jan 1942 in Ashley County, AR.
Children of JEFFIE HAMMOCK and CHARLES ROBERTS are:
543.   i.   RUTH[11] ROBERTS, b. 15 Jul 1894, Ashley County, AR; d. 20 May 1986, Ashley County, AR.
544.   ii.   CLAUD CYRUS ROBERTS, b. 14 Mar 1896, Ashley Co., AR; d. 21 Mar 1950, Ashley County, AR.
545.   iii. SYLVESTER ALFRED ROBERTS, b. 05 May 1898, Ashley Co., AR; d. 10 Nov 1978, Orange Co., FL.
         iv.   LILLIAN ROBERTS, b. 1900, Ashley Co., AR; d. 1900, Ashley Co., AR.
546.   v.   WILLIAM TRACY ROBERTS, b. 15 Jan 1902, Ashley Co., AR; d. 26 Aug 1963, Big Springs, TX.
547.   vi.   VIRGIL ASBERRY ROBERTS, b. 09 May 1904, Ashley Co., AR; d. 18 Oct 1984, Dallas Co., TX.
548.   vii. HATTIE MAE ROBERTS, b. 10 Sep 1906, Ashley Co., AR; d. 18 Dec 1924, Ashley County, AR.
         viii. J. C. ROBERTS, b. 1909, Ashley County, AR; d. 1910, Ashley County, AR.
549.   ix.   CLARA BELL ROBERTS, b. 11 Nov 1911, Ashley Co., AR; d. 18 May 1993, Ashley Co., AR.
550.   x.   JESSE WILLARD ROBERTS, b. 03 May 1917, Ashley Co., AR; d. 03 Nov 1981, Ashley County, AR.

Key Source: Lois Hagood, *The Elusive Ancestor* (Crossett, AR, 1992).

480. VIRGINIA MARGARET "JENNY"[10] HAMMOCK *(ALFRED WASHINGTON "DOCK"[9] HAMMACK, SIMEON J.[8], WILLIAM T.[7], ROBERT HAMMACK[6] JR., ROBERT HAMMACK[5] SR., WILLIAM "THE ELDER"[4] HAMMACK, WILLIAM "O"[3], JOHN[2] HAMMOCKE, ? JOHN[1] HAMMOT)* was born 19 Feb 1886 in Ashley County, AR, and died 23 Feb 1917 in Ashley County, AR. She married (1) WILLIAM M. FERGUSON Abt. 1904 in Ashley County, AR. He was born Abt. 1865 in Texas, and died Abt. 1909 in Ashley County, AR. She married (2) W. D. PEDEN Abt. 1913 in Ashley Co., AR. He was born Abt. 1860 in AR, and died Aft. 1920 in Ashley County, AR.
Children of VIRGINIA HAMMOCK and WILLIAM FERGUSON are:
551.   i.   BENNIE[11] FERGUSON, b. 30 Oct 1905, Ashley County, AR; d. 03 Oct 1964, Monticello, Drew County, AR.

552.   ii.   VERGIE MAE FERGUSON, b. 1908, Ashley Co., AR.

553.   iii. LILLIE BELL FERGUSON, b. 03 Sep 1909, Ashley Co., AR; d. 1988, Ashley Co., AR.

Children of VIRGINIA HAMMOCK and W. PEDEN are:

554.   iv.   WALTER DAVID[11] PEDEN, b. 09 Dec 1914, Ashley County, AR; d. Aft. 1953, Kansas City, KS.

555.   v.   MARTHA AGNES PEDEN, b. 1917, Ashley Co., AR; d. Aft. 1942, Pulaski Co., AR.

Key Source: Lois Hagood, *The Elusive Ancestor* (Crossett, AR, 1992).

481. LOUANNA[10] SMITH *(MARTHA[9] HAMMACK, SIMEON J.[8], WILLIAM T.[7], ROBERT HAMMACK[6] JR., ROBERT HAMMACK[5] SR., WILLIAM "THE ELDER"[4] HAMMACK, WILLIAM "O"[3], JOHN[2] HAMMOCKE, ? JOHN[1] HAMMOT)* was born Abt. 1869 in Madison Co., MS, and died Aft. 1910 in Yazoo Co., Mississippi. She married SAM J. CAGLE 20 Dec 1890 in Madison Co., MS. He was born Abt. 1869 in Mississippi, and died Aft. 1920 in Richland Parish, LA.

Children of LOUANNA SMITH and SAM CAGLE are:

         i.   EUNICE[11] CAGLE, b. Jan 1894, Madison Co., MS; d. Aft. 1910, Yazoo Co., Mississippi.

         ii.   IRA CAGLE, b. Nov 1894, Madison Co., MS; d. Aft. 1920, Richland Parish, LA.

         iii. CLIFFORD CAGLE, b. Nov 1898, Madison Co., MS; d. Aft. 1910, Yazoo Co., Mississippi.

         iv.   MAY CAGLE, b. Abt. 1904, Madison Co., MS; d. Aft. 1920, Richland Parish, LA.

         v.   ELSEY CAGLE, b. Aft. 1906, Madison Co., MS; d. Aft. 1920, Richland Parish, LA.

         vi.   ELVY CAGLE, b. Abt. 1908, Madison Co., MS; d. Aft. 1920, Richland Parish, LA.

Key Source: 1900 Madison Co., MS, Census, p. 147; 1910 Yazoo Co., MS, Census, p. 22; 1920 Richland Parish, LA, Census, p. 31.

482. LESLIE L.[10] HAMMACK *(GEORGE W. T.[9], SIMEON J.[8], WILLIAM T.[7], ROBERT HAMMACK[6] JR., ROBERT HAMMACK[5] SR., WILLIAM "THE ELDER"[4] HAMMACK, WILLIAM "O"[3], JOHN[2] HAMMOCKE, ? JOHN[1] HAMMOT)* was born Nov 1871 in Calhoun Co., MS, and died Bet. 1931 - 1961 in Calhoun Co., MS. He married SARAH FRANCES PARKER Abt. 1896 in Calhoun Co., MS. She was born 15 May 1876 in MS, and died Aft. 1930 in Calhoun Co., MS.

Children of LESLIE HAMMACK and SARAH PARKER are:

         i.   EDWIN FRANCIS[11] HAMMACK, b. Nov 1897, Calhoun Co., MS; d. Aft. 1930, Calhoun Co., MS; m. LEE MINOR.

         ii.   MARY LEE HAMMACK, b. Abt. 1902, Calhoun Co., MS; d. Aft. 1910, Calhoun Co., MS.

556.   iii. GEORGE HAMMACK, b. 08 May 1911, Calhoun Co., MS; d. Dec 1983, Jefferson Co., AL.

Key Sources: 1900 Calhoun Co., MS, Census, p. 247; 1910 Calhoun Co., MS, Census, p. 116; Family records of Felix Maben Hammack, Bend, OR.

483. BARBARA[10] HAMMACK *(GEORGE W. T.[9], SIMEON J.[8], WILLIAM T.[7], ROBERT HAMMACK[6] JR., ROBERT HAMMACK[5] SR., WILLIAM "THE ELDER"[4] HAMMACK, WILLIAM "O"[3], JOHN[2] HAMMOCKE, ? JOHN[1] HAMMOT)* was born 16 Sep 1874 in Calhoun Co., MS, and died 20 Sep 1961 in Calhoun Co., MS. She married (1) WALTER GABLE Abt. 1892 in Calhoun Co., MS. He was born Abt. 1870 in Mississippi, and died Abt. 1896 in Calhoun Co., MS. She married (2) J. M. TUCKER Aft. 1900 in Calhoun Co., MS. He was born 1859 in Mississippi, and died 1940 in Calhoun Co., MS.

Children of BARBARA HAMMACK and WALTER GABLE are:

         i.   GRAFTON[11] GABLE, b. 21 Oct 1892, Calhoun Co., MS; d. Aft. 1961, Calhoun Co., MS.

         ii.   WESLEY GABLE, b. 02 Apr 1895, Calhoun Co., MS; d. 05 Jun 1918, Calhoun Co., MS.

Key Source: "Mrs. J. M. Tucker," *Calhoun Monitor*, 28 September 1961.

484. ELLA ELIZABETH[10] HAMMACK *(GEORGE W. T.[9], SIMEON J.[8], WILLIAM T.[7], ROBERT HAMMACK[6] JR., ROBERT HAMMACK[5] SR., WILLIAM "THE ELDER"[4] HAMMACK, WILLIAM "O"[3],*

JOHN[2] *HAMMOCKE, ? JOHN[1] HAMMOT)* was born 07 Jul 1878 in Calhoun Co., MS, and died 13 Mar 1947 in Tallahatchie Co., MS. She married JACOB ALBERT LOMENICK 19 Aug 1906 in Alcorn Co., MS. He was born 18 Dec 1879 in Hamilton Co., TN, and died 28 Dec 1956 in Sunflower Co., MS.
Children of ELLA HAMMACK and JACOB LOMENICK are:

      i.   JAMES WALTER[11] LOMENICK, b. 25 May 1907, Mississippi; d. Jan 1977, De Soto Co., MS; m. MARGARET LOUISE WILLIAMS.

557.   ii.   OTIS EUGENE LOMENICK, b. 05 Nov 1911, Mississippi; d. 05 Aug 1980, St. Tammany Parish, LA.

558.   iii.   MALCOLM ALBERT LOMENICK, b. 14 Mar 1916, Mississippi; d. 03 Jan 1996, Crittenden Co., AR.

Key Sources: 1920 Colbert Co., AL, Census, p. 237; Social Security Death Index; Family Records of Felix Maben Hammack, Bend, OR.

485. SARA[10] HAMMACK *(GEORGE W. T.[9], SIMEON J.[8], WILLIAM T.[7], ROBERT HAMMACK[6] JR., ROBERT HAMMACK[5] SR., WILLIAM "THE ELDER"[4] HAMMACK, WILLIAM "O"[3], JOHN[2] HAMMOCKE, ? JOHN[1] HAMMOT)* was born 11 Aug 1880 in Calhoun Co., MS, and died 24 Apr 1973 in Hillsborough Co., FL. She married JAMES T. BRACHT Aft. 1900 in Calhoun Co., MS. He was born 15 May 1875 in Kentucky, and died 21 Dec 1953 in Hamilton Co., OH.
Children of SARA HAMMACK and JAMES BRACHT are:

559.   i.   JAMES T.[11] BRACHT, b. 19 Oct 1914, Colbert Co., AL; d. 13 Dec 1994, Hamilton Co., OH.

      ii.   DOROTHY MAXINE BRACHT, b. 2 July 1916, Colbert Co., AL; d. 6 June 1999, Hillsborough Co., FL, m. [------] COY.

Key Sources: Ohio Death Certificate of James T. Bracht; Florida Death Certificate of Sara H. Bracht; "James T. Bracht," *Cincinnati Post*, 14 December 1994; "Sara H. Bracht," *Tampa Tribune*, 25 April 1973.

486. JESSE G.[10] HAMMACK *(GEORGE W. T.[9], SIMEON J.[8], WILLIAM T.[7], ROBERT HAMMACK[6] JR., ROBERT HAMMACK[5] SR., WILLIAM "THE ELDER"[4] HAMMACK, WILLIAM "O"[3], JOHN[2] HAMMOCKE, ? JOHN[1] HAMMOT)* was born 10 Jun 1882 in Calhoun Co., MS, and died 08 May 1959 in Calhoun Co., MS. He married DEBBIE SWINDOLL 1910 in Calhoun Co., MS. She was born 10 Jun 1889 in Calhoun Co., MS, and died 20 Sep 1946 in Calhoun Co., MS.
Children of JESSE HAMMACK and DEBBIE SWINDOLL are:

560.   i.   CLARICE[11] HAMMACK, b. Abt. 1914, Tallahatchie Co., Mississippi; d. Aft. 1946, Tallahatchie Co., Mississippi.

      ii.   MARY ALICE HAMMACK, b. Abt. 1922, Tallahatchie Co., Mississippi; d. Aft. 1946, Tallahatchie Co., Mississippi; m. S. A. MAHAFFEY.

     iii.   INFANT HAMMACK, b. 27 Mar 1911, Calhoun Co., MS; d. 27 Mar 1911, Calhoun Co., MS.

Key Sources: 1920 Tallahatchie Co., MS, Census, p. 250; "Mrs. J. G. Hammack," *Calhoun Monitor*, 2 October 1946.

487. MARY CLEVIE[10] HAMMACK *(GEORGE W. T.[9], SIMEON J.[8], WILLIAM T.[7], ROBERT HAMMACK[6] JR., ROBERT HAMMACK[5] SR., WILLIAM "THE ELDER"[4] HAMMACK, WILLIAM "O"[3], JOHN[2] HAMMOCKE, ? JOHN[1] HAMMOT)* was born 23 Nov 1885 in Calhoun Co., MS, and died 07 Mar 1939 in Calhoun Co., MS. She married ARTHUR EUGENE PARKER Abt. 1902 in Calhoun Co., MS. He was born 18 Apr 1881 in Calhoun Co., MS, and died 08 Feb 1942 in Grenada Co., MS.
Children of MARY HAMMACK and ARTHUR PARKER are:

      i.   MAX[11] PARKER, b. Abt. 1904, Calhoun Co., MS; d. Aft. 1942, Calhoun Co., MS; m. MARGUERITE O'NEAL, 23 Dec 1933, Calhoun Co., MS.

561.   ii.   MYRTLE IRIS PARKER, b. 28 Jun 1905, Calhoun Co., MS; d. 24 Aug 1997, Calhoun City, MS.
Key Sources: 1910 Calhoun Co., MS, Census, p. 141; "Mr. A. E. Parker," *Calhoun Monitor*, 12 February 1942.

488. FRANCIS FOLSOM[10] HAMMACK *(GEORGE W. T.*[9]*, SIMEON J.*[8]*, WILLIAM T.*[7]*, ROBERT HAMMACK*[6] *JR., ROBERT HAMMACK*[5] *SR., WILLIAM "THE ELDER"*[4] *HAMMACK, WILLIAM "O"*[3]*, JOHN*[2] *HAMMOCKE, ? JOHN*[1] *HAMMOT)* was born 15 Aug 1890 in Calhoun Co., MS, and died 16 Dec 1968 in Tallahatchie Co., MS. He married MARJORIE RUTH MILES 09 Mar 1916 in Calhoun Co., MS. She was born 07 Mar 1898 in Banner, Calhoun County, MS, and died 29 Jun 1976 in Tutwiler, Tallahatchie County, MS.
Children of FRANCIS HAMMACK and MARJORIE MILES are:
562.   i.   WALTER AUSTELL[11] HAMMACK, b. 05 Dec 1916, Tutwiler, Tallahatchie County, MS; d. 07 Aug 1996, Memphis, TN.
563.   ii.   CHARLES RAY HAMMACK, b. 25 Jul 1921, Tutwiler, Tallahatchie County, MS; d. 17 Jan 1992, Tuscaloosa, AL.
564.   iii.   BOBBIE NELL HAMMACK, b. 28 Jan 1929, Tutwiler, Tallahatchie County, MS.
Key Source: Family records of Bobbie Nell Hammack Hood, Duncan, MS.

489. THOMAS COLUMBUS[10] HAMMACK *(FELIX L.*[9]*, LEWIS M.*[8] *HAMMOCK, WILLIAM T.*[7] *HAMMACK, ROBERT HAMMACK*[6] *JR., ROBERT HAMMACK*[5] *SR., WILLIAM "THE ELDER"*[4] *HAMMACK, WILLIAM "O"*[3]*, JOHN*[2] *HAMMOCKE, ? JOHN*[1] *HAMMOT)* was born 16 Dec 1860 in Jones Co., GA, and died 18 Dec 1936 in Jones Co., GA. He married (1) MARY LEE LANE 28 Feb 1882 in Jones Co., GA. She was born 27 Sep 1862 in Jones Co., GA, and died 18 Jan 1892 in Jones Co., GA. He married (2) IDA AMANDA BOSTICK Abt. 1892 in Jones Co., GA. She was born 18 Oct 1869 in Jones Co., GA, and died 02 Jun 1952 in Jones Co., GA.
Children of THOMAS HAMMACK and MARY LEE LANE are:
        i.   BERTA[11] HAMMACK, b. Abt. August 1883, Jones Co., GA; d. Aft. 1900, Jones Co., GA.
        ii.   HATTIE HAMMACK, b. Abt. August 1885, Jones Co., GA; d. Aft. 1900, Jones Co., GA.
        iii. THOMAS HAMMACK, b. Abt. July 1888, Jones Co., GA; d. Aft. 1900, Jones Co., GA.
        iv.   GLENN HAMMACK, b. Abt. February 1892, Jones Co., GA; d. Aft. 1900, Jones Co., GA.
    Children of THOMAS HAMMACK and IDA BOSTICK are:
        v.   MARY LOU HAMMACK, b. Abt. March 1894, Jones Co., GA; d. Aft. 1900, Jones Co., GA.
        vi.   ELIZABETH HAMMACK, b. Abt. February 1896, Jones Co., GA; d. Aft. 1900, Jones Co., GA.
        vii. FELIX LEWIS HAMMACK, b. Abt. June 1898, Jones Co., GA; d. Aft. 1920, Jones Co., GA; m. REBECCA SMITH.
        viii. ETHEL HAMMACK, b. Abt. 1902, Jones Co., GA; d. Aft. 1920, Jones Co., GA.
        ix.   FRANCES HAMMACK, b. Abt. 1904, Jones Co., GA; d. Aft. 1920, Jones Co., GA.
Key Source: 1900 Jones Co., GA, Census, p. 135; 1910 Jones Co., GA, Census, p. 291; 1920 Jones Co., GA, Census, p. 129.

490. FELIX WILBORN[10] HAMMOCK, JR. *(FELIX WILBORN*[9]*, MANSEL W.*[8]*, WILLIAM T.*[7]*, ROBERT HAMMACK*[6] *JR., ROBERT HAMMACK*[5] *SR., WILLIAM "THE ELDER"*[4] *HAMMACK, WILLIAM "O"*[3]*, JOHN*[2] *HAMMOCKE, ? JOHN*[1] *HAMMOT)* was born 09 Apr 1862 in Crawford Co., GA, and died 24

Apr 1940 in Monroe Co., GA. He married MARION HILL FITZPATRICK. She was born 07 Nov 1865 in Crawford Co., GA, and died 06 Dec 1955 in Monroe Co., GA.
Children of FELIX HAMMOCK and MARION FITZPATRICK are:

     i.   MAUDE[11] HAMMOCK, b. August 1890, Crawford Co., GA; d. Aft. 1900, Crawford Co., GA.

    ii.   ANNIE HAMMOCK, b. August 1893, Crawford Co., GA; d. Aft. 1910, Monroe Co., GA.

   iii.   SUSIE HAMMOCK, b. 1888, Crawford Co., GA; d. Bef. 1900, Crawford Co., GA.

   iv.   RUTH AMANDA HAMMOCK, b. 15 Oct 1895, Crawford Co., GA; d. Aft. 1910, Monroe Co., GA.

    v.   SARAH ETHEL HAMMOCK, b. 1898, Crawford Co., GA; d. Bef. 1900, Crawford Co., GA.

   vi.   FELIX WILBORN HAMMOCK II, b. 1901, Monroe Co., GA; d. 1902, Monroe Co., GA.

  vii.   HENRY MANSEL HAMMOCK, b. 1903, Monroe Co., GA; d. Aft. 1920,Monroe Co., GA.

 viii.   MARION HILL HAMMOCK, b. 1906, Monroe Co., GA; d. Aft. 1920, Monroe Co., GA.

Key Sources: 1900 Crawford Co., GA, Census, p. 127; 1910 Monroe Co., GA, Census, p. 291; 1920 Monroe Co., GA, Census, p. 141.

491. WILLIAM[10] HAMMACK *(JAMES MANSEL[9], MANSEL W.[8], WILLIAM T.[7], ROBERT HAMMACK[6] JR., ROBERT HAMMACK[5] SR., WILLIAM "THE ELDER"[4] HAMMACK, WILLIAM "O"[3], JOHN[2] HAMMOCKE, ? JOHN[1] HAMMOT)* was born Abt. 1867 in Crawford Co., GA, and died Bet. 1880 - 1895 in Crawford Co., GA. He married NETTIE [------] Abt. 1888 in Crawford Co., GA. She was born 1870 in Crawford Co., GA, and died Aft. 1900 in Crawford Co., GA. NETTIE HAMMACK married (2) WILLIE RIGDON.
Child of WILLIAM HAMMACK and NETTIE [------] is:

     i.   CLARA[11] HAMMACK, b. May 1890, Crawford Co., GA; d. Aft. 1900, Crawford Co., GA.

Key Source: 1900 Crawford Co., GA, Census, p. 136.

492. JESSE[10] HAMMACK *(JOHN[9], JOHN[8], JOHN[7], JOHN[6], RICHARD[5], RICHARD[4], WILLIAM "O"[3], JOHN[2] HAMMOCKE, ? JOHN[1] HAMMOT)* was born Abt. 1814 in Grainger Co., TN, and died Aft. 1880 in Union Co., TN. He married (1) CATHERINE [------] Abt. 1834 in Grainger Co., TN. She was born Abt. 1814 in TN, and died Bet. 1860 - 1870 in Claiborne Co., TN. He married (2) MARY Aft. 1860 in Claiborne Co., TN. She was born Abt. 1833 in TN, and died Aft. 1870 in Union Co., TN.
Children of JESSE HAMMACK and CATHERINE [------] are:

     i.   ISAAC H.[11] HAMMACK, b. Abt. 1835, Grainger Co., TN.

    ii.   ANNA J. HAMMACK, b. Abt. 1838, Grainger Co., TN.

Key Sources: 1850 Grainger Co., TN, Census, p. 260; 1860 Claiborne Co., TN, Census, p. 367; 1870 Union Co., TN, Census, p. 290; 1880 Union Co., TN, Census, p. 241.

493. MARTIN[10] HAMMACK *(JOHN[9], JOHN[8], JOHN[7], JOHN[6], RICHARD[5], RICHARD[4], WILLIAM "O"[3], JOHN[2] HAMMOCKE, ? JOHN[1] HAMMOT)* was born Abt. 1817 in Grainger Co., TN, and died Aft. 1880 in \. He married (1) NANCY [------] Abt. 1835 in Grainger Co., TN. She was born Abt. 1816 in Grainger Co., TN, and died Bef. 1870 in Grainger Co., TN. He married (2) JUDA [------] Abt. 1870 in Union Co., TN. She was born Abt. 1815 in TN, and died Aft. 1880 in Grainger Co., TN.
Children of MARTIN HAMMACK and NANCY [------] are:

     i.   JAMES[11] HAMMACK, b. Abt. 1836, TN; d. Aft. 1870, Union Co., TN; m. MARY BERTRAM, 16 Nov 1860, Grainger Co., TN.

    ii.   JACKSON HAMMACK, b. Abt. 1838, Grainger Co., TN; d. Bet. 1860 - 1870, TN.

   iii.   WILLIAM HAMMACK, b. Abt. 1839, Grainger Co., TN; d. Aft. 1880, Union Co., TN.

iv. WASHINGTON HAMMACK, b. Abt. 1841, Grainger Co., TN; d. Aft. 1860, Union Co., TN.

v. BETSY HAMMACK, b. Abt. 1843, Grainger Co., TN; d. Aft. 1860, Union Co., TN.

vi. WINNY HAMMACK, b. Abt. 1844, Grainger Co., TN; d. Aft. 1864, Union Co., TN; m. JOHN BEELER, Abt. 1864, Union Co., TN.

Key Sources: 1850 Grainger Co., TN, Census, p. 264; 1860 Union Co., TN, Census, p. 430; 1870 Grainger Co., TN, Census, p. 149; 1870 Union Co., TN, Census, p. 214; 1880 Grainger Co., TN, Census, p. 241.

494. PETER[10] HAMMACK *(NOAH[9], WILLIAM[8], JOHN[7], JOHN[6], RICHARD[5], RICHARD[4], WILLIAM "O"[3], JOHN[2] HAMMOCKE, ? JOHN[1] HAMMOT)* was born Abt. 1840 in Indiana, and died Aft. 1880 in LaClede Co., MO. He married SARAH [------] Abt. 1868 in Illinois. She was born Abt. 1845 in Wisconsin, and died Aft. 1880 in LaClede Co., MO.

Children of PETER HAMMACK and SARAH [------] are:

i. JOHN[11] HAMMACK, b. Abt. 1868, Illinois; d. Aft. 1880, LaClede Co., MO.

ii. LIZZIE HAMMACK, b. Abt. 1870, Illinois; d. Aft. 1880, LaClede Co., MO.

iii. CHARLES HAMMACK, b. Abt. 1878, Kansas; d. Aft. 1880, LaClede Co., MO.

Key Source: 1880 LaClede Co., MO, Census, p. 102.

495. WYATT H.[10] HAMMACK *(LACE J.[9], TALIAFERRO[8], JOHN[7], RICHARD[6], RICHARD[5], RICHARD[4], WILLIAM "O"[3], JOHN[2] HAMMOCKE, ? JOHN[1] HAMMOT)* was born Abt. 1851 in Wayne Co., IL, and died Aft. 1880 in Wayne Co., IL. He married MARY [------] Abt. 1876 in Wayne Co., IL. She was born Abt. 1856 in IL, and died Aft. 1880 in Wayne Co., IL.

Children of WYATT HAMMACK and MARY [------] are:

i. JAMES[11] HAMMACK, b. Abt. 1877, Wayne Co., IL; d. Aft. 1880, Wayne Co., IL.

ii. CHARITY HAMMACK, b. Abt. 1878, Waync Co., IL; d. Aft. 1880, Wayne Co., IL.

iii. ADELBERT HAMMACK, b. Abt. 1880, Wayne Co., IL; d. Aft. 1880, Wayne Co., IL.

Key Source: 1880 Wayne Co., IL, Census, p. 12.

496. DANIEL[10] HAMMACK *(GEORGE[9], JOHN[8], DANIEL[7], RICHARD[6], RICHARD[5], RICHARD[4], WILLIAM "O"[3], JOHN[2] HAMMOCKE, ? JOHN[1] HAMMOT)* was born Abt. 1843 in Indiana, and died Aft. 1870 in Washington Co., NE. He married ADELINE [------] Abt. 1868 in Nebraska. She was born Abt. 1850 in Iowa, and died Aft. 1870 in Washington Co., NE.

Child of DANIEL HAMMACK and ADELINE [------] is:

i. HATTIE[11] HAMMACK, b. Abt. 1869, Nebraska.

Key Source: 1870 Washington Co., NE, Census, p. 426.

497. WILLIAM THOMAS[10] HAMMACK *(WILLIAM HENRY[9], COLEMAN[8], LEWIS[7], RICHARD[6], RICHARD[5], RICHARD[4], WILLIAM "O"[3], JOHN[2] HAMMOCKE, ? JOHN[1] HAMMOT)* was born Abt. 1848 in Franklin Co., MO, and died Aft. 1892 in Baxter Co., AR. He married (1) MARY ELIZABETH GREENSTREET Abt. 1866 in Missouri. She was born Abt. 1845 in Kentucky, and died Aft. 1880 in Pulaski Co., MO. He married (2) MARGARET ANNE KAYSINGER BOAZ 1892 in Baxter Co., AR.

Children of WILLIAM HAMMACK and MARY GREENSTREET are:

i. WILLIAM HENRY[11] HAMMACK, b. Abt. 1866, Pulaski Co., MO.

ii. ZACHARIAH MEDFORD HAMMACK, b. Abt. 1867, Pulaski Co., MO.

iii. ELIJAH B. HAMMACK, b. 1871, Pulaski Co., MO; m. ELIZABETH BOAZ, 19 Feb 1893, Baxter Co., AR.

iv. GEORGE THOMAS HAMMACK, b. Abt. 1872, Pulaski Co., MO; d. Aft. 1880, Pulaski Co., MO.

v.   MILLIE JANE HAMMACK, b. Abt. 1874, Pulaski Co., MO; d. Aft. 1880, Pulaski Co., MO.

vi.   EDWARD LAWRENCE HAMMACK, b. 13 Feb 1875, Pulaski Co., MO; d. Aft. 1880, Pulaski Co., MO.

vii. ALLEN FRANK HAMMACK, b. Abt. 1876, Pulaski Co., MO; d. 1929.

viii. DAVID HAMMACK, b. 18 Jul 1879, Pulaski Co., MO; d. 1929.

ix.   SAMUEL HAMMACK.

x.   JAMES MITCHELL HAMMACK.

xi.   JOHN M. HAMMACK, b. Abt. 1870.

Child of WILLIAM HAMMACK and MARGARET BOAZ is:

xii. MARY[11] HAMMACK, b. Abt. 1896, Baxter Co., AR.

Key Sources: 1880 Pulaski Co., MO, Census, p. 393; 1900 Baxter Co., AR, Census.

Generation No. 11

498. MINNIE E.[11] HAMMACK *(JAMES WILBURN[10], WILLIAM T. H.[9], SIMEON J.[8], WILLIAM T.[7], ROBERT HAMMACK[6] JR., ROBERT HAMMACK[5] SR., WILLIAM "THE ELDER"[4] HAMMACK, WILLIAM "O"[3], JOHN[2] HAMMOCKE, ? JOHN[1] HAMMOT)* was born 27 Sep 1871 in Madison Co., MS, and died 16 Sep 1952 in Hinds Co., MS. She married CLAUDE WAVERLY LORANCE. He was born 28 Nov 1874 in Hinds Co., MS, and died 24 Oct 1937 in Hinds Co., MS.

Children of MINNIE HAMMACK and CLAUDE LORANCE are:

i.   CLARENCE W.[12] LORANCE, b. 19 Oct 1904, Mississippi; d. 29 Nov 1955, Mississippi; m. PATTIE ELKINS; b. 06 Nov 1903, Mississippi; d. 16 Jul 1993, Mississippi.

ii.   CATHERINE LORANCE, b. Abt. 1906, Madison Co., MS; d. Aft. 1920, Madison Co., MS.

iii. ARTHUR LORANCE, b. Abt. 1908, Madison Co., MS; d. Aft. 1920, Madison Co., MS.

iv.   LOUISE LORANCE, b. 06 Sep 1909, Mississippi; d. 13 Mar 1986, Mississippi; m. EVERETT S. GOOCH; b. 19 Dec 1916, Mississippi; d. 19 May 1980, Mississippi.

v.   CAROL LORANCE, b. Abt. 1914, Madison Co., MS; d. Aft. 1910, Madison Co., MS.

Key Source: 1910 Madison Co., MS, Census, p. 193; 1920 Madison Co., MS, Census, p. 103.

499. FREDERICK WILLIAM[11] HAMMACK *(JAMES WILBURN[10], WILLIAM T. H.[9], SIMEON J.[8], WILLIAM T.[7], ROBERT HAMMACK[6] JR., ROBERT HAMMACK[5] SR., WILLIAM "THE ELDER"[4] HAMMACK, WILLIAM "O"[3], JOHN[2] HAMMOCKE, ? JOHN[1] HAMMOT)* was born 24 Jan 1874 in Madison Co., MS, and died 18 Nov 1924 in Flora, Madison County, MS. He married EVA MCDOWELL Abt. 1904 in Madison Co., MS. She was born 06 Aug 1879 in Madison Co., MS, and died 12 Feb 1946 in Flora, Madison County, MS.

Children of FREDERICK HAMMACK and EVA MCDOWELL are:

565. i.   FREDERICK TABOR[12] HAMMACK, b. 08 Apr 1905, Madison Co., MS; d. 12 Nov 1955, Flora, Madison County, MS.

566. ii.   FRANCES V. HAMMACK, b. 19 Sep 1906, Madison Co., MS; d. 27 Feb 1976, Flora, Madison County, MS.

567. iii. FREDERICK WILLIAM HAMMACK, JR., b. 16 Jan 1918, Madison Co., MS; d. 11 Nov 1994, Flora, Madison County, MS.

Key Sources: 1920 Madison Co., MS, Census, p. 102; Social Security Death Index; Telephone Interview with Louise Lane Hammack, July 1996.

500. LENA M.[11] HAMMACK *(JAMES WILBURN[10], WILLIAM T. H.[9], SIMEON J.[8], WILLIAM T.[7], ROBERT HAMMACK[6] JR., ROBERT HAMMACK[5] SR., WILLIAM "THE ELDER"[4] HAMMACK, WILLIAM "O"[3], JOHN[2] HAMMOCKE, ? JOHN[1] HAMMOT)* was born 12 Feb 1876 in Madison Co., MS, and died 14 March 1928, Fort Worth, Tarrant Co., TX. She married JOHN SAMUEL HAMMACK 17

Jan 1900 in Madison Co., MS, son of WILSON H. HAMMACK (313) and MARTHA BAKER. He was born 12 Feb 1880 in Hinds Co., MS, and died 17 March 1943, Fort Worth, Tarrant Co., TX.

Children of LENA HAMMACK and JOHN HAMMACK are:

     i. WILSON H.[12] HAMMACK, b. 8 August 1901, Hinds Co., MS; d. 10 November 1957, Tarrant Co., TX.

    ii. WILLIAM E. HAMMACK, b. Abt. 1903, Hinds Co., MS; d. Aft. 1910, Hinds Co., MS.

   iii. RALPH E. HAMMACK, b. Abt. 1903, Hinds Co., MS; d. Aft. 1910, Hinds Co., MS.

   iv. CHARLES H. HAMMACK, b. Abt. 1907, Hinds Co., MS; d. Aft. 1930, Tarrant Co., TX.

Key Source: 1910 Hinds Co., MS, Census, p. 28; Texas Death Certificates for John Samuel Hammack, Lena Hammack, Wilson Hines Hammack, Joseph Wilson Hammack. Wilson Hines Hammack married Mary Wright. In the 1930 Tarrant Co., TX, Census, he was enumerated with sons Raymond, age 7; Joseph, age 6; and Gregory, age 2. Joseph Wilson Hammack was born 9 September 1923 in Fort Worth, Tarrant Co., TX, and died 13 September 1948 in Ackerly, Martin Co., TX. He was a petroleum engineer and was buried in Fort Worth, Texas. Charles H. Hammack and wife Lillian, age 23, and daughter Betty Charles, age 1 3/12, were enumerated in the 1930 Tarrant Co., TX, census.

501. CHARLES CLIFTON[11] HAMMACK *(JAMES WILBURN[10], WILLIAM T. H.[9], SIMEON J.[8], WILLIAM T.[7], ROBERT HAMMACK[6] JR., ROBERT HAMMACK[5] SR., WILLIAM "THE ELDER"[4] HAMMACK, WILLIAM "O"[3], JOHN[2] HAMMOCKE, ? JOHN[1] HAMMOT)* was born Abt. 1878 in Madison Co., MS, and died Aft. 1920 in Madison Co., MS. He married MAUDE L. ? Abt. 1901 in Madison Co., MS. She was born 29 Dec 1876 in Mississippi, and died 03 Mar 1960 in Hinds Co., MS.

Children of CHARLES HAMMACK and MAUDE ? are:

     i. HERSCHEL M.[12] HAMMACK, b. Abt. 1902, Madison Co., MS; d. Aft. 1910, Madison Co., MS.

    ii. HELEN E. HAMMACK, b. Abt. 1904, Madison Co., MS; d. Aft. 1920, Madison Co., MS.

   iii. RAY W. HAMMACK, b. Abt. 1905, Madison Co., MS; d. Aft. 1920, Madison Co., MS.

   iv. CHARLES ALTON HAMMACK, b. 11 Nov 1906, Madison Co., MS; d. 15 Sep 1963, Madison Co., MS.

    v. ALBERT SIDNEY HAMMACK, b. Abt. 1910, Madison Co., MS; d. Aft. 1920, Madison Co., MS.

   vi. OLIVE HAMMACK, b. 26 Jan 1913, Madison Co., MS; d. 27 Oct 1986, Madison Co., MS.

  vii. JEFFIE HAMMACK, b. 17 Aug 1915, Madison Co., MS; d. 10 Jul 1998, Shelby Co., TN; m. KENNETH F. WISSNER; b. 20 Jan 1914, Mississippi; d. 01 Jun 1989, Madison Co., MS.

Key Source: 1910 Madison Co., MS, Census, p. 187; 1920 Madison Co., MS, Census, p. 104.

502. ETHEL[11] HAMMACK *(JOHN ASA[10], WILLIAM T. H.[9], SIMEON J.[8], WILLIAM T.[7], ROBERT HAMMACK[6] JR., ROBERT HAMMACK[5] SR., WILLIAM "THE ELDER"[4] HAMMACK, WILLIAM "O"[3], JOHN[2] HAMMOCKE, ? JOHN[1] HAMMOT)* was born 12 Jul 1878 in Madison Co., MS, and died Aug 1966 in Madison Co., MS. She married H. W. O'NEAL 13 Dec 1899 in Madison Co., MS. He was born 06 Mar 1876 in Hinds Co., MS, and died 09 Dec 1903 in Madison Co., MS.

Child of ETHEL HAMMACK and H. O'NEAL is:

     i. CORILLE[12] O'NEAL, b. 27 Jan 1901, Madison Co., MS; d. 2000, Madison Co., MS; m. ELON ELBERT LANE; b. 10 Dec 1896, Madison Co., MS; d. 02 Jan 1981, Madison Co., MS.

    ii. INEZ O'NEAL, b. Abt. 1903, Madison Co., MS; d. Aft. 1910, Madison Co., MS.

Key Source: 1910 Madison Co., MS, Census, p. 104.

503. IMOGENE[11] HAMMACK *(JOHN ASA[10], WILLIAM T. H.[9], SIMEON J.[8], WILLIAM T.[7], ROBERT HAMMACK[6] JR., ROBERT HAMMACK[5] SR., WILLIAM "THE ELDER"[4] HAMMACK, WILLIAM "O"[3],*

JOHN[2] HAMMOCKE, ? JOHN[1] HAMMOT) was born Oct 1879 in Madison Co., MS, and died 1951 in Madison Co., MS. She married WILL ALEXANDER COX Abt. 1901 in Madison Co., MS. He was born 1875 in Mississippi, and died 1942 in Madison Co., MS.

Children of IMOGENE HAMMACK and WILL COX are:

 i. WILL ALEXANDER[12] COX, JR, b. 27 Aug 1903, Madison Co., MS.
 ii. EARNEST HAMPTON COX, b. 05 Jul 1905, Madison Co., MS.
 iii. ETHLYN COX, b. 14 Feb 1907, Madison Co., MS.
 iv. JOHN ASA COX, b. 24 Aug 1909, Madison Co., MS; d. 1990, Madison Co., MS.
 v. CORA AUGUSTA COX, b. 16 Feb 1911, Madison Co., MS; d. Aft. 1994, Madison Co., MS; m. [------] SEARLE.
 vi. JAMES HARVEY COX, b. Abt. 1913, Madison Co., MS; d. Aft. 1994, Madison Co., MS.

Key Source: 1920 Hinds Co., MS, Census, p. 95.

504. WILLIAM HOWARD[11] HAMMACK *(GEORGE THOMAS[10], WILLIAM T. H.[9], SIMEON J.[8], WILLIAM T.[7], ROBERT HAMMACK[6] JR., ROBERT HAMMACK[5] SR., WILLIAM "THE ELDER"[4] HAMMACK, WILLIAM "O"[3], JOHN[2] HAMMOCKE, ? JOHN[1] HAMMOT)* was born 12 Oct 1882 in Madison County, MS, and died 13 Sep 1937 in Madison County, MS. He married MARY KATIE GARY 09 Dec 1903 in Madison Co., MS. She was born 05 Apr 1887 in Madison County, MS, and died 19 Jun 1972 in Madison County, MS.

Children of WILLIAM HAMMACK and MARY GARY are:

 i. WILLIAM C.[12] HAMMACK, b. 12 Apr 1905, Madison County, MS; d. 23 May 1906, Madison County, MS.
 ii. HERMAN J. HAMMACK, b. 08 Sep 1906, Madison County, MS; d. 01 Sep 1982, Madison County, MS; m. RUTHIE [--------]; b. 18 Aug 1920, Mississippi; d. 20 Feb 1986, Madison Co., MS.
 iii. MARION COLUMBUS HAMMACK, b. 25 Dec 1908, Madison County, MS; d. 10 Nov 1940, Madison County, MS.
 iv. ROBERT CLIVE HAMMACK, b. 17 Jan 1910, Madison County, MS; d. 24 Jan 1997, Hinds County, MS; m. VERA A. GILL; b. 05 Jan 1917, Mississippi; d. 10 Apr 1993, Hinds Co., MS.
 v. ADELAIDE HAMMACK, b. 23 Nov 1911, Madison County, MS; d. Aft. 1997, Hinds Co., MS.
 vi. HOWARD HAMMACK, b. 09 Dec 1913, Madison County, MS; d. 19 Dec 1942, Madison County, MS.
 vii. WEBSTER HAMMACK, b. 23 Oct 1915, Madison County, MS; d. Aft. 1970, Madison County, MS.

Key Sources: 1910 Madison Co., MS, Census, p. 286; 1920 Madison Co., MS, Census, p. 104.

505. LILLIAN G.[11] HAMMACK *(GEORGE THOMAS[10], WILLIAM T. H.[9], SIMEON J.[8], WILLIAM T.[7], ROBERT HAMMACK[6] JR., ROBERT HAMMACK[5] SR., WILLIAM "THE ELDER"[4] HAMMACK, WILLIAM "O"[3], JOHN[2] HAMMOCKE, ? JOHN[1] HAMMOT)* was born 15 Feb 1885 in Hinds County, MS, and died Aft. 1930 in Copiah County, MS. She married JOHN T. ROBEY 22 Jan 1913 in Hinds Co., MS.

Child of LILLIAN HAMMACK and JOHN ROBEY is:

 i. FRED[12] ROBEY, b. Abt. 1914, Mississippi; d. Abt. 1934, During college years.

Key Source: 1920 Winston Co., MS, Census, p. 34.

506. MABEL E.[11] HAMMACK *(GEORGE THOMAS[10], WILLIAM T. H.[9], SIMEON J.[8], WILLIAM T.[7], ROBERT HAMMACK[6] JR., ROBERT HAMMACK[5] SR., WILLIAM "THE ELDER"[4] HAMMACK, WILLIAM "O"[3], JOHN[2] HAMMOCKE, ? JOHN[1] HAMMOT)* was born 06 Jul 1889 in Hinds County, MS,

and died Aft. 1930 in Hinds County, MS. She married WALTON JACKSON HARPER 17 Jul 1907 in Hinds Co., MS.
Children of MABEL HAMMACK and WALTON HARPER are:

       i.   FLORA[12] HARPER, b. Abt. 1910, Copiah Co., MS; m. ? RENO.

568.   ii. ISAAC CORNELIUS HARPER, b. Abt. 1910, Copiah Co., MS.

Key Source: 1920 Hinds Co., MS, Census, p. 237.

507. MARION CLAIBORNE[11] HAMMACK *(GEORGE THOMAS[10], WILLIAM T. H.[9], SIMEON J.[8], WILLIAM T.[7], ROBERT HAMMACK[6] JR., ROBERT HAMMACK[5] SR., WILLIAM "THE ELDER"[4] HAMMACK, WILLIAM "O"[3], JOHN[2] HAMMOCKE, ? JOHN[1] HAMMOT)* was born 01 Jul 1891 in Texas, and died 01 Jul 1967 in Gatesville, Copiah County, MS. He married TINEY BELL DEAN 09 Jul 1911, daughter of JOHN DEAN and SARAH TAYLOR. She was born 19 Apr 1897 in Florence, Mississippi, and died 23 Sep 1980 in Hopewell, Copiah Co., MS..
Children of MARION HAMMACK and TINEY DEAN are:

       i.   MARGUERITE CELIDA[12] HAMMACK, b. 17 Feb 1914, Copiah Co., MS; m. JAMES ALVIN WALTERS, 03 Jun 1936; d. 29 May 1991.

569.   ii. MYRTIE MONELL HAMMACK, b. 01 Nov 1916, Copiah Co., MS.

570.   iii. TINEY BELLE HAMMACK, b. 30 Apr 1920, Copiah Co., MS.

571.   iv. MARION CLAIBORNE HAMMACK, JR., b. 09 Sep 1924, Copiah Co., MS.

572.   v. WILBUR CLYDE HAMMACK, b. 23 Sep 1926, Copiah Co., MS; d. 18 Jun 1992, Mississippi.

573.   vi. WINFRED CARROL HAMMACK, b. 18 May 1931, Copiah Co., MS.

574. vii. FRANCES JEANNETTE HAMMACK, b. 22 Jul 1936, Copiah Co., MS.

Key Sources: 1920 Copiah Co., MS, Census, p. 231; Family records of Felix Maben Hammack, Bend, OR.

508. THOMAS CLIVE[11] HAMMACK *(GEORGE THOMAS[10], WILLIAM T. H.[9], SIMEON J.[8], WILLIAM T.[7], ROBERT HAMMACK[6] JR., ROBERT HAMMACK[5] SR., WILLIAM "THE ELDER"[4] HAMMACK, WILLIAM "O"[3], JOHN[2] HAMMOCKE, ? JOHN[1] HAMMOT)* was born 01 Jul 1891 in Texas, and died Aft. 1944 in Mississippi. He married (1) AMY JULIA ROBERTSON 23 Jul 1914 in Louisiana. He married (2) LESSIE [--------] Aft. 1920.
Children of THOMAS HAMMACK and AMY ROBERTSON are:

575.   i.   CARY THOMAS[12] HAMMACK.

576.   ii. MILDRED LEOLA HAMMACK.

577.   iii. DORIS HAMMACK.

Children of THOMAS HAMMACK and LESSIE [--------] are:

     iv. LEON[12] HAMMACK, m. JOYCE MARTIN, 1968.

      v. RUDOLPH CARROLL HAMMACK, m. BARBARA FUQUA, 1962.

Key Source: Family records of Felix Maben Hammack, Bend, OR.

509. IVA VIOLA[11] HAMMACK *(GEORGE THOMAS[10], WILLIAM T. H.[9], SIMEON J.[8], WILLIAM T.[7], ROBERT HAMMACK[6] JR., ROBERT HAMMACK[5] SR., WILLIAM "THE ELDER"[4] HAMMACK, WILLIAM "O"[3], JOHN[2] HAMMOCKE, ? JOHN[1] HAMMOT)* was born 14 Feb 1898 in Hinds County, MS, and died Aft. 1930 in Hinds County, MS. She married HOWARD SMITH 10 May 1919 in Copiah Co., MS.
Children of IVA HAMMACK and HOWARD SMITH are:

       i.   RUTH HELEN[12] SMITH.

      ii. KATHLEEN SMITH.

    iii. FRANCES SMITH.
    iv. CARROL SMITH.
    v. THOMAS SMITH.
Key Source: Family records of Felix Maben Hammack, Bend, OR.

510. EMOGENE[11] HAMMACK *(GEORGE THOMAS[10], WILLIAM T. H.[9], SIMEON J.[8], WILLIAM T.[7], ROBERT HAMMACK[6] JR., ROBERT HAMMACK[5] SR., WILLIAM "THE ELDER"[4] HAMMACK, WILLIAM "O"[3], JOHN[2] HAMMOCKE, ? JOHN[1] HAMMOT)* was born 20 Sep 1900 in Mississippi, and died 28 Aug 1937 in Copiah County, MS. She married (1) E. HOMER WATSON 19 Feb 1920 in Copiah Co., MS. She married (2) BERT DONALDSON 04 Apr 1931 in Copiah Co., MS.
Children of EMOGENE HAMMACK and E. WATSON are:
    i. VIOLA[12] WATSON.
    ii. HUNTER WATSON.
Child of EMOGENE HAMMACK and BERT DONALDSON is:
    iii. DAISY[12] DONALDSON.
Key Source: Family records of Felix Maben Hammack, Bend, OR.

511. ALBERT E. "PRINCE"[11] HAMMACK *(GEORGE THOMAS[10], WILLIAM T. H.[9], SIMEON J.[8], WILLIAM T.[7], ROBERT HAMMACK[6] JR., ROBERT HAMMACK[5] SR., WILLIAM "THE ELDER"[4] HAMMACK, WILLIAM "O"[3], JOHN[2] HAMMOCKE, ? JOHN[1] HAMMOT)* was born 05 May 1903 in Mississippi, and died Aft. 1920 in Copiah County, MS. He married HATTIE BELLE KNIGHT 26 Apr 1920 in Copiah Co., MS.
Children of ALBERT HAMMACK and HATTIE KNIGHT are:
    i. ALMA[12] HAMMACK.
    ii. BETTY HAMMACK.
    iii. VIVIAN HAMMACK.
    iv. JESSIE HAMMACK.
Key Source: Family records of Felix Maben Hammack, Bend, OR.

512. AUDREY ELAINE[11] HAMMACK *(GEORGE THOMAS[10], WILLIAM T. H.[9], SIMEON J.[8], WILLIAM T.[7], ROBERT HAMMACK[6] JR., ROBERT HAMMACK[5] SR., WILLIAM "THE ELDER"[4] HAMMACK, WILLIAM "O"[3], JOHN[2] HAMMOCKE, ? JOHN[1] HAMMOT)* was born 02 Apr 1906 in Mississippi, and died Aft. 1940 in Copiah County, MS. She married KENNETH C. ANDERSON 26 Dec 1926 in Copiah Co., MS.
Child of AUDREY HAMMACK and KENNETH ANDERSON is:
    i. JACQUELINE[12] ANDERSON, m. ROBERT BRISTER.
Key Source: Family records of Felix Maben Hammack, Bend, OR.

513. KATIE M.[11] COLLUM *(SIMON CICERO[10], MARY JANE[9] HAMMACK, SIMEON J.[8], WILLIAM T.[7], ROBERT HAMMACK[6] JR., ROBERT HAMMACK[5] SR., WILLIAM "THE ELDER"[4] HAMMACK, WILLIAM "O"[3], JOHN[2] HAMMOCKE, ? JOHN[1] HAMMOT)* was born 09 Mar 1878 in Navarro Co., TX, and died 06 Apr 1952 in Bell Co., TX. She married JAMES M. CHURCH. He was born Abt. 1870 in Texas, and died bet. 1920 - 1930 in Navarro Co., TX.
Child of KATIE COLLUM and JAMES CHURCH is:
    i. CHRISTINE[12] CHURCH, b. Abt. 1912, Navarro Co., TX; d. Aft. 1930, Navarro Co., TX.
Key Sources: 1920 Navarro Co., TX, Census, p. 198; 1920 Navarro Co., TX, Census, p. 136.

514. DAISEY[11] COLLUM *(SIMON CICERO[10], MARY JANE[9] HAMMACK, SIMEON J.[8], WILLIAM T.[7], ROBERT HAMMACK[6] JR., ROBERT HAMMACK[5] SR., WILLIAM "THE ELDER"[4] HAMMACK,*

WILLIAM "O"[3], JOHN[2] HAMMOCKE, ? JOHN[1] HAMMOT) was born 12 Apr 1881 in Navarro Co., TX, and died 14 Dec 1936 in Navarro Co., TX. She married SIDNEY F. STORY Abt. 1910 in Navarro Co., TX. He was born Abt. 1880 in Texas, and died Aft. 1930 in Navarro Co., TX.

Children of DAISEY COLLUM and SIDNEY STORY are:

      i.   PAULINE[12] STORY, b. Abt. 1917, Navarro Co., TX; d. Aft. 1930, Navarro Co., TX.

      ii.   DANIEL A. STORY, b. Abt. 1921, Navarro Co., TX; d. Aft. 1930, Navarro Co., TX.

Key Source: 1930 Navarro Co., TX, Census, p. 67; Texas Death Certificate of Daisey Collum Story.

515. MARY (MAYME)[11] COLLUM *(ALFRED EUGENE[10], MARY JANE[9] HAMMACK, SIMEON J.[8], WILLIAM T.[7], ROBERT HAMMACK[6] JR., ROBERT HAMMACK[5] SR., WILLIAM "THE ELDER"[4] HAMMACK, WILLIAM "O"[3], JOHN[2] HAMMOCKE, ? JOHN[1] HAMMOT)* was born 21 Sep 1877 in Mississippi, and died 22 Oct 1942 in Hardeman Co., TX. She married THOMAS G. JOHNSTON Abt. 1900 in Navarro Co., TX. He was born Abt. 1873 in Texas, and died Aft. 1910 in Navarro Co., TX.

Children of MARY COLLUM and THOMAS JOHNSTON are:

      i.   GEL[12] JOHNSTON, b. Abt. 1901, Texas; d. Aft. 1910, Navarro Co., TX.

      ii.   DAVE J. JOHNSTON, b. Abt. 1905, Texas; d. Aft. 1930, Navarro Co., TX.

Key Sources: 1910 Navarro Co., TX, Census, p. 157; 1920 Navarro Co., TX, Census, p. 123; 1930 Navarro Co., TX, Census, p. 92; Texas Death Certificate of Mary Collum Johnston.

516. THOMAS EATMON[11] DOOLITTLE *(SAREPTA ANN ELIZABETH[10] HAMMACK, CHARLES M.[9], SIMEON J.[8], WILLIAM T.[7], ROBERT HAMMACK[6] JR., ROBERT HAMMACK[5] SR., WILLIAM "THE ELDER"[4] HAMMACK, WILLIAM "O"[3], JOHN[2] HAMMOCKE, ? JOHN[1] HAMMOT)* was born 10 May 1869 in Calhoun Co., MS, and died 04 Sep 1954 in Slate Springs, Calhoun Co., MS. He married (1) LEILA GENTRY. She was born 11 Feb 1871 in Calhoun Co., MS, and died 07 Feb 1933 in Calhoun Co., MS. He married (2) THEO D. MITCHELL Abt. 1893 in Calhoun Co., MS. She was born 03 Oct 1874 in Mississippi, and died 07 Jul 1909 in Calhoun Co., MS.

Children of THOMAS DOOLITTLE and THEO MITCHELL are:

      i.   BESSIE T.[12] DOOLITTLE, b. 20 Mar 1895, Calhoun Co., MS; d. Aft. 1920, Calhoun Co., MS; m. JAMES ELLIS MCCORD; b. 10 Nov 1876, Calhoun Co., MS; d. 27 Oct 1955, Calhoun Co., MS.

578.   ii.   SAMUEL BOYD DOOLITTLE, b. 26 Sep 1897, Calhoun Co., MS; d. 29 Dec 1963, Slate Springs, Calhoun Co., MS.

579.   iii.   MAX DOOLITTLE, b. Aug 1898, Calhoun Co., MS; d. Aft. 1954, Calhoun Co., MS.

      iv.   THOMAS EVERETT DOOLITTLE, b. 25 Nov 1900, Calhoun Co., MS; d. 23 Sep 1966, Shelby Co., TN; m. LOUISE MCGAHEY EDMONDSON.

      v.   LOTTIE RUTH DOOLITTLE, b. 31 Jul 1906, Calhoun Co., MS; d. 26 Sep 1906, Calhoun Co., MS.

Key Sources: 1920 Calhoun Co., MS, Census, p. 208; "T. E. Doolittle," *Calhoun Monitor-Herald*, 9 September 1954.

517. JAMES WILLIAM[11] DOOLITTLE *(SAREPTA ANN ELIZABETH[10] HAMMACK, CHARLES M.[9], SIMEON J.[8], WILLIAM T.[7], ROBERT HAMMACK[6] JR., ROBERT HAMMACK[5] SR., WILLIAM "THE ELDER"[4] HAMMACK, WILLIAM "O"[3], JOHN[2] HAMMOCKE, ? JOHN[1] HAMMOT)* was born 21 Jun 1871 in Calhoun Co., MS, and died 06 Mar 1949 in Calhoun Co., MS. He married DORA DEAN DENTON Abt. 1895 in Calhoun Co., MS. She was born 02 Nov 1876 in Calhoun Co., MS, and died 03 May 1944 in Calhoun Co., MS.

Children of JAMES DOOLITTLE and DORA DENTON are:

580.   i.   DELORES[12] DOOLITTLE, b. Apr 1897, Calhoun Co., MS; d. Aft. 1949, Calhoun Co., MS.

ii.   WILLIE A. DOOLITTLE, b. Sep 1898, Calhoun Co., MS; d. Aft. 1949, Shelby, MS; m. RUTHIE PRYOR.

Key Sources: 1920 Calhoun Co., MS, Census, p. 207; "J. W. Doolittle," *Calhoun Monitor*, 10 March 1949.

518. CALVIN CHARLES[11] DOOLITTLE *(SAREPTA ANN ELIZABETH[10] HAMMACK, CHARLES M.[9], SIMEON J.[8], WILLIAM T.[7], ROBERT HAMMACK[6] JR., ROBERT HAMMACK[5] SR., WILLIAM "THE ELDER"[4] HAMMACK, WILLIAM "O"[3], JOHN[2] HAMMOCKE, ? JOHN[1] HAMMOT)* was born 1876 in Calhoun Co., MS, and died Aft. 1949 in Rogers, AR. He married ADDIE LOU PARKER Abt. 1902 in Calhoun Co., MS. She was born Abt. 1883 in Mississippi, and died Aft. 1920 in Calhoun Co., MS.
Children of CALVIN DOOLITTLE and ADDIE PARKER are:

i.   ORIS[12] DOOLITTLE, b. Abt. 1903, Calhoun Co., MS; d. Aft. 1920, Calhoun Co., MS.
ii.   PARKER DOOLITTLE, b. Abt. 1908, Calhoun Co., MS; d. Aft. 1920, Calhoun Co., MS.

Key Source: 1920 Calhoun Co., MS, Census, p. 207.

519. MAYBELLE[11] DOOLITTLE *(SAREPTA ANN ELIZABETH[10] HAMMACK, CHARLES M.[9], SIMEON J.[8], WILLIAM T.[7], ROBERT HAMMACK[6] JR., ROBERT HAMMACK[5] SR., WILLIAM "THE ELDER"[4] HAMMACK, WILLIAM "O"[3], JOHN[2] HAMMOCKE, ? JOHN[1] HAMMOT)* was born 17 Feb 1880 in Calhoun Co., MS, and died 20 Oct 1967 in Calhoun Co., MS. She married JOHN MILLER HOLLAND 1900 in Calhoun Co., MS. He was born 26 Aug 1879 in Calhoun Co., MS, and died 10 Oct 1954 in Calhoun Co., MS.
Children of MAYBELLE DOOLITTLE and JOHN HOLLAND are:

i.   TROY[12] HOLLAND, b. Abt. 1903, Calhoun Co., MS; d. Aft. 1967, Calhoun Co., MS; m. EDNA HOLLINGSWORTH, 26 Jan 1929, Calhoun Co., MS.
ii.   MARY E. HOLLAND, b. 14 Dec 1904, Calhoun Co., MS; d. 24 Apr 1908, Calhoun Co., MS.
581.   iii.   HENRY HAVEN HOLLAND, b. 02 Oct 1905, Calhoun Co., MS; d. Aft. 1967, Calhoun Co., MS.
582.   iv.   MILLER DOOLITTLE HOLLAND, b. 04 Apr 1908, Calhoun Co., MS; d. Aft. 1967, Calhoun Co., MS.

Key Sources: 1920 Calhoun Co., MS, Census, p. 207; "Mrs. J. M. Holland," *Calhoun Monitor*, 26 October 1967.

520. GEORGIA ANN[11] DOOLITTLE *(SAREPTA ANN ELIZABETH[10] HAMMACK, CHARLES M.[9], SIMEON J.[8], WILLIAM T.[7], ROBERT HAMMACK[6] JR., ROBERT HAMMACK[5] SR., WILLIAM "THE ELDER"[4] HAMMACK, WILLIAM "O"[3], JOHN[2] HAMMOCKE, ? JOHN[1] HAMMOT)* was born 1884 in Calhoun Co., MS, and died 1950 in Vardaman, MS. She married FINNER R. CARVER. He was born 1882, and died 1961.
Child of GEORGIA DOOLITTLE and FINNER CARVER is:
583.   i.   FINNER[12] CARVER, b. 28 Jan 1919, Calhoun Co., MS.

Key Sources: 1910 Calhoun Co., MS, Census, p. 111; 1920 Calhoun Co., MS, Census, p. 207.

521. LESTER[11] HAMMACK *(CHARLES[10], CHARLES M.[9], SIMEON J.[8], WILLIAM T.[7], ROBERT HAMMACK[6] JR., ROBERT HAMMACK[5] SR., WILLIAM "THE ELDER"[4] HAMMACK, WILLIAM "O"[3], JOHN[2] HAMMOCKE, ? JOHN[1] HAMMOT)* was born Apr 1891 in Calhoun Co., MS, and died Aft. 1920 in Sunflower Co., MS. He married PEARL [--------] Abt. 1911 in Mississippi. She was born Abt. 1891 in Mississippi, and died Aft. 1920 in Sunflower Co., MS.
Children of LESTER HAMMACK and PEARL [--------] are:

i.   RUBIE[12] HAMMACK, b. Abt. 1912, Sunflower Co., MS; d. Aft. 1920, Sunflower Co., MS.

ii. HELLON HAMMACK, b. Abt. 1914, Sunflower Co., MS; d. Aft. 1920, Sunflower Co., MS.
iii. W. L. HAMMACK, b. Abt. 1916, Sunflower Co., MS; d. Aft. 1920, Sunflower Co., MS.
iv. BLANCHE HAMMACK, b. Abt. 1919, Sunflower Co., MS; d. Aft. 1920, Sunflower Co., MS.

Key Source: 1920 Sunflower Co., MS, Census, p. 280.

522. CHARLES RANDOLPH[11] WASSON *(NAOMI[10] HAMMACK, CHARLES M.[9], SIMEON J.[8], WILLIAM T.[7], ROBERT HAMMACK[6] JR., ROBERT HAMMACK[5] SR., WILLIAM "THE ELDER"[4] HAMMACK, WILLIAM "O"[3], JOHN[2] HAMMOCKE, ? JOHN[1] HAMMOT)* was born 04 Jul 1895 in Sunflower Co., MS, and died 30 Dec 1960 in Greenville, MS. He married JEWELL SHARP 21 Dec 1921 in Sunflower Co., MS. She was born 07 Apr 1901 in Sunflower Co., MS.
Children of CHARLES WASSON and JEWELL SHARP are:
584. i. CHARLES DOUGLAS[12] WASSON, b. 22 Apr 1927, Sunflower Co., MS.
585. ii. DENNIS CAMPBELL WASSON, b. 02 Jul 1932, Sunflower Co., MS.
586. iii. EUNICE DELORES WASSON, b. 12 Jun 1938, Sunflower Co., MS.
iv. EULA ELOISE WASSON, b. 12 Jun 1938, Sunflower Co., MS; m. WILLIAM SHANNON HANABLE, 22 Jul 1967, Sunflower Co., MS; b. 16 Dec 1938, Sewickley, PA.

Key Source: 1900 Sunflower Co., MS, Census, p. 217; 1910 Sunflower Co., MS, Census, p. 130; 1920 Sunflower Co., MS, Census, p. 94; S. F. Brewster, *Data on Wasson Families and Allied Lines* (unpublished, 1973), pp. 138-140, housed in Eudora Welty Library, Jackson, MS.

523. CHARLIE FRANKLIN[11] SANDERFORD *(AMANDA V.[10] TAYLOR, SARAH ANN E.[9] HAMMACK, SIMEON J.[8], WILLIAM T.[7], ROBERT HAMMACK[6] JR., ROBERT HAMMACK[5] SR., WILLIAM "THE ELDER"[4] HAMMACK, WILLIAM "O"[3], JOHN[2] HAMMOCKE, ? JOHN[1] HAMMOT)* was born 16 Mar 1873 in Madison Co., MS, and died 05 Dec 1922 in Henderson Co., TX. He married TENNESSEE LEE YOUNG Abt. 1895 in Henderson Co., TX. She was born Apr 1876 in Tennessee, and died 03 Oct 1963 in Henderson Co., TX.
Children of CHARLIE SANDERFORD and TENNESSEE YOUNG are:
587. i. LAWRENCE J.[12] SANDERFORD, b. May 1897, Texas; d. Aft. 1930, Henderson Co., TX.
ii. ROBERT M. SANDERFORD, b. Nov 1899, Texas; d. Aft. 1920, Henderson Co., TX.
iii. WILLIE SANDERFORD, b. Abt. 1902, Texas; d. Aft. 1920, Henderson Co., TX.
iv. JEFFIE SANDERFORD, b. Abt. 1905, Texas; d. Aft. 1930, Henderson Co., TX; m. [-----] DOVER; d. Bef. 1930, Henderson Co., TX.
v. HENRY F. SANDERFORD, b. 15 Jul 1907, Texas; d. 19 Dec 1977, Henderson Co., TX; m. LEONA [------]; b. Abt. 1913, Texas; d. Aft. 1930, Henderson Co., TX.
vi. JOHN T. SANDERFORD, b. Abt. 1910, Texas; d. Aft. 1920, Henderson Co., TX.

Key Sources: Texas Death Certificate of Charlie Sanderford; 1920 Henderson Co., TX, p. 117.

524. ROBERT M.[11] SANDERFORD *(AMANDA V.[10] TAYLOR, SARAH ANN E.[9] HAMMACK, SIMEON J.[8], WILLIAM T.[7], ROBERT HAMMACK[6] JR., ROBERT HAMMACK[5] SR., WILLIAM "THE ELDER"[4] HAMMACK, WILLIAM "O"[3], JOHN[2] HAMMOCKE, ? JOHN[1] HAMMOT)* was born Apr 1875 in Madison Co., MS, and died Aft. 1920 in Ellis Co., TX. He married SARAH C. [------] Abt. 1905 in Texas. She was born Abt. 1881 in Texas, and died Aft. 1920 in Ellis Co., TX.
Children of ROBERT SANDERFORD and SARAH [------] are:
i. ARTHUR J.[12] SANDERFER, b. Abt. 1903, Texas; d. Aft. 1910, Jack Co., TX.
ii. ELZIE C. SANDERFER, b. Abt. 1906, Texas; d. Aft. 1920, Ellis Co., TX.
iii. LINNIE SANDERFER, b. Abt. 1912, Texas; d. Aft. 1920, Ellis Co., TX.
iv. MATTIE SANDERFER, b. Abt. 1916, Texas; d. Aft. 1920, Ellis Co., TX.

Key Source: 1920 Ellis Co., TX, Census, p. 268.

525. GEORGE CLEVELAND[11] HAMMACK *(WILLIAM SIMMS[10], JOHN T.[9], SIMEON J.[8], WILLIAM T.[7], ROBERT HAMMACK[6] JR., ROBERT HAMMACK[5] SR., WILLIAM "THE ELDER"[4] HAMMACK, WILLIAM "O"[3], JOHN[2] HAMMOCKE, ? JOHN[1] HAMMOT)* was born 26 Oct 1884 in Hinds County, Mississippi, and died 17 Nov 1963 in Hinds County, Mississippi. He married MARY ALMEDIA BANKSTON 19 Feb 1911 in Hinds County, Mississippi, daughter of JOHN BANKSTON and ABI O'NEAL. She was born 03 Apr 1894 in Hinds County, Mississippi, and died 09 Dec 1974 in Hinds County, Mississippi.

Children of GEORGE HAMMACK and MARY BANKSTON are:

588.   i.   SADIE LUCILLE[12] HAMMACK, b. 21 Feb 1912, Hinds County, MS; d. 16 Nov 1996, Monroe, LA.
589.   ii.   WILLIAM BANKSTON HAMMACK, b. 24 Oct 1913, Hinds County, MS; d. 10 Apr 1989, Jackson, MS.
590.   iii.   MARY MILDRED HAMMACK, b. 07 Aug 1915, Hinds County, MS; d. 11 Dec 2003, Mansfield, LA.
591.   iv.   EDGAR HENDRICKS HAMMACK, b. 20 Oct 1917, Hinds County, MS; d. 28 Dec 1986, Atlanta, GA.
592.   v.   GEORGE CLEVELAND HAMMACK, JR., b. 17 May 1922, Hinds County, MS.
593.   vi.   JAMES WILSON HAMMACK, b. 28 May 1924, Hinds County, MS.
594.   vii.   DANIEL CLEMENT HAMMACK, b. 13 Apr 1926, Hinds County, MS.
595.   viii. FELIX MABEN HAMMACK, b. 05 Mar 1928, Hinds County, Mississippi.
596.   ix.   CELESTE ALMEDIA HAMMACK, b. 24 Mar 1932, Hinds County, MS; d. 12 Oct 1951, Near Alexandria, LA.
597.   x.   ALLIE JO HAMMACK, b. 01 Nov 1934, Hinds County, MS; d. 11 Oct 1966, Memphis, TN.

Key Sources: 1910 Hinds Co., MS, Census, p. 167; 1920 Hinds Co., MS, Census, p. 102; Family records of Felix Maben Hammack, Bend, OR.

526. ROBERT FELIX[11] HAMMACK *(WILLIAM SIMMS[10], JOHN T.[9], SIMEON J.[8], WILLIAM T.[7], ROBERT HAMMACK[6] JR., ROBERT HAMMACK[5] SR., WILLIAM "THE ELDER"[4] HAMMACK, WILLIAM "O"[3], JOHN[2] HAMMOCKE, ? JOHN[1] HAMMOT)* was born 15 Oct 1885 in Hinds County, MS, and died 02 Apr 1949. He married KATIE CAMPBELL 24 Mar 1910, daughter of WILLIAM CAMPBELL and MARY O'NEAL. She was born 08 Feb 1889, and died 22 Sep 1979 in Yazoo County, MS.

Children of ROBERT HAMMACK and KATIE CAMPBELL are:

          i.   MARGARET ELIZABETH[12] HAMMACK, b. 16 Aug 1915; d. 30 Jun 1988, Hinds County, MS; m. (1) DEWEY LUCE HARTHCOCK, 10 Nov 1936; d. 16 Dec 1959; m. (2) HENRY T HARDY, 30 Dec 1960; d. 30 Dec 1980.
598.   ii.   RUBY COOMBS HAMMACK, b. 06 Sep 1926, Yazoo County, MS.
599.   iii.   MARY KATHERINE HAMMACK, b. 21 Nov 1929, Yazoo County, MS.

Key Sources: 1920 Yazoo Co., MS, Census, p. 63; Family records of Felix Maben Hammack, Bend, OR.

527. DRURY BROWN "DOOLEY"[11] HAMMACK *(WILLIAM SIMMS[10], JOHN T.[9], SIMEON J.[8], WILLIAM T.[7], ROBERT HAMMACK[6] JR., ROBERT HAMMACK[5] SR., WILLIAM "THE ELDER"[4] HAMMACK, WILLIAM "O"[3], JOHN[2] HAMMOCKE, ? JOHN[1] HAMMOT)* was born 11 Sep 1889 in Hinds County, MS, and died 23 Apr 1962 in Hinds County, MS. He married MARY ANN TANNER 21 Feb 1916, daughter of JOHN TANNER and MARTHA THURMAN. She was born 28 Aug 1898, and died 07 Jan 1968.

Children of DRURY HAMMACK and MARY TANNER are:

600.   i.   WILLIE BELL[12] HAMMACK, b. 16 Dec 1916, Hinds County, MS; d. 21 Oct 1990.
601.   ii.   ETHEL MAE HAMMACK, b. 29 Oct 1917, Hinds County, MS.

602.   iii.   THOMAS CLIFTON "PETE" HAMMACK, b. 14 Feb 1919, Hinds County, MS.
603.   iv.   MARTHA ELIZABETH HAMMACK, b. 21 Jan 1922, Hinds County, MS.
604.   v.   DEWEY LEON HAMMACK, b. 06 Dec 1923, Hinds County, MS; d. 06 Sep 1973.
        vi.   ANNIE GRACE HAMMACK, b. 16 May 1926, Hinds County, MS; m. WILLIAM RUSSELL.
        vii.   MINNIE LEE HAMMACK, b. 13 Aug 1930; m. ALLEN MOORE, 05 Apr 1969; b. 12 Dec 1912; d. 26 Aug 1974.
605.   viii.   JAMES MARLIN HAMMACK, b. 01 Sep 1936; d. 29 Jun 1974.
Key Sources: 1920 Hinds Co., MS, Census, p. 120; Family records of Felix Maben Hammack, Bend, OR.

528. CLARA BELLE[11] HAMMACK *(WILLIAM SIMMS[10], JOHN T.[9], SIMEON J.[8], WILLIAM T.[7], ROBERT HAMMACK[6] JR., ROBERT HAMMACK[5] SR., WILLIAM "THE ELDER"[4] HAMMACK, WILLIAM "O"[3], JOHN[2] HAMMOCKE, ? JOHN[1] HAMMOT)* was born 10 Apr 1892 in Hinds County, MS, and died 27 Apr 1989 in Hinds County, MS near Brownsville. She married ALGEY LOUIS BURGESS 17 Jun 1918 in Hinds County, MS, son of JOHN R. BURGESS. He was born 11 Feb 1890, and died 07 Feb 1959 in Hinds County, MS near Brownsville.
Children of CLARA HAMMACK and ALGEY BURGESS are:
606.   i.   WILBURN LOUIS[12] BURGESS, b. 27 Oct 1923, Hinds County, MS.
607.   ii.   FRANCIS NORMAN BURGESS, b. 18 Oct 1926, Hinds County, MS.
Key Sources: 1920 Hinds Co., MS, Census, p. 103; Family records of Felix Maben Hammack, Bend, OR.

529. DOLLIE CLIFFORD[11] HAMMACK *(WILLIAM SIMMS[10], JOHN T.[9], SIMEON J.[8], WILLIAM T.[7], ROBERT HAMMACK[6] JR., ROBERT HAMMACK[5] SR., WILLIAM "THE ELDER"[4] HAMMACK, WILLIAM "O"[3], JOHN[2] HAMMOCKE, ? JOHN[1] HAMMOT)* was born 01 Mar 1894 in Hinds County, MS near Brownsville, and died 09 Oct 1977 in Hinds County, MS near Brownsville. She married HARLEY CLEVELAND BURGESS 11 Feb 1912, son of JONATHAN BURGESS and ELIZABETH CROTWELL. He was born 26 May 1893, and died 04 Feb 1980 in Hinds County, MS near Brownsville.
Children of DOLLIE HAMMACK and HARLEY BURGESS are:
608.   i.   ROSALIE[12] BURGESS, b. 15 Apr 1913, Hinds County, MS near Brownsville.
609.   ii.   MERLE BURGESS, b. 03 Sep 1917, Madison County, MS near Flora.
Key Sources: 1920 Hinds Co., MS, Census, p. 103; Family records of Felix Maben Hammack, Bend, OR.

530. EDD BROWN[11] HAMMACK *(WILLIAM SIMMS[10], JOHN T.[9], SIMEON J.[8], WILLIAM T.[7], ROBERT HAMMACK[6] JR., ROBERT HAMMACK[5] SR., WILLIAM "THE ELDER"[4] HAMMACK, WILLIAM "O"[3], JOHN[2] HAMMOCKE, ? JOHN[1] HAMMOT)* was born 24 Dec 1897 in Hinds County, MS, and died May 1981 in Jackson, MS. He married M. MARJORIE HARDY 23 Dec 1933. She died Abt. 1983.
Child of EDD HAMMACK and M. HARDY is:
        i.   JAMES EDWARD[12] HAMMACK, b. 20 May 1941; d. Abt. 26 Jul 1994, Jackson, MS.
Key Source: Family records of Felix Maben Hammack, Bend, OR.

531. MYRTLE LOUISE[11] HAMMACK *(JOHN ROBERT[10], JOHN T.[9], SIMEON J.[8], WILLIAM T.[7], ROBERT HAMMACK[6] JR., ROBERT HAMMACK[5] SR., WILLIAM "THE ELDER"[4] HAMMACK, WILLIAM "O"[3], JOHN[2] HAMMOCKE, ? JOHN[1] HAMMOT)* was born 15 Nov 1896 in Bismarck, ND, and died 08 Sep 1978 in Bengough, Sask. She married JACOB JEROME (JACK) TELENGA 29 Jun 1914. He was born 23 Jan 1889 in Rockford, Illinois, and died 10 Jan 1957 in Bengough, Sask.
Children of MYRTLE HAMMACK and JACOB TELENGA are:
610.   i.   VICTORIA LENA[12] TELENGA, b. 20 Dec 1915, Turtle Lake, McLean County, ND; d. 10 Oct 1981, Ceylon, Sask.

611.   ii.   GEORGINA E. TELENGA, b. 26 Mar 1918, Paisley Brook, Sask.; d. 27 Mar 1999, Regina, Sask.
612.   iii. FLORENCE TELENGA, b. 19 Nov 1923, Big Beaver, Sask.
613.   iv.   FLOYD TELENGA, b. 30 Jul 1926, Big Beaver, Sask; d. 26 Dec 1976, Lethbridge, Alta..
614.   v.   JEROME TELENGA, b. 05 Jun 1934, Big Beaver, Sask; d. 24 Jan 1999, Regina, Sask.
615.   vi.   GLORIA TELENGA, b. 27 Feb 1940, Coronach, Sask.

Key Source: Family records of Jonas Hammack, Bend, OR.

532. ROMEY[11] HAMMACK *(JOHN ROBERT[10], JOHN T.[9], SIMEON J.[8], WILLIAM T.[7], ROBERT HAMMACK[6] JR., ROBERT HAMMACK[5] SR., WILLIAM "THE ELDER"[4] HAMMACK, WILLIAM "O"[3], JOHN[2] HAMMOCKE, ? JOHN[1] HAMMOT)* was born 11 Aug 1898 in ND, and died 01 Oct 1976 in Minot, ND. He married AGNES GUNDERSON.

Children of ROMEY HAMMACK and AGNES GUNDERSON are:
            i.   LAFAYETTE[12] HAMMACK.
            ii.   BLANCHE HAMMACK.

Key Source: Family records of Jonas Hammack, Bend, OR.

533. HARRY HERBERT[11] HAMMACK *(JOHN ROBERT[10], JOHN T.[9], SIMEON J.[8], WILLIAM T.[7], ROBERT HAMMACK[6] JR., ROBERT HAMMACK[5] SR., WILLIAM "THE ELDER"[4] HAMMACK, WILLIAM "O"[3], JOHN[2] HAMMOCKE, ? JOHN[1] HAMMOT)* was born 28 Aug 1900 in Bismarck, ND, and died 02 Nov 1936 in Kenmare, Ward County, ND. He married WALLENA "LENA" WATTERUDE 05 Aug 1922 in Bowbells, Burke County, ND. She was born 24 Oct 1903 in Fergus Falls, MN, and died 02 Jul 1965 in Eden Prairie, MN.

Children of HARRY HAMMACK and WALLENA WATTERUDE are:
616.   i.   DALE MCDONALD[12] HAMMACK, b. 15 Nov 1924, Columbus, ND.
617.   ii.   ALOHA DELPHINE HAMMACK, b. 25 Feb 1928, Columbus, Burke County, ND; d. 11 Mar 1987, St. Louis Park, MN.

Key Source: Family records of Jonas Hammack, Bend, OR.

534. EUGENE[11] HAMMACK *(JOHN ROBERT[10], JOHN T.[9], SIMEON J.[8], WILLIAM T.[7], ROBERT HAMMACK[6] JR., ROBERT HAMMACK[5] SR., WILLIAM "THE ELDER"[4] HAMMACK, WILLIAM "O"[3], JOHN[2] HAMMOCKE, ? JOHN[1] HAMMOT)* was born 25 Jul 1905 in Stanton, ND, and died 26 Feb 1986 in Stanley, ND. He married FLORA ALBERS. She was born 31 May 1908 in Illinois.

Children of EUGENE HAMMACK and FLORA ALBERS are:
618.   i.   CLAYTON DARREL "CLAY"[12] HAMMACK, b. 01 Jun 1931.
            ii.   DON HAMMACK, b. 10 Mar 1933.
619.   iii. PATRICIA HAMMACK, b. 19 Nov 1941.

Key Source: Family records of Jonas Hammack, Bend, OR.

535. WILBON[11] HAMMACK *(JOHN ROBERT[10], JOHN T.[9], SIMEON J.[8], WILLIAM T.[7], ROBERT HAMMACK[6] JR., ROBERT HAMMACK[5] SR., WILLIAM "THE ELDER"[4] HAMMACK, WILLIAM "O"[3], JOHN[2] HAMMOCKE, ? JOHN[1] HAMMOT)* was born 28 Sep 1907 in Ruso, McLean County, ND, and died 1987 in Portland, OR. He married MARGARET MAY, daughter of JULIUS MAY. She was born 1912 in Stanley, ND, and died 20 Sep 1995 in Portland, OR.

Children of WILBON HAMMACK and MARGARET MAY are:
            i.   ROGER WILBON[12] HAMMACK, b. 22 Nov 1936; d. 1955.
            ii.   GAIL HAMMACK, b. 24 May 1939; m. (1) ? ACKERMAN, Abt. 1959; m. (2) RON COWAN, Abt. 1988.

Key Source: Family records of Jonas Hammack, Bend, OR.

536. JONAS ALAN[11] HAMMACK *(JOHN ROBERT[10], JOHN T.[9], SIMEON J.[8], WILLIAM T.[7], ROBERT HAMMACK[6] JR., ROBERT HAMMACK[5] SR., WILLIAM "THE ELDER"[4] HAMMACK, WILLIAM "O"[3], JOHN[2] HAMMOCKE, ? JOHN[1] HAMMOT)* was born 02 Oct 1914 in Big Bend, Mercer County, ND. He married ANNIE BILODEAU 28 Oct 1939 in Bend, Oregon, daughter of ARTHUR BILODEAU and HELEN LECKBAND. She was born 31 Dec 1921 in Seattle, Washington, and died 19 Jul 1992 in Tumalo, Oregon.

Children of JONAS HAMMACK and ANNIE BILODEAU are:

620.   i.   ROSE[12] HAMMACK, b. 17 Feb 1943, Redmond, Oregon.

        ii.   ALAN HAMMACK, b. 13 Jul 1945, Bend, Oregon; m. (1) PARR NORTON, Portland, Oregon; m. (2) SANDY ROGERS, Abt. 1976.

        iii.   PATRICK HAMMACK, b. 21 Mar 1947, Bend, Oregon; m. CONNIE KELLUM.

Key Source: Family records of Jonas Hammack, Bend, OR.

537. GRANVILLE[11] NOLAN *(GERTRUDE A.[10] HAMMACK, FELIX WILBORN[9], SIMEON J.[8], WILLIAM T.[7], ROBERT HAMMACK[6] JR., ROBERT HAMMACK[5] SR., WILLIAM "THE ELDER"[4] HAMMACK, WILLIAM "O"[3], JOHN[2] HAMMOCKE, ? JOHN[1] HAMMOT)* was born Apr 1891 in Calhoun Co., MS, and died Aft. 1930 in Webster Co., MS. He married BERTHA [------] Abt. 1915 in Calhoun Co., MS. She was born Abt. 1895 in Mississippi, and died Aft. 1930 in Webster Co., MS.

Children of GRANVILLE NOLAN and BERTHA [------] are:

        i.   J. W.[12] NOLAN, b. Abt. 1915, Calhoun Co., MS; d. Aft. 1930, Webster Co., MS.

        ii.   MARY NOLAN, b. Abt. 1920, Webster Co., MS; d. Aft. 1930, Webster Co., MS.

        iii.   JAMES P. NOLAN, b. Abt. 1922, Webster Co., MS; d. Aft. 1930, Webster Co., MS.

Key Sources: 1920 Webster Co., MS, Census, p. 246; 1930 Webster Co., MS, Census, p. 75.

538. WILLIAM ROSCOE[11] DAVIS *(BETSY ANN[10] HAMMACK, FELIX WILBORN[9], SIMEON J.[8], WILLIAM T.[7], ROBERT HAMMACK[6] JR., ROBERT HAMMACK[5] SR., WILLIAM "THE ELDER"[4] HAMMACK, WILLIAM "O"[3], JOHN[2] HAMMOCKE, ? JOHN[1] HAMMOT)* was born 13 Jul 1893 in Calhoun Co., MS, and died 04 Aug 1959 in Calhoun Co., MS. He married BERTHA MAY VANCE Abt. 1916 in Calhoun Co., MS. She was born 02 Dec 1892 in Calhoun Co., MS, and died 19 Apr 1946 in Sabougla, Calhoun Co., MS.

Children of WILLIAM DAVIS and BERTHA VANCE are:

        i.   WILLIAM ROSCOE DAVIS[12] JR., b. 01 Dec 1917, Calhoun Co., MS; d. 17 Oct 1918, Calhoun Co., MS.

621.   ii.   JAMES VANCE DAVIS, b. 18 Mar 1919, Calhoun Co., MS.

622.   iii.   WILLIAM ROSCOE DAVIS JR., b. 16 May 1927, Calhoun Co., MS.

Key Sources: 1920 Calhoun Co., MS, Census, p. 211; Family records of William Roscoe Davis, Jr., Grenada, MS.

539. ERNEST F.[11] HAMMOCK *(FELIX A.[10], ALFRED WASHINGTON "DOCK"[9] HAMMACK, SIMEON J.[8], WILLIAM T.[7], ROBERT HAMMACK[6] JR., ROBERT HAMMACK[5] SR., WILLIAM "THE ELDER"[4] HAMMACK, WILLIAM "O"[3], JOHN[2] HAMMOCKE, ? JOHN[1] HAMMOT)* was born 1900 in Ashley County, AR, and died Aft. 1920 in Ashley County, AR. He married ICIE M. [------] Abt. 1920 in Arkansas. She was born 08 Sep 1903 in Arkansas, and died 18 Feb 1955 in Ashley County, AR.

Children of ERNEST HAMMOCK and ICIE [------] are:

        i.   ERVIN[12] HAMMOCK.

        ii.   PRESTON HAMMOCK.

        iii.   CHARLES HAMMOCK.

        iv.   ALBERT HAMMOCK.

        v.   MACARTHUR HAMMOCK.

      vi.   ERNESTINE HAMMOCK.

      vii. NELLIE HAMMOCK.

    viii. JEFFIE HAMMOCK.

      ix. SARAH HAMMOCK.

623.   x. JOHN ALFRED HAMMOCK, b. 29 Apr 1922, Ashley Co., AR; d. Apr 1978, Ashley Co., AR.

      xi. S. T. HAMMOCK, b. 1926, Ashley County, AR; d. 1978, Ashley County, AR.

     xii. DOCK HAMMOCK, b. 1933, Ashley County, AR; d. 1976, Ashley County, AR.

Key Source: Lois Hagood, *The Elusive Ancestor* (Crossett, AR, 1992); Lois Hagood, "C. W. Roberts Family," in Robert A. and Mary I. Carpenter, *Reflections of Ashley County* (Dallas, TX, 1988), F544.

540. WILLIE B.[11] HAMMOCK *(FELIX A.[10], ALFRED WASHINGTON "DOCK"[9] HAMMACK, SIMEON J.[8], WILLIAM T.[7], ROBERT HAMMACK[6] JR., ROBERT HAMMACK[5] SR., WILLIAM "THE ELDER"[4] HAMMACK, WILLIAM "O"[3], JOHN[2] HAMMOCKE, ? JOHN[1] HAMMOT)* was born 1902 in Ashley Co., AR, and died Aft. 1920 in Ashley Co., AR. She married WILLIAM "BILL" SMITH.
Children of WILLIE HAMMOCK and WILLIAM SMITH are:

624.   i. FRANCES[12] SMITH.

      ii. MARJORIE SMITH.

625.   iii. VIRGINIA SMITH.

626.   iv. BETTI SMITH.

Key Source: Lois Hagood, *The Elusive Ancestor* (Crossett, AR, 1992); Lois Hagood, "C. W. Roberts Family," in Robert A. and Mary I. Carpenter, *Reflections of Ashley County* (Dallas, TX, 1988), F544.

541. JAMES PELL[11] HAMMOCK *(FELIX A.[10], ALFRED WASHINGTON "DOCK"[9] HAMMACK, SIMEON J.[8], WILLIAM T.[7], ROBERT HAMMACK[6] JR., ROBERT HAMMACK[5] SR., WILLIAM "THE ELDER"[4] HAMMACK, WILLIAM "O"[3], JOHN[2] HAMMOCKE, ? JOHN[1] HAMMOT)* was born 31 Jul 1907 in Ashley Co., AR, and died 02 Jan 1981 in Monticello, AR. He married PAULINE GREGORY, daughter of LEE GREGORY and MINNIE WRIGHT. She was born 28 Jan 1927.
Children of JAMES HAMMOCK and PAULINE GREGORY are:

627.   i. ANNIE MAE[12] HAMMOCK, b. 09 Aug 1944, Montrose, AR.

628.   ii. JAMES ALFORD HAMMOCK, b. 18 May 1946, Montrose, AR.

629.   iii. EDITH P HAMMOCK, b. 30 Oct 1947, Montrose, AR; d. 22 Mar 2003, Monticello, AR.

     iv. FRANCES HELEN HAMMOCK, b. 23 Sep 1948, Dermott, AR.

      v. ELIZABETH DIANE HAMMOCK, b. Aug 1949, Montrose, AR; d. 12 Sep 1949, Montrose, AR.

     vi. BETTY JO HAMMOCK, b. 23 Mar 1950, Monticello, AR.

    vii. CARL EDWARD HAMMOCK, b. 25 Mar 1952, Monticello, AR; d. 24 Jan 1957, Monticello, AR.

   viii. ANNIE JEANETTE HAMMOCK, b. 12 May 1953, Monticello, AR.

     ix. HAROLD LEE HAMMOCK, b. 26 Jun 1954, Monticello, AR.

Key Source: Lois Hagood, *The Elusive Ancestor* (Crossett, AR, 1992); Lois Hagood, "C. W. Roberts Family," in Robert A. and Mary I. Carpenter, *Reflections of Ashley County* (Dallas, TX, 1988), F544.

542. GERTRUDE[11] MORMON *(BETTIE[10] HAMMOCK, ALFRED WASHINGTON "DOCK"[9] HAMMACK, SIMEON J.[8], WILLIAM T.[7], ROBERT HAMMACK[6] JR., ROBERT HAMMACK[5] SR., WILLIAM "THE ELDER"[4] HAMMACK, WILLIAM "O"[3], JOHN[2] HAMMOCKE, ? JOHN[1] HAMMOT)* was born 18 Sep 1888 in Ashley Co., AR, and died 09 Dec 1975 in Ashley Co., AR. She married TOM DILLON.
Children of GERTRUDE MORMON and TOM DILLON are:

i.   PATRICK[12] DILLON.
ii. HAWKINS DILLON.
iii. JOHN DILLON.
iv. MATTIE OPAL DILLON.
v.   BETTI DILLON.
vi. T. R. DILLON.

Key Source: Lois Hagood, *The Elusive Ancestor* (Crossett, AR, 1992); Lois Hagood, "C. W. Roberts Family," in Robert A. and Mary I. Carpenter, *Reflections of Ashley County* (Dallas, TX, 1988), F544.

543. RUTH[11] ROBERTS (*JEFFIE JANE[10] HAMMOCK, ALFRED WASHINGTON "DOCK"[9] HAMMACK, SIMEON J.[8], WILLIAM T.[7], ROBERT HAMMACK[6] JR., ROBERT HAMMACK[5] SR., WILLIAM "THE ELDER"[4] HAMMACK, WILLIAM "O"[3], JOHN[2] HAMMOCKE, ? JOHN[1] HAMMOT*) was born 15 Jul 1894 in Ashley County, AR, and died 20 May 1986 in Ashley County, AR. She married WILLIAM THOMAS HONEYCUTT, SR. 12 Oct 1913 in Ashley County, AR, son of THOMAS HONEYCUTT and MARGARET JOHNSTON. He was born 04 Nov 1892 in Arkansas, and died 01 Jul 1968 in Boulder City, NV.
Children of RUTH ROBERTS and WILLIAM HONEYCUTT are:

      i.   INFANT[12] HONEYCUTT, b. 18 Sep 1914, Ashley Co., AR; d. 18 Sep 1914, Ashley Co., AR.
630. ii. OLIVIA HONEYCUTT, b. 21 Sep 1915, Ashley County, AR; d. 20 May 1949, Ashley Co., AR.
631. iii. WILLIAM THOMAS HONEYCUTT, JR., b. 28 Jan 1917, Ashley County, AR; d. 06 Oct 1992, Ouachita Co., AR.
632. iv. LOIS RUTH HONEYCUTT, b. 23 Feb 1919, Ashley County, AR; d. 23 Jun 1996, Ashley County, AR.

Key Source: Lois Hagood, *The Elusive Ancestor* (Crossett, AR, 1992); Lois Hagood, "C. W. Roberts Family," in Robert A. and Mary I. Carpenter, *Reflections of Ashley County* (Dallas, TX, 1988), F544.

544. CLAUD CYRUS[11] ROBERTS (*JEFFIE JANE[10] HAMMOCK, ALFRED WASHINGTON "DOCK"[9] HAMMACK, SIMEON J.[8], WILLIAM T.[7], ROBERT HAMMACK[6] JR., ROBERT HAMMACK[5] SR., WILLIAM "THE ELDER"[4] HAMMACK, WILLIAM "O"[3], JOHN[2] HAMMOCKE, ? JOHN[1] HAMMOT*) was born 14 Mar 1896 in Ashley Co., AR, and died 21 Mar 1950 in Ashley County, AR. He married ADDIE E. STOVER 06 Jul 1919 in Ashley Co., AR, daughter of MCMILLON STOVER and FLORENCE TACKETT.
Children of CLAUD ROBERTS and ADDIE STOVER are:
633. i.   MARGARET LAVENIAL[12] ROBERTS, b. 13 Jul 1920, Ashley Co., AR; d. 22 Jun 1980, Ashley Co., AR.
634. ii. LAVONIA JOYCE ROBERTS, b. 31 May 1926, Ashley Co., AR.
635. iii. ELIZABETH LANE ROBERTS, b. 27 Jul 1930, Ashley Co., AR.

Key Source: Lois Hagood, *The Elusive Ancestor* (Crossett, AR, 1992); Lois Hagood, "C. W. Roberts Family," in Robert A. and Mary I. Carpenter, *Reflections of Ashley County* (Dallas, TX, 1988), F544.

545. SYLVESTER ALFRED[11] ROBERTS (*JEFFIE JANE[10] HAMMOCK, ALFRED WASHINGTON "DOCK"[9] HAMMACK, SIMEON J.[8], WILLIAM T.[7], ROBERT HAMMACK[6] JR., ROBERT HAMMACK[5] SR., WILLIAM "THE ELDER"[4] HAMMACK, WILLIAM "O"[3], JOHN[2] HAMMOCKE, ? JOHN[1] HAMMOT*) was born 05 May 1898 in Ashley Co., AR, and died 10 Nov 1978 in Orange Co., FL. He married IRMA JO MACHEN 18 Jun 1930 in Ashley Co., AR, daughter of GUM MACHEN and ELIZABETH NOBEL. She was born 16 Apr 1903 in Ashley Co., AR, and died 08 Aug 1985 in Orange Co., FL.

Child of SYLVESTER ROBERTS and IRMA MACHEN is:
636.   i.   BARBARA JANE[12] ROBERTS, b. 05 Feb 1939, Ashley Co., AR.
Key Source: Lois Hagood, *The Elusive Ancestor* (Crossett, AR, 1992); Lois Hagood, "C. W. Roberts Family," in Robert A. and Mary I. Carpenter, *Reflections of Ashley County* (Dallas, TX, 1988), F544.

546. WILLIAM TRACY[11] ROBERTS *(JEFFIE JANE[10] HAMMOCK, ALFRED WASHINGTON "DOCK"[9] HAMMACK, SIMEON J.[8], WILLIAM T.[7], ROBERT HAMMACK[6] JR., ROBERT HAMMACK[5] SR., WILLIAM "THE ELDER"[4] HAMMACK, WILLIAM "O"[3], JOHN[2] HAMMOCKE, ? JOHN[1] HAMMOT)* was born 15 Jan 1902 in Ashley Co., AR, and died 26 Aug 1963 in Big Springs, TX. He married OLLIE ADELE THOMAS, daughter of CLYDE E. THOMAS, SR.. She was born 05 Jun 1912 in Lampasas, TX.
Children of WILLIAM ROBERTS and OLLIE THOMAS are:
637.   i.   REBA JEAN[12] ROBERTS, b. 29 Oct 1929, Big Springs, TX.
638.   ii.   DONNIE JANE ROBERTS, b. 11 Jul 1930, Big Springs, TX.
639.   iii. MARY KATHERINE ROBERTS, b. 03 Mar 1934, Big Springs, TX.
Key Source: Lois Hagood, *The Elusive Ancestor* (Crossett, AR, 1992); Lois Hagood, "C. W. Roberts Family," in Robert A. and Mary I. Carpenter, *Reflections of Ashley County* (Dallas, TX, 1988), F544.

547. VIRGIL ASBERRY[11] ROBERTS *(JEFFIE JANE[10] HAMMOCK, ALFRED WASHINGTON "DOCK"[9] HAMMACK, SIMEON J.[8], WILLIAM T.[7], ROBERT HAMMACK[6] JR., ROBERT HAMMACK[5] SR., WILLIAM "THE ELDER"[4] HAMMACK, WILLIAM "O"[3], JOHN[2] HAMMOCKE, ? JOHN[1] HAMMOT)* was born 09 May 1904 in Ashley Co., AR, and died 18 Oct 1984 in Dallas Co., TX. He married GRACE EVELYN FRANKLIN Abt. 1935 in Madel, OK. She was born 05 Aug 1908 in Sadler, TX, and died 14 Oct 1982 in Dallas, TX.
Children of VIRGIL ROBERTS and GRACE FRANKLIN are:
640.   i.   MARTHA ANN[12] ROBERTS, b. 29 Apr 1937, Dallas, TX.
641.   ii.   JANE FRANKLIN ROBERTS, b. 22 Mar 1942, Dallas, TX.
Key Source: Lois Hagood, *The Elusive Ancestor* (Crossett, AR, 1992); Lois Hagood, "C. W. Roberts Family," in Robert A. and Mary I. Carpenter, *Reflections of Ashley County* (Dallas, TX, 1988), F544.

548. HATTIE MAE[11] ROBERTS *(JEFFIE JANE[10] HAMMOCK, ALFRED WASHINGTON "DOCK"[9] HAMMACK, SIMEON J.[8], WILLIAM T.[7], ROBERT HAMMACK[6] JR., ROBERT HAMMACK[5] SR., WILLIAM "THE ELDER"[4] HAMMACK, WILLIAM "O"[3], JOHN[2] HAMMOCKE, ? JOHN[1] HAMMOT)* was born 10 Sep 1906 in Ashley Co., AR, and died 18 Dec 1924 in Ashley County, AR. She married BROOKLYN KELLEY Abt. 1922 in Ashley Co., AR, son of IKE KELLEY and EULA DOSS.
Child of HATTIE ROBERTS and BROOKLYN KELLEY is:
642.   i.   EDWARD LAVERNE[12] KELLEY, b. 05 Oct 1924, Ashley County, AR.
Key Source: Lois Hagood, *The Elusive Ancestor* (Crossett, AR, 1992); Lois Hagood, "C. W. Roberts Family," in Robert A. and Mary I. Carpenter, *Reflections of Ashley County* (Dallas, TX, 1988), F544.

549. CLARA BELL[11] ROBERTS *(JEFFIE JANE[10] HAMMOCK, ALFRED WASHINGTON "DOCK"[9] HAMMACK, SIMEON J.[8], WILLIAM T.[7], ROBERT HAMMACK[6] JR., ROBERT HAMMACK[5] SR., WILLIAM "THE ELDER"[4] HAMMACK, WILLIAM "O"[3], JOHN[2] HAMMOCKE, ? JOHN[1] HAMMOT)* was born 11 Nov 1911 in Ashley Co., AR, and died 18 May 1993 in Ashley Co., AR. She married LESLIE CLYDE JOHNSON 13 Feb 1936 in Strong, AR.
Children of CLARA ROBERTS and LESLIE JOHNSON are:
643.   i.   VRELAN CLYDE[12] JOHNSON, b. 25 May 1922, Ashley Co., AR.
644.   ii.   TRAVIS FLOYD JOHNSON, b. 12 Nov 1924, Ashley Co., AR.
645.   iii. JAMES RUSSELL JOHNSON, b. 13 Apr 1938, Ashley Co., AR.

Key Source: Lois Hagood, *The Elusive Ancestor* (Crossett, AR, 1992); Lois Hagood, "C. W. Roberts Family," in Robert A. and Mary I. Carpenter, *Reflections of Ashley County* (Dallas, TX, 1988), F544.

550. JESSE WILLARD[11] ROBERTS *(JEFFIE JANE[10] HAMMOCK, ALFRED WASHINGTON "DOCK"[9] HAMMACK, SIMEON J.[8], WILLIAM T.[7], ROBERT HAMMACK[6] JR., ROBERT HAMMACK[5] SR., WILLIAM "THE ELDER"[4] HAMMACK, WILLIAM "O"[3], JOHN[2] HAMMOCKE, ? JOHN[1] HAMMOT)* was born 03 May 1917 in Ashley Co., AR, and died 03 Nov 1981 in Ashley County, AR. He married MARY LOUISE WATSON 13 Aug 1937 in Ashley Co., AR, daughter of WILLIAM WATSON and EVA HIGHEN.
Child of JESSE ROBERTS and MARY WATSON is:
646.   i.   LINDA CAROLYN[12] ROBERTS, b. 24 Mar 1944, Ashley Co., AR.

Key Source: Lois Hagood, *The Elusive Ancestor* (Crossett, AR, 1992); Lois Hagood, "C. W. Roberts Family," in Robert A. and Mary I. Carpenter, *Reflections of Ashley County* (Dallas, TX, 1988), F544.

551. BENNIE[11] FERGUSON *(VIRGINIA MARGARET "JENNY"[10] HAMMOCK, ALFRED WASHINGTON "DOCK"[9] HAMMACK, SIMEON J.[8], WILLIAM T.[7], ROBERT HAMMACK[6] JR., ROBERT HAMMACK[5] SR., WILLIAM "THE ELDER"[4] HAMMACK, WILLIAM "O"[3], JOHN[2] HAMMOCKE, ? JOHN[1] HAMMOT)* was born 30 Oct 1905 in Ashley County, AR, and died 03 Oct 1964 in Monticello, Drew County, AR. He married HATTIE MILES. She was born 04 Mar 1910 in Leland, MS, and died 17 Dec 1984 in Drew Co., AR.
Children of BENNIE FERGUSON and HATTIE MILES are:
   i.   CHRISTINE[12] FERGUSON, b. 21 Sep 1936, Drew Co., AR; m. CLEVE KENDALL, 24 Dec 1953.
   ii.   BEN FRANK (BUD) FERGUSON, b. 21 Nov 1938, Drew Co., AR; m. REBECCA SHINN.
   iii.   ELEANOR EMMAGENE (PEGGY) FERGUSON, b. 19 Aug 1943, Drew Co., AR; m. KEITH BURKE.
   iv.   ROBERT FERGUSON, b. 04 Aug 1945, Drew Co., AR; m. NANCY ?.
   v.   HATTIE MAE FERGUSON, b. 08 Jan 1948, Drew Co., AR; m. HARRY WOODS.

Key Source: Lois Hagood, *The Elusive Ancestor* (Crossett, AR, 1992); Lois Hagood, "C. W. Roberts Family," in Robert A. and Mary I. Carpenter, *Reflections of Ashley County* (Dallas, TX, 1988), F544.

552. VERGIE MAE[11] FERGUSON *(VIRGINIA MARGARET "JENNY"[10] HAMMOCK, ALFRED WASHINGTON "DOCK"[9] HAMMACK, SIMEON J.[8], WILLIAM T.[7], ROBERT HAMMACK[6] JR., ROBERT HAMMACK[5] SR., WILLIAM "THE ELDER"[4] HAMMACK, WILLIAM "O"[3], JOHN[2] HAMMOCKE, ? JOHN[1] HAMMOT)* was born 1908 in Ashley Co., AR. She married CLIFTON DOUGLAS.
Children of VERGIE FERGUSON and CLIFTON DOUGLAS are:
647.   i.   WAYMON[12] DOUGLAS.
   ii.   NANCY MARY DOUGLAS.
648.   iii.   CHARLOTTE ANN DOUGLAS.
649.   iv.   THAD ANDERSON DOUGLAS, b. 1930.

Key Source: Lois Hagood, *The Elusive Ancestor* (Crossett, AR, 1992); Lois Hagood, "C. W. Roberts Family," in Robert A. and Mary I. Carpenter, *Reflections of Ashley County* (Dallas, TX, 1988), F544.

553. LILLIE BELL[11] FERGUSON *(VIRGINIA MARGARET "JENNY"[10] HAMMOCK, ALFRED WASHINGTON "DOCK"[9] HAMMACK, SIMEON J.[8], WILLIAM T.[7], ROBERT HAMMACK[6] JR., ROBERT HAMMACK[5] SR., WILLIAM "THE ELDER"[4] HAMMACK, WILLIAM "O"[3], JOHN[2] HAMMOCKE, ? JOHN[1] HAMMOT)* was born 03 Sep 1909 in Ashley Co., AR, and died 1988 in Ashley Co., AR. She married SEARCY HARMON.
Children of LILLIE FERGUSON and SEARCY HARMON are:

     i. LOIS PERNICEY[12] HARMON.

    ii. LAVERNE HARMON.

   iii. PAULENE HARMON.

   iv. JAMES HARMON.

    v. DEAN HARMON.

   vi. LAMAR HARMON.

  vii. LEON HARMON.

 viii. TROY HARMON.

   ix. DAVID HARMON.

Key Source: Lois Hagood, *The Elusive Ancestor* (Crossett, AR, 1992); Lois Hagood, "C. W. Roberts Family," in Robert A. and Mary I. Carpenter, *Reflections of Ashley County* (Dallas, TX, 1988), F544.

554. WALTER DAVID[11] PEDEN *(VIRGINIA MARGARET "JENNY"[10] HAMMOCK, ALFRED WASHINGTON "DOCK"[9] HAMMACK, SIMEON J.[8], WILLIAM T.[7], ROBERT HAMMACK[6] JR., ROBERT HAMMACK[5] SR., WILLIAM "THE ELDER"[4] HAMMACK, WILLIAM "O"[3], JOHN[2] HAMMOCKE, ? JOHN[1] HAMMOT)* was born 09 Dec 1914 in Ashley County, AR, and died Aft. 1953 in Kansas City, KS. He married MARY EVA FOX 09 Feb 1936 in Ashley County, AR.

Children of WALTER PEDEN and MARY FOX are:

     i. WALTER DEAN[12] PEDEN, b. 09 Mar 1937, Boydell, AR.

    ii. MARY VIRGINIA PEDEN, b. 27 Sep 1938, Boydell, AR.

   iii. JOHN EDWARD PEDEN, b. 29 Sep 1940, Boydell, AR.

   iv. WILLIAM J. PEDEN, b. 19 Jun 1943, Boydell, AR.

    v. CATHERINE LORAINE PEDEN, b. 05 Feb 1946, Boydell, AR.

   vi. EVELYN ALLENE PEDEN, b. 17 Feb 1948, Boydell, AR.

  vii. VALERIE PEDEN, b. 17 Oct 1953, Kansas City, KS.

Key Source: Lois Hagood, *The Elusive Ancestor* (Crossett, AR, 1992); Lois Hagood, "C. W. Roberts Family," in Robert A. and Mary I. Carpenter, *Reflections of Ashley County* (Dallas, TX, 1988), F544.

555. MARTHA AGNES[11] PEDEN *(VIRGINIA MARGARET "JENNY"[10] HAMMOCK, ALFRED WASHINGTON "DOCK"[9] HAMMACK, SIMEON J.[8], WILLIAM T.[7], ROBERT HAMMACK[6] JR., ROBERT HAMMACK[5] SR., WILLIAM "THE ELDER"[4] HAMMACK, WILLIAM "O"[3], JOHN[2] HAMMOCKE, ? JOHN[1] HAMMOT)* was born 1917 in Ashley Co., AR, and died Aft. 1942 in Pulaski Co., AR. She married ERNEST J. KELLEY.

Children of MARTHA PEDEN and ERNEST KELLEY are:

650.   i. JIMMY NEAL[12] KELLEY, b. 23 May 1938, Pulaski Co., AR.

651.   ii. RITA JUNE KELLEY, b. 17 Oct 1942, Pulaski Co., AR.

Key Source: Lois Hagood, *The Elusive Ancestor* (Crossett, AR, 1992); Lois Hagood, "C. W. Roberts Family," in Robert A. and Mary I. Carpenter, *Reflections of Ashley County* (Dallas, TX, 1988), F544.

556. GEORGE[11] HAMMACK *(LESLIE L.[10], GEORGE W. T.[9], SIMEON J.[8], WILLIAM T.[7], ROBERT HAMMACK[6] JR., ROBERT HAMMACK[5] SR., WILLIAM "THE ELDER"[4] HAMMACK, WILLIAM "O"[3], JOHN[2] HAMMOCKE, ? JOHN[1] HAMMOT)* was born 08 May 1911 in Calhoun Co., MS, and died Dec 1983 in Jefferson Co., AL. He married PEARL WATKINS. She was born 22 Jun 1909 in Mississippi, and died 22 Mar 1996 in Jefferson Co., AL.

Children of GEORGE HAMMACK and PEARL WATKINS are:

     i. JANE[12] HAMMACK, b. Abt. 1932, Mississippi; m. HARRY BEACHAM.

    ii. B. LESLIE HAMMACK, b. 07 Mar 1934, Mississippi.

   iii. MARY FRANCES HAMMACK, b. 06 Feb 1936, Mississippi; m. ? HAWKINS.

Key Source: Family records of Bobbie Nell Hammack Hood, Duncan, MS.

557. OTIS EUGENE[11] LOMENICK *(ELLA ELIZABETH[10] HAMMACK, GEORGE W. T.[9], SIMEON J.[8], WILLIAM T.[7], ROBERT HAMMACK[6] JR., ROBERT HAMMACK[5] SR., WILLIAM "THE ELDER"[4] HAMMACK, WILLIAM "O"[3], JOHN[2] HAMMOCKE, ? JOHN[1] HAMMOT)* was born 05 Nov 1911 in Mississippi, and died 05 Aug 1980 in St. Tammany Parish, LA. He married EUGENIE BRIANT. She was born 29 Jul 1915 in Louisiana, and died 10 Apr 2003 in St. Tammany Parish, LA.

Children of OTIS LOMENICK and EUGENIE BRIANT are:
     i.   OTIS EUGENE[12] LOMENICK.
     ii.   STEPHEN LOMENICK.
     iii.   CYNTHIA LOMENICK, m. [----] DURTSCHE.
     iv.   MICHELLE LOMENICK, m. [-----] MITCHELL.

Key Source: "Eugenie Briant Lomenick," *Times Picayune*, 11 April 2003.

558. MALCOLM ALBERT[11] LOMENICK *(ELLA ELIZABETH[10] HAMMACK, GEORGE W. T.[9], SIMEON J.[8], WILLIAM T.[7], ROBERT HAMMACK[6] JR., ROBERT HAMMACK[5] SR., WILLIAM "THE ELDER"[4] HAMMACK, WILLIAM "O"[3], JOHN[2] HAMMOCKE, ? JOHN[1] HAMMOT)* was born 14 Mar 1916 in Mississippi, and died 03 Jan 1996 in Crittenden Co., AR. He married MELISSA RUTH MCCAIN 24 Jan 1938 in Sunflower Co., MS. She was born 04 Nov 1921 in Sunflower Co., MS, and died 10 Feb 1992 in Crittenden Co., AR.

Children of MALCOLM LOMENICK and MELISSA MCCAIN are:
     i.   DONALD D.[12] LOMENICK.
     ii.   DAUGHTER LOMENICK.
     iii.   DAUGHTER LOMENICK.

Key Source: Family records of Bobbie Nell Hammack Hood, Duncan, MS.

559. JAMES T.[11] BRACHT *(SARA[10] HAMMACK, GEORGE W. T.[9], SIMEON J.[8], WILLIAM T.[7], ROBERT HAMMACK[6] JR., ROBERT HAMMACK[5] SR., WILLIAM "THE ELDER"[4] HAMMACK, WILLIAM "O"[3], JOHN[2] HAMMOCKE, ? JOHN[1] HAMMOT)* was born 19 Oct 1914 in Colbert Co., AL, and died 13 Dec 1994 in Hamilton Co., OH. He married EVELYN BUFFINGTON. She was born 16 Jun 1916 in Ohio, and died 02 Jan 2004 in Hamilton Co., OH.

Children of JAMES BRACHT and EVELYN BUFFINGTON are:
     i.   JAMES L.[12] BRACHT, m. LOIS [------].
652.   ii.   LINDA BRACHT.

Key Source: "Evelyn Bracht," *Cincinnati Post*, 5 January 2004.

560. CLARICE[11] HAMMACK *(JESSE G.[10], GEORGE W. T.[9], SIMEON J.[8], WILLIAM T.[7], ROBERT HAMMACK[6] JR., ROBERT HAMMACK[5] SR., WILLIAM "THE ELDER"[4] HAMMACK, WILLIAM "O"[3], JOHN[2] HAMMOCKE, ? JOHN[1] HAMMOT)* was born Abt. 1914 in Tallahatchie Co., Mississippi, and died Aft. 1946 in Tallahatchie Co., Mississippi. She married ROBERT SMITH.

Children of CLARICE HAMMACK and ROBERT SMITH are:
     i.   LILLIAN[12] SMITH, b. Abt. 1935.
     ii.   DOROTHY SMITH, b. Abt. 1938.

Key Source: Family records of Bobbie Nell Hammack Hood, Duncan, MS.

561. MYRTLE IRIS[11] PARKER *(MARY CLEVIE[10] HAMMACK, GEORGE W. T.[9], SIMEON J.[8], WILLIAM T.[7], ROBERT HAMMACK[6] JR., ROBERT HAMMACK[5] SR., WILLIAM "THE ELDER"[4] HAMMACK, WILLIAM "O"[3], JOHN[2] HAMMOCKE, ? JOHN[1] HAMMOT)* was born 28 Jun 1905 in Calhoun Co., MS, and died 24 Aug 1997 in Calhoun City, MS. She married CELL ROANE LOVORN, SR..

Children of MYRTLE PARKER and CELL LOVORN are:

     i. ROANE[12] LOVORN, JR..

     ii. TOM LOVORN.

Key Source: "A. E. Parker," *Calhoun Monitor*, 12 February 1942; Family records of Bobbie Nell Hammack Hood, Duncan, MS.

562. WALTER AUSTELL[11] HAMMACK *(FRANCIS FOLSOM[10], GEORGE W. T.[9], SIMEON J.[8], WILLIAM T.[7], ROBERT HAMMACK[6] JR., ROBERT HAMMACK[5] SR., WILLIAM "THE ELDER"[4] HAMMACK, WILLIAM "O"[3], JOHN[2] HAMMOCKE, ? JOHN[1] HAMMOT)* was born 05 Dec 1916 in Tutwiler, Tallahatchie County, MS, and died 07 Aug 1996 in Memphis, TN. He married ERNESTINE KNIGHT.

Children of WALTER HAMMACK and ERNESTINE KNIGHT are:

     i. RAY ALLEN[12] HAMMACK, b. Abt. 1940.

     ii. RODNEY HAMMACK, b. Abt. 1946.

Key Source: Family records of Bobbie Nell Hammack Hood, Duncan, MS.

563. CHARLES RAY[11] HAMMACK *(FRANCIS FOLSOM[10], GEORGE W. T.[9], SIMEON J.[8], WILLIAM T.[7], ROBERT HAMMACK[6] JR., ROBERT HAMMACK[5] SR., WILLIAM "THE ELDER"[4] HAMMACK, WILLIAM "O"[3], JOHN[2] HAMMOCKE, ? JOHN[1] HAMMOT)* was born 25 Jul 1921 in Tutwiler, Tallahatchie County, MS, and died 17 Jan 1992 in Tuscaloosa, AL. He married ELLEN DANIEL Abt. 1946.

Children of CHARLES HAMMACK and ELLEN DANIEL are:

     i. JEFF[12] HAMMACK.

     ii. PATTI HAMMACK, m. ? HALLEAD.

     iii. TERRI HAMMACK, m. ? MORRISON.

Key Source: Family records of Bobbie Nell Hammack Hood, Duncan, MS.

564. BOBBIE NELL[11] HAMMACK *(FRANCIS FOLSOM[10], GEORGE W. T.[9], SIMEON J.[8], WILLIAM T.[7], ROBERT HAMMACK[6] JR., ROBERT HAMMACK[5] SR., WILLIAM "THE ELDER"[4] HAMMACK, WILLIAM "O"[3], JOHN[2] HAMMOCKE, ? JOHN[1] HAMMOT)* was born 28 Jan 1929 in Tutwiler, Tallahatchie County, MS. She married GEORGE ADAM HOOD 23 Mar 1951 in Mississippi.

Child of BOBBIE HAMMACK and GEORGE HOOD is:

     i. MARJORIE NELL[12] HOOD, b. 24 Sep 1952, Dallas Co., TX.

Key Source: Family records of Bobbie Nell Hammack Hood, Duncan, MS.

Generation No. 12

565. FREDERICK TABOR[12] HAMMACK *(FREDERICK WILLIAM[11], JAMES WILBURN[10], WILLIAM T. H.[9], SIMEON J.[8], WILLIAM T.[7], ROBERT HAMMACK[6] JR., ROBERT HAMMACK[5] SR., WILLIAM "THE ELDER"[4] HAMMACK, WILLIAM "O"[3], JOHN[2] HAMMOCKE, ? JOHN[1] HAMMOT)* was born 08 Apr 1905 in Madison Co., MS, and died 12 Nov 1955 in Flora, Madison County, MS. He married LOUISE LANE, daughter of ELIAS LANE and EDNA CHAPMAN. She was born 01 Apr 1905 in Madison Co., MS, and died 08 Aug 1959 in Flora, Madison County, MS.

Child of FREDERICK HAMMACK and LOUISE LANE is:

     i. FREDERICK TABOR[13] HAMMACK, JR., b. 15 Jul 1931, Madison Co., MS; d. 08 Jul 1953, Flora, Madison County, MS.

Key Source: Telephone Interview with Helen Wren Hammack, Flora, MS, July 1996.

566. FRANCES V.[12] HAMMACK *(FREDERICK WILLIAM[11], JAMES WILBURN[10], WILLIAM T. H.[9], SIMEON J.[8], WILLIAM T.[7], ROBERT HAMMACK[6] JR., ROBERT HAMMACK[5] SR., WILLIAM "THE*

ELDER"[4] *HAMMACK, WILLIAM "O"*[3], *JOHN*[2] *HAMMOCKE, ? JOHN*[1] *HAMMOT)* was born 19 Sep 1906 in Madison Co., MS, and died 27 Feb 1976 in Flora, Madison County, MS. She married EDWARD CLORE. He was born 29 Dec 1907 in Mississippi, and died 07 Jan 1975 in Madison Co., MS.

Children of FRANCES HAMMACK and EDWARD CLORE are:

    i.   CARA[13] CLORE.

    ii. EVANNE CLORE.

Key Source: Telephone Interview with Helen Wren Hammack, Flora, MS, July 1996.

567. FREDERICK WILLIAM[12] HAMMACK, JR. *(FREDERICK WILLIAM*[11], *JAMES WILBURN*[10], *WILLIAM T. H.*[9], *SIMEON J.*[8], *WILLIAM T.*[7], *ROBERT HAMMACK*[6] *JR., ROBERT HAMMACK*[5] *SR., WILLIAM "THE ELDER"*[4] *HAMMACK, WILLIAM "O"*[3], *JOHN*[2] *HAMMOCKE, ? JOHN*[1] *HAMMOT)* was born 16 Jan 1918 in Madison Co., MS, and died 11 Nov 1994 in Flora, Madison County, MS. He married HELEN WREN. She was born 16 Nov 1915 in Mississippi, and died 26 May 2002 in Madison Co., MS.

Children of FREDERICK HAMMACK and HELEN WREN are:

    i.   FREDERICK WILLIAM[13] HAMMACK III, b. 09 Nov 1949, Madison Co., MS; d. 07 Nov 1992, Madison Co., MS.

    ii. WREN HAMMACK, m. EDWARD H. GREGORY III.

Key Source: Telephone Interview with Helen Wren Hammack, Flora, MS, July 1996.

568. ISAAC CORNELIUS[12] HARPER *(MABEL E.*[11] *HAMMACK, GEORGE THOMAS*[10], *WILLIAM T. H.*[9], *SIMEON J.*[8], *WILLIAM T.*[7], *ROBERT HAMMACK*[6] *JR., ROBERT HAMMACK*[5] *SR., WILLIAM "THE ELDER"*[4] *HAMMACK, WILLIAM "O"*[3], *JOHN*[2] *HAMMOCKE, ? JOHN*[1] *HAMMOT)* was born Abt. 1910 in Copiah Co., MS. He married LULA SOLOMON. She was born in Lucedale, MS.

Child of ISAAC HARPER and LULA SOLOMON is:

653.   i.   NORMAN EDMOND[13] HARPER.

Key Source: Family records of Felix Maben Hammack, Bend, OR.

569. MYRTIE MONELL[12] HAMMACK *(MARION CLAIBORNE*[11], *GEORGE THOMAS*[10], *WILLIAM T. H.*[9], *SIMEON J.*[8], *WILLIAM T.*[7], *ROBERT HAMMACK*[6] *JR., ROBERT HAMMACK*[5] *SR., WILLIAM "THE ELDER"*[4] *HAMMACK, WILLIAM "O"*[3], *JOHN*[2] *HAMMOCKE, ? JOHN*[1] *HAMMOT)* was born 01 Nov 1916 in Copiah Co., MS. She married JOHN CLIFFORD BOMMER 16 Oct 1940 in Crystal Springs, MS.

Children of MYRTIE HAMMACK and JOHN BOMMER are:

    i.   RITA GAIL[13] BOMMER.

    ii. TRINA YVETTE BOMMER.

Key Source: Family records of Felix Maben Hammack, Bend, OR.

570. TINEY BELLE[12] HAMMACK *(MARION CLAIBORNE*[11], *GEORGE THOMAS*[10], *WILLIAM T. H.*[9], *SIMEON J.*[8], *WILLIAM T.*[7], *ROBERT HAMMACK*[6] *JR., ROBERT HAMMACK*[5] *SR., WILLIAM "THE ELDER"*[4] *HAMMACK, WILLIAM "O"*[3], *JOHN*[2] *HAMMOCKE, ? JOHN*[1] *HAMMOT)* was born 30 Apr 1920 in Copiah Co., MS. She married JAMES RHODEN HALL 01 Jun 1940 in Mississippi. He was born 25 Nov 1916 in Mississippi.

Children of TINEY HAMMACK and JAMES HALL are:

    i.   LINDA CAROL[13] HALL, b. 05 Oct 1943, Mississippi; m. ROBERT L. MOORER.

    ii. ERROL KEITH HALL, b. 08 Jun 1946, Mississippi; m. (1) SUSAN GAYLE HANKS; m. (2) ELIZABETH ANNE PITTMAN SAMPLEY.

Key Source: Family records of Felix Maben Hammack, Bend, OR.

571. MARION CLAIBORNE[12] HAMMACK, JR. *(MARION CLAIBORNE*[11], *GEORGE THOMAS*[10], *WILLIAM T. H.*[9], *SIMEON J.*[8], *WILLIAM T.*[7], *ROBERT HAMMACK*[6] *JR., ROBERT HAMMACK*[5] *SR.,*

WILLIAM "THE ELDER"[4] HAMMACK, WILLIAM "O"[3], JOHN[2] HAMMOCKE, ? JOHN[1] HAMMOT) was born 09 Sep 1924 in Copiah Co., MS. He married (1) MAXINE KEYES 01 Jul 1944 in Mississippi. He married (2) MYRNA RICE Aft. 1950.

Children of MARION HAMMACK and MAXINE KEYES are:

      i.   CHERYL DIANE[13] HAMMACK.

      ii. KERRY KEYES HAMMACK.

      iii. LISA HAMMACK.

Child of MARION HAMMACK and MYRNA RICE is:

      iv. MISTY[13] HAMMACK.

Key Source: Family records of Felix Maben Hammack, Bend, OR.

572. WILBUR CLYDE[12] HAMMACK *(MARION CLAIBORNE[11], GEORGE THOMAS[10], WILLIAM T. H.[9], SIMEON J.[8], WILLIAM T.[7], ROBERT HAMMACK[6] JR., ROBERT HAMMACK[5] SR., WILLIAM "THE ELDER"[4] HAMMACK, WILLIAM "O"[3], JOHN[2] HAMMOCKE, ? JOHN[1] HAMMOT)* was born 23 Sep 1926 in Copiah Co., MS, and died 18 Jun 1992 in Mississippi. He married (1) IVA CLIBURN 11 Jul 1947. He married (2) BEVERLY DAVIS Aft. 1950. He married (3) INEZ HARRISON Aft. 1955.

Child of WILBUR HAMMACK and IVA CLIBURN is:

      i.   MICHAEL[13] HAMMACK.

Child of WILBUR HAMMACK and BEVERLY DAVIS is:

      ii. CATHY DARLENE[13] HAMMACK.

Child of WILBUR HAMMACK and INEZ HARRISON is:

      iii. WILLIAM CHARLES[13] HAMMACK.

Key Source: Family records of Felix Maben Hammack, Bend, OR.

573. WINFRED CARROL[12] HAMMACK *(MARION CLAIBORNE[11], GEORGE THOMAS[10], WILLIAM T. H.[9], SIMEON J.[8], WILLIAM T.[7], ROBERT HAMMACK[6] JR., ROBERT HAMMACK[5] SR., WILLIAM "THE ELDER"[4] HAMMACK, WILLIAM "O"[3], JOHN[2] HAMMOCKE, ? JOHN[1] HAMMOT)* was born 18 May 1931 in Copiah Co., MS. He married FAY HOWARD 27 Jan 1951 in Mississippi.

Children of WINFRED HAMMACK and FAY HOWARD are:

      i.   LAURIE[13] HAMMACK, m. ROBERT BULLEN.

      ii. JOAN HAMMACK, m. JAMES ERWIN.

      iii. SUSAN HAMMACK, m. MARK HARDEE.

Key Source: Family records of Felix Maben Hammack, Bend, OR.

574. FRANCES JEANNETTE[12] HAMMACK *(MARION CLAIBORNE[11], GEORGE THOMAS[10], WILLIAM T. H.[9], SIMEON J.[8], WILLIAM T.[7], ROBERT HAMMACK[6] JR., ROBERT HAMMACK[5] SR., WILLIAM "THE ELDER"[4] HAMMACK, WILLIAM "O"[3], JOHN[2] HAMMOCKE, ? JOHN[1] HAMMOT)* was born 22 Jul 1936 in Copiah Co., MS. She married ARTHUR HAROLD NASH 17 Dec 1955 in Mississippi.

Children of FRANCES HAMMACK and ARTHUR NASH are:

      i.   BARRY LEN[13] NASH, m. CATHY [--------].

      ii. ERIC DWAYNE NASH, m. (1) JANIE WEBB; m. (2) CHERYL STRONG.

      iii. HAROLD SCOTTIE NASH, m. (1) RENEE MCKINNON; m. (2) PAULA JENNINGS.

Key Source: Family records of Felix Maben Hammack, Bend, OR.

575. CARY THOMAS[12] HAMMACK *(THOMAS CLIVE[11], GEORGE THOMAS[10], WILLIAM T. H.[9], SIMEON J.[8], WILLIAM T.[7], ROBERT HAMMACK[6] JR., ROBERT HAMMACK[5] SR., WILLIAM "THE ELDER"[4] HAMMACK, WILLIAM "O"[3], JOHN[2] HAMMOCKE, ? JOHN[1] HAMMOT)* He married JEWELL KNOX 1939.

Children of CARY HAMMACK and JEWELL KNOX are:

     i.   CARY STEPHEN[13] HAMMACK.

    ii.   RALPH HAMMACK.

Key Source: Family records of Felix Maben Hammack, Bend, OR.

576. MILDRED LEOLA[12] HAMMACK *(THOMAS CLIVE[11], GEORGE THOMAS[10], WILLIAM T. H.[9], SIMEON J.[8], WILLIAM T.[7], ROBERT HAMMACK[6] JR., ROBERT HAMMACK[5] SR., WILLIAM "THE ELDER"[4] HAMMACK, WILLIAM "O"[3], JOHN[2] HAMMOCKE, ? JOHN[1] HAMMOT)* She married LINDEN LEA 1938.

Children of MILDRED HAMMACK and LINDEN LEA are:

     i.   RICHARD LAWRENCE[13] LEA.

    ii.   AMY LINDA LEA.

Key Source: Family records of Felix Maben Hammack, Bend, OR.

577. DORIS[12] HAMMACK *(THOMAS CLIVE[11], GEORGE THOMAS[10], WILLIAM T. H.[9], SIMEON J.[8], WILLIAM T.[7], ROBERT HAMMACK[6] JR., ROBERT HAMMACK[5] SR., WILLIAM "THE ELDER"[4] HAMMACK, WILLIAM "O"[3], JOHN[2] HAMMOCKE, ? JOHN[1] HAMMOT)* She married H. G. HOOD, JR. 1944.

Children of DORIS HAMMACK and H. HOOD are:

     i.   KENNETH CLIVE[13] HOOD.

    ii.   MARION FAYE HOOD.

Key Source: Family records of Felix Maben Hammack, Bend, OR.

578. SAMUEL BOYD[12] DOOLITTLE *(THOMAS EATMON[11], SAREPTA ANN ELIZABETH[10] HAMMACK, CHARLES M.[9], SIMEON J.[8], WILLIAM T.[7], ROBERT HAMMACK[6] JR., ROBERT HAMMACK[5] SR., WILLIAM "THE ELDER"[4] HAMMACK, WILLIAM "O"[3], JOHN[2] HAMMOCKE, ? JOHN[1] HAMMOT)* was born 26 Sep 1897 in Calhoun Co., MS, and died 29 Dec 1963 in Slate Springs, Calhoun Co., MS. He married MAUDE M. [------]. She was born 18 Aug 1898 in Calhoun Co., MS, and died 09 Dec 1979 in Slate Springs, Calhoun Co., MS.

Children of SAMUEL DOOLITTLE and MAUDE [------] are:

     i.   TOM WALTER[13] DOOLITTLE.

    ii.   DONALD DOOLITTLE.

Key Source: Genealogical records of Imogene Springer, Calhoun City, MS, July 1996.

579. MAX[12] DOOLITTLE *(THOMAS EATMON[11], SAREPTA ANN ELIZABETH[10] HAMMACK, CHARLES M.[9], SIMEON J.[8], WILLIAM T.[7], ROBERT HAMMACK[6] JR., ROBERT HAMMACK[5] SR., WILLIAM "THE ELDER"[4] HAMMACK, WILLIAM "O"[3], JOHN[2] HAMMOCKE, ? JOHN[1] HAMMOT)* was born Aug 1898 in Calhoun Co., MS, and died Aft. 1954 in Calhoun Co., MS. He married BLUNDIE DENLEY.

Child of MAX DOOLITTLE and BLUNDIE DENLEY is:

     i.   LARRY[13] DOOLITTLE.

Key Source: Genealogical records of Imogene Springer, Calhoun City, MS, July 1996.

580. DELORES[12] DOOLITTLE *(JAMES WILLIAM[11], SAREPTA ANN ELIZABETH[10] HAMMACK, CHARLES M.[9], SIMEON J.[8], WILLIAM T.[7], ROBERT HAMMACK[6] JR., ROBERT HAMMACK[5] SR., WILLIAM "THE ELDER"[4] HAMMACK, WILLIAM "O"[3], JOHN[2] HAMMOCKE, ? JOHN[1] HAMMOT)* was born Apr 1897 in Calhoun Co., MS, and died Aft. 1949 in Calhoun Co., MS. She married LESTER B. MAWK 11 Mar 1924 in Calhoun Co., MS.

Child of DELORES DOOLITTLE and LESTER MAWK is:

654.   i.   JAMES BECKWITH[13] MAWK, b. 19 Feb 1925, Calhoun Co., MS.
Key Source: Fox, Doolittle, Holland, and Mawk Family Records, Calhoun City Public Library, Calhoun City, MS.

581. HENRY HAVEN[12] HOLLAND (*MAYBELLE[11] DOOLITTLE, SAREPTA ANN ELIZABETH[10] HAMMACK, CHARLES M.[9], SIMEON J.[8], WILLIAM T.[7], ROBERT HAMMACK[6] JR., ROBERT HAMMACK[5] SR., WILLIAM "THE ELDER"[4] HAMMACK, WILLIAM "O"[3], JOHN[2] HAMMOCKE, ? JOHN[1] HAMMOT)* was born 02 Oct 1905 in Calhoun Co., MS, and died Aft. 1967 in Calhoun Co., MS. He married LOTTIE MARIE DOSS 03 Feb 1926 in Calhoun Co., MS. She was born 17 Aug 1906 in Calhoun Co., MS.
Children of HENRY HOLLAND and LOTTIE DOSS are:
655.   i.   MYRA MARIE[13] HOLLAND, b. 27 Jun 1929, Calhoun Co., MS.
656.   ii. MABLE KATHRYN HOLLAND, b. 24 Aug 1931, Calhoun Co., MS.
657.   iii. HENRY HAVEN HOLLAND, b. 22 Mar 1938, Calhoun Co., MS.
Key Source: Fox, Doolittle, Holland, and Mawk Family Records, Calhoun City Public Library, Calhoun City, MS.

582. MILLER DOOLITTLE[12] HOLLAND (*MAYBELLE[11] DOOLITTLE, SAREPTA ANN ELIZABETH[10] HAMMACK, CHARLES M.[9], SIMEON J.[8], WILLIAM T.[7], ROBERT HAMMACK[6] JR., ROBERT HAMMACK[5] SR., WILLIAM "THE ELDER"[4] HAMMACK, WILLIAM "O"[3], JOHN[2] HAMMOCKE, ? JOHN[1] HAMMOT)* was born 04 Apr 1908 in Calhoun Co., MS, and died Aft. 1967 in Calhoun Co., MS. He married LOLA SKELTON 03 Mar 1928 in Calhoun Co., MS. She was born 27 Aug 1912 in Calhoun Co., MS.
Children of MILLER HOLLAND and LOLA SKELTON are:
658.   i.   MARY ELIZABETH[13] HOLLAND, b. 17 Mar 1931, Calhoun Co., MS.
659.   ii. HENRY MEEK HOLLAND, b. 28 Jan 1933, Calhoun Co., MS.
660.   iii. JOHN MILLER HOLLAND, b. 18 Jun 1936, Calhoun Co., MS.
661.   iv. JAMES SKELTON HOLLAND, b. 25 Sep 1947, Grenada, MS.
Key Source: Fox, Doolittle, Holland, and Mawk Family Records, Calhoun City Public Library, Calhoun City, MS.

583. FINNER[12] CARVER (*GEORGIA ANN[11] DOOLITTLE, SAREPTA ANN ELIZABETH[10] HAMMACK, CHARLES M.[9], SIMEON J.[8], WILLIAM T.[7], ROBERT HAMMACK[6] JR., ROBERT HAMMACK[5] SR., WILLIAM "THE ELDER"[4] HAMMACK, WILLIAM "O"[3], JOHN[2] HAMMOCKE, ? JOHN[1] HAMMOT)* was born 28 Jan 1919 in Calhoun Co., MS. He married MARY EVELYN SHAW 14 Jun 1941 in Calhoun Co., MS. She was born 05 Aug 1921 in Calhoun Co., MS.
Children of FINNER CARVER and MARY SHAW are:
662.   i.   KEITH SHAW[13] CARVER, b. 10 Oct 1946, Nashville, TN.
        ii. JOHN FINNER CARVER, b. 12 Nov 1947, Nashville, TN.
Key Source: Fox, Doolittle, Holland, and Mawk Family Records, Calhoun City Public Library, Calhoun City, MS.

584. CHARLES DOUGLAS[12] WASSON (*CHARLES RANDOLPH[11], NAOMI[10] HAMMACK, CHARLES M.[9], SIMEON J.[8], WILLIAM T.[7], ROBERT HAMMACK[6] JR., ROBERT HAMMACK[5] SR., WILLIAM "THE ELDER"[4] HAMMACK, WILLIAM "O"[3], JOHN[2] HAMMOCKE, ? JOHN[1] HAMMOT)* was born 22 Apr 1927 in Sunflower Co., MS. He married VIRGINIA NOBLE 18 Nov 1953 in Shaw, MS. She was born 26 Aug 1934 in Washington Co., MS.
Children of CHARLES WASSON and VIRGINIA NOBLE are:
        i.   CHARLOTTE ANNE[13] WASSON, b. 12 Apr 1954, Greenville, MS.

    ii.   CHARLES DOUGLAS WASSON, b. 16 Sep 1956, Greenville, MS.

    iii. WAYNE NOBLE WASSON, b. 14 Jun 1970, Greenville, MS.

Key Source: Samuel F. Brewster, Sr., *Data on Wasson Families and Allied Lines* (unpublished, 1973). This volume is housed in the Eudora Welty Library, Jackson, MS.

585. DENNIS CAMPBELL[12] WASSON *(CHARLES RANDOLPH[11], NAOMI[10] HAMMACK, CHARLES M.[9], SIMEON J.[8], WILLIAM T.[7], ROBERT HAMMACK[6] JR., ROBERT HAMMACK[5] SR., WILLIAM "THE ELDER"[4] HAMMACK, WILLIAM "O"[3], JOHN[2] HAMMOCKE, ? JOHN[1] HAMMOT)* was born 02 Jul 1932 in Sunflower Co., MS. He married DELORES KATHLEEN BRANDT 02 Sep 1955 in Phoenix, AZ. She was born 10 Dec 1933 in Sunflower Co., MS.

Children of DENNIS WASSON and DELORES BRANDT are:

    i.   ELIZABETH ANN[13] WASSON, b. 07 May 1956, Phoenix, AZ.

    ii.   CAROL DENESE WASSON, b. 05 Mar 1958, Phoenix, AZ.

    iii. JANET ELAINE WASSON, b. 23 Apr 1960, Phoenix, AZ.

    iv. MICHAEL SCOTT WASSON, b. 27 Sep 1963, Phoenix, AZ.

Key Source: Samuel F. Brewster, Sr., *Data on Wasson Families and Allied Lines* (unpublished, 1973). This volume is housed in the Eudora Welty Library, Jackson, MS.

586. EUNICE DELORES[12] WASSON *(CHARLES RANDOLPH[11], NAOMI[10] HAMMACK, CHARLES M.[9], SIMEON J.[8], WILLIAM T.[7], ROBERT HAMMACK[6] JR., ROBERT HAMMACK[5] SR., WILLIAM "THE ELDER"[4] HAMMACK, WILLIAM "O"[3], JOHN[2] HAMMOCKE, ? JOHN[1] HAMMOT)* was born 12 Jun 1938 in Sunflower Co., MS. She married AVEN BETHAY WILLIAMS, JR. 22 Nov 1960 in Greenville, MS. He was born 28 Jan 1934 in Quitman Co., MS.

Children of EUNICE WASSON and AVEN WILLIAMS are:

    i.   DIANNE ELOISE[13] WILLIAMS, b. 24 Jul 1961, Greenville, MS.

    ii.   TED WASSON WILLIAMS, b. 24 Oct 1963, Greenville, MS.

Key Source: Samuel F. Brewster, Sr., *Data on Wasson Families and Allied Lines* (unpublished, 1973). This volume is housed in the Eudora Welty Library, Jackson, MS.

587. LAWRENCE J.[12] SANDERFORD *(CHARLIE FRANKLIN[11], AMANDA V.[10] TAYLOR, SARAH ANN E.[9] HAMMACK, SIMEON J.[8], WILLIAM T.[7], ROBERT HAMMACK[6] JR., ROBERT HAMMACK[5] SR., WILLIAM "THE ELDER"[4] HAMMACK, WILLIAM "O"[3], JOHN[2] HAMMOCKE, ? JOHN[1] HAMMOT)* was born May 1897 in Texas, and died Aft. 1930 in Henderson Co., TX. He married GENEVA [------] Abt. 1925 in Henderson Co., TX. She was born Abt. 1900 in Texas, and died Aft. 1930 in Henderson Co., TX.

Child of LAWRENCE SANDERFORD and GENEVA [------] is:

    i.   ORIS E.[13] SANDERFER, b. Abt. 1927, Henderson Co., TX.

Key Source: 1930 Henderson Co., TX, Census, p. 40.

588. SADIE LUCILLE[12] HAMMACK *(GEORGE CLEVELAND[11], WILLIAM SIMMS[10], JOHN T.[9], SIMEON J.[8], WILLIAM T.[7], ROBERT HAMMACK[6] JR., ROBERT HAMMACK[5] SR., WILLIAM "THE ELDER"[4] HAMMACK, WILLIAM "O"[3], JOHN[2] HAMMOCKE, ? JOHN[1] HAMMOT)* was born 21 Feb 1912 in Hinds County, MS, and died 16 Nov 1996 in Monroe, LA. She married FLETCHER ALTON BABB 20 Aug 1933 in Lake Providence, LA. He was born 30 Dec 1905 in Marianna, AR, and died 04 Mar 1982 in Lake Providence, LA.

Children of SADIE HAMMACK and FLETCHER BABB are:

663.   i.   MARY KATHERINE[13] BABB, b. 17 Jul 1934, East Carroll Parish, LA.

664.   ii.   ALMEDIA LEE BABB, b. 12 Aug 1936.

665.   iii. CAROLYN BABB, b. 28 Jun 1938.

666.   iv. FRANCES ANN BABB, b. 29 Jun 1945.

667.   v.   SADIE RUTH BABB, b. 30 Mar 1950, Lake Providence, LA.
668.   vi.   JOHN ALTON BABB, b. 28 Jul 1952.
Key Source: Family records of Felix Maben Hammack, Bend, OR.

589. WILLIAM BANKSTON[12] HAMMACK *(GEORGE CLEVELAND[11], WILLIAM SIMMS[10], JOHN T.[9], SIMEON J.[8], WILLIAM T.[7], ROBERT HAMMACK[6] JR., ROBERT HAMMACK[5] SR., WILLIAM "THE ELDER"[4] HAMMACK, WILLIAM "O"[3], JOHN[2] HAMMOCKE, ? JOHN[1] HAMMOT)* was born 24 Oct 1913 in Hinds County, MS, and died 10 Apr 1989 in Jackson, MS. He married ALINE JOSIE LANCASTER 26 Jul 1937 in Yazoo City, MS. She was born 08 May 1918.
Children of WILLIAM HAMMACK and ALINE LANCASTER are:
669.   i.   MARY ANN[13] HAMMACK, b. 28 Jul 1938, Hinds County, MS.
        ii.   CAROL KAY HAMMACK, b. 24 May 1944; m. JAMES KIRKLAND.
670.   iii. WILLIAM BANKSTON HAMMACK, JR., b. 21 Apr 1949, Hinds County, MS.
Key Source: Family records of Felix Maben Hammack, Bend, OR.

590. MARY MILDRED[12] HAMMACK *(GEORGE CLEVELAND[11], WILLIAM SIMMS[10], JOHN T.[9], SIMEON J.[8], WILLIAM T.[7], ROBERT HAMMACK[6] JR., ROBERT HAMMACK[5] SR., WILLIAM "THE ELDER"[4] HAMMACK, WILLIAM "O"[3], JOHN[2] HAMMOCKE, ? JOHN[1] HAMMOT)* was born 07 Aug 1915 in Hinds County, MS, and died 11 Dec 2003 in Mansfield, LA. She married THOMAS JOSEPH SITTON 11 Apr 1937 in Lake Providence, LA, son of THOMAS SITTON and MARY NOTHOFER. He was born 22 Mar 1914 in East Carroll Parish, LA, and died 07 Oct 2003 in West Carroll Parish, LA.
Children of MARY HAMMACK and THOMAS SITTON are:
671.   i.   DOROTHY LUCILLE[13] SITTON, b. 29 Dec 1939, East Carroll Parish, LA.
672.   ii.   MARY ELIZABETH SITTON, b. 05 Nov 1943, Lake Providence, LA.
673.   iii. JOSEPH PAUL SITTON, b. 03 Aug 1948.
674.   iv.   THOMAS STRIBLING SITTON, b. 03 Mar 1952.
Key Source: Family records of Felix Maben Hammack, Bend, OR.

591. EDGAR HENDRICKS[12] HAMMACK *(GEORGE CLEVELAND[11], WILLIAM SIMMS[10], JOHN T.[9], SIMEON J.[8], WILLIAM T.[7], ROBERT HAMMACK[6] JR., ROBERT HAMMACK[5] SR., WILLIAM "THE ELDER"[4] HAMMACK, WILLIAM "O"[3], JOHN[2] HAMMOCKE, ? JOHN[1] HAMMOT)* was born 20 Oct 1917 in Hinds County, MS, and died 28 Dec 1986 in Atlanta, GA. He married (1) AVIS MYRDELL MCFARLAND 15 Feb 1940 in Clinton, MS, daughter of WESLEY MCFARLAND and MARGARET CREEKMORE. She was born 02 Jul 1924 in Dekalb, Kemper Co., MS. He married (2) MARIAM FRANKLIN Abt. 1980.
Children of EDGAR HAMMACK and AVIS MCFARLAND are:
675.   i.   JOHN EUGENE[13] HAMMACK, b. 15 May 1941, Hinds County, MS.
676.   ii.   EDGAR HENDRICKS HAMMACK JR., b. 17 May 1954.
Key Source: Family records of Felix Maben Hammack, Bend, OR.

592. GEORGE CLEVELAND[12] HAMMACK, JR. *(GEORGE CLEVELAND[11], WILLIAM SIMMS[10], JOHN T.[9], SIMEON J.[8], WILLIAM T.[7], ROBERT HAMMACK[6] JR., ROBERT HAMMACK[5] SR., WILLIAM "THE ELDER"[4] HAMMACK, WILLIAM "O"[3], JOHN[2] HAMMOCKE, ? JOHN[1] HAMMOT)* was born 17 May 1922 in Hinds County, MS. He married (1) MARGARET MITCHELL GOODE 02 Nov 1946 in Lake Providence, LA, daughter of O. GOODE and VIVIAN BLANTON. She was born 26 Apr 1926. He married (2) FRANCES EMMA REYNOLDS 13 Aug 1983 in Jackson, MS, daughter of EARLE REYNOLDS and EMMA RABB. She was born 07 Jan 1923 in Jacksonville, FL.
Children of GEORGE HAMMACK and MARGARET GOODE are:

      i.   GEORGE CLEVELAND[13] HAMMACK III, b. 13 Feb 1948, Lake Providence, LA; d. 28 Nov 1994, Los Angeles, CA.

677.   ii.   ANNETTE HAMMACK, b. 22 Jan 1950.

678.   iii.   DAVID MITCHELL HAMMACK, b. 28 Oct 1959.

Key Source: Family records of Felix Maben Hammack, Bend, OR.

593. JAMES WILSON[12] HAMMACK *(GEORGE CLEVELAND[11], WILLIAM SIMMS[10], JOHN T.[9], SIMEON J.[8], WILLIAM T.[7], ROBERT HAMMACK[6] JR., ROBERT HAMMACK[5] SR., WILLIAM "THE ELDER"[4] HAMMACK, WILLIAM "O"[3], JOHN[2] HAMMOCKE, ? JOHN[1] HAMMOT)* was born 28 May 1924 in Hinds County, MS. He married MARTHA JOHNSTON 20 Jun 1948 in Lake Providence, LA, daughter of WALTER JOHNSTON and DELMA BYRD. She was born 28 Nov 1917 in Bogue Chitto, Lincoln Co., MS.

Children of JAMES HAMMACK and MARTHA JOHNSTON are:

      i.   DAPHNE JEAN[13] HAMMACK, b. 11 May 1949.

     ii.   JAMES WILSON HAMMACK JR., b. 11 May 1951.

    iii.   LISA JOY HAMMACK, b. 04 Aug 1958.

    iv.   MARCUS CHARLES HAMMACK, b. 04 Aug 1959, Jackson, Hinds County, MS.; d. 10 Dec 1992, Touro Infirmary in New Orleans, LA.

Key Source: Family records of Felix Maben Hammack, Bend, OR.

594. DANIEL CLEMENT[12] HAMMACK *(GEORGE CLEVELAND[11], WILLIAM SIMMS[10], JOHN T.[9], SIMEON J.[8], WILLIAM T.[7], ROBERT HAMMACK[6] JR., ROBERT HAMMACK[5] SR., WILLIAM "THE ELDER"[4] HAMMACK, WILLIAM "O"[3], JOHN[2] HAMMOCKE, ? JOHN[1] HAMMOT)* was born 13 Apr 1926 in Hinds County, MS. He married (1) VIOLA MARIE SULLIVAN 01 Jul 1949 in Vicksburg, MS. She was born 11 Aug 1928, and died 18 Aug 1993 in Tallulah, LA. He married (2) MARY CHRISTINE JORDAN 30 Jun 1984 in East Carroll Parish, LA, daughter of ALBERT JORDAN and FRANCES THAMES. She was born 17 May 1934 in West Carroll Parish, LA.

Children of DANIEL HAMMACK and VIOLA SULLIVAN are:

679.   i.   DANIEL CLEMENT HAMMACK[13] JR., b. 19 Aug 1950, Lake Providence, LA.

680.   ii.   JANET CELESTE HAMMACK, b. 04 Sep 1954.

681.   iii.   PAMELA LOUISE HAMMACK, b. 20 Jul 1958, Lake Providence, LA.

Key Source: Family records of Felix Maben Hammack, Bend, OR.

595. FELIX MABEN[12] HAMMACK *(GEORGE CLEVELAND[11], WILLIAM SIMMS[10], JOHN T.[9], SIMEON J.[8], WILLIAM T.[7], ROBERT HAMMACK[6] JR., ROBERT HAMMACK[5] SR., WILLIAM "THE ELDER"[4] HAMMACK, WILLIAM "O"[3], JOHN[2] HAMMOCKE, ? JOHN[1] HAMMOT)* was born 05 Mar 1928 in Hinds County, Mississippi. He married MARY ANN DAY 31 Aug 1952 in Union Parish, Louisiana. She was born 03 Nov 1931 in Union Parish, Louisiana.

Children of FELIX HAMMACK and MARY DAY are:

682.   i.   CHARLOTTE CHRISTMAS[13] HAMMACK, b. 26 Jul 1953, Louisville, Jefferson Co., KY.

683.   ii.   DENISE HAMMACK, b. 05 Sep 1955, Memphis, Shelby Co., TN.

684.   iii.   PHILIP STEVEN HAMMACK, b. 01 Feb 1958, Albany, Linn County, Oregon.

    iv.   FREDERICK NATHAN HAMMACK, b. 18 Dec 1958, Albany, Linn County, Oregon.

Key Source: Family records of Felix Maben Hammack, Bend, OR.

596. CELESTE ALMEDIA[12] HAMMACK *(GEORGE CLEVELAND[11], WILLIAM SIMMS[10], JOHN T.[9], SIMEON J.[8], WILLIAM T.[7], ROBERT HAMMACK[6] JR., ROBERT HAMMACK[5] SR., WILLIAM "THE ELDER"[4] HAMMACK, WILLIAM "O"[3], JOHN[2] HAMMOCKE, ? JOHN[1] HAMMOT)* was born 24 Mar

1932 in Hinds County, MS, and died 12 Oct 1951 in Near Alexandria, LA. She married LLOYD
LEBANE CLEMENT 01 Jan 1950 in Lake Providence, LA. He was born 31 Jan 1931.
Child of CELESTE HAMMACK and LLOYD CLEMENT is:
685.   i.   ELIZABETH GAYLE[13] CLEMENT, b. 13 Jul 1950.
Key Source: Family records of Felix Maben Hammack, Bend, OR.

597. ALLIE JO[12] HAMMACK *(GEORGE CLEVELAND*[11]*, WILLIAM SIMMS*[10]*, JOHN T.*[9]*, SIMEON J.*[8]*,
WILLIAM T.*[7]*, ROBERT HAMMACK*[6] *JR., ROBERT HAMMACK*[5] *SR., WILLIAM "THE ELDER"*[4]
HAMMACK, WILLIAM "O"[3]*, JOHN*[2] *HAMMOCKE, ? JOHN*[1] *HAMMOT)* was born 01 Nov 1934 in
Hinds County, MS, and died 11 Oct 1966 in Memphis, TN. She married FRANK HERMAN SCHULTE
01 Sep 1957 in Lake Providence, LA, son of FRANK SR. and BERTHA LOENNEKE. He was born 01
Oct 1927 in Cape Girardeau, MO, and died Abt. 2002 in Memphis, Shelby Co., TN.
Children of ALLIE HAMMACK and FRANK SCHULTE are:
        i.   FREDERICK BERNARD[13] SCHULTE, b. 04 Jan 1963.
686.   ii.   LAURA ANN SCHULTE, b. 07 Feb 1964, Memphis, TN.
687.   iii. EMILY IRENE SCHULTE, b. 25 May 1965, Memphis, TN.
Key Source: Family records of Felix Maben Hammack, Bend, OR.

598. RUBY COOMBS[12] HAMMACK *(ROBERT FELIX*[11]*, WILLIAM SIMMS*[10]*, JOHN T.*[9]*, SIMEON J.*[8]*,
WILLIAM T.*[7]*, ROBERT HAMMACK*[6] *JR., ROBERT HAMMACK*[5] *SR., WILLIAM "THE ELDER"*[4]
HAMMACK, WILLIAM "O"[3]*, JOHN*[2] *HAMMOCKE, ? JOHN*[1] *HAMMOT)* was born 06 Sep 1926 in
Yazoo County, MS. She married CHARLES BUFORD VAUGHAN 03 Jul 1945 in Yazoo County, MS.
Children of RUBY HAMMACK and CHARLES VAUGHAN are:
688.   i.   CATHRYN ELIZABETH[13] VAUGHAN, b. 03 May 1946, Yazoo County, MS.
689.   ii.   CORA CHARLEEN VAUGHAN, b. 01 Aug 1949, Yazoo County, MS.
Key Source: Family records of Felix Maben Hammack, Bend, OR.

599. MARY KATHERINE[12] HAMMACK *(ROBERT FELIX*[11]*, WILLIAM SIMMS*[10]*, JOHN T.*[9]*, SIMEON
J.*[8]*, WILLIAM T.*[7]*, ROBERT HAMMACK*[6] *JR., ROBERT HAMMACK*[5] *SR., WILLIAM "THE ELDER"*[4]
HAMMACK, WILLIAM "O"[3]*, JOHN*[2] *HAMMOCKE, ? JOHN*[1] *HAMMOT)* was born 21 Nov 1929 in
Yazoo County, MS. She married WILLIAM AUGUSTUS DAVIS 10 Apr 1948 in Yazoo County, MS.
Children of MARY HAMMACK and WILLIAM DAVIS are:
690.   i.   ROBERT DEWEY[13] DAVIS, b. 02 Dec 1951, Yazoo City, MS.
691.   ii.   MARY JOAN DAVIS, b. 14 Nov 1954, Yazoo County, MS.
692.   iii. WILLIAM TIMOTHY DAVIS, b. 08 Nov 1963, Yazoo County, MS.
Key Source: Family records of Felix Maben Hammack, Bend, OR.

600. WILLIE BELL[12] HAMMACK *(DRURY BROWN "DOOLEY"*[11]*, WILLIAM SIMMS*[10]*, JOHN T.*[9]*,
SIMEON J.*[8]*, WILLIAM T.*[7]*, ROBERT HAMMACK*[6] *JR., ROBERT HAMMACK*[5] *SR., WILLIAM "THE
ELDER"*[4] *HAMMACK, WILLIAM "O"*[3]*, JOHN*[2] *HAMMOCKE, ? JOHN*[1] *HAMMOT)* was born 16 Dec
1916 in Hinds County, MS, and died 21 Oct 1990. She married TRAVIS H. PACE. He was born 08 Aug
1920, and died 10 Oct 1979.
Children of WILLIE HAMMACK and TRAVIS PACE are:
693.   i.   GLORIA JEAN[13] PACE, b. 11 Aug 1941.
694.   ii.   ANNA DEAN PACE, b. 22 Apr 1943.
Key Source: Family records of Felix Maben Hammack, Bend, OR.

601. ETHEL MAE[12] HAMMACK *(DRURY BROWN "DOOLEY"*[11]*, WILLIAM SIMMS*[10]*, JOHN T.*[9]*,
SIMEON J.*[8]*, WILLIAM T.*[7]*, ROBERT HAMMACK*[6] *JR., ROBERT HAMMACK*[5] *SR., WILLIAM "THE*

ELDER"⁴ HAMMACK, WILLIAM "O"³, JOHN² HAMMOCKE, ? JOHN¹ HAMMOT) was born 29 Oct 1917 in Hinds County, MS. She married T. W. HUMPHRIES Abt. 1939 in Monroe, LA. He was born 30 Jun 1914.

Children of ETHEL HAMMACK and T. HUMPHRIES are:

    i.   ANN¹³ HUMPHRIES, b. 22 Jul 1939; m. (1) ? SEAB; m. (2) ? GRAHAM.

    ii.   LINDA HUMPHRIES, b. 21 Apr 1943; m. ? THORNTON.

    iii.   TOMMY HUMPHRIES, b. 09 Jun 1954.

Key Source: Family records of Felix Maben Hammack, Bend, OR.

602. THOMAS CLIFTON "PETE"¹² HAMMACK *(DRURY BROWN "DOOLEY"¹¹, WILLIAM SIMMS¹⁰, JOHN T.⁹, SIMEON J.⁸, WILLIAM T.⁷, ROBERT HAMMACK⁶ JR., ROBERT HAMMACK⁵ SR., WILLIAM "THE ELDER"⁴ HAMMACK, WILLIAM "O"³, JOHN² HAMMOCKE, ? JOHN¹ HAMMOT)* was born 14 Feb 1919 in Hinds County, MS. He married HILDA BURTON 16 Jun 1950. She was born 19 Jun 1929.

Children of THOMAS HAMMACK and HILDA BURTON are:

    i.   JAMES DOUGLAS¹³ HAMMACK, b. 10 Jul 1951.

695. ii.   THOMAS CHRISTOPHER HAMMACK, b. 25 Dec 1959.

Key Source: Family records of Felix Maben Hammack, Bend, OR.

603. MARTHA ELIZABETH¹² HAMMACK *(DRURY BROWN "DOOLEY"¹¹, WILLIAM SIMMS¹⁰, JOHN T.⁹, SIMEON J.⁸, WILLIAM T.⁷, ROBERT HAMMACK⁶ JR., ROBERT HAMMACK⁵ SR., WILLIAM "THE ELDER"⁴ HAMMACK, WILLIAM "O"³, JOHN² HAMMOCKE, ? JOHN¹ HAMMOT)* was born 21 Jan 1922 in Hinds County, MS. She married ROBERT FERNWOOD PALFREY 15 Sep 1944 in Pike County, MS. He was born 05 Dec 1923.

Children of MARTHA HAMMACK and ROBERT PALFREY are:

    i.   MARCIA LYNN¹³ PALFREY, b. 10 Jan 1948, Jones County, MS; m. JERRY E. JACOB, 01 Sep 1966, Jackson County, MS.

    ii.   ROBERT FERNWOOD PALFREY, JR., b. 05 Dec 1952, Escambia County, FL; m. BETTY WISE, Tallapoosa County, AL.

    iii.   DOUGLAS NEAL PALFREY, b. 01 Sep 1955, Escambia County, FL.

Key Source: Family records of Felix Maben Hammack, Bend, OR.

604. DEWEY LEON¹² HAMMACK *(DRURY BROWN "DOOLEY"¹¹, WILLIAM SIMMS¹⁰, JOHN T.⁹, SIMEON J.⁸, WILLIAM T.⁷, ROBERT HAMMACK⁶ JR., ROBERT HAMMACK⁵ SR., WILLIAM "THE ELDER"⁴ HAMMACK, WILLIAM "O"³, JOHN² HAMMOCKE, ? JOHN¹ HAMMOT)* was born 06 Dec 1923 in Hinds County, MS, and died 06 Sep 1973.

Child of DEWEY LEON HAMMACK is:

    i.   MARLIN DWAYNE¹³ HAMMACK, b. 22 Feb 1956.

Key Source: Family records of Felix Maben Hammack, Bend, OR.

605. JAMES MARLIN¹² HAMMACK *(DRURY BROWN "DOOLEY"¹¹, WILLIAM SIMMS¹⁰, JOHN T.⁹, SIMEON J.⁸, WILLIAM T.⁷, ROBERT HAMMACK⁶ JR., ROBERT HAMMACK⁵ SR., WILLIAM "THE ELDER"⁴ HAMMACK, WILLIAM "O"³, JOHN² HAMMOCKE, ? JOHN¹ HAMMOT)* was born 01 Sep 1936, and died 29 Jun 1974. He married MAMIE WOODS. She was born 17 Jun 1938.

Children of JAMES HAMMACK and MAMIE WOODS are:

    i.   CATHY¹³ HAMMACK, b. 07 Oct 1959.

    ii.   JAMES MARLIN HAMMACK, JR., b. 22 Sep 1960.

    iii.   DAVID HAMMACK, b. 11 Jun 1962.

    iv.   BETH HAMMACK, b. 11 Oct 1963.

Key Source: Family records of Felix Maben Hammack, Bend, OR.

606. WILBURN LOUIS[12] BURGESS *(CLARA BELLE[11] HAMMACK, WILLIAM SIMMS[10], JOHN T.[9], SIMEON J.[8], WILLIAM T.[7], ROBERT HAMMACK[6] JR., ROBERT HAMMACK[5] SR., WILLIAM "THE ELDER"[4] HAMMACK, WILLIAM "O"[3], JOHN[2] HAMMOCKE, ? JOHN[1] HAMMOT)* was born 27 Oct 1923 in Hinds County, MS. He married BOBBIE DUKES 30 Aug 1941 in Madison County, MS, daughter of ROBERT DUKES and SKEET. She was born 24 Sep 1925 in Hinds County, MS.
Children of WILBURN BURGESS and BOBBIE DUKES are:
696.   i.   MYRTAL DIANE[13] BURGESS, b. 14 Aug 1946.
697.   ii.   WILBURN LOUIS BURGESS, JR, b. 15 Oct 1948, Hinds County, MS.
Key Source: Family records of Felix Maben Hammack, Bend, OR.

607. FRANCIS NORMAN[12] BURGESS *(CLARA BELLE[11] HAMMACK, WILLIAM SIMMS[10], JOHN T.[9], SIMEON J.[8], WILLIAM T.[7], ROBERT HAMMACK[6] JR., ROBERT HAMMACK[5] SR., WILLIAM "THE ELDER"[4] HAMMACK, WILLIAM "O"[3], JOHN[2] HAMMOCKE, ? JOHN[1] HAMMOT)* was born 18 Oct 1926 in Hinds County, MS. He married DOROTHY D. FREEMAN 08 Jun 1951 in Hinds County, MS. She was born 04 Jul 1929 in Chicago, IL.
Children of FRANCIS BURGESS and DOROTHY FREEMAN are:
        i.   FRANCIS NORMAN[13] BURGESS, JR., b. 05 Jun 1954; m. MICHELLE WHITTLEY.
698.   ii.   GEORGE A. BURGESS, b. 26 Sep 1957.
        iii. AMIE L. BURGESS, b. 16 Sep 1967.
Key Source: Family records of Felix Maben Hammack, Bend, OR.

608. ROSALIE[12] BURGESS *(DOLLIE CLIFFORD[11] HAMMACK, WILLIAM SIMMS[10], JOHN T.[9], SIMEON J.[8], WILLIAM T.[7], ROBERT HAMMACK[6] JR., ROBERT HAMMACK[5] SR., WILLIAM "THE ELDER"[4] HAMMACK, WILLIAM "O"[3], JOHN[2] HAMMOCKE, ? JOHN[1] HAMMOT)* was born 15 Apr 1913 in Hinds County, MS near Brownsville. She married WALTER WHITFIELD RUSSELL in Yazoo City, MS. He was born 31 Dec 1914, and died 02 Aug 1952.
Children of ROSALIE BURGESS and WALTER RUSSELL are:
        i.   INA CLAIRE[13] RUSSELL, b. 11 Nov 1946; m. CLIFTON LEE MCMILLIAN, 20 Aug 1977; b. 19 Feb 1940.
699.   ii.   WAYNE WHITFIELD RUSSELL, b. 11 Feb 1952.
Key Source: Family records of Felix Maben Hammack, Bend, OR.

609. MERLE[12] BURGESS *(DOLLIE CLIFFORD[11] HAMMACK, WILLIAM SIMMS[10], JOHN T.[9], SIMEON J.[8], WILLIAM T.[7], ROBERT HAMMACK[6] JR., ROBERT HAMMACK[5] SR., WILLIAM "THE ELDER"[4] HAMMACK, WILLIAM "O"[3], JOHN[2] HAMMOCKE, ? JOHN[1] HAMMOT)* was born 03 Sep 1917 in Madison County, MS near Flora. She married PHILLIP ABNER RUSSELL 01 Mar 1937 in Hinds County, MS. He was born 06 Jan 1912, and died 12 Apr 1994.
Children of MERLE BURGESS and PHILLIP RUSSELL are:
700.   i.   HELEN ROSALIE[13] RUSSELL.
701.   ii.   PHILLIP ABNER RUSSELL, JR., b. 15 May 1939.
Key Source: Family records of Felix Maben Hammack, Bend, OR.

610. VICTORIA LENA[12] TELENGA *(MYRTLE LOUISE[11] HAMMACK, JOHN ROBERT[10], JOHN T.[9], SIMEON J.[8], WILLIAM T.[7], ROBERT HAMMACK[6] JR., ROBERT HAMMACK[5] SR., WILLIAM "THE ELDER"[4] HAMMACK, WILLIAM "O"[3], JOHN[2] HAMMOCKE, ? JOHN[1] HAMMOT)* was born 20 Dec 1915 in Turtle Lake, McLean County, ND, and died 10 Oct 1981 in Ceylon, Sask. She married JOHN MORROW MURRAY 25 Sep 1936 in Plentywood, MT, son of DAVID MURRAY and MARY MCELROY. He was born 29 Jul 1904 in Oil City, Pennsylvania, and died 03 Jan 1977 in Ceylon, Sask.
Children of VICTORIA TELENGA and JOHN MURRAY are:

i. EDWIN JOHN[13] MURRAY, b. 1936, Ceylon, Sask; m. JULIA ANN RISTOW, 18 Aug 1962.

702. ii. DARLENE ANNETTE MURRAY, b. 1940, Ceylon, Sask.

Key Source: Family records of Jonas Hammack, Bend, OR.

611. GEORGINA E.[12] TELENGA *(MYRTLE LOUISE[11] HAMMACK, JOHN ROBERT[10], JOHN T.[9], SIMEON J.[8], WILLIAM T.[7], ROBERT HAMMACK[6] JR., ROBERT HAMMACK[5] SR., WILLIAM "THE ELDER"[4] HAMMACK, WILLIAM "O"[3], JOHN[2] HAMMOCKE, ? JOHN[1] HAMMOT)* was born 26 Mar 1918 in Paisley Brook, Sask., and died 27 Mar 1999 in Regina, Sask. She married ROY GEORGE HENRY 10 May 1945 in Plentywood, MT. He was born 25 Jun 1918 in Buffalo Gap, Sask., and died 22 Jan 1986.

Children of GEORGINA TELENGA and ROY HENRY are:

i. DELPHAINE[13] HENRY, b. 10 Jun 1947; m. RAYMOND STOSKI, 05 Aug 1967.

703. ii. LARRY GEORGE HENRY, b. 1954; d. 15 Apr 1994, Regina, Sask..

Key Source: Family records of Jonas Hammack, Bend, OR.

612. FLORENCE[12] TELENGA *(MYRTLE LOUISE[11] HAMMACK, JOHN ROBERT[10], JOHN T.[9], SIMEON J.[8], WILLIAM T.[7], ROBERT HAMMACK[6] JR., ROBERT HAMMACK[5] SR., WILLIAM "THE ELDER"[4] HAMMACK, WILLIAM "O"[3], JOHN[2] HAMMOCKE, ? JOHN[1] HAMMOT)* was born 19 Nov 1923 in Big Beaver, Sask. She married VERNON HIBBARD 19 Nov 1947 in Plentywood, MT.

Children of FLORENCE TELENGA and VERNON HIBBARD are:

704. i. GLENN[13] HIBBARD, b. 19 Jun 1950.

705. ii. WANDA HIBBARD, b. 04 Aug 1954.

Key Source: Family records of Jonas Hammack, Bend, OR.

613. FLOYD[12] TELENGA *(MYRTLE LOUISE[11] HAMMACK, JOHN ROBERT[10], JOHN T.[9], SIMEON J.[8], WILLIAM T.[7], ROBERT HAMMACK[6] JR., ROBERT HAMMACK[5] SR., WILLIAM "THE ELDER"[4] HAMMACK, WILLIAM "O"[3], JOHN[2] HAMMOCKE, ? JOHN[1] HAMMOT)* was born 30 Jul 1926 in Big Beaver, Sask, and died 26 Dec 1976 in Lethbridge, Alta. He married VERA DAHL 03 Jul 1950 in Minton, Sask.

Children of FLOYD TELENGA and VERA DAHL are:

i. DALE[13] TELENGA, m. CELESTE JOANNE MARTEL, 14 Aug 1971.

ii. SHARLENE TELENGA, m. JERRY WOZNICZKO, 18 May 1974.

706. iii. LINDA ANN TELENGA.

Key Source: Family records of Jonas Hammack, Bend, OR.

614. JEROME[12] TELENGA *(MYRTLE LOUISE[11] HAMMACK, JOHN ROBERT[10], JOHN T.[9], SIMEON J.[8], WILLIAM T.[7], ROBERT HAMMACK[6] JR., ROBERT HAMMACK[5] SR., WILLIAM "THE ELDER"[4] HAMMACK, WILLIAM "O"[3], JOHN[2] HAMMOCKE, ? JOHN[1] HAMMOT)* was born 05 Jun 1934 in Big Beaver, Sask, and died 24 Jan 1999 in Regina, Sask. He married EVELYN DAVEY 24 May 1963 in Strasbourg, Sask. She was born 28 Apr 1939 in Strasbourg, Saskatchewan.

Children of JEROME TELENGA and EVELYN DAVEY are:

707. i. HAROLD[13] TELENGA, b. 11 Apr 1964.

708. ii. MICHELE TELENGA, b. 26 Dec 1967.

iii. SHELDON TELENGA, b. 21 Feb 1973.

Key Source: Family records of Jonas Hammack, Bend, OR.

615. GLORIA[12] TELENGA *(MYRTLE LOUISE[11] HAMMACK, JOHN ROBERT[10], JOHN T.[9], SIMEON J.[8], WILLIAM T.[7], ROBERT HAMMACK[6] JR., ROBERT HAMMACK[5] SR., WILLIAM "THE ELDER"[4]*

HAMMACK, WILLIAM "O"[3], JOHN[2] HAMMOCKE, ? JOHN[1] HAMMOT) was born 27 Feb 1940 in Coronach, Sask. She married (1) NORVAL THOMPSON 15 Jul 1960 in Big Beaver, Sask. She married (2) BRUCE F. PATCHETT 27 Dec 1985.
Child of GLORIA TELENGA and NORVAL THOMPSON is:
709.   i.   BRADLEY ROSS[13] THOMPSON, b. 21 Nov 1965, Calgary, Alta.
Key Source: Family records of Jonas Hammack, Bend, OR.

616. DALE MCDONALD[12] HAMMACK *(HARRY HERBERT[11], JOHN ROBERT[10], JOHN T.[9], SIMEON J.[8], WILLIAM T.[7], ROBERT HAMMACK[6] JR., ROBERT HAMMACK[5] SR., WILLIAM "THE ELDER"[4] HAMMACK, WILLIAM "O"[3], JOHN[2] HAMMOCKE, ? JOHN[1] HAMMOT)* was born 15 Nov 1924 in Columbus, ND. He married (1) PAULE MAURICETTE ROBERT Abt. 1945 in France. She was born 19 Dec 1924 in Saint Quentin, France. He married (2) FLORENCE SCHRIER 26 Aug 1972.
Children of DALE HAMMACK and PAULE ROBERT are:
        i.   CRAIG KEITH[13] HAMMACK, b. 12 Oct 1950, Kalamazoo, MI.
710.   ii.   BRUCE ALLAN HAMMACK, b. 15 May 1952, Kalamazoo, MI.
711.   iii. JACQUELINE DALE HAMMACK, b. 29 Mar 1954.
Key Source: Family records of Jonas Hammack, Bend, OR.

617. ALOHA DELPHINE[12] HAMMACK *(HARRY HERBERT[11], JOHN ROBERT[10], JOHN T.[9], SIMEON J.[8], WILLIAM T.[7], ROBERT HAMMACK[6] JR., ROBERT HAMMACK[5] SR., WILLIAM "THE ELDER"[4] HAMMACK, WILLIAM "O"[3], JOHN[2] HAMMOCKE, ? JOHN[1] HAMMOT)* was born 25 Feb 1928 in Columbus, Burke County, ND, and died 11 Mar 1987 in St. Louis Park, MN. She married ORLAN ANDREW GORMAN. He was born 25 Sep 1925 in Kenmare, Ward County, ND.
Children of ALOHA HAMMACK and ORLAN GORMAN are:
712.   i.   STEVEN GREGORY[13] GORMAN, b. 30 Apr 1949, Kenmare, Ward County, ND.
713.   ii.   JILL RENEE GORMAN, b. 03 May 1951, Kenmare, Ward County, ND.
        iii. JACK GORMAN, b. 10 May 1954, Minneapolis, MN.
Key Source: Family records of Jonas Hammack, Bend, OR.

618. CLAYTON DARREL "CLAY"[12] HAMMACK *(EUGENE[11], JOHN ROBERT[10], JOHN T.[9], SIMEON J.[8], WILLIAM T.[7], ROBERT HAMMACK[6] JR., ROBERT HAMMACK[5] SR., WILLIAM "THE ELDER"[4] HAMMACK, WILLIAM "O"[3], JOHN[2] HAMMOCKE, ? JOHN[1] HAMMOT)* was born 01 Jun 1931. He married JULIA LYNN, daughter of HAROLD LYNN and INEZ SMITH. She was born 30 Nov 1948.
Children of CLAYTON HAMMACK and JULIA LYNN are:
714.   i.   BRADFORD[13] HAMMACK, b. 03 Feb 1953.
        ii.   SANDRA, b. 18 Jul 1959.
Key Source: Family records of Jonas Hammack, Bend, OR.

619. PATRICIA[12] HAMMACK *(EUGENE[11], JOHN ROBERT[10], JOHN T.[9], SIMEON J.[8], WILLIAM T.[7], ROBERT HAMMACK[6] JR., ROBERT HAMMACK[5] SR., WILLIAM "THE ELDER"[4] HAMMACK, WILLIAM "O"[3], JOHN[2] HAMMOCKE, ? JOHN[1] HAMMOT)* was born 19 Nov 1941. She married GORDON WILHELMI.
Child of PATRICIA HAMMACK and GORDON WILHELMI is:
        i.   DAVID[13] WILHELMI, m. RHONDA.
Key Source: Family records of Jonas Hammack, Bend, OR.

620. ROSE[12] HAMMACK *(JONAS ALAN[11], JOHN ROBERT[10], JOHN T.[9], SIMEON J.[8], WILLIAM T.[7], ROBERT HAMMACK[6] JR., ROBERT HAMMACK[5] SR., WILLIAM "THE ELDER"[4] HAMMACK,*

WILLIAM "O"³, JOHN² HAMMOCKE, ? JOHN¹ HAMMOT) was born 17 Feb 1943 in Redmond, Oregon. She married (1) TIM WAKEFIELD. She married (2) JAMES A GALLANT.

Children of ROSE HAMMACK and TIM WAKEFIELD are:

715.   i.   JEFFREY DALE¹³ WAKEFIELD, b. 03 Jul 1967.

       ii.   JENNY DEANN WAKEFIELD, b. 09 Jan 1970; d. 10 Mar 1972.

      iii.   SCOTT EDWARD WAKEFIELD, b. 19 Jul 1973.

716.   iv.   AMY MARIE WAKEFIELD, b. 25 Jun 1975.

Key Source: Family records of Jonas Hammack, Bend, OR.

621. JAMES VANCE¹² DAVIS *(WILLIAM ROSCOE¹¹, BETSY ANN¹⁰ HAMMACK, FELIX WILBORN⁹, SIMEON J.⁸, WILLIAM T.⁷, ROBERT HAMMACK⁶ JR., ROBERT HAMMACK⁵ SR., WILLIAM "THE ELDER"⁴ HAMMACK, WILLIAM "O"³, JOHN² HAMMOCKE, ? JOHN¹ HAMMOT)* was born 18 Mar 1919 in Calhoun Co., MS. He married MIRIAM LOUISE GARY 28 Jan 1939 in Mississippi.

Child of JAMES DAVIS and MIRIAM GARY is:

717.   i.   BEVERLY JAYNE¹³ DAVIS, b. 17 Sep 1947, Mississippi.

Key Source: Family records of William Roscoe Davis, Jr., Grenada, MS.

622. WILLIAM ROSCOE DAVIS¹² JR. *(WILLIAM ROSCOE¹¹ DAVIS, BETSY ANN¹⁰ HAMMACK, FELIX WILBORN⁹, SIMEON J.⁸, WILLIAM T.⁷, ROBERT HAMMACK⁶ JR., ROBERT HAMMACK⁵ SR., WILLIAM "THE ELDER"⁴ HAMMACK, WILLIAM "O"³, JOHN² HAMMOCKE, ? JOHN¹ HAMMOT)* was born 16 May 1927 in Calhoun Co., MS. He married JESSIE MARIE WILLIAMSON 21 Jul 1949 in Grenada, MS.

Child of WILLIAM JR. and JESSIE WILLIAMSON is:

718.   i.   NANCY REA¹³ DAVIS, b. 22 Feb 1953, Grenada Co., MS.

Key Source: Family records of William Roscoe Davis, Jr., Grenada, MS.

623. JOHN ALFRED¹² HAMMOCK *(ERNEST F.¹¹, FELIX A.¹⁰, ALFRED WASHINGTON "DOCK"⁹ HAMMACK, SIMEON J.⁸, WILLIAM T.⁷, ROBERT HAMMACK⁶ JR., ROBERT HAMMACK⁵ SR., WILLIAM "THE ELDER"⁴ HAMMACK, WILLIAM "O"³, JOHN² HAMMOCKE, ? JOHN¹ HAMMOT)* was born 29 Apr 1922 in Ashley Co., AR, and died Apr 1978 in Ashley Co., AR.

Child of JOHN ALFRED HAMMOCK is:

       i.   PATRICIA DIANE¹³ HAMMOCK, b. 13 Jun 1955, Warren, AR; d. 17 Oct 2004, Monticello, AR; m. DAVID SANSON.

Key Source: Lois Hagood, *The Elusive Ancestor* (Crossett, AR, 1992); Lois Hagood, "C. W. Roberts Family," in Robert A. and Mary I. Carpenter, *Reflections of Ashley County* (Dallas, TX, 1988), F544.

624. FRANCES¹² SMITH *(WILLIE B.¹¹ HAMMOCK, FELIX A.¹⁰, ALFRED WASHINGTON "DOCK"⁹ HAMMACK, SIMEON J.⁸, WILLIAM T.⁷, ROBERT HAMMACK⁶ JR., ROBERT HAMMACK⁵ SR., WILLIAM "THE ELDER"⁴ HAMMACK, WILLIAM "O"³, JOHN² HAMMOCKE, ? JOHN¹ HAMMOT)* She married HOLLIS JOHNSON.

Children of FRANCES SMITH and HOLLIS JOHNSON are:

       i.   CHARLES¹³ JOHNSON.

      ii.   WILLIE ANNETTE JOHNSON.

Key Source: Lois Hagood, *The Elusive Ancestor* (Crossett, AR, 1992); Lois Hagood, "C. W. Roberts Family," in Robert A. and Mary I. Carpenter, *Reflections of Ashley County* (Dallas, TX, 1988), F544.

625. VIRGINIA¹² SMITH *(WILLIE B.¹¹ HAMMOCK, FELIX A.¹⁰, ALFRED WASHINGTON "DOCK"⁹ HAMMACK, SIMEON J.⁸, WILLIAM T.⁷, ROBERT HAMMACK⁶ JR., ROBERT HAMMACK⁵ SR.,*

WILLIAM "THE ELDER"[4] HAMMACK, WILLIAM "O"[3], JOHN[2] HAMMOCKE, ? JOHN[1] HAMMOT) She married ERNSTON ALLISON.

Children of VIRGINIA SMITH and ERNSTON ALLISON are:

      i.   BILLY[13] ALLISON.

      ii. JIMMY ALLISON.

     iii. MARGARET ANN ALLISON.

     iv. PAULA ALLISON.

      v. WANDA ALLISON.

Key Source: Lois Hagood, *The Elusive Ancestor* (Crossett, AR, 1992); Lois Hagood, "C. W. Roberts Family," in Robert A. and Mary I. Carpenter, *Reflections of Ashley County* (Dallas, TX, 1988), F544.

626. BETTI[12] SMITH *(WILLIE B.[11] HAMMOCK, FELIX A.[10], ALFRED WASHINGTON "DOCK"[9] HAMMACK, SIMEON J.[8], WILLIAM T.[7], ROBERT HAMMACK[6] JR., ROBERT HAMMACK[5] SR., WILLIAM "THE ELDER"[4] HAMMACK, WILLIAM "O"[3], JOHN[2] HAMMOCKE, ? JOHN[1] HAMMOT)* She married PAT SHELTON.

Children of BETTI SMITH and PAT SHELTON are:

      i.   LINDA[13] SHELTON.

      ii. CARL SHELTON.

     iii. RAYMOND SHELTON.

Key Source: Lois Hagood, *The Elusive Ancestor* (Crossett, AR, 1992); Lois Hagood, "C. W. Roberts Family," in Robert A. and Mary I. Carpenter, *Reflections of Ashley County* (Dallas, TX, 1988), F544.

627. ANNIE MAE[12] HAMMOCK *(JAMES PELL[11], FELIX A.[10], ALFRED WASHINGTON "DOCK"[9] HAMMACK, SIMEON J.[8], WILLIAM T.[7], ROBERT HAMMACK[6] JR., ROBERT HAMMACK[5] SR., WILLIAM "THE ELDER"[4] HAMMACK, WILLIAM "O"[3], JOHN[2] HAMMOCKE, ? JOHN[1] HAMMOT)* was born 09 Aug 1944 in Montrose, AR. She married (1) DONALD E. ELLIOTT. She married (2) BOBBY GENE ENDSLEY. She married (3) DONALD ROSS HIGH.

Children of ANNIE HAMMOCK and DONALD ELLIOTT are:

719.   i.   ANNIE JEANETTE[13] ELLIOTT, b. 24 May 1961, Monticello, AR.

         ii. JAMES E. ELLIOTT, b. 14 Jul 1962, Monticello, AR.

720.   iii. KENNETH RAY ELLIOTT, b. 14 Feb 1963, Monticello, AR.

721.   iv. JUDY KAY ELLIOTT, b. 11 Mar 1965, Monticello, AR.

Children of ANNIE HAMMOCK and BOBBY ENDSLEY are:

722.   v. BOBBY WAYNE[13] ENDSLEY, b. 29 Mar 1966, Monticello, AR.

723.   vi. LARRY GENE ENDSLEY, b. 27 Nov 1968, Dermott, AR.

       vii. JACK A. ENDSLEY, b. 11 Jul 1970, Houston, TX.

Key Source: Lois Hagood, *The Elusive Ancestor* (Crossett, AR, 1992); Lois Hagood, "C. W. Roberts Family," in Robert A. and Mary I. Carpenter, *Reflections of Ashley County* (Dallas, TX, 1988), F544.

628. JAMES ALFORD[12] HAMMOCK *(JAMES PELL[11], FELIX A.[10], ALFRED WASHINGTON "DOCK"[9] HAMMACK, SIMEON J.[8], WILLIAM T.[7], ROBERT HAMMACK[6] JR., ROBERT HAMMACK[5] SR., WILLIAM "THE ELDER"[4] HAMMACK, WILLIAM "O"[3], JOHN[2] HAMMOCKE, ? JOHN[1] HAMMOT)* was born 18 May 1946 in Montrose, AR. He married (1) LUELLA JAMES. He married (2) RUTHIE REAP.

Children of JAMES HAMMOCK and LUELLA JAMES are:

      i.   JAMES WESLEY[13] HAMMOCK, b. 24 Jan 1966, Monticello, AR; d. 25 Jul 1966, Monticello, AR.

      ii. BETTY LOU HAMMOCK, b. 09 May 1967, Monticello, AR.

     iii. CHARLES ALFORD HAMMOCK, b. 15 Mar 1969, Monticello, AR.

Children of JAMES HAMMOCK and RUTHIE REAP are:

iv. THOMAS JAMES[13] HAMMOCK, b. 25 Feb 1982, Monticello, AR.

v. BECKY JO HAMMOCK, b. 07 Dec 1983, Monticello, AR.

vi. JAMES W. HAMMOCK, b. 19 Sep 1988, Monticello, AR.

Key Source: Lois Hagood, *The Elusive Ancestor* (Crossett, AR, 1992); Lois Hagood, "C. W. Roberts Family," in Robert A. and Mary I. Carpenter, *Reflections of Ashley County* (Dallas, TX, 1988), F544.

629. EDITH P[12] HAMMOCK *(JAMES PELL[11], FELIX A.[10], ALFRED WASHINGTON "DOCK"[9] HAMMACK, SIMEON J.[8], WILLIAM T.[7], ROBERT HAMMACK[6] JR., ROBERT HAMMACK[5] SR., WILLIAM "THE ELDER"[4] HAMMACK, WILLIAM "O"[3], JOHN[2] HAMMOCKE, ? JOHN[1] HAMMOT)* was born 30 Oct 1947 in Montrose, AR, and died 22 Mar 2003 in Monticello, AR. She married (1) HOWARD ARRINGTON. She married (2) LARRY GENE POE. She married (3) ALVY LEE KAISER.

Children of EDITH HAMMOCK and HOWARD ARRINGTON are:

i. MARY PAULETTE[13] ARRINGTON, b. 12 Oct 1966, New Orleans, LA.

ii. MARY ANN ARRINGTON, b. 28 Jun 1968, Monticello, AR.

Children of EDITH HAMMOCK and LARRY POE are:

iii. LARRY GENE[13] POE, JR., b. 12 May 1971, Monticello, AR.

iv. ANNIE J. POE, b. 25 Dec 1972, Monticello, AR.

Key Source: Lois Hagood, *The Elusive Ancestor* (Crossett, AR, 1992); Lois Hagood, "C. W. Roberts Family," in Robert A. and Mary I. Carpenter, *Reflections of Ashley County* (Dallas, TX, 1988), F544.

630. OLIVIA[12] HONEYCUTT *(RUTH[11] ROBERTS, JEFFIE JANE[10] HAMMOCK, ALFRED WASHINGTON "DOCK"[9] HAMMACK, SIMEON J.[8], WILLIAM T.[7], ROBERT HAMMACK[6] JR., ROBERT HAMMACK[5] SR., WILLIAM "THE ELDER"[4] HAMMACK, WILLIAM "O"[3], JOHN[2] HAMMOCKE, ? JOHN[1] HAMMOT)* was born 21 Sep 1915 in Ashley County, AR, and died 20 May 1949 in Ashley Co., AR. She married EDWARD DUELL TANNER in Warren, AR, son of A. TANNER and AUDREY SINGLETON. He was born 04 May 1917.

Child of OLIVIA HONEYCUTT and EDWARD TANNER is:

724. i. DONNA RUTH[13] TANNER, b. 11 Aug 1941, Ouachita Co., AR.

Key Source: Lois Hagood, *The Elusive Ancestor* (Crossett, AR, 1992); Lois Hagood, "C. W. Roberts Family," in Robert A. and Mary I. Carpenter, *Reflections of Ashley County* (Dallas, TX, 1988), F544.

631. WILLIAM THOMAS[12] HONEYCUTT, JR. *(RUTH[11] ROBERTS, JEFFIE JANE[10] HAMMOCK, ALFRED WASHINGTON "DOCK"[9] HAMMACK, SIMEON J.[8], WILLIAM T.[7], ROBERT HAMMACK[6] JR., ROBERT HAMMACK[5] SR., WILLIAM "THE ELDER"[4] HAMMACK, WILLIAM "O"[3], JOHN[2] HAMMOCKE, ? JOHN[1] HAMMOT)* was born 28 Jan 1917 in Ashley County, AR, and died 06 Oct 1992 in Ouachita Co., AR. He married BESSIE ELIZABETH DOMANSKI 13 Feb 1941 in Smackover, AR, daughter of THADIUS DOMANSKI and MANILA WILLIAMS. She was born 24 Sep 1923 in Arcadia, Bienville Parish, LA.

Children of WILLIAM HONEYCUTT and BESSIE DOMANSKI are:

725. i. JANICE CAROLYN[13] HONEYCUTT, b. 07 Feb 1942, Ouachita Co., AR.

726. ii. GARY RANDAL HONEYCUTT, b. 01 Jan 1947, Ouachita Co., AR.

Key Source: Lois Hagood, *The Elusive Ancestor* (Crossett, AR, 1992); Lois Hagood, "C. W. Roberts Family," in Robert A. and Mary I. Carpenter, *Reflections of Ashley County* (Dallas, TX, 1988), F544.

632. LOIS RUTH[12] HONEYCUTT *(RUTH[11] ROBERTS, JEFFIE JANE[10] HAMMOCK, ALFRED WASHINGTON "DOCK"[9] HAMMACK, SIMEON J.[8], WILLIAM T.[7], ROBERT HAMMACK[6] JR., ROBERT HAMMACK[5] SR., WILLIAM "THE ELDER"[4] HAMMACK, WILLIAM "O"[3], JOHN[2] HAMMOCKE, ? JOHN[1] HAMMOT)* was born 23 Feb 1919 in Ashley County, AR, and died 23 Jun 1996 in Ashley

County, AR. She married MANSEL HAGOOD 03 Feb 1940 in Ouachita Co., AR, son of JOHN HAGOOD and WINNIE NORREL. He was born 13 Apr 1913 in Arkansas, and died 20 Sep 1975 in Ouachita Co., AR.

Child of LOIS HONEYCUTT and MANSEL HAGOOD is:

727.	i.	DONALD MANSEL[13] HAGOOD, b. 23 Jul 1964, DeQueen, Sevier County, AR.

Key Source: Lois Hagood, *The Elusive Ancestor* (Crossett, AR, 1992); Lois Hagood, "C. W. Roberts Family," in Robert A. and Mary I. Carpenter, *Reflections of Ashley County* (Dallas, TX, 1988), F544.

633. MARGARET LAVENIAL[12] ROBERTS *(CLAUD CYRUS[11], JEFFIE JANE[10] HAMMOCK, ALFRED WASHINGTON "DOCK"[9] HAMMACK, SIMEON J.[8], WILLIAM T.[7], ROBERT HAMMACK[6] JR., ROBERT HAMMACK[5] SR., WILLIAM "THE ELDER"[4] HAMMACK, WILLIAM "O"[3], JOHN[2] HAMMOCKE, ? JOHN[1] HAMMOT)* was born 13 Jul 1920 in Ashley Co., AR, and died 22 Jun 1980 in Ashley Co., AR. She married JOE ADAMS 28 May 1943 in Ashley Co., AR.

Children of MARGARET ROBERTS and JOE ADAMS are:

728.	i.	RHODA JO[13] ADAMS, b. 03 Sep 1944, Ashley Co., AR.
	ii.	DENNIS DALE ADAMS, b. 20 Oct 1948, Ashley Co., AR.

Key Source: Lois Hagood, *The Elusive Ancestor* (Crossett, AR, 1992); Lois Hagood, "C. W. Roberts Family," in Robert A. and Mary I. Carpenter, *Reflections of Ashley County* (Dallas, TX, 1988), F544.

634. LAVONIA JOYCE[12] ROBERTS *(CLAUD CYRUS[11], JEFFIE JANE[10] HAMMOCK, ALFRED WASHINGTON "DOCK"[9] HAMMACK, SIMEON J.[8], WILLIAM T.[7], ROBERT HAMMACK[6] JR., ROBERT HAMMACK[5] SR., WILLIAM "THE ELDER"[4] HAMMACK, WILLIAM "O"[3], JOHN[2] HAMMOCKE, ? JOHN[1] HAMMOT)* was born 31 May 1926 in Ashley Co., AR. She married DIBRELL HELTON 1947 in Crossett, Ashley County, AR.

Children of LAVONIA ROBERTS and DIBRELL HELTON are:

729.	i.	KENNETH[13] HELTON, b. 21 Feb 1948.
	ii.	DEBRA HELTON, b. 06 Sep 1952.
	iii.	BARRY HELTON, b. 23 Nov 1956; m. KAREN PETTY.
	iv.	REGINALD HELTON, b. 30 Sep 1958; m. MARIE SPARKS, 28 Jun 1986.

Key Source: Lois Hagood, *The Elusive Ancestor* (Crossett, AR, 1992); Lois Hagood, "C. W. Roberts Family," in Robert A. and Mary I. Carpenter, *Reflections of Ashley County* (Dallas, TX, 1988), F544.

635. ELIZABETH LANE[12] ROBERTS *(CLAUD CYRUS[11], JEFFIE JANE[10] HAMMOCK, ALFRED WASHINGTON "DOCK"[9] HAMMACK, SIMEON J.[8], WILLIAM T.[7], ROBERT HAMMACK[6] JR., ROBERT HAMMACK[5] SR., WILLIAM "THE ELDER"[4] HAMMACK, WILLIAM "O"[3], JOHN[2] HAMMOCKE, ? JOHN[1] HAMMOT)* was born 27 Jul 1930 in Ashley Co., AR. She married PAUL HARVEY PALSER. He was born 24 Jul 1927 in Nebraska.

Children of ELIZABETH ROBERTS and PAUL PALSER are:

730.	i.	REBECCA LANE[13] PALSER, b. 13 Oct 1951.
	ii.	RONALD PAUL PALSER, b. 24 Jun 1954.
731.	iii.	ELIZABETH GRACE PALSER, b. 22 May 1955.
	iv.	MICHELLE RENEE PALSER, b. 24 Jan 1969; m. THOMAS CHRISTOPHER MILLER, 25 Aug 1990.

Key Source: Lois Hagood, *The Elusive Ancestor* (Crossett, AR, 1992); Lois Hagood, "C. W. Roberts Family," in Robert A. and Mary I. Carpenter, *Reflections of Ashley County* (Dallas, TX, 1988), F544.

636. BARBARA JANE[12] ROBERTS *(SYLVESTER ALFRED[11], JEFFIE JANE[10] HAMMOCK, ALFRED WASHINGTON "DOCK"[9] HAMMACK, SIMEON J.[8], WILLIAM T.[7], ROBERT HAMMACK[6] JR., ROBERT HAMMACK[5] SR., WILLIAM "THE ELDER"[4] HAMMACK, WILLIAM "O"[3], JOHN[2] HAMMOCKE, ?*

JOHN[1] *HAMMOT)* was born 05 Feb 1939 in Ashley Co., AR. She married RONALD BRUCE KEENE 27 Aug 1966 in Crossett, Ashley County, AR.

Children of BARBARA ROBERTS and RONALD KEENE are:

> i. LISA MARIE[13] KEENE, b. 11 Feb 1970, Ashley Co., AR; m. RAUL ROMOCATIZ, 28 Apr 1994.
>
> ii. BRYCE ROBERTS KEENE, b. 26 Feb 1974, Ashley Co., AR.

Key Source: Lois Hagood, *The Elusive Ancestor* (Crossett, AR, 1992); Lois Hagood, "C. W. Roberts Family," in Robert A. and Mary I. Carpenter, *Reflections of Ashley County* (Dallas, TX, 1988), F544.

637. REBA JEAN[12] ROBERTS *(WILLIAM TRACY*[11]*, JEFFIE JANE*[10] *HAMMOCK, ALFRED WASHINGTON "DOCK"*[9] *HAMMACK, SIMEON J.*[8]*, WILLIAM T.*[7]*, ROBERT HAMMACK*[6] *JR., ROBERT HAMMACK*[5] *SR., WILLIAM "THE ELDER"*[4] *HAMMACK, WILLIAM "O"*[3]*, JOHN*[2] *HAMMOCKE, ? JOHN*[1] *HAMMOT)* was born 29 Oct 1929 in Big Springs, TX. She married THOMAS ROSS BAILEY 01 Jun 1952. He was born 1928.

Children of REBA ROBERTS and THOMAS BAILEY are:

> i. THOMAS G.[13] BAILEY, b. 23 Dec 1956; m. BEVERLY MASSEY.
>
> ii. JAMES ROBERT BAILEY, b. 24 Nov 1959.

Key Source: Lois Hagood, *The Elusive Ancestor* (Crossett, AR, 1992); Lois Hagood, "C. W. Roberts Family," in Robert A. and Mary I. Carpenter, *Reflections of Ashley County* (Dallas, TX, 1988), F544.

638. DONNIE JANE[12] ROBERTS *(WILLIAM TRACY*[11]*, JEFFIE JANE*[10] *HAMMOCK, ALFRED WASHINGTON "DOCK"*[9] *HAMMACK, SIMEON J.*[8]*, WILLIAM T.*[7]*, ROBERT HAMMACK*[6] *JR., ROBERT HAMMACK*[5] *SR., WILLIAM "THE ELDER"*[4] *HAMMACK, WILLIAM "O"*[3]*, JOHN*[2] *HAMMOCKE, ? JOHN*[1] *HAMMOT)* was born 11 Jul 1930 in Big Springs, TX. She married DAN RAY BYRNE 27 Mar 1948 in Big Springs, TX.

Children of DONNIE ROBERTS and DAN BYRNE are:

> 732. i. DAN RAY[13] BYRNE, JR., b. 30 Nov 1948, El Paso, TX.
>
> 733. ii. WILLIAM ROBERT BYRNE, b. 01 Jul 1950, Big Springs, TX.
>
> iii. KIM ELAINE BYRNE, b. 07 Oct 1961, Corpus Christi, TX; m. JEFF HUNT, 01 Aug 1979, Corpus Christi, TX.

Key Source: Lois Hagood, *The Elusive Ancestor* (Crossett, AR, 1992); Lois Hagood, "C. W. Roberts Family," in Robert A. and Mary I. Carpenter, *Reflections of Ashley County* (Dallas, TX, 1988), F544.

639. MARY KATHERINE[12] ROBERTS *(WILLIAM TRACY*[11]*, JEFFIE JANE*[10] *HAMMOCK, ALFRED WASHINGTON "DOCK"*[9] *HAMMACK, SIMEON J.*[8]*, WILLIAM T.*[7]*, ROBERT HAMMACK*[6] *JR., ROBERT HAMMACK*[5] *SR., WILLIAM "THE ELDER"*[4] *HAMMACK, WILLIAM "O"*[3]*, JOHN*[2] *HAMMOCKE, ? JOHN*[1] *HAMMOT)* was born 03 Mar 1934 in Big Springs, TX. She married EDWARD EUGENE HOLLY 14 May 1955 in Big Springs, TX.

Children of MARY ROBERTS and EDWARD HOLLY are:

> i. KAREN CELESTE[13] HOLLY, b. 16 May 1957, Big Springs, TX.
>
> ii. KELLY ANN HOLLY, b. 14 Oct 1959, Big Springs, TX; m. LARRY BLAINE GRILLE.

Key Source: Lois Hagood, *The Elusive Ancestor* (Crossett, AR, 1992); Lois Hagood, "C. W. Roberts Family," in Robert A. and Mary I. Carpenter, *Reflections of Ashley County* (Dallas, TX, 1988), F544.

640. MARTHA ANN[12] ROBERTS *(VIRGIL ASBERRY*[11]*, JEFFIE JANE*[10] *HAMMOCK, ALFRED WASHINGTON "DOCK"*[9] *HAMMACK, SIMEON J.*[8]*, WILLIAM T.*[7]*, ROBERT HAMMACK*[6] *JR., ROBERT HAMMACK*[5] *SR., WILLIAM "THE ELDER"*[4] *HAMMACK, WILLIAM "O"*[3]*, JOHN*[2] *HAMMOCKE, ? JOHN*[1] *HAMMOT)* was born 29 Apr 1937 in Dallas, TX. She married (1) ERNEST ADOLPH SCHWEIZER. She married (2) RICHARD ALVA NELSON.

Children of MARTHA ROBERTS and ERNEST SCHWEIZER are:
> i. HEIDI MARIE[13] SCHWEIZER, b. 14 Jun 1966.
> ii. SCOTT ROBERTS SCHWEIZER, b. 26 May 1969.

Key Source: Lois Hagood, *The Elusive Ancestor* (Crossett, AR, 1992); Lois Hagood, "C. W. Roberts Family," in Robert A. and Mary I. Carpenter, *Reflections of Ashley County* (Dallas, TX, 1988), F544.

641. JANE FRANKLIN[12] ROBERTS *(VIRGIL ASBERRY[11], JEFFIE JANE[10] HAMMOCK, ALFRED WASHINGTON "DOCK"[9] HAMMACK, SIMEON J.[8], WILLIAM T.[7], ROBERT HAMMACK[6] JR., ROBERT HAMMACK[5] SR., WILLIAM "THE ELDER"[4] HAMMACK, WILLIAM "O"[3], JOHN[2] HAMMOCKE, ? JOHN[1] HAMMOT)* was born 22 Mar 1942 in Dallas, TX. She married (1) JERRY RAY DOUGLAS. She married (2) RICHARD HATLEY.
Children of JANE ROBERTS and JERRY DOUGLAS are:
> i. JERRY[13] DOUGLAS.
> ii. KENNETH ROBERTS DOUGLAS.

Key Source: Lois Hagood, *The Elusive Ancestor* (Crossett, AR, 1992); Lois Hagood, "C. W. Roberts Family," in Robert A. and Mary I. Carpenter, *Reflections of Ashley County* (Dallas, TX, 1988), F544.

642. EDWARD LAVERNE[12] KELLEY *(HATTIE MAE[11] ROBERTS, JEFFIE JANE[10] HAMMOCK, ALFRED WASHINGTON "DOCK"[9] HAMMACK, SIMEON J.[8], WILLIAM T.[7], ROBERT HAMMACK[6] JR., ROBERT HAMMACK[5] SR., WILLIAM "THE ELDER"[4] HAMMACK, WILLIAM "O"[3], JOHN[2] HAMMOCKE, ? JOHN[1] HAMMOT)* was born 05 Oct 1924 in Ashley County, AR. He married MARY LOUISE SEIFERS 24 Nov 1942 in Ashley Co., AR.
Children of EDWARD KELLEY and MARY SEIFERS are:
> i. JOHN ALLEN[13] KELLEY, b. 20 Jan 1944; m. PEGGY BROWN.
> ii. JOAN CAROLYN KELLEY, b. 07 Apr 1947; m. (1) GARY WILLIAMS; m. (2) BRIAN WRAXALL.
> iii. DEBRA LYNN KELLEY, b. 26 Nov 1950; m. (1) JAMES WHITE; m. (2) CLIFF GILLAND.
> iv. DAVID KENT KELLEY, b. 20 Feb 1955; m. JANE SULLIVAN.
> v. PATRICK KEVIN KELLEY, b. 10 Jul 1964; m. EYNE SWAIN.

Key Source: Lois Hagood, *The Elusive Ancestor* (Crossett, AR, 1992); Lois Hagood, "C. W. Roberts Family," in Robert A. and Mary I. Carpenter, *Reflections of Ashley County* (Dallas, TX, 1988), F544.

643. VRELAN CLYDE[12] JOHNSON *(CLARA BELL[11] ROBERTS, JEFFIE JANE[10] HAMMOCK, ALFRED WASHINGTON "DOCK"[9] HAMMACK, SIMEON J.[8], WILLIAM T.[7], ROBERT HAMMACK[6] JR., ROBERT HAMMACK[5] SR., WILLIAM "THE ELDER"[4] HAMMACK, WILLIAM "O"[3], JOHN[2] HAMMOCKE, ? JOHN[1] HAMMOT)* was born 25 May 1922 in Ashley Co., AR. He married EDITH ELIZABETH RICKMAN.
Children of VRELAN JOHNSON and EDITH RICKMAN are:
> i. ADA ELLON[13] JOHNSON, b. 20 Mar 1941, Ashley Co., AR; m. JOHNNY MACK JOHNSON.
> ii. SARAH ELIZABETH JOHNSON, b. 18 Nov 1943, Ashley Co., AR; m. JOHNNY FAYE CARTER, 20 May 1961, Crossett, Ashley County, AR.
> iii. GWENNYETH ANN JOHNSON, b. 27 Jul 1947, Ashley Co., AR; m. AUBREY L. STEPHENSON, 05 Jun 1964, Crossett, Ashley County, AR.
> iv. LELAN GLENN JOHNSON, b. 18 Nov 1949, Ashley Co., AR; m. GEORGIA MARIE WILDER, Crossett, Ashley County, AR.

Key Source: Lois Hagood, *The Elusive Ancestor* (Crossett, AR, 1992); Lois Hagood, "C. W. Roberts Family," in Robert A. and Mary I. Carpenter, *Reflections of Ashley County* (Dallas, TX, 1988), F544.

644. TRAVIS FLOYD[12] JOHNSON *(CLARA BELL[11] ROBERTS, JEFFIE JANE[10] HAMMOCK, ALFRED WASHINGTON "DOCK"[9] HAMMACK, SIMEON J.[8], WILLIAM T.[7], ROBERT HAMMACK[6] JR., ROBERT HAMMACK[5] SR., WILLIAM "THE ELDER"[4] HAMMACK, WILLIAM "O"[3], JOHN[2] HAMMOCKE, ? JOHN[1] HAMMOT)* was born 12 Nov 1924 in Ashley Co., AR. He married SARAH BROWN 31 May 1953 in Ruston, LA. She was born 16 May 1934.
Children of TRAVIS JOHNSON and SARAH BROWN are:
    i. CYNTHIA LOU[13] JOHNSON, b. 18 Oct 1956, Ouachita Co., AR.
    ii. BETH LAFRAN JOHNSON, b. 21 Oct 1960, Pine Bluff, AR; m. RICK COOK.
Key Source: Lois Hagood, *The Elusive Ancestor* (Crossett, AR, 1992); Lois Hagood, "C. W. Roberts Family," in Robert A. and Mary I. Carpenter, *Reflections of Ashley County* (Dallas, TX, 1988), F544.

645. JAMES RUSSELL[12] JOHNSON *(CLARA BELL[11] ROBERTS, JEFFIE JANE[10] HAMMOCK, ALFRED WASHINGTON "DOCK"[9] HAMMACK, SIMEON J.[8], WILLIAM T.[7], ROBERT HAMMACK[6] JR., ROBERT HAMMACK[5] SR., WILLIAM "THE ELDER"[4] HAMMACK, WILLIAM "O"[3], JOHN[2] HAMMOCKE, ? JOHN[1] HAMMOT)* was born 13 Apr 1938 in Ashley Co., AR. He married BARBARA REED.
Children of JAMES JOHNSON and BARBARA REED are:
    i. DEBRA SUE[13] JOHNSON, b. 03 Dec 1965, Pine Bluff, AR.
    ii. LISA KAY JOHNSON, b. 15 May 1968, Pine Bluff, AR.
    iii. JAMIE DIANE JOHNSON, b. 02 Sep 1970, Pine Bluff, AR.
Key Source: Lois Hagood, *The Elusive Ancestor* (Crossett, AR, 1992); Lois Hagood, "C. W. Roberts Family," in Robert A. and Mary I. Carpenter, *Reflections of Ashley County* (Dallas, TX, 1988), F544.

646. LINDA CAROLYN[12] ROBERTS *(JESSE WILLARD[11], JEFFIE JANE[10] HAMMOCK, ALFRED WASHINGTON "DOCK"[9] HAMMACK, SIMEON J.[8], WILLIAM T.[7], ROBERT HAMMACK[6] JR., ROBERT HAMMACK[5] SR., WILLIAM "THE ELDER"[4] HAMMACK, WILLIAM "O"[3], JOHN[2] HAMMOCKE, ? JOHN[1] HAMMOT)* was born 24 Mar 1944 in Ashley Co., AR. She married (1) PAUL MCKAY 01 Sep 1964 in Ashley Co., AR. She married (2) PHILLIP WAYNE LAMB 07 Mar 1982 in Ashley Co., AR.
Children of LINDA ROBERTS and PHILLIP LAMB are:
    i. PHILLIP ALFRED ELLIOT[13] LAMB, b. 06 Jan 1984, Pulaski Co., AR.
    ii. JOHNATHAN WILLARD DEVEN LAMB, b. 13 Feb 1988, India.
Key Source: Lois Hagood, *The Elusive Ancestor* (Crossett, AR, 1992); Lois Hagood, "C. W. Roberts Family," in Robert A. and Mary I. Carpenter, *Reflections of Ashley County* (Dallas, TX, 1988), F544.

647. WAYMON[12] DOUGLAS *(VERGIE MAE[11] FERGUSON, VIRGINIA MARGARET "JENNY"[10] HAMMOCK, ALFRED WASHINGTON "DOCK"[9] HAMMACK, SIMEON J.[8], WILLIAM T.[7], ROBERT HAMMACK[6] JR., ROBERT HAMMACK[5] SR., WILLIAM "THE ELDER"[4] HAMMACK, WILLIAM "O"[3], JOHN[2] HAMMOCKE, ? JOHN[1] HAMMOT)* He married (1) LAVOTICA KELLEBREW. He married (2) DOROTHY WYMAN.
Child of WAYMON DOUGLAS and LAVOTICA KELLEBREW is:
    i. BRUCE[13] DOUGLAS.
Child of WAYMON DOUGLAS and DOROTHY WYMAN is:
    ii. APRIL[13] DOUGLAS.
Key Source: Lois Hagood, *The Elusive Ancestor* (Crossett, AR, 1992); Lois Hagood, "C. W. Roberts Family," in Robert A. and Mary I. Carpenter, *Reflections of Ashley County* (Dallas, TX, 1988), F544.

648. CHARLOTTE ANN[12] DOUGLAS *(VERGIE MAE[11] FERGUSON, VIRGINIA MARGARET "JENNY"[10] HAMMOCK, ALFRED WASHINGTON "DOCK"[9] HAMMACK, SIMEON J.[8], WILLIAM T.[7],*

ROBERT HAMMACK[6] JR., ROBERT HAMMACK[5] SR., WILLIAM "THE ELDER"[4] HAMMACK, WILLIAM "O"[3], JOHN[2] HAMMOCKE, ? JOHN[1] HAMMOT) She married WALTER MONROE WIGLEY.

Children of CHARLOTTE DOUGLAS and WALTER WIGLEY are:
>   i. MARY ANN[13] WIGLEY.
>   ii. JOY LYNETTE WIGLEY.

Key Source: Lois Hagood, *The Elusive Ancestor* (Crossett, AR, 1992); Lois Hagood, "C. W. Roberts Family," in Robert A. and Mary I. Carpenter, *Reflections of Ashley County* (Dallas, TX, 1988), F544.

649. THAD ANDERSON[12] DOUGLAS *(VERGIE MAE[11] FERGUSON, VIRGINIA MARGARET "JENNY"[10] HAMMOCK, ALFRED WASHINGTON "DOCK"[9] HAMMACK, SIMEON J.[8], WILLIAM T.[7], ROBERT HAMMACK[6] JR., ROBERT HAMMACK[5] SR., WILLIAM "THE ELDER"[4] HAMMACK, WILLIAM "O"[3], JOHN[2] HAMMOCKE, ? JOHN[1] HAMMOT)* was born 1930. He married PATRICIA LEE FARMER.

Children of THAD DOUGLAS and PATRICIA FARMER are:
>   i.   THAD ANDERSON[13] DOUGLAS, JR..
>   ii. DEBRA DIANNE DOUGLAS.
>   iii. DEANNA LEE DOUGLAS.

Key Source: Lois Hagood, *The Elusive Ancestor* (Crossett, AR, 1992); Lois Hagood, "C. W. Roberts Family," in Robert A. and Mary I. Carpenter, *Reflections of Ashley County* (Dallas, TX, 1988), F544.

650. JIMMY NEAL[12] KELLEY *(MARTHA AGNES[11] PEDEN, VIRGINIA MARGARET "JENNY"[10] HAMMOCK, ALFRED WASHINGTON "DOCK"[9] HAMMACK, SIMEON J.[8], WILLIAM T.[7], ROBERT HAMMACK[6] JR., ROBERT HAMMACK[5] SR., WILLIAM "THE ELDER"[4] HAMMACK, WILLIAM "O"[3], JOHN[2] HAMMOCKE, ? JOHN[1] HAMMOT)* was born 23 May 1938 in Pulaski Co., AR. He married NETA LANORE CASE 10 Jun 1961 in Clinton, Hinds County, MS.

Children of JIMMY KELLEY and NETA CASE are:
>   i. PHILLIP NEAL[13] KELLEY, b. 24 Jun 1962; m. SERITA ABERNATHY.
>   ii. KEVIN KENT KELLEY, b. 02 Dec 1968.

Key Source: Lois Hagood, *The Elusive Ancestor* (Crossett, AR, 1992); Lois Hagood, "C. W. Roberts Family," in Robert A. and Mary I. Carpenter, *Reflections of Ashley County* (Dallas, TX, 1988), F544.

651. RITA JUNE[12] KELLEY *(MARTHA AGNES[11] PEDEN, VIRGINIA MARGARET "JENNY"[10] HAMMOCK, ALFRED WASHINGTON "DOCK"[9] HAMMACK, SIMEON J.[8], WILLIAM T.[7], ROBERT HAMMACK[6] JR., ROBERT HAMMACK[5] SR., WILLIAM "THE ELDER"[4] HAMMACK, WILLIAM "O"[3], JOHN[2] HAMMOCKE, ? JOHN[1] HAMMOT)* was born 17 Oct 1942 in Pulaski Co., AR. She married TOMMY J. THOMPSON 26 Jan 1961 in Pulaski Co., AR.

Children of RITA KELLEY and TOMMY THOMPSON are:
>   i.   INFANT[13] THOMPSON, b. 14 Oct 1964.
>   ii. TERRI RENA THOMPSON, b. 22 Feb 1966; d. 06 Mar 1974.
>   iii. KELLY ANN THOMPSON, b. 05 May 1970.

Key Source: Lois Hagood, *The Elusive Ancestor* (Crossett, AR, 1992); Lois Hagood, "C. W. Roberts Family," in Robert A. and Mary I. Carpenter, *Reflections of Ashley County* (Dallas, TX, 1988), F544.

652. LINDA[12] BRACHT *(JAMES T.[11], SARA[10] HAMMACK, GEORGE W. T.[9], SIMEON J.[8], WILLIAM T.[7], ROBERT HAMMACK[6] JR., ROBERT HAMMACK[5] SR., WILLIAM "THE ELDER"[4] HAMMACK, WILLIAM "O"[3], JOHN[2] HAMMOCKE, ? JOHN[1] HAMMOT)* She married KENT MOREHEAD.

Child of LINDA BRACHT and KENT MOREHEAD is:
>   i. RON[13] MOREHEAD.

Key Source: "Evelyn Bracht," *Cincinnati Post*, 5 January 2004.

Generation No. 13

653. NORMAN EDMOND[13] HARPER *(ISAAC CORNELIUS[12], MABEL E.[11] HAMMACK, GEORGE THOMAS[10], WILLIAM T. H.[9], SIMEON J.[8], WILLIAM T.[7], ROBERT HAMMACK[6] JR., ROBERT HAMMACK[5] SR., WILLIAM "THE ELDER"[4] HAMMACK, WILLIAM "O"[3], JOHN[2] HAMMOCKE, ? JOHN[1] HAMMOT)*
Child of NORMAN EDMOND HARPER is:
     i.   MARIA[14] HARPER, m. ? PRICE.
Key Source: Family Records of Felix Maben Hammack, Bend, OR.

654. JAMES BECKWITH[13] MAWK *(DELORES[12] DOOLITTLE, JAMES WILLIAM[11], SAREPTA ANN ELIZABETH[10] HAMMACK, CHARLES M.[9], SIMEON J.[8], WILLIAM T.[7], ROBERT HAMMACK[6] JR., ROBERT HAMMACK[5] SR., WILLIAM "THE ELDER"[4] HAMMACK, WILLIAM "O"[3], JOHN[2] HAMMOCKE, ? JOHN[1] HAMMOT)* was born 19 Feb 1925 in Calhoun Co., MS. He married CELIA RUTH DOLER. She was born 21 Jan 1924 in Calhoun Co., MS, and died 28 Aug 1985 in Calhoun Co., MS.
Children of JAMES MAWK and CELIA DOLER are:
734.   i.   JAMES DOLER[14] MAWK, b. 02 Apr 1946, Houston, MS.
     ii. THOMAS DEAN MAWK, b. 12 Feb 1954, Houston, MS.
Key Source: Fox, Doolittle, Holland, and Mawk Family Records, Calhoun City Public Library, Calhoun City, MS.

655. MYRA MARIE[13] HOLLAND *(HENRY HAVEN[12], MAYBELLE[11] DOOLITTLE, SAREPTA ANN ELIZABETH[10] HAMMACK, CHARLES M.[9], SIMEON J.[8], WILLIAM T.[7], ROBERT HAMMACK[6] JR., ROBERT HAMMACK[5] SR., WILLIAM "THE ELDER"[4] HAMMACK, WILLIAM "O"[3], JOHN[2] HAMMOCKE, ? JOHN[1] HAMMOT)* was born 27 Jun 1929 in Calhoun Co., MS. She married GEORGE LACEY VANLANDINGHAM 08 Jun 1949 in Calhoun Co., MS. He was born 09 Jul 1925 in Calhoun Co., MS.
Children of MYRA HOLLAND and GEORGE VANLANDINGHAM are:
735.   i.   PAMELA[14] VANLANDINGHAM, b. 20 Feb 1950, Greenwood, MS.
736.   ii. GEORGE LACEY VANLANDINGHAM, b. 22 Feb 1954, Greenwood, MS.
     iii. ROBERT STEVEN VANLANDINGHAM, b. 31 Aug 1960, Greenwood, MS.
Key Source: Fox, Doolittle, Holland, and Mawk Family Records, Calhoun City Public Library, Calhoun City, MS.

656. MABLE KATHRYN[13] HOLLAND *(HENRY HAVEN[12], MAYBELLE[11] DOOLITTLE, SAREPTA ANN ELIZABETH[10] HAMMACK, CHARLES M.[9], SIMEON J.[8], WILLIAM T.[7], ROBERT HAMMACK[6] JR., ROBERT HAMMACK[5] SR., WILLIAM "THE ELDER"[4] HAMMACK, WILLIAM "O"[3], JOHN[2] HAMMOCKE, ? JOHN[1] HAMMOT)* was born 24 Aug 1931 in Calhoun Co., MS. She married JAMES CURTIS GUNN 03 Jul 1950 in Mississippi. He was born 08 Aug 1927 in Walnet, MS.
Children of MABLE HOLLAND and JAMES GUNN are:
     i.   TOMMY CURTIS[14] GUNN, b. 29 Aug 1951, Ripley, MS.
     ii. GLORIA ANN GUNN, b. 11 Mar 1954, Ripley, MS.
Key Source: Fox, Doolittle, Holland, and Mawk Family Records, Calhoun City Public Library, Calhoun City, MS.

657. HENRY HAVEN[13] HOLLAND *(HENRY HAVEN[12], MAYBELLE[11] DOOLITTLE, SAREPTA ANN ELIZABETH[10] HAMMACK, CHARLES M.[9], SIMEON J.[8], WILLIAM T.[7], ROBERT HAMMACK[6] JR., ROBERT HAMMACK[5] SR., WILLIAM "THE ELDER"[4] HAMMACK, WILLIAM "O"[3], JOHN[2] HAMMOCKE, ? JOHN[1] HAMMOT)* was born 22 Mar 1938 in Calhoun Co., MS. He married DOROTHY ANNE WALKER 18 Apr 1964 in Mississippi. She was born 23 Aug 1944 in Drew, MS.
Children of HENRY HOLLAND and DOROTHY WALKER are:
     i.   HENRY WADE[14] HOLLAND, b. 21 Nov 1965, Mississippi.
    ii.   SHANNON KEITH HOLLAND, b. 11 Oct 1971, Mississippi.
Key Source: Fox, Doolittle, Holland, and Mawk Family Records, Calhoun City Public Library, Calhoun City, MS.

658. MARY ELIZABETH[13] HOLLAND *(MILLER DOOLITTLE[12], MAYBELLE[11] DOOLITTLE, SAREPTA ANN ELIZABETH[10] HAMMACK, CHARLES M.[9], SIMEON J.[8], WILLIAM T.[7], ROBERT HAMMACK[6] JR., ROBERT HAMMACK[5] SR., WILLIAM "THE ELDER"[4] HAMMACK, WILLIAM "O"[3], JOHN[2] HAMMOCKE, ? JOHN[1] HAMMOT)* was born 17 Mar 1931 in Calhoun Co., MS. She married ROBERT BLAIN GARY 27 Jan 1951 in Mississippi.
Children of MARY HOLLAND and ROBERT GARY are:
     i.   ROBERT DENNIS[14] GARY, b. 18 Jun 1957, Clarksdale, MS.
    ii.   STEVEN ALAN GARY, b. 31 May 1960, Oxford, MS.
Key Source: Fox, Doolittle, Holland, and Mawk Family Records, Calhoun City Public Library, Calhoun City, MS.

659. HENRY MEEK[13] HOLLAND *(MILLER DOOLITTLE[12], MAYBELLE[11] DOOLITTLE, SAREPTA ANN ELIZABETH[10] HAMMACK, CHARLES M.[9], SIMEON J.[8], WILLIAM T.[7], ROBERT HAMMACK[6] JR., ROBERT HAMMACK[5] SR., WILLIAM "THE ELDER"[4] HAMMACK, WILLIAM "O"[3], JOHN[2] HAMMOCKE, ? JOHN[1] HAMMOT)* was born 28 Jan 1933 in Calhoun Co., MS. He married SARAH JANE SHEWMAKE 16 Jul 1955 in Mississippi. She was born 07 Jan 1935 in Derma, MS.
Children of HENRY HOLLAND and SARAH SHEWMAKE are:
     i.   MELANIE BETH[14] HOLLAND, b. 29 Jul 1956, Aberdeen, MS.
    ii.   MICHAEL TIP HOLLAND, b. 21 Jan 1959, Oklahoma City, OK.
   iii.   MELISSA KAY HOLLAND, b. 26 Nov 1961, Oklahoma City, OK; d. 19 Dec 1961, Oklahoma City, OK.
Key Source: Fox, Doolittle, Holland, and Mawk Family Records, Calhoun City Public Library, Calhoun City, MS.

660. JOHN MILLER[13] HOLLAND *(MILLER DOOLITTLE[12], MAYBELLE[11] DOOLITTLE, SAREPTA ANN ELIZABETH[10] HAMMACK, CHARLES M.[9], SIMEON J.[8], WILLIAM T.[7], ROBERT HAMMACK[6] JR., ROBERT HAMMACK[5] SR., WILLIAM "THE ELDER"[4] HAMMACK, WILLIAM "O"[3], JOHN[2] HAMMOCKE, ? JOHN[1] HAMMOT)* was born 18 Jun 1936 in Calhoun Co., MS. He married GLENDA ROSE HAMILTON 28 May 1955 in Mississippi. She was born 29 Jun 1938 in Dublin, MS.
Children of JOHN HOLLAND and GLENDA HAMILTON are:
     i.   BELINDA[14] HOLLAND, b. 24 Jan 1957, Fort Worth, TX.
    ii.   TERRI LYNN HOLLAND, b. 05 May 1958, Dallas, TX.
   iii.   JOANNA HOLLAND, b. 03 Apr 1965, Berlin, Germany.
Key Source: Fox, Doolittle, Holland, and Mawk Family Records, Calhoun City Public Library, Calhoun City, MS.

661. JAMES SKELTON[13] HOLLAND *(MILLER DOOLITTLE[12], MAYBELLE[11] DOOLITTLE, SAREPTA ANN ELIZABETH[10] HAMMACK, CHARLES M.[9], SIMEON J.[8], WILLIAM T.[7], ROBERT HAMMACK[6] JR.,*

ROBERT HAMMACK[5] SR., WILLIAM "THE ELDER"[4] HAMMACK, WILLIAM "O"[3], JOHN[2] HAMMOCKE, ? JOHN[1] HAMMOT) was born 25 Sep 1947 in Grenada, MS. He married (1) MARJORIE ANN BLANSETT 03 Dec 1965 in Mississippi. She was born 05 Jun 1947 in Red Bluffs, CA. He married (2) NORMA CHRISTINE HUGHES 01 Feb 1974 in Mississippi. She was born 07 Mar 1951 in Oklahoma City, OK.

Children of JAMES HOLLAND and MARJORIE BLANSETT are:

     i.   KIMBERLY DEE[14] HOLLAND, b. 15 May 1967, Houston, MS.

    ii.   CHRISTOPHER BARRETT HOLLAND, b. 07 Feb 1972, Houston, MS.

Key Source: Fox, Doolittle, Holland, and Mawk Family Records, Calhoun City Public Library, Calhoun City, MS.

662. KEITH SHAW[13] CARVER *(FINNER[12], GEORGIA ANN[11] DOOLITTLE, SAREPTA ANN ELIZABETH[10] HAMMACK, CHARLES M.[9], SIMEON J.[8], WILLIAM T.[7], ROBERT HAMMACK[6] JR., ROBERT HAMMACK[5] SR., WILLIAM "THE ELDER"[4] HAMMACK, WILLIAM "O"[3], JOHN[2] HAMMOCKE, ? JOHN[1] HAMMOT)* was born 10 Oct 1946 in Nashville, TN. He married LONELLA JANE BARCROFT 10 Aug 1968 in Tennessee. She was born 11 Oct 1948 in Fort Walton Beach, FL.

Child of KEITH CARVER and LONELLA BARCROFT is:

     i.   KEITH SHAW[14] CARVER, JR., b. 16 Jun 1970, Jackson, TN.

Key Source: Fox, Doolittle, Holland, and Mawk Family Records, Calhoun City Public Library, Calhoun City, MS.

663. MARY KATHERINE[13] BABB *(SADIE LUCILLE[12] HAMMACK, GEORGE CLEVELAND[11], WILLIAM SIMMS[10], JOHN T.[9], SIMEON J.[8], WILLIAM T.[7], ROBERT HAMMACK[6] JR., ROBERT HAMMACK[5] SR., WILLIAM "THE ELDER"[4] HAMMACK, WILLIAM "O"[3], JOHN[2] HAMMOCKE, ? JOHN[1] HAMMOT)* was born 17 Jul 1934 in East Carroll Parish, LA. She married THEODORE SODEN BULL 06 Jun 1954 in Lake Providence, LA, son of THEODORE BULL and MILDRED SODEN. He was born 12 Oct 1931 in Trenton, NJ, and died 16 Jun 1992 in San Antonio, TX.

Children of MARY BABB and THEODORE BULL are:

737.   i.   THEODORE ALTON[14] BULL, b. 20 Apr 1955, Greenville, SC.

738.   ii.   THOMAS CLARENCE BULL, b. 21 Nov 1956, Greenville, SC.

739.   iii.   LEAH KATHERINE BULL, b. 17 Nov 1958, Greenville, SC.

740.   iv.   LORILYN RUTH BULL, b. 07 Oct 1962, Boonton, NJ.

     v.   JOANNA CELESTE BULL, b. 16 Aug 1980, Livingston, NJ; m. JOSHUA LEE ROWLEY; b. 30 Jan 1980, Chattanooga, TN.

Key Source: Family records of Felix Maben Hammack, Bend, OR.

664. ALMEDIA LEE[13] BABB *(SADIE LUCILLE[12] HAMMACK, GEORGE CLEVELAND[11], WILLIAM SIMMS[10], JOHN T.[9], SIMEON J.[8], WILLIAM T.[7], ROBERT HAMMACK[6] JR., ROBERT HAMMACK[5] SR., WILLIAM "THE ELDER"[4] HAMMACK, WILLIAM "O"[3], JOHN[2] HAMMOCKE, ? JOHN[1] HAMMOT)* was born 12 Aug 1936. She married WILLIAM BERNARD LUEG, JR 25 Dec 1960 in Lake Providence, LA, son of WILLIAM LUEG and GERTRUDE CARLSON. He was born 05 Feb 1936.

Children of ALMEDIA BABB and WILLIAM LUEG are:

     i.   WILLIAM ALTON[14] LUEG, b. 10 May 1962, Houston, TX.

    ii.   JEFFREY ALLEN LUEG, b. 01 Apr 1964, Dallas, TX.

741.   iii.   ANDREA KATHERINE LUEG, b. 26 Jul 1966, Dallas, TX.

Key Source: Family records of Felix Maben Hammack, Bend, OR.

665. CAROLYN[13] BABB *(SADIE LUCILLE[12] HAMMACK, GEORGE CLEVELAND[11], WILLIAM SIMMS[10], JOHN T.[9], SIMEON J.[8], WILLIAM T.[7], ROBERT HAMMACK[6] JR., ROBERT HAMMACK[5] SR.,*

WILLIAM "THE ELDER"⁴ HAMMACK, WILLIAM "O"³, JOHN² HAMMOCKE, ? JOHN¹ HAMMOT) was born 28 Jun 1938. She married EDMUND C GLOVER 06 Apr 1961 in West Point, GA, son of CLIFFORD GLOVER and LOUISE LILES. He was born 1938.

Children of CAROLYN BABB and EDMUND GLOVER are:

742.   i.   SARAH FRANCES¹⁴ GLOVER, b. 20 Jun 1968, Langdale, AL.

        ii.   VIRGINIA ANN GLOVER, b. 17 May 1975, Langdale, AL; m. LANCE TANKERSLEY, 03 Apr 2004, Savannah, GA; b. 22 Mar 1972, Clearwater, FL.

Key Source: Family records of Felix Maben Hammack, Bend, OR.

666. FRANCES ANN¹³ BABB *(SADIE LUCILLE¹² HAMMACK, GEORGE CLEVELAND¹¹, WILLIAM SIMMS¹⁰, JOHN T.⁹, SIMEON J.⁸, WILLIAM T.⁷, ROBERT HAMMACK⁶ JR., ROBERT HAMMACK⁵ SR., WILLIAM "THE ELDER"⁴ HAMMACK, WILLIAM "O"³, JOHN² HAMMOCKE, ? JOHN¹ HAMMOT)* was born 29 Jun 1945. She married (1) CALVIN HUNTER MCFADDEN 16 Aug 1971 in First Methodist Church, Lake Providence, LA, son of WAVE MCFADDEN and LUCILLE WILLIAMS. He was born 12 Mar 1944 in Kansas City, MO. She married (2) JOHN CHRISTOPHER LAWLER 14 Feb 1993 in Clairmont Presbyterian Church, Decatur, GA, son of ALBERT LAWLER and LILLIAN LATTIMER. He was born 07 Oct 1947 in Rome, GA.

Children of FRANCES BABB and CALVIN MCFADDEN are:

743.   i.   CALVIN HUNTER¹⁴ MCFADDEN, JR., b. 06 Sep 1973.

        ii.   EMILY RUTH MCFADDEN, b. 09 Apr 1978.

Key Source: Family records of Felix Maben Hammack, Bend, OR.

667. SADIE RUTH¹³ BABB *(SADIE LUCILLE¹² HAMMACK, GEORGE CLEVELAND¹¹, WILLIAM SIMMS¹⁰, JOHN T.⁹, SIMEON J.⁸, WILLIAM T.⁷, ROBERT HAMMACK⁶ JR., ROBERT HAMMACK⁵ SR., WILLIAM "THE ELDER"⁴ HAMMACK, WILLIAM "O"³, JOHN² HAMMOCKE, ? JOHN¹ HAMMOT)* was born 30 Mar 1950 in Lake Providence, LA. She married JOHN BERNARD PENA 07 Apr 1979 in Monroe, LA, son of CLAUDE PENA and RUTH PASSWATER. He was born 04 Aug 1951 in Laredo, TX.

Children of SADIE BABB and JOHN PENA are:

744.   i.   WILLIAM FLETCHER¹⁴ PENA, b. 05 Apr 1973, Lake Providence, LA.

        ii.   STEPHEN BENJAMIN PENA, b. 11 Dec 1979, Houston, TX.

        iii. AMY RUTH PENA, b. 11 Apr 1984, Houston, TX; m. JOSHUA G. ARNOLD; b. Victoria, TX.

Key Source: Family records of Felix Maben Hammack, Bend, OR.

668. JOHN ALTON¹³ BABB *(SADIE LUCILLE¹² HAMMACK, GEORGE CLEVELAND¹¹, WILLIAM SIMMS¹⁰, JOHN T.⁹, SIMEON J.⁸, WILLIAM T.⁷, ROBERT HAMMACK⁶ JR., ROBERT HAMMACK⁵ SR., WILLIAM "THE ELDER"⁴ HAMMACK, WILLIAM "O"³, JOHN² HAMMOCKE, ? JOHN¹ HAMMOT)* was born 28 Jul 1952. He married CLAUDIA J CREWS 31 May 1975 in Lake Providence, LA, daughter of W. CREWS and G. HOPKINS. She was born 15 Nov 1953 in Oak Grove, LA.

Children of JOHN BABB and CLAUDIA CREWS are:

745.   i.   NICHOLAS JOEL¹⁴ BABB, b. 17 Feb 1979, Greenville, MS.

        ii.   SARAH GRACE BABB, b. 04 Oct 1985, Monroe, LA.

        iii. JONATHAN THOMAS BABB, b. 24 May 1989, Natchez, MS.

Key Source: Family records of Felix Maben Hammack, Bend, OR.

669. MARY ANN¹³ HAMMACK *(WILLIAM BANKSTON¹², GEORGE CLEVELAND¹¹, WILLIAM SIMMS¹⁰, JOHN T.⁹, SIMEON J.⁸, WILLIAM T.⁷, ROBERT HAMMACK⁶ JR., ROBERT HAMMACK⁵ SR., WILLIAM "THE ELDER"⁴ HAMMACK, WILLIAM "O"³, JOHN² HAMMOCKE, ? JOHN¹ HAMMOT)* was

born 28 Jul 1938 in Hinds County, MS. She married JIMMY CLYDE LEE, JR 21 Jun 1957, son of JAMES LEE and TEXIE THORNHILL. He was born 04 Aug 1938 in Jackson, MS.
Children of MARY HAMMACK and JIMMY LEE are:

746.   i.   DEBRA CELESTE[14] LEE, b. 02 Oct 1960, Jackson, MS.

747.   ii.   PATRICIA DIANNE LEE, b. 20 May 1962, Jackson, MS.

Key Source: Family records of Felix Maben Hammack, Bend, OR.

670. WILLIAM BANKSTON[13] HAMMACK, JR. *(WILLIAM BANKSTON[12], GEORGE CLEVELAND[11], WILLIAM SIMMS[10], JOHN T.[9], SIMEON J.[8], WILLIAM T.[7], ROBERT HAMMACK[6] JR., ROBERT HAMMACK[5] SR., WILLIAM "THE ELDER"[4] HAMMACK, WILLIAM "O"[3], JOHN[2] HAMMOCKE, ? JOHN[1] HAMMOT)* was born 21 Apr 1949 in Hinds County, MS. He married SARAH DIANNE CAMPBELL, daughter of SILAS CAMPBELL and MARGARET ROBERTSON. She was born 04 Jan 1950 in Hinds County, MS.
Children of WILLIAM HAMMACK and SARAH CAMPBELL are:

       i.   JOSEPH DAVID[14] WHITE, b. 22 Oct 1967.

      ii.   JENNIFER MICHELLE HAMMACK, b. 29 Apr 1972, Hinds County, MS; m. ALLEN WAYNE VAUGHN, 15 May 1993, Philadelphia, MS.

    iii.   JELENA MARGARET HAMMACK, b. 29 Apr 1972, Hinds County, MS; m. RONALD SCOTT MCLAIN, 20 Apr 1996, Negril, Jamaica.

Key Source: Family records of Felix Maben Hammack, Bend, OR.

671. DOROTHY LUCILLE[13] SITTON *(MARY MILDRED[12] HAMMACK, GEORGE CLEVELAND[11], WILLIAM SIMMS[10], JOHN T.[9], SIMEON J.[8], WILLIAM T.[7], ROBERT HAMMACK[6] JR., ROBERT HAMMACK[5] SR., WILLIAM "THE ELDER"[4] HAMMACK, WILLIAM "O"[3], JOHN[2] HAMMOCKE, ? JOHN[1] HAMMOT)* was born 29 Dec 1939 in East Carroll Parish, LA. She married JAMES DONALD WHITE 26 Aug 1961 in Lake Providence, LA, son of BRAD WHITE and BERNADINE THIELS. He was born 01 May 1939 in Rapides Parish, LA.
Children of DOROTHY SITTON and JAMES WHITE are:

748.   i.   DONNA MARIE[14] WHITE, b. 12 Jan 1963, Caddo Parish, LA.

      ii.   DAVID JAMES WHITE, b. 03 Oct 1965, Webster Parish, LA; m. LINDA ELOISE FORD, 01 Jun 1991, Ruston, LA.

749.   iii.   MARK ALLAN WHITE, b. 19 Nov 1967, Webster Parish, LA.

750.   iv.   BRAD THOMAS WHITE, b. 18 Feb 1973, Webster Parish, LA.

      v.   JEFFREY DONALD WHITE, b. 13 Sep 1975, Clark Co., AR.

Key Source: Family records of Felix Maben Hammack, Bend, OR.

672. MARY ELIZABETH[13] SITTON *(MARY MILDRED[12] HAMMACK, GEORGE CLEVELAND[11], WILLIAM SIMMS[10], JOHN T.[9], SIMEON J.[8], WILLIAM T.[7], ROBERT HAMMACK[6] JR., ROBERT HAMMACK[5] SR., WILLIAM "THE ELDER"[4] HAMMACK, WILLIAM "O"[3], JOHN[2] HAMMOCKE, ? JOHN[1] HAMMOT)* was born 05 Nov 1943 in Lake Providence, LA. She married DAVID ARTHUR WIENS 19 Jun 1971 in Corvallis, OR, son of HENRY WIENS and KATHERINE DEGARMO. He was born 18 Jul 1940 in Pocatello, ID.
Children of MARY SITTON and DAVID WIENS are:

751.   i.   JENNIFER MARIE[14] WIENS, b. 12 Mar 1972, Corvallis, OR.

      ii.   JANELLE TERESA WIENS, b. 08 Apr 1979, Oak Grove, LA; m. JAMIN RAY BROWER; b. 28 Aug 1977, Anderson, Madison County, IN.

    iii.   NATHAN DAVID WIENS, b. 04 Aug 1985, Monroe, LA.

Key Source: Family records of Felix Maben Hammack, Bend, OR.

673. JOSEPH PAUL[13] SITTON *(MARY MILDRED[12] HAMMACK, GEORGE CLEVELAND[11], WILLIAM SIMMS[10], JOHN T.[9], SIMEON J.[8], WILLIAM T.[7], ROBERT HAMMACK[6] JR., ROBERT HAMMACK[5] SR., WILLIAM "THE ELDER"[4] HAMMACK, WILLIAM "O"[3], JOHN[2] HAMMOCKE, ? JOHN[1] HAMMOT)* was born 03 Aug 1948. He married SUZANNE MARIE VOGT, daughter of DONALD VOGT and ROSE WINTER. She was born 27 Dec 1955 in LaMarque, TX.
Children of JOSEPH SITTON and SUZANNE VOGT are:
  i.   MELISSA JOANN[14] SITTON, b. 18 Apr 1977, Lake Providence, LA.
  ii. STEPHEN PAUL SITTON, b. 23 Aug 1980, Lake Providence, LA; d. 24 May 2003, Ruston, LA.
Key Source: Family records of Felix Maben Hammack, Bend, OR.

674. THOMAS STRIBLING[13] SITTON *(MARY MILDRED[12] HAMMACK, GEORGE CLEVELAND[11], WILLIAM SIMMS[10], JOHN T.[9], SIMEON J.[8], WILLIAM T.[7], ROBERT HAMMACK[6] JR., ROBERT HAMMACK[5] SR., WILLIAM "THE ELDER"[4] HAMMACK, WILLIAM "O"[3], JOHN[2] HAMMOCKE, ? JOHN[1] HAMMOT)* was born 03 Mar 1952. He married (1) MICHAEL ANNE SUMRALL, daughter of CARL SUMRALL and DOROTHY SULLIVAN. She was born in Lake Providence, LA. He married (2) CRYSTAL BETH DOLAN 09 Jul 1988, daughter of IVAN DOLAN and DULCENA MANN. She was born 11 Jun 1947.
Children of THOMAS SITTON and MICHAEL SUMRALL are:
752.   i.   CHRISTOPHER THOMAS[14] SITTON, b. 27 Sep 1974, Lake Providence, LA.
       ii. JOHN MICHAEL SITTON, b. 15 May 1978, Lake Providence, LA.
Key Source: Family records of Felix Maben Hammack, Bend, OR.

675. JOHN EUGENE[13] HAMMACK *(EDGAR HENDRICKS[12], GEORGE CLEVELAND[11], WILLIAM SIMMS[10], JOHN T.[9], SIMEON J.[8], WILLIAM T.[7], ROBERT HAMMACK[6] JR., ROBERT HAMMACK[5] SR., WILLIAM "THE ELDER"[4] HAMMACK, WILLIAM "O"[3], JOHN[2] HAMMOCKE, ? JOHN[1] HAMMOT)* was born 15 May 1941 in Hinds County, MS. He married IRENE STORMENT 15 Jul 1965 in Jackson, MS. She was born 04 Apr 1942 in Jackson, MS.
Child of JOHN HAMMACK and IRENE STORMENT is:
  i.   ADAM[14] HAMMACK, b. 01 Oct 1981, Jackson, MS.
Key Source: Family records of Felix Maben Hammack, Bend, OR.

676. EDGAR HENDRICKS HAMMACK[13] JR. *(EDGAR HENDRICKS[12] HAMMACK, GEORGE CLEVELAND[11], WILLIAM SIMMS[10], JOHN T.[9], SIMEON J.[8], WILLIAM T.[7], ROBERT HAMMACK[6] JR., ROBERT HAMMACK[5] SR., WILLIAM "THE ELDER"[4] HAMMACK, WILLIAM "O"[3], JOHN[2] HAMMOCKE, ? JOHN[1] HAMMOT)* was born 17 May 1954. He married SHELIA AMONS 22 Aug 1981 in Mize, MS. She was born 12 Nov 1955 in Mize, MS.
Children of EDGAR JR. and SHELIA AMONS are:
  i.   MARGARET ANNE[14] HAMMACK, b. 04 May 1984, Jackson, MS.
  ii. ALEX EDGAR HAMMACK, b. 07 Apr 1986, Jackson, MS.
Key Source: Family records of Felix Maben Hammack, Bend, OR.

677. ANNETTE[13] HAMMACK *(GEORGE CLEVELAND[12], GEORGE CLEVELAND[11], WILLIAM SIMMS[10], JOHN T.[9], SIMEON J.[8], WILLIAM T.[7], ROBERT HAMMACK[6] JR., ROBERT HAMMACK[5] SR., WILLIAM "THE ELDER"[4] HAMMACK, WILLIAM "O"[3], JOHN[2] HAMMOCKE, ? JOHN[1] HAMMOT)* was born 22 Jan 1950. She married (1) FRANK SANTOS Abt. 1973. She married (2) BRIAN WILLIAM MARTELLO Abt. 1993.
Children of ANNETTE HAMMACK and FRANK SANTOS are:
  i.   DAVID JOSEPH[14] SANTOS, b. 14 Feb 1975, Lowell, MA.

ii. JENNIFER LYNN SANTOS, b. 27 Apr 1977, Lowell, MA.
Key Source: Family records of Felix Maben Hammack, Bend, OR.

678. DAVID MITCHELL[13] HAMMACK *(GEORGE CLEVELAND[12], GEORGE CLEVELAND[11], WILLIAM SIMMS[10], JOHN T.[9], SIMEON J.[8], WILLIAM T.[7], ROBERT HAMMACK[6] JR., ROBERT HAMMACK[5] SR., WILLIAM "THE ELDER"[4] HAMMACK, WILLIAM "O"[3], JOHN[2] HAMMOCKE, ? JOHN[1] HAMMOT)* was born 28 Oct 1959. He married REBECCA ROSE EDWARD. She was born 10 Dec 1964 in Eglin Air Force Base, Florida.
Children of DAVID HAMMACK and REBECCA EDWARD are:
    i. DAVID MICAH[14] HAMMACK, b. 20 Oct 1984.
    ii. MATTHEW RYAN HAMMACK, b. 10 May 1986.
    iii. JASON NICHOLAS HAMMACK, b. 25 Sep 1987.
    iv. CONSTANCE ELIZABETH HAMMACK, b. 02 Oct 1988.
Key Source: Family records of Felix Maben Hammack, Bend, OR.

679. DANIEL CLEMENT HAMMACK[13] JR. *(DANIEL CLEMENT[12] HAMMACK, GEORGE CLEVELAND[11], WILLIAM SIMMS[10], JOHN T.[9], SIMEON J.[8], WILLIAM T.[7], ROBERT HAMMACK[6] JR., ROBERT HAMMACK[5] SR., WILLIAM "THE ELDER"[4] HAMMACK, WILLIAM "O"[3], JOHN[2] HAMMOCKE, ? JOHN[1] HAMMOT)* was born 19 Aug 1950 in Lake Providence, LA. He married GLORIA ANN BURRIS 26 Nov 1971 in Evadale, TX, daughter of CECIL BURRIS and FLORIA CANNON. She was born 10 Apr 1950 in Bunkie, LA.
Children of DANIEL JR. and GLORIA BURRIS are:
753.   i. CRYSTAL REBECCA[14] HAMMACK, b. 28 May 1973, Houston, TX.
    ii. MISTY MICHELLE HAMMACK, b. 29 Apr 1977, Houston, TX.
Key Source: Family records of Felix Maben Hammack, Bend, OR.

680. JANET CELESTE[13] HAMMACK *(DANIEL CLEMENT[12], GEORGE CLEVELAND[11], WILLIAM SIMMS[10], JOHN T.[9], SIMEON J.[8], WILLIAM T.[7], ROBERT HAMMACK[6] JR., ROBERT HAMMACK[5] SR., WILLIAM "THE ELDER"[4] HAMMACK, WILLIAM "O"[3], JOHN[2] HAMMOCKE, ? JOHN[1] HAMMOT)* was born 04 Sep 1954. She married CHARLES LEROY NOLAN 23 Jan 1976 in Tallulah, LA. He was born 21 May 1955.
Children of JANET HAMMACK and CHARLES NOLAN are:
    i. CHRISTOPHER DANIEL[14] NOLAN, b. 20 Jul 1976.
    ii. MATTHEW CHARLES NOLAN, b. 06 Mar 1984.
    iii. SPENCER SCOTT NOLAN, b. 29 Jul 1985.
Key Source: Family records of Felix Maben Hammack, Bend, OR.

681. PAMELA LOUISE[13] HAMMACK *(DANIEL CLEMENT[12], GEORGE CLEVELAND[11], WILLIAM SIMMS[10], JOHN T.[9], SIMEON J.[8], WILLIAM T.[7], ROBERT HAMMACK[6] JR., ROBERT HAMMACK[5] SR., WILLIAM "THE ELDER"[4] HAMMACK, WILLIAM "O"[3], JOHN[2] HAMMOCKE, ? JOHN[1] HAMMOT)* was born 20 Jul 1958 in Lake Providence, LA. She married CHARLES RANDY JOHNSON 13 Feb 1976 in Lake Providence, LA, son of WILLIAM JOHNSON and MYTICE BRODDON. He was born 14 Feb 1954 in Panama City, FL.
Children of PAMELA HAMMACK and CHARLES JOHNSON are:
    i. KIMBERLY MICHELLE[14] JOHNSON, b. 15 Jul 1976; m. TERRY ROGER PLESS, 25 Feb 1993.
    ii. KENDRA NICHOLE JOHNSON, b. 20 Jun 1979.
    iii. CHARLES RANDY JOHNSON II, b. 19 Oct 1988.
    iv. WILLIAM JACKSON JOHNSON II, b. 21 Aug 1992.

Key Source: Family records of Felix Maben Hammack, Bend, OR.

682. CHARLOTTE CHRISTMAS[13] HAMMACK *(FELIX MABEN*[12]*, GEORGE CLEVELAND*[11]*, WILLIAM SIMMS*[10]*, JOHN T.*[9]*, SIMEON J.*[8]*, WILLIAM T.*[7]*, ROBERT HAMMACK*[6] *JR., ROBERT HAMMACK*[5] *SR., WILLIAM "THE ELDER"*[4] *HAMMACK, WILLIAM "O"*[3]*, JOHN*[2] *HAMMOCKE, ? JOHN*[1] *HAMMOT)* was born 26 Jul 1953 in Louisville, Jefferson Co., KY. She married JOHN ROBERT NITCHER 28 Jul 1973 in Albany, Oregon, son of CORLISS NITCHER and MARY HALVERSON. He was born 21 Jan 1952 in Albany, Oregon.
Children of CHARLOTTE HAMMACK and JOHN NITCHER are:
     i.   CHRISTINA HOPE[14] NITCHER, b. 19 Sep 1974.
    ii.   DAVID ALAN NITCHER, b. 16 Feb 1978.
   iii.   STEVEN LEE NITCHER, b. 13 Jan 1979.
Key Source: Family records of Felix Maben Hammack, Bend, OR.

683. DENISE[13] HAMMACK *(FELIX MABEN*[12]*, GEORGE CLEVELAND*[11]*, WILLIAM SIMMS*[10]*, JOHN T.*[9]*, SIMEON J.*[8]*, WILLIAM T.*[7]*, ROBERT HAMMACK*[6] *JR., ROBERT HAMMACK*[5] *SR., WILLIAM "THE ELDER"*[4] *HAMMACK, WILLIAM "O"*[3]*, JOHN*[2] *HAMMOCKE, ? JOHN*[1] *HAMMOT)* was born 05 Sep 1955 in Memphis, Shelby Co., TN. She married DARRYL G. FINCH 03 Jan 1976 in Nacogdoches, TX, son of THOMAS FINCH and MARY NEWELL. He was born 26 Apr 1954 in Camden, AR.
Children of DENISE HAMMACK and DARRYL FINCH are:
        i.   JULIA DAY[14] FINCH, b. 13 Jun 1977.
754.   ii.   EMILY NEWELL FINCH, b. 18 May 1979.
Key Source: Family records of Felix Maben Hammack, Bend, OR.

684. PHILIP STEVEN[13] HAMMACK *(FELIX MABEN*[12]*, GEORGE CLEVELAND*[11]*, WILLIAM SIMMS*[10]*, JOHN T.*[9]*, SIMEON J.*[8]*, WILLIAM T.*[7]*, ROBERT HAMMACK*[6] *JR., ROBERT HAMMACK*[5] *SR., WILLIAM "THE ELDER"*[4] *HAMMACK, WILLIAM "O"*[3]*, JOHN*[2] *HAMMOCKE, ? JOHN*[1] *HAMMOT)* was born 01 Feb 1958 in Albany, Linn County, Oregon. He married MARIA LILIA CHRISTINE B. CANUTO 12 Jul 2003 in Naga City, Philippines, daughter of EFREN CANUTO and LILIA BOREBOR. She was born 15 Dec 1971 in Pili, Philippines.
Child of PHILIP HAMMACK and MARIA CANUTO is:
     i.   LILANN MARIA[14] HAMMACK, b. 02 Dec 2005.
Key Source: Family records of Felix Maben Hammack, Bend, OR.

685. ELIZABETH GAYLE[13] CLEMENT *(CELESTE ALMEDIA*[12] *HAMMACK, GEORGE CLEVELAND*[11]*, WILLIAM SIMMS*[10]*, JOHN T.*[9]*, SIMEON J.*[8]*, WILLIAM T.*[7]*, ROBERT HAMMACK*[6] *JR., ROBERT HAMMACK*[5] *SR., WILLIAM "THE ELDER"*[4] *HAMMACK, WILLIAM "O"*[3]*, JOHN*[2] *HAMMOCKE, ? JOHN*[1] *HAMMOT)* was born 13 Jul 1950. She married ? CAUSEY.
Child of ELIZABETH CLEMENT and ? CAUSEY is:
     i.   ELIZABETH CELESTE[14] CAUSEY.
Key Source: Family records of Felix Maben Hammack, Bend, OR.

686. LAURA ANN[13] SCHULTE *(ALLIE JO*[12] *HAMMACK, GEORGE CLEVELAND*[11]*, WILLIAM SIMMS*[10]*, JOHN T.*[9]*, SIMEON J.*[8]*, WILLIAM T.*[7]*, ROBERT HAMMACK*[6] *JR., ROBERT HAMMACK*[5] *SR., WILLIAM "THE ELDER"*[4] *HAMMACK, WILLIAM "O"*[3]*, JOHN*[2] *HAMMOCKE, ? JOHN*[1] *HAMMOT)* was born 07 Feb 1964 in Memphis, TN. She married TOM CARROLL 11 Feb 1989 in Memphis, TN, son of THOMAS CARROLL and STEPHANIE ELASSER. He was born 25 Mar 1961 in Greenville, SC.
Children of LAURA SCHULTE and TOM CARROLL are:
     i.   DANIEL THOMAS[14] CARROLL, b. 11 Jun 1991, San Diego, CA.

    ii.   EMILY GRACE CARROLL, b. 31 Oct 1992, Norfolk, VA.

    iii. RACHEL ANN CARROLL, b. 17 Dec 1994, Monterey, CA.

    iv. MEGAN JOY CARROLL, b. 13 Nov 1998, Norfolk, VA.

Key Source: Family records of Felix Maben Hammack, Bend, OR.

687. EMILY IRENE[13] SCHULTE *(ALLIE JO[12] HAMMACK, GEORGE CLEVELAND[11], WILLIAM SIMMS[10], JOHN T.[9], SIMEON J.[8], WILLIAM T.[7], ROBERT HAMMACK[6] JR., ROBERT HAMMACK[5] SR., WILLIAM "THE ELDER"[4] HAMMACK, WILLIAM "O"[3], JOHN[2] HAMMOCKE, ? JOHN[1] HAMMOT)* was born 25 May 1965 in Memphis, TN. She married BRIAN THOMAS SHERRILL 07 May 1994 in Norfolk, VA, son of RAYMOND SHERRILL and FREIDA BATHMANN. He was born 11 Dec 1956 in Corona, CA.

Children of EMILY SCHULTE and BRIAN SHERRILL are:

    i.   LARA NICOLE[14] SHERRILL, b. 17 Jun 1996.

    ii. JUSTIN NICHOLAS SHERRILL, b. 10 Jan 1998, Hampton, VA.

    iii. KRISTINA HOPE SHERRILL, b. 10 Oct 2000, Fairfax, VA.

    iv. MICAH BRIAN SHERRILL, b. 07 Sep 2003, Warrenton, VA.

Key Source: Family records of Felix Maben Hammack, Bend, OR.

688. CATHRYN ELIZABETH[13] VAUGHAN *(RUBY COOMBS[12] HAMMACK, ROBERT FELIX[11], WILLIAM SIMMS[10], JOHN T.[9], SIMEON J.[8], WILLIAM T.[7], ROBERT HAMMACK[6] JR., ROBERT HAMMACK[5] SR., WILLIAM "THE ELDER"[4] HAMMACK, WILLIAM "O"[3], JOHN[2] HAMMOCKE, ? JOHN[1] HAMMOT)* was born 03 May 1946 in Yazoo County, MS. She married CLARK JOHNSON 19 Sep 1964 in Yazoo County, MS.

Children of CATHRYN VAUGHAN and CLARK JOHNSON are:

    i.   ELIZABETH VAUGHAN[14] JOHNSON, b. 16 Jul 1965.

    ii. JEFFREY UPTON JOHNSON, b. 01 Jul 1969.

Key Source: Family records of Felix Maben Hammack, Bend, OR.

689. CORA CHARLEEN[13] VAUGHAN *(RUBY COOMBS[12] HAMMACK, ROBERT FELIX[11], WILLIAM SIMMS[10], JOHN T.[9], SIMEON J.[8], WILLIAM T.[7], ROBERT HAMMACK[6] JR., ROBERT HAMMACK[5] SR., WILLIAM "THE ELDER"[4] HAMMACK, WILLIAM "O"[3], JOHN[2] HAMMOCKE, ? JOHN[1] HAMMOT)* was born 01 Aug 1949 in Yazoo County, MS. She married CHARLES WISTER NICHOLS, JR 16 Nov 1974.

Child of CORA VAUGHAN and CHARLES NICHOLS is:

    i.   ALLISON VAUGHAN[14] NICHOLS, b. 26 Jul 1976.

Key Source: Family records of Felix Maben Hammack, Bend, OR.

690. ROBERT DEWEY[13] DAVIS *(MARY KATHERINE[12] HAMMACK, ROBERT FELIX[11], WILLIAM SIMMS[10], JOHN T.[9], SIMEON J.[8], WILLIAM T.[7], ROBERT HAMMACK[6] JR., ROBERT HAMMACK[5] SR., WILLIAM "THE ELDER"[4] HAMMACK, WILLIAM "O"[3], JOHN[2] HAMMOCKE, ? JOHN[1] HAMMOT)* was born 02 Dec 1951 in Yazoo City, MS. He married BETTY BROOME 12 Mar 1976 in Jackson, MS. She was born in Jackson, MS.

Children of ROBERT DAVIS and BETTY BROOME are:

    i.   BRADLEY ALEXANDER[14] DAVIS, b. 29 Jun 1977, Jackson, MS.

    ii. SCOTT ANDERSON DAVIS, b. 01 Aug 1980, Jackson, MS.

    iii. ADAM ROBERT DAVIS, b. 03 Feb 1984, Jackson, MS.

    iv. TODD OWEN DAVIS, b. 17 Jul 1986, Jackson, MS.

Key Source: Family records of Felix Maben Hammack, Bend, OR.

691. MARY JOAN[13] DAVIS *(MARY KATHERINE[12] HAMMACK, ROBERT FELIX[11], WILLIAM SIMMS[10], JOHN T.[9], SIMEON J.[8], WILLIAM T.[7], ROBERT HAMMACK[6] JR., ROBERT HAMMACK[5] SR., WILLIAM "THE ELDER"[4] HAMMACK, WILLIAM "O"[3], JOHN[2] HAMMOCKE, ? JOHN[1] HAMMOT)* was born 14 Nov 1954 in Yazoo County, MS. She married WILLIAM CHARLES CREEL 28 Dec 1974 in Yazoo County, MS. He was born in Yazoo County, MS.

Children of MARY DAVIS and WILLIAM CREEL are:

     i.   AMY CATHERINE[14] CREEL, b. 05 Jul 1977, Greenville, MS.

     ii. STEVEN CHARLES CREEL, b. 27 Mar 1980, Greenville, MS.

     iii. BRIAN JUSTIN CREEL, b. 24 Sep 1987, Greenville, MS.

Key Source: Family records of Felix Maben Hammack, Bend, OR.

692. WILLIAM TIMOTHY[13] DAVIS *(MARY KATHERINE[12] HAMMACK, ROBERT FELIX[11], WILLIAM SIMMS[10], JOHN T.[9], SIMEON J.[8], WILLIAM T.[7], ROBERT HAMMACK[6] JR., ROBERT HAMMACK[5] SR., WILLIAM "THE ELDER"[4] HAMMACK, WILLIAM "O"[3], JOHN[2] HAMMOCKE, ? JOHN[1] HAMMOT)* was born 08 Nov 1963 in Yazoo County, MS. He married MARTHA SHIRLEY 15 Nov 1986 in Jackson, MS. She was born in Quitman, MS.

Children of WILLIAM DAVIS and MARTHA SHIRLEY are:

     i.   JORDAN MARY[14] DAVIS, b. 05 Oct 1990, Jackson, MS.

     ii. MACI MARGARET DAVIS, b. 07 Nov 1994.

Key Source: Family records of Felix Maben Hammack, Bend, OR.

693. GLORIA JEAN[13] PACE *(WILLIE BELL[12] HAMMACK, DRURY BROWN "DOOLEY"[11], WILLIAM SIMMS[10], JOHN T.[9], SIMEON J.[8], WILLIAM T.[7], ROBERT HAMMACK[6] JR., ROBERT HAMMACK[5] SR., WILLIAM "THE ELDER"[4] HAMMACK, WILLIAM "O"[3], JOHN[2] HAMMOCKE, ? JOHN[1] HAMMOT)* was born 11 Aug 1941. She married ? LUCKET.

Child of GLORIA PACE and ? LUCKET is:

     i.   RICHARD K.[14] LUCKET, b. 05 Jun 1970.

Key Source: Family records of Felix Maben Hammack, Bend, OR.

694. ANNA DEAN[13] PACE *(WILLIE BELL[12] HAMMACK, DRURY BROWN "DOOLEY"[11], WILLIAM SIMMS[10], JOHN T.[9], SIMEON J.[8], WILLIAM T.[7], ROBERT HAMMACK[6] JR., ROBERT HAMMACK[5] SR., WILLIAM "THE ELDER"[4] HAMMACK, WILLIAM "O"[3], JOHN[2] HAMMOCKE, ? JOHN[1] HAMMOT)* was born 22 Apr 1943. She married ? CACKRELL.

Children of ANNA PACE and ? CACKRELL are:

     i.   JAMES WAYNE[14] CACKRELL, b. 02 Apr 1968.

     ii. TRAVIS NEWTON CACKRELL, b. 09 Jun 1971.

Key Source: Family records of Felix Maben Hammack, Bend, OR.

695. THOMAS CHRISTOPHER[13] HAMMACK *(THOMAS CLIFTON "PETE"[12], DRURY BROWN "DOOLEY"[11], WILLIAM SIMMS[10], JOHN T.[9], SIMEON J.[8], WILLIAM T.[7], ROBERT HAMMACK[6] JR., ROBERT HAMMACK[5] SR., WILLIAM "THE ELDER"[4] HAMMACK, WILLIAM "O"[3], JOHN[2] HAMMOCKE, ? JOHN[1] HAMMOT)* was born 25 Dec 1959. He married JO METHVIN 07 Dec 1985. She was born 23 Apr 1963.

Children of THOMAS HAMMACK and JO METHVIN are:

     i.   CARLEY DEVIN[14] HAMMACK.

     ii. CHRISTOPHER DREW HAMMACK, b. 04 Feb 1991.

Key Source: Family records of Felix Maben Hammack, Bend, OR.

696. MYRTAL DIANE[13] BURGESS *(WILBURN LOUIS[12], CLARA BELLE[11] HAMMACK, WILLIAM SIMMS[10], JOHN T.[9], SIMEON J.[8], WILLIAM T.[7], ROBERT HAMMACK[6] JR., ROBERT HAMMACK[5] SR., WILLIAM "THE ELDER"[4] HAMMACK, WILLIAM "O"[3], JOHN[2] HAMMOCKE, ? JOHN[1] HAMMOT)* was born 14 Aug 1946. She married KENNON BROUSSARD 20 May 1972 in Lafayette, LA.
Child of MYRTAL BURGESS and KENNON BROUSSARD is:
      i. ROBERT KENNON[14] BROUSSARD, b. 16 Oct 1974, Houma, LA.
Key Source: Family records of Felix Maben Hammack, Bend, OR.

697. WILBURN LOUIS[13] BURGESS, JR *(WILBURN LOUIS[12], CLARA BELLE[11] HAMMACK, WILLIAM SIMMS[10], JOHN T.[9], SIMEON J.[8], WILLIAM T.[7], ROBERT HAMMACK[6] JR., ROBERT HAMMACK[5] SR., WILLIAM "THE ELDER"[4] HAMMACK, WILLIAM "O"[3], JOHN[2] HAMMOCKE, ? JOHN[1] HAMMOT)* was born 15 Oct 1948 in Hinds County, MS. He married DELORES MARINA NEIL in Memphis, TN. She was born 23 Jun 1948 in Memphis, TN.
Children of WILBURN BURGESS and DELORES NEIL are:
      i. ALTON LOUIS[14] BURGESS, b. 18 Mar 1970, Hinds County, MS; m. DAWN SMITH, 06 Jun 1994, Memphis, TN.
     ii. WILLIAM NEIL BURGESS, b. 06 Nov 1973.
    iii. MARY JENNIFER BURGESS, b. 10 Jul 1976.
Key Source: Family records of Felix Maben Hammack, Bend, OR.

698. GEORGE A.[13] BURGESS *(FRANCIS NORMAN[12], CLARA BELLE[11] HAMMACK, WILLIAM SIMMS[10], JOHN T.[9], SIMEON J.[8], WILLIAM T.[7], ROBERT HAMMACK[6] JR., ROBERT HAMMACK[5] SR., WILLIAM "THE ELDER"[4] HAMMACK, WILLIAM "O"[3], JOHN[2] HAMMOCKE, ? JOHN[1] HAMMOT)* was born 26 Sep 1957. He married TONYA SMITH 01 Jun 1985 in Hinds County, MS. She was born in Brandon, MS.
Children of GEORGE BURGESS and TONYA SMITH are:
      i. TAYLOR RENA[14] BURGESS, b. 15 Mar 1990.
     ii. PAYTON ALAN BURGESS, b. 31 Mar 1991.
    iii. BRETT AUSTIN BURGESS, b. 08 Mar 1994.
Key Source: Family records of Felix Maben Hammack, Bend, OR.

699. WAYNE WHITFIELD[13] RUSSELL *(ROSALIE[12] BURGESS, DOLLIE CLIFFORD[11] HAMMACK, WILLIAM SIMMS[10], JOHN T.[9], SIMEON J.[8], WILLIAM T.[7], ROBERT HAMMACK[6] JR., ROBERT HAMMACK[5] SR., WILLIAM "THE ELDER"[4] HAMMACK, WILLIAM "O"[3], JOHN[2] HAMMOCKE, ? JOHN[1] HAMMOT)* was born 11 Feb 1952. He married CAROL AUDRY POLK 30 Jun 1979. She was born 01 Sep 1951.
Child of WAYNE RUSSELL and CAROL POLK is:
      i. RANDI HOPE[14] RUSSELL, b. 16 Mar 1984.
Key Source: Family records of Felix Maben Hammack, Bend, OR.

700. HELEN ROSALIE[13] RUSSELL *(MERLE[12] BURGESS, DOLLIE CLIFFORD[11] HAMMACK, WILLIAM SIMMS[10], JOHN T.[9], SIMEON J.[8], WILLIAM T.[7], ROBERT HAMMACK[6] JR., ROBERT HAMMACK[5] SR., WILLIAM "THE ELDER"[4] HAMMACK, WILLIAM "O"[3], JOHN[2] HAMMOCKE, ? JOHN[1] HAMMOT)* She married GREG BREWTON 24 Jun 1966.
Children of HELEN RUSSELL and GREG BREWTON are:
      i. JASON CARTER[14] BREWTON, b. 25 Sep 1969.
     ii. RACHEL JEAN BREWTON, b. 17 Nov 1970.
Key Source: Family records of Felix Maben Hammack, Bend, OR.

701. PHILLIP ABNER[13] RUSSELL, JR. *(MERLE[12] BURGESS, DOLLIE CLIFFORD[11] HAMMACK, WILLIAM SIMMS[10], JOHN T.[9], SIMEON J.[8], WILLIAM T.[7], ROBERT HAMMACK[6] JR., ROBERT HAMMACK[5] SR., WILLIAM "THE ELDER"[4] HAMMACK, WILLIAM "O"[3], JOHN[2] HAMMOCKE, ? JOHN[1] HAMMOT)* was born 15 May 1939. He married (1) UNKNOWN. He married (2) DIANE PASSONS SANDERS 23 Jun 1979.
Children of PHILLIP RUSSELL and UNKNOWN are:
> i. TAMMY IRENE[14] RUSSELL, b. 25 May 1963.
> ii. TERRY LYNN RUSSELL, b. 21 Jun 1965.
> iii. KENNETH ALAN RUSSELL, b. 05 Nov 1968.

Children of PHILLIP RUSSELL and DIANE SANDERS are:
> iv. MICHAEL[14] SANDERS, b. 1960; d. 22 Jun 1980.
> v. DORINDA SANDERS, b. 25 Jul 1962.

Key Source: Family records of Felix Maben Hammack, Bend, OR.

702. DARLENE ANNETTE[13] MURRAY *(VICTORIA LENA[12] TELENGA, MYRTLE LOUISE[11] HAMMACK, JOHN ROBERT[10], JOHN T.[9], SIMEON J.[8], WILLIAM T.[7], ROBERT HAMMACK[6] JR., ROBERT HAMMACK[5] SR., WILLIAM "THE ELDER"[4] HAMMACK, WILLIAM "O"[3], JOHN[2] HAMMOCKE, ? JOHN[1] HAMMOT)* was born 1940 in Ceylon, Sask. She married (1) DOUGLAS MCEWEN 1958. She married (2) DENNIS BARRATT 1987.
Children of DARLENE MURRAY and DOUGLAS MCEWEN are:
755.   i. HAL MURRAY[14] MCEWEN, b. 1960, Bengough, Sask.
> ii. SHAWNA LEE MCEWEN, b. 1964, Bengough, Sask.
756.   iii. KIPP DOUGLAS MCEWEN, b. 1966.

Key Source: Family records of Jonas Hammack, Bend, OR.

703. LARRY GEORGE[13] HENRY *(GEORGINA E.[12] TELENGA, MYRTLE LOUISE[11] HAMMACK, JOHN ROBERT[10], JOHN T.[9], SIMEON J.[8], WILLIAM T.[7], ROBERT HAMMACK[6] JR., ROBERT HAMMACK[5] SR., WILLIAM "THE ELDER"[4] HAMMACK, WILLIAM "O"[3], JOHN[2] HAMMOCKE, ? JOHN[1] HAMMOT)* was born 1954, and died 15 Apr 1994 in Regina, Sask.. He married DEBBIE BARTSHEWSKI 1973.
Children of LARRY HENRY and DEBBIE BARTSHEWSKI are:
757.   i. HOLLIE[14] HENRY, b. 16 Jun 1973.
> ii. JODIE HENRY, b. 20 Jul 1978.

Key Source: Family records of Jonas Hammack, Bend, OR.

704. GLENN[13] HIBBARD *(FLORENCE[12] TELENGA, MYRTLE LOUISE[11] HAMMACK, JOHN ROBERT[10], JOHN T.[9], SIMEON J.[8], WILLIAM T.[7], ROBERT HAMMACK[6] JR., ROBERT HAMMACK[5] SR., WILLIAM "THE ELDER"[4] HAMMACK, WILLIAM "O"[3], JOHN[2] HAMMOCKE, ? JOHN[1] HAMMOT)* was born 19 Jun 1950. He married SHARON MACK 24 Jul 1971. She was born 13 Aug 1951.
Children of GLENN HIBBARD and SHARON MACK are:
758.   i. KIMBERLY[14] HIBBARD, b. 18 Feb 1971.
> ii. KRISTY HIBBARD, b. 10 May 1975.
> iii. BRADLEY HIBBARD, b. 05 Oct 1976.
> iv. CHERIE HIBBARD, b. 26 Jun 1979.

Key Source: Family records of Jonas Hammack, Bend, OR.

705. WANDA[13] HIBBARD *(FLORENCE[12] TELENGA, MYRTLE LOUISE[11] HAMMACK, JOHN ROBERT[10], JOHN T.[9], SIMEON J.[8], WILLIAM T.[7], ROBERT HAMMACK[6] JR., ROBERT HAMMACK[5]*

SR., WILLIAM "THE ELDER"⁴ HAMMACK, WILLIAM "O"³, JOHN² HAMMOCKE, ? JOHN¹ HAMMOT) was born 04 Aug 1954.

Child of WANDA HIBBARD is:

     i.   TYRELL¹⁴ HIBBARD, b. 02 Aug 1972; d. 14 May 2002.

Key Source: Family records of Jonas Hammack, Bend, OR.

706. LINDA ANN¹³ TELENGA *(FLOYD¹², MYRTLE LOUISE¹¹ HAMMACK, JOHN ROBERT¹⁰, JOHN T.⁹, SIMEON J.⁸, WILLIAM T.⁷, ROBERT HAMMACK⁶ JR., ROBERT HAMMACK⁵ SR., WILLIAM "THE ELDER"⁴ HAMMACK, WILLIAM "O"³, JOHN² HAMMOCKE, ? JOHN¹ HAMMOT)* She married MICHAEL JOHN LATURNUS 09 Apr 1977. He died Aug 2003.

Children of LINDA TELENGA and MICHAEL LATURNUS are:

     i.   MATTHEW¹⁴ LATURNUS.

    ii.   SCOTT LATURNUS.

Key Source: Family records of Jonas Hammack, Bend, OR.

707. HAROLD¹³ TELENGA *(JEROME¹², MYRTLE LOUISE¹¹ HAMMACK, JOHN ROBERT¹⁰, JOHN T.⁹, SIMEON J.⁸, WILLIAM T.⁷, ROBERT HAMMACK⁶ JR., ROBERT HAMMACK⁵ SR., WILLIAM "THE ELDER"⁴ HAMMACK, WILLIAM "O"³, JOHN² HAMMOCKE, ? JOHN¹ HAMMOT)* was born 11 Apr 1964. He married TRINA MOONEY 31 Jul 1993. She was born 08 Oct 1971.

Child of HAROLD TELENGA and TRINA MOONEY is:

     i.   CAMDON¹⁴ TELENGA.

Key Source: Family records of Jonas Hammack, Bend, OR.

708. MICHELE¹³ TELENGA *(JEROME¹², MYRTLE LOUISE¹¹ HAMMACK, JOHN ROBERT¹⁰, JOHN T.⁹, SIMEON J.⁸, WILLIAM T.⁷, ROBERT HAMMACK⁶ JR., ROBERT HAMMACK⁵ SR., WILLIAM "THE ELDER"⁴ HAMMACK, WILLIAM "O"³, JOHN² HAMMOCKE, ? JOHN¹ HAMMOT)* was born 26 Dec 1967. She married EVAN RECKNELL 07 Aug 1992. He was born Jul 1955.

Children of MICHELE TELENGA and EVAN RECKNELL are:

     i.   BRODY¹⁴ RECKNELL, b. 05 Jun 1991.

    ii.   BRETT RECKNELL, b. 02 Jun 1993.

Key Source: Family records of Jonas Hammack, Bend, OR.

709. BRADLEY ROSS¹³ THOMPSON *(GLORIA¹² TELENGA, MYRTLE LOUISE¹¹ HAMMACK, JOHN ROBERT¹⁰, JOHN T.⁹, SIMEON J.⁸, WILLIAM T.⁷, ROBERT HAMMACK⁶ JR., ROBERT HAMMACK⁵ SR., WILLIAM "THE ELDER"⁴ HAMMACK, WILLIAM "O"³, JOHN² HAMMOCKE, ? JOHN¹ HAMMOT)* was born 21 Nov 1965 in Calgary, Alta.. He married DEANNE MCFARLANE. She was born 22 Apr 1967 in Calgary, Alta..

Children of BRADLEY THOMPSON and DEANNE MCFARLANE are:

     i.   BREANNE DAWN¹⁴ THOMPSON, b. 25 May 1990.

    ii.   BRITTANY RAE THOMPSON, b. 13 Dec 1991.

Key Source: Family records of Jonas Hammack, Bend, OR.

710. BRUCE ALLAN¹³ HAMMACK *(DALE MCDONALD¹², HARRY HERBERT¹¹, JOHN ROBERT¹⁰, JOHN T.⁹, SIMEON J.⁸, WILLIAM T.⁷, ROBERT HAMMACK⁶ JR., ROBERT HAMMACK⁵ SR., WILLIAM "THE ELDER"⁴ HAMMACK, WILLIAM "O"³, JOHN² HAMMOCKE, ? JOHN¹ HAMMOT)* was born 15 May 1952 in Kalamazoo, MI. He married SUCKI CHOI.

Children of BRUCE HAMMACK and SUCKI CHOI are:

     i.   JENNIFER¹⁴ HAMMACK, b. Sep 1977.

    ii.   JAYSON DALE HAMMACK, b. Sep 1981.

Key Source: Family records of Jonas Hammack, Bend, OR.

711. JACQUELINE DALE[13] HAMMACK *(DALE MCDONALD[12], HARRY HERBERT[11], JOHN ROBERT[10], JOHN T.[9], SIMEON J.[8], WILLIAM T.[7], ROBERT HAMMACK[6] JR., ROBERT HAMMACK[5] SR., WILLIAM "THE ELDER"[4] HAMMACK, WILLIAM "O"[3], JOHN[2] HAMMOCKE, ? JOHN[1] HAMMOT)* was born 29 Mar 1954. She married RANDY GRANDE.
Child of JACQUELINE HAMMACK and RANDY GRANDE is:
      i. DUSTIN[14] GRANDE, b. Feb 1982.
Key Source: Family records of Jonas Hammack, Bend, OR.

712. STEVEN GREGORY[13] GORMAN *(ALOHA DELPHINE[12] HAMMACK, HARRY HERBERT[11], JOHN ROBERT[10], JOHN T.[9], SIMEON J.[8], WILLIAM T.[7], ROBERT HAMMACK[6] JR., ROBERT HAMMACK[5] SR., WILLIAM "THE ELDER"[4] HAMMACK, WILLIAM "O"[3], JOHN[2] HAMMOCKE, ? JOHN[1] HAMMOT)* was born 30 Apr 1949 in Kenmare, Ward County, ND. He married DIANE HACKEL.
Children of STEVEN GORMAN and DIANE HACKEL are:
      i. PAUL[14] GORMAN.
     ii. ANNIE GORMAN.
Key Source: Family records of Jonas Hammack, Bend, OR.

713. JILL RENEE[13] GORMAN *(ALOHA DELPHINE[12] HAMMACK, HARRY HERBERT[11], JOHN ROBERT[10], JOHN T.[9], SIMEON J.[8], WILLIAM T.[7], ROBERT HAMMACK[6] JR., ROBERT HAMMACK[5] SR., WILLIAM "THE ELDER"[4] HAMMACK, WILLIAM "O"[3], JOHN[2] HAMMOCKE, ? JOHN[1] HAMMOT)* was born 03 May 1951 in Kenmare, Ward County, ND. She married LLOYD ALAN DEVANEY. He was born 07 Oct 1949.
Child of JILL GORMAN and LLOYD DEVANEY is:
      i. BRITT RENEE[14] DEVANEY, b. 07 Oct 1988, Chicago, IL.
Key Source: Family records of Jonas Hammack, Bend, OR.

714. BRADFORD[13] HAMMACK *(CLAYTON DARREL "CLAY"[12], EUGENE[11], JOHN ROBERT[10], JOHN T.[9], SIMEON J.[8], WILLIAM T.[7], ROBERT HAMMACK[6] JR., ROBERT HAMMACK[5] SR., WILLIAM "THE ELDER"[4] HAMMACK, WILLIAM "O"[3], JOHN[2] HAMMOCKE, ? JOHN[1] HAMMOT)* was born 03 Feb 1953. He married KERRY MCGINTY. She was born 13 Aug 1952.
Children of BRADFORD HAMMACK and KERRY MCGINTY are:
      i. GABRIEL[14] HAMMACK, b. 18 May 1976.
     ii. CHERISH HAMMACK, b. 14 Aug 1977.
Key Source: Family records of Jonas Hammack, Bend, OR.

715. JEFFREY DALE[13] WAKEFIELD *(ROSE[12] HAMMACK, JONAS ALAN[11], JOHN ROBERT[10], JOHN T.[9], SIMEON J.[8], WILLIAM T.[7], ROBERT HAMMACK[6] JR., ROBERT HAMMACK[5] SR., WILLIAM "THE ELDER"[4] HAMMACK, WILLIAM "O"[3], JOHN[2] HAMMOCKE, ? JOHN[1] HAMMOT)* was born 03 Jul 1967. He married DEBERA RIDER 29 Sep 1995.
Child of JEFFREY WAKEFIELD and DEBERA RIDER is:
      i. RASHAEL[14] WAKEFIELD, b. 14 Oct 1992.
Key Source: Family records of Jonas Hammack, Bend, OR.

716. AMY MARIE[13] WAKEFIELD *(ROSE[12] HAMMACK, JONAS ALAN[11], JOHN ROBERT[10], JOHN T.[9], SIMEON J.[8], WILLIAM T.[7], ROBERT HAMMACK[6] JR., ROBERT HAMMACK[5] SR., WILLIAM "THE ELDER"[4] HAMMACK, WILLIAM "O"[3], JOHN[2] HAMMOCKE, ? JOHN[1] HAMMOT)* was born 25 Jun

1975. She married FRANKLIN ANTHONY COOK 09 May 1998, son of FRANKLIN COOK and BONNIE. He was born 02 Jul 1974.

Child of AMY WAKEFIELD and FRANKLIN COOK is:

    i.   JONAS ANTHONY[14] COOK, b. 26 Jul 2004.

Key Source: Family records of Jonas Hammack, Bend, OR.

717. BEVERLY JAYNE[13] DAVIS *(JAMES VANCE[12], WILLIAM ROSCOE[11], BETSY ANN[10] HAMMACK, FELIX WILBORN[9], SIMEON J.[8], WILLIAM T.[7], ROBERT HAMMACK[6] JR., ROBERT HAMMACK[5] SR., WILLIAM "THE ELDER"[4] HAMMACK, WILLIAM "O"[3], JOHN[2] HAMMOCKE, ? JOHN[1] HAMMOT)* was born 17 Sep 1947 in Mississippi. She married THOMAS EDWARD LINN 19 Aug 1967.

Children of BEVERLY DAVIS and THOMAS LINN are:

    i.   DAVIS EDWARD[14] LINN, b. 09 Feb 1969.

    ii. HEATHER LEIGH LINN, b. 08 May 1970.

Key Source: Family records of William Roscoe Davis, Jr., Grenada, MS.

718. NANCY REA[13] DAVIS *(WILLIAM ROSCOE DAVIS[12] JR., WILLIAM ROSCOE[11] DAVIS, BETSY ANN[10] HAMMACK, FELIX WILBORN[9], SIMEON J.[8], WILLIAM T.[7], ROBERT HAMMACK[6] JR., ROBERT HAMMACK[5] SR., WILLIAM "THE ELDER"[4] HAMMACK, WILLIAM "O"[3], JOHN[2] HAMMOCKE, ? JOHN[1] HAMMOT)* was born 22 Feb 1953 in Grenada Co., MS. She married RONALD RALPH GRANHOLM 12 Jul 1975 in Grenada, MS.

Child of NANCY DAVIS and RONALD GRANHOLM is:

    i.   ERIC DAVIS[14] GRANHOLM, b. 05 Mar 1980, Grenada Co., MS.

Key Source: Family records of William Roscoe Davis, Jr., Grenada, MS.

719. ANNIE JEANETTE[13] ELLIOTT *(ANNIE MAE[12] HAMMOCK, JAMES PELL[11], FELIX A.[10], ALFRED WASHINGTON "DOCK"[9] HAMMACK, SIMEON J.[8], WILLIAM T.[7], ROBERT HAMMACK[6] JR., ROBERT HAMMACK[5] SR., WILLIAM "THE ELDER"[4] HAMMACK, WILLIAM "O"[3], JOHN[2] HAMMOCKE, ? JOHN[1] HAMMOT)* was born 24 May 1961 in Monticello, AR. She married (1) HERMAN DELL AUSTIN. She married (2) DAVID SANSON.

Children of ANNIE ELLIOTT and HERMAN AUSTIN are:

759.   i.   HERMAN DELL[14] AUSTIN, JR., b. 29 Mar 1979, Big Spring, TX.

760.   ii. AMANDA LYNN AUSTIN, b. 25 May 1980, Big Spring, TX.

    iii. ROBERT LEE AUSTIN, b. 20 Aug 1982, Monticello, AR.

Child of ANNIE ELLIOTT and DAVID SANSON is:

    iv. MARIE[14] SANSON, b. 30 Apr 1986, Monticello, AR.

Key Source: Lois Hagood, *The Elusive Ancestor* (Crossett, AR, 1992); Lois Hagood, "C. W. Roberts Family," in Robert A. and Mary I. Carpenter, *Reflections of Ashley County* (Dallas, TX, 1988), F544.

720. KENNETH RAY[13] ELLIOTT *(ANNIE MAE[12] HAMMOCK, JAMES PELL[11], FELIX A.[10], ALFRED WASHINGTON "DOCK"[9] HAMMACK, SIMEON J.[8], WILLIAM T.[7], ROBERT HAMMACK[6] JR., ROBERT HAMMACK[5] SR., WILLIAM "THE ELDER"[4] HAMMACK, WILLIAM "O"[3], JOHN[2] HAMMOCKE, ? JOHN[1] HAMMOT)* was born 14 Feb 1963 in Monticello, AR. He married (1) STEPHANIE CARRINGTON. He married (2) CINDY JUDKINS.

Child of KENNETH ELLIOTT and STEPHANIE CARRINGTON is:

    i.   JUSTIN RAY[14] ELLIOTT, b. 30 Sep 1986, Monticello, AR; d. 30 Sep 1986, Pine Bluff, AR.

Child of KENNETH ELLIOTT and CINDY JUDKINS is:

    ii. ERIC WAYNE[14] ELLIOTT, b. 27 Nov 1988, Monticello, AR.

Key Source: Lois Hagood, *The Elusive Ancestor* (Crossett, AR, 1992); Lois Hagood, "C. W. Roberts Family," in Robert A. and Mary I. Carpenter, *Reflections of Ashley County* (Dallas, TX, 1988), F544.

721. JUDY KAY[13] ELLIOTT *(ANNIE MAE[12] HAMMOCK, JAMES PELL[11], FELIX A.[10], ALFRED WASHINGTON "DOCK"[9] HAMMACK, SIMEON J.[8], WILLIAM T.[7], ROBERT HAMMACK[6] JR., ROBERT HAMMACK[5] SR., WILLIAM "THE ELDER"[4] HAMMACK, WILLIAM "O"[3], JOHN[2] HAMMOCKE, ? JOHN[1] HAMMOT)* was born 11 Mar 1965 in Monticello, AR. She married JAMES HANNEY.
Child of JUDY ELLIOTT and JAMES HANNEY is:
    i.   JOHN DAVID[14] HANNEY, b. 26 Aug 1984, Dermott, AR.

Key Source: Lois Hagood, *The Elusive Ancestor* (Crossett, AR, 1992); Lois Hagood, "C. W. Roberts Family," in Robert A. and Mary I. Carpenter, *Reflections of Ashley County* (Dallas, TX, 1988), F544.

722. BOBBY WAYNE[13] ENDSLEY *(ANNIE MAE[12] HAMMOCK, JAMES PELL[11], FELIX A.[10], ALFRED WASHINGTON "DOCK"[9] HAMMACK, SIMEON J.[8], WILLIAM T.[7], ROBERT HAMMACK[6] JR., ROBERT HAMMACK[5] SR., WILLIAM "THE ELDER"[4] HAMMACK, WILLIAM "O"[3], JOHN[2] HAMMOCKE, ? JOHN[1] HAMMOT)* was born 29 Mar 1966 in Monticello, AR. He married LINDA MANN.
Child of BOBBY ENDSLEY and LINDA MANN is:
    i.   JESSICA LYNN[14] ENDSLEY, b. 20 Feb 1994, Houston, TX.

Key Source: Lois Hagood, *The Elusive Ancestor* (Crossett, AR, 1992); Lois Hagood, "C. W. Roberts Family," in Robert A. and Mary I. Carpenter, *Reflections of Ashley County* (Dallas, TX, 1988), F544.

723. LARRY GENE[13] ENDSLEY *(ANNIE MAE[12] HAMMOCK, JAMES PELL[11], FELIX A.[10], ALFRED WASHINGTON "DOCK"[9] HAMMACK, SIMEON J.[8], WILLIAM T.[7], ROBERT HAMMACK[6] JR., ROBERT HAMMACK[5] SR., WILLIAM "THE ELDER"[4] HAMMACK, WILLIAM "O"[3], JOHN[2] HAMMOCKE, ? JOHN[1] HAMMOT)* was born 27 Nov 1968 in Dermott, AR. He married (1) ANGELA REEVES. He married (2) ANGELA OWENS.
Children of LARRY ENDSLEY and ANGELA REEVES are:
    i.   ASHLAND NICOLE[14] ENDSLEY, b. 09 Nov 1994, Monticello, AR.
    ii. DUSTY MASON ENDSLEY, b. 15 Sep 1995, Monticello, AR.
    iii. ZACHARY TAYLOR ENDSLEY, b. 18 Jan 1997, Monticello, AR.

Children of LARRY ENDSLEY and ANGELA OWENS are:
    iv. CHRISTOPHER BLAKE[14] ENDSLEY, b. 31 Jan 1991, Warren, AR.
    v. COLE ENDSLEY, b. 02 Mar 1993, Little Rock, AR.

Key Source: Lois Hagood, *The Elusive Ancestor* (Crossett, AR, 1992); Lois Hagood, "C. W. Roberts Family," in Robert A. and Mary I. Carpenter, *Reflections of Ashley County* (Dallas, TX, 1988), F544.

724. DONNA RUTH[13] TANNER *(OLIVIA[12] HONEYCUTT, RUTH[11] ROBERTS, JEFFIE JANE[10] HAMMOCK, ALFRED WASHINGTON "DOCK"[9] HAMMACK, SIMEON J.[8], WILLIAM T.[7], ROBERT HAMMACK[6] JR., ROBERT HAMMACK[5] SR., WILLIAM "THE ELDER"[4] HAMMACK, WILLIAM "O"[3], JOHN[2] HAMMOCKE, ? JOHN[1] HAMMOT)* was born 11 Aug 1941 in Ouachita Co., AR. She married JOHN WHITMORE BIRD IV 19 Apr 1962, son of JOHN BIRD and RUTH WILLIAM. He was born 1940.
Children of DONNA TANNER and JOHN BIRD are:
    i.   JOHN RICHARD[14] BIRD, b. 25 Oct 1963, Ouachita Co., AR.
    ii. LAURA ELIZABETH BIRD, b. 13 Dec 1970, Morris Co., TX.

Key Source: Lois Hagood, *The Elusive Ancestor* (Crossett, AR, 1992); Lois Hagood, "C. W. Roberts Family," in Robert A. and Mary I. Carpenter, *Reflections of Ashley County* (Dallas, TX, 1988), F544.

725. JANICE CAROLYN[13] HONEYCUTT *(WILLIAM THOMAS[12], RUTH[11] ROBERTS, JEFFIE JANE[10] HAMMOCK, ALFRED WASHINGTON "DOCK"[9] HAMMACK, SIMEON J.[8], WILLIAM T.[7], ROBERT HAMMACK[6] JR., ROBERT HAMMACK[5] SR., WILLIAM "THE ELDER"[4] HAMMACK, WILLIAM "O"[3], JOHN[2] HAMMOCKE, ? JOHN[1] HAMMOT)* was born 07 Feb 1942 in Ouachita Co., AR. She married (1) ROBERT CHARLES (ROB) GILLESPIE 1960 in Arkansas. She married (2) THOMAS JOSEPH SANDY 27 Dec 1985 in Youngstown, OH. He was born 11 Apr 1954 in Youngstown, OH.
Children of JANICE HONEYCUTT and ROBERT GILLESPIE are:
    i.   ROBERT CHARLES[14] GILLESPIE III, b. 20 Mar 1961, Washington, D.C..
    ii. TIFFANY ANN GILLESPIE, b. 01 Feb 1969, Columbus, OH.
Key Source: Lois Hagood, *The Elusive Ancestor* (Crossett, AR, 1992); Lois Hagood, "C. W. Roberts Family," in Robert A. and Mary I. Carpenter, *Reflections of Ashley County* (Dallas, TX, 1988), F544.

726. GARY RANDAL[13] HONEYCUTT *(WILLIAM THOMAS[12], RUTH[11] ROBERTS, JEFFIE JANE[10] HAMMOCK, ALFRED WASHINGTON "DOCK"[9] HAMMACK, SIMEON J.[8], WILLIAM T.[7], ROBERT HAMMACK[6] JR., ROBERT HAMMACK[5] SR., WILLIAM "THE ELDER"[4] HAMMACK, WILLIAM "O"[3], JOHN[2] HAMMOCKE, ? JOHN[1] HAMMOT)* was born 01 Jan 1947 in Ouachita Co., AR. He married JANICE MCGAUGH 15 Oct 1966 in Arkansas, daughter of ALVIN MCGAUGH and AUDRA FINCER. She was born 26 Oct 1948 in Texarkana, Bowie County, TX.
Children of GARY HONEYCUTT and JANICE MCGAUGH are:
    i.   URSULA ANN[14] HONEYCUTT, b. 28 May 1967, Ashley Co., AR.
    ii. GARY RANDAL HONEYCUTT, JR., b. 31 Oct 1969, Ashley Co., AR.
Key Source: Lois Hagood, *The Elusive Ancestor* (Crossett, AR, 1992); Lois Hagood, "C. W. Roberts Family," in Robert A. and Mary I. Carpenter, *Reflections of Ashley County* (Dallas, TX, 1988), F544.

727. DONALD MANSEL[13] HAGOOD *(LOIS RUTH[12] HONEYCUTT, RUTH[11] ROBERTS, JEFFIE JANE[10] HAMMOCK, ALFRED WASHINGTON "DOCK"[9] HAMMACK, SIMEON J.[8], WILLIAM T.[7], ROBERT HAMMACK[6] JR., ROBERT HAMMACK[5] SR., WILLIAM "THE ELDER"[4] HAMMACK, WILLIAM "O"[3], JOHN[2] HAMMOCKE, ? JOHN[1] HAMMOT)* was born 23 Jul 1964 in DeQueen, Sevier County, AR. He married JERRI ANN BUCK 10 Jul 1987 in Ashley County, AR, daughter of RODGER BUCK and BONNI WAGLEY. She was born 19 Jan 1967 in Prescott, Nevada County, AR.
Child of DONALD HAGOOD and JERRI BUCK is:
    i.   BRITTANY ANN[14] HAGOOD, b. 19 Jan 1989, Drew Co., AR.
Key Source: Lois Hagood, *The Elusive Ancestor* (Crossett, AR, 1992); Lois Hagood, "C. W. Roberts Family," in Robert A. and Mary I. Carpenter, *Reflections of Ashley County* (Dallas, TX, 1988), F544.

728. RHODA JO[13] ADAMS *(MARGARET LAVENIAL[12] ROBERTS, CLAUD CYRUS[11], JEFFIE JANE[10] HAMMOCK, ALFRED WASHINGTON "DOCK"[9] HAMMACK, SIMEON J.[8], WILLIAM T.[7], ROBERT HAMMACK[6] JR., ROBERT HAMMACK[5] SR., WILLIAM "THE ELDER"[4] HAMMACK, WILLIAM "O"[3], JOHN[2] HAMMOCKE, ? JOHN[1] HAMMOT)* was born 03 Sep 1944 in Ashley Co., AR. She married JAMES MCCORKLE.
Children of RHODA ADAMS and JAMES MCCORKLE are:
    i.   BRENT[14] MCCORKLE.
    ii. BROCK MCCORKLE.
Key Source: Lois Hagood, *The Elusive Ancestor* (Crossett, AR, 1992); Lois Hagood, "C. W. Roberts Family," in Robert A. and Mary I. Carpenter, *Reflections of Ashley County* (Dallas, TX, 1988), F544.

729. KENNETH[13] HELTON *(LAVONIA JOYCE[12] ROBERTS, CLAUD CYRUS[11], JEFFIE JANE[10] HAMMOCK, ALFRED WASHINGTON "DOCK"[9] HAMMACK, SIMEON J.[8], WILLIAM T.[7], ROBERT HAMMACK[6] JR., ROBERT HAMMACK[5] SR., WILLIAM "THE ELDER"[4] HAMMACK, WILLIAM "O"[3], JOHN[2] HAMMOCKE, ? JOHN[1] HAMMOT)* was born 21 Feb 1948. He married KATHY WASHAM 19 Dec 1972.
Children of KENNETH HELTON and KATHY WASHAM are:
    i.   JENNIFER[14] HELTON.
    ii. BECKY HELTON.
    iii. KEITH HELTON.
    iv. JOHN BARRY HELTON.
Key Source: Lois Hagood, *The Elusive Ancestor* (Crossett, AR, 1992); Lois Hagood, "C. W. Roberts Family," in Robert A. and Mary I. Carpenter, *Reflections of Ashley County* (Dallas, TX, 1988), F544.

730. REBECCA LANE[13] PALSER *(ELIZABETH LANE[12] ROBERTS, CLAUD CYRUS[11], JEFFIE JANE[10] HAMMOCK, ALFRED WASHINGTON "DOCK"[9] HAMMACK, SIMEON J.[8], WILLIAM T.[7], ROBERT HAMMACK[6] JR., ROBERT HAMMACK[5] SR., WILLIAM "THE ELDER"[4] HAMMACK, WILLIAM "O"[3], JOHN[2] HAMMOCKE, ? JOHN[1] HAMMOT)* was born 13 Oct 1951. She married ROBERT DENNIS ROGERS 04 Jan 1973.
Children of REBECCA PALSER and ROBERT ROGERS are:
    i.   ANGELA LANE[14] ROGERS, b. 15 Dec 1976.
    ii. CHRISTOPHER ROBERT ROGERS, b. 02 Nov 1979.
Key Source: Lois Hagood, *The Elusive Ancestor* (Crossett, AR, 1992); Lois Hagood, "C. W. Roberts Family," in Robert A. and Mary I. Carpenter, *Reflections of Ashley County* (Dallas, TX, 1988), F544.

731. ELIZABETH GRACE[13] PALSER *(ELIZABETH LANE[12] ROBERTS, CLAUD CYRUS[11], JEFFIE JANE[10] HAMMOCK, ALFRED WASHINGTON "DOCK"[9] HAMMACK, SIMEON J.[8], WILLIAM T.[7], ROBERT HAMMACK[6] JR., ROBERT HAMMACK[5] SR., WILLIAM "THE ELDER"[4] HAMMACK, WILLIAM "O"[3], JOHN[2] HAMMOCKE, ? JOHN[1] HAMMOT)* was born 22 May 1955. She married JERYL LYNN NANCE 11 Aug 1976.
Children of ELIZABETH PALSER and JERYL NANCE are:
    i.   DEENEE ELIZABETH[14] NANCE, b. 28 Dec 1980.
    ii. KRISTI LYNN NANCE, b. 13 May 1982.
    iii. DUSTIN THOMAS NANCE, b. 26 Nov 1983.
Key Source: Lois Hagood, *The Elusive Ancestor* (Crossett, AR, 1992); Lois Hagood, "C. W. Roberts Family," in Robert A. and Mary I. Carpenter, *Reflections of Ashley County* (Dallas, TX, 1988), F544.

732. DAN RAY[13] BYRNE, JR. *(DONNIE JANE[12] ROBERTS, WILLIAM TRACY[11], JEFFIE JANE[10] HAMMOCK, ALFRED WASHINGTON "DOCK"[9] HAMMACK, SIMEON J.[8], WILLIAM T.[7], ROBERT HAMMACK[6] JR., ROBERT HAMMACK[5] SR., WILLIAM "THE ELDER"[4] HAMMACK, WILLIAM "O"[3], JOHN[2] HAMMOCKE, ? JOHN[1] HAMMOT)* was born 30 Nov 1948 in El Paso, TX. He married CAROLYN WILLIAMS 22 May 1971 in El Paso, TX.
Children of DAN BYRNE and CAROLYN WILLIAMS are:
    i.   PATRICIA COLLEEN[14] BYRNE, b. 06 Jan 1974, Austin, TX.
    ii. SHANNON MICHELLE BYRNE, b. 06 Jul 1976, Big Springs, TX.
    iii. MEGAN KATHERINE BYRNE, b. 11 Mar 1980, Corpus Christi, TX.
Key Source: Lois Hagood, *The Elusive Ancestor* (Crossett, AR, 1992); Lois Hagood, "C. W. Roberts Family," in Robert A. and Mary I. Carpenter, *Reflections of Ashley County* (Dallas, TX, 1988), F544.

733. WILLIAM ROBERT[13] BYRNE *(DONNIE JANE[12] ROBERTS, WILLIAM TRACY[11], JEFFIE JANE[10] HAMMOCK, ALFRED WASHINGTON "DOCK"[9] HAMMACK, SIMEON J.[8], WILLIAM T.[7], ROBERT HAMMACK[6] JR., ROBERT HAMMACK[5] SR., WILLIAM "THE ELDER"[4] HAMMACK, WILLIAM "O"[3], JOHN[2] HAMMOCKE, ? JOHN[1] HAMMOT)* was born 01 Jul 1950 in Big Springs, TX. He married ROBBIE JANE WALKER 26 Mar 1975 in Big Springs, TX.
Children of WILLIAM BYRNE and ROBBIE WALKER are:
    i. KERRI BETH[14] BYRNE, b. 30 Nov 1977, Portland, TX.
    ii. TRACY ROBERTS BYRNE, b. 01 Aug 1979, Portland, TX.
    iii. WILLIAM KENT BYRNE, b. 12 Sep 1982, Portland, TX.
Key Source: Lois Hagood, *The Elusive Ancestor* (Crossett, AR, 1992); Lois Hagood, "C. W. Roberts Family," in Robert A. and Mary I. Carpenter, *Reflections of Ashley County* (Dallas, TX, 1988), F544.

Generation No. 14

734. JAMES DOLER[14] MAWK *(JAMES BECKWITH[13], DELORES[12] DOOLITTLE, JAMES WILLIAM[11], SAREPTA ANN ELIZABETH[10] HAMMACK, CHARLES M.[9], SIMEON J.[8], WILLIAM T.[7], ROBERT HAMMACK[6] JR., ROBERT HAMMACK[5] SR., WILLIAM "THE ELDER"[4] HAMMACK, WILLIAM "O"[3], JOHN[2] HAMMOCKE, ? JOHN[1] HAMMOT)* was born 02 Apr 1946 in Houston, MS. He married CAROLYN JEAN JONES 10 Sep 1967 in Mississippi. She was born 10 Dec 1946 in Grenada, MS.
Children of JAMES MAWK and CAROLYN JONES are:
    i. TORREY LANE[15] MAWK, b. 02 Feb 1970, Oxford, MS.
    ii. CARRIE DIONNE MAWK, b. 09 Sep 1974, Oxford, MS.
Key Source: Fox, Doolittle, Holland, and Mawk Family Records, Calhoun City Public Library, Calhoun City, MS.

735. PAMELA[14] VANLANDINGHAM *(MYRA MARIE[13] HOLLAND, HENRY HAVEN[12], MAYBELLE[11] DOOLITTLE, SAREPTA ANN ELIZABETH[10] HAMMACK, CHARLES M.[9], SIMEON J.[8], WILLIAM T.[7], ROBERT HAMMACK[6] JR., ROBERT HAMMACK[5] SR., WILLIAM "THE ELDER"[4] HAMMACK, WILLIAM "O"[3], JOHN[2] HAMMOCKE, ? JOHN[1] HAMMOT)* was born 20 Feb 1950 in Greenwood, MS. She married TIMOTHY H. TRONE 29 Dec 1975 in Calhoun Co., MS.
Children of PAMELA VANLANDINGHAM and TIMOTHY TRONE are:
    i. JAMES T.[15] TRONE, b. 22 Jun 1977, Mississippi.
    ii. MATTHEW VAN TRONE, b. 25 Jun 1980, Mississippi.
    iii. MARK HOLLAND TRONE, b. 02 Sep 1984, Mississippi.
Key Source: Fox, Doolittle, Holland, and Mawk Family Records, Calhoun City Public Library, Calhoun City, MS.

736. GEORGE LACEY[14] VANLANDINGHAM *(MYRA MARIE[13] HOLLAND, HENRY HAVEN[12], MAYBELLE[11] DOOLITTLE, SAREPTA ANN ELIZABETH[10] HAMMACK, CHARLES M.[9], SIMEON J.[8], WILLIAM T.[7], ROBERT HAMMACK[6] JR., ROBERT HAMMACK[5] SR., WILLIAM "THE ELDER"[4] HAMMACK, WILLIAM "O"[3], JOHN[2] HAMMOCKE, ? JOHN[1] HAMMOT)* was born 22 Feb 1954 in Greenwood, MS. He married MARCIA BROWN 12 Mar 1977 in Mississippi.
Children of GEORGE VANLANDINGHAM and MARCIA BROWN are:
    i. BRIAN[15] VANLANDINGHAM, b. 24 Feb 1983, Mississippi.
    ii. LAUREN MCKEE VANLANDINGHAM, b. 09 Sep 1986, Mississippi.
Key Source: Fox, Doolittle, Holland, and Mawk Family Records, Calhoun City Public Library, Calhoun City, MS.

737. THEODORE ALTON[14] BULL *(MARY KATHERINE[13] BABB, SADIE LUCILLE[12] HAMMACK, GEORGE CLEVELAND[11], WILLIAM SIMMS[10], JOHN T.[9], SIMEON J.[8], WILLIAM T.[7], ROBERT HAMMACK[6] JR., ROBERT HAMMACK[5] SR., WILLIAM "THE ELDER"[4] HAMMACK, WILLIAM "O"[3], JOHN[2] HAMMOCKE, ? JOHN[1] HAMMOT)* was born 20 Apr 1955 in Greenville, SC. He married CHERYL BARKER 26 Jun 1976, daughter of LEO BARKER and MARY MOORE.
Children of THEODORE BULL and CHERYL BARKER are:
- i. MARISA KATHERINE[15] BULL, b. 12 Mar 1978, Englewood Cliffs, NJ; m. SIMON PETER NANCE, 24 Jun 2000; b. 27 Sep 1978, El Paso, TX.
- ii. RACHEL AMANDA BULL, b. 06 Jan 1981, Englewood, NJ.
- iii. AMY LYNN BULL, b. 10 Apr 1984, Hyannis, MA.

Key Source: Family records of Felix Maben Hammack, Bend, OR.

738. THOMAS CLARENCE[14] BULL *(MARY KATHERINE[13] BABB, SADIE LUCILLE[12] HAMMACK, GEORGE CLEVELAND[11], WILLIAM SIMMS[10], JOHN T.[9], SIMEON J.[8], WILLIAM T.[7], ROBERT HAMMACK[6] JR., ROBERT HAMMACK[5] SR., WILLIAM "THE ELDER"[4] HAMMACK, WILLIAM "O"[3], JOHN[2] HAMMOCKE, ? JOHN[1] HAMMOT)* was born 21 Nov 1956 in Greenville, SC. He married CHERYL ANN VEASEMAN 03 Apr 1987 in Lakewood, CO, daughter of KENNETH VEASEMAN and PAT GATH.
Children of THOMAS BULL and CHERYL VEASEMAN are:
- i. HANNAH JEAN[15] BULL, b. 18 Oct 1989, Portland, OR.
- ii. CADY SAVANNAH BULL, b. 19 Mar 1994, Wheat Ridge, CO.
- iii. TYLER JORDAN BULL, b. 30 Aug 1997, Wheat Ridge, CO.

Key Source: Family records of Felix Maben Hammack, Bend, OR.

739. LEAH KATHERINE[14] BULL *(MARY KATHERINE[13] BABB, SADIE LUCILLE[12] HAMMACK, GEORGE CLEVELAND[11], WILLIAM SIMMS[10], JOHN T.[9], SIMEON J.[8], WILLIAM T.[7], ROBERT HAMMACK[6] JR., ROBERT HAMMACK[5] SR., WILLIAM "THE ELDER"[4] HAMMACK, WILLIAM "O"[3], JOHN[2] HAMMOCKE, ? JOHN[1] HAMMOT)* was born 17 Nov 1958 in Greenville, SC. She married DOUGLAS CHARLES ROTHROCK 22 Dec 1979 in Harrisburg, PA, son of CHARLES ROTHROCK and CAROL WALLS.
Children of LEAH BULL and DOUGLAS ROTHROCK are:
- i. BENJAMIN CHARLES[15] ROTHROCK, b. 19 Dec 1980, Lewistown, PA.
- ii. ZACHARY OWEN ROTHROCK, b. 08 Apr 1982, Lewistown, PA.
- iii. MEREDITH ELISE ROTHROCK, b. 13 Jan 1987, Lewistown, PA.

Key Source: Family records of Felix Maben Hammack, Bend, OR.

740. LORILYN RUTH[14] BULL *(MARY KATHERINE[13] BABB, SADIE LUCILLE[12] HAMMACK, GEORGE CLEVELAND[11], WILLIAM SIMMS[10], JOHN T.[9], SIMEON J.[8], WILLIAM T.[7], ROBERT HAMMACK[6] JR., ROBERT HAMMACK[5] SR., WILLIAM "THE ELDER"[4] HAMMACK, WILLIAM "O"[3], JOHN[2] HAMMOCKE, ? JOHN[1] HAMMOT)* was born 07 Oct 1962 in Boonton, NJ. She married GREGORY JAMES MILLER 28 May 1983, son of JAMES MILLER and EVA LEHMAN.
Children of LORILYN BULL and GREGORY MILLER are:
- i. SUSAN ELIZABETH[15] MILLER, b. 15 Apr 1985, Allentown, PA.
- ii. REBECCA KATHERINE MILLER, b. 18 Jan 1988, Allentown, PA.
- iii. ESTHER RUTH MILLER, b. 07 Apr 1995, Kingston, PA.

Key Source: Family records of Felix Maben Hammack, Bend, OR.

741. ANDREA KATHERINE[14] LUEG *(ALMEDIA LEE[13] BABB, SADIE LUCILLE[12] HAMMACK, GEORGE CLEVELAND[11], WILLIAM SIMMS[10], JOHN T.[9], SIMEON J.[8], WILLIAM T.[7], ROBERT*

HAMMACK[6] JR., ROBERT HAMMACK[5] SR., WILLIAM "THE ELDER"[4] HAMMACK, WILLIAM "O"[3], JOHN[2] HAMMOCKE, ? JOHN[1] HAMMOT) was born 26 Jul 1966 in Dallas, TX. She married (1) GARY LYN DURBIN 1989 in Arlington, TX. She married (2) GEORGE ROVNY 11 Jun 1999 in Arlington, TX, son of GEORGE ROVNY and CONNIE. He was born 14 May 1961 in Erie, PA.
Children of ANDREA LUEG and GARY DURBIN are:
    i.   BENJAMIN GARETH[15] DURBIN, b. 10 Mar 1991, Arlington, TX.
    ii. RACHEL ALEXANDRIA DURBIN, b. 24 Oct 1994, Arlington, TX.
Children of ANDREA LUEG and GEORGE ROVNY are:
    iii. ISAAC[15] ROVNY, b. 10 Mar 2000, Arlington, TX; d. 10 Mar 2000, Arlington, TX.
    iv. REBECCA ROSE ROVNY, b. 29 Jan 2001, Arlington, TX.
Key Source: Family records of Felix Maben Hammack, Bend, OR.

742. SARAH FRANCES[14] GLOVER *(CAROLYN[13] BABB, SADIE LUCILLE[12] HAMMACK, GEORGE CLEVELAND[11], WILLIAM SIMMS[10], JOHN T.[9], SIMEON J.[8], WILLIAM T.[7], ROBERT HAMMACK[6] JR., ROBERT HAMMACK[5] SR., WILLIAM "THE ELDER"[4] HAMMACK, WILLIAM "O"[3], JOHN[2] HAMMOCKE, ? JOHN[1] HAMMOT)* was born 20 Jun 1968 in Langdale, AL. She married GREGORY CLARK STEPHENS 21 Aug 1987, son of ROGER STEPHENS and JOANN WHITE STEPHENS.
Children of SARAH GLOVER and GREGORY STEPHENS are:
    i.   LILY LOUISE[15] STEPHENS, b. 05 Sep 1995, LaGrange, GA.
    ii. ANDREW GLOVER STEPHENS, b. 31 Mar 1999, LaGrange, GA.
Key Source: Family records of Felix Maben Hammack, Bend, OR.

743. CALVIN HUNTER[14] MCFADDEN, JR. *(FRANCES ANN[13] BABB, SADIE LUCILLE[12] HAMMACK, GEORGE CLEVELAND[11], WILLIAM SIMMS[10], JOHN T.[9], SIMEON J.[8], WILLIAM T.[7], ROBERT HAMMACK[6] JR., ROBERT HAMMACK[5] SR., WILLIAM "THE ELDER"[4] HAMMACK, WILLIAM "O"[3], JOHN[2] HAMMOCKE, ? JOHN[1] HAMMOT)* was born 06 Sep 1973. He married PATTI TAYLOR, daughter of KEITH TAYLOR and DONNA BARMORE. She was born 08 Sep 1974.
Children of CALVIN MCFADDEN and PATTI TAYLOR are:
    i.   MARY CLAIRE[15] MCFADDEN, b. 30 Jun 2002, Monroe, LA.
    ii. MCKENZIE RAE MCFADDEN, b. 30 Mar 2004, Monroe, LA.
Key Source: Family records of Felix Maben Hammack, Bend, OR.

744. WILLIAM FLETCHER[14] PENA *(SADIE RUTH[13] BABB, SADIE LUCILLE[12] HAMMACK, GEORGE CLEVELAND[11], WILLIAM SIMMS[10], JOHN T.[9], SIMEON J.[8], WILLIAM T.[7], ROBERT HAMMACK[6] JR., ROBERT HAMMACK[5] SR., WILLIAM "THE ELDER"[4] HAMMACK, WILLIAM "O"[3], JOHN[2] HAMMOCKE, ? JOHN[1] HAMMOT)* was born 05 Apr 1973 in Lake Providence, LA. He married KERRI K. GREEN, daughter of JOHN GREEN and HELEN REYNOLDS. She was born 05 Jan 1973 in Cheyenne, WY.
Child of WILLIAM PENA and KERRI GREEN is:
    i.   ABIGALE KRISTINE[15] PENA, b. 12 Dec 2002, Austin, TX.
Key Source: Family records of Felix Maben Hammack, Bend, OR.

745. NICHOLAS JOEL[14] BABB *(JOHN ALTON[13], SADIE LUCILLE[12] HAMMACK, GEORGE CLEVELAND[11], WILLIAM SIMMS[10], JOHN T.[9], SIMEON J.[8], WILLIAM T.[7], ROBERT HAMMACK[6] JR., ROBERT HAMMACK[5] SR., WILLIAM "THE ELDER"[4] HAMMACK, WILLIAM "O"[3], JOHN[2] HAMMOCKE, ? JOHN[1] HAMMOT)* was born 17 Feb 1979 in Greenville, MS. He married MARJORIE JANE CONNOLLY. She was born 04 Jan 1980.
Children of NICHOLAS BABB and MARJORIE CONNOLLY are:
    i.   ALEXANDER NEIL[15] CONNOLLY, b. 26 Sep 1998.

    ii. MATTHEW OWEN BABB, b. 06 Jul 2001.
    iii. GWENDOLYN NIKE BABB, b. 29 May 2004.
Key Source: Family records of Felix Maben Hammack, Bend, OR.

746. DEBRA CELESTE[14] LEE *(MARY ANN[13] HAMMACK, WILLIAM BANKSTON[12], GEORGE CLEVELAND[11], WILLIAM SIMMS[10], JOHN T.[9], SIMEON J.[8], WILLIAM T.[7], ROBERT HAMMACK[6] JR., ROBERT HAMMACK[5] SR., WILLIAM "THE ELDER"[4] HAMMACK, WILLIAM "O"[3], JOHN[2] HAMMOCKE, ? JOHN[1] HAMMOT)* was born 02 Oct 1960 in Jackson, MS. She married (1) RICKY HANCOCK 11 Oct 1980. She married (2) JERRY SHOEMAKER Abt. 1990.
Child of DEBRA LEE and RICKY HANCOCK is:
    i. JAMES DEREK[15] HANCOCK, b. 28 Feb 1986, Jackson, MS.
Child of DEBRA LEE and JERRY SHOEMAKER is:
    ii. LINDSEY JADE[15] SHOEMAKER, b. 19 Jul 1991, Jackson, MS.
Key Source: Family records of Felix Maben Hammack, Bend, OR.

747. PATRICIA DIANNE[14] LEE *(MARY ANN[13] HAMMACK, WILLIAM BANKSTON[12], GEORGE CLEVELAND[11], WILLIAM SIMMS[10], JOHN T.[9], SIMEON J.[8], WILLIAM T.[7], ROBERT HAMMACK[6] JR., ROBERT HAMMACK[5] SR., WILLIAM "THE ELDER"[4] HAMMACK, WILLIAM "O"[3], JOHN[2] HAMMOCKE, ? JOHN[1] HAMMOT)* was born 20 May 1962 in Jackson, MS. She married MICHAEL DAVID MAY 16 Aug 1980.
Children of PATRICIA LEE and MICHAEL MAY are:
    i. MICHAEL JASON[15] MAY, b. 05 Jul 1983, Jackson, MS.
    ii. KRISTI DIANNE MAY, b. 18 Apr 1985, Jackson, MS.
Key Source: Family records of Felix Maben Hammack, Bend, OR.

748. DONNA MARIE[14] WHITE *(DOROTHY LUCILLE[13] SITTON, MARY MILDRED[12] HAMMACK, GEORGE CLEVELAND[11], WILLIAM SIMMS[10], JOHN T.[9], SIMEON J.[8], WILLIAM T.[7], ROBERT HAMMACK[6] JR., ROBERT HAMMACK[5] SR., WILLIAM "THE ELDER"[4] HAMMACK, WILLIAM "O"[3], JOHN[2] HAMMOCKE, ? JOHN[1] HAMMOT)* was born 12 Jan 1963 in Caddo Parish, LA. She married GARRY STEVEN BURRY 06 Aug 1988 in Arkadelphia, AR.
Children of DONNA WHITE and GARRY BURRY are:
    i. STEPHANIE MARIE[15] BURRY, b. 17 Nov 1991, Louisville, Jefferson Co., KY.
    ii. ALISON CLAIRE BURRY, b. 22 Mar 1994, Louisville, Jefferson Co., KY.
Key Source: Family records of Felix Maben Hammack, Bend, OR.

749. MARK ALLAN[14] WHITE *(DOROTHY LUCILLE[13] SITTON, MARY MILDRED[12] HAMMACK, GEORGE CLEVELAND[11], WILLIAM SIMMS[10], JOHN T.[9], SIMEON J.[8], WILLIAM T.[7], ROBERT HAMMACK[6] JR., ROBERT HAMMACK[5] SR., WILLIAM "THE ELDER"[4] HAMMACK, WILLIAM "O"[3], JOHN[2] HAMMOCKE, ? JOHN[1] HAMMOT)* was born 19 Nov 1967 in Webster Parish, LA. He married PENNY GAYLE TROTTER 21 Mar 1992 in Magnolia, AR.
Children of MARK WHITE and PENNY TROTTER are:
    i. JACOB THOMAS[15] WHITE, b. 31 Jan 1995, Minden, LA.
    ii. SPENCER LAWLESS WHITE, b. 05 Nov 1996, Minden, LA.
Key Source: Family records of Felix Maben Hammack, Bend, OR.

750. BRAD THOMAS[14] WHITE *(DOROTHY LUCILLE[13] SITTON, MARY MILDRED[12] HAMMACK, GEORGE CLEVELAND[11], WILLIAM SIMMS[10], JOHN T.[9], SIMEON J.[8], WILLIAM T.[7], ROBERT HAMMACK[6] JR., ROBERT HAMMACK[5] SR., WILLIAM "THE ELDER"[4] HAMMACK, WILLIAM "O"[3],*

JOHN² HAMMOCKE, ? JOHN¹ HAMMOT) was born 18 Feb 1973 in Webster Parish, LA. He married GWEN.

Child of BRAD WHITE and GWEN is:

    i. BRAYDEN THOMAS¹⁵ WHITE, b. 18 Feb 2005.

Key Source: Family records of Felix Maben Hammack, Bend, OR.

751. JENNIFER MARIE¹⁴ WIENS *(MARY ELIZABETH¹³ SITTON, MARY MILDRED¹² HAMMACK, GEORGE CLEVELAND¹¹, WILLIAM SIMMS¹⁰, JOHN T.⁹, SIMEON J.⁸, WILLIAM T.⁷, ROBERT HAMMACK⁶ JR., ROBERT HAMMACK⁵ SR., WILLIAM "THE ELDER"⁴ HAMMACK, WILLIAM "O"³, JOHN² HAMMOCKE, ? JOHN¹ HAMMOT)* was born 12 Mar 1972 in Corvallis, OR. She married (1) ROBERT JAMES STILES 14 Feb 1993. He was born 03 Nov 1971 in Jacksonville, AR. She married (2) EDWARD LYNN LEWIS 06 Jan 2001 in Ouachita Parish, LA. He was born 17 Jun 1970 in Florida.

Child of JENNIFER WIENS and ROBERT STILES is:

    i. BRANDON MICHAEL¹⁵ STILES, b. 02 May 1993, Little Rock, AR.

Child of JENNIFER WIENS and EDWARD LEWIS is:

    ii. ABIGAIL NICOLE¹⁵ LEWIS, b. 08 Apr 2002, Fayetteville, NC.

Key Source: Family records of Felix Maben Hammack, Bend, OR.

752. CHRISTOPHER THOMAS¹⁴ SITTON *(THOMAS STRIBLING¹³, MARY MILDRED¹² HAMMACK, GEORGE CLEVELAND¹¹, WILLIAM SIMMS¹⁰, JOHN T.⁹, SIMEON J.⁸, WILLIAM T.⁷, ROBERT HAMMACK⁶ JR., ROBERT HAMMACK⁵ SR., WILLIAM "THE ELDER"⁴ HAMMACK, WILLIAM "O"³, JOHN² HAMMOCKE, ? JOHN¹ HAMMOT)* was born 27 Sep 1974 in Lake Providence, LA. He married AMY ELIZABETH ALLEN.

Children of CHRISTOPHER SITTON and AMY ALLEN are:

    i. MARY MADELINE¹⁵ SITTON, b. 22 Jun 2001, Shreveport, LA.

    ii. CLAUDIA CATHERINE SITTON, b. 19 May 2005.

Key Source: Family records of Felix Maben Hammack, Bend, OR.

753. CRYSTAL REBECCA¹⁴ HAMMACK *(DANIEL CLEMENT HAMMACK¹³ JR., DANIEL CLEMENT¹² HAMMACK, GEORGE CLEVELAND¹¹, WILLIAM SIMMS¹⁰, JOHN T.⁹, SIMEON J.⁸, WILLIAM T.⁷, ROBERT HAMMACK⁶ JR., ROBERT HAMMACK⁵ SR., WILLIAM "THE ELDER"⁴ HAMMACK, WILLIAM "O"³, JOHN² HAMMOCKE, ? JOHN¹ HAMMOT)* was born 28 May 1973 in Houston, TX. She married CHARLES WAYNE WELLS 16 Mar 1990 in Houston, TX. He was born 20 May 1970 in Oneida, NY.

Children of CRYSTAL HAMMACK and CHARLES WELLS are:

    i. CAITLIN MORGAN¹⁵ WELLS, b. 22 Jul 1990, Houston, TX.

    ii. CHELSEA MEGAN WELLS, b. 09 Feb 1993, Houston, TX.

Key Source: Family records of Felix Maben Hammack, Bend, OR.

754. EMILY NEWELL¹⁴ FINCH *(DENISE¹³ HAMMACK, FELIX MABEN¹², GEORGE CLEVELAND¹¹, WILLIAM SIMMS¹⁰, JOHN T.⁹, SIMEON J.⁸, WILLIAM T.⁷, ROBERT HAMMACK⁶ JR., ROBERT HAMMACK⁵ SR., WILLIAM "THE ELDER"⁴ HAMMACK, WILLIAM "O"³, JOHN² HAMMOCKE, ? JOHN¹ HAMMOT)* was born 18 May 1979. She married MIKE ELBERT WILLIAMS 20 Jan 2002 in Houston, TX, son of CHARLES WILLIAMS and KAREN MCCARTNEY.

Child of EMILY FINCH and MIKE WILLIAMS is:

    i. SAMANTHA MCCARTNEY¹⁵ WILLIAMS, b. 07 Oct 2004.

Key Source: Family records of Felix Maben Hammack, Bend, OR.

755. HAL MURRAY[14] MCEWEN *(DARLENE ANNETTE*[13] *MURRAY, VICTORIA LENA*[12] *TELENGA, MYRTLE LOUISE*[11] *HAMMACK, JOHN ROBERT*[10]*, JOHN T.*[9]*, SIMEON J.*[8]*, WILLIAM T.*[7]*, ROBERT HAMMACK*[6] *JR., ROBERT HAMMACK*[5] *SR., WILLIAM "THE ELDER"*[4] *HAMMACK, WILLIAM "O"*[3]*, JOHN*[2] *HAMMOCKE, ? JOHN*[1] *HAMMOT)* was born 1960 in Bengough, Sask. He married LAURA PARADUN 1982.

Children of HAL MCEWEN and LAURA PARADUN are:

     i.   PAMELA[15] JANE MCEWEN, b. 1981.

     ii. MELISSA LYNN MCEWEN, b. 1983.

     iii. JOSHUA DOUGLAS MCEWEN, b. 1989.

Key Source: Family records of Jonas Hammack, Bend, OR.

756. KIPP DOUGLAS[14] MCEWEN *(DARLENE ANNETTE*[13] *MURRAY, VICTORIA LENA*[12] *TELENGA, MYRTLE LOUISE*[11] *HAMMACK, JOHN ROBERT*[10]*, JOHN T.*[9]*, SIMEON J.*[8]*, WILLIAM T.*[7]*, ROBERT HAMMACK*[6] *JR., ROBERT HAMMACK*[5] *SR., WILLIAM "THE ELDER"*[4] *HAMMACK, WILLIAM "O"*[3]*, JOHN*[2] *HAMMOCKE, ? JOHN*[1] *HAMMOT)* was born 1966. He married HEATHER FANCOURT 1988.

Children of KIPP MCEWEN and HEATHER FANCOURT are:

     i.   CRYSTAL BILLIE[15] JEAN MCEWEN, b. Aug 1988.

     ii. DUNCAN JAMES MCEWEN, b. Dec 1993.

     iii. MARINA VICTORIA MCEWEN, b. 25 Jun 1995.

Key Source: Family records of Jonas Hammack, Bend, OR.

757. HOLLIE[14] HENRY *(LARRY GEORGE*[13]*, GEORGINA E.*[12] *TELENGA, MYRTLE LOUISE*[11] *HAMMACK, JOHN ROBERT*[10]*, JOHN T.*[9]*, SIMEON J.*[8]*, WILLIAM T.*[7]*, ROBERT HAMMACK*[6] *JR., ROBERT HAMMACK*[5] *SR., WILLIAM "THE ELDER"*[4] *HAMMACK, WILLIAM "O"*[3]*, JOHN*[2] *HAMMOCKE, ? JOHN*[1] *HAMMOT)* was born 16 Jun 1973.

Child of HOLLIE HENRY is:

     i.   CODEY[15] ANN HENRY, b. 23 Oct 1993.

Key Source: Family records of Jonas Hammack, Bend, OR.

758. KIMBERLY[14] HIBBARD *(GLENN*[13]*, FLORENCE*[12] *TELENGA, MYRTLE LOUISE*[11] *HAMMACK, JOHN ROBERT*[10]*, JOHN T.*[9]*, SIMEON J.*[8]*, WILLIAM T.*[7]*, ROBERT HAMMACK*[6] *JR., ROBERT HAMMACK*[5] *SR., WILLIAM "THE ELDER"*[4] *HAMMACK, WILLIAM "O"*[3]*, JOHN*[2] *HAMMOCKE, ? JOHN*[1] *HAMMOT)* was born 18 Feb 1971.

Child of KIMBERLY HIBBARD is:

     i.   JASMINE[15] HIBBARD, b. 22 Aug 1994.

Key Source: Family records of Jonas Hammack, Bend, OR.

759. HERMAN DELL[14] AUSTIN, JR. *(ANNIE JEANETTE*[13] *ELLIOTT, ANNIE MAE*[12] *HAMMOCK, JAMES PELL*[11]*, FELIX A.*[10]*, ALFRED WASHINGTON "DOCK"*[9] *HAMMACK, SIMEON J.*[8]*, WILLIAM T.*[7]*, ROBERT HAMMACK*[6] *JR., ROBERT HAMMACK*[5] *SR., WILLIAM "THE ELDER"*[4] *HAMMACK, WILLIAM "O"*[3]*, JOHN*[2] *HAMMOCKE, ? JOHN*[1] *HAMMOT)* was born 29 Mar 1979 in Big Spring, TX. He married TANYA SHORES.

Child of HERMAN AUSTIN and TANYA SHORES is:

     i.   DYLAN MCCLAIN[15] AUSTIN, b. 03 Feb 2000, Little Rock, AR.

Key Source: Lois Hagood, *The Elusive Ancestor* (Crossett, AR, 1992); Lois Hagood, "C. W. Roberts Family," in Robert A. and Mary I. Carpenter, *Reflections of Ashley County* (Dallas, TX, 1988), F544.

760. AMANDA LYNN[14] AUSTIN *(ANNIE JEANETTE*[13] *ELLIOTT, ANNIE MAE*[12] *HAMMOCK, JAMES PELL*[11]*, FELIX A.*[10]*, ALFRED WASHINGTON "DOCK"*[9] *HAMMACK, SIMEON J.*[8]*, WILLIAM T.*[7]*,

ROBERT HAMMACK[6] JR., ROBERT HAMMACK[5] SR., WILLIAM "THE ELDER"[4] HAMMACK, WILLIAM "O"[3], JOHN[2] HAMMOCKE, ? JOHN[1] HAMMOT) was born 25 May 1980 in Big Spring, TX.
Child of AMANDA LYNN AUSTIN is:

      i.   DESHON ALEXANDER[15] AUSTIN, b. 24 Jul 2003.

Key Source: Lois Hagood, *The Elusive Ancestor* (Crossett, AR, 1992); Lois Hagood, "C. W. Roberts Family," in Robert A. and Mary I. Carpenter, *Reflections of Ashley County* (Dallas, TX, 1988), F544.

Appendix 4:
Hammack Mysteries: Unidentified Hammacks and Hammocks

This section summarizes known information about Hammacks and Hammocks whom, in most instances, it has not been possible to place conclusively in the previous summary. Most of these individuals are in fact descendants of the immigrant William Hammack of Richmond County, Virginia, but there is not enough information to place them in their proper position within the family pedigree. The Connecticut Hammick family were not descendants of William Hammack of Richmond County, Virginia (although they likely connect to the Hammicks of Ermington, Devonshire, England), and the Rudolph Hammack family of Augusta County probably were not, either. Likewise, it is possible that certain of the Midwestern Hammack families belonged to a different lineage. There is little doubt, however, that the overwhelming majority of individuals bearing the Hammack and Hammock surnames from Virginia southward to Texas were members of this particular family.

A. Hammack of Athens Co., OH

1840 Ohio Census, Athens County, Rome Township, page 353:
     A. Hammock   120001-102010001

Able and Jacob Hammack of Clarke Co., Indiana

One Jacob Hammock served as a soldier in Holmes' New Jersey Militia during the American Revolution. He may be the man enumerated as over age 45 in the 1820 census below.

1820 Indiana Census, Clarke County, page 30:

     Able Hammick   000100-101   Jacob Hammick   101001-21101

Note that Jacob Hammack (born before 1775) was apparently the father of Abel; the name Jacob is also found in the Frederick Co., VA, family.

Abraham Hammock (c. 1815, GA -- aft. 1880, Drew Co., AR), m. c. 1843, Martha [-------].

1850 Drew Co., Arkansas, p. 80,[1839] HH 78/78: Abraham Hammock, age 35, Farmer, $480, GA; Martha, 25, AL; John, 6, AR; Jasper, 5, AR; Josephine, 4, AR; Elijah, 1, AR; Edward, 1, AR.[1840] This family was living next to James and Elizabeth Bussey, both natives of GA.

1860 Drew Co., AR, Census, Prairie Township, p. 150: HH 437/437: William Hamock, 36, Farmer, $1600/$500, AL; M. A., 33, female, NC; M. J., 5, female, AR; Caroline, 4, female, AR; E. E., 2, female, AR.

1860 Drew Co., AR, Census, Clear Creek Township, p. 215: HH 803/803: A. Hammock, 46, Farmer, GA; M. A., 38, female, AL; John, 18, AL; Jasper, 17, AL; Josephine, 15, AL; Edward E., 10, AL; H. L., 10, AL; George T., 6, AL.

[1839] HFH, 2: 54, indicates that Abraham's wife was Martha Van Landingham. HFH lists the six children as John, Jasper, Edward, Rufus, Leila, and Josephine, and states that these families lived around Monticello, Dermott, and Monroe, Louisiana. Ernest Hammock became a Monticello Lawyer and was a Lieutenant in the Spanish-American War. William Hammock became a prominent railroad official.

[1840] HFH, 2: 137, speculates that this was Edward Abraham Hammack who moved to Roff, Oklahoma.

1900 Drew Co., Ark., Census, 12-15-8-3: John Hammack, November 1841, AR; Lizzie, July 1844, SC; Ernest, February 1871, AR; Letia F., March 1877, AR; Johnnie, November 1875, AR; Charley, October 1880, AR. HFH identifies this family as John and Sarah Elizabeth Roddy Hammock, with offspring: Willie R. Hammock (26 September 1867 --); Ernest G. Hammock (12 February 1871 --); Johnny A. Hammock (1 November 1875 --).

1900 Drew Co., Ark., Census, 12-75-13-17: William R. Hammock, September 1863, AR; Vashti, April 1871, AR; Elizabeth, March 1873, AR; Janie, July 1896, AR.

1900 Monticello Co., Ark, Census, 12-75-16-17: T. Ed Hammack, June 1850, AR; Alice S., December 1852, SC; Blanche, February 1874, AR; Walter B., March 1881, AR; Cestena, March 1884, AR; Paul, August 1885, AR; Robert, January 1896, AR; Maude Bussey, January 1873, AR, Daughter.

1900 Prairie Co., Ark., Census, 31-101-5-78: R. M. Hammack, November 1860, AR; L. W., August 1861, AR, Wife; Garner, June 1886, AR; Hugh, April 1898, AR; Josephine, November 1844, AR, Sister.

Asa C. Hammock (c. 1820, GA -- aft. 1860, GA).

He may have been the Asa C. Hammock who is said to have married Mary Ann Samples on 22 July 1841 in Alabama. He was apparently living in Macon County, Alabama, in 1843, at which time he subscribed to a local newspaper called *The Macon Republican*.[1841]

1860 Pierce Co., GA, Census, Blackshear PO, HH 125/129: A. C. Hamock, 40, male, Teacher, Vocal Music, GA; Sarah, 35, GA; Susannah, 6, GA; Nancy, 4, GA; Benjamin F., 1, GA.

A. J. and George Ann Maddox Hammack

This man has now been identified as Alfonso J. "Forney" Hammack, son of Jeremiah and Martha Hammack of Chambers Co., AL. He was shown there aged 12 at the time of the 1860 census.

A. J. Hammack (23 June 1849, AL - 25 June 1893, Williamson Co., TX, bur. near Jarrell, TX, Old Corn Hill Cemetery), m. Georgia Ann Maddox (5 March 1850 - 28 February 1940, Williamson Co., TX, bur. near Jarrell, TX, Old Corn Hill Cemetery).[1842] Buried with them is Robert Earl Hamack (17 January 1878 -- 8 December 1910).[1843]

1870 White Co., AR, Census, Rosebud PO, Marshall Township, p. 391, HH 60/60: A. J. Hammack, 21, Farmer, AL; G. A., 19, Keeping House, AL. They were living next to the family of G. W. and M. E. Mattox, aged 50 and 47, natives of Georgia, with several children born in Alabama.

1880 White Co., AR, Census, Marshall PO, HH 20/20: ____ Hammack, 31, AL/GA/GA; Ann, 30, AL/GA/GA; Minnie, 6 8/12, AR/AL/AL; Mattie, 5 7/12, AR/AL/AL; Earl, 2 5/12, Son, AR/AL/AL.

[1841] *Tap Roots*, Vol. 7, No. 1 (July 1969), p. 50.

[1842] Texas Death Certificate Number 6283 shows that she was widow of A. J. Hammack and daughter of George Maddox. Texas Death Certificate Number 9347 shows that Robert Early Hammack (1876-1910) was a son of Forney Hammack and Georgia Maddox. Texas Death Certificate Number 45731 shows that Lindsey Brown Hammack (1880-1951) was a son of A. J. Hammack and Georgia Maddox. Texas Death Certificate Number 82826 shows that Virginia Ruth Van Ness (1882-1964) was a daughter of A. J. Hammack and Georgia Maddox. Texas Death Certificate Number 3423 shows that Minnie Lou Hammack Temple (1872-1939) was a daughter of A. J. Hammack and Georgia Maddox.

[1843] See HFH, 2: 56.

1900 Bell Co., TX, Census, HH 288/261: Georgia Hammack, March 1852, 48, AL/AL/AL; Earl, January 1878, AR/AL/AL; Brown, January 1879, 20, AR/AL/AL; Virgie, July 1882, AR/AL/AL; Jessie, September 1890, TX/AL/AL.

Allison Willis Whatley "Lance" Hammack (c. 1819, GA --).

The late June Hannah believed that Allison W. W. Hammack was a son of James and Lucy (Hammack) Hammack and a grandson of John and Mary Ann Lewis Hammack and of Robert and Millenor Jackson Hammack. No documentation has been discovered to prove this suggestion.

1850 CHAMBERS CO., ALA, P. 412, HH 423/423: Lance Hammock, 31, Farmer, $300, GA; Emily, 23, GA.

1860 CHAMBERS CO., AL, p. 965, Southern Division, HH 558/558: Allison W. Hammock, 40, Overseer, $300, GA; Emily, 31, GA; Mary F., 9, AL; John, 8, AL; Epsey, 5, AL; James M., 3, AL; Martha A., 1, AL. NOTE that Lance was at this time living near the family of Jeremiah and Martha McKinney Hammack.

Survey of Cemeteries in Chambers Co., Ala. (Chattahoochee Valley Historical Society, Inc. Pub. 1014, 1983), Swint and Hammack Cemetery, S6 NW ¼, Township 23, Range 28: S. E. Hammack (15 July 1855-7 August 1912); A. W. W. Hammack (1828-1899); three infant children of Mr. and Mrs. W. B. Crowder; Emily Goggans Hammack (No Dates); Joe S. Hammack (1 September 1888-12 September 1888); Mrs. Martha E. Swint (3 April 1859-9 February 1892); Fredie Hammack (14 February 1894-15 February 1894).

Anna Hammock

1821 GA Land Lottery: Anna Hammock of Harris's District, Early County, drew land lot 204, land district 4, Monroe County.

Ann Hammack of Laurens Co., GA

In 1840, the only Hammack enumerated in Laurens was Reddick P. Hammack; he and his wife had no offspring at that time. Ann was living in the 49th Division in 1850 and was enumerated on page 237. She was 7 years old and was living with William Warren, age 25, and wife Margaret, age 18. The Warrens had one daughter, Mary Jane, age 2. James Warren, age 20, was living with them. All persons in the household were born in Georgia.

Archibald D. Hammock (31 March 1821, GA – 6 February 1909, Fannin Co., TX) of Georgia, Alabama, and Texas. Archibald D. Hammock married Martha J. McDaniel on 14 June 1843, in Alabama. He married (2) Mary [-----] (1 January 1836 – 23 June 1923, Fannin Co., TX).

In Lowndes Co., AL, HH 300/300, p. 107, was A. D. Hammock, age 27, Shoemaker, GA, with family: Margaret J., 20, GA; Laura, 4, AL; Derabia (male), 1, AL; Octavia, 1, AL. He was living in Columbus, Muscogee Co., GA, in 1870 as Archibald Hammock, shoe maker.

1860 Dallas Co., AL, Athens PO, HH 223/218: A. D. Hammock, 37, Shoe & Boot Maker, $4500/$1000, GA; Elizabeth, 29, AL; Laura, 13, AL; Araibia, 10, AL; Octavia, 10, AL; A. D., 9, male, AL; Philip G., 7, AL; Enos C., 4, AL; Wilburn W., 11/12, AL; Robert Boothe, 5, AL.

1870 Muscogee Co., GA, Census: Archibald D. Hammock, 47, GA, 6th Ward. He was aged 47, a boot and shoe maker with property worth $100, and born in Georgia. Wife Mary was aged 31 and keeping house. Son Walter was aged 11 and going to school, as was William Melton, a 14 year old boy living with the family.

1870 Dallas Co., TX, Census, p. 385, Dallas PO, HH 910/903: Michael Fagan, 45, Shoemaker, $0/$350, Ireland; Luticia, 35, Keeps House, SC; A. D. Hammock, 20, Shoemaker, AL; Sarah, 23, SC.

1880 Fannin Co., TX, p. 314, HH 83/197: A. D. Hammock, 56, Boot and Shoe Maker, GA/Unknown/GA; Mary, 42, GA/SC/GA; Octavia Brown, 30, Boarder, AL/GA/AL. Also living with them were several black servants and laborers.

1880 Fannin Co., TX, Census, p. 312: A. D. Hammock, 29, Boot Maker, AL/GA/GA; Luda P., 26, Keeping House, TX/AL/TN; Georgia Miller, 9, TX/AL/TX; Laura Hammock, 9, TX/AL/GA; Eddie Miller, 5, TX/AL/TX; Ruth Hammock, 5, TX/AL/GA; Peggy Maples, 50, black, TN/--/--. Georgia, Laura, Eddie, and Ruth are shown as sons and daughters; apparently A.D. had married a widow named Luda Miller as his second wife.

Texas Death Certificate Number 12514 shows that Archibald D. Hammock, born 14 March, 1851, Lowndes Co., AL, died March 13, 1935, in Denton, Denton Co., TX. Hammock had married Delia Drinkwater. Shown as a son of Archibald D. Hammock, he was buried in Bonham, Texas. Informant for the death certificate was Robert Hammack of Port Natchez, Texas.

Becky Hammack

Becky Hammack, m. 18 July, 1846, Claiborne Co., TN, Latan Rannins.

Benjamin Hammock (c. 1800, GA --) of Randolph Co., GA

1850 Randolph Co., GA, Census, 8th District, p. 402, HH 5/5: Benjamin Hammock, 49, Farmer, $1,000, GA; Margaret, 41, GA; William J., 15, GA; W. C., 14, female, GA; E. E., 12, female, GA; T. T., 5, female, GA; Francis, 3, female, GA; Luiza, 3/12, GA.

Calvin Hammack (c. 1815, TN --).

1850 Fulton Co., Arkansas, Census, p. 164, HH 46/46: Calvin Hammack, 15, TN, living with George Grisson, 33, Farmer, VA; Catherine, 40, VA; Evaline, 7, TN; William, 4, AR; Noah, 3, AR; Ann, 2, AR.

Caroline Hammock and Henry E. Miller

Caroline Hammock married Henry E. Miller on 31 December 1857 in Yazoo Co., MS. The 1860 Yazoo Co., MS, Census, HH 996/890, showed John Warmack, 50, Merchant, $2000/$9000, GA; S. M., 40, female, MS; William Q., 25, Merchant, MS; M. J. Boyd, 17, female, MS; Lucy, 12, female, MS; B. F Sherrard, 14, MS. In HH 997/891 was H. E. Miller, 31, male, Saddler, $500/$7000, Germany; C. Miller, 18, female, MS; H. E. Miller, 2, male, MS; John Cusnt, 30, Saddler, Austria; F. Hancock, 17, MS; J. Moyer, 33, Couch Maker, Switzerland; A. C. Houston, 27, NC; J. J. Clague, 32, Coach Smith, Ohio; Daniel McGuire, 26, Coach Painter, Ireland; T. Tune, 30, Laborer, Ireland; John Mack, 35, Laborer, Ireland; J. F. Meyer, 21, Grocery Keeper, Ind.; A. J. Gill, 26, Pilot, Alabama. The Millers were still in Yazoo in 1870 and 1880. It may be that Warmack was incorrectly transcribed as Hammock in the Yazoo County marriage record for this couple.

Cassandra Hammack of Montgomery Co., AL

1870 Montgomery Co., AL, Census, Mt. Meigs PO, p. 346, HH 2075/2080: Nancy Clemens, 71, At Home, $2945/$400, SC; J. Wesley, 15, AT School, AL.

Catherine Hammock Thompson of Grayson Co., VA

Catherine Hammock Thompson, widow of William Hammock and Robert Thompson, moved from Albemarle County, Virginia, to Grayson Co., VA, where she died testate about 1820. Estimates, based on the birth of her children by her second husband Robert Thompson, suggest that she was probably born about 1738 and that she married Thompson no later than about 1761. Robert Thompson was a widower when he married Catherine, and he died testate in Albemarle County, Virginia, about 1787. By his first marriage, he had a son Bartlett Thompson. This name is significant, since Robert Hammock of Surry Co., NC, also named a son Bartlett Hammock. Catherine's will mentions one son by her first marriage, Robert Hammock, who was still living when she wrote her will. A court suit filed in Grayson County following Catherine's death (T. J. Michie, *Virginia Reports, Jefferson – 33 Grattan, 1730-1880, Volumes 4, 5, and 6 Randolph* (Charlottesville, VA, 1903), 4 Rand., 157-159, pp. 77-78) establishes that Catherine's son was Robert Hammock who was living in Surry Co., NC, in 1820.

Catherine's husband William Hammock (d. by 1760-1761) fits to have been a son of either William Hammack (34) or of Richard Hammack, Jr. (35), sons of Richard Hammack, Sr., of Richmond, Westmoreland, and Louisa Counties. He would thus have been a first or second cousin of the Robert (116), son of John and Mary Martin Hammack, who was originally suspected to have been the man who settled in Surry County.

C. M. and Margaret Hammock of Baltimore Co., MD

1850 Baltimore Co., MD, Census, 3rd Ward, p. 301, HH 184/215: C. M. Hammock, 27, Boot and Shoemaker, VA; Margaret, 20, MD; Francis, 4/12, male, MD.

1880 Baltimore Co., MD, Census, Homestead District, p. 288, HH 682/725: Margret Hammack, 50, Keeping House, MD/MD/MD; George, 23, Paper Carrier, MD/MD/MD; William, 20, Paper Carrier, MD/MD/MD; Estella, 14, At School, MD/MD/MD; Alice, 11, At School.

1900 Baltimore Co., MD, Census, 8th Ward, p. 85, HH 219/249: Margaret A. Hammock, March 7, 1830, MD/CT/MD; George F., April 13, 1856, MD/MD/MD; William E., October 4, 1860, MD/MD/MD;

Estella, November 2, 1863, MD/MD/MD; Amelia, April 5, 1863, MD/MD/MD; James W., July 29, 1853, MD/MD/MD; Alice, August 15, 1868, MD/MD/MD; Katie Estella, January 28, 1885, MD/MD/MD; Carrie, April 8, 1892, MD/MD/MD; Martha, May 25, 1894, MD/MD/MD. Margaret was a widow, and 5 of her 10 children were then living; William and Amelia had been married for 16 years, and all four of their children were then living. James W. Hammock was a widower, and Kate, Carrie, and Martha were Margaret's granddaughters. Margaret was an invalid. George and William were day laborers. Estella was a book folder. James W. was a can maker, and Alice worked sewing. Kate was a book folder, and Carrie had a broken spine and was an invalid.

Charity Hammack Chambers

Charity Hammack married David Chambers on 6 January 1848 in Jones Co., GA. The 1850 Jones Co., GA, Census, HH 663/663, showed: David Chambers, 21, Overseer, GA; Charity, 27, GA; William T., 1, GA. In HH 662 was Louisa Ussery. In HH 659 was Robert Chambers, age 28. In HH 658 were Thomas Hammond, 30; Mary Hammond, 70; Elizabeth Hammond, 45; and William Chambers, 18. In HH 650 were William G. and Sophia Maddox, and in HH 649 was Mary Hammack, age 31.

1860 Jasper Co., MS, Census, Garlandville PO, HH 243/243: David Chambers, 28, Farmer, $0/$100, GA; Charity, 30, D.H.W., GA; W. F., 12, male, GA; J. S., 7, male, GA; M. A., 5, female, GA; R. S., 1, male, GA. [NOTE that in 1840, Joseph Chambers was living in Hammock's District, Jones County, p. 120, near John Ussery.]

1870 Jasper Co., MS, Census, Garlandville PO, HH 73/88: David Chambers, 39, Farmer, $500/$380, GA; Charity, 47, Keeping House, GA; Joseph, 18, GA; Martha, 16, GA.

Chatham Co., NC, Hammack and Hammock Families

NOTE: I have theorized that at least some of these Hammacks descend from William Hammack, son of John and Mary Martin Hammack, of Albemarle Co., VA. This family moved to Overton Co., TN.

1800 NC Census Index: John and William Hammock, Chatham County, p. 203.

1810 NC Census Index: William Hammack, Chatham County, p. 191.

1820 NC Census Index: William Hammock, Chatham County, p. 31.

1830 NC Census Index:

John Hammock	Chatham County	439
John Hammock	Stokes County	259
William Hammock	Chatham County	440

1840 NC Census Index:

John Hammock	Chatham County	193
John Hammock	Stokes County	133
William Hammock	Chatham County	171

Christiana Hammack and Joe Rollins

Christiana Hammack married Joe Rollins in 1892 in Madison Co., MS.

1870 Madison Co., MS, Census, Police Division No. 2, Vernon, MS, HH 364: Joseph Rollins, 41, MS; Sarah, 35, VA; and children, including Joseph, 3 months, MS. The Rollins family was in HH 364 with William and Amanda Taylor Sanderford in HH 377. Hence, they were in the Vernon Community, where the family of William T. H. Hammack lived.

In 1900, these families were living in Beat 2, Madison Co., MS, near William M. Hammock, 49, GA. Christina Rollins was age 31, born in MS with father born in GA and mother in MS. The census indicates that she and Joe Rollins were black, as were several other nearby Rollins families.

Conecuh and Escambia County, Alabama, Hammac Families.

Three Hammac men – believed by descendants to have been brothers – settled in Conecuh and Escambia Counties, Alabama, prior to 1840. These men were Joshua Hammac, born in 1805 in Georgia; Robert Hammac, born about 1810 in Georgia; and George Hammack, born in 1812 in Tennessee. Descendants believe that they had a sister, Mary Hammac Kent Townsend, who was born between 1804 and 1810 in Georgia.

I have speculated that these Hammacs might have been children of Jesse Hammack of Jefferson Co., GA, for several reasons. The first is that several families who lived near the Hammacs in South Alabama had also come from Jefferson and Burke Counties into southern Alabama at about the same time. A second factor is the connection with Tennessee. One Jesse Hammack was living in Tennessee in 1820 with a large family; he is otherwise unidentified and could be the Jesse who disappeared from Jefferson County, Georgia, about 1807. After the War of 1812, a large number of Tennessee settlers began moving into Alabama, and Jesse and his family might have moved southward to reconnect with family and friends in southern Alabama. This is speculation only, but it may be significant that the name Jesse does appear in the South Alabama family on multiple occasions.

I have also tentative placed Jesse as the father of Willoughby Hammack who was born about 1805 in Georgia and who later lived in Tennessee and Kentucky and perhaps of Hugh Hammack who was born about 1810 in Georgia and later lived in Kentucky. Henry Franklin Hammack speculated that Hugh and Willoughby of Tennessee and Kentucky were brothers and connected to the family of Hugh Hammack of Wilkes County, Georgia. He also speculated that Willoughby Hammock of Newton and Jasper Counties, Georgia (born about 1768) was Hugh's son. Henry Franklin Hammack apparently was basing these connections only on common names: Willoughby (born about 1768)'s son Thomas named a son Hugh Jack Hammock, and then the names Willoughby and Hugh appear in Tennessee and Kentucky with a Georgia connection. One problem with this theory is that there is no evidence that Hugh Hammack, who was living in Surry County, North Carolina, in the 1770s, had children, although he may have. Hugh Hammack (1732-1783) settled in Wilkes County, Georgia, and apparently died soon after he moved there, without acquiring property. Nothing has been found to indicate that he left a widow or offspring, although he may have done so.

I have speculated, based on his appearance on tax records in the same community as other Hammacks in the 1790s, that Willoughby may have been a son of John and Mary Ann Hammack, that Mary Ann was a Lewis before her marriage, and that Willoughby may have been named for her relative Willoughby Lewis. The given name Willoughby was common in Richmond and Northumberland Counties, Virginia, where Willoughby Allerton had been a prominent early settler and government official. A number of area families seem to have named offspring for him. Thus, it is possible that two different groups of Hammacks could have used the given name Willoughby for different reasons. Willoughby Hammock (born about 1768) appears in Clarke County, Georgia, with a Robert Hammock from about 1800 to about 1806. Born by about 1779, this Robert may have been Willoughby's younger brother. Given that John Hammack wrote his will in 1776 and died soon afterwards, if Mary Ann Hammack was expecting a child when John died, that child might have been born in 1777 or 1778 and could be the Robert who appeared with Willoughby in Clarke County.

In addition to the mystery of the origins of Willoughby and Robert Hammack of Clarke County, there was a John Hammock who appeared in nearby Franklin County, Georgia, from about 1800 to about 1806. This John was probably also born in the 1770s. I have speculated that he might belong to one of the Tennessee Hammack families that originated in western Virginia, but without additional information, it is impossible to tell.

John Hammack, son of Benedict Hammack, moved with his sons to Burke County, Georgia, from Edgecombe Co., NC. This group – which used the given names Samuel, John, Jesse, and Emanuel – seems to have accounted for most of the south Georgia, north Florida, and south Alabama Hammack and Hammock families. As noted, I have speculated that John's son Jesse was the father of the Conecuh and Escambia County, Alabama, Hammac siblings.

It is worth noting that Joshua Hammac (1805-1890) had a son Willoby Hammac (1838-1862) as well as a son Jesse Hammac (c. 1830 – after 1860). His brother George Hammac (c. 1812 – after 1860) also had a son Jesse Hammac (c. 1843 -).

Based on my study of the early Georgia Hammacks and Hammocks, there seem only a few possible origins for the men discussed above. In addition to the factors already mentioned, my thinking has been shaped in part by the survival of the registration lists for Georgia's 1805 land lottery, which constitute a fairly complete listing of all adult males twenty-one years of age or over living in Georgia in 1802 as well as of widows with minor children and minor orphans whose father was dead and mother dead or remarried in that year. Hence, the listing should include the father of Willoughby Hammock of Kentucky (born about 1805 in Georgia) and of the South Alabama Hammacs (the eldest known one of whom was born in the 1803-1805 period) if he was over twenty-one years of age in 1802. The following individuals were shown: Benjamin of Lincoln County (son of Benedict); Daniel of Washington County (unidentified); Elijah of Wilkes County (son of John, Sr.); Mrs. Elizabeth (widow of Samuel) of Lincoln County (daughter-in-law of John, Sr.); Emanuel of Jefferson County (probable son of John and grandson of Benedict, Sr.); James of Wilkes County (son of John and Mary Ann and son-in-law of Robert and Millenor); Jesse of Jefferson County (probable son of John and grandson of Benedict, Sr.); John of Franklin County (unidentified); John of Jefferson County (probable son of John and grandson of Benedict, Sr.); John of Lincoln's County (otherwise known as John C., son of Benedict, Jr.); John of Harden's Creek, Wilkes County (son of Robert and Millenor); John, Jr., of Wilkes County (son of John Sr.); John of Wilkes County (otherwise known as John Sr., who died in Lincoln County, son of John and Mary Ann); Lewis of Harden's Creek, Wilkes County (son of Robert and Millenor); Lewis of Wilkes County (son of John and Mary Ann); Mrs. Milly (Millenor Jackson, widow of Robert) of Wilkes County; Paschal of Lincoln County (shown as Hammett, and son of John, Sr.); Robert of Clarke County (probable brother of Willoughby, and possible son of John and Mary Ann); Robert of Wilkes County (son of Benedict, Jr.); Robert of Harden's Creek, Wilkes County (son of Robert and Millenor); Samuel of Jefferson County (probable son of John and grandson of Benedict, Sr.); Thomas of Wilkes County (son of John and Mary Ann); William of Lincoln County (son of John, Sr.); William of Wilkes County (son of Benedict, Sr.); William of Wilkes County (son of John and Mary Ann); William of Harden's Creek, Wilkes County (son of Robert and Millenor); Willoughby of Clarke County (probable brother of Robert and possible son of John and Mary Ann). Based on my research, this list seems to include every known adult Hammack or Hammock male living in Georgia in the period 1803-1805.

Of this group, the issue of the following men cannot be conclusively documented at this point: Daniel of Washington; Elijah of Wilkes; James of Wilkes; Jesse of Jefferson; John of Franklin; Lewis of Wilkes; Paschal of Lincoln; Robert of Clarke; Samuel of Jefferson; William of Wilkes (son of Benedict, Sr.). It is possible with a fair degree of certainty to exclude all of the other men. Further, based on the research discussed elsewhere in this volume, known facts seem to exclude Elijah of Wilkes, James of Wilkes, Lewis of Wilkes, Paschal of Lincoln, and William of Wilkes. Good records exist of these men as well as good circumstantial evidence (based on the 1820 and 1830 census, tax digests, deed records, and Hammocks and Hammacks associated with them) about who their children probably were.

We are thus left with the following prime possibilities: Daniel of Washington; Jesse of Jefferson; John of Jefferson; Robert of Clarke; and Samuel of Jefferson. The long-deceased Hugh (d. 1783) and William (c. 1726 – c. 1808) of Wilkes were of an age to have possibly fathered the Willoughby (born about 1768), Robert (born by about 1778), and John (born by about 1778) but not any of the children born after 1800. Hence, as candidates for father of the unidentified South Alabama Hammacs and of Willoughby and Hugh of Tennessee and Kentucky, the most likely possibilities seem to have been Daniel (Washington County), Jesse (Jefferson County), John (Jefferson County); John (Franklin County); Robert (Clarke County); and Samuel (Jefferson County). Daniel seems to have remained in Washington County until at least 1827 and can probably be eliminated. Based on my own research, the most likely candidates seem to have been Jesse, the two Johns, or Robert of Clarke County.

In general, therefore, I offer the following general conclusions:

1. Willoughby and Robert could have been sons of John and Mary Ann Hammack. John was a nephew of Robert and Ann Lambert Hammack, who probably helped rear him. This connection and the Lewis connection could account for both the names Hugh and Willoughby.

2. Willoughby and Robert could be sons of Hugh Hammack (c. 1732 – c. 1783, son of Robert and Ann Lambert Hammack), if he married and had offspring. John Hammock of Jackson County could also have been a son. This possibility remains more speculative than the others, since nothing exists to prove that Hugh left descendants. If Hugh did leave heirs, it may be that the Amelia Hammack later found as a widow in Washington County was his wife. There could also be a connection to Daniel Hammock who lived in Washington County from about 1802 to about 1827. Robert and Willoughby left Clarke County, Georgia, about 1806; Willoughby left a clear trail, but Robert did not. He may have died young and without children. He could perhaps have been the husband of Catherine Hammock who appeared in Walton County, Georgia, in 1820. Or he could have moved into Tennessee and Alabama, becoming the father of some of the aforementioned Hammacks and Hammacs whose identities are less than certain.

3. Willoughby and Robert could possibly tie to the Hammacks of Burke and Jefferson Counties, although Willoughby first appears near the present-day boundary between Wilkes and Warren Counties in the late-1780s at the same time that this other group of Hammacks was settling in the Burke County area. If this were the case, for some reason they moved north and west while the rest of John's family moved southward.

4. In theory, these men could tie to the family of William Hammock (son of Benedict and brother of John of Burke County) who married Betty Ann Hames and died about 1808 in Wilkes County. Only two of William's offspring, William and Charity, born in 1760 and about 1763, have been conclusively identified. There could perhaps have been other children who have not been identified.

Based on the available evidence, it appears to the author most likely that the Hammacs of Conecuh and Escambia Counties connect in some way to the Jefferson County, Georgia, Hammack family and that Willoughby and Robert Hammock connect in some way to the family of John and Mary Ann Hammack. This points to an origin in the Benedict Hammack family line for one group and in the William and Christian Middleton Hammack family line for the other group. The mysterious Jesse Hammack who may have moved from Jefferson Co., GA, to Tennessee seems a strong possibility to have produced the Conecuh and Escambia County family, given the fact that George W. Hammac was said to have been born in Tennessee in 1812. Still, Willoughby's "brother" Robert Hammock should be studied carefully.

More research should be done as new records become accessible to prove or disprove this theory and hopefully to clarify the connection to Willoughby and Robert Hammock and to conclusively establish their origins as well.

Daniel Hammack of Washington Co., GA

1805 Georgia Land Lottery Registration: Daniel Hammack, Washington County.

1807 Georgia Land Lottery: Daniel Hammack, Pace's District, Washington County, drew land lot 10, land district 11, Wilkinson County. This land later fell into Montgomery County.

This man is unplaced, but also found in Washington County is the following person:

Georgia Land Patents: Grant to AMELIA HAMMOCK on 15 Oct., 1795, 100 acres in Washington County, GA, bound on east by Benefield's land, northwest by Smith's land and said Hill Creek, west by Dickson's land and south east by William's land. Signed: George Matthews, Governor of Georgia. Amelia is called "her" and so is definitely a woman.

1827 Georgia Land Lottery: Daniel Hammack and Sarah Hammack participated in the lottery as residents of Washington County.

In 1850, members of the Jefferson Co., GA, Hammock family are found in Washington County; in 1860, an 80 year old Sarah Hammock, otherwise unidentified, was enumerated in Washington County.

Daniel B. Hammock (c. 1809 -- aft. 1860) of Williamson Co., TN

1840 TN Census: Daniel B. Hammock, Williamson County, p. 118.

1850 Williamson Co., TN, Census, HH 95/278: Daniel B. Hammock, 41, TN; Nancy, 41, TN; John, 17, TN; James, 15, TN; Elizabeth, 13, TN; Andrew J., 11, TN; Jane, 9, TN; Sarah, 7, TN; Elijah T., 5, TN; Amos D., 1, TN.

1860 Williamson Co., TN, Census, HH 330/319: Daniel Hammock, 50, Farmer, $300, TN; Nancy, 50, TN; John, 27, TN; James, 24, TN; Jane, 19, TN; Andrew Hammock, 21, TN; Sarah, 18, TN; Eliza H., 16, TN; Amos H., 12, TN.

Elizabeth Hammock of Twiggs Co., GA

1850 Twiggs Co., GA, Census, 4th Division, p. 199: E. Hammock, 47, female, GA; Lanner, 16, female, GA; Francis, 14, female, GA; Littleberry H., 12, female (but actually male), GA; Elizabeth, 9, female, GA. Elizabeth was living near Elender Hughes, 75, GA; Haden Hughes, 40, GA; and A. B. Hughes, 40, GA.

1860 TWIGGS CO., GA. p. 404. 355th GMD (NOTE that GMD 355 is in northern Twiggs, directly across the line from Bibb County and directly south of Jones County, which it borders), HH 558/558: Elizabeth Hammock, 55, Farmer, $1000/$1704, GA; Haywood, 21, Day Laobrer, GA; Susan F., 22, GA; Elizabeth, 20, GA.

E. R. Hammock (c . 1820, GA – aft. 1850, Winston Co., MS)

1860 WINSTON CO., MS, CENSUS, LOUISVILLE, HH 72: E. R. Hammock, 40, female, School Teacher, $0/$1500, GA, living with John S. Miller, 55, Farmer, GA, $25,000/$75,000, SC, and wife A. J., 37, GA. The Millers had five children, aged 14 to 4, all born in Mississippi. Also in the household were W. A. Mosely, 17, MS: B. H. Roberts, 16, SC; and C. H. Grigg, 24, GA.

Edy Hammack

22 July, 1856: Will of Jonathan Smith of Fayette County, proven on 7 December 1857, names daughter Edy Hammock.

Elijah Hamrick

One Elijah Hamrick was enumerated in Tippah Co., MS, 2nd District, p. 418, in 1850; he was enumerated in HH 381. The name is Hamrick, and he and his family were natives of NC.

Elisha Hammack (c. 1833, KY --)

1850 Claiborne Parish, LA, Census, p. 134, HH 589/589: Elisha Hammack, 27, Laborer, KY; Nancy, 26, AR; Margaret E., 7, AR; James K. P., 1, MO.

1860 LaFayette Co., AR, Census, Beech Township, Rondo Post Office, p. 80, HH 560/560: Elisha Hammack, 38, Farmer, $200/$744, KY; Nancy, 35, AR; James K. P., 15, MO.

Eliza Hammack (c. 1812, GA --) and Joseph Cates (c. 1806, GA --)

Eliza Hammack married Joseph Cates on 6 November 1829 in Newton Co., GA.

1860 Calhoun Co., AR, Census, Hampton PO, HH 357/351: Joseph Cates, 54, Farmer, $1600/$1500, SC; Eliza, 48, GA; Charles, 20, Farmer, GA; Louisa, 18, GA; Joseph, 16, Farmer, AR; Martin, 13, AR; Georgiana, 11, AR; Harrison, 9, AR; Niece, 7, AR; Major, 5, AR. Major Cates and his family were still living in Locust Bayou, Calhoun Co., AR, in 1880.

Eliza Hammack (c. 1830, AL --) of Robertson Co., TX

1870 Robertson Co., TX, Census, p. 242, Bremond PO, HH 1036/1036: Eliza Hammock, 40, Boarding House, AL; Robert, 16, AL; Gus, 8, GA. NOTE that in 1860, one James P. Hammock, 21, GA, a laborer, was residing in Robertson County.

E. Hammack of Decatur Co., GA

1860 Decatur Co., GA, Census, p. 252, HH 1046/1046, Bainbridge PO: Robert Smith, 50; Mary, 30; Wesley, 8; Elizabeth, 4; Richard, 1; Eliza, 8; E. Hammock, 21, female, House Domestic. All members of the household were born in GA. Smith's estate was valued at $2000/$10,000.

Elizabeth Hammich of Hamilton Co., OH

1850 Hamilton Co., Ohio, Census, HH 2290/2294: Elizabeth Hammich, 26, Germany; Nicolas, 7, OH; Fred, 6, OH; Tomas, 4, OH; Phillipena, 1, OH; Thomas Hammock, 34, Germany.

Elizabeth Hamack (c. 1773, PA --) of Madison Co., IL

Columbiana Co., OH, is directly west of Beaver Co., PA, and lies along the boundary between OH and PA. No Hammacks were shown in the 1820 Ohio census index, but one Elizabeth Hammack was shown on page 358 of the 1830 Columbiana census, living in Beaver Township:

Elizabeth Hammock, 1 male aged 20-30; 1 female aged 10-15; 1 female aged 15-20; 1 female aged 50-60; 1 female aged 60-70.

This Elizabeth fits in terms of age to be the seventy-seven year old Elizabeth Hammack found in Madison Co., IL, in 1850; she was a native of Pennsylvania. She could connect, perhaps, to Jacob Hammock, Revolutionary soldier of New Jersey, or Thomas Hammock, Revolutionary soldier of Connecticut.

1850 Madison Co., IL, p. 391, HH 127: Isaac E. Wanrach, 49, Carpenter, $1,000, PA; Frederick C., 25, Potter, TN; Thomas, 13, IL; Susan, 10, IL; George L., 9, IL; Minerva C., 6, IL; Elizabeth Hamack, 77, PA.

No Hammacks or Hammocks are found in Madison County indices for 1860-1880.

Elizabeth Hammack (1780/90 --) of Switzerland Co., IN

1830 Indiana Census Index, p. 45: Elizabeth Hammack, Switzerland County: 1 male aged 10-15; 1 male aged 15-20; 1 male aged 20-25; 1 female aged 5-10; 1 female aged 40-50. Elizabeth was aged 40-50 and born 1780-1790. She may belong to the Kentucky or Virginia Hammacks. Switzerland County is located in the southern portion of Indiana.

Elizabeth Hammack and Mitchell Pierce

Elizabeth Hammack married Mitchell Pierce on 18 June 1835 in Bibb Co., GA. James Hammack, Johnston Hammack, and Lewis Hammack were all living in Bibb County in the early 1830s.

1850 Upson Co., GA, Census: Mitchell Pierce, 41, Overseer, Massachusetts; Elizabeth, 35, GA; Thomas, 14, GA; John, 10, GA; Davis, 9, GA; Henry, 7, GA; Harper, 6, GA; Elizabeth, 2, GA.

1860 Talbot Co., GA, Census, Centre PO, GMD 688 (this district is in the SW corner, near Muscogee and Marion Counties), HH 290/290: Mitchell Pearce, 49, Overseer, $200, GA; Elizabeth, 42, TN; Elizabeth, 11, GA. (NOTE that there are Hollis and Amos families in this neighborhood.)

1870 Upson Co., GA, Census, Thomaston PO, HH 1420/1420: Mitchell Pearce, 68, Farm Hand, $150, GA; Bettie, 56, Keeping House, GA; Bettie, 20, At Home, GA; John, 30, Farm Hand, GA; Mary, 23, Farm hand, GA; Isabella Starling, 17, Farm Hand, GA.

1880 Talbot Co., GA, Census, GMD 685, HH 159/160: Mitchell Pearce, 83, Works VA/VA/__; Elizabeth, 22, Daughter, Keeping House, GA/GA/GA.

Elizabeth J. Hammack (c. 1825, MO --) of Searcy Co., AR

1860 Scott Co., AR, Census, Mountain Township, p. 719, HH 104/103: Elizabeth J. Hammock, 35, $300/$300, MO; Louisa, 11, MO; Eliza, 9, MO; Levisa, 7, MO; Jasper, 5, MO; Mary J., 1, MO.

Scott County joins Sebastian to the north and west and Polk and Montgomery to the south. Mountain Township is in south central Scott County. Hot Springs County joins Montgomery County to the south and east.

NOTE that in Hot Springs County, Valley Township, in 1910 was Jasper P. Hammock, 53, AR/TN/TN; wife Mary; son Thomas F.; and daughter Alice. IN HH 39/40, next door, was George M., 29, AR/AR/AR; Bela C., 27, TN/TN/TN; May T., 5; Junia C., 3; Ida E., 7/12; and three unmarried sisters-in-law, surnamed Boon. Jasper was still in Hot Springs County in 1920.

Elizabeth Hammack (c. 1829, AL --) of Navarro Co., TX

1880 Navarro Co., TX, Census, p. 499, in household of Joseph and Maggie Ennis, natives of NY and OH: Elizabeth Hammock, 51, Keeping House, AL/NC/SC; Walter W. Hammock, 20, Printer, AL/GA/AL; George Hammock, 18, Railroad, GA/GA/AL; Annie Mashbern, 31, GA/NC/NC.

1900 Bexar Co., TX, Census, San Antonio, HH 112/128: Walter Hammock, June 1860, 39, GA/GA/GA; Anna, March 1859, TX/AL/AL; Mary, August 1875, TX/GA/TX; Robert, August 1883, TX/GA/TX; Ira P. Palmer, December 1876, MO/OH/MO.

Elizabeth Hammack and William Jones

Elizabeth Hammack married William Jones on 6 December 1821 in Jefferson Co., GA.

Elizabeth Hammack and D. Dunn

Elizabeth Hammack married D. Dunn on 23 February 1854 in Paulding Co., GA. There was a David Dunn, 26, AL, with wife Elizabeth, 25, SC, and two small children living in Blount Co., AL, in 1860.

Elizabeth Hammack and Anderson Jarrell

Elizabeth Hammack married Anderson Jarrell on 30 December 1839 in Newton Co., GA.

Elizabeth Hammock Green

People of Jones Co., GA, Volume 5, pp. 24-25: James Benjamin Green (1755-1802), married Elizabeth (Betty) Hammock, and lived in Hancock and Telfair Counties. They supposedly came to the Wilkes and Elbert County area initially from Brunswick Co., VA.

Eliza Hammack (c. 1845, GA --) of Ware Co., GA

1860 Ware Co., GA, Census, p. 129, HH 108/108: Eliza Hammack, age 15, GA, living with Dr. William B. Folks, 29, $1500/$2500, GA; his wife Mary J., 30, GA; and their offspring.

Ella Hammock (c. 1856, GA --), Taylor Hammack (c. 1858, GA --) and Kate Hammack (c. 1862, GA --)

1870 Muscogee Co., GA, Census, Ward 2, HH 284: Mary Gilmore, 20, Keeping House, GA; Ella Hammock, 14, Works in Cotton Factory, GA; Taylor, 12, GA; Kate, 8, GA; Lizzie Gilmore, 8/12, AL. In HH 220/315, Ward 4, was Macon Hammock, 16, female, white, AL, a Domestic Servant who was living with Warner R. and Amanda Kent and their family.

Ellen Hammack of Washington, D.C.

1870 Washington, D.C., Census, HH 2249/2495: Peter Murphy, 50, Laborer, Ireland; Catherine, 70, Keeping House, Ireland; Ellen Hammack, 40, Virginia.

F. A. Hammock (c. 1832 --) and George Hamm0ck (c. 1831 --) of Butler Co., AL

1860 Butler Co., AL, Census, HH 1205/1205: G. H. Hammock, 24, Laborer, $200, AL; S. A., 25, GA; W. W. Y., 4, male, AL. In HH 1433/1433 were: F. A. Hammock, 28, female, GA, with family of G. B. Knowing, 35, GA, and A. M. Knowling, 25, GA, and two children. They were living in Butler Springs.

1880 Butler Co., AL, Census, Oaky Streak PO, HH 370/371: George Hammock, 49, Farmer, AL; Sarah, 49, Keeping House, AL; Elizabeth, 18, AL; William Wadford, 24, Laborer, AL.

F. R. Hammock (c. 1815, VA --) of Virginia, Georgia, and Mississippi

1860 Monroe Co., Mississippi Census, HH 411/411: F. R. Hammock, 45, female, $500/$1,000, VA; R. L., 19, male, Bookkeeper, GA. In HH 253/253 of the same enumeration was Isham Hammock, 33, Overseer, MS, who was working on the plantation of Lucinda Brooks, 55, Farmer, GA. The Brooks estate was valued at $5130/$11680.

Fanny Hammock (c. 1790, SC --) of Hart Co., GA

Fanny Hammock, a free woman of color, was enumerated in Franklin Co., GA, in 1840. she was found on page 301 of the census, GMD 370. She was aged 36-55. At the time of the 1860 census, Fanny was living in Hart Co., GA. She was then 70 years old and a native of SC. She was listed as a spinster in the census.

Francis Hammack (c. 1847, OH --) of Ohio

1850 Green Co., Ohio, Census, HH 821/821: Francis Hammack, 3, male, OH, was living with Henry G. McKing, 22, Plasterer, OH, and Eliza J. McKing, 22, OH.

George Hammick

The only Hammick or Hammock shown in Maryland census indices before 1850 was George Hammick, shown in Frederick Co., MD, in 1830. He was enumerated on page 150. There is nothing at present to link him to the Virginia family.

G. Hammock of Johnson Co., TX

1880 Johnson Co., TX, Census, Precinct 5, p. 346: G. Hammack, 35, AR/AR/AR; Mary C., 34, TN/TN/TN, Keeping House; Robert, 11, TX/AR/TN; Mary E., 9, TX/AR/TN; Joseph H., 8, TX/AR/TN; William Thomas, 4, TX/AR/TN; Green H., 2, TX/AR/TN; D., 4/12, TX/AR/TN.

Texas Death Certificate 54,992 shows that Green Berry Hammack, Jr., was born 15 June 1877 in Johnson Co., TX, and died 12 December 1948 in Round Rock, Williamson Co., TX. He was a son of Green Berry Hammack, Sr., and Mary Davis, a native of Tennessee. Greenberry was buried in Ponds Springs, TX. Texas Death Certificate Number 33,871 shows that Mary Elizabeth Carpenter (1869-1939) was a daughter of William Green Hammack, a native of England, and Mary E. Davis, a native of Tennessee. She was buried in Rosemound Cemetery.

Greensville Hamock

1840 Virginia Census Index: Greensville Hamock, Patrick County, p. 49. Greensville *Hancock* was enumerated in Patrick Co., VA, in 1850, p. 388, so the rendering Hamock was probably a mistake.

The Hammack Heirs of Catherine Simmons

Catherine Hammack Simmons was a daughter of John and Mary Ann Hammack and a sister of John Hammack of Lincoln County, James Hammack of Jones and Bibb Counties, Lewis Hammack of Jones and Bibb Counties, William Hammack of Wilkes and Ware Counties, Thomas Hammack of Wilkes County, and perhaps Willoughby Hammack of Jasper County. Catherine died at the home of Mansel W. Hammack, son of William T. and Mary Felts Hammack, who was a distant cousin and a nephew of Lucy Hammack, first wife of Catherine's brother James Hammack.

Catherine left her estate to three nephews and two nieces. It is not clear from the division that these heirs were siblings, however, but it would appear that they were. All of them link to Bibb Co., GA, or Pike Co., GA, which suggests a link with either Lewis Hammack or James Hammack, both of whom have many unidentified offspring.

It must be the case, however, that Catherine provided for her "favorite" nieces and nephews, not for all of them, for both James and Lewis had additional offspring who were not included in this division.

Note that the heirs of Daniel Hammack received $9.14 as their share of his portion when he died without children. Multiplied by nine, this amount is $82.26 (the amount claimed by Silas Hammack as his portion of Catherine's estate) and by eight it is $73.12 1/2 (the amount claimed by Mary Hammack Wright as her portion of Catherine's estate). It would appear that Daniel's share may have been redistributed among the other heirs of Catherine Simmons, including Fanny English's children.

Based on census data, Fanny Hammack English was born about 1803; Mary Hammack Wright about 1811; Joshua Hammack about 1817; Daniel Hammack about 1821; and Silas Hammack (perhaps) about 1827.

The following abstracts of legal documents refer to this matter:

- Will of Catharine Simmons. "I wish after my death have which effects I leave to so divided that each named person may have an equal share out of two hundred and fifty dollars, that is to say, *Silas M. Hammack, Daniel Hammack, Mary Wright and her four children, and the balance that I may have to be divided equal between Fanny English and William English and all the children that she may have younger than said William.*" Test: J. K. Simmons. Signed: Catharine (X) Simmons. Georgia, Crawford County. Court of Ordinary Term, 1852. The within being produced in open court was proven upon the oath of John K. Simmons, the witness thereto. It is ordered that the same be admitted to probate and that this order be entered on the minutes. James J. Ray, ordinary. Georgia, Crawford County. No Executor being named in the will of Catharine Simmons, It is ordered by this Court that Mansel W. Hammack be and he is hereby appointed administrator cum annexo testamento of the estate of said Catharine, upon complying with the statute in such cases made provided. (Crawford Co., GA, Will Book 2, p. 124-25.)

- January, 1852. Mansel W. Hammack through his attorneys Culverhouse and Ingraham filed an objection to granting of letters to John K. Simmons and says that the said Catherine Simmons is indebted to the said Mansel W. Hammack and that she died at his home and that he is kin to the said deceased, that the said John K. Simmons is neither a creditor nor next of kin to the deceased and therefore is not entitled to said letters. (Crawford Co., GA, Inferior Court Minutes, 1838-49, p. 104.) [NOTE: This suggests that Mansel W. Hammack was a blood relation of Catherine Simmons, whereas John K. Simmons was not; Catherine apparently had no children, so John K. Simmons was apparently her stepson.]

- 2 Feb., 1852. Mansel W. Hammack appointed administrator of Katherine Simmons. A citation having been published in the Georgia Macon Telegraph and no objections filed. Joel Curtis, Allen G. Simmons, T. D. Hammack, W. C. Cleveland and Ephraim Johnson appointed appraisers. (Crawford Co., Ga, Inferior Court Minutes, 1838-49, p. 95.)

- 1 March, 1852. The will of Katherine Simmons, deceased, was proven and admitted to record. No executor was named or appointed in said Will. Mansel W. Hammack and John K. Simmons filed separate applications for letters of administration. Court decided that Mansel W. Hammack was entitled to said letters he having given bond and security for $2,000. (Crawford Co., GA, Inferior Court Minutes, 1838-49.)

- 1 March, 1852. Washington C. Cleveland, Ephraim Johnson, Allen G. Simmons, Joel Carter and Talbot D. Hammack appointed appraisers of estate of Katherine Simmons. (Crawford Co., GA, Inferior Court Minutes, 1838-49, p. 102.)

- 7 June, 1852, Crawford Co., GA. Washington C. Cleveland, Ephraim Johnson and Tolbert D. Hammack as Appraisers (sworn 2 March, 1852, by Amos V. Dreher, JP) returned an appraisement of estate of Catharine Simmons. Included were notes on John K. Simmons, one payable on demand and give 17 Feb., 1848, for $600.62, one for $10 give 9 Jan., 1849, and another for $50 given 8 Nov., 1849. Other items were household and returned at $24.72. The appraisers also made a recommendation to the Court of Ordinary that Mansel W. Hammack be allowed $150 for his care and trouble in the last illness of said deceased..."she living with him the last year before her death and being very old required personal attention the most of the time and for the last three months most entirely confined to the bed and had to be attended to almost as an infant child." (Crawford Co., GA, Returns Book F, p. 291.)

- 7 June, 1852. Mansel W. Hammack as administrator returned the sale of personal property sold 27 March, 1852. Some 20 items were sold for less than $20. Purchasers were: Elizabeth Brown; Anderson Grant; Marian Hammack; George Moore; and Milton Brown. (Crawford Co., GA, Returns Book F, p. 299.)

- 10 January, 1853. Mansel W. Hammack as administrator of Catherine Simmons, deceased, allowed the sum of $150 as an item to his credit in his first annual return. Said amount being for the care and attention performed by himself and his family and servants for the deceased, including her board and illness at his home. (Crawford Co., GA, Inferior Court Minutes, 1838-49, p. 145.)

- January, 1858. Mansel W. Hammack, administrator of Katherine Simmons. Return includes receipt dated 9 Feb., 1850, in which Thomas English signs for Frances English and William English and the younger children of the said Francis for $80.72. Also for $9.14 "being his wife's part of legacy of Daniel Hammack, deceased, which she is entitled to as sister and heir of said Daniel Hammack." Voucher 5, Crawford County, Gillis Wright for $73.12 1/2 in full of legacy of his wife Mary Wright and children and $9.14 as sister and heir of Daniel Hammack. Signed: Gillis (X) Wright, Mary (X) Wright. Voucher 6, receipt of Silas M. Hammack for $82.26, and of Joshua (X) Hammack by agent Silas M. Hammack, who are heirs to Daniel's part of the legacy. Return also mentions that Silas M. Hammack walled up the grave of said Catherine Simmons. (Crawford Co., GA, Returns Book I, p. 53.)

Heirs of Catherine Simmons, perhaps all siblings:

1. Daniel Hammock (c. 1821 -- by 1859). NOTE that Silas was an heir of Daniel Hammack.

2 June, 1849. Daniel Hammock to Silas M. Hammock, 50 a., LL 244, LD 8, Pike Co., GA. (Pike Co., GA, DB H, p. 393.)

5 Jan., 1849. Daniel Hammack to Hubbard T. Parteem, 101.25 a., LL 243, LD 8, Pike Co., GA. (Pike Co., GA, DB H, p. 497.)

14 June, 1850. Daniel Hammack to Benj. Hurtsfield, 120 a., LL 244, LD 8, Pike Co., GA. (Pike Co., GA, DB H, p. 621.)

2. Silas Hammack. NOTE that Silas was an heir of Daniel.. He may have been born about 1827 in Georgia.

29 Dec., 1858. Silas Hammock to Josephus R. Ansley, LL 244, LD 8, Pike Co., GA. (Pike Co., GA, DB L, p. 557.)

3. Joshua Hammack (c. 1809/17 -- aft. 1850, Macon Co., GA), m. 2 April 1835, Bibb Co., GA, Rebecca Smith. Note that Catherine Simmons's estate settlement identifies Joshua as an heir of Daniel.

1840 Bibb Co., GA, Census, p. 94: Joshua Hammock: 1m 30-40; 1f 0-5; 1f 15-20.

1850 MACON CO., GA, District 770 p. 117, Joshua J. Hammock, 33, GA; Rebecca, 40, GA; Elizabeth A., 14, GA; Isabella McKinzie, 35, GA; Ann E., 15, GA.

4. Mary Hammack (c. 1811 -- after 1850, Pike Co., GA), m. Gillis Wright (c. 1805 -- after 1850, Pike Co., GA), son of George and Sarah Bridges Wright.

1840 Pike Co., GA, Census, p. 145 (GMD 592, NW Pike): Gillis Wright, 1 male 15-20, 1 male 20-305; 2 females 5-10, 2 females 10-15, 1 female 20-30.

1850 Pike Co., GA, Census, HH 2 and HH 3, p. 123, 68th Subdivision: George Wright, 77, Laborer, SC; Sarah, 75, SC. In HH 3: Gills Wright, 45, GA; Mary, 39, GA; Martha A., 19, GA; Elizabeth, 17, GA; Catherine, 15, GA; Daniel Hammock, 29, GA.

5. Frances Hammack (c. 1806 --), m. Thomas English.

1850 Bibb Co., GA, Census, GMD 482 (NOTE: This district borders Crawford County to the west and Monroe County to the north, and is the district where James Hammack was living in 1830): HH 106: Thomas English, 48, no occupation shown, $500, GA; Frances, 44, GA; Georgia, 15, GA; William T., 13, GA; James, 11, GA; John, 6, GA; William, 4, GA; Catherine, 88, NC.[1844]

Henry J. Hammock (c. 1814, GA --) of Georgia and Upshur Co., TX

This couple may have been the Henry Hammock who married Elizabeth Griggs on 20 December 1835 in Jones Co., GA.

1850 Upshur Co., TX, Census, 6 December 1850, HH 251/251: H. J. Hammock[1845], 36, Farmer, $300, GA; E., 36, female, GA; E., 16, female, GA; M. H., 14, female, AL; M., 12, female, AL; N., 8, female, TX; J., 4, male, TX; S., 2, female, TX.

1860 Upshur Co., TX, Pittsburg PO, HH 480/467, near Carpenter and Cope families: E. Hammock, 45, farmer, GA; John, 14, TX; Arabella, 12, TX; William, 9, TX; H., 22, Laborer, AL, $0/$75; B. H. Mapp, 20, Laborer, GA.

John, son of H. and Elizabeth, may be the following man, who was shown in 1880:

1880 Wood Co., TX, Census, Precinct 4, p. 355: John W. Hammock, 34, Farmer, TX/AL/GA; Josephine, 18, Keeping House, AR/TN/IL; Jack Clinton, 17, Works on Farm, TX/GA/GA, Nephew.

Henry C. Hammock or Hammacker (1850, IL --).

1850 Ogle Co., IL, Census, HH 4/4: Henry C. Hammock, 0/12, in HH of Abram Hamaker, 37, Miller, $800, PA, and wife Elizabeth, 34, PA; John, 14, PA; Mary, 12, PA; Abraham, 10, OH; Webster, 8, OH; Nancy, 6, OH; Eliza, 4, OH; William Filoney, 42, Wood Cutter, PA; Robert Meek, 23, Miller, PA; William Jones, 28, Lawyer, PA.

NOTE that Pennsylvania indices from 1790-1804 show no Hammacks or Hammocks but several Hammaker families.

[1844] Is it possible that this is actually the elusive Catherine Simmons? She was clearly alive in 1850 but has not yet been located in the Georgia census reports. Also note Silas Hancock in HH 107. This name clearly reads "Hancock," but it is worth noting that Silas Hammock was alive in 1850 and has not been located in any Georgia census return. Hammock and Hammack have often been read as Hancock, and there are instances in which documents referring to members of the Hammock family clearly record the name as Hancock.

[1845] This name is indexed as A. J. Hammock but appears to be H. J. Hammock.

Hugh Hammock (c. 1813, GA --) of Georgia and Kentucky

Hugh Hammock married 19 Jan., 1835, Caldwell Co., KY, Rebecca Patterson.[1846]

1850 Livingston Co., KY, Census, p. 324, HH 15/15: Hugh Hammack, 37, GA; Rebecca, 39, TN; Jane, 13, KY; Catherine, 10, KY; Jennet, 8, Ky; James D., 6, KY; William C., 3, KY. [The index shows Henry Hammack on this page but does not show Hugh. I assume that the transcriber misread Hugh as Henry.] HFH, 2: 190, indicates that he may have had a son Robert Ashton Hammack, who moved from Christian Co., KY, to Springfield, TN.

1870 Caldwell Co., KY, Census, HH 130/121: Rebecca Hammock, 62, Keeping House, TN; M. A., 18, female, Without Occupation, KY; Jane Frazer, 33, Without Occupation, KY; J. R., 12, Farm Laborer, IL; M. K., 9, female, At Home, KY; Jennett Manning, 28, Without Occupation, KY; M. A., 8, female, At Home, TN.

Idileann Hammack of Wilkes Co., GA

1850 Wilkes Co., GA, Census, 94th Subdivision, p. 351: Idileann Hammack, 20, female, GA, living with James M. Howard, 23, GA; his wife Francis, 24, GA; and their two children.

Isaac Hammack of Connecticut

The 1670 Connecticut census showed no Hammack families. Isaac Hammack and family were living in Connecticut before 1800.

From D. L. Jacobus, *Families of Ancient New Haven*, p. 718: Isaac Hammock, alias Douglas, of New Haven, died c. 1812. He married (1) Esther (-- 27 Oct., 1792), m. (2) 1 Sept., 1795, Hannah Shapla [Chappell?], m. (3) Lucinda [---] (-- 16 October 1821, New Haven, CT, bur. Hampden Plains Cemetery, aged 49).[1847] Nine of his children were baptized at the house of Widow Atwater at the Hay Scale. He was the father of:[1848]

(1) Samuel; resided Cheshire; m. 12 Apr., 1825, Harriet Eaton of Southington;

(2) George; m. 24 Dec., 1797, Lois [---]; she divorced him in 1810;

(3) Bathsheba (c. 1773, bapt. 16 Jan., 1794, age 21 --). She may have married, 24 July 1796, Aaron Alford, of Hartford.[1849]

(4) Hannah (c. 1776, bapt. 16 Jan., 1794, age 16 --);

(5) daughter (c. 1773 -- 4 Jan., 1778, age 4);

(6) Rebecca (c. 1780, bapt. 16 Jan., 1794, age 14 --), m. (1) 1 June, 1799, Harry Smith of New Haven,

---

[1846] Other Caldwell County Hammock marriages are for members of the family of William Hammock (1761-1850), later of Union Co., KY: Jeremiah Hammock to Polly Sullivant, 18 Jan., 1831; Minney Hammock to Joseph Gregory 7 Jan., 1812; Ruth Hammock to Charles Sullivant, 9 Jan., 1810; and possibly Nancy Hammock to Benjamin Lewis, 20 Dec., 1850.

[1847] D. L. Jacobus, *Families of Ancient New Haven*, p. 1797.

[1848] See D. L. Jacobus, *Families of Ancient New Haven*, p. 718.

[1849] L. B. Barbour, *Families of Early Hartford*.

who divorced her in 1802; m. (2) 7 Feb., 1803, William Gowen, of Boston, MA; m. (3) [----] Lisbon;

(7) Stephen (c. 1783, bapt. 16 Jan., 1794, age 10 --);

(8) Amelia (c. 1785, bapt. 16 Jan., 1794 -- bef. 1812), m. 27 Aug., 1807, Benj. Applewhite;

(9) Elisha (c. 1786, bapt. 16 Jan., 1794, age 8 -- d. s. p.);

(10) Isaiah (c. 1788, bap. 16 Jan., 1794, age 7 --);

(11) Esther (c. 1790, bapt. 16 Jan., 1794, age 4 --);

(12) Grace (c. 1791, bapt. 16 Jan., 1794, age 3 --).

The following individuals were shown in Connecticut census records:

1830 Index:	Stephen Hammick	Hartford	p. 124	Southing. Co.
	Samuel J. Hammick	Cheshire	p. 101	New Haven Co.
1840 Index:	Henry Hamick	Hartford	p. 405	Southing. Co.
	Samuel J. Hamick	Cheshire	p. 197	New Haven Co.
	Striffin Hamick	Hartford	p. 407	Southing. Co.
1850 Index:	Charles Hamick	Cheshire	p. 82	New Haven Co.
	Henry Hamick	Hartford	p. 92	Southing. Co.
	Samuel Hammick	Cheshire	p. 92	New Haven Co.
	Lewis Hammik	Cheshire	p. 81	New Haven Co.
	Stephen Hammik	Cheshire	p. 82	New Haven Co.

From *Cheshire (CT) Vital Records*:

Harriet E. Hammock m. 18 Aug., 1850, Benjamin H. Beebe.
Lois E. Hammock, of Cheshire, m. 6 June, 1846, Edward S. Steele, of New Britain.
Samuel Hammock, of Cheshire, m. 12 Apr., 1825, Harriet Eaton, of Southington.

Isaac Hammack of Arkansas

The 1840 Arkansas census index showed Isaac Hamack in Petit Jean, Conway County. Upon examination, this name was revealed to be that of **Isaac Wamack**.

J. Hammock (c. 1811, GA --) of Russell Co., AL

1860 Russell Co., AL, Census, Dover PO, HH 1132/1130: J. Hammack, 49, Farmer, $500/$8,000, GA; S., 26, Female; John, 2, male, all born in GA.

1870 Lee Co., AL, Census, Smith's Station, HH 106/106: J. Hamock, 59, male, GA; S., 36, female, GA; J., 9, male, AL; E., 5, female, AL; E., 3, female, AL.
NOTE: This man was the correct age to have been the John Hammock who was enumerated in Macon Co., AL, in 1850; if so, however, something must have happened to his first family enumerated in 1850.

J. H. Hammack of MS

J. H. Hammock married Mary Crenshaw 26 October 1858 in Tippah Co., MS.

J. M. Hammack (c. 1849, GA --) of Grimes Co., TX

1880 Grimes Co., TX, Census, Plantersville, ED 64, p. 120: J. M. Hammach, 30, Farmer, GA/GA/GA; Paulina, 25, Keeping House, TX/Prussia/--; Mattie, 2, TX/GA/TX; J. A., 9/12, TX/GA/TX.

The 1900 Grimes Co., TX, Census, Precinct 4, HH 88/88, shows J. H. Hammack, October 1849, 50, GA/GA/GA; Pauline, December 1856, TX/Germany/MS; Jim, August 1879, TX; Lena, December 1884, TX; Sallie, February 1892, TX; Gussie, August 1892, TX; A. S. September 1895, TX; Johnny, November 1896, TX; Josie, September 1898, TX. J. H. and Pauline had been married for 23 years; 8 of their 12 children were then living.

The 1910 Grimes Co., TX, Census, Precinct 4, HH 122/123, shows this family as John L. Hammock, 60, GA/GA/GA; Pauline, 52, TX/Germany/MS; Gussie, 19, TX; Albert S., 17, TX; Johnnie, 15, female, TX; Jose, 12, female, TX. John and Pauline had been married for 33 years; 7 of their 11 children were then living.

Texas Death Certificates for Sallie Hammack Patterson (1887-1965), Albert S. Hammack (1893-1965), Johnnie Hammack Hanks (1894-1947), and James Gus Hammack (1879-1953) indicate that the proper names for this couple were John L. Hammack and Paulina Maywald (or Mayward).

James Uriah Hammack of Columbia Co., AR

Uriah Hammack married Artemessia Tye on 13 April 1853 in Barbour Co., AL. The family moved to Columbia Co., AR, about 1860, and Uriah apparently died there between 1870 and 1880. I have tentatively identified Uriah as a son of Thomas Hammack of Barbour Co., AL.

1860 Columbia Co., AR, Census, HH 268/270, Clay Township: J. U. Hammack, 32, Farmer, GA; A. E., 22, GA; John T., 6, AL; James W., 3, AL; Mary F., 2, AL; D. V., 6/12, female, AR. Next door, in HH 269/271, was John Tye, 47, NC, with wife Mary, 47, SC. Children were James H., 16, GA; Emija W., 15, AL; Serena F., 13, AL; John W., 12, AL; and Seletha E., 9, AL. John Tye had been living in Barbour Co., AL, at the time of the 1850 census.

1870 Columbia Co., AR, Census, Clay Township, HH 40/41: James V. Hammock, 53, $400/$150, GA; Artemisha, 35, GA; John T., 14, GA; James W., 13, AL; Delila, 8, AR; Henrietta, 6, AR; Frances, 1, AR.[1850]

1880 Columbia Co., AR, Census, Clay Township, HH 62: J. T. Hammack, 25; Dillia L., 20, Sister; Sarah H., 15, Sister; Adda E., 12, Sister; Ellah J., 10, Sister; Martha A., 8, Sister. J. T. was born in Alabama; the others were born in Arkansas. The children listed their father as a native of GA and their mother as a native of AL.

1. John T. Hammack (c. 1854, AL --), m. 10 September 1879, Columbia Co., AR, Jane Oglesby.

[1850] This name appears to be Hamrock and is indexed that way, but this is clearly the same family.

1900 Columbia Co., Ark., Census, 7-46-12-73: John Hammack, February 1855, AL; Franklin Scott, July 1818, GA.

2. James W. Hammack (c. 1857, AL --), m. 9 December 1875, Columbia Co., AR, Mary T. Rush.

3. Mary F. Hammack (c. 1858, AL --).

4. Delila L. Hammack (c. 1860, AR --). She married James S. Bishop on 12 May 1881, Columbia Co., AR.

5. Sarah Henrietta Hammack (c. 1864, AR --). She may have been the Tiney Hammack who married 5 September 1888, Columbia Co., AR, to H. R. Powers.

6. Adda Frances Hammack (c. 1869, AR --). She probably m. 26 January 1890, Columbia Co., AR, E. S. Gooch.

7. Ellah J. Hammack (c. 1870, AR --).

8. Martha A. Hammack (c. 1872, AR --). She might be the Anna Hammack who married D. W. A. Banion in December 1890, Columbia Co., AR.

Unidentified Columbia Co., AR, Marriages: Rebecca Hammack to Matthew Smith, 9 September 1867.

James Hancock of Sumter Co., GA

This name appears to be James Hamock in the 1860 census; the 1870 Sumter Co., GA, Census and the 1880 Butler Co., AL, Census clearly show this family as Hancock.

1860 Sumter Co., GA, Census, p. 442, HH 616/623: James Hamock, 49, Farmer, $2,000/$500, SC; Nancy, 37, GA; Nancy, 15, GA; Permelia, 13, GA; Francis S., 11, GA; M. G., 9, GA; Sarah A. S., 7, GA; J. W., 5, male, GA; Anna B., 2, GA/

1870 Sumter Co., GA, Census, p. 314, HH 564/562: James Hancock, 59, Farmer, $3,000/$1,000, SC; Nancy, 46, Keeps House, GA; Frances, 20, At Home, GA; Martha, 17, At Home, GA; Sarah, 15, At School, GA; John, 10, At School, GA; Belle, 9, At School, GA; Thomas, 7, At School, GA; Alice, 4, GA; Julia, 2, GA; Pamelia Smith, 22, Seamstress, GA; Maggie, 3, GA; Thomas, 6/12, GA; John Hancock, 79, Retired Farmer, 79, GA.

Fannie Hancock married Lee Butts 16 July 1876 in Alabama; she died on 3 May 1892 in Jefferson Co., AL. The family was in Butler Co., AL, in 1880, HH 352/352, living next to Lee and Elizabeth Butts. James was aged 69 and Nancy age 55. Son John W. was aged 21.

James Lewis Hammock (c. 1835, GA -- aft. 1880, Lee Co., AL) and
Elizabeth Jane Martin of Russell Co., AL

The Alabama Death Certificates of James William Hammock (1863-1938), George Edd Hammock (1870-1951), and Sarah Elizabeth Hammock Kelly (1878-1958) identify their parents as James Lewis Hammock and Elizabeth Jane Martin Hammock. Jane Martin, age 10, appears with her siblings John (age 18), Benjamin (age 16), and Ransom (age 12) in the 1850 Coosa Co., AL, Census; they were enumerated in the household of Thomas Martin, age 65, a Pennsylvania native, and Agnes Martin, age 60, a North Carolina native. In 1860, T. B. Martin, age 78, a native of Dublin , Ireland, was enumerated in HH 80/798, Opelika, Russell Co., AL, with wife Agnes, age 60, a North Carolina native, and B. A. Martin, age 24, and Ransom Martin, age 22. In 1870, Ransom (age 30) and Agnes (age 70, identified as "Aga") were living with John Martin (age 49) and wife Nancy (age 43).

1860 Russell Co., AL, Census, p. 1012, Watoola: James Hammack, 25, Day Labor, $50, GA;[1851] Jane, 19, GA; J. T., 2, male, AL; S. E., 1/12, female, AL. Martin researchers indicate that Jane was the youngest daughter of Thomas B. Martin (1782, Ireland -- aft. 1860, AL) and Agnes Culpepper, who were living in Coosa Co., AL, by 1850.

1870 Lee Co., AL, Census, Opelika PO, p. 392: J. Hammock, 33, Farming, GA; Jane, 23, Keeping House, GA; Walter, 13, AL; Missouri, 11, AL; James, 9, AL; Laura, 5, AL; Caroline, 2, AL.

1880 Lee Co., AL, Census, Beat 7, HH 109/111: James Hammack, 56, GA/GA/VA; Jane, 40, GA; Missouri, 18, AL;[1852] Walton, 21, AL; James, 16, AL; Laura, 14, AL; Caroline, 12, AL; George, 9, AL; Melissa, 7, AL; Elizabeth, 5, AL; Franklin, 2, AL; Aggie Martin, 78, NC/NC/NC, Mother-in-law.

James and William Hammock of Lawrence Co., AR

Ephraim Hammack of Madison Co., KY, is claimed by HFH as father of William Hamock and presumably of James Hammock also. In terms of migration and chronology, these men fit to be sons of Benjamin Hammack of Union Co., KY, and IL.

1820 Union Co., KY, Census
    William Hammock   201201-1001
    skip 4
    Benjamin Hammock   120010-2001

This suggests that Benjamin had one son born 1810-1820 and two sons born 1804-1810. He also had two daughters born 1810-1820. In Pulaski County was John Hammock (20001-101).

1850 Lawrence Co., AR, Census, p. 214, BLACK ROCK TWP, HH 332/332: James Hammack, 23, Farmer, $100, IL; Caroline, 20, IL; Elizabeth Walters, 10, AR. In HH 337/337 were: William Hamock, 29, Farmer, $300, KY; Mary A., 22, TN; William R., 3, AR; James M., 2, AR; John W. Bush, 16, Farmer, IL.

1860 Lawrence Co., AR, Marion Township, Stranger Home Post Office, p. 129, HH 128/135: William Hammock, 40, Farmer, $1000/$650, IL; Mary A., 34, TN; Wm. Benjamin, 13, AR; James M., 11, AR;

[1851] Descendants claim that he was James Lewis Hammack.
[1852] She was called "Pink". George was George Edward. Elizabeth was Sarah Elizabeth. James was James William. Walter was Thomas Walter. Laura (1866, Lee Co., AL) married William Rodgers on 22 February 1885 in Tallapoosa Co., AL.

Emily F., 7, AR; Mary E., 2, AR; Louisa, 2, AR; Jasper N., 2/12, AR; Isaac Johnson, 24, Laborer, IL.

William appears in the 1870 Marion Co., AR, Census, Independence Township, Whitesville PO, HH 15/25: William Hammack, 50, Farmer, $800/$500, KY; Mary, 43, Keeping House, KY; Monroe, 21, Farmer, AR; Mary E., 12, AR; Louiza A., 12, AR; Margaret, 8, AR; Thomas E., 6, AR; Henry E., 4, AR.

William was in Baxter Co., AR, in 1880, p. 254, HH 1/1: Wm. Hammock, 60, Farmer, 60, KY/KY/KY; Arminda, 38, House Keeping, AL/--/--; Mollie, 21, AR/KY/IL; Ann, 17, AR/KY/IL; Thomas, 16, AR/KY/IL; Henrietta, 14, AR/KY/IL; Katharine, 8, AR/KY/AL; Mattie, 6, AR/KY/AL; Robert, 3, AR/KY/AL; Jennie, 1, AR/KY/AL.

1900 Marion Co., Ark., Census, 25-80-6-55: Thomas E. Hammack, March 1864, AR; Louisa A., September 1863, AR; Mary S., October 1886, AR; William B., September 1889, AR; Lucy F., April 1892, AR; Boany (?), September 1894, Son, AR; Benjamin Quary, March 1876, MO, brother-in-law or father-in-law.

Henry Franklin Hammack, 2: 28, includes this family: William Hammack left his home in Madison Co., Kentucky, when aged 18. He was married first to an unknown lady born about 1827. His second wife was Armenda Cooper, mother of Robert Henry Hammack and grandmother of Thomas E. Hammack (born 1906). This William Hammack was a son of an earlier Ephraim Hammack.

"Thomas E. Hammack copied the following from his grandfather William Hammack's old Bible family record: William Hammack, born about 1820, died July 22, 1887. Ephraim of Kentucky, forefather, married August, 1844, Lawrence Co., AR, Mary Ann Bush, born January 19, 1827, died October 23, 1870. 12 children: William Benjamin (1847-1866); James Monroe (1848 --); John DePhthah (1850-1851); Stephen Malachi (1852-1852); Emily Francis (1853-1865); Sarah Elizabeth (1856-1865); Mary Emiline (1858-1886); Louisa Angeline (1858-1884); Jasper Newton (1860 --); Margaret Ann (1862-1925); Thomas Edward (1864-1956); and Henrietta (1866-1930). Thomas Edward and wife Louise later lived in Seminole, OK. James Monroe and wife Sarah lived in Baxter Co., AR."

According to HFH, William and Mary Ann Bush Hammack were born in Kentucky but died in Baxter Co., AR. He ran away from KY at age 18, first going to IL, and then to AR. His own mother died when he was a small boy, his father married again, and his stepmother was not good to him. He had several brothers and sisters in KY. William Benjamin married Arminda Cooper, born 24 August 1843, AL, died 8 May 1928. The family eventually moved from Baxter County to Wagoner Co., OK. Children of William Benjamin and Arminda were: Irena Catherine, born 30 May 1872, wife of Romey Deatherage; Martha Jane Hammack, 30 November 1873, wife of Abner Johnson Deatherage (1874-1958); Robert Henry, 27 February 1877 - 2 October 1946, husband of Leaner Kasinger; Nancy Janette Hammack (24 March 1879 - 24 May 1958), wife of George Robert Deatherage (16 February 1875 -- 22 April 1941); George Washington 13 January 1883 -- 11 January 1913, husband of Maggie Williams; Albert Marion 21 August 1883 -- 14 June 1940, husband of Daisy Hart.[1853]

James Hammack (c. 1828, GA --) of Georgia and Texas

1850 Bexar Co., TX, The Cibilo Creeks, Comanche Spring and Leon Creeks, 22 November 1850, p. 334, HH 197/197: Edward D. Westfall, 29, Farmer, $750, Indiana; Josephus Blanchard, 26, Indiana; James Hammock, 22, Farmer, GA.

[1853] Additional generations of these families are found in HFH, 2: 229-230.

NOTE that there was also a John Hammack, 26, TN, shown in Bexar County in 1850; in his household was a Joseph Blanchard, 30, MS. It may be that John and James and Josephus and Joseph were the same individuals.

James Hammack (c. 1803, KY --) of Sullivan Co., IN

James Hammack is said to have married Lavina Smock, daughter of Heinrich Smock (born 28 February 1775, Adams Co., PA) and Anna DeBaun.

1850 Sullivan Co., Indiana, Census, p. 277, HH 102/102: James Hammoch, Farmer, KY; Levina, 50, KY; Isaiah, 18, IN; Sarah, 17, IN; Nancy, 16, IN; Mary, 13, IN; Levina, 10, IN; Indian, 8, female, IN; Syntha, 5, IN; Anne, 3, IN; Agnes, 3, IN (twin); Charity, 1, IN.

Isaiah married Sarah Walden on 21 October 1856 in Vigo Co., IN. Sarah married Samuel Harmon on 8 April 1853 in Sullivan Co., IN. Nancy married Isaiah Adams on 28 April 1853 in Sullivan Co., IN. Mary married Zachariah Eggers on 17 December 1857 in Vigo Co., IN. Lavina married Isaiah Adams on 20 August 1857 in Vigo Co., IN. Indiana married Jeremiah Adams on 9 September 1865 in Vigo Co., IN. Cynthia married Nathan Robert Terry on 7 July 1864 in Sullivan County. She died in 1873. Anna married Nathan Robert Terry on 9 December 1873 in Sullivan County. She died in 1923.

1860 Sullivan Co., IN, Census, Curry Township, HH 1280/1280: Sarah Hamack, 41, Seamstress, KY; Levina, 18, IL; Ann, 16, IN; Daniel, 13, Mary E., 9, IN; Caroline, 8, IN; James J., 4, IN.

1860 Sullivan Co., IN, Census, HH 1171/1171: James Hammick, 52, Farm Laborer, KY; Levina, 48, KY; Indiana, 18, IN; Cintha, 15, IN; Agness, 14, IN; Anna, 14, IN; Charity, 12, IN; Emirene, 6, IN.

1880 Sullivan Co., IN, Farmersburg - Curry Township, HH 193/194: Sarah Hammack, 63, Keeping House, KY/PA/VA; Levina, 38, IL/KY/KY; James, 24, IN/KY/KY; Tenia, 7, granddaughter, IN/KY/KY.

1900 Sullivan Co., IN, Census, Curry Township, HH 74/74: James Hammack, March 1856, IN/GA/KY; Levina, July 1843, IN/GA/KY, Sister; James F., April 1884, IL/IN/IL, Nephew.

James and George Hammack of Putnam Co., IN

The index to the 1840 Putnam Co., IN, census shows two Hammacks in Putnam County, Homer on page 304 and Hannah on page 388. Homer has not been located. The entry for Hannah was located and transcribed; it is not clear that her surname is Hammack, however. It might have been Hamrick or Hannick.

1840 Indiana Census Index:

Homer Hammack   Putnam   p. 304
Hannah Hammack   Putnam   p. 388

This name is spelled with an "I" and may actually be Hamrick. Hannah's household included two males aged 10-15; 1 female aged 5-10; and one female aged 40-50.

1850 Putnam Co., Indiana, Census, Jefferson Township, HH 144/144: James Hammock, 35, VA, $700; Lucinda, 36, VA; John M., 12, IN; Nancy E., 10, IN; Catherine, 4, IN; Henry T., 3, IN; Samuel, 1, IN.

Note that this James was living near George Hammack of the William and Jane Long Hammack family.

James P. Hammock (1839, GA--) of Robertson Co., TX, and GA

1860 Robertson Co., TX, Census, Wheelock PO, p. 180, HH 32/32: James P. Hammock, 21, Laborer, GA, in HH of Josephus and Catherine Cavitt, natives of TN and AL.

Others in the household included Robert Williams, 18, AL; William Langley, 35, AL; Josephine Summerville, 14, TX; and Peter Acrews, 30, TN. On page 180, also in Wheelock, HH 452/452, was James Hammock, 22, Farm Laborer, GA, in the household of George Singleton, 21, Farm laborer, GA, and wife Zilpha, 18, GA. Also in the household was Ella, 8/12, GA.

James Hammack (c. 1822, TN --) of Tennessee and Kentucky

1850 Wayne Co., KY, Census, p. 266, HH 370/377: James Hammack, 28, Laborer, $300, TN; Teletha, 29, KY; John N., 2, KY; Samuel E., 3/12, KY.

1860 Wayne Co., KY, Census, p. 239, Mill Springs PO, 7 June 1860, HH 69/68: James Hammack, 38, Black Smith, $300, TN; Telitha, 39, KY; John W., 12, KY; Thomas J., KY; Jeremiah S., 4, KY; James K., 1/365, KY.

James Hammack (c. 1858, GA --) of Throckmorton Co., TX

1880 Throckmorton Co., TX, Census, p. 300, ED 181: James Hammock, age 22, GA, was living with John A. and Sarah A. Matthews, natives of LA and TX.

James H. Hammock (c. 1863, GA --) of Macon Co., GA

This man may have been in Twiggs Co., GA, in 1880. 1880 Twiggs Co., GA, Census shows Mary Hammock, 18, and James Hammock, 17, as grandchildren of William Barnes, 68, GA/NC/NC. Barnes was living in GMD 323, Twiggs Co., GA, p. 3B, in 1880.

Oglethorpe City Cemetery, Macon Co., GA:

> James H. Hammock, b. 4-10-1862, d. 10-10-1925.
> Nancy Hammock, d. 5-4-1937.
> Bertie Hammock, wife of J. R. Bray, 1897-1925

The 1910 census showed James H., 38; Nancy, 35; Bertie, 11; and Clarence, 9. They were living in HH 119/121, Macon Co., GA, GMD 1070.

Georgia Death Certificates, 1914-1927, show the following deaths for men named James Hammock: William James P. Hammock, son of William Hammock, born April 1857, Paulding Co., GA, died 30 January 1924, Haralson Co., GA; James Hammock, born 10 April 1870, Georgia, died 18 October 1926, Sumter Co., GA, husband of Nancy Hammock, son of Blue Hammock and Margie Roberts; Henry Daniel Hammock, born 1872, Washington Co., GA, died 22 April 1924, Laurens Co., GA, son of Jim Hammock and Mariah Page; James William Hammock, born 17 May 1863, GA, died 27 May 1925, Bibb Co., GA, parents not shown; James B. Hammack, born 14 October 1856, Houston Co., GA, died 23 November 1923, Bibb Co., GA, son of James Hammack and Martha Emmerson; Mrs. A. S. Martin, born 10 October

1863, GA, died 2 May 1925, Bibb Co., GA, son of James Hammack and Annie J. Cranford. If the date of death for James H. Hammack is correct, none of these men can be him.

James M. Hammock and Vianna Sims

James and James M. Hammack participated in the 1827 Georgia Land Lottery. James M. Hammock married Vianna Sims on 16 January 1834 in Pike Co., GA.

Jane and Mary Hammett

This family appears as Hammock in 1860 but as Hammett in 1850. Significantly, in 1850 they were living only two households from Martin Hammock (HH 1833/1917), which seems to suggest that he name really was Hammett. No references to any of these people have been found after 1860.

1850 Grainger Co., TN, Census, HH 1831/1915: Jane Hammett, 65, VA; Mary Beltoner, 32, TN; William, 14, TN; Jane, 13, TN; Sally A., 9, TN; Narcissa, 7, TN; Betsy, 4, TN; Joseph P., 9/12, TN; Rhoda Hammett, 17, B, TN.

1860 Grainger Co., TN, Census, Rutledge PO, HH 1443/1443: Mary Hammack, 42, Spinster, $50, TN; William, 25, Laborer, TN; Jane, 22, TN; Sarah A., 19, TN; Narcissa, 17, TN; Elizabeth, 14, TN; Joseph, 11, TN; Artilda, 7, TN; Jane, 77, Unknown.

Jane Hammick Thompson

Jane Hammick, m. 27 Dec., 1823, Jefferson Co., TN, Isaac Thompson.

Jeff Hammack (c. 1824, AL --) of Kemper Co., MS

1870 Kemper Co., MS, Census, Scooba, 20 August 1870, p. 333: Jeff Hammack, 46, Farmer, AL; Eaphiann, 51, GA; Anna, 21, MS; Susan, 12, At Home, MS; Leavy, 17, male, Farm Hand, MS; Anderson, 31, Farm Hand, 0/$200, AL. This name is difficult to read and could be Hammett.

Jeremiah Hamrick (c. 1810, GA --).

Although indexed as Hammick, this name appears to be Hamrick. This man was actually Jeremiah Hamrick (c. 1810 – c. 1852), son of Peter and Elizabeth Goldman Hamrick of Lincoln Co., GA, and husband of Sarah Beall.[1854]

1850 Carroll Co., MS, Census, Southern Division, HH 276: Jeremiah Hamrick, 40, $400, GA; Sarah, 35, GA; John, 12, MS.

Jeremiah Hammack of Bibb Co., GA

Jeremiah and Johnston Hammack of Bibb Co., GA, are probably sons of Lewis and Elizabeth Hammack of Bibb Co., GA. The relationship has not been proven, however.

[1854] Note that there was a connection of sorts here. His aunt, Nancy Hamrick, married Austin Moncrief; their son, William Moncrief, married Elizabeth Hammock, granddaughter of John Hammack, Sr., of Lincoln County. David Moncrief had also married Sarah Pollard, a sister of James Hammack's wife Mary Pollard.

Jeremiah Hammack was married by 1830, at which time he may have had two or three children. If he were no more than thirty in 1830, it seems unlikely that he was the father of all of the children in his household. He may have married an older woman, perhaps a widow, who had children of her own. Bibb County is southeast of Butts County, separated from it by Monroe County (which borders Jones). It seems likely that the Jeremiah enumerated in Bibb County is the man who died about 1832 in Butts County. Butts Co., GA, Wills, Administration of Estates, 1826-1841, pp. 186-187, indicated that the inventory of Jeremiah Hammack was recorded 25 July 1832 and valued at $182.43 ¾. A return was recorded 10 February 1834 and dated 1 January 1834. No heirs were mentioned.[1855]

Districts 716 and 564 were part of the city of Macon; district 519 borders Monroe County and district 482, which borders both Monroe and Crawford Counties.

1830 Bibb Co., GA, Census:

p. 50.	Jeremiah Hammack	1m 10-15 1m 20-30	2f 5-10 2f 10-15 1f 40-50	GMD 716
	Johnston Hammack	1m 10-15 1m 20-30	1f 5-10 1f 20-30	GMD 716
p. 55.[1856]	Johnston Hammack	1m 10-15 1m 20-30	1f 5-10 1f 20-30	GMD 564
p. 61	James Hammack	1m 0-5 2m 5-10 3m 10-15 1m 15-20 1m 50-60	1f 0-5 1f 5-10 1f 30-40	GMD 482
	David Moncrief	1m 20-30	1f 0-5 1f 15-20[1857]	
p. 70	Lewis Hammack	1m 5-10 1m 10-15 1m 50-60	1f 0-5 2f 10-15 1f 15-20 1f 40-50	GMD 519

Johnson Hammack married Esther Chesser in Jasper County[1858] on 27 August 1822 and is said to have married Susannah Hammack Stringfield, his cousin, in 1830 in Alabama. Johnson Hammack was living in Ellis's District, Crawford County, Georgia, in 1827, when he drew land lot 111, land district 6, Carroll County, in the state land lottery. Carroll Co., GA, DB B, p. 149, shows that Benjamin Merrell, sheriff, sold this land to Paul T. Rodgers for $10.00 on 4 October 1830 "to satisfy a suit in Justice Court, Bibb Co., Rushing Rogers vs. Johnson Hammack, owner of the land." William L. Parr and Hiram Wright witnessed the deed.

Johnson Hammack was in western Georgia or eastern Alabama by 1840. The *Columbus Enquirer*, issue of 9 Dec., 1840, carried the following notice: "Macon Co., AL: $500 Reward offered for capture of Johnson Hammock, murderer of Absolom Echols, offered by James W. Echols, of Waverly Hall, GA." This Johnson Hammack is apparently the John Hammack, 47, GA, who was enumerated in the Alabama

[1855] See Butts Co., GA, Wills, Administration of Estates, 1826-1841, pp. 252-253.
[1856] This seems to be the same man, enumerated erroneously for a second time.
[1857] David Moncrief married Sarah Pollard on 5 September 1827 in Bibb Co., GA.
[1858] Jasper County is directly north of Jones County; Bibb County is directly south of Jones County.

State Penitentiary, Coosa Co., AL, in 1850; he had been in jail for murder since 1842.[1859] If it occurred at all, his marriage to Susannah Hammack Stringfield apparently did not last; by 1840 she was living in Brazoria Co., TX, where she had married again and was known as Susan Hughes. Susannah had many relatives in Macon Co., AL, which may have influenced Johnston Hammack's decision to move there.

Joel Hammock or Hamrick

1830 Virginia Census Index, Nicholas County: Joel Hamnock, p. 179. The 1820 index showed Joel Hamrick in Nicholas, along with Benjamin, Benjamin, Sr., Enoch, Tilson and William Hamrick, all on p. 205. In 1850, Joel Hamrick was in Braxton, p. 177, along with several other Hamricks, including Benjamin, in Braxton, and another Benjamin in Nicholas County. This man was Joel Hamrick (1770 – c. 1860), son of Benjamin and Mary Sias Hamrick of Prince William Co., VA.

Joel W. Hammack

Joel W. Hammock married Emily Hardin 28 July 1876 in Tallapoosa Co., AL.

John Hamick of Germany and Maryland

1860 Baltimore Co., MD, Census, 20th Ward, p. 468, HH 888/1037: John Hamick, 45, Shoemaker, $500/$100, Hesse Cassie; Josepha, 45, Hesse Cassie; Catherine, 17, MD; John, 16, Apprentice, MD; Joseph, 11, MD; Alfred, 8, MD.

John Hammock of Franklin Co., GA

This man was born by 1779, if not earlier. He was alive as late as 1805. What became of him is unclear. At the time of the 1805 land lottery, several men named John were eligible to draw: John of Franklin County; John of Jefferson County; John of Lincoln County; John of Harden's Creek, Wilkes County; John Sr., of Wilkes County; John, Jr., of Wilkes County. This suggests that John of Franklin County was an altogether different man. Since it is known that Daniel and Mary Martin Hammack of Tennessee lived in Franklin and Jackson County in the 1790s, it may be that John also belonged to the Virginia – Tennessee family.

1800 Franklin Co., GA, Tax Digest: John Hammock, no land, Epperson's District, p. 35.

1802 Franklin Co., GA, Tax Digest: John Hammock, no land, poll tax only, p. 103. Neighboring surnames included Apperson and Vineyard.

1803 Franklin Co., GA, Tax Digest: John Hammock, 125 acres, Indian Creek, granted James Worker, p. 138.

1805 Franklin Co., GA, Tax Digest, John Hammock, 271 acres, granted James Worker, joining D. Duff and James Worker, Indian Creek, p. 138.

1805: John Hammock was entitled to draw in the state land lottery and was then a resident of Franklin

---

[1859] One Johnston *Wamack* was living in Murray Co., GA, by 1840, where he was enumerated on page 267 in GMD 824. His household contained one male aged 20-30, one female aged 0-5, and one female aged 20-30.

County.

No clear record of this man has been found after 1805.

John G. Hammock of Ohio

1840 Lawrence Co., OH, Census: Jno. G. Hammock. This man's household contained one male aged 0-5; 1 male aged 15-20; 1 male aged 40-50; 1 female aged 0-5; 2 females aged 5-10; 2 females aged 10-15; 1 female aged 30-40.[1860]

John L. Hammack (c. 1822, GA --) of Muscogee Co., GA

John married Frances Painter in Upson Co., GA, in 1837.

1840 Upson Co., GA, Census, GMD 561, p. 53: John Hammock, 1 male 20-30; 1 female 0-5; 1 female 15-20. Nearby families included Crawford Martin, Wm. Snead, Benjamin Goodroe, Samuel Bell, John Bell.

1850 MUSCOGEE p. 329 Columbus (4 Nov), HH 616: John L. Hammock, 28, Carpenter, GA; Frances, 26, GA; Nancy C., 11, GA; Elizabeth, 9, GA; John L., 3, GA; James P., 10/12, GA.

1860 Muscogee Co., GA, Census, Columbus PO, HH 494/494 and 495/495: Francis Hammack, 37, $0/$100, GA; James, 22, GA; Elizabeth, 19, GA; John, 14, GA; James, 10, GA; Mary, 7, GA; Mrs. Painter, 83, GA.

1870 Muscogee Co., GA, Census, Columbus PO, 2nd Ward, HH 7/8: Frances Hammock, 48, GA; Fannie, 28, GA; Lou, 27, GA; John, 22, Fisherman, GA; James, 18, Fisherman, GA; Mary, 15, At Home, GA; Annie, 9, GA.

1880 Muscogee Co., GA, Vol. 17, ED 53, Sheet 22, Line 35: Francis Hammack, 64, GA; James, 24, GA; Mary, 20, GA; Eva, 4, GA.

NOTE: J. M. Hammack who was in Texas in 1880 appears in 1900 as John L. Hammack, and the death certificates of four of his children also give his name as John L. Hammack. Perhaps he connects to this family.

John M. Hameak (c. 1842, AL --).

John M. Hameaks was shown in Lee Co., AL, in 1880, HH 461, Beat 10: John M. Hameaks, 38, AL; Fannie, 33, AL; Albert, 17; James, 13; Susan E., 11; Sarah E., 7; Stroud, 2; Nancy, 67, GA, Mother.

John Hammock of Beartown, Deer Lodge Co., Montana

1870 Deer Lodge Co., Montana, Census, p. 28, HH 43: John Hammock, 33, Miner, AR.

[1860] This entry is difficult to read and is indexed as William Hammock, but it appears to be Jno. G. Hammock.

John Hammack of Escambia Co., FL

1840: John Hammack, Escambia County, p. 23.

John Hammack (bef. 1779 --) of Franklin Co., GA

The identity of this John Hammack is uncertain; he could be the son of Robert and Millenor or the son of John of Lincoln. He could be an unidentified John Hammack.

John Hammock, 1800 Franklin County, GA, Tax Digest, p. 34.
John Hammack, 1805 Georgia Land Lottery, Franklin Co., GA.

John Hammock (c. 1824, TN or AL --) of Tennessee and Texas

1850 Bexar Co., TX, San Antonio, p. 273, HH 695/695: Alfred Wolf, 49, Clerk, West Indies; J. C. Pulley, 28, Attorney at Law, Canada; A. J. McClellan, 30, merchant, $5000, Ireland; Charles F. King, 39, $500, New Hampshire; John Hammock, 26, Ranging Co., TN; Joseph C. Blanchard, 30, Ranging Co., MS. NOTE: This John Hammock was of the same approximate age as John Hammock, age 35, AL, who appears as an overseer for C. Stringfellow in Brazoria Co., TX, in 1860. The Stringfellow connection would suggest that this man is a member of the family of John Hammack of Lincoln Co., GA.

John Hammock (c. 1829, KY --) of Bourbon Co., KY

1850 Bourbon Co., KY, Census, p. 227: John Hammock, 21, Painter, KY, in HH of Wm. D. Griffing, 30, Pedlar, KY, with wife Norah, 44, KY, and family.

John Hammock (c. 1812, SC or GA --) of Macon Co., AL

1850 Macon Co., AL, Census, HH 1577: John Hammock, 38, SC; Eliza, 30, SC; James, 8, AL; Sarah, 6, AL; John, 4, AL; William, 2, AL.

John Hammock (c. 1859, GA --) of DeKalb Co., GA

The 1870 DeKalb Co., GA, Census, HH 434/434, Barns District, showed John Hammock, 11, Farm Laborer, GA, living with Braxton and Anna Drake, 52 and 50, both natives of Georgia.

John Hamuck or Hamrick of Jasper Co., GA

1820 Jasper Co., GA, Census, shows a man whose name is indexed as John Hamuck but who appears upon inspection to have been John Hamrick: 3 males aged 0-5; 1 male aged 15-20; 1 male aged 20-30; 2 females aged 0-5; 1 female aged 5-10; 2 females aged 10-15; 1 female aged 15-20.

John Hammack or Hamrick of Irwin Co., GA

1820 Irwin County, GA, Census, p. 232, shows an individual whose name could have been John Hamick, Hamrick, or Hamnok: 3m 0-10; 1m 18-26; 1m 26-45; 2f 0-10; 1f 10-16; 2f 16-26; 1f 26-45. This man was probably really John Hamrick.

John Hammack (c. 1859, GA --) of Pulaski Co., GA

John Hammack was enumerated on page 331 of Pulaski Co., GA, in 1860, HH 687/860. He was an 11 year old boy living with William Cone's family: William Cone, 60 Farming, $1200./$600, SC; Susan, 48, Wife, GA; Absalom Brayrnt, 33, Black Smith, $1000/$500, NC; John Hammock, 11, GA; Jane, 17, Laborer, GA.

John Hammack (or Hamrick) and Nancy Todd

John Hammack or Hamrick married Nancy Todd on 26 April 1811 in Wilkes Co., GA. Hamrick researchers claim that this was Rev. John Hamrick (c. 1774, Prince William Co., VA -- 30 January 1836, Upson Co., GA), son of Benjamin Hamrick and Fannie Burchett, who fathered four children by Martha Mosely and then another six by Nancy Todd. He died in 1836 in Upson County. Nancy died 17 January 1867 in Upson Co., GA.

John L. Hammack (c. 1820, VA --) of Maryland and Washington, D.C.

1850 Charles Co., MD, Census, Hill Top District, p. 239, HH 394/394: John L. Hammock, 30, Farmer, $2,000, MD; Emeline, 25, MD; Cynthia Skinner, 65, MD; William F. Hammock, 5, MD; John P., 4, MD; Homer B., 2, MD;[1861] Elnana, 1, female, MD.

1860 Charles Co., MD, Census, Hill Top District, p. 710, HH 635/630, living next to John and Ellen Barnes: John Hancock, 38, Farmer, $18,000, VA; Emma, 36, MD; John, 16, MD; Wellamina, 15, female; Frances Posey, 14, female; Henrietta Posey, 30, female; William Davis, 24, male; Homer Hancock, 13, MD; Emma, 11, MD; Charrelconett, 10, female, MD; Ricarda, 7, female, MD; Estella, 5, female, MD; Julia A., 3, female. Note that William and Julian are both shown as females, and that the name is twice written as Hancock rather than Hammock. It would seem that the enumerator was either recopying rough notes when he made this entry or that he did not actually visit the household himself.

1870 Charles Co., MD, Census, Doncaster PO, p. 48, HH 642/643: E. Hammock, 50, Keeping House, $2000/$300, MD; H. B., 21, Farmer, MD; E. E., 20, female, MD; C. M., 17, female, MD; L. R., 16, female, MD; E. A., 12, female, MD; J. L., 11, male, MD. In HH 643/654 were W. F. Hammack, 24, Farmer, MD, and M. J., 28, Keeping House, MD. There were several Barnes families enumerated in this neighborhood.

1880 Washington, D.C., Census, p. 277, HH 136/177: William F. Hammack, 35, Street Car, MD/VA/MD; Jane M., 34, Keeping House, MD/MD/MD; John S., 8, Attending School, MD/MD/MD; Emma, 5, MD/MD/MD; Harry C. F., 2, MD/MD/MD; Joseph Barnes, 26, Street Car, MD/MD/MD. HH 136/179: Emline Hammack, 65, MD/MD/MD, living with Jennie Boynton, 33, Keeping House, DC/MD/MD; George, 8, DC/DC/DC; and Maggie, 6, DC/DC/DC.

1880 Charles Co., MD, Census, 3rd District, HH 362/366: Homer Hammack, 32, Farmer, MD/MD/MD; Sarah M., 30, MD/MD/MD; Marcella, 2, MD/MD/MD; Bensen, 9/12, MD/MD/MD. HH 363/367: E. A. Hammack, 63, Keeping House, MD/MD/MD; Recarda, 23, MD/MD/MD; Ernestina, 23, MD/MD/MD; Julian, 21, MD/MD/MD; Lousia B. Hammack, 79, Sister-in-law, VA/VA/VA.

1900 Washington, D. C., Soundex, 7-78-19-51/31, 6th Street: Emma R. Hammack, 35, February 1865,

---

[1861] Homer B. Hammack, age 73, was still living in Charles Co., MD, in 1920.

MD: Marceline, 32, February 1868, MD; James Rutland, 38, February 1862, NY, Lodger. Although the age does not match, this may be William F.'s daughter Emma.

1900 Washington, D.C., Soundex, 9-101-19-65: Jane M. Hammack, 53, September 1846, MD; John L., 25, March 1875, MD; Pearl E., 23, March 1877, MD; Harry T., 21, November 1878, MD; Ernestine, 18, September 1881, DC; Albert C. Gardiner, 27, February 1873, Kansas, Renter. Jane was the widow of William F. Hammack.

1900 Washington, D. C., Soundex, 4-37-17-21, Pennsylvania Avenue: Emma L. Hammack, 43, February 1857, MD; Katherine S., January 1877, MD; Mary C., December 1879, MD; Helen M., December 1881, MD; Frank S., August 1884, MD. Emma may be the sister of William F. Hammack.

1900 Washington, D.C., Soundex, 9-109-21-68: Julian L. Hammack, May 1860, MD; Isabelle M., February 1840, NY; Julian C., November 1891, DC; Marcella, March 1880, MD, Niece; Charles W. Henry, January 1865, OH, Boarder. Julian was the brother of William F. Hammack.

John T. Hammack (c. 1831, GA --) of Harris Co., TX

This man may have be identical with the Thomas Hammack found in Louisiana in 1860. Both families had connections with mulattoes, and John T. Hammack was the same approximate age as Thomas Hammack.

1880 Harris Co., TX, p. 149, ED 76: John T. Hammock, 49, Hack Driver, GA/GA/GA; Louisa, 23, TX/--/--, Mulatto; John, 6/12, TX/GA/TX, Mulatto; Lula, 3, TX/GA/TX, Mulatto.

Texas Death Certificate Number 3073 shows that John William Hammock, identified as Negro, died 9 January 1944, age 61, and that he was a son of John Hammock and Louisa Brandon. His birthdate is given as January 9, 1873 (indicating that he was actually age 71). The death certificate states that he was born in Houston, Harris Co., TX, and lived there for his entire life. His father was born in Alabama and his mother in Texas; John William Hammock was buried in Olive Wood Cemetery in Houston.

John W. Hammack (c. 1805 -- 1860/70, Crawford Co., GA), m. 17 March, 1831, Crawford Co., GA, Cenia Walton (c. 1807 -- aft. 1870, prob. Crawford Co., GA).

The identity of John W. Hammack is uncertain. His proximity in 1860 to the family of Susan Hammack Fowler, daughter of Talbot D. Hammack, suggests that he was closely related to the other Crawford Co., GA, Hammack families. He may have come from the families of James and Lewis Hammack, who appear in the 1830 Bibb Co., GA, census.

1840 Crawford Co., GA, Census, p. 375: John Hammack, 1 male 0-5; 1 male 30-40; 1 female 0-5; 1 female 20-30.

1850 Crawford Co., GA, Census, HH 556/556: Jno. Hammock, 45, GA; S., 43, female, GA; E., 13, female, GA; E., 10, male, GA; E., 6, female, GA.

1860 Crawford Co., GA, Census, Knoxville PO, p. 918, HH 387/376: John Hammack, 56, Farmer, $500/$100, GA; Sena, 53, GA; Melvina, 15, GA. Note: John B. Fowler and his wife Susan Hammack Fowler, daughter of Talbot D. Hammack, were living next door in HH 387/377.

1870 Crawford Co., GA, Census, GMD 577, p. 417, HH 581/591: Elizabeth Nichols, 34, Keeping House, $0/$100, GA; John, 15, At School; Jefferson, 12, At School; Sarah, 10; Ellen, 9; Sena Hammack, 65, At home.

Issue of John W. and Sena Walton Hammack:

1. Sarah Elizabeth Hammack (1837 -- aft. 1870), m. 17 Nov., 1853, Crawford Co., GA, James A. Nichols.

1860 Crawford Co., GA, Census, HH 391/381: James A. Nichols, 27, Farmer, $1000, GA; Sarah E., 23, Ga; John W., 5, GA; Jefferson, 2, GA; Sarah E., 6/12, GA. The following were neighbors: Joseph H. Wright (384), Allen Beckham (385), John and Sena Hammack (386), John B. and Susan Fowler (387), Vinson and Elizabeth Nichols (388), and Daniel and Mary Nichols (389).

2. E. Hammack (1840 -- married or deceased by 1860 census).

3. E. Melvina Hammack (c. 1845 --). She may be Margaret Adna Elvira Hammack (1843 - 1882) who married James Long. They were living in Crawford Co., GA, at the time of the 1880 census.

Joshua Hammocker (c. 1822, AL --).

1860 Pontotoc Co. Chesterville, p. 217, HH 1426/1426: Joshua Hammocker, 38, Farmer, $100, AL; Charlotte, 31, SC; John, 4, MS; Joshua, 1, MS.

John McNeal and Julia Ann Hammock

John McNeal is shown to have married Julia Ann Hammock on 3 November 1839 in Jones County; the 1840 Jones County census, page 127, shows that he was aged 20-30 with wife aged 15-20. Note that on the same page appeared Eliza and Susannah Wammock, suggesting that perhaps his wife could have been a Wammock rather than a Hammock or Hammack before marriage.

David and Charity (Hammock) Chambers are found in Jasper Co., MS, in 1860 and 1870. A John McNeal, a native of Georgia, is also found in the same county in those reports:

1860 Jasper Co., MS, Census, Turnerville PO, HH 929/934: John McNeal, 39, farmer, $2,000/$3,800, GA; M. J., 30, Doing House Work, MS: E. M., 11, female, MS; L. A., 9, female, MS; S. E., 6, female, MS; J. J., 2, male, MS.

In Sumter Co., GA, in 1870, Samuel McNeil was living with his grandmother, Nancy Feagin Hammack, formerly of Jones County, Georgia. This suggests that Julia Hammack McNeil was her daughter. It is possible that Julia died and that John McNeil moved west afterwards.

Ketura Hammack

This family was transcribed by Ruth Land Hatten as Hammack; upon checking the original census document, it became clear that this name was Hannah.

1900 Yazoo Co., MS, Census, 111-5-38: Ketura Hannah, February 1861, 39, MS; Henry, October 1886, MS; William, April 1888, MS; Brown, October 1889, MS; Annie, May 1891, MS; Myrtle, October 1892, MS; Nettie, October 1894, MS; Mattie, April 1896, MS; Mary, May 1897, MS; Thomas Milner,

December 1878, 21, MS.

L. T. Hammack (c. 1829, GA --).

1850 Ashley Co., AR, Census, p. 34, Mill Creek Township, HH 142: L. T. Hammack, 21, Farmer, GA; Elizabeth, 42, GA; Talitha, 8, GA; Robert, 18, Laborer, GA; Mary, 4, GA.

NOTE that in 1860, an R. B. Hammack, 27, GA, and a Messer Hammack, 31, GA, were enumerated in adjacent households in Franklin Co., AL. Note also that Arkansas marriage records indicate that Ritha Hammack married James Cates on 31 August 1831 and resided in Ashley Co., AR. Ritha may have been deceased by 1850, when James Cates, a widower, age 54 and born in North Carolina, was enumerated in HH 33/33, White Township, Ashley Co., AR. Cates's children ranged in age from William J. F., age 21, to Ann, age 8.

Laura Hammack Rogers

Laura Hammock married William M. Rodgers 22 July 1885 in Tallapoosa Co., AL.

Levi and John Hammock of Echols Co., GA

No subsequent or previous references to these individuals have been found; they may have had another surname -- Hannah or Hamrick -- that resembled Hammack.

1870 Echols Co., GA, Census, Statenville PO, HH 356/356: John Hammock, 51, Laboring on Farm, FL; Pollie, 62, Keeping House, GA; Mollie, 14, FL; Jackson, 22, At Home, FL. In HH 363/365 were: Levi Hammock, 72, Farm Laborer, GA; Mary, 51, Keeping House, GA; Ella M., 16, At Home, GA.

Lewis Hammock of Claiborne Co., TN

I had initially suspected a connection between this family and that of Martin and Sarah Janeway Hammack of Claiborne Co., TN. It does not appear, however, that a close connection existed.

Lewis Hammack (c. 1820/1821, TN -- aft. 1850, Claiborne Co., TN). The 1850 Claiborne Co., TN, Census, shows, HH 105/452: Lewis Hammock, 29, TN; Eliza, 27, TN; Andrew J., 5, TN;[1862] Charity E., 4, TN; Daniel R., 1, TN. Lewis died 17 March 1865, during the American Civil War, and was buried in Georgia.

Andrew Jackson Hammack (3 June 1840, TN -- 19 January 1907, Jefferson, White Co., AR), identified by Henry Franklin Hammack as Lewis's son, m. 1863, Sarah Peppers. He moved from Palmer and Taylorsville, IL, to Arkansas about 1900. Their children were: Mary (1864 - infancy); Albert (1866 -- infancy); Orpha (1870-1872); Lucy Ollie (1867-1948); , wife of James A. Killman; and Charles Benjamin (11 August 1877 -- aft. 1955).

1880 Christian Co., IL, Census, Morrisonville PO, p. 659, HH 191/199: Andrew J. Hammack, 37, Hardware Merchant, TN/--/--; Sarah, 32, Keeping House, OH/IN/VA; Lucy Ollie, 13, Attending School, IL; Charles D., 3, IL.

[1862] This may be the Andrew J. Hammack, son of Lewis Hammack, who later lived in McRae, Arkansas.

Andrew J. Hammack moved to McRae, Arkansas. He first moved into Kentucky and then Southern Illinois. According to Henry Franklin Hammack, this family claimed a close kinship with Judge Lewis Hammack of Pinckneyville, Illinois.

Reverend Robert Hammack (1845-1926) of Tennessee and Kentucky also claimed a near kinship with Andrew Jackson Hammack and, according to Henry Franklin Hammack, visited his family on several occasions. Reverend Robert Hammack was a son of William and Rachel Murphy Hammack of Grainger Co., TN, and Laurel Co., KY, and a grandson of William and Sarah Brock Hammack of Grainger Co., TN, a great-grandson of John and Nancy Maples Hammack, and a great-great-grandson of John and Mary Martin Hammack.

Judge Lewis Hammack, born about 1825, Warren Co., TN, with whom the Andrew Jackson Hammacks also claimed kin, was a son of Benjamin Hammack and Sarah Hull of Madison Co., KY, and Marion and Perry Counties, IL. Benjamin is believed to have been a son of Lewis and Keziah Daniel Hammack and a grandson of Richard and Mary Witcher Hammack. This Richard was a brother of John Hammack who married Mary Martin. Hence, the probability seems very great that Lewis Hammack (d. 1865) and his son Andrew Jackson Hammack of McRae, Arkansas, were descendants of Richard Hammack, son of William "O" Hammack. Exactly how they fit into that family has not been discovered, however.

See Henry Franklin Hammack, 2: 190, 322. Andrew Jackson Hammack of McRae had a son Charles Benjamin Hammack who died 10 October 1958, age 81, in North Little Rock, Arkansas. He indicated that Andrew Jackson's father Lewis died at Andersonville during the Civil War.

Lewis C. Hamock of Perry Co., MO

Lewis C. Hamock appears in the index to the 1840 Missouri Census; the index shows that he was enumerated on page 7 of the Perry County census. The actual census contains an ink spill across the name of Lewis C. Hamock and across the enumerated data. The name is not at all clear. It might actually be Lewis C. HANCOCK. He was aged 15-20 with a female aged 20-30. There may also have been a male aged 20-30, but there is a stain over the appropriate column that is difficult to read.

Little B. Hammack (c. 1802, GA --).

1850 Lee Co., GA, Census, p. 278, 50th Division, HH 112/112: Little B. Hammok, 48, Farmer, $200, GA; Mary, 35, GA; Jane, 16, GA; James D., 14, GA; Nancy D., 10, GA; William H. H., 9, GA; Sarah E., 6, GA; Berry L., 2, GA; Sarah Davis, 40, GA. NOTE that this name could have been Hammack or Wammack.

Louisa Hammack of Washington, D. C.

1850 Washington, D. C., Census, pp. 77, 135, and Book 2, p. 115: HH 950/1051, Louisa Hammack, 39, VA, in HH of D. O. Hare, 39, Engineer, $1600, VA, and Mary, 29, VA, and family. Louisa was apparently a sister of John Hammack of Charles Co., MD. In 1880 she was aged 79 and living in Charles Co., MD, with John's widow and family.

Lucy Hammack (c. 1832, KY --).

1850 Crittendon Co., KY, Census, Wappanocca Township, p. 364, HH 96/96, showed Lucy Hammack, 18, KY, in HH of Samuel Daniels, 27, VA and wife Susan, 23, TN. Included were three children, aged 8 months to 5 years, born in Arkansas and Kentucky.

Luther Hammack

1870 Jasper Township, Jasper Co., MO, Census, Carthage PO, p. 39, HH 12/12: Luther Hammack, 42, Farmer, $5000, NY; Rachel, 30, KH, OH; James, 15, IO; Luther, 10, Kansas; Richard, 8, Kansas; Francis, 6, Kansas; Alice, 4, Kansas; Fanny, 3, MO; Charles, 1/12, MO.

Lydia Hammack and Jesse Hendricks

Lydia Hammack married Jesse Hendricks on 29 December 1849 in Troup Co., GA. Although indexed as Hammock, family members maintain that this was Lydia Hammett (10 September 1820 -- 10 September 1899), daughter of William Hammett, Sr., and Syntha Strozier Hammett. Her birth is given in William Hammett's family Bible; she later m. (2) Robert Brown.

Mahala Hammick Bales

Mahala J. Hammick married 31 May, 1845, Jefferson Co., TN, Inman Bales.

Margaret Hammock (c. 1813, NC --) of Baldwin Co., AL

1860 Baldwin Co., AL, HH 11/10: Stephen Hammock, 28, AL; Eliza, 22, FL; Margaret E., 8, AL; John R., 6, AL: Sarah T., 3, AL; Francis, 11/12, AL.[1863] Note that one Stephen Hammock, age 20, was in the household of Eady Hammock in Conecuh Co., AL, in 1850. Living next to this Stephen in HH 12/11 was Margaret Hammoc, 47, NC; John T. Hammoc, 24, AL.

In Baldwin County in 1870 was Charles Hammock, age 8, AL, living with Elijah and Elizabeth (Vickery) Wilson, who had married 1 April 1861. Also in the county was John Hammock, age 14, AL, a Domestic Servant, living with Gustavus and Sarah Schmitd. Both are shown in 1880, and Charles was in Baldwin County as late as 1920. In 1880, John was 24, AL/AL/GA, living with Samuel and Mary (Vickery) Crane, aged 68 and 45; he is listed as a nephew. Charles, in 1880, was still living with Elijah and Elizabeth Wilson; he is listed as a nephew.

It would appear that Eliza Hammock, Mary Crane, and Elizabeth Wilson may have been relatives, perhaps sisters.

Maria Hammack of Alleghany Co., PA

1850 Pennsylvania Census Index: Maria Hammack, Alleghany Co., PA, Pittsburg District, p. 116.

[1863] Note that in HH 9 was William Wilson, age 24, and in HH 10 was Charles Wilson, age 23. Living with Charles Wilson and wife Josephine was Eda Hancock, 46, Day Laborer, Georgia. It is not clear whether the name was Hancock or Hamock. In HH 11 was Stephen Hammoc. In HH 12 was Margaret Hammoc. In HH 40/33 was Samuel S. Carne, 47, CT, Carpenter; Mary Vickery, 27, NC; Elizabeth, 6, AL: John, 4, AL; Leonard Carne, 2, AL; Samuel Crane, 7/12, AL. The 1870 Baldwin census, HH 2/2, showed Samuel Crane, 60, CT, and Mary, 40, FL, with several children, aged 15 to 2. Elijah Wilson, 46, AL, and Elizabeth Wilson, 42, FL, with a large family of offspring, were in Township 3 South, HH 2/2.

One Charles Wilson (b. 1827) married Josephine Hammock; he may have been a brother of Elijah who married Elizabeth Vickery. Elizabeth Vickery married Elijah Wilson in 1844 in Escambia Co., FL.

Marion Hammack and Jeremiah Matthews

Marion Hammack married Jeremiah Matthews, on 5 Jan., 1853, in Upson Co., GA.

Jeremiah had apparently been previously married. Buried in the Trice Cemetery, Upson Co., GA, is Nancy Hudson Trice, wife of Jerry Matthews, b. 16 Dec., 1816, d. 5 Dec., 1851, m. 16 March, 1833. Jeremiah Mathews was born 16 April 1812 and died 3 May 1882. Descendants indicate that he and Nancy had at least six children, born 1834 to 1849. Note that in the 1860 Upson Co., GA, Census, Double Bridges PO, HH 355/321, was J. B. Mathews, 38, Sawyer, $100, GA. In HH 359/325 was Emeline Talley Hammack, and in HH 362 was G. W. Hammock. Martha Hammock was in HH 363. William Jameson and his large family were in HH 350/316. In 1870, one Jerry Matthews, 60, GA, was living in HH 1506/1524, Harris Co., GA; his wife was Emma, age 62. James and Tyrus Jemison, aged 21 and 15, were living with the family.

Martha Hamock of Des Moines Co., IO

1850 Iowa Census Index, Des Moines Co., p. 510, HH 1932: Martha Hamock, 14, Germany, living with Antone Durlemire, 27, Plasterer, $200, Germany; Eretta, 29, Germany; Jane, 1/12, Iowa; William Sebower, 22, Germany.

Martin Hancock of Bedford Co., TN

The 1830 Bedford Co., TN, Census, p. 123, showed: Martin Hammock, 1male 5-10; 1 male 30-40; 2 females 0-5; 2 females 5-10; 1 female 20-30. This name has been transcribed and indexed as Hammock, but the compiler read it as Hancock when viewing the actual census. This is apparently Martin Hancock, Jr. (1799, Wilson Co., TN -- c. 1880, Bedford Co., TN), son of Martin Hancock (1761, NC -- 1835, Wilson Co., TN) and wife Elizabeth.

Mary Hammack of Marion Co., TX

1880 Marion Co., TX, Census, ED 85, p. 378: Mary Hammock, 21, Housekeeper, TX/TN/VA. Mary was living with the family of Goodwin Harris, 36, TN, and Sallie S. Harris, 27, AL.

Mary Hammack (c. 1812, GA --) of Montgomery Co., AL

1850 Montgomery Co., AL, Census, p. 167, HH 231: John H. Burnley, 24, Farmer, GA; Mary A. Hammock, 38, GA; Rebecca, 7, AL; Benjamin F., 5, AL. Nearby were other Burnleys, the oldest being HH 233/233, Samuel Burnley, 73, Farmer, $5000, GA, and Mary Ann Owens, 78, GA. Samuel Burnley, born 1776, Liberty Co., GA, married Ann Brannon at Midway, Liberty Co., GA, in 1803; their daughter Rebecca Burnley, born 1819, McIntosh Co., GA, married Thomas R. Porter on 8 October 1837 in Montgomery Co., AL. They removed to Upshur Co., TX.

Mary Hammack of Upson Co., GA

The 1840 Upson Co., GA, Census, p. 25, shows an individual whose name appears to be Marry Hammock with the following family: 1 male 5-10; 1 female 5-10; 2 females 10-15; 1 female 15-20; 1 female 40-50. This enumeration suggests a woman born about 1800 who probably married about 1820 and had offspring born about 1834 (female), 1836 (female), 1838 (female), 1840 (female), and 1845 (male). This family has not yet been identified. The family was living in GMD 470, which joins Crawford and Monroe Counties. One possibility is that this is Mary Pollard Hammack, widow of James Hammack, but the census data do not appear to match those from the 1830 Bibb County census.

Mary Hammock Wade (c. 1820, GA -- aft. 1880)

Mary m. (1) [------] Hammock and (2) 10 April 1862, Tallapoosa Co., AL, James Wade. She had at least one child, James Hammock, born about 1836.

1880 Tallapoosa Co., AL, Census, HH 68/110: Mary Wade, 60; James Hammock, 44, son. Other surnames included Donald, Smith, Williams, and Britt. Both were names of Georgia.

This James may be the James M. Hammock who married Selia Boatright on 16 December 1868 in Tallapoosa Co., AL. He appears in Tallapoosa Co., AL, Precinct 12, HH 343/344, in 1900: James M. Hammock, January 1838, 62, widowed, male, white, GA/GA/GA; James M., February 1881, 19, AL/GA/AL, son.

Mary Hammock and William McCormick

Mary Hammock married William McCormick on 27 August 1848 in Tallapoosa Co., AL.

1870 Tallapoosa Co., AL, Census, Youngsville, HH 237/240: Mary McCormack, 46, farming, $300/$250, AL; William, 18, AL; Millie, 16, AL; Ellen, 11, AL.

Mary Hammack and Luke White

Mary Hammack married Luke White on 11 June 1845 in Monroe Co., MS.

1860 Monroe Co., MS, Census, Aberdeen PO, HH 474/474: Mary White, 36, GA; James, 12, MS; Sarah E., 10, MS: Fannie, 8, MS; Henry Henderson, 25, NY.

Mary Ann Hammock and Ely Miles

Mary Ann Hammock married Ely Y. Miles on 17 May 1844 in Yazoo Co., MS.

Ely Y. Miles (1820, GA -- 1900, MS) married (1) Mary Ann Hammock and (2) 8 May 1851, Winston Co., MS, Martha J. Kemp. He and Mary Ann Hammock were the parents of: Caswell Monroe Miles (7 August 1844, Winston Co., MS); William B. P. Miles (January 1847, MS); Joseph Obie Miles (1848, MS); and James M. Miles (1850, MS). He had six children by his second marriage. Mary Hammock Miles died in 1850.

Mary's children lived and died in Winston Co., MS. Some researchers believe that her name was Mary Ann Hardy, not Hammock. At the time of the 1850 Winston Co., MS, Census, 22nd Subdivision, p. 351, Roll 382, the family was shown in this way: John Hardy, 56, NC; Esther, 50, GA; Caswell Miles, 6, MS; William, 4, MS; Joseph, 2, MS; James, 5/12, MS.

Mary Hammack and Peter Sperry

Mary died 24 November 1836 in Ross Co., OH; she married Peter Sperry (January 1760 -- 29 May 1838), who also died in Ross Co., OH.

Mary Harris Hammack

1870 Morgan Co., GA, Census, HH 1066/1066: Thomas O. Harris, 79, Farmer, $500/$225, VA; Mary F. Hammack, 29, Keeping House, GA.

At the time of the 1860 Morgan census, Thomas was living in HH 248/248. He was age 70, a farmer, and a native of Virginia. His property was valued at $1000/$1500. In his household were Mary, 22, GA; Susan, 20, GA, Alonzo, 18, GA; and Lucy, 16, GA.

Massachusetts Hammacks

1830 Index: No Hammacks or similar spellings

1840 Index:	N. S. Hamak	Worcester Co.	134	
	Nathan Hamak	Worcester Co.	134	
	John Hammack	Middlesex Co.	127	Charleston

1850 Index: No Hammacks or similar spellings

Mattidas Hammack and James B. Thompson

Matilda Hammack (1813 -- 1883, Cass Co., TX, bur. Pearl Hill Cemetery) married James B. Thompson (1810 -- 1880, Center Grove Cemetery, Cass Co., TX) on 20 June 1833 in Talbot Co., GA.

1860 Cass Co., TX, Census, Linden PO, HH 98/101: J. B. Thompson, 50, farmer, $1000/$400, GA; M., 47, GA; A. M. E., 20, female, GA; J., 17, female, GA; M. C., 10, female, AL; N. D., 6, female, AL. Their daughter Nancy D. Thompson (1853, AL --) married Thomas Washington Simmons (1 October 1852, SC --) in Cass Co., TX; she had six children between 1874 and 1885 -- Walter, Mary Ellen, James Franklin, Susan Elnor, Hattie, and Annie Eliza. Another daughter, Mary, married William Bailey Gholson, a native of Butler Co., AL, in Cass Co., TX.

Micajah Hammack of Wilkes Co., GA

1850 Wilkes Co., GA, Census, 94th Subdivision, p. 315, HH 421/417, near John W. Strozier, Parker Callaway, and James Huling: Micajah Hamok, 52, Farmer, GA; Elizabeth, 28, GA; Susannah L., 19, GA; Elizabeth, 12, GA; Mary, 10, GA; John, 8, GA; Lucinda, 6, GA; James, 1, GA. Note that this name does appear to read Micajah Hamok; Wilkes County marriages, however, show that Micajah Hancock married Elizabeth Lane on 4 August 1847.

Michael S. Hammack and Sarah Williams

Michael S. Hammack married Sarah Williams on 22 September 1836 in Talbot Co., GA.

Michael may belong to the John Hammock family or to the Joshua Hammock family. The following reference probably pertains to him: Newton Co July 1843 Term-Court of Ordinary, "It appearing to the Court that **Jesse Hammock** was appointed Administrator on the estate of **Michael Hammock**, deceased, by the Court of Harris County and that he is desirous of removing the business of the said estate to this County. It is therefore ordered that he give bond for the sum of $400 with **David Crawford** and **James M. Smith** as securities." Michael apparently died prior to July 1843 and had at that time been married for about six years. No further records of him have been found.

Nancy Hammick of Union Co., KY

1850 Union Co., KY, Census, p. 518, HH 821/821: Nancy Hammick, 57, $300, NC, living with Joseph French, 30, Laborer, France; J. Lynn, 60, Laborer, KY; John Hall, 25, Laborer, KY; Catherine Miller, 49, OH; James Edwards, 40, Boat Caulker, KY; A. Dickinson, 15, KY.

Nancy Hammack and Jesse Eubanks

Nancy Hammack married Jesse Eubanks on 24 December 1854 in Paulding Co., GA, which is directly west of Cobb County.

1860 Paulding Co., GA, Census, Dallas PO, HH 702/702: Jesse Eubanks, 45, Farmer, $350/$300, SC; Nancy, 40, GA; Thomas, 18, Farm Labor, SC; Rosa D., 17, SC; John, 16, SC; Drewsila, 4, SC; Caledonia, 3, GA.

1870 Paulding Co., GA, Census, Dallas PO, HH 230/230: Jesse Eubanks, 57, Farmer, $400/$150, GA; Nancy, 41, Keeping House, GA; Elizabeth, 14, GA.

Narcissa Hammack of Hood Co., TX

Elijah Hammack married Naricssa Luton. She had m. (1) John D. Hall, (2) Henry Grissom, (3) Elijah Hammock. She m. (4) John M. Taylor. All of her husbands were widowers.

Narcissa was a daughter of Jesse M. Luton and Mary P. Sims, who were living in Henderson Co., TX, by 1850.

1880 Hood Co., TX, Precinct 1, p. 18: Narcissa Hammock, 42, TN/TN/TN; Nora, 9, TX/--/--; Edwin, 7, TX/--/--; Nancy, 5, TX/--/--; Alice J., 2, TX/--/--; James M. Sims, 36, TN/TN/TN, Nephew.

1880 Hood Co., TX, Precinct 1, p. 12: Bettie Hammack, 11, TX/--/--. Bettie was living with Ben and Mattie Sargent and their son William; she is listed as Ben Sargent's sister-in-law. Sargent was 28, a native of GA, with both parents born in GA. Mattie was 17 and a native of TX; the birthplaces of her parents were omitted.[1864]

Narcissa Hammack of Lee Co., AL

John M. Hammock (c. 1833, GA --), m. Narcissa J. [-----] (c. 1837, GA --).

1860 Dale Co., AL, Census, HH 882/882: John M. Hammock, 27, Mechanic, $90/$600, GA; Narcissa J., 23, GA; Simeon H., 2, AL.

1880 Lee Co., AL, Census, Beat 2, HH 28/29: Narcissa Hammack, 42, Restraunter, AL/GA/GA; Remesis, 8, AL/AL/AL; Pearl, 6, AL/AL/AL.

[1864] Mattie J. Hammock was born 11 February 1862 in Van Zandt Co., TX. She died 30 June 1925. She married Benjamin Tate Sargent on 5 June 1852. They lived at Granbury, Hood Co., TX, where seven children were born between 1880 and 1894.

Remesis Hammack was enumerated in Montgomery Co., AL, in 1900. According to the index at www.heritagequestonline.com, Remesis (then spelled Remesus) was the only person in the United States with this name. He was in Montgomery County living with Laura A. Hicks (age 38), her niece Mary Cranford (age 25), and several different boarders, surnamed Dennis and Updike. Remesus A. Hammock was 28 years old, born November 1871 in Alabama, with a father born in GA and a mother born in AL. By 1910, Remesus was in Denver Co., CO, where he was working as an electrical engineer. He was still living there in 1920. In 1910 he had wife Anna G., 30, and daughters Marie M., 7, AL, and Agnes R., 6, AL. All three were still living in 1920.

Nathaniel Hammock

Nathaniel Hammock married 29 January 1824, Madison Co., AL, Elizabeth A. Hightower. Although indexed as Hamock, this person was actually Nathaniel Hancock (29 December 1802, Onslow Co., NC -- 19 June 1854, Bossier Parish, LA), who married Elizabeth Hightower (16 November 1801, VA --). They were in Limestone Co., AL, in 1838 when son Richard was born.

New York Hammacks

1830 Index:	Isaiah Hammick	Delaware County, p. 128, Meredith Twp.
1850 Index:	Eliz. Hammick	Delaware County, p. 63, Franklin.
	John Hammick	Albany County, p. 188, Albany.
	Benjamin Hamick	Charles County, p. 237, Harmony.

Obediah Hancock

1840 Virginia Census Index: Wythe County, Obediah Hamock, p. 106. Obediah *Hancock* was enumerated in Wythe Co., VA, in 1850, p. 336.

Polly Hemock and John Ruby

Some researchers maintain that Polly Hemock married 22 January 1824, Madison Co., AL, John Ruby. Ruby family researchers indicate, however, that John William Ruby (1800, PA -- 1854, Tate Co., MS) married Polly Hancock on 14 January 1824 in Madison Co., AL; they were parents of Joshua Green Ruby, born 1824, Madison Co., AL. Polly died, and John married Narcissa King on 11 November 1830 in Madison Co., AL.

Rebecca Hammack of Tallapoosa Co., AL

There is a Troup Co., GA, marriage record for John Hammoc, Jr., and Rebecca Fletcher on 11 April 1839. Could this be the same Rebecca who appears in the following record from the 1850 Tallapoosa Co., AL, Census, p. 79: Rebecca Hammock, 30, GA; John, 14, GA; Bird P., 11, GA.

Sarah Hammack (c. 1832, NC --) of Randolph Co., NC

1850 Guilford Co., NC, Census, p. 420, HH 691/691: Sarah Hammock, 18, Randolph Co., NC, living with Norus Mendenhall, Physician, in a house with twenty or so girls, most of whom were shown as students.

R. B. and Messer Hammock

1860 Franklin Co., AL, Census, HH 829/829: R. B. Hammock, 27, Day Labor, GA; Caroline, 23, TN; James W., 2, TN. The same census showed, in HH 830/830: Messer Hammock, 31, Day Labor, GA; Jane Hammock, 27, MS; Catharine Hammack, 7, AL; James, 5, GA; Thomas, 4, GA; Andy C., 1, AL. Messer married Ellen Jane Hill. (Note that this young son is Thomas Boston Hammock (1855-1937) who married (1) Elizabeth Byrd and (2) Nanny E. Fields; there was another son, William Frank Hammock, born in 1862, AL, who was living with John T. Gassaway at the time of the 1880 Franklin Co., AL, Census).

At the time of the 1880 census, Andrew Hammock, 20, was living with a Boggs family, as was Thomas Hammock, 22, and his wife Mary A. Hammock, 15. Mary A. Hammock is shown as the daughter of Boggs.

Thomas and family were in Hardin Co., TN, by 1880. They were living in HH 270/292: Thomas B. Hammock, March 1860, 39, AL/AL/AL; Nannie, May, 1877, 23, AL/AL/AL; Noel B., April 1886, 14, TN/AL/TN; James F., December 1887, TN/AL/TN; Benjamin P., August 1897, 2, Indian Territory/AL/TN. Thomas and family were still in Hardin County in 1910, by which time he had several additional children: David H., age 9, TN; Thomas J., age 6, AR; Cornie, age 4, TN; Ludie A., age 2 5/12, TN. Living next door, in HH 149/151, was James W. Hammock, 22, TN; wife Cora, 19, TN; and daughter Katie W., 1 7/12, TN.

Note that R. B., Sarah, and James W. all appear again in HH 712/712. He was aged 28; Sarah was 21; and James W. was 3. The birthplaces are the same in both enumerations. The family was enumerated in Frankfort both times.

Descendants claim that James Washington Hammock was born 9 September 1855 in Franklin Co., AL, and died 6 November 1927 in Irene, Hill Co., TX. He married Dutch Went Treadwell, daughter of James Harris Treadwell and Sarah Alabama French, who was born 5 August 1865 in Oklahoma and died 10 June 1924 in Waco, McLennan Co., TX. They were the parents of Henry Augustus Hammock (3 May 1885); James Rudolph Hammock (June 1888); George Hester Hammock (13 March 1890); Lutie Eloda Hammock (December 1892); Ira Jewell Hammock (December 1893); Dutch Hammock (December 1895); Dovie Hammock (February 1898); Sweetie Hammock (16 January 1900 --); Cody Hammock (10 August 1903 --); Kenneth Hammock; and Sarah Addie Hammock.

Dutch and James W. are said to have married in Oklahoma in 1884. They were living in Precinct 8, Hill Co., TX, in 1900; the 1900 census showed Games as a Georgia native with both parents born in Georgia. Duch was shown as a native of TX with father born in GA and mother in AL. All children were shown as natives of TX.

Richard D. Hammock

Richard D. Hammock, 40th GA Volunteer Infantry, Company F, Captured 16 May 1863, Baker's Creek, DE, and died July 1863, Fort Delaware, Delaware City, DE.

Robert Hambuck

The 1840 Arkansas census index shows Robert Hambuck living in Union Township, white Co., AR, in 1840, enumerated on page 246. This name was actually that of Robert Hambrick (10101-110001).

Robert Hammock of Clarke County, GA

This man, born by 1780, had a very close association with Willoughby Hammock. Willoughby appears in Franklin County in 1795 signing a bond with Jacob Laphrode as executor of one John Moore. It is possible that Robert was Willoughby's younger brother who did not come of age until about 1801.

1799: Willeby Hammack was taxed on page 40 of the Jackson County digest; Robert's name does not appear in the index, suggesting he was not yet of age or had not yet come to the area.

1801: Willoughby and Robert Hammock were taxed in Jackson Co., GA, pp. 4-5.

1802: Robert Hamock, poll; Williby Hamock, 202 acres, granted Maruberry, adjacent Easley, Clarke County, Apalatchee River, and 100 acres, granted Phillips, adjacent Hanbach, Clark County, Apalatchee River. Clarke County Tax Digest, p. 23.

1803: Robert Hammack, poll; Isaac Hamby, poll; Williby Hambrich, 202 acres and 700 acres.

1804: Willoughby Hammack was taxed with 202 acres in Clarke County; near him appear the names Robert Hamby, Isaac Hamby, and William Hamby. Clarke County Tax Digest, p. 69.

1805: Robert Hammock registered for Georgia Land Lottery in Clarke County, Registration Number 234, near Willoughby Hammock, registration number 232. Note that Robert, son of Benedict, appears in Wilkes County in this year, as does Robert, son of Robert and Millenor.

1805: Robert and Williby Hammock taxed in Clarke County, pp. 9-10. Robert Hammack paid poll tax only, while Williby was taxed with 202 acres granted Marbury.

1806: Robert and Williby Hammock taxed in Captain Williams's District, Clarke County, p. 136. Robert paid poll tax. Isaac Autry's name appeared between those of Williby and Robert. Williby paid tax on 199 acres granted Marbury and joining William Kelly.

1807: Robert and Willoby Hammock were taxed in Captain Robertson's District, Clarke County, p. 157. Robert paid poll tax only, while Willoby was taxed with 516 acres granted Marbury on Appalatchee River. Neighboring surnames included Bankston, Loyd, Tankersley, and McClendon. Most of these names later appeared in Clarke, Morgan, and Walton Counties.

16 December 1807: Willoughby Hammack purahxes 202.5 acres in LL 12, LD 11, from Isaac and Mary Tucker for $300; Eliajh Gentry, Arter Bearden, and David Neal witnessed the deed. See Jasper Co., GA, DB 1, pp. 526-527.

28 April 1808: Willeby Hammack purchases land in Randolph (later Jasper) Co., GA, in LL 36, LD 18, from Gilbert Gay with Thomas Paxton, Joseph Dixon, and Alexander McKey as witnesses. See Jasper Co., GA, DB 1, p. 476.

19 September 1809: Robert Hamnott of Randolph Co., GA, purchases land in LL 215, LD 19, for $400 from William Phillips of Randolph County, 202.5 acres, located on Murder Creek. Jesse Evans and Solomon Stricklin witnessed the deed. Jasper Co., GA, DB 1, p. 447. Note that on 4 July 1809, one William Hamnott witnessed a power of attorney, along with Jane Phillips and William Phillips, from Captain Isaac Phillips of Randolph County to Captain Gilbert Gray of Randolph County to recover a

slave woman left in the care of William Tarvin. Jasper Co., GA, DB 1, pp. 502-503. Note that Willoughby Hammack had purchased land from Gilbert Gay in 1808.

10 October 1809: Willoby Hammock of Randolph County purchases 105 acres in LL 181, LD 19, from Roderick Easley of Clarke County. Jasper Co., GA, DB 1, p. 525.

Jasper County tax digests for this period have not survived. As a result, it has not been possible to determine if Robert Hammack moved to Jasper County (perhaps his name was shown incorrectly in the above deed as Hamnott?). Robert was born by about 1779 and died after 1807; he could have moved into Walton Co., GA, Tennessee and Kentucky, or southern Alabama, where there is some difficulty placing Hammack, Hammock, and Hammac families, or he could have died childless. More research should be undertaken to determine what became of him.

Robert Hammock and Jane Perry of Crawford Co., GA

CRAWFORD COUNTY, GA, MARRIAGE BOOKS SHOW THE FOLLOWING:[1865]

James E. Hammock to Elizabeth Whittington, 19 December 1841.
Robert Hamock to Mary Jane Perry, 19 December 1844.
Sarah Hamock to Mark F. Perry, 27 January 1850.

NOTE that James was probably born about 1820, Robert about 1822, and Sarah about 1830. These individuals have not been identified, and it is not clear whether their surname was actually Hammack or another, such as Hancock, that is sometimes mistaken for it.

Roxa, James, and John Hammack of Cass Co., TX

These individuals were a mystery for some time but have now been identified. The research began with the following information:

1880 Cass Co., TX, Census, ED 12, p. 142: William F. Martin, 36, Farmer, GA/GA/GA; Wilanta, 40, Keeping House, GA/GA/GA; Emma, 14, At Home, GA/GA/GA; Colquitt, 12, Works on Farm, GA/GA/GA; Ida, 10, GA/GA/GA; William, 3, TX/GA/GA; Roxa Hammack, 24, At Home, GA/GA/GA; James W. Hammack, 20, Works on Farm, GA/GA/GA; John J. Hammack, 18, Works on Farm, GA/GA/GA. The three Hammacks are listed as step-children of William Martin.

Descendants claim that Roxie Elizabeth Hammack (1855, GA -- 10 January 1920, Hughes Spring, Cass Co., TX) married James Samuel Fletcher (1844-1917) on 29 December 1881 in Cass Co., TX. They were living in Cass Co., TX, in 1900. Also living nearby was William F. Martin, a widower, who was living with is daughter Ada L. Terry. The Texas Death Index indicated that Ada Lee Terry (1872-1956) died in Cass Co., TX, and that she was a daughter of William Martin and Welindy Katherine Woodall.

The 1860 Twiggs Co., GA, Census, HH 363/363, showed William J. Hammock, 25, Farmer, $1800/$950, GA; Wylantie C., 20; Roxie A. E., 5; Mary A. M., 2; and James W. S., age 4/12. Living with the family was Caroline Ryal, age 9. In HH 366/366 was William F. Martin, age 17, son of James W. Martin, age

[1865] William R. Henry, comp., *Marriage Records of Crawford County, Georgia: Marriage Books "A-1, A-2, A-2C, A-4, B, C, & 5.", 1823-1899. Other Marriage Records, 1825-1873 from Other Probate Court Records, The Macon Messenger, & Loose Files at State Archives* (Warner Robins, Ga.: Central Georgia Genealogical Society, Inc. 1989).

42, GA. These families were living in GMD 355 Twiggs Co., GA, which lies on the boundary between Twiggs and Bibb Counties and is just south of Jones Co., GA.[1866]

William J. Hammack was a son of James Hammack of Twiggs Co., GA. The family was enumerated in Twiggs Co., GA, in the 1850 census, p. 164, HH 98/98: James Hammack, 43, Farmer, $4000, GA; Ann J., 23, GA; Amanda, 18, GA; Louisa, 17, GA; William J., 15, Farmer, GA; Jain, 13, GA; James M., 11, GA; Masoura, 9, GA; John A., 6, GA; Albert J., 4, GA; Henry J., 2, GA; Elijah F., 1, GA; A. Bruford, 25, Farmer, male, GA.

William J. Hammock died during the American Civil War on 25 June 1862 at King's School House, Virginia, and Wylantie married (2) her neighbor William F. Martin. They were living in Texas by 1870. They were enumerated in Hickory Hill District, Davis Co., TX, p. 33, HH 55/55, at the time of the 1870 Census: William F. Martin, 27, GA, Farmer; Willanta, 30, GA; Roxey Hamock, 14, Georgia; Mary Hamock, 12, Georgia; James Hamock, 10, Georgia; John Hamock, 8, Georgia; Emma Martin, 5, Georgia; Colquit Martin, 3, Georgia; and Ida Martin, 3/12, Texas.

Of the other children of William J. and Wylantie Woodall Hammack, James W. may have been living in Ward 8, Sabine Parish, LA, in 1910, HH 9/12, where he was enumerated as follows: James W. Hammack, 50, married 24, GA/GA/GA; Helen, 40, married 24, 6/6, TX/KY/GA; Maud, 23, TX; Lerah, 20, TX; Nona, 18, TX; Thomas W., 15, TX; Herbert, 13, TX; Jimmie, 7, female, TX.

John J. Hammack, youngest of the Hammack siblings, died 29 January 1936 in Pittsburg, TX. His death certificate showed that he was born 28 December 1861 in Alabama and that he was buried in Willow Oak Cemetery. His mother's name was given as Amanda Hammack, and no father's name was indicated. Wife Sallie Hammock supplied information for the certificate. She was born in 1862 in Mississippi and died 27 January 1948 in Gilmer, Upshur Co., TX, but was buried in Willow Oak Cemetery. John J. Hammack was living in Pittsburg, Camp Co., TX, at the time of the 1920 census, where he was shown as John J. D. Hammack, age 58, GA, with wife Sallie, age 58, MS. In 1910, the family was living in Upshur Co., TX. John J. Hammack was age 48, GA, with wife Sallie, age 49, MS. Two of their four children were then living. In the household was son William J. Hammack, age 24, widower, with his infant daughter Virlie B., age 2, TX. At the time of the 1900 Upshur Co., TX, Census, John D. Hammack, born December 1861, GA, was shown with Wife Sarah A., born May 1861, MS, and children Manda W., born December 1885, TX, and William, born May 1887, TX.[1867]

S. Hammack of Logan Co., KY

Published census indices show S. Hammack enumerated on page 33 of the 1820 Logan Co., KY, census. No such person has been located on the actual census.

Samuel Hammack (abt. 1830-aft. 1860) of Muscogee County

[1866] Wylanta Catherine Woodall Hammack Martin was apparently a daughter of James W. Woodall of Bibb and Twiggs Counties. He was enumerated in HH 535/435 in Twiggs County in 1860, age 46, with wife Mary age 42, and son James W. F., age 15. They were enumerated in Bibb Co., GA, HH 82/84, in 1850 as James Woodall, 36; Mary, 30; Catherine, 10; Mary A., 7; and James F., 6. They were living in GMD 514, which is on the boundary of Bibb, Jones, and Twiggs Counties.

[1867] TX Death Certificates show that Willie Jackson Hammack died 3 February 1919 in Ewell Upshur Co., TX, and that he was a son of J. J. Hammack, a native of Georgia, and Sallie Hodge, a native of Choctaw Co., MS. He was 32 years old, and the informant for the certificate was his father, J. J. Hammack, of Pittsburgh, TX. Amanda Wylanda Hammack Arnold, born 14 December 1884 in Hughes Springs, Cass Co., TX, died 26 September 1959 in Longview, Gregg Co., TX. Her death certificate shows that she was a daughter of John Hammack and Sarah Hodges and that she was buried in Gilmer City Cemetery, Gilmer, Upshur Co., TX.

Some believe that Samuel Hammack was a son of James Hammack and Mary Pollard. He married 8 July 1843, Muscogee Co., GA, Rebecca A. Pearson.

1860 Muscogee Co., GA, Census, Shingle Hill, Columbus, p. 322, HH 190/190: Samuel Hammock, 30, $1,000/$100, AL; Rebecca, 25, GA; Thomas J., 16, GA; Andrew J., 14, GA; Sarah F., 12, GA; Samuel, 7, GA;[1868] Rebecca, 4, GA; Mary A., 2, GA.

Sarah Hammock and Thomas Johnson

Sarah Hammock married Thomas Johnson 12 December 1867 in Tallapoosa Co., AL.

Sarah Hammack and William Gresham

Sarah Hammack married William Gresham on 19 May 1850 in Wilkes County, Georgia.

Seaborn Hammack of Alabama

1850 Perry Co., AL, Census, Plantersville, HH 50: Jacob Hammock, 53, Farmer, $620, GA; Hannah, 52, GA; Lewis J., 28, GA; Catherine, 27, AL; Jacob W., 11, AL; Martha, 9, AL.

Note that this Jacob Hammack had married Hannah Jones on 28 January 1817 in Jones Co., GA, and was a son of Lewis Hammack and a grandson of Robert and Millenor Jackson Hammack. Hannah was living in Mississippi in 1860 with son Lewis, although some family members returned to Crawford Co., GA, after Jacob died about 1850. In the next household appeared the following:

1850 Perry Co., AL, Census, Plantersville, HH 51: Seaborn Hammock, 50, GA, Farmer, $1,500; Sarah J., 28, NC; John, 19, AL; James, 17, AL; Henry, 15, AL; Susan S., 11, AL; Thomas, 3, AL; William, 1, AL.

Jacob Hammack was living in Dallas Co., AL, in 1840 (census p. 52), while Seaborn Hamick was living in Perry Co., AL (census p. 254), in the same year:

> Seaborne Hamick (or Harrick)
> 1 m under 5 1 f under 5
> 2 m 5/10 1 f 10/15
> 1 m 10/15 1 f 15/20
> 1 m 15/20 1 f 20/30
> 1 m 40/50 1 f 30/40

This man is a mystery. His close physical proximity with Jacob Hammack suggests a link to the Lewis Hammack family. Another Seaborn Hammack, son of Robert and Nancy Combs Hammack, was in Wilkes County from before 1800 until he moved in the 1840s to Coweta Co., GA. This man does not appear to have been in that area. One Seaborn Hamoik of Burney's District, Jasper Co., GA, drew LL 167, LD 12, Henry County, at the time of the 1821 Georgia Land Lottery. He has not been traced.

[1868] Samuel James Hammock was born 10 March 1850; he married Laura Corbitt in 1892, Wood Co., TX. She was born 3 May 1876. Samuel James died 22 July 1936 in Amarillo, Potter Co., TX. Laura died 5 June 1960 in Sunset, Wise Co., TX. They were parents of several children, all born in Wood County, TX: Mary Rosalee; Virgil James; Lillie Ann; Ovie; Lizzie Florence; Claudie William; Jesse Bee; Lollie Rebecca; Maude Ella.

Susan Hammack and William James Graham

Susan Hammock married William James Graham 8 April 1855, Upson Co., GA. Individuals researching this family indicate that the name should be Susan Hancock. The 1860 Upson Co., GA, Census, Thomaston PO, HH 220/199, showed: Wm. Graham, 27, Overseer, $80, GA; Susan, 24, GA; T. S. Graham, 4, GA; E. H. Hancock, 28, female, Serving, GA. The family was still in Upson in 1870.

Thomas Hammack (c. 1830, GA --).

1860 Calcasieu Parish, LA, Census, p. 180, HH 400/420: Thomas Hammock, 30, Blacksmith, $250, GA; Nancy, 27, AL; George, 8, LA; William, 5, LA; Susan, 3, LA; Ann, 1, LA; Nancy Hodge, 20, LA.

At the time of the 1870 Calcasieu Parish, LA, census, Polly Hammock, 34, LA, was found in Lake Charles PO, HH 368/368. With her was George Hammack, age 12, LA. William, age 11, was in Lake Charles, HH 590/590, as a servant for James Nicholson. The 1880 census gave William's age was 22; he was in the 3rd ward of Calcasieu with a 15-year old wife named Minerva.

Thomas J. Hammack of Erath Co., TX

1880 Erath Co., TX, Census, ED 152, p. 74: Thomas J. Hammack, 24, Farming, TX/GA/KY; Martha M., 20, Keeping House, TX/TN/TN.

1900 Erath Co., TX, Census, JP-4, HH 317/333: Thomas Hammack, February 1856, 44, TX/GA/AL; Mollie, January 1860, 40, TX/TX/TX; m. 22 years; 1 of 2 children living.

1910 Erath Co., TX, Census, JP-4, HH 215/215: Mattie M. Hammack, 50, Widowed, Mother-in-law, TX/US/US, living with Albert L. McAlley, 30, TX, and wife Rebecca, 28, TX. The McAlleys had four children, all then living.

Also in Erath County in 1880, Precinct 4, HH 143/143, were: Thomas J. Hamic, 35, Farming, AR/__/__; Sarah J., 33, AL/__/AL; Mary M., 12, TX; William T,. 10, TX; James C., 9, TX; Charles 5, TX; John T., 3, TX; Frances L. E., 3/12, February, TX. The 1900 census of Precinct 4, Erath Co., TX, HH 49/65 showed: Thos. J. Hamic, November 1844, 55, AR/AL/AL; S. J., April 1847, 53, AL/AR/AR, married 33 years, 8 of 8 children living; Charlie, June 1874, 25, TX; George, October 1883, TX; Annie, June 1899, TX; Mollie Tutt, June 1867, TX, Widowed, Daughter.

Troup County Hammacks

These names have been listed in published indices as Hammack, but on close inspection they appear to be Hannah. This identification (Hannah) matches location of some of these same individuals in the 1870 and 1880 census reports also.

1860 Troup Co., GA, LaGrange, GA, p. 327, 18 July (film very dim and difficult to read), HH 1056/983: N. B. Hannah, 31, Mechanic, GA; J. B., 25, female, GA; S. A., 8, male, GA; M. R., 6, female, GA.

1860 Troup Co., GA, Census, LaGrange, GA, HH 1057/984: J. R. Hannah, 32, Mechanic, GA; S. E., 30, female, GA; J. R., 12, male, GA; W. T., 11, male, GA; L.A., 8, male, GA; J. M., 6, male, GA; S. A., 5, female, GA; J. H., 9/12, male, GA.

1860 Troup Co., GA, Census, LaGrange, GA, HH 1058/965: William Hannah, 54, Mechanic, SC; M. R., 54, SC.

The 1870 Troup census, HH 227/235, shows William Hannah, 64, Butcher, $1000/$200, GA; Malinda, 64, Keeping House, GA; Alford, 40, Day Work, GA. There were five Liman children living with the family. William, age 74, was still alive in Troup in 1880; George Lynam was living with him. Also in LaGrange was Leroy Hannah, age 28, and wife Mary, 26. The 1870 Troup Census, HH 698/629, O'Neal's Mill, shows James Hanner, 43, GA; Sophonia, 40, GA; Matthew, 15, GA; Doliska, 13, GA; Dalton, 10, GA; Anna, 9, GA; Augustus, 5, GA; Minnie, 2, GA; and Leroy, 17, GA.

Tump Hammack

Roscoe Davis recalled hearing of Tump Hammack as a relative, but her identity is not certain.

1905: Bethel Baptist Church minutes record death of Tump Hammack. Tump is unidentified. The name appears on the list of female members.

W. H. Hemmick of Alexandria Co., VA, m. Caroline Tatsapaugh

1850 Alexandria Co., VA, Census: Benjamin Hammack, p. 310, HH 651: John Tatsapaugh, 60, Merchant, VA; Charles R., 22, VA; John P., 20, VA; Joseph W., 18, VA; W. H. Hemmick,[1869] 24, MD, no occupation; Caroline, 26, VA; Rowland F., 4, VA; George Fore, 21, VA, black.

William Hammack of Macon Co., AL

This William Hammack was enumerated in Macon Co., AL, in 1850, aged 35, with wife Mary, aged 30, and six children:

1. Sarah Hammack (c. 1838, GA – aft. 1850, Macon Co., AL).
2. William Hammack (c. 1840, GA – aft. 1850, Macon Co., AL).
3. James Hammack (c. 1842, GA – aft. 1850, Macon Co., AL).
4. Eliza Hammack (c. 1844, AL – aft. 1850, Macon Co., AL).
5. Jane Hammack (c. 1846, AL – aft. 1850, Macon Co., AL).
6. John Hammack (c. 1848, AL – aft. 1850, Macon Co., AL).

Based upon the location in which he was living, this William was probably a grandson of John Hammack of Lincoln County, Georgia, but his precise placement in that family is unknown.

William Hammock (c. 1816, TN --) of Pike Co., AR

1850 Pike Co., AR, Census, Missouri Township, p. 197, HH 276/276: William Hammock, 34, Farmer, TN; Mary, 30, TN; W. J., 9, male, AL; Thomas J., 6, male, AR; Hester A., 4, female, AR; John M., 2, male, AR. In HH 280/280 was Moses Brock, 47, TN, and wife Mahala. NOTE that Pike is SW of Hot Springs near the present day boundary between Arkansas, Oklahoma, and Texas. In HH 275/275 was Moses Brock, 34, TN;

[1869] William H. Hemmick m. 21 August, 1848, Alexandria, VA, Caroline R. Tatsapaugh, daughter of John Tatsapaugh. Bondsmen: William H. Hemmick, John Tatsapaugh. From T. Michael Miller, *Alexandria and Alexandria (Arlington) Co., VA, Ministers Returns and Marriage Bonds, 1801-1852.*

Kezziar, 32, GA; William F., 2, AR; and Lenard N., 2/12, AR.[1870] Moses Brock (1803-1888) was from Grainger Co., TN and a son of George Brock and Amy Dyer; he married Zipporah Dennis there in 1822 and Mahala Dyer there in 1833. Eleven children were born in Grainger County between 1823 and 1842. He was a first cousin of Sarah Brock (daughter of Moses Brock and Susannah Dyer) who married William Hammock in 1801 in Grainger County. Scattered throughout the neighborhood in 1850 are several other Dyer and Brock families from Tennessee living in close proximity to William Hammock.

William Hammick of Paulding Co., GA

William was enumerated with his family on page 832 of the 1860 Paulding County census. They were living in HH 871/871: William Hammick, 41, Farmer, $600/$200, TN; Dilpha, 40, GA; Richard, 17, Farm Laborer, GA; Sarah, 12, GA; James N., 4, GA. This name is difficult to read and was either Hammick or Hamrick.

William Hamock or Hancock of Tattnall County, GA

1820 Tattnall Co., GA, Census, p. 117:

Emanuel Hammock	1m 0-10	4f 0-10
	1m 10-16	1f 10-16
	1m 26-45	1f 26-45
Wm. Hamock (or Hancock)	2m 0-10	3f 0-10
	1m 26-45	3 (or 5) f 10-16
		1f 26-45

This William was probably surnamed Hancock, for no references to a William Hammock before or afterwards have been located in Tattnall County.

William Hammack of Lee Co., AL

This man was apparently the son of William and Rutha Hammack and the grandson of John Hammack of Lincoln Co., GA.

1870 Lee Co., AL, Census, Loachapoka PO, HH 192/192: W. B. Hammick, 53, Farming, $3000/$1000, GA; Sarah, 45, H. Keeping, GA; S. E., 17, female, AL; W. D., 17, male, AL; Pasch, 15, male, AL; J. D., 12, male, AL; W. W., 10, male, AL: R. E. L., 7, male, AL; J. C., 5, male, AL; E. E., 2, female, AL.

1880 Lee Co., AL, Census, Beat 5, p. 129, Loachapoka, HH 256/294: William Hammack, 60, GA/GA/GA; Elizabeth, 50, GA/GA/GA; Eugene, 25, female, AL/GA/GA; John, 20, AL/GA/GA; Wesley, 19, AL/GA/GA; Lee, 17, AL/GA/GA; Inez, 10, AL/GA/GA; Joe, 12, AL/GA/GA; Paschal, 23, AL/GA/GA.

The history of this family is greatly clarified by F. W. Johnson and E. W. Winkler, *A History of Texas and Texans* (5 vols., 1914), 4: 2091-2093:

> REV. WILLIAM D. HAMMACK. The life record of Rev. "William D. Hammack since his coming to Kaufman county in 1874, is one notable not alone for his achievements in the fields of agriculture and finance, but also for his long and zealous service in the work of his Master. Coming here with but little save his youthful strength of heart, ambition and determination to win, he has accumulated a

---

[1870] Note that Sarah Brock Hammock had a brother named Leonard Brock, son of Moses Brock. Moses who married Keziah is believed to have been a son of Sarah Hammock's brother Leonard Brock.

handsome financial competency and has gained also what few men achieve, the esteem and love of those with whom he has passed so many years. Rev. Hammack was born in Lee county, Alabama, February 15, 1853, and was reared on a small farm and in an upright though humble home. His father was William B. Hammack, who owned a few slaves and identified himself with Alabama in the flush of young manhood. He was born in Georgia in 1826, and it is believed that he left his native state about the year 1840, although the early separation of our subject from his parents and his continued living apart from them precluded his acquiring data regarding the identity of his forebears of the intimate facts of his immediate family. William B. Hammack married a neighbor girl, Miss Susan Ligon, and they passed their lives within a quarter of a mile of where they established their first home. Mr. Hammack, in .some manner, acquired a liberal education, for he taught school in young manhood and was fitted for equal competition with his fellow farmers in the race of life. He entered the Confederate army while the war between the south and north was in progress and was with General Pemberton's troops when they surrendered at Vicksburg in 1863. He was a supporter of democratic principles, and in his religious belief was a devout Missionary Baptist. He and his wife were the parents of the following children: Eugenia, who married Robert Short and died at Columbus, Georgia; William D., whose name introduces this review; Pascal H., who died at Abilene, Texas; John D., who is carrying on operations on the old family home in Alabama; Lee, who resides at Columbus, Georgia; Villis W., who passed away at Crandall, Texas; Joseph, who died at Abilene, Texas; and Inez, who is the wife of Robert McKinney, of Young county, Texas.

William D. Hammack was urged by the spirit of empire to seek the West in his youth. He left home with the blessings of his parents at the age of nineteen years and went by rail from Loachapoka, Alabama, to New Orleans, where he took passage on a Mississippi steamer for Jefferson, Texas, reaching that point after some ten days of travel. He and his companion, Robert McKinney, who subsequently became his brother-in-law, boarded a Dallas freight ox-wagon at Jefferson and spent about ten days covering the distance between that old historic town and the future metropolis at the forks of the Trinity. Their destination was Collin county, where Mr. McKinney's people lived, and the morning following his arrival Mr. Hammack started the serious part of his independent career.

As a beginning, Mr. Hammack accepted employment with a farmer, Henry Smith, in Dallas county, at nine dollars a month, and remained with him for a period of three months. His next employer was J. E. Garrett, who appreciated his services to the extent of paying him twenty-five dollars for two months' work, and the next eix months he spent with William Housley, at twenty dollars per month, which concluded his first year of life in Texas. During these several months he improved an opportunity looking toward a life companionship, and in November, 1873, when but twenty years of age, be married.

Mr. Hammack began the year 1874 as a hand at twenty dollars per month and board for " the two" with Joe Sullivan and closed the year with the suggestion of a "nest-egg" which made an end of his career as a farm laborer. In 1874 he rented land in that locality and in the fall moved into Kaufman county with his few family effects and his one horse, which later he had the misfortune to lose. The next two years he worked on shares with P. E. Yates, and but of his profits equipped himself with a team, and, for the first time, exercised some independence as a farmer. He then began renting land for the "third and fourth" and continued it until 1885, when, having accumulated a small bunch of cattle and a little surplus money, he moved to Hamilton county, Texas, with the hope of becoming, some da}', a cattle baron of Central Texas. Just what happened to alter his plans so suddenly does not appear, but within ten months after his departure from Kaufman county he was back here, minus his stock and some of his money, but, with commendable perseverance, ready to recuperate his losses behind the plow. Subsequently he bargained for a small tract of land three miles north of Crandall, a property containing fifty-, five acres, which he could have purchased some years before at five dollars an acre—and for which he had possessed the money—but for which he now paid thirty dollars an acre, giving five notes for the balance of the purchase money. The little house on the farm sheltered his family and served as his home, with its changes and its successor, for many years, and here he witnessed some of the most prosperous years of his active life. He brought the tract all under cultivation, purchased the five notes as they came due, added other lands to his tax values from time to time and eventually accumulated two hundred and fifty acres, which, with other material possessions, form the substantial character of his holdings at the present time.

In 1899 Mr. Hammack moved into Crandall and for a few years remained in active conduct of his rural affairs from this point. He was one of the early settlers of the new towns, and built his home and a brick business house as his contribution to the development of the community. He is vice president of the First National Bank of Crandall and a member of its official board. While he has accomplished with much credit the task of rearing and educating his family, he has not neglected the spiritual side of man's nature. He was reared in a home where Christian influence prevailed, but his own conversion was delayed until 1874, when at a meeting at Big Springs, near Dallas, his heart was touched under the preaching of Rev. Lockhart and he surrendered and offered his services in some manner to the forces striving against sin. A voice called him to preach, and he qualified by ordination in 1887 at the Mount Calvary church, north of Crandall. He entered actively into the work of pastor and into the auxiliary work of the church and filled several charges about the country, including a service of eight years as pastor of the church where he was ordained. He continued the work until 1910, when his physical condition rendered him incapable of effective and efficient service and he abandoned active connection with the ministry as well as his business affairs. He was a member of the East Fork Baptist Association, which co-operated with the Church party during the split in the Baptist church of Texas.

Mr. Hammack married Miss Mary E. Rogers, whose father spent his last years and died in Scott County, Texas. She was born near Forrest. Mississippi, in 1854, and she and her husband became the parents of the following children: Russell P., a farmer of Kaufman County, who married Maggie McShann; Henry M., who is engaged in farming near Kemp, Texas; John D., a resident of Groesbeck. Texas, who married Lula Tyra; and Martha, who is Mrs. J. W. Webb, of Bosque County, Texas. The mother of these children died in 1892. On January 4, 1893, in Kaufman county, Mr. Hammack married the second time, Mrs. J. M. Yates, who was Ruth Seaberry; a daughter of Oliver and Susan (Harper) Seaberry, native of Georgia. The father was a prominent planter and farmer. By her first marriage the present Mrs. Hammack had seven children, five of whom are living, two dying in infancy. Although retired from active participation in business affairs, Mr. Hammack still evinces a keen interest in all that affects the welfare of his community, where his well-known integrity, probity and force of character give him a distinct influence in the forming of public opinion.

William B. Hammack married Susannah Liggon on 13 April 1848 in Chambers Co., AL. Nowel N. Liggon witnessed the marriage. Texas Death Certificate 20304 shows that William David Hammack, born 15 February 1853, son of William Hammack and Susie Liggen, died on 24 September and was buried 25 September 1915 in Crandall, Kaufman Co., TX. Informant was his son John Hammack, of Crandall.

1880 Kaufman Co., TX, Census, District 35, Precinct 2, p. 70: William Hammack, 25, Farming, AL/AL/AL; Mary, 25, Keeping House, MS/MS/AL; Russell, 6, At Home, TX/AL/MS; Martha, 5, At Home, TX/AL/MS; Henry, 3, TX/AL/MS.

William was still living in Kaufman County in 1900; he was shown as W. D. Hammack and was enumerated with his second wife, Ruth.

William D. Hammack was the father of : Henry Marsailes Hammack (1876-1944), Russell Hammack (1873-1962), Maggie Hammack McShane, John D. Hammack (1883-1927), and Martha Hammack Webb. This family remained in Kaufman Co., TX.

William J. Hammack of Lowndes Co., MS

1840 Mississippi Census: William J. Hammuck, Lowndes County, p. 191. William was aged 30-40 and had no other individuals in his household.

William Hammack of Jefferson Co., IL

1830 Illinois Census Index: William Hammack, Jefferson Co., IL, p. 224. William's household included 2 males aged 20-30; 1 female aged 15-20; 1 female aged 30-40.

William Hammack of Jackson Co., MS

1900 Jackson Co., MS, Census, Beat 1 NE, 38-4-68: William Hammock, October 1860, AL; Caroline, January 1867, AL; William F. Downing, 70, AL; Edgar Williams, 14, AL. William Downing is listed as of no relation to the Hammocks.

William E. Hammock and Martha Moore

"Other Marriage Records, 1825-1873," Crawford Co., GA, Marriages, pp. 98, 103:

William E. Hammack to Martha Moore, 20 Apr., 1849, *Macon Messenger.*

William Hammack of Baltimore Co., MD

The 1860 Baltimore Co., MD, Census, 12th Ward, p. 945, HH 1547/1791 shows Elizabeth Wright, 57, MD; Mary A. Audl, 30, MD; Emanuel Thomas, 28, MD; Francis Smith, 30, Tailor, MD: and *William Hammack, 9, MD.*

William Hammacks of New Jersey and Maryland

1860 Baltimore Co., MD, Census, Reisterstown PO, 4th District, p. 153, HH 70/65: William Hammacks, 50, Laborer, NJ; Mary, 45, NJ; George N., 21, VA; Isaac, 19, TN; Eli, 16, TN; Mary J., 11, MD; William, 8, MD; Francis M., 6, MD; 3 boarders.

Willoughby Hammack of Georgia and Kentucky

1850 Caldwell Co., KY, Census, p. 315, HH 519/519: Willoughby Hammack, 46, Farmer, GA; Jane, 42, KY; Nancy, 17, Caldwell County, KY; Mary, 12, TN; Jason, 10, TN; Marion, 8, TN; Thomas, 3, TN. According to HFH, 2: 1919, Marion married Mary S. Walker and Thomas married Nettie Sarden.

Wilson H. Hammock of Hines County, Mississippi

I have speculated in the genealogical report that Wilson H. Hammock might have been a son of Jacob and Hannah Hammack of Georgia, Alabama, and Mississippi. He has not been conclusively identified. He was living in Union Parish, LA, in 1853, where he was postmaster of the Shiloh Post Office (Charles R. Rode, United States Post Office Directory and Postal Guide, New York, 1853) and was living in central Alabama by the early 1860s, when he served in Lewis's Battalion, Company D, Alabama Cavalry, during the Civil War. He was living in Hinds County, Mississippi, during the 1870s and remained there for the rest of his life. His family's later association with the family of William T. H. Hammack suggests that he might be closely related to the Jones County – Crawford County, Georgia, Hammack group, but more research should be done. The family of Thomas and Matilda Hammock of Chambers County, Alabama, had several connections to Union Parish, Louisiana, and also used the name Wilson on one occasion.

Zachariah Hammock

Zachariah Hammack was a son of J. T. Hammock who married Martha Ingram on 27 March 1871 in Johnson Co., TX. His grandparents Solomon Crosby Ingram and Elizabeth Payne had moved from Georgia to Jefferson Co., AL, to MS, AR, and TX. Martha Ingram Hammock m. (2) [------] Stephen sand (3) 18 November 1885, Johnson Co., TX, M. L. Benton.

1880 Johnson Co., TX, Census, Precinct 5, p. 348: Z. Hammock, 8, TX/GA/GA. Z. is shown as a grandson of S. and E. Ingram, natives of GA and NC. Other grandchildren included Fannie Stevens and Effie McNeal. Several members of the household were born in AR.

Texas Death Certificate Number 92142 shows that Zachariah Abraham Hammock died 14 December 1969, age 98, in Wichita Falls and was a son of Martha Ingram Hammock. He was born July 1, 1871, in Granbury, Texas.

Rudolph Hammack of Virginia

Rudolph Hammack (by c. 1743 -- bef. 10 November 1783, Frederick Co., VA), m. Elizabeth [--------] (c. 1743 – aft. c. 1806, Frederick Co., VA).

Rudolph's origins are uncertain. He could connect to the family of William Hammack of Richmond County, but that seems doubtful. He may have been of German origin and might have been an immigrant to the American colonies himself. There was a Jacob Hammock who served as a Revolutionary soldier in New Jersey, a Thomas Hammock who did so in Connecticut, and an Isaac Hammock who was living in Connecticut in the years just after the Revolution ended. Perhaps Rudolph connects to one of these groups.

From my own research, there is only one reference to Rudolph Hammack, progenitor of this line, in Frederick Co., VA, Deeds up to 1789:

> Frederick Co., VA, DB 13, p. 126: 31 July, 1769, Isaac Riddle and George Bowman, acting executor of the Last Will and Testament of George Bowman, deceased, to Rudy Hammack, of Frederick Co., VA, for 5 shillings, 400 acres, on a branch of the North Shenandoah and Crooked Run. Wit: John Worth, Abraham Bowman, Joseph Bowman.

1787 Virginia Census (Yantis):

FREDERICK CO.

Elizabeth Hammock* self	0	0	0	5	12

1800 Frederick Co., VA, Tax List (*The Virginia Genealogist*, 23:266):

Rudy Hammack	1-3
Elizabeth Hammack	1-3

1820 Virginia Census Index:

Hampshire County	Jacob Hammack, p. 224A, and John Hammock, p. 266A.

1830 Virginia Census Index

Frederick County	Jacob Hammock p. 62	Eastern Division
	Samuel S. Hammock p. 62	Eastern Division
Hampshire County	Jacob Hammak	p. 24
	Samuel Hammack	p. 28

1840 Virginia Census Index:

Hampshire County	Jacob Hammack p. 176	
	Jane Hammack	p. 197
	John Hammack	p. 176
Warren County	Jacob Hammilk	p. 185
	Jacob Hammick	p. 185

Descendants of Rudolph Hammack:

1. John Hammack (c. 1765, VA -- aft. 1850, Hampshire Co., VA), m. 18 April 1788, Frederick Co., VA, Catherine Cline (c. 1763, VA -- aft. 1850, Hampshire Co., VA).

Kerns, *Historical Records of Old Frederick and Hampshire Counties, VA* (Revised, Bowie, MD: Heritage Books, Inc., 1992), pp. 38, shows that in 1813 John Hammack was one of fifteen horse breeders in Hamsphire Co., VA.

1850 Hampshire Co., VA, Census, HH 232/232: John Hammack[1871], 85, Farmer, $1,500, VA; Catherine, 87, VA.

John's will was written 7 August 1782 and proved 24 April 1854 in Hampshire Co., VA. Children named in his will were:

1-1. Abraham Hammack (c. 1806, Frederick Co., VA -- aft. 1850, Hampshire Co., VA).

1850 Hampshire Co., VA, Census, HH 233/233: Abraham Hammack, 44, Farmer, VA; Maria, 40, VA; Sarah Ann, 20, VA; John, 18, Laborer, VA; Abraham, 14, VA; Harriett J., 13, VA; Isaac, 5, VA.

1860 Hampshire Co., VA, Census, Hanging Rock PO, p. 1, HH 6/6: Abraham Hammack, 53, Farmer, $2,500/$690, VA; Maria, 47, VA; Isaac, 18, Farmer, OH. In HH 5/5: John Hammack, Jr., 29, Miller, $84, VA; Ann J., 22, VA; James M., 3, VA; John F., 1, VA.

1870 Hampshire Co., WV, Census, Bloomery Township, p. 454, HH 37/37: Maria Hammack, 65, FA, living with the family of Amos and Eliza Johnson, age 63 and 59, both natives of VA.

1-1-1. Sarah Ann Hammack (c. 1830, VA --).
1-1-2. John Hammack (c. 1832, VA --).

1870 Hampshire Co., WV, Census, Capon Township, p. 480, HH 215/213: John Hammack, 37, Farm laborer, VA; Ann J., 27, Keeping House, VA; James M., 12, At Home, VA; John F., 9, VA; Susan E., 7, VA; Amanda C., 6, WV; Jonathan J., 3, WV; Charles E. B., 1, WV.

1-1-3. Abraham Hammack (c. 1835, VA --).
1-1-4. Harriett J. Hammack (c. 1837, VA --).
1-1-5. Isaac Hammack (c. 1845, VA or OH --).

1870 Saline Co., MO, Census, Grand Pass Township, HH 114/119: Isaac Hammack, 25, $900/$220, OH; Eliza, 30, KH, VA; William L., 1, MO.

1880 Macon Co., MO, Census, Lingo PO, p. 561, HH 57/57: Isaac Hammack, 35, Farmer, OH/VA/VA; Eliza, 38, KH, VA/VA/VA; John W., 6, MO; Albert M., 2, MO; Ida V., 3/12, MO; Minnie M., 3/12, MO.

[1871] As per the census, this John was born c. 1765 in Virginia. Henry Franklin Hammack, *Wandering Back*, p. 114, identifies him as son of Rudolph Hammack who died c. 1783, Frederick Co., VA, and as an older brother of Jacob Hammack (1772 --) who settled in Warren Co., VA. HFH also states that John first purchased land in Hampshire County in 1796.
   John Hammack dated his will in Hampshire Co., VA, 7 Aug., 1852, proved 24 Apr., 1854, naming wife Catherine and sons Abraham, Jacob and Samuel and daughters Sarah Secrist and Rebecca Yonley.

1-2. Jacob Hammack (c. 1800 -- 18 November 1845, age 44 years, 5 months, 6 days, bur. Hammack Cemetery, Sedan, WV), m. Elizabeth D. Wise (c. 1800 -- 29 January 1869, age 68 years, 2 months, bur. Hammack Cemetery, Sedan, WV).[1872]

1850 Hampshire Co., VA, Census, HH 213/213: Elizabeth Hammack, 50, $13,000, VA; Anthony, 31, Manufacturer, $3,000, VA; William, 26, VA; John, 23, VA; James Cade, 17, VA; Charles Conner, 27, Tailor, VA; Charles Thomas, 18, Laborer, VA.

1860 Hampshire Co., VA, Census, Hanging Rock PO, p. 5, HH 4/4: John Hammack, 34, Manufacturer, $21,300/$6,000, VA; Elizabeth, 60, VA. There were several other individuals -- surnamed McGuire, Slouaker, Nolt, and Pugh -- who appeared to be working with the family.

1-2-1. Anthony Hammack (c. 1819, VA -- aft. 1860, Macon Co., MO), m. Rhody [----].

1860 Macon Co., MO, Census, HH 915/917: A. Hammock, 41, Miller, VA; Rhody, 35, VA; Sarah, 1, MO.

1880 Macon Co., MO, Census, Lyda PO, HH 54/55: John Roan, 63, Farmer and Preacher, NC/NC/NC; Rhoda, 53, KH, VA/VA/VA; VIRGINIA HAMMACK, 18, Step-daughter, School, MO/VA/VA.

1-2-2. William Hammack (7 February 1824, Hampshire Co., VA -- aft. 1883, MO), m. Maria Saville.

1900 Chariton Co., MO, Census, p. 221, Sudbury PO, HH 138/1389: William Hammack, February 1824, VA/VA/VA; Sophronia, January 1848, married 3 years, MO/KY/VA; Mattie A., May 1879, MO/VA/VA; Jennie L., May 1881, MO/VA/VA; Annie M., December 1883, MO/VA/VA.

HFH, 2: 83, cites "A History of Randolph and Macon Counties, MO"[1873]: "William Hammack was one of the earliest settlers in Macon county, coming there in the fall of 1851 overland in a buggy, accompanied by his mother, from West Virginia. He engaged in farming and was a miller and stock raiser and prospered through the years. In 1884, his farm land holdings in Macon and Chariton Counties amounted to upwards of 2,000 acres. William Hammack was born in Hampshire County, West Virginia, February 7, 1824, a son of Jacob and Elizabeth (Wise) Hammack. His wife, to whom he was married in February, was Miss Maria Saville of West Virginia. This good lady died December 19, 1883, leaving six daughters, Emma E., Mary E., Mattie A., Sarah M., Virginia Lee, and Fannie M."

1860 Macon Co., MO, Census, Russell Township, HH 879/880: Wm. Hammock, 36, Farmer, $32,000/$2,600, VA; Jessie Smith, 25, Laborer, $825, VA; Jno. Buster, 18, Laborer, MO.

1870 Macon Co., MO, Census, p. 259, Russell Township, HH 265/270: William Hammock, 46, Farmer, $21,200/$12,000, VA; Mariah, 20, Keeping House, VA. In HH 266/271 were: Roda Hammock, 42, Keeping House, $17,500/$8,000, VA; Missouri, 11, MO; Virginia, 9, MO.

1-2-3. John Hammack (c. 1827 -- 10 February 1865, Hampshire Co., VA, age 39, bur. Hammack Cemetery, Old Poston Mill, North River, Sedan, WV).[1874]

[1872] Kerns, *Historical Records of Old Frederick and Hampshire Counties, VA* (Revised, Bowie, MD: Heritage Books, Inc., 1992), pp. 38.

[1873] Published 1884, pp. 995-996.

[1874] Kerns, *Historical Records of Old Frederick and Hampshire Counties, VA* (Revised, Bowie, MD: Heritage Books, Inc., 1992), pp. 38,

1-3. Samuel Hammack (-- will written 30 July 1832, proved 27 August 1832, VA), m. Jane [-----] (living 1832).

1-3-1. William Thornton Hammack. He may be the William T. Hammack who appears 1870-1880 in Barton Co., MO.

1870 Barton Township, Barton Co., MO, HH 12/12: William Hammack, 40, $900/$785, VA; Annie E., 25, Keeping House, MO; Samuel F., 4, MO; William F., 1, MO.

1880 Barton City Township, Barton Co., MO, HH 55/58: W. T. Hammack, 50, VA/VA/MD; Anna E., 34, MO/VA/VA; Sam. F., 14, MO/VA/MO; Frank W., 11, MO/VA/MO; Ella Hill, 17, Servant, KY/KY/KY; John Hill, 1/12, Son, MO/UN/KY.

1900 Madison Co., MS, Census, Canton, Cameron St., 63-20-54: Frank Hammack, July 1873, MO; Lenora, July 1878, IA; Maud, April 1897, MS; P. Carl, July 1899, MS; Annie, November 1849, Mother, MO; Olive, Sister, IL. Frank Hammack m. Nora Gailey, 28 Dec 1896, Madison Co., Miss.

1910 Orleans Parish, New Orleans, Precinct 7, HH 76/76: Annie Hammock, 64, Widowed, 3/1, MO/KY/VA, and Frank, 40, Widowed, MO/VA/MO, living as boarders with Nellie and George Frantz.

1920 Orleans Parish, New Orleans, Precinct 7, HH 268/307: Frank W. Hammack, 51, MO/MO/VA; Annie, 35, LA/IRE/OH; Annie Gibson, 80, Mother-in-Law, VA/VA/VA.

1-3-2. Harriett Ann Hammack. *History and Biography, Counties of White and Pulaski, IN* (Chicago, 1883), p. 380, indicates that Harriet A. Hammock, a native of Hampshire Co., VA, married in 1844 Vaus Dobbins, born 1 November 1819, Hampshire Co., VA, son of Samuel and Sarah (Mitchell) Dobbins. They had ten children and resided in Big Creek Township, White Co., IN.

1-3-3. Mary Hammack.
1-3-4. Catherine Hammack.

1-4. Sarah Hammack (1790 -- 1881), m. 16 August 1810, John Henry Secrist (1782 -- 16 September 1856, from blood poisoning), son of Frederick Secrist (1754 -- 1834, Hampshire Co., VA) and Catherine Switzer (1754 -- 1822).[1875]

John Henry and Sarah Hammack Secrist moved in 1814 to Guernsey Co., Ohio. They were the parents of 11 children. According to Kerns, Frederick Co., VA, Order Book 14, p. 197, shows that Henry Secrist, father of Frederick and grandfather of John Henry, took a naturalization oath with many other German immigrants to the Shenandoah Valley.

1-5. Rebecca Hammack Yonley.

2. Jacob Hammack (9 February 1772, Frederick Co., VA --), m. October 1807, Frederick Co., VA, Catherine DeLong (4 May 1787, VA -- aft. 1850, Warren Co., VA).

[1875] See Kerns, Frederick Co., VA, Settlement and Some First Families of Back Creek Valley, 1730-1830 (Baltimore: Gateway Press, Inc., 1995), p. 237.

1850 Warren Co., VA, Census, p. 26, HH 370/377: Catherine Hammack, 64, Farmer, $3,572, VA;[1876] Jacob, 34, VA; Samuel, 33, VA; Joseph L., 31, VA; Cornelius, 20, VA; Sarah J., 21, VA; Theodocia Watson, 23, VA.

1860 Warren Co., VA, Census, Buckton PO, p. 1055, HH 825/725: C. Hammack, 74, female, Farming, $3,000/$1,000, VA; Samuel, 41, Farmer, VA; Sarah, 29, VA; George Martin, 15, VA. Several black servants were living with the family also.

John, Samuel, and William E. settled in Hampshire County, Virginia, near Romney.

Offspring:[1877]

2-1. Rudolph Hammack (26 October 1808 -- 1838/1840, Frederick Co., VA). He may have been the Rudolph Hammack who married Nancy Foley (c. 1805 -- c. 1874) on 15 March 1832 in Frederick Co., VA. Nancy Foley Hammack m. (2) Jacob Clapsaddle (c. 1793 - c. 1849). By her second marriage, she was the mother of Bertha Clapsaddle, Byrd Clapsaddle, and Marcus A. Clapsaddle.

1850 Warren Co., VA, Census, p. 22, HH 313/320: William S. Hammack, 17, Farmer, VA; John R., 16, VA. The Hammacks were living with Nancy Clapsaddle, 43, VA; Sarah E., 18, VA; Bertha Clapsaddle,[1878] 8, VA; Marcus A., 6, VA.

NOTE: In the 1860 Warren Co., VA, Census, Waterlick PO, p. 1042, HH 731/644: Wm. S. Hammack, 25, Merchant, $0/$1200, VA; Eliza Jane, 23, VA; Peter S. Hyde, 25, Merchant, $400/$3000, VA. In Front Royal, HH 791/697, were: Nancy Clapsaddle, 54, Farming, $4500/$214, VA; S. E. Hammick, 28, VA; Jno. R., 25, RR Hand, VA; Byrd Clapsaddle, 18, Farm hand, VA.

2-1-1. Sarah E. Hammack (c. 1833 --).

2-1-2. William S. Hammack (c. 1835 -- aft. 1860, Waterlick, Warren Co., VA), m. Eliza Jane [------]. William S. may have died between 1860 and 1860; Eliza was living with his brother John R. Hammack in 1870.

2-1-3. John R. Hammack (c. 1836 -- aft. 1870, Front Royal, Warren Co., VA), m. Alice [------].

1870 Warren Co., VA, Census, Front Royal PO, p. 420, HH 329/304: Jno. R. Hammock, 35, Farmer, $800/$400, VA; Eliza J., 30, Keeping House, VA; Alice, 28, "In this Family, VA; Joseph , 6, At Home, VA. IN HH 321/305 was Nancy Clapsaddle, 65, Keeping House, $1400/$475, VA, with Bird, 27, VA; Marcus A., 26, VA; Margaret, 24, VA; and Nancy N., 2/12, VA.

2-2. John W. Hammack (29 January 1810 --).

[1876] This family is detailed in Henry Franklin Hammack, *Wandering Back*, pp. 13-17, 28, 71-74, 88, 113-119, 146, 267-269, 308-309. In addition to Jacob, other children named in Rudolph's will were sons Rudolph (Rudy) and John and daughters Nancy Moyers, Mary Sperry and Elizabeth Hammack. John Hammack, evidently the son of Rudolph, was in Hampshire Co., VA, in 1850.

[1877] HFH, 2: 308.

[1878] Born in March of 1843, Byrd Clapsaddle was the third child and eldest son of Jacob Clapsaddle (c. 1793 - c. 1849) and Nancy Foley (c. 1805 - c. 1874). The other siblings were Bertha (c. 1842) and Marcus A. (c. 1845). Jacob Clapsaddle (Klebsattel) came to Virginia from Pennsylvania and was of German descent. Nancy Foley had married Rudolph Hammack on 13 March 1832 in Frederick Co., VA. They had three children -- Sarah, William, and John. Rudolph died between 1838 and 1840, and Nancy married Jacob Clapsaddle between 1838 and 1841.

2-3. William Ephraim Hammack (17 April 1 1812 --).

William and Barbara A. Hammick appeared in HH 1803/1832, Middletown, Frederick Co., VA, in 1850: William Hammick, 37, Miller, VA; Barbara A., 34, VA; Mary S., 7, VA; Peter J., 5, VA; Sarah A., 4, VA; John W., 2, VA; Samuel C., 1, VA; Barbara C., 8, VA.

1860 Hampshire Co., VA, Census, Bloomery PO, p. 46, HH 2/3: William E. Hammack, 47, $5000/$1130, VA; Barbara A., 44, VA; Barbara C., 18, VA; Mary E., 17, VA Peter J., 15, VA; Sarah A., 14, VA; John W., 13, VA; Samuel C., 10, VA; James B., 8, VA; Martha E., 7, VA; Edmonia M., 1, VA.

1870 Hampshire Co., WV, Census, Bloomery PO, p. 452, HH 15/15: William Hammack, 58, Farmer, $4000/$1200, VA; Barbara A., 55, Keeping House, VA; Peter J., 25, Farm Hand, VA; John W., 23, Farm Hand, VA; Samuel C., 21, Farm hand, VA; James B., 19, Farm Hand, VA; Mary E., 26, At Home, VA; Martha E., 17, At Home, VA; Edmonia M., 12, At Home, VA.

2-3-1. Barbara C. Hammack, born 30 December 1841.
2-3-2. Mary Elizabeth Hammack, born 19 February 1843.
2-3-3. Peter Jacob Hammack, born 23 February 1845.

2-3-3-1. William Madison Hammack, born 11 March 1875. He was the father of Clarence G. Hammack (10 December 1897-) and Frederick M. Hammack.

2-3-3-2. Henry Wilson Hammack, born 23 January 1877.
2-3-3-3. Neil Hammack.
2-3-3-4. Johnnie Hammack.

2-3-4. Sarah Ann Hammack (23 March 1846 -).
2-3-5. John William Hammack (5 April 1847 -).
2-3-6. Samuel Cornelius Hammack (2 March 1849 -).
2-3-7. Martha Eleanor Hammack (2 October 1852 -).
2-3-8. James Benjamin Hammack (16 January 1854 -).
2-3-9. Edmonia Marcelia Hammack (24 December 1858 -).

2-4. Elizabeth M. Hammack (12 May 1813 --).

2-5. Jacob Hammock (22 March 1815 - 28 March 1882, Frederick Co., VA, bur. Ridings Chapel Methodist Church), m. Mary Ann Larrick (19 March 1831 – 8 March 1914, Frederick Co., VA, bur. Ridings Chapel Methodist Church).

1860 Frederick Co., VA, Census, Back Creek Valley PO, p. 624, HH 35/33: Jacob Hammack, 45, Farmer, $0/$475, VA; Mary A., 29, Housewifery, VA; Catharine B., 8, VA; James W., 6, VA; Asa C., 4, VA; Severena M., 2, VA.

1870 Warren Co., VA, Census, Front Royal PO, p. 453, HH 37/36: Jacob Hammack, 55, Farmer, $1600/$550, VA; Mary A., 40, VA; Catherine R., 18, AT Home, VA; Jas. W., 16, Farm laborer, VA; Asa C., 14, Farm Laborer, VA; Sevarina M., 12, At Home, VA; David W., 6, AT Home, VA; Collin J., 4, AT Home, VA; John D., 2, At Home, VA. Members of the family of John D. Hammock (1868-1941) used the Hammock spelling.

2-5-1. Catherine Rebecca Hammock Settles (24 December 1851 --).

2-5-2. James William Hammock (20 March 1854 --), m. Jennie Barrow.

2-5-3. Asa Cornelius Hammock (19 April 1856 --).

2-5-4. Severine Muse Hammock (22 March 1858).

2-5-5. Minnie Hammock (12 November 1861 --), m. Scott Larrick.

2-5-6. David Wesley Hammock (26 September 1854 --), m. Sallie Barrow.

2-5-7. Colonel Jacob Hammock (13 February 1866 --).

2-5-8. John D. Hammock (21 May 1868 --).

2-5-9. Ellen Louvenia Hammock (28 October 1870 --), unmarried.

2-5-10. Daniel Isaac Hammock (21 June 1874 -- 22 April 1946), m. 17 September 1907, Winchester, VA, Lizzie Lee Stokes (12 May 1879 -- 10 June 1945).

2-6. Samuel Hammack (31 July 1816 --). Some have suggested that he was Samuel Cornelius Hammack and that he wrote his will 30 July 1832, proved 27 August 1832.

1860 Warren Co., VA, Census, Middletown PO, HH 826/726 (next door to Catherine Hammack): Jos. Hammick, 39, Farmer, 0/$175, VA; Sarah A., 24, VA; Elma, 3, VA; Miller G., 1, VA.

1870 Warren Co., VA, Census, Front Royal, p. 453, HH 40/40: Samuel A. Hammack, 53, Farmer, $1,500/$500, VA; Eliza J., 33, Keeping House, VA; Laura L., 8/12, At Home, VA. Several servants were living with the family, as well as Jenny Cline, 37, "In this Family," VA, and her son Clarence, age 3/12, VA.

2-7. Joseph Leroy Hammack (5 February 1818 -- 3 December 1908, Warren Co., VA)[1879], husband of Sara A. Ridings (4 December 1832 -- 31 January 1892)

1870 Warren Co., VA, Census, Front Royal PO, p. 452, HH 28/28: Joseph Hammock, 51, Farmer, $2,250/$600, VA; Sarah A., 34, Keeping House, VA; Emma J., 14, At Home, VA; Idea B., 12, female, AT Home, VA; Mary E., 9, AT Home, VA; Joseph A., 7, AT Home, VA; Sarah A., 5, At Home, VA; Mary E., 3, At Home, VA; Lucy, 7/12, AT Home, VA.

2-8. Daniel Nathaniel (9 January 1820 -- 3 December 1895), m. 8 January 1852, Amanda C. Larrick (20 August 1832 -- 1904). The 1850 Frederick Co., VA, Census, Middletown, HH 1809/1838 showed Daniel M. Hammick, 32, Miller, VA, living with the family of David J. Miller, a 34 year old farmer.

1860 Frederick Co., VA, Census, Back Creek Valley PO, p. 625, HH 44/42: Daniel M. Hammack, 40, Miller, $3000/$705, V A; Amanda C., 28, Housewifery, VA; Maria A., 8, VA; Mary C., 7, VA; Margaret S., 4, VA; John W. Chapman, 14, Domestic, VA.

1870 Frederick Co., VA, Census, Back Creek Township, p. 16, HH 243/238: Daniel N. Hammack, 50, farmer, $5000/$580, VA; Amanda E., 38, Keeping House, VA; Maurice A., 17, At Home, VA, female; Mary C., 15, At Home, VA; Margaret S., At Home, VA.

2-8-1. Marvis Arbella Hammack (15 January 1853 --), unmarried.

2-8-2. Mary Catherine Hammack (19 June 1854 -- 10 October 1893).

2-8-3. Margaret Susan Hammack (9 October 1855 --), wife of Isaac Frye.

2-9. Catherine J. Hammack Hammack (25 Dec., 1821 --).

[1879] Children at his death were Nellie Hammond and Lucy Funkhouser of Strasburg, Maude Cuppett of Uniontown, PA, Cora and Sallie Hammack of Reliance, and Ashby Hammack, also of Reliance. Another daughter was Ida Wyndam.

2-10. Orato Hammack Hammack (2 Feb., 1823 --).

2-11. Martha A. Hammack (22 Apr., 1825 --). She may have m. 11 September 1849, Warren Co., VA, Simon Peter Smith.

2-12. Abraham Hammack (1827 --).

2-13. Sarah Hammack (1828 --).

2-14. Cornelius B. Hammack (5 June, 1830 --).

1860 Shenandoah Co., VA, Census, Woodstock PO, p. 860, HH 243/243: Cornelius B. Hammack, 29, Minister, $200, VA; Mary E., 28, VA.

1870 Augusta Co., VA, Census, Mt. Sidney PO, p. 376, HH 379/386: Cornelius B. Hammack, 40, Minister of Gospel, $0/$1,000, VA; Mary E., 31, Keeping House, VA; Abraham S., 4, VA; Lydia A. C., 1, VA.

3. Rudolph Hammack (by c. 1778, Frederick Co., VA -- c. 1803, Frederick Co., VA)., m. Ann (Nancy) Shambaugh (2 August 1778, Bucks Co., PA -- 8 July 1847, Warren Co., VA), who m. (2) 22 September 1812, Frederick Co., VA, John Crampton.

The will of Ann Shambaugh Crampton lists her deceased daughter Elizabeth, wife of Rudolph Hammock, and her children: Samuel S. Hammock, Daniel hammock, Mary Cline (wife of James Cline) and Elizabeth Rodgers (wife of John S. Rodgers). Elizabeth married John S. Rodgers in 1818; they had Ann Margaret; Samuel R. (1821); Hada E. (1827); Elisabeth C. (1832); and Mary A. (1834). Ann Shambaugh Crampton wrote her will 10 November 1846 in Warren Co., VA.

Will of Daniel Shambaugh refers to daughter Ann Hammock; in the distribution she is called Ann Hammock alias Crampton. As Ann Hammock, on 22 September 1812 in Frederick Co., VA, she married John Crampton with Jacob Shambeck as her bondsman. "The will of Ann Crampton lists her deceased daughter Elizabeth, dec. md. to Rudolph Hammock, dec., and Elizabeth's children -- Samuel S. Hammock, Daniel Hammock, Mary Cline (Wife of James), and Elizabeth Rodgers (wife of John S. Rodgers).

Daniel Shambaugh was born 10 April 1753 in Bucks Co., PA; he died 10 June 1837 in Reliance, Warren Co., VA. he wrote his will in December 1836 (Will Book 12, p. 12). He was a son of George Shambaugh and Elisabeth Boehm, Pennsylvania Germans. He married about 1775 in Bucks Co., PA, Catharina Hendricks. they were the parents of Ann Shambaugh (2 August 1778 -- 8 July 1847).

24 January 1803: Appraisement of estate of Rudolph Hamick (Frederick Co., VA, Will Book 7, p. 112).

January 1803: Account of estate of Rudolph Hammak with Daniel Shambough administrator (Frederick Co., VA, Will Book 7, p. 231).

1810 Frederick Co., VA, Census: Nancy Hammock.

1820 Frederick Co., VA, Census: Nancy Crampton.

1830 Frederick Co., VA, Census: In household of John Rogers.

1840 Warren Co., VA, Census: In household of John S. Rogers.

3-1. Elizabeth Hammock (c. 1798, VA -- aft. 1870, Warren Co., VA), m. 10 September 1818, Frederick Co., VA, John S. Rogers.

3-2. Daniel S. Hammack (c. 1800, VA -- aft. 1850, OH), m. 22 September 1826, Frederick Co., VA, Elizabeth Ann Taylor.

One Daniel S. Hammack married Elizabeth Ann Taylor on 22 September 1826 in Frederick Co., VA. They apparently moved to Ohio between 1830 and 1840. They were found in Auglaize Co., OH, in 1850. Daniel is shown in Frederick Co., VA, in 1803 as an orphan.

1850 Ohio Census, Auglaize Co., OH, p. 320, Clay Township, HH 386/386: D. S. Hammack, 50, Farmer, $1,000, VA; Elizabeth, 45, VA; Mary, 14, OH; Daniel, 13, OH; Martha, 12, OH; Abigail, 10, OH; Eme Eliza, 7, OH; Samantha, 4, OH.

3-2. Samuel Shambaugh Hammack (14 July 1800, VA -- 18 October 1876, Fairfield Co., OH, bur. Asbury Cemetery), m. Louisa Mauk (c. 1805, VA -- aft. 1850, Fairfield Co., OH, bur. Asbury Cemetery). Samuel S. Hammack married Louisa Mauk on 23 November 1824 in Frederick Co., VA.[1880]

1850 Fairfield Co., Ohio, Census, HH 1243: S. S. Hammack, 47, Farmer, $8,725, VA; Louisa, 45, VA; Michael R., 23, Miller, VA; Daniel R., 20, Farmer, VA; Mary E., 19, VA; Louisa, 16, OH; Amanda, 14, OH; Samuel H., 10, OH.

HFH, p. 267, states that Samuel Shambaugh Hammack (14 July, 1800, prob. Frederick Co., VA -- 18 Oct., 1876, Asbury Cemetery, Fairfield Co., OH), m. Louisa Mauk in Frederick Co., VA, and had six children, all born in VA.

3-2-1. Michael Rudolph Hammack (9 October 1825, Frederick Co., VA -- 5 August 1893, Fairfield Co., OH), m. 1852, Nancy E. Wiseman.

They had six children, all born in Lancaster, OH: Charles W., Edwin C., Ella L., Elizabeth P., Orrisn S., and Henry Clay. Henry Clay Hammack was born 31 October 1875 and died 14 May 1948; he married Florence Richmond in 1898, and they had four children, all born in Lima, OH: Pauline E., Doran Alexander, Clay R., and Janice C. HFH discusses later generations of this family.

3-2-2. Daniel Hammack (c. 1830, Frederick Co., VA -- aft. 1880, Fairfield Co., OH), m. 10 January 1858, Fairfield Co., OH, Mary C. Renshaw.

3-3-3. Samuel Hammack (c. 1840, Fairfield Co., OH -- aft. 1880, Clark Co., IL), m. Rebecca A. Nichols.

1880 Clark Co., IL, Census, Casey Township, HH 175/180: S. H. Hammock, 40, OH/VA/VA., Farming; Katie, 15, OH; Hattie, 10, IN; Maudie, 6, IL; Onie, 3, IL.

3-3-4. Louisa Hammack (c. 1834, Fairfield Co., OH -- aft. 1880, Fairfield Co., OH), m. Solomon Beery.

3-3-5. Mary Hammack (c. 1831, Frederick Co., VA -- aft. 1880, Fairfield Co., OH), m. 1 January 1854, Fairfield Co., OH, Samuel H. Anderson.

3-3-6. Amanda Hammack (c. 1836, Frederick Co., VA -- aft. 1880, Clark Co., IL). As Amanda Hammack, 43, "Mother-in-law," OH/VA/VA, she was enumerate din HH 186/181, Clark Co., IL, in 1880, with John M. Miller, age 19, OH; wife Dora L., 19, OH; and Myra A., 9/12, IL.

3-4. Mary Hammack (c. 1803, Frederick Co., VA -- 16 April 1890, Kline's Mill, Frederick Co., VA), m. 29

[1880] HFH, 2: 267.

January 1827, Frederick Co., VA, James Russell Kline (1 May 1805, VA -- 1869, Frederick Co., VA).

4. Nancy Hammack Moyers. She is identified in Frederick Co., VA, Deed Book 30, p. 213, 1 December 1806, as the wife of Gasper Moyers (whose name also appears as Myers and Miers).

5. Mary Hammack Sperry. She is identified in Frederick Co., VA, Deed Book 30, p. 213, 1 December 1806, as wife of Peter Sperry.

6. Elizabeth Hammack. She is identified in Frederick Co., VA, Deed Book 30, p. 213, 1 December 1806, as wife of John Barrett. (Note that John's surname was difficult to read and could be incorrectly transcribed.)

Unidentified, but probable members of this group:

1850 Roanoke Co., VA, Census, pp. 290-291, HH 425: Charles Calvert, 35, Tailor, VA; Catherine, 24, VA; children; and Jacob V. Hammock, 20, Tailor, VA. In HH 440: George Gish, 67, Farmer, $5,250, PA; Elizabeth, 54, PA; children; and Catherine Hammock, 17, VA.

1880 McDonough Co., IL, Census, Industry PO, HH 7/7: Wm. Hammack, 40, farmer, OH/VA/VA/ Tennessee, 39, KH, OH/OH/OH; Florence, 2, At Home, IL/OH/OH.

Charlemagne, King of the Franks and Emperor of the West, lived from 742 A.D. to 814 A.D. The greatest monarch of his time, by 800 A.D. he ruled an empire that stretched from central Italy northwards to Denmark and from eastern Germany westward to the Atlantic Ocean. On Christmas Day 800 A.D., Pope Leo III crowned Charlemagne Emperor of the Romans, an event that led in time to the creation of the Holy Roman Empire. Charlemagne established a royal dynasty that included many future Kings of France and Germany as well as Holy Roman Emperors. Notable descendants included Emperor Henry, Duke of Saxony, Brunswick, and Zelle, known as the Fowler, and Hugh Capet, King of France. In a later generation, King Henry of France married Anna, daughter of Jaroslav the Wise, Grand Prince of Kiev, introducing Russian and Swedish ancestry into the bloodline. After the Norman Conquest of England in 1066, several of Charlemagne's later descendants helped colonize England. They often married into noble Anglo-Saxon families, and many later royal and noble Anglo-Norman families in England, including the Plantagenents, claimed descent from Charlemagne.

England's de Clare family descended from Charlemagne through a maternal bloodline in the family's French ancestry. Richard de Clare (1153-1217), Earl of Hertford, married Amice, Countess of Gloucester, whose mother's family had come from Normandy; their son Gilbert became Earl of both Gloucester and Hertford before dying in 1230.

Richard de Clare, a Magna Carta signer (as discussed in Appendix 2), was a direct ancestor of Christopher Calthorpe, a native of Norfolk, England and an early settler of Virginia. Through the Calthorpe lineage, members of the Mississippi Brown, Cates, and Hammack families trace their ancestry to Charlemagne.

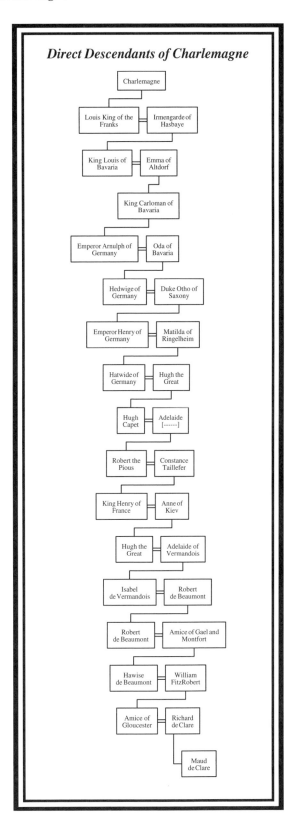

Direct Descendants of Charlemagne

Direct Descendants of Richard de Clare

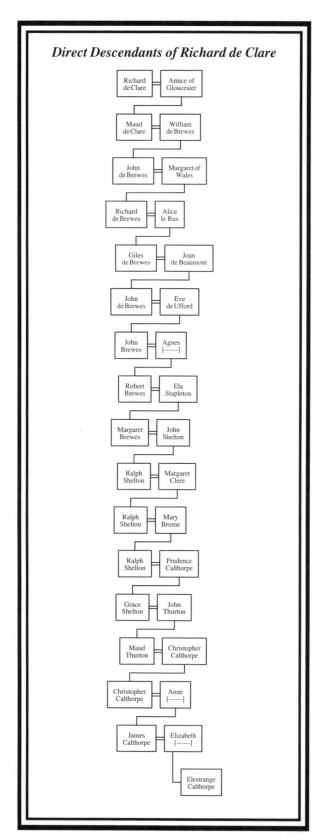

Descendants of James Calthorpe

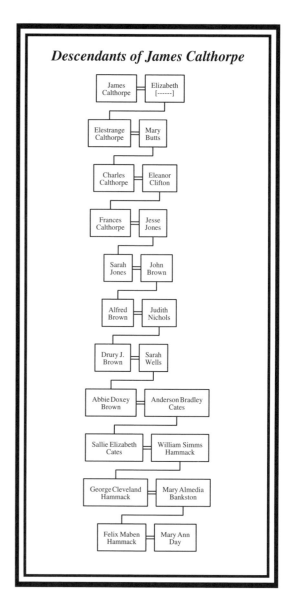

Sources: From Charlemagne to Richard de Clare, see Redlich, Langston, and Buck, *Pedigrees of Some of the Emperor Charlemagne's Descendants* (3 vols., Baltimore, 1941-1972). From de Clare to Christopher Calthorpe, see Richardson and Everingham, *Magna Carta Ancestry* (Baltimore, 2005). From Calthorpe to France Calthorpe Jones, see J. F. Dorman, *Adventurers of Purse and Person, 1607-1624/5* (3 vols., 4th ed., Alexandria, VA, 2005-2007). From Frances Calthorpe Jones, see herein, pp. 291-333.

Bibliography

I. Primary Sources.

A. Unpublished.

1. England.

Devonshire Lay Subsidy, 1655, 57 (PRO: E 179/245/11).

Ermington Parish Register Transcripts, 1603-1850 (Microfilm, The Genealogical Society of Utah).

Prerogative Court of Canterbury, The National Archives, Kew, Richmond, Surrey, England:

Will of Henry Hammack, Mariner, Probate 11/416.

Will of Anne Carter, Probate 11/306.

2. United States of America.

a. Alabama.

Washington County.

Washington Co., AL, Deed Book A, Microfilm, ADAH.

Alabama Confederate Pension Applications, ADAH.

Card File Index to Early Alabama Residents, Gary, ADAH, citing.

U.S. Land Records, Receiver's Office, Milledgeville, GA, 1817-1818.

U. S. Land Records, Receiver's Office, Cahaba, AL, 1818.

b. Arkansas.

Sebastian County.

Amos Family File, Fort Smith Public Library, Fort Smith, AR.

Arkansas State Records:

Arkansas Confederate Pension Applications, Arkansas History Commission, Little Rock, AR.

Alfred Hammack Pension Application.

1912 Census of Confederate Veterans, Arkansas History Commission, Little Rock, AR.

c. Georgia.

Bibb County.

Bibb Co., GA, Deed Books A-C, Microfilm, GDAH.

Clarke County.

Clarke County. Clarke Co., GA, Deed Books A-L, Microfilm, GDAH.

Columbia County.

Columbia Co., GA, Deed Book P, Microfilm, GDAH.

1806 Columbia Co., GA, Tax Digest, Microfilm, GDAH.

Crawford County.

Crawford Co., GA, Annual Returns, Books A-U, Microfilm, GDAH.

Crawford Co., GA, Deed Books A-U, 27, Microfilm, GDAH.

Crawford Co., GA, Inferior Court Minutes,1830-1849, Microfilm, GDAH.

Crawford Co., GA, Inferior Court Records, County and Ordinary Purposes, 1830-1846, Microfilm, GDAH.

Crawford Co., GA, Superior Court Loose Papers, GDAH.

Crawford Co., GA, Will Books A-B, 1-3, Microfilm, GDAH.

Mt. Carmel Baptist Church Records, Microfilm, GDAH.

Greene County.

Greene Co., GA, Deed Books AA – NN.

Greene Co., GA, Deed Book 1.

Greene Co., GA, Estate Divisions and Annual Returns, 1822-1829.

Greene Co., GA, Executors and Administrators Book G, Microfilm, GDAH.

Greene Co., GA, Miscellaneous Records Book A, 1787-1801, Microfilm, GDAH.

Greene Co., GA, Ordinary Estate Records, Unbound, 1790-1843, Greene Co., GA, Probate Court, Greensboro, GA.

Wooten O'Neal File.

John Stephens File.

James Stewart.

Greene Co., GA, Tax Digests, 1788-1850, Microfilm, GDAH.

Greene Co., GA, Will Books A-D, Microfilm, GDAH.

Hancock County.

Hancock Co., GA, Deed Books A-N, Microfilm, GDAH.
Hancock Co., GA, Direct Index to Real Estate Conveyances, Microfilm, GDAH.
Hancock Co., GA, Will Book M, 1824-1828, Microfilm, GDAH.
Hancock Co., GA, Tax Digests, 1793-1820, Microfilm, GDAH.
Powelton Baptist Church Records, Membership Lists, 1786-1852, Microfilm, GDAH.

Henry County.
Henry Co., GA, Deed Book J, Microfilm, GDAH.

Jefferson County.
1796-1810 Jefferson Co., GA, Tax Digests, Microfilm, GDAH.

Jones County.
Jones Co., GA, Annual Returns, A-H, Microfilm, GDAH.
Jones Co., GA, Deed Books A-Z, Microfilm, GDAH.
Jones Co., GA, Will Books A-D, Microfilm, GDAH.
Jones Co., GA, Tax Digests, 1811-1855, Microfilm, GDAH.

Lincoln County.
Lincoln Co., GA, Will Books A-D, Microfilm, GDAH.

Macon County.
Macon Co., GA, Deed Book A, Microfilm, GDAH.
Macon Co., GA, Annual Returns Book A, Microfilm, GDAH.
1852 Macon Co., GA, Tax Digest, Microfilm, GDAH.

Morgan County.
Morgan Co., GA, Deed Books A-K, GG.
Morgan Co., GA, Will Books A-C.
1811-1829 Morgan Co., GA, Tax Digests, Microfilm, GDAH.

Newton County.
Newton Co., GA, Deed Books A-I.

Pike County.
Pike Co., GA, Deed Book E, Microfilm, GDAH.
1831 Pike Co., GA, Tax Digest, Microfilm, GDAH.

Putnam County.
Putnam Co., GA, Deed Books A-D, Microfilm, GDAH.
1815 Putnam Co., GA, Tax Digest, Microfilm, GDAH.
Putnam Co., GA, Miscellaneous Book Q, Microfilm, GDAH.
Putnam Co., GA, Will Books A-C, Microfilm, GDAH.

Talbot County.
Talbot Co., GA, Deed Book A, Microfilm, GDAH.
Talbot Co., GA, Will Book A, Microfilm, GDAH.

Taliaferro County.
Taliaferro Co., GA, Annual Returns, Book A, 1823-1850.
Taliaferro Co., GA, Deed Books A-J, 1.
1834 Taliaferro Co., GA, Poor School Minutes, Microfilm, GDAH.
Taliaferro Co., GA, Tax Digests, 1827-1860, Microfilm, GDAH.
Taliaferro Co., GA, Inventories, Appraisals, Sales, and Divisions of Estates, Book B, 1834-1850.
Taliaferro Co., GA, Will Books 1-3.

Taylor County.
Taylor Co., GA, Deed Book D, Microfilm, GDAH.

Walton County.
Walton Co., GA, Deed Books A-B.

Warren County.
Warren Co., GA, Deed Books A-C, Microfilm, GDAH.

Wilkes County.
Wilkes Co., GA, Deed Books AA-ZZ, Microfilm, GDAH.
Wilkes Co., GA, Deed Books AAA-ZZZ, Microfilm, GDAH.
Wilkes Co., GA, Loose Estate Papers, Microfilm, GDAH:
Robert Hammack File.
Thomas Hammack File.

Wilkes Co., GA, Poor Fund Distribution, 1816-1825, Miscellaneous Minutes, Overseers of the
    Poor.
Minutes of Phillip's Mill Baptist Church, Wilkes Co., GA, Microfilm, GDAH.
Georgia, State, Colonial, and Confederate Records:
Georgia Confederate Service Records, Microfilm, GDAH.
Georgia Land Grant Books B, EEE, HHH, NNN, Microfilm, GDAH.
Georgia Land Plat Book C, Microfilm, GDAH.
1805 Georgia Land Lottery Papers, Registration Lists, GDAH.
1807 Georgia Land Lottery Papers, Fortunate Drawers, GDAH.
1820 Georgia Land Lottery Papers, Fortunate Drawers, GDAH.
1821 Georgia Land Lottery Papers, Fortunate Drawers, GDAH.
1827 Georgia Land Lottery Papers, Fortunate Drawers, GDAH.
Simpson Moore Family Bible, Microfilm, GDAH.
d. Kentucky.
Christian County.
    1798-1803 Christian Co., KY, Tax Lists, Kentucky State Library and Archives, Frankfort, KY.
e. Louisiana.
    Louisiana Confederate Service Records, Microfilm, Louisiana State Archives, Baton Rouge, LA.
f. Maryland.
    Dorchester Co., MD, Accounts, Liber 22, Microfilm, Maryland Hall of Records, Annapolis, MD.
g. Mississippi.
Calhoun County.
    Calhoun Co., MS, Land Abstract Books.
    Calhoun Co., MS, Deed Book R.
    1879, 1883, 1887, 1902 Calhoun Co., MS, Land Tax Lists, MDAH.
    1860, 1884-1885, 1903-1907 Calhoun Co., MS, Personal Property Tax Lists, MDAH.
    Bethel Baptist Church Minutes, Transcription, Calhoun City Library, Calhoun City, MS.
Choctaw County.
    1863 Choctaw Co., MS, Personal Property Tax Roll, MDAH.
    Old Concord Baptist Church Records, Transcription, Calhoun City Library, Calhoun City, MS.
Copiah County.
    Copiah Co., MS, Estate Books A-L.
    Copiah Co., MS, Court of Chancery, Loose Estate Files:
    Drury J. Brown Papers, Boxes 374, 446.
    1841 Copiah Co., MS, Personal Property Tax Roll, Mississippi Department of Archives and
        History, Jackson, MS.
Hinds County.
    Hinds Co., MS, Annual Reports Book 4-5.
    Hinds Co., MS, Deed BooksG, 5-8, 10, 13, 17-26, 30, 48, 54-61, 64, 67-68, 70-72, 75-76.
    Hinds Co., MS Probate Minutes Book 2-4.
    1833-1834 Hinds Co., MS, Tax Lists, Microfilm, MDAH.
    Hinds Co., MS, Chancery Court, Loose Papers, Raymondville, MS.
    Estate Files, John F. Cates
    Estate Files, Sarah Nichols
    Estate Files, Wright Nichols
Lauderdale County.
    Lauderdale Co., MS, Deed Book I/J, Microfilm, MDAH.
    Lauderdale Co., MS, Deed Book Z, Microfilm, MDAH.
    1838-1850 Lauderdale Co., MS, Tax Lists, Microfilm, MDAH.
Madison County.
    Madison Co., MS, Deed Books AAA-PPP, 9-10, 67-75.
    1861, 1868 Madison Co., MS, Personal Property Tax List, MDAH.
    1887 Madison Co., MS, Land Tax List, MDAH.
Smith County.
    1853-1857 Smith Co., MS, Tax Rolls, Microfilm, MDAH.
Webster County.

Philadelphia Baptist Church Minutes, Transcription, Calhoun City Library, Calhoun City, MS.

Mississippi State and Confederate Records:

Mississippi Death Certificates, Microfilm, MDAH.

Mississippi Confederate Service Records, Microfilm, MDAH.

Mississippi Confederate Widows's Pensions, MSDAH.

Abbie D. Brown Cates, Hinds County.

Mary Gary, Madison County.

Georgia O'Neal, Hinds County.

Vertical Files, Mississippi Department of Archives and History, Jackson, MS:

Judith Cates Chancery Notice, 1877, Cates Vertical File.

h. North Carolina.

Bertie County.

Bertie Co., NC, Deed Books A – P, L-2, Microfilm, NCDAH.

Bute County.

Bute Co., NC, Deed Book A, Microfilm, NCDAH.

Caswell County.

Caswell Co., NC, Deed Books A-J, M, N, Q.

Caswell Co., NC, Will Books A-C.

Caswell Co., NC, Estate Books B-C.

1777-1798 Caswell County, NC, Tax Lists, NCDAH.

Chatham County.

Chatham Co., NC, Court Minutes, 1790-1792, Microfilm, NCDAH.

Craven County.

Craven Co., NC, Deed Book 5, Microfilm, NCDAH.

Edgecombe County.

Edgecombe Co., NC, Deed Books 1-6, Microfilm, NCDAH.

Granville County.

Granville Co., NC, Deed Book L, Microfilm, NCDAH.

Iredell County.

1815 Iredell Co., NC, Tax List, NCDAH.

Johnston County.

Johnston Co., NC, Deed Books A-K, Microfilm, NCDAH.

Mecklenburg County.

Mecklenburg Co., NC, Will Book F, Microfilm, NCDAH.

Onslow County.

Onslow Co., NC, Deed Books I-J, Microfilm, NCDAH.

Orange County.

Orange Co., NC, Deed Books 1-5.

Orange Co., NC, Inventories, Accounts of Sales, 1758-1785.

Orange Co., NC, Records Book 1, 1752-1761.

Orange Co., NC, Will Books A – G.

Perquimans District.

1712-1720 Perquimans District, NC, Tax Lists, NCDAH.

Person County.

Person Co., NC, Deed Books A-K, N, R.

Person Co., NC, Estate Book, 1807-1811.

Person Co., NC, Estates, Book 1811-1815.

Person Co., NC, Estate Book 1815-1819.

Person Co., NC, Estate Book, 1820-1823.

Person Co., NC, Estate Book, 1831-1837.

Person Co., NC, Estate Book, 1838-1841.

Person Co., NC, Guardians' Accounts, Book A.

Person Co., NC, Guardians' Accounts, Book B.

Person Co., NC, Inventories, Wills, and List of Tithables, 1835-1837.

Person Co., NC, Record Books 5-7, 11.

1794 -1823 Person Co., NC, Tax Lists, NCDAH.

Flat River Primtive Baptist Church Minutes, 1786-1890, Microfilm, Person County, NC, Library.

Wheeley's Primitive Baptist Church Minutes, Person Co., NC, Library.

Pitt County.

Pitt Co., NC, Deed Book B, Microfilm, NCDAH.

Pitt Co., NC, Grant Book G, 1779-1784, NCDAH.

Rockingham County.

Rockingham Co., NC, Deed Books A-C, Microfilm, NCDAH.

Rowan County.

Rowan Co., NC, Deed Books 4-5, 9, Microfilm, NCDAH.

Tyrell County.

Tyrell Co., NC, Deed Book 1, Microfilm, NCDAH.

North Carolina State and Colonial Records:

North Carolina Land Patent Books 5-23, NCDAH.

Original Will Records, NCDAH:

Will of John Stevens, Johnston County, 1777.

Will of Francis Stringer, Craven County, 1745.

Secretary of State, Office of Granville Proprietary Land Office Papers, NCDAH.

Bankson, Laurance, Orange County.

1786 NC State Census:

Surry County.

i. Pennsylvania.

Philadelphia Deed Book E-7, Microfilm, Church of Jesus Christ of Latter Day Saints.

Minutes of Warrington, PA, Monthly Meeting, Department of Records, Yearly Meeting of Religious Society of Friends, Philadelphia, PA.

j. South Carolina.

Edgefield County.

Edgefield Co., SC, Deed Books 13-16, 21-22, Microfilm, SCDAH.

Edgefield Co., SC, Probate Court, Loose Estate Files, Edgefield, SC.

Michael Burkhalter File.

Samuel Gardner File.

William Stringer File.

Laurens County.

Laurens Co., SC, Deed Books A-H, Laurens Co., SC, Court House, Laurens, SC.

Newberry County.

Newberry Co., SC, Deed Books A-H, Microfilm, SCDAH.

Newberry Co., SC, Probate Court, Loose Estate Files, Newberry, SC.

William Gary File.

Bush River Baptist Church Records, 1771-1921, Microfilm, Southern Baptist Historical Library and Archives, Nashville, TN.

Spartanburg County.

Spartanburg Co., SC, Deed Books A-I, N, O, S, Microfilm, SCDAH.

Spartanburg Co., SC, Probate Court, Loose Estate Files, Spartanburg, SC.

Isaac Cantrell File.

Union County.

Union Co., SC, Deed Books A-D, Union Co., SC, Court House, Union, SC.

South Carolina, State and Colonial Records:

SCDAH Records Series S213184, Microfilm, Vol. 17.

SCDAH Records Series S213019, Microfilm, Vols. 29, 33.

SCDAH Records Series S111001, Microfilm, Vols. 12-13.

SCDAH Records Series S108092, Microfilm, Accounts Audited of Claims Growing Out of the American Revolution, Reels 80, 135.

SCDAH Records Series S213190, Microfilm, Vols. 5-17.

k. Tennessee.

Grainger County.

1804, 1805, and 1809 Grainger Co., TN, Tax Lists, Microfilm, Tennessee State Library and

Archives, Nashville, TN.

Knox County.

1812 Knox Co., TN, Tax List, Tennessee State Library and Archives, Nashville, TN.

Tennessee State and Confederate Records:

Tennessee Confederate Pension Applications, Tennessee State Library and Archives, Nashville, TN.

l. Texas.

Texas Death Index, 1903-1975, Texas State Archives, Austin, TX.

m. Virginia.

Albemarle County.

Albemarle Co., VA, Deed Books 1-7, Microfilm, LVA.

Albemarle Co., VA, 1785 Personal Property Tax List, Microfilm, LVA.

Amelia County.

Amelia Co., VA, Deed Books 1-16, Microfilm, LVA.

Amelia Co., VA, Order Books, 1-6, Microfilm, LVA.

1762, 1763, 1764 Tithable Lists, LVA.

Bedford County.

Bedford Co., VA, Will Book 1, Microfilm, LVA.

Brunswick County.

Brunswick Co., VA, Deed Books 1-13, Microfilm, LVA.

Brunswick Co., VA, Order Book 2, Microfilm, LVA.

Brunswick Co., VA, Will Books 1-6, Microfilm, LVA.

Campbell County.

Campbell Co., VA, Deed Books 1-3, Microfilm, LVA.

Caroline County.

Caroline Co., VA, Order Books, 1732-1746, Microfilm, LVA.

Essex County.

Essex Co., VA, Deeds and Wills, Books 13-17, Microfilm, LVA.

Essex Co., VA, Order Books, 1695-1699, 1716-1723, Microfilm, LVA.

Goochland County.

Goochland Co., VA, Deed Books 9-13, Microfilm, LVA.

Goochland Co., VA, Order Book 1769, Microfilm, LVA.

Isle of Wight County.

Isle of Wight Co., VA, Deeds, Wills, Etc., Great Book, 1715-1726, Microfilm, LVA.

Louisa County.

Louisa Co., VA, Deed Books A-C, Microfilm, LVA.

Louisa Co.., VA, Will Book A, Microfilm, LVA.

Lancaster County.

Lancaster Co., VA, Order Books 1656-1666, 1666-1680, Microfilm, LVA.

Lunenburg County.

Lunenburg Co., VA, Deed Book 1-20, Microfilm, LVA.

Lunenburg Co., VA, Order Books, 1-16, Microfilm, LVA.

Lunenburg Co., VA, Will Book 4, Microfilm, LVA.

Lunenburg Co., VA, Tithable Lists, 1744-1782, Library of Virginia, Richmond, VA.

Lunenburg Co., VA, Personal Property and Land Tax Lists, 1782-1820, Microfilm, Library of Virginia, Richmond, VA.

Mecklenburg County.

Mecklenburg Co., VA, Deed Books 2-3, Microfilm, LVA.

Norfolk County.

Norfolk Co., VA, Records Books 1-4, Microfilm, LVA.

Northumberland County.

Northumberland Co., VA, Order Book 5, Microfilm, LVA.

Northumberland Co., VA, Records, 1652-55, Microfilm, LVA.

Northumberland Co., VA, Record Book 1652-58, Microfilm, LVA.

Northumberland Co., VA, Deeds & Wills, 1706-20, Microfilm, LVA.

Northumberland Co., VA, Record Book, 1658-62, Microfilm, LVA.

Northumberland Co., VA, Record Book 1662-66, Microfilm, LVA.
Northumberland Co., VA, Records Books 3, 15, Microfilm, LVA.
Northumberland Co., VA, 1678-1713, Microfilm, LVA.
Northumberland Co., VA, Deeds & Orders, 1650-52, Microfilm, LVA.
Northumberland Co., VA, Record Book, 1652-58, Microfilm, LVA.
Northumberland Co., VA, Record Book, 1658-62, Microfilm, LVA.
Northumberland Co., VA, Record Book 17, Microfilm, LVA.

Orange County.
Orange Co., VA, Order Book, 1747-1757, Microfilm, LVA.

Pittsylvania County.
Pittsylvania County, VA, Deed Books 1-2, Microfilm, LVA.
Pittsylvania Co., VA, Order Book 38, Microfilm, LVA.
Pittsylvania Co., VA, Personal Property and Land Tax Lists, 1782-1810, Microfilm, LVA.

Prince Edward County.
Prince Edward Co., VA, Deed Books 1-2, Microfilm, LVA.

Prince George County.
Prince George Co., VA, Deeds, Etc., 1713-1728, Microfilm, LVA.

Princess Anne County.
Princess Anne Co., VA, Deed Book 3, Microfilm, LVA.

Rappahannock County (Old).
Rappahannock County Deed Book 3, 1663-1668, Microfilm, LVA.
Rappahannock County Deed Book, 1672-1676, Microfilm, LVA.
Rappahannock County Deeds & Wills, 1677-1682, Microfilm, LVA.
Rappahannock County Deed Book 1682-1686, Microfilm, LVA.
Rappahannock County Orders, 1683-1686, Microfilm, LVA.
Rappahannock County Orders, 1686-1692, Microfilm, LVA.
Rappahannock County Orders, 1692-1695, Microfilm, LVA.
Rappahannock County Deeds, Wills, Inventories, Etc., 1656-1664, Microfilm, LVA.
Rappahannock County Deeds, & C., 1663-1668, Microfilm, LVA.
Rappahannock County Deeds & C, 1668-1672, Microfilm, LVA.
Rappahannock County Deeds, Wills, Inventories, Etc., 1672-1676, Microfilm, LVA.
Rappahannock County Records, 1677-1687, Microfilm, LVA.
Rappahannock County Deeds, Wils, Inventories, Etc., No. 7, 1682-1688, Microfilm, LVA.
Rappahannock County Deed Book No. 8, 1688-1692, Microfilm, LVA.
Rappahannock County Wills, Deeds, Etc., No. 1, 1665-1677, Microfilm, LVA.
Rappahannock County Wills, No. 2, 1677-1682, Microfilm, LVA.

Richmond County.
Richmond County Account Book 1, Microfilm, LVA.
Richmond County Deeds, No. 1, 1692-1693, Microfilm, LVA.
Richmond County Deeds, No. 2, 1693-1697, Microfilm, LVA.
Richmond County Deed Book, No. 3, 1697-1704, Microfilm, LVA.
Richmond County Deed Book, No. 4, 1705-1708, Microfilm, LVA.
Richmond County Deed Book, No. 5, 1708-1711, Microfilm, LVA.
Richmond County Deed Book, No. 6, 1711-1714, Microfilm, LVA.
Richmond County Deed Book, No. 7, 1714-1720, Microfilm, LVA.
Richmond County Deed Book, No. 8, 1720-1733, Microfilm, LVA.
Richmond County Deed Book, No. 9, 1734-1741, Microfilm, LVA.
Richmond County Deed Book, No. 10, 1741-1750, Microfilm, LVA.
Richmond County Deed Book, No. 11, 1750-1757, Microfilm, LVA.
Richmond County Deed Book, No. 12, 1757-1768, Microfilm, LVA.
Richmond County Deed Book, No. 13, 1768-1774, Microfilm, LVA.
Richmond County Deed Book, NO. 14, 1772-1779, Microfilm, LVA.
Richmond County Deed Book, No. 15, 1779-1788, Microfilm, LVA.
Richmond County Deed Book, No. 16, 1788-1793, Microfilm, LVA.
Richmond County Deed Book, No. 17, .1793-1802, Microfilm, LVA.
Richmond County Deed Book, No. 18, 1802-1810, Microfilm, LVA.

Richmond County Deed Book, No. 19, 1810-1815, Microfilm, LVA.
Richmond County Deed Book, NO. 20, 1815-1820, Microfilm, LVA.
Richmond County Deed Book, No. 21, 1820-1825, Microfilm, LVA.
Richmond County Deed Book, No. 23, 1828-1832, Microfilm, LVA.
Richmond County Deed Book, No. 24, 1835-1840, Microfilm, LVA.
Richmond County Deed Book, No. 25, 1839-1842, Microfilm, LVA.
Richmond County Deed Book, No. 26, 1842-1846, Microfilm, LVA.
Richmond County Deed Book, No. 27, 1846-1850, Microfilm, LVA.
Richmond County Orders, 1692-1694, Microfilm, LVA.
Richmond County Orders, 1694-1699, Microfilm, LVA.
Richmond County Orders, Book 3, 1699-1704, Microfilm, LVA.
Richmond County Orders, Book 4, 1704-1708, Microfilm, LVA.
Richmond County Orders, Book 5, 1708-1711, Microfilm, LVA.
Richmond County Orders, Book 6, 1711-1716, Microfilm, LVA.
Richmond County Orders, Book 7, 1716-1717, Microfilm, LVA.
Richmond County Orders, Book 8, 1718-1721, Microfilm, LVA.
Richmond County Orders, Book 9, 1721-1732, Microfilm, LVA.
Richmond County Orders, Book 10, 1732-1739, Microfilm, LVA.
Richmond County Orders, Book 11, 1739-1746, Microfilm, LVA.
Richmond County Orders, Book 12, 1746-1752, Microfilm, LVA.
Richmond County Orders, Book 13, 1752-1755, Microfilm, LVA.
Richmond County Orders, Book 14, 1756-1762, Microfilm, LVA.
Richmond County Orders, Book 15, 1762-1765, Microfilm, LVA.
Richmond County Orders, Book 16, 1765-1769, Microfilm, LVA.
Richmond County Orders, Book 17, 1769-1773, Microfilm, LVA.
Richmond County Orders, Book 19, 1773-1776, 1784-1786, Microfilm, LVA.
Richmond County Orders, Book 18, 1776-1784, Microfilm, LVA.
Richmond County Orders, Book 20, 1784-1789, Microfilm, LVA.
Richmond County Orders, Book 21, 1789-1794, Microfilm, LVA.
Richmond County Order Book, 1793-1794, Microfilm, LVA.
Richmond County Orders, 1795, Microfilm, LVA.
Richmond County Orders, 1809-1810, Microfilm, LVA.
Richmond County Orders, 1814-1816, Microfilm, LVA.
Richmond County Order Book, No. 24, 1816-1820, Microfilm, LVA.
Richmond County Order Book, NO. 25, 1820-1822, Microfilm, LVA.
Richmond County Order Book, No. 26, 1822-1825, Microfilm, LVA.
Richmond County Order Book, No. 27, 1825-1832, Microfilm, LVA.
Richmond County Order Book No. 28, 1832-1837, Microfilm, LVA.
Richmond County Order Book, 1837-1844, Microfilm, LVA.
Richmond County Order Book, No. 29, 1844-1850, Microfilm, LVA.
Richmond County Wills and Inventories, 1699-1709, Microfilm, LVA.
Richmond County Wills and Inventories, 1709-1717, Microfilm, LVA.
Richmond County Will Book, No. 4, 1717-1725, Microfilm, LVA.
Richmond County Will Book, No. 5, 1725-1753, Microfilm, LVA.
Richmond County Will Book, No. 6, 1753-1767, Microfilm, LVA.
Richmond County Will Book, No. 7, 1767-1787, Microfilm, LVA.
Richmond County Will and Inventories, NO. 8, 1789-1794, Microfilm, LVA.
Richmond County Will Book, No. 9, 1794-1822, Microfilm, LVA.
Richmond County Will Book, NO. 10, 1822-1846, Microfilm, LVA.
Richmond County Will Book, No. 11, 1846-1879, Microfilm, LVA.
Richmond County Will Book, No. 12, 1879-1908, Microfilm, LVA.
Richmond County Poll List, Huntington Library, Huntington, CA, from negative photostats at
    the Library of Virginia, and Richmond Co., VA, Account Book I, pp. 174-177.
Richmond Co., VA, Personal Property Tax Lists, 1782-1850, Microfilm, LVA.
Southampton County.
Southampton Co., VA, Deed Book 5, Microfilm, LVA.

Southampton Co., VA, Will Books 1-3, Microfilm, LVA.

Surry County.

Surry Co., VA, Court Records Book 4, 1682-1691.

Surry Co., VA, Court Records Book 6, 1701-1711.

Surry Co., VA, Will Books 5-6.

Sussex County.

Sussex Co., VA, Deed Books A-E.

Sussex Co., VA, Will Books A-C.

Westmoreland County.

Westmoreland County Deeds and Wills, No. 1, 1653-1671, Microfilm, LVA.

Westmoreland County Deeds, Wills, Etc., 1661-1662, Microfilm, LVA.

Westmoreland County Deeds, Patents, Etc., 1665-1677, Microfilm, LVA.

Westmoreland County Deeds and Wills, No. 2, 1691-1699, Microfilm, LVA.

Westmoreland County Deeds and Wills, No. 3, 1701-1707, Microfilm, LVA.

Westmoreland County Deeds and Wills, No. 4, 1707-1709, Microfilm, LVA.

Westmoreland County Deeds and Wills, No. 5, 1712-1717, Microfilm, LVA.

Westmoreland County Deeds and Wills, No. 6, 1716-1720, Microfilm, LVA.

Westmoreland County Deeds and Wills, No. 7, 1720-1722, Microfilm, LVA.

Westmoreland County Deeds and Wills, No. 8, 1723-1738, Microfilm, LVA.

Westmoreland County Deeds and Wills, No. 9, 1738-1744, Microfilm, LVA.

Westmoreland County Deeds and Wills, No. 10, 1744-1748, Microfilm, LVA.

Westmoreland County Deeds and Wills, No. 11, 1748-1753, Microfilm, LVA.

Westmoreland County Deeds, 1706-1804, Index, Microfilm, LVA.

Westmoreland County Order Book, 1690-1698, Microfilm, LVA.

Westmoreland County Order Book, 1698-1705, Microfilm, LVA.

Westmoreland County Order Book, 1705-1721, Microfilm, LVA.

Westmoreland County Order Book, 1721-1731, Microfilm, LVA.

Westmoreland County Order Book, 1731-1739, Microfilm, LVA.

Westmoreland County Order Book, 1739-1743, Microfilm, LVA.

Westmoreland County Order Book, 1743-1747, Microfilm, LVA.

Westmoreland County Order Book, 1747-1750, Microfilm, LVA.

York County.

York Co., VA, Deeds and Bonds, Book 3, Microfilm, John D. Rockefeller Library, Colonial Williamsburg, Williamsburg, VA.

Virginia State and Colonial Records:

George Connally Family Bible, LVA.

Northern Neck Land Grants Books, Microfilm, LVA.

Register of Albemarle Parish, Surry and Sussex Counties, VA, LVA.

Register and Vestry Book of St. Peter's Parish, New Kent Co., VA, LVA.

Virginia Land Patent Books 1-38, LVA.

n. United States Census.

1790 U. S. Census:

Caswell and Surry Counties, NC.

Edgefield and Orangeburg Districts, SC.

1800 U.S. Census:

Caswell and Johnston Counties, NC.

Edgefield County, SC.

1810 U.S. Census:

Caldwell Co., KY.

Caswell and Chatham Counties, NC.

Grainger Co., TN.

1820 U.S. Census:

Jasper, Jones, Morgan, Tattnall, Walton, and Wilkes Counties, GA.

Union Co., KY.

Caswell, Chatham, and Person Counties, NC.

Bedford, Davidson, and Sumner Counties, TN.

Pittsylvania Co., VA.

1830 U. S. Census:

Monroe and Perry Counties, AL.

Bibb, Clarke, Crawford, Habersham, Hancock, Jackson, Jones, Monroe, Newton, Talbot, Taliaferro, Twiggs, Walton, Ware, and Wilkes Counties, GA.

Gallatin Co., IL.

Union Co., KY.

Copiah and Hinds Counties, MS.

Chatham and Person Counties, NC.

Jefferson Co., TN; Overton Co., TN; Smith and Sumner Counties, TN.

1840 U.S. Census:

Barbour, Conecuh and Shelby Counties, AL.

Crawford, Early, Houston, Jones, Macon, Marion, Newton, Stewart, Talbot, Taliaferro, Tattnall, Twiggs, and Wilkes Counties, Georgia.

Chatham Co., NC.

Overton, Smith, and Sumner Counties, TN.

1850 U.S. Census:

Barbour, Bibb, Clarke, Conecuh, Russell, Sumter, and Tallapoosa Counties, AL.

Carroll, Crawford, Greene, Harris, Houston, Jones, Macon, Muscogee, Newton, Randolph, Sumter, Talbot, Taliaferro, and Tattnall Counties.

Saline Co., IL.

LaClede Co., MO.

Copiah, Choctaw, Hinds, Lauderdale, and Yazoo Counties, MS.

Macon and Overton Counties, TN.

Monroe Co., VA.

1860 U.S. Census:

Barbour, Bibb, Clarke, Lowndes, Pike, Russell, and Tallapoosa Counties, AL.

Hot Spring Co., AR.

Carroll, Crawford, Jasper, Jones, Muscogee, Newton, Pike, Randolph, Schley, and Warren Counties, GA.

Saline and Pope Counties, IL.

Henry Co., IN.

Choctaw (Population, Slave, and Agricultural Schedules), Copiah, Hinds, Lauderdale, Madison, and Smith Counties, MS.

San Augustine Co., TX.

1870 U.S. Census:

Barbour, Pike, Russell, Talladega, and Tallapoosa Counties, AL.

Pulaski Co., AR.

Crawford, Jones, Muscogee, Newton, and Sumter Counties, GA.

Pope and Saline Counties, IL.

Madison County, IN.

Sabine Parish, LA.

Calhoun (Population and Agricultural Schedules), Hinds, Holmes, Madison and Scott Counties, MS.

Robertson and Rusk Counties, TX.

1880 U.S. Census:

Calhoun, Lee, and Pike Counties, GA.

Newton, Pike, and Rockdale Counties, GA.

Pope County, IL.

Hancock and Henry Counties, IN.

Sabine Parish, LA.

Calhoun (Population and Agricultural Schedules), Hinds, Issaquena, Lauderdale, and Madison (Population and Agricultural Schedules) Counties, MS.

Navarro and Rusk Counties, TX.

1880 Mississippi Mortality Schedule, Madison County.

1900 U.S. Census:

Los Angeles Co., CA.

Sabine Parish, LA.

Calhoun, Hinds, Madison, and Sunflower Counties, MS.

McLean County, ND.

Rusk and Titus Counties, TX.

1910 U.S. Census:

Ashley Co., AR.

Calhoun, Hinds, and Madison Counties, MS.

Natchitoches and Sabine Parishes, LA.

McLean Co., ND.

Washita Co., OK.

Navarro Co., TX.

1920 U.S. Census:

Ashley Co, AR.

Calhoun, Hinds, Madison, and Sunflower Counties, MS.

Mercer Co., ND.

Custer Co., OK.

o. United States of America.

Revolutionary War Pension Applications, Microfilm, National Archives, Washington, D.C.

John Fuller, R3835.

Jane Bailey Jackson, W3823/BLWT 3672/160-55.

Dempsey Jordan, W4462.

David Moore, S16980.

Henry Stewart, S31982.

William Whitefield, S38466.

B. Published.

1. Books and Articles.

A Collection of Memorials Concerning Divers Deceased Ministers and others of the People called Quakers in Pennsylvania (Philadelphia, PA, 1824).

Abercrombie, Janice L., and Richard Slatten, eds. *Virginia Revolutionary Public Claims* (3 vols., Athens, LA, 1992).

Acker, M. W. *Franklin Co., GA, Court of Ordinary Records, 1787-1849* (Birmingham, AL, 1989).

Abbe, M. H., and L. W. Parr. *Clarke Co., GA, Tax Digests, 1802-1830* (3 vols., Athens, GA, 2005-2006).

Abbott, F. M. *History of the People of Jones Co., GA* (16 vols., Macon, GA, 1977).

Andrea, Leonardo. The Leonardo Andrea Genealogical Collection for South Carolina, South Caroliniana Library, The University of South Carolina, Stringer File.

Baldwin, J. *Maryland Calendar of Wills, 1635-1743* (8 vols., Baltimore, MD, 1904-1928).

Bannerman, W. B., ed. *The Registers of St. Olave, Hart Street, London, 1563-1700* (Harleian Society, Vol. 96; London, England, 1916).

Bell, L. C. *Register of Charles Parish, York Co., VA: History and Register of Births, 1648-1789, and Deaths, 1665-1787* (Richmond, VA, 1932).

Bell, M. B. *Colonial Bertie Co., NC, Deed Books, A-H, 1720-1757* (Easley, SC, 1977).

Bell, R. *The Book of Ulster Surnames* (Belfast, Ireland, 1988).

Biographical Souvenir of the States of Georgia and Florida (Chicago, IL, 1889).

Bennett, W. D. *Orange Co., NC, Records* (19 vols., Raleigh, NC, 1987 -).

Billings, Warren. *The Old Dominion in the Seventeenth-Century* (Chapel Hill, NC, and Williamsburg, VA, 1975).

Bradley, S. A. *Craven Co., NC, Wills, Deeds, Inventories* (2 vols., Lawrenceville, VA, 2001).

Brantley, K. J., ed. *Records of the Church of Christ at Williams Creek, 1787-1840* (Powder Springs, GA, 1995).

Breen, T. H., J. H. Lewis, and K. Schlessinger, "Motive for Murder: A Servant's Life in Virginia, 1678," *William and Mary Quarterly*, 3rd. Ser., xl (1983): 116-117.

Bruno, J. L. *Newton County, GA, Estate Records, 1822-1900* (2 vols., Covington, GA, 1996).

Bryan, M. G. *Passports Issued by Governors of Georgia, 1785 to 1820* (Washington, DC, 1977).

Burr, B. F. *Tyrell Co., NC, Minutes, Court of Pleas and Quarter Sessions, 1735-1754* (Nacogdoches Co., TX, 1981).

Carlyon-Britton, P. *The Register of Hanham and Oldland, Gloucestershire, 1584-1681* (The Parish Register Society, v. 63; Exeter, England, 1908).

Chalkley, L. *Chronicles of the Scotch-Irish Settlement in Virginia: Extracted from the Original Court Records of Augusta County, 1745-1800* (3 vols., repr., Baltimore, MD, 1999).

Clark, M. J. *American Militia in the Frontier Wars, 1790-1796* (Baltimore, MD, 2003).

Clay, J. W., ed. *Dugdale's Visitation of Yorkshire, 1665-1666, With Additions* (3 vols., Exeter, England, 1917).

Davidson, G. G., ed. *Historical Collections of the Georgia Chapters, Daughters of the American Revolution, Records of Richmond County, Georgia (formerly Saint Paul's Parish)* (Macon, GA, 1929).

Davis, E. T. *Wills and Administrations of Surry Co., VA, 1671-1750* (Baltimore, MD, 1980).

Davis, R. S., Jr., and J. E. Dorsey. *Lincoln County Genealogy and History* (Swainsboro, GA, 1987).

Davis, R. S., Jr. *Georgia Citizens and Soldiers of the American Revolution* (Easley, SC, 1999).

Quaker Records in Georgia: Wrightsborough 1772-1793, Friendsborough, 1776-1777 (Augusta, GA, 1986).

The Wilkes Co. Papers, 1773-1833 (Easley, SC, 1979).

Dorman, J. F., ed. *Westmoreland Co., VA, Deeds and Wills No. 2, 1691-1699* (Washington, DC, 1965).

Evans, Tad. *Greene Co., GA, Newspaper Clippings, 1852-1873* (2 vols., Savannnah, GA, 1995).

Evans, Tad. *Jones Co., GA, Newspaper Abstracts, 1810-1888* (2 vols., Savannah, GA, 2001).

Evans, T. G., ed. *Collections of the New York Genealogical and Biographical Society, Volume II: Baptisms from 1639 to 1730 in the Reformed Dutch Church in New Amsterdam and New York* (New York, NY, 1901).

Farmer, M. M. *Morgan Co., GA, Deed Books A-G, 1808-1820* (Dallas, TX, 2002).

Fleet, B. *Virginia Colonial Abstracts: The Original 34 Volumes Reprinted in 3* (Baltimore, MD, 1988).

Forrest, C. W. *Hinds Co., MS, Will Book I, 1822-57* (Jackson, MS, 1959).

Fothergill, A. B. *Wills of Westmoreland Co., VA, 1654-1800* (Richmond, VA, 1925).

Gammon, David B. *Abstracts of Wills of Bertie Co., NC, 1722-1774* (Raleigh, NC, 1990).

Records of Estates, Bertie Co., NC, 1728-1744, 1762-1790 (Raleigh, NC, 1986).

Tax Lists of Warren County, NC, 1779-1790 (Raleigh, NC, 1994).

Graham, J. S. *A History of Clarke County* (Birmingham, AL, 1923).

Gray, Gertrude E. *Northern Neck Land Grants, 1694-1862* (4 vols., Baltimore, MD, 1987-2008).

Grimes, J. B. *Abstract of North Carolina Wills, 1690-1760* (Raleigh, NC, 1910).

Gwynn, Z. H. *Abstracts of Wills and Estate Records of Granville Co., NC, 1746-1808* (Rocky Mount, NC, 1973).

Court Minutes of Granville Co., NC, 1746-1820 (Rocky Mount, NC, 1977).

Hahn, Marilyn Davis. *Old Cahaba Land Office Records & Military Warrants, 1817-1853* (Easley, SC, 1981).

Old Sparta & Elba Land Office Records and Military Warrants, 1822-1860 (Easley, S.C., 1983).

Harvey, W. *The Visitation of Norfolk in the Year 1563, ed. by Brigadier General Bulwer* (2 vols., Norwich, England, 1895).

Harris, V. M. *Ancient, Curious, and Famous Wills* (Boston, MA, 1911).

Hart, L. H., III. *Surry Co., VA, Wills, Estates and Inventories, 1730-1800* (Easley, SC, 1983).

Haun, W. P. *Bertie Co., NC, Court Minutes, 1740-1762* (7 vols., Durham, NC, 1976 -).

Chowan Co., NC, County Court Minutes Pleas & Quarter Sessions, 1730-1754 (3 vols., Durham, NC, 1983).

Craven Co., NC, Deed and Will Abstracts (3 vols., Durham, NC, 1996).

Craven Precinct, North Carolina, Precinct County Court Minutes (9 vols., Durham, NC, 1978).

Johnston Co., NC, Deeds (6 vols., Durham, NC, 1980-)

Old Albemarle County, North Carolina, Perquimans Precinct, Births, Marriages, Deaths, and Flesh Marks, 1659-1820 (Durham, NC, 1980).

Orange Co., NC, Court Minutes, 1752-1761 (Durham, NC, 1991).

Perquimans Co., NC, Deed Abstracts, 1681-1729 (Durham, NC, 1989).

Headley, R. *Wills of Richmond Co., VA* (Baltimore, MD, 1983).

Hendrix, G. C. *The Jury Lists of SC, 1778-1779* (Baltimore, MD, 1975).

Hinshaw, W. W. *Encyclopedia of American Quaker Genealogy* (6 vols., Ann Arbor, MI, 1936-1950).

Hofmann, Margaret. *Abstracts of Deeds, Edgecombe Precinct, N.C., 1732-58* (Weldon, NC, 1969).

Colony of North Carolina, 1735-1764: Abstracts of Land Patents (Raleigh, NC, 1982).

The Granville District of North Carolina, 1748-63: Abstracts of Land Grants (5 vols., Weldon, NC, 1988-1995).

Holcomb, Brent H. *Bute Co., NC, Court Minutes, 1767-1779* (Columbia, SC, 1988).

Newberry Co., SC, Deed Abstracts, 1785-1806 (3 vols., Columbia, SC, 1999-2000).

Petitions for Land form South Carolina Council Journals (7 vols., Columbia, SC, 1998).

Hudson, Frank Parker. *Wilkes Co., GA, Tax Records, 1785-1805* (2 vols., Atlanta, GA, 1996).

Hyde, L. *The Essays of Henry D. Thoreau* (London, England, 2002).

"Jeremiah Hammack Family Bible," *Tap Roots*, Vol. 7, No. 3 (1970): 123-125.

Jones, W. K. *The Douglas Register: Detailed Register of Births, Marriages, and Deaths as Kept by the Rev. William Douglas, from 1750 to 1797* (Richmond, VA, 1928).

Jordan, Estelle G. *Abstracts of Charles Co., MD, Court and Land Records, 1685-1694* (Baltimore, MD, 2007).

Kelsey, M., N. G. Floyd, G. G. Parsons, *Marriages and Death Notices from the "South Western Baptist" Newspaper* (Bowie, MD, 1995).

King, G. H. S. *Marriages of Richmond Co., VA, 1668-1853* (Fredericksburg, VA, 1964).

The Registers of North Farnham Parish, 1663-1814, and Lunenburg Parish, 1783-1800, Richmond Co., VA (Fredericksburg, VA, 1966).

Kratovil, J. S. *Index to War of 1812 Service Records for Volunteer Soldiers from Georgia* (Atlanta, GA, 1986).

Linn, J. W. *Abstracts of the Minutes of the Court of Pleas and Quarter Sessions, Rowan County, North Carolina, 1753-1762* (Salisbury, NC, 1977).

Abstracts of the Minutes of the Court of Pleas and Quarter Sessions, Rowan County, North Carolina, 1763-1774 (Salisbury, NC, 1979).

Rowan Co., NC, Tax Lists, 1757-1800: Annotated Transcriptions (Rowan, NC, 1995).

Lucas, S. E., Jr., ed., *Index to the Headright and Bounty Grants of Georgia, 1756-1909* (Vidalia, GA, 1970).

Some Georgia County Records (7 vols., Easley, SC, 1977-).

Marsh, H. and T. *Land Deed Genealogy of Hancock County, GA* (Easley, SC, 1997)

Metcalfe, W. C. *The Visitation of Northamptonshire, 1564, 1618-19* (London, England, 1887).

Midgley, L. M., ed. *Ministers' Accounts of the Earldom of Cornwall, 1296-1297*, 2 vols. (Camden Society, 3rd ser., vols. 66, 68, 1942-1945).

Miller, T. L., ed. *Bounty and Donation Land Grants of Texas, 1835-1888* (Austin, TX, and London, England, 1967).

Moss, B. G. *Roster of South Carolina Patriots in the American Revolution* (Baltimore, MD, 1983).

Nugent, N. M. *Cavaliers and Pioneers: Abstracts of Virginia Land Patents and Grants* (3 vols., Richmond, VA, 1929-1934).

Osborn, George C., ed. "Notes and Documents: My Confederate History -- Clay Sharkey," *The Journal of Mississippi History*, Vol. 4 (1942): 225-232.

Potter, D. W. *Passports of Southeastern Pioneers, 1770-1823: Indian, Spanish, and other Land Passports for Tennessee, Kentucky, Georgia, Mississippi, Virginia, North and South Carolina* (Baltimore, MD, 1982).

Pruitt, A. B. *Abstracts of Land Entries: Caswell Co., NC, 1778-95, 1841-1863, and Person Co., NC, 1792-1795* (Raleigh, NC, 1990).

Abstracts of Land Warrants of Guilford Co., NC, 1778-1932 (Raleigh, NC, 1989).

Craven Co., NC, Deed Books 2, 3, &4 (1708-1765) (Whitakers, NC, 2004).

Rockingham Co., NC, Land Warrants: 1778-1929 (Raleigh, NC, 2001).

Spartanburg County-District, South Carolina, Deed Abstracts, Books A-T, 1785-1827 (Easley, SC, 1988).

"Revolutionary War Public Service Claims," *The Virginia Genealogist*, Vol. 30 (1986), No. 4.

Rye, W., ed. *The Visitacion of Norfolk, Made and Taken by William Hervey, Clarenceux King of Arms, Anno 1563, Enlarged with Another Visitacion Made by Clarenceux Cocke, with Many Other Descents; and Also the Visitation Made by John Raven, Richmond, Anno 1613* (Harleian Society, Publications, v. 32; London, England, 1891).

Saunders, T. *The Colonial and State Records of North Carolina* (26 vols., Raleigh, NC, 1886-1907).

Shields, Ruth H. *Abstracts of the Minutes of the Court of Pleas and Quarter Sessions of Orange Co., NC,*

1752-1766 (Chapel Hill, NC, 1965).

Orange Co., NC, Court Minutes (Chapel Hill, 1965).

Smith, Sarah Quinn. *Early Georgia Wills and Settlements of Estates: Wilkes County* (Washington, GA, 1959).

Southern Historical Association. *Memoirs of Georgia* (2 vols., Atlanta, GA, 1895).

Thaxton, Donna B., and C. Stanton Thaxton, eds. *Georgia Indian Depredation Claims* (Americus, GA, 1988).

Thomas, A. *Laurens Co., GA, Legal Records, 1807-1857* (2 vols., Roswell, GA, 1991).

Tucker, James, ed., "William Hammack Family Bible," *Tap Roots*, Vol. 24, No. 1 (July 1986), pp. 3-5.

Turner, F. P. *Greene Co., GA, Land Records, Deeds, 1785-1810* (Fernandina Beach, FL, 1997).

U.S. War Department, *The War of the Rebellion: A Compilation of the Official Records of the Union and Confederate Armies* (53 vols., Washington, DC, 1880-1901).

Virginia Transportation Research Council, *Historic Records of Virginia: Augusta County Road Orders, 1745-1769* (Charlottesville, VA, 1998).

Webster, I. B. *Rockingham Co., NC, Deed Abstracts, 1785-1800* (Madison, NC, 1973).

Weisiger, B. B., III. *Charles City Co., VA, Wills and Deeds, 1725-31* (Richmond, VA, 1984).

Charles City Co., VA, Records, 1737-1774, with several 17th Century Fragments (Richmond, VA, 1986).

Henrico Co., VA, Deeds, 1677-1774 (4 vols., Richmond, VA, 1985 -).

Henrico Co., VA, Wills, 1654-1737 (Richmond, VA, 1976).

Prince George Co., VA, Records, 1733-92 (Richmond, VA, 1975).

Prince George Co., VA, Wills and Deeds, 1713-28 (Richmond, VA, 1973).

Wells, C. *Edgefield Co., SC, Deed Books 36-38* (Baltimore, MD, 2007).

Whitten, J. *Abstracts of Bedford Co., VA, Wills, Inventories, and Accounts, 1754-1787* (Dallas, TX, 1968).

Wingo, E. B. *Norfolk Co., VA, Tithables, 1730-1750* (Norfolk, VA, 1974).

Wooley, J. E. and V. *Edgefield Co., SC, Wills, 1787-1836* (Greenville, SC, 1991).

2. Newspapers.

The Calhoun Monitor-Herald.
The Cookeville (TN) Herald-Citizen.
The Georgia Journal.
The Hinds County Gazette.
The Madison County Herald.
The Gospel Manager.
The Smithfield (NC) Herald.
The South Western Baptist Newspaper.
The Washington Chronicle.
The Weatherford (OK) News.
The Weekly American Banner.

3. Electronic.

International Genealogical Index, Version 5.0, The Church of Jesus Christ of Latter-Day Saints.

1841 Census of England Database (The National Archives, Kew, Richmond, Surrey, TW9 4DU.

4. DNA Studies.

Mitchell family DNA Study: http://www.familytreedna.com/public/Mitchell.

II. Secondary Sources

1. Books and Articles.

Addison, W. *Understanding English Surnames* (London, England, 1978).

Allen, C. "Hannah (Collett) Lanier," *The American Genealogist*, Vol. 77, No. 4 (October 2002), p. 322-326.

Austin, J. H. *The Georgians: Genealogies of Pioneer Settlers* (Baltimore, MD, 1984).

Avant, D. A. *Some Southern Colonial Families* (Tallahassee, FL, 1982).

Ayers, E. L. *The Promise of the New South: Life After Reconstruction* (Oxford, England, 1993).

Baber, Adin. *Nancy Hanks of "Undistinguished families, second families"* (Bloomington, IN, 1959).

Nancy Hanks, The Destined Mother of a President (Glendale, CA, 1963).

Ball, T. W. *A Glance Into The Great South-East or Clarke County, Alabama, and Its Surroundings, From 1540 to 1877* (Grove Hill, AL, 1882).

Bardlsey, C. W. *A Dictionary of English and Welsh Surnames With Special American Instances* (London, England, 1901).

Bartley, N. V. *The Creation of Modern Georgia* (2d. ed., Athens, GA, 1990).

Barton, William E. *The Lineage of Lincoln* (Indianapolis, IN, 1929).

Beeman, R. *The Evolution of the Southern Backcountry: A Case Study of Lunenburg Co., VA 1746-1832* (Philadelphia, PA, 1984).

Bell, R. M. *The Alexander Stephens Family: Pennsylvania-Georgia* (Washington, PA, 1981).

Blassingame, J. W. *The Slave Community: Plantation Life in the Antebellum South* (New York, NY, and Oxford, England, 1972).

Bloom, K. J. *The Mississippi Valley's Great Yellow Fever Epidemic of 1878* (Baton Rouge, LA, 1993).

Boddie, J. B. *Historical Southern Families* (23 vols., Redwood City, CA, 1957-).

Seventeenth-Century Isle of Wight (Chicago, IL, 1938).

Boles, J. *The South Through Time* (New York, NY, 1995).

Bouvier, John. *A Law Dictionary Adapted to the Constitution and Laws of the United States of America and of the Several States of the American Union* (Philadelphia, PA, 1856).

Brandenberger, Evelyn Duke, and Clara Jackson Martin, "The Jacksons of Lower Virginia," *The Virginia Genealogist*, 33 (1990): 224-230.

Brayton, J. A. "A Royal Descent For Christopher Calthorpe of York Co., VA," *The Virginia Genealogist*, pp. 67-70.

"The Ancestry of Edward Jones of Isle of Wight County, Virginia," *The Virginia Genealogist*, Vol. 45, No. 1 (January-March 2001): 67.

Brents, J. A. *The Patriots and Guerillas of East Tennessee and Kentucky...including Sketches of Noted Guerillas and Distinguished Patriots* (New York, NY, 1863).

Brewer, H. "Entailing Aristocracy in Colonial Virginia: 'Ancient Feudal Restraints' and Revolutionary Reform," *William and Mary Quarterly*, 3rd. Ser., Vol. 54, No. 2 (April 1997), pp. 307-346.

Brieger, James W. *Hometown Mississippi* (2nd ed., no publisher, no date).

Breen, T. H., ed. "'Baubles of Britain': The American and Consumer Revolutions of the Eighteenth Century," in P. D. Morgan, ed., *Diversity and Unity in Early North America* (London, England, 1993).

Tobacco Culture: The Mentality of the Great Tidewater Planters on the Eve of the Revolution (Princeton, NJ, 1985).

Brown, D. *Bury My Heart at Wounded Knee: An Indian History of the American West* (New York, NY, 1970; repr., New York, NY, 2001).

Brown, R. H. *The Republic in Peril: 1812* (New York, NY, 1971).

Brown, K. M. *Good Wives, Nasty Wenches, and Anxious Patiarchs: Gender, Race, and Power in Colonial Virginia* (Chapel Hill, NC, and London, England, 1996).

Carroll County Heritage Book Committee, *The Heritage of Carroll Co., GA, 1826-2001* (Waynesville, NC, 2002).

Carter, Arthur C. *Carter and Kinsmen: Folmar - Rodgers - Sanders - Bryan* (Montgomery, AL, 1990).

Carson, C., N. F. Barka, W. M. Kelso, G. W. Stone, D. Upton, "Impermanent Architecture in the Southern American Colonies," *Winterthur Portfolio* 16 (1981), pp. 135-196.

Chipman, D. E. *Spanish Texas, 1519-1821* (Austin, TX, 1992).

Clement, M. C. *Lanier: Her Name* (Chatham, VA, 1954).

Cooper, W. J., and T. E. Terrill, *The American South: A History* (2 vols., 4th ed., Lanham, MD, 2008).

Cressy, D. *Birth, Marriage, and Death: Ritual, Religion, and the Life Cycle in Tudor and Stuart England* (Oxford, England, 1997).

Cressy, D. "The Protestation Oath Protested, 1641 and 1642," *The Historical Journal*, 45 (2002): 251-279.

Cruse, J. B. *Battles of the Red River War* (College Station, TX, 2008).

Dorman, J. F., and M. J. Hiden, eds. *Adventurers of Purse and Person in Virginia, 1607-1624* (3rd. ed., Richmond, VA, 1987).

Doolittle, W. F. *The Doolittle Family in America* (Cleveland, OH, 1901).

Doolittle, W. F. *Doolittle Family in America* (revised ed., Cleveland, OH, 1922).

Doughtie, B. M. *The Mackeys (Variously Spelled) and Allied Families* (Decatur, GA, 1957).

Edelblute, C., R. Freshwater and H. Freshwater, *Freshwater Families: Research and Genealogy* (2nd ed., Richmond, VA, 1990).

Elmore, L. *An Elmore Odyssey* (Layton, UT, 1989).

Everton, W. M., et al. *The Handy Book for Genealogists* (7th ed., Logan, UT, 1981).

Faris, David. *Plantagenet Ancestry of Seventeenth-Century Colonists* (Boston, MA, 1999).

Plantagenet Ancestry of Seventeenth-Century Colonists: The Descent from the Later Plantagenet Kings of England (Baltimore, MD, 1996).

Faust, D. G. *Republic of Suffering: Death and the American Civil War* (New York, NY, 2009).

Fentress County Historical Society, *History of Fentress Co., Tennessee* (Dallas, TX, 1987).

Fincher, E.D., and A. W. Fincher, *Fincher in the USA, 1683-1900* (Greenville, SC, 1981).

First Families of Tennessee, *First Families of Tennessee: A Register of Early Settlers and Their Present Day Descendants* (Knoxville, TN, 2000).

Fischer, D. H. *Albion's Seed: Four British Folkways in America* (Oxford, England, 1989).

Foner, E. *Reconstruction: American's Unfinished Revolution, 1863-1877* (New York, NY, 1988).

Freeman, P., and E. P. Harper, *Twenty-One Southern Families: Notes and Genealogies* (Atlanta, GA, 1985).

Futhey, J.S., and G. Cope, *The History of Chester Co., PA* (Philadelphia, PA, 1881).

Gillis, M. B. *Gillis and Other Pioneer Families of Georgia, Second Edition, Ancestral Families of the Author* (Glenview, IL, 2000).

Gnann, P. R., A. G. LeBey, M. L. Lassiter, et. al., *Georgia Salzburgers and Allied Families* (4 vols., Greenville, SC, 1956-2003).

Goodwyn, L. *The Populist Moment: A Short History of the Agrarian Revolt* (Oxford, England, 1978).

Griffin, Patrick. *The People With No Name: Ireland's Ulster Scots, America's Scots-Irish, and the Creation of a British Atlantic World, 1689-1764* (Princeton, NJ, 2001).

Hagood, Lois. *The Elusive Ancestor* (Crossett, AR, 1992).

Haigler, Anne Martin. *Bankston Cousins* (Florissant, MO, 1998).

Haley, J. L. *The Buffalo War: The History of the Red River Indian Uprising of 1874* (Austin, TX, 1998).

Hall, William K. *Descendants of Nicholas Perkins of Virginia* (Ann Arbor, MI, 1957).

Hammack, H. F. *Wandering Back* (2 vols., Beebe, AR, 1954-1961).

Harrison, B. *The Bassanos, Italian Musicians at the English Court, 1531-1664* (La Canada, CA, 1991).

Hathaway, J. R. B. *The North Carolina Historical and Genealogical Register*, Vol. 1 (1900).

Heal, F., and C. Holmes, *The Gentry in England and Wales, 1500-1700* (Basingstoke, England, 1994).

Heinemann, R. L., J. G. Kolp, A. S. Parent, Jr., and W. G. Shade, *Old Dominion, New Commonwealth: A History of Virginia, 1607-2007* (Charlottesville, VA, and London, England, 2007).

Hild, M. *Greenbackers, Knights of Labor, and Populists: Farmer-Labor Insurgency in the Late Nineteenth-Century South* (Athens, GA, and London, England, 2007).

Hoffecker, C. E., R. Waldron, L. E. Williams, and B. E. Benson, *New Sweden in America* (Newark, NJ, and London, England, 1995).

Holton, W. *Forced Founders: Indians, Debtors, Slaves, and the Making of the American Revolution in Virginia* (Chapel Hill, NC, and London, England, 1999).

Howe, D. W. *What God Hath Wrought: The Transformation of America, 1815-1848* (Oxford, England, 2009).

Isaac, R. *The Transformation of Virginia, 1740-1790* (New York, NY, 1982).

Ingersoll, L. *Lanier: A Genealogy of the family who came to Virginia and their French Ancestors in London* (Washington, DC, 1965).

Jackson, J. G. *My Search for John Stephen Jackson: His Ancestors and Descendants* (Easley, SC, 2006).

Jackson, W. J. *Ancestral Notebook of Jackson and Related Families* (Fort Lauderdale, FL, 1973).

Jordan, Robert A. *Jordan Journal: History of the George and Arthur Jordan Families of Virginia, North Carolina, Indiana from 1634* (Evansville, IN, 1996).

Knight, T. D. *Early Moore Families of Wilkes, Jones, Greene, Hancock, and Taliaferro Counties, Georgia: The Quest to Identify Elizabeth Jane Moore Hammack* (unpublished manuscript, 2004).

Lamb, G. *Orkney Surnames* (Edinburgh, Scotland, 1981).

Kolbe, J. Christian. *The Library of Virginia, Research Notes Number 17: Colonial Tithables* (Richmond, VA, 2001).

"Land Lottery System," The New Georgia Encyclopedia (*http://www.georgiaencyclopedia.org*), Retrieved 15 May 2009.

Lasocki, D., and R. Prior, *The Bassanos, Venetian Musicians and InstrumentMakers in England, 1531-1665* (Aldershot, England, 1995).

Lee-Warner, Rev. James. "The Calthropes of Burnham," *Norfolk Archaeology*, v. 9 (1884), pp. 1-19.

Lenoir County Heritage Commission, *The Heritage of Lenoir County, North Carolina* (Kinston, NC, 1981).

Litwack, L. *Been in the Storm So Long: The Aftermath of Slavery* (New York, NY, 1979).

Long, Daniel R. *John Lewis, "The Lost Pioneer," His Ancestors and Descendants (1670 - 1970)* (Baltimore, MD, 1971).

Leyburn, J. G. *The Scotch-Irish: A Social History* (Chapel Hill, NC, 1962).

Lloyd, Daniel B. *The Middletons and Kindred Families of Southern Maryland* (Bethesda, MD, 1975).

McCall, E. T. *McCall-Tidwell and Allied Families* (Atlanta, GA, 1931).

McCall, K. S. *A Study of One McCall Family in the Nineteenth Century: Georgia, Mississippi, Louisiana, and Texas* (Ardmore, OK, 1979).

McSwain, E. D. *Some Ancestors and Descendants of Richard Parker, Chirurgeon, Born in Cornwall, 1629, Died in Virginia, Ca. 1680, and Many Other Parker Records* (Macon, GA, 1980).

McKinley, R. *The Surnames of Oxfordshire* (London, England, 1977).

Mead, C. L. *The Land Between Two Rivers: Madison Co., MS* (Jackson, MS, 1987).

Middleton, R. *Colonial America: A History* (3rd ed., Malden, MA, 2002).

Miller, N. C. and G. L. *Allens of the South States* (Baltimore, MD, 1989).

Millican, P. "The Gawdys of Norfolk and Suffolk," in *Original Papers of the Norfolk and Norwich Archeological Society*, 26 (Norwich, England, 1946): 335-347, and 27 (Norwich, England, 1947): 30-43, 70-73.

K. F. Mitchell, *Early Southern Fullers* (Easley, SC, 2004).

Monod, P. K. *Jacobitism and the English People, 1688-1788* (Cambridge, England, and New York, NY, 1993).

Morgan, E. S. *American Slavery, American Freedom: The Ordeal of Colonial Virginia* (New York, NY, 1975).

Naipaul, V. S. *A Turn in the South* (New York, NY, 1989).

NSDAR, *DAR Patriot Index, Centennial Edition* (3 vols., Washington, DC, 1990).

Newton Co., GA, Historical Society, *History of Newton Co., GA* (Covington, GA, 1988).

Nottingham, C. W., and E. Hannah, *History of Upson County, Georgia* (Macon, GA, 1930).

Nuss, W. E. *My Hammock Family, 1656-: A History of the Ancestors and Descendants of George Bartlett William Hammock (1825-1862)* (Cullman, AL, 1997).

Omohundro, G. P. *Ancestors and Descendants of Brice Wiseman Hammack* (Santa Ana, CA, 1986).

Owen, Thomas M. *History and Genealogies of Old Granville Co., NC, 1746-1800* (Greenville, SC, 1993).

Padel, O.J. *Cornish Place-Name Elements* (London, England, 1985). This volume was published as volumes LVI-LVII of the *English Place Name Society* series.

Pagan, J. R., *Anne Orthwood's Bastard* (Oxford, 2004).

"Law and Society in Restoration Virginia" (D. Phil. Thesis, University of Oxford, 1996).

Paschal, R. L. P. *Some Paschal Ancestors, Descendants and Allied Families* (Wolfe City, TX, 1969).

Perry, J. R. *The Formation of a Society on Virginia's Eastern Shore, 1615-1655* (Chapel Hill, NC, and London, England, 1990).

Rakove, Jack. *James Madison and the Creation of the American Republic* (3rd ed., New York, NY, 2007).

Ramsey, R. W. *Carolina Cradle: Settlement of the Northwest Carolina Frontier, 1747-1762* (Chapel Hill, NC, 1964).

Ray, W. S. *Index to Hathaway's Register* (Baltimore, MD, 1956).

Reaney, P.H., and R. M. Wilson, *A Dictionary of English Surnames* (Oxford, England, 1997).

Remini, R. V. *Andrew Jackson and His Indian Wars* (New York, NY, 2001).

Andrew Jackson (New York, NY, 1969).

Richardson, D., and K. G. Everingham, eds., *Magna Carta Ancestry: A Study in Colonial and Medieval Ancestry* (Baltimore, MD, 2005).

Plantagenet Ancestry: A Study in Colonial and Medieval Families (Baltimore, MD, 2004).

Risjord, N. R. *Representative Americans: The Revolutionary Generation* (Lanham, MD, 2001).

Representative Americans: The Romantics (Lanham, MD, and Oxford, England, 2001).

Roberts, Gary B. *Ancestors of American Presidents* (Santa Clarita, CA, 1995).

Rowland, Dunbar. *The Mississippi Official and Statistical Register of 1908* (Jackson, MS, 1908).

Rozier, John. *The Houses of Hancock, 1785-1865* (Decatur, GA, 1996).

Rutman, D. B. and A. H. *A Place in Time: Middlesex Co., VA, 1650-1750* (New York, NY, and Oxford, England, 1984).

Saggus, C. D. *Agrarian Arcadia: Anglo-Virginian Planters of Wilkes County, Georgia* (Washington, GA, 1996).

Shine, J. W. *Shine Family in Europe and America* (Sault St. Marie, MI, 1917).

Shivers, Forrest. *The Land Between: A History of Hancock County, Georgia, to 1940* (Spartanburg, SC, 1990).

Smith, E. W. *The History of Hancock Co., GA* (Sparta, GA, 1974).

Sparrow, W. K., and C. B. Alexander. *"First of Patriots and the Best of Men": Richard Caswell in Public Life* (Kinston, NC, 2007).

St. George, R. "'Heated' Speech and Literacy in Seventeenth-Century New England," in D. G. Allen and D. D. Hall, *Seventeenth-Century New England* (Boston, MA, 1985), pp. 275-322.

Stone, Lawrence. *The Family, Sex, and Marriage in England, 1500-1800* (London, England, 1977).

Sturgill, David A. *Who Was Nancy Hanks Lincoln* (Piney Creek, NC, 1995).

Tisdale, R. *Meet the Tisdales: Descendants of John Tisdale of Taunton, Massachusetts, 1634-1980* (Baltimore, MD, 1981).

Tomlinson, G. S. *The Descendants of Richard and Janey Burch of King and Queen County, Virginia, and Person County, North Carolina: A Collaborated Genealogy* (Senatobia, MS, 1994).

Torrence, C., ed. *The Edward Pleasants Valentine Papers: Abstracts of 17th- and 18th-Century Virginia Records Relating to 34 Families* (4 vols., repr., Baltimore, MD, 1979).

Torrence, C. *Old Somerset on the Eastern Shore of Maryland: A Study in Foundations and Founders* (Richmond, VA, 1935).

Ulrich, L. T. *Good Wives: Image and Reality in the Lives of Women in Northern New England, 1650-1750* (New York, NY, 1982).

Updike, Ethel S. *Gary Family of England to Virginia to South Carolina* (Salt Lake City, UT, 1976).

Vicksburg National Military Park Commission, *Indiana at Vicksburg* (Vicksburg, MS, 1911).

Washington, G. S. H. L. *The Earliest Washingtons and Their Anglo-Scottish Connections* (Cambridge, England, 1964).

Way, G. *Scottish Clan and Family Encyclopedia* (Glasgow, Scotland, 1994).

Weis, Frederick L. *Ancestral Roots of Sixty Colonists Who Came to New England Between 1623 and 1650* (6th ed., W. L. Sheppard, Jr., ed., Baltimore, MD, 1988).

Weisiger, Minor T. *The Library of Virginia, Research Notes Number 3: Using Personal Property Tax Records in the Archives at the Library of Virginia* (Richmond, VA, 2001).

Wellington, W. W. *Cemeteries of Madison Co., MS* (Canton, MS, 1995).

Wertenbaker, T. J. *The Planters of Colonial Virginia* (Princeton, NJ, 1922).

Whatley, George F. *The Families of Whatley, Persons, Roop and Fields* (St. Petersburg, FL, 1989).

Whitelaw, R. T. *Virginia's Eastern Shore: A History of Accomack and Northampton Counties* (2 vols., Richmond, VA, 1951).

Wilkinson, M. M. *Genealogy of the Wilkinson and Allied Families* (Shelby, MS, 1949).

Williams, Carolyn White. *History of Jones County, Georgia: For One Hundred Years, Specifically 1807-1907* (Macon, GA, 1957).

Williams, Carolyn White, and T. B. White. *History of Greene County, Georgia, 1786-1886* (Macon, GA, 1961).

Wilson, M. I. *Nicholas Lanier: Master of the King's Music* (Aldershot, England, 1994).

Wood, M. S. W. *Stevens-Davis and Allied Families: A Memorial Volume of History, Biography, and Genealogy* (Macon, GA, 1957).

Woodward, C. V. *Origins of the New South, 1877-1913* (Baton Rouge, LA, 1951).

Reunion and Reaction: The Compromise of 1877 and the End of Reconstruction (Oxford, England, 1991).

Wright, T. R. B., L. Washington, R. H. McKim, and G. W. Beale. *Westmoreland Co., VA* (Richmond, VA, 1912).

Wynne, A. E. *Southern Lineages: Records of Thirteen Families* (Aberdeen, MS, 1940).

NAME INDEX

The following Name Index compiled by Picton Press contains a total of 13,446 entries. Women are indexed whenever possible under both their maiden and married name(s). Maiden names are given in parentheses, thus Mary (Smith) Jones. When the maiden name is unknown, it is given thus: Mary (--) Jones. As always, readers are cautioned to check under all conceivable spellings.

Picton Press   12 January 2011

[UNKNOWN]
Bettie, 732
John, 732
Lucy, 725
Mary, 732
S M, 725
William Q, 725
ABBOTT
Agnes, 358
ABERNATHY
Serita, 694
ACES
Roxalano, 560
ACHELLY
Mary, 408
ACKERMAN
--, 666
Gail (Hammack), 666
ACREE
Elizabeth (O'Neal), 383
Nathaniel, 383
Olive, 392
ACREWS
Peter, 746
ADAMS
Augustus, 537
Caleb, 135-136, 536
Dennis Dale, 690
Elizabeth Anna, 537
Emeline, 537
George F, 563
Indiana (Hammoch), 745
Isaiah, 745
Jeremiah, 745
Joe, 690
John W, 537
Joshua, 537
Lavina (Hammoch), 745
Lively, 530
Margaret Lavenial (Roberts), 690
Martha, 537
Martha Jane, 586

Mary Ann, 537
Nancy (Hammoch), 745
Nettie (Rogers), 536
Nipper, 537
Rhoda Jo, 690, 711
Sallie, 527
Sarah Jane, 537
Sarah Jane (Hammack), 563
William, 537
AINSWORTH
Martha Jane, 610
ALBERS
Flora, 666
ALEXANDER
Margaret, 648
ALFORD
Aaron, 739
Bathsheba (Hammack), 739
ALLDAY
Johnnie Elizabeth, 643
ALLEN
Amy Elizabeth, 717
Elizabeth, 411
Elizabeth (Walker), 412
Elizabeth (West), 412
Elizabeth (Young?), 412
James A, 626
Martha J (Hammack), 626
Mary (Owen), 412
Mary Ann (Amos), 544
Nancy, 412
Robert, 412
Thomas Bryant, 544
William, 412
ALLERTON
Willoughby, 727
ALLISON
Billy, 688
Ernston, 688
Jimmy, 688
Margaret Ann, 688
Paula, 688

Virginia (Smith), 687-688
Wanda, 688
ALLUMS
Rhoda, 595
AMONS
Sheila, 700
AMOS
Ada E, 610
Ada Lee, 611
Adaline Ariadne (McBride), 535
Ala "Aler" Emeline, 611
Alexander Zachariah, 611
Amy Archina (Oldham), 611
Annie (Bentley), 544
Anny (Bentley), 504
Arsula Jane (Calhoun), 611
Beverly, 544
Beverly C, 504
Caroline F, 504
Caroline J (Harper), 504
Catherine, 609
Catherine Elizabeth, 612
Celeste, 610
Cora (Haley), 611
Daniel, 504
David W, 610
Donie, 610
Elizabeth, 481, 511, 544
Elizabeth C (Harper), 504
Elizabeth Jane, 610
Ella L, 612
Emeline (Miles), 610
Eugenia Augusta, 612
Frances Elizabeth Catherine, 610
Frances Mary "Mollie" (Moore), 612
George, 504, 544
George Burkett, 612
George W, 535
George Washington, 159-160, 504, 544, 611
Helen (Mullins), 613
Henry D, 504

HAMMACK/ HAMMOCK (continued)

Melvina, 630, 753
Meredith, 625
Meredith Stanton, 517
Messer, 755, 763
Micajah, 760(2)
Michael, 34, 36, 38, 464, 466, 469,
    473, 482, 512, 541, 573, 629,
    676, 760
Michael R, 783
Michael Rudolph, 783
Michael S, 535, 760
Mildred, 508, 628
Mildred (Lambert), 85, 87, 110, 236,
    472
Mildred Leola, 659, 677
Miles Jefferon, 619
Miles Jefferson "Jeff", 618
Millenor, 728
Millenor (--), 751
Millenor (Jackson), 121, 216, 239,
    246, 428, 433, 477, 723, 767
Miller G, 781
Milley, 482
Millie, 556
Millie (Smallwood), 601
Millie Ann, 541
Millie Ann (Hayes), 586
Millie Jane, 656
Milly, 471, 479-480, 496, 529-530
Milly Ann (Smallwood), 639
Milly C (--), 565
Milly Quarles (Oakley), 556
Minerva, 622
Minerva (--), 768
Minerva Jane (Walker), 567
Minnie, 722, 781
Minnie E, 641, 656
Minnie Lee, 665
Minnie Lou, 636
Minnie M, 776
Missouri, 532, 577, 593
Missouri "Dink", 525
Misty, 676
Misty Michelle, 701
Mitchell W, 619
Mollie, 744, 755, 768
Mollie (Pride), 522
Mollie J (Woodman), 579
Molly, 477
Molly (--), 551, 638-639
Molly (Mann), 593
Molly (Scutt), 499
Monroe, 744
Morgan, 522
Morgan Brown, 487, 521
Morgan M, 587
Moses, 492, 528
Myrna (Rice), 676
Myrtie Monell, 659, 675
Myrtle, 638, 641
Myrtle Louise, 647, 665

N, 738
Nancy, 136(2), 460, 471, 476, 481,
    487, 489-490, 497, 501-502,
    509, 520-522, 525-526, 532,
    536, 538, 553, 555, 559, 561,
    567, 578, 586-587, 593, 619,
    624, 628-629, 632-633, 722,
    730-731, 738, 742, 745, 761(2),
    773, 782, 784
Nancy "Anna", 497
Nancy (--), 496, 526, 558, 571, 631,
    654, 742, 746, 768
Nancy (Anna), 477
Nancy (Bolton), 559
Nancy (Brown), 97-98, 113-114,
    487
Nancy (Burrows), 527, 532
Nancy (Combs), 476, 489, 767
Nancy (Cotterrell), 625
Nancy (Cromwell), 521
Nancy (Decker), 622
Nancy (Ellrod), 577
Nancy (Ezell), 193, 195
Nancy (Faust), 616
Nancy (Feagin), 154, 540, 754
Nancy (Foley), 779
Nancy (Green), 561
Nancy (Jackson), 567, 581
Nancy (Laughton), 573
Nancy (Maple), 756
Nancy (Maples), 507, 557
Nancy (McCall), 529
Nancy (McClung), 518
Nancy (Miller), 496
Nancy (Parks), 567
Nancy (Poythress), 519
Nancy (Prunty), 509
Nancy (Scott), 572
Nancy (Sercy), 533
Nancy (Todd), 752(2)
Nancy (Whatley), 534
Nancy (Williams), 526
Nancy (Wood), 552
Nancy A, 565
Nancy Ann, 492, 568
Nancy Barbara, 637
Nancy C, 531, 750
Nancy D, 756
Nancy E, 553, 593, 618-619, 745
Nancy E (Fields), 763
Nancy E (Hammock), 618-619
Nancy E (Magill), 522
Nancy Eliza (Ezell), 599
Nancy Ellen (Johnson), 607
Nancy Ellen (Jones), 568
Nancy Ellen (Parr), 570
Nancy I Victoria, 586
Nancy J, 554, 573, 624
Nancy J (Copeland), 556
Nancy Jane, 558, 572, 631
Nancy Janette, 585, 744
Nancy Katherine (Collins), 518

Nancy Levicy, 519
Nancy M, 592
Nancy Margaret, 569
Nancy R, 633
Nancy Rebecca, 603
Nancy Virginia, 553
Nannie, 763
Nannie (--), 634
Nannie C, 554
Naomi, 597, 645
Napolean B, 551, 627
Napoloen Bonaparte, 595
Narcissa, 747
Narcissa (Lutton), 761
Narcissa J (--), 761
Nathan, 623
Nathan Bussey, 596
Nathaniel, 628, 762
Neil, 780
Nellie, 668
Nellie B (--), 617
Nettie, 654
Nettie (--), 654
Nettie (Sarden), 773
Newton Evans, 622
Nicholas, 469
Nicholas Thomas V, 554
Nina (Smith), 594
Noah, 558, 621-622
Noel B, 763
Nona, 766
Nora, 761
Nora (Gailey), 778
Nottley Scott, 632
Obediah, 762
Octavia, 723
Ola Hicks, 600
Olive, 657, 778
Oliver, 564, 629
Ollie (--), 590
Onie, 783
Orato Hammack, 782
Orlena H, 607
Orpha, 755
Orphie, 597
Orra (--), 630
Orrisn S, 783
Oscar, 587
P Carl, 778
Pachal, 770
Palmer, 580
Pamela Antoinette (Porter), 634
Pamela Louise, 681, 701
Parr (Norton), 667
Parthena (Hundley), 531
Parthena Ann (Ray), 556
Pascal H, 771
Pasch, 770
Paschal, 484, 513-514, 575, 728-729
Paschall, 491
Paschall H, 576
Patricia, 666, 686

HAMMACK/ HAMMOCK (continued)

Russell Grant, 637
Russell P, 635
Ruth, 474, 487, 506, 522, 559, 724
Ruth (--), 773
Ruth (Phillips), 556
Ruth (Seaberry), 772
Ruth Amanda, 654
Ruth J, 521
Ruth Seaberry (Yates), 635
Ruth Sutes (Lassiter), 633
Rutha (--), 513, 770
Ruthe (Reap), 688
Ruthie (--), 658
Ruthy B, 575
S, 738, 740(2), 753, 766
S A, 622, 734
S E, 723, 770, 779
S H, 783
S S, 783
S T, 668
Sadie Lucile, 211
Saide Lucille, 664, 679
Salley (Harvey), 557
Sallie, 614, 629, 638, 741
Sallie (--), 766(2)
Sallie (Adams), 527
Sallie (Barrow), 781
Sallie (Hodge), 636
Sallie E (--), 645
Sallie Elizabeth (Cates), 205-211,
    217, 432-433, 445, 447, 459,
    646
Sallie H, 587
Sally, 501, 516, 552, 625
Sally (Dial), 522
Sally (Sharp), 557
Sally Ann (--), 559
Sally S, 592, 640
Samantha, 783
Samantha (White), 607
Samantha Jane (Kantzler), 632
Samuel, 469, 473, 475, 482-483,
    491, 513, 526, 554, 558, 571,
    623, 656, 728-729, 739-739,
    740(2), 745, 766-766, 767(2),
    775, 778-779, 781, 783
Samuel A, 781
Samuel Abisha, 632
Samuel C, 780(2)
Samuel Cornelius, 780-781
Samuel E, 746
Samuel F, 778
Samuel H, 783
Samuel J, 587, 740
Samuel Moreman, 574, 634
Samuel P, 511
Samuel S, 775, 782-783
Samuel Shambaugh, 783
Samule L, 635
Sandra, 686
Sandy (Rogers), 667

Sara, 198, 600, 652
Sara (Brock), 558
Sara A (Ridings), 781
Sara E, 561, 588
Sarah, 155(3), 190(2), 466, 477-478,
    484, 490-491, 493, 496,
    507-508, 515, 521-522, 525,
    527, 549, 554, 556, 564,
    570-571, 577, 601, 615, 621,
    623-624, 631, 668, 724, 730(2),
    745(2), 751, 762(2), 765, 767(2),
    769-770, 777-779, 782
Sarah "Sally" (--), 501
Sarah (--), 475, 477, 483, 490-491,
    526, 554, 563, 570, 578,
    619-620, 655, 722, 734, 744,
    755
Sarah (Ashley), 560
Sarah (Brock), 756, 770
Sarah (Campbell), 615
Sarah (Cloyd), 569
Sarah (Daniel), 518
Sarah (Goodman), 572
Sarah (Hull), 572, 756
Sarah (Janeway), 558, 755
Sarah (Lay), 196-198
Sarah (Meese), 564
Sarah (Peppers), 755
Sarah (Sikes), 516
Sarah (Smith), 558
Sarah (Smock), 567
Sarah (Tanner), 622
Sarah (Ussery), 536
Sarah (Walden), 745
Sarah (Weeden), 632
Sarah (Williams), 535, 760
Sarah A, 747, 780-781
Sarah A (--), 533, 766, 781(2)
Sarah A L, 591
Sarah A L (Winstead), 551
Sarah A S, 742
Sarah Addie, 763
Sarah Allinda, 533
Sarah Analiza, 593
Sarah Ann, 564, 571-572, 624, 627,
    776, 780
Sarah Ann "Sally" (Lane), 571
Sarah Ann (Miller), 568
Sarah Ann (Prichett), 517
Sarah Ann (Smith), 587
Sarah Ann E, 540, 595, 598
Sarah Ann R, 519
Sarah C, 498, 542
Sarah C (Welch), 564
Sarah Caroline (Downing), 527
Sarah Catherine, 579
Sarah Catherine Bayne, 541, 604,
    613
Sarah Dianne (Campbell), 699
Sarah Dorothy, 522
Sarah E, 553, 570, 577, 619, 756
Sarah E (--), 619

Sarah E (Flynt), 524
Sarah E (Hudson), 571
Sarah Eleanor, 562
Sarah Elizabeth, 569, 585, 743-744,
    754
Sarah Elizabeth (Roddy), 722
Sarah Ellen, 519, 553
Sarah Elmira (Lowe), 638
Sarah Ethel, 654
Sarah F, 767
Sarah Frances (Parker), 651
Sarah H, 741
Sarah Henrietta, 580, 742
Sarah Henrietta (Hammack), 742
Sarah J, 554, 625, 767, 779
Sarah J (--), 554
Sarah J (Clark), 559
Sarah J (Emmerson), 591
Sarah J P (Wesson), 526
Sarah Jane, 563
Sarah Jane (Crawford), 592
Sarah Jane (Curtis), 597
Sarah Jane (Lay), 600
Sarah M, 777
Sarah M (--), 752
Sarah Margaret, 583
Sarah N, 618
Sarah P, 502
Sarah Pope, 585
Sarah T, 757
Sarah V, 517
Sarepta (Curtis), 187, 190
Sarepta Ann Elizabeth, 597, 644
Seaborn, 489, 524, 586, 767(2)
Seaborn T, 616
Selia (Boatright), 759
Sena, 753-754
Sena (--), 754
Seneca, 627
Seneca Watts, 563, 626
Serilda J (Bramblett), 569
Sevarina M, 780
Severena M, 780
Severine Muse, 781
Sharron, 591
Sheila (Amons), 700
Sidney W, 193, 599, 648
Silas, 601, 735-737
Silas M, 737
Simeon, 163-164, 199, 215, 432,
    463, 513, 577, 596
Simeon J, 498, 540
Simeon S, 599
Simeon Wiley, 517
Sinthy, 558, 623
Solomon Wadkins, 528
Sophia, 501, 625
Sophia (--), 555
Sophia Jane (Bray), 633
Sophronia (--), 777
Spencer, 508, 564, 629-630
St Clair "Sink", 560, 625

HARRIS (continued)
Goodwin, 758
Jane, 574
John, 555
Julia A, 591-592
Lucy, 760
Mary, 760
Mary F, 534
Mary F (Hammack), 760
Mary N, 618
Melinda (Hammock), 555
Sallie S, 758
Singelton, 592
Susan, 760
Thomas O, 760
HARRISON
Inez, 676
Mary, 383
HART
Daisy, 585, 744
HARTHCOCK
Dewey Luce, 664
Margaret Elizabeth (Hammack), 664
HARTHEAD
Rebecca, 621
HARTSFIELD
Virginia, 606
HARVEY
Betsy, 502
Lula, 402
Salley, 557
HASKINS
George Tara, 582
Jenny Drusilla (Hammock), 582
HASLELOCK
Johanna, 17(4)
HASTY
Absalom, 534
Martha (Hammock), 534
HATFIELD
Susan, 627
HATLEY
Jane Franklin (Roberts), 692
Richard, 692
HATTAWAY
Lucy J, 546
HATTEN
Ruth Land, 754
HAVENS
Louvenia, 554
Mary Katherine, 554
HAWKINS
--, 672
Ellen S (Hammac), 589
Harriett Louise, 588
Mary Frances (Hammack), 672
Olivia (O'Neal), 402
W M, 589
William LaFayette, 402
HAY
Sarah, 324

HAYES
Christopher Lowery, 566
Mary, 408
Mary Ann Malinda (Hammack), 566
Millie Ann, 586
HAYNES
Joe, 563
Lafayette, 563
Louisa Ann (Hammack), 563
Martha Catherine (Hammack), 563
HAZARD
Betsey (Austin), 552
Joseph, 552
HAZELWOOD
Katey, 502
HEAD
Frances Elizabeth Catherine (Amos), 610
Sarah Millanda (Amos), 610
Thomas Edmund, 610
HEARD
Adaline E, 491
HEATH
Cathrena, 356
HEDRICK
Mary, 628
Rosey Ann, 628
HELCHEY
Aeltje, 346
HELPER
Jacob Cyrus, 560
Polly (Hammack), 560
HELTON
Barry, 690
Becky, 712
Debra, 690
Dibrell, 690
Jennifer, 712
John Barry, 712
Karen (Petty), 690
Kathy (Washam), 712
Keith, 712
Kenneth, 690, 712
Lavonia Joyce (Roberts), 690
Marie (Sparks), 690
Reginald, 690
HEMMECK
Jane, 468
William, 468
HEMMICK
Caroline (Tatsapaugh), 769
George Fore, 769
Rowland F, 769
W H, 769
HEMOCK
Polly, 762
HENDERSON
Henry, 759
Mary, 369(2)
Peggy, 422
Ruth, 371

HENDRICKS
Anne (Linville), 352
Catharina, 782
Henry, 349, 352
Jese, 757
John, 345, 349
Lydia (Hammack), 757
Rebecca (Groesbeck) Wells, 345
HENDRICKSON
Aeltje (Helchey), 346
Albertus, 346
HENRY
Charles W, 753
Codey Ann, 718
Debbie (Bartshewsi), 706
Delphaine, 685
Georgina E (Telenga), 685
Hollie, 706, 718
Jodi, 706
Larry George, 685, 706
Roy George, 685
HENSON
--, 517
Sarah V (Hammock), 517
HESTER
Elijah, 328
HESTON
John, 544
Sarah T (Amos), 544
HIATT
Rachel, 568
HIBBARD
Bradley, 706
Cherie, 706
Florence (Telenga), 685
Glenn, 685, 706
Jasmine, 718
Kimberly, 706, 718
Kristy, 706
Sharon (Mack), 706
Tyrell, 707
Vernon, 685
Wanda, 685, 706-707
HICKS
Laura A, 762
HICKSON
Rebecca (Hammock), 532
Timothy, 532
HIGGINS
Emeline (Adams), 537
William A, 537
HIGH
Annie Mae (Hammock), 688
Donald Ross, 688
HIGHEN
Eva, 671
HIGHTOWER
Elizabeth, 762
Elizabeth A, 762
Josephine (Hammack), 553
Vianna R, 587
William J, 553

SELLARS (continued)
Rachel, 505-506
SELMAN
Martha (Grant), 331
SERCY
Nancy, 533
SHAMBAUGH
Ann, 782
Ann "Nancy", 782
Catharina (Hendricks), 782
Daniel, 782
Elisabeth (Boehm), 782
George, 782
SHAPLA/CHAPPELL
Hannah, 739
SHARP
Jewell, 663
Sally, 557
SHAW
Abina, 539
Mary Evelyn, 678
SHELTON
Betti (Smith), 688
Carl, 688
Linda, 688
Pat, 688
Raymond, 688
SHEPHERD
Frances M, 585
Nancy A, 602
Solomon, 341
Susnanah (Farquhar), 341
SHEPPARD
Dovie L, 640
Rosanna, 407
SHERMAN
Elizabeth, 305
family, 305
Margaret C, 622
SHERRARD
B F, 725
SHERRER
Mary Ann (Hammock), 574
Richard S, 574
SHERRILL
Brian Thomas, 703
Emily Irene (Schulte), 703
Freida (Bathmann), 703
Justin Nicholas, 703
Kristina Hope, 703
Lara Nicole, 703
Micah Brian, 703
Raymond, 703
SHEWIN
Hannah, 409
Sarah (Martin), 409
William, 409
SHEWMAKE
Sarah Jane, 696
SHIFLET
Emma Lodaski, 517

SHINE
Daniel, 417
John, 419
SHIRLEY
Martha, 704
SHOEMAKER
Debra Celeste (Lee), 716
Jerry, 716
SHORES
Tanya, 718
SHORT
Eugenia (Hammack), 576, 771
Robert, 576, 771
SHORTER
James, 383
Patsy (O'Neal), 383
SHULTE
Allie Jo (Hammack), 212
Frank Herman, 212
SIAS
Mary, 749
SIBLEY
Mary Jane, 638
SIKES
Sarah, 516
SIMMONS
Allen G, 736
Annie Eliza, 760
Calvin Green, 565
Catherine, 736-737
Catherine (Hammack), 119, 157
Caty (Hammack), 474
Frances, 528
Gilly Harriet (Hammack), 565
Hattie, 760
J K, 736
James A, 588
James Franklin, 760
John K, 736
Katherine, 736-737
Lucinda (Hammac), 588
Mary Ellen, 760
Nancy D (Thompson), 760
Susan Elnor, 760
Thomas Washington, 760
Walter, 760
William, 119, 157, 474
SIMPSON
Joseph, 248
Louisa M, 607
Mary (Wheeler), 248
Samuel, 419
SIMS
Elizabeth (Hammack), 584
James, 584
James M, 761
Mary P, 761
Mildred, 493
Vianna, 747
SINCLAIR
Elizabeth Ann, 617
George, 617

SINGLETON
Audrey, 689
Ella, 746
George, 746
Zilpha (--), 746
SITTON
Amy Elizabeth (Allen), 717
Christopher, 700
Christopher Thomas, 717
Claudia Catherine, 717
Crystal Beth (Dolan), 700
Dorothy Lucille, 680, 699
family, 211
John Michael, 700
Joseph Paul, 680, 700
Mary (Nothoffer), 680
Mary Elizabeth, 680, 699
Mary Madeline, 717
Mary Mildred (Hammack), 211, 680
Melissa Joann, 700
Michael Anne (Sumrall), 700
Stephen Paul, 700
Suzanne Marie (Vogt), 700
Thomas, 680
Thomas Joseph, 211, 680
Thomas Stribling, 680, 700
SKELTON
Lola, 678
SKINNER
Cynthia, 752
SLATER
George, 425-426
John, 423, 425
John D, 426
Levi, 425
Nancy, 423
Sarah (Bowman), 426
Susannah (Gardner), 425
SLAY
Martha Elizabeth, 306
SLAYDEN
Sarah Evans, 493
SLEVELL
Elizabeth, 466
SLOCUMB
Alice E, 609
Charles, 609
James W, 609
John, 609
Melissa G (Bryant), 609
Perry L, 609
William, 609
SLOUAKER
--, 777
SMALLWOOD
Aaron Augustus, 639
Catherine (Wood), 590
Elijah, 590
Eliza (Poole), 590
Emily (Combs), 525, 529
Jacob W, 590
John T, 639